Introduction to Information Systems

Supporting and Transforming Business

Ninth Edition

R. KELLY RAINER JR.

BRAD PRINCE

WILEY

EDITORIAL DIRECTOR	Michael McDonald
EDITOR	Courtney Jordan
INSTRUCTIONAL DESIGNER	Wendy Ashenberg
EDITORIAL ASSISTANT	Kali Ridley
SENIOR MARKETING MANAGER	Maureen Shelburne
PRODUCTION EDITOR	Rachel Conrad
SENIOR PRODUCT DESIGNER	Thomas Nery
PRODUCTION MANAGEMENT SERVICES	Lumina Datamatics, Inc.
COVER ILLUSTRATION	© Alaris/Shutterstock,
	© ProStockStudio/Shutterstock

This book was typeset in 9.5/12 Source Sans Pro at Lumina Datamatics.

Founded in 1807, John Wiley & Sons, Inc. has been a valued source of knowledge and understanding for more than 200 years, helping people around the world meet their needs and fulfill their aspirations. Our company is built on a foundation of principles that include responsibility to the communities we serve and where we live and work. In 2008, we launched a Corporate Citizenship Initiative, a global effort to address the environmental, social, economic, and ethical challenges we face in our business. Among the issues we are addressing are carbon impact, paper specifications and procurement, ethical conduct within our business and among our vendors, and community and charitable support. For more information, please visit our website: www.wiley.com/go/citizenship.

Evaluation copies are provided to qualified academics and professionals for review purposes only, for use in their courses during the next academic year. These copies are licensed and may not be sold or transferred to a third party. Upon completion of the review period, please return the evaluation copy to Wiley. Return instructions and a free of charge return shipping label are available at www.wiley.com/go/returnlabel. If you have chosen to adopt this textbook for use in your course, please accept this book as your complimentary desk copy. Outside of the United States, please contact your local representative.

EPUB ISBN: 9781119767503

The inside back cover will contain printing identification and country of origin if omitted from this page. In addition, if the ISBN on the back cover differs from the ISBN on this page, the one on the back cover is correct.

Library of Congress Cataloging-in-Publication Data

Names: Rainer, R. Kelly, Jr., 1949- author. | Prince, Brad, 1978- author.
Title: Introduction to information systems : supporting and transforming business / R. Kelly Rainer Jr., Brad Prince.
Description: Eighth edition. | Hoboken, NJ : Wiley, [2020] | Includes index.
Identifiers: LCCN 2019035278 (print) | LCCN 2019035279 (ebook) | ISBN 9781119761464 (paperback) |
    ISBN 9781119796985 (adobe pdf) | ISBN 9781119767503 (epub)
Subjects: LCSH: Information technology. | Computer networks. | Management information systems.
Classification: LCC T58.5 .R35 2020 (print) | LCC T58.5 (ebook) | DDC 658.4/038011—dc23
LC record available at https://lccn.loc.gov/2019035278
LC ebook record available at https://lccn.loc.gov/2019035279

Printed in the United States of America.

SKY10033210_020822

The entire focus of this book is to help students become informed users of information systems and information technology. In general, informed users receive increased value from organizational information systems and technologies. We hope to help students do just that.

What Do Information Systems Have to Do with Business?

This edition of Rainer and Prince's *Introduction to Information Systems* will answer this question for you. In every chapter, you will see how real global businesses use technology and information systems to increase their profitability, gain market share, develop and improve their customer relations, and manage their daily operations. In other words, you will learn how information systems provide the foundation for all modern organizations, whether they are public sector, private section, for-profit, or not-for-profit. We have several goals for all business majors, particularly undergraduates. First, we want to teach you how to use information technology to help you master your current or future jobs to help ensure the success of your organizations. Second, we want you to become *informed users* of information systems and information technology. Third, we want you to understand the digital transformation that your organization will likely be undergoing. The digital transformation of organizations is the acceleration of existing business processes and the development of new processes and business models. In this way, organizations can capitalize on the capabilities and opportunities of various technologies to improve performance. Examples of these technologies include Big Data, cloud computing, artificial intelligence, the Internet of Things, mobile computing, and commerce. We address each of these in our book. To accomplish these goals, we focus on not merely *learning* the concepts of information technology but rather on *applying* those concepts to perform business more effectively and efficiently. We concentrate on placing information systems in the context of business, so that you will more readily grasp the concepts we present in the text.

Pedagogical Structure

Various pedagogical features provide a structured learning system that reinforces the concepts through features such as chapter-opening organizers, section reviews, study aids, frequent applications, and hands-on exercises and activities.

Chapter-opening organizers include the following pedagogical features:

- **Chapter Outline:** Lists the major concepts covered in each chapter.
- **Learning Objectives:** Provide an overview of the key learning goals that students should achieve after reading the chapter.
- **Opening Cases:** With the exception of Chapter 8, chapter-opening cases address a business problem faced by actual organizations and how they employ information systems and information technology to solve these issues. The cases generally consist of a description of the problem, an overview of the IS solutions implemented, and a presentation of the results of the implementation. Each case closes with discussion questions so that students can further explore the concepts presented in the case.

Chapter 8's opening case addresses how pro-democracy protesters in Hong Kong have used a variety of technologies that make it easier and safer for them to communicate and collaborate. These technologies include mesh networks, encrypted messaging apps, a Reddit-like forum, and online anonymity measures. An important aspect of this case for students is that information systems impact societies as a whole, not just organizations.

Study aids are provided throughout each chapter. These include the following:

- IT's About Business cases provide real-world applications, with questions that relate to concepts covered in the text. Icons relate these sections to the specific functional areas in the text.
- Highlighted examples interspersed throughout the text illustrate the use (and misuse) of IT by real-world organizations, thus making the conceptual discussion more concrete.
- Tables list key points or summarize different concepts.
- End-of-section reviews (Before You Go On...) prompt students to pause and test their understanding of basic concepts before moving on to the next section.

End-of-chapter study aids provide extensive opportunity for the reader to review:

- What's in IT for Me? is a unique chapter summary section that demonstrates the relevance of topics for different functional areas (accounting, finance, marketing, production/operations management, and human resources management).

- The chapter Summary, keyed to learning objectives listed at the beginning of the chapter, enables students to review the major concepts covered in the chapter.

- The end-of-chapter Glossary facilitates studying by listing and defining all the key terms introduced in the chapter.

- Closing cases in each chapter address a business problem faced by actual companies and how they used IS to solve these issues. The cases generally consist of a description of the problem, an overview of the IS solution implemented, and a presentation of the results of that implementation. Each case is followed by discussion questions so that students can further explore the concepts presented in the case.

Hands-on exercises and activities require the reader to do something with the concepts they have studied. These include the following:

- Apply the Concept Activities: This book's unique pedagogical structure is designed to keep students actively engaged with the course material. Reading material in each chapter subsection is supported by an "Apply the Concept" activity that is directly related to a chapter objective. These activities include links to online videos and articles and other hands-on activities that require students to immediately apply what they have learned. Each Apply the Concept has the following elements:
  - Background (places the activity in the context of relevant reading material)
  - Activity (a hands-on activity that students carry out)
  - Deliverable (various tasks for students to complete as they perform the activity)
- Discussion Questions and Problem-Solving Activities: Provide practice through active learning. These exercises are hands-on opportunities to apply the concepts discussed in the chapter.

Key Features

We have been guided by the following goals that we believe will enhance the teaching and learning experience.

What's in IT for Me? Theme

We emphasize the importance of information systems by calling attention in every chapter to how that chapter's topic relates to each business major. Icons guide students to relevant issues for their specific functional area—accounting (ACC), finance (FIN), marketing (MKT), production operations management (POM), human resources management (HRM), and management information systems (MIS). Chapters conclude with a detailed summary (entitled "What's in IT for Me?") of how key concepts in the chapter relate to each functional area.

Active Learning

We recognize the need to actively involve students in problem solving, creative thinking, and capitalizing on opportunities. Therefore, we have included in every chapter a variety of hands-on exercises, activities, and mini-cases, including exercises that require students to use software application tools. Through these activities and an interactive website, we enable students to apply the concepts they learn.

Diversified and Unique Examples from Different Industries

Extensive use of vivid examples from large corporations, small businesses, and government and not-for-profit organizations enlivens the concepts from the chapter. The examples illustrate everything from the capabilities of information systems, to their cost and justification and the innovative ways that corporations are using IS in their operations. Small businesses have been included to recognize the fact that many students will work for small- to mid-sized companies, and some will even start their own small business. In fact, some students may already be working at local businesses, and the concepts they are learning in class can be readily observed or put into practice in their jobs. Each chapter constantly highlights the integral connection between business and IS. This connection is especially evident in the chapter-opening and closing cases, the "IT's About Business" boxes, and the highlighted examples.

Successes and Failures

Many textbooks present examples of the successful implementation of information systems, and our book is no exception. However, we go one step beyond by also providing numerous examples of IS failures, in the context of lessons that can be learned from such failures. Misuse of information systems can be very expensive.

Global Focus

An understanding of global competition, partnerships, and trading is essential to success in a modern business environment. Therefore, we provide a broad selection of international cases and examples. We discuss the role of information systems in facilitating export and import, the management of international companies, and electronic trading around the globe.

Innovation and Creativity

In today's rapidly changing business environment, creativity and innovation are necessary for a business to operate effectively and profitably. Throughout our book, we demonstrate how information systems facilitate these processes.

Focus on Ethics

With corporate scandals appearing in the headlines almost daily, ethics and ethical questions have come to the forefront of businesspeople's minds. In addition to devoting an entire chapter to ethics and privacy (Chapter 3), we have included examples and cases throughout the text that focus on business ethics.

A Guide to Icons in This Book

As you read this book, you will notice a variety of icons interspersed throughout the chapters.

These icons highlight material relating to different functional areas. MIS concepts are relevant to all business careers, not just careers in IT. The functional area icons help students of different majors quickly pick out concepts and examples of particular relevance to them. Below is a quick reference of these icons:

ACCT **For the Accounting Major** highlights content relevant to the functional area of accounting.

FIN **For the Finance Major** highlights content relevant to the functional area of finance.

MKT **For the Marketing Major** highlights content relevant to the functional area of marketing.

POM **For the Production/Operations Management Major** highlights content relevant to the functional area of production/operations management.

HRM **For the Human Resources Major** highlights content relevant to the functional area of human resources.

MIS **For the MIS Major** highlights content relevant to the functional area of MIS.

What's New in Rainer *Introduction to Information Systems*, 9e

The new edition includes all new or updated chapter opening cases, chapter closing cases, and IT's About Business.

Highlights of Rainer 9e (or New Material)

Digital Transformation of Organizations

More than likely, students will go to work for companies that are undergoing digital transformation. We emphasize digital transformation and the information technologies that drive such transformations (see Chapter 1's opening case, IT's About Business 1.1, IT's About Business 1.2, IT's About Business 1.3, and Chapter 1's closing case). The technologies that drive digital transformation include Big Data (see Chapter 5), broadband Internet access (see Chapter 6), wireless and mobile computing (see Chapter 8), the Internet of Things (see Chapter 8), social computing (see Chapter 9), business analytics (see Chapter 12), agile systems development methods (see Chapter 13), cloud computing (see Technology Guide 3), and artificial intelligence (see Chapter 14).

Artificial Intelligence

In our all-new Chapter 14, we address the critically important topic of artificial intelligence.

- We first carefully define AI in terms of the tasks that humans perform, rather than how humans think. We then compare the capabilities of natural intelligence and artificial intelligence.
- We differentiate between weak AI and strong AI.
- We define supervised machine learning, semi-supervised machine learning, reinforcement learning, unsupervised machine learning, and deep learning.
- We address bias in machine-learning systems.
- We define neural networks and how they function.
- We discuss various applications of AI, including computer vision, natural language processing, robotics, speech recognition, and intelligent agents.
- We provide a thorough discussion of AI applications in the functional areas, including accounting, finance, marketing, production/operations management, human resource management, and MIS.

Business Analytics

In Chapter 12, we expanded our discussion of the difference between analytics and statistics, added real-world scenarios that allow students to apply the business analytics process (Figure 12.3), and added a discussion of Google Analytics.

Social Computing

In Chapter 9, we added a section called "Problems with Social Computing." We address three serious issues with social media platforms. First, they allow almost anyone to publish any content. Second, the platforms employ psychological measures to keep visitors on their sites longer. Third, third-party entities employ various means to spread their messages. Our discussion includes bots, cyborgs, trolls, troll farms, fake news, and deepfakes, as well as the infinite scroll and randomly scheduled rewards.

E-Business and E-Commerce

In Chapter 7, we provide an expanded discussion of blockchain technology. We provide examples of the use of blockchains, including cryptocurrencies such as Bitcoin, the energy grid, digital content creators (e.g., music and journalism), and along supply chains.

Telecommunications and Networking

In Chapter 6, we provide an expanded discussion of the evolution of the Web, from Web 1.0 to Web 5.0.

Hardware

- In Technology Guide 1, we added a new section addressing augmented reality (AR), virtual reality (VR), and mixed reality (MR). We provide numerous real-world examples of AR, VR, and MR.
- We added a brief discussion of why Moore's Law is slowing down.
- We also added brief discussions of graphics processing units and quantum computing.

Cloud Computing

- In Technology Guide 3, we added a new section comparing the "Big Three" cloud computing vendors: Amazon Web Services, Microsoft Azure, and the Google Cloud Platform.
- We also added a discussion of multi–cloud computing environments.

Online Resources

This text also facilitates the teaching of an introductory IS course by providing extensive support materials for instructors and students. Go to www.wiley.com to access the Student and Instructor websites.

Instructor's Manual

The Instructor's Manual includes a chapter overview, teaching tips and strategies, answers to all end-of-chapter questions, supplemental mini-cases with essay questions and answers, and experiential exercises that relate to particular topics.

Test Bank

The Test Bank is a comprehensive resource for test questions. It contains multiple-choice, true/false, short answer, and essay questions for each chapter. The multiple-choice and true/false questions are labeled according to difficulty: easy, medium, or hard.

Computerized Test Bank

Wiley provides complimentary software to generate print exams or to import test bank questions into standard LMS formats. The assessment items available in this software are a subset of those in the WileyPLUS question banks. See the assignment banks in WileyPLUS for the complete catalog of assessment items related to your adopted text.

PowerPoint Presentations

The PowerPoint presentations consist of a series of slides for each chapter of the text, are designed around the text content, and incorporate key points from the text and all text illustrations as appropriate.

Weekly Updates

Weekly updates, harvested from around the Web by David Firth of the University of Montana, provide you with the latest IT news and issues. These are posted every Monday morning throughout the year at http://wileyinformationsystemsupdates.com and include links to articles and videos as well as discussion questions to assign or use in class.

OfficeGrader

OfficeGrader is an Access-based VBA macro that enables automatic grading of Office assignments. The macros compare Office files and grade them against a master file. OfficeGrader is available for Word, Access, Excel, and PowerPoint for Office 2010 and Office 2013. For more information, contact your Wiley sales representative or visit the book companion site and click on "OfficeGrader."

WileyPlus

WileyPLUS helps instructors:

- Save time by automating grading of practice, homework, quizzes, and exams
- Create a focused and personalized course that reflects their teaching style
- Quickly identify and understand student learning trends to improve classroom engagement
- Improve their course year over year using WileyPLUS data

Instructor Resources include:

- Lecture Videos—The authors provide an extensive series of lecture videos, ranging in length from 3 minutes to 10 minutes. The videos explain key concepts throughout the book, with each clip addressing a single concept. In this way, the lecture videos reinforce key concepts in the text without being confusing to the students. (*Note:* This feature is only available in WileyPLUS.)

- Data Analytics & Business Module—With the emergence of data analytics transforming the business environment, Wiley has partnered with business leaders in the Business-Higher Education Forum (BHEF) to identify the competencies graduates need to be successful in their careers. As a result, WileyPLUS includes a new data analytics module with industry-validated content that prepares operations management students for a changing workforce. (*Note:* This feature is only available in WileyPLUS.)
- Activity Links and Starter Files—Apply the Concept activities link out to the Web, providing videos for students to view and use in the activities. When appropriate, students are provided with starter files to complete as part of the deliverable.
- Database Activity Solution Files—Every database activity in the book comes with a solution file that can be used in the Office Grader Application or by an individual to grade the students' submissions.
- Database Activity Starter Files—When appropriate, students are provided with starter files to complete as part of the deliverable.
- Instructor's Manual—This guide contains detailed solutions to all questions, exercises, and problems in the textbook.
- Practice Quizzes—These quizzes give students a way to test themselves on course material before exams. Each chapter exam contains fill-in-the-blank, application, and multiple-choice questions that provide immediate feedback with the correct answer.
- Reading Quizzes—These quizzes reinforce basic concepts from the reading.

- Spreadsheet Activity Solution Files—Every spreadsheet activity in the book comes with a solution file that can be used in the Office Grader Application or by an individual to grade the students' submissions.

Student Resources include:

- Video Lectures—The authors are featured in these video lectures, which provide explanations of key concepts throughout the book. (*Note:* This feature is only available in WileyPLUS.)
- Practice Quizzes—These quizzes give students a way to test themselves on course material before exams. Each chapter exam contains fill-in-the-blank, application, and multiple-choice questions that provide immediate feedback with the correct answer.
- *Microsoft Office 2013/2016/2019 Lab Manual & Instructor Resources*—by Ed Martin, CUNY-Queensborough is a thorough introduction to the Microsoft Office products of Word, Excel, Access, and PowerPoint with screenshots that show students step-by-step instructions on basic MS Office tasks.

Wiley Custom

This group's services allow you to:

- Adapt existing Wiley content and combine texts
- Incorporate and publish your own materials
- Collaborate with our team to ensure your satisfaction

Wiley Custom Select

Wiley Custom Select allows you to build your own course materials using selected chapters of any Wiley text and your own material if desired. For more information, contact your Wiley sales representative or visit **http://customselect.wiley.com**.

Brief Contents

Contents

CHAPTER 1

Introduction to Information Systems

CHAPTER OUTLINE	LEARNING OBJECTIVES
1.1 Why Should I Study Information Systems?	1.1 Identify the reasons why being an informed user of information systems is important in today's world.
1.2 Overview of Computer-Based Information Systems	1.2 Describe the various types of computer-based information systems in an organization.
1.3 How Does IT Impact Organizations?	1.3 Discuss ways in which information technology can affect managers and nonmanagerial workers.
1.4 Importance of Information Systems to Society	1.4 Identify positive and negative societal effects of the increased use of information technology.

Opening Case

MIS POM The Digital and Physical Transformation of Grocery Stores

The Problem

In 1916, Piggly Wiggly invented the full-service grocery store that we know today. The grocer launched the shopping cart, checkout lanes, browsable aisles, and price tags on items, all of which were technological disruptions at that time. Significantly, customers buy groceries today in almost the same way that they did in 1916. They travel to a brick-and-mortar store, select products off the shelves, and self-deliver their products to their homes.

The modern grocery business is huge and complex, has very small profit margins, and is intensely competitive. The global volume of grocers is approximately $6 trillion annually. In the United States, the industry volume totals some $700 billion per year and represents roughly half of all retail sales. In May 2020 the United States was home to more than 32,000 chain supermarket physical locations and almost 7,000 independent locations.

Although many grocery stores now offer online services, overall the industry has concentrated on operating with physical locations for two main reasons. First, many shoppers prefer to select their own products, especially meat, produce, and other perishable goods. Second, few grocers find it profitable to invest in the highly efficient, large-scale cold chains required to make home deliveries. A *cold chain* is a temperature-controlled supply chain that maintains a low-temperature range to preserve and extend the shelf life of products, particularly food and pharmaceuticals.

Competitive pressures, technological advances, and evolving consumer attitudes and behaviors are transforming the grocery industry. In addition, the COVID 19 pandemic brought new demands on grocers as these essential businesses had to adapt to meet new social distancing requirements and increased demand for contact-less shopping.

To address these trends, stores are deploying *omnichannel strategies*. This strategy encompasses physical environments such as storefronts as well as digital environments such as electronic commerce, mobile applications, and social media. Omnichannel enables customers to seamlessly engage with a company through multiple channels at one time. The question becomes: How should grocers most effectively enter the online market?

Online-grocery startups first appeared in the late 1990s. Notable examples were Webvan and HomeGrocer. Neither company survived the dot-com bubble, which was the result of excessive speculation in

Internet-related companies in the late 1990s. In January 2020, roughly half of book and music sales occurred online, along with 40 percent of consumer electronics sales, 30 percent of apparel sales, and 20 percent of furniture purchases. In contrast, only 3 percent of grocery sales occurred online at that time. By mid-2020, online grocery sales had increased to 12.5 percent of all purchases.

A Number of Solutions

The grocery industry is implementing many solutions, both physical and digital, in its transformation. For clarity, we can classify these solutions along the supply chain of grocery stores (see Chapter 11): supply-chain solutions for managing their vendors (upstream), in-store solutions, and delivery solutions (downstream).

Supply-chain solutions. Grocery stores typically source goods from hundreds of separate vendors. The largest stores stock up to 50,000 items. Consequently, the industry must manage its supply chains effectively and efficiently. Supply chain management software and automated warehouses help in this process.

- *Supply chain management software*: Walmart, the largest grocer in the United States, is an example of superior supply chain management. In 1983, Walmart began using bar codes in conjunction with its point-of-sale system to track products. In 1992, the retailer deployed Retail Link, its sophisticated supply chain management system. By sharing point-of-sale data from Walmart stores with suppliers, Retail Link tightly integrated Walmart and its suppliers. Other grocers have only recently begun to deploy these technologies.

- *Automated warehouses*: In 2012, Amazon acquired Kiva Systems, a manufacturer of warehouse robots with an accompanying inventory system. The concept behind Kiva was to use robots to bring items to humans rather than have humans find items in a warehouse and take them to a packing point (a process called *picking*). Today, Amazon has more than 200,000 robots in its warehouses transporting bins, picking items, and stacking pallets.

In-store solutions. Grocery stores deploy many technologies. These technologies include electronic labels on products, Internet of Things (IoT) sensors, smart shelves, radio-frequency identification (RFID) tags on products, personalized advertisements, cashierless checkout, facial recognition checkout, and robots.

- *Electronic labels* will eliminate paper bar codes on each item and enable stores to change all the prices in a store within minutes, a process called *digital pricing*. In 2018, Kroger deployed the Enhanced Display for Grocery Environment (EDGE), which displays prices, advertisements, nutritional data, and coupon availability.

- *Internet of Things sensors* have many uses in supermarkets. For example, they can measure the weight of products on a store's smart shelves. Also, they are valuable in measuring and controlling the temperature of products.

- *Smart shelves* are wirelessly connected shelves that have weight sensors. The sensors report on the quantity of items on the shelves, thus enabling stores, grocers' warehouses, and vendors to practice real-time inventory management. The sensors communicate with *product RFID tags* to report misplaced items that do not belong on certain shelves. RFID tags provide more information on products than bar codes, and they enable cashierless checkout.

Smart shelves can interact with apps on customers' smartphones to offer *personalized advertisements*. Additionally, if customers use the store's app to create a shopping list, then the smart shelves can interact with their lists and show them where to find the items they want.

- *Facial recognition* aims to simplify and accelerate the checkout process even more. Customers scan their items at an automated checkout booth, have their identity checked by scanning their faces and matching the scans to their online shopping account, and then enter their mobile phone number to complete the transaction. Chinese supermarket chain 7Fresh (owned by Chinese e-commerce firm **JD.com**) is using this technology.

- Industry analysts note that almost half of in-store tasks could be automated. *Robots* can answer shoppers' questions, suggest products based on a shopper's previous purchases, track inventory, keep track of expiration dates, stock shelves, pick and pack products for delivery, clean up spills, and even assemble sandwiches and salads.

Retailers are using some or all of these technologies to launch *cashierless checkout options* for several reasons, including the high costs associated with cashiers (about 30 percent of store's labor costs), customer frustration with slow checkout lanes, and the demand for contactless shopping brought on by the COVID 19 pandemic. Retailers are offering self-checkout (also known as self-service checkout and as semi-attended customer-activated terminal, SACAT). The customer performs the job of the cashier themselves by scanning the items' barcodes, weighing produce on digital scales, placing the groceries in an electronically monitored bagging area, and then paying for the items themselves.

Cashierless stores (called *scan and go*) take this process a step further using a combination of ceiling mounted cameras and shelf-weight sensors to automatically track customers as they move about a store and the items they place in their carts. Once a customer has finished shopping, they can walk out of the store without needing to scan any item or interact with a cashier. Examples of cashierless stores are Amazon Go, Ahold Delhaize's "tap to go," and China's BingoBox, a chain of unstaffed convenience stores.

Let's look more closely at Amazon Go. To enter the store, customers scan the Amazon Go app at entry turnstiles. From that moment, cameras and sensors identify them by their Amazon account as they shop. Taking an item off the smart shelf adds it to the customer's virtual cart. Putting an item back on the shelf removes it from the customer's cart. When customers are finished shopping, they simply leave the store. Amazon then sends them an email receipt and charges their Amazon account.

Delivery solutions. Online grocery systems have difficulty telling shoppers exactly what is in stock, what they might like, and what substitutions exist. The online systems also require inventory pickers and delivery personnel. Unfortunately, the industry's narrow profit margins make it difficult to assume the added costs of these employees. Grocery delivery can occur in several ways.

Delivery at the store. Customers can order online, go to the store, and pick up their products inside the store, at a drive-through, or curbside, a process called *click-and-collect*. Click-and-collect does not require delivery, thereby keeping costs down.

Delivery to customers. As noted, delivery to customers involves additional costs for grocers. To keep these costs to a minimum, grocers have been investing in drop density analytics, warehouse location, automation, and subscription business models.

With delivery to customers, grocers must analyze *drop density*, which is the number of deliveries made per trip. Lower drop density—that is, fewer deliveries per trip—results in higher delivery costs.

To increase drop density, a grocer can provide delivery service to specific communities only at specified times each week. A Dutch grocer, Picnic (**www.picnic.app**), has achieved a drop density of 14 deliveries per hour with this model.

Another solution is pooled deliveries, where grocers collaborate with their competitors or with other businesses. In China, an app links some 50 companies with thousands of independent drivers to deliver goods. The app contains profiles and user ratings of drivers, and indicates whether they are available and will help to unpack items. The app provides drivers with trip planners and route maps. Early trials have indicated that this approach could reduce retailers' delivery costs by 30 percent.

Amazon, Walmart, and Instacart are the largest competitors in the online grocery space. Let's take a look at their delivery services. Keep in mind that Kroger, Albertson's, and Target also offer delivery services.

Amazon Prime Now (**www.amazon.com**) delivers fresh foods directly from Whole Foods stores. (Amazon purchased Whole Foods in 2017.) Another Amazon service, AmazonFresh, delivers groceries only from Amazon fulfillment centers.

As of February 2021, Walmart offered same-day delivery from some 2,000 stores. Walmart Plus, offered from 1,400 stores, offers free shipping with no order minimum, free delivery from a local store, member pricing on fuel, and mobile scan and go.

Instacart (**www.instacart.com**)—the largest independent grocery-delivery service—is available in all 50 U.S. states and all 10 Canadian provinces in partnership with more than 350 retailers that operate more than 25,000 grocery stores.

Farmstead (**www.farmsteadapp.com**) is a same-day, locally sourced grocery startup based in San Francisco that employs a subscription service. Launched in 2016, the company does not charge for delivery, and it focuses on fresh products.

Farmstead uses machine learning (see Chapter 14) to determine the best routes for its fleet of contracted drivers, who make multiple deliveries per outing.

Farmstead also uses machine learning for picking and managing their produce. The grocer captures data on every product it carries, including sell-by dates and how fast inventory moves. It then inputs these data into a machine-learning model that determines exactly how much stock to buy.

- *Store goods closer to customers.* Another strategy to make deliveries cheaper is to store goods closer to where people live. For example, a company called Fabric (**http://getfabric.com**) has built several micro-fulfillment centers in dense urban areas that can deliver e-commerce orders to customers in less than an hour. These centers, known as *dark stores*, are not open to the public. Instead, they are organized solely for order fulfillment.

As another example, startup Takeoff Technologies (**www.takeoff.com**) is building small (10,000 square feet) micro-fulfillment centers in unused space inside supermarkets. (A typical Kroger supermarket contains roughly 160,000 square feet.) Customers place orders through established grocers, and Takeoff fulfills the orders locally and quickly, utilizing robotic picking and artificial intelligence.

Some stores are opening smaller locations that offer a smaller selection of products but are more convenient to customers. For example, by May 2020 Target had added 100 small-format stores with plans to open more, and Amazon had plans to open 12 small grocery stores in the Los Angeles area.

- *Driverless vehicles and drones.* Grocers are also exploring driverless vehicles and drone deliveries for last-mile delivery. These technologies are expensive to implement, and they require customers to be home at the scheduled time of delivery. For example, Kroger has partnered with Nuro (**http://nuro.ai**), a company that makes self-driving cars, to pilot a grocery delivery service in Scottsdale, Arizona, and Houston, Texas.

Results

In 2019, online sales accounted for about 3 percent of the U.S. grocery market, totaling about $29 billion. Analysts predict that online sales could exceed 22 percent by 2025, as major grocers invest in automation and innovative operations to solve challenges in fulfillment and last-mile delivery.

As a result of the COVID-19 pandemic, more Americans than ever before are ordering groceries online, either for delivery or pickup. From January to May 2020, Instacart's order volume increased by 150 percent, and new downloads of its app had increased by 700 percent. In response, the company hired 300,000 new personal shoppers, its name for the gig workers who pick and deliver groceries. A gig worker is an independent contractor who does not receive the benefits that an employee receives, such as workers' compensation and health and retirement plans.

Amazon grocery orders increased by 5,000 percent during the COVID-19 lockdown. The company hired 175,000 new delivery and operations employees, but it had to limit new grocery sign-ups until it could ramp up its service.

However, some grocers are resisting digital transformation as they maintain their focus on the preferences and demands of their current customer base. For example, on March 1, 2019, Trader Joe's discontinued its delivery services in New York City, stating that its stores were already close to customers and that the firm was unwilling to pass on delivery costs to them.

Sources: Compiled from I. Bogost, "The Supermarket after the Pandemic," *The Atlantic*, April 17, 2020; S. Begley, et al., "Digital Disruption at the Grocery Store," *McKinsey Consulting*, February, 2020; S. Ivry, "Can Grocery Stores Survive the Age of Big Tech?" *Food52*, October 6, 2019; R. Kestenbaum, "Turmoil Is Coming to the Grocery Business and Industry Leaders Don't Want to Talk about It," *Forbes*, October 2, 2019; C. Walton, "Grocery Stores of the Future Will Likely Share These 3 Important Characteristics," *Forbes*, September 8, 2019; G. Szatvanyi, "5 Trends Shaping the Grocery Store of the Future," *Grocery Dive*, July 3, 2019; "4 Trends Disrupting Brick-and-Mortar Grocery," *Winsight Grocery Business*, June 21, 2019; T. Stanger, "What's the Difference between AmazonFresh and Amazon Prime Now?" *Consumer Reports*, June 7, 2019; "11 Predictions for the Future of Grocery," *Produce Retailer*, May 28, 2019; K. Tyko, "Walmart Takes Shot in Shipping Wars by Announcing Free 'Next Day' Delivery," *USA Today*, May 14, 2019; "Automation in Retail: An Executive Overview for Getting Ready," *McKinsey Consulting*, May 2019; K. Alldredge et al., "'Power Partnerships': Manufacturer-Retailer Collaborations that Work," *McKinsey Consulting*, May 2019; N. Taylor, "Is This What the Future of Grocery Will Look Like?" *Winsight Grocery Business*, April 16, 2019; J. Dumont, "Trader Joe's Exits Grocery Delivery in NYC," *Grocery Dive*, January 31, 2019; D. Kuijpers, et al., "Reviving Grocery Retail: Six Imperatives," *McKinsey Consulting*, December 2018; A. Chua, "Cash Not Accepted at Honestbee's First Brick-and-Mortar Chop Space," *Today*, October 17, 2018; B. Ladd, "Takeoff Technologies Launches the World's First Robotic Supermarket," *Forbes*, October 2, 2018; L. Bu, Y. Li, and M. Shao, "An 'Uber' for Chinese E-Commerce," *McKinsey Consulting*, January 2017.

Questions

1. Provide examples to describe the physical transformations undertaken by the grocery industry.

2. Provide examples to describe the digital transformations undertaken by the grocery industry.

3. Which transformations are more important for the grocery industry: physical or digital? Support your answer.

4. Explain why implementing these physical and digital transformations is a strategic necessity for the grocery industry.

Introduction

Before we proceed, we need to define information technology and information systems. **Information technology (IT)** refers to any computer-based tool that people use to work with information and support an organization's information and information-processing needs. An **information system (IS)** collects, processes, stores, analyzes, and disseminates information for a specific purpose.

IT has far-reaching effects on individuals, organizations, and our planet. Although this text is largely devoted to the many ways in which IT is transforming modern organizations, you will also learn about the significant impacts of IT on individuals and societies, the global economy, and our physical environment. IT is making our world smaller, enabling more and more people to communicate, collaborate, and compete, thereby leveling the playing field.

The COVID-19 pandemic forced people to depend on IT in new ways and demonstrated how far-reaching technology can be. Specifically, IT has come to the forefront of electronic commerce, distance education, and politics (consider social media and the 2020 elections). As you will see, we draw attention to IT's impact on the pandemic throughout this book.

This text focuses on the successful applications of IT in organizations; that is, how organizations can use IT to solve business problems and achieve competitive advantage in the marketplace. However, not all business problems can be solved with IT. Therefore, you must continue to develop your business skills!

When you graduate, either you will start your own business or you will work for an organization, whether it is public sector, private sector, for-profit, or not-for-profit. Your organization will have to survive and compete in an environment that has been radically transformed by information technology. This environment is global, massively interconnected, intensely competitive, 24/7/365, real-time, rapidly changing, and information-intensive. To compete successfully, your organization must use IT effectively.

As you read this chapter and this text, keep in mind that the information technologies you will learn about are important to businesses of all sizes. No matter which area of business you major in, which industry you work for, or the size of your company, you will benefit from learning about IT. Who knows? Maybe you will use the tools you learn about in this class to make your great idea a reality by becoming an entrepreneur and starting your own business!

The modern environment is intensely competitive not only for your organization, but for you as well. You must compete with human talent from around the world. Therefore, you personally will have to make effective use of IT.

Accordingly, this chapter begins with a discussion of three reasons why you should become knowledgeable about IT. Next, it distinguishes among data, information, and knowledge, and it differentiates computer-based information systems from application programs. Finally, it considers the impacts of information systems on organizations and on society in general.

1.1 Why Should I Study Information Systems?

Author Lecture Videos are available exclusively in *WileyPLUS*.
Apply the Concept activities are available in the Appendix and in *WileyPLUS*.

Your use of IT makes you part of the most connected generation in history: you have grown up online; you are, quite literally, never out of touch; you use more information technologies (in the form of digital devices) for more tasks; and you are bombarded with more information than any generation in history. The *MIT Technology Review* refers to you as *Homo conexus*. Information technologies are so deeply embedded in your lives that your daily routines would be almost unrecognizable to a college student just 20 years ago.

Essentially, you practice *continuous computing*, surrounded by a movable information network. This network is created by constant communication among the digital devices you carry and wear (for example: laptops, tablets, smartphones, and wearables); the wired and wireless networks that you access as you move about; and Web-based tools for finding information and communicating and collaborating with other people. Your network enables you to pull information about virtually anything from anywhere at any time, and to push your own ideas back to the Web, from wherever you are, via a mobile device. Think of everything you do online, often with your smartphone: register for classes; take classes (not just at your university); access class syllabi, information, PowerPoints, and lectures; research class papers and presentations; conduct banking; pay your bills; research, shop, and purchase products from companies and other people; sell your "stuff"; search for, and apply for, jobs; make your travel reservations (hotel, airline, rental car); create your own blog and post your own podcasts and videos to it; design your own page on Facebook and LinkedIn; make and upload videos to YouTube; take, edit, and print your own digital photographs; stream music and movies to your personal libraries; use RSS feeds to create your personal electronic newspaper; text and Tweet your friends and family throughout your day; send Snaps; order a ride from Uber or Lyft; track the location and arrival time of the next campus bus; select a place or room to rent on Airbnb; and many other activities. (*Note*: If any of these terms are unfamiliar to you, don't worry. You will learn about everything mentioned here in detail later in this text.)

Let's put the preceding paragraph in perspective. What would a typical day for you be like if you had no access to computing devices of any kind, including your phone? This scenario also means that you have no access to the Internet.

The Informed User—You!

So, the question is: Why should you learn about information systems and information technology? After all, you can comfortably use a computer (or other electronic devices) to perform many activities, you have been surfing the Web for years, and you feel confident that you can manage any IT application that your organization's MIS department installs. Let's look at three reasons why you should learn about ISs and IT.

MIS The first reason to learn about information systems and information technology is to become an **informed user**; that is, a person knowledgeable about ISs and IT. In general, informed users obtain greater value from whichever technologies they use. You will enjoy many benefits from being an informed user of IT, including:

- You will benefit more from your organization's IT applications because you will understand what is "behind" those applications (see **Figure 1.1**). That is, what you see on your computer screen is brought to you by your MIS department, who are operating "behind" your screen.

FIGURE 1.1   **MIS provides what users see and use on their computers.**

iStock.com/Slawomir Fajer

- You will be in a position to enhance the quality of your organization's IT applications with your input.
- Even as a new graduate, you will quickly be in a position to recommend—and perhaps to help select—which IT applications your organization will use.
- Being an informed user will keep you abreast of both new information technologies and rapid developments in existing technologies. Remaining "on top of things" will help you to anticipate the impacts that "new and improved" technologies will have on your organization and to make recommendations regarding the adoption and use of these technologies.
- You will understand how using IT can improve your organization's performance and teamwork as well as your own productivity.
- If you have ideas of becoming an entrepreneur, then being an informed user will help you to utilize IT when you start your own business.

The second reason to learn about ISs and IT is that the organization you join will undoubtedly be undergoing a digital transformation. In fact, digital transformation has become one of the most important strategies for organizations. A December 2019 survey by *Forbes* magazine noted that 70 percent of companies surveyed had a digital transformation strategy in place or were working on such a strategy, and 27 percent of companies stated that digital transformation was a matter of survival.

Digital transformation is the business strategy that leverages IT to dramatically improve employee, customer, and business partner relationships; to support continuous improvement in business operations and business processes; and to develop new business models and businesses. The information technologies that drive digital transformation include:

- Big Data (see Chapter 5);
- Business Analytics (see Chapter 12);
- Broadband Internet access (see Chapter 6);
- Mobile Computing (see Chapter 8);
- The Internet of Things (see Chapter 8);
- Social Computing (see Chapter 9);
- Agile Systems Development methods (see Chapter 13);
- Cloud Computing (see Technology Guide 3);
- Artificial Intelligence (see Chapter 14);

You see examples of digital transformation throughout this chapter. In fact, IT's About Business 1.1 shows how broadband Internet access and mobile computing transformed the country of Vietnam.

The third reason to learn about ISs and IT is that managing the IS function within an organization is no longer the exclusive responsibility of the IS department. Rather, users now play key roles in every step of this process. The overall objective in this text is to provide you with the necessary information to contribute immediately to managing the IS function in your organization. In short, our goal is to help you become a very informed user!

IT Offers Career Opportunities

MIS Because IT is vital to the operation of modern businesses, it offers many employment opportunities. The demand for traditional IT staff—programmers, business analysts, systems analysts, and designers—is substantial. In addition, many well-paid jobs exist in areas such as the Internet and electronic commerce (e-commerce), mobile commerce (m-commerce), network security, telecommunications, and multimedia design.

The IS field includes the people in various organizations who design and build information systems, the people who use those systems, and the people responsible for managing those systems. At the top of the list is the chief information officer (CIO).

The CIO is the executive in charge of the IS function. In most modern organizations, the CIO works with the chief executive officer (CEO), the chief financial officer (CFO), and other senior

IT's About Business 1.1

MIS **FIN** **MKT** The Digital Transformation of Vietnam

The Problem

In 1975, Vietnam reunified after having been at war for 30 years. At that time, the country was isolated from the international community due to the Cold War, and it faced a U.S. economic embargo. As a result, it was one of the poorest countries in the world. By the mid-1980s, Vietnam's per capita gross domestic product (GDP) was only between $200 and $300. The country's economy exhibited small-scale production, low labor productivity, and insufficient supplies of food and consumer goods.

The Solution

In 1986, the Vietnamese government began to transition from its highly centralized, planned economy to a market-based economy. The government decided to maintain some centralized government planning but also provide free market incentives, such as encouraging people to establish private businesses.

These reforms also helped to transform the country's telecommunications industry, which was the key technological driver behind Vietnam's digital transformation. From 1945 until 1985, the Communist Party had controlled the country's telecommunications industry. In this capacity it restricted access to telecommunications services to high-ranking government officials.

Vietnam's telecommunications transformation occurred slowly. As late as 1995 the country had only 3.8 telephones per 100 people. Furthermore, the Vietnamese people had to pay 3–4 times more than average global telecommunications prices for telecom services. Further, the government continued to restrict competition from foreign telecommunications companies.

In the early 2000s, Vietnam finally began to encourage foreign investment in the development of its telecommunications infrastructure. Specifically, the government designated Siemens, a German-based multinational corporation, to build the entire Vietnamese microwave system. The government also increased the number of primary telecommunications links across the country, and it ensured that all provinces were connected to Vietnam's three major cities—Hanoi, Da Nang, and Ho Chi Minh City (formerly Saigon), with fiber-optic cable and microwave links.

Following these developments, mobile networks began to emerge. Today, the five major companies in Vietnam's mobile market are Viettel Mobile, MobiFone, VinaPhone, VietnamMobile, and Gmobile.

A modern telecommunications infrastructure is changing the way the Vietnamese people conduct business, manufacture goods, entertain themselves, shop, manage their finances, and communicate. Let's take a closer look at five businesses that have benefited from Vietnam's digital transformation: Appota, Tiki, Skinlosophy, and Timo.

Appota

Founded in 2011, Appota (**www.appota.com**) is one of the top three game publishers in Vietnam. The firm has developed an e-wallet for gaming purchases, and its apps include a Wi-Fi password-sharing facility, a book reader, news, movies, comics, and other forms of entertainment. The company also has a business-to-business advertising group, and it is planning to expand its mobile payments operations.

Appota took advantage of the rapid growth of smartphones in Vietnam by operating only in the mobile space. The company has more than 50 million users and more than 5 million monthly active users.

Appota's next venture was to develop physical products that function via smartphones. For example, in 2019 the company launched a smart lock, operated by an app, that secures everything from front doors to suitcases.

Tiki

Tiki (**http://tiki.vn**), launched in 2010, is an online bookseller that specializes in English-language titles. Today, the firm is one of the top electronic-commerce platforms in Vietnam as well as the fastest growing. Tiki's growth has paralleled the rapid expansion of electronic commerce in Vietnam. Each month, Tiki ships 4.5 million items from a large selection of consumer goods. Tiki's best sellers are consumer electronics. In addition, sales of lifestyle and fashion products are increasing rapidly.

With an average of 17 million monthly customer visits, logistics is critical. Tiki maintains 33 warehouses in 13 cities, and it offers its customers a two-hour delivery option. However, although many Vietnamese people are moving to cities, almost two-thirds of the population still lives in rural areas. Delivery to remote areas typically takes longer and costs more.

Tiki's customers currently pay for more than half of their purchases with cash on delivery. The company wants digital payments to become more widely adopted. Digital payments enable sellers to be paid more quickly. In addition, Tiki delivery personnel do not have to handle cash. Fortunately for Tiki, the use of e-wallets is expanding at 28 percent per year in Vietnam, so the number of digital transactions will continue to grow.

Skinlosophy

As recently as 2010, Vietnam's beauty market had two major types of brands. The first type—international brands—consisted of sophisticated, science-based, well-designed, packaged, and marketed beauty products. The second type consisted of homegrown Vietnamese beauty products. Skinlosophy (http://skinlosophy.vn) is working to combine the benefits of both types by using scientific processes to purify herbal ingredients traditionally grown in Asia. The firm's traditional ingredients include green tea, red ginseng, silk, and lingzhi mushrooms.

Skinlosophy designs their products for use in Vietnam's hot, humid climate. Their products are dry to the touch, do not clog pores, and "feel nonexistent on the skin." Their most popular products are cleansers, acne remedies, and skin formulas. Significantly, 80 percent of the firm's sales are online, primarily to professional women between the ages of 22 and 30. By May 2020 Skinlosophy employed 20 people and sold, on average, more than 1,000 products per week.

Timo

Opened in 2016, Timo (http://timo.vn) was Vietnam's first digital bank. Timo Hangouts serve as bank branches. Instead of a traditional branch with tellers, however, Hangouts have coffee shops and are used to open accounts or simply to meet with friends. By May 2020 Timo had more than 500,000 customers.

Timo is appealing to consumers for several reasons. First, nearly every transaction, including money transfers, payments, making a deposit or a withdrawal, and managing accounts, can be done remotely through the bank's mobile app. Customers need to meet a Timo Care Representative in person at a Hangout only when they open an account. Second, Timo provides nearly all of its services for free. Finally, customers can conveniently buy insurance products and invest directly through the app.

The Results

Vietnam's population in 2020 was 97 million with an average age of 31. In May 2020, the country had 66 million Internet users for a market penetration of 68 percent. Moreover, 96 percent of users accessed the Internet via mobile devices.

The development of Vietnam's telecommunications infrastructure has increased Internet access for its citizens and has been the key to the rapid development of Vietnam's digital economy. According to analysts, 88 percent of urban and 38 percent of rural households now have digital access. Further, 95 percent of Vietnam's urban population owns a smartphone, as do 69 percent of the country's rural population.

In 2019, Vietnam's GDP had grown to $255 billion. In early 2020, the country's per capita GDP had increased dramatically from $200 to $300 to more than $6,000. By early 2020, more than 45 million people had risen out of poverty as the country developed industries that spanned textiles, agriculture, furniture, plastics, paper, tourism, and telecommunications.

Vietnam has evolved into one of the most digital of all economies in Southeast Asia. In May 2020, the country's digital economy was valued at USD $12 billion. Further, it was the second fastest-growing digital economy in the region after Indonesia. Analysts estimate that by 2025 the value of the country's digital economy will reach USD $43 billion.

Further, in May 2020, Vietnam's mobile e-commerce market value exceeded $3 billion. A 2019 report by Google and the Mobile Marketing Association identified Vietnam as a "mobile-first market" with more than 51 million smartphones, representing more than 80 percent of the population aged 15 and older. Further, network coverage is extensive. The Vietnamese population has access to 3G (third-generation wireless) and 4G (fourth-generation wireless) even in rural and mountainous areas.

Unfortunately, the news is not all positive, as digital technologies can be used to monitor citizens. Vietnam's government has been widely criticized for its surveillance of citizens and restrictions on freedom of speech. In fact, the Vietnamese government's approach to human rights and privacy is questionable. Press freedom is one of the worst in the world, and the government increasingly monitors Vietnamese citizens online.

For example, the Vietnamese government arrested blogger Nguyen Ngoc Nhu Quynh on October 10, 2016, and sentenced her to 10 years in prison. The government contended that she conducted "anti-State propaganda."

Nguyen was known by her blogging pseudonym Me Nam, which translates to "Mother Mushroom." Her blog was often critical

of the government, and it addressed such issues as land confiscation, freedom of speech, and police brutality. In October 2018 Nguyen arrived in the United States, where she had been granted asylum following her release from prison in Vietnam.

Sources: S. Lazarus, "How New Technology Is Transforming Vietnam's Economy," *CNN*, April 6, 2020; S. Lazarus, "Vietnamese Beauty Brand Skinlosophy Fuses Tradition with Technology," *CNN Style*, March 25, 2020; "Vietnam Takes a Leap in Digital Transformation with Foreign Participation," *Vietnam.net Global*, January 6, 2020; "Vietnam Internet Statistics 2019," *Vnetwork.vn*, November 11, 2019; "The World Bank in Vietnam: Overview," *The World Bank*, October 18, 2019; "How Much Do Our Wardrobes Cost to the Environment," *The World Bank*, September 23, 2019; "Vietnam's Digital Bank Timo Celebrates Its Third Birthday," *Fintechnews Vietnam*, June 28, 2019; E. McKirdy, "'Stalinist' Vietnamese Cybersecurity Law Takes Effect, Worrying Rights Groups ad Online Campaigners," *CNN*, January 2, 2019; "E-Commerce Payments Trends: Vietnam," *J.P. Morgan Global Payment Trends*, 2019; "The State of Mobile in Rural Vietnam Report," *Google and the Mobile Marketing Association*, 2019; "Vietnamese Economic Outline," *Santander Trade Markets*, 2019; "e-Conomy SEA 2018: Southeast Asia's Internet Economy Hits an Inflection Point," *Google-Temasek*, November 2018; E. McKirdy, "Vietnamese Activist 'Mother Mushroom' Freed from Prison, Granted Asylum in the U.S.," *CNN*, October 18, 2018; P. Vanham, "The Story of Vietnam's Economic Miracle," *World Economic Forum*, September 11, 2018; S. Ray, "Vietnam and Its Telecom Sector: How the Country Answered the Call for Reform," *Yourstory.com*, November 16, 2017; E. McKirdy, "Vietnamese Blogger Mother Mushroom Jailed for 10 Years," *CNN*, June 29, 2017; J. Hookway, "Vietnam's Mobile Revolution Catapults Millions into the Digital Age," *The Wall Street Journal*, June 12, 2015.

Questions

1. Information technologies do not always lead transformation in organizations (or countries).
   a. Explain how the policies of the Vietnamese government led to the digital transformation of the country.
   b. Consider the Royal Spirit Group's DBW factory. Provide examples of both technological and nontechnological initiatives that drove the factory's sustainable operations.
   c. Consider Appota, Tiki, Skinlosophy, and Timo. Did technological initiatives drive each company's success? If so, provide examples of such initiatives for each company.

2. Explain how the development of the telecommunications infrastructure (fiber-optic cables and wireless) was a key driver of the country's digital transformation.

3. Why was Vietnam's digital transformation a strategic necessity for the country? Consider examples from the country's economic development in your answer.

executives. Therefore, he or she actively participates in the organization's strategic planning process. In today's digital environment, the IS function has become increasingly strategic within organizations. As a result, although most CIOs still rise from the IS department, a growing number are coming up through the ranks in the business units (e.g., marketing, finance). Regardless of your major, you could become the CIO of your organization one day. This is another reason to be an informed user of information systems!

Table 1.1 provides a list of IT jobs, along with a description of each one. For further details about careers in IT, see **www.linkedin.com**, **www.computerworld.com/category/careers/**, and **www.monster.com**.

Career opportunities in IS are strong and are projected to remain strong over the next 10 years. The *U.S. News & World Report* listed its "25 best jobs of 2020" and Glassdoor listed its

TABLE 1.1   Information Technology Jobs

Position	Job Description
Chief Information Officer	Highest-ranking IS manager; responsible for all strategic planning in the organization
IS Director	Manages all systems throughout the organization and the day-to-day operations of the entire IS organization
Information Center Manager	Manages IS services such as help desks, hotlines, training, and consulting
Applications Development Manager	Coordinates and manages new systems development projects
Project Manager	Manages a particular new systems development project
Systems Analyst	Interfaces between users and programmers; determines information requirements and technical specifications for new applications
Operations Manager	Supervises the day-to-day operations of the data and/or computer center
Programming Manager	Coordinates all applications programming efforts
Social Media Manager	Coordinates all social media development efforts and all social media monitoring and response efforts
Business Analyst	Focuses on designing solutions for business problems; interfaces closely with users to demonstrate how IT can be used innovatively
Systems Programmer	Creates the computer code for developing new systems software or maintaining existing systems software
Applications Programmer	Creates the computer code for developing new applications or maintaining existing applications
Emerging Technologies Manager	Forecasts technology trends; evaluates and experiments with new technologies
Network Manager	Coordinates and manages the organization's voice and data networks
Database Administrator	Manages the organization's databases and oversees the use of database-management software
Auditing or Computer Security Manager	Oversees the ethical and legal use of information systems
Webmaster	Manages the organization's website
Web Designer	Creates websites and pages

"50 best jobs in America for 2020." Glassdoor (**www.glassdoor.com**) is a website where current and former employees anonymously review companies. Let's take a look at these rankings. (Note that the rankings differ because the magazine and Glassdoor used different criteria in their research.) As you can see, jobs suited for MIS majors appear in both lists, many of them quite high. The job rankings are as follows:

U.S. News & World Report (out of 25)

#1 Software Developer

#12 IT Manager

#23 Web Developer

Glassdoor (out of 50)

#1 User Interface Designer	#26 Business Analyst
#2 Java Developer	#27 Systems Engineer
#3 Data Scientist	#29 Scrum Master
#4 Product Manager	#32 Software Developer
#5 DevOps Engineer	#33 Cloud Engineer
#6 Data Engineer	#46 Automation Engineer
#7 Software Engineer	#49 Network Engineer
#18 Applications Engineer	

Not only do IS careers offer strong job growth, but the pay is excellent as well. The Bureau of Labor Statistics, an agency within the Department of Labor that is responsible for tracking and analyzing trends relating to the labor market, notes that the median salary in 2019 for "computer and information systems managers" was approximately $146,360, and predicted that the profession would grow by an average of 11 percent per year through 2026.

In addition, LinkedIn analyzed thousands of profiles of members who graduated between 2018 and 2019. LinkedIn collected salary information using the LinkedIn Salary tool. It discovered that of the 10 highest-paying entry-level jobs, 7 were in the technology industry. These jobs include:

Job	Median Starting Salary
#1 Data Scientist	$95,000
#2 Software Engineer	$90,000
#6 User Experience Designer	$73,000
#7 IT Consultant	$72,000
#8 Java Developer	$72,000
#9 Systems Engineer	$70,000
#10 Software Developer	$68,600

Managing Information Resources

Managing information systems in modern organizations is a difficult, complex task. Several factors contribute to this complexity. First, information systems have enormous strategic value to organizations. Firms rely on them so heavily that, in some cases, when these systems are not working (even for a short time), the firm cannot function. (This situation is called "being hostage to information systems.") Second, information systems are very expensive to acquire, operate, and maintain.

A third factor contributing to the difficulty in managing information systems is the evolution of the management information systems (MIS) function within the organization. When businesses first began to use computers in the early 1950s, the MIS department "owned" the only computing resource in the organization: the mainframe. At that time, end users did not interact directly with the mainframe.

MIS In contrast, in the modern organization, computers are located in all departments, and almost all employees use computers in their work. This situation, known as *end user computing*, has led to a partnership between the MIS department and the end users. The MIS department now acts as more of a consultant to end users, viewing them as customers. In fact, the main function of the MIS department is to use IT to solve end users' business problems.

MIS As a result of these developments, the responsibility for managing information resources is now divided between the MIS department and the end users. This arrangement raises several important questions. Which resources are managed by whom? What is the role of the MIS department, its structure, and its place within the organization? What is the appropriate relationship between the MIS department and the end users? Regardless of who is doing what, it is essential that the MIS department and the end users work in close cooperation.

There is no standard way to divide responsibility for developing and maintaining information resources between the MIS department and the end users. Instead, that division depends on several factors: the size and nature of the organization, the amount and type of IT resources, the organization's attitudes toward computing, the attitudes of top management toward computing, the maturity level of the technology, the amount and nature of outsourced IT work, and even the countries in which the company operates. Generally speaking, the MIS department is responsible for corporate-level and shared resources, and the end users are responsible for departmental resources. **Table 1.2** identifies both the traditional functions and various new, consultative functions of the MIS department.

So, where do the end users come in? Take a close look at Table 1.2. Under the traditional MIS functions, you will see two functions for which you provide vital input: managing systems development and infrastructure planning. Under the consultative MIS functions, in contrast, you exercise the primary responsibility for each function, while the MIS department acts as your advisor.

TABLE 1.2 The Changing Role of the Information Systems Department

Traditional Functions of the MIS Department

Managing systems development and systems project management

- As an end user, you will have critical input into the systems development process. You will learn about systems development in Chapter 13.

Managing computer operations, including the computer center

Staffing, training, and developing IS skills

Providing technical services

Infrastructure planning, development, and control

- As an end user, you will provide critical input about the IS infrastructure needs of your department.

New (Consultative) Functions of the MIS Department

Initiating and designing specific strategic information systems

- As an end user, your information needs will often mandate the development of new strategic information systems.

You will decide which strategic systems you need (because you know your business needs and requirements better than the MIS department does), and you will provide input into developing these systems.

Incorporating the Internet and electronic commerce into the business

- As an end user, you will be primarily responsible for effectively using the Internet and electronic commerce in your business. You will work with the MIS department to accomplish these tasks.

Managing system integration, including the Internet, intranets, and extranets

- As an end user, your business needs will determine how you want to use the Internet, your corporate intranets, and extranets to accomplish your goals. You will be primarily responsible for advising the MIS department on the most effective use of the Internet, your corporate intranets, and extranets.

Educating non-MIS managers about IT

- Your department will be primarily responsible for advising the MIS department on how best to educate and train your employees about IT.

Educating the MIS staff about the business

- Communication between the MIS department and business units is a two-way street. You will be responsible for educating the MIS staff on your business, its needs and requirements, and its goals.

Partnering with business unit executives

- Essentially, you will be in a partnership with the MIS department. You will be responsible for seeing that this partnership is one "between equals" and ensuring its success.

Managing outsourcing

- Outsourcing is driven by business needs. Therefore, the outsourcing decision resides largely with the business units (i.e., with you). The MIS department, working closely with you, will advise you on technical issues such as communications bandwidth and security.

Proactively using business and technical knowledge to see innovative ideas about using IT

- Your business needs will often drive innovative ideas about how to effectively use information systems to accomplish your goals. The best way to bring these innovative uses of IS to life is to partner closely with your MIS department. Such close partnerships have amazing synergies!

Creating business alliances with business partners

- The needs of your business unit will drive these alliances, typically along your supply chain. Again, your MIS department will act as your advisor on various issues, including hardware and software compatibility, implementing extranets, communications, and security.

Before you go on...

1. Rate yourself as an informed user. (Be honest; this isn't a test!)
2. Explain the benefits of being an informed user of information systems.
3. Discuss the various career opportunities offered in the IT field.

1.2 Overview of Computer-Based Information Systems

Organizations refer to their management information systems functional area by several names, including the MIS Department, the Information Systems (IS) Department, the Information Technology (IT) Department, and the Information Services Department. Regardless of the name, however, this functional area deals with the planning for—and the development, management, and use of—information technology tools to help people perform all the tasks related to information processing and management. Recall that **information technology** relates to any computer-based tool that people use to work with information and support the information and information-processing needs of an organization.

As previously stated, an **information system** collects, processes, stores, analyzes, and disseminates information for a specific purpose. The purpose of information systems has been defined as getting the right information to the right people, at the right time, in the right amount, and in the right format. Because information systems are intended to supply useful information, we need to differentiate between information and two closely related terms: data and knowledge (see **Figure 1.2**).

Data items refer to an elementary description of things, events, activities, and transactions that are recorded, classified, and stored but are not organized to convey any specific meaning. Data items can be numbers, letters, figures, sounds, and images. Examples of data items are collections of numbers (e.g., 3.11, 2.96, 3.95, 1.99, 2.08) and characters (e.g., B, A, C, A, B, D, F, C).

Information refers to data that have been organized so that they have meaning and value to the recipient. For example, a grade point average (GPA) by itself is data, but a student's name coupled with his or her GPA is information. The recipient interprets the meaning and draws conclusions and implications from the information. Consider the examples of data provided in the preceding paragraph. Within the context of a university, the numbers could be grade point averages, and the letters could be grades in an Introduction to MIS class.

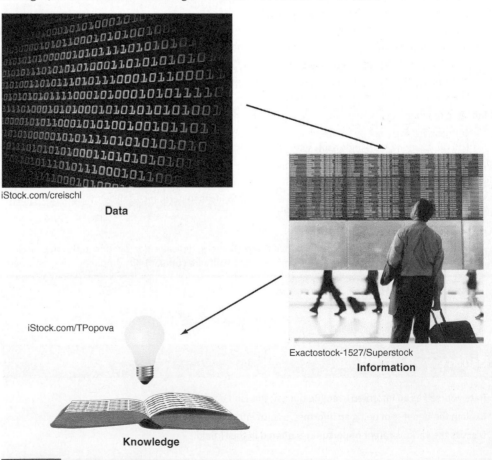

iStock.com/creischl
Data

iStock.com/TPopova

Exactostock-1527/Superstock
Information

Knowledge

 FIGURE 1.2   **Data, information, and knowledge.**

Knowledge consists of data and/or information that have been organized and processed to convey understanding, experience, accumulated learning, and expertise as they apply to a current business problem. For example, suppose that a company recruiting at your school has found over time that students with grade point averages over 3.0 have experienced the greatest success in its management program. Based on this accumulated knowledge, that company may decide to interview only those students with GPAs over 3.0. This is an example of knowledge because the company utilizes information—GPAs—to address a business problem—hiring successful employees. As you can see from this example, organizational knowledge, which reflects the experience and expertise of many people, has great value to all employees.

Consider this example:

Data	Information	Knowledge
[No context]	[University context]	
3.16	3.16 + John Jones = GPA	* Job prospects
2.92	2.92 + Sue Smith = GPA	* Graduate school prospects
1.39	1.39 + Kyle Owens = GPA	* Scholarship prospects
3.95	3.95 + Tom Elias = GPA	

Data	Information	Knowledge
[No context]	[Professional baseball pitcher context]	
3.16	3.16 + Corey Kluber = ERA	
2.92	2.92 + Chris Sale = ERA	* Keep pitcher, trade pitcher, or send pitcher to minor leagues
1.39	1.39 + Clayton Kershaw = ERA	* Salary/contract negotiations
3.95	3.95 + Shane Bieber = ERA	

GPA = Grade point average (higher is better)

ERA = Earned run average (lower is better); ERA is the number of runs per nine innings that a pitcher surrenders.

You see that the same data items with no context can have entirely different meanings in different contexts.

Now that you have a clearer understanding of data, information, and knowledge, let's shift our focus to computer-based information systems. As you have seen, these systems process data into information and knowledge that you can use.

A **computer-based information system (CBIS)** is an information system that uses computer technology to perform some or all of its intended tasks. Although not all information systems are computerized, today most are. For this reason the term "information system" is typically used synonymously with "computer-based information system." The basic components of computer-based information systems are listed below. The first four are called **information technology components**. **Figure 1.3** illustrates how these four components interact to form a CBIS.

- **Hardware** consists of devices such as the processor, monitor, keyboard, and printer. Together, these devices accept, process, and display data and information.
- **Software** is a program or collection of programs that enable the hardware to process data.
- A **database** is a collection of related files or tables containing data.
- A **network** is a connecting system (wireline or wireless) that enables multiple computers to share resources.
- **Procedures** are the instructions for combining the above components to process information and generate the desired output.
- *People* use the hardware and software, interface with it, or utilize its output.

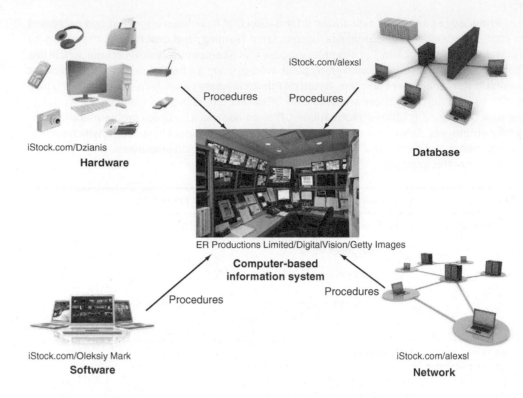

iStock.com/Dzianis
Hardware

iStock.com/alexsl

Procedures   Procedures

ER Productions Limited/DigitalVision/Getty Images
Computer-based information system

Database

iStock.com/Oleksiy Mark
Software

Procedures   Procedures

iStock.com/alexsl
Network

FIGURE 1.3 Computer-based information systems consist of hardware, software, databases, networks, procedures, and people.

Figure 1.4 illustrates how these components are integrated to form the wide variety of information systems found within an organization. Starting at the bottom of the figure, you see that the IT components of hardware, software, networks (wireline and wireless), and databases form the **information technology platform**. IT personnel use these components to develop information systems, oversee security and risk, and manage data. These activities cumulatively are called **information technology services**. The IT components plus IT services comprise the organization's **information technology infrastructure**. At the top of the pyramid are the various organizational information systems.

Computer-based information systems have many capabilities. **Table 1.3** summarizes the most important ones.

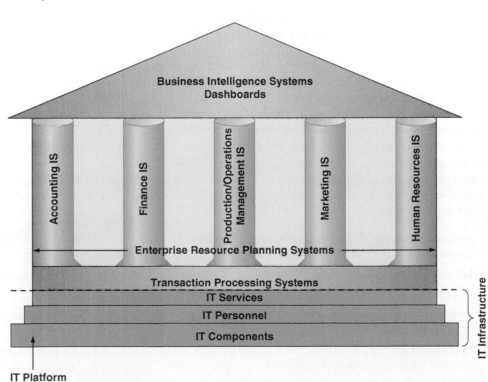

Business Intelligence Systems
Dashboards

Accounting IS
Finance IS
Production/Operations Management IS
Marketing IS
Human Resources IS

Enterprise Resource Planning Systems

Transaction Processing Systems
IT Services
IT Personnel
IT Components

IT Infrastructure

IT Platform

FIGURE 1.4 Information technology inside your organization.

TABLE 1.3   **Major Capabilities of Information Systems**

Perform high-speed, high-volume numerical computations.
Provide fast, accurate communication and collaboration within and among organizations.
Store huge amounts of information in an easy-to-access yet small space.
Allow quick and inexpensive access to vast amounts of information worldwide.
Analyze and interpret vast amounts of data quickly and efficiently.
Automate both semiautomatic business processes and manual tasks.

Information systems perform these various tasks via a wide spectrum of applications. An **application** (or **app**) is a computer program designed to support a specific task or business process. (A synonymous term is **application program**.) Each functional area or department within a business organization uses dozens of application programs. For instance, the human resources department sometimes uses one application for screening job applicants and another for monitoring employee turnover. The collection of application programs in a single department is usually referred to as a **departmental information system** (also known as a **functional area information system (FAIS)**). For example, the collection of application programs in the human resources area is called the human resources information system (HRIS). There are collections of application programs—that is, departmental information systems—in the other functional areas as well, such as accounting, finance, marketing, and production/operations.

The importance of information systems cannot be understated. In fact, a 2016 report from the Software Alliance shows that information systems added more than *$1 trillion of value* to the United States gross domestic product.

Types of Computer-Based Information Systems

Modern organizations employ many different types of information systems. Figure 1.4 illustrates the different types of information systems that function *within* a single organization, and **Figure 1.5** shows the different types of information systems that function *among* multiple

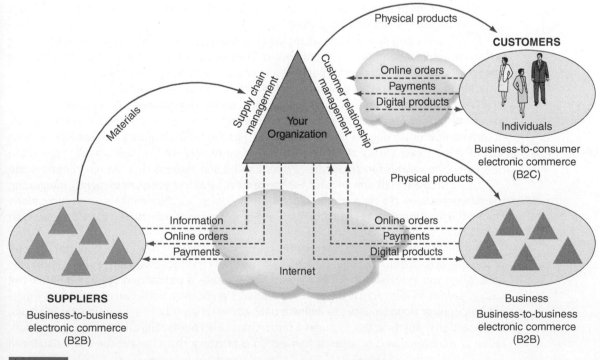

FIGURE 1.5   **Information systems that function among multiple organizations.**

organizations. You will study transaction processing systems, management information systems, and enterprise resource planning systems in Chapter 10. You will learn about customer relationship management (CRM) systems in Chapter 11 and supply chain management (SCM) systems in Chapter 11.

In the next section you will learn about the numerous and diverse types of information systems employed by modern organizations. You will also read about the types of support these systems provide.

Breadth of Support of Information Systems   Certain information systems support parts of organizations, others support entire organizations, and still others support groups of organizations. This section addresses all of these systems.

Recall that each department or functional area within an organization has its own collection of application programs, or information systems. These functional area information systems are the supporting pillars for the information systems located at the top of Figure 1.4, namely, business intelligence systems and dashboards. As the name suggests, each FAIS supports a particular functional area within the organization. Examples are accounting IS, finance IS, production/operations management (POM) IS, marketing IS, and human resources IS.

ACCT **FIN** Consider these examples of IT systems in the various functional areas of an organization. In finance and accounting, managers use IT systems to forecast revenues and business activity, to determine the best sources and uses of funds, and to perform audits to ensure that the organization is fundamentally sound and that all financial reports and documents are accurate.

MKT In sales and marketing, managers use information technology to perform the following functions:

- *Product analysis*: Developing new goods and services
- *Site analysis*: Determining the best location for production and distribution facilities
- *Promotion analysis*: Identifying the best advertising channels
- *Price analysis*: Setting product prices to obtain the highest total revenues

Marketing managers also use IT to manage their relationships with their customers.

POM In *manufacturing*, managers use IT to process customer orders, develop production schedules, control inventory levels, and monitor product quality. They also use IT to design and manufacture products. These processes are called *computer-assisted design (CAD)* and *computer-assisted manufacturing (CAM)*.

HRM Managers in *human resources* use IT to manage the recruiting process, analyze and screen job applicants, and hire new employees. They also employ IT to help employees manage their careers, to administer performance tests to employees, and to monitor employee productivity. Finally, they rely on IT to manage compensation and benefits packages.

Two information systems that support the entire organization, **enterprise resource planning (ERP) systems** and transaction processing systems, are designed to correct a lack of communication among the functional area ISs. For this reason, Figure 1.4 shows ERP systems spanning the FAISs. ERP systems were an important innovation because organizations often developed the various functional area ISs as stand-alone systems that did not communicate effectively (if at all) with one another. ERP systems resolve this problem by tightly integrating the functional area ISs via a common database. In doing so, they enhance communications among the functional areas of an organization. For this reason, experts credit ERP systems with greatly increasing organizational productivity.

A **transaction processing system (TPS)** supports the monitoring, collection, storage, and processing of data from the organization's basic business transactions, each of which generates data. When you are checking out at Walmart, for example, a transaction occurs each time the cashier swipes an item across the bar code reader. Significantly, within an organization, different functions or departments can define a transaction differently. In accounting, for example, a transaction is anything that changes a firm's chart of accounts. The information system definition of a transaction is broader: a transaction is anything that changes the firm's database.

The chart of accounts is only part of the firm's database. Consider a scenario in which a student transfers from one section of an Introduction to MIS course to another section. This move would be a transaction to the university's information system, but not to the university's accounting department (the tuition would not change).

The TPS collects data continuously, typically in *real time*—that is, as soon as the data are generated—and it provides the input data for the corporate databases. TPSs are considered critical to the success of any enterprise because they support core operations. Significantly, nearly all ERP systems are also TPSs, but not all TPSs are ERP systems. In fact, modern ERP systems incorporate many functions that previously were handled by the organization's functional area information systems. You study both TPSs and ERP systems in detail in Chapter 10.

ERP systems and TPSs function primarily within a single organization. Information systems that connect two or more organizations are referred to as **interorganizational information systems (IOSs)**. IOSs support many interorganizational operations, of which *supply chain management* is the best known. An organization's **supply chain** is the flow of materials, information, money, and services from suppliers of raw materials through factories and warehouses to the end customers.

Note that the supply chain in Figure 1.5 shows physical flows, information flows, and financial flows. Digitizable products are those that can be represented in electronic form, such as music and software. Information flows, financial flows, and digitizable products go through the Internet, whereas physical products are shipped. For example, when you order a computer from **www.dell.com**, your information goes to Dell via the Internet. When your transaction is completed (that is, your credit card is approved and your order is processed), Dell ships your computer to you. (We discuss supply chains in more detail in Chapter 11.)

Electronic commerce (e-commerce) systems are another type of interorganizational information system. These systems enable organizations to conduct transactions, called business-to-business (B2B) electronic commerce, and customers to conduct transactions with businesses, called business-to-consumer (B2C) electronic commerce. Figure 1.5 illustrates B2B and B2C electronic commerce. Electronic commerce systems are so important that we discuss them in detail in Chapter 7, with additional examples interspersed throughout the text. IT's About Business 1.2 shows how various technologies have enabled Lemonade Insurance to grow rapidly via e-commerce.

IT's About Business 1.2

MIS **FIN** **Lemonade Disrupts the Insurance Industry**

Traditional insurance companies. The business model of insurance companies involves pooling (combining) funds from many insured entities to pay for the losses that some of the entities may incur. That is, insurers pool risk from individual entities and redistribute it across a larger group of entities. Insurers protect insured entities from risk for a fee, which is the insurance premium. The premium depends on the frequency with which an event might occur and the severity of that event.

The essential task of any insurer is to price risk and then charge the customer a premium for assuming that risk. When a customer files a claim, the company must process the claim, check it for accuracy, and submit payment. Before paying a claim, insurance companies use an adjusting process to filter out fraudulent claims and minimize the risk of loss to the company.

Most insurance companies generate revenue in three ways. First, they charge premiums in exchange for insurance coverage. Second, they reinvest those premiums into other investments. Finally, to save money, they keep their administrative expenses as low as possible. Unfortunately, the public often believes that traditional insurers try to save money by denying legitimate claims.

Some companies engage in reinsurance to reduce risk. *Reinsurance* is insurance that insurers purchase to protect themselves from excessive losses as a result of high exposure to a risk. Reinsurance is an integral component of insurance companies' efforts to avoid default due to excessive, unexpected payouts. For example, a hurricane makes landfall in Florida, causing billions of dollars in damages. An insurance company that sold many homeowners' policies might not be able to cover the losses. Instead, that company spreads parts of the coverage to other insurance companies (reinsurance), thereby spreading the cost of risk among many insurance companies.

Lemonade. Launched in 2015, Lemonade Insurance Company (**www.lemonade.com**) is a U.S. property and casualty insurance company that offers renters and home insurance policies for homes, apartments, co-ops, and condominiums. The company operates in 26 states and Washington, D.C., as well as in Germany and the Netherlands. Lemonade is a regulated insurance carrier, meaning that the firm must maintain cash reserves equal to at least a third of its revenue.

Lemonade acts as an insurance carrier rather than a broker. An *insurance carrier* is the company that holds your insurance policy. In contrast, *insurance brokers* work directly with clients to help find policies that meet their needs. *Insurance underwriters* evaluate risks and decide the specific terms and costs associated with those policies.

Acting as a carrier means that Lemonade does not sell policies backed by traditional insurers the way competitors Hippo (**www.hippo.com**) and Jetty (**www.jetty.com**) do. Rather, the insurer retains claim liabilities on its own balance sheet. The firm underwrites its own policies and is reinsured at Lloyd's of London.

Lemonade uses technology in developing its electronic commerce business model. Using artificial intelligence algorithms, a desktop and mobile app, and behavioral economics, Lemonade is disrupting the traditional insurance industry. The company delivers insurance policies and handles claims using chatbots. The chatbot guides customers through the application process by asking a series of questions and producing a quote very quickly. A *chatbot* is a software application that conducts an online chat conversation with a customer via text or text-to-speech instead of direct contact with a human agent. (We discuss chatbots in Chapter 7.)

Lemonade uses its algorithms to approve applicants, price risk, and determine whether a claim should be paid, all without human involvement. (Lemonade states that it pays 30 percent of its claims this way.) If a claim is not instantly approved, then a human claims representative reviews it. Lemonade's technologies enable the company to offer policies at a very low price. For example, renters' insurance starts at $5 per month, and homeowners' insurance starts at $25 per month.

Demonstrating the value of its algorithms, Lemonade paid one customer's claim for his stolen Canada Goose parka in three seconds. That was the time that it took Lemonade's claims algorithms to run 18 antifraud algorithms and send bank instructions to deposit $729 in the man's account.

Lemonade's business model is paperless and has no brokers, and is low-cost, easy to interact with, and trustworthy. The insurer's model differs from those of traditional insurance companies in that the insurer takes 25 percent of insurance premium revenue for administrative costs and potential profits. The company uses the other 75 percent to pay customer claims, purchase reinsurance (lessening some risk), and pay taxes and fees. They donate any remaining funds from the 75 percent (called leftover premiums) to charities that customers choose in the firm's annual Giveback program. As of May 2020 the Giveback program was partnering with almost 100 nonprofit organizations.

Lemonade maintains that its Giveback program is designed to solve the conflicts of interest that are inherent in traditional insurance. Every dollar that insurance companies pay out in claims is a dollar less to their bottom line. According to Lemonade, this fact creates distrust between insurers and their customers. By introducing charities into its model, Lemonade contends that it has changed its customers' incentives. That is, if they file false claims, they are not hurting an insurance company, but a charitable cause that they selected.

Significantly, the Giveback program has elicited fascinating customer behavior. Even after their claims have been paid, some Lemonade customers contact the firm to admit that their goods have been found and they want to return the money. They cite Giveback as their motivation.

Lemonade has also rewritten the insurance policy itself. Similar to the policies of traditional insurers, the firm's original policy was 40 pages long and difficult to understand. Lemonade's Policy 2.0 provides their customers with a clear and easy way to understand what their policy does and does not cover.

Interestingly, Lemonade has open-sourced its policy on GitHub (**http://github.com**), a web-based platform for version control. This site simplifies the process of working with other people and makes it easy to collaborate on projects. Anyone, from state legislators, to consumer advocacy groups, to Lemonade competitors, to interested customers, can make edits and contributions to the policy. Lemonade retains final control of this process.

Like all insurance companies, Lemonade must conform to certain regulations. Much of the language in typical insurance policies is legally required to be in the document. As a result, Lemonade is working with regulators to allow Policy 2.0 to be sold, and that process differs from state to state and country to country.

At the end of 2017, Lemonade's loss ratio—the amount it pays in claims divided by the premiums it collects—was an unsustainable 166 percent, compared to 65–70 percent for large insurers. Two years later, this ratio had dropped to 73 percent. The reason for the decline was that Lemonade had collected increasing amounts of customer data, which it utilized to refine its algorithms.

By May 2020 Lemonade claimed a 0.1 percent share of the combined homeowners' and renters' insurance markets, compared with 19 percent for State Farm and 10 percent for Allstate, according to data from 17 states collected by the Insurance Information Institute. Although a tiny company, on the crowdsourced insurance company review site Clearsurance (**www.clearsurance.com**), Lemonade ranked second in customer satisfaction for renters' insurance, behind only USAA. By May 2020 the startup had received $480 million in several rounds of funding, and financial analysis firm Demotech (**www.demotech.com**) rated Lemonade's financial stability as A-Exceptional.

It is important to note that while Lemonade promises speed and convenience, traditional insurance companies do not tend to draw out the claims process. Furthermore, although Lemonade can offer great prices, customers can also find competitive prices at traditional insurers. The price of insurance depends on many factors, so it is important to obtain quotes from multiple insurers before you decide on a company.

Sources: Compiled from M. Gallo, "Lemonade Review: We Tested an Insurance Company Designed for People Who Hate to Talk on the Phone," *Chicago Tribune*, May 18, 2020; M. High, "How Is Digital Technology Disrupting Insurtech?" *FinTech Magazine*, May 4, 2020; M. High, "Next Generation Financial Services: Technology and Disruption," *FinTech Magazine*, April 28, 2020; "Lemonade Launches in the Netherlands," *Bloomberg*, April 2, 2020; A. Aziz, "The Power of Purpose: How Lemonade Is Disrupting Insurance with Goodness (and a New Foundation)," *Forbes*, March 9, 2020; J. Crook, "Lemonade Is Getting into Pet Insurance," *TechCrunch*, February 4, 2020; C. Morris, "Americans Will Spend $75 Billion on Their Pets This Year," *Fortune*, December 16, 2019; S. Ross, "What Is the Main Business Model for Insurance Companies?," *Investopedia.com*, June 25, 2019; J. Kauflin and K. Stoller, "Brokers Begone," *Forbes*, May 31, 2019; A. Simpson, "Lemonade Proposes Open Source Insurance Policy for All to Change, Adopt," *Insurance Journal*, May 21, 2018; J. Crook, "Lemonade Wants to Rewrite the Insurance Policy Itself," *TechCrunch*, May 16, 2018; L. Howard, "Insurance Flipsides: Countering the Industry's Negative Perception Problem," *Insurance Journal*, May 10, 2018; S. Jenks, "Pet Insurance Is the Latest Work Perk," *New York Times*, June 7, 2017; **www.lemonade.com**, accessed May 25, 2020.

Questions

1. Discuss some of the problems with traditional insurance companies that Lemonade is trying to solve.

2. Provide three examples of how Lemonade uses information technologies to develop and support its business model.

3. What steps should traditional insurance companies take to compete with Lemonade? Provide examples to support your answer.

Support for Organizational Employees   So far, you have concentrated on information systems that support specific functional areas and operations. Now you will learn about information systems that typically support particular employees within the organization.

Clerical workers, who support managers at all levels of the organization, include bookkeepers, secretaries, electronic file clerks, and insurance claim processors. *Lower-level managers* handle the day-to-day operations of the organization, making routine decisions such as assigning tasks to employees and placing purchase orders. *Middle managers* make tactical decisions, which deal with activities such as short-term planning, organizing, and control.

Knowledge workers are professional employees such as financial and marketing analysts, engineers, lawyers, and accountants. All knowledge workers are experts in a particular subject area. They create information and knowledge, which they integrate into the business. Knowledge workers, in turn, act as advisors to middle managers and executives. Finally, *executives* make decisions that deal with situations that can significantly change the manner in which business is conducted. Examples of executive decisions are introducing a new product line, acquiring other businesses, and relocating operations to a foreign country.

Functional area information systems summarize data and prepare reports, primarily for middle managers, but sometimes for lower-level managers as well. Because these reports typically concern a specific functional area, report generators (RPGs) are an important type of functional area IS.

Business analytics (BA) systems (also known as **business intelligence (BI) systems**) provide computer-based support for complex, nonroutine decisions, primarily for middle managers and knowledge workers. (They also support lower-level managers, but to a lesser extent.) These systems are typically used with a data warehouse, and they enable users to perform their own data analysis. You will learn about BA systems in Chapter 12.

Expert systems (ESs) attempt to duplicate the work of human experts by applying reasoning capabilities, knowledge, and expertise within a specific domain. They have become valuable in many application areas, primarily but not exclusively areas involving decision making. For example, navigation systems use rules to select routes, but we do not typically think of these systems as expert systems. Significantly, expert systems can operate as stand-alone systems or be embedded in other applications. We examine ESs in greater detail in Chapter 14.

Dashboards (also called **digital dashboards**) are a special form of IS that support all managers of the organization. They provide rapid access to timely information and direct access to structured information in the form of reports. Dashboards that are tailored to the information needs of executives are called *executive dashboards*. Chapter 12 provides a thorough discussion of dashboards.

Table 1.4 provides an overview of the different types of information systems used by organizations.

TABLE 1.4   **Types of Organizational Information Systems**

Type of System	Function	Example
Transaction processing system	Processes transaction data from terminal	Walmart checkout point-of-sale business events
Enterprise resource planning	Integrates all functional areas of the organization	Oracle, SAP system
Functional area IS	Supports the activities within a specific functional area	System for processing payroll
Decision support system	Provides access to data and analysis tools	"What-if" analysis of changes in budget
Expert system	Mimics human expert in a particular area and makes decisions	Credit card approval analysis
Dashboards	Present structured, summarized information about aspects of business important to executives	Status of sales by product
Supply chain management system	Manages flows of products, services, and information among organizations	Walmart Retail Link system connecting suppliers to Walmart
Electronic commerce system	Enables transactions among organizations and between organizations and customers	www.dell.com

Before you go on...

1. What is a computer-based information system?
2. Describe the components of computer-based information systems.
3. What is an application program?
4. Explain how information systems provide support for knowledge workers.
5. As we move up the organization's hierarchy from clerical workers to executives, how does the type of support provided by information systems change?

1.3   How Does IT Impact Organizations?

Author Lecture Videos are available exclusively in *WileyPLUS*.
Apply the Concept activities are available in the Appendix and in *WileyPLUS*.

Throughout this text you will encounter numerous examples of how IT affects various types of organizations. These examples will make you aware of just how important IT actually is to organizations. In fact, for the vast majority of organizations, if their information systems fail, then they cease operations until the problems are found and fixed. Consider the following examples.

- Bluelink (**http://bluelink.org**) is a technology company that develops mobile apps designed to register, organize, and mobilize voters. During the 2020 Iowa Democratic caucuses, the company's app (IowaReporterApp) failed. As a result, the results of the caucuses were delayed as officials had to manually count the votes.

- In November 2019 a British Airways software problem caused pilots to be unable to file their flight plans. The outage led to delays that snowballed into cancellations, affecting flights to and from London's Gatwick and Heathrow airports. Pilots were forced to plot their courses on old-fashioned charts and thousands of passengers were stuck on the ground for up to 24 hours before the system was restored.

This section provides an overview of the impact of IT on modern organizations. As you read this section, you will learn how IT will affect you as well.

IT Impacts Entire Industries

As of mid-2020, the technology required to transform industries through software had been developed and integrated and could be delivered globally. In addition, software tools and Internet-based services enabled companies in many industries to launch new software-powered startups without investing in new infrastructure or training new employees. For example, in 2000, operating a basic Internet application cost businesses approximately $150,000 per month. By mid-2020, operating that same application in Amazon's cloud could cost as little as $100 per month, depending on the amount of data traffic to and from the website. (We discuss cloud computing in Technology Guide 3.)

In essence, software is impacting every industry, and every organization must prepare for these impacts. Let's examine a few examples of software disruption across several industries. Many of these examples focus on two scenarios: (1) industries where software disrupted the previous market-leading companies and (2) industries where a new company (or companies) used software to achieve a competitive advantage.

The Book Industry.   In mid-2020, the largest book publisher and bookseller in the United States was Amazon, a software company. Amazon's core capability is its software engine, which can sell virtually anything online without building or maintaining any retail stores. Now even books themselves have become software products, known as electronic (or digital) books, or e-books. In 2020, physical books accounted for approximately 81 percent of total book sales, and electronic books accounted for approximately 19 percent of total book sales. Keep in mind that electronic book sales increased from 0 percent in 1994 when Amazon was founded to 19 percent 26 years later.

Interestingly, according to the 2018 Academic Student Ebook Experience Survey, 74 percent of respondents said that they preferred print books when reading for pleasure. Furthermore, 68 percent said that they preferred print books for assigned readings.

The Music Industry. Total U.S. album sales peaked at 785 million in 2000, which was the year after Napster was created. Napster was a service that allowed anyone with a computer and a reasonably fast Internet connection to download and trade music for free. From 2000 to 2018, the major music labels (companies) worked diligently to eliminate illegal downloading and sharing, begun by Napster in 2001. Despite these efforts, however, album sales continued to decline.

However, by 2019 music fans had shifted from illegal downloads to paid streaming platforms such as Spotify (**www.spotify.com**), Apple Music (**www.music.apple.com**), Amazon Prime (**www.amazon.com**), and Pandora (**www.pandora.com**), which generally charge $5 to $10 per month for unlimited access to millions of songs. Even though the record labels receive only about 0.3 cents each time a song is streamed, these small amounts are significant. In 2019, the global record industry reported revenues of $21.5 billion, with streaming generating $11.4 billion.

The Video Industry. Blockbuster—which rented and sold videos and ancillary products through its chain of stores—was the industry leader until it was disrupted by a software company, Netflix (**www.netflix.com**). By the first quarter, 2020, Netflix had the largest global subscriber base of any video service, with 167 million subscribers. Meanwhile, Blockbuster declared bankruptcy in February 2011 and was acquired by satellite television provider Dish Network (**www.dish.com**) a month later. In May 2020, only one Blockbuster store—located in Bend, Oregon—was still open.

MIS **The Software Industry.** Incumbent software companies such as Oracle and Microsoft are increasingly threatened by software-as-a-service (SaaS) products—for example, Salesforce (**www.salesforce.com**) and Android, an open-source operating system. (We discuss operating systems in Technology Guide 2 and SaaS in Technology Guide 3.)

The Video Game Industry. Today, the fastest growing entertainment companies are video game makers—again, software. Examples are Zynga (**www.zynga.com**), the creator of FarmVille; Rovio (**www.rovio.com**), the maker of Angry Birds; and Minecraft (**www.minecraft .net**), now owned by Microsoft (**www.microsoft.com**).

The Photography Industry. Software disrupted this industry years ago. Today it is virtually impossible to buy a mobile phone that does not include a software-powered camera. In addition, people can upload photos automatically to the Internet for permanent archiving and global sharing. Leading photography companies include Instagram (**www.instagram .com**), Shutterfly (**www.shutterfly.com**), Snapfish (**www.snapfish.com**), and Flickr (**www .flickr.com**). Meanwhile, Kodak, the longtime market leader—whose name was almost synonymous with cameras—declared bankruptcy in January 2012.

MKT **The Marketing Industry.** Today's largest direct marketing companies include Facebook (**www.facebook.com**), Google (**www.google.com**), and Amazon (**www.amazon .com**). All of these companies are using software to disrupt the retail marketing industry.

HRM **The Recruiting Industry.** LinkedIn (**www.linkedin.com**) is disrupting the traditional job-recruiting industry. For the first time, employees and job searchers can maintain their résumés on a publicly accessible website that interested parties can search in real time.

FIN **The Financial Services Industry.** Software has transformed the financial services industry. Practically every financial transaction—for example, buying and selling stocks—is now performed by software. Also, many of the leading innovators in financial services are software companies. See our discussion of FinTech in Chapter 7.

The Motion Picture Industry. The process of making feature-length computer-generated films has become incredibly IT intensive. Studios require state-of-the-art information technologies, including massive numbers of servers, sophisticated software, and an enormous amount of storage (all described in Technology Guide 1).

Consider DreamWorks Animation (**www.dreamworks.com**), a motion picture studio that creates animated feature films, television programs, and online virtual worlds. For a single motion picture, the studio manages more than 500,000 files and 300 terabytes (a terabyte is 1 trillion bytes) of data, and it uses about 80 million central processing unit (CPU; described in Technology Guide 1) hours. As DreamWorks executives state, "In reality, our product is data that looks like a movie. We are a digital manufacturing company."

Software is also disrupting industries that operate primarily in the physical world. Consider these examples:

- *The Automobile Industry*: In modern cars, software is responsible for running the engine, controlling safety features, entertaining passengers, guiding drivers to their destinations, and connecting the car to mobile, satellite, and GPS networks. Other software functions include Wi-Fi receivers, which turn your car into a mobile hot spot; software, which helps maximize fuel efficiency; and ultrasonic sensors, which enable some models to parallel park automatically.

  The next step is to network all vehicles together, a necessary step toward the next major breakthrough: self-driving or driverless cars. Google, Tesla (**www.tesla.com**), Apple, and all of the major automobile companies are now developing driverless vehicles.

- *The Agriculture Industry*: Agriculture is increasingly powered by software, including satellite analysis of soils linked to per-acre seed-selection software algorithms. In addition, precision agriculture makes use of automated, driverless tractors controlled by global positioning systems (GPS) and software. *Precision agriculture* is an approach to farm management that uses information technology to ensure that crops receive exactly what they need—for example, water, fertilizer, and pesticides—for optimum health and productivity. (See IT's About Business 1.3.)

- *The Fashion Industry*: Women have long "borrowed" special-occasion dresses from department stores, buying them and then returning them after wearing them for one evening. Now, Rent the Runway (**www.renttherunway.com**) has redefined the fashion business, making expensive clothing available to more women than ever before. The firm is also disrupting traditional physical retailers. After all, why buy a dress when you can rent one for a very low price? Some department stores feel so threatened by Rent the Runway that they have reportedly told vendors that they will remove floor merchandise if it ever shows up on that company's website.

- *The Legal Profession*: Today, electronic discovery (e-discovery) software applications can analyze documents in a fraction of the time that human lawyers would take, at a fraction of the cost. For example, Blackstone Discovery (**www.blackstonediscovery.com**) helped one company analyze 1.5 million documents for less than $100,000. That company estimated that the process would have cost $1.5 million had it been performed by lawyers.

  Law firms are now beginning to use a new artificial intelligence software package called ROSS (**www.rossintelligence.com**). For example, law firm BakerHostetler has hired ROSS to serve as a legal researcher in bankruptcy cases. In May 2020 ROSS offered its full set of features, unlimited searches, and access to its entire database of U.S. federal and state cases for prices starting at $69 per month per user.

IT Reduces the Number of Middle Managers

HRM IT makes managers more productive, and it increases the number of employees who can report to a single manager. Thus, IT ultimately decreases the number of managers and experts. It is reasonable to assume, therefore, that in coming years organizations will have fewer managerial levels and fewer staff and line managers. If this trend materializes, promotional opportunities will decrease, making promotions much more competitive. Bottom line: pay attention in school!

IT Changes the Manager's Job

One of the most important tasks of managers is making decisions. A major consequence of IT has been to change the manner in which managers make their decisions. In this way, IT ultimately has changed managers' jobs.

IT often provides managers with near-real-time information, meaning that managers have less time to make decisions, making their jobs even more stressful. Fortunately, IT also provides many tools—for example, business analytics applications such as dashboards, search engines, and intranets—to help managers handle the volumes of information they must deal with on an ongoing basis.

So far in this section, we have been focusing on managers in general. Now let's focus on you. Due to advances in IT, you will increasingly supervise employees and teams who are geographically dispersed. Employees can work from anywhere at any time, and teams can consist of employees who are literally dispersed throughout the world. Information technologies such as telepresence systems (discussed in Chapter 6) can help you manage these employees even though you do not often see them face-to-face. For these employees, electronic or "remote" supervision will become the norm. Remote supervision places greater emphasis on completed work and less emphasis on personal contacts and office politics. You will have to reassure your employees that they are valued members of the organization, thereby diminishing any feelings they might have of being isolated and "out of the loop."

Will IT Eliminate Jobs?

One major concern of every employee, part-time or full-time, is job security. Relentless cost-cutting measures in modern organizations often lead to large-scale layoffs. Put simply, organizations are responding to today's highly competitive environment by doing more with less. Regardless of your position, then, you consistently will have to add value to your organization and make certain that your superiors are aware of this value.

Many companies have responded to difficult economic times, increased global competition, demands for customization, and increased consumer sophistication by increasing their investments in IT. In fact, as computers continue to advance in terms of intelligence and capabilities, the competitive advantage of replacing people with machines is increasing rapidly. This process frequently leads to layoffs. At the same time, however, IT creates entirely new categories of jobs, such as electronic medical record-keeping and nanotechnology.

IT Impacts Employees at Work

Many people have experienced a loss of identity because of computerization. They feel like "just another number" because computers reduce or eliminate the human element present in non-computerized systems.

The Internet threatens to exert an even more isolating influence than have computers and television. Encouraging people to work and shop from their living rooms could produce some unfortunate psychological effects, such as depression and loneliness.

HRM **IT Impacts Employees' Health and Safety.**   Although computers and information systems are generally regarded as agents of "progress," they can adversely affect individuals' health and safety. In fact, the average American worker spends seven hours per day in front of some type of screen (consider laptops, tablets, smartphones, computers, and televisions). Let's consider two issues associated with IT: job stress and long-term use of the keyboard.

An increase in an employee's workload and/or responsibilities can trigger *job stress*. Although computerization has benefited organizations by increasing productivity, it also has created an ever-expanding workload for some employees. Some workers feel overwhelmed and have become increasingly anxious about their job performance. These feelings of stress and anxiety can actually diminish rather than improve workers' productivity while jeopardizing their physical and mental health. Management can help alleviate these problems by providing training, redistributing the workload among workers, and hiring more workers.

On a more specific level, the long-term use of keyboards can lead to *repetitive strain injuries* such as backaches and muscle tension in the wrists and fingers. *Carpal tunnel syndrome* is a particularly painful form of repetitive strain injury that affects the wrists and hands.

Designers are aware of the potential problems associated with the prolonged use of computers. To address these problems, they continually attempt to design a better computing environment. The science of designing machines and work settings that minimize injury and illness is called *ergonomics*. The goal of ergonomics is to create an environment that is safe, well lit, and comfortable. Examples of ergonomically designed products are antiglare screens that alleviate problems of fatigued or damaged eyesight and chairs that contour the human body to decrease backaches. **Figure 1.6** displays some sample ergonomic products.

HRM **IT Provides Opportunities for People with Disabilities.** Computers can create new employment opportunities for people with disabilities by integrating speech-recognition and vision-recognition capabilities. For example, individuals who cannot type can use a voice-operated keyboard, and individuals who cannot travel can work at home.

Going further, adaptive equipment for computers enables people with disabilities to perform tasks they normally would not be able to do. For example, the Web and graphical user interfaces (GUIs; e.g., Windows) can be difficult for people with impaired vision to use. To address this problem, manufacturers have added audible screen tips and voice interfaces, which essentially restore the functionality of computers to the way it was before GUIs became standard.

Other devices help improve the quality of life in more mundane, but useful, ways for people with disabilities. Examples are a two-way writing telephone, a robotic page turner, a hair brusher, and a hospital-bedside video trip to the zoo or the museum. Several organizations specialize in IT designed for people with disabilities.

Media Bakery

Media Bakery

Media Bakery

Media Bakery

FIGURE 1.6 **Ergonomic products protect computer users.**

1.4 | Importance of Information Systems to Society

This section explains in greater detail why IT is important to society as a whole. Other examples of the impact of IT on society appear throughout the text.

> **Author Lecture Videos** are available exclusively in *WileyPLUS*.
> **Apply the Concept** activities are available in the Appendix and in *WileyPLUS*.

IT Affects Our Quality of Life

IT has significant implications for our quality of life. The workplace can be expanded from the traditional 9-to-5 job at a central location to 24 hours a day at any location. IT can provide employees with flexibility that can significantly improve the quality of leisure time, even if it doesn't increase the total amount of leisure time.

From the opposite perspective, however, IT also can place employees on "constant call," which means they are never truly away from the office, even when they are on vacation. In fact, surveys reveal that the majority of respondents take their laptops and smartphones on their vacations, and 100 percent take their cell phones. Going further, the majority of respondents did some work while vacationing, and almost all of them checked their e-mail regularly.

The Robot Revolution Is Here Now

Once restricted largely to science fiction, robots that can perform practical tasks are now a reality. Two major types of robot are industrial robots and collaborative robots, or cobots.

An *industrial robot* is an automated, programmable machine used in manufacturing operations. Applications for industrial robots include welding, painting, assembly, disassembly, packaging and labeling, palletizing, and many others. *Collaborative robots*, or *cobots*, are machines designed to be used in collaborative applications where there are interactions with humans within a shared space. Applications for cobots include providing information in public spaces, transporting materials and products within a building, inspection of goods, patrolling perimeters, securing facilities, and many others. Now let's look at the differences between the two types.

POM **Industrial robots versus cobots.**   Cobots are designed to work alongside human employees, while industrial robots perform work in place of those employees. A cobot can assist employees with work that may be too dangerous, strenuous, or tedious for them to accomplish on their own. This assistance can create a safer, more efficient workplace without eliminating factory jobs. In contrast, industrial robots are used to automate the manufacturing process almost entirely without human help on the manufacturing floor. This process can free employees for more meaningful tasks that are less mundane and less prone to repetitive-motion injuries.

Cobots are also more easily programmable than industrial robots because they are capable of "learning" on the job. A factory worker can re-program a cobot simply by moving the cobot's arms along a desired path. At that point, the cobot will "remember" the new movement and be able to repeat it on its own. Industrial robots cannot be so easily reprogrammed and require an engineer to write new software for any changes in the process that the robot is to perform.

Industrial robots are designed for heavy manufacturing, while cobots are designed for light manufacturing. Industrial robots require safety cages to keep humans out of the workspace, while cobots are safe enough to function around people and do not require the same type of safety infrastructure that industrial robots require. Last but certainly not least, industrial robots are much more expensive ($100,000 to $150,000) than cobots ($35,000 to $50,000).

Cobots have become increasingly common on factory floors, in hospital corridors, and in farm fields. Amazon Robotics is an excellent example of cobots in a distribution center.

Traditionally, companies moved goods around their distribution centers with human-operated conveyors or with human-operated machines such as forklifts. That is, orders would enter the distribution center and humans would locate, pick, and pack the items for shipment.

Amazon Robotics, formerly Kiva Systems, reversed the process with cobots. In the new approach, the company stores items on portable storage units. When an order enters the company database, software locates the closest cobot to the item and directs it to retrieve that item. The cobots navigate around the distribution center by following bar code stickers on the floor. Each cobot has sensors that read the bar codes and prevent collisions. When the cobot reaches the correct storage unit, it slides underneath it and lifts it off the ground through a corkscrew action. The cobot then carries the storage units to a human operator who picks the item(s).

The bottom line with this system is that, rather than humans going to the items, the cobots bring the items to the humans. The system is much more efficient and accurate than the traditional one.

Drones.   A *drone* is an unmanned aerial vehicle (UAV) (a flying robot, if you will) that either is controlled by pilots from the ground or autonomously follows a preprogrammed mission. Commercial drones function in a variety of business purposes, in contrast to drones used by hobbyists for recreational purposes.

An interesting use of drones is in the fight against deforestation. A good example of this process is in Yangon, Myanmar, where Dendra Systems (**www.dendra.io**) is working with a non-profit organization called Worldview International Foundation (**http://wif.foundation**) to plant mangrove saplings. Dendra, formerly BioCarbon Engineering, is a startup company that makes drones to plant trees and grasses.

Drones first fly over the area to be planted, map it, and collect data about the topography and soil conditions. Dendra integrates these data with satellite data of the area and determines the best locations to plant seeds. Once the company analyzes the data, drones fire biodegradable pods filled with germinated seeds and nutrients into the ground at the preselected locations. Over the next months, drones fly over the planted areas and monitor how the mangroves are growing.

Autonomous Vehicles.   An autonomous, or self-driving, car (essentially a robot car) is a vehicle that is capable of sensing its environment and moving safely to its destination with little or no human input. When you think about autonomous vehicles, consider these statistics:

- Human error accounts for more than 90 percent of automobile accidents.
- Each year more than 6 million vehicle accidents are reported to law enforcement.
- In 2019, a total of 38,800 Americans and 1.35 million people worldwide died in automobile accidents.
- The average car in the United States is used two hours per day, which is only 8 percent of the time. Therefore, a car owner owns a rapidly depreciating asset that is idle the vast majority of the time.

These statistics offer compelling reasons for autonomous vehicles, and the development of these vehicles is proceeding rapidly. Leading autonomous vehicle companies are Waymo (**www.waymo.com**), GM Cruise (**https://getcruise.com**), and Ford Autonomous (**www.ford.com**).

There is some bad news, however. Several fatalities have been reported with Tesla automobiles on full autopilot (self-driving mode). Whether these deaths were caused by the automobiles is under investigation.

It probably will be a long time before we see robots making decisions by themselves, handling unfamiliar situations, and interacting with people. Nevertheless, robots are extremely helpful in various environments, particularly those that are repetitive, harsh, or dangerous to humans. Consider the use of robots in hospitals during the COVID-19 pandemic.

The Emergence of Cognitive Computing: IBM Watson

MIS IBM Watson (**www.ibm.com/watson**) is a suite of enterprise-ready artificial intelligence services, applications, and software tools. Watson integrates advanced natural language processing, information retrieval, knowledge representation and reasoning, and machine learning technologies in order to answer open-domain (general) questions. IBM has labeled the type of processing demonstrated by Watson as *cognitive computing*. Watson has four primary capabilities:

- The ability to understand human language, with all of its nuance and ambiguity;
- The ability to learn and absorb information;
- The ability to formulate hypotheses;
- The ability to understand the context of a question.

By mid-2020, organizations in at least 20 industries were using Watson in a variety of applications. IT's About Business 1.3 illustrates how a number of technologies, including robots, drones, autonomous vehicles, and artificial intelligence, are transforming the agriculture industry.

IT's About Business 1.3

POM The Agriculture Industry's Transformations

Global agriculture, critical to all of us, is a $5 trillion industry. In addition, the increasing global population is placing ever greater demands on agriculture.

Agriculture has experienced transformations throughout its history. The first transformation was the introduction of mechanized agriculture, which began during the Industrial Revolution of the 19th century. Farm mechanization is the process of using powered machinery to perform farm jobs previously carried out by humans and animals. As a result, farming productivity increased markedly while becoming much less labor intensive.

The second agricultural transformation, called the Green Revolution, dates to the 1950s and 1960s. During this period agriculture benefitted from new chemical fertilizers and synthetic herbicides and pesticides. The chemical fertilizers provided crops with extra nutrients, and the herbicides and pesticides controlled weeds, killed insects, and prevented diseases. Also during this period, scientists used genetic modification to develop high-yield crops. As a result of these innovations, agricultural productivity again rapidly increased.

The third agricultural transformation, *precision agriculture*, is a process designed to apply the precise and correct amounts of inputs such as water, fertilizer, pesticides, and herbicides at the correct time in the correct place to maximize crop yields. This process also targets environmental impacts and has become critical to sustainable agriculture.

Precision agriculture uses a number of technologies such as global positioning systems (GPS; see Chapter 8), digital imagery (see Chapter 6), sensors (see Chapter 8), robotics, drones, autonomous vehicles, and artificial intelligence (we discuss these last four technologies in Chapter 14). Communications among these technologies uses fifth-generation (5G) wireless technology (see Chapter 8), expected to be widely deployed by 2020. Let's examine these technologies.

Global positioning systems. GPS allow farmers to construct precise maps of their fields. These maps enable farmers to accurately navigate to specific locations in their fields to collect soil samples or to monitor various crop conditions.

Digital imagery. Precision agriculture uses geospatial technologies—for example, images from satellites and drones integrated with GPS coordinates—to map specific areas that vary in crop and soil conditions. Farmers can then match inputs—water, seed, fertilizer, herbicides, and pesticides—to those areas by applying them at variable rates. *Variable-rate technology* is the process of applying these inputs in precise amounts at precise locations across a field without manually changing the settings on the equipment or having to make multiple passes over a field.

These specific areas in fields are depicted with zone maps and prescription maps. Zone maps display the difference between healthy and stressed plants by representing the amount of light they are reflecting. Prescription maps tell farmers how much input to apply to each small area of a field. Precision farming has become so precise that farmers today are able to treat individual plants.

Sensors. A sensor is a device that detects or measures and then records a physical property. In agriculture, sensors help farmers monitor and optimize crops and keep up with changing environmental factors. In essence, sensors enable farmers to understand their crops at a very small scale. Drones and farm equipment can carry sensors, and farmers can place stationary sensors in and around their fields.

Sensors measure various soil properties such as chemical composition, compactness, and temperatures at various depths. Environmental sensors measure air temperature, rainfall, leaf wetness, wind speed and direction, dew point temperature, solar radiation, and atmospheric pressure. Animal sensors enable farmers to identify each cow and to track each cow's activity level, health, and the optimal time for breeding.

Robotics. A wide variety of robots are being utilized in precision agriculture. Let's take a look at some of them.

- A robot named TerraSentia navigates a field by generating laser pulses to scan its environment. The robot produces a detailed map of a field, from the size and health of the plants to the number and quality of ears each corn plant will produce by the end of the season. The robot also measures plant height, stem diameter, and the total number of grain- and fruit-producing plants.

- Agrobot (**www.agrobot.com**) uses imaging technology to assess a strawberry's ripeness before it harvests the particular fruit.

- The Oz weeding robot by Naio Technologies has a camera capable of identifying weeds that sprout between rows of crops like broccoli and cauliflower. One machine replaces 11 workers.

- A robot from Abundant Robotics (**www.abundantrobotics.com**) recognizes when an apple is ready for harvesting and then picks the apple without bruising the fruit.

- In a processing plant, a pair of robots have arms that end with a round suction head. They grip five-pound packages of shredded lettuce and place them into boxes moving along a conveyor belt. Next, larger robots lift and stack the filled boxes.

- Robots can be equipped with sensors for pest control. When the robot detects a concentration of insects that exceeds the critical limit (typically set by the insecticide manufacturer), it sprays the affected area.

Drones. An agricultural drone is an unmanned aerial vehicle used to help optimize farming operations, increase crop production, and monitor crop health and growth. Drones carry sensors and digital cameras that provide farmers with a detailed picture of their fields. Specifically, drones can perform soil and field analysis, plant seeds, monitor crops, spray crops (down to individual plants), map crops precisely, and monitor irrigation and livestock.

Autonomous vehicles. GPS systems and artificial intelligence are underlying technologies for autonomous (self-driving) farm equipment such as tractors, combines, and harvesters. Although self-driving is the ultimate goal, as of May 2020 the equipment still required a human driver. If farming machinery were to become fully autonomous and be equipped with precisely accurate maps of fields, it could then function on a continuous (24/7/365) basis without a human operator.

One company, Bear Flag (**www.bearflagrobotics.com**), is developing autonomous tractors. The firm is integrating sensors and software into existing equipment from major manufacturers to allow farmers to automate many of their most common tasks, such as spraying and mowing in orchards.

Artificial intelligence (AI). Precision agriculture generates vast amounts of data, which AI helps to analyze. Let's look at an example.

In 2016, IBM bought the Weather Company and then integrated that firm's weather data into its IBM Watson Decision Platform for Agriculture. (We discuss IBM Watson in the next section.) The platform analyzes data from satellite imagery and from sensors on farm equipment that monitor seed counts, nutrient levels, and fertilizer flow, among other variables of interest to farmers. The system provides hyperlocal—meaning a very small geographical area—six-month weather predictions based on satellite and atmospheric conditions. The system also provides management models for corn, soybeans, wheat, barley, and other crops.

The platform furnishes farmers with a dashboard of controls. For instance, a farmer inspecting field conditions can take an image from a smartphone, upload it to the decision platform, and receive a diagnosis of crop health along with suggested remedies if needed.

And the result of these agricultural transformations? In 1800, about 90 percent of the U.S. workforce was involved with agriculture. By 1900, that number had declined to just under 40 percent. Today, 1 percent of American workers are in agriculture.

Significantly, despite the rapid decline in the number of U.S. workers employed in agriculture, agricultural productivity has vastly increased. In 1800, one farmer could produce slightly more food than was needed to support a family. By 1930, each farmer produced enough food to feed about 26 people. In the 1960s, each farmer was able to feed about 155 people. Today, each farmer can feed 265 people.

Sources: Compiled from L. Calderone, "Satellite Imaging for Agriculture," *Agritech Tomorrow*, April 23, 2020; J. de Koff, "Beginner's Guide to Agricultural Drones," *Future Farming*, April 14, 2020; "How to Improve Farm Productivity with Satellite Technology in 2020," *AgPro*, February 27, 2020; K. Sheikh, "A Growing Presence on the Farm," *New York Times*, February 13, 2020; A. Meola, "Smart Farming in 2020: How IoT Sensors Are Creating a More Efficient Precision Agriculture Industry," *Business Insider*, January 24, 2020; P. Melgares, "Robots, Drones Becoming Workhorses for Agriculture," *AgFax*, January 3, 2020; S. Verma, "5 Unparalleled Advantages Offered by IoT to Farming Business," *Data Science Central*, November 13, 2019; J. Wilson, "How High Tech Is Transforming One of the Oldest Jobs: Farming," *New York Times*, September 6, 2019; K. Sheikh, "A New Way to Fight Crop Diseases, with a Smartphone," *New York Times*, July 30, 2019; K. Walch, "How AI Is Transforming Agriculture," *Forbes*, July 5, 2019; V. Kuprenko, "IoT in Agriculture: Why It Is a Future of Connected Farming World," *The IoT Magazine*, June 21, 2019; L. Bandoim, "How Self-Driving Tractors and AI Are Changing Agriculture," *Forbes*, April 27, 2019; T. Maddox, "Agriculture 4.0," *TechRepublic*, December 12, 2018; M. Jordan, "As Immigrant Farmworkers Become More Scarce, Robots Replace Humans," *New York Times*, November 20, 2018.

Questions

1. We addressed eight technologies that are transforming the agriculture industry. Provide examples of how these technologies work together synergistically in this transformation.

2. Discuss the impact of the transformation of the agriculture industry as our planet's population continues to increase. Provide examples to support your answer.

IT Impacts Health Care

IT has brought about major improvements in health care delivery. Medical personnel use IT to make better and faster diagnoses and to monitor critically ill patients more accurately. IT has also streamlined the process of researching and developing new drugs. Expert systems now help doctors diagnose diseases, and machine vision is enhancing the work of radiologists. Surgeons use virtual reality to plan complex surgeries. They also employ surgical robots to perform long-distance surgery. Finally, doctors discuss complex medical cases via videoconferencing. New computer simulations re-create the sense of touch, allowing doctors-in-training to perform virtual procedures without risking harm to an actual patient.

Information technology can be applied to improve the efficiency and effectiveness of healthcare. Among the thousands of other health care applications, administrative systems are critically important. These systems perform functions ranging from detecting insurance fraud to creating nursing schedules to performing financial and marketing management.

The Internet contains vast amounts of useful medical information. Despite the fact that this information exists on the Internet, physicians caution against self-diagnosis. Rather, people should use diagnostic information obtained from Google and medical websites such as WebMD (**www.webmd.com**) only to ask questions of their physicians.

One of the earliest applications of IBM Watson was in the field of medicine. Watson is able to analyze vast amounts of medical data and provide insights.

Although some health data are structured—for example, blood pressure readings and cholesterol counts—the vast majority are unstructured. These data include textbooks, medical journals, patient records, and nurse and physician notes. In fact, modern medicine entails so much unstructured data that their rapid growth has surpassed the ability of health care practitioners to keep up. IBM emphasizes that Watson is *not* intended to replace health care professionals. Rather, its purpose is to assist them in avoiding medical errors and fine-tuning their medical diagnoses.

By mid-2020, Watson had digested millions of medical and scientific articles as well as information from thousands of clinical trials collected form clinicaltrials.gov, the federal government's public database. Watson can read, and remember, patient histories, monitor the latest drug trials, examine the potency of new therapies, and closely follow state-of-the-art guidelines that help doctors choose optimal treatments for their patients. Watson can also analyze images such as magnetic resonance imaging (MRI) scans and radiographs (X-rays). To exploit these capabilities, two top-ranked hospitals are collaborating with Watson in the field of oncology (cancer care): Memorial Sloan Kettering (**www.mskcc.org**) and the Mayo Clinic (**www.mayoclinic.org**).

Before you go on...

1. What are some of the quality-of-life improvements made possible by IT? Has IT had any negative effects on our quality of life? If so, then explain, and provide examples.

2. Describe the robotic revolution, and consider its implications for humans. How do you think robotics will affect your life in the future?

3. Explain how IT has improved health care practices. Has the application of IT to health care created any problems or challenges? If so, then explain, and provide examples.

What's in IT for me?

In Section 1.2, we discussed how IT supports each of the functional areas of the organization. Here we examine the MIS function.

MIS For the MIS Major

The MIS function directly supports all other functional areas in an organization. That is, the MIS function is responsible for providing the information that each functional area needs in order to make decisions. The overall objective of MIS personnel is to help users improve performance and solve business problems using IT. To accomplish this objective, MIS personnel must understand both the information requirements and the technology associated with each functional area. Given their position, however, they must think "business needs" first and "technology" second.

Summary

1.1 Identify the reasons why being an informed user of information systems is important in today's world.

The benefits of being an informed user of IT include the following:

- You will benefit more from your organization's IT applications because you will understand what is "behind" those applications.
- You will be able to provide input into your organization's IT applications, thus improving the quality of those applications.
- You will quickly be in a position to recommend or to participate in the selection of IT applications that your organization will use.
- You will be able to keep up with rapid developments in existing information technologies, as well as the introduction of new technologies.
- You will understand the potential impacts that "new and improved" technologies will have on your organization. Consequently, you will be qualified to make recommendations concerning their adoption and use.
- You will play a key role in managing the information systems in your organization.
- You will be in a position to use IT if you decide to start your own business.

1.2 Describe the various types of computer-based information systems in an organization.

- Transaction processing systems (TPS) support the monitoring, collection, storage, and processing of data from the organization's basic business transactions, each of which generates data.
- Functional area information systems (FAISs) support a particular functional area within the organization.
- Interorganizational information systems (IOSs) support many interorganizational operations, of which supply chain management is the best known.
- Enterprise resource planning (ERP) systems correct a lack of communication among the FAISs by tightly integrating the functional area ISs via a common database.
- Electronic commerce (e-commerce) systems enable organizations to conduct transactions with other organizations (called business-to-business (B2B) electronic commerce), and with customers (called business-to-consumer (B2C) electronic commerce).

- Business intelligence (BI) systems provide computer-based support for complex, nonroutine decisions, primarily for middle managers and knowledge workers.
- Expert systems (ESs) attempt to duplicate the work of human experts by applying reasoning capabilities, knowledge, and expertise within a specific domain.

1.3 Discuss ways in which information technology can affect managers and nonmanagerial workers.

Potential IT impacts on managers:

- IT may reduce the number of middle managers.
- IT will provide managers with real-time or near real-time information, meaning that managers will have less time to make decisions.
- IT will increase the likelihood that managers will have to supervise geographically dispersed employees and teams.

Potential IT impacts on nonmanagerial workers:

- IT may eliminate jobs.
- IT may cause employees to experience a loss of identity.
- IT can cause job stress and physical problems, such as repetitive stress injury.

1.4 List positive and negative societal effects of the increased use of information technology.

Positive societal effects:

- IT can provide opportunities for people with disabilities.
- IT can provide people with flexibility in their work (e.g., work from anywhere, anytime).
- Robots will take over mundane chores.
- IT will enable improvements in health care.

Negative societal effects:

- IT can cause health problems for individuals.
- IT can place employees on constant call.
- IT can potentially misinform patients about their health problems.

Chapter Glossary

application (or app)   A computer program designed to support a specific task or business process.

business analytics systems   See **business intelligence systems**

business intelligence (BI) systems   Systems that provide computer-based support

for complex, nonroutine decisions, primarily for middle managers and knowledge workers.

computer-based information system (CBIS)   An information system that uses computer technology to perform some or all of its intended tasks.

dashboard   A special form of IS that supports all managers of the organization by providing rapid access to timely information and direct access to structured information in the form of reports.

data items   An elementary description of things, events, activities, and transactions that are recorded, classified, and stored but are not organized to convey any specific meaning.

database A collection of related files or tables containing data.

digital transformation The business strategy that leverages IT to dramatically improve employee, customer, and business partner relationships; support continuous improvement in business operations and business processes; and develop new business models and businesses.

electronic commerce (e-commerce) systems A type of interorganizational information system that enables organizations to conduct transactions, called business-to-business (B2B) electronic commerce, and customers to conduct transactions with businesses, called business-to-consumer (B2C) electronic commerce.

enterprise resource planning (ERP) systems Information systems that correct a lack of communication among the functional area ISs by tightly integrating the functional area ISs via a common database.

expert systems (ES) An attempt to duplicate the work of human experts by applying reasoning capabilities, knowledge, and expertise within a specific domain.

functional area information systems (FAISs) (departmental information system) ISs that support a particular functional area within the organization.

hardware A device such as a processor, monitor, keyboard, or printer. Together, these devices accept, process, and display data and information.

information Data that have been organized so that they have meaning and value to the recipient.

information system (IS) A system that collects, processes, stores, analyzes, and disseminates information for a specific purpose.

information technology (IT) Any computer-based tool that people use to work with information and support the information and information-processing needs of an organization.

information technology components Hardware, software, databases, and networks.

information technology infrastructure IT components plus IT services.

information technology platform The name given to the combination of the IT components of hardware, software, networks (wireline and wireless), and databases.

information technology services Activities performed by IT personnel using IT components; specifically, developing information systems, overseeing security and risk, and managing data.

informed user A person who is knowledgeable about information systems and information technology.

interorganizational information systems (IOSs) Information systems that connect two or more organizations.

knowledge Data and/or information that have been organized and processed to convey understanding, experience, accumulated learning, and expertise as they apply to a current problem or activity.

knowledge workers Professional employees such as financial and marketing analysts, engineers, lawyers, and accountants, who are experts in a particular subject area and who create information and knowledge, which they integrate into the business.

network A connecting system (wireline or wireless) that enables multiple computers to share resources.

procedures The set of instructions for combining hardware, software, database, and network components in order to process information and generate the desired output.

software A program or collection of programs that enable the hardware to process data.

supply chain The flow of materials, information, money, and services from suppliers of raw materials through factories and warehouses to the end customers.

transaction processing system (TPS) A system that supports the monitoring, collection, storage, and processing of data from the organization's basic business transactions, each of which generates data.

Discussion Questions

1. Would your university be a good candidate for digital transformation? Why or why not? Support your answer.

2. If you responded yes, then what types of digital initiatives should your university undertake to transform itself?

3. Describe a business that you would like to start. Discuss how information technology could: (a) help you find and research an idea for a business, (b) help you formulate your business plan, and (c) help you finance your business.

4. Your university wants to recruit high-quality high school students from your state. Provide examples of (a) the data that your recruiters would gather in this process, (b) the information that your recruiters would process from these data, and (c) the types of knowledge that your recruiters would infer from this information.

5. Can the terms data, information, and knowledge have different meanings for different people? Support your answer with examples.

6. Information technology makes it possible to "never be out of touch." Discuss the pros and cons of always being available to your employers and clients (regardless of where you are or what you are doing).

7. Robots have the positive impact of being able to relieve humans from working in dangerous conditions. What are some negative impacts of robots in the workplace?

8. Is it possible to endanger yourself by accessing too much medical information on the Web? Why or why not? Support your answer.

9. Describe other potential impacts of IT on societies as a whole.

10. What are the major reasons why it is important for employees in all functional areas to become familiar with IT?

11. Given that information technology is impacting every industry, what does this mean for a company's employees? Provide specific examples to support your answer.

12. Given that information technology is impacting every industry, what does this mean for students attending a college of business? Provide specific examples to support your answer.

13. Is the vast amount of medical information on the Web a good thing? Answer from the standpoint of a patient and from the standpoint of a physician.

Problem-Solving Activities

1. Visit some websites that offer employment opportunities in IT. Prominent examples are: **www.linkedin.com**, **www.dice.com**, **www .monster.com**, **www.collegerecruiter.com**, **www.careerbuilder.com**, **www.jobcentral.com**, **www.job.com**, **www.career.com**, **www .simplyhired.com**, and **www.truecareers.com**. Compare IT salaries to salaries offered to accountants, marketing personnel, financial personnel, operations personnel, and human resources personnel. For other information on IT salaries, check *Computerworld*'s annual salary survey.

2. Go to **www.ups.com**.

   a. Find out what information is available to customers before they send a package.

   b. Find out about the "package tracking" system.

   c. Compute the cost of delivering a box, weighing 40 pounds, from your hometown to Long Beach, California (or to Lansing, Michigan, if you live in or near Long Beach). Compare the fastest delivery against the least cost. How long did this process take? Look into the business services offered by UPS. How do they make this process easier when you are a business customer?

3. Search the Web for information about the Department of Homeland Security (DHS). Examine the available information, and comment on the role of information technologies in the department.

4. Access **www.irobot.com**, and investigate the company's Education and Research Robots. Surf the Web for other companies that manufacture robots, and compare their products with those of iRobot.

Closing Case

`MIS` `POM` Digital Transformation of Equipment Manufacturers Has Negative Consequences

Digital transformation has caused equipment manufacturers to fundamentally change their business models. In the past, these manufacturers generated revenue one time, with each sale. Today, they embed software and sensors (see the Internet of Things in Chapter 8) into their products that enable equipment to communicate with other equipment, with their users, and with the manufacturers themselves.

Analyzing the data that the software and sensors provide, the manufacturers are able to offer additional services after each sale, creating more continuous revenue flows from each customer. Let's take a closer look at two major equipment manufacturers in different industries: John Deere (Deere; **www.deere.com**) in agriculture and Medtronic (**www.medtronic.com**) in health care.

Founded in 1837, Deere is the largest agricultural equipment manufacturer in the world, with 2019 global revenues of $39 billion. Software and sensors in Deere equipment enable the machines to steer themselves, creating more accurate paths with less overlap. As a result, farmers can work longer with less fatigue. The technologies also enable farmers to monitor and operate machinery, check crop health, and monitor environmental conditions. In essence, farmers use the data generated by these technologies to plant, spray, fertilize, and harvest at optimal times.

Further, self-monitoring sensors implanted in the equipment can detect when it is not operating properly. Deere can then recommend preventive maintenance (a function of predictive analytics; see Chapter 12), thereby reducing the possibility of expensive downtime.

Medtronic, founded in 1949, is the largest medical equipment manufacturer in the world, with 2019 global revenues of $30.5 billion. Consider Medtronic ventilators, which, in May 2020, had come to the forefront of global needs during the COVID-19 pandemic.

Software and sensors in the ventilators monitor patients' breathing and the amount of oxygen that patients are receiving. The ventilators also gather and analyze data from self-monitoring sensors to detect when they are not operating properly. When necessary, the ventilator can recommend preventive maintenance, thereby reducing the possibility of negative outcomes for patients.

A Negative Consequence of the Digital Transformation of Equipment Manufacturers

Unfortunately, the equipment manufacturers' digital transformations have led to a serious, negative consequence. The companies are making it difficult for customers and independent repair shops and technicians to repair today's equipment, which operates on copyright-protected software.

As a result, farmers who buy Deere tractors and hospitals that buy Medtronic equipment cannot repair their equipment themselves. Instead, they must work with company-approved technicians, who may take time to arrive and can be expensive. Essentially, Deere sells their tractors to farmers and Medtronic sells medical equipment to hospitals, and both companies use software to control every aspect of the equipment use after the sale.

Consequently, many farmers and hospitals are supporting "right to repair" legislation. Such bills, which have been proposed in 22 states, contain two basic elements.

- They allow owners to repair their equipment themselves without voiding warranties or agreements.

- They require equipment manufacturers such as Deere and Medtronic to offer the diagnostic tools, manuals, and other supplies that farmers need to fix their own machines.

As expected, Deere and Medtronic oppose this legislation.

Interestingly, Apple also opposes the right-to-repair legislation. Apple argues that the bills could result in poor repair work or make consumers vulnerable to hackers. Right-to-repair advocates respond that Apple, which offers iPhone repair services at every Apple store, wants to maintain control of its share of the approximately $4 billion smartphone-repair business.

The equipment-manufacturers controversy had its beginning in the debate over jailbreaking iPhones and other high-tech devices. *Jailbreaking* refers to the process of bypassing the restrictions that Apple puts on its operating system and taking full control of the device. The legal question underlying this controversy centers on the Digital Millennium Copyright Act (DMCA) of 1998.

The Digital Millennium Copyright Act (DMCA) is a U.S. copyright law that criminalizes the production and dissemination of technology, devices, or services intended to circumvent measures that control access to copyrighted works as well as the act of circumventing an access control. The DMCA was originally meant to prevent people from pirating music and movies, but it has arguably been taken advantage of by companies selling a wide variety of devices that contain software.

After the passage of the DMCA, regulators considered whether there should be exceptions to the law. In such cases, consumers might have the right to circumvent *technical protection measures* (TPMs) intended to protect intellectual property and the rights of intellectual property holders. The U.S. Copyright Office subsequently exempted 27 classes of intellectual property from TPMs. Class 21 covers a variety of types of motor vehicles, including mechanized farm equipment, and Class 27 covers networked medical devices.

Deere and Medtronic have noted that the exemptions are for the equipment owners themselves, but they prevent owners from transferring the right to modify software "to third parties, such as repair shops or hackers." The manufacturers argue further that they need to control access to their equipment's software to ensure that their machines operate properly and safely and to preserve product warranties.

After the Copyright Office granted the exemptions, the manufacturers began to require their customers to sign an updated end-user license agreement (EULA) that restricted their ability to repair or modify their equipment, in essence requiring them to use certified diagnostic and repair software. In response, farmers and hospitals contend that, despite the exemptions, Deere and Medtronic maintain tight control over how their customers service their equipment. Violation of the EULAs would be considered a breach of contract, meaning that Deere and Medtronic would have to sue their own customers if they want to enforce these agreements.

Farmers note that this problem poses a threat to their livelihood if their tractor breaks at an inopportune time. One farmer stated that he does not have time to wait for a dealership employee to come to his farm and repair his tractor, particularly at harvest time. The farmer went on to claim that almost all repairs on new equipment require software downloads. Significantly, a Massachusetts law already guarantees the same type of access to passenger vehicle software that right-to-repair advocates want from agricultural equipment manufacturers.

Hospitals contend that this problem could not only cause a loss of income, but it could present a serious threat to their patients if medical equipment breaks at an inopportune time. As with farmers, hospitals simply do not have the time to wait for certified technicians to make needed repairs.

Interestingly, in 2018 the U.S. Food and Drug Administration (FDA; **www.fda.gov**) asserted "the continued availability of third-party entities to service and repair medical devices is critical to the functioning of the U.S. healthcare system." More recently, as the COVID-19 pandemic led to critical shortages of ventilators, hospitals had even greater need of keeping the ventilators that they do have in operating order. Therefore, hospitals had even greater urgency to be able to repair the ventilators themselves.

The question remains: What is the disconnect between the FDA's 2018 statement and the fact that manufacturers still oppose right-to-repair? In an unfortunate example from Italy, manufacturers threatened to sue volunteers who 3D-printed parts for ventilators that could not be obtained from any other source. The parts from the manufacturer cost $11,000, and the 3D-printed parts cost $1! As of mid-September 2020 it was unclear if the original manufacturer had actually proceeded with the lawsuit.

Sources: Compiled from J. Koebler, "Hospitals Need to Repair Ventilators. Manufacturers Are Making That Impossible," *Motherboard*, March 18, 2020; G. Moody, "Volunteers 3D-Print Unobtainable $11,000 Valve for $1 to Keep COVID-19 Patients Alive; Original Manufacturer Threatens to Sue," *Techdirt*, March 17, 2020; P. Waldman and L. Mulvany, "Who Really Owns a John Deere?" *BusinessWeek*, March 9, 2020; J. List, "John Deere and Nebraska's Right to Repair," *Hackaday*, March 9, 2020; R. Jensen, "Hackers, Farmers, and Doctors Unite! Support for Right to Repair Laws Slowly Grows," *Ars Technica*, June 20, 2019; A. Minter, "U.S. Farmers Are Being Bled by the Tractor Monopoly," *Bloomberg.com*, April 23, 2019; A. Shah, "Who Has the Right to Repair Your Farm or Medical Tools?" *ASME.org*, April 16, 2019; J. Hirsch, "As Farmers Fight for the Right to Repair Their Tractors, an Antitrust Movement Gains Steam," *The Counter*, April 8, 2019; K. Wiens and E. Chamberlain, "John Deere Just Swindled Farmers out of Their Right to Repair," *Wired*, September 19, 2018; D. Swinhoe, "How Tractor Seller John Deere Became a Technology Company," *IDG Connect*, June 5, 2018; D. Newman, "Top Six Digital Transformation Trends in Agriculture," *Forbes*, May 14, 2018; J. Hightower, "John Deere Is Against the Right to Repair Its Equipment," *AlterNet*, August 1, 2017; J. Roberts, "One Controversial Thing Tractors and iPhones Have in Common," *Fortune*, June 29, 2017; A. Fitzpatrick, "Hand Me that Wrench: Farmers and Apple Fight over the Toolbox," *Time*, June 22, 2017; A. Ebrahimzadeh, "Will Farmers or 3rd Party Repair Shops Sue John Deere for Allegedly Contractually Prohibiting Unlicensed Tractor Repairs?," *aeesq.com*, May 8, 2017; J. Bloomberg, "John Deere's Digital Transformation Runs Afoul of Right-to-Repair Movement," *Bloomberg BusinessWeek*, April 30, 2017; D. Grossman, "There's a Thriving John Deere Black Market as Farmers Fight for 'Right to Repair'," *Popular Mechanics*, March 22, 2017; M. Reilly, "A Fight over Tractors in America's Heartland Comes Down to Software," *MIT Technology Review*, March 22, 2017; J. Koebler, "Why American Farmers Are Hacking Their Tractors with Ukrainian Firmware," *Motherboard*, March 21, 2017; C. Perlman, "From Product to Platform: John Deere Revolutionizes Farming," *Harvard Business School Digital Innovation and Transformation*, February 26, 2017; "How John Deere Turned Technology into Business Transformation," **www.digitalsocialstrategy.org**, December 10, 2016; K. Wiens, "How Copyright Law Stifles Your Right to Tinker with Tech," *MIT Technology Review*, July 26, 2016; K. Wiens, "We Can't Let John Deere Destroy the Very Idea of Ownership," *Wired*, April 21, 2015; **www.deere.com**, accessed May 2, 2020; **www.medtronic.com**, accessed May 2, 2020.

Questions

1. Describe how Deere's and Medtronic's digital transformations changed their business models.

2. Discuss why Deere's and Medtronic's digital transformations are "not all good news."

Look ahead to Chapter 3 for the next three questions:

3. Discuss the ethicality and the legality of the end-user license agreements that the two companies require their customers to sign.

4. Discuss the ethicality and the legality of customers who use unlicensed shops to repair their equipment using hacked software.

5. The fundamental tenets of ethics include responsibility, accountability, and liability. Discuss each of these tenets as it applies to John Deere's actions and Medtronic's actions toward their customers.

CHAPTER 2

Organizational Strategy, Competitive Advantage, and Information Systems

Opening Case

MIS The Coronavirus Pandemic Magnifies the Digital Divide

Background

The United States has a long history of bringing utility access to all Americans. To illustrate this point, let's consider three government actions: the Rural Electrification Administration (REA), the Communications Act of 1934, and the Telecommunications Act of 1996.

In the early 1930s, when President Franklin D. Roosevelt established the REA, 90 percent of U.S. farmers lived without electricity. The cost of installing electric lines to the country's most remote areas was prohibitive for profit-seeking businesses. Therefore, the REA provided loans to rural electric cooperatives to construct their electric networks. By the end of the 1940s, most farms in the United States had electricity.

In hindsight, it is clear that Americans should have access to electricity. The country's economic and social well-being depend on it.

With the Communications Act of 1934, the U.S. government provided a universal service guarantee that mandates that every resident have a baseline level of telecommunications services. The government recognized that telephone services provide a vital link to emergency services, government services, and surrounding communities. Because of the universal service guarantee, providers frequently must offer and maintain—even at a loss—expensive copper twisted-pair phone lines in rural areas to support small populations. The carriers are compensated for these costs through a tax on customers' phone bills, called the Universal Service Fund. Again, in hindsight it is clear that universal access to telecommunications service—today, broadband access to the Internet—is essential to the nation's prosperity. Advocates of universal broadband Internet access contend that broadband Internet is not a luxury but a right of all 21st century Americans.

The overall objective of the Telecommunications Act of 1996 was to provide higher-quality services for consumers. The act wanted to ensure that all Americans are connected to the Internet, regardless of their income.

The 1996 act recognized that broadband Internet access provides many significant benefits, in the areas of public health, telework, and education. The coronavirus pandemic has magnified the importance of the digital divide, particularly in these areas. **Digital divide** refers to the gap between people who have access to modern information and communications technologies, and those who have restricted access, limited access, or no access.

- *Public health*: Rural areas suffer from a shortage of physicians and hospitals. Being able to conduct a video conference with a physician, nurse practitioner, or nurse without having to drive miles to an office or a hospital can literally save lives.
- *Teleworking*: Being able to work from home provides flexibility to workers. Teleworking has received far more attention during the COVID-19 pandemic.

For example, an unemployed person who has Internet access at home will be employed seven weeks faster than a person who does not. In addition, he or she will earn more than $5,000 in additional income annually, according to an analysis of data from the Bureau of Labor Statistics (BLS; **www.bls.gov**).

- *Education*: Before the coronavirus pandemic, 70 percent of primary and secondary school teachers assigned homework online. The *homework gap*, referring to children who cannot do online homework because they do not have reliable broadband access, is now extending to higher education.

Significantly, students are 7 percent more likely to earn a high school diploma and attend college when they are connected to the Internet at home. Furthermore, these students will earn more than $2 million more over their lifetimes.

The Problem

As of May 2020 the United States still had a persistent digital divide. The divide was once only a problem of Internet access. Today, it encompasses access speed and connection quality.

To effectively use modern Internet, people must have a broadband connection, which the FCC defines as the ability to download data at 25 megabits per second (Mbps) and to upload data at 3 Mbps. In addition, consumers must have a consistent Internet connection; that is, a connection that does not fluctuate unpredictably.

Let's consider two questions:

(1) How big is the digital divide?

(2) Whom does the digital divide impact the most?

Question #1: In 2020 the FCC reported that approximately 16 million Americans did not have consistent broadband Internet access. Further, many people could not obtain broadband service because they lived in an area where it was not cost effective for providers to provide such access.

However, industry analysts contend that the number of Americans without reliable broadband service is much higher than what the FCC reports. For example, a 2019 Microsoft study found that almost 163 million Americans were not using the Internet at broadband speeds. Two serious problems in the way the FCC gathers its data account for the large disparity in these statistics.

First, the FCC asks Internet providers if they are "providing or could provide, without an extraordinary commitment of resources, broadband service to an area." If the answer is yes to either (providing or could provide), then the FCC considers that area to have broadband access. As a result, many places are counted as having broadband access when they not only have no such access, but providers have no plans to provide it anytime soon.

Second, the FCC bases its data on census blocks, which are the smallest units used by the U.S. Census Bureau. A *census block* is a statistical area bounded by visible features such as roads, streams, and railroad tracks, and by nonvisible boundaries such as streets, roads, transmission lines, property lines, city, township, school district, county limits, and line-of-sight extensions of roads. In rural areas, these blocks can be very large. If broadband access is delivered to a single customer in that block, then the FCC counts the entire block as having access.

For example, in 2019 the FCC stated that 100 percent of Ferry County, Washington, residents had broadband Internet access. However, local officials contended that very few residents of the rural county had broadband access and that those who did were using broadband in their businesses. In fact, Microsoft data indicated that only 2 percent of Ferry County residents were using broadband Internet.

Question #2: The problem with the digital divide is that Americans who live in rural areas are more likely than Americans who live in urban areas to lack reliable broadband Internet access. The Rural Broadband Association (**www.ntca.org**) cites a 2016 study from the Hudson Institute that found that nearly 70 percent of the economic impact of broadband Internet access went to urban rather than rural economies.

Consider workers, veterans, and retirees who face economic and health challenges. The pandemic caused the closing of government benefits offices that assist these people at the same time that government websites were crashing due to surges in traffic. Even if government websites could meet the challenge, few agencies have established online or remote options for citizens who must meet with civil servants for hearings and other official proceedings.

For example, although some states have enacted measures to make unemployment insurance readily available by allowing people to apply online without going to an office, this process requires reliable Internet access. People must be able to access and fill out forms online, sign the forms online, and submit them online.

Covid's Impact on the Digital Divide

Although the Internet has provided the opportunity for many people to experience some sort of normalcy during the pandemic, millions of Americans do not have reliable broadband Internet access. Unfortunately, underserved areas and communities have not been able to access health care or transition to an online workplace or school environment. We now examine the impact of the digital divide during the coronavirus pandemic in the areas of telehealth, telework, and distance education.

Telehealth

Telehealth is the distribution of health-related services and information via electronic information and telecommunications technologies. Telehealth enables long-distance patient and health-care professional contact, care, advice, reminders, intervention, monitoring, and education.

Jane Fox, a social worker in a rural town, uses telehealth technology to help psychiatrists evaluate their patients. Unfortunately, she cannot work from home because her broadband Internet connection is too unreliable. She cannot afford to lose her connection in the middle of a telehealth videoconference. As a result, she must drive 35 miles to the closest hospital to videoconference with patients and psychiatrists.

During the pandemic, people seeking medical care were cautioned to avoid hospitals and physicians' offices in favor of video or phone calls with their healthcare professionals. However, conducting video sessions with these professionals requires broadband Internet access.

The Centers for Disease Control and Prevention (CDC) estimates that 60 percent of Americans have chronic health conditions and cannot simply stop seeing their physicians. Telehealth is the obvious solution, especially for older adults who face the greatest risk from the coronavirus. Unfortunately, many of these individuals do not have broadband Internet access at home.

The federal government took some steps to accelerate access to telehealth services by expanding Medicare coverage to phone and video consultations and modifying the rules that prevent health-care workers in one state from practicing in another. One coronavirus stimulus package also included $200 million to increase connectivity for rural health-care providers and improve telehealth options for veterans. However, physicians will have to start using such technology to make it widely available for patients.

Telework

Telework is the practice of performing your job away from the office. During the coronavirus pandemic, telework came to mean working from home while socially distancing. To be able to telework effectively, employees must have a computer, laptop, or phone, and, most importantly, a consistent broadband connection. Without these technologies, telework is very difficult, if not impossible.

According to the BLS, under normal circumstances about 7 percent of U.S. employees have a flexible workplace, meaning that they have the option of working part-time or full-time from home. White-collar workers are much more likely to have a telework option. Roughly 22 percent of employees with jobs in management, business, or finance can telework, compared to only 1 percent of service workers.

When we take race and ethnicity into account, 37 percent of Asian employee and 30 percent of Caucasian employees have a telework option, compared with 20 percent of Black employees and 16 percent of Hispanic employees, according to the BLS. In June 2020 the U.S. unemployment rate had reached 11.1 percent and was highest among the Black and Hispanic populations.

Distance Education

As of May 2020 many school districts and universities had closed for physical classes through the end of the school year. These institutions implemented distance learning policies so that students could continue their lessons via the Internet. Unfortunately, the shift to distance education was not smooth, and it highlighted the problems stemming from the digital divide.

As an example, one rural school in California switched to distance learning and discovered that 42 of its 168 students—that is, 25 percent—did not have *any* Internet connection at home. As a result, teachers lost touch with some of those students. Furthermore, some areas did not have a reliable cellular signal, meaning that students could not go online using free Internet services offered by their schools during the pandemic.

To enable students to access the Internet, education officials in South Carolina and Texas dispatched school buses equipped as Wi-Fi hotspots to rural and low-income neighborhoods. Another school in Texas set up a stationary Wi-Fi hotspot in the parking lot of its football stadium where students could park and connect. In Prince George County in Virginia, the school district distributed laptops to students who did not have a computer at home and paid for Internet access for students who did not have it.

In South Dakota, one district printed out hard copies of work for students who did not have broadband Internet access. Families picked up and dropped off students' work at the school. After families turned in completed work, teachers waited 72 hours to grade it to ensure that any coronavirus on the schoolwork had died.

Stopgap "Solutions"

Many libraries, schools, and other municipal buildings are leaving their Wi-Fi connections on overnight because they are the only source of connectivity in their towns. Also, in April 2020 Google announced it would provide free Wi-Fi to 100,000 rural California families through the end of the school year, plus 4,000 Chromebook laptops for students.

Eight of the nation's major Internet service providers (ISPs) have announced various steps to improve broadband access and connectivity during the pandemic. Providers are raising caps on data bandwidth or offering two months of free broadband to households with students.

The FCC stated that more than 650 broadband Internet providers, telephone companies, and trade associations signed its Keep Americans Connected pledge not to terminate internet service over pandemic-related financial troubles, to waive late fees, and to allow free access to Wi-Fi services. Offers from ISPs are available only in locations where those companies already provided service.

In 2017, Microsoft began its Airband Initiative, a five-year commitment to bring broadband access to underserved Americans by using TV white space devices and other low-cost wireless technologies. These devices detect the presence of existing but unused areas of airwaves and utilize them to transmit wireless internet signals. By mid-2020, the Airband Initiative reached people in 25 states.

Closing the digital divide is a step toward shrinking the persistent gaps in economic opportunity, educational achievement, and health outcomes in the United States. According to Deloitte Consulting, it would take a $150 billion investment in fiber-optics infrastructure to modernize rural broadband across the country. Improving broadband Internet access requires political will and incentives for private telecommunications companies to build broadband networks in remote communities that offer minimal profit.

One possible "benefit" of the pandemic is a broader recognition of how central to our society broadband Internet access has become. Policymakers must realize that normal supply-and-demand economics do not work with critical infrastructure. (Recall our discussion earlier in this case about U.S. policy for providing electricity, telephone service, and Internet access to all Americans.)

Sources: Compiled from A. Gilreath, "Without In-Person Classes, Many Students Have Essentially Gone Missing, Teachers Say," *USA Today*, May 4, 2020; G. Sohn, "During the Pandemic, the FCC Must Provide Internet for All," *Wired*, April 28, 2020; Y. Baig, "Digital Divide Leaves Rural and Poor Sonoma County Students with No Internet Connection," *The Press Democrat*, April 13, 2020; A. Holpuch, "U.S.'s Digital Divide 'Is Going to Kill People' as Covid-19 Exposes Inequalities," *The Guardian*, April 13, 2020; K. Finley, "When School Is Online, the Digital Divide Grows Greater," *Wired*, April 9, 2020; D. Goldstein, A. Popescu, and N. Hannah-Jones, "As School Moves Online, Many Students Stay Logged Out," *New York Times*, April 8, 2020; E. Mansfield and S. Conlon, "Coronavirus for Kids without Internet: Quarantined Worksheets, Learning in Parking Lots," *USA Today*, April 4, 2020; D. Castro, "Coronavirus Pandemic Exposes Why America's Digital Divide Is Dangerous," *USA Today*, April 1, 2020; C. Merrefield, "Rural Broadband in the Time of Coronavirus," *Journalist's Resource*, March 30, 2020; V. Bekiempis, "Pandemic Response Lays Bare America's Digital Divide," *The Guardian*, March 21, 2020; L. Poon, "Coronavirus Exposes How Bad America's Homework Gap Really Is," *CityLab*, March 20, 2020; D. Truong, "As Classes Move Online, What Happens to Students without Internet or Computers?" *WAMU Radio Station*, March 18, 2020; N. Turner-Lee, "What the Coronavirus Reveals about the Digital Divide between Schools and Communities," *Brookings.edu*, March 17, 2020; M. Vasquez, "Trump Administration Lays out New Health, Economic Steps to Combat Virus," *CNN*, March 17, 2020; D. Truong, "D.C. Is Spending Millions to Get Tablets in the Hands of All Students," *WAMU Radio Station*, March 6, 2020; J. Busby and J. Tanberk, "FCC Reports Broadband Unavailable to 21.3 Million Americans, BroadbandNow Study Indicates 42 Million Do Not

Have Access," *BroadbandNow Research*, February 3, 2020; F. Donovan, "Broadband Internet Expansion Key to Telehealth in Rural Areas," *HIT Infrastructure*, September 20, 2019; K. Bode, "Better Broadband Lowers Unemployment Rates," *Motherboard*, June 6, 2019; S. Meinrath et al., "Broadband Availability and Access in Rural Pennsylvania," *The Center for Rural Pennsylvania*, June 2019; "2019 Broadband Deployment Report," *Federal Communications Commission*, May 29, 2019; J. Kahan, "It's Time for a New Approach for Mapping Broadband Data to Better Serve Americans," Microsoft.com blog, April 8, 2019; S. Lohr, "Digital Divide Is Wider than We Think, Study Says," *New York Times*, December 4, 2018; B. Smith, "The Rural Broadband Divide: An Urgent National Problem that We Can Solve," Microsoft.com blog, December 3, 2018; C. Aguh, "How the 'Digital Divide' Is Holding the U.S. Economy Back," *VentureBeat*, February 10, 2018; "Rural American Has a Serious Internet Problem," *The Week*, June 15, 2017; A. Dellinger, "Is Internet Access a Right? Americans Split on Belief If Internet Access Is a Right or Privilege," *International Business Times*, May 7, 2017; M. Anderson, "Digital Divide Persists Even as Lower-Income Americans Make Gains in Tech Adoption," *Pew Research Center*, March 22, 2017; G. Galvin, "States Struggle to Bridge Digital Divide," *U.S. News and World Report*, March 16, 2017; D. West and J. Karsten, "Rural and Urban America Divided by Broadband Access," *Brookings*, July 18, 2016; H. Kuttner, "The Economic Impact of Rural Broadband," *Hudson Institute*, April 20, 2016.

Questions

1. Describe some impacts on individuals and families (not mentioned in the case) resulting from a lack of Internet access.
2. Is affordable broadband Internet access strategically important to cities? Why or why not? Support your answer.
3. Is affordable broadband Internet access strategically important to the United States? Why or why not? Support your answer.
4. Does everyone deserve access to affordable high-speed Internet, just as they have for water, sewers, electricity, and telephone service? That is, is broadband Internet access a right or a privilege? Support your answer.

Introduction

Organizations operate in the incredible complexity of the modern high-tech world. As a result, they are subject to myriad business pressures. Information systems are critically important in helping organizations respond to business pressures and in supporting organizations' global strategies. As you study this chapter, you will see that any information system can be *strategic*, meaning it can provide a competitive advantage if it is used properly. The chapter-opening case, as well as all the other cases in this chapter, illustrate how information technology (IT) can provide a competitive advantage to organizations.

Competitive advantage refers to any assets that provide an organization with an edge against its competitors in some measure such as cost, quality, or speed. A competitive advantage helps an organization control a market and accrue larger-than-average profits. Significantly, both strategy and competitive advantage take many forms.

Although many companies use technology in very expensive ways, an entrepreneurial spirit coupled with a solid understanding of what IT can do for you will provide competitive advantages to entrepreneurs just as it does for Wall Street CIOs. As you study this chapter, think of the small businesses in your area that are utilizing popular technologies in interesting and novel ways. Have any of them found an innovative use for Twitter? Facebook? Amazon? PayPal? Square? Zoom? If not, then can you think of any businesses that would benefit from employing these technologies?

This chapter is important for you for several reasons. First, the business pressures we address in the chapter will affect your organization. Just as important, however, they also will affect *you*. Therefore, you must understand how information systems can help you—and eventually your organization—respond to these pressures.

Acquiring a competitive advantage is also essential for your organization's survival. Many organizations achieve competitive advantage through the efforts of their employees. Therefore, becoming knowledgeable about strategy and how information systems affect strategy and competitive position will help you throughout your career.

This chapter encourages you to become familiar with your organization's strategy, mission, and goals and to understand its business problems and how it makes (or loses) money. It will help you understand how information technology contributes to organizational strategy. Furthermore, you likely will become a member of business or IT committees that decide (among many other things) how to use existing technologies more effectively and whether to adopt new ones. After studying this chapter, you will be able to make immediate contributions in these committees.

Essentially, organizations consist of a large number of diverse business processes. In this chapter, you will first learn about the different types of business processes and the support that information systems provide for all business processes.

The need for organizations to optimize their business processes has led to efforts such as business process improvement (BPI), business process reengineering (BPR), and business process management (BPM). You will learn how organizations address these important efforts and the key role that information systems play in supporting and enabling these efforts.

Next, you will see how information systems enable organizations to respond to business pressures. Finally, you will learn how information systems help organizations acquire competitive advantages in the marketplace.

2.1 Business Processes

A **business process** is an ongoing collection of related activities that create a product or a service of value to the organization, its business partners, and its customers. The process involves three fundamental elements:

- *Inputs:* Materials, services, and information that flow through and are transformed as a result of process activities
- *Resources:* People and equipment that perform process activities
- *Outputs:* The product or a service created by the process

If the process involves a customer, then that customer can be either internal or external to the organization. A manager who is the recipient of an internal reporting process is an example of an internal customer. In contrast, an individual or a business that purchases the organization's products is the external customer of the fulfillment process.

Successful organizations measure their process activities to evaluate how well they are executing these processes. Two fundamental metrics that organizations employ in assessing their processes are efficiency and effectiveness. *Efficiency* focuses on doing things well in the process; for example, progressing from one process activity to another without delay or without wasting money or resources. *Effectiveness* focuses on doing the things that matter; that is, creating outputs of value to the process customer—for example, high-quality products.

Many processes cross functional areas in an organization. For example, product development involves research, design, engineering, manufacturing, marketing, and distribution. Other processes involve only a single functional area. **Table 2.1** identifies the fundamental business processes performed in an organization's functional areas.

Cross-Functional Processes

All the business processes in Table 2.1 fall within a single functional area of the company. However, many other business processes, such as procurement and fulfillment, cut across multiple functional areas; that is, they are cross-functional business processes, meaning that no single functional area is responsible for their execution. Rather, multiple functional areas collaborate to perform the process. For a cross-functional process to be successfully completed, each functional area must execute its specific process steps in a coordinated, collaborative way. To clarify this point, let's take a look at the procurement and fulfillment of **cross-functional processes**. We discuss these processes in greater detail in Chapter 10.

POM The *procurement process* includes all of the tasks involved in acquiring needed materials externally from a vendor. Procurement comprises five steps that are completed in three different functional areas of the firm: warehouse, purchasing, and accounting.

ACCT The process begins when the warehouse recognizes the need to procure materials, perhaps due to low inventory levels. The warehouse documents this need with a purchase requisition, which it sends to the purchasing department (step 1). In turn, the purchasing department identifies a suitable vendor, creates a purchase order based on the purchase requisition, and sends the order to the vendor (step 2). When the vendor receives the purchase order, it ships the materials, which are received in the warehouse (step 3). The vendor then sends an invoice, which is received by the accounting department (step 4). Accounting sends payment to the vendor, thereby completing the procurement process (step 5).

TABLE 2.1 Examples of Business Processes

ACCT Accounting Business Processes

Managing accounts payable	Managing invoice billings
Managing accounts receivable	Managing petty cash
Reconciling bank accounts	Producing month-end close
Managing cash receipts	Producing virtual close

FIN Finance Business Processes

Managing account collection	Producing property tax assessments
Managing bank loan applications	Managing stock transactions
Producing business forecasts	Generating financial cash-flow reports
Applying customer credit approval and credit terms	

MKT Marketing Business Processes

Managing post-sale customer follow-up	Handling customer complaints
Collecting sales taxes	Handling returned goods from customers
Applying copyrights and trademarks	Producing sales leads
Using customer satisfaction surveys	Entering sales orders
Managing customer service	Training sales personnel

POM Production/Operations Management Business Processes

Processing bills of materials	Managing quality control for finished goods
Processing manufacturing change orders	Auditing for quality assurance
Managing master parts list and files	Receiving, inspecting, and stocking parts and materials
Managing packing, storage, and distribution	Handling shipping and freight claims
Processing physical inventory	Handling vendor selection, files, and inspections
Managing purchasing	

HRM Human Resources Business Processes

Applying disability policies	Producing performance appraisals and salary adjustments
Managing employee hiring	Managing resignations and terminations
Handling employee orientation	Applying training and tuition reimbursement
Managing files and records	Managing travel and entertainment
Applying health-care benefits	Managing workplace rules and guidelines
Managing pay and payroll	Overseeing workplace safety

MIS Management Information Systems Business Processes

Antivirus control	Applying electronic mail policy
Computer security issues incident reporting	Generating Internet use policy
Training computer users	Managing service agreements and emergency services
Computer user and staff training	Applying user workstation standards
Applying disaster recovery procedures	Managing the use of personal software

POM **ACCT** The *fulfillment process* is concerned with processing customer orders. Fulfillment is triggered by a customer purchase order that is received by the sales department. Sales then validates the purchase order and creates a sales order. The sales order communicates data related to the order to other functional areas within the organization, and it tracks the progress of the order. The warehouse prepares and sends the shipment to the customer. Once accounting is notified of the shipment, it creates an invoice and sends it to the customer. The customer then makes a payment, which accounting records.

An organization's business processes can create a competitive advantage if they enable the company to innovate or to execute more effectively and efficiently than its competitors. They can also be liabilities, however, if they make the company less responsive and productive. Consider the airline industry. It has become a competitive necessity for all of the airlines to offer electronic ticket purchases through their websites. To provide competitive advantage, however, these sites must be highly responsive and they must provide both current and accurate information on flights and prices. An up-to-date, user-friendly site that provides fast answers to user queries will attract customers and increase revenues. In contrast, a site that provides outdated or inaccurate information, or has a slow response time, will hurt rather than improve business.

Clearly, good business processes are vital to organizational success. But how can organizations determine if their business processes are well designed? The first step is to document the process by describing its steps, its inputs and outputs, and its resources. The organization can then analyze the process and, if necessary, modify it to improve its performance.

To understand this point, let's consider the e-ticketing process. E-ticketing consists of four main process activities: searching for flights, reserving a seat, processing payment, and issuing an e-ticket. These activities can be broken down into more detailed process steps. The result may look like the process map in **Figure 2.1**. Note that different symbols correspond to different

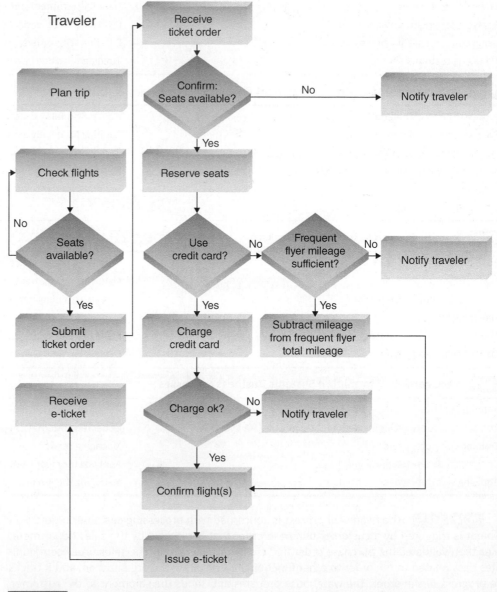

 FIGURE 2.1   **Business process for ordering an e-ticket from an airline website.**

types of process steps. For example, rectangles (steps) are activities that are performed by process resources (reserve seats, issue e-ticket). Diamond-shaped boxes indicate decisions that need to be made (seats available?). Arrows are used as connectors between steps; they indicate the sequence of activities.

These symbols are important in the process flowchart (which is similar to a programming flowchart). Other symbols may be used to provide additional process details. For example, D-shaped boxes are used instead of rectangles when a waiting period is part of a process, ovals can show start and stop points, and process resources can be attached to activities with resource connector lines or included as an annotation or property for each activity box.

The customers of the process are travelers planning a trip, and the process output is an e-ticket. Travelers provide inputs to the process: the desired travel parameters to begin the search, the frequent flyer miles number, and their credit card information. Also, a computerized reservation system that stores information for many airlines provides some of the process inputs such as the seat availability and prices. The resources used in the process are the airline website, the computerized reservation system, and, if the customer calls the airline call center at any time during the process, the call center system and the human travel agents. The process creates customer value by efficiently generating an output that meets the customer search criteria—dates and prices. The performance of the process depends on efficiency metrics such as the time required to purchase an e-ticket, from the moment the customer initiates the ticket search until he or she receives the e-ticket. Effectiveness metrics include customer satisfaction with the airline website. Finally, the performance of the process may be affected if the quality or the timeliness of the inputs is low—for example, if the customer enters the wrong dates—or if the process resources are not available—for example, if the website crashes before the purchase is finalized.

Information Systems and Business Processes

MIS An information system (IS) is a critical enabler of an organization's business processes. Information systems facilitate communication and coordination among different functional areas, and allow easy exchange of, and access to, data across processes. Specifically, ISs play a vital role in three areas:

- Executing the process
- Capturing and storing process data
- Monitoring process performance

In this section, you will learn about each of these roles. In some cases, the role is fully automated—that is, it is performed entirely by the IS. In other cases, the IS must rely on the manager's judgment, expertise, and intuition. IT's About Business 2.1 shows how NASCAR uses information technology to streamline its prerace process.

MIS **Executing the Process.**   An IS helps organizations execute processes efficiently and effectively. ISs are typically embedded into the processes, and they play a critical role in executing the processes. In other words, an IS and the processes are usually intertwined. If the IS does not work, the process cannot be executed. An IS helps execute processes by informing people when it is time to complete a task by providing the necessary data to complete the task and, in some cases, by providing the means to complete the task.

In the procurement process, for example, the IS generates the purchase requisitions and then informs the purchasing department that action on these requisitions is needed. The accountant will be able to view all shipments received to match an invoice that has been received from a supplier and verify that the invoice is accurate. Without the IS, these steps, and therefore the process, cannot be completed. For example, if the IS is not available, how will the warehouse know which orders are ready to pack and ship?

IT's About Business 2.1

MIS   NASCAR Uses IT in its Prerace Inspection

The National Association for Stock Car Auto Racing (NASCAR; **www .nascar.com**) is a family-owned-and-operated business that governs multiple auto racing events. One of NASCAR's key business processes is the prerace inspection of the cars. The rationale for prerace inspection is to ensure that all cars are as evenly matched as possible.

Prerace inspection begins two days before a race. Each car on the entry list for a particular race must pass a thorough inspection to compete. Here is how the process works.

In the first inspection, NASCAR officials assess whether a car meets NASCAR requirements—height off the ground at the front and the back of the car, weight, fuel tank capacity, and many other factors. Cars that meet these requirements are cleared to practice, and they qualify for the race.

If a car does not pass the first inspection, then NASCAR allows that team to fix the problem and undergo a second inspection. However, the team is sent to the end of the line. This process can cause a backup of cars waiting to be cleared before the race. In the past, NASCAR would let a team with a violation keep its spot in line while it fixed the problem, essentially jumping ahead of teams still waiting to undergo their initial inspection. That situation left crew chiefs with little incentive to repair violations. If the repair did not fix the violation, they would simply try again.

After the first inspection, each team has two days before the race to work on their cars. After each team qualifies, NASCAR conducts a second, post-qualifying inspection. On race morning, all cars are inspected one final time.

Historically, NASCAR officials performed the prerace inspection by walking to each inspection station and visually observing each car. Moreover, they recorded their observations on paper. These forms contained more than 100 items clustered in categories depending on the kind of inspection. The form would remain with each vehicle as it went through the inspection process. Each season, NASCAR used roughly 25,000 sheets of paper for inspections.

In September 2014, NASCAR implemented an app from Microsoft that incorporates everything from the paper form, but in a more useful format. Each vehicle is displayed on a dashboard that tracks its stages through the inspection process. The dashboard also uses color-coded flags to highlight violations. Officials can be alerted to any pending issues for each vehicle, and they can access the NASCAR rulebook at the press of a digital button. They can also add digital notes and photographs to detail any infractions. In addition, the app enables officials to determine whether prerace inspections are completed on time. Finally, the race director can use his tablet to monitor each inspection station, identify which cars have been cited for violations, and learn the status of every car.

The Microsoft app simplified the prerace inspection process. Consider, for example, that the paper form needed a NASCAR official's signature on every item. In contrast, the app by default assumes every item's status is good unless otherwise noted by officials.

The app stored a large amount of data. Information on the prerace inspections of all vehicles was collected in real time. Consequently, NASCAR officials could spot problems to help make the races fair for everyone.

NASCAR began using a new inspection system for the 2018 racing season. The new process, developed by Hawk-Eye Innovations (**www.hawkeyeinnovations.com**), uses 17 cameras and 8 projectors to create a three-dimensional map of each car. Each map is then compared to each manufacturer's standard, as depicted by a computer-aided drawing (CAD) from that manufacturer. Areas of the car's body in compliance appear in green; areas of the body outside the allowable tolerance display in red. The entire process takes approximately three minutes per car. The new process, driven by technology, is far faster and more efficient than the previous process, and it stores much more data about each car.

For traditional race weekends, two prequalifying inspection failures result in the loss of 15 minutes of practice and an ejected crew member, typically the car chief. For two-day enhanced race weekends that feature impounded race cars and an inspection process after time trials, one failure after qualifying results in having to start at the rear of the field.

The prerace inspection process has resulted in several notable penalties. For example, nine cars failed inspection prior to the Gander RV 400 race at Pocono Raceway in July 2019. In February 2020 reigning Daytona 500 winner Denny Hamlin dropped to the rear of the field after his No. 11 Joe Gibbs Racing Toyota failed prerace inspection twice before the Daytona 500. In May 2020 the Joe Gibbs Racing team's Toyota failed the prerace inspection twice at Darlington Raceway, forcing defending NASCAR Cup Series champion Kyle Busch to the rear of the field for the Real Heroes 400 race.

Sources: Compiled from "Kyle Busch to Drop to the Rear after JGR No. 18 Fails Pre-Race Inspection Twice at Darlington," *NASCAR.com*, May 17, 2020; "No. 11 of Denny Hamlin Fails Pre-Race Inspection, Will Drop to Rear for 2020 Daytona 500," *NASCAR.com,* February 16, 2020; "Multiple Cars Fail Pre-Race Inspection at Pocono Raceway," *NASCAR. com*, July 28, 2019; M. Weaver, "NASCAR's New Disqualification Policy Explained," *Autoweek*, February 7, 2019; Z. Albert, "Competition Model for 2019 Adds Disqualifications, Alters Post-Race Inspection," *NASCAR. com*, February 4, 2019; Z. Albert, "New 2018 Inspection Process Aims to 'Create a Level Playing Field'," *NASCAR.com*, February 1, 2018; S. Choney, "NASCAR Levels the Playing Field by Bringing the Latest Technology into an American Tradition," Microsoft.com blog, June 27, 2016; N. Linhart, "NASCAR App Improves Inspection Efficiency," *Charlotte Sun Times*, February 10, 2015; J. Gluck, "App Improves NASCAR Inspection Process," *USA Today*, February 8, 2015; "A Day at the Track for a NASCAR Race," *NASCAR.com,* January 5, 2015; "Going Through Inspections," *NASCAR.com*, January 5, 2015; J. Richter, "NASCAR Pre-Race Inspection? There's an App for That," *Fox Sports*, October 23, 2014; T. Bradley, "NASCAR Turns to Microsoft and Windows 8 to Streamline Race Operations," *Forbes*, October 21, 2014; J. Hammond, "NASCAR Inspections a Work in Progress," *Fox Sports*, April 16, 2013; **www.nascar.com**, accessed June 1, 2020.

Questions

1. Discuss why prerace inspection is a business process for NASCAR.
2. Describe the various benefits that the old app provided to NASCAR.
3. Describe the advantages of the new (2018) app over the previous app.
4. Refer to Section 2.3. Is the app a strategic information system for NASCAR? Why or why not? Support your answer.

In the fulfillment process, the IS will inform people in the warehouse that orders are ready for shipment. It also provides them with a listing of what materials must be included in the order and where to find those materials in the warehouse.

MIS Capturing and Storing Process Data.

Processes create data such as dates, times, product numbers, quantities, prices, and addresses, as well as who did what, when, and where. IS captures and stores these data, commonly referred to as *process data* or *transaction data.* Some of these data are generated and automatically captured by the IS. These are data related to who completes an activity, when, and where. Other data are generated outside the IS and must be entered into it. This data entry can occur in various ways, ranging from manual entry to automated methods involving data in forms such as bar codes and RFID tags that can be read by machines.

In the fulfillment process, for example, when a customer order is received by mail or over the phone, the person taking the order must enter data such as the customer's name, what the customer ordered, and how much he or she ordered. Significantly, when a customer order is received through the firm's website, then all customer details are captured by the IS. Data such as the name of the person entering the data (who), at which location the person is completing the task (where), and the date and time (when) are automatically included by the IS when it creates the order. The data are updated as the process steps are executed. When the order is shipped, the warehouse will provide data about which products were shipped and in what quantities, and the IS will automatically include data related to who, when, and where.

An important advantage of using an IS compared to a manual system or multiple functional area information systems is that the data need to be entered into the system only once. Furthermore, once they are entered, other people in the process can easily access them, and there is no need to reenter them in subsequent steps.

The data captured by the IS can provide immediate feedback. For example, the IS can use the data to create a receipt or to make recommendations for additional or alternative products.

MIS Monitoring Process Performance.

A third contribution of IS is to help monitor the state of the various business processes. That is, the IS indicates how well a process is executing. The IS performs this role by evaluating information about a process. This information can be created at either the *instance level* (i.e., a specific task or activity) or at the *process level* (i.e., the process as a whole).

For example, a company might be interested in the status of a particular customer order. Where is the order within the fulfillment process? Was the complete order shipped? If so, when? If not, then when can we expect it to be shipped? Or, for the procurement process, when was the purchase order sent to the supplier? What will be the cost of acquiring the material? At the process level, the IS can evaluate how well the procurement process is being executed by calculating the lead time, or the time between sending the purchase order to a vendor and receiving the goods, for each order and each vendor over time.

Not only can the IS help monitor a process, but it can also detect problems with the process. The IS performs this role by comparing the information with a standard—that is, what the company expects or desires—to determine if the process is performing within expectations. Management establishes standards based on organizational goals.

If the information provided by the IS indicates that the process is not meeting the standards, then the company assumes that some type of problem exists. Some problems can be routinely and automatically detected by the IS, whereas others require a person to review the information and make judgements. For example, the IS can calculate the expected date that a specific order will be shipped and determine whether this date will meet the established standard. Or, the IS can calculate the average time taken to fill all orders over the past month and compare this information with the standard to determine if the process is working as expected.

POM Monitoring business processes, then, helps detect problems with these processes. These problems are very often really symptoms of a more fundamental problem. In such cases, the IS can help diagnose the cause of the symptoms by providing managers with additional detailed information. For example, if the average time to process a customer order appears to have increased over the previous month, this problem could be a symptom of a more basic problem.

HRM A manager can then drill down into the information to diagnose the underlying problem. To accomplish this task, the manager can request a breakdown of the information by type of product, customer, location, employees, day of the week, time of day, and so on. After reviewing this detailed information, the manager might determine that the warehouse has experienced an exceptionally high employee turnover rate over the last month and that the delays are occurring because new employees are not sufficiently familiar with the process. The manager might conclude that this problem will work itself out over time, in which case there is nothing more to be done. Alternatively, the manager could conclude that the new employees are not being adequately trained and supervised. In this case, the company must take actions to correct the problem. The following section discusses several methodologies that managers can use to take corrective action when process problems are identified.

Robotic Process Automation

Robotic process automation (RPA) is a system that enables enterprises to automate business processes and tasks that historically were carried out by employees. Companies that employ RPA develop software "robots"—known as *bots*—that automate the steps in a business process. Let's consider a variety of RPA scenarios.

MKT *Customer service*: Modern customers are accustomed to quick responses that solve their problems. Automated customer care bots can examine queries and route them to the correct customer care agent. Bots can also offer initial responses to customers without human intervention.

POM *Invoice processing*: RPA bots can automate the entire process from receipt to payment. The bots can automate receiving the invoice from the supplier, entering the invoice data, checking the invoice for correctness, and generating payments, thus minimizing human involvement.

POM *Sales orders*: RPA bots can automate tasks such as generating sales quotes and sales orders, monitoring the status of the order, generating invoices, generating payment terms and methods, monitoring returns, and generating refunds. Interestingly, RPA bots can monitor returns and generate refunds very quickly, which improves the customer experience and positively impacts the company's reputation.

HRM *Payroll*: RPA bots can verify that employee data are consistent across multiple systems, validate timesheets, load earnings and deductions in calculating the amount of payment, create the paycheck, administer benefits, and make any necessary reimbursements.

POM *Price comparison*: All businesses make purchases. In the purchasing process, companies perform research about pricing in order to make informed decisions. RPA bots compare prices from different vendors as well as product attributes and quality.

POM *Manage customer information*: In May 2020 Takeda Pharmaceuticals (**www.takeda .com**) was recruiting patients for a clinical trial of a COVID-19 treatment. It normally took the firm several weeks to collect the volunteers' information, determine who would be suitable for the trial, and prepare the paperwork. Takeda used RPA bots to create patient files, select data input fields, and cut and paste text. As a result, the firm finished each person's paperwork in days instead of weeks.

HRM *Processing HR information*: Businesses generate large amounts of employee data, which RPA bots can collect and organize. These data include employee history with the company, payroll, and level of training.

HRM *Recruitment*: RPA bots can source resumes from different platforms such as LinkedIn, assess candidate qualifications, and filter spam and unqualified applications.

Before you go on...

1. What is a business process?
2. Describe several business processes carried out at your university.
3. Define a cross-functional business process and provide several examples of such processes.
4. Pick one of the processes described in Question 2 or 3 and identify its inputs, outputs, customer(s), and resources. How does the process create value for its customer(s)?
5. What is robotic process automation? Provide examples of its use in organizations.

2.2 Business Process Improvement, Business Process Reengineering, and Business Process Management

Excellence in executing business processes is widely recognized as the underlying basis for all significant measures of competitive performance in an organization. Consider the following measures, for example:

- *Customer satisfaction*: The result of optimizing and aligning business processes to fulfill customers' needs, wants, and desires
- *Cost reduction*: The result of optimizing operations and supplier processes
- *Cycle and fulfillment time reduction*: The result of optimizing the manufacturing and logistics processes
- *Quality*: The result of optimizing the design, development, and production processes
- *Differentiation*: The result of optimizing the marketing and innovation processes
- *Productivity*: The result of optimizing each individual's work processes

The question is: How does an organization ensure business process excellence?

In their book *Reengineering the Corporation*, first published in 1993, Michael Hammer and James Champy argued that to become more competitive, American businesses needed to radically redesign their business processes to reduce costs and increase quality. The authors further asserted that information technology is the key enabler of such change. This radical redesign, called **business process reengineering (BPR)**, is a strategy for making an organization's business processes more productive and profitable. The key to BPR is for enterprises to examine their business processes from a "clean sheet" perspective and then determine how they can best reconstruct those processes to improve their business functions. BPR's popularity was propelled by the unique capabilities of information technology, such as automation and standardization of many process steps and error reduction due to improved communication among organizational information silos.

Although some enterprises have successfully implemented BPR, many organizations found this strategy too difficult, too radical, too lengthy, and too comprehensive. The impact on employees, on facilities, on existing investments in information systems, and even on organizational culture was overwhelming. Despite the many failures in BPR implementation, however, businesses increasingly began to organize work around business processes rather than individual tasks. The result was a less radical, less disruptive, and more incremental approach, called *business process improvement (BPI)*.

BPI focuses on reducing variation in the process outputs by searching for root causes of the variation in the process itself (e.g., a broken machine on an assembly line) or among the process inputs (e.g., a decline in the quality of raw materials purchased from a certain supplier). BPI is usually performed by teams of employees that include a process expert—usually the process

Author Lecture Videos are available exclusively in *WileyPLUS*.
Apply the Concept activities are available in the Appendix and in *WileyPLUS*.

owner (the individual manager who oversees the process)—as well as other individuals who are involved in the process. These individuals can be involved directly; for example, the workers who actually perform process steps. Alternatively, these individuals can be involved indirectly; for example, customers who purchase the outputs from the process.

Six Sigma is a popular methodology for BPI initiatives. Its goal is to ensure that the process has no more than 3.4 defects per million outputs by using statistical methods to analyze the process. (A defect is defined as a faulty product or an unsatisfactory service.) Six Sigma was developed by Motorola in the 1980s, and it is now used by companies worldwide, thanks in part to promotional efforts by early adopters such as GE. Six Sigma is especially appropriate for manufacturing environments, in which product defects can be easily defined and measured. Over the years, the methodology has been modified so that it focuses less on defects and more on customer value. As a result, it can now be applied to services as well as to products. Today, Six Sigma tools are widely used in financial services and health care institutions as components of process-improvement initiatives.

Regardless of the specific methodology you use, a successful BPI project generally follows five basic phases: define, measure, analyze, improve, and control (DMAIC).

- In the *define phase*, the BPI team uses a graphical process diagram to document the existing "as is" process activities, process resources, and process inputs and outputs. The team also documents the customer requirements for the process output, together with a description of the problem to be addressed.

- In the *measure phase*, the BPI team identifies relevant process metrics, such as time and cost, to generate one output (product or service) and collects data to understand how metrics evolve over time. Sometimes the data already exist, in which case the team can extract them from the IS that supports the process. Other times, however, the BPI team must combine operational process data already stored in the company's IS systems with other data sources, such as customer and employee observations, interviews, and surveys.

- In the *analysis phase*, the BPI team examines the "as is" process diagram and the collected data to identify problems with the process (e.g., decreasing efficiency or effectiveness) and their root causes. If possible, the team should also benchmark the process; that is, compare its performance with that of similar processes in other companies, or other areas of the organization. The team can employ IT applications such as statistical analysis software or simulation packages in this phase.

  Using process simulation software during the analysis phase provides two benefits. First, it enables a process manager to quickly simulate a real situation (e.g., with a certain number of people undertaking activities) for a specific amount of time (e.g., a working day, a week, or a month). The manager can then estimate the process performance over time without having to observe the process in practice. Second, it allows the manager to create multiple scenarios; for example, using a different number of resources in the process or using a different configuration for the process steps. Process simulation software can also provide a number of outputs regarding a process, including the time used by all resources to execute specific activities, the overall cycle time of a process, the identification of resources that are infrequently used, and the bottlenecks in the process. Simulating a process provides a risk-free and inexpensive test of an improvement solution that does not need to be conducted with real resources.

- In the *improve phase*, the BPI team identifies possible solutions for addressing the root causes of the problem, maps the resulting "to be" process alternatives, and selects and implements the most appropriate solution. Common ways to improve processes are eliminating process activities that do not add value to the output and rearranging activities in a way that reduces delays or improves resource use. The organization must be careful, however, not to eliminate internal *process controls*—those activities that safeguard company resources, guarantee the accuracy of its financial reporting, and ensure adherence to rules and regulations.

- In the *control phase*, the team establishes process metrics and monitors the improved process after the solution has been implemented to ensure the process performance remains stable. An IS system can be very useful for this purpose.

Although BPI initiatives do not deliver the huge performance gains promised by BPR, many organizations prefer them because they are less risky and less costly. BPI focuses on delivering quantifiable results—and if a business case cannot be made, the project is not continued. All employees can be trained to apply BPI techniques in their own work to identify opportunities for improvement. Thus, BPI projects tend to be performed more from the bottom up, in contrast to BPR projects, which involve top-down change mandates. BPI projects take less time overall, and even if they are unsuccessful, they consume fewer organizational resources than BPR projects. However, if incremental improvements through BPI are no longer possible, or if significant changes occur in the firm's business environment, then the firm should consider BPR projects. One final consideration is that over time, employees can become overstretched or lose interest if the company undertakes too many BPI projects and does not have an effective system to manage and focus the improvement efforts.

POM To sustain BPI efforts over time, organizations can adopt **business process management (BPM)**, a management system that includes methods and tools to support the design, analysis, implementation, management, and continuous optimization of core business processes throughout the organization. BPM integrates disparate BPI initiatives to ensure consistent strategy execution.

Important components of BPM are process modeling and business activity monitoring. BPM begins with *process modeling*, which is a graphical depiction of all of the steps in a process. Process modeling helps employees understand the interactions and dependencies among the people involved in the process, the information systems they rely on, and the information they require to optimally perform their tasks. Process modeling software can support this activity. IT's About Business 2.2 shows how Chevron has employed BPR, BPI, and BPM.

IT's About Business 2.2

POM **MIS** BPR, BPI, and BPM at Chevron

Chevron (**www.chevron.com**), one of the world's largest oil and gas companies, and its subsidiaries are involved in exploring and producing oil and natural gas, as well as in manufacturing, transporting, and distributing petrochemical products, including gasoline and refined products. In 2013, Chevron employed more than 60,000 people worldwide, produced the equivalent of more than 2.6 million barrels of oil every day, and garnered more than $230 billion in sales. Chevron has initiated several process reengineering and improvement efforts over the years, evolving from BPR to BPI and eventually to BPM, as described next.

In 1995, Chevron's output was less than half of its current amount, producing roughly 1 million barrels of oil per day across six plants. The company had three major departments: Refining, Marketing, and Supply and Distribution (S&D). Management determined that they needed to improve their supply chain (see Chapter 11) to better integrate their multiple internal processes. A key figure in this initiative was Vice President Peter McCrea, who had a strong idea for dramatically improving performance. McCrea was convinced that Chevron had to reengineer the company's core processes from beginning to end: from the acquisition of crude oil to the distribution of final products to Chevron customers.

To accomplish this task, Chevron adopted a holistic approach. The company collaborated with a consulting firm to create a model of the existing processes. The objective was to radically improve these processes to align with Chevron's business goals. In other words, Chevron's strategy was not to concentrate on the existing processes to identify specific areas to improve. Rather, the project identified the desired outputs and then worked backward by examining the supporting processes, using BPR. As an added benefit, this holistic approach led the company to examine the interdependencies among processes used in different business units. This approach ultimately improved the company's overall performance. In a 1996 report, Chevron claimed the BPR project saved the company $50 million.

This complex BPR effort was initially followed by several smaller, employee-driven BPI initiatives. For example, in 1998, six Chevron employees initiated a project to improve water treatment processes at a company plant in California. As a result of their efforts, operating costs fell by one-third. Their success inspired other employees to initiate BPI projects in Indonesia, Angola, and other locations by using the Six Sigma improvement methodology. Although some managers were able to demonstrate the benefits of BPI at the local level, it was not until 2006 that these efforts achieved companywide recognition and corporate backing. In that year, Lean Six Sigma, which combines statistical process analysis with techniques to eliminate waste and improve process flow, became Chevron's preferred improvement methodology. Since Chevron implemented Lean Six Sigma, company employees have initiated hundreds of BPI projects worldwide, resulting in significant savings. From 2008 to 2010 alone, Chevron reported more than $1 billion in BPI benefits. To support these internal improvement efforts, Chevron convinced its suppliers to participate in its BPI initiatives.

To coordinate these various BPI efforts, Chevron has adopted a unified BPM approach that involves standardizing processes across the entire company and consolidating process information within a central repository. Chevron estimates that only 20 percent of its processes can be fully automated—the rest involve a combination of manual and automated steps. Thus, process standardization involves not only supporting activities that can be automated but also ensuring that relevant employees are familiar with the standards for manual activities. To familiarize employees with these processes, Chevron implemented Nimbus (**nimbus.tibco.com**), a business process management suite (BPMS) that acts as a repository of standard companywide rules and procedures. Nimbus can also provide employees with detailed work instructions.

Let's use shipping as an example of a process in which the BPMS could shine. Shipping was executed in different ways in locations throughout Asia, Europe, and the United States. To establish uniform company standards, Chevron employed a BPI approach.

The company documented its processes as they existed across different geographical locations, identified best practices, and combined these practices into a common process. It then detailed these new policies and procedures and distributed them to managers through the company's Web-based BPMS.

Chevron has a companywide management system that focuses on operational excellence, and BPM is a key part of that system. All Chevron operating companies and business units must implement continuous improvement processes using carefully defined guidelines, metrics, and targets that are reviewed and adapted every year. Chevron's metrics focus on process efficiency, safety, risk, and the environment. The commitment to continuous improvement is part of Chevron's corporate culture. All employees participate in operational excellence activities, and managers receive specific operational excellence training.

Operational excellence is especially crucial during difficult economic times. For example, in the fourth quarter of 2014, Chevron's net income was $3.5 billion, down nearly 30 percent from the same period in 2013. This decline resulted primarily from the steep drop in crude oil prices. However, the results probably would have been worse without the operational excellence initiatives. Chevron's CEO noted that the lower crude oil prices were partially offset by increased operational efficiency in the company's downstream operations—that is, refining oil products and delivering them to customers. This increased efficiency was a product of the company's ongoing BPR, BPI, and BPM efforts. These efforts appear to be paying off: by 2017 Chevron's net income had increased dramatically to $9.2 billion.

Sources: Compiled from "Operational Excellence," *Chevron.com*, March 2012; "Chevron—Using Nimbus Control Software to Manage Processes," *Finding FindingPetroleum.com*, September 23, 2010; "Chevron Wins Boston Strategies International's 2010 Award for Lean Six Sigma Implementation in Oil and Gas Operations," *Bostonstrategies .com*, September 22, 2010; E. Schmidt, "From the Bottom Up: Grassroots Effort Finds Footing at Chevron," *isixsigma.com*, March 1, 2010; R. Parker, "Business Process Improvement: A Talk with Chevron's Jim Boots," *Ebizq.net*, August 26, 2009; P. Harmon, *Business Process Management*, Elsevier, Burlington, MA, 2007; **www.chevron.com**, accessed June 1, 2020.

Questions

1. Discuss the primary advantages of BPR at Chevron.
2. Why did Chevron adopt BPI?
3. How did Chevron apply BPM in its operations?

Business activity monitoring (BAM) is a real-time approach for measuring and managing business processes. Companies use BAM to monitor their business processes, identify failures or exceptions, and address these failures in real time. Furthermore, because BAM tracks process operations and indicates whether they succeed or fail, it creates valuable records of process behaviors that organizations can use to improve their processes.

BPM activities are often supported by *business process management suites (BPMS)*. A BPMS is an integrated set of applications that includes a repository of process information such as process maps and business rules, tools for process modeling, simulation, execution, coordination across functions, and reconfiguration in response to changing business needs as well as process-monitoring capabilities.

Gartner (**www.gartner.com**), a leading IT research and advisory firm, states that companies need to focus on developing and mastering BPM skills throughout the organization. Gartner notes that high-performing companies use BPM technologies such as real-time process monitoring, visualization, analytics, and intelligent automated decision making to support intelligent business operations.

Another promising emerging trend is *social BPM.* This technology enables employees to collaborate using social media tools on wired and mobile platforms, both internally across functions and externally with stakeholders (such as customers or subject-area experts), to exchange process knowledge and improve process execution.

BPM initially helps companies improve profitability by decreasing costs and increasing revenues. Over time, BPM can create a competitive advantage by improving organizational flexibility—making it easy to adapt to changing business conditions and to take advantage of new opportunities. BPM also increases customer satisfaction and ensures compliance with rules and regulations. In all cases, the company's strategy should drive the BPM effort.

Before you go on...

1. What is business process reengineering?
2. What is business process improvement?
3. What is business process management?

2.3 | Business Pressures, Organizational Responses, and Information Technology Support

Modern organizations compete in a challenging environment. To remain competitive, they must react rapidly to problems and opportunities that arise from extremely dynamic conditions. In this section, you examine some of the major pressures confronting modern organizations and the strategies that organizations employ to respond to these pressures.

Author Lecture Videos are available exclusively in *WileyPLUS*.
Apply the Concept activities are available in the Appendix and in *WileyPLUS*.

Business Pressures

The **business environment** is the combination of social, legal, economic, physical, and political factors in which businesses conduct their operations. Significant changes in any of these factors are likely to create business pressures on organizations. Organizations typically respond to these pressures with activities supported by IT. **Figure 2.2** illustrates the relationships among business pressures, organizational performance and responses, and IT support. You will learn about three major types of business pressures: market, technology, and societal pressures.

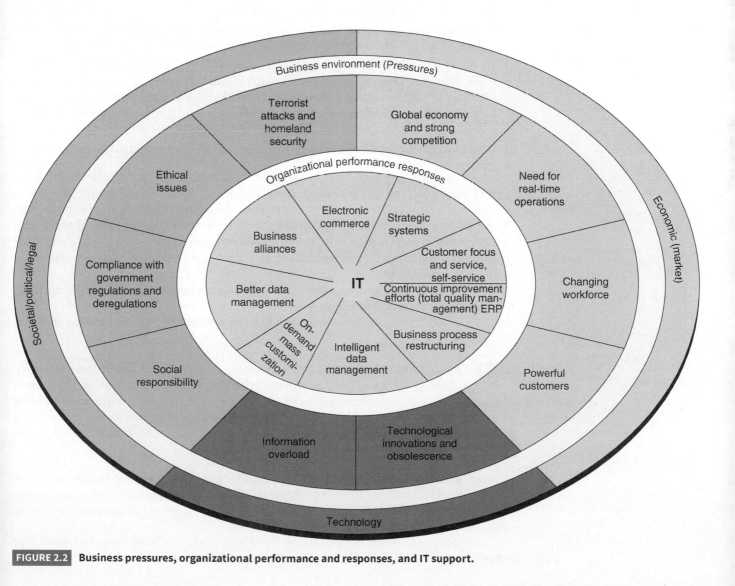

FIGURE 2.2   Business pressures, organizational performance and responses, and IT support.

MKT **Market Pressures.** Market pressures are generated by the global economy, intense competition, the changing nature of the workforce, and powerful customers. Let's look more closely at each of these factors.

Globalization. **Globalization** is the integration and interdependence of economic, social, cultural, and ecological facets of life, made possible by rapid advances in information technology. Today, individuals around the world are able to connect, compute, communicate, collaborate, and compete everywhere and anywhere, any time, and all the time; to access limitless amounts of information, services, and entertainment; to exchange knowledge; and to produce and sell goods and services. People and organizations can now operate without regard to geography, time, distance, or even language barriers. The bottom line? Globalization is markedly increasing competition.

These observations highlight the importance of market pressures for you. Simply put, you and the organizations you join will be competing with people and organizations from all over the world.

Let's consider some examples of globalization:

- Multinational corporations operate on a global scale, with offices and branches located worldwide.
- Many automobile manufacturers use parts from other countries, such as a car being assembled in the United States with parts coming from Japan, Germany, or Korea.
- The World Trade Organization (WTO; **www.wto.org**) supervises international trade.
- Regional agreements such as the United States–Mexico–Canada Agreement (USMCA) have contributed to increased world trade and increased competition. In September 2018 the three countries reached an agreement to replace the North American Free Trade Agreement (NAFTA) with the USMCA. The three countries had ratified the USMCA by March 2020.
- The European Union (EU) is an economic and political union of 27 countries that are located in Europe. Following general elections in 2017 and 2019, Parliament ratified the withdrawal agreement, and the United Kingdom left the European Union on January 31, 2020. The withdrawal was known as Brexit.
- The rise of India and China as economic powerhouses has increased global competition.

One important pressure that businesses in a global market must contend with is the cost of labor, which varies significantly among countries. In general, labor costs are higher in developed countries such as the United States and Japan than in developing countries such as Bangladesh and El Salvador. Also, developed countries usually offer greater benefits, such as healthcare, to employees, driving the cost of doing business even higher. Therefore, many labor-intensive industries have moved their operations to countries with low labor costs. IT has made such moves much easier to implement.

However, manufacturing overseas is no longer the bargain it once was, and manufacturing in the United States is no longer as expensive. For example, manufacturing wages in China have increased from $3.60 per hour in 2018 to $5.64 per hour in 2020, an increase of almost 60 percent.

HRM **The Changing Nature of the Workforce.** The workforce, particularly in developed countries, is becoming more diversified. Increasing numbers of women, single parents, minorities, and persons with disabilities are now employed in all types of positions. IT is easing the integration of these employees into the traditional workforce. IT is also enabling people to work from home, which can be a major benefit for parents with young children and for people confronted with mobility or transportation issues.

Powerful Customers. Consumer sophistication and expectations increase as customers become more knowledgeable about the products and services they acquire. Customers can use the Internet to find detailed information about products and services, to compare prices, and to purchase items at electronic auctions.

Organizations recognize the importance of customers and they have increased their efforts to acquire and retain them. Modern firms strive to learn as much as possible about their customers to better anticipate and address their needs. This process, called *customer intimacy*, is an important component of *customer relationship management (CRM)*, an organization-wide effort toward maximizing the customer experience. You will learn about CRM in Chapter 11.

MIS **Technology Pressures.**   The second category of business pressures consists of those pressures related to technology. Two major technology-related pressures are technological innovation and information overload.

Technological Innovation and Obsolescence.
New and improved technologies rapidly create or support substitutes for products, alternative service options, and superb quality. As a result, today's state-of-the-art products may be obsolete tomorrow. For example, how fast are new versions of your smartphone being released? How quickly are electronic versions of books, magazines, and newspapers replacing traditional hard copy versions? These changes force businesses to keep up with consumer demands.

Consider the rapid technological innovation of the Apple iPad (**www.apple.com/ipad**).

- Apple released its first iPad in April 2010.
- Apple released its iPad Mini in November 2012.
- In November 2013 Apple released its iPad Air.
- In November 2015 Apple released its iPad Pro.
- In 2019, Apple released the latest versions of its iPad (7th generation), iPad Mini (5th generation), and iPad Air (3rd generation).
- In 2020, Apple released the latest version of its iPad Pro (4th generation).

One manifestation of technological innovation is "bring your own device (BYOD)." BYOD refers to the policy of permitting employees to bring personally owned mobile devices (laptops, tablet computers, and smartphones) to the workplace and to use those devices to connect to the corporate network as well as for personal use. The academic version of BYOD involves students' using personally owned devices in educational settings to connect to their school's network.

MIS The rapid increase in BYOD represents a huge challenge for IT departments. Not only has IT lost the ability to fully control and manage these devices, but employees are now demanding that they be able to conduct company business from multiple personal devices.

The good news is that BYOD has increased worker productivity and satisfaction. In fact, some employees with BYOD privileges actually work longer hours with no additional pay. The bad news is security concerns. Many companies with BYOD policies have experienced an increase in *malware* (malicious software, discussed in Chapter 4). Furthermore, there is an increased risk of losing sensitive proprietary information. Such information might not be securely stored on a personal mobile device, which can be lost or stolen.

Information Overload.
The amount of information available on the Internet doubles approximately every year, and much of it is free. The Internet and other telecommunications networks are bringing a flood of information to managers. To make decisions effectively and efficiently, managers must be able to access, navigate, and use these vast stores of data, information, and knowledge. Information technologies such as search engines (discussed in Chapter 6) and data mining (Chapter 12) provide valuable support in these efforts.

Societal, Political, and Legal Pressures.
The third category of business pressures includes social responsibility, government regulation/deregulation, spending for social programs, spending to protect against terrorism, and ethics. This section will explain how all of these elements affect modern businesses. We start with social responsibility.

Social Responsibility.
Social issues that affect businesses and individuals range from the state of the physical environment, to company and individual philanthropy, to education. Some corporations and individuals are willing to spend time and money to address various social problems. These efforts are known as **organizational social responsibility** or **individual social responsibility**.

One critical social problem is the state of the physical environment. A growing IT initiative, called *green IT*, addresses some of the most pressing environmental concerns. IT is instrumental in organizational efforts to "go green" in three areas:

1. *Facilities design and management.* Organizations are creating more environmentally sustainable work environments. Many organizations are pursuing Leadership in Energy and Environmental Design (LEED) certification from the U.S. Green Building Council, a nonprofit group that promotes the construction of environmentally friendly buildings. One impact of this development is that IT professionals are expected to help create green facilities.

2. *Carbon management.* As companies try to reduce their carbon footprints, they are turning to IT executives to develop the systems needed to monitor carbon throughout the organization and its supply chain, which can be global in scope. Therefore, IT employees need to become knowledgeable about embedded carbon and how to measure it in the company's products and processes.

3. *International and U.S. environmental laws.* IT executives must deal with federal and state laws and international regulations that impact everything from the IT products they buy to how they dispose of them to their company's carbon footprint.

IT's About Business 2.3 illustrates the precarious nature of our physical environment today. The case addresses how conservationists are using various technologies in an attempt to save the Great Barrier Reef in Australia.

IT's About Business 2.3

MIS   Saving Australia's Great Barrier Reef

Coral reefs are home to one-fourth of the world's marine species, and they provide one-sixth of the animal protein that humans consume. In fact, coral reefs have been nicknamed the "rainforests of the sea" for their beauty and their biodiversity. The structure of coral reefs also buffers shorelines against waves, storms, and floods.

In particular, the Great Barrier Reef (**www.barrierreef.org**), a UNESCO World Heritage Site, is home to one of the earth's most diverse ecosystems. The reef is the size of Germany, and more than 9,000 species of fish, whales, dolphins, turtles, mollusks, plankton, and soft and hard coral live there. In addition, the reef attracts more than 2 million tourists every year.

Coral polyps—tiny, soft-bodied, translucent animals that are related to jellyfish—build coral reefs. The algae that the polyps host give them their incredible colors along with most of their nutrients. Unfortunately, the reef's coral has rapidly deteriorated as a result of a process called *bleaching*.

Bleaching takes place when abnormal conditions—such as increased sea temperatures—cause the coral to expel the very small algae that live there. When this happens, the corals bleach, or turn white. If bleaching is severe enough, then it will kill coral.

The reef's first mass bleaching event happened in 1998. Subsequent outbreaks occurred in 2002, 2016, 2017, and 2020. Coral populations can recover from bleaching events, but the process can take a decade or longer. As of May 2020, approximately half of the Great Barrier Reef was already dead. Finding ways to address this environmental catastrophe has been extremely challenging. Fortunately, however, researchers are making progress using various technologies including drones, artificial intelligence, robots, underwater loudspeakers, and sun shields. Let's take a closer look at these technologies.

Drones

With so much coral to regrow, it is difficult to decide which parts of the reef should be addressed first. Traditionally, underwater surveys and NASA satellite imagery have been the primary methods used to collect data about the state of the reef. Both of these methods have drawbacks.

In-water surveys are typically inefficient because they provide limited amounts of data. Conversely, satellite images can provide large amounts of data, but they can be difficult to understand due to low resolution or cloud coverage.

To overcome these limitations, scientists at Southern Cross University in Australia developed the RangerBot, the world's first vision-based, autonomous underwater drone designed specifically for coral reef environments. Launched in September 2019, the RangerBot eliminates coral-eating crown-of-thorns starfish, monitors the reef for health indicators, and maps underwater areas.

The RangerBot carries a hyperspectral camera. These cameras collect and process data from across the electromagnetic spectrum, which is beyond the visual spectrum that humans can see. The visual range of humans is 400–700 nanometers (billionths of a meter), while a hyperspectral camera can capture data between 300 – 1000 nanometers.

Hyperspectral drone images mitigate the cloud coverage or resolution issues of satellite images. These images differentiate among coral, sand, and algae. In addition, they identify the type of coral and the precise levels of coral bleaching. Scientists integrate the drone camera data with previously collected data from in-water surveys.

Researchers have also developed the LarvalBot, a drone that was derived from the RangerBot. LarvalBots deliver larvae coral to reefs for reseeding. Users operate the drones via an iPad and direct them where to drop millions of coral spawn into the reef.

The coral spawning process entails capturing the spawn and growing it in floating cages for five to seven days. When the spawn is ready to settle, LarvalBots or human divers distribute it. Prior to the LarvalBots, coral respawning used only divers who worked in 400-square-metre spaces. With the drones, researchers are respawning areas of one square kilometer.

Artificial Intelligence

Reef conservationists are facing new challenges in interpreting data captured by drone cameras. In comparison to the 30–40 data points collected by underwater survey images, a single hyperspectral image can gather more than 4,000 data points about a particular area of coral. Consequently, a single drone flight can gather thousands of gigabytes of raw data that must be processed and analyzed. To be able to utilize the drones' full potential, scientists used machine learning to develop computer vision algorithms to help interpret the data (see Chapter 14).

Conservationists also face challenges about how to distribute coral spawn efficiently when the amount of spawn is limited. They have to determine the most suitable area to grow coral spawn to maximize resettlement. To meet these challenges, they use computer vision algorithms to distinguish healthy coral reef systems from unhealthy areas.

Interestingly, as recently as 2015 drone systems cost about $500,000 (Australian dollars). As of May 2020 the cost had diminished to roughly $100,000. Processing the image data now takes two or three days; five years ago it required three to four weeks. The cost of the drones and the speed of processing drone data are excellent examples of Moore's Law in action (see Technology Guide 1).

Robots

Scientists have developed and deployed a solar- and wave-powered robot called the Wave Glider to patrol the reef. The robot is unmanned and autonomous, transmitting data in near real time 24/7/365. Scientists around the world can access its mission data by phone or laptop.

The Wave Glider uses multibeam sonar to create a computerized three-dimensional model of the entire reef. The technique bounces sound pulses off the seabed and measures the time that it takes for the echo to return. Because scientists know the speed of sound in water, they can accurately calculate the depth of whatever the sound has hit, either coral or the sea floor. Therefore, the sonar reveals the shape of the reef in detail.

Underwater Loudspeakers

Researchers discovered that the quietness of damaged coral reefs was keeping fish away. As a result, they placed underwater loudspeakers to play recorded sounds of healthy reefs in an effort to lure young fish to live in areas where coral had become degraded. The sounds doubled the total number of fish coming to the experimental areas of reef and increased the number of species by 50 percent.

Sun Shields

University of Melbourne scientists have developed an ultra-thin sun shield—the biodegradable film is 50,000 times thinner than a human hair—that floats of top of the water during heat waves to protect the coral underneath. The film can reduce the light exposure, a necessary ingredient for bleaching, by up to 30 percent.

And the bottom line? Scientists assert that if the world can hold global warming to an increase of 1.5 degrees Celsius, then they might be able to stabilize global reefs. At that temperature level, the world would still have functional reefs that support fisheries and tourism. If the world warms by 3 degrees Celsius, however, then we will lose most of the coral reefs around the world.

Sources: Compiled from P. Budgen, "Australia, Strategies to Save the Great Barrier Reef Show There's Still Hope," *Lifegate*, May 6, 2020; G. Readfern, "Rescuing the Great Barrier Reef: How Much Can Be Saved, and How Can We Do It?" *The Guardian*, April 5, 2020; A. Frangoul, "How Researchers Are Trying to Save the Great Barrier Reef," *CNBC*, February 21, 2020; E. Madin, et al., "Emerging Technologies and Coral Reef Conservation: Opportunities, Challenges, and Moving Forward," *Frontiers in Marine Science*, December 10, 2019; A. Kooser, "Underwater Loudspeakers Could Help Restore Damaged Coral Reefs," *CNET*, November 29, 2019; C. Kwan, "How AI and Drones Are Trying to Save the Great Barrier Reef," *TechRepublic*, June 26, 2019; "This Robot Is Delivering Coral Babies to the Great Barrier Reef," *EcoWatch*, January 13, 2019; "Scientists Turn to Technology to Save Coral Reefs," *Financial Times*, April 18, 2018; P. Ward," The Technologies Protecting the Great Barrier Reef, *Culture Trip,* March 29, 2018; J. Bisset, "Mapping the Great Barrier Reef with Cameras, Drones, and NASA Tech," *CNET*, October 24, 2017; www.barrierreef.org, accessed May 28, 2020.

Questions

1. Why is saving the Great Barrier Reef strategically important to Australia and our planet? Provide examples to support your answer.

2. Describe why conservationists must integrate machine learning with their use of drones in their efforts to save the Great Barrier Reef.

Continuing our discussion of social responsibility, social problems all over the world may be addressed through corporate and individual philanthropy. In some cases, questions arise as to what percentage of contributions actually goes to the intended causes and recipients and what percentage goes to the charity's overhead. Another problem that concerns contributors is that they often exert little influence over the selection of the projects their contributions will support. The Internet can help address these concerns and facilitate generosity and connection. Consider the following examples:

- *PatientsLikeMe* (**www.patientslikeme.com**), or any of the thousands of message boards dedicated to infertility, cancer, and various other ailments. People use these sites and message boards to obtain information about health care decisions based on volunteered information, while also receiving much-needed emotional support from strangers.

- **FIN** *Kiva* (**www.kiva.org**): Kiva is a nonprofit enterprise that provides a link between lenders in developed countries and entrepreneurs in developing countries. Users pledge interest-free loans rather than tax-deductible donations. Kiva directs 100 percent of the loans to borrowers.

- *DonorsChoose* (**www.donorschoose.org**): DonorsChoose is an education-oriented website that functions entirely within the United States. Users make donations to public schools rather than loans. The website addresses the huge problem of underfunded public schools.

Still another social problem that affects modern business is the digital divide. The **digital divide** refers to the wide gap between those individuals who have access to information and communications technologies and those who do not. This gap exists both within and among countries. As you see in this chapter's opening case, the coronavirus pandemic has emphasized the problems caused by the digital divide.

One well-known project to narrow the divide is the One Laptop per Child (OLPC) project (**www.onelaptopperchild.org**). OLPC is a nonprofit association dedicated to developing an inexpensive laptop aimed at revolutionizing how the world educates its children. In 2020, the price of OLPC's laptop remained approximately $230. (This price includes educational software loaded on the laptop.) However, there are many other costs associated with these laptops, including shipping, solar chargers, maintenance, and training. Some international users contend that the actual cost of one laptop is therefore approximately $450.

Compliance with Government Regulations.

Another major source of business pressures is government regulations regarding health, safety, environmental protection, and equal opportunity. Businesses tend to view government regulations as expensive constraints on their activities. In general, government deregulation intensifies competition.

In the wake of numerous corporate scandals, the U.S. government passed many new laws, including the Sarbanes-Oxley Act, the USA PATRIOT Act, the Gramm-Leach-Bliley Act, and the Health Insurance Portability and Accountability Act (HIPAA). Organizations must be in compliance with the regulations contained in these statutes. The process of becoming and remaining compliant is expensive and time consuming. In almost all cases, organizations rely on IT support to provide the necessary controls and information for compliance.

Protection against Terrorist Attacks.

Since September 11, 2001, organizations have been under increased pressure to protect themselves against terrorist attacks, both physical attacks and cyberattacks. Employees who are in the military reserves have also been called up for active duty, creating personnel problems. Information technology can help protect businesses by providing security systems and possibly identifying patterns of behavior associated with terrorist activities, including cyberattacks (discussed in Chapter 4). For a good example of a firm that provides this protection, see Palantir (**www.palantir.com**).

An example of protection against terrorism is the Department of Homeland Security's (DHS) Office of Biometric Identity Management (OBIM) program. (We discuss biometrics in Chapter 4.) OBIM (**www.dhs.gov/obim**) is a network of biometric screening systems such as fingerprint and iris and retina scanners that ties into government databases and watch lists to check the identities of millions of people entering the United States. The system is now operational in more than 300 locations, including major international ports of entry by air, sea, and land.

Ethical Issues.

Ethics relates to general standards of right and wrong. *Information ethics* relates specifically to standards of right and wrong in information processing practices. Ethical issues are very important because, if handled poorly, they can damage an organization's image and destroy its employees' morale. The use of IT raises many ethical issues, ranging from monitoring email to invading the privacy of millions of customers whose data are stored in private and public databases. Chapter 3 covers ethical issues in detail.

Unfortunately, not all organizations use information technology ethically. IT's about Business 2.4 provides an example of such a situation.

IT's About Business 2.4

MIS Houston Astros Caught Stealing Signs

Sign stealing is a baseball practice where one team tries to learn the signs of its opponent. Signs can be sent from catchers to pitchers, from dugouts to catchers, from infielders to other infielders, or from base coaches to batters or runners. In games, the team at bat and the team in the field constantly exchange signs.

Figuring out what signs mean can give a team a competitive advantage. The biggest advantage is when one team discovers what signs mean between the opposing catcher and pitcher. In that way, the batter can know if the next pitch will be a fastball or a breaking ball (curve or slider). If a team knows which signs are being given to the pitcher, that knowledge negates the biggest advantage that the pitcher has over a batter; namely, the element of surprise.

Sign stealing has long been an accepted tradition in baseball. Some early accounts of sign stealing go back to the 1870s when the Hartford Dark Blues, a charter member of the National League, were accused of using a telegraph pole outside the ballpark to steal opponents' signs. The Blues allegedly hired a man to climb the pole and use binoculars to steal signs. From his perch, he would signal the Blues's bench with the next pitch.

Historically, players and coaches have attempted to steal their opponents' signs by watching the other team and trying to recognize patterns or sequences. Stealing signs is legal if teams do it visually. However, it is illegal if teams use cameras, binoculars, or electronic devices of any type. Team replay assistants, who help notify managers when to challenge a call on the field, have access only to the live game broadcast. All other TV monitors available to players and coaches show the live game broadcast on an eight-second delay.

Since the 2014 season, Major League Baseball (MLB; **www .mlb.com**) has allowed managers one chance per game to challenge a call on the field—but not balls and strikes—using a video replay system. Each team has a video replay review room. A center field camera generates the videos. That camera was used by the Astros' replay room, whose operators were supposed to help manager A. J. Hinch decide whether to challenge an umpire's call.

The Sign-Stealing Scheme

A number of teams had suspicions that the Astros were stealing signs. However, the scheme did not become public until November 2019, when former Astros pitcher Mike Fiers informed Ken Rosenthal and Evan Drellich of *The Athletic* about it. The revelation led to an MLB investigation. The league discovered that the Astros had used the center field camera feed to steal opponents' signs. Here is how the Astros scheme worked.

At the beginning of the 2017 season, when the Astros won the World Series, employees in the Astros' video replay review room began to use the live game feed from the center field camera to attempt to decode and transmit opposing teams' sign sequences— that is, which sign flashed by the catcher is the actual sign—for use when an Astros runner was on second base. Once they decoded the sign sequence, a player in the video replay review room would act as a "runner" to relay the information to the dugout. The person in the dugout would notify the players in the dugout or signal the sign sequence to the runner on second base, who in turn would decipher the catcher's sign and signal to the batter from second base.

Then, Alex Cora, the Astros' bench coach, began to call the replay review room on the replay phone to obtain the sign information. On at least some occasions, the employees in the replay review room communicated the sign sequence information by text message, which was received on the smartwatch of a staff member on the bench, or in other cases on a cell phone stored nearby.

Two months into the 2017 season, a group of players discussed how the team could improve on decoding signs and sending the signs to the batter. MLB investigators charged that Cora arranged for a video room technician to install a monitor displaying the center field camera feed immediately outside the Astros' dugout. One or more players watched the live feed. Then, after decoding the sign, a player would bang a nearby trash can with a bat to communicate the upcoming pitch type to the batter. Generally, one or two bangs corresponded to certain off-speed pitches, while no bang corresponded to a fastball.

The trashcan banging practice ended before the 2018 season, but the Astros' replay review room staff continued the sign-stealing scheme for at least part of the 2018 season. The scheme ended during the 2018 season when, according to Astros' players, they believed that other teams had learned about the scheme and how to defeat it.

The Astros also deployed a computer software program called Codebreaker to steal signs from opposing catchers to pitchers. Using the center field camera, a staffer would log the stolen signs into a spreadsheet and then run an algorithm to determine an opponent's sign sequencing and what all the signs meant. Houston's front office joked that the program came from the team's "dark arts" department.

Results

MLB commissioner Rob Manfred suspended A. J. Hinch and Jeff Luhnow (the Astros' general manager) for the 2020 season. Manfred also stripped the Astros of their first- and second-round selections in the 2020 and 2021 MLB drafts, and he fined the franchise $5 million. However, he declined to vacate the Astros' 2017 championship. Shortly after Hinch and Luhnow's suspensions were announced, Astros owner Jim Crane fired them both.

According to the MLB commissioner's report, Alex Cora was the architect of the sign-stealing scheme. Significantly, Cora left the Astros after the 2017 season to manage the Boston Red Sox in 2018 and 2019. After the scandal became public, he and the Red Sox "mutually agreed to part ways" in January 2020. In addition, Carlos Beltran, who played for the Astros in 2017, had been hired by the New York Mets as their manager in November 2019. He stepped down as the Mets' manager on January 16, 2020.

Sources: Compiled from S. Gardner, "Evan Gattis Admits 2017 Houston Astros 'Cheated Baseball and Cheated Fans,'" *USA Today*, April 2, 2020; N. Vigdor, "The Houston Astros Cheating Scandal Explained," *New York Times*, February 28, 2020; J. Bogage, "What Is Sign Stealing? Making Sense of Major League Baseball's Latest Scandal," *The Washington Post*, February 14, 2020; D. Sheinin, "Astros Say They Are Sorry but Draw a Line When It Comes to Questioning 2017 World Series Title," *The Washington Post*, February 13, 2020; M. Kennedy, "Houston Astros Apologize for Sign-Stealing, but Provide Fuel for Critics," *NPR.org*, February 13, 2020; "Everything You Need to Know about MLB's Sign-Stealing Scandal," *ESPN.com*, February 13, 2020; J. Diamond, "'Dark Arts' and 'Codebreaker': The Origins of the Houston Astros Cheating Scheme," *The Wall Street Journal*, February 7, 2020; L. Pope and T. Bannon, "8 Things to Know about the Astros' Sign-Stealing Scandal,

Including a Former White Sox Pitcher's Early Suspicions," *Chicago Tribune*, January 17, 2020; J. Passan, "Astros' Jeff Luhnow, AJ Hinch Fired for Sign Stealing," *ESPN.com*, January 13, 2020; B. Nightengale, "MLB Hands Down Historic Punishment to Astros for Sign Stealing," *USA Today*, January 13, 2020; D. Waldstein, "Former Astros Pitcher Says Team Electronically Stole Signs in 2017," *New York Times*, November 12, 2019; M. Fiers and K. Rosenthal, "The Astros Stole Signs Electronically in 2017—Part of a Much Broader Issue for Major League Baseball," *The Athletic*, November 12, 2019; P. Dickson, *The Hidden Language of Baseball: How Signs and Sign Stealing Have Influenced the Course of Our National Pastime*, Lincoln: University of Nebraska Press, 2003; **www.mlb.com**, accessed May 27, 2020.

Questions

1. Describe how the Astros used technology in the team's sign-stealing scheme.

2. Describe how the Astros used non-technological means in the team's sign-stealing scheme.

3. Information technologies, particularly wireless technologies, continue to rapidly improve. Will such improvements lead to more schemes designed to gain a competitive advantage in baseball? Why or why not? Provide examples to support your answer.

Clearly, then, the pressures on organizations are increasing, and organizations must be prepared to take responsive actions if they are to succeed. You will learn about these organizational responses in the next section.

Organizational Responses

Organizations are responding to the various pressures just discussed by implementing IT such as strategic systems, customer focus, make-to-order and mass customization, and e-business. This section explores each of these responses.

Strategic Systems. Strategic systems provide organizations with advantages that enable them to increase their market share and profits to better negotiate with suppliers and to prevent competitors from entering their markets. IT's About Business 2.5 provides an example of how strategically important information systems can be to an organization. As you will see, many information systems are so strategically important to organizations that if they are inadequate, or fail altogether, their organizations are at risk of failing as well.

IT's About Business 2.5

MIS MKT NFL Stadiums Deploy Technology to Attract Fans

National Football League (NFL; **www.nfl.com**) teams and their stadiums are competing with large, high-definition televisions in the homes of their fans. The teams and stadiums must offer an experience that exceeds that of fans who watch the games from the comfort of their homes.

NFL fan expectations have increased when it comes to wireless connectivity in stadiums. To keep fans coming to live events, NFL stadiums must provide very fast Wi-Fi connections (see Chapter 8) inside and outside the stadiums. Fans want to connect and communicate with people inside the stadiums as well as outside them. They also want to download information to enhance their experience and share it with friends. NFL stadiums are having to provide more network data capacity to accommodate fans using 12-megapixel cameras to capture images and videos that they upload to social media platforms.

Stadium visitors also engage with venue-specific apps and services. These services include the ability to order food from your seat, to determine the length of the closest bathroom line, to watch instant replays, to upgrade your seat location after you arrive at the stadium, to watch video replays, and even to view behind-the-scenes footage available only to fans in the stadium who are using the stadium or team app.

To provide the services and functions that fans demand, stadiums typically have some 2,000 Wi-Fi access points, 2,000 Bluetooth beacons, and fiber-optic backbone networks (see Chapter 6) that provide almost 100 gigabits per second (Gbps) of available internet bandwidth. In NFL stadiums, the Wi-Fi adoption rate by fans increased from 18 percent in 2013 to 45 percent in 2019. In addition, the average bandwidth transferred increased from 1.9 terabytes in 2015 to 4.6 terabytes in 2019.

Let's take a closer look at the technologies employed by NFL stadiums and teams. These technologies include wireless access points, mobile tickets, Wi-Fi 6, augmented reality, cashless transactions, biometric screening, and beacons.

Wireless access points. NFL stadium technology requires many wireless access points. (A wireless access point is a transmitter with an antenna that allows other Wi-Fi devices to connect to a wired local area network and the internet.) Some stadiums place these points under seats so they will be closer to stadium visitors to increase Wi-Fi coverage. Under-seat access points are not always the best option because they are more expensive to install and maintain. Another option is to put access points on handrails and hide them under a sign or panel for aesthetic purposes. Access points improve connectivity in stadiums by ensuring that each spot in the stadium has wireless coverage.

Mobile Tickets: In the past, paper tickets were anonymous. A fan could buy a ticket and then give it to a friend to go to the game. As a result, stadiums and teams did not really know who actually came to a game. During the 2019–2020 season, NFL stadiums introduced the digital mobile ticket.

By putting mobile tickets on people's phones, stadiums decreased the wait times at entrances. Further, the stadium and the team learn who is at the game. This knowledge enables them to market more effectively to the people who come to the games. They also know what time the fans arrived, what they ate, and what they purchased. These data are important for targeted marketing such as personalized offers for merchandise.

Wi-Fi 6. The NFL is planning to transition to Wi-Fi 6 by the 2022 season. Wi-Fi 6 is the next generation standard for wireless fidelity. The biggest benefits of Wi-Fi 6 are its fast speed and its ability to support many devices and applications on a single network. Wi-Fi 6 speeds are estimated to be about 30 percent faster than Wi-Fi 5.

SoFi Stadium, where the Los Angeles Chargers and Los Angeles Rams will play starting in 2020, will have Wi-Fi 6. The indoor-outdoor stadium in Inglewood, California, will seat up to 100,000 people and was set to open in July 2020. Super Bowl LVI in 2022 will take place in SoFi stadium, as will the opening and closing ceremonies of the 2028 Los Angeles Olympic Games. The new stadium will have more than 2,500 Wi-Fi 6 access points, providing four times more bandwidth than earlier versions of Wi-Fi and promising that everyone in the stadium can be on their phones at the same time.

Augmented Reality. (See Technology Guide 1.) The Dallas Cowboys use augmented reality (AR) in the team's "Pose with the Pros" app. Fans attending the game participate in an AR experience that enables them to take photos with their favorite Cowboys players. A Samsung Galaxy S10 5G smartphone uses AR technology to superimpose the players' images into the shot. Then a camera snaps a photo of the fan with the players. The Cowboys noted that the app gathered more than 50 million social media impressions. (An impression occurs when one person views a particular content on a social media website.)

Cashless transactions. In 2019, Mercedes-Benz Stadium, home of the Atlanta Falcons, began using a cashless system (e.g., credit cards, phone apps) at most food and refreshment stands and kiosks. The Falcons contend that the system shortens lines and improves hygiene standards as staff no longer have to handle cash. Improved hygiene is of particular importance during the coronavirus pandemic.

Biometric screening. Stadiums are beginning to use biometric screening (see Chapter 4) to shorten wait times in lines at the stadium entrances and at concession stands. For example, CenturyLink Field, home of the Seattle Seahawks, has begun using CLEAR's technology (see **www.clearme.com**). Instead of traditional identification documents, CLEAR uses facial and fingerprint recognition to identify people. Fans at the stadium must only enroll one time at a kiosk to be able to use "fast lanes" at stadium entrances and concessions.

Beacons. Beacons are small wireless transmitters that use low-energy Bluetooth technology to send signals to nearby devices (see Chapter 8). Stadiums and teams are using beacons' accurate location capabilities to deliver targeted personalized messages, alerts, and offers on mobile devices. How do stadiums use beacons? Consider the following examples:

- Finding and upgrading seats: Beacons help fans to find their seats quickly and easily. Stadiums can also target people who are waiting in line to go to cheaper seats, or they can offer fans on-the-spot discounted upgrades on better seating.

- Beacons situated next to refreshment stands can register how many people with the app are waiting in line. By making this information available to fans in the app, stadiums can direct fans to refreshment stands with shorter wait times.

- Beacons can create additional revenue for stadiums via mobile sales of merchandise or food. For instance, beacons enable fans to use the stadium app to order food right from their seats.

Sources: Compiled from Z. Kerravala, "The NFL Knows a Lot about Deploying High-Capacity WiFi Networks," *Network World*, February 11, 2020; T. Maddox, "Super Bowl 2020: How 5G Will Help Keep Fans Safe at the Game," *TechRepublic,* January 31, 2020; T. Maddox, "Super Bowl 54: 49ers and Chiefs Matchup Will Be the First 5G Super Bowl in History," *TechRepublic*, January 31, 2020; C. Reichert, "NFL's Biggest Stadium Will Open with Wi-Fi 6," *CNET*, November 1, 2019; S. Ogus, "Dallas Cowboys Use Augmented Reality in Popular New Fan Activation 'Pose with the Pros,'" *Forbes*, September 13, 2019; "These Are the NFL Stadiums that Give Fans the Best and Worst Experiences," *Gameday News*, September 12, 2019; B. Fischer, "The More Fun League: NFL Aims for Better Fan Experience," *Sports Business Journal*, August 19, 2019; L. Bradley, "Top 5 Tech Trends Transforming In-Stadium Fan Experience," *Medium.com*, July 22, 2019; C. Arkenberg, et. al, "Redesigning Stadiums for a Better Fan Experience, *Deloitte,* June 27, 2019; T. Maddox, "Super Bowl 53 Is Poised to Make Digital History," *TechRepublic*, January 30, 2019; T. Maddox, "How Verizon and AT&T Are Preparing for Super Bowl 53," *TechRepublic*, January 31, 2019; M. Spencer, "How the NFL and Its Stadiums Became Leaders in WiFi Technology and Monetizing Apps," *Chat Sports*, January 9, 2019; N. Mallik, "How Stadiums Can Use Beacons to Enhance Fans' Experiences," *beaconstac.com*, May 31, 2018; T. Maddox, "How the NFL and Its Stadiums Became Leaders in Wi-Fi, Monetizing Apps, and Customer Experience," *TechRepublic*, August 25, 2016; **www.nfl.com**, accessed May 30, 2020.

Questions

1. Consider all of the technologies discussed in this case. Taken together, are they strategically important to NFL stadiums and NFL teams? Why or why not? Provide specific examples to support your answer.

2. Look ahead to the next section and apply the five forces of Porter's Competitive Forces Model to each technology discussed in this case (individually). Which forces are most applicable to each technology? Support your answer.

MKT **Customer Focus.**   Organizational attempts to provide superb customer service can make the difference between attracting and retaining customers versus losing them to competitors. Numerous IT tools and business processes have been designed to keep customers happy. Recall that a *business process* is a collection of related activities that produce a product or a service of value to the organization, its business partners, and its customers. Consider

Amazon, for example. When you visit Amazon's website any time after your first visit, the site welcomes you back by name, and it presents you with information about items that you might like, based on your previous purchases. In another example, Dell guides you through the process of purchasing a computer by providing information and choices that help you make an informed buying decision.

POM **Make-to-Order and Mass Customization.**   **Make-to-order** is a strategy of producing customized (made to individual specifications) products and services. The business problem is how to manufacture customized goods efficiently and at a reasonably low cost. Part of the solution is to change manufacturing processes from mass production to mass customization. In mass production, a company produces a large quantity of identical items. An early example of mass production was Henry Ford's Model T, for which buyers could pick any color they wanted—as long as it was black.

Ford's policy of offering a single product for all of its customers eventually gave way to *consumer segmentation*, in which companies provide standard specifications for different consumer groups, or segments. Clothes manufacturers, for example, design their products in different sizes and colors to appeal to different customers. The next step was *configured mass customization*, in which companies offer features that allow each shopper to customize his or her product or service with a range of components. Examples are ordering a car, a computer, or a smartphone, for which the customer can specify which features he or she wants.

In the current strategy, known as **mass customization**, a company produces a large quantity of items, but it customizes them to match the needs and preferences of individual customers. Mass customization is essentially an attempt to perform make-to-order on a large scale. Examples are:

- NikeID (**www.nikeid.com**) allows customers to design their footwear.
- M&M candies: My M&M (**www.mms.com**) allows customers to add photos, art, and messages to candy.
- Dell (**www.dell.com**) and HP (**www.hp.com**) allow customers to exactly specify the computer they want.

E-Business and E-Commerce.

Conducting business electronically is an essential strategy for companies that are competing in today's business environment. *Electronic commerce (EC or e-commerce)* describes the process of buying, selling, transferring, or exchanging products, services, or information through computer networks, including the Internet. *E-business* is a somewhat broader concept. In addition to the buying and selling of goods and services, e-business also refers to servicing customers, collaborating with business partners, and performing electronic transactions within an organization. Chapter 7 focuses extensively on this topic. In addition, e-commerce applications appear throughout the text.

You now have a general overview of the pressures that affect companies in today's business environment and the responses that these companies choose to manage these pressures. To plan for the most effective responses, companies formulate strategies. In the new digital economy, these strategies rely heavily on information technology, especially strategic information systems. You examine these topics in the next section.

Before you go on...

1. What are the characteristics of the modern business environment?
2. Discuss some of the pressures that characterize the modern global business environment.
3. Identify some of the organizational responses to these pressures. Are any of these responses specific to a particular pressure? If so, then which ones?

2.4 # Competitive Advantage and Strategic Information Systems

A *competitive strategy* is a statement that identifies a business's approach to compete, its goals, and the plans and policies that will be required to carry out those goals (Porter, 1985).[1] A strategy, in general, can apply to a desired outcome, such as gaining market share. A competitive strategy focuses on achieving a desired outcome when competitors want to prevent you from reaching your goal. Therefore, when you create a competitive strategy, you must plan your own moves, but you must also anticipate and counter your competitors' moves.

Through its competitive strategy, an organization seeks a competitive advantage in an industry. That is, it seeks to outperform its competitors in a critical measure such as cost, quality, and time-to-market. Competitive advantage helps a company function profitably within a market and generate higher-than-average profits.

Competitive advantage is increasingly important in today's business environment, as you will note throughout the text. In general, the *core business* of companies has remained the same. That is, information technologies simply offer tools that can enhance an organization's success through its traditional sources of competitive advantage, such as low cost, excellent customer service, and superior supply chain management. **Strategic information systems (SISs)** provide a competitive advantage by helping an organization to implement its strategic goals and improve its performance and productivity. Any information system that helps an organization either achieve a competitive advantage or reduce a competitive disadvantage qualifies as a strategic information system.

Porter's Competitive Forces Model

The best-known framework for analyzing competitiveness is Michael Porter's **competitive forces model** (Porter, 1985). Companies use Porter's model to develop strategies to increase their competitive edge. Porter's model also demonstrates how IT can make a company more competitive.

Porter's model identifies five major forces that can endanger or enhance a company's position in a given industry. **Figure 2.3** highlights these forces. Although the Web has changed the

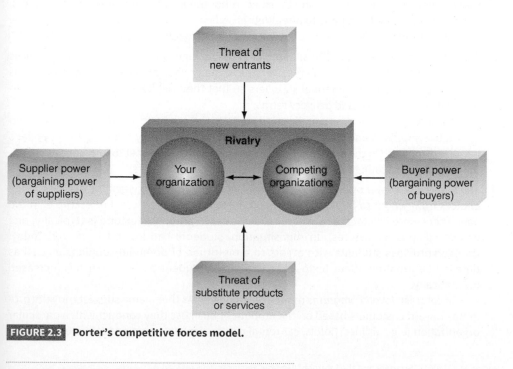

FIGURE 2.3 **Porter's competitive forces model.**

[1]Porter, M.E. (1985) *Competitive Advantage*, Free Press, New York.

nature of competition, it has not changed Porter's five fundamental forces. In fact, what makes these forces so valuable as analytical tools is that they have not changed for centuries. Every competitive organization, no matter how large or small, or which business it is in, is driven by these forces. This observation applies even to organizations that you might not consider competitive, such as local governments. Although local governments are not for-profit enterprises, they compete for businesses to locate in their districts, for funding from higher levels of government, for employees, and for many other things.

Significantly, Porter (2001)[2] concludes that the *overall* impact of the Web is to increase competition, which generally diminishes a firm's profitability. Let's examine Porter's five forces and the ways that the Web influences them.

1. *The threat of entry of new competitors.* The threat that new competitors will enter your market is high when entry is easy and low when there are significant barriers to entry. An **entry barrier** is a product or service feature that customers have learned to expect from organizations in a certain industry. An organization that seeks to enter the industry must offer this feature to survive in the marketplace. There are many types of entry barriers. Consider, for example, legal requirements such as admission to the bar to practice law or obtaining a license to serve liquor, where only a certain number of licenses are available.

   Suppose you want to open a gasoline station. To compete in that industry, you would have to offer pay-at-the-pump service to your customers. Pay-at-the-pump is an IT-based barrier to entering this market because you must offer it for free. The first gas station that offered this service gained first-mover advantage and established barriers to entry. This advantage did not last, however, because competitors quickly offered the same service and thus overcame the entry barrier.

   For most firms, the Web *increases* the threat that new competitors will enter the market because it sharply reduces traditional barriers to entry, such as the need for a sales force or a physical storefront. Today, competitors frequently need only to set up a website. This threat of increased competition is particularly acute in industries that perform an *intermediation role*, which is a link between buyers and sellers (e.g., stock brokers and travel agents), as well as in industries in which the primary product or service is digital (e.g., the music industry). The geographical reach of the Web also enables distant competitors to compete more directly with an existing firm.

   In some cases, however, the Web increases barriers to entry. This scenario occurs primarily when customers have come to expect a nontrivial capability from their suppliers. For example, the first company to offer Web-based package tracking gained a competitive advantage from that service. Competitors were forced to follow suit.

2. *The bargaining power of suppliers.* Supplier power is high when buyers have few choices from whom to buy and low when buyers have many choices. Therefore, organizations would rather have more potential suppliers so that they will be in a stronger position to negotiate price, quality, and delivery terms.

   The Internet's impact on suppliers is mixed. On the one hand, it enables buyers to find alternative suppliers and to compare prices more easily, thereby reducing the supplier's bargaining power. On the other hand, as companies use the Internet to integrate their supply chains, participating suppliers prosper by locking in customers.

3. *The bargaining power of customers (buyers).* Buyer power is high when buyers have many choices from whom to buy and low when buyers have few choices. For example, in the past, there were few locations where students could purchase textbooks (typically, one or two campus bookstores). In this situation, students had low buyer power. Today, the Web provides students with access to a multitude of potential suppliers as well as detailed information about textbooks. As a result, student buyer power has increased dramatically.

   In contrast, *loyalty programs* reduce buyer power. As their name suggests, loyalty programs reward customers based on the amount of business they conduct with a particular organization (e.g., airlines, hotels, car rental companies). Information technology enables

---

[2]Porter, M.E. (2001) "Strategy and the Internet," *Harvard Business Review*, March.

companies to track the activities and accounts of millions of customers, thereby reducing buyer power. That is, customers who receive perks from loyalty programs are less likely to do business with competitors. (Loyalty programs are associated with customer relationship management, which you will study in Chapter 11.)

4. *The threat of substitute products or services.* If there are many alternatives to an organization's products or services, then the threat of substitutes is high. Conversely, if there are few alternatives, then the threat is low. Today, new technologies create substitute products very rapidly. For example, customers can purchase wireless telephones instead of landline telephones, Internet music services instead of traditional CDs, and ethanol instead of gasoline for their cars.

   Information-based industries experience the greatest threat from substitutes. Any industry in which digitized information can replace material goods (e.g., music, books, software) must view the Internet as a threat because the Internet can convey this information efficiently and at low cost and high quality.

   Even when there are many substitutes for their products, however, companies can create a competitive advantage by increasing switching costs. *Switching costs* are the costs, in money and time, imposed by a decision to buy elsewhere. For example, contracts with smartphone providers typically include a substantial penalty for switching to another provider until the term of the contract expires (quite often, two years). This switching cost is monetary.

   As another example, when you buy products from Amazon, the company develops a profile of your shopping habits and recommends products targeted to your preferences. If you switch to another online vendor, then that company will need time to develop a profile of your wants and needs. In this case, the switching cost involves time rather than money.

5. *The rivalry among existing firms in the industry.* The threat from rivalry is high when there is intense competition among many firms in an industry. The threat is low when the competition involves fewer firms and is not as intense.

   In the past, proprietary information systems—systems that belong exclusively to a single organization—have provided strategic advantage to firms in highly competitive industries. Today, however, the visibility of Internet applications on the Web makes proprietary systems more difficult to keep secret. In simple terms, when I see my competitor's new system online, I will rapidly match its features to remain competitive. The result is fewer differences among competitors, which leads to more intense competition in an industry.

   To understand this concept, consider the highly competitive grocery industry, in which Walmart, Kroger, Safeway, and other companies compete essentially on price. Some of these companies have IT-enabled loyalty programs in which customers receive discounts and the store gains valuable business intelligence on customers' buying preferences. Stores use this business intelligence in their marketing and promotional campaigns. (You will learn about business intelligence in Chapter 12.)

   Grocery stores are also experimenting with RFID to speed up the checkout process, track customers through the store, and notify customers of discounts as they pass by certain products. Grocery companies also use IT to tightly integrate their supply chains for maximum efficiency and thus reduce prices for shoppers.

   Established companies can also gain a competitive advantage by allowing customers to use data from the company's products to improve their own performance. For example, Babolat (**www.babolat.com**), a manufacturer of sports equipment, has developed its Babolat Play Pure Drive system. The system has sensors embedded into the handle of its tennis rackets. A smartphone app uses the data from the sensors to monitor and evaluate ball speed, spin, and impact location to give tennis players valuable feedback.

   Competition is also being affected by the extremely low variable cost of digital products. That is, once a digital product has been developed, the cost of producing additional units approaches zero. Consider the music industry as an example. When artists record music, their songs are captured in digital format. Physical products, such as CDs or DVDs of the songs for sale in music stores, involve costs. The costs of a physical distribution channel are much higher than those involved in delivering the songs digitally over the Internet.

In fact, in the future, companies might give away some products for free. For example, some analysts predict that commissions for online stock trading will approach zero because investors can search the Internet for information to make their own decisions regarding buying and selling stocks. At that point, consumers will no longer need brokers to give them information that they can obtain themselves, virtually for free.

Porter's Value Chain Model

Organizations use Porter's competitive forces model to design general strategies. To identify specific activities in which they can use competitive strategies for greatest impact, they use his value chain model (1985). A **value chain** is a sequence of activities through which the organization's inputs, whatever they are, are transformed into more valuable outputs, whatever they are. The **value chain model** identifies points for which an organization can use information technology to achieve a competitive advantage (see **Figure 2.4**).

According to Porter's value chain model, the activities conducted in any organization can be divided into two categories: primary activities and support activities. **Primary activities** relate to the production and distribution of the firm's products and services. These activities create value for which customers are willing to pay. The primary activities are buttressed by **support activities**. Unlike primary activities, support activities do not add value directly to the firm's products or services. Rather, as their name suggests, they contribute to the firm's competitive advantage by supporting the primary activities.

Next, you will see examples of primary and support activities in the value chain of a manufacturing company. Keep in mind that other types of firms, such as transportation, health care, education, retail, and others, have different value chains. The key point is that *every* organization has a value chain.

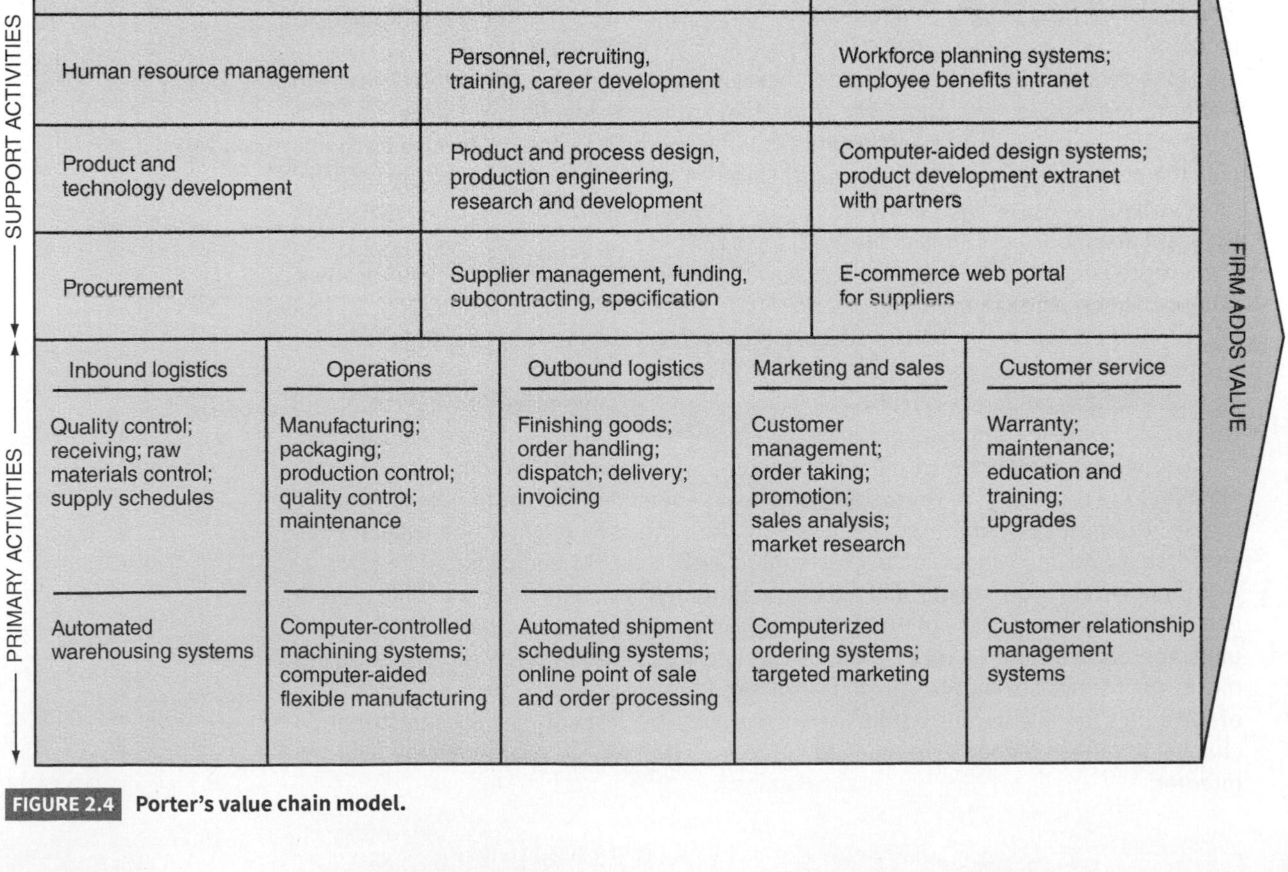

FIGURE 2.4   **Porter's value chain model.**

In a manufacturing company, primary activities involve purchasing materials, processing the materials into products, and delivering the products to customers. Manufacturing companies typically perform five primary activities in the following sequence:

1. Inbound logistics (inputs)
2. Operations (manufacturing and testing)
3. Outbound logistics (storage and distribution)
4. Marketing and sales
5. Services

As work progresses in this sequence, value is added to the product in each activity. Specifically, the following steps occur:

1. The incoming materials are processed (in receiving, storage, and so on) in activities called *inbound logistics.*
2. The materials are used in operations, in which value is added by turning raw materials into products.
3. These products are prepared for delivery (packaging, storing, and shipping) in the outbound logistics activities.
4. Marketing and sales sell the products to customers, increasing product value by creating demand for the company's products.
5. Finally, the company performs after-sales service for the customer, such as warranty service or upgrade notification, adding further value.

As noted earlier, these primary activities are buttressed by support activities. Support activities consist of the following:

1. The firm's infrastructure (accounting, finance, management)
2. Human resources management
3. Product and technology development (R&D)
4. Procurement

Each support activity can be applied to any or all of the primary activities. The support activities can also support one another.

A firm's value chain is part of a larger stream of activities, which Porter calls a **value system**. A value system, or an *industry value chain*, includes the suppliers that provide the inputs necessary to the firm along with their value chains. After the firm creates products, these products pass through the value chains of distributors (which also have their own value chains), all the way to the customers. All parts of these chains are included in the value system. To achieve and sustain a competitive advantage, and to support that advantage with information technologies, a firm must understand every component of this value system.

Strategies for Competitive Advantage

Organizations continually try to develop strategies to counter the five competitive forces identified by Porter. You will learn about five of those strategies here. Before we go into specifics, however, it is important to note that an organization's choice of strategy involves trade-offs. For example, a firm that concentrates only on cost leadership might not have the resources available for research and development, leaving the firm unable to innovate. As another example, a company that invests in customer happiness (customer orientation strategy) will experience increased costs.

Companies must select a strategy and then stay with it, because a confused strategy cannot succeed. This selection, in turn, decides how a company will use its information systems. A new information system that can improve customer service but will increase costs slightly will be welcomed at a high-end retailer such as Nordstrom's, but not at a discount store such as Walmart. The following list presents the most commonly used strategies. **Figure 2.5** provides an overview of these strategies.

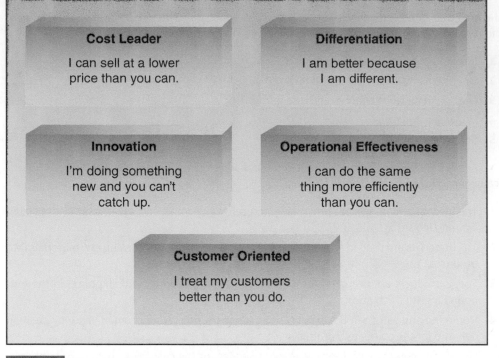

FIGURE 2.5   Strategies for competitive advantage.

1. *Cost leadership strategy*. Produce products and services at the lowest cost in the industry. An example is Walmart's automatic inventory replenishment system, which enables the company to reduce inventory storage requirements. As a result, Walmart stores use floor space only to sell products and not to store them, thereby reducing inventory costs.

2. *Differentiation strategy*. Offer different products, services, or product features than your competitors. Southwest Airlines, for example, has differentiated itself as a low-cost, short-haul express airline. This has proved to be a winning strategy for competing in the highly competitive airline industry.

3. *Innovation strategy*. Introduce new products and services, add new features to existing products and services, or develop new ways to produce them. A classic example is the introduction of automated teller machines (ATMs) by Citibank. The convenience and cost-cutting features of this innovation gave Citibank a huge advantage over its competitors. Like many innovative products, the ATM changed the nature of competition in the banking industry. Today, an ATM is a competitive *necessity* for any bank. Another excellent example is Apple's rapid introduction of innovative products.

4. *Operational effectiveness strategy*. Improve the manner in which a firm executes its internal business processes so that it performs these activities more effectively than its rivals. Such improvements increase quality, productivity, and employee and customer satisfaction while decreasing time to market.

5. *Customer orientation strategy*. Concentrate on making customers happy. Web-based systems are particularly effective in this area because they can create a personalized, one-to-one relationship with each customer. Amazon (**www.amazon.com**), Apple (**www.apple .com**), and Starbucks (**www.starbucks.com**) are classic examples of companies devoted to customer satisfaction.

Business–Information Technology Alignment

The best way for organizations to maximize the strategic value of IT is to achieve business–information technology alignment. In fact, the holy grail of organizations is business–information technology alignment, or strategic alignment (which we will call simply *alignment*). **Business-information technology alignment (business–IT alignment)** is the tight integration of the

IT function with the organization's strategy, mission, and goals. That is, the IT function directly supports the business objectives of the organization. There are six characteristics of excellent alignment:

1. Organizations view IT as an engine of innovation that continually transforms the business, often creating new revenue streams.
2. Organizations view their internal and external customers and their customer service function as supremely important.
3. Organizations rotate business and IT professionals across departments and job functions.
4. Organizations provide overarching goals that are completely clear to each IT and business employee.
5. Organizations ensure that IT employees understand how the company makes (or loses) money.
6. Organizations create a vibrant and inclusive company culture.

Unfortunately, many organizations fail to achieve this type of close alignment. In fact, according to a McKinsey and Company survey on IT strategy and spending, approximately 27 percent of the IT and business executives who participated agreed that their organization had adequate alignment between IT and the business. Given the importance of business and IT alignment, why do so many organizations fail to implement this policy? The major reasons are:

- Business managers and IT managers have different objectives
- The business and IT departments are ignorant of the other group's expertise
- A lack of communication

Put simply, business executives often know little about information technology, and IT executives understand the technology but may not understand the real needs of the business. One solution to this problem is to foster a collaborative environment in organizations so that business and IT executives can communicate freely and learn from each other.

Businesses can also use enterprise architecture to foster alignment. Originally developed as a tool to organize a company's IT initiatives, the enterprise architecture concept has evolved to encompass both a technical specification (the information and communication technologies and the information systems used in an organization) and a business specification (a collection of core business processes and management activities).

Before you go on...

1. What are strategic information systems?
2. According to Porter, what are the five forces that could endanger a firm's position in its industry or marketplaces?
3. Describe Porter's value chain model. Differentiate between Porter's competitive forces model and his value chain model.
4. What strategies can companies use to achieve competitive advantage?
5. What is business–IT alignment?
6. Provide examples of business–IT alignment at your university, regarding student systems. (*Hint*: What are the "business" goals of your university with regard to student registration, fee payment, grade posting, and so on?)

What's in IT for me?

For All Business Majors

All of the functional areas of any organization are literally composed of a variety of business processes, as we can see from the examples discussed in this chapter. Regardless of your major, you will be involved in a variety of business processes from your first day on the job. Some of these processes you will perform by yourself; some will involve only your group, team, or department; and some will involve several (or all) functional areas of your organization.

It is important for you to be able to visualize processes, understand the inputs and outputs of each process, and know the "customer" of each process. If you can accomplish these things, then you will contribute to making processes more efficient and effective. This often means incorporating information technology in the process. It is also important for you to understand how each process fits into your organization's strategy.

In addition, all functional areas in any organization must work together in an integrated fashion for the firm to respond adequately to business pressures. These responses typically require each functional area to employ a variety of information systems to support, document, and manage cross-functional business processes. In today's competitive global marketplace, it is more critical than ever that these responses be timely and accurate.

It is also essential that all functional areas work together for the organization to achieve a competitive advantage in its marketplace. Again, the functional areas use a variety of strategic information systems to achieve this goal.

You have seen why companies must be concerned with strategic advantage. But why is this chapter so important for you? There are several reasons. First, the business pressures you have learned about have an impact on your organization, but they also affect you as an individual. So, it is critical that you understand how information systems can help you, and eventually your organization, to respond to these pressures.

Achieving a competitive advantage is also essential for your organization's survival. In many cases, you, your team, and all your colleagues will be responsible for creating a competitive advantage. Therefore, having general knowledge about strategy and about how information systems affect the organization's strategy and competitive position will help you in your career.

You also need a basic knowledge of your organization's strategy, mission, and goals, as well as its business problems and how it makes (or loses) money. You now know how to analyze your organization's strategy and value chain, as well as the strategies and value chains of your competitors. You also have acquired a general knowledge of how information technology contributes to organizational strategy. This knowledge will help you to do your job more effectively, to be promoted more quickly, and to contribute significantly to the success of your organization.

Summary

2.1 Discuss ways in which information systems enable cross-functional business processes and processes for a single functional area.

A business process is an ongoing collection of related activities that produce a product or a service of value to the organization, its business partners, and its customers. Examples of business processes in the functional areas are managing accounts payable, managing accounts receivable, managing after-sale customer follow-up, managing bills of materials, managing manufacturing change orders, applying disability policies, employee hiring, computer user and staff training, and applying Internet use policy. The procurement and fulfillment processes are examples of cross-functional business processes.

2.2 Compare and contrast business process reengineering and business process management to determine the different advantages and disadvantages of each.

Business process reengineering (BPR) is a radical redesign of business processes that is intended to improve the efficiency and effectiveness of an organization's business processes. The key to BPR is for enterprises to examine their business processes from a "clean sheet" perspective and then determine how they can best reconstruct those processes to improve their business functions. Because BPR proved difficult to implement, organizations have turned to business process management. Business process management (BPM) is a management technique that includes methods and tools to support the design, analysis, implementation, management, and optimization of business processes.

2.3 Identify effective IT responses to different kinds of business pressures.

- *Market pressures*: An example of a market pressure is powerful customers. Customer relationship management is an effective IT response that helps companies achieve customer intimacy.

- *Technology pressures*: An example of a technology pressure is information overload. Search engines and business intelligence applications enable managers to access, navigate, and use vast amounts of information.

- *Societal, political, and legal pressures*: An example of a societal, political, or legal pressure is social responsibility, such as the state of the physical environment. Green IT is one response that is intended to improve the environment.

2.4 Describe the strategies that organizations typically adopt to counter Porter's five competitive forces.

Porter's five competitive forces:

1. *The threat of entry of new competitors*: For most firms, the Web increases the threat that new competitors will enter the market by reducing traditional barriers to entry. Frequently, competitors need only to set up a website to enter a market. The Web can also increase barriers to entry, as when customers come to expect a nontrivial capability from their suppliers.

2. *The bargaining power of suppliers*: The Web enables buyers to find alternative suppliers and to compare prices more easily, thereby reducing suppliers' bargaining power. From a different perspective, as companies use the Web to integrate their supply chains, participating suppliers can lock in customers, thereby increasing suppliers' bargaining power.

3. *The bargaining power of customers (buyers)*: The Web provides customers with incredible amounts of choices for products, as well as information about those choices. As a result, the Web increases buyer power. However, companies can implement loyalty programs in which they use the Web to monitor the activities of millions of customers. Such programs reduce buyer power.

4. *The threat of substitute products or services*: New technologies create substitute products very rapidly, and the Web makes information about these products available almost instantly. As a result, industries (particularly information-based industries) are in great danger from substitutes (e.g., music, books, newspapers, magazines, software). However, the Web also can enable a company to build in switching costs, so that it will cost customers time or money to switch from your company to that of a competitor.

5. *The rivalry among existing firms in the industry*: In the past, proprietary information systems provided strategic advantage for firms in highly competitive industries. The visibility of Internet applications on the Web makes proprietary systems more difficult to keep secret. Therefore, the Web makes strategic advantage more short-lived.

The five strategies are as follows:

1. *Cost leadership strategy*—Produce products and services at the lowest cost in the industry

2. *Differentiation strategy*—Offer different products, services, or product features

3. *Innovation strategy*—Introduce new products and services, put new features in existing products and services, or develop new ways to produce them

4. *Operational effectiveness strategy*—Improve the manner in which internal business processes are executed so that a firm performs similar activities better than its rivals

5. *Customer orientation strategy*—Concentrate on making customers happy

Chapter Glossary

business environment   The combination of social, legal, economic, physical, and political factors in which businesses conduct their operations.

business–information technology alignment   The tight integration of the IT function with the strategy, mission, and goals of the organization.

business process   A collection of related activities that create a product or a service of value to the organization, its business partners, and its customers.

business process management   A management technique that includes methods and tools to support the design, analysis, implementation, management, and optimization of business processes.

business process reengineering   A radical redesign of a business process that improves its efficiency and effectiveness, often by beginning with a "clean sheet" (i.e., from scratch).

competitive advantage   An advantage over competitors in some measure such as cost, quality, or speed; leads to control of a market and to larger-than-average profits.

competitive forces model   A business framework devised by Michael Porter that analyzes competitiveness by recognizing five major forces that could endanger a company's position.

cross-functional processes   No single functional area is responsible for a process's execution.

digital divide   The gap between those who have access to information and communications technology and those who do not.

entry barrier   Product or service feature that customers expect from organizations in a certain industry; an organization trying to enter this market must provide this product or service at a minimum to be able to compete.

globalization   The integration and interdependence of economic, social, cultural, and ecological facets of life, enabled by rapid advances in information technology.

individual social responsibility   See **organizational social responsibility**.

make-to-order   The strategy of producing customized products and services.

mass customization   A production process in which items are produced in large quantities but are customized to fit the desires of each customer.

organizational social responsibility (also individual social responsibility)   Efforts by organizations to solve various social problems.

primary activities   Those business activities related to the production and distribution of the firm's products and services, thus creating value.

strategic information systems (SISs)   Systems that help an organization gain a competitive advantage by supporting its strategic goals and increasing performance and productivity.

support activities   Business activities that do not add value directly to a firm's product or service under consideration but support the primary activities that do add value.

value chain   A sequence of activities through which the organization's inputs, whatever they are, are transformed into more valuable outputs, whatever they are.

value chain model   Model that shows the primary activities that sequentially add value to the profit margin; also shows the support activities.

value system   A stream of activities that includes the producers, suppliers, distributors, and buyers, all of whom have their own value chains.

Discussion Questions

1. Consider the student registration process at your university:

   a. Describe the steps necessary for you to register for your classes each semester.

   b. Describe how information technology is used (or is not used) in each step of the process.

2. Why is it so difficult for an organization to actually implement business process reengineering?

3. Explain why IT is both a business pressure and an enabler of response activities that counter business pressures.

4. What does globalization mean to you in your choice of a major? In your choice of a career? Will you have to be a "lifelong learner"? Why or why not?

5. What might the impact of globalization be on your standard of living?

6. Is IT a strategic weapon or a survival tool? Discuss.

7. Why might it be difficult to justify a strategic information system?

8. Describe the five forces in Porter's competitive forces model and explain how increased access to high-speed Internet has affected each one.

9. Describe Porter's value chain model. What is the relationship between the competitive forces model and the value chain model?

10. Describe how IT can be used to support different value chains for different companies.

11. Discuss the idea that an information system by itself can rarely provide a sustainable competitive advantage.

Problem-Solving Activities

1. Surf the Internet for information about the Department of Homeland Security. Examine the available information, and comment on the role of information technologies in the department.

2. Experience mass customization by designing your own shoes at **www.nike.com**, your car at **www.jaguar.com**, your business card at **www.iprint.com**, and your diamond ring at **www.bluenile.com**. Summarize your experiences.

3. Access **www.go4customer.com**. What does this company do, and where is it located? Who are its customers? Provide examples of how a U.S. company would use its services.

4. Access the website of Walmart China (**www.walmartchina.com/english/index.htm**). How does Walmart China differ from your local Walmart (consider products, prices, services, and so on)? Describe these differences.

5. Apply Porter's value chain model to Costco (**www.costco.com**). What is Costco's competitive strategy? Who are Costco's major competitors? Describe Costco's business model. Describe the tasks that Costco must accomplish for each primary value chain activity. How would Costco's information systems contribute to Costco's competitive strategy, given the nature of its business?

6. Apply Porter's value chain model to Dell (**www.dell.com**). What is Dell's competitive strategy? Who are Dell's major competitors? Describe Dell's business model. Describe the tasks that Dell must accomplish for each primary value chain activity. How would Dell's information systems contribute to Dell's competitive strategy, given the nature of its business?

Closing Case

MIS **POM** **MKT** **The Car Rental Industry**

The Business Problem

Car rental companies began by renting cars to travelers at airports. The business model of these companies historically has been to purchase or lease large fleets of vehicles at the lowest possible price, rent them to customers for income, and then sell them either directly to the public or at auction. The industry grew rapidly; by 2019 it had achieved a global revenue of approximately $90 billion.

Enterprise (**www.enterprise.com**), Hertz (**www.hertz.com**), and Avis Budget (**www.avisbudgetgroup.com**) are the three largest (in order) U.S. airport-based car rental companies by market share. In 2019 they owned a combined 94 percent share of the $32 billion U.S. rental market. Each company encompasses multiple brands:

- Enterprise Holdings: Enterprise, National Car Rental, Alamo, and Enterprise CarShare
- Hertz Global Holdings: Hertz, Thrifty, and Dollar Rent A Car
- Avis Budget Group: Avis, Budget, Payless Car Rental, Zipcar

Despite its large revenues, however, the car rental industry is experiencing a number of problems:

- Until recently, the traditional process of renting a car has been time-consuming, inefficient, and irritating to customers. Customers wait to get off their planes, wait to claim their baggage, and then proceed to curbside where they wait to board a shuttle to the rental car lot. At the lot, they wait in line, speak with a representative, manually fill out forms, and receive the car keys. Then they must go to the lot and find the car.

- These companies all offer vehicles from the same manufacturers and therefore have difficulty differentiating themselves.

- A few decades ago, car rental companies were the only solution to people's need to access a vehicle without owning one. Today, people have many more options to meet their mobility needs. Car rental companies compete with ride-hailing services such as Uber and Lyft, as well as with peer-to-peer car-sharing services such as GetAround and Turo.

Ride-hailing services have had the greatest impact on car rental companies. In 2019, digital marketing firm Epsilon (**http://us.epsilon.com**) analyzed travel transactions for 2017 and 2018. The company found that the majority of previous car rental customers had decreased their spending on rental cars, and about half of them had stopped renting cars altogether.

In general, there are the three types of ground transportation for business travelers: ride hailing, rental cars, and taxis. According to Certify (**www.certify.com**), a provider of online travel and expense management for companies, business travelers use Uber and Lyft approximately 72 percent of the time, rental cars 22 percent of the time, and taxis about 5 percent.

Peer-to-peer car-sharing companies enable private car owners to rent out their vehicles. The companies take a percentage of the total cost of the rental from the people who rent out their cars, and they provide insurance for owners and renters. Customers book rentals, chat with car owners, arrange pickup and drop-off spots, and make payments directly through the companies' apps.

To address their problems, car rental companies are investing in technology, offering more vehicle choice, and providing personalized service and much more efficient pickup and return processes. In addition, these firms want to diversify their income streams while increasing customer satisfaction.

A Number of Possible Solutions

MKT **Improving the customer experience with online apps.** As noted previously, car rental companies have had poor customer service processes in the past. In order to make the rental process as seamless as possible, car rental companies have developed sophisticated mobile apps. In 2020, almost 70 percent of car rentals were made online via apps.

The apps contain data on drivers, including name, address, driver's license number, and payment details. With these data, the apps enable customers to easily sign in via their e-mail or social network. Customers can quickly and easily make or change a reservation, receive confirmation and details of the current rental and all upcoming rentals, receive receipts, and have the option to cancel the booking. The apps make the check-in and drop-off processes much faster and easier. Further, to ensure that customers can quickly find the car that best meets their needs, the apps also have pages for each type of car that include the car description, images, features, rental rules, and availability.

Avis was the first rental car company to introduce split payment functionality in its mobile app. The company surveyed travelers nationwide and found that 87 percent were likely to mix business and leisure in the same trip. Accordingly, Split My Bill provides travelers with the ability to split car rental payments between two credit cards or forms of payment. Customers have the option to split their payment by total bill amount, rental days, or additions such as SiriusXM radio. Customers can also charge vehicle upgrade costs to a second form of payment during their rental period.

And the result of investment in its mobile app? In December 2019, consumer insights firm J.D. Power awarded Avis with its top rental car travel app for receiving the highest score in the firm's U.S. Travel App Satisfaction Study.

MIS **Connected cars.** Car rental companies are connecting their vehicles to the internet. For example, by the end of 2019 Avis had connected more than 200,000 of its vehicles to the internet, and it planned to connect all 600,000 of its cars by the end of 2020.

Each car contains sensors that monitor certain variables, from the car's exact location in case the driver needs roadside assistance, to fuel levels, tire pressure, and brake pad condition. The sensors also enable the driver to remotely lock and unlock a vehicle and flash the lights. The companies' goals are to improve driver safety, reduce maintenance costs, ensure that their cars spend more time on the road, and generate new sources of revenue from selling ads and services.

For a car to make a profit for a rental company, it must be rented out at least 82 percent of the time. If car rental companies can monitor a car's performance in real time, then they can avoid spending money servicing cars that do not need it. In addition, they can reduce the chances of a breakdown that would take a car out of service and irritate customers.

Location tracking also helps these companies generate more revenue-earning days out of their fleets. For example, when cars are towed and impounded because of parking violations, renters often walk away. This situation leaves the car rental companies to handle the problem, which includes finding the lot in which the car is impounded. To address this problem, car rental operators have set up *geofencing* —a virtual perimeter for a real-world geographic area—around the largest impound lots in the United States. As a result, they no longer have to wait for impound workers to contact them. Geofencing has reduced the average recovery time for an impounded car by half, to six days.

Connected cars also enable these firms to broaden their customer bases by placing their cars closer to more drivers. They hope to become less reliant on airport locations, where they earn approximately 70 percent of their revenue. Additionally, car rental companies are working with retailers, mall developers, and city planners to create self-service, counter-free hubs where people can pick up and drop off a car.

For example, Avis is using this model in Kansas City, Missouri, where all its 5,000 cars are connected. Avis is sharing live car-location data to help city planners refine their digital traffic flow models. In that way, city planners can more effectively determine which roads are used most frequently, and they can schedule repairs more efficiently. In return, the city has provided dedicated parking places for Avis cars.

MIS **Autonomous vehicles.** Industry analysts expect that autonomous vehicles will be attractive to the lucrative business traveler market. McKinsey believes that business travelers will want self-driving rental cars, which will enable them to work on the way to their destinations. Business travelers make up roughly 40 percent of car rental company customers.

Car rental companies have been planning to be in this market from its beginnings by partnering with autonomous vehicle companies: Enterprise and Voyage (**www.voyage.auto**), Hertz and Aptiv (**www.aptiv.com**), and Avis and Waymo (**www.waymo.com**).

POM **Fleet management.** Car rental companies operate huge networks of garages, and they possess expertise in maintaining, repairing, and cleaning cars. As a result, these firms sell fleet management services to other companies, including autonomous vehicle makers.

For example, Waymo's driverless taxis need to be on the road as much as possible during each 24-hour day. Therefore, these cars must be serviced and cleaned much more frequently than typical cars. All of the Big Three car rental companies have outstanding fleet-management operations.

In Phoenix, Avis is servicing Waymo's fleet of 600 self-driving Chrysler Pacifica minivans. Avis handles tasks such as oil changes, tire rotations, and cleaning, while Waymo maintains the autonomous vehicles' digital systems. Avis's deal with Waymo provides added revenue without the large fixed cost that comes from actually owning cars. At the same time, Waymo avoids the expense of managing maintenance.

Car sharing. Although car sharing accounts for only 1 percent of the revenues of car rental companies, these companies have car-sharing brands. These units help them prepare for a future with more counter-free locations for their rental fleets. Key car-sharing brands are Zipcar (Avis), Enterprise CarShare, and Hertz 24/7.

Resale retail. Rental car companies sell their cars after a few years. Unfortunately, the weak second-hand market has reduced industry profits. To better control the timing and location of those sales, the Big Three are building their own physical used car sales lots.

These firms rotate their vehicles out of their rental fleets while the vehicles are still under the original manufacturer's warranty, and they sell them through their sales programs. The cars in these programs are certified, meaning that they have passed a rigorous multipoint, bumper-to-bumper inspection process by certified mechanics. They usually offer 12-month, 12,000-mile warranties (which cost extra).

Value-added services. In 2018, Hertz launched Hertz+, a platform on its website that offers its customers access to more than 130,000 global experiences. These experiences include exclusive events, tours, and other travel opportunities. Hertz+ works with **PlacePass.com**, a technology company that helps companies access the market for in-destination experiences.

Avis has deployed an open software development system that allows ride-hailing services, digital mapmakers, city planners, and other potential partners to share data with Avis's app. This system has produced revenue for Avis. For example, a department store could pay Avis a fee, in return for which Avis would embed ads in its app to steer users to the store's website. The app could also literally steer customers to the physical store. For example, an Avis customer who forgot to pack a needed article of clothing could be taken to a physical store by his or her self-driving rental car.

The Results

According to J.D. Power, customer satisfaction with rental car companies reached record highs in 2019. Based on a 1000-point scale, Hertz scored 856, Enterprise 855, and Avis 833, with an industry average of 843. The small 23-point difference between Hertz and Avis highlights the competition in the industry.

Unfortunately, the COVID-19 pandemic has damaged the entire travel industry, including car rental companies. As of May 2020, car rental reservations at airport locations had declined between 50 and 75 percent, according to the American Car Rental Association. Neighborhood branch locations experienced a smaller decline in reservations than airport locations did. One possible reason for the smaller decline is people involved in accidents need an insurance replacement vehicle.

Car rental firms began to furlough employees in March 2020. By May, they had begun to lay off employees. For instance, on April 20, Hertz announced that it would lay off 10,000 of its 29,000 employees in its North American operation.

And the bottom line? Regardless of the uncertainty that the car rental industry faces, the U.S. Department of Homeland Security (DHS) has declared the industry essential, and it remains open for business.

In May 2020, Hertz filed for bankruptcy, a victim of the coronavirus pandemic. By declaring bankruptcy, Hertz maintained that it intended to stay in business while restructuring its debts and emerging a financially healthier company.

Sources: Compiled from C. Isidore, "Hertz Files for Bankruptcy," *CNN Business*, May 22, 2020; M. Zinn, "Car Rental Industry Braces for Impact from Coronavirus," *News-Press*, May 2, 2020; M. Goldstein, "Hertz Car Rental Suffers Massive Layoffs, Stock Drop from COVID-19 Pandemic," *Forbes*, April 24, 2020; "Avis Budget Group Surpasses 200,000 Connected Vehicle Mark," *Avis Budget Group Press Release*, December 16, 2019; A. Levy, "Lyft Announces Car Rental Service; Hertz and Avis Shares Plunge," *CNBC,* December 13, 2019; "Introducing Lyft Rentals," *Lyft Blog*, December 12, 2019; I. Carey, "Hertz Rises Where Avis Falls in Crowded Landscape for Rides," *Skift*, November 8, 2019; I. Carey, "Hertz Continues to Outshine Avis with Tech Investments for Operations," *Skift*, November 7, 2019; "Increasing Competition Drives Rental Car Companies to Achieve Record High Satisfaction," *J.D. Power Press Release*, October 16, 2019; D. Lubinsky, "'Complete' Tech Transformation for Rental Companies," *Auto Remarketing*, August 14, 2019; A. Shah, "Avis Revamps IT to Stay Relevant in Changing Industry," *Wall Street Journal*, July 3, 2019; "Avis Car Rental Enhances Mobile App Experience with New Split Payment Feature," *Avis Budget Group Press Release*, June 3, 2019; "Car Rental Companies: Evolving with Consumer Needs," *Invers*, May 27, 2019; A. Sheivachman, "Avis and Hertz Struggle to Find Path to Car Rental Profit," *Skift*, May 7, 2019; P. Wahba, "A Fork in the Road for Avis," *Fortune*, November 1, 2018; C. Elliott, "Car Rental Companies Are in a 'Transformative' Stage. Here's What That Means for You," *Forbes*, September 23, 2018; P. LaMonica, "Avis Will Start Providing Rental Cars to Lyft Drivers," *CNN Business*, August 6, 2018; W. Richter, "Numbers Are in: Uber, Lyft v. Rental Cars & Taxis in the U.S. in Q2," *Wolf Street*, July 29, 2018; H. Shaban and P. Holley, "GM Launches a Peer-to-Peer Car-Sharing Service," *The Washington Post*, July 24, 2018; A. Griswold, "Startups Like Uber Decimated Taxi Companies. Rental Cars Are Next," *Quartz*, May 10, 2018; P. Holley, "Airbnb for Cars Is Here. And the Rental Car Giants Are Not Happy," *The Washington Post*, March 30, 2018; "Avis Now Provides More Features on Mobile App," *Auto Rental News*, July 12, 2016; **www.avisbudgetgroup.com**, **www.hertz.com**, **www.enterprise.com**, accessed April 10, 2020.

Questions

1. This case has addressed a number of possible solutions for the problems afflicting the car rental industry.

   a. Which solution do you think had the greatest strategic impact on the industry? Provide specific examples to support your answer.

   b. Which solution do you think has the least strategic impact on the industry? Provide specific examples to support your answer.

2. Apply the five forces of Porter's Competitive Forces Model to each possible solution discussed in this case (individually). Which forces are most applicable to each solution? Support your answers.

CHAPTER 3

Ethics and Privacy

CHAPTER OUTLINE	LEARNING OBJECTIVES
3.1 Ethical Issues	**3.1** Define ethics, and explain its three fundamental tenets and the four categories of ethical issues related to information technology.
3.2 Privacy	**3.2** Discuss at least one potential threat to the privacy of the data stored in each of three places that store personal data.

Opening Case

MIS Student Tracking Apps

Colleges across the United States are using short-range Bluetooth sensors on smartphones and campuswide Wi-Fi networks (see Chapter 8) to track hundreds of thousands of students more precisely than ever before. Schools use these technologies to monitor students' academic performance, analyze their conduct, and assess their mental health.

Three companies providing these tracking technologies are SpotterEDU (**www.spotteredu.com**), Degree Analytics (**www.degreeanalytics.com**), and Life360 (**www.life360.com**). School and company officials claim that location monitoring can increase student success. They contend that if they know more about where students are, they can intervene before problems arise.

SpotterEDU. SpotterEDU monitors students' attendance by "pinpointing students within a classroom until they leave." The app automatically notifies professors if a student skips a class or shows up more than a few minutes late. While the app notes whether students are in the classroom during class times, the company claims that its app does not have global positioning system (GPS) tracking. Therefore, it cannot locate students anywhere but in their classrooms.

School officials give SpotterEDU their students' full schedules. The system can then e-mail a professor or adviser automatically if a student skips class or walks in more than two minutes late. The app also notes if students left early or stepped out for a break. At some schools, advisers text students if they do not show up within five minutes of the beginning of class.

Individual professors choose whether to use the app. If the professors use it, then students in those classes cannot opt out and must install the software on their phones.

SpotterEDU CEO Rick Carter contends that his company developed the app as a way to monitor student athletes. He notes that many schools already pay class checkers to make certain that athletes attend classes so they remain eligible to play.

Interestingly, SpotterEDU's terms of use state that its data are not guaranteed to be "accurate, complete, correct, adequate, useful, timely, reliable or otherwise." Regardless of that statement, Carter claimed that, as of May 2020, almost 40 schools were using his app.

Carter asserts that the real value for school officials is that they can split students into groups, such as "out-of-state students," for further review. When asked why an official would want to segregate out data on student groups, Carter replied that many colleges already do so to uncover patterns in academic retention and performance.

Students' attendance and tardiness can be scored into a point system that some professors use for grading. Carter noted that schools could use the data to take action against truant students, such as taking back scholarship funds.

Degree Analytics (DA). Schools also employ the Degree Analytics app, which uses Wi-Fi check-ins to track the movements of some 200,000 students attending 19 state universities, private colleges, and other schools. Degree Analytics claims to monitor more than just attendance. By logging the time a student spends in different parts of the campus, company algorithms search for patterns in student behaviour. For instance, a student avoiding the cafeteria might suffer from food insecurity or an eating disorder, and a student skipping class might be depressed.

A DA algorithm can also divide the student body into groups such as "full-time freshmen" or "commuter students." The algorithm then compares each student to "normal" behavior, as defined by data that DA has collected about their peers. The system also generates a "risk score" for students based on factors such as how much time they spend in public areas such as campus cafeterias or the gym. Students who spend less time than average with others are noted, and the company alerts school officials in case they want to pursue intervention.

Significantly, behavioral scientists are highly skeptical of these advertised capabilities, asserting they are largely untested and unproven in their abilities to pinpoint students' behavioral "problems."

Virginia Commonwealth University (VCU; **www.vcu.edu**) deployed a Degree Analytics pilot program to monitor a set of courses required of all freshmen. Students could opt out by clicking "no" on a link that asked whether they want to help "support student success, operations, and security." VCU students contended that they were frustrated to first learn of the system in a short e-mail concerning a "new attendance tool" and were given only two weeks before the opt-out deadline passed. Students quickly spread the opt-out link across social media, while the student newspaper raised doubts about the program's secrecy and mission. Nearly 60 percent of VCU students refused to participate in the program.

Life360. Some parents wish their children experienced even closer supervision. They argue that the tracking companies should share their data with parents, particularly if the parents are paying for their children's college educations. The Life360 app is not just for college students. The company reports that some 18 million people around the world use it.

Life360 (**www.life360.com**) is a tracking app that parents use to monitor their children—everything from where they are to how fast they are driving. The app enables parents to monitor communications and control how much time their children spend on apps and games. For instance, some parents will give their children the keys to the car only if they consent to being monitored by a paid version of the app that tracks driving speed.

Interestingly, one video with more than 500,000 views instructs teens on how to change their phone settings to trick the app into freezing their location. Other social media posts from college students show how the app can extend overcontrolling parenting even into young adulthood. In fact, on message boards such as r/insaneparents and r/raisedbynarcissists, teens and young adults are sharing the darker side effects of these technologies.

One college sophomore's parents call him whenever they see something on the app that makes them suspect he is doing something they would not like. Another student claimed that her parents insist that she leave Life360 turned on at all times while she is at college as a condition of paying for her to attend.

Life360's CEO defends the app, citing several examples of tracking services that help parents find their children in emergency situations. Essentially, people using the app must weigh the safety and security of their loved ones against their privacy.

When parents and children already have a relationship that includes a degree of privacy, trust, and independence, the decrease in privacy resulting from tracking apps need not necessarily seem overwhelming. However, the American Civil Liberties Union has expressed privacy concerns regarding the tracking apps.

Many educators warn that the apps are useless for students who do not own smartphones and coercive for students who do. They also contend that the apps are unnecessary for professors, who can take attendance by utilizing the pop quizzes and random checks they have always used. Some educators argue that the apps are intrusive and significantly reduce students' privacy. They further contend that increased monitoring undermines students' independence and development toward being on their own as adults.

Students disagree on whether campus-tracking systems constitute a breach of privacy. In fact, some students argue that they have nothing to hide. However, students tend to agree that the technology is becoming widespread and they cannot really do anything about it.

Sources: Compiled from D. Belkin, "No Place to Hide: Colleges Track Students, Everywhere," *Wall Street Journal*, March 5, 2020; S. Hollister, "U.S. Colleges Are Trying to Install Location Tracking Apps on Students' Phones," *The Verge*, January 28, 2020; Z. Schermele, "Education Technology: Schools Are Using Apps to Collect Student Data, Track Attendance," *Teen Vogue*, January 27, 2020; A. Kesel, "University of Missouri Students Will Now Be Required to Install Location Tracking App," *The Mind Unleashed*, January 27, 2020; M. Williams and S. Terada, "Invasive or Helpful? MU Using Students' Phones to Track if They Are in Class or Not," *Kansas City Star*, January 21, 2020; T. Cushing, "Tracking College Students Everywhere They Go on Campus Is the New Normal," *Techdirt.com*, December 31, 2019; D. Harwell, "Colleges Are Turning Students' Phones into Surveillance Machines, Tracking the Locations of Hundreds of Thousands," *The Washington Post*, December 24, 2019; T. Nash, "Majority of VCU Students Refuse to Participate in Wi-Fi Tracking Program," *Muckrock*, December 4, 2019; A. Ohlheiser, "'Don't Leave Campus': Parents Are Now Using Tracking Apps to Watch Their Kids at College," *The Washington Post*, October 22, 2019; L. Gardner, "Students Under Surveillance," *The Chronicle of Higher Education*, October 13, 2019; J. Barshay and S. Aslanian, "Under a Watchful Eye," *apmreports.org*, August 6, 2019; C. Gartenberg, "Chinese Schools Are Using 'Smart Uniforms' to Track Their Students' Locations," *The Verge*, December 28, 2018; **www.spotteredu.com**, accessed June 3, 2020; **www.degreeanalytics.com**, accessed June 3, 2020; **www.life360.com**, accessed June 3, 2020.

Questions

1. Discuss the ethicalilty and legality of student-tracking apps.

2. The fundamental tenets of ethics include responsibility, accountability, and liability. Discuss each of these tenets as it applies to student-tracking apps.

3. Would you opt out if your university decided to use a student-tracking app? Why or why not?

Introduction

You will encounter numerous ethical and privacy issues in your career, many of which will involve IT in some manner. The two issues are closely related to each other and also to IT, and both raise significant questions involving access to information in the digital age. The answers to these questions are not straightforward. In fact, IT has made finding answers to these questions even more difficult.

Consider student-tracking apps in the chapter opening case. Are these apps legal? Are they ethical? In a further example, suppose your organization decides to adopt social computing technologies (which you will study in Chapter 9) to include business partners and customers in new product development. You will be able to analyze the potential privacy and ethical implications of implementing these technologies.

This chapter provides insights into how to respond to ethical and privacy issues. Furthermore, it will help you to make immediate contributions to your company's code of ethics and its privacy policies. You will also be able to provide meaningful input concerning the potential ethical and privacy impacts of your organization's information systems on people within and outside the organization.

All organizations, large and small, must be concerned with ethics. In particular, small business (or start-up) owners face a very difficult situation when their employees have access to sensitive customer information. There is a delicate balance between access to information and the appropriate use of that information. This balance is best maintained by hiring honest and trustworthy employees who abide by the organization's code of ethics. Ultimately, this issue leads to another question: Does the small business, or a start-up, even have a code of ethics to fall back on in this type of situation?

3.1 Ethical Issues

Ethics refers to the principles of right and wrong that individuals use to make choices that guide their behavior. Deciding what is right or wrong is not always easy or clear-cut. Fortunately, there are many frameworks that can help us make ethical decisions.

Author Lecture Videos are available exclusively in *WileyPLUS*.
Apply the Concept activities are available in the Appendix and in *WileyPLUS*.

Ethical Frameworks

There are many sources for ethical standards. Here we consider five widely used standards: the utilitarian approach, the rights approach, the fairness approach, the common good approach, and the deontology approach. There are many other sources, but these five are representative.

The *utilitarian approach* states that an ethical action is the one that provides the most good or does the least harm. The ethical corporate action would be the one that produces the greatest good and does the least harm for all affected parties—customers, employees, shareholders, the community, and the physical environment.

The *rights approach* maintains that an ethical action is the one that best protects and respects the moral rights of the affected parties. Moral rights can include the rights to make one's own choices about what kind of life to lead, to be told the truth, not to be injured, and to enjoy a degree of privacy. Which of these rights people are actually entitled to—and under what circumstances—is widely debated. Nevertheless, most people acknowledge that individuals are entitled to some moral rights. An ethical organizational action would be one that protects and respects the moral rights of customers, employees, shareholders, business partners, and even competitors.

The *fairness approach* posits that ethical actions treat all human beings equally, or, if unequally, then fairly, based on some defensible standard. For example, most people might believe it is fair to pay people higher salaries if they work harder or if they contribute a greater amount to the firm. However, there is less certainty regarding CEO salaries that are hundreds or thousands of times larger than those of other employees. Many people question whether this huge disparity is based on a defensible standard or whether it is the result of an imbalance of power and hence is unfair.

The *common good approach* highlights the interlocking relationships that underlie all societies. This approach argues that respect and compassion for all others are the basis for ethical actions. It emphasizes the common conditions that are important to the welfare of everyone. These conditions can include a system of laws, effective police and fire departments, healthcare, a public educational system, and even public recreation areas.

Finally, the *deontology approach* states that the morality of an action is based on whether that action itself is right or wrong under a series of rules, rather than based on the consequences of that action. An example of deontology is the belief that killing someone is wrong, even if it was in self-defense.

If we combine these five standards, we can develop a general framework for ethics (or ethical decision making). This framework consists of five steps:

1. Recognize an ethical issue:

   Could this decision or situation damage someone or some group?

   Does this decision involve a choice between a good and a bad alternative?

   Does this issue involve more than simply legal considerations? If so, then in what way?

2. Get the facts:

   What are the relevant facts of the situation?

   Do I have sufficient information to make a decision?

   Which individuals or groups have an important stake in the outcome?

   Have I consulted all relevant persons and groups?

3. Evaluate alternative actions:

   Which option will produce the most good and do the least harm? (the utilitarian approach)

   Which option best respects the rights of all stakeholders? (the rights approach)

   Which option treats people equally or proportionately? (the fairness approach)

   Which option best serves the community as a whole, and not just some members? (the common good approach)

4. Make a decision and test it:

   Considering all the approaches, which option best addresses the situation?

5. Act and reflect on the outcome of your decision:

   How can I implement my decision with the greatest care and attention to the concerns of all stakeholders?

   How did my decision turn out, and what did I learn from this specific situation?

Now that we have created a general ethical framework, we will focus specifically on ethics in the corporate environment.

Ethics in the Corporate Environment

Many companies and professional organizations develop their own codes of ethics. A **code of ethics** is a collection of principles intended to guide decision making by members of the organization. For example, the Association for Computing Machinery (**www.acm.org**), an organization of computing professionals, has a thoughtful code of ethics for its members (see **www.acm.org/code-of-ethics**).

Keep in mind that different codes of ethics are not always consistent with one another. Therefore, an individual might be expected to conform to multiple codes. For example, a person who is a member of two large professional computing-related organizations may be simultaneously required by one organization to comply with all applicable laws and by the other organization to refuse to obey unjust laws.

Fundamental tenets of ethics include:

- **Responsibility** means that you accept the consequences of your decisions and actions.
- **Accountability** refers to determining who is responsible for actions that were taken.
- **Liability** is a legal concept that gives individuals the right to recover the damages done to them by other individuals, organizations, or systems.

Before you go any further, it is critical that you realize that what is *unethical* is not necessarily *illegal*. For example, a bank's decision to foreclose on a home can be technically legal, but it can raise many ethical questions. In many instances, then, an individual or organization faced with an ethical decision is not considering whether to break the law. As the foreclosure example illustrates, however, ethical decisions can have serious consequences for individuals, organizations, and society at large. This chapter's closing case addresses the legality and ethicality of Grubhub's business practices.

ACCT **FIN** We have witnessed a large number of extremely poor ethical decisions, not to mention outright criminal behavior, at many organizations. During 2001 and 2002, three highly publicized fiascos occurred at Enron, WorldCom, and Tyco. At each company, executives were convicted of various types of fraud for using illegal accounting practices. These actions led to the passage of the Sarbanes–Oxley Act in 2002. Sarbanes–Oxley requires publicly held companies to implement financial controls and company executives to personally certify financial reports.

Then, the subprime mortgage crisis exposed unethical lending practices throughout the mortgage industry. The crisis also highlighted pervasive weaknesses in the regulation of the U.S. financial industry as well as the global financial system. It ultimately contributed to a deep recession in the global economy. Along these same lines, financier Bernie Madoff was convicted in 2009 of operating a Ponzi scheme and sentenced to 150 years in federal prison. Several of Madoff's employees were also convicted in 2014.

Unfortunately, ethical misbehavior continued. Consider Wells Fargo bank (**www .wellsfargo.com**). In 2016, authorities found that bank employees had created approximately 2 million fake customer checking and credit card accounts without their knowledge. Bank employees had created the accounts under pressure from supervisors to meet daily account quotas. The bank then charged customers at least $1.5 million in fees for the fake accounts. Not only were the bank's victims charged overdraft and maintenance fees, but their credit scores were lowered for not staying current on accounts that they did not even know about.

Wells Fargo fired some 5,300 employees. The bank was also ordered to pay $185 million in fines, which is a very small amount compared to the $5.6 billion that the bank earned in the second quarter of 2016. Furthermore, in October 2016, Wells Fargo CEO John Stumpf stepped down from his position.

In June 2018 Wells Fargo was again accused of misconduct by the Securities and Exchange Commission (SEC, **www.sec.gov**). The SEC said that the bank collected large fees by "improperly encouraging" brokerage clients to actively trade high-fee debt products that were intended to be held to maturity. The bank agreed to pay a $4 million penalty and to return to clients $930,377 of fees it gained from the transactions plus $178,064 of interest.

MIS Avast (**www.avast.com**) is a computer-security company based in the Czech Republic. Some 400 million people around the world use the firm's software. In 2019, researchers found that the company used browser extensions (small software programs that customize the browsing experience) to watch everything their customers did online. Avast then sold that data to corporate customers as "insights." Clients included Google, Microsoft, PepsiCo, and McKinsey.

Advancements in information technologies have generated a new set of ethical problems. Computer processing power doubles roughly every 18 months, meaning that organizations are more dependent than ever on their information systems. Organizations can store increasing amounts of data at decreasing costs. As a result, they can maintain more data on individuals for longer periods of time. Going further, computer networks, particularly the Internet, enable organizations to collect, integrate, and distribute enormous amounts of information on individuals, groups, and institutions. These developments have created numerous ethical problems concerning the appropriate collection and use of customer information, personal privacy, and the protection of intellectual property. As IT's About Business 3.1 illustrates, Google is being closely scrutinized in the United States and around the world for its data collection and analysis practices.

Ethics and Information Technology

All employees have a responsibility to encourage ethical uses of information and information technology. Many of the business decisions you will face at work will have an ethical dimension. Consider the following decisions that you might have to make:

- **HRM** Should organizations monitor employees' Web surfing and email?
- **MKT** Should organizations sell customer information to other companies?
- **HRM** Should organizations audit employees' computers for unauthorized software or illegally downloaded music or video files?

IT's About Business 3.1

MIS **MKT** **Google and Your Privacy**

Google's Business Problem

The contract between consumers and Google and many other technology companies is that the companies provide services for free in return for the use of consumers' data. Analysis of consumer data enables content publishers and website and app developers to monetize their products and advertisers to reach their audiences.

Google does have a privacy policy. Without this policy, the company could not collect much of the personal data that it currently does. The policy is a contract in which consumers give "informed consent" to the collection of their personal data.

The more consumer data that Google collects and analyzes, the more precisely the company can target its ads, and the higher the likelihood that these ads will encourage consumers to make purchases. For example, Google can determine the number of online and offline (physical store) purchases generated by digital ad campaigns, a goal that marketing experts describe as the "Holy Grail" of online advertising. Specifically, Google can inform a company how many shoppers viewed a particular ad and then later visited a store and purchased the product displayed in the ad.

In 2013, the general public became much more aware of their lack of online privacy when Edward Snowden, the former U.S. National Security Agency contractor, leaked highly classified information from the National Security Agency (NSA; **www.nsa.gov**), publicly revealing the extensiveness of government surveillance. Snowden included Google among the data sources utilized by British and U.S. intelligence agencies.

Consumers now realize that thousands of companies know their identity by what they do online. Further, they know that their online profiles can potentially reveal extremely private information about them.

Although consumers are aware that Google creates online profiles, they typically do not appreciate the extent of the data that Google collects. Google collects consumers' search histories, web pages visited, the Internet Service Provider (ISP) that each visitor is using, login data, IP addresses of the visitor's device (Internet Protocol; see Chapter 6), purchase activities, geolocations, email content, friends' data, videos watched, cookies, and much, much more. Google uses this data to personalize advertisements, from which it derives most of its revenue.

Today, Google is integrating data from billions of credit card transaction records with location data to prove that its online ads are prompting people to make purchases, even when the transactions occur offline in physical stores. (It is important to note that Google is not the only company performing these analyses. Facebook, for example, and numerous other firms do so as well.)

Google also purchases data from data brokers to make individual profiles even more comprehensive. Data brokers collect data about individuals from public records and private sources, including census and change-of-address records, motor vehicle and driving records, user-contributed material to social networking sites, magazine subscriptions, telephone records, media

and court reports, voter registration lists, consumer purchase histories, most-wanted lists and terrorist watch lists, bank card transaction records, healthcare authorities, and web-browsing histories.

Google does not just offer services such as search, maps, Gmail, and various apps. The company also has an extensive tracker network with third-party trackers embedded in almost 80 percent of the top websites today.

A *third-party tracker* is a piece of computer code embedded in a web page by, for example, Google, that is typically invisible to consumers. This code collects data on consumer visits to a web page without the consumer's knowledge. Each tracker exposes some personal data to Google. When Google embeds the same tracker in many websites, the company has formed a *tracker network*. Tracker networks help to develop extensive individual profiles.

Industry researchers allege that Google uses "secret web-tracking pages." Specifically, they assert that Google uses a tracker containing web-browsing information, location, and other data, and sends that information and data to advertising companies via web pages that "showed no content." This process could allow companies that purchase ads to match a user's Google profile and web activity to profiles from other companies, which violates Google's own ad-buying rules. Significantly, cookies require the user's permission, but hidden webpages do not.

Google's problem: Does the technology giant violate its users' privacy? This problem has become serious enough that rival browsers are challenging Google by emphasizing their attention to user privacy. These browsers are:

- Brave (**www.brave.com**) does not collect any data about your online activity. Brave automatically blocks third-party trackers and all advertising cookies.

- Firefox (**https://www.mozilla.org/en-US/firefox/new/**) is the third most popular browser on the internet, behind Google's Chrome and Apple's Safari. Firefox automatically blocks third-party trackers and all advertising cookies.

- Tor browser (**www.torproject.org**) encrypts your web activities three times and sends them to three Tor servers before you reach your desired website. With Tor encryption, each server has access to only one set of instructions, so no server has access to both your IP address and the website you are visiting. This process makes it impossible for Tor to keep any records about your online activity. Further, every time you close your session, the browser deletes all cookies and browsing history.

- DuckDuckGo (**www.duckduckgo.com**) does not have a standalone desktop browser, which means that it is a solution only if you using your smartphone or tablet. Deleting your entire browsing history requires tapping a single button. The browser automatically blocks ads and third-party trackers.

The Results

On June 2, 2020, a class action suit was filed against Google in the United States, accusing the company of invading the privacy of millions of consumers without their knowledge by tracking internet use even when the consumers were using Google's private browsing mode. The suit charged that Google tracks consumers through Google Analytics, Google Ad Manager, and various other application and website plug-ins.

According to the plaintiffs, this data collection is almost always performed without consumers' knowledge, as Google does not require websites to disclose up-front that Google is collecting visitors' data. As a result, the suit accuses Google of collecting the personal data of individuals without their consent. The suit concluded: "Google's practices infringe upon users' privacy; intentionally deceive consumers; give Google and its employees power to learn intimate details about individuals' lives, interests, and internet usage; and make Google 'one stop shopping' for any government, private, or criminal actor who wants to undermine individuals' privacy, security, or freedom."

Google is also facing litigation in the State of Arizona, Australia, and the United Kingdom for allegedly conducting deceptive and misleading tracking practices. In addition, the U.S. Department of Justice (**www.doj.gov**) and other state attorneys general are likely to file antitrust lawsuits against Google sometime in the summer of 2020.

In response, Google contends that all users who sign into Google's services consent to Google's sharing their data with third parties. As noted above, this process is called informed consent.

Sources: Compiled from M. Burgess, "Google Got Rich from Your Data. DuckDuckGo Is Fighting Back," *Wired*, June 8, 2020; C. Kwan, "Google Faces Class Action for Allegedly Tracking Private Browsing Activity," *ZDNet*, June 3, 2020; C. Kwan, "Google Sued by Arizona AG for Alleged Deceptive Tracking Practices," *ZDNet*, May 28, 2020; T. Romm, "Google Likely to Face Federal, State Antitrust Lawsuits in Coming Months, Sources Say," *Washington Post*, May 15, 2020; L. Newman, "The Fractured Future of Browser Privacy," *Wired*, January 30, 2020;

J. Abu-Ghazaleh, "Why Google Gets Away with so Much," *OneZero*, January 17, 2020; D. Bohn, "Google to 'Phase Out' Third-Party Cookies in Chrome, but Not for Two Years," *The Verge*, January 14, 2020; R. Koch, "Most Secure Browser for Your Privacy in 2020," *ProtonMail*, December 9, 2019; T. Herrera, "You're Tracked Everywhere You Go Online. Use this Guide to Fight Back," *The New York Times*, November 24, 2019; "Australian Regulator Files Privacy Suit against Google Alleging Location Data Misuse," *CNBC*, October 29, 2019; E. Bott, "How to Replace Each Google Service with a More Privacy-Friendly Alternative," *The Ed Bott Report*, October 22, 2019; L. Newman, "Google Tightens Its Voice Assistant Rules Amid Privacy Backlash," *Wired*, September 23, 2019; J. Wakefield, "Google's 'Secret Web Tracking Pages' Explained," *BBC News*, September 5, 2019; C. Jee, "Your're Very Easy to Track Down, Even When Your Data Has Been Anonymized," *MIT Technology Review*, July 23, 2019; D. Nield, "All the Ways Google Tracks You—and How to Stop It," *Wired*, May 27, 2019; T. Haselton and M. Graham, "Google Uses Gmail to Track a History of Things You Buy—and It's Hard to Delete," *CNBC*, May 17, 2019; B. Barrett, "Security News this Week: Oh, Great, Google Tracks What You Buy Online with Gmail," *Wircd*, May 10, 2019; L. Goode, "Google's New Privacy Features Put the Responsibility on Users," *Wired*, May 8, 2019; E. Dreyfuss, "Google Tracks You Even If Location History's Off," *Wired*, August 13, 2018; A. Kieler, "Google's Tracking of Offline Spending Sparks Call for Federal Investigation," *The Consumerist*, July 31, 2017; L. Tung, "Google: We'll Track Your Offline Credit Card Use to Show that Online Ads Work," *ZDNet*, May 24, 2017; R. Kilpatrick, "Google's New Feature Can Match Ad Clicks with In-Store Purchases," *Fortune*, May 23, 2017; "What Are the Biggest Tracker Networks and What Can I Do about Them?," *Quora*, January 1, 2017; **www.google.com**, accessed June 11, 2020.

Questions

1. Discuss the ethicality and legality of Google's data collection and analysis methods. Be sure to include "informed consent" in your discussion.

2. The fundamental tenets of ethics include responsibility, accountability, and liability. Discuss each of these tenets as it applies to Google's data collection and analysis methods.

The diversity and ever-expanding use of IT applications have created a variety of ethical issues. These issues fall into four general categories: privacy, accuracy, property, and accessibility.

1. *Privacy issues* involve collecting, storing, and disseminating information about individuals.
2. *Accuracy issues* involve the authenticity, fidelity, and correctness of information that is collected and processed.
3. *Property issues* involve the ownership and value of information.
4. *Accessibility issues* revolve around who should have access to information and whether they should pay a fee for this access.

Table 3.1 lists representative questions and issues for each of these categories. Online Ethics Cases also presents 14 scenarios that raise ethical issues. These scenarios will provide a context for you to consider situations that involve ethical or unethical behaviour.

Many of the issues and scenarios discussed in this chapter involve privacy as well as ethics. In the next section, you will learn about privacy issues in more detail.

TABLE 3.1   A Framework for Ethical Issues

Privacy Issues

What information about oneself should an individual be required to reveal to others?

What kinds of surveillance can an employer use on its employees?

What types of personal information can people keep to themselves and not be forced to reveal to others?

What information about individuals should be kept in databases, and how secure is the information there?

Accuracy Issues

Who is responsible for the authenticity, fidelity, and accuracy of the information collected?

How can we ensure that the information will be processed properly and presented accurately to users?

How can we ensure that errors in databases, data transmissions, and data processing are accidental and not intentional?

Who is to be held accountable for errors in information, and how should the injured parties be compensated?

Property Issues

Who owns the information?

What are just and fair prices for its exchange?

How should we handle software piracy (illegally copying copyrighted software)?

Under what circumstances can one use proprietary databases?

Can corporate computers be used for private purposes?

How should experts who contribute their knowledge to create expert systems be compensated?

How should access to information channels be allocated?

Accessibility issues

Who is allowed to access information?

How much should companies charge for permitting access to information?

How can access to computers be provided for employees with disabilities?

Who will be provided with the equipment needed for accessing information?

What information does a person or an organization have a right to obtain, under what conditions, and with what safeguards?

Before you go on...

1. What does a code of ethics contain?
2. Identify and discuss the fundamental tenets of ethics.

Author Lecture Videos are available exclusively in *WileyPLUS*.
Apply the Concept activities are available in the Appendix and in *WileyPLUS*.

 **Privacy**

In general, **privacy** is the right to be left alone and to be free of unreasonable personal intrusions. **Information privacy** is the right to determine when, and to what extent, information about you can be gathered or communicated to others. Privacy rights apply to individuals, groups, and institutions. The right to privacy is recognized today in all the U.S. states and by the federal government, either by statute or in common law.

Privacy can be interpreted quite broadly. However, court decisions in many countries have followed two rules fairly closely:

1. The right of privacy is not absolute. Privacy must be balanced against the needs of society.
2. The public's right to know supersedes the individual's right of privacy.

These two rules illustrate why determining and enforcing privacy regulations can be difficult.

As we discussed earlier, rapid advances in information technologies have made it much easier to collect, store, and integrate vast amounts of data on individuals in large databases. On an average day, data about you are generated in many ways: surveillance cameras located on toll roads, on other roadways, in busy intersections, in public places, and at work; credit card transactions; telephone calls (landline and cellular); banking transactions; queries to search engines; and government records (including police records). These data can be integrated to produce a **digital dossier**, which is an electronic profile of you and your habits. The process of forming a digital dossier is called **profiling.** (See IT's About Business 3.1 for an excellent example of profiling.)

Data aggregators, such as LexisNexis (**www.risk.lexisnexis.com**), ChoicePoint (**www .choicepoint.com**), and Acxiom (**www.acxiom.com**), are prominent examples of profilers. These companies collect public data such as real estate records and published telephone numbers, in addition to nonpublic information such as Social Security numbers; financial data; and police, criminal, and motor vehicle records. They then integrate these data to form digital dossiers on most adults in the United States. They ultimately sell these dossiers to law enforcement agencies and companies that conduct background checks on potential employees. They also sell them to companies that want to know their customers better, a process called *customer intimacy.*

Electronic Surveillance

According to the American Civil Liberties Union (ACLU), tracking people's activities with the aid of information technology has become a major privacy-related problem. The ACLU notes that this monitoring, or **electronic surveillance**, is rapidly increasing, particularly with the emergence of new technologies. Electronic surveillance is conducted by employers, the government, and other institutions.

Americans today live with a degree of surveillance that would have been unimaginable just a few years ago. For example, surveillance cameras track you at airports, subways, banks, and other public venues. Inexpensive digital sensors are also now everywhere. They are incorporated into laptop webcams, video-game motion sensors, smartphone cameras, utility meters, passports, and employee ID cards. Step out your front door and you could be captured in a high-resolution photograph taken from the air or from the street by Google or Microsoft as they update their mapping services. Drive down a city street, cross a toll bridge, or park at a shopping mall, and your license plate can be recorded and time-stamped.

Emerging technologies such as low-cost digital cameras, motion sensors, and biometric readers are helping to increase the monitoring of human activity. The costs of storing and using digital data are also rapidly decreasing. The result is an explosion of sensor data collection and storage.

A special problem arises with smartphones that are equipped with global positioning system (GPS) sensors. These sensors routinely *geotag* photos and videos, embedding images with the longitude and latitude of the location shown in the image. Thus, you could be inadvertently supplying criminals with useful intelligence by posting personal images on social networks or photo-sharing websites. These actions would show the criminals exactly where you live and when you are there. You could be providing government agencies with useful information as well. IT's About Business 3.2 addresses pervasive government surveillance with a look at China's Social Credit System.

IT's About Business 3.2

MIS **FIN**   China's Social Credit System

In China, cash has long dominated transactions. As recently as 2011, only one-third of Chinese citizens had a bank account. As a result, the country did not have the chance to develop credit histories. The use of cash and the lack of credit histories meant that people could default on loans or sell poor or counterfeit goods with few repercussions. The question became: Whom could you trust?

In 2015, the Chinese government began to address this question by allowing eight companies to run trial credit scores. One of the companies is Ant Financial Services Group (**www.antgroup.com**), an affiliate company of the Alibaba Group (**www.alibaba.com**). Ant developed a credit scoring and loyalty program operated by Credit Sesame (**http://creditsesame.com**). Sesame determines credit scores by analyzing "a thousand variables" across multiple data sets. The company takes into account a broad range of behaviors, both financial and social.

Extending its 2015 initiative, the Chinese government is developing a national reputation system, called the Social Credit System (SCS), which is designed to regulate both citizen and corporate behavior based on a point system. By the end of 2020, the government intends to standardize the assessment of citizens' and businesses' economic and social reputations, or their "social credit."

Some observers contend that the Chinese government does not see its role in the SCS as an assigner of scores, but rather as a record keeper and data sharer. Its job essentially is to consolidate government files into a central database of social credit records. It then provides state agencies, city governments, banks, industry associations, and the general public with data on individuals and companies so that they can make their own social credit evaluations.

Data Inputs into the SCS

Data inputs into the SCS are extensive. They include data from court documents, government and corporate records, and, in some cases, citizen observers. For financial data, the SCS resembles credit scoring systems employed in other countries, such as FICO (**www.fico.com**) scores in the United States. However, China's SCS not only analyzes financial information but also includes broader aspects of a person's life, such as their purchase history, political activities, and interactions with others. (Recall the data that Sesame Credit analyzes above.) In April 2019, the People's Bank of China announced the launch of a new version of the Personal Credit Report, which collects and analyzes more detailed and comprehensive personal information.

The Chinese government is also employing various technologies to gather data about its citizens. The government closely monitors Internet usage, and it censors the Internet. Further, the government assigns a unique ID to each person that is linked to each person's cell phone number and online activity.

Facial-recognition technology is increasingly widespread across China, with few restraints on how it can be used to track and monitor citizens. Under a 2019 law, Chinese citizens who buy new mobile phones or register new mobile phone services must have their faces scanned.

The Current State of the SCS

As of September 2019 the central government had not issued a social credit score to any Chinese citizen. Nevertheless, some citizens are receiving these scores because the central government is encouraging cities to use social credit data to independently develop their own scoring systems for local residents. As of May 2020 multiple social credit systems were in use in China: the judicial system, the local government system, the financial credit system, and the commercial credit-rating system.

The judicial system. In 2013, the Supreme People's Court (SPC) of China started a blacklist of people who the government alleged did not comply with court judgments; for example, by not paying fines or by failing to formally apologize to someone they are found to have wronged.

Local governments. In December 2017 the National Development and Reform Commission and the People's Bank of China selected "model cities" to pilot the SCS. The Chinese government found that these pilots were successful in their handling of blacklists and redlists, the primary mechanism of the SCS. People on the blacklist have exhibited negative behaviors, while people on the redlist have demonstrated positive ones. As of 2019, local governments in many Chinese provinces had initiated more than 40 Social Credit System experiments.

The financial system. The Chinese government has authorized some private Chinese companies to conduct pilots of the SCS. Citizens can opt out of these systems at any time upon request.

The commercial-credit rating system. For businesses, the SCS serves as a market regulation mechanism. The goal is to establish a self-enforcing regulatory system fueled by Big Data (see Chapter 5) in which businesses exercise "self-restraint." The basic idea is that with a functional credit system in place, companies will comply with government policies and regulations to avoid having their scores lowered by disgruntled employees, customers, or clients.

Punishments and Rewards

The Chinese government analyzes data to discourage negative behaviours and encourage positive ones. Negative behaviours include:

- Playing loud music
- Eating in public transportation
- Violating traffic rules such as jaywalking and running red lights
- Failing to correctly sort personal waste (improper recycling)
- Not returning library books on time
- Cheating in national, provincial, or municipal examinations
- Committing traffic violations
- Cheating on online video games
- Failing to pay bills promptly
- Not keeping dogs on a leash in public places
- Smoking in nonsmoking areas

Positive behaviors include donating blood, donating to charity, volunteering for community services, and paying taxes correctly and on time.

Examples of punishments. One municipal court released an app that displayed a "map of deadbeat debtors" within 500 meters of a user's location. The app also encouraged users to report debtors who they believed could repay their debts.

The central government appears to be sharing blacklists with technology platforms. This action prevents blacklisted citizens from booking flights or purchasing train tickets online. By July 2019, according to the National Development and Reform Commission of China, nearly 30 million air tickets as well as 6 million high-speed rail tickets had been denied to people on the blacklist.

Local governments are asking social media companies to help in public shaming initiatives. In one city, the social media app TikTok partnered with the local court to broadcast photos of blacklisted people between videos, like a digital mugshot. In another city, blacklisted people and entities are displayed on a map within the messaging app WeChat. Other cities display mugshots of blacklisted individuals on large LED screens on buildings, or they show the images before the movie in movie theaters.

Some cities have banned children of blacklisted citizens from attending private schools and even universities. In some locales, if you call a blacklisted person on the phone, you will hear a siren and a recorded message saying: "Warning, this person is on the blacklist. Be careful, and urge them to repay their debts." When a blacklisted person crosses certain intersections in Beijing, facial-recognition technology projects their face and ID number on massive electronic billboards.

Still other punishments include slow Internet connections, exclusion from high-prestige work, and exclusion from five-star hotels. In general, it takes two to five years to be removed from the blacklist. However, early removal is possible if the blacklisted person has demonstrated enough positive behaviors.

Examples of rewards. In contrast to blacklisted individuals, people with high social credit scores may receive rewards such as preferential treatment and less waiting time at hospitals and government agencies, discounts at hotels, greater likelihood of receiving employment offers, easier access to loans and lower interest rates on those loans, discounts for car- and bike-sharing services, discounts on utilities, fast-tracked visa applications, and free health checkups.

In addition, some cities reward individuals for helping authorities enforce restrictions of religious practices. Examples are forcing practitioners of Falun Gong (a religious movement) to renounce their beliefs and reporting on Uyghurs who publicly pray, fast during Ramadan, or perform other Islamic practices. Uyghurs are a minority ethnic group native to the Xinjiang Autonomous Region in northwest China.

Personal credit scores can also be used on social and couples' platforms. For example, China's biggest matchmaking service, Baihe (**http://baihe.com**), allows its users to publish their own social credit score. As expected, users with higher social credit scores are in higher demand than those with lower scores.

Companies with good social credit scores enjoy benefits such as good credit conditions, lower tax rates, and more investment opportunities. Companies with low social credit scores face unfavorable conditions for new loans, high tax rates, investment restrictions, and fewer chances to participate in publicly funded projects.

A Final Word

To say the least, the SCS is extremely controversial. Supporters of the SCS claim that the system helps to regulate social behavior, improve personal and corporate "trustworthiness," and promote traditional moral values. Opponents contend that it oversteps the rule of law and infringes on the legal rights of individuals and organizations, particularly the right to privacy as well as personal dignity. Further, opponents assert that the SCS may become a tool for comprehensive government surveillance and for suppression of dissent against the Chinese government.

Sources: Compiled from M. Hvistendahl, "How a Chinese AI Giant Made Chatting—and Surveillance—Easy," *Wired*, May 10, 2020; B. Betz, "What Is China's Social Credit System?" *Fox News*, May 4, 2020; K. Schaefer, "The Apps of China's Social Credit System," *ub.triviumchina.com*, October 14, 2019; L. Matsakis, "How the West Got China's Social Credit System Wrong," *Wired*, July 29, 2019; D. Carroll, "China Embraces Its Surveillance State. The U.S. Pretends It Doesn't Have One," *Quartz*, July 23, 2019; I. Cockerell, "Inside China's Massive Surveillance Operations," *Wired*, May 9, 2019; S. Liao, "China Banned Millions of People with Poor Social Credit from Transportation in 2018," *The Verge*, March 1, 2019; S. Sacks and L. Laskai, "China's Privacy Conundrum," *Slate*, February 7, 2019; "Beijing to Judge Every Resident Based on Behavior by End of 2020," *Bloomberg News*, November 21, 2018; A. Ma, "China Has Started Ranking Citizens with a Creepy 'Social Credit' System," *Business Insider*, October 29, 2018; C. Lowe, "The World's First Mass Surveillance System Is Now Online," *Legacy Research Group*, August 22, 2018.

Questions

1. Discuss the ethicality and the legality of China's Social Credit System.

2. The fundamental tenets of ethics include responsibility, accountability, and liability. Discuss each of these tenets as it applies to China's Social Credit System.

MIS Another example of how new devices can contribute to electronic surveillance is facial recognition technology (see Chapter 4). Just a few years ago, this software worked only in very controlled settings such as passport checkpoints. However, this technology can now match faces even in regular snapshots and online images. IT's About Business 3.3 provides an example of how advances in facial recognition technologies can negatively impact privacy.

Photo tagging is the process of assigning names to images of people. Facial recognition software then indexes facial features. Once an individual in a photo is tagged, the software searches for similar facial features in untagged photos. This process allows the user to quickly group photos in which the tagged person appears. Significantly, the individual is not aware of this process.

IT's About Business 3.3

MIS Clearview AI

Facial recognition technology has always been controversial because it contributes to a loss of privacy. Police departments have used facial recognition tools for roughly 20 years, but for the most part they could search only government-provided images such as mug shots and driver's license photos.

In recent years, however, facial recognition algorithms have become much more accurate. Until now, this technology has been used carefully, due primarily to privacy concerns. In fact, some technology companies capable of releasing these types of systems have not done so.

For example, Facebook built an internal facial recognition app that allowed employees to identify their colleagues and friends just by pointing their phone cameras at them. Facebook did not release the app publicly, and the company claims to have discontinued the app. Google also developed facial recognition technology and withheld it. In June 2020, IBM announced that it would no longer offer or develop facial recognition technology because the firm opposes the technology's potential use for "mass surveillance, racial profiling, and violations of basic human rights and freedom." That same month Amazon banned police from using its facial recognition product, called Rekognition (**http://aws.amazon.com/rekognition**), for one year.

Clearview AI (**http://clearview.ai**) has developed a new facial recognition app. Users can take a picture of a person, upload it, and see public photos of that person, along with links to where those photos appeared. The app uses a database of more than 3 billion images that Clearview claims to have scraped from Facebook, YouTube, Venmo, Instagram, Twitter, employment websites, news websites, educational websites, and millions of other sites. The practice of extracting images from a website is known as *image scraping*.

Clearview uses a neural network (see Chapter 14) to convert all images into mathematical formulas based on many measures of facial geometry. A *neural network* is a group of virtual neurons placed in layers, which work in parallel to simulate the way the human brain works, although in a greatly simplified form. For example, one measure is how far apart a person's eyes are, and another is the distance from a person's forehead to his or her chin. Clearview clusters all photos with similar formulas into "neighborhoods." When a user uploads a photo of a face into Clearview's system, the company converts the face into a formula and then displays all of the scraped photos stored in that formula's neighborhood, along with the links to the sites from which those images came.

Researchers have found that Clearview has provided its facial-recognition software to more than 2,200 federal agencies—including the FBI, Immigration and Customs Enforcement (ICE), the Department of Justice, and the Department of Homeland Security (DHS)—police departments, private companies (e.g., Macy's, Best Buy, and Kohl's), and other organizations (e.g., the National Basketball Association). Evidence shows that the company has also provided its technology to users in Saudi Arabia and the United Arab Emirates, countries with questionable records on civil liberties and human rights. Significantly, hackers stole Clearview AI's entire client list in February 2020.

Researchers have also discovered that the company has allowed wealthy individuals, such as Clearview investors and friends, to use its app. For example, one billionaire allegedly used the app to identify a man who was dating his daughter. When asked by reporters, Clearview declined to provide a list of all of the organizations, governments, and individuals using its app.

The Good News

Clearview claims that organizations have used its app to help solve shoplifting, identity theft, credit card fraud, murder, and child sexual exploitation cases. For instance, one police department used Clearview to solve the case of one man shooting another. A bystander recorded the crime on a phone, so the police had an image of the gunman's face to upload to Clearview's app. They immediately got a match and arrested the man. He had appeared in a video that someone had posted on social media, and his name was included in a caption on the video. A spokesman for the police noted that the suspect did not have a driver's license and had not been arrested as an adult, so his image was not in any government databases. The spokesman claimed that the suspect probably would not have been identified without the Clearview app's ability to search social media for his face.

Other police departments used Clearview to identify:

- A person accused of sexually abusing a child when the person's face appeared in the mirror of another person's gym photo
- The person behind a series of mailbox thefts in Atlanta, Georgia
- An unidentified man found dead on a city sidewalk
- Suspects in multiple identity fraud cases at several banks

A Florida detective had previously relied on a state-provided facial recognition tool, called FACES, which analyzes more than 30 million Florida mug shots and Department of Motor Vehicle photos. Clearview's database of images is much larger than FACES, and, unlike FACES, Clearview's algorithm does not require photos of people looking straight at the camera. With Clearview, users can upload imperfect photos, including people wearing a hat or glasses, as well as profiles or partial images. The detective uploaded photos to Clearview from cold cases and identified more than 30 suspects, none of whom were identified from FACES.

The Bad News

Performance. The Clearview app does not always work. Most of the photos in Clearview's database are taken at eye level. In contrast, most of the images that the police upload are taken by surveillance cameras mounted on ceilings or high on walls. Clearview contends that high angles are "wrong for good face recognition." The app also has a tendency to delivery false matches for women and people of color.

Accuracy. Possibly as a result of these performance problems, Clearview has not consistently reported the accuracy of its app. In one instance, the firm maintained that its app finds matches up to 75 percent of the time. In another report, it claimed to have "accuracy finding a match out of 1 million faces" almost 99 percent of the time. Specifically, the company is not clear how often the app provides false positives, which can result in arresting the wrong person.

Further, Clearview's app has not been tested by an independent party such as the National Institute of Standards and Technology (**www.nist.gov**), a federal agency that conducts a vendor testing program that rates the performance of facial recognition algorithms. Clearview contends that its app has been reviewed and certified by an "independent panel" of experts. However, the company has not identified those experts or indicated when the review and certification occurred.

Legal Issues. Representatives of numerous organizations, particularly social media sites, have asserted that their policies prohibit image scraping. In fact, Twitter explicitly bans the use of its data for facial recognition. Because social media sites prohibit people from scraping users' images, Clearview is violating the sites' terms of service.

Major Internet platforms, including LinkedIn, Twitter, Facebook, Venmo, Google, and YouTube, have sent cease-and-desist letters to Clearview. The company has acknowledged that it received the letters, and it stated that its "attorneys are responding appropriately." In an interview in February 2020, the company's CEO emphasized that there is a First Amendment right to public information.

In May 2020 the American Civil Liberties Union (ACLU; **www.aclu.org**) sued Clearview, asserting that the company's app and database of images violated the privacy of Illinois residents. The ACLU stated it was suing to stop the firm's "unlawful surreptitious capture and storage of millions of Illinoisans' sensitive biometric identifiers." The lawsuit alleges that Clearview violated the state's Biometric Information Privacy Act, a 2008 law that prevents companies from collecting or storing fingerprints or scans of citizens' faces without their consent. Significantly, the ACLU is not seeking monetary damages. Instead, it wants Clearview to delete the images it has already captured and to stop capturing them in the future. Clearview is facing similar lawsuits in New York, California, Virginia, and Vermont.

In response, Clearview hired former U.S. solicitor general Paul Clement to address concerns about the app's legality. In an August 2019 memo, Clement asserted that law enforcement agencies "do not violate the federal Constitution or relevant existing state biometric and privacy laws when using Clearview for its intended purpose." He further wrote that the authorities do not have to inform defendants that they were identified with Clearview as long as the app is not the sole basis for obtaining an arrest warrant.

What Should Users Do? If Clearview does have your photos, is there anything you can do about that? According to Clearview's privacy policy, users have certain rights. However, the policy states that the "right to erasure"—deleting your information from their platform—is available only under certain conditions. Clearview's CEO, Hoan Ton-That, acknowledged that the company had received erasure requests—although he would not say how many—and was "processing removal requests for persons in jurisdictions that impose that legal requirement." Ironically, to make such requests, users must confirm their identity by sending in a photo of themselves on a government ID.

Ton-That further asserted that his company uses only publicly available images. If you change your privacy setting in Facebook so that search engines cannot link to your profile, then your Facebook photos will not be included in their database. However, if your profile has already been scraped, then it is too late. Clearview keeps all of the images that it has scraped even if they are deleted later or taken down. He did say that his company was working on a tool that would let people request that images be removed if these images had been taken down from the website of origin.

The Next Application? The *New York Times* analyzed the computer code underlying the Clearview app. The code can integrate the app with augmented reality (AR) glasses. Therefore, users would potentially be able to identify every person they saw. The app could identify activists at a protest rally or a stranger on a bus, revealing not just their names but where they live, what they do, and whom they know. Clearview asserts that it has no plans to release this AR functionality.

Final Thoughts

The State of New Jersey and some large cities, including San Francisco, Oakland, and Berkeley in California, as well as Somerville and Boston in Massachusetts, have prohibited police from using facial recognition technology. However, legal scholars believe that a federal mandate is necessary.

Woodrow Hartzog, a professor of law and computer science at Northeastern University, views Clearview as the latest proof that facial recognition should be banned in the United States at the federal level. He noted that industry efforts not to release such risky technology are no longer effective because the technology is so lucrative. He contends that any benefits from the technology will be outweighed by accompanying, damaging impacts on personal privacy.

It is more than likely that many more companies will develop facial recognition apps. A privacy professor at Stanford Law School, Al Gidari, noted, "There is no monopoly on math." He continued, "Absent a very strong federal privacy law, we're all screwed."

Sources: Compiled from C. Haskins and R. Mac, "Boston Just Banned Its Government from Using Facial Recognition Technology," *BuzzFeed*, June 24, 2020; N. Statt, "Amazon Bans Police from Using Its Facial Recognition Technology for the Next Year," *The Verge*, June 10, 2020; I. Togoh, "IBM Will No Longer Offer or Develop Facial Recognition Software in Pursuit of Racial Justice Reform," *Forbes*, June 9, 2020; S. Ovide, "A Case for Banning Facial Recognition," *The New York Times*, June 9, 2020; R. Mac and C. Haskins, "The ACLU Is Suing Clearview AI to Stop 'Privacy-Destroying Face Surveillance'," *BuzzFeed*, May 28, 2020; R. Heilweil, "The World's Scariest Facial Recognition Company, Explained," *Vox*, May 8, 2020; N. Statt, "Clearview AI to Stop Selling Controversial Facial Recognition App to Private Companies," *The Verge*, May 7, 2020; C. Vazquez and A. Torres, "Detectives Use Facial Recognition Technology to Find Rapper in Wynwood Shooting," *WPLG Local 10 News*, March 6, 2020; K. Hill, "Before Clearview Became a Police Tool, It Was a Secret Plaything of the Rich," *The New York Times*, March 5, 2020; R. Mac, C. Haskins, and L. McDonald, "Clearview's Facial Recognition App Has Been Used by the Justice Department, ICE, Macy's, Walmart, and the NBA," *BuzzFeed*, February 27, 2020; A. Ng, "Clearview AI's Entire Client List Stolen in Data Breach," *CNET*, February 26, 2020; B. Gilbert, "Amazon Sells Facial Recognition Software to Police All Over the U.S., but Has No Idea How Many Departments Are Using It," *Business Insider*, February 21, 2020; K. Hill and G. Dance, "Clearview's Facial Recognition App Is Identifying Child Victims of Abuse," *The New York Times*, February 10, 2020; J. Snow, "Hey Clearview, Your Misleading PR Campaign Doesn't Make Your Face Surveillance Product Any Less Dystopian," *ACLU.org*, February 10, 2020; D. O'Sullivan, "This Man Says He's Stockpiling Billions of Our Photos," *CNN Business*, February 10, 2020; R. Heilweil, "Why We Don't Know as Much as We Should about Police Surveillance Technology," *Vox*, February 5, 2020; T. Schuba, "CPD Using Controversial Facial Recognition Program that Scans Billions of Photos from Facebook, Other Sites," *Chicago Sun Times*, January 29, 2020; K. Hill, "New Jersey Bars Police from Using Clearview Facial Recognition App," *The New York Times*, January 24, 2020; R. Mac, C. Haskins, and L. McDonald, "Clearview AI Says Its Facial Recognition Software Identified a Terrorism Suspect. The Cops Say That's Not True," *BuzzFeed*, January 23, 2020; K. Hill, "The Secretive Company that Might End Privacy as We Know It," *The New York Times*, January 18, 2020; M. Cruz and K. Brieskom, "Florida Law Enforcement Agencies Use Facial Recognition to Identify Alleged Thief," *WFTV*, December 27, 2019; S. Ghaffary, "How to Avoid a Dystopian Future of Facial Recognition in Law Enforcement," *Vox*, December 10, 2019; Q. Wong, "Facebook Built a Facial Recognition App for Employees," *CNET*, November 22, 2019; S. Ghaffary, "San Francisco's Facial Recognition Technology Ban, Explained," *Vox*, May 14, 2019; B. Bosker, "Facial Recognition: The One Technology Google Is Holding Back," *Huffington Post*, December 6, 2017; **https://clearview.ai**, accessed June 9, 2020.

Questions

1. Discuss the ethicality and the legality of Clearview AI's facial recognition software.

2. The fundamental tenets of ethics include responsibility, accountability, and liability. Discuss each of these tenets as it applies to Clearview's facial recognition software.

3. In your opinion, do the benefits of facial recognition systems outweigh the dangers to your privacy? Support your answer.

Why is tagging important? The reason is that once you are tagged in a photo, that photo can be used to search for matches across the entire Internet or in private databases, including databases fed by surveillance cameras. How could this type of surveillance affect you? As one example, a car dealer can take a picture of you when you step onto the car lot. He or she could then quickly profile you (find out information about where you live, your employment, etc.) on the Web to achieve a competitive edge in making a sale. Even worse, a stranger in a restaurant could photograph you with a smartphone and then go online to profile you for reasons of his or her own. One privacy attorney has asserted that losing your right to anonymity would have a chilling effect on where you go, whom you meet, and how you live your life.

Drones are presenting additional surveillance concerns. Low-cost drones with high-performance cameras can be used for persistent aerial surveillance. Since the beginning of modern aviation, landowners have had rights to the airspace above their property up to 500 feet. However, to regulate small, low-flying drones, the Federal Aviation Administration (FAA; **www.faa.gov**) has assumed authority all the way down to the ground.

Consider this example. You see a drone flying about 100 feet above your backyard and you suspect that it is spying on you. Who is flying it? Whom are you going to sue? And if you do sue, how are you going to prove that the drone was spying on you?

The FAA is responsible for addressing drone-related privacy concerns. The Federal Trade Commission (FTC; **www.ftc.gov**), the U.S. government's primary consumer privacy agency, is also exploring the drone privacy issue.

HRM   The scenarios we just considered deal primarily with your personal life. However, electronic surveillance has become a reality in the workplace as well. In general, employees have very limited legal protection against surveillance by employers. The law supports the right of employers to read their employees' e-mail and other electronic documents and to monitor their employees' Internet use. Today, more than three-fourths of organizations routinely monitor their employees' Internet usage. Two-thirds of them also use software to block connections to inappropriate websites, a practice called *URL filtering*. Furthermore, organizations are installing monitoring and filtering software to enhance security by blocking malicious software and to increase productivity by discouraging employees from wasting time.

MIS   In one organization, the chief information officer (CIO) monitored roughly 13,000 employees for three months to determine the type of traffic they engaged in on the network. He then forwarded the data to the chief executive officer (CEO) and the heads of the human resources and legal departments. These executives were shocked at the questionable websites the employees were visiting, as well as the amount of time they were spending on those sites. The executives quickly decided to implement a URL filtering product.

In general, surveillance is a concern for private individuals regardless of whether it is conducted by corporations, government bodies, or criminals. As a nation, the United States is still struggling to define the appropriate balance between personal privacy and electronic surveillance, especially in situations that involve threats to national security.

Personal Information in Databases

Modern institutions store information about individuals in many databases. Perhaps the most visible locations of such records are credit-reporting agencies. Other institutions that store personal information include banks and financial institutions; cable TV, telephone, and utility companies; employers; mortgage companies; hospitals; schools and universities; retail establishments; government agencies (Internal Revenue Service, your state, your municipality); and many others.

There are several concerns about the information you provide to these record keepers. Some of the major concerns are as follows:

- Do you know where the records are?
- Are the records accurate?
- Can you change inaccurate data?
- How long will it take to make a change?
- Under what circumstances will the personal data be released?

- How are the data used?
- To whom are the data given or sold?
- How secure are the data against access by unauthorized people?

Information on Internet Bulletin Boards, Newsgroups, and Social Networking Sites

Every day we see more and more *electronic bulletin boards, newsgroups,* and *electronic discussions* such as chat rooms and *social networking sites* (discussed in Chapter 9). These sites appear on the Internet, within corporate intranets, and on blogs. A *blog,* short for "weblog," is an informal, personal journal that is frequently updated and is intended for general public reading. How does society keep owners of bulletin boards from disseminating information that may be offensive to readers or simply untrue? This is a difficult problem because it involves the conflict between freedom of speech on the one hand and privacy on the other. This conflict is a fundamental and continuing ethical issue in the United States and throughout the world.

There is no better illustration of the conflict between free speech and privacy than the Internet. Many websites contain anonymous, derogatory information on individuals, who typically have little recourse in the matter. The vast majority of U.S. firms use the Internet in examining job applications, including searching on Google and on social networking sites. Consequently, derogatory information contained on the Internet can harm a person's chances of being hired.

Privacy Codes and Policies

Privacy policies (or **privacy codes**) are an organization's guidelines for protecting the privacy of its customers, clients, and employees. In many corporations, senior management has begun to understand that when they collect vast amounts of personal information, they must protect it. Many organizations also give their customers some voice in how their information is used by providing them with opt-out choices. The **opt-out model** of informed consent permits the company to collect personal information until the customer specifically requests that the data not be collected. Privacy advocates prefer the **opt-in model** of informed consent, which prohibits an organization from collecting any personal information unless the customer specifically authorizes it.

One privacy tool available to consumers is the *Platform for Privacy Preferences* (P3P), a protocol that automatically communicates privacy policies between an electronic commerce website and visitors to that site. P3P enables visitors to determine the types of personal data that can be extracted by the sites they visit. It also allows visitors to compare a site's privacy policy to the visitors' preferences or to other standards, such as the Federal Trade Commission's (FTC) Fair Information Practices Standard or the European Directive on Data Protection.

Table 3.2 provides a sampling of privacy policy guidelines. The last section, "Data Confidentiality," refers to security, which we consider in Chapter 4. All of the good privacy intentions in the world are useless unless they are supported and enforced by effective security measures.

Despite privacy codes and policies, and despite opt-out and opt-in models, guarding whatever is left of your privacy is becoming increasingly difficult. This problem is illustrated in IT's About Business 3.1, 3.2, and 3.3 as well as this chapter's open and closing cases.

International Aspects of Privacy

As the number of online users has increased globally, governments throughout the world have enacted a large number of inconsistent privacy and security laws. This highly complex global legal framework is creating regulatory problems for companies. Approximately 50 countries have some form of data protection laws. Many of these laws conflict with those of other countries, or they require specific security measures. Other countries have no privacy laws at all.

The absence of consistent or uniform standards for privacy and security obstructs the flow of information among countries (*transborder data flows*). The European Union (EU), for one,

TABLE 3.2   Privacy Policy Guidelines: A Sampler

Data Collection

- Data should be collected on individuals only for the purpose of accomplishing a legitimate business objective.
- Data should be adequate, relevant, and not excessive in relation to the business objective.
- Individuals must give their consent before data pertaining to them can be gathered. Such consent may be implied from the individual's actions (e.g., applications for credit, insurance, or employment).

Data Accuracy

- Sensitive data gathered on individuals should be verified before they are entered into the database.
- Data should be kept current, where and when necessary.
- The file should be made available so that the individual can ensure that the data are correct.
- In any disagreement about the accuracy of the data, the individual's version should be noted and included with any disclosure of the file.

Data Confidentiality

- Computer security procedures should be implemented to ensure against unauthorized disclosure of data. These procedures should include physical, technical, and administrative security measures.
- Third parties should not be given access to data without the individual's knowledge or permission, except as required by law.
- Disclosures of data, other than the most routine, should be noted and maintained for as long as the data are maintained.
- Data should not be disclosed for reasons incompatible with the business objective for which they are collected.

has taken steps to not only overcome this problem but also to protect the rights of individuals. The EU data protection laws are stricter than the U.S. laws and therefore could create problems for the U.S.-based multinational corporations, which could face lawsuits for privacy violations.

On May 25, 2018, the *General Data Protection Regulation* (GDPR), the world's strongest data protection laws, went into effect in the European Union. The GDPR replaces the 1995 data protection directive.

The GDPR modernizes laws that protect the personal information of individuals because previous data protection laws across Europe could not keep pace with rapid technological changes. The GDPR changes how businesses and public sector organizations manage the information of their customers. The regulation also increases the rights of individuals and gives them more control over their own information.

The GDPR covers both personal data and sensitive personal data. *Personal data* includes information that can be used to identify a person, such as a name, address, Internet Protocol (IP) address, and many other pieces of information. *Sensitive personal data* encompasses genetic data, racial information, information about religious and political views, sexual orientation, and trade union membership, among others.

The GDPR applies to *data controllers*, which are the organizations that have relationships with data subjects, and *data processors*, which are organizations that work for data controllers and process personal data on the controllers' behalf. The GDPR defines a *natural person* as a living human being and a *data subject* as a human being whose data an organization has or processes.

The GDPR states that data controllers and data processors should keep minimal data on each data subject, secure it properly, ensure that it is accurate, and retain the data for only as long as it is needed. The GDPR also covers individuals' rights, which include:

- The right to know what organizations are doing with their data
- The right to ask, at any time, for copies of all the data that organizations have about them
- The right to know an organization's justification why it has their data and how long it is planning to keep it

- The right to have their data corrected, if needed
- The right to have their data deleted. This provision is called the "right to be forgotten"

The GDPR provides the ability for regulators to fine businesses that do not comply with the regulation. Specifically, regulators can fine an organization:

- If it does not correctly process an individual's data
- If it experiences a security breach
- If it is required to have, but does not have, a data protection officer

The transfer of data into and out of a nation without the knowledge of either the authorities or the individuals involved raises a number of privacy issues. Whose laws have jurisdiction when records are stored in a different country for reprocessing or retransmission purposes? For example, if data are transmitted by a Polish company through a U.S. satellite to a British corporation, which country's privacy laws control the data, and at what points in the transmission? Questions like these will become more complicated and frequent as time goes on. Governments must make an effort to develop laws and standards to cope with rapidly changing information technologies to solve some of these privacy issues.

The United States and the European Union share the goal of protecting their citizens' privacy, but the United States takes a different approach. To bridge the different privacy approaches, the U.S. Department of Commerce, in consultation with the European Union, developed a "safe harbor" framework to regulate the way that the U.S. companies export and handle the personal data (e.g., names and addresses) of European citizens. In 2016, the European Commission and the U.S. Department of Commerce established the EU-US Privacy Shield, a new legal framework for transatlantic data flows, put in place to replace Safe Harbor.

Before you go on…

1. Describe the issue of privacy as it is affected by IT.
2. Discuss how privacy issues can impact transborder data flows.

What's in IT for me?

ACCT For the Accounting Major

Public companies, their accountants, and their auditors have significant ethical responsibilities. Accountants now are being held professionally and personally responsible for increasing the transparency of transactions and assuring compliance with Generally Accepted Accounting Principles (GAAP). In fact, regulatory agencies such as the Securities and Exchange Commission (SEC) and the Public Company Accounting Oversight Board (PCAOB) require accounting departments to adhere to strict ethical principles.

FIN For the Finance Major

As a result of global regulatory requirements and the passage of Sarbanes–Oxley, financial managers must follow strict ethical guidelines. They are responsible for full, fair, accurate, timely, and understandable disclosure in all financial reports and documents that their companies submit to the SEC and in all other public financial reports. Furthermore, financial managers are responsible for compliance with all applicable governmental laws, rules, and regulations.

MKT For the Marketing Major

Marketing professionals have new opportunities to collect data on their customers; for example, through business-to-consumer electronic commerce (discussed in Chapter 7). Business ethics clearly mandate that these data should be used only within the company and should not be sold to anyone else. Marketers do not want to be sued for invasion of privacy over data collected for their marketing database.

Customers expect their data to be properly secured. However, profit-motivated criminals want that data. Therefore, marketing managers must analyze the risks of their operations. Failure to protect corporate and customer data will cause significant public relations problems and outrage customers. Customer relationship management (discussed in Chapter 11) operations and tracking customers' online buying habits can expose unencrypted data to misuse or result in privacy violations.

POM **For the Production/Operations Management Major**

POM professionals decide whether to outsource (or offshore) manufacturing operations. In some cases, these operations are sent overseas to countries that do not have strict labor laws. This situation raises serious ethical questions. For example: Is it ethical to hire employees in countries with poor working conditions in order to reduce labor costs?

HRM **For the Human Resource Management Major**

Ethics is critically important to HR managers. HR policies define the appropriate use of information technologies in the workplace.

Questions such as the following can arise: Can employees use the Internet, e-mail, or chat systems for personal purposes while at work? Is it ethical to monitor employees? If so, then how, how much, and how often? HR managers must formulate and enforce such policies while at the same time maintaining trusting relationships between employees and management.

MIS **For the MIS Major**

Ethics might be more important for MIS personnel than for anyone else in the organization, because these individuals have control of the organization's information assets. They also have control over a huge amount of employees' personal information. As a result, the MIS function must be held to the highest ethical standards.

Summary

3.1 Describe ethics, its three fundamental tenets, and the four categories of ethical issues related to information technology.

Ethics refers to the principles of right and wrong that individuals use to make choices that guide their behavior.

Fundamental tenets of ethics include responsibility, accountability, and liability. Responsibility means that you accept the consequences of your decisions and actions. Accountability refers to determining who is responsible for actions that were taken. Liability is a legal concept that gives individuals the right to recover the damages done to them by other individuals, organizations, or systems.

The major ethical issues related to IT are privacy, accuracy, property (including intellectual property), and access to information. Privacy may be violated when data are held in databases or transmitted over networks. Privacy policies that address issues of data collection, data accuracy, and data confidentiality can help organizations avoid legal problems.

3.2 Discuss at least one potential threat to the privacy of the data stored in each of three places that store personal data.

Privacy is the right to be left alone and to be free of unreasonable personal intrusions. Threats to privacy include advances in information technologies, electronic surveillance, personal information in databases, Internet bulletin boards, newsgroups, and social networking sites. The privacy threat in Internet bulletin boards, newsgroups, and social networking sites is that you might post too much personal information that many unknown people can see.

Chapter Glossary

accountability   A tenet of ethics that refers to determining who is responsible for actions that were taken.

code of ethics   A collection of principles intended to guide decision making by members of an organization.

digital dossier   An electronic description of an individual and his or her habits.

electronic surveillance   Tracking people's activities with the aid of computers.

ethics   The principles of right and wrong that individuals use to make choices to guide their behaviors.

information privacy   The right to determine when, and to what extent, personal information can be gathered by or communicated to others.

liability   A legal concept that gives individuals the right to recover the damages done to them by other individuals, organizations, or systems.

opt-in model   A model of informed consent in which a business is prohibited from collecting any personal information unless the customer specifically authorizes it.

opt-out model   A model of informed consent that permits a company to collect personal information until the customer specifically requests that the data not be collected.

privacy   The right to be left alone and to be free of unreasonable personal intrusions.

privacy codes   See **privacy policies.**

privacy policies (or privacy codes)   An organization's guidelines for protecting the privacy of customers, clients, and employees.

profiling   The process of forming a digital dossier.

responsibility   A tenet of ethics in which you accept the consequences of your decisions and actions.

Discussion Questions

1. In 2008, the Massachusetts Bay Transportation Authority (MBTA) obtained a temporary restraining order barring three Massachusetts Institute of Technology (MIT) students from publicly displaying what they claimed to be a way to get "free subway rides for life." Specifically, the 10-day injunction prohibited the students from revealing vulnerabilities of the MBTA's fare card. The students were scheduled to present their findings in Las Vegas at the DEFCON computer hacking conference. Were the students' actions legal? Were their actions ethical? Discuss your answer from the students' perspective and then from the perspective of the MBTA.

2. Frank Abagnale, the criminal played by Leonardo DiCaprio in the motion picture *Catch Me If You Can*, ended up in prison. After he left prison, however, he worked as a consultant to many companies on matters of fraud.

   a. Why do these companies hire the perpetrators (if caught) as consultants? Is this a good idea?

   b. You are the CEO of a company. Discuss the ethical implications of hiring Frank Abagnale as a consultant.

3. Access various search engines to find information relating to the use of drones (unmanned aerial vehicles (UAVs)) for electronic surveillance purposes in the United States.

   a. Take the position favoring the use of drones for electronic surveillance.

   b. Take the position against the use of drones for electronic surveillance.

4. Research the Volkswagen "Diesel Dupe." The fundamental tenets of ethics include responsibility, accountability, and liability. Discuss each of these tenets as it applies to the Volkswagen scandal.

5. Research the Facebook–Cambridge Analytica scandal.

   a. Discuss the legality and the ethicality of Facebook in the Facebook–Cambridge Analytica incident.

   b. Discuss the legality and the ethicality of Cambridge Analytica in the Facebook–Cambridge Analytica incident.

   c. Describe how each of the fundamental tenets of ethics (responsibility, accountability, and liability) applies to Facebook and then to Cambridge Analytica in this incident.

5. Research Quizlet (**www.quizlet.com**).

   a. Discuss the ethicality of students' use of Quizlet (and similar apps) for exams.

   b. If students discover that the actual exam questions were on Quizlet, discuss the ethicality of them not telling the professor.

Problem-Solving Activities

1. An information security manager routinely monitored Web surfing among her company's employees. She discovered that many employees were visiting the "sinful six" websites. (*Note*: The "sinful six" are websites with material related to pornography, gambling, hate, illegal activities, tastelessness, and violence.) She then prepared a list of the employees and their surfing histories and gave the list to management. Some managers punished their employees. Some employees, in turn, objected to the monitoring, claiming that they should have a right to privacy.

   a. Is monitoring of Web surfing by managers ethical? (It is legal.) Support your answer.

   b. Is employee Web surfing on the "sinful six" ethical? Support your answer.

   c. Is the security manager's submission of the list of abusers to management ethical? Why or why not?

   d. Is punishing the abusers ethical? Why or why not? If yes, then what types of punishment are acceptable?

   e. What should the company do in this situation? (*Note*: There are a variety of possibilities here.)

2. Access the Computer Ethics Institute's website at **www.cpsr.org/issues/ethics/cei**. The site offers the "Ten Commandments of Computer Ethics." Study these rules and decide whether any others should be added.

3. Access the Association for Computing Machinery's code of ethics for its members (**www.acm.org/code-of-ethics**). Discuss the major points of this code. Is this code complete? Why or why not? Support your answer.

4. Access **https://odimpact.org/case-united-states-eightmaps.html**. Is the use of data on this website illegal? Unethical? Support your answer.

5. The Electronic Frontier Foundation (**www.eff.org**) has a mission of protecting rights and promoting freedom in the "electronic frontier." Review the organization's suggestions about how to protect your online privacy, and summarize what you can do to protect yourself.

6. Access your university's guidelines for ethical computer and Internet use. Are there limitations as to the types of websites that you can visit and the types of material you can view? Are you allowed to change the programs on the lab computers? Are you allowed to download software from the lab computers for your personal use? Are there rules governing the personal use of computers and e-mail?

7. Access **www.albion.com/netiquette/corerules.html**. What do you think of this code of ethics? Should it be expanded? Is it too general?

8. Access **www.cookiecentral.com** and **www.epubliceye.com**. Do these sites provide information that helps you protect your privacy? If so, then explain how.

9. Do you believe that a university should be allowed to monitor e-mail sent and received on university computers? Why or why not? Support your answer.

Closing Case

MIS **MKT** **FIN**   **Restaurant Owners versus Grubhub**

Restaurant owners. Many restaurant owners sign up for Grubhub's (www.grubhub.com) online delivery platform because they value its services. Grubhub handles delivery orders and displays restaurant menus to new customers in exchange for a commission on each order placed through the platform. This service enables restaurants to reach customers who want to order online without having to build and manage their own websites. Further, the platform's marketing services can replace old-fashioned advertising strategies such as hand-delivering take-out menus.

Grubhub charges anywhere from a 3 to 15 percent commission fee depending on whether a restaurant makes their own deliveries. However, if a customer orders from a restaurant through the Grubhub app or through a non-associated website (discussed below), Grubhub can bill for an additional 20 percent commission on a single order.

Over time, however, restaurant owners began to notice that their profits were decreasing even though their sales were stable. They also discovered that Grubhub's commission fees had been increasing. According to the owners, Grubhub's response was to suggest that if the restaurants paid higher fees for marketing promotions, then their search rankings would rise. If they did not, then their restaurants could fall lower on Grubhub's web page, and they could lose sales.

In addition to higher fees, restaurant owners had three problems with the Grubhub platform: (1) Grubhub's buying Web domain names of existing restaurants, (2) phone fees, and (3) non-partnered restaurants. We examine each of these issues below.

Buying web domain names. Restaurant owners began to develop their own websites so that they could offer online orders and use a local delivery service that offered a flat monthly rate and no commission fee. However, a serious problem surfaced. Grubhub already owned the web domains that matched many restaurants' names. In fact, researchers found that as of May 2019 Grubhub had registered 34,000 websites.

Many owners contended that they had never given Grubhub permission to register their restaurants' names. In fact, the owners believe that Grubhub purchased their restaurants' Web domains to prevent the restaurants from building their own websites, a process called cybersquatting. *Cybersquatting* is the act of registering, trafficking in, or using a domain name in bad faith. The domain names that Grubhub purchased resemble the landing pages of the actual restaurants, complete with menus, online ordering forms, and phone numbers, despite the fact that these domains are not actually associated with the restaurants themselves. These domains are known as *non-associated websites*. Although these websites look like the real restaurant websites, they link only to Grubhub.

Phone fees. The Grubhub app and the non-associated websites also displayed phone numbers that Grubhub controlled to ensure it was receiving its commission. The process worked like this: Grubhub would set up and promote a unique phone number for restaurants listed on their platform. Allegedly, when a customer called a restaurant using that number and the phone call lasted longer than 45 seconds, Grubhub would assume that the customer had placed an order. The platform would then take credit for the "order" and charge the restaurant $5 to $9 per call, even if an order had not actually been placed. The problem was that customers often call restaurants to make reservations, to ask about the status of an order, or for other reasons

besides actually ordering food. Not surprisingly, Grubhub's system results in restaurants being charged with unnecessary additional fees. Restaurant owners sued Grubhub over phone orders, alleging that the company was charging fees for bogus phone calls that did not directly result in an order.

Non-partnered restaurants. Industry analysts noted that Grubhub had listings on its platform for restaurants that it did not partner with. Grubhub had been allowing customers to order food with its app from restaurants that had not signed up to be on Grubhub or its subsidiaries' platforms. To make matters worse, Grubhub announced that if a restaurant did not want to appear on its platform, then it would need to directly ask Grubhub to be removed.

A large number of restaurant owners complained, resulting in government agencies investigating Grubhub's actions for potential anticompetitive behaviour. In addition, U.S. senator Chuck Schumer called on Grubhub to pay restaurants back for bogus phone fees, and he asked the company to cooperate with the U.S. Small Business Administration's probe into the platform's business practices.

Grubhub. In response to restaurant owners' complaints and various investigations, Grubhub stated: "Grubhub has never cybersquatted. As a service to our restaurants, we have created microsites for them as another source of orders and to increase their online brand presence. Additionally, we have registered domains on their behalf, consistent with our restaurant contracts. We no longer provide that service, and it has always been our practice to transfer the domain to the restaurant as soon as they request it."

Grubhub CEO Matt Maloney asserted that restaurants using its food delivery platform had explicitly agreed to Web domain purchases and the creation of websites advertising their businesses. He stated further that Grubhub had a "very clear provision in every one of our restaurant contracts saying that we would provide this service to bring them more orders."

Maloney also maintained that Grubhub had (1) discontinued the practice of automatically creating websites for restaurants in 2018, (2) charged restaurants substantially less for orders received via those websites than for orders placed directly through the Grubhub app, and (3) turned ownership of the websites over to the restaurants upon their request.

Some reporters who were covering this controversy stated that the contract language between Grubhub and restaurants appeared to support some of Maloney's assertions. For example, the second item in the terms of service signed by restaurant owners states that Grubhub "may create, maintain and operate a microsite ('MS') and obtain the URL for such MS on restaurant's behalf."

In response to its critics, in early 2020 Grubhub announced a new plan. First, the platform would extend the time period in which restaurants can review all phone orders from 60 to 120 days. Second, the platform launched a new website to make it easier for restaurants to request direct control of any URLs registered as part of their contract with Grubhub. Third, the platform began to facilitate round-table events to create more direct dialogue with its restaurant partners.

And the bottom line? In the food delivery industry, DoorDash (www.doordash.com) leads with 35 percent of consumer spending, followed by Uber Eats with 28.8 percent, then Grubhub at 21.7 percent. Despite the controversy, Grubhub did report an increase in active diners, growing 28 percent to 22.6 million in 2019 compared to 17.7 million in 2018. Furthermore, Grubhub reported a total revenue of $1.3 billion in 2019. In June 2020 Just Eat Takeaway (**www.justeattakea-way.com**) purchased Grubhub for $7.3 billion.

Sources: Compiled from L. Chapman and N. Drozdiak, "Grubhub to Be Acquired for $7.3 Billion as Food Delivery Wars Heat Up," *Fortune*, June 10, 2020; J. Littman, "Grubhub Adds 150K Non-Partnered Restaurants as Controversy Grows," *Restaurant Dive*, February 7, 2020; N. Garun, "Grubhub's New Growth Hack Is Listing Restaurants that Didn't Agree to Be Listed," *The Verge*, January 30, 2020; J. Settembre, "DoorDash, Grubhub Skewered by Small Restaurants for Posting Menus," *FOX Business*, January 21, 2020; A. Kelso, "Grubhub Threatened with Legislative Action if It Doesn't Fix Phone Order Issues," *Restaurant Dive*, November 14, 2019; A. Rigie, "This Is How Grubhub Is Hurting Your Favorite Restaurants and Why You Should Care," *Forbes*, August 21, 2019; A. Kelso, "Grubhub Updates Call Fee, Web Domain Policies after Backlash," *Restaurant Dive*, August 2, 2019; J. Cutchin, "Facing Fury over 'Fake Websites,' Grubhub Says Restaurants Have It Wrong," *Los Angeles Times*, July 2, 2019; J. Zhang, "Grubhub Says It Didn't Create Fake Websites without Restaurants' Permission," *Eater.com*, July 2, 2019; C. Brown, "Grubhub Is Buying Up Thousands of Restaurant Web Addresses," *New Food Economy*, June 28, 2019; N. Garun, "Grubhub Is Using Thousands of Fake Websites to Upcharge Commission Fees from Real Businesses," *The Verge*, June 28, 2019; L. Fickenscher and K. Dugan, "Grubhub Repays One Eatery $10K over Fee Protest," *New York Post*, June 24, 2019; K. Dugan and L. Fickenscher, "City Council to Investigate Grubhub's Restaurant-Killing Fees," *New York Post*, June 9, 2019; D. Suzanne-Mayer, "Lawsuit Accuses Grubhub of Charging Restaurants for Bogus Phone Calls," *The Takeout*, May 20, 2019; K. Dugan and L. Fickenscher, "Grubhub Charging Us even When Our Customers Don't Order: Restaurant Owners," *New York Post*, May 19, 2019; C. Hetrick, "Philadelphia Restaurant Alleges Grubhub Charged Eateries Millions for 'Sham' Phone Orders," *Chicago Tribune*, March 14, 2019; **www.grubhub.com**, accessed June 3, 2020.

Questions

1. Discuss the ethicality and the legality of each of Grubhub's business practices: registering domain names, phone fees, and nonpartnered restaurants.

2. The fundamental tenets of ethics include responsibility, accountability, and liability. Discuss each of these tenets as it applies to Grubhub's business practices in this case.

CHAPTER 4

Information Security

CHAPTER OUTLINE	LEARNING OBJECTIVES
4.1 Introduction to Information Security	4.1 Identify the five factors that contribute to the increasing vulnerability of information resources and provide specific examples of each factor.
4.2 Unintentional Threats to Information Systems	4.2 Compare and contrast human mistakes and social engineering and provide a specific example of each one.
4.3 Deliberate Threats to Information Systems	4.3 Discuss the 10 types of deliberate attacks.
4.4 What Organizations Are Doing to Protect Information Resources	4.4 Describe the three risk mitigation strategies and provide an example of each one in the context of owning a home.
4.5 Information Security Controls	4.5 Identify the three major types of controls that organizations can use to protect their information resources and provide an example of each one.

Opening Case

MIS FIN Data Breaches

From the beginning of 2019 until mid-2020, data breaches exposed approximately *17 billion records*, including usernames, passwords, debit and credit card numbers, home addresses, phone numbers, and other types of sensitive data. The first quarter of 2020 set the record for data breaches, with more than 8 billion records stolen. Some data breaches result from sophisticated nation-state espionage operations; others are carried out by online criminals who plan to sell the stolen data.

Attackers have typically stolen and aggregated consumer data that they have used to break into people's accounts, steal their money, blackmail them, or impersonate them. In fact, according to Experian (**www.experian.com**), more than 30 percent of data breach victims later experience identity theft.

In June 2020 attackers took data thefts to a new level. They integrated previously breached databases into a vast, unprecedented collection of *2.2 billion* unique usernames and associated passwords and were selling them on the Dark Web. The *Dark Web* is a part of the Internet that is not visible to search engines and requires the use of an anonymizing browser such as Tor to be accessed.

Because the data came from old leaks, security professionals hope that users change their passwords when they are notified about a breach. Taken together, these massive databases create real risk to individuals by enabling identity theft, credential theft, phishing and spear phishing attacks, credential stuffing, and other attacks. We discuss these attacks later in this chapter. We now take a look at some recent data breaches.

Wishbone

In May 2020 a hacker put up for sale the data on 40 million users registered on Wishbone (**www.wishbone.io**), a mobile app that lets users compare two items in a simple voting poll. According to the seller's claims and a sample of the data published online, the Wishbone data included usernames, emails, phone numbers, city, state, and country, as well as hashed passwords. To produce a *hashed password*, organizations apply an algorithm to the real password to turn plaintext into an unintelligible series of numbers, symbols, and letters. Unfortunately, security researchers revealed that the Wishbone passwords were in a weak hashing format that can be cracked using freely available online tools.

Wawa

Founded in 1964, Wawa, Inc. (**www.wawa.com**) is a U.S. chain of convenience stores and gasoline stations located along the East Coast. In December 2019 Wawa disclosed a major security breach, stating that hackers had inserted malicious software, known as *malware*, on the company's point-of-sale systems. The breach impacted all 860 of Wawa's convenience retail stores, and the malware had operated from March 4 until December 12, 2019. The attackers stole data on 30 million U.S. customers as well as more than 1 million non-U.S. cardholders. On January 27, 2020, a Dark Web marketplace known as Joker's Stash began selling card data from the breach.

The retailer further stated that the data included debit and credit card numbers, expiration dates, and cardholder names, but not debit card PINs, credit card CVV2 numbers, or other personal information. However, security researchers concluded that the Wawa data actually did include CVV2 numbers. A CVV2 number is a three- or four-digit number printed on the back or front of credit cards, debit cards, and prepaid cards that you provide for security purposes when making a purchase online or over the phone.

Verifications.io

Email validation companies are an important component of the email marketing industry. These firms do not send out marketing emails for themselves. Instead, they check their customers' mailing lists to ensure that the email addresses contained in them are valid.

This process entails sending a message to the email address and confirming that it was delivered. Mainstream email marketing firms often outsource the process rather than face the risk of being blacklisted by spam filters or lowering their online reputation scores. In early 2019, security researchers discovered an unprotected, publicly accessible database belonging to Verifications.io, an email validation firm. The data contained 809 million records of detailed, plaintext marketing data.

The data consisted of 2 billion unencrypted records. These records contained 763 million unique email addresses, as well as names, phone numbers, physical addresses, genders, dates of birth, personal mortgage amounts, interest rates, various social media accounts associated with email addresses, and characterizations of people's credit scores (such as average, above average, and so on). The data did not include Social Security numbers or credit card numbers.

Verifications.io responded that the database contained data gathered from public sources, asserting that the company was not liable for any negative consequences caused by its data leak. That being said, the company took its website and the database offline the same day that the security researchers reported the problem.

People Data Labs and Oxydata

People Data Labs (PDL; **www.peopledatalabs.com**) and Oxydata (**www.oxydata.io**) are data brokers. A *data broker* collects and integrates data from a variety of sources—public records, census and change of address records, motor vehicle and driving records, user-contributed material to social media websites, media and court reports, voter registration lists, consumer purchase histories, bank card transaction records, Web-browsing histories, and many other sources—and then sells the data to other organizations.

PDL claims to have data for sale on more than 1.5 billion people around the world, including personal email addresses, LinkedIn addresses, Facebook addresses and IDs, and phone numbers. Oxydata claims to have similar data on 380 million people in 85 industries and 195 countries.

In October 2019 security researchers found approximately 1.2 billion records of consumer data on an unsecured, easily accessible server. The data contained 50 million unique home and cell phone numbers; associated social media profiles from Facebook, Twitter, LinkedIn, and Github; work histories seemingly scraped from LinkedIn; and 622 million unique email addresses. The data did not contain sensitive data such as passwords, credit card numbers, or Social Security numbers.

Security researchers asserted that the data appeared to come from PDL and Oxydata. PDL responded that they did not know how the data appeared on the exposed server. Oxydata maintained that, although the data on the exposed server could have come from one of its customers, it definitely was not leaked from the Oxydata database.

The researchers did not know who actually collected the data or if the data in fact were stolen. They reported the exposure to the Federal Bureau of Investigation (FBI). Within a few hours, an unknown person(s) took the server and the exposed data offline.

Neither data broker could rule out the possibility that one of their customers had mishandled their data. Further, the two firms could have left the data exposed themselves. This situation emphasizes the security and privacy issues inherent in the business of collecting, buying, and selling data. What is important here is that huge volumes of data are being collected, aggregated, stored, and commercialized without the knowledge of the data owners. Who are these owners? They are all of us!

Final thoughts: Damage from data breaches impacts not only consumers but companies as well. Wishbone, Wawa, and People Data Labs are facing class action lawsuits over their respective data breaches. As of July 2020 it appeared that Verifications.io had gone out of business. At that time, there was no evidence of a lawsuit against Oxydata.

Sources: Compiled from "All Data Breaches in 2019 & 2020—An Alarming Timeline," *SelfKey Blog*, June 7, 2020; J. Lugo, "Wishbone App Breached, Affecting More than 40 Million Users," *Security Boulevard*, June 3, 2020; C. Cimpanu, "Hacker Leaks 40 Million User Records from Popular Wishbone App," *ZDNet*, May 20, 2020; A. Culafi, "Payment Cards from Wawa Data Breach Found on Dark Web," *TechTarget*, January 30, 2020; "2020 Q1 Report," *RiskBased Security*, 2020; "Wawa Says Data Breach Affected Thousands over 10 Months," *Associated Press*, December 20, 2019; C. Cimpanu, "Wawa Says POS Malware Incident Impacts 'Potentially All Locations'," *ZDNet*, December 19, 2019; L. Newman, "1.2 Billion Records Found Exposed on a Single Server," *Wired*, November 22, 2019; L. Dignan, "Nation State Actors, Affiliates behind Increasing Amount of Data Breaches," *ZDNet*, May 8, 2019; M. Tatham, "Identity Theft Statistics," *Experian*, March 15, 2018; R. Schultz, "Email Vendor Verifications.io Seems to Be out of Business Following Breach," *Email Marketing Daily*, March 15, 2019; D. Winder, "(Updated) 2 Billion Unencrypted Records Leaked in Marketing Data Breach—What to Do Next," *Forbes*, March 10, 2019; L. Newman, "An Email Marketing Company Left 809 Million Records Exposed Online," *Wired*, March 7, 2019; A. Greenberg, "Hackers Are Passing around a Megaleak of 2.2 Billion Records," *Wired*, January 30, 2019.

Questions

1. What is the common problem in all the of data breaches discussed in this case? Hint: Consider user credentials.

2. How would you solve the common problem in all of these data breaches?

3. Place yourself as a victim in any of these data breaches. What should you do when you are notified (or when you believe) that your personal data have been compromised?

Introduction

The cases in this chapter provide several lessons. First, it is difficult, if not impossible, for organizations to provide perfect security for their data. Second, there is a growing danger that countries are engaging in economic cyberwarfare. Third, it appears that it is impossible to secure the Internet. Information security impacts each and every one of us. This chapter's opening case illustrates that our personally identifiable, private data are not secure.

The solutions for these and other related issues are not clear. As you learn about information security in the context of information technology, you will acquire a better understanding of these issues, their importance, their relationships, and their trade-offs. Keep in mind that the issues involved in information security impact individuals and small organizations as well as large organizations.

Information security is especially important to small businesses. Large organizations that experience an information security problem have greater resources to both resolve and survive the problem. In contrast, small businesses have fewer resources and therefore can be more easily crippled by a data breach.

When properly used, information technologies can have enormous benefits for individuals, organizations, and entire societies. In Chapters 1 and 2 you read about diverse ways in which IT has made businesses more productive, efficient, and responsive to consumers. You also explored fields such as medicine and philanthropy in which IT has improved people's health and well-being. Unfortunately, bad actors can misuse information technologies, often with devastating consequences. Consider the following scenarios:

- Individuals can have their personal data and subsequently their identities stolen.
- Organizations can have customer information stolen, leading to financial losses, erosion of customer confidence, and legal actions.
- Countries face the threats of *cyberterrorism* and *cyberwarfare*, terms for Internet-based attacks. Cyberwarfare is a critical problem for the U.S. government. In fact, President Obama signed a cyberwarfare directive in October 2012 that, for the first time, laid out specific ground rules for how and when the U.S. military can carry out offensive and defensive cyber operations against foreign threats. The directive emphasized the U.S. government's focus on cybersecurity as a top priority, a focus that continues to grow in importance.

Clearly, the misuse of information technologies has come to the forefront of any discussion of IT. In fact, according to security analysts, cybercrime will cost the world approximately $6 trillion per year by 2021.

With organizations facing the loss or theft of 17 billion records since the beginning of 2019 (see this chapter's opening case), they must be aware of the full financial impact that a data breach will have. According to IBM Security's annual study of the financial impact of data breaches in organizations, the average cost of a breach in the United States is about $8 million, more than double the worldwide average cost. While less common, breaches of more than 1 million records cost companies an average of $42 million in losses and breaches of 50 million records cost companies $388 million. The average length of a breach was 279 days, with companies taking 206 days to first identify the breach after it occurs and an additional 73 days to contain the breach.

FIN The direct costs of a data breach include hiring forensic experts, notifying customers, setting up telephone hotlines to field queries from concerned or affected customers, offering free credit monitoring, and providing discounts for future products and services. The more intangible costs of a breach include the loss of business from increased customer turnover—called *customer churn*—and decreases in customer trust.

HRM Unfortunately, employee negligence causes many data breaches, meaning that organizational employees are a weak link in information security. It is therefore very important for you to learn about information security so that you will be better prepared when you enter the workforce.

4.1 | Introduction to Information Security

Security can be defined as the degree of protection against criminal activity, danger, damage, or loss. Following this broad definition, **information security** refers to all of the processes and policies designed to protect an organization's information and information systems (IS) from unauthorized access, use, disclosure, disruption, modification, or destruction. You have seen that information and information systems can be compromised by deliberate criminal actions and by anything that can impair the proper functioning of an organization's information systems.

Before continuing, let's consider these key concepts. Organizations collect huge amounts of information, and they employ numerous information systems that are subject to myriad threats. A **threat** to an information resource is any danger to which a system may be exposed. The **exposure** of an information resource is the harm, loss, or damage that can result if a threat compromises that resource. An information resource's **vulnerability** is the possibility that a threat will harm that resource.

Today, five key factors are contributing to the increasing vulnerability of organizational information resources, making it much more difficult to secure them:

1. Today's interconnected, interdependent, wirelessly networked business environment
2. Smaller, faster, cheaper computers and storage devices
3. Decreasing skills necessary to be a computer hacker
4. International organized crime taking over cybercrime
5. Lack of management support

The first factor is the evolution of the IT resource from mainframe-only to today's highly complex, interconnected, interdependent, wirelessly networked business environment. The Internet now enables millions of computers and computer networks to communicate freely and seamlessly with one another. Organizations and individuals are exposed to a world of untrusted networks and potential attackers. In general, a *trusted network* is any network within your organization, and an *untrusted network* is any network external to your organization. Also, wireless technologies enable employees to compute, communicate, and access the Internet anywhere and at any time. Significantly, wireless is an inherently unsecure broadcast communications medium.

The second factor reflects the fact that modern computers and storage devices—for example, thumb drives or flash drives—continue to become smaller, faster, cheaper, and more portable, with greater storage capacity. These characteristics make it much easier to steal or lose a computer or a storage device that contains huge amounts of sensitive information. Also, far more people are able to afford powerful computers and connect inexpensively to the Internet, thus raising the potential of an attack on information assets.

The third factor is that the computing skills necessary to be a hacker are *decreasing*. The reason is that the Internet contains information and computer programs called *scripts* that users with limited skills can download and use to attack any information system that is connected to the Internet. (Security experts can also use these scripts for legitimate purposes, such as testing the security of various systems.)

The fourth factor is that international organized crime is taking over cybercrime. **Cybercrime** refers to illegal activities conducted over computer networks, particularly the Internet. Consulting company Accenture (**www.accenture.com**) maintains that groups of well-organized criminal organizations have taken control of a global billion-dollar crime network. The network, powered by skillful hackers, targets known software security weaknesses. These crimes are typically nonviolent; however, they are quite lucrative. Consider, for example, that losses from armed robberies average hundreds of dollars and those from white-collar crimes can average tens of thousands of dollars. In contrast, losses from computer crimes can average hundreds of thousands of dollars. Furthermore, computer crimes can be committed from anywhere in the world at any time, effectively providing an international safe haven for cybercriminals.

The fifth, and final, factor is lack of management support. For the entire organization to take security policies and procedures seriously, senior managers must set the tone. Unfortunately, senior managers often do not do so. Ultimately, however, lower-level managers may be even more important. These managers are in close contact with employees every day and are thus in a better position to determine whether employees are following security procedures.

Author Lecture Videos are available exclusively in *WileyPLUS*.
Apply the Concept activities are available in the Appendix and in *WileyPLUS*.

IT's About Business 4.1

MIS Thieves Steal 100 Luxury Vehicles from Car2Go

Car2Go was a car-sharing service available in six North American cities. Car2Go did not charge recurring membership fees, nor did it charge for gas. After paying a $35 joining fee, members rented cars for a fixed fee of 41 cents per minute, or $14.99 per hour.

With the map on the Car2Go app, customers could find cars on the streets and in designated lots around a city. They waved their RFID-enabled membership card over the windshield, and the doors unlocked. The keys and a credit card for refueling were kept in the glove compartment. Customers could leave the car anywhere in the Home Area—that is, Car2Go's operating area in a particular city—and they did not have to refuel it.

Car2Go's executive team in Europe, where fraud rates were much lower than in the United States, wanted to make it easier for people to sign up for the service. In the past, the company required all customers to undergo background checks conducted manually by humans. These checks took one to two days to complete, which irritated some customers. Therefore, in April 2019 the service stopped requiring these checks.

Within a week after dopping these requirements, the company reported that about 20 people had set up approximately 80 bogus accounts in Chicago, using fake or stolen credit cards as their payment methods. In several instances, hackers with lists of stolen email addresses and passwords had written computer programs to locate car-sharing accounts using those fake credentials.

Almost immediately, there was an increase in rentals for Car2Go's Mercedes CLA sedans and GLA sport utility vehicles. These rentals lasted much longer than Car2Go's average 90-minute rental. In fact, many of the Mercedes were not returned at all. Instead, employees at Car2Go headquarters in Austin, Texas, watched on a digital map as many of their cars gathered in West Chicago, a neighborhood just outside the company's coverage area.

Car2Go sent several workers to retrieve the vehicles, only to find that thieves had them. Some of the thieves blocked the vehicles to prevent repossession, and others threatened the employees. Car2Go was able to remotely disable vehicles, but the confusing situation made it difficult to know which cars to actually disable. At the same time that Car2Go was noticing the increase in rentals, Facebook ads featuring short-term Mercedes rentals began to target Chicagoans. Two days later, Car2Go suspended operations in Chicago because the company could not distinguish its legitimate customers from the thieves.

Car2Go asked the Chicago Police Department for help. According to the police, all of the stolen cars had functioning GPS trackers and license plates that started with the letter AX. Further, many still had visible Car2Go stickers on them. As a result, officers were able to quickly arrest almost two dozen joyriders. Many of them claimed that they had innocently rented the vehicles from people in the neighborhood without realizing that anything was wrong. The only person charged with a felony had phony credit cards in his possession.

In total, more than 100 cars were compromised. All of them were eventually recovered, though some only after they were stripped of doors, seats, and other parts. In response, Car2Go reinstated its original policy of manually reviewing new accounts. The company subsequently reported that it had not experienced any serious issues in the following two months.

In spring 2019, Car2Go and DriveNow merged to become Share Now (**www.share-now.com**). In December 2019 Daimler announced that Share Now would no longer operate in North America, effective February 29, 2020. Daimler noted that a key strategy for Share Now was to move to electric vehicles and that North America did not have the infrastructure (i.e., charging stations) to support that strategy. Share Now made no mention of security concerns contributing to its decision to cease operations in North America.

Sources: Compiled from "How to Protect against Hacks on Car Sharing Services," *Upstream.com*, 2020; R. Pegoraro, "An Elegy for Car2Go, the Smarter Zipcar Rival that Lost Its Way," *Fast Company*, December 21, 2019; A. Migdal, "Hundreds of Thousands of Car2Go Members to Lose Service as Company Pulls out of North America," *CBC News*, December 18, 2019; A. Hawkins, "Share Now, Formerly Car2Go, Is Leaving North America," *The Verge*, December 18, 2019; L. Zimberoff, "How a Rental App Lost Control of Its Cars," *Bloomberg Businessweek*, July 15, 2019; J. Brustein, "Mercedes Thieves Showed Just How Vulnerable Car-Sharing Can Be," *Bloomberg Businessweek*, July 11, 2019; D. Solomon, "Thefts of Austin-Based Car2Go Rentals Show the Vulnerability of Our App-Based World," *Texas Monthly*, April 21, 2019; "21 People Arrested in Car2Go Fraud Incident that Caused App to Temporarily Suspend Its Service in Chicago," *CBS News Chicago*, April 19, 2019; "Car2Go and DriveNow Merge to Become Share Now," *New Mobility*, March 4, 2019; "More Members, More Rentals: Car2Go Has Successful Financial Year 2018," *Car2Go Press Release*, January 10, 2019; E. Kovacs, "Car Sharing Apps Vulnerable to Hacker Attacks: Kaspersky," *Security Week*, July 25, 2018; **www.share-now.com**, accessed July 5, 2020.

Questions

1. How could Daimler executives have tested their decision to eliminate background checks before fully implementing it?

2. Consider yourself a Daimler executive. Rather than eliminating the background checks altogether, would it be possible to redesign the process so that it took much less time? If so, how would you have done this?

3. Describe how hacking played a role in the theft of luxury vehicles from Car2Go.

Management can also make decisions that lead to problems. IT's About Business 4.1 shows how a management decision adversely impacted Car2Go. As you read this case, note that not all security problems are caused by high-tech wizardry.

Before you go on...

1. Define information security.
2. Differentiate among a threat, an exposure, and a vulnerability.
3. Why are the skills needed to be a hacker decreasing?

4.2 Unintentional Threats to Information Systems

Information systems are vulnerable to many potential hazards and threats, as you can see in **Figure 4.1**. The two major categories of threats are unintentional threats and deliberate threats. This section discusses unintentional threats, and the next section addresses deliberate threats.

Unintentional threats are acts performed without malicious intent that nevertheless represent a serious threat to information security. A major category of unintentional threats is human error.

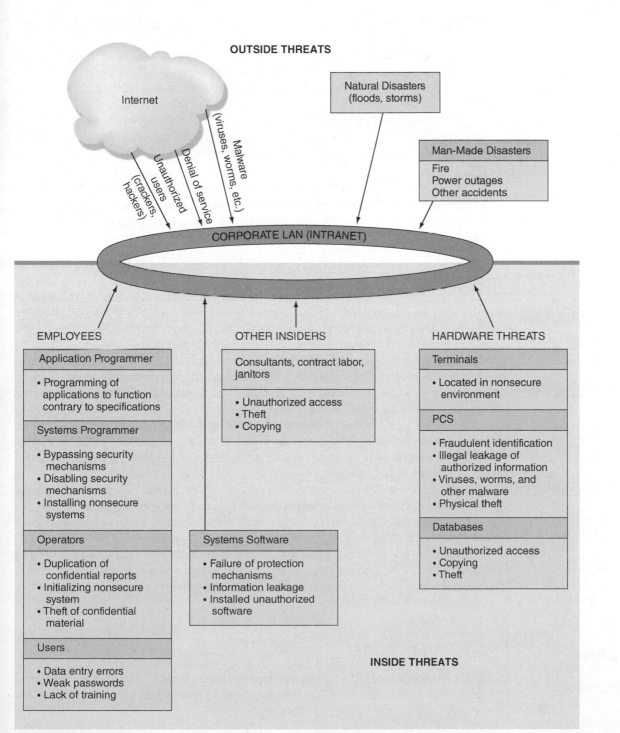

FIGURE 4.1 Security threats.

Human Errors

`HRM` Organizational employees span the breadth and depth of the organization, from mail clerks to the CEO, and across all functional areas. There are two important points to be made about employees. First, the higher the level of employee, the greater the threat he or she poses to information security. This is true because higher-level employees typically have greater access to corporate data, and they enjoy greater privileges on organizational information systems. Second, employees in two areas of the organization pose especially significant threats to information security: human resources and information systems. Human resources employees generally have access to sensitive personal information about all employees. Likewise, IS employees not only have access to sensitive organizational data, but they also frequently control the means to create, store, transmit, and modify those data. Consider these two examples.

- `MIS` `POM` For 10 years, a Siemens contractor created spreadsheets that the company used to manage equipment orders. The spreadsheets contained custom macros that enabled Siemens to automate inventory and order management. The contractor embedded logic bombs that would trigger after a certain date and crash the spreadsheets. Each time the spreadsheets would crash, Siemens would call him and he would "fix the problem" for a fee.

  The scheme fell apart when he was out of town and had to give his password for the spreadsheets to Siemens IT staff so that they could use the spreadsheets to fill an urgent order. They found the logic bombs and the police arrested the contractor.

- `MKT` A marketing and software company in the United Kingdom terminated an IT employee. After he left, he could still access the company's systems because he had stolen a fellow employee's login credentials. He then deleted each of the firm's 23 Amazon Web Services servers. As a result, the firm said that it lost "big contracts with some clients" totaling about $700,000. The perpetrator was sentenced to two years in prison.

Other relevant employees include contract labor, consultants, and janitors and guards. Contract labor, such as temporary hires, may be overlooked in information security arrangements. However, these employees often have access to the company's network, information systems, and information assets. Consultants, although technically not employees, perform work for the company. Depending on the nature of their work, they may also have access to the company's network, information systems, and information assets.

Finally, janitors and guards are the most frequently ignored people in information security systems. Companies frequently outsource their security and janitorial services. As with contractors, then, these individuals work for the company although they technically are not employees. Moreover, they are usually present when most—if not all—other employees have gone home. They typically have keys to every office, and nobody questions their presence in even the most sensitive parts of the building. In fact, an article from *2600: The Hacker Quarterly* (**www.2600.com**) described how to get a job as a janitor for the purpose of gaining physical access to an organization.

Human errors or mistakes by employees pose a serious problem. These errors are typically the result of laziness, carelessness, or a lack of awareness concerning information security. This lack of awareness arises from poor education and training efforts by the organization. Human mistakes manifest themselves in many different ways, as illustrated in **Table 4.1**.

The human errors you have just studied, although unintentional, are committed entirely by employees. However, employees also can make unintentional mistakes in response to actions by an attacker. Attackers often employ social engineering to induce individuals to make unintentional mistakes and disclose sensitive information.

Social Engineering

Social engineering is an attack in which the perpetrator uses social skills to trick or manipulate legitimate employees into providing confidential company information such as passwords. The

TABLE 4.1   Human Mistakes

Human Mistake	Description and Examples
Carelessness with computing devices (e.g., laptops, tablets, smartphones)	Losing or misplacing devices, leaving them in taxis, and so on
Carelessness with computing devices	Losing or misplacing these devices, or using them carelessly so that malware is introduced into an organization's network
Opening questionable e-mails	Opening e-mails from someone unknown, or clicking on links embedded in e-mails (see *phishing attack* in Table 4.2)
Careless Internet surfing	Accessing questionable websites; can result in malware and alien software being introduced into the organization's network
Poor password selection and use	Choosing and using weak passwords (see *strong passwords* in the "Authentication" section later in this chapter)
Carelessness with one's office	Leaving desks and filing cabinets unlocked when employees go home at night; not logging off the company network when leaving the office for any extended period of time
Carelessness using unmanaged devices	Unmanaged devices are those outside the control of an organization's IT department and company security procedures. These devices include computers belonging to customers and business partners, computers in the business centers of hotels, and so on.
Carelessness with discarded equipment	Discarding old computer hardware and devices without completely wiping the memory; includes computers, smartphones, BlackBerry® units, and digital copiers and printers
Careless monitoring of environmental hazards	These hazards, which include dirt, dust, humidity, and static electricity, are harmful to the operation of computing equipment

most common example of social engineering occurs when the attacker impersonates someone else on the telephone, such as a company manager or an IS employee. The attacker claims he forgot his password and asks the legitimate employee to give him a password to use. Other common ploys include posing as an exterminator, an air conditioning technician, or a fire marshal. Examples of social engineering abound.

In one company, a perpetrator entered a company building wearing a company ID card that looked legitimate. He walked around and put up signs on bulletin boards reading "The help desk telephone number has been changed. The new number is 555-1234." He then exited the building and began receiving calls from legitimate employees thinking they were calling the company help desk. Naturally, the first thing the perpetrator asked for was each caller's username and password. He now had the information necessary to access the company's information systems.

Two other social engineering techniques are tailgating and shoulder surfing. *Tailgating* is a technique designed to allow the perpetrator to enter restricted areas that are controlled with locks or card entry. The perpetrator follows closely behind a legitimate employee and, when the employee gains entry, the attacker asks him or her to "hold the door." *Shoulder surfing* occurs when a perpetrator watches an employee's computer screen over the employee's shoulder. This technique is particularly successful in public areas such as in airports and on commuter trains and airplanes.

4.3 Deliberate Threats to Information Systems

There are many types of deliberate threats to information systems. We provide a list of 10 common types for your convenience:

1. Espionage or trespass
2. Information extortion
3. Sabotage or vandalism
4. Theft of equipment or information
5. Identity theft
6. Compromises to intellectual property
7. Software attacks
8. Alien software
9. Supervisory control and data acquisition (SCADA) attacks
10. Cyberterrorism and cyberwarfare

Espionage or Trespass

Espionage or trespass occurs when an unauthorized individual attempts to gain illegal access to organizational information. It is important to distinguish between competitive intelligence and industrial espionage. Competitive intelligence consists of legal information-gathering techniques, such as studying a company's website and press releases, attending trade shows, and similar actions. In contrast, industrial espionage crosses the legal boundary.

Information Extortion

Information extortion occurs when an attacker either threatens to steal, or actually steals, information from a company. The perpetrator demands payment for not stealing the information, for returning stolen information, or for agreeing not to disclose the information. An increasingly serious type of information extortion is ransomware.

Ransomware, or digital extortion, blocks access to a computer system or encrypts an organization's data until the organization pays a sum of money. Victims are told to pay the ransom, usually in Bitcoin. Attackers typically use the anonymizing Tor network (**www.torproject.org**).

Ransomware attacks are growing rapidly. In 2020 ransomware attacks extorted approximately $20 billion globally. As bad as these figures look, the reality is probably worse. Experts estimate that fewer than 25 percent of ransomware attacks are reported. Significantly, security analysts note that over half of the companies compromised by ransomware pay the ransom.

Methods of Attack. Most commonly, ransomware attacks use spear phishing and whaling attacks. These emails are carefully tailored to look as convincing as possible, so they appear no different from any other email the victim might receive.

Some ransomware developers distribute ransomware to any hacker who wants to use it. This process is called *ransomware-as-a-service*. In this type of ransomware, the original creators publish the software on the Dark Web, allowing other criminals to use the code in return for receiving 40 to 50 percent of each ransom paid.

Rather than threatening to delete encrypted data, some cybercriminals are beginning to threaten to release it to the public, a strategy known as *doxxing*. For organizations that deal with private and sensitive customer data, such as financial services, hospitals, and law firms, such attacks can have severe consequences. In addition to the impact to brand reputation, regulations such as the Health Information Portability and Accountability Act (HIPAA) require customer notifications and other activities that can quickly total hundreds of thousands of dollars. Compared to other industry segments, personal health information is 50 times more valuable than financial information on the Dark Web.

The Costs of Ransomware.

Direct costs are the ransom payment. Indirect costs include the cost of recovering files from backup and restoring encrypted systems, business interruption, loss of reputation, liability (lawsuits), loss of data, investments in additional cybersecuritry software, additional staff training, and increased cyber insurance (particularly covering ransomware attacks).

Protection against Ransomware.

There are many steps that organizations can take to protect itself against ransomware infections.

- Perhaps most importantly, all organizations must provide education and training so that users are aware of phishing, spear phishing, and whaling attacks and do not click on any suspicious emails or links in emails.

- Organizations must install the latest versions of software and apply patches immediately.

- Organizations must back up crucial data and information often, preferably through an encrypted cloud-based storage company or an online backup service. Examples are iDrive (**www.idrive.com**) and Carbonite (**www.carbonite.com**). Important: the backup data storage must be connected to your system only when you are backing up the data.

- Organizations should employ *anti-ransomware software*. Packages such as Acronis Ransomware Protection (**www.acronis.com**) and Malwarebytes Anti-Ransomware Beta (**www.malwarebytes.com**) use two methods to defeat ransomware. First, they detect the digital signatures of known malware to recognize it going forward. This approach does not work if the software has not yet encountered a particular type of malware.

  Second, they detect malware by its behavior. These programs monitor the activity of apps, and they quarantine processes that perform suspicious actions, such as generating an encryption key or starting to encrypt files. This method is more effective at detecting and stopping ransomware than simply searching for malware signatures because it can detect new threats as well as known threats.

- Organizations should utilize the *No More Ransom* initiative (**www.nomoreransom.org**). The portal offers information and advice on how to avoid falling victim to ransomware as well as free decryption tools for various types of ransomware to help victims retrieve their encrypted data. The portal is updated as often as possible to ensure that tools are available to fight the latest forms of ransomware. The platform is available in multiple languages, and more than 100 partners across the public and private sectors support the initiative.

  As of July 2020 No More Ransom offered 138 decryption tools covering many families of ransomware. These tools had deprived cybercriminals of at least $108 million in ransoms.

- Organizations should also be aware that individual security companies regularly release decryption tools to counter the ongoing evolution of ransomware. Many of these companies post updates about these tools on their company blogs as soon as they have cracked the malware's code.

IT's About Business 4.2 provides examples of ransomware. As you read this case, pay special attention to how each organization responded to the ransomware attack.

IT's About Business 4.2

MIS **FIN** **Ransomware Is Alive and Well**

Unfortunately, examples of successful ransomware attacks abound. These attacks can seriously affect both the organizations involved and the organizations' customers and business partners. In this case, we take a look at several ransomware attacks, paying particular attention to the organizations' responses and the results of the attacks.

Universities

On August 21, 2020, the University of Utah (**www.utah.edu**) revealed that it paid a ransomware gang just over $450,000. The university asserted that the hackers encrypted only a very small amount of its data and that its IT staff restored the data from backups. However, when the gang threatened to release student-related data online, the university agreed to pay the ransom.

On June 1, 2020, a ransomware attack encrypted a limited number of servers within the University of California San Francisco's (UCSF; **www.ucsf.edu**) School of Medicine. The attackers revealed some data as proof of their actions in their demand for a ransom payment.

The attackers first demanded $3 million. After conducting negotiations with UCSF on the Dark Web, they agreed to lower that total to $1.14 million. When the university transferred 116.4 bitcoins to the hackers, it received a decryption tool to unlock the data encrypted in the attack.

UCSF did not specify which data were affected. The university did state that it did not believe that patient medical records were exposed. The incident also did not affect patient care delivery operations or COVID-19-related work.

Norsk Hydro ASA

Norsk Hydro ASA (**www.hydro.com**) is a Norwegian aluminum and renewable energy company with operations in 50 countries. In June 2019 an employee opened an infected email from a trusted customer, resulting in a ransomware attack on the company. The hackers crippled 22,000 computers across 170 sites around the world.

Law enforcement agencies consider the company's response to be the "gold standard" answer to hackers. Norsk did not respond to the attackers at all, not even to ask what the ransom would be. Instead, they opted to restore their data from trusted backup servers. Additionally, Norsk was completely open and transparent with everyone about what had happened. Here is what Norsk did.

The entire workforce, consisting of 35,000 employees, turned to pen and paper. The firm switched production lines that shaped molten metal to manual functions. In some cases, retired workers came back to help their colleagues operate the lines "the old-fashioned way." In some cases, though, production lines did have to stop. When Norsk recovered, it had spent roughly $70 million.

The City of New Orleans

On December 13, 2019, the City of New Orleans experienced a ransomware attack. In response, Mayor LaToya Cantrell declared a city-wide state of emergency. The city's IT department shut down all city servers and ordered all employees to shut down their computers and disconnect from Wi-Fi. In total, the city shut down most of its government systems and more than 4,000 government computers. Fortunately, the attack did not impact the city's 911 service, police department, fire department, and emergency medical services.

Further, the city did not believe that any employee information was compromised.

New Orleans IT officials stated that it would take months before the city was able to rebuild its systems. The city did not disclose whether it had paid a ransom.

The attack cost New Orleans at least $7 million in financial damages. The city was able to recover $3 million from a cyber insurance policy it had purchased prior to the incident. Following the attack the city increased its cyber insurance coverage to $10 million.

There have been many cases where smaller companies decided to shut down, lacking the funds to (a) pay a ransom demand to retrieve their data and (b) rebuild their IT infrastructure. Here are two recent examples.

The Heritage Company

The Heritage Company, an Arkansas-based telemarketing firm, experienced a ransomware attack at the beginning of October 2019. CEO Sandra Franecke reported that the company lost "hundreds of thousands of dollars" as a result of the incident. IT recovery efforts were not successful, and the firm's leadership halted operations and left more than 300 employees without jobs.

Brookside Ear Nose and Throat & Hearing Service

In April 2019 Brookside Ear Nose and Throat (ENT) & Hearing Service in Battle Creek, Michigan, experienced a ransomware attack when a virus injected itself into the practice's electronic medical system. The virus deleted and overwrote every medical record, bill, and appointment, including backup data files. The virus did leave behind a duplicate of the deleted files, which could be unlocked with a password. The attackers promised to provide that password for $6,500 in U.S. currency wired to an account.

The practice's two ENT surgeons refused to pay the ransom. They felt that there was no guarantee that the password would work or that the malware would not show up again. Lacking medical and billing records, the doctors closed the business on April 1, 2019, and retired about a year before they had planned.

Sources: Compiled from C. Cimpanu, "University of Utah Pays $457,000 to Ransomware Gang," *ZDNet*, August 21, 2020; M. Novinson, "The 11 Biggest Ransomware Attacks of 2020 (So Far)," *CRN*, June 30, 2020; "UCSF Hospital Paid $1.14 Million in Bitcoin after Ransomware Attack," *Coindesk*, June 30, 2020; D. Winder, "The University of California Pays $1 Million Ransom Following Cyber Attack," *Forbes*, June 29, 2020; J. Tidy, "How Hackers Extorted $1.14 Million from University of California, San Francisco," *BBC News*, June 29, 2020; A. Scroxton, "Facilities Firm ISS World Crippled by Ransomware Attack," *Computer Weekly*, February 20, 2020; D. Kobialka, "New Orleans Mayor: Ransomware Attack Cost City $7 Million," *MSSP Alert*, January 16, 2020; C. Cimpanu, "Company Shuts Down because of Ransomware, Leaves 300 without Jobs just before Holidays," *ZDNet*, January 3, 2020; D. Kobialka, "New Orleans Ransomware Attack Update: City to Raise Cyber Insurance to $10 Million," *MSSP Alert*, December 24, 2019; D. Winder, "New Orleans Declares State of Emergency Following Cyber Attack," *Forbes*, December 14, 2019; Z. Zorz, "Danish Company Demant Expects to Suffer Huge Losses Due to Cyber Attack," *Help Net Security*, October 1, 2019; C. Cimpanu, "Ransomware Incident to Cost Danish Company a Whopping $95 Million," *ZDNet*, September 30, 2019; J. Tidy, "How a Ransomware Attack Cost One Firm £45m," *BBC News*, June 25, 2019; J. Carlson, "All of Records Erased, Doctor's Office Closes after Ransomware Attack," *Star Tribune*, April 6, 2019.

Sabotage or Vandalism

Sabotage and vandalism are deliberate acts that involve defacing an organization's website, potentially damaging the organization's image and causing its customers to lose faith. One form of online vandalism is a hacktivist or cyberactivist operation. These are cases of high-tech civil disobedience to protest the operations, policies, or actions of an organization or government agency. For example, in February 2020 Anonymous, a decentralized hacktivist movement, hacked the United Nations Department of Economic and Social Affairs (**www.un.org/development/desa**). The group created a web page for Taiwan, a country that had not had a seat at the UN since 1971. The hacked page featured a Taiwan independence flag and the Anonymous logo.

Theft of Equipment or Information

Computing devices and storage devices are becoming smaller yet more powerful with vastly increased storage. Common examples are laptops, iPads, smartphones, digital cameras, thumb drives, and iPods. As a result, these devices are becoming easier to steal and easier for attackers to use to steal information. In fact, not all attacks on organizations involve sophisticated software.

Table 4.1 points out that one type of human mistake is carelessness with laptops and other small computers such as tablets and, particularly, smartphones. In fact, many computing devices have been stolen because of such carelessness. The cost of a stolen device includes the loss of data, the loss of intellectual property, device replacement, legal and regulatory costs, investigation fees, and lost productivity.

One form of theft, known as *dumpster diving*, involves rummaging through commercial or residential trash to find discarded information. Paper files, letters, memos, photographs, IDs, passwords, credit cards, and other forms of information can be found in dumpsters. Unfortunately, many people never consider that the sensitive items they throw in the trash might be recovered and used for fraudulent purposes.

Dumpster diving is not necessarily theft, because the legality of this act varies. Because dumpsters are usually located on private premises, dumpster diving is illegal in some parts of the United States. Even in these cases, however, these laws are enforced with varying degrees of rigor.

Identity Theft

Identity theft is the deliberate assumption of another person's identity, usually to gain access to his or her financial information or to frame him or her for a crime. Techniques for illegally obtaining personal information include the following:

- Stealing personal data in computer databases
- Infiltrating organizations that store large amounts of personal data; for example, data aggregators such as Acxiom (**www.acxiom.com**)

- Impersonating a trusted organization in an electronic communication (phishing)
- Stealing mail or dumpster diving

Consider this identity-theft scheme in May 2020. With 40 million Americans filing for jobless benefits as a result of the COVID-19 pandemic, criminals targeted outdated computer systems in some state unemployment offices. A Nigerian crime ring called Scattered Canary used stolen password data and Social Security numbers to file false unemployment claims in Washington and several other states.

The criminals stole approximately $650 million from Washington. When the state detected the breach in June 2020, officials were able to recover $333 million of the money. The damage was so extensive that the state used its National Guard to examine nearly 200,000 claims for fraud.

Recovering from identity theft is costly, time consuming, and burdensome. Victims also report problems in obtaining credit and obtaining or holding a job, as well as adverse effects on insurance or credit rates. Victims also state that it is often difficult to remove negative information from their records, such as their credit reports.

Compromises to Intellectual Property

Protecting intellectual property is a vital issue for people who make their livelihood in knowledge fields. **Intellectual property** is the property created by individuals or corporations that is protected under *trade secret*, *patent*, and *copyright* laws.

A **trade secret** is an intellectual work, such as a business plan, that is a company secret and is not based on public information. An example is the formula for Coca-Cola. A **patent** is an official document that grants the holder exclusive rights on an invention or a process for a specified period of time. **Copyright** is a statutory grant that provides the creators or owners of intellectual property with ownership of the property, also for a designated period. Current U.S. laws award patents for 20 years and copyright protection for the life of the creator plus 70 years. Owners are entitled to collect fees from anyone who wants to copy their creations. It is important to note that these are definitions under U.S. law. There is some international standardization of copyrights and patents, but it is far from total. Therefore, there can be discrepancies between U.S. law and other countries' laws.

The most common intellectual property related to IT deals with software. In 1980, the U.S. Congress amended the Copyright Act to include software. The amendment provides protection for the *source code* and *object code* of computer software, but it does not clearly identify what is eligible for protection. For example, copyright law does not protect fundamental concepts, functions, and general features such as pull-down menus, colors, and icons. However, copying a software program without making payment to the owner—including giving a disc to a friend to install on his or her computer—is a copyright violation. Not surprisingly, this practice, called **piracy**, is a major problem for software vendors. The BSA (**www.bsa.org**) Global Software Piracy Study found that the commercial value of software theft totals billions of dollars per year.

Software Attacks

Software attacks have evolved from the early years of the computer era, when attackers used malicious software—called **malware**—to infect as many computers worldwide as possible, to the profit-driven, Web-based attacks of today. Modern cybercriminals use sophisticated, blended malware attacks, typically through the Web, to make money.

Software attacks target all Internet-connected devices, even smart televisions. As increasing numbers of Internet of Things devices (see Chapter 8) are installed, they provide billions of new targets for cybercriminals to target. As a result, hackers could hold your connected home or connected car hostage. There is even the potential that hackers could infect medical devices, thereby putting lives directly at risk.

Table 4.2 displays a variety of software attacks. These attacks are grouped into three categories: remote attacks requiring user action, remote attacks requiring no user action, and software attacks initiated by programmers during the development of a system.

TABLE 4.2　Types of Software Attacks

Type	Description
Remote Attacks Requiring User Action	
Virus	Segment of computer code that performs malicious actions by attaching to another computer program
Polymorphic virus	Segment of computer code that modifies itself (i.e., changes its computer code) to avoid detection by anti-malware systems, while keeping its same functionality
Worm	Segment of computer code that performs malicious actions and will replicate, or spread, by itself (without requiring another computer program)
Phishing attack	Attacks that use deception to acquire sensitive personal information by masquerading as official looking emails or instant messages
Spear phishing attack	Phishing attacks target large groups of people. In spear phishing attacks, the attackers find out as much information about an individual as possible to improve their chances that phishing techniques will be successful and obtain sensitive, personal information.
Whaling attack	Attack that targets high-value individuals such as senior executives in an attempt to steal sensitive information from a company such as financial data or personal details about employees
Remote Attacks Needing No User Action	
Denial-of-service attack	An attacker sends so many information requests to a target computer system that the target cannot manage them successfully and typically ceases to function (crashes).
Distributed denial-of-service attack	An attacker first takes over many computers, typically by using malicious software. These computers are called *zombies* or **bots**. The attacker uses these bots—which form a **botnet**—to deliver a coordinated stream of information requests to a target computer, causing it to crash.
Attacks by a Programmer Developing a System	
Trojan horse	Software programs that hide in other computer programs and reveal their designed behavior only when they are activated
Back door	Typically a password, known only to the attacker, that allows him or her to access a computer system at will, without having to go through any security procedures (also called a *trap door*)
Logic bomb	A segment of computer code that is embedded within an organization's existing computer programs and is designed to activate and perform a destructive action at a certain time or date

Not all cybercriminals are sophisticated, however. For example, a student at a U.S. university was sentenced to one year in prison for using keylogging software (discussed later in this chapter) to steal 750 fellow students' passwords and vote himself and four of his fraternity brothers into the student government's president and four vice president positions. The five positions would have brought the students a combined $36,000 in stipends.

The student was caught when university security personnel noticed strange activity on the campus network. Authorities identified the computer used in the activity from its IP address. On this computer, which belonged to the student in question, authorities found a PowerPoint presentation detailing the scheme. Authorities also found research on his computer, with queries such as "how to rig an election" and "jail time for keylogger."

Once the university caught on to the scheme, the student reportedly turned back to hacking to try to get himself out of trouble. He created new Facebook accounts in the names of actual classmates, going as far as conducting fake conversations between the accounts to try to deflect the blame. Those actions contributed to the one-year prison sentence, which the judge imposed even after the student pleaded guilty and requested probation.

Consider another example. In July 2019 the FBI and the bank Capital One (**www .capitalone.com**) announced a huge data breach. Data stolen in the breach included 106 million credit card applications and compromised data such as names, addresses, phone numbers, email addresses, dates of birth, 140,000 Social Security numbers, 80,000 bank account numbers, and some credit scores. The breach affected over 100 million Americans and 6 million Canadians. The bank stated that responding to the incident would cost between $100 million and $150 million.

On July 17, 2019, an unidentified person notified Capital One that the data had been posted on a GitHub account. The FBI examined the account and discovered the account owner's full name and résumé. Not only that, but the suspect posted about her actions on Slack and Twitter. A search of her bedroom found "files and items" that referenced Capital One. Authorities charged her with computer fraud and wire fraud.

Alien Software

Many personal computers have alien software, or *pestware*, running on them that the owners are unaware of. **Alien software** is clandestine software that is installed on your computer through duplicitous methods. It typically is not as malicious as viruses, worms, or Trojan horses, but it does use up valuable system resources. It can also enable other parties to track your Web surfing habits and other personal behaviors.

The vast majority of pestware is **adware**—software that causes pop-up advertisements to appear on your screen. Adware is common because it works. According to advertising agencies, for every 100 people who close a pop-up ad, 3 click on it. This "hit rate" is extremely high for Internet advertising.

Spyware is software that collects personal information about users without their consent. Three common types of spyware are stalkerware, keystroke loggers, and screen scrapers.

Stalkerware is spyware used to monitor people close to the perpetrator. Victims typically do not know the stalkerware is on their device unless they run an antivirus scan. Developers of stalkerware market their apps as child safety or anti-theft tools. However, these apps can easily be used for the purpose of spying on a partner.

This software has powerful surveillance functions which include: keylogging; making screenshots; monitoring Internet activity; recording location; recording video and phone calls; and intercepting app communications made via Skype, Facebook, WhatsApp, and iMessage, as well as others. Most stalkerware apps are not available on official app stores. Installation does not necessarily require access to the victim's device. Rather, a perpetrator can send the intended victim an innocuous-seeming download, such as a picture.

Keystroke loggers, also called *keyloggers*, record both your individual keystrokes and your Web browsing history. The purposes range from criminal—for example, theft of passwords and sensitive personal information such as credit card numbers—to annoying—for example, recording your Internet search history for targeted advertising.

Companies have attempted to counter keyloggers by switching to other forms of identifying users. For example, at some point all of us have been forced to look at wavy, distorted letters and type them correctly into a box. That string of letters is called a *CAPTCHA*, and it is a test. The point of CAPTCHA is that computers cannot (yet) accurately read those distorted letters. Therefore, the fact that you can transcribe them means that you are probably not a software program run by an unauthorized person, such as a spammer. As a result, attackers have turned to *screen scrapers*, or *screen grabbers*. This software records a continuous "movie" of a screen's contents rather than simply recording keystrokes.

Spamware is pestware that uses your computer as a launch pad for spammers. **Spam** is unsolicited e-mail, usually advertising for products and services. When your computer is infected with spamware, e-mails from spammers are sent to everyone in your e-mail address book, but they appear to come from you.

Not only is spam a nuisance, but it wastes time and money. Spam costs U.S. companies billions of dollars every year. These costs arise from productivity losses, clogged email systems, additional storage, user support, and antispam software. Spam can also carry viruses and worms, making it even more dangerous.

A new tool from DoNotPay (**www.donotpay.com**) offers help in unsubscribing from email lists. To use most subscription management tools, such as Unroll.me, you have to grant the service access to your email account, so that it can analyze your messages.

DoNotpay's antispam service works differently. You just forward your spam emails to spam@donotpay.com and a bot (software robot) will automatically unsubscribe you from that mailing list. In that way, DoNotPay does not need access to your account and only sees emails that you want it to manage.

Going further, DoNotPay will check if there is currently a class action settlement against the organization that sent you the email. If there is, you can instruct DoNotPay to automatically claim any compensation for which you are eligible on your behalf. If your claim is successful, you will receive payment. DoNotPay is not involved in the payment transaction.

Cookies are small amounts of information that websites store on your computer, temporarily or more or less permanently. In many cases, cookies are useful and innocuous. For example, some cookies are passwords and user IDs that you do not want to retype every time you access the website that issued the cookie. Cookies are also necessary for online shopping because merchants use them for your shopping carts.

Tracking cookies, however, can be used to track your path through a website, the time you spend there, what links you click on, and other details that the company wants to record, usually for marketing purposes. Tracking cookies can also combine this information with your name, purchases, credit card information, and other personal data to develop an intrusive profile of your spending habits.

Most cookies can be read only by the party that created them. However, some companies that manage online banner advertising are, in essence, cookie-sharing rings. These companies can track information such as which pages you load and which ads you click on. They then share this information with their client websites, which may number in the thousands.

Supervisory Control and Data Acquisition (SCADA) Attacks

SCADA refers to a large-scale distributed measurement and control system. SCADA systems are used to monitor or to control chemical, physical, and transport processes such as those used in oil refineries, water and sewage treatment plants, electrical generators, and nuclear power plants. Essentially, SCADA systems provide a link between the physical world and the electronic world.

SCADA systems consist of multiple sensors, a master computer, and communications infrastructure. The sensors connect to physical equipment. They read status data such as the open/closed status of a switch or a valve, as well as measurements such as pressure, flow, voltage, and current. They control the equipment by sending signals to it, such as opening or closing a switch or a valve or setting the speed of a pump. The sensors are connected in a network, and each sensor typically has an Internet address (Internet Protocol, or IP, address, discussed in Chapter 6). If attackers gain access to the network, then they can cause serious damage, such as disrupting the power grid over a large area or upsetting the operations of a large chemical or nuclear plant. Such actions could have catastrophic results. Consider these examples in May and June 2020.

- China requires foreign companies to choose between several tax-reporting software packages. Security analysts discovered that the most widely used package contained a backdoor that could allow malicious actors to conduct network reconnaissance or attempt to take remote control of company systems.
- North Korean state hackers sent COVID-19–themed phishing emails to more than 5 million businesses and individuals in Singapore, Japan, the United States, South Korea, India, and the UK in an attempt to steal personal and financial data.
- North Korean state hackers compromised one of India's nuclear power plants. The Nuclear Power Corporation of India stated that the malware only infected the plant's administrative network but did not reach its internal network, which controls the plant's nuclear reactors.

- Security experts discovered bugs placed by Iranian state hackers in a large number of enterprise virtual private network servers, including those sold by Pulse Secure (**www.pulsesecure.net**), Palo Alto Networks (**www.paloaltonetworks.com**), Fortinet (**www.fortinet.com**), and Citrix (**www.citrix.com**). The bugs are designed to plant backdoors in companies around the world.
- Japan's defense ministry announced it was investigating a large-scale cyber attack against Mitsubishi Electric (**www.mitsubishielectric.com**) that could have compromised details of new state-of-the-art missile designs.
- Israeli hackers disrupted operations at an Iranian port for several days, causing massive backups and delays. Officials characterized the attack as a retaliation against a failed Iranian hack in April targeting the command and control systems of Israeli water distribution systems.

Cyberterrorism and Cyberwarfare

Cyberterrorism and **cyberwarfare** refer to malicious acts in which attackers use a target's computer systems, particularly through the Internet, to cause physical, real-world harm or severe disruption, often to carry out a political agenda. These actions range from gathering data to attacking critical infrastructure; for example, through SCADA systems. We treat the two types of attacks as synonymous here, even though cyberterrorism is typically carried out by individuals or groups, whereas cyberwarfare is carried out by nation-states or non-state actors such as terrorists.

Before you go on...

1. Why has the theft of computing devices become more serious over time?
2. What are the three types of software attacks?
3. Define alien software and explain why it is a serious problem.
4. What is a SCADA system? Why can attacks against SCADA systems have catastrophic consequences?

4.4 What Organizations Are Doing to Protect Information Resources

Author Lecture Videos are available exclusively in *WileyPLUS*.
Apply the Concept activities are available in the Appendix and in *WileyPLUS*.

Why is stopping cybercriminals such a challenge? **Table 4.3** illustrates the many major difficulties involved in protecting information. Because organizing an appropriate defense system is so important to the entire enterprise, it is one of the major responsibilities of any prudent CIO as well as of the functional managers who control information resources. In fact, IT security is the business of *everyone* in an organization.

In addition to the problems listed in Table 4.3, another reason why information resources are difficult to protect is that the online commerce industry is not particularly willing to install safeguards that would make completing transactions more difficult or complicated. As one example, merchants could demand passwords or personal identification numbers for all credit card transactions. However, these requirements might discourage people from shopping online. For credit card companies, it is cheaper to block a stolen credit card and move on than to invest time and money prosecuting cybercriminals.

The final reason why information resources are difficult to protect is that it is extremely difficult to catch perpetrators. However, it is possible to catch attackers, albeit with great effort, time, and expense, as this chapter's closing case illustrates.

Organizations spend a great deal of time and money protecting their information resources. Before doing so, they perform risk management.

TABLE 4.3   **Difficulties in Protecting Information Resources**

Hundreds of potential threats exist.
Computing resources may be situated in many locations.
Many individuals control or have access to information assets.
Computer networks can be located outside the organization, making them difficult to protect.
Rapid technological changes make some controls obsolete as soon as they are installed.
Many computer crimes are undetected for a long period of time, so it is difficult to learn from experience.
People tend to violate security procedures because the procedures are inconvenient.
The amount of computer knowledge necessary to commit computer crimes is usually minimal. As a matter of fact, a potential criminal can learn hacking, free, from the Internet.
The costs of preventing hazards can be very high. Therefore, most organizations simply cannot afford to protect themselves against all possible hazards.
It is difficult to conduct a cost-benefit justification for controls before an attack occurs because it is difficult to assess the impact of a hypothetical attack.

A **risk** is the probability that a threat will impact an information resource. The goal of **risk management** is to identify, control, and minimize the impact of threats. In other words, risk management seeks to reduce risk to acceptable levels.

FIN The Enterprise Risk Management (ERM) framework guides risk management in the enterprise. ERM is a risk-based approach to managing an enterprise that integrates internal control, the Sarbanes–Oxley Act mandates, and strategic planning. ERM consists of several steps:

- Determine the relationship of risk to organizational goals.
- Differentiate between risks and opportunities.
- Assess risk, which involves three steps: (1) assess the value of each asset being protected, (2) estimate the probability that each asset will be compromised, and (3) compare the probable costs of the asset's being compromised with the costs of protecting that asset. The organization then considers how to mitigate the risk.

    Risk mitigation has two functions: (1) implementing controls to prevent identified threats from occurring, and (2) developing a means of recovery if the threat becomes a reality. The three most common risk mitigation strategies are:

    Risk acceptance: Accept the potential risk, continue operating with no controls, and absorb any damages that occur.

    Risk transference: Transfer the risk by using other means to compensate for the loss, such as by purchasing insurance.

    Risk limitation: Limit the risk by implementing controls that minimize the impact of the threat.

- Implement controls.
- Evaluate the controls. Examine the costs of implementing adequate control measures against the value of those control measures. If the costs of implementing a control are greater than the value of the asset being protected, the control is not cost effective. Organizations evaluate controls through information systems auditing.

    Companies implement security controls to ensure that information systems function properly. These controls can be installed in the original system, or they can be added after a system is in operation. Installing controls is necessary but not sufficient to provide adequate security. People who are also responsible for security need to answer questions such as: Are all controls installed as intended? Are they effective? Has any breach of security occurred? If so, what actions are required to prevent future breaches?

    These questions must be answered by independent and unbiased observers. Such observers perform the task of *information systems auditing*. In an IS environment, an **audit** is an examination of information systems, their inputs, outputs, and processing.

Created by the International Systems Audit and Control Association (ISACA; **www.isaca .org**), COBIT 5 provides a framework for IT security and IT auditing. The framework's intent is to align IT with business objectives and manage risk. The COBIT 5 framework is based on five principles, the first three of which apply most directly to security issues.

1. Meeting stakeholder needs: A system should be in place that addresses enterprise information security requirements. The system should include metrics for the number of clearly defined key security roles and the number of security-related incidents reported.

2. Covering the enterprise end-to-end: A security plan should be accepted and communicated throughout the organization. This process includes the level of stakeholder satisfaction with the plan, the number of security solutions that are different from those in the plan, and the number of security solutions deviating from the enterprise security architecture that can lead to security gaps and possibly increase the time needed to resolve security or compliance issues.

3. Applying a single, integrated framework: Information security solutions are implemented throughout the organization. The solutions include the number of services and solutions that align with the security plan and security incidents caused by noncompliance with the security plan.

4. Enabling a holistic approach

5. Separating governance from management

Before you go on...

1. Identify and discuss several reasons why it is difficult to protect information resources.
2. Compare and contrast risk management and risk analysis.

4.5 | Information Security Controls

Author Lecture Videos are available exclusively in *WileyPLUS*.
Apply the Concept activities are available in the Appendix and in *WileyPLUS*.

To protect their information assets, organizations implement **controls**, or defense mechanisms (also called *countermeasures*). These controls are designed to protect all of the components of an information system, including data, software, hardware, and networks. Because there are so many diverse threats, organizations use layers of controls, or *defense-in-depth.*

Controls are intended to prevent accidental hazards, deter intentional acts, detect problems as early as possible, enhance damage recovery, and correct problems. Before you study controls in more detail, it is important to emphasize that the single most valuable control is user education and training. Effective and ongoing education makes every member of the organization aware of the vital importance of information security.

In this section, you will learn about three major types of controls: physical controls, access controls, and communications controls. **Figure 4.2** illustrates these controls. In addition to applying controls, organizations plan for business continuity in case of a disaster, and they periodically audit their information resources to detect possible threats. You will study these topics in this section as well.

Physical Controls

Physical controls prevent unauthorized individuals from gaining access to a company's facilities. Common physical controls include walls, doors, fencing, gates, locks, badges, guards, and alarm systems. More sophisticated physical controls include pressure sensors, temperature sensors, and motion detectors. One shortcoming of physical controls is that they can be inconvenient to employees.

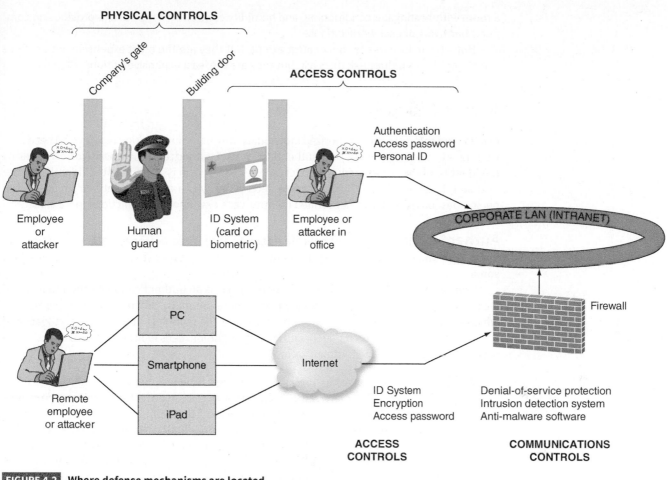

FIGURE 4.2   Where defense mechanisms are located.

Guards deserve special mention because they have very difficult jobs, for at least two reasons. First, their jobs are boring and repetitive and generally do not pay well. Second, if guards perform their jobs thoroughly, the other employees may harass them, particularly if they slow up the process of entering the facility.

Organizations also implement physical security measures that limit computer users to acceptable login times and locations. These controls also limit the number of unsuccessful login attempts, and they require all employees to log off their computers when they leave for the day. They also set the employees' computers to automatically log off the user after a certain period of disuse.

A basic security strategy for organizations is to be prepared for any eventuality. A critical element in any security system is a *business continuity plan*, also known as a *disaster recovery plan*.

Business continuity is the chain of events linking planning to protection and to recovery. The purpose of the business continuity plan is to provide guidance to people who keep the business operating after a disaster occurs. Employees use this plan to prepare for, respond to, and recover from events that affect the security of information assets. The objective is to restore the business to normal operations as quickly as possible following an attack. The plan is intended to ensure that critical business functions continue.

In the event of a major disaster, organizations can employ several strategies for business continuity. These strategies include hot sites, warm sites, and cold sites. A *hot site* is a fully configured computer facility with all of the company's services, communications links, and physical plant operations. A hot site duplicates computing resources, peripherals, telephone systems, applications, and workstations. A *warm site* provides many of the same services and options as the hot site. However, it typically does not include the actual applications the company needs. A warm site includes computing equipment such as servers, but it often does not include user workstations. A *cold site* provides only rudimentary services and facilities, such as a building or a room with heating, air conditioning, and humidity control. This type of site provides no computer hardware or user workstations.

Hot sites reduce risk to the greatest extent, but they are the most expensive option. Conversely, cold sites reduce risk the least, but they are the least expensive option.

Access Controls

Access controls restrict unauthorized individuals from using information resources. These controls involve two major functions: authentication and authorization. **Authentication** confirms the identity of the person requiring access. After the person is authenticated (identified), the next step is authorization. **Authorization** determines which actions, rights, or privileges the person has, based on his or her verified identity. Let's examine these functions more closely.

Authentication.   To authenticate (identify) authorized personnel, an organization can use one or more of the following methods: something the user is, something the user has, something the user does, or something the user knows.

Something the user is, also known as **biometrics**, is an authentication method that examines a person's innate physical characteristics. There are many different types of biometrics, which include fingerprint scanning, retinal scanning, iris scanning, analysis of heartbeats and body temperature, voice recognition, and facial recognition. Let's look at examples of how organizations use biometrics for authentication.

- **POM** Your voice changes as you age, becoming a little rougher each year. Nuance Communications Gatekeeper (**www.nuance.com**), a voice biometrics tool, analyzes the caller's voice "roughness" and other "micro-characteristics" that humans cannot hear to confirm that an older person is calling. Nuance customer Telefonica (**www.telefonica.com**) uses the tool to help with increased contact center volume during the COVID-19 pandemic. When the tool identifies an older person, the company routes them to priority customer service with shorter wait times and protocols to prevent fraudulent account takeover.

- **FIN** At Barclays Bank (**www.barclays.co.uk**), over 65 percent of calls are now handled by voice recognition, providing enrolled customers much faster, easier access to account services. Rather than spending five minutes providing passwords, PINs, and answering security questions, Barclays' customers spend just 20 seconds verifying their identities with voice recognition.

- **FIN** Security personnel were watching activity in a bank branch. Biometric sensors had detected unusual heartbeats and body heat patterns from new customers who had entered to open an account. It turns out that those "customers" had entered the United States days before as human cargo on a ship from another country. A criminal gang was using them to orchestrate financial fraud. The sensors had detected telltale signs of stress, alerting bank personnel to the attempted fraud.

Note that some applications of facial recognition increase security where others can lead to increased surveillance by governments with subsequent loss of personal privacy. (See IT's About Business 3.2, IT's About Business 3.3, and IT's About Business 4.3).

Something the user has is an authentication mechanism that includes regular identification (ID) cards, smart ID cards, and tokens. *Regular ID cards*, or *dumb cards*, typically have the person's picture and often his or her signature. *Smart ID cards* have an embedded chip that stores pertinent information about the user. (Smart ID cards used for identification differ from smart cards used in electronic commerce, which you learn about in Chapter 7. Both types of card have embedded chips, but they are used for different purposes.) *Tokens* have embedded chips and a digital display that presents a login number that the employees use to access the organization's network. The number changes with each login.

Something the user does is an authentication mechanism that includes voice and signature recognition. In *voice recognition*, the user speaks a phrase—for example, his or her name and department—that has previously been recorded under controlled conditions. The voice recognition system matches the two voice signals. In *signature recognition*, the user signs his or her name, and the system matches this signature with one previously recorded under controlled,

IT's About Business 4.3

MIS A Facial Recognition Failure

In January 2020 Robert Williams was arrested by officers of the Detroit Police Department. The officers charged Williams with stealing $3,800 in watches from a store called Shinola 15 months earlier. Williams had an alibi, and he denied the charges.

The police took Williams to a detention center, where they took his his mug shot, fingerprints, and DNA. They held him for 30 hours before he was released on a $1,000 personal bond.

The next day, the police showed Williams an image from a surveillance video taken in the store. The image was of a heavyset man dressed in black and wearing a red St. Louis Cardinals cap standing in front of a watch display. Williams denied that the image was of him.

Here is how the process played out. The shoplifting incident occurred in October 2018. A loss-prevention contractor for the store reviewed the surveillance video and sent a copy to the Detroit police. The following March a digital image examiner for the Michigan State Police uploaded a "probe image"—a still image from the video, showing the man in the Cardinals cap—to the state's facial recognition database. The system would have mapped the man's face and searched for similar ones among 49 million photos.

A company called DataWorks Plus (www.dataworksplus.com) provides the facial recognition technology for the state. The software incorporates components developed by NEC (www.necam.com) and Rank One Computing (www.rankone.io). In 2019 the federal government conducted a study of more than 100 facial recognition systems including algorithms from both companies. The study found that facial recognition systems in general were biased, falsely identifying African-American and Asian-American faces 10 to 100 times more often than Caucasian faces.

After the digital image examiner ran her search of the probe image, the state system would have provided a row of images generated by NEC and a row from Rank One, along with confidence scores for each image. A *confidence score* is the probability that the man's image from the store video matched an image from the photos in the police database. Williams's driver's license photo was among the matches. The examiner sent this photo to the Detroit police as an "Investigative Lead Report." The police file states, "This document is not a positive identification. It is an investigative lead only, and it is not probable cause for arrest."

After receiving the "match," investigators looked for evidence that would corroborate the case against Williams. Reporters noted that the police did not check Williams's phone for location data. They also failed to check whether Williams had an alibi or if he owned the clothing that the suspect was wearing. Instead, the police asked the loss-prevention contractor, who was not in the store at the time of the incident, if Williams was the man in the surveillance footage. She identified him, which prompted the arrest.

Two weeks after Williams's arrest, the prosecutor moved to dismiss the charges, but "without prejudice," meaning that Williams could be charged again. A spokesperson for the prosecutor revealed that a second witness had been at the store during the incident but had not been asked to look at a photo lineup. The spokesperson continued that if the individual made an identification in the future, then the prosecutor's office would decide whether to issue charges again.

Shortly after the prosecutor made these statements, the American Civil Liberties Union (ACLU; www.aclu.org) of Michigan filed a complaint with the city, requesting an absolute dismissal of the case, an apology, and the removal of Williams's information from Detroit's criminal databases. In response to the complaint and the case's publicity, the Wayne County prosecutor's office announced that Williams could have both the case and his fingerprint data expunged. The prosecutor stated, "We apologize. This does not in any way make up for the hours that Mr. Williams spent in jail."

Williams's case is the first known instance of mistaken charges filed as a result of facial recognition software. His case became even more noteworthy when in June 2020 Detroit's police chief admitted that facial recognition technology used by the department misidentifies suspects about 96 percent of the time.

Sources: Compiled from T. Lee, "Detroit Police Chief Cops to 96-Percent Facial Recognition Error Rate," *Ars Technica*, June 30, 2020; S. Ovide, "When the Police Think Software Is Magic," *The New York Times*, June 25, 2020; "Man Wrongfully Arrested Because Face Recognition Can't Tell Black People Apart," *ACLU*, June 24, 2020; S. Fussell, "A Flawed Facial-Recognition System Sent this Man to Jail," *Wired*, June 24, 2020; B. Allyn, "'The Computer Got It Wrong': How Facial Recognition Led to False Arrest of Black Man," *NPR*, June 24, 2020; K. Hill, "Wrongfully Accused by an Algorithm," *The New York Times*, June 24, 2020; S. Ovide, "A Case for Banning Facial Recognition," *The New York Times*, June 9, 2020; P. Grother, M. Ngan, and K. Hanaoka, "Face Recognition Vendor Test," *National Institute of Standards and Technology*, December 2019; T. Simonite, "The Best Algorithms Struggle to Recognize Black Faces Equally," *Wired*, July 22, 2019; A. Harmon, "As Cameras Track Detroit's Residents, a Debate Ensues over Racial Bias," *The New York Times*, July 8, 2019; "London's Police's Face Recognition System Gets It Wrong 81% of the Time," *MIT Technology Review*, July 4, 2019; S. Levin, "Half of US Adults Are Recorded in Police Facial Recognition Databases, Study Says," *The Guardian*, October 18, 2016.

Questions

1. Was the mistaken arrest of Mr. Williams the fault of the facial recognition technology itself, the process in which the technology was employed, the police investigation itself, or some combination of all three? Support your answer with specific examples.

2. Given that we badly need to replace user authentication with username and password credentials, are you comfortable having facial recognition technology used to authenticate you? (For example, using facial recognition to unlock your iPhone.) Why or why not?

3. Refer to Chapter 14. How do we remove bias from facial recognition technology algorithms?

monitored conditions. Signature recognition systems also match the speed and the pressure of the signature.

Something the user knows is an authentication mechanism that includes passwords and passphrases. **Passwords** present a huge information security problem in all organizations. Most of us have to remember numerous passwords for different online services, and we typically must choose complicated strings of characters to make them harder to guess. Passwords must effectively manage the tradeoff between convenience and security. For example, if passwords are 50 characters in length and include special symbols, they might keep your computer and its files safe, but they would be impossible to remember.

We have all bought into the idea that a password is sufficient to protect our data, as long as it is sufficiently elaborate. In reality, however, passwords by themselves can no longer protect us, regardless of how unique or complex we make them. In fact, security experts refer to passwords and PINs as a "double fail." First, they are easily stolen or hacked and easily forgotten. Second, they provide very poor security and a terrible customer experience at the same time.

Attackers employ a number of strategies to obtain our passwords, no matter how strong they are. They can guess them, steal them (with phishing or spear phishing attacks), crack them using brute force computation, or obtain them online. (*Brute force password cracking* means that a computer system tries all possible combinations of characters until a password is discovered.) Given these problems with passwords, what are users and businesses supposed to do?

To identify authorized users more efficiently and effectively, organizations are implementing more than one type of authentication, a strategy known as *multifactor authentication.* This system is particularly important when users log in from remote locations.

Single-factor authentication, which is notoriously weak, commonly consists simply of a password. Two-factor authentication consists of a password plus one type of biometric identification, such as a fingerprint. Three-factor authentication is any combination of three authentication methods.

Multifactor authentication is useful for several reasons. For example, voice recognition is effective when a user calls from an office but is less optimal when calling from a crowded subway or busy street. Similarly, fingerprint and iris scanners are effective when users are not busy with other tasks, but less than optimal when users are driving.

Multifactor authentication enables increasingly powerful security processes. For example, a quick fingerprint scan in a mobile banking app could enable a customer to access their account balance or perform other low-level functions. However, a request to transfer money, pay bills, or apply for a line of credit would trigger a request for voice or iris recognition. In most cases, the more factors the system uses, the more reliable it is. However, stronger authentication is also more expensive, and, as with strong passwords, it can be irritating to users.

Several initiatives are under way to improve the authentication process under the auspices of the Fast Identity Online (FIDO) alliance (**https://fidoalliance.org**). FIDO is an industry consortium that was created to address the inability of strong authentication devices to work together and the problems that users face in creating and remembering multiple usernames and passwords.

The concept underlying FIDO is that identifiers such as a person's fingerprint, iris scan, and the unique identifier of any USB device or contactless ring will not be sent over the Internet. Rather, they will be checked locally. The only data that will be transferred over the Internet are cryptographic keys that cannot be reverse-engineered to steal a person's identity. Let's consider Google's Trust API.

Google has announced a new way of securing Android apps called Trust API. Rather than using standard passwords, Trust API uses biometrics such as facial recognition, your typing pattern, and even how you walk to help determine that you are who you say you are. Each metric contributes to an overall "trust score" that will let you unlock your apps. The program will run in the background of an Android phone, using the phone's sensors to continuously monitor the user's behavior. If the trust score falls below a certain threshold, then a user might be prompted to provide additional authentication.

If you must use passwords, make them *strong passwords*, which are more difficult for hackers to discover. However, most of the standards that we use to determine the strength of passwords are wrong, according to Bill Burr, a former employee of the National Institute of Standards and Technology (NIST) and the man responsible for originally publishing the standards.

Burr asserted that long, easy-to-remember passphrases were the most valuable. A **passphrase** is a series of characters that is longer than a password but is still easy to memorize. Examples of passphrases are "maytheforcebewithyoualways" and "thisisasgoodasitgets."

In place of passwords and passphrases, security experts recommend the use of password managers. *Password managers* are software packages that provide users with the capability to generate unique, long, complex, easily changed passwords for their online accounts. These packages also offer the secure, encrypted storage of these passwords in either a local or cloud-based password vault. Users must provide a single master password to access the vault. By using a password manager, users do not have to memorize different passwords for all their online accounts.

However, if hackers access the password to the vault, then they have access to all the user's accounts. Therefore, many password managers provide two-factor authentication for additional security.

Authorization.   After users have been properly authenticated, the rights and privileges to which they are entitled on the organization's systems are established in a process called *authorization*. A **privilege** is a collection of related computer system operations that a user is authorized to perform. Companies typically base authorization policies on the principle of **least privilege**, which posits that users be granted the privilege for an activity only if there is a justifiable need for them to perform that activity.

Communications Controls

Communications controls (also called **network controls**) secure the movement of data across networks. Communications controls consist of firewalls, anti-malware systems, whitelisting and blacklisting, encryption, virtual private networks (VPNs), transport layer security (TLS), and employee monitoring systems.

Firewalls.   A **firewall** is a system that prevents a specific type of information from moving between untrusted networks, such as the Internet, and private networks, such as your company's network. Put simply, firewalls prevent unauthorized Internet users from accessing private networks. All messages entering or leaving your company's network pass through a firewall. The firewall examines each message and blocks those that do not meet specified security rules.

Firewalls range from simple, for home use, to very complex for organizational use. **Figure 4.3(a)** illustrates a basic firewall for a home computer. In this case, the firewall is implemented as software on the home computer. **Figure 4.3(b)** shows an organization that has implemented an external firewall, which faces the Internet, and an internal firewall, which

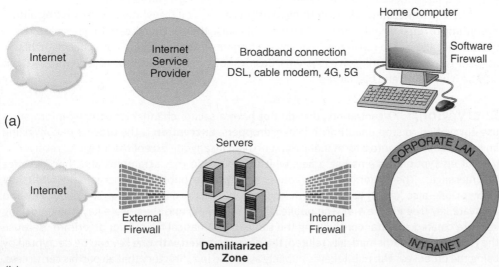

FIGURE 4.3   (a) **Basic firewall for a home computer. (b) Organization with two firewalls and a demilitarized zone.**

faces the company network. Corporate firewalls typically consist of software running on a computer dedicated to the task. A **demilitarized zone (DMZ)** is located between the two firewalls. Messages from the Internet must first pass through the external firewall. If they conform to the defined security rules, they are then sent to company servers located in the DMZ. These servers typically handle web page requests and e-mail. Any messages designated for the company's internal network—for example, its intranet—must pass through the internal firewall, again with its own defined security rules, to gain access to the company's private network.

The danger from viruses and worms is so severe that many organizations are placing firewalls at strategic points *inside* their private networks. In this way, if a virus or worm does get through both the external and internal firewalls, then the internal damage may be contained.

Anti-malware Systems.

Anti-malware systems, also called *antivirus* or *AV*, software, are software packages that attempt to identify and eliminate viruses and worms, and other malicious software. AV software is implemented at the organizational level by the IS department. Hundreds of AV software packages are currently available. Among the best known are Norton AntiVirus (**www.broadcom.com**), McAfee VirusScan (**www.mcafee.com**), and Trend Micro Maximum Security (**www.trendmicro.com**).

Anti-malware systems are generally reactive. Whereas firewalls filter network traffic according to categories of activities that are likely to cause problems, anti-malware systems filter traffic according to a database of specific problems. These systems create definitions, or signatures, of various types of malware and then update these signatures in their products. The anti-malware software then examines suspicious computer code to determine whether it matches a known signature. If the software identifies a match, then it removes the code. For this reason, organizations regularly update their malware definitions.

Because malware is such a serious problem, the leading vendors are rapidly developing anti-malware systems that function proactively as well as reactively. These systems evaluate behavior rather than relying entirely on signature matching. In theory, therefore, it is possible to catch malware before it can infect systems.

It is important to note that organizations must not rely only on anti-malware systems. The reason is that new types of malware are appearing too rapidly for such systems to keep pace. Therefore, multifactor authentication is critically important.

Whitelisting and Blacklisting.

A report by the Yankee Group (**www.451research .com**), a technology research and consulting firm, stated that 99 percent of organizations had installed anti-malware systems, but 62 percent still suffered malware attacks. As we have seen, anti-malware systems are usually reactive, and malware continues to infect companies.

One solution to this problem is **whitelisting**. Whitelisting is a process in which a company identifies the software that it will allow to run on its computers. Whitelisting permits acceptable software to run, and it either prevents any other software from running or lets new software run only in a quarantine environment until the company can verify its validity.

Whereas whitelisting allows nothing to run unless it is on the whitelist, **blacklisting** allows everything to run unless it is on the blacklist. A blacklist, then, includes certain types of software that are not allowed to run in the company environment. For example, a company might blacklist peer-to-peer file sharing on its systems. Besides software, people, devices, and websites can also be whitelisted and blacklisted.

Encryption.

Organizations that do not have a secure channel for sending information use encryption to stop unauthorized eavesdroppers. **Encryption** is the process of converting an original message into a form that cannot be read by anyone except the intended receiver.

All encryption systems use a key, which is the code that scrambles and then decodes the messages. The majority of encryption systems use public-key encryption. **Public-key encryption**—also known as *asymmetric encryption*—uses two different keys: a public key and a private key (see **Figure 4.4**). The public key (locking key) and the private key (the unlocking key) are created simultaneously using the same mathematical formula or algorithm. Because the two keys are mathematically related, the data encrypted with one key can be decrypted by using the other key. The public key is publicly available in a directory that all parties can access. The private key is kept secret, never shared with anyone, and never sent across the Internet. In this system, if Hannah wants to send a message to Harrison, she first obtains Harrison's public

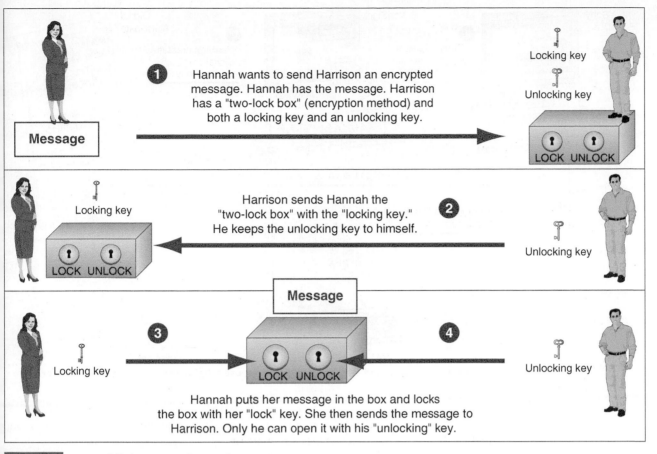

FIGURE 4.4   **How public-key encryption works.**

key (locking key), which she uses to encrypt her message (put the message in the "two-lock box"). When Harrison receives Hannah's message, he uses his private key to decrypt it (open the box).

Although this arrangement is adequate for personal information, organizations that conduct business over the Internet require a more complex system. In these cases, a third party, called a **certificate authority**, acts as a trusted intermediary between the companies. The certificate authority issues digital certificates and verifies the integrity of the certificates. A **digital certificate** is an electronic document attached to a file that certifies that the file is from the organization it claims to be from and has not been modified from its original format. As you can see in **Figure 4.5**, Sony requests a digital certificate from VeriSign, a certificate authority, and it uses this certificate when it conducts business with Dell. Note that the digital certificate contains an identification number, the issuer, validity dates, and the requester's public key. For examples of certificate authorities, see **www.entrust.com**, **www.verisign.com**, **www .cybertrust.com**, **www.secude.com**, and **www.thawte.com**.

Virtual Private Networking.   A **virtual private network (VPN)** is a private network that uses a public network (usually the Internet) to connect users. VPNs essentially integrate the global connectivity of the Internet with the security of a private network and thereby extend the reach of the organization's networks. VPNs are called *virtual* because they have no separate physical existence. They use the public Internet as their infrastructure. They are created by using logins, encryption, and other techniques to enhance the user's *privacy*, which we defined in Chapter 3 as the right to be left alone and to be free of unreasonable personal intrusion.

VPNs have several advantages. First, they allow remote users to access the company network. Second, they provide flexibility. That is, mobile users can access the organization's network from properly configured remote devices. Third, organizations can impose their security policies through VPNs. For example, an organization may dictate that only corporate e-mail applications are available to users when they connect from unmanaged devices.

To provide secure transmissions, VPNs use a process called *tunneling*. **Tunneling** encrypts each data packet to be sent and places each encrypted packet inside another packet. In this

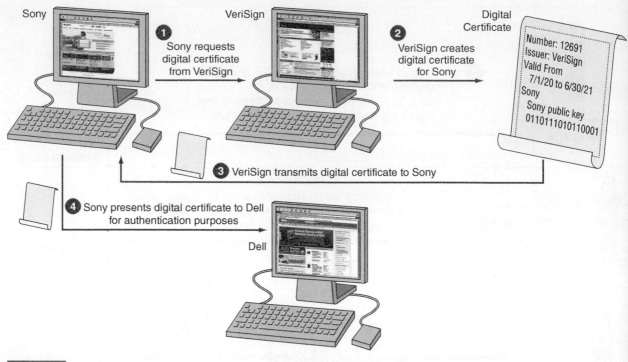

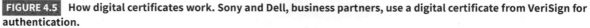

FIGURE 4.5 How digital certificates work. Sony and Dell, business partners, use a digital certificate from VeriSign for authentication.

manner, the packet can travel across the Internet with confidentiality, authentication, and integrity. **Figure 4.6** illustrates a VPN and tunneling.

Transport Layer Security.

Transport layer security (TLS), formerly called **secure socket layer (SSL)**, is an encryption standard used for secure transactions such as credit card purchases and online banking. TLS encrypts and decrypts data between a Web server and a browser end to end.

TLS is indicated by a URL that begins with "https" rather than "http," and it often displays a small padlock icon in the browser's status bar. Using a padlock icon to indicate a secure connection and placing this icon in a browser's status bar are artifacts of specific browsers. Other browsers use different icons; for example, a key that is either broken or whole. The important thing to remember is that browsers usually provide visual confirmation of a secure connection.

HRM Employee Monitoring Systems.

Many companies are taking a proactive approach to protecting their networks against what they view as one of their major security threats, namely, employee mistakes. These companies are implementing **employee monitoring systems**, which scrutinize their employees' computers, e-mail activities, and Internet

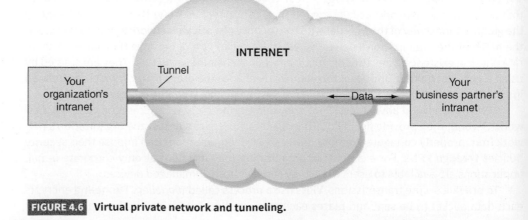

FIGURE 4.6 Virtual private network and tunneling.

surfing activities. These products are useful to identify employees who spend too much time surfing on the Internet for personal reasons, who visit questionable websites, or who download music illegally. Vendors that provide monitoring software include Veriato (**www.veriato.com**) and Forcepoint (**www.forcepoint.com**).

Before you go on...

1. What is the single most important information security control for organizations?
2. Differentiate between authentication and authorization. Which of these processes is always performed first?
3. Compare and contrast whitelisting and blacklisting.
4. What is the purpose of a disaster recovery plan?

What's in IT for me?

ACCT For the Accounting Major

Public companies, their accountants, and their auditors have significant information security responsibilities. Accountants are now being held professionally responsible for reducing risk, assuring compliance, eliminating fraud, and increasing the transparency of transactions according to Generally Accepted Accounting Principles (GAAP). The SEC and the Public Company Accounting Oversight Board (PCAOB), among other regulatory agencies, require information security, fraud prevention and detection, and internal controls over financial reporting. Forensic accounting, a combination of accounting and information security, is one of the most rapidly growing areas in accounting today.

FIN For the Finance Major

Because information security is essential to the success of organizations today, it is no longer the concern only of the CIO. As a result of global regulatory requirements and the passage of the Sarbanes–Oxley Act, responsibility for information security also lies with the CEO and CFO. Consequently, all aspects of the security audit, including the security of information and information systems, are a key concern for financial managers.

CFOs and treasurers are also increasingly involved with investments in information technology. They know that a security breach of any kind can have devastating financial effects on a company. Banking and financial institutions are prime targets for computer criminals. A related problem is fraud involving stocks and bonds that are sold over the Internet. Finance personnel must be aware of both the hazards and the available controls associated with these activities.

MKT For the Marketing Major

Marketing professionals have new opportunities to collect data on their customers; for example, through business-to-consumer electronic commerce. Customers expect their data to be properly secured. However, profit-motivated criminals want those data. Therefore, marketing managers must analyze the risk of their operations. Failure to protect corporate and customer data will cause significant public relations problems and make customers very angry. It can also lead to lawsuits, and it could cause companies to lose customers to competitors. CRM operations and tracking customers' online buying habits can expose data to misuse (if they are not encrypted) or result in privacy violations.

POM For the Production/Operations Management Major

Every process in a company's operations—inventory purchasing, receiving, quality control, production, and shipping—can be disrupted by an IT security breach either in the company or at a business partner. Any weak link in supply chain management or enterprise resource management systems puts the entire chain at risk. Companies may be held liable for IT security failures that impact other companies.

HRM For the Human Resource Management Major

HR managers have responsibilities to secure confidential employee data. They must also ensure that all employees explicitly verify that they understand the company's information security policies and procedures.

MIS For the MIS Major

The MIS function provides the security infrastructure that protects the organization's information assets. This function is critical to the success of the organization, even though it is almost invisible until an attack succeeds. All application development, network deployment, and introduction of new information technologies have to be guided by IT security considerations. MIS personnel must customize the risk exposure security model to help the company identify security risks and prepare responses to security incidents and disasters.

Senior executives of publicly held companies look to the MIS function for help in meeting Sarbanes–Oxley Act requirements, particularly in detecting "significant deficiencies" or "material weaknesses" in internal controls and remediating them. Other functional areas also look to the MIS function to help them meet their security responsibilities.

Summary

4.1 Identify the five factors that contribute to the increasing vulnerability of information resources, and specific examples of each factor.

The five factors are the following:

- Today's interconnected, interdependent, wirelessly networked business environment.
  - *Example*: The Internet
- Smaller, faster, cheaper computers and storage devices
  - *Examples*: Netbooks, thumb drives, iPads
- Decreasing skills necessary to be a computer hacker
  - *Example*: Information system hacking programs circulating on the Internet
- International organized crime taking over cybercrime
  - *Example*: Organized crime has formed transnational cybercrime cartels. Because it is difficult to know exactly where cyberattacks originate, these cartels are extremely hard to bring to justice.
- Lack of management support
  - *Example*: Suppose that your company spent $10 million on information security countermeasures last year, and they did not experience any successful attacks on their information resources. Short-sighted management might conclude that the company could spend less during the next year and obtain the same results. Bad idea.

4.2 Compare and contrast human mistakes and social engineering, along with specific examples of each one.

Human mistakes are unintentional errors. However, employees can also make unintentional mistakes as a result of actions by an attacker, such as social engineering. *Social engineering* is an attack through which the perpetrator uses social skills to trick or manipulate a legitimate employee into providing confidential company information.

An example of a human mistake is tailgating. An example of social engineering is when an attacker calls an employee on the phone and impersonates a superior in the company.

4.3 Discuss the 10 types of deliberate attacks.

The 10 types of deliberate attacks are the following:

Espionage or trespass occurs when an unauthorized individual attempts to gain illegal access to organizational information.

Information extortion occurs when an attacker either threatens to steal, or actually steals, information from a company. The perpetrator demands payment for not stealing the information, for returning stolen information, or for agreeing not to disclose the information.

Sabotage and vandalism are deliberate acts that involve defacing an organization's website, possibly causing the organization to lose its image and experience a loss of confidence by its customers.

Theft of equipment and information is becoming a larger problem because computing devices and storage devices are becoming smaller yet more powerful with vastly increased storage, making these devices easier and more valuable to steal.

Identity theft is the deliberate assumption of another person's identity, usually to gain access to his or her financial information or to frame him or her for a crime.

Preventing *compromises to intellectual property* is a vital issue for people who make their livelihood in knowledge fields. Protecting intellectual property is particularly difficult when that property is in digital form.

Software attacks occur when malicious software penetrates an organization's computer system. Today, these attacks are typically profit-driven and Web-based.

Alien software is clandestine software that is installed on a computer through duplicitous methods. It is typically not as malicious as viruses, worms, or Trojan horses, but it does use up valuable system resources.

Supervisory control and data acquisition refers to a large-scale distributed measurement and control system. SCADA systems are used to monitor or control chemical, physical, and transport processes. A *SCADA attack* attempts to compromise such a system to cause damage to the real-world processes that the system controls.

With both *cyberterrorism* and *cyberwarfare*, attackers use a target's computer systems, particularly through the Internet, to cause physical, real-world harm or severe disruption, usually to carry out a political agenda.

4.4 Describe the three risk-mitigation strategies and examples of each one in the context of owning a home.

The three risk-mitigation strategies are the following:

Risk acceptance, in which the organization accepts the potential risk, continues operating with no controls, and absorbs any damages that occur. If you own a home, you may decide not to insure it. Thus, you are practicing risk acceptance. Clearly, this is a bad idea.

Risk limitation, in which the organization limits the risk by implementing controls that minimize the impact of threats. As a homeowner, you practice risk limitation by putting in an alarm system or cutting down weak trees near your house.

Risk transference, in which the organization transfers the risk by using other means to compensate for the loss, such as by purchasing insurance. The vast majority of homeowners practice risk transference by purchasing insurance on their houses and other possessions.

4.5 Identify the three major types of controls that organizations can use to protect their information resources, along with an example of each one.

Physical controls prevent unauthorized individuals from gaining access to a company's facilities. Common physical controls include walls, doors, fencing, gates, locks, badges, guards, and alarm systems. More sophisticated physical controls include pressure sensors, temperature sensors, and motion detectors.

Access controls restrict unauthorized individuals from using information resources. These controls involve two major functions: authentication and authorization. Authentication confirms the identity of the person requiring access. An example is biometrics. After the person is authenticated (identified), the next step is authorization. Authorization determines which actions, rights, or privileges the person has, based on his or her verified identity. Authorization is generally based on least privilege.

Communications (network) controls secure the movement of data across networks. Communications controls consist of firewalls, anti-malware systems, whitelisting and blacklisting, encryption, virtual private networking, secure socket layer, and vulnerability management systems.

Chapter Glossary

access controls   Controls that restrict unauthorized individuals from using information resources and are concerned with user identification.

adware   Alien software designed to help pop-up advertisements appear on your screen.

alien software   Clandestine software that is installed on your computer through duplicitous methods.

anti-malware systems (antivirus software)   Software packages that attempt to identify and eliminate viruses, worms, and other malicious software.

audit   An examination of information systems, their inputs, outputs, and processing.

authentication   A process that determines the identity of the person requiring access.

authorization   A process that determines which actions, rights, or privileges the person has, based on verified identity.

biometrics   The science and technology of authentication (i.e., establishing the identity of an individual) by measuring the subject's physiological or behavioral characteristics.

blacklisting   A process in which a company identifies certain types of software that are not allowed to run in the company environment.

bot   A computer that has been compromised by, and under the control of, a hacker.

botnet   A network of computers that have been compromised by, and under control of, a hacker, who is called the botmaster.

business continuity   The chain of events linking planning to protection and to recovery.

certificate authority   A third party that acts as a trusted intermediary between computers (and companies) by issuing digital certificates and verifying the worth and integrity of the certificates.

communications controls (also network controls)   Controls that deal with the movement of data across networks.

controls   Defense mechanisms (also called *countermeasures*).

cookies   Small amounts of information that websites store on your computer, temporarily or more or less permanently.

copyright   A grant from a governmental authority that provides the creator of intellectual property with ownership of it for a specified period of time, currently the life of the creator plus 70 years.

cybercrime   Illegal activities executed on the Internet.

cyberterrorism   A premeditated, politically motivated attack against information, computer systems, computer programs, and data that results in violence against noncombatant targets by subnational groups or clandestine agents.

cyberwarfare   War in which a country's information systems could be paralyzed from a massive attack by destructive software.

demilitarized zone (DMZ)   A separate organizational local area network that is located between an organization's internal network and an external network, usually the Internet.

denial-of-service attack   A cyberattack in which an attacker sends a flood of data packets to the target computer with the aim of overloading its resources.

digital certificate   An electronic document attached to a file certifying that the file is from the organization it claims to be from and has not been modified from its original format or content.

distributed denial of service (DDoS) attack   A denial of service attack that sends a flood of data packets from many compromised computers simultaneously.

employee monitoring systems   Systems that monitor employees' computers, e-mail activities, and Internet surfing activities.

encryption   The process of converting an original message into a form that cannot be read by anyone except the intended recipient.

exposure   The harm, loss, or damage that can result if a threat compromises an information resource.

firewall   A system (either hardware, software, or a combination of both) that prevents a specific type of information from moving between untrusted networks, such as the Internet, and private networks, such as your company's network.

identity theft   Crime in which someone uses the personal information of others to create a false identity and then uses it fraudulently.

information security   Protecting an organization's information and information systems from unauthorized access, use, disclosure, disruption, modification, or destruction.

intellectual property   The intangible property created by individuals or corporations, which is protected under trade secret, patent, and copyright laws.

least privilege   A principle that users be granted the privilege for some activity only if there is a justifiable need to grant this authorization.

logic bombs   Segments of computer code embedded within an organization's existing computer programs.

malware   Malicious software such as viruses and worms.

network controls   See **communications controls**.

passphrase   A series of characters that is longer than a password but is still easy to memorize.

password   A private combination of characters that only the user should know.

patent   A document that grants the holder exclusive rights on an invention or process for a specified period of time, currently 20 years.

phishing attack   An e-mail attack that uses deception to fraudulently acquire sensitive personal information by masquerading as an official looking e-mail.

physical controls   Controls that restrict unauthorized individuals from gaining access to a company's computer facilities.

piracy   Copying a software program (other than freeware, demo software, etc.) without making payment to the owner.

privilege   A collection of related computer system operations that can be performed by users of the system.

public-key encryption   (also called *asymmetric encryption*) A type of encryption that uses two different keys: a public key and a private key.

ransomware   (or digital extortion) Malicious software that blocks access to a computer system or encrypts an organization's data until the organization pays a sum of money.

risk   The likelihood that a threat will occur.

risk management   A process that identifies, controls, and minimizes the impact of threats, in an effort to reduce risk to manageable levels.

secure socket layer (SSL)   See **transport layer security**

security   The degree of protection against criminal activity, danger, damage, or loss.

social engineering   Getting around security systems by tricking computer users inside a company into revealing sensitive information or gaining unauthorized access privileges.

spam   Unsolicited e-mail.

spamware   Alien software that uses your computer as a launch platform for spammers.

spear phishing   An attack in which the perpetrators find out as much information about an individual as possible to improve their chances that phishing techniques will obtain sensitive, personal information.

spyware   Alien software that can record your keystrokes or capture your passwords.

threat   Any danger to which an information resource may be exposed.

trade secret   Intellectual work, such as a business plan, that is a company secret and is not based on public information.

transport layer security (TLS)   An encryption standard used for secure transactions such as credit card purchases and online banking.

Trojan horse   A software program containing a hidden function that presents a security risk.

tunneling   A process that encrypts each data packet to be sent and places each encrypted packet inside another packet.

virtual private network (VPN)   A private network that uses a public network (usually the Internet) to securely connect users by using encryption.

virus   Malicious software that can attach itself to (or "infect") other computer programs without the owner of the program being aware of the infection.

vulnerability   The possibility that an information resource will be harmed by a threat.

whitelisting   A process in which a company identifies acceptable software and permits it to run, and either prevents anything else from running or lets new software run in a quarantined environment until the company can verify its validity.

worm   Destructive programs that replicate themselves without requiring another program to provide a safe environment for replication.

Discussion Questions

1. Why are computer systems so vulnerable?

2. Why should information security be a prime concern to management?

3. Is security a technical issue? A business issue? Both? Support your answer.

4. Compare information security in an organization with insuring a house.

5. Why are authentication and authorization important to e-commerce?

6. Why is cross-border cybercrime expanding rapidly? Discuss possible solutions.

7. What types of user authentication are used at your university or place of work? Do these measures seem to be effective? What if a higher level of authentication were implemented? Would it be worth it, or would it decrease productivity?

8. Why are federal authorities so worried about SCADA attacks?

Problem-Solving Activities

1. A critical problem is assessing how far a company is legally obligated to go in order to secure personal data. Because there is no such thing as perfect security (i.e., there is always more that one can do), resolving this question can significantly affect cost.

    a. When are security measures that a company implements sufficient to comply with its obligations?

    b. Is there any way for a company to know if its security measures are sufficient? Can you devise a method for any organization to determine if its security measures are sufficient?

2. Enter **www.scambusters.org**. Find out what the organization does. Learn about e-mail scams and website scams. Report your findings.

4. Visit **www.dhs.gov** (Department of Homeland Security). Search the site for "National Strategy to Secure Cyberspace" and write a report on their agenda and accomplishments to date.

5. Enter **www.alltrustnetworks.com** and other vendors of biometrics. Find the devices they make that can be used to control access into information systems. Prepare a list of products and major capabilities of each vendor.

6. Software piracy is a global problem. Access the following websites: **www.bsa.org** and **www.microsoft.com/piracy**. What can organizations do to mitigate this problem? Are some organizations dealing with the problem better than others?

7. Investigate the Sony PlayStation Network hack that occurred in April 2011.

    a. What type of attack was it?

    b. Was the success of the attack due to technology problems at Sony, management problems at Sony, or a combination of both? Provide specific examples to support your answer.

    c. Which Sony controls failed?

    d. Could the hack have been prevented? If so, how?

    e. Discuss Sony's response to the hack.

    f. Describe the damages that Sony incurred from the hack.

8. Investigate the Equifax hacks in 2017.

    a. What type of attack was it?

    b. What actions should Equifax have taken to prevent the breaches? Provide specific examples to support your answer.

    c. Place yourself as a victim in the Equifax breaches. What should you do when you are notified (or when you think) that your personal data has been compromised?

    d. In light of the Equifax breaches, should all consumers have the option to opt out of credit bureaus? Why or why not?

Closing Case

MIS Successful Operations against Cybercrime

European Authorities and Encrochat

Beginning in 2017, an international coalition of law enforcement agencies infiltrated a chat platform used by organized crime syndicates. The suspects all communicated through Encrochat, an encrypted service that required specialized phones to operate. Investigators did not try to break the encryption. Instead, they installed malware on the phones themselves that allowed officials to read messages before they were encrypted and sent.

The suspects used modified Android phones that Encrochat advertised as guaranteeing "perfect anonymity." Encrochat physically removed the GPS, camera, USB, and microphone functions from the phones so that users could not be recorded or traced through the devices. Further, the company installed dual operating systems on each device—standard Android as well as the Encrochat system—so the phones could appear as normal devices. The phones also had a function that allowed them to be wiped completely when a user entered a certain PIN.

Authorities monitored and investigated more than 100 million messages in real time sent between Encrochat users, leading to arrests in the United Kingdom, Norway, Sweden, France, and the Netherlands. By July 3, 2020, UK agencies had arrested 746 suspects and seized 77 guns, 2 metric tons of drugs, 28 million illicit pills, 55 "high value" cars, and more than $67 million in cash. Dutch agencies had arrested more than 100 suspects and seized more than 8,000 kilograms of cocaine, 1,200 kilograms of crystal meth, dozens of guns and luxury cars, and almost $22.5 million in cash.

After attempting to recover from the attack, Encrochat determined that the attack originated from a nation-state. The company decided to shut down and advised users to power off and physically dispose of their phones.

Almost immediately after the arrests began, other encrypted phone companies started to advertise for Encrochat customers. A company called Omerta offered 10 percent off to "communicate with impunity."

Microsoft and the Necurs Botnet

In March 2020 Microsoft and partners from 35 countries disrupted a botnet, called Necurs, behind the world's largest cybercrime network. The botnet was behind stock scams, fake pharmaceutical spam emails, "Russian dating" scams, and financial malware and ransomware distribution. Authorities believe that Russian cybercriminals operated the botnet.

To disrupt Necurs, Microsoft analyzed a technique that the botnet used to generate new domains through an algorithm. The firm then predicted more than 6 million domains that would be created in the next two years. It reported these domains to registries around the world, enabling authorities to block them.

FBI and WeLeakInfo

The website Have I Been Pwned (**www.haveibeenpwned.com**) maintains a massive database of leaked user credentials so that victims can see if they are impacted. The criminal versions of this website are sites such as WeLeakInfo, which takes that same data breach data and sells them for very low prices to hackers who want to exploit exposed user credentials. In January 2020 the FBI (**www.fbi.gov**) seized WeLinkInfo, which had brokered 12 billion records.

Dutch and Northern Irish police arrested two men in connection with the website. The FBI had previously taken down LeakedSource, which operated similarly to WeLeakInfo. However, other comparable sites remained online.

U.S. Department of Justice and Child Pornography Website

In October 2019 the U.S. Department of Justice (DOJ) (**www.justice.gov**) announced that it had taken down the massive Dark Web child pornography site Welcome to Video, which was a Tor network-based site that accepted Bitcoin. The site had operated from June 2015 until March 2018, generating and distributing exploitative content. Note: The delay from March 2018 until October 2019 emphasizes the length of time often necessary to prepare a criminal case.

The takedown resulted from investigators tracing Bitcoin transactions. The investigation began by examining illegal transactions involving virtual currency on the Dark Web. By following the funds on a blockchain (discussed in Chapter 7), investigators uncovered the extent of users on the Welcome to Video site.

Authorities gathered evidence in two ways: they examined the Welcome to Video website, and they followed the money. When they examined the website, they found two unconcealed Internet Protocol (IP) addresses (see Chapter 6) managed by a South Korean Internet service provider. The IP addresses were assigned to an account that provided service to the site operator's home address.

To follow the money, agents sent small amounts of Bitcoin—roughly $125 to $290—to the Bitcoin wallets that Welcome to Video listed for payments. Because the Bitcoin blockchain leaves all transactions visible and verifiable, the agents could observe the virtual currency in these wallets being transferred to another wallet. They learned from a Bitcoin exchange that the second wallet was registered to the site's operator with his personal phone number and one of his personal email addresses. Agents found the physical server in his home that was running the website, along with more than 1 million addresses of the site's users.

A U.S. federal grand jury indicted the site's operator. South Korean officials had already arrested him on separate charges related to child sexual abuse, and he was serving his sentence there.

Officials around the world arrested a total of 337 Welcome to Video users in 23 U.S. states, Washington D.C., and 11 other countries. Authorities seized 250,000 unique videos. These authorities, in conjunction with the National Center for Missing and Exploited Children, analyzed the videos and rescued at least 23 children who were being abused by site participants. Investigators continue to analyze the videos to identify more children and perpetrators of exploitation.

U.S. Department of Justice and BEC Scammers

Business email compromise (BEC) schemes involve creating compelling scam emails, often purporting to be from senior executives. These emails trick employees, customers, or vendors into wiring payment for goods or services to alternate bank accounts. BEC scammers are well known to quickly adapt to major global news themes and use them to legitimize their fake emails. For example, they quickly integrated COVID-19 pandemic themes into their messages.

The FBI has noted that between June 2016 and July 2019 there have been more than 166,000 domestic and international reports of email fraud resulting in more than $26 billion in losses. A large proportion of BEC scams originates from the West African nation of Nigeria. The scams have been reported in all 50 U.S. states and in 177 countries. BEC schemes include traditional email scamming, tax fraud, check fraud, gift card scams, and many others.

In September 2019 the U.S. Department of Justice (**www.justice.gov**) announced the arrests of 281 suspects in connection with BEC scams and wire fraud. The action was the largest of its kind to date against this type of scammer. The investigation took four months to carry out across 10 countries, and it resulted in the seizure of almost $4 million in cash. In all, 167 arrests were carried out in Nigeria, 74 in the United States, 18 in Turkey, and 15 in Ghana, plus several more in other countries.

French Authorities, Avast, and the Retadup Malware Gang

In August 2019 antivirus company Avast (**www.avast.com**) and the French National Gendarmerie announced that they had taken down the IT infrastructure of the Retadup malware gang. Retadup malware had infected Windows personal computers and servers across more than 140 countries, with the majority of the infections occurring in Latin America. Significantly, more than 85 percent of the infected machines had no antivirus software installed.

The gang used the processing power of the infected machines to mine for monero cryptocurrency, an illegal process called cryptojacking. *Cryptojacking* is the unauthorized use of any computing device by cybercriminals to mine for cryptocurrency.

In March 2019 security analysts at Avast traced an increase in stealthy cryptocurrency mining infections to a type of malware called Retadup. The analysts also studied the command-and-control communications used to control infected computers. Avast alerted France's national cybercrime investigation team, C3N, that servers in France appeared to be hosting the majority of the command-and-control infrastructure for distributing the malware and controlling infected machines. C3N secured judicial cooperation with the FBI, and in July 2019 authorities seized control of the servers in both France and the United States. Avast researchers had discovered a design flaw in Retadup's command-and-control communications protocol. This flaw enabled authorities to instruct the malware to delete itself from all 850,000 infected computers.

Security researchers from data breach monitoring service and prevention service Under the Breach (**www.underthebreach.com**) were able to track down the Retadup author's real world identity. However, as of September 2020 it was unclear if authorities had arrested anyone who was involved in this operation.

Sources: Compiled from J. Cox, "How Police Secretly Took over a Global Phone Network for Organized Crime," *Motherboard*, July 2, 2020; K. Cox, "Police Infiltrate Encrypted Phones, Arrest Hundreds in Organized Crime Bust," *Ars Technica*, July 2, 2020; F. Abbasi, "COVID-19 Themed BEC Scams," *Trustwave*, April 15, 2020; J. Murdock, "Botnet Linked to Criminals in Russia that Infected 9 Million Computers to Spew Spam and Malware Is Disrupted," *Newsweek*, March 11, 2020; C. Fisher, "Microsoft Disrupts a Botnet that Infected 9 Million Computers," *Engadget*, March 10, 2020; B. Barrett, "How Microsoft Dismantled the Infamous Necurs Botnet," *Wired*, March 10, 2020; C. Cimpanu, "FBI Seizes WeLeakInfo, a Website that Sold Access to Breached Data," *ZDNet*, January 17, 2020; B. Barrett, "FBI Takes Down Site with 12 Billion Stolen Records," *Wired*, January 10, 2020; P. LeBlanc, "Justice Department Announces Takedown of the 'Largest' Darknet Child Pornography Site," *CNN*, October 16, 2019; L. Newman, "How a Bitcoin Trail Led to a Massive Dark Web Child-Porn Site Takedown," *Wired*, October 16, 2019; L. Newman, "281 Alleged Email Scammers Arrested in Massive Global Sweep," *Wired*, September 18, 2019; M. Schwartz, "Police Trick Malware Gang into Disinfecting 850,000 Systems," *Bank Info Security*, August 28, 2019; C. Cimpanu, "Avast and French Police Take over Botnet and Disinfect 850,000 Computers," *ZDNet*, August 28, 2019; "A Multimillion-Dollar Criminal Crypto-Mining Ecosystem Has Been Uncovered," *MIT Technology Review*, March 25, 2019.

Questions

1. Describe the various methods that authorities used in the vignettes in this case to stop illegal cyberactivity and apprehend suspects.

2. Were these methods technical, behavioral, or a combination of both? Provide examples to support your answer.

CHAPTER 5

Data and Knowledge Management

Opening Case

MIS Our Genetic Data: A Double-Edged Sword

Personal data is an umbrella term referring to our names, addresses, phone numbers, Social Security numbers, and health and financial records, along with social media posts, location data, search-engine queries, and a myriad of other personal details. These data are highly sensitive because their misuse impacts all of us so severely: for example, identity theft, extortion, financial loss, loss of privacy, and many other negative consequences.

A major challenge associated with keeping our personal data safe is that a variety of entities collect them. In some instances, companies collect, analyze, and sell our personal data without our knowledge or consent. Recall our discussion of data aggregators in Chapter 3.

Sometimes, we provide our data willingly and knowingly, even though the specifics appear in lengthy, hard-to-read terms-of-service agreements. For example, with Google and Facebook, the consumer can use each platform's functions for free in return for allowing the companies to monetize our data by targeting us with advertisements.

In recent years, scientists have been able to discover genetic data, which is the most personal type of data for each of us. *Genetic data* refers to the inherited characteristics located in our chromosomal deoxyribonucleic acid (DNA) or ribonucleic acid (RNA). Each of us has a unique genome, which comprises our complete set of DNA, including all of our genes. As with all of our personal data, the problems with our genetic data are: Who has collected it? Who is collecting it now? Who has it? What are they doing with it?

As a result of patients taking a more proactive role in their health care, direct-to-consumer (DTC) laboratory testing is becoming increasingly popular. DTC genetic tests allow consumers to access information about their genetics without involving their health-care professionals.

As of July 2020 the International Society of Genetic Genealogy (**www.isogg.org**) listed 33 DTC companies that are performing genetic testing. More than 12 million people around the world have utilized the services of one of these companies, such as 23andMe (**www.23andme .com**). How does this process work? Basically, you send a vial of saliva along with a fee to 23andMe. In return, you receive a report that includes (a) the proportion of your DNA that comes from each of 45 global genetic populations, (b) the origins of your maternal and paternal ancestors, and (c) a feature that allows you to connect with DNA relatives, if you opt in. The report also contains health-care information such as DNA that might not affect your health but could affect the health of your children as well as how your DNA can influence your chances of contracting certain diseases.

In 2010, GEDmatch (**www.gedmatch.com**) was founded to help amateur and professional genealogists and adoptees searching for birth parents. Users could upload their DNA profiles from DTC companies to identify relatives who had also uploaded their profiles. Participants could hide their names by using aliases. Each account, however, had to include an associated email address. GEDmatch provided results such as the closest matches to a user's DNA and the estimated number of generations to a common ancestor. By December 2019 more than 1 million people had uploaded their profiles to the site.

Solving Crimes (The Good News)

The police began using GEDmatch to solve crimes, particularly cold cases. A cold case is an unsolved criminal investigation which remains active pending the discovery of new evidence. Until the authorities began using commercial genetic databases to assist with their detective work, the only DNA officially available to them were records of DNA samples provided by individuals involved with the justice system; that is, suspects and convicted criminals. This process of using commercial genetic databases led to an ongoing debate regarding public safety versus privacy concerns—in essence, the good news and the bad news about the use of our genetic data. Let's look closely at forensic genealogy.

Forensic genealogy is the practice of analyzing genetic data from DTC companies or from companies such as GEDmatch for the purpose of identifying suspects or victims in criminal cases. Forensic genealogy uses *genetic genealogy*, which is the use of DNA tests in combination with traditional genealogical methods to infer biological relationships between and among individuals. Traditional genealogical methods include the study of families and family history by conducting oral interviews and researching records such as birth and marriage certificates, census data, and newspaper obituaries. The process combines data from those techniques with data from modern sources such as social media platforms, particularly Facebook.

To use forensic genealogy, law enforcement agencies have uploaded crime-scene DNA data to genetic companies to locate possible relatives of potential suspects. Genealogy experts then assemble family trees and analyze demographic identifiers. One company, Parabon NanoLabs (**www.parabon-nanolabs.com**), is a leader in the use of forensic genealogy as an investigative tool.

After law enforcement agencies have identified potential suspects through forensic genealogy, they use conventional investigative methods such as comparing present physical features to past eyewitness statements and police sketches. This process can often narrow down the choices to a few candidates.

Solving Cold Cases - Example 1

In 1987 a young woman left her family home for what was supposed to be a quick trip with her boyfriend. They did not return the next day, as planned. After several days, her body was found. She had been shot. Two days later, his body was found 75 miles away. He had been strangled. Police found the van they were driving in a third location.

The police collected a semen sample from the woman's pants. By 1994, DNA analysis had advanced to the point that the semen could produce a genetic profile of the suspect. In 2003, investigators uploaded the profile to CODIS, the FBI's criminal DNA database. The investigators hoped for a match, but CODIS did not return one.

In 2017, a detective who was examining the department's cold cases heard that there was a way to obtain more information from DNA. He contacted Parabon. Genealogists there used the 30-year-old DNA sample and found two of the eventual suspect's second cousins: one on his father's side of the family, and one on his mother's side. The firm's lead genealogist used newspaper archives and marriage records to build a family tree dating back to the two cousins' great-grandparents. She then found a particular couple who lived about 7 miles from where the boyfriend's body was found.

The genealogist concentrated on that couple's only son—who would have been 24 at the time of the murders—as a suspect. Next, an undercover officer who had begun watching the suspect picked up a cup that had fallen off his truck. The DNA from the cup and the DNA from a cheek swab provided by the suspect once in custody matched the DNA gathered 30 years before. He was convicted and sentenced to serve two life sentences concurrently. As of July 2020 he was appealing the verdict.

Solving Cold Cases - Example 2

The trail of the Golden State Killer had gone cold decades ago. The police linked him to more than 50 rapes and at least 12 murders from 1976 to 1986 but he eluded all attempts to find him. However, the police had retrieved a DNA sample from one of the crime scenes and had carefully preserved it over the years.

When the police heard about GEDmatch, they uploaded the suspect's DNA sample. After four months of close examination, GEDmatch provided matches to relatives of the suspect, although not the suspect himself. Because the site did provide family trees, genealogists were able to find third cousins of the suspect. After examining the family tree to find a common ancestor of the third cousins, they proceeded back down the tree to identify a likely suspect. In addition to the DNA evidence, some of his victims had described him as a 5'9", 165-pound white male, characteristics that matched his features.

In April 2018 the police arrested the suspect, who was then 72 years old and a former police officer. His DNA matched the sample taken in an earlier crime. In June 2020 he pled guilty to several counts of first-degree murder and in August the court sentenced him to 11 consecutive life sentences without the possibility of parole.

Privacy Concerns (The Bad News)

The use of open-source genetic databases has ignited a debate regarding the Fourth Amendment. This amendment states that a warrant is required in situations that violate an individual's reasonable expectations of privacy. Given the sensitivity of information surrounding commercial genetic databases, especially regarding familial associations, courts have asserted that individuals are subject to protection under the Fourth Amendment.

Privacy advocates protested that law enforcement agencies were accessing the entire GEDmatch database without the informed consent of the users. As a result, GEDmatch began to require its customers to specifically opt in to allow law enforcement agencies to access their genetic data. The agencies objected, claiming that GEDmatch's policy change would make it much more difficult to identify suspects and solve cold cases using genetic genealogy.

In September 2019 the U.S. Department of Justice (**www.justice .gov**) released interim guidelines stating that federal investigators could use forensic genealogy to discover suspects only in serious crimes such as murder and rape. The guidelines also stated that federal investigators must have a search warrant to collect DNA samples from a suspect's relatives, who must have previously opted in to allow law enforcement agencies to access their genetic data. Because the DOJ is a federal agency, these guidelines did not apply to state or local law enforcement agencies.

In December 2019 forensic for-profit DNA analysis company Verogen (www.verogen.com) bought GEDmatch. Verogen's CEO asserted that the site would focus on solving crimes, not just connecting family members through their DNA. He further stated that current and future users would have the ability to opt out of criminal DNA searches and that Verogen would fight "future attempts to access the data of those who have not opted in."

Forensic genealogists then began using Family Tree DNA (www.familytreedna.com) due to the increased difficulty involved in obtaining genetic profiles from Verogen. Family Tree's policy dictates that customers are automatically opted in unless they choose to opt out.

Sources: Compiled from S. Bradbury, "Killer Sentenced to Life in Prison in 1980 Colorado Cold Case Solved with DNA," *The Denver Post*, July 1, 2020; J. Chamary, "How Genetic Genealogy Helped Catch the Golden State Killer," *Forbes*, June 30, 2020; H. Murphy and T. Arango, "Joseph DeAngelo Pleads Guilty in Golden State Killer Cases," *New York Times*, June 29, 2020; S. Gilgore, "The Reston Company Cracking Cold Police Cases Is Coming to Your TV," *Washington Business Journal*, May 6, 2020; E. Ruiz, "40-Year-Old Cold Case Solved with New Genetic Genealogy Technology," *The Denver Channel*, March 6, 2020; D. Geiger, "Trucker Pleads Guilty to 21-Year-Old Woman's 40-Year-Old Cold Case Murder," Oxygen.com, February 25, 2020; "GEDmatch Sold, Will Serve as 'Molecular Witness' for Police," *The Crime Report*, December 10, 2019; H. Murphy, "Genealogy Sites Have Helped Identify Suspects. Now They've Helped Convict One." *New York Times*, July 1, 2019; "GEDmatch Puts DNA Database Off-Limits to Police: Will Cold Cases Get Colder?" *The Crime Report*, May 22, 2019; P. Aldhous, "This Genealogy Database Helped Solve Dozens of Crimes. But Its New Privacy Rules Will Restrict Access by Cops," *BuzzFeed News*, May 19, 2019; P. Aldhous, "The Arrest of a Teen on an Assault Charge Has Sparked New Privacy Fears about DNA Sleuthing," *BuzzFeed*, May 14, 2019; J. Lepola, "A Closer Look at Solving Crimes with the Help of Genetic Genealogy," *Sinclair Broadcast Group*, May 14, 2019; L. Matsakis, "The Wired Guide to Personal Data (and Who Is Using It)," *Wired*, February 15, 2019; "The Genomic Data Challenges of the Future," *The Medical Futurist*, October 27, 2018; D. Barry, T. Arango, and R. Oppel, "The Golden State Killer Left a Trail of Horror with Taunts and Guile," *New York Times*, April 28, 2018; G. Kolata and H. Murphy, "The Golden State Killer Is Tracked through a Thicket of DNA, and Experts Shudder," *New York Times*, April 27, 2018.

Questions

1. Should we be willing to sacrifice our privacy to solve crimes? In other words, does the end justify the means?

2. You are a candidate for a position at a company. Discuss the positive and negative consequences of that company having access to your DNA results.

3. Would you be willing to have your DNA results made available to law enforcement agencies to help in solving a criminal case? Why or why not? Support your answer.

Introduction

Information technologies and systems support organizations in managing—that is, acquiring, organizing, storing, accessing, analyzing, and interpreting—data. As you noted in Chapter 1, when these data are managed properly, they become *information* and then *knowledge*. Information and knowledge are invaluable organizational resources that can provide any organization with a competitive advantage.

So, just how important are data and data management to organizations? From confidential customer information (see this chapter's opening case) to intellectual property to financial transactions to social media posts, organizations possess massive amounts of data that are critical to their success. Of course, to benefit from these data, they need to manage it effectively. This type of management, however, comes at a huge cost. According to Symantec's (www.symantec.com) State of Information survey, digital information costs organizations worldwide more than $1 trillion annually. In fact, it makes up roughly *half* of an organization's total value. The survey found that large organizations spend an average of $40 million annually to maintain and use data, and small-to-medium-sized businesses spend almost $350,000.

This chapter examines the processes whereby data are transformed first into information and then into knowledge. Managing data is critical to all organizations. Few business professionals are comfortable making or justifying business decisions that are not based on solid information. This is especially true today, when modern information systems make access to that information quick and easy. For example, there are information systems that format data in a way that managers and analysts can easily understand. Consequently, these professionals can access these data themselves and then analyze the data according to their needs. The result is useful *information*. Managers can then apply their experience to use this information to address a business problem, thereby producing *knowledge*. Knowledge management, enabled by information technology, captures and stores knowledge in forms that all organizational employees can access and apply, thereby creating the flexible, powerful "learning organization."

Organizations store data in databases. Recall from Chapter 1 that a *database* is a collection of related data files or tables that contain data. We discuss databases in Section 5.2, focusing on the relational database model. In Section 5.6, we take a look at the fundamentals of relational database operations.

Clearly, data and knowledge management are vital to modern organizations. But, why should *you* learn about them? The reason is that you will play an important role in the development of database applications. The structure and content of your organization's database depend on how users (meaning you) define your business activities. For example, when database developers in the firm's MIS group build a database, they use a tool called *entity-relationship (ER) modeling*. This tool creates a model of how users view a business activity. When you understand how to create and interpret an ER model, then you can evaluate whether the developers have captured your business activities correctly.

Keep in mind that decisions about data last longer, and have a broader impact, than decisions about hardware or software. If decisions concerning hardware are wrong, then the equipment can be replaced relatively easily. If software decisions turn out to be incorrect, they can be modified, though not always painlessly or inexpensively. Database decisions, in contrast, are much harder to undo. Database design constrains what the organization can do with its data for a long time. Remember that business users will be stuck with a bad database design, while the programmers who created the database will quickly move on to their next projects.

Furthermore, consider that databases typically underlie the enterprise applications that users access. If there are problems with organizational databases, then it is unlikely that any applications will be able to provide the necessary functionality for users. Databases are difficult to set up properly and to maintain. They are also the component of an information system that is most likely to receive the blame when the system performs poorly and the least likely to be recognized when the system performs well. This is why it is so important to get database designs right the first time—and you will play a key role in these designs.

You might also want to create a small personal database using a software product such as Microsoft Access. If so, you will need to be familiar with at least the basics of the product.

After the data are stored in your organization's databases, they must be accessible in a form that helps users make decisions. Organizations accomplish this objective by developing *data warehouses.* You should become familiar with data warehouses because they are invaluable decision-making tools. We discuss data warehouses in Section 5.4.

You will also make extensive use of your organization's knowledge base to perform your job. For example, when you are assigned a new project, you will likely research your firm's knowledge base to identify factors that contributed to the success (or failure) of previous, similar projects. We discuss knowledge management in Section 5.5.

You begin this chapter by examining the multiple challenges involved in managing data. You then study the database approach that organizations use to help address these challenges. You turn your attention to Big Data, which organizations must manage in today's business environment. Next, you study data warehouses and data marts, and you learn how to use them for decision making. You conclude the chapter by examining knowledge management.

5.1   Managing Data

Author Lecture Videos are available exclusively in *WileyPLUS.*
Apply the Concept activities are available in the Appendix and in *WileyPLUS.*

All IT applications require data. These data should be of high quality, meaning that they should be accurate, complete, timely, consistent, accessible, relevant, and concise. Unfortunately, the process of acquiring, keeping, and managing data is becoming increasingly difficult.

The Difficulties of Managing Data

Because data are processed in several stages and often in multiple locations, they are frequently subject to problems and difficulties. Managing data in organizations is difficult for many reasons.

1. The amount of data is increasing exponentially with time. Much historical data must be kept for a long time, and new data are added rapidly. For example, to support millions of

customers, large retailers such as Walmart must manage many petabytes of data. (A petabyte is approximately 1,000 terabytes, or trillions of bytes; see Technology Guide 1.)

2. Data are also scattered throughout organizations, and they are collected by many individuals using various methods and devices. These data are frequently stored in numerous servers and locations and in different computing systems, databases, formats, and human and computer languages.

   MIS Organizations have developed information systems for specific business processes, such as transaction processing, supply chain management, and customer relationship management. The ISs that specifically support these processes impose unique requirements on data, which leads to repetition and conflicts across the organization. For example, the marketing function might maintain information on customers, sales territories, and markets. These data might be duplicated within the billing or customer service functions. This arrangement can produce inconsistent data within the enterprise. Inconsistent data prevent a company from developing a unified view of core business information—data concerning customers, products, finances, and so on—across the organization and its information systems. This situation refers to data silos.

   A **data silo** is a collection of data held by one group that is not easily accessible by other groups. Data silos hinder the process of gaining actionable insights from organizational data, create barriers to an overall view of the enterprise and its data, and delay digital transformation efforts (see Chapter 1). One major method to remove data silos is through cloud data management (see Technology Guide 3 for a complete discussion of cloud computing).

3. Another problem is that data are generated from multiple sources: internal sources (for example, corporate databases and company documents); personal sources (for example, personal thoughts, opinions, and experiences); and external sources (for example, commercial databases, government reports, and corporate websites).

   Some of these data sources are in the form of *data streams*, which are data that are continuously generated by point-of-sale systems, clickstream data, social media, and sensors. We take a brief look at these data streams here.

   - **POM** *Point-of-sale data*. Organizations capture data from each customer purchase with their POS systems. Clerks (or customers themselves using self-checkout) use bar code scanners to scan each item purchased. POS systems collect data in real time, such as the name, product identification number, and unit price of each item; the total amount of all items purchased; the sales tax on that amount; the payment method used; a time stamp of the purchase; and many other data points.

   - **MKT** *Clickstream data*. Clickstream data are those data that visitors and customers produce when they visit a website and click on hyperlinks (described in Chapter 6). Clickstream data include the terms that the visitor to the website entered into a search engine to reach that website, all links that users click, how long they spend on each page, if they click the "back" button, if they add or remove items from a shopping cart, and many other data points.

   - **MKT** *Social media data*. Social media data (also called social data) are the data collected from individuals' activity on social media websites, including Facebook, YouTube, LinkedIn, Twitter, and many others. These data include shares, likes and dislikes, ratings, reviews, recommendations, comments, and many other examples.

   - *Sensor data*. The Internet of Things (IoT; see Chapter 8) is a system in which any object, natural or manmade, contains internal or external wireless sensor(s) that communicate with each other without human interaction. Each sensor monitors and reports data on physical and environmental conditions around it, such as temperature, sound, pressure, vibration, and movement. Sensors can also control physical systems, such as opening and closing a valve and adjusting the fuel mixture in your car. (See our discussion of supervisory control and data acquisition (SCADA) systems in Chapter 4.)

As with all technology, being able to collect massive amounts of data from many different sources is a double-edged sword. IT's About Business 5.1 shows how a startup company helps organizations make sense of the vast amounts of data available to them.

IT's About Business 5.1

MIS FIN What to Do with All that Data?

Today, capturing data is easy, and storing those data is relatively inexpensive. For this reason, an increasing number of companies are turning to Enigma to help them make sense of their data.

Founded in 2011, Enigma (**www.enigma.com**) is a data management and business intelligence company that specializes in data integration and analytics. The firm can rapidly make sense of multiple disconnected, disparate public and private data sources for a variety of uses. The company collects, cleans, organizes, integrates, and analyzes data from thousands of sources around the world with the use of machine learning algorithms (see Chapter 14).

Enigma differentiates itself from other platforms such as Amazon, Google, and Facebook. The company asserts that these firms apply machine learning to Big Data to "get people to click on things." In contrast, Enigma defines its mission as fundamentally changing how businesses function by collecting data from diverse sources and modeling how the world operates with machine learning algorithms.

The company began by collecting publicly available data, such as Federal Aviation Administration flight logs (**www.faa.gov**), university research publications, business filings, shipping manifests, the Census Bureau (**www.census.gov**), the Federal Communications Commission (**www.fcc.gov**), the Federal Election Commission (**www.fec.gov**), the Internet Revenue Service (**www.irs.gov**), the U.S. Customs & Border Protection agency (CBP; **www.cbp.gov**), and building permits.

The company then moved on to complex, hard-to-find data. For example, using Freedom of Information Act (FOIA) requests, they were able to access the CBP's Automated Manifest System to track every container ship arriving in the United States, including the importer and the ship's port of call. From the National Fire Incident Reporting System (**www.nfirs.fema.gov/NFIRSWeb/login**), they retrieved the cause and location of every fire in the country. To address energy, they collected oil well data from the Railroad Commission of Texas (**www.rrc.state.tx.us**), founded in 1891 to establish tariffs. From New York City's Metropolitan Transportation Authority (**www.new.mta.info**), they were able to access years of rail incident and injury data.

At the same time Enigma was accessing numerous disparate data sources, it was also developing machine learning algorithms to integrate data from these sources and analyze those data for insights. Let's look at several examples.

- **FIN** Consider the financial services industry. Banks integrate Enigma's data with customer data stored in their own systems to help them recognize fraud more quickly. For instance, Enigma helps American Express with its anti-money-laundering operations.

  As another example, to help banks accurately identify the best candidates for small business loans, Enigma integrates property tax filing data with state business filings and Uniform Commercial Code liens to produce credit ratings for each candidate.

- Pharmaceutical companies use Enigma's data and insights to improve drug safety. Specifically, Enigma has collected data on every molecule used by the U.S. pharmaceutical industry, as well as all drug trials, patent filings, and adverse events.

- **FIN** If a hedge fund wants to determine which restaurant chains have the potential to grow the fastest, Enigma can check FCC logs for radio licenses, which are required to open drive-through windows.

- Insurers ask Enigma to perform risk assessment. For example, if insurers want to avoid underwriting in risky fire zones, Enigma integrates and analyzes data sets on emergency call logs and building permits.

  MetLife (**www.metlife.com**) is one of the largest global providers of insurance, annuities, and employee benefit programs, with 90 million customers located in 60 countries. The company's insurance group integrates Enigma data gathered from public health systems and universities with its own data to improve its underwriting process. *Underwriting* is the process of accepting liability under an insurance policy, thus guaranteeing payment in case loss or damage occurs. MetLife's $588 billion investment management group is using Enigma data to quantify how the quality of restaurants, parks, and community event spaces affects real estate prices.

- Consider voter registration data in the United States, a public data set. These data are difficult to access and equally difficult to structure. Enigma works with this data set to help companies in the consumer packaged goods (CPG) industry place products such as drinks and soups. The startup bases their recommendations on where people live, their driving distance from businesses, and many other data points.

Not all of Enigma's machine learning algorithms target profits. For example, the firm has volunteered its applications toward studying the gender salary gap across 558 occupations. It has discovered that some of the most serious disparities occur in accounting, retail, and sales.

Enigma is also working with Polaris (**www.polarisproject .org**), a nonprofit, nongovernmental organization (NGO) that combats and prevents slavery and human trafficking. Interestingly, Enigma works with banks in this area, helping them catch people, because banks are required by regulations to do so, and banks incur liabilities when human traffickers conduct transactions in their networks.

Enigma notes that it has always been difficult for banks to share data, principally due to privacy concerns. Therefore, Enigma, along with Polaris, has deployed a crowdsourcing tool that many banks are using to share information on slavery and human trafficking. The tool is private to the banking industry because Enigma and Polaris do not want suspected traffickers to discover details about it.

As of July 2020 Enigma had integrated 100,000 data sets in more than 100 countries, organized data on 30 million small businesses, and accumulated 140 billion data points on the U.S. population. Analysts estimate the firm's valuation to be $750 million with annual revenue around $30 million.

Sources: Compiled from E. Williams, "Where Insights Meet Privacy: Privacy-Preserving Machine Learning," *Forbes*, July 2, 2020; "10 Emerging Tech Companies Showcase Inventive Products and Services," *Business Wire*, June 25, 2020; R. Sarfin, "Data Integration and Machine Learning: 3 Real-World Use Cases," *Syncsort*, August 6, 2019; D. Costa, "How Enigma Is Using Big Data to Fight Human Trafficking," *PC Magazine*, June 10, 2019; A. Gara, "Data's Cartographers," *Forbes*, February

28, 2019; "Angel Nguyen Swift: It Is All about the Data," *ACAMS Today*, January 24, 2019; "Why We're Joining the Fight against Human Trafficking," *Medium.com*, December 4, 2018; "BB&T Announces Fintech Investment in Enigma," *PR Newswire*, September 18, 2018; A. Patnaik, "Data Integration and Machine Learning: A Natural Synergy," *tdwi.org*, August 18, 2017; M. Richardson, "Using Machine Learning Techniques to Automate Data Integration," *IT Toolbox*, May 31, 2017; **www.enigma .com**, accessed July 14, 2020.

Questions

(look ahead to Section 5.2 for the definitions of structured and unstructured data)

1. Provide examples of structured data that Enigma collects and analyzes.
2. Provide examples of unstructured data that Enigma collects and analyzes.

4. Adding to these problems is the fact that new sources of data such as blogs, podcasts, tweets, Facebook posts, YouTube videos, texts, and RFID tags and other wireless sensors are constantly being developed, and the data these technologies generate must be managed. Also, the data become less current over time. For example, customers move to new addresses or they change their names, companies go out of business or are bought, new products are developed, employees are hired or fired, and companies expand into new countries.

5. Data are also subject to *data rot.* Data rot refers primarily to problems with the media on which the data are stored. Over time, temperature, humidity, and exposure to light can cause physical problems with storage media and thus make it difficult to access data. The second aspect of data rot is that finding the machines needed to access the data can be difficult. For example, it is almost impossible today to find 8-track players to listen to music on. Consequently, a library of 8-track tapes has become relatively worthless, unless you have a functioning 8-track player or you convert the tapes to a more modern medium such as DVDs.

6. Data security, quality, and integrity are critical, yet they are easily jeopardized. Legal requirements relating to data also differ among countries as well as among industries, and they change frequently.

7. **ACCT** **FIN** Two other factors complicate data management. First, federal regulations— for example, the Sarbanes–Oxley Act of 2002—have made it a top priority for companies to better account for how they are managing information. Sarbanes–Oxley requires that (1) public companies evaluate and disclose the effectiveness of their internal financial controls, and (2) independent auditors for these companies agree to this disclosure. The law also holds CEOs and CFOs personally responsible for such disclosures. If their companies lack satisfactory data management policies and fraud or a security breach occurs, then the company officers could be held liable and face prosecution.

   Second, companies are drowning in data, much of which are unstructured. As you have seen, the amount of data is increasing exponentially. To be profitable, companies must develop a strategy for managing these data effectively. (See IT's About Business **5.1**.)

8. An additional problem with data management is Big Data. Big Data is so important that we devote Section 5.3 to this topic.

Data Governance

To address the numerous problems associated with managing data, organizations are turning to data governance. **Data governance** is an approach to managing information across an entire organization. It involves a formal set of business processes and policies that are designed to ensure that data are handled in a certain, well-defined fashion. That is, the organization follows unambiguous rules for creating, collecting, handling, and protecting its information. The objective is to make information available, transparent, and useful for the people who are authorized to access it, from the moment it enters an organization until it becomes outdated and is deleted.

One strategy for implementing data governance is master data management. **Master data management** is a process that spans all of an organization's business processes and applications. It provides companies with the ability to store, maintain, exchange, and synchronize a consistent, accurate, and timely "single version of the truth" for the company's master data.

Master data are a set of core data, such as customer, product, employee, vendor, geographic location, and so on, that span the enterprise's information systems. It is important to distinguish between master data and transactional data. **Transactional data**, which are generated and captured by operational systems, describe the business's activities, or *transactions*. In contrast, master data are applied to multiple transactions, and they are used to categorize, aggregate, and evaluate the transactional data.

Let's look at an example of a transaction. You (Mary Jones) purchase one Samsung 42-inch LCD television, part number 1234, from Bill Roberts at Best Buy, for $2,000, on April 20, 2017. In this example, the master data are "product sold," "vendor," "salesperson," "store," "part number," "purchase price," and "date." When specific values are applied to the master data, then a transaction is represented. Therefore, transactional data would be, respectively, "42-inch LCD television," "Samsung," "Bill Roberts," "Best Buy," "1234," "$2,000," and "April 20, 2017."

An example of master data management is Dallas, Texas, which implemented a plan for digitizing the city's public and private records, such as paper documents, images, drawings, and video and audio content. The master database can be used by any of the 38 government departments that have appropriate access. The city is also integrating its financial and billing processes with its customer relationship management program. (You will learn about customer relationship management in Chapter 11.)

How will Dallas use this system? Imagine that the city experiences a water-main break. Before it implemented the system, repair crews had to search City Hall for records that were filed haphazardly. Once the workers found the hard-copy blueprints, they would take them to the site and, after examining them manually, would decide on a plan of action. In contrast, the new system delivers the blueprints wirelessly to the laptops of crews in the field, who can magnify or highlight areas of concern to generate a rapid response. This process reduces the time it takes to respond to an emergency by several hours.

Along with data governance, organizations use the database approach to efficiently and effectively manage their data. We discuss the database approach in Section 5.2.

Before you go on...

1. What are some of the difficulties involved in managing data?
2. Define *data governance*, *master data*, and *transactional data*.

5.2   The Database Approach

Author Lecture Videos are available exclusively in *WileyPLUS*.
Apply the Concept activities are available in the Appendix and in *WileyPLUS*.

From the mid-1950s, when businesses first adopted computer applications, until the early 1970s, organizations managed their data in a *file management environment*. This environment evolved because organizations typically automated their functions one application at a time. Therefore, the various automated systems developed independently from one another, without any overall planning. Each application required its own data, which were organized in a data file.

A **data file** is a collection of logically related records. In a file management environment, each application has a specific data file related to it. This file contains all of the data records the application requires. Over time, organizations developed numerous applications, each with an associated application-specific data file.

For example, imagine that most of your information is stored in your university's central database. In addition, however, a club to which you belong maintains its own files, the athletics department has separate files for student athletes, and your instructors maintain grade data on their personal computers. It is easy for your name to be misspelled in one of these databases or files. Similarly, if you move, then your address might be updated correctly in one database or file but not in the others.

Using databases eliminates many problems that arose from previous methods of storing and accessing data, such as file management systems. Databases are arranged so that one set

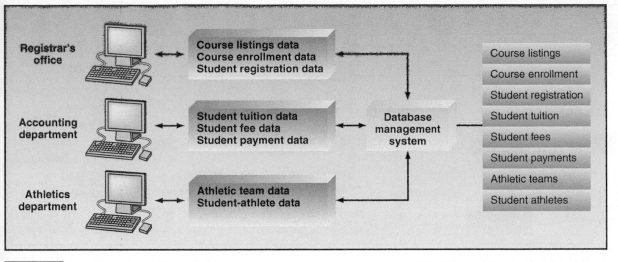

of software programs—the database management system—provides all users with access to all of the data. (You will study database management systems later in this chapter.) Database systems minimize the following problems:

- *Data redundancy*: The same data are stored in multiple locations.
- *Data isolation*: Applications cannot access data associated with other applications.
- *Data inconsistency*: Various copies of the data do not agree.

Database systems also maximize the following:

- *Data security*: Because data are "put in one place" in databases, there is a risk of losing a lot of data at one time. Therefore, databases must have extremely high security measures in place to minimize mistakes and deter attacks.
- *Data integrity*: Data meet certain constraints; for example, there are no alphabetic characters in a Social Security number field.
- *Data independence*: Applications and data are independent of one another; that is, applications and data are not linked to each other, so all applications are able to access the same data.

Figure 5.1 illustrates a university database. Note that university applications from the registrar's office, the accounting department, and the athletics department access data through the database management system.

A database can contain vast amounts of data. To make these data more understandable and useful, they are arranged in a hierarchy. We take a closer look at this hierarchy in the next section.

The Data Hierarchy

Data are organized in a hierarchy that begins with bits and proceeds all the way to databases (see **Figure 5.2**). A **bit** (*binary digit*) represents the smallest unit of data a computer can process. The term *binary* means that a bit can consist only of a 0 or a 1. A group of eight bits, called a **byte**, represents a single character. A byte can be a letter, a number, or a symbol. A logical grouping of characters into a word, a small group of words, or an identification number is called a **field**. For example, a student's name in a university's computer files would appear in the "name" field, and her or his Social Security number would appear in the "Social Security number" field. Fields can contain data other than text and numbers, such as an image, or any other type of multimedia. Examples are a motor vehicle department's licensing database that contains a driver's photograph, or a field that contains a voice sample to authorize access to a secure facility.

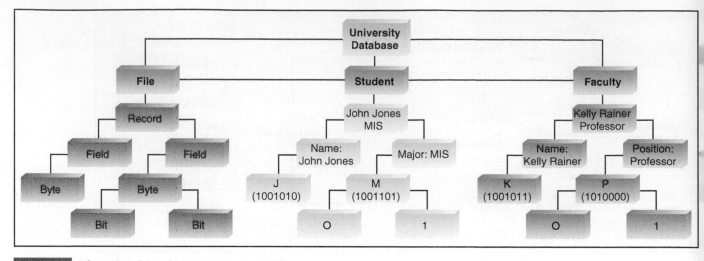

FIGURE 5.2 Hierarchy of data for a computer-based file.

A logical grouping of related fields, such as the student's name, the courses taken, the date, and the grade, comprises a **record**. In the Apple iTunes Store, a song is a field in a record, with other fields containing the song's title, its price, and the album on which it appears. A logical grouping of related records is called a data file or a **table**. For example, a grouping of the records from a particular course, consisting of course number, professor, and students' grades, would constitute a data file for that course. Continuing up the hierarchy, a logical grouping of related files constitutes a *database*. Using the same example, the student course file could be grouped with files on students' personal histories and financial backgrounds to create a student database. In the next section, you will learn about relational database models.

The Relational Database Model

A **database management system (DBMS)** is a set of programs that provide users with tools to create and manage a database. Managing a database refers to the processes of adding, deleting, accessing, modifying, and analyzing data that are stored in a database. An organization can access these data by using query and reporting tools that are part of the DBMS or by utilizing application programs specifically written to perform this function. DBMSs also provide the mechanisms for maintaining the integrity of stored data, managing security and user access, and recovering information if the system fails. Because databases and DBMSs are essential to all areas of business, they must be carefully managed.

There are a number of different database architectures, but we focus on the relational database model because it is popular and easy to use. Other database models—for example, the hierarchical and network models —are the responsibility of the MIS function and are not used by organizational employees. Popular examples of relational databases are Microsoft Access and Oracle.

Most business data—especially accounting and financial data—traditionally were organized into simple tables consisting of columns and rows. Tables enable people to compare information quickly by row or column. Users can also retrieve items rather easily by locating the point of intersection of a particular row and column.

The **relational database model** is based on the concept of two-dimensional tables. A relational database generally is not one big table—usually called a *flat file*—that contains all of the records and attributes. Such a design would entail far too much data redundancy. Instead, a relational database is usually designed with a number of related tables. Each of these tables contains records (listed in rows) and attributes (listed in columns).

To be valuable, a relational database must be organized so that users can retrieve, analyze, and understand the data they need. A key to designing an effective database is the data model. A **data model** is a diagram that represents entities in the database and their relationships. An **entity** is a person, a place, a thing, or an event—such as a customer, an employee, or a product—about which an organization maintains information. Entities can typically be identified in the user's work environment. A record generally describes an entity. An **instance** of an entity refers to each row in a relational table, which is a specific, unique representation of the entity. For example, your university's student database contains an entity called "student." An instance of the student entity would be a particular student. Thus, you are an instance of the student entity in your university's student database.

Each characteristic or quality of a particular entity is called an **attribute**. For example, if our entities were a customer, an employee, and a product, entity attributes would include customer name, employee number, and product color.

Consider the relational database example about students diagrammed in **Figure 5.3**. The table contains data about the entity called students. As you can see, each row of the table corresponds to a single student record. (You have your own row in your university's student database.) Attributes of the entity are student name, undergraduate major, grade point average, and graduation date. The rows are the records on Sally Adams, John Jones, Jane Lee, Kevin Durham, Juan Rodriguez, Stella Zubnicki, and Ben Jones. Of course, your university keeps much more data on you than our example shows. In fact, your university's student database probably keeps hundreds of attributes on each student.

Every record in the database must contain at least one field that uniquely identifies that record so that it can be retrieved, updated, and sorted. This identifier field (or attribute) is called the **primary key**. For example, a student record in a U.S. university would use a unique student number as its primary key. (*Note:* In the past, your Social Security number served as the primary key for your student record. However, for security reasons, this practice has been discontinued.) In Figure 5.3, Sally Adams is uniquely identified by her student ID of 012345.

In some cases, locating a particular record requires the use of secondary keys. A **secondary key** is another field that has some identifying information but typically does not identify the record with complete accuracy. For example, the student's major might be a secondary key if a user wanted to identify all of the students majoring in a particular field of study. It should not be the primary key, however, because many students can have the same major. Therefore, it cannot uniquely identify an individual student.

A **foreign key** is a field (or group of fields) in one table that uniquely identifies a row of another table. A foreign key is used to establish and enforce a link between two tables. We discuss foreign keys in Section 5.6.

Organizations implement databases to efficiently and effectively manage their data. There are a variety of operations that can be performed on databases. We look at three of these operations in detail in Section 5.6: query languages, normalization, and joins.

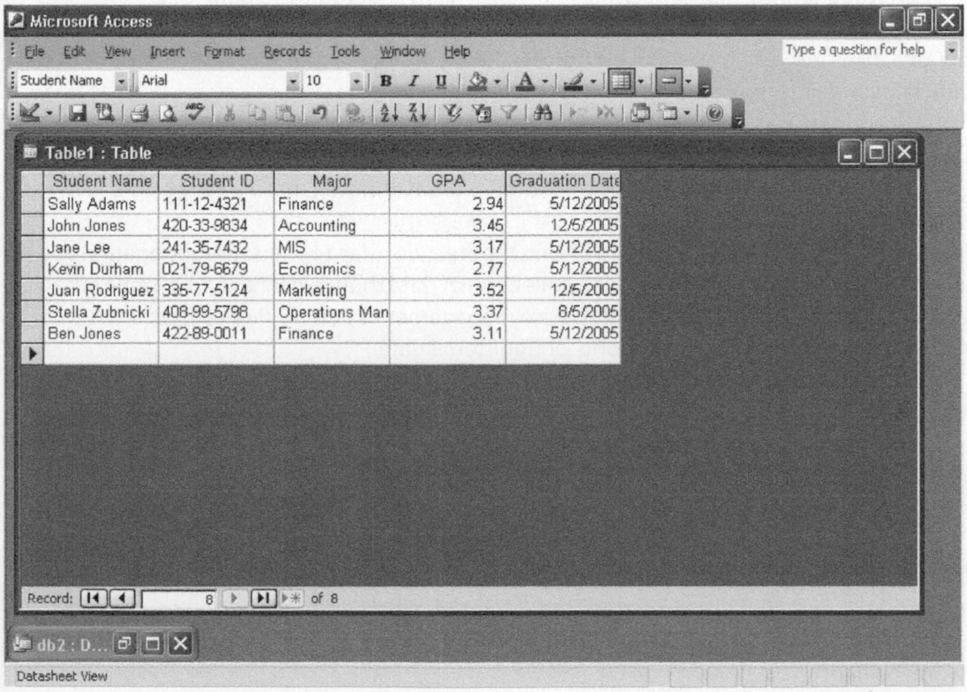

Student Name	Student ID	Major	GPA	Graduation Date
Sally Adams	111-12-4321	Finance	2.94	5/12/2005
John Jones	420-33-9834	Accounting	3.45	12/5/2005
Jane Lee	241-35-7432	MIS	3.17	5/12/2005
Kevin Durham	021-79-6679	Economics	2.77	5/12/2005
Juan Rodriguez	335-77-5124	Marketing	3.52	12/5/2005
Stella Zubnicki	408-99-5798	Operations Man	3.37	8/5/2005
Ben Jones	422-89-0011	Finance	3.11	5/12/2005

FIGURE 5.3 **Student database example.**

As we noted earlier in this chapter, organizations must manage huge quantities of data. Such data consist of structured and unstructured data and are called Big Data (discussed in Section 5.3). **Structured data** is highly organized in fixed fields in a data repository such as a relational database. Structured data must be defined in terms of field name and type (e.g., alphanumeric, numeric, and currency). **Unstructured data** refers to data that do not reside in a traditional relational database. Examples of unstructured data are e-mail messages, word processing documents, videos, images, audio files, PowerPoint presentations, Facebook posts, Tweets, Snaps, ratings and recommendations, and web pages. Industry analysts estimate that 80 to 90 percent of the data in an organization are unstructured. To manage Big Data, many organizations are using special types of databases, which we also discuss in Section 5.3.

Because databases typically process data in real time (or near real time), it is not practical to allow users access to the databases. After all, the data will change while the user is looking at them! As a result, data warehouses have been developed to allow users to access data for decision making. You will learn about data warehouses in Section 5.4.

Before you go on...

1. What is a data model?
2. What is a primary key? A secondary key?
3. What is an entity? An attribute? An instance?
4. What are the advantages and disadvantages of relational databases?

5.3 Big Data

Author Lecture Videos are available exclusively in *WileyPLUS*.
Apply the Concept activities are available in the Appendix and in *WileyPLUS*.

We are accumulating data and information at an increasingly rapid pace from many diverse sources. In fact, organizations are capturing data about almost all events, including events that, in the past, firms never used to think of as data at all—for example, a person's location, the vibrations and temperature of an engine, and the stress at numerous points on a bridge—and then analyzing those data.

Organizations and individuals must process a vast amount of data that continues to increase dramatically. According to IDC (a technology research firm; **www.idc.com**), the world generates over one zettabyte (10^{21} bytes) of data each year. Furthermore, the amount of data produced worldwide is increasing by 50 percent each year.

As recently as the year 2000, only 25 percent of the stored information in the world was digital. The other 75 percent was analog; that is, it was stored on paper, film, vinyl records, and the like. By 2020, the amount of stored information in the world was more than 98 percent digital and less than 2 percent nondigital.

As we discussed at the beginning of this chapter, we refer to the superabundance of data available today as Big Data. **Big Data** is a collection of data that is so large and complex that it is difficult to manage using traditional database management systems. (We capitalize *Big Data* to distinguish the term from large amounts of traditional data.)

Essentially, Big Data is about predictions (see Predictive Analytics in Chapter 12). Predictions do not come from "teaching" computers to "think" like humans. Instead, predictions come from applying mathematics to huge quantities of data to infer probabilities. Consider these examples:

- The likelihood that an e-mail message is spam
- The likelihood that the typed letters "teh" are supposed to be "the"
- The likelihood that the direction and speed of a person jaywalking indicates that he will make it across the street in time, meaning that a self-driving car need only slow down slightly

Big Data systems perform well because they contain huge amounts of data on which to base their predictions. Moreover, these systems are configured to improve themselves over time by searching for the most valuable signals and patterns as more data are input.

Defining Big Data

It is difficult to define Big Data. Here we present two descriptions of the phenomenon. First, the technology research firm Gartner (**www.gartner.com**) defines Big Data as diverse, high-volume, high-velocity information assets that require new forms of processing in order to enhance decision making, lead to insights, and optimize business processes. Second, the Big Data Institute (TBDI; **https://thebigdatainstitute.wordpress.com**) defines Big Data as vast datasets that:

- Exhibit variety;
- Include structured, unstructured, and semistructured data;
- Are generated at high velocity with an uncertain pattern;
- Do not fit neatly into traditional, structured, relational databases; and
- Can be captured, processed, transformed, and analyzed in a reasonable amount of time only by sophisticated information systems.

Big Data generally consists of the following:

- Traditional enterprise data—for example, customer information from customer relationship management systems, transactional enterprise resource planning data, Web store transactions, operations data, and general ledger data.
- Machine-generated/sensor data—for example, smart meters; manufacturing sensors; sensors integrated into smartphones, automobiles, airplane engines, and industrial machines; equipment logs; and trading systems data.
- Social data—for example, customer feedback comments; microblogging sites such as Twitter; and social media sites such as Facebook, YouTube, and LinkedIn.
- Images captured by billions of devices located throughout the world, from digital cameras and camera phones to medical scanners and security cameras.

Let's take a look at a few specific examples of Big Data:

- Facebook's 2.45 billion users upload more than 350 million new photos every day. They also click a "like" button or leave a comment more than 5 billion times every day. Facebook's data warehouse stores more than 300 petabytes of data, and the platform receives 600 terabytes of incoming data per day.
- The 2 billion users of Google's YouTube service upload more than 300 hours of video per minute. Google itself processes on average more than 70,000 search queries per second.
- In July 2020 industry analysts estimated that Twitter users sent some 550 million tweets per day.
- Autonomous cars generate up to 20 terabytes of data per car per day.

Characteristics of Big Data

Big Data has three distinct characteristics: volume, velocity, and variety. These characteristics distinguish Big Data from traditional data:

1. *Volume*: We have noted the huge volume of Big Data. Consider machine-generated data, which are generated in much larger quantities than nontraditional data. For example, sensors in a single jet engine can generate 10 terabytes of data in 30 minutes. (See our discussion of the Internet of Things in Chapter 8.) With more than 25,000 airline flights per day, the daily volume of data from just this single source is incredible. Smart electrical meters, sensors in heavy industrial equipment, and telemetry from automobiles compound the volume problem.

2. *Velocity*: The rate at which data flow into an organization is rapidly increasing. Velocity is critical because it increases the speed of the feedback loop between a company, its customers, its suppliers, and its business partners. For example, the Internet and mobile technology enable online retailers to compile histories not only on final sales, but on their customers' every click and interaction. Companies that can quickly use that information—for example, by recommending additional purchases—gain competitive advantage.

3. *Variety*: Traditional data formats tend to be structured and relatively well described, and they change slowly. Traditional data include financial market data, point-of-sale transactions, and much more. In contrast, Big Data formats change rapidly. They include satellite imagery, broadcast audio streams, digital music files, web page content, scans of government documents, and comments posted on social networks.

Irrespective of their source, structure, format, and frequency, Big Data are valuable. If certain types of data appear to have no value today, it is because we have not yet been able to analyze them effectively. For example, several years ago when Google began harnessing satellite imagery, capturing street views, and then sharing these geographical data for free, few people understood its value. Today, we recognize that such data are incredibly valuable because analyses of Big Data yield deep insights. We discuss analytics in detail in Chapter 12.

Issues with Big Data

Despite its extreme value, Big Data does have issues. In this section, we take a look at data integrity, data quality, and the nuances of analysis that are worth noting.

Big Data Can Come from Untrusted Sources.   As we discussed earlier, one of the characteristics of Big Data is variety, meaning that Big Data can come from numerous, widely varied sources. These sources may be internal or external to the organization. For example, a company might want to integrate data from unstructured sources such as e-mails, call center notes, and social media posts with structured data about its customers from its data warehouse. The question is, how trustworthy are those external sources of data? For example, how trustworthy is a Tweet? The data may come from an unverified source. Furthermore, the data itself, reported by the source, may be false or misleading.

Big Data Is Dirty.   *Dirty data* refers to inaccurate, incomplete, incorrect, duplicate, or erroneous data. Examples of such problems are misspelling of words, and duplicate data such as retweets or company press releases that appear multiple times in social media.

Suppose a company is interested in performing a competitive analysis using social media data. The company wants to see how often a competitor's product appears in social media outlets as well as the sentiments associated with those posts. The company notices that the number of positive posts about the competitor is twice as great as the number of positive posts about itself. This finding could simply be a case of the competitor pushing out its press releases to multiple sources; in essence, blowing its own horn. Alternatively, the competitor could be getting many people to retweet an announcement.

Big Data Changes, Especially in Data Streams.   Organizations must be aware that data quality in an analysis can change, or the data themselves can change, because the conditions under which the data are captured can change. For example, imagine a utility company that analyzes weather data and smart-meter data to predict customer power usage. What happens when the utility is analyzing these data in real time and it discovers that data are missing from some of its smart meters?

Managing Big Data

Big Data makes it possible to do many things that were previously much more difficult; for example, to spot business trends more rapidly and accurately, to prevent disease, to track crime, and so on. When Big Data is properly analyzed, it can reveal valuable patterns and information that were previously hidden because of the amount of work required to discover them. Leading corporations, such as Walmart and Google, have been able to process Big Data for years, but only at great expense. Today's hardware, cloud computing (see Technology Guide 3), and open-source software make processing Big Data affordable for most organizations.

For many organizations the first step toward managing data was to integrate information silos into a database environment and then to develop data warehouses for decision making. An *information silo* is an information system that does not communicate with other related information systems in an organization. After they completed this step, many organizations turned their attention to the business of information management—making sense of their rapidly expanding data. In recent years, Oracle, IBM, Microsoft, and SAP have spent billions of dollars purchasing software firms that specialize in data management and business analytics. (You will learn about business analytics in Chapter 12.)

In addition to existing data management systems, today many organizations employ NoSQL databases to process Big Data. Think of them as "not only SQL" (structured query language) databases. (We discuss SQL in section 5.6.)

As you have seen in this chapter, traditional relational databases such as Oracle and MySQL store data in tables organized into rows and columns. Recall that each row is associated with a unique record, and each column is associated with a field that defines an attribute of that account.

In contrast, NoSQL databases can manipulate structured as well as unstructured data as well as inconsistent or missing data. For this reason, NoSQL databases are particularly useful when working with Big Data. Hadoop and MapReduce are particularly useful when analyzing massive databases.

Hadoop (**http://hadoop.apache.org**) is not a type of database. Rather, it is a collection of programs that allow people to store, retrieve, and analyze very large data sets using massively parallel processing. *Massively parallel processing* is the coordinated processing of an application by multiple processors that work on different parts of the application, with each processor utilizing its own operating system and memory. As such, Hadoop enables users to access NoSQL databases, which can be spread across thousands of servers, without a reduction in performance. For example, a large database application that could take 20 hours of processing time on a centralized relational database system might take only a few minutes when using Hadoop's parallel processing.

MapReduce refers to the software procedure of dividing an analysis into pieces that can be distributed across different servers in multiple locations. MapReduce first distributes the analysis (map) and then collects and integrates the results back into a single report (reduce).

Many products use NoSQL databases, including Cassandra (**http://cassandra.apache .org**), CouchDB (**http://couchdb.apache.org**), and MongoDB (**www.mongodb.org**). Let's take a look at how eHarmony uses Redis's (**www.redis.io**) in-memory NoSQL database. An in-memory database is a DBMS that primarily relies on main memory (see Technology Guide 1) for data storage, in contrast to DBMSs that use hard-drive storage.

eHarmony (**www.eharmony.com**) uses Oracle's DBMS for cold data and Redis for hot data. *Cold data* refers to the storage of relatively inactive data that does not have to be accessed frequently or rapidly. *Hot data* refers to data that must be accessed frequently and rapidly. The eHarmony matching system applies analytics in near real time to quickly pair a candidate with a best-case potential match. Quickly serving up compatible matches requires rapid searches of personality trait data (i.e., Redis used with hot data). eHarmony's back-end business operations do not require high-speed access to data and therefore use Oracle with cold data.

Putting Big Data to Use

Modern organizations must manage Big Data and gain value from it. They can employ several strategies to achieve this objective.

Making Big Data Available.

Making Big Data available for relevant stakeholders can help organizations gain value. For example, consider open data in the public sector. Open data are accessible public data that individuals and organizations can use to create new businesses and solve complex problems. In particular, government agencies gather vast amounts of data, some of which are Big Data. Making those data available can provide economic benefits. In fact, an Open Data 500 study at the GovLab at New York University discovered 500 examples of U.S.-based companies whose business models depend on analyzing open government data.

Enabling Organizations to Conduct Experiments.

Big Data allows organizations to improve performance by conducting controlled experiments. For example, Amazon (and many other companies such as Google and LinkedIn) constantly experiments by offering slightly different looks on its website. These experiments are called A/B experiments, because each experiment has only two possible outcomes. Here is an example of an A/B experiment at Etsy (**www.etsy.com**), an online marketplace for vintage and handmade products.

MKT When Etsy analysts noticed that one of its web pages attracted customer attention but failed to maintain it, they looked more closely at the page and discovered that it had few "calls to action." (A call to action is an item, such as a button, on a web page that enables a customer to do something.) On this particular Etsy page, customers could leave, buy, search, or click on two additional product images. The analysts decided to show more product images on the page.

Consequently, one group of visitors to the page saw a strip across the top of the page that displayed additional product images. Another group saw only the two original product images. On the page with additional images, customers viewed more products and, significantly, bought more products. The results of this experiment revealed valuable information to Etsy.

Microsegmentation of Customers.

Segmentation of a company's customers means dividing them into groups that share one or more characteristics. Microsegmentation simply means dividing customers up into very small groups, or even down to the individual customer.

MKT For example, Paytronix Systems (**www.paytronix.com**) provides loyalty and rewards program software for thousands of different restaurants. Paytronix gathers restaurant guest data from a variety of sources beyond loyalty and gift programs, including social media. Paytronix analyzes this Big Data to help its restaurant clients microsegment their guests. Restaurant managers are now able to more precisely customize their loyalty and gift programs. Since they have taken these steps, they are noting improved profitability and customer satisfaction in their restaurants.

POM Creating New Business Models.

Companies are able to use Big Data to create new business models. For example, a commercial transportation company operated a substantial fleet of large long-haul trucks. The company recently placed sensors on all of its trucks. These sensors wirelessly communicate sizeable amounts of information to the company, a process called *telematics*. The sensors collect data on vehicle usage—including acceleration, braking, cornering, and so on—in addition to driver performance and vehicle maintenance.

By analyzing this Big Data, the company was able to improve the condition of its trucks through near-real-time analysis that proactively suggested preventive maintenance. The company was also able to improve the driving skills of its operators by analyzing their driving styles.

The transportation company then made its Big Data available to its insurance carrier. Using this data, the insurance carrier was able to perform a more precise risk analysis of driver behavior and the condition of the trucks. The carrier then offered the transportation company a new pricing model that lowered its premiums by 10 percent due to safety improvements enabled by analysis of the Big Data.

Organizations Can Analyze More Data.

In some cases, organizations can even process all of the data relating to a particular phenomenon, so they do not have to rely as much on sampling. Random sampling works well, but it is not as effective as analyzing an entire dataset. Random sampling also has some basic weaknesses. To begin with, its accuracy depends on ensuring randomness when collecting the sample data. However, achieving such randomness is problematic. Systematic biases in the process of data collection can cause results to be highly inaccurate. For example, consider political polling using landline phones. This sample tends to exclude people who use only cell phones. This bias can seriously skew the results because cell phone users are typically younger and more liberal than people who rely primarily on landline phones.

Big Data Used in the Functional Areas of the Organization

In this section, we provide examples of how Big Data is valuable to various functional areas in the firm.

HRM **Human Resources.**   Employee benefits, particularly health care, represent a major business expense. Consequently, some companies have turned to Big Data to better manage these benefits. Caesars Entertainment (**www.caesars.com**), for example, analyzes health-insurance claim data for its 65,000 employees and their covered family members. Managers can track thousands of variables that indicate how employees use medical services, such as the number of emergency room visits and whether employees choose a generic or brand name drug.

Consider the following scenario. Data revealed that too many employees with medical emergencies were being treated at hospital emergency rooms rather than at less expensive urgent-care facilities. The company launched a campaign to remind employees of the high cost of emergency room visits, and they provided a list of alternative facilities. Subsequently, 10,000 emergencies shifted to less expensive alternatives, for a total savings of $4.5 million.

Big Data is also having an impact on *hiring*. An example is Catalyst IT Services (**www .catalyte.io**), a technology outsourcing company that hires teams for programming jobs. Traditional recruiting is typically too slow, and hiring managers often subjectively choose candidates who are not the best fit for the job. Catalyst addresses this problem by requiring candidates to fill out an online assessment. It then uses the assessment to collect thousands of data points about each candidate. In fact, the company collects more data based on *how* candidates answer than on *what* they answer.

For example, the assessment might give a problem requiring calculus to an applicant who is not expected to know the subject. How the candidate responds—laboring over an answer, answering quickly and then returning later, or skipping the problem entirely—provides insight into how that candidate might deal with challenges that he or she will encounter on the job. That is, someone who labors over a difficult question might be effective in an assignment that requires a methodical approach to problem solving, whereas an applicant who takes a more aggressive approach might perform better in a different job setting.

The benefit of this Big Data approach is that it recognizes that people bring different skills to the table and there is no one-size-fits-all person for any job. Analyzing millions of data points can reveal which attributes candidates bring to specific situations.

As one measure of success, employee turnover at Catalyst averages about 15 percent per year, compared with more than 30 percent for its U.S. competitors and more than 20 percent for similar companies overseas.

MKT **Product Development.**   Big Data can help capture customer preferences and put that information to work in designing new products. For example, Ford Motor Company (**www.ford.com**) was considering a "three blink" turn indicator that had been available on its European cars for years. Unlike the turn signals on its U.S. vehicles, this indicator flashes three times at the driver's touch and then automatically shuts off.

Ford decided that conducting a full-scale market research test on this blinker would be too costly and time consuming. Instead, it examined auto-enthusiast websites and owner forums to discover what drivers were saying about turn indicators. Using text-mining algorithms, researchers culled more than 10,000 mentions and then summarized the most relevant comments.

The results? Ford introduced the three-blink indicator on the new Ford Fiesta in 2010, and by 2013 it was available on most Ford products. Although some Ford owners complained online that they have had trouble getting used to the new turn indicator, many others defended it. Ford managers note that the use of text-mining algorithms was critical in this effort because they provided the company with a complete picture that would not have been available using traditional market research.

POM **Operations.**   For years, companies have been using information technology to make their operations more efficient. Consider United Parcel Service (UPS). The company has long relied on data to improve its operations. Specifically, it uses sensors in its delivery vehicles that can, among other things, capture the truck's speed and location, the number of times it is placed in Reverse, and whether the driver's seat belt is buckled. These data are uploaded at the end of each day to a UPS data center, where they are analyzed overnight. By combining

GPS information and data from sensors installed on more than 46,000 vehicles, UPS reduced fuel consumption by 8.4 million gallons, and it cut 85 million miles off its routes.

MKT **Marketing.**   Marketing managers have long used data to better understand their customers and to target their marketing efforts more directly. Today, Big Data enables marketers to craft much more personalized messages.

The United Kingdom's InterContinental Hotels Group (IHG; **www.ihg.com**) gathered details about the members of its Priority Club rewards program, such as income levels and whether members prefer family-style or business-traveler accommodations. The company then consolidated all this information with information obtained from social media into a single data warehouse. Using its data warehouse and analytics software, the hotelier launched a new marketing campaign. Where previous marketing campaigns generated, on average, between 7 and 15 customized marketing messages, the new campaign generated more than 1,500. IHG rolled out these messages in stages to an initial core of 12 customer groups, each of which is defined by 4,000 attributes. One group, for example, tends to stay on weekends, redeem reward points for gift cards, and register through IHG marketing partners. Using this information, IHG sent these customers a marketing message that alerted them to local weekend events.

The campaign proved to be highly successful. It generated a 35 percent higher rate of customer conversions, or acceptances, than previous similar campaigns.

POM **Government Operations.**   Consider the United Kingdom. According to the INRIX Traffic Scorecard, although the United States has the worst congestion on average, London topped the world list for metropolitan areas. In London, drivers wasted an average of 101 hours per year in gridlock. Congestion is bad for business. The INRIX study estimated that the cost to the U.K. economy would be £307 billion between 2013 and 2030.

Congestion is also harmful to urban resilience, negatively affecting both environmental and social sustainability in terms of emissions, global warming, air quality, and public health. As for the livability of a modern city, congestion is an important component of the urban transport user experience (UX).

Calculating levels of UX satisfaction at any given time involves solving a complex equation with a range of key variables and factors: total number of transport assets (road and rail capacity, plus parking spaces), users (vehicles, pedestrians), incidents (roadwork, accidents, breakdowns), plus expectations (anticipated journey times and passenger comfort).

The growing availability of Big Data sources within London—for example, traffic cameras and sensors on cars and roadways—can help to create a new era of smart transport. Analyzing this Big Data offers new ways for traffic analysts in London to "sense the city" and enhance transport via real-time estimation of traffic patterns and rapid deployment of traffic management strategies.

Before you go on...

1. Define Big Data.
2. Describe the characteristics of Big Data.
3. Describe how companies can use Big Data to a gain competitive advantage.

5.4   Data Warehouses and Data Marts

Author Lecture Videos are available exclusively in *WileyPLUS*.
Apply the Concept activities are available in the Appendix and in *WileyPLUS*.

Today, the most successful companies are those that can respond quickly and flexibly to market changes and opportunities. A key to this response is the effective and efficient use of data and information by analysts and managers. The challenge is to provide users with access to corporate data so they can analyze the data to make better decisions. Let's consider an example. If the manager of a local bookstore wanted to know the profit margin on used books at her store, then she could obtain that information from her database using SQL or query-by-example (QBE).

QBE is a method of creating database queries that allows the user to search for documents based on an example in the form of a selected string of text or in the form of a document name or a list of documents. However, if she needed to know the trend in the profit margins on used books over the past 10 years, then she would have to construct a very complicated SQL or QBE query.

This example illustrates several reasons why organizations are building data warehouses and data marts. First, the bookstore's databases contain the necessary information to answer the manager's query, but the information is not organized in a way that makes it easy for her to find what she needs. Therefore, complicated queries might take a long time to answer, and they also might degrade the performance of the databases. Second, transactional databases are designed to be updated. This update process requires extra processing. Data warehouses and data marts are read-only. Therefore, the extra processing is eliminated because data already contained in the data warehouse are not updated. Third, transactional databases are designed to access a single record at a time. In contrast, data warehouses are designed to access large groups of related records.

To solve these problems, companies are using a variety of tools with data warehouses and data marts to make it easier and faster for users to access, analyze, and query data. You will learn about these tools in Chapter 12 on business analytics.

Describing Data Warehouses and Data Marts

In general, data warehouses and data marts support business analytics applications. As you will see in Chapter 12, business analytics encompasses a broad category of applications, technologies, and processes for gathering, storing, accessing, and analyzing data to help business users make better decisions. A **data warehouse** is a repository of historical data that are organized by subject to support decision makers within the organization.

Because data warehouses are so expensive, they are used primarily by large companies. A **data mart** is a low-cost, scaled-down version of a data warehouse that is designed for the end-user needs in a strategic business unit (SBU) or an individual department. Data marts can be implemented more quickly than data warehouses, often in less than 90 days. Furthermore, they support local rather than central control by conferring power on the user group. Typically, groups that need a single or a few business analytics applications require only a data mart rather than a data warehouse.

The basic characteristics of data warehouses and data marts include the following:

- *Organized by business dimension or subject.* Data are organized by subject—for example, by customer, vendor, product, price level, and region. This arrangement differs from transactional systems, where data are organized by business process such as order entry, inventory control, and accounts receivable.

- *Use online analytical processing.* Typically, organizational databases are oriented toward handling transactions. That is, databases use *online transaction processing* (OLTP), where business transactions are processed online as soon as they occur. The objectives are speed and efficiency, which are critical to a successful Internet-based business operation. In contrast, data warehouses and data marts, which are designed to support decision makers but not OLTP, use online analytical processing (OLAP), which involves the analysis of accumulated data by end users. We consider OLAP in greater detail in Chapter 12.

- *Integrated.* Data are collected from multiple systems and are then integrated around subjects. For example, customer data may be extracted from internal (and external) systems and then integrated around a customer identifier, thereby creating a comprehensive view of the customer.

- *Time variant.* Data warehouses and data marts maintain historical data; that is, data that include time as a variable. Unlike transactional systems, which maintain only recent data (such as for the last day, week, or month), a warehouse or mart may store years of data. Organizations use historical data to detect deviations, trends, and long-term relationships.

- *Nonvolatile.* Data warehouses and data marts are nonvolatile—that is, users cannot change or update the data. Therefore, the warehouse or mart reflects history, which, as we just saw, is critical for identifying and analyzing trends. Warehouses and marts are updated, but through IT-controlled load processes rather than by users.

- *Multidimensional.* Typically, the data warehouse or mart uses a multidimensional data structure. Recall that relational databases store data in two-dimensional tables. In contrast, data warehouses and marts store data in more than two dimensions. For this reason, the data are said to be stored in a **multidimensional structure**. A common representation for this multidimensional structure is the *data cube.*

The data in data warehouses and marts are organized by *business dimensions*, which are subjects such as product, geographic area, and time period that represent the edges of the data cube. If you look ahead to **Figure 5.6** for an example of a data cube, you see that the product dimension is composed of nuts, screws, bolts, and washers; the geographic area dimension is composed of East, West, and Central; and the time period dimension is composed of 2016, 2017, and 2018. Users can view and analyze data from the perspective of these business dimensions. This analysis is intuitive because the dimensions are presented in business terms that users can easily understand.

A Generic Data Warehouse Environment

The environment for data warehouses and marts includes the following:

- Source systems that provide data to the warehouse or mart
- Data-integration technology and processes that prepare the data for use
- Different architectures for storing data in an organization's data warehouse or data marts
- Different tools and applications for the variety of users. (You will learn about these tools and applications in Chapter 12.)
- **Metadata** (data about the data in a repository), data quality, and governance processes that ensure that the warehouse or mart meets its purposes

Figure 5.4 depicts a generic data warehouse or data mart environment. Let's drill down into the component parts.

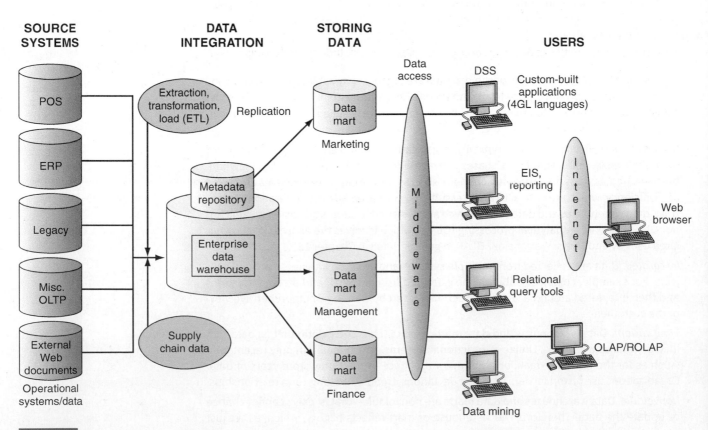

FIGURE 5.4   **Data warehouse framework.**

Source Systems.   There is typically some "organizational pain point"—that is, a business need—that motivates a firm to develop its BI capabilities. Working backward, this pain leads to information requirements, BI applications, and requirements for source system data. These data requirements can range from a single source system, as in the case of a data mart, to hundreds of source systems, as in the case of an enterprise-wide data warehouse.

Modern organizations can select from a variety of source systems, including operational/transactional systems, enterprise resource planning (ERP) systems, website data, third-party data (e.g., customer demographic data), and more. The trend is to include more types of data (e.g., sensing data from RFID tags). These source systems often use different software packages (e.g., IBM, Oracle), and they store data in different formats (e.g., relational, hierarchical).

A common source for the data in data warehouses is the company's operational databases, which can be relational databases. To differentiate between relational databases and multidimensional data warehouses and marts, imagine your company manufactures four products—nuts, screws, bolts, and washers—and has sold them in three territories—East, West, and Central—for the previous three years—2019, 2020, and 2021. In a relational database, these sales data would resemble **Figure 5.5**(a) through (c). In a multidimensional database, in contrast, these data would be represented by a three-dimensional matrix (or data cube), as depicted in **Figure 5.6**. This matrix represents sales *dimensioned by* products, regions, and year. Notice that Figure 5.5(a) presents only sales for 2016. Sales for 2017 and 2018 are presented in Figure 5.5(b) and (c), respectively. **Figure 5.7**(a) through (c) illustrates the equivalence between these relational and multidimensional databases.

Unfortunately, many source systems that have been in use for years contain "bad data"—for example, missing or incorrect data—and they are poorly documented. As a result, data-profiling software should be used at the beginning of a warehousing project to better understand the data. Among other things, this software can provide statistics on missing data, identify possible primary and foreign keys, and reveal how derived values—for example, column 3 = column 1 + column 2—are calculated. Subject area database specialists such as marketing and human resources personnel can also assist in understanding and accessing the data in source systems.

Organizations need to address other source systems issues as well. For example, many organizations maintain multiple systems that contain some of the same data. These enterprises need to select the best system as the source system. Organizations must also decide how granular, or detailed, the data should be. For example, does the organization need daily sales figures or data for individual transactions? The conventional wisdom is that it is best to store data at a highly granular level because someone will likely request those data at some point.

(a) 2019

Product	Region	Sales
Nuts	East	50
Nuts	West	60
Nuts	Central	100
Screws	East	40
Screws	West	70
Screws	Central	80
Bolts	East	90
Bolts	West	120
Bolts	Central	140
Washers	East	20
Washers	West	10
Washers	Central	30

(b) 2020

Product	Region	Sales
Nuts	East	60
Nuts	West	70
Nuts	Central	110
Screws	East	50
Screws	West	80
Screws	Central	90
Bolts	East	100
Bolts	West	130
Bolts	Central	150
Washers	East	30
Washers	West	20
Washers	Central	40

(c) 2021

Product	Region	Sales
Nuts	East	70
Nuts	West	80
Nuts	Central	120
Screws	East	60
Screws	West	90
Screws	Central	100
Bolts	East	110
Bolts	West	140
Bolts	Central	160
Washers	East	40
Washers	West	30
Washers	Central	50

FIGURE 5.5   **Relational databases.**

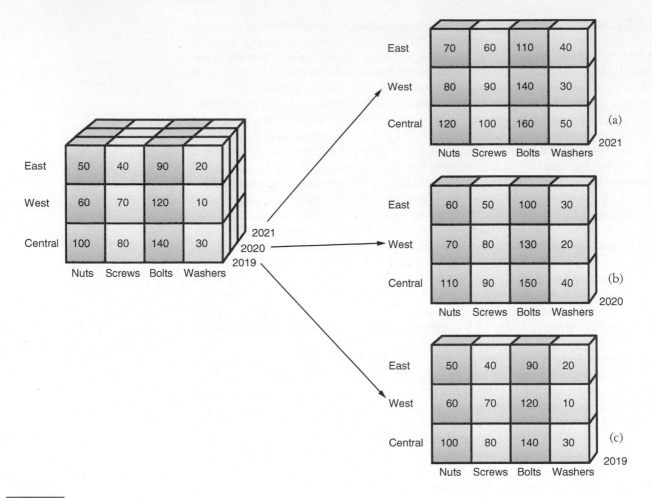

Data cube.

Data Integration.   In addition to storing data in their source systems, organizations need to *extract* the data, *transform* them, and then *load* them into a data mart or warehouse. This process is often called ETL, although the term *data integration* is increasingly being used to reflect the growing number of ways that source system data can be handled. For example, in some cases, data are extracted, loaded into a mart or warehouse, and then transformed (i.e., ELT rather than ETL).

Data extraction can be performed either by handwritten code such as SQL queries or by commercial data-integration software. Most companies employ commercial software. This software makes it relatively easy to (1) specify the tables and attributes in the source systems that are to be used; (2) map and schedule the movement of the data to the target, such as a data mart or warehouse; (3) make the required transformations; and, ultimately, (4) load the data.

After the data are extracted, they are transformed to make them more useful. For example, data from different systems may be integrated around a common key, such as a customer identification number. Organizations adopt this approach to create a 360-degree view of all of their interactions with their customers. As an example of this process, consider a bank. Customers can engage in a variety of interactions: visiting a branch, banking online, using an ATM, obtaining a car loan, and more. The systems for these touch points—defined as the numerous ways that organizations interact with customers, such as e-mail, the Web, direct contact, and the telephone—are typically independent of one another. To obtain a holistic picture of how customers are using the bank, the bank must integrate the data from the various source systems into a data mart or warehouse.

Product	Region	Sales
Nuts	East	50
Nuts	West	60
Nuts	Central	100
Screws	East	40
Screws	West	70
Screws	Central	80
Bolts	East	90
Bolts	West	120
Bolts	Central	140
Washers	East	20
Washers	West	10
Washers	Central	30

2019

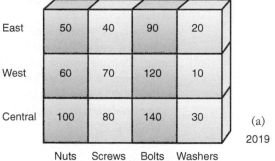

(a)
2019

Product	Region	Sales
Nuts	East	60
Nuts	West	70
Nuts	Central	110
Screws	Easl	50
Screws	West	80
Screws	Central	90
Bolts	East	100
Bolts	West	130
Bolts	Central	150
Washers	East	30
Washers	West	20
Washers	Central	40

2020

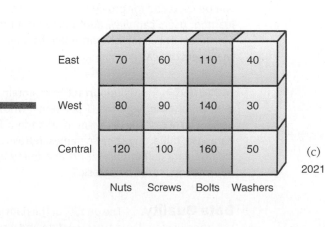

(b)
2020

Product	Region	Sales
Nuts	East	70
Nuts	West	80
Nuts	Central	120
Screws	East	60
Screws	West	90
Screws	Central	100
Bolts	East	110
Bolts	West	140
Bolts	Central	160
Washers	East	40
Washers	West	30
Washers	Central	50

2021

(c)
2021

FIGURE 5.7   Equivalence between relational and multidimensional databases.

Other kinds of transformations also take place. For example, format changes to the data may be required, such as using *male* and *female* to denote gender, as opposed to 0 and 1 or M and F. Aggregations may be performed, say on sales figures, so that queries can use the summaries rather than recalculating them each time. Data-cleansing software may be used to clean up the data; for example, eliminating duplicate records for the same customer.

Finally, data are loaded into the warehouse or mart during a specified period known as the "load window." This window is becoming smaller as companies seek to store ever-fresher data in their warehouses. For this reason, many companies have moved to real-time data warehousing, where data are moved using data-integration processes from source systems to the data warehouse or mart almost instantly. For example, within 15 minutes of a purchase at Walmart, the details of the sale have been loaded into a warehouse and are available for analysis.

Storing the Data.   Organizations can choose from a variety of architectures to store decision-support data. The most common architecture is *one central enterprise data warehouse*, without data marts. Most organizations use this approach because the data stored in the warehouse are accessed by all users, and they represent the single version of the truth.

Another architecture is *independent data marts.* These marts store data for a single application or a few applications, such as marketing and finance. Organizations that employ this architecture give only limited thought to how the data might be used for other applications or by other functional areas in the organization. Clearly this is a very application-centric approach to storing data.

The independent data mart architecture is not particularly effective. Although it may meet a specific organizational need, it does not reflect an enterprise-wide approach to data management. Instead, the various organizational units create independent data marts. Not only are these marts expensive to build and maintain, but they often contain inconsistent data. For example, they may have inconsistent data definitions such as: What is a customer? Is a particular individual a potential or a current customer? They might also use different source systems, which can have different data for the same item, such as a customer address (if the customer had moved). Although independent data marts are an organizational reality, larger companies have increasingly moved to data warehouses.

Still another data warehouse architecture is the *hub and spoke.* This architecture contains a central data warehouse that stores the data plus multiple dependent data marts that source their data from the central repository. Because the marts obtain their data from the central repository, the data in these marts still comprise the *single version of the truth* for decision-support purposes.

The dependent data marts store the data in a format that is appropriate for how the data will be used and for providing faster response times to queries and applications. As you have learned, users can view and analyze data from the perspective of business dimensions and measures. This analysis is intuitive because the dimensions are presented in business terms that users can easily understand.

Metadata.   It is important to maintain data about the data, known as *metadata*, in the data warehouse. Both the IT personnel who operate and manage the data warehouse and the users who access the data require metadata. IT personnel need information about data sources; database, table, and column names; refresh schedules; and data-usage measures. Users' needs include data definitions, report and query tools, report distribution information, and contact information for the help desk.

Data Quality.   The quality of the data in the warehouse must meet users' needs. If it does not, then users will not trust the data and ultimately will not use it. Most organizations find that the quality of the data in source systems is poor and must be improved before the data can be used in the data warehouse. Some of the data can be improved with data-cleansing software. The better, long-term solution, however, is to improve the quality at the source system level. This approach requires the business owners of the data to assume responsibility for making any necessary changes to implement this solution.

To illustrate this point, consider the case of a large hotel chain that wanted to conduct targeted marketing promotions using zip code data it collected from its guests when they checked in. When the company analyzed the zip code data, they discovered that many of the zip codes were 99999. How did this error occur? The answer is that the clerks were not asking customers for their zip codes, but they needed to enter something to complete the registration process. A short-term solution to this problem was to conduct the marketing campaign using city and state data instead of zip codes. The long-term solution was to make certain the clerks entered the actual zip codes. The latter solution required the hotel managers to assume responsibility for making certain their clerks entered the correct data.

Governance.

To ensure that BI is meeting their needs, organizations must implement *governance* to plan and control their BI activities. Governance requires that people, committees, and processes be in place. Companies that are effective in BI governance often create a senior-level committee composed of vice presidents and directors who (1) ensure that the business strategies and BI strategies are in alignment, (2) prioritize projects, and (3) allocate resources. These companies also establish a middle management–level committee that oversees the various projects in the BI portfolio to ensure that these projects are being completed in accordance with the company's objectives. Finally, lower-level operational committees perform tasks such as creating data definitions and identifying and solving data problems. All of these committees rely on the collaboration and contributions of business users and IT personnel.

Users.

Once the data are loaded in a data mart or warehouse, they can be accessed. At this point, the organization begins to obtain business value from BI; all of the prior stages constitute creating BI infrastructure.

There are many potential BI users, including IT developers; frontline workers; analysts; information workers; managers and executives; and suppliers, customers, and regulators. Some of these users are *information producers,* whose primary role is to create information for other users. IT developers and analysts typically fall into this category. Other users—including managers and executives—are *information consumers*, because they use information created by others.

Companies have reported hundreds of successful data-warehousing applications. You can read client success stories and case studies at the websites of vendors such as NCR Corp. (**www.ncr.com**) and Oracle (**www.oracle.com**). For a more detailed discussion, visit the Data Warehouse Institute (**http://tdwi.org**). The benefits of data warehousing include the following:

- End users can access needed data quickly and easily through Web browsers because these data are located in one place.
- End users can conduct extensive analysis with data in ways that were not previously possible.
- End users can obtain a consolidated view of organizational data.

These benefits can improve business knowledge, provide competitive advantage, enhance customer service and satisfaction, facilitate decision making, and streamline business processes.

Despite their many benefits, data warehouses have some limitations. IT's About Business 5.2 points out these limitations and considers an emerging solution; namely, data lakes.

IT's About Business 5.2

MIS Data Lakes

Most large organizations have an enterprise data warehouse (EDW), which contains data from other enterprise systems such as customer relationship management (CRM), inventory, and sales transaction systems. With EDWs, organizations maintain the data using traditional databases, meaning that the EDW is built upon labeled rows and columns of data. EDWs are the primary mechanism in many organizations for performing analytics, reporting, and operations.

Despite their benefits to organizations, EDWs do have problems. Specifically, they require organizations to design the data model—called the schema—before they load any data into the EDW. A *database schema* defines the structure of both the database and the data contained in that database. For example, in the case of relational databases, the schema specifies the tables and fields of the database. The schema also describes the content and structure of the physical data stored. These descriptions are called *metadata*.

As a result, EDWs are relatively inflexible and can answer only a limited number of questions. It is therefore difficult for business analysts and data scientists who rely on EDWs to ask ad hoc questions of the data.

It is also difficult for EDWs to manage new sources of data, such as streaming data from sensors (see the Internet of Things in Chapter 8), and social media data such as blog postings, ratings, recommendations, product reviews, Tweets, photographs, and video clips.

EDWs are also too rigid to be effective with Big Data, with its huge data volumes, broad variety of data, and high data velocity. As a result of these problems, organizations have begun to realize that EDWs cannot meet all of their business needs.

The emergence of systems such as Apache Hadoop (**http://hadoop.apache.org**) has enabled organizations to implement parallel searches on large data repositories to greatly speed up operations on the data. Hadoop provided the impetus for the creation of data lakes.

A **data lake** is a central repository that stores all of an organization's data, regardless of the source or format of those data. Data lakes receive data in any format, both structured and unstructured. Also, the data do not have to be consistent. For example, organizations might have the same type of information in different data formats, depending on where the data originate.

Organizations typically use Hadoop to build their data lakes. They can then employ a variety of storage and processing tools to extract value quickly from these data lakes and to inform key business decisions.

Organizations do not transform the data before entering them into the data lake as they would for an EDW. In fact, the structure of the data is not known when the data are fed into the data lake. Rather, it is discovered only when the data are read, meaning that users do not model the data until they actually use it. This process is more flexible, and it makes it easier for users to discover new data and to enter new data sources into the data lake.

Data lakes provide many benefits for organizations:

- Organizations can derive value from unlimited types of data.
- Organizations have no limits on how they can query the data.
- Organizations do not create data silos. Instead, data lakes provide a single, unified view of data across the organization.

To load data into a data lake, organizations should take these steps:

- Define the incoming data from a business perspective.
- Document the context, origin, and frequency of the incoming data.
- Classify the security level (public, internal, sensitive, restricted) of the incoming data.
- Document the creation, usage, privacy, regulatory, and encryption business rules that apply to the incoming data.
- Identify the owner (sponsor) of the incoming data.
- Identify the data steward(s) who monitor and maintain the datasets.

After organizations follow these steps, they load all the data into a large table. Each piece of data—whether a customer's name, a photograph, or a Facebook post—is placed in an individual cell. It does not matter where in the data lake that cell is located, where the data came from, or their format, because metadata tags connect all of the data. Organizations can add or change these tags as requirements evolve. Further, they can assign multiple tags to the same piece of data. Because the rules for storing the data do not need to be defined in advance, there is no need for expensive and time-consuming data modeling.

Organizations can also protect sensitive information by specifying who has access to the data in each cell, and under what circumstances, as the data are loaded. For example, a retail operation might make cells containing customers' names and contact data available to sales and customer service. At the same time, however, it might make the cells containing more sensitive, personally identifiable information or financial data available only to the finance department. In that way, when users run queries on the data, their access rights restrict which data they can view.

It is very important to note that organizations use both EDWs and data lakes. To understand this arrangement, let's distinguish between "small data" and "Big Data" questions. A small data question would be: What is the total revenue for the northeast region in 2020? This question is easily and quickly answered by an EDW because the data are well defined.

A Big Data question would be: Describe the detailed customer relationship over the past three years for a high-value customer who has moved her business to another firm. This question is a much better fit for a data lake because the variables are not clear from the outset and will probably include unstructured data such as email messages and audio clips. This query would be very difficult to answer with an EDW.

Many firms use data lakes as a holding area for data that it does not plan to use immediately but that may be valuable later. An example is archiving data for regulatory data-retention requirements. In another example, companies might use their data lakes to test assumptions on massive volumes of data and then extract and load the most useful data into their EDWs for decision making.

There are many examples of data lakes in practice. Let's take a look at how L'Oréal (**www.lorealparisusa.com**) employs its data lake.

POM **MKT** L'Oréal, a 100-year-old cosmetics industry leader, owns more than 40 brands and must analyze a vast amount of data, including 7 billion products manufactured annually, 50 million data points created each day, and 500 patents filed each year. The firm relies on scientists and marketing professionals to work together to create several thousand new formulas every year. The company must also ensure that its products are safe for humans. This process requires analyzing data about product formulas and raw materials in addition to what consumers think of the new formulas.

To accomplish its goals, L'Oréal employed Talend (**www .talend.com**), a leading cloud-based data integration company, to create a data lake on Microsoft Azure. The platform integrates structured laboratory data with varying, often raw, unstructured data, such as images of models using L'Oréal cosmetics. The data are available in real time, and the data lake is refreshed several times every day.

ACCT   L'Oréal developed its first application for the finance department to address the economic management of research. The application's dashboards displayed all of the key performance indicators for research-related activities and their associated costs, such as tests for product certification.

L'Oréal's next application addressed research into the impact of its products on the human microbiome, which consists of the genetic material of all of the microbes—bacteria, fungi, protozoa, and viruses—that live on and inside the human body. Another application involves products that can counter the effects of pollution on the skin.

Sources: Compiled from A. Thusoo, "Data Lakes and Data Warehouses: The Two Sides of a Modern Cloud Data Platform," *Forbes*, July 7, 2020; C. Foot, "Key Factors for Successful Data Lake Implementation,"

TechTarget, July 6, 2020; V. Combs, "L'Oréal's New Data Lake Holds 100 Years of Product Development Research," *TechRepublic*, October 30, 2019; "Essential Guide to Data Lakes," *Matillion*, 2019; S. Wooledge, "Data Lakes and Data Warehouses: Why You Need Both," *Arcadia Data*, October 11, 2018; T. King, "Three Key Data Lake Trends to Stay on Top of This Year," *Solutions Review*, May 11, 2018; T. Olavsrud, "6 Data Analytics Trends that Will Dominate 2018," *CIO*, March 15, 2018; P. Tyaqi and H. Demirkan, "Data Lakes: The Biggest Big Data Challenges," *Analytics Magazine*, September/October 2017; M. Hagstroem, M. Roggendorf, T. Saleh, and J. Sharma, "A Smarter Way to Jump into Data Lakes," *McKinsey and Company*, August 2017; P. Barth, "The New Paradigm for Big Data Governance," *CIO*, May 11, 2017; N. Mikhail, "Why Big Data Kills Businesses," *Fortune*, February 28, 2017; "Architecting Data Lakes," *Zaloni*, February 21, 2017; D. Kim, "Successful Data Lakes: A Growing Trend," *The Data Warehousing Institute*, February 16, 2017; L. Hester, "Maximizing Data Value with a Data Lake," *Data Science Central*, April 20, 2016.

Questions

1. Discuss the advantages and disadvantages of enterprise data warehouses.

2. Describe the advantages and disadvantages of data lakes.

3. Why don't organizations use enterprise data warehouses for managing Big Data?

Before you go on...

1. Differentiate between data warehouses and data marts.
2. Describe the characteristics of a data warehouse.
3. What are three possible architectures for data warehouses and data marts in an organization?

5.5 Knowledge Management

As we have noted throughout this text, data and information are vital organizational assets. Knowledge is a vital asset as well. Successful managers have always valued and used intellectual assets. These efforts may not have been systematic, however, and they may not have ensured that knowledge was shared and dispersed in a way that benefited the overall organization. Moreover, industry analysts estimate that most of a company's knowledge assets are not housed in relational databases. Instead, they are dispersed in e-mail, word processing documents, spreadsheets, presentations on individual computers, and in people's heads. This arrangement makes it extremely difficult for companies to access and integrate this knowledge. The result frequently is less effective decision making.

Author Lecture Videos are available exclusively in *WileyPLUS*.
Apply the Concept activities are available in the Appendix and in *WileyPLUS*.

Concepts and Definitions

Knowledge management (KM) is a process that helps organizations manipulate important knowledge that comprises part of the organization's memory, usually in an unstructured format. For an organization to be successful, knowledge, as a form of capital, must exist in a format that can be exchanged among persons. It must also be able to grow.

Knowledge.   In the information technology context, knowledge is distinct from data and information. As you learned in Chapter 1, data are a collection of facts, measurements, and statistics; information is organized or processed data that are timely and accurate.

Knowledge is information that is *contextual*, *relevant*, and *useful*. Simply put, knowledge is information in action. **Intellectual capital** (or **intellectual assets**) is another term for knowledge.

To illustrate, a bulletin listing all of the courses offered by your university during one semester would be considered *data*. When you register, you process the data from the bulletin to create your schedule for the semester. Your schedule would be considered *information*. Awareness of your work schedule, your major, your desired social schedule, and characteristics of different faculty members could be construed as *knowledge*, because it can affect the way you build your schedule. You see that this awareness is contextual and relevant (to developing an optimal schedule of classes) as well as useful (it can lead to changes in your schedule). The implication is that knowledge has strong experiential and reflective elements that distinguish it from information in a given context. Unlike information, knowledge can be used to solve a problem.

Numerous theories and models classify different types of knowledge. In the next section, we will focus on the distinction between explicit knowledge and tacit knowledge.

Explicit and Tacit Knowledge.   **Explicit knowledge** deals with more objective, rational, and technical knowledge. In an organization, explicit knowledge consists of the policies, procedural guides, reports, products, strategies, goals, core competencies, and IT infrastructure of the enterprise. In other words, explicit knowledge is the knowledge that has been codified (documented) in a form that can be distributed to others or transformed into a process or a strategy. A description of how to process a job application that is documented in a firm's human resources policy manual is an example of explicit knowledge.

In contrast, **tacit knowledge** is the cumulative store of subjective or experiential learning. In an organization, tacit knowledge consists of an organization's experiences, insights, expertise, know-how, trade secrets, skill sets, understanding, and learning. It also includes the organizational culture, which reflects the past and present experiences of the organization's people and processes, as well as the organization's prevailing values. Tacit knowledge is generally imprecise and costly to transfer. It is also highly personal. Finally, because it is unstructured, it is difficult to formalize or codify, in contrast to explicit knowledge. A salesperson who has worked with particular customers over time and has come to know their needs quite well would possess extensive tacit knowledge. This knowledge is typically not recorded. In fact, it might be difficult for the salesperson to put into writing, even if he or she were willing to share it.

Knowledge Management Systems

The goal of knowledge management is to help an organization make the most productive use of the knowledge it has accumulated. Historically, management information systems have focused on capturing, storing, managing, and reporting explicit knowledge. Organizations now realize they need to integrate explicit and tacit knowledge into formal information systems. **Knowledge management systems (KMSs)** refer to the use of modern information technologies—the Internet, intranets, extranets, and databases—to systematize, enhance, and expedite knowledge management both within one firm and among multiple firms. KMSs are intended to help an organization cope with turnover, rapid change, and downsizing by making the expertise of the organization's human capital widely accessible.

Organizations can realize many benefits with KMSs. Most importantly, they make *best practices*—the most effective and efficient ways accomplishing business processes—readily available to a wide range of employees. Enhanced access to best-practice knowledge improves overall organizational performance. For example, account managers could make available their tacit knowledge about how best to manage large accounts. The organization could then use this knowledge when it trains new account managers. Other benefits include enhanced customer service, more efficient product development, and improved employee morale and retention.

At the same time, however, implementing effective KMSs presents several challenges. First, employees must be willing to share their personal tacit knowledge. To encourage this behavior, organizations must create a knowledge management culture that rewards employees who add their expertise to the knowledge base. Second, the organization must continually maintain and upgrade its knowledge base. Specifically, it must incorporate new knowledge and delete old, outdated knowledge. Finally, companies must be willing to invest in the resources needed to carry out these operations.

The KMS Cycle

A functioning KMS follows a cycle that consists of six steps (see **Figure 5.8**). The reason the system is cyclical is that knowledge is dynamically refined over time. The knowledge in an effective KMS is never finalized because the environment changes over time and knowledge must be updated to reflect these changes. The cycle works as follows:

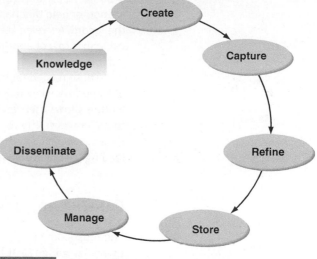

FIGURE 5.8 **The knowledge management system cycle.**

1. *Create knowledge.* Knowledge is created as people determine new ways of doing things or develop know-how. Sometimes external knowledge is brought in.

2. *Capture knowledge.* New knowledge must be identified as valuable and be presented in a reasonable way.

3. *Refine knowledge.* New knowledge must be placed in context so that it is actionable. This is where tacit qualities (human insights) must be captured along with explicit facts.

4. *Store knowledge.* Useful knowledge must then be stored in a reasonable format in a knowledge repository so that other people in the organization can access it.

5. *Manage knowledge.* Like a library, the knowledge must be kept current. Therefore, it must be reviewed regularly to verify that it is relevant and accurate.

6. *Disseminate knowledge.* Knowledge must be made available in a useful format to anyone in the organization who needs it, anywhere and any time.

Before you go on...

1. What is knowledge management?
2. What is the difference between tacit knowledge and explicit knowledge?
3. Describe the knowledge management system cycle.

5.6 Appendix: Fundamentals of Relational Database Operations

There are many operations possible with relational databases. In this section, we discuss three of these operations: query languages, normalization, and joins.

As you have seen in this chapter, a relational database is a collection of interrelated two-dimensional tables consisting of rows and columns. Each row represents a record, and each column (or field) represents an attribute (or characteristic) of that record. Every record in the database must contain at least one field that uniquely identifies that record so that it can be retrieved, updated, and sorted. This identifier field, or group of fields, is called the *primary key*.

Author Lecture Videos are available exclusively in *WileyPLUS*. **Apply the Concept** activities are available in the Appendix and in *WileyPLUS*.

In some cases, locating a particular record requires the use of secondary keys. A *secondary key* is another field that has some identifying information, but typically does not uniquely identify the record. A *foreign key* is a field (or group of fields) in one table that matches the primary key value in a row of another table. A foreign key is used to establish and enforce a link between two tables.

These related tables can be joined when they contain common columns. The uniqueness of the primary key tells the DBMS which records are joined with others in related tables. This feature allows users great flexibility in the variety of queries they can make. Despite these features, however, the relational database model has some disadvantages. Because large-scale databases can be composed of many interrelated tables, the overall design can be complex, leading to slow search and access times.

Query Languages

The most commonly performed database operation is searching for information. **Structured query language (SQL)** is the most popular query language used for interacting with a database. SQL allows people to perform complicated searches by using relatively simple statements or key words. Typical key words are SELECT (to choose a desired attribute), FROM (to specify the table or tables to be used), and WHERE (to specify conditions to apply in the query).

To understand how SQL works, imagine that a university wants to know the names of students who will graduate cum laude (but not magna or summa cum laude) in December 2005. (Refer to Figure 5.3 in this chapter.) The university IT staff would query the student relational database with an SQL statement such as:

SELECT Student_Name

FROM Student_Database

WHERE Grade_Point_Average > = 3.40 and Grade_Point_Average < 3.60.

The SQL query would return John Jones and Juan Rodriguez.

Another way to find information in a database is to use *query by example (QBE)*. In QBE, the user fills out a grid or template—also known as a *form*—to construct a sample or a description of the data desired. Users can construct a query quickly and easily by using drag-and-drop features in a DBMS such as Microsoft Access. Conducting queries in this manner is simpler than keying in SQL commands.

Entity–Relationship Modeling

Designers plan and create databases through the process of **entity–relationship modeling** using an **entity–relationship (ER) diagram**. There are many approaches to ER diagramming. You will see one particular approach here. The good news is that if you are familiar with one version of ER diagramming, then you will be able to easily adapt to any other version.

ER diagrams consist of entities, attributes, and relationships. To properly identify entities, attributes, and relationships, database designers first identify the business rules for the particular data model. **Business rules** are precise descriptions of policies, procedures, or principles in any organization that stores and uses data to generate information. Business rules are derived from a description of an organization's operations, and help to create and enforce business processes in that organization. Keep in mind that *you* determine these business rules, not the MIS department.

Entities are pictured in rectangles, and relationships are described on the line between two entities. The attributes for each entity are listed, and the primary key is underlined. The **data dictionary** provides information on each attribute, such as its name; if it is a key, part of a key, or a non-key attribute; the type of data expected (alphanumeric, numeric, dates, etc.); and valid values. Data dictionaries can also provide information on why the attribute is needed in the database; which business functions, applications, forms, and reports use the attribute; and how often the attribute should be updated.

ER modeling is valuable because it allows database designers to communicate with users throughout the organization to ensure that all entities and the relationships among the entities are represented. This process underscores the importance of taking all users into account when designing organizational databases. Notice that all entities and relationships in our example are labeled in terms that users can understand.

Relationships illustrate an association between entities. The *degree of a relationship* indicates the number of entities associated with a relationship. A *unary relationship* exists when an association is maintained within a single entity. A *binary relationship* exists when two entities are associated. A *ternary relationship* exists when three entities are associated. In this chapter, we discuss only binary relationships because they are the most common. Entity relationships may be classified as one-to-one, one-to-many, or many-to-many. The term *connectivity* describes the relationship classification.

Connectivity and cardinality are established by the business rules of a relationship. *Cardinality* refers to the maximum number of times an instance of one entity can be associated with an instance in the related entity. Cardinality can be mandatory single, optional single, mandatory many, or optional many. **Figure 5.9** displays the cardinality symbols. Note that there are four possible cardinality symbols: mandatory single, optional single, mandatory many, and optional many.

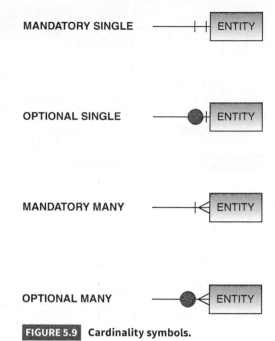

FIGURE 5.9   **Cardinality symbols.**

Let's look at an example from a university. An *entity* is a person, place, or thing that can be identified in the users' work environment. For example, consider student registration at a university. Students register for courses, and they also register their cars for parking permits. In this example, STUDENT, PARKING PERMIT, CLASS, and PROFESSOR are entities. Recall that an instance of an entity represents a particular student, parking permit, class, or professor. Therefore, a particular STUDENT (James Smythe, 8023445) is an instance of the STUDENT entity; a particular parking permit (91778) is an instance of the PARKING PERMIT entity; a particular class (76890) is an instance of the CLASS entity; and a particular professor (Margaret Wilson, 390567) is an instance of the PROFESSOR entity.

Entity instances have *identifiers*, or *primary keys*, which are attributes (attributes and identifiers are synonymous) that are unique to that entity instance. For example, STUDENT instances can be identified with Student Identification Number, PARKING PERMIT instances can be identified with Permit Number, CLASS instances can be identified with Class Number, and PROFESSOR instances can be identified with Professor Identification Number.

Entities have **attributes**, or properties, that describe the entity's characteristics. In our example, examples of attributes for STUDENT are Student Name and Student Address. Examples of attributes for PARKING PERMIT are Student Identification Number and Car Type. Examples of attributes for CLASS are Class Name, Class Time, and Class Place. Examples of attributes for PROFESSOR are Professor Name and Professor Department. (Note that each course at this university has one professor—no team teaching.)

Why is Student Identification Number an attribute of both the STUDENT and PARKING PERMIT entity classes? That is, why do we need the PARKING PERMIT entity class? If you consider all of the interlinked university systems, the PARKING PERMIT entity class is needed for other applications, such as fee payments, parking tickets, and external links to the state Department of Motor Vehicles.

Let's consider the three types of binary relationships in our example.

In a *one-to-one (1:1)* relationship, a single-entity instance of one type is related to a single-entity instance of another type. In our university example, STUDENT–PARKING PERMIT is a 1:1 relationship. The business rule at this university represented by this relationship is: students may register only one car at this university. Of course, students do not have to register a car at all. That is, a student can have only one parking permit but does not need to have one.

Note that the relationship line on the PARKING PERMIT side shows a cardinality of optional single. A student can have, but does not have to have, a parking permit. On the STUDENT side

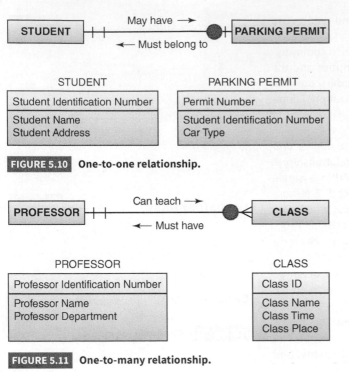

FIGURE 5.10 One-to-one relationship.

FIGURE 5.11 One-to-many relationship.

of the relationship, only one parking permit can be assigned to one student, resulting in a cardinality of mandatory single. See **Figure 5.10**.

The second type of relationship, *one-to-many (1:M)*, is represented by the CLASS–PROFESSOR relationship in **Figure 5.11**. The business rule at this university represented by this relationship is: at this university, there is no team teaching. Therefore, each class must have only one professor. On the other hand, professors may teach more than one class. Note that the relationship line on the PROFESSOR side shows a cardinality of mandatory single. In contrast, the relationship line on the CLASS side shows a cardinality of optional many.

The third type of relationship, *many-to-many (M:M)*, is represented by the STUDENT–CLASS relationship. Most database management systems do not support many-to-many relationships. Therefore, we use *junction* (or *bridge*) *tables*, so that we have two one-to-many relationships. The business rule at this university represented by this relationship is: students can register for one or more classes, and each class can have one or more students (see **Figure 5.12**). In this example, we create the REGISTRATION table as our junction table. Note that Student ID and Class ID are foreign keys in the REGISTRATION table.

Let's examine the following relationships:

- The relationship line on the STUDENT side of the STUDENT–REGISTRATION relationship shows a cardinality of optional single.
- The relationship line on the REGISTRATION side of the STUDENT–REGISTRATION relationship shows a cardinality of optional many.
- The relationship line on the CLASS side of the CLASS–REGISTRATION relationship shows a cardinality of optional single.
- The relationship line on the REGISTRATION side of the CLASS–REGISTRATION relationship shows a cardinality of optional many.

Normalization and Joins

To use a relational database management system efficiently and effectively, the data must be analyzed to eliminate redundant data elements. **Normalization** is a method for analyzing and reducing a relational database to its most streamlined form to ensure minimum redundancy, maximum data integrity, and optimal processing performance. Data normalization is a methodology for organizing attributes into tables so that redundancy among the non-key attributes is eliminated. The result of the data normalization process is a properly structured relational database.

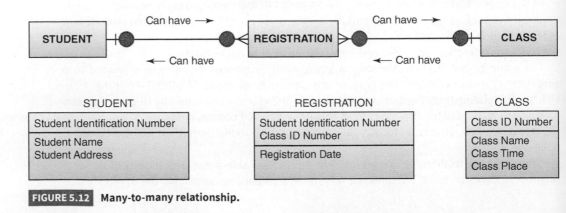

FIGURE 5.12 Many-to-many relationship.

Order Number	Order Date	Customer ID	Customer F Name	Customer L Name	Customer Address	Zip Code	Pizza Code	Pizza Name	Quantity	Price	Total Price
1116	9/1/14	16421	Rob	Penny	123 Main St.	37411	P	Pepperoni	1	$11.00	$41.00
							MF	Meat Feast	1	$12.00	
							V	Vegetarian	2	$9.00	
1117	9/2/14	17221	Beth	Jones	41 Oak St.	29416	HM	Ham and Mushroom	3	$10.00	$56.00
							MF	Meat Feast	1	$12.00	
							TH	The Hawaiian	1	$14.00	

FIGURE 5.13   **Raw data gathered from orders at the pizza shop.**

Data normalization requires a list of all the attributes that must be incorporated into the database and a list of all of the defining associations, or functional dependencies, among the attributes. **Functional dependencies** are a means of expressing that the value of one particular attribute is associated with a specific single value of another attribute. For example, for Student Number 05345 at a university, exactly one Student Name, John C. Jones, is associated with it. That is, Student Number is referred to as the determinant because its value *determines* the value of the other attribute. We can also say that Student Name is functionally dependent on Student Number.

As an example of normalization, consider a pizza shop. This shop takes orders from customers on a form. Figure 5.13 shows a table of nonnormalized data gathered by the pizza shop. This table has two records, one for each order being placed. Because there are several pizzas on each order, the order number and customer information appear in multiple rows. Several attributes of each record have null values. A null value is an attribute with no data in it. For example, Order Number has four null values. Therefore, this table is not in first normal form. The data drawn from that form is shown in **Figure 5.13**.

In our example, ORDER, CUSTOMER, and PIZZA are entities. The first step in normalization is to determine the functional dependencies among the attributes. The functional dependencies in our example are shown in **Figure 5.14**.

In the normalization process, we will proceed from nonnormalized data, to first normal form, to second normal form, and then to third normal form. (There are additional normal forms, but they are beyond the scope of this book.)

Figure 5.15 demonstrates the data in *first normal form*. The attributes under consideration are listed in one table and primary keys have been established. Our primary keys are Order Number, Customer ID, and Pizza Code. In first normal form, each ORDER has to repeat the order number, order date, customer first name, customer last name, customer address, and customer zip code. This data file contains repeating groups and describes multiple entities. That is, this relation has data redundancy, a lack of data integrity, and the flat file would be difficult to use in various applications that the pizza shop might need.

Consider the table in Figure 5.15 and notice the very first column (labeled Order Number). This column contains multiple entries for each order—three rows for Order Number 1116 and three rows for Order Number 1117. These multiple rows for an order are called *repeating groups*. The table in Figure 5.15 also contains multiple entities: ORDER, CUSTOMER, and PIZZA. Therefore, we move on to second normal form.

To produce second normal form, we break the table in **Figure 5.15** into smaller tables to eliminate some of its data redundancy. Second normal form does not allow partial functional dependencies. That is, in a table in second normal form, every

Order Number	$\longrightarrow$	Order Date
Order Number	$\longrightarrow$	Quantity
Order Number	$\longrightarrow$	Total Price
Customer ID	$\longrightarrow$	Customer F Name
Customer ID	$\longrightarrow$	Customer L Name
Customer ID	$\longrightarrow$	Customer Address
Customer ID	$\longrightarrow$	Zip Code
Customer ID	$\longrightarrow$	Total Price
Pizza Code	$\longrightarrow$	Pizza Name
Pizza Code	$\longrightarrow$	Price

FIGURE 5.14   **Functional dependencies in pizza shop example.**

Order Number	Order Date	Customer ID	Customer F Name	Customer L Name	Customer Address	Zip Code	Pizza Code	Pizza Name	Quantity	Price	Total Price
1116	9/1/14	16421	Rob	Penny	123 Main St.	37411	P	Pepperoni	1	$11.00	$41.00
1116	9/1/14	16421	Rob	Penny	123 Main St.	37411	MF	Meat Feast	1	$12.00	$41.00
1116	9/1/14	16421	Rob	Penny	123 Main St.	37411	V	Vegetarian	2	$9.00	$41.00
1117	9/2/14	17221	Beth	Jones	41 Oak St.	29416	HM	Ham and Mushroom	3	$10.00	$56.00
1117	9/2/14	17221	Beth	Jones	41 Oak St.	29416	MF	Meat Feast	1	$12.00	$56.00
1117	9/2/14	17221	Beth	Jones	41 Oak St.	29416	TH	The Hawaiian	1	$14.00	$56.00

FIGURE 5.15 First normal form for data from pizza shop.

non-key attribute must be functionally dependent on the entire primary key of that table. **Figure 5.16** shows the data from the pizza shop in second normal form.

If you examine Figure 5.16, you will see that second normal form has not eliminated all the data redundancy. For example, each Order Number is duplicated three times, as are all customer data. In *third normal form*, non-key attributes are not allowed to define other non-key attributes. That is, third normal form does not allow transitive dependencies in which one non-key attribute is functionally dependent on another. In our example, customer information

Order Number	Order Date	Customer ID	Customer F Name	Customer L Name	Customer Address	Zip Code	Total Price
1116	9/1/14	16421	Rob	Penny	123 Main St.	37411	$41.00
1116	9/1/14	16421	Rob	Penny	123 Main St.	37411	$41.00
1116	9/1/14	16421	Rob	Penny	123 Main St.	37411	$41.00
1117	9/2/14	17221	Beth	Jones	41 Oak St.	29416	$56.00
1117	9/2/14	17221	Beth	Jones	41 Oak St.	29416	$56.00
1117	9/2/14	17221	Beth	Jones	41 Oak St.	29416	$56.00

Order Number	Pizza Code	Quantity
1116	P	1
1116	MF	1
1116	V	2
1117	HM	3
1117	MF	1
1117	TH	1

Pizza Code	Pizza Name	Price
P	Pepperoni	$11.00
MF	Meat Feast	$12.00
V	Vegetarian	$9.00
HM	Ham and Mushroom	$10.00
TH	The Hawaiian	$14.00

FIGURE 5.16 Second normal form for data from pizza shop.

ORDER

Order Number	Order Date	Customer ID	Total Price
1116	9/1/14	16421	$41.00
1117	9/2/14	17221	$56.00

CUSTOMER

Customer ID	Customer F Name	Customer L Name	Customer Address	Zip Code
16421	Rob	Penny	123 Main St.	37411
17221	Beth	Jones	41 Oak St.	29416

ORDER-PIZZA

Order Number	Pizza Code	Quantity
1116	P	1
1116	MF	1
1116	V	2
1117	HM	3
1117	MF	1
1117	TH	1

PIZZA

Pizza Code	Pizza Name	Price
P	Pepperoni	$11.00
MF	Meat Feast	$12.00
V	Vegetarian	$9.00
HM	Ham and Mushroom	$10.00
TH	The Hawaiian	$14.00

FIGURE 5.17   **Third normal form for data from pizza shop.**

depends both on Customer ID and Order Number. **Figure 5.17** shows the data from the pizza shop in third normal form. Third normal form structure has these important points:

- It is completely free of data redundancy.
- All foreign keys appear where needed to link related tables.

Let's look at the primary and foreign keys for the tables in third normal form:

- *The ORDER relation*: The primary key is Order Number and the foreign key is Customer ID.
- *The CUSTOMER relation*: The primary key is Customer ID.
- *The PIZZA relation*: The primary key is Pizza Code.
- *The ORDER–PIZZA relation*: The primary key is a composite key, consisting of two foreign keys, Order Number and Pizza Code.

Now consider an order at the pizza shop. The tables in third normal form can produce the order in the following manner by using the join operation (see **Figure 5.18**). The **join operation** combines records from two or more tables in a database to obtain information that is located in different tables. In our example, the join operation combines records from the four normalized tables to produce an ORDER. Here is how the join operation works:

- The ORDER relation provides the Order Number (the primary key), Order Date, and Total Price.
- The primary key of the ORDER relation (Order Number) provides a link to the ORDER–PIZZA relation (the link numbered 1 in **Figure 5.18**).

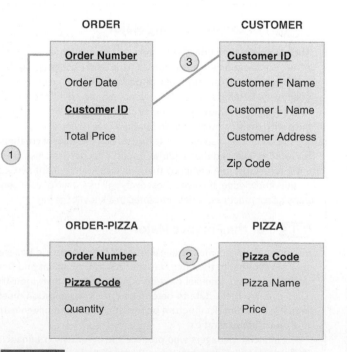

FIGURE 5.18   **The join process with the tables of third normal form to produce an order.**

- The ORDER–PIZZA relation supplies the Quantity to ORDER.
- The primary key of the ORDER–PIZZA relation is a composite key that consists of Order Number and Pizza Code. Therefore, the Pizza Code component of the primary key provides a link to the PIZZA relation (the link numbered 2 in Figure 5.18).
- The PIZZA relation supplies the Pizza Name and Price to ORDER.
- The Customer ID in ORDER (a foreign key) provides a link to the CUSTOMER relation (the link numbered 3 in Figure 5.18).
- The CUSTOMER relation supplies the Customer FName, Customer LName, Customer Address, and Zip Code to ORDER.

At the end of this join process, we have a complete ORDER. Normalization is beneficial when maintaining databases over a period of time. One example is the likelihood of having to change the price of each pizza. If the pizza shop increases the price of the Meat Feast from $12.00 to $12.50, this process is one easy step in Figure 5.18. The price field is changed to $12.50 and the ORDER is automatically updated with the current value of the price.

Before you go on...

1. What is structured query language?
2. What is query by example?
3. What is an entity? An attribute? A relationship?
4. Describe one-to-one, one-to-many, and many-to-many relationships.
5. What is the purpose of normalization?
6. Why do we need the join operation?

What's in IT for me?

ACCT For the Accounting Major

The accounting function is intimately concerned with keeping track of an organization's transactions and internal controls. Modern databases enable accountants to perform these functions more effectively. Databases help accountants manage the flood of data in today's organizations so that they can keep their firms in compliance with the standards imposed by Sarbanes–Oxley.

Accountants also play a role in justifying the costs of creating a knowledge base and then auditing its cost-effectiveness. Also, if you work for a large CPA company that provides management services or sells knowledge, then you most likely will use some of your company's best practices, which are stored in a knowledge base.

FIN For the Finance Major

Financial managers make extensive use of computerized databases that are external to the organization, such as CompuStat and Dow Jones, to obtain financial data on organizations in their industry. They can use these data to determine if their organization meets industry benchmarks in return on investment, cash management, and other financial ratios.

Financial managers who produce the organization's financial status reports are also closely involved with Sarbanes–Oxley. Databases help these managers comply with the law's standards.

MKT For the Marketing Major

Databases help marketing managers access data from the organization's marketing transactions, such as customer purchases, to plan targeted marketing campaigns and to evaluate the success of previous campaigns. Knowledge about customers can make the difference between success and failure. In many databases and knowledge bases, the vast majority of information and knowledge concerns customers, products, sales, and marketing. Marketing managers regularly use an organization's knowledge base, and they often participate in creating that base.

POM For the Production/Operations Management Major

Production/operations personnel access organizational data to determine optimal inventory levels for parts in a production process. Past production data enable production/operations management (POM) personnel to determine the optimal configuration for assembly lines. Firms also collect quality data that inform them not only about the quality of finished products but also about quality issues with incoming raw materials, production irregularities, shipping and logistics, and after-sale use and maintenance of the products.

Knowledge management is extremely important for running complex operations. The accumulated knowledge regarding scheduling, logistics, maintenance, and other functions is very valuable. Innovative ideas are critical for improving operations, and they can be supported by knowledge management.

HRM For the Human Resources Management Major

Organizations maintain extensive data on employees including gender, age, race, current and past job descriptions, and performance evaluations. HR personnel access these data to provide reports to government agencies regarding compliance with federal equal opportunity guidelines. HR managers also use these data to evaluate hiring practices and salary structures and to manage any discrimination grievances or lawsuits brought against the firm.

Databases help HR managers provide assistance to all employees as companies turn over more and more decisions about health care and retirement planning to the employees themselves. The employees can use the databases for help in selecting the optimal mix among these critical choices.

HR managers also need to use a knowledge base frequently to find out how past cases were handled. Consistency in how employees are treated not only is important, but it also protects the company against legal actions. In addition, training for building, maintaining, and using the knowledge system is sometimes the responsibility of the HR department. Finally, the HR department might be responsible for compensating employees who contribute their knowledge to the knowledge base.

MIS For the MIS Major

The MIS function manages the organization's data as well as the databases. MIS database administrators standardize data names by using the data dictionary. This process ensures that all users understand which data are in the database. Database personnel also help users access needed data and generate reports with query tools.

What's in IT for me? (Appendix: Section 5.6)

For all Business Majors

All business majors will have to manage data in their professional work. One way to manage data is through the use of databases and database management systems. It is likely that you will need to obtain information from your organization's databases. You will probably use structured query language to obtain this information. Further, as your organization plans and designs its databases, it will most likely use entity–relationship diagrams. You will provide much of the input to these diagrams. For example, you will describe the entities that you use in your work, the attributes of those entities, and the relationships among them. You will also help database designers as they normalize database tables by describing how the normalized tables relate to one another (e.g., through the use of primary and foreign keys). Finally, you will assist database designers as they plan their join operations to provide you with the information that you need when that information is stored in multiple tables.

Summary

5.1 Discuss ways that common challenges in managing data can be addressed using data governance.

The following are three common challenges in managing data:

- Data are scattered throughout organizations and are collected by many individuals using various methods and devices. These data are frequently stored in numerous servers and locations and in different computing systems, databases, formats, and human and computer languages.
- Data come from multiple sources.
- Information systems that support particular business processes impose unique requirements on data, which results in repetition and conflicts across an organization.

One strategy for implementing data governance is master data management. Master data management provides companies with the ability to store, maintain, exchange, and synchronize a consistent, accurate, and timely "single version of the truth" for the company's core master data. Master data management manages data gathered from across an organization, data from multiple sources, and data across business processes within an organization.

5.2 Discuss the advantages and disadvantages of relational databases.

Relational databases enable people to compare information quickly by row or column. Users also can easily retrieve items by finding the point of intersection of a particular row and column. However, large-scale relational databases can be composed of numerous interrelated tables, making the overall design complex, with slow search and access times.

5.3   Define Big Data and its basic characteristics.

Big Data is composed of high-volume, high-velocity, and high-variety information assets that require new forms of processing in order to enhance decision making, lead to insights, and optimize business processes. Big Data has three distinct characteristics that distinguish it from traditional data: volume, velocity, and variety.

- *Volume*: Big Data consists of vast quantities of data.
- *Velocity*: Big Data flows into an organization at incredible speeds.
- *Variety*: Big Data includes diverse data in differing formats.

5.4   Explain the elements necessary to successfully implement and maintain data warehouses.

To successfully implement and maintain a data warehouse, an organization must:

- Link source systems that provide data to the warehouse or mart.
- Prepare the necessary data for the data warehouse using data integration technology and processes.
- Decide on an appropriate architecture for storing data in the data warehouse or data mart.
- Select the tools and applications for the variety of organizational users.
- Establish appropriate metadata, data quality, and governance processes to ensure that the data warehouse or mart meets its purposes.

5.5   Describe the benefits and challenges of implementing knowledge management systems in organizations.

Organizations can realize many benefits with KMSs, including:

- Best practices are readily available to a wide range of employees
- Improved customer service
- More efficient product development
- Improved employee morale and retention

Challenges to implementing KMSs include:

- Employees must be willing to share their personal tacit knowledge.

- Organizations must create a knowledge management culture that rewards employees who add their expertise to the knowledge base.
- The knowledge base must be continually maintained and updated.
- Companies must be willing to invest in the resources needed to carry out these operations.

5.6   Understand the processes of querying a relational database, entity-relationship modeling, and normalization and joins.

The most commonly performed database operation is requesting information. *Structured query language* is the most popular query language used for this operation. SQL allows people to perform complicated searches by using relatively simple statements or key words. Typical key words are SELECT (to specify a desired attribute), FROM (to specify the table to be used), and WHERE (to specify conditions to apply in the query).

Another way to find information in a database is to use *query by example.* In QBE, the user fills out a grid or template—also known as a *form*—to construct a sample or a description of the data desired. Users can construct a query quickly and easily by using drag-and-drop features in a DBMS such as Microsoft Access. Conducting queries in this manner is simpler than keying in SQL commands.

Designers plan and create databases through the process of **entity–relationship modeling**, using an **entity–relationship diagram**. ER diagrams consist of entities, attributes, and relationships. Entities are pictured in boxes, and relationships are represented as lines. The attributes for each entity are listed, and the primary key is underlined.

ER modeling is valuable because it allows database designers to communicate with users throughout the organization to ensure that all entities and the relationships among the entities are represented. This process underscores the importance of taking all users into account when designing organizational databases. Notice that all entities and relationships in our example are labeled in terms that users can understand.

Normalization is a method for analyzing and reducing a relational database to its most streamlined form to ensure minimum redundancy, maximum data integrity, and optimal processing performance. When data are *normalized*, attributes in each table depend only on the primary key.

The *join operation* combines records from two or more tables in a database to produce Information that is located in different tables.

Chapter Glossary

attribute   Each characteristic or quality of a particular entity.

Big Data   A collection of data so large and complex that it is difficult to manage using traditional database management systems.

bit   A binary digit—that is, a 0 or a 1.

business rules   Precise descriptions of policies, procedures, or principles in any organization that stores and uses data to generate information.

byte   A group of eight bits that represents a single character.

database management system (DBMS)   The software program (or group of programs) that provide access to a database.

data dictionary   A collection of definitions of data elements; data characteristics that use the data elements; and the individuals, business functions, applications, and reports that use these data elements.

data file (also table)   A collection of logically related records.

data governance   An approach to managing information across an entire organization.

data lake   A central repository that stores all of an organization's data, regardless of their source or format.

data mart   A low-cost, scaled-down version of a data warehouse that is designed for the end-user needs in a strategic business unit (SBU) or a department.

data model A diagram that represents entities in the database and their relationships.

data silo A collection of data held by one group that is not easily accessible by other groups.

data warehouse A repository of historical data that are organized by subject to support decision makers in the organization.

entity Any person, place, thing, or event of interest to a user.

entity–relationship (ER) diagram Document that shows data entities and attributes and relationships among them.

entity–relationship (ER) modeling The process of designing a database by organizing data entities to be used and identifying the relationships among them.

explicit knowledge The more objective, rational, and technical types of knowledge.

field A characteristic of interest that describes an entity.

foreign key A field (or group of fields) in one table that uniquely identifies a row (or record) of another table.

functional dependency A means of expressing that the value of one particular attribute is associated with, or determines, a specific single value of another attribute.

instance Each row in a relational table, which is a specific, unique representation of the entity.

intellectual capital (or intellectual assets) Other terms for knowledge.

join operation A database operation that combines records from two or more tables in a database.

knowledge management (KM) A process that helps organizations identify, select, organize, disseminate, transfer, and apply information and expertise that are part of the organization's memory and that typically reside within the organization in an unstructured manner.

knowledge management systems (KMSs) Information technologies used to systematize, enhance, and expedite intra- and interfirm knowledge management.

master data A set of core data, such as customer, product, employee, vendor, geographic location, and so on, that spans an enterprise's information systems.

master data management A process that provides companies with the ability to store, maintain, exchange, and synchronize a consistent, accurate, and timely "single version of the truth" for the company's core master data.

multidimensional structure Storage of data in more than two dimensions; a common representation is the data cube.

normalization A method for analyzing and reducing a relational database to its most streamlined form to ensure minimum redundancy, maximum data integrity, and optimal processing performance.

primary key A field (or attribute) of a record that uniquely identifies that record so that it can be retrieved, updated, and sorted.

query by example To obtain information from a relational database, a user fills out a grid or template—also known as a *form*—to construct a sample or a description of the data desired.

record A grouping of logically related fields.

relational database model Data model based on the simple concept of tables in order to capitalize on characteristics of rows and columns of data.

relationships Operators that illustrate an association between two entities.

secondary key A field that has some identifying information, but typically does not uniquely identify a record with complete accuracy.

structured data Highly organized data in fixed fields in a data repository such as a relational database that must be defined in terms of field name and type (e.g., alphanumeric, numeric, and currency).

structured query language The most popular query language for requesting information from a relational database.

table A grouping of logically related records.

tacit knowledge The cumulative store of subjective or experiential learning, which is highly personal and hard to formalize.

transactional data Data generated and captured by operational systems that describe the business's activities, or transactions.

unstructured data Data that do not reside in a traditional relational database.

Discussion Questions

1. Is Big Data really a problem on its own, or are the use, control, and security of the data the true problems? Provide specific examples to support your answer.

2. What are the implications of having incorrect data points in your Big Data? What are the implications of incorrect or duplicated customer data? How valuable are decisions that are based on faulty information derived from incorrect data?

3. Explain the difficulties involved in managing data.

4. What are the problems associated with poor-quality data?

5. What is master data management? What does it have to do with high-quality data?

6. Explain why master data management is so important in companies that have multiple data sources.

7. Describe the advantages and disadvantages of relational databases.

8. Explain why it is important to capture and manage knowledge.

9. Compare and contrast tacit knowledge and explicit knowledge.

10. Draw the entity–relationship diagram for a company that has departments and employees. In this company, a department must have at least one employee, and company employees may work in only one department.

11. Draw the entity–relationship diagram for library patrons and the process of checking out books.

12. You are working at a doctor's office. You gather data on the following entities: PATIENT, PHYSICIAN, PATIENT DIAGNOSIS, and TREATMENT. Develop a table for the entity PATIENT VISIT. Decide on the primary keys and/or foreign keys that you want to use for each entity.

13. Read the article: S. Kliff and M. Sanger-Katz, "Bottleneck for U.S. Coronavirus Response: The Fax Machine," *New York Times*, July 13, 2020. Describe which of the problems in managing data (Section 5.1) are being emphasized by the COVID-19 pandemic.

Problem-Solving Activities

1. Access various employment websites (e.g., **www.monster.com** and **www.dice.com**) and find several job descriptions for a database administrator. Are the job descriptions similar? What are the salaries offered in these positions?

2. Access the websites of several real estate companies. Find the sites that take you through a step-by-step process for buying a home, that provide virtual reality tours of homes in your price range (say, $200,000 to $250,000) and location, that provide mortgage and interest rate calculators, and that offer financing for your home. Do the sites require that you register to access their services? Can you request that an e-mail be sent to you when properties you might be interested in become available? How does the process outlined influence your likelihood of selecting this company for your real estate purchase?

3. It is possible to find many websites that provide demographic information. Access several of these sites and see what they offer. Do the sites differ in the types of demographic information they offer? If so, how? Do the sites require a fee for the information they offer? Would

demographic information be useful to you if you wanted to start a new business? If so, how and why?

4. Search the web for uses of Big Data in homeland security. Specifically, read about the spying by the U.S. National Security Agency (NSA). What role did technology and Big Data play in this questionable practice?

5. Search the Web for the article "Why Big Data and Privacy Are Often at Odds." What points does this article present concerning the delicate balance between shared data and customer privacy?

6. Access the websites of IBM (**www.ibm.com**), Microsoft (**www.microsoft.com**), and Oracle (**www.oracle.com**), and trace the capabilities of their latest data management products, including web connections.

7. Access the website for the Gartner Group (**www.gartner.com**). Examine the company's research studies pertaining to data management. Prepare a report on the state of the art.

8. Diagram a knowledge management system cycle for a fictional company that sells customized T-shirts to students.

Closing Case

MIS **The Democratic Party Upgrades Its Data Repository and Its Data**

Until 2011, the Democratic Party (**www.democrats.org**) stored data in multiple databases, making it difficult for campaigns to integrate the data to form a holistic profile of voters and issues important to those voters. In 2011, the party deployed Vertica (**www.vertica.com**), an analytics database, as its central data repository. Vertica enabled the party to store every state's voter file, every door knock and phone call that organizers made, and all commercially available data that campaigns collected. Using Vertica, the successful 2012 Obama reelection campaign was able to analyze the data to target potential voters with outreach and advertising at an individual level instead of placing them into broad categories such as urban voters or soccer moms.

After 2012, a lack of maintenance caused problems with Vertica. As a result, the party had to devote an increasing amount of resources to address these problems. A key problem with the system involved data. After 2012, the party began to collect rapidly increasing amounts of data, which Vertica was unable to manage. The data were poorly labeled, inconsistent, incorrect, and contained missing values such as voter phone numbers and addresses.

To compound this problem, Vertica's interface was not intuitive. It was difficult for Democratic Party personnel with limited experience in data analytics to use. As a result, state and local campaigns did not derive much value from the system. One analyst stated that you had to know or have participated in a prior campaign to understand where the really good data were and how to effectively access and use them. Such poor-quality data had consequences. For example, analysts noted that party operatives had a habit of knocking on dead people's doors.

Vertica also predated cloud-based systems. Therefore, the party had to deploy servers that could not manage the terabytes of data flowing into them. Further, the servers could not manage the

thousands of data analysts trying to access data in the final days before an election.

As a result, in the months before the 2016 election, presidential candidate Hillary Clinton's team struggled with the system. It often crashed for 16 hours at a time during the campaign. In fact, the campaign had dozens of computer engineers on call 24 hours per day, ready to restart the system each time it went down.

Having witnessed the critical role that poor data and an unreliable database had played in their unsuccessful 2016 presidential election, the Democrats realized that they had to improve their data infrastructure. To accomplish this task, the party hired a new chief technology officer, who divided his 40-person IT staff into two teams. One team would maintain Vertica just long enough to get through Election Day 2018. The other team would build a new system to replace Vertica.

Up through the 2018 midterm elections, one team of party engineers continued to provide constant maintenance to keep Vertica operational. Even with their efforts, Vertica crashed for 10 hours one night just prior to voting.

A major goal for the other team was to develop a more stable platform that did not require the party to maintain its own servers. The party raised $5 million from donors explicitly for this project.

Accordingly, the team developed a new data repository called the Data Warehouse. The new system uses Google's analytics tool, BigQuery, a cloud-based platform capable of handling massive data sets at the scale and speed necessary for modern campaigns. Further, the Data Warehouse is more reliable and more intuitive for smaller campaigns, whose operatives generally do not have experience in data analytics.

Creating a data exchange. The Federal Election Commission (FEC) prohibits coordination between campaigns and outside groups. This ruling has traditionally prevented the candidate's campaign and its super PAC (political action committee) from comparing or inter-mingling the data collected by each entity. A *super PAC* is a type of independent committee that raises unlimited sums of money from cor-porations, unions, and/or individuals but is not permitted to contribute to or coordinate directly with parties or candidates.

In 2011, the Republicans found a way around that rule by creat-ing a third-party organization called the Data Trust. This company is outside the Republican Party and acts as a data repository. Multiple Republican groups license their data to the trust, which allows other groups such as PACs to pay for access to it without violating FEC regu-lations. Democrats, quite correctly, viewed the Data Trust as a compet-itive advantage for the Republican Party.

The Democrat's Data Warehouse helped the party achieve one of its primary goals before the 2020 elections: the creation of its data exchange. The exchange allows the party and other political groups to share their data for the first time, without violating campaign finance laws. The Democrat's exchange is modeled on the Republican Party's GOP Data Trust.

Somewhat surprisingly, Democratic officials who manage their states' voter files were initially reluctant to give up control of their data. The party had to come up with a compromise. The Democratic National Committee (DNC) would house the data. The data exchange would track only who provides the data, the data they provide, who accesses the data, and the data they access.

Democratic operatives also had concerns about whether the Data Warehouse would be accessible enough to campaign staffers who do not have any SQL coding skills, because the system requires some pro-gramming skills. Therefore, it was critical for the Data Warehouse team to build tools that enabled the average field staffer to easily access and analyze the data stored in the Data Warehouse. In fact, the Democratic Party has developed a number of tools based on the Data Warehouse.

The Blueprint tool. One of these tools, called Blueprint, helps campaigns and state parties, particularly those with limited technical expertise, to access voter data to better target their campaign efforts. Blueprint increased the Democratic Party's digital capabilities at a time when campaigning in person is extremely difficult, if not impossible, due to the COVID-19 pandemic. It helps campaigns decide whom to call, text, e-mail, and target with digital advertisements.

Rather than having to search through the party's voter database themselves, Blueprint enables campaign workers at every level to access data such as voters' addresses, ethnicity, and voting history in a specific area. Blueprint is especially valuable for down-ballot can-didates, who often do not have in-house technical teams focused on analyzing data to mobilize prospective voters and volunteers. The term *down-ballot* refers to a candidate who is relatively low-profile and local compared to a more prominent candidate whose name appears higher on the ballot.

The party piloted Blueprint in several states, including Texas. Using this tool, in March 2020 the Texas Democratic Party introduced a new model that scores every Texas voter from 1 to 100 according to how likely they are to vote for a Democratic candidate. This model helps the state party more efficiently identify and target undecided

voters. Texas used Blueprint's data to make its scoring system more effective. The Data Warehouse and Blueprint allowed them to access demographic and consumer data that they did not already have. These data included voters' ethnicity, neighborhood, and income.

The voter registration tool. In June 2020 the party deployed another new tool to help Democratic campaign workers and state par-ties contact voters who, unknowingly, had been either purged from active voter rolls or designated as inactive voters. The party hopes that the tool will be valuable in states that removed voters who either had not voted recently or had not responded to mailings from the state. (States justify these policies by claiming that they protect against fraudulent voting.) The tool allows campaigns and state parties to recognize these voters and collect their names, phone numbers, and addresses. The campaigns can then target them with calls, text mes-sages, and mail.

The new voter file. The COVID-19 pandemic severely limited traditional door-to-door canvassing. As a result, campaigns need to increase the efficiency of virtual canvassing. In July 2020 the Demo-cratic Party deployed a new voter file model, designed to predict the likelihood that a person will (a) have a working cell phone number and (b) respond positively to a text message. The party wants to make its voter outreach efforts more productive by giving volunteers accurate cell phone numbers and preventing them from texting wrong or dis-connected numbers.

Sources: Compiled from J. Turman, "DNC Hopes to Reach More Voters with New Voter File Model," *CBS News*, July 10, 2020; D. Merica, "Dem-ocrats Roll out New Tool to Combat Voter Purges," *CNN*, June 16, 2020; E. Birnbaum and I. Lapowsky, "New DNC Data Tool Aims to Give and Edge to Campaigns Light on Tech Expertise," *Protocol*, April 9, 2020; I. Lapowsky, "'We've Had People Panicking:' Tech Startups Scramble to Take the 2020 Race Digital," *Protocol*, April 1, 2020; M. Nickelsburg, "DNC's New Tech Leader Talks about What Went Wrong in 2016 and How Dems Are Preparing for 2020," *GeekWire*, July 29, 2019; B. Mitchell, "The Revo-lution Will Be Online: How Democrats Are Trying to Catch Up to Trump," *CNET*, June 3, 2019; J. Easley, "Inside the DNC's Plan to Defeat Trump," *The Hill*, May 31, 2019; R. Cramer, "Want the Voter File? Campaigns Will Have to Pay, Record Videos and Fundraise for the DNC to Get It," *Buzz-Feed*, May 4, 2019; I. Lapowsky, "Inside the Democrats' Plan to Fix Their Crumbling Data Operation," *Wired*, April 2, 2019; "DNC Rolls out New Data Warehouse," **Democrats.org**, April 2, 2019; B. Barrow, "Howard Dean to Head New Democratic Voter Data Exchange," *Associated Press*, February 13, 2019; I. Lapowsky, "Democrats Uber-ized Activism. Can It Win Them the Midterms?" *Wired*, November 6, 2018; **www.democrats.org**, accessed July 13, 2020.

Questions

1. Are the data contained in the Data Warehouse Big Data? Provide specific examples to support your answer.

2. Are the data contained in the Data Warehouse structured? Provide specific examples to support your answer.

3. Describe another application that the Democratic Party could develop for the Data Warehouse.

CHAPTER 6

Telecommunications and Networking

CHAPTER OUTLINE	LEARNING OBJECTIVES
6.1 What Is a Computer Network?	6.1 Compare and contrast the major types of networks.
6.2 Network Fundamentals	6.2 Describe wireline communications media and transmission technologies.
6.3 The Internet and the World Wide Web	6.3 Describe the most common methods for accessing the Internet.
6.4 Network Applications: Discovery	6.4 Explain the impact that discovery network applications have had on business and everyday life.
6.5 Network Applications: Communication	6.5 Explain the impact that communication network applications have had on business and everyday life.
6.6 Network Applications: Collaboration	6.6 Explain the impact that collaboration network applications have had on business and everyday life.
6.7 Network Applications: Educational	6.7 Explain the impact that educational network applications have had on business and everyday life.

Opening Case

MIS The Splinternet

For most of its relatively short history, the Internet has had very limited centralized planning and governance. In general, the Internet today enables users to exchange ideas and information instantaneously and with minimal supervision, regardless of national boundaries.

The modern, open Internet also provides a platform that nations can use to undertake information warfare, manipulate one another's citizens, and/or project their interests past their own national borders. Many nations frame their Internet access policies to balance the destabilizing effects of the Internet against its benefits for economic development, trade, productivity, and intellectual and cultural exchange. Even liberal democracies must strike a balance between a managed Internet and an open Internet. In Britain and South Korea, for example, Internet service providers (ISPs) are required by law to limit access to pornography.

As a result, a global splinternet is forming. The *splinternet*, also known as *Internet balkanization*, is a loosely connected set of national Internets. There are many reasons for the emergence of the splinternet.

Some countries are unhappy with the Western coalition that has traditionally controlled the Internet and its governance. For example, the actual operations of the Internet *domain name system* (DNS) are conducted by a wide variety of organizations, but a majority of the "root servers" that function as the Internet's foundational layer are operated by groups in the United States. The DNS is basically an Internet phone book. For instance, when you type "google.com" into your browser, your computer uses the DNS to translate this domain name into an IP address, which identifies the correct server on the Internet to send your request.

Many countries are unhappy with the fact that the Internet was developed and engineered to ensure that no one can prevent anyone from sending anything to anyone. One reason is that these countries want to have more control over dissent. Another is that they are nervous about malicious software reaching military installations and critical power and water grids via the open Internet. (Recall our discussion of SCADA attacks in Chapter 4.)

Another catalyst for nations to develop national Internet control occurred in 2013 when Edward Snowden, a contractor with the U.S. National Security Agency (NSA), leaked a number of classified documents. These documents revealed that the NSA, through its PRISM program, had been collecting information from global users of Google, Facebook, Apple, Microsoft, and Yahoo, including many national political leaders like Angela Merkel of Germany and Dilma Rousseff of Brazil. These revelations caused Brazil to pass the Marco Civil da Internet law, which requires global companies to comply with Brazilian laws concerning data protection. Other nations have taken similar actions.

Countries are using laws and regulatory powers within their jurisdictions to impose limits on digital activities. Specifically, many countries want to maintain sovereignty over their national data by implementing measures such as data privacy regulations and restrictions on data they deem inappropriate. As of August 2020 more than 30 regions or nations were imposing data sovereignty regulations including the European Union (the General Data Protection Regulation or GDPR), Brazil, China, and India.

These policies particularly impact social media platforms such as Facebook and Twitter. These companies have users in almost every country, and governments are increasingly insisting that they comply with local laws and cultural norms regarding access and content. Let's take a closer look at the leading proponents of the splinternet.

China

China opted out of the open Internet by embedding a homegrown ISP and DNS infrastructure in the early 2000s. In addition, the country permitted very few entry and exit points to be built from the global Internet within its borders. China, therefore, has fewer digital borders to monitor.

China's Internet is enclosed by Golden Shield, a censorship and surveillance project operated by the country's Ministry of Public Security. One of the more notable components of Golden Shield is the Great Firewall of China, a series of legislative and technological actions that restrict citizens' access to foreign services like Google, Facebook, and the *New York Times*. China does not allow privately operated foreign Internet platforms, including many social media platforms that can promote dissent, opposition, or subversive ideas, to operate within its borders.

The firewall also selectively blocks certain Internet addresses, words, phrases, IP addresses, and so on, as defined by the government. Although formidable, the firewall is not perfect because virtual private networks (VPNs) and censorship avoidance software such as Tor can circumvent it.

China is also seeking to export its version of the Internet throughout Southeast Asia and Africa. According to the International Institute for Strategic Studies (**www.iiss.org**), China is engaged in some 80 telecommunications projects around the world. These projects are contributing to a growing Chinese-owned global network. Analysts note that China provides the technological infrastructure along with example laws for citizen surveillance and the necessary training for countries to use in deploying a Chinese version of the Internet. China is selling the concept as an alternative to a Western Internet that some countries perceive as too open.

Russia

Russia first proposed disconnecting from the global Internet in 2014. In December 2018 the Russian parliament passed a law requiring the country's ISPs to provide the technical means to disconnect from the rest of the world and reroute Internet traffic internally through exchange points managed by Roskomnadzor, Russia's telecommunications and media regulator. *Exchange points* are physical locations where ISPs connect with one another to exchange traffic.

In May 2019 Russian president Vladimir Putin signed the law, which took effect on November 1. The following month the Russian government announced that it had completed a multiday test of its national Internet, known as RuNet. This announcement strongly implied that RuNet had successfully disconnected from the global Internet.

According to the Kremlin, the purpose of the disconnection is to make Russia's Internet independent and easier to defend against attacks from abroad. However, outside observers contend that the move is part of Russia's long tradition of trying to control the flow of information among its citizens.

Russia will have many problems if it decides to actually implement RuNet.

- The country initially welcomed the global Internet and has a multitude of entry and exit connections. It will be very difficult for Russia to identify the myriad access points that its citizens use to get online, including their laptops, smartphones, and iPads. Some Russians will use servers abroad, such as Google's Public DNS, which Russia will not be able to duplicate. Therefore, the connection will fail when a Russian citizen tries to access these servers.

- If the authorities implement RuNet and require their ISPs to use it, Russian users might not notice that a website that is censored unless they actively try to access that site. For example, a user trying to connect to Facebook.com could be redirected to vk.com, a Russian social media service that strongly resembles Facebook. Russian users will not be pleased as they wonder how much the information on vk.com is censored by their government.

- The Internet is an essential component of the global economy. Therefore, disconnecting would seriously damage Russia's economy. For example, although many cloud vendors mirror (duplicate) their content in different regions, none of the major cloud services (Microsoft, Google, and Amazon Web Services) maintains data centers in Russia. As a result, Russia could have to create its own cloud service.

- Many Russian ISPs carry traffic on behalf of other ISPs, with reciprocal arrangements that these ISPs carry traffic for Russian ISPs. If Russia implements its disconnection project incorrectly, then a large amount of traffic going in and out of the country will simply be lost.

- The disconnection process will be technically difficult and very expensive.

- The idea is not popular with the general public.

- Even if a disaster does not occur—such as banking, hospital, or aviation facilities failing to connect—many websites could stop working. Most web pages rely on multiple servers to function, which may exist in different parts of the world. If Russia disconnects, then users may no longer have access to these servers.

As of October 2020 the question of whether the Kremlin intends to fully cut Russia off from the global Internet remained unresolved.

Other countries

Not all countries fall completely into the category of the "global and open Internet" or a "sovereign and controlled Internet." Since 2015, several countries called *digital deciders*—Israel, Brazil, Ukraine, South Korea, and India, among others—have moved toward a more sovereign and controlled Internet. Their reasons vary, but several of those countries are in similar situations. Specifically, Ukraine, Israel, and South Korea, which exist in perpetual states of conflict, have discovered that their adversaries are weaponizing the Internet against them. Brazil has not forgotten the Snowden revelations.

Further, an increasing number of Western countries are reconsidering what sovereignty on the Internet means. In the aftermath of election meddling in many countries, most notably the United States, and the well-documented practice by Russian operatives of creating discord on Western social media, many Western policymakers have become convinced that an open and free Internet can actually harm democracy itself.

Results

The splinternet is already a threat to businesses that operate in multiple countries. If a business does nothing to respond, it may find its applications and services cut off from valuable customers in certain countries and regions. Further, firms will face large fines if they fail to comply with national and local Internet regulations.

To determine whether your company is at risk, consider these questions:

- Does the company have an international data strategy?
- Can the company manage data movement specific to certain regions, including the EU? India? China? Russia? Other regions?
- Can the company quickly respond to important national or regional regulatory changes?
- Can the company avoid being blocked from operating in other nations or regions by instantly changing their data management settings?

If firms cannot answer "yes" to each of these questions, then their international operations are at risk. Consequently, they must modernize their IT operations and data mobility strategy to align with the new splinternet reality.

Sources: Compiled from L. Newman, "Russia Takes a Big Step toward Internet Isolation," *Wired*, January 5, 2020; C. Cimpanu, "Russia Successfully Disconnected from the Internet," *ZDNet*, December 23, 2019; "Russia's Law that Lets It Disconnect from the Internet Comes into Force Today," *MIT Technology Review*, November 1, 2019; Z. Doffman, "Putin Begins Installing Equipment to Cut Russia's Access to World Wide Web," *Forbes*, September 24, 2019; T. Merritt, "Top 5 Things to Know about the Splinternet," *TechRepublic*, October 7, 2019; J. Kim, "The Splinternet Is Here and Your Company Needs to Be Ready," *TheNextWeb*, June 10, 2019; J. Sherman, "Russian and Iran Plan to Fundamentally Isolate the Internet," *Wired*, June 6, 2019; J. Roberts, "The Splinternet Is Growing," *Fortune*, May 29, 2019; "Iran Says Its Internet Almost Ready to Shield Country from 'Harmful' Internet," *Radio Farda*, May 20, 2019; S. Adee, "Russia Is the Latest Country to Try to Find Ways to Police Its Online Borders, Sparking the End of the Internet as We Know It," *BBC News*, May 15, 2019; N. Hodge and M. Ilyushina, "Putin Signs Law to Create an Independent Russian Internet," *CNN*, May 1, 2019; C. Jee, "Russia Wants to Cut Itself off from the Global Internet. Here's What That Really Means," *MIT Technology Review*, March 21, 2019; "Russia Must Build Own Internet in Case of Foreign Disruption: Putin," *Reuters*, February 20, 2019; L. Matsakis, "What Happens if Russia Cuts Itself off from the Internet," *Wired*, February 12, 2019; K. Finley, "California Could Soon Have Its Own Version of the Internet," *Wired*, December 29, 2018; R. Morgus, J. Woolbright, and J. Sherman, "The Digital Deciders," *New America*, October 23, 2018; M. Daoudi, "Beware the SplinterNet—Why Three Recent Events Should Have Businesses Worried," *Forbes*, July 12, 2018; D. Alba, "The World May Be Headed for a Fragmented 'Splinternet'," *Wired*, July 7, 2017; B. Moscowitz, "The Reasons Why a Free and Open Internet Could Spell the Web's Downfall," *Quartz Media*, April 4, 2017.

Questions

1. What are the advantages of the splinternet to a nation? Provide examples to support your answer.
2. What are the disadvantages of the splinternet to a nation? Provide examples to support your answer.
3. What are the advantages of the splinternet to you as an individual? Provide examples to support your answer.
4. What are the disadvantages of the splinternet to you as an individual? Provide examples to support your answer.

Introduction

In addition to networks being essential in your personal lives, there are three fundamental points about network computing you need to know. First, in modern organizations computers do not work in isolation. Rather, they constantly exchange data with one another. Second, this exchange of data—facilitated by telecommunications technologies—provides companies with many significant advantages. Third, this exchange can take place over any distance and over networks of any size.

Without networks, the computer on your desk would be merely another productivity-enhancement tool, just as the typewriter once was. The power of networks, however, turns your computer into an amazingly effective tool for accessing information from thousands of sources, thereby making both you and your organization more productive. Regardless of the type of organization (profit/not-for-profit, large/small, global/local) or industry (manufacturing, financial services, health care), networks in general, and the Internet in particular, have transformed—and will continue to transform—the way we do business.

Networks support new and innovative ways of doing business, from marketing to supply chain management to customer service to human resources management. In particular, the Internet and private intranets—a network located within a single organization that uses Internet software and TCP/IP protocols—have enormous impacts on our lives, both professionally and personally.

For all organizations regardless of size, having a telecommunications and networking system is no longer just a source of competitive advantage. Rather, it is necessary for survival.

Computer networks are essential to modern organizations for many reasons. First, networked computer systems enable organizations to become more flexible so they can adapt to rapidly changing business conditions. Second, networks allow companies to share hardware, computer applications, and data across the organization and among different organizations. Third, networks make it possible for geographically dispersed employees and workgroups to share documents, ideas, and creative insights. This sharing encourages teamwork, innovation, and more efficient and effective interactions. Networks are also a critical link between businesses, their business partners, and their customers.

Clearly, networks are essential tools for modern businesses. But why do *you* need to be familiar with networks? The simple fact is that if you operate your own business or you work in a business, then you cannot function without networks. You will need to communicate rapidly with your customers, business partners, suppliers, employees, and colleagues. Until about 1990, you would have used the postal service or the telephone system with voice or fax capabilities for business communication. Today, however, the pace of business is much faster—almost real time. To keep up with this incredibly fast pace, you will need to use computers, e-mail, messaging, the Internet, smartphones, and other mobile devices. Furthermore, all these technologies will be connected through networks to enable you to communicate, collaborate, and compete on a global scale.

Networking and the Internet are the foundations for commerce in the 21st century. Recall that one key objective of this book is to help you become an informed user of information systems. Knowledge of networking is an essential component of modern business literacy.

We simply cannot overemphasize the global importance of the Internet. It has been said that the Internet is truly the nervous system of our world.

In fact, having fast (broadband) access to the Internet is a prerequisite for success for many people. For instance, in 2017, New York City sued Verizon for allegedly failing to provide adequate fiber-optic services to the city. In July 2018 Verizon reached a deal with New York State regulators to expand its high-speed Internet services in New York City and repair its existing telephone infrastructure.

In that same year, New York Attorney General Eric Schneiderman filed a lawsuit alleging that Charter Communications (now Spectrum; **www.spectrum.com**) defrauded New York customers by failing to deliver the Internet speeds and performance levels promised to them. Spectrum is an American telecommunications company that provides cable, telephone, and television services. In March 2019 Spectrum began paying out $62.5 million to customers over the Internet speed lawsuit.

You begin this chapter by learning what a computer network is and by identifying the various types of networks. You then study network fundamentals. You next turn your attention to the basics of the Internet and the World Wide Web. You conclude by examining the many network applications available to individuals and organizations—that is, what networks help you do.

6.1 What Is a Computer Network?

A **computer network** is a system that connects computers and other devices (e.g., printers) through communications media so that data and information can be transmitted among them. Voice and data communication networks are continually becoming faster—that is, their bandwidth is increasing—and cheaper. **Bandwidth** refers to the transmission capacity of a network; it is stated in bits per second. Bandwidth ranges from narrowband (relatively low transmission capacity) to broadband (relatively high network capacity).

Author Lecture Videos are available exclusively in *WileyPLUS*.
Apply the Concept activities are available in the Appendix and in *WileyPLUS*.

The telecommunications industry itself has difficulty defining the term *broadband*. The Federal Communications Commission's (FCC) rules define **broadband** as the transmission capacity of a communications medium (discussed later in this chapter) faster than 25 megabits per second (Mbps) for download—the transmission speed for material coming to you from an Internet server, such as a movie streamed from Netflix—and 3 Mbps for upload—the transmission speed for material that you upload to an Internet server such as a Facebook post or YouTube video.

Interestingly, some Federal Communications Commission (FCC; **www.fcc.gov**) members feel that the definition of broadband should be increased to 100 Mbps for download. The definition of broadband remains fluid, however, and it will undoubtedly continue to change to reflect greater transmission capacities in the future.

You are likely familiar with certain types of broadband connections such as *digital subscriber line (DSL)* and cable to your homes and dorms. DSL and cable fall within the range of transmission capacity mentioned here and are thus defined as broadband connections.

The various types of computer networks range from small to worldwide. They include (from smallest to largest): personal area networks (PANs), local area networks (LANs), metropolitan area networks (MANs), wide area networks (WANs), and the ultimate WAN, the Internet. PANs are short-range networks—typically a few meters—that are used for communication among devices close to one person. They can be wired or wireless. (You will learn about wireless PANs in Chapter 8.) MANs are relatively large networks that cover a metropolitan area. MANs fall between LANs and WANs in size. WANs typically cover large geographical areas; in some cases, they can span the entire planet and reach from Earth to Mars and beyond.

Local Area Networks

Regardless of their size, networks represent a compromise among three objectives: speed, distance, and cost. Organizations typically must select two of the three. To cover long distances, organizations can have fast communication if they are willing to pay for it, or inexpensive communication if they are willing to accept slower speeds. A third possible combination of the three trade-offs is fast, inexpensive communication with distance limitations. This is the idea behind local area networks.

A **local area network (LAN)** connects two or more devices in a limited geographical region, usually within the same building, so that every device on the network can communicate with every other device. Most LANs today use Ethernet (discussed later in this chapter). **Figure 6.1**

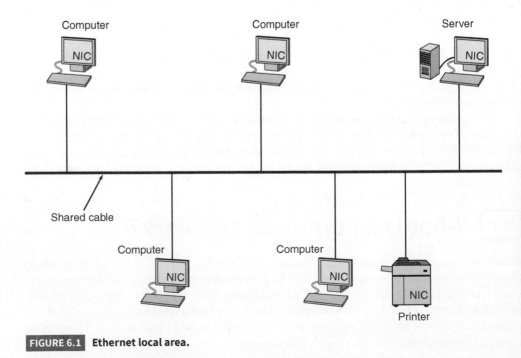

FIGURE 6.1 Ethernet local area.

illustrates an Ethernet LAN that consists of four computers, a server, and a printer, all of which connect through a shared cable. Every device in the LAN has a *network interface card (NIC)* that allows the device to physically connect to the LAN's communications medium. This medium is typically unshielded twisted-pair wire (UTP).

Although it is not required, many LANs have a **file server** or **network server**. The server typically contains various software and data for the network. It also houses the LAN's network operating system, which manages the server and routes and manages communications on the network.

Wide Area Networks

When businesses have to transmit and receive data beyond the confines of the LAN, they use wide area networks. The term *wide area network* did not even exist until local area networks appeared. Before that time, what we call a wide area network today was simply called a network.

A **wide area network (WAN)** is a network that covers a large geographical area. WANs typically connect multiple LANs. They are generally provided by common carriers such as telephone companies and the international networks of global communications services providers. Examples of these providers include AT&T (**www.att.com**) in the United States, Deutsche Telekom in Germany (**www.telekom.com**), and NTT Communications in Japan.

WANs have large capacities, and they typically combine multiple channels (e.g., fiber-optic cables, microwave, and satellite). WANs also contain **routers**—communications processors that route messages from a LAN to the Internet, across several connected LANs, or across a WAN such as the Internet. The Internet is an example of a WAN.

Enterprise Networks

Organizations today have multiple LANs and may have multiple WANs. All of these networks are interconnected to form an **enterprise network**. **Figure 6.2** displays a model of enterprise computing. Note that the enterprise network in the figure has a backbone network. Corporate **backbone networks** are high-speed central networks to which multiple smaller networks (such as LANs and smaller WANs) connect. The LANs are called *embedded LANs* because they connect to the backbone WAN.

Unfortunately, traditional networks can be rigid and lack the flexibility to keep pace with increasing business networking requirements. The reason for this problem is that the functions of traditional networks are distributed across physical routers and devices (i.e., hardware). Therefore, to implement changes, each network device must be configured individually. In some cases, devices must be configured manually. *Software-defined networks (SDN)* are an emerging technology that is becoming increasingly important to help organizations manage their data flows across their enterprise networks. With SDN, decisions that control how network traffic flows across network devices are managed centrally by software. The software dynamically adjusts data flows to meet business and application needs.

Think of traditional networks as the road system of a city in 1920. Data packets are the cars that travel through the city. A traffic officer (physical network devices) controls each intersection and directs traffic by recognizing the turn signals and the size and shape of the vehicles passing through the intersection. The officers can direct only the traffic at their intersection. They do not know the overall traffic volume in the city nor do they know traffic movement across the city. Therefore, it is difficult to control the city's traffic patterns as a whole and to manage peak-hour traffic. When problems occur, the city must communicate with each individual officer by radio.

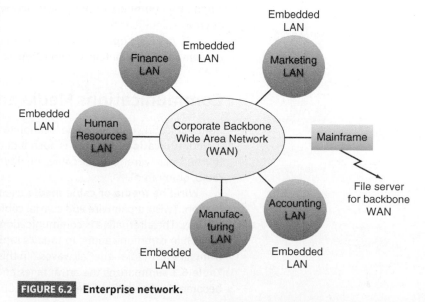

FIGURE 6.2 Enterprise network.

Now think of SDN as the road system of a modern city. Each traffic officer is replaced by a traffic light and a set of electronic vehicle counters, which are connected to central monitoring and control software. With this system, the city's traffic can be instantly and centrally controlled. The control software can direct traffic differently at various times of the day (say, rush hours). The software monitors traffic flow and automatically changes the traffic lights to help traffic flow through the city with minimal disruption.

Before you go on...

1. What are the primary business reasons for using networks?
2. What are the differences between LANs and WANs?
3. Describe an enterprise network.

6.2 Network Fundamentals

Author Lecture Videos are available exclusively in *WileyPLUS*.
Apply the Concept activities are available in the Appendix and in *WileyPLUS*.

In this section, you will learn the basics of how networks actually operate. You begin by studying wireline communications media, which enable computers in a network to transmit and receive data. You conclude this section by looking at network protocols and the types of network processing.

Today, computer networks communicate through *digital signals*, which are discrete pulses that are either on or off, representing a series of *bits* (0s and 1s). This quality allows digital signals to convey information in a binary form that can be interpreted by computers.

The U.S. public telephone system (called the "plain old telephone system" or POTS) was originally designed as an analog network to carry voice signals or sounds in an analog wave format. *Analog signals* are continuous waves that transmit information by altering the amplitude and frequency of the waves. POTS require *dial-up modems* to convert signals from analog to digital and vice versa. Dial-up modems are almost extinct in most parts of the developed world today.

Cable modems are modems that operate over coaxial cable—for example, cable TV. They offer broadband access to the Internet or to corporate intranets. Cable modem speeds vary widely. Most providers offer bandwidth between 1 and 6 million bits per second (Mbps) for downloads (from the Internet to a computer) and between 128 and 768 thousand bits per second (Kbps) for uploads. Cable modem services share bandwidth among subscribers in a locality. That is, the same cable line connects to many households. Therefore, when large numbers of neighbors access the Internet at the same time, cable speeds can decrease significantly.

DSL modems operate on the same lines as voice telephones and dial-up modems. DSL modems always maintain a connection, so an Internet connection is immediately available.

Communications Media and Channels

Communicating data from one location to another requires some form of pathway or medium. A **communications channel** is such a pathway. It is comprised of two types of media: cable (twisted-pair wire, coaxial cable, or fiber-optic cable) and broadcast (microwave, satellite, radio, or infrared).

Wireline media or **cable media** use physical wires or cables to transmit data and information. Twisted-pair wire and coaxial cables are made of copper, and fiber-optic cable is made of glass. The alternative is communication over **broadcast media** or **wireless media.** The key to mobile communications in today's rapidly moving society is data transmissions over electromagnetic media—the "airwaves." In this section, you will study the three wireline channels. **Table 6.1** summarizes the advantages and disadvantages of each of these channels. You will become familiar with wireless media in Chapter 8.

TABLE 6.1   Advantages and Disadvantages of Wireline Communications Channels

Channel	Advantages	Disadvantages
Twisted-pair wire	Inexpensive Widely available Easy to work with	Slow (low bandwidth) Subject to interference Easily tapped (low security)
Coaxial cable	Higher bandwidth than twisted-pair Less susceptible to electromagnetic interference	Relatively expensive and inflexible Easily tapped (low to medium security) Somewhat difficult to work with
Fiber-optic cable	Very high bandwidth Relatively inexpensive Difficult to tap (good security)	Difficult to work with (difficult to splice)

Twisted-Pair Wire.   The most prevalent form of communications wiring, **twisted-pair wire**, is used for almost all business telephone wiring. As the name suggests, it consists of strands of copper wire twisted in pairs (see **Figure 6.3**). Twisted-pair wire is relatively inexpensive to purchase, widely available, and easy to work with. However, it also has some significant disadvantages. Specifically, it is relatively slow for transmitting data, it is subject to interference from other electrical sources, and it can be easily tapped by unintended recipients to gain unauthorized access to data.

Coaxial Cable.   Coaxial cable (**Figure 6.4**) consists of insulated copper wire. Compared with twisted-pair wire, it is much less susceptible to electrical interference, and it can carry much more data. For these reasons, it is commonly used to carry high-speed data traffic as well as television signals (thus the term *cable TV*). However, coaxial cable is more expensive and more difficult to work with than twisted-pair wire. It is also somewhat inflexible.

Fiber Optics.   Fiber-optic cable (**Figure 6.5**) consists of thousands of very thin filaments of glass fibers that transmit information through pulses of light generated by lasers. The fiber-optic cable is surrounded by cladding, a coating that prevents the light from leaking out of the fiber.

Fiber-optic cables are significantly smaller and lighter than traditional cable media. They can also transmit far more data, and they provide greater security from interference and tapping. Fiber-optic cable is typically used as the backbone for a network, whereas twisted-pair wire and coaxial cable connect the backbone to individual devices on the network. As of August 2020 approximately 750,000 miles of 380 undersea fiber-optic cables carry over 99.5 percent of all transoceanic data. In 2016, FASTER, the aptly named 5,600-mile undersea fiber-optic cable

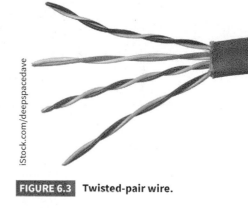

iStock.com/deepspacedave

FIGURE 6.3   **Twisted-pair wire.**

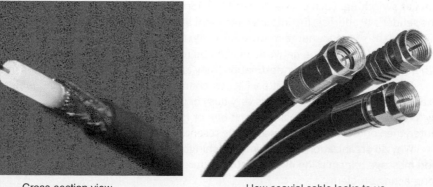

GIPhotoStock/Science Source

Cross-section view

How coaxial cable looks to us

iStock.com/piotr_malczyk

FIGURE 6.4   **Two views of coaxial cable.**

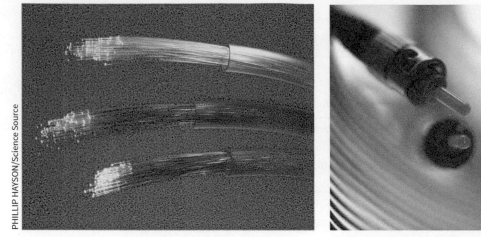

FIGURE 6.5   **Two views of fiber-optic cable.**

Cross-section view   How fiber-optic cable looks to us

connecting Japan and the United States, became operational. FASTER is purported to be able to transmit data at 60 terabits (trillions of bits) per second across the Pacific Ocean.

Network Protocols

Computing devices that are connected to the network must access and share the network to transmit and receive data. These devices are often referred to as *nodes* of the network. They work together by adhering to a common set of rules and procedures—known as a **protocol**—that enable them to communicate with one another. The two major protocols are the Ethernet and Transmission Control Protocol/Internet Protocol.

Ethernet.   A common LAN protocol is **Ethernet**. Many organizations use 100-gigabit Ethernet, through which the network provides data transmission speeds of 100 gigabits (100 billion bits) per second. The 400-gigabit Ethernet began entering service in 2018.

Transmission Control Protocol/Internet Protocol.   The **Transmission Control Protocol/Internet Protocol (TCP/IP)** is the protocol of the Internet. TCP/IP uses a suite of protocols, the primary ones being the Transmission Control Protocol (TCP) and the Internet Protocol (IP). The TCP performs three basic functions: (1) it manages the movement of data packets (see further on) between computers by establishing a connection between the computers, (2) it sequences the transfer of packets, and (3) it acknowledges the packets that have been transmitted. The **Internet Protocol (IP)** is responsible for disassembling, delivering, and reassembling the data during transmission.

Before data are transmitted over the Internet, they are divided into small, fixed bundles called *packets.* The transmission technology that breaks up blocks of text into packets is called **packet switching**. Each packet carries the information that will help it reach its destination—the sender's IP address, the intended recipient's IP address, the number of packets in the message, and the sequence number of the particular packet within the message. Each packet travels independently across the network and can be routed through different paths in the network. When the packets reach their destination, they are reassembled into the original message.

It is important to note that packet-switching networks are reliable and fault tolerant. For example, if a path in the network is very busy or is broken, packets can be dynamically ("on the fly") rerouted around that path. Also, if one or more packets do not get to the receiving computer, then only those packets need to be resent.

Why do organizations use packet switching? The main reason is to achieve reliable end-to-end message transmission over sometimes-unreliable networks that may have short-acting or long-acting problems.

The packets use the TCP/IP protocol to carry their data. TCP/IP functions in four layers (see **Figure 6.6**). The *application layer* enables client application programs to access the other

Email: Sending a Message via SMTP (Simple Mail Transfer Protocol)	Application	Email: Message received
Break Message into packets and determine order	Transport	Packets reordered and replaced (if lost)
Assign sending and receiving IP addresses and apply to each packet	Internet	Packets routed through internal network to desired IP address
Determine path across network/Internet to intended destination	Network Interface	Receipt of packets

FIGURE 6.6 The four layers of the TCP/IP reference model.

layers, and it defines the protocols that applications use to exchange data. One of these application protocols is the **Hypertext Transfer Protocol (HTTP)**, which defines how messages are formulated and how they are interpreted by their receivers. (We discuss hypertext in Section 6.3.) The *transport layer* provides the application layer with communication and packet services. This layer includes TCP and other protocols. The *Internet layer* is responsible for addressing, routing, and packaging data packets. The IP is one of the protocols in this layer. Finally, the *network interface layer* places packets on, and receives them from, the network medium, which can be any networking technology.

Two computers using TCP/IP can communicate even if they use different hardware and software. Data sent from one computer to another proceed downward through all four layers, beginning with the sending computer's application layer and going through its network interface layer. After the data reach the receiving computer, they travel up the layers.

TCP/IP enables users to send data across sometimes-unreliable networks with the assurance that the data will arrive in uncorrupted form. TCP/IP is very popular with business organizations because of its reliability and the ease with which it can support intranets and related functions.

Let's look at an example of packet switching across the Internet. **Figure 6.7** illustrates a message being sent from New York City to Los Angeles over a packet-switching network. Note that the different colored packets travel by different routes to reach their destination in Los Angeles, where they are reassembled into the complete message.

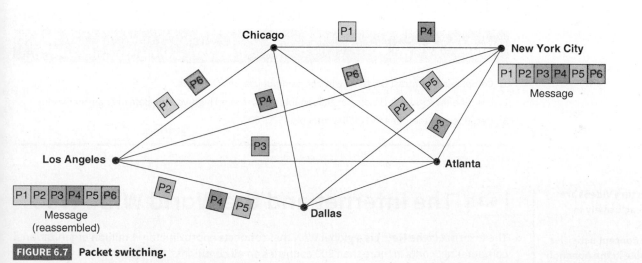

FIGURE 6.7 Packet switching.

Types of Network Processing

Organizations typically use multiple computer systems across the firm. **Distributed processing** divides processing work among two or more computers. This process enables computers in different locations to communicate with one another through telecommunications links. A common type of distributed processing is client/server processing. A special type of client/server processing is peer-to-peer processing.

Client/Server Computing.   **Client/server computing** links two or more computers in an arrangement in which some machines, called **servers**, provide computing services for user PCs, called **clients**. Usually, an organization performs the bulk of its processing or application and data storage on suitably powerful servers that can be accessed by less powerful client machines. The client requests applications, data, or processing from the server, which acts on these requests by "serving" the desired commodity.

Client/server computing leads to the ideas of "fat" clients and "thin" clients. As discussed in Technology Guide 1, *fat clients* have large storage and processing power and therefore can run local programs (such as Microsoft Office) if the network goes down. In contrast, *thin clients* may have no local storage and only limited processing power. Thus, they must depend on the network to run applications. For this reason, they are of little value when the network is not functioning.

Peer-to-Peer Processing.   **Peer-to-peer (P2P) processing** is a type of client/server distributed processing in which each computer acts as *both* a client and a server. Each computer can access (as assigned for security or integrity purposes) all files on all other computers.

There are three basic types of peer-to-peer processing. The first type accesses unused CPU power among networked computers. An application of this type is SETI@home (**http://setiathome.ssl.berkeley.edu**). These applications are from open-source projects, and they can be downloaded at no cost.

The second form of peer-to-peer is real-time, person-to-person collaboration, such as Microsoft SharePoint Workspace. This product provides P2P collaborative applications that use buddy lists to establish a connection and allow real-time collaboration within the application.

The third peer-to-peer category is advanced search and file sharing. This category is characterized by natural language searches of millions of peer systems. It enables users to discover other users, not just data and web pages. One example of this category is BitTorrent.

BitTorrent (**www.bittorrent.com**) is an open-source, free, peer-to-peer file-sharing application that simplifies the problem of sharing large files by dividing them into tiny pieces, or "torrents." BitTorrent addresses two of the biggest problems of file sharing: (1) downloading bogs down when many people access a file at once, and (2) some people leech, meaning they download content but refuse to share it. BitTorrent eliminates the bottleneck by enabling all users to share little pieces of a file at the same time—a process called *swarming*. The program prevents leeching because users must upload a file while they download it. Thus, the more popular the content, the more efficiently it travels over a network.

Before you go on...

1. Compare and contrast the three wireline communications channels.
2. Describe the various technologies that enable users to send high-volume data over any network.
3. Describe the Ethernet and TCP/IP protocols.

Author Lecture Videos are available exclusively in *WileyPLUS*.
Apply the Concept activities are available in the Appendix and in *WileyPLUS*.

6.3   The Internet and the World Wide Web

The **Internet ("the Net")** is a global WAN that connects approximately 1 million organizational computer networks in more than 200 countries on all continents. It has become so widespread that it features in the daily routine of some 5 billion people.

The computers and organizational nodes on the Internet can be of different types and makes. They are connected to one another by data communications lines of different speeds. The primary network connections and telecommunications lines that link the nodes are referred to as the **Internet backbone**. For the Internet, the backbone is a fiber-optic network that is operated primarily by large telecommunications companies.

Many people mistakenly assume that Internet traffic (data transmissions) occurs wirelessly. However, only 1 percent of Internet traffic is carried by satellites. So, what does the Internet actually look like?

The Internet is quite tangible, consisting of underwater cables that total almost 750,000 miles in length. These cables, which range in thickness from a garden hose to about three inches in diameter, come onshore at cable landing points.

From these points, the cables are buried underground and make their way to large data centers. (We discuss data centers in Technology Guide 3.) In the United States, most of these underground cables are located along major roads and railways. In fact, one of the world's most concentrated hubs in terms of Internet connectivity is located in lower Manhattan in New York City.

As a network of networks, the Internet enables people to access data in other organizations and to communicate, collaborate, and exchange information seamlessly around the world quickly and inexpensively. Thus, the Internet has become a necessity for modern businesses.

The Internet grew out of an experimental project of the Advanced Research Project Agency (ARPA) of the U.S. Department of Defense. The project began in 1969 as the *ARPAnet*. Its purpose was to test the feasibility of a WAN over which researchers, educators, military personnel, and government agencies could share data, exchange messages, and transfer files.

Today, Internet technologies are being used both within and among organizations. An **intranet** is a network that uses Internet protocols so that users can take advantage of familiar applications and work habits. Intranets support discovery (easy and inexpensive browsing and search), communication, and collaboration inside an organization.

In contrast, an **extranet** connects parts of the intranets of different organizations. It also enables business partners to communicate securely over the Internet using virtual private networks (VPNs) (explained in Chapter 4). Extranets offer limited accessibility to the intranets of participating companies, as well as necessary interorganizational communications. They are widely used in the areas of business-to-business (B2B) electronic commerce (see Chapter 7) and supply chain management (SCM) (see Chapter 11).

No central agency manages the Internet. Instead, the costs of its operation are shared among hundreds of thousands of nodes. Thus, the cost for any one organization is small. Organizations must pay a small fee if they wish to register their names, and they need to install their own hardware and software to operate their internal networks. Organizations are obliged to move any data or information that enters their organizational network, regardless of the source, to their destination, at no charge to the senders. The senders, of course, pay the telephone bills for using either the backbone or regular telephone lines.

Accessing the Internet

You can access the Internet in several ways. From your place of work or your university, you can use your organization's LAN. A campus or company backbone connects all of the various LANs and servers in the organization to the Internet. You can also log on to the Internet from your home or on the road, using either wireline or wireless connections.

Connecting through an Online Service.   You can access the Internet by opening an account with an Internet service provider. An **Internet service provider (ISP)** is a company that provides Internet connections for a fee. Large ISPs include Comcast (**www.xfinity.com**), AT&T (**www.att.com**), Spectrum (**www.spectrum.com**), and Verizon (**www.verizon.com**).

ISPs connect to one another through **network access points (NAPs).** NAPs are exchange points for Internet traffic. They determine how traffic is routed. NAPs are key components of the Internet backbone. **Figure 6.8** displays a schematic of the Internet. The white links at the top of the figure represent the Internet backbone; the brown dots where the white links meet are the NAPs.

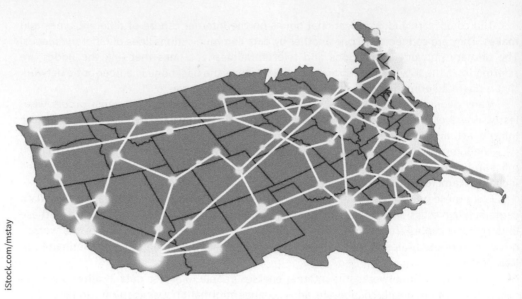

iStock.com/mstay

FIGURE 6.8 Internet (backbone in white).

Connecting through Other Means.

There have been several attempts to make access to the Internet cheaper, faster, and easier. For example, terminals known as Internet kiosks have been located in public places like libraries and airports (and even in convenience stores in some countries) for use by people who do not have their own computers. Accessing the Internet from smartphones and tablets is common, and fiber-to-the-home (FTTH) is growing rapidly. FTTH involves connecting fiber-optic cable directly to individual homes. **Table 6.2** summarizes the various means of connecting to the Internet. Satellite connections and Google Fiber are worth noting in more detail.

Connecting through satellite.

See our discussion in Section 8.1.

Google Fiber (FTTH).

Google Fiber (**http://fiber.google.com**) is a service that provides fiber-to-the-home. In August 2020 Google Fiber was available in 27 metropolitan areas in the U.S., in direct competition with cable Internet providers. Google Fiber offers download speeds of 1 gigabit per second (1 Gbps) and costs approximately $70 per month.

Google Fiber competitors have responded to Google's initiatives. For example, AT&T offers its 1 Gbps GigaPower service in approximately 80 U.S. metropolitan areas for $40 per month.

Addresses on the Internet.

Each computer on the Internet has an assigned address, called the **Internet Protocol (IP) address** that distinguishes it from all other computers. The IP address consists of sets of numbers in four parts, separated by dots. For example, the IP address of one computer might be 135.62.128.91. You can access a website by typing this number in the address bar of your browser.

TABLE 6.2   **Internet Connection Methods**

Service	Description
Dial-up	Still used in the United States where broadband is not available
DSL	Broadband access through telephone companies
Cable modem	Access over your cable TV coaxial cable. Can have degraded performance if many of your neighbors are accessing the Internet at once.
Satellite	Access where cable and DSL are not available
Wireless	Very convenient, and WiMAX will increase the use of broadband wireless
Fiber-to-the-home (FTTH)	Expensive and usually placed only in new housing developments

Currently, there are two IP addressing schemes. The first scheme, IPv4, was the most widely used. IP addresses using IPv4 consist of 32 bits, meaning that there are 2^{32} possibilities for IP addresses, or 4,294,967,295 distinct addresses. Note that the IP address in the preceding paragraph (135.62.128.91) is an IPv4 address. At the time that IPv4 was developed, there were not as many computers that needed addresses as there are today. Therefore, a new IP addressing scheme has been developed, IPv6, because we have run out of available IPv4 addresses.

IP addresses using IPv6 consist of 128 bits, meaning that there are 2^{128} possibilities for distinct IP addresses, which is an unimaginably large number. IPv6, which is replacing IPv4, will accommodate the rapidly increasing number of devices that need IP addresses, such as smartphones and devices that constitute the Internet of Things (see Section 8.4).

IP addresses must be unique so that computers on the Internet know where to find one another. The Internet Corporation for Assigned Names and Numbers (ICANN) (**www.icann.org**) coordinates these unique addresses throughout the world, working on behalf of an international "multistakeholder community" composed primarily of technology companies.

Because numeric IP addresses are difficult to remember, most computers have names as well. ICANN accredits certain companies called *registrars* to register these names, which are derived from the **domain name system (DNS)**. **Domain names** consist of multiple parts, separated by dots, that are read from right to left. For example, consider the domain name *business.auburn.edu.* The rightmost part (or zone) of an Internet name is its top-level domain (TLD). The letters *edu* in business.auburn.edu indicate that this is an educational site. The following are popular U.S. TLDs:

.com	commercial sites
.edu	educational sites
.mil	military government sites
.gov	civilian government sites
.org	organizations

To conclude our domain name example, *auburn* is the name of the organization (Auburn University), and *business* is the name of the particular machine (server) within the organization to which the message is being sent.

A top-level domain (TLD) is the domain at the highest level in the hierarchical Domain Name System of the Internet. The top-level domain names are located in the root zone (rightmost zone) of the name. Management of most TLDs is delegated to responsible organizations by ICANN. ICANN operates the Internet Assigned Numbers Authority (IANA), which is in charge of maintaining the DNS root zone. Today, IANA distinguishes the following groups of TLDs:

- Country-code top-level domains (ccTLD): Two-letter domains established for countries or territories. For example, *de* stands for Germany, *it* for Italy, and *ru* for Russia.

- Internationalized country code top-level domains (IDN ccTLD): These are ccTLDs in non-Latin character sets (e.g., Arabic or Chinese).

- Generic top-level domains (gTLD): Top-level domains with three or more characters. gTLDs initially consisted of .gov, .edu, .com, .mil, .org, and .net. In late 2000, ICANN introduced .aero, .biz, .coop, .info, .museum, .name, and .pro.

The Future of the Internet

Researchers assert that if Internet bandwidth is not improved rapidly, then within a few years the Internet will be able to function only at a much-reduced speed. The Internet is sometimes too slow for data-intensive applications such as full-motion video files (movies) and large medical files (X-rays). The Internet is also unreliable and is not secure. As a result, Internet2 has been developed by many U.S. universities collaborating with industry and government. **Internet2** develops and deploys advanced network applications such as remote medical diagnosis, digital libraries, distance education, online simulation, and virtual laboratories. It is designed to be fast, always on, everywhere, natural, intelligent, easy, and trusted. Note that Internet2 is not a separate physical network from the Internet. For more details, see **www .internet2.edu**.

The World Wide Web

Many people equate the Internet with the World Wide Web. However, they are not the same thing. The Internet functions as a transport mechanism, whereas the World Wide Web is an application that uses those transport functions. Other applications, such as e-mail, also run on the Internet.

The **World Wide Web** (**the Web** or **WWW**) is a system of universally accepted standards for storing, retrieving, formatting, and displaying information through a client/server architecture. The Web handles all types of digital information, including text, hypermedia, graphics, and sound. It uses graphical user interfaces (GUIs) (explained in Technology Guide 2), so it is very easy to navigate. However, the web that we are familiar with is only a small part of the entire web, as you see in IT's About Business 6.1.

Hypertext is the underlying concept defining the structure of the World Wide Web. Hypertext is the text displayed on a computer display or other electronic device with references, called *hyperlinks*, to other text that the reader can immediately access, or where text can be revealed progressively at additional levels of details. A **hyperlink** is a connection from a hypertext file or document to another location or file, typically activated by clicking on a highlighted word or image on the screen, or by touching the screen.

Organizations that wish to offer information through the Web must establish a *home page*, which is a text and graphical screen display that usually welcomes the user and provides basic

---

IT's About Business 6.1

MIS   The Surface Web, the Deep Web, and the Dark Web

The *surface web*—also known as the *visible web* or the *clearnet*—is the collection of websites that we are all familiar with and use constantly. Surface websites are indexed by traditional search engines. They track user data, deploy cookies, and share Internet Protocol data. Examples of surface web content are YouTube, Wikipedia, and basically everything that we can see on the results page of any search engine. Estimates are that the surface web comprises 10–16 percent of the information that is on the Internet.

The *deep web* refers to the collection of websites that cannot be indexed by traditional search engines. Deep web content does not appear on the results pages of search engines because it exists behind passwords, firewalls, and paywalls and it requires credentials to access. Deep web content includes databases, webmail pages, registration-required content, online banking pages, medical and financial records, personal files, and other forms of untracked Internet communication. Estimates are that the deep web comprises 80–90 percent of information on the Internet.

Finally, the *Dark Web* is a network of websites, servers, forums, and communication tools that require encryption technologies to access and therefore cannot be indexed on traditional search engines. Compared to the surface web and the deep web, the Dark Web comprises a very small amount of information. Security experts estimate that there are between 10,000 and 100,000 active sites.

To access Dark Web sites, users must employ Tor, an acronym for The Onion Router. Tor is free, open-source software that helps keep the source and destination of Internet traffic anonymous by sending each computer's IP address through a network of similarly encrypted IP addresses. Each computer knows only the immediate sender and the next recipient.

Users can also employ Tails, a portable and disposable Linux-based operating system that operates from a flash drive. Tails adds a layer of security to activities on the Dark Web. Despite Tor and Tails, however, there is no guarantee of complete anonymity on the Dark Web.

People and organizations use the Dark Web for both legitimate and criminal purposes. Criminals exploit the Dark Web's anonymity to sell guns, drugs, people (slavery), and stolen data.

On the positive side, organizations such as the United Nations, the Electronic Frontier Foundation, and news organizations use the Dark Web to protect dissidents, informants, and sources in oppressive countries. That is, the Dark Web provides a safe haven for whistleblowers, activists, and journalists who need to share sensitive information but cannot do so publicly for fear of political persecution or retribution by their governments or employers.

Other legitimate Dark Web users include corporate IT departments and law enforcement agencies. Corporations monitor and search the Dark Web for stolen data and compromised accounts. Law enforcement agencies hunt criminals on the Dark Web. For example, the United Nations law enforcement department, the Office on Drugs and Crime, monitors the Dark Web and shares data with both the public and global police organizations such as Europol and the FBI.

Sources: Compiled from A. Spadafora, "Your Personal Details Are Almost Certainly for Sale on the Dark Web Now," *TechRadar*, July 11, 2020; "What's the Dark Web & How to Access It in 3 Easy Steps," *vpnMentor*, June 17, 2020; A. Holmes, "The Dark Web Turns 20 This Month." *Business Insider*, March 21, 2020; P. O'Neill, "A Dark Web Tycoon Pleads Guilty. But How Was He Caught?" *MIT Technology Review*, February 8, 2020; "Everything You Need to Know about the Dark Web in 2020," *Broadbandsearch.com*, 2020; "Dark Web Monitoring: The Good, the Bad, and the Ugly," *Photon Research*, September 11, 2019; "Double Blow to Dark Web Marketplaces," *Europol*, May 3, 2019; L. Whitney, "How Criminals Use Fraud Guides from the Dark Web to Scam Organizations and Individuals," *TechRepublic*, April 17, 2019; R. Gehl, "Illuminating the Dark Web," *The Conversation*, October 31, 2018; D. Patterson, "Dark Web: A Guide for Business Professionals," *TechRepublic*, October 26, 2018.

Questions

1. Discuss the advantages and disadvantages of the surface web.
2. Discuss the advantages and disadvantages of the deep web.
3. Discuss the advantages and disadvantages of the Dark Web.

information on the organization that has established the page. In most cases, the home page will lead users to other pages. All the pages of a particular company or individual are collectively known as a **website**. Most web pages provide a way to contact the organization or the individual. The person in charge of an organization's website is its *webmaster*. (Note: *Webmaster* is a gender-neutral title.)

To access a website, the user must specify a **uniform resource locator (URL)** which points to the address of a specific resource on the web. For example, the URL for Microsoft is **http://www.microsoft.com**. Recall that HTTP stands for *hypertext transport protocol*. The remaining letters in this URL—**www.microsoft.com**—indicate the domain name that identifies the web server that stores the website.

Users access the Web primarily through software applications called browsers. **Browsers** provide a graphical front end that enables users to point and click their way across the web, a process called *surfing*. Web browsers became a means of universal access because they deliver the same interface on any operating system on which they run. As of July 2019, Google Chrome was the leading browser, followed by Apple Safari, Firefox, Microsoft Internet Explorer, and Microsoft Edge.

The World Wide Web has evolved since Professor Tim Berners-Lee wrote the original computer code for it in 1999. IT's About Business 6.2 examines this evolution from Web 0.0 to Web 5.0 and closes with a new form of the Web developed by Professor Berners-Lee.

IT's About Business 6.2

MIS   The Evolution of the World Wide Web

Each new version of the World Wide Web has transformed the ways in which users interact with data, information, organizations, and one another. The Web has also transformed the ways in which organizations conduct business. Let's examine how the Web has evolved since its invention in 1989.

Web 0.0: The Development of the Web (1989–1990)

In 1989, Tim Berners-Lee, a British scientist at the European Organization for Nuclear Research (CERN), invented the World Wide Web—the first Web browser—and the fundamental protocols and algorithms that enabled the Web to expand globally. His original specifications of uniform resource locators (URLs), hypertext transport protocol (HTTP), and hypertext markup language (HTML) were the basic building blocks of the Web. The Web was introduced to the public in 1990.

Web 1.0: The Read-Only Web (1990–2000)

Web 1.0 presented users with information, which typically was presented by organizations to users. For example, firms used static websites to display product information and directions to their closest brick-and-mortar store location.

This version of the Web was where users searched and found information. It was called the Read-Only Web because it was generally not interactive and users were basically content consumers.

By 1999 there were approximately 3 million static websites. The massive amounts of information available on these websites led to the creation of Web browsers—for example, Mosaic, Netscape Navigator, Opera, and Internet Explorer—and search engines—for example, Yahoo and Google.

The first shopping cart applications appeared during Web 1.0. *Shopping carts* on ecommerce retailers' sites make it easier for consumers to purchase a product or service. Carts accept customers' payments and distribute the payment information to the merchant, payment processor, and other parties. Amazon, founded in 1994, and eBay, founded in 1995, were early adopters of shopping carts.

Web 2.0: The Social (Read-Write) Web (2000–2010)

Whereas Web 1.0 connected users with information, Web 2.0 connected people with people. Internet users became participants and were able to interact with one another and with websites. They could collaborate on ideas, share information, and generate or create information that would be available to other users around the world. By 2006 there were approximately 85 million websites.

Web 2.0 is called the Read–Write Web because users were able to create and upload content. It is also called the Social Web because users could interact with one another and upload the content that they created to social media websites.

During this period, companies began to realize the benefits of community interaction with their websites. Web 2.0 enabled users to create and upload content on many platforms including:

- Blogs: In 1999, LiveJournal and Blogger launched as blogging platforms.
- Crowdsourced websites: Encyclopedia Wikipedia launched in 2001.
- Social media websites: MySpace launched in 2003, Facebook in 2004, and Twitter in 2006.
- Video-streaming websites: YouTube launched in 2005.

Web 3.0: The Semantic (Read–Write–Execute) Web (2010–2020)

Web 3.0 is known as the Semantic Web because it attempts to represent knowledge in a format that allows computers to automatically reach conclusions and make decisions utilizing certain reasoning capabilities. By 2014 the Web contained more than 1 billion websites.

Two major applications underlie Web 3.0: semantic markup and web services. *Semantic markup* is a method of structuring HTML so that HTML provides the meaning of the information in web pages and web applications rather than just its appearance. A *web service* is an application designed to support machine-to-machine interaction over the Internet.

By combining semantic markup and web services, Web 3.0 provides for machine-readable content, developed so that applications can directly interact with one another. Web applications can also interpret information for humans. For example, Google can understand a user's search history, and Amazon can understand a user's previous purchases. This feature enables both websites to provide personalized advertisements and suggestions. However, Web 3.0 applications such as these could not provide context to information, understand relevance, or make more complex decisions.

Users can access Web 3.0 content with multiple applications from wherever they are. Further, because every device is connected to the Web, services can be used everywhere. These features have led to Web 3.0 also being called the "portable, personal, mobile" Web.

Web 3.0 websites began to use sensor-driven, machine-readable content, called the Internet of Things (IoT; see Chapter 8). For example, smart appliances with IoT technology contain embedded sensors enabling them to connect to the Web. These appliances can perform tasks without human involvement. So, if you leave your "smart" stove on when you leave your house, the stove will wait for a certain period of time and then alert you on your phone. You can turn off the stove from that app. Your "smart" refrigerator can note expiration dates of items and alert you when an expiration date is approaching. If you are leaving work, the refrigerator can alert you to pick up that item from the grocery store on your way home.

As we look at Web 4.0 and Web 5.0 as of October 2020, keep in mind that we are speculating because these versions of the Web are still being developed.

Web 4.0: The Symbiotic Web (2020–2030)

Web 4.0 is the open intelligent web, often characterized as the Web OS. That is, the entire Web acts a single operating system where information flows from any one point to any other point.

Web 4.0 is also known as the *symbiotic web*. The goal of the symbiotic web is to enable humans and machines to interact in symbiosis. A *symbiotic relationship* between humans and machines is one in which humans and machines improve each other. Humans have capabilities such as compassion, intuition, and value judgement. Machines demonstrate learning, discovery, and fact checking. These capabilities complement and magnify each other.

Web 4.0 will interact with users in the same way that humans communicate with one another. Users will be able to meet and interact virtually on the Web through the use of avatars. An *avatar* is a graphical representation of a user that may take either a 2D form, such as an icon, or a 3D form, as in games or virtual worlds.

Web 5.0 (2030 and beyond)

Web 5.0, referred to as the *telepathic web*, could emerge with technologies such as neural (brain) implants. These implants could give humans the ability to communicate with the Web through their thoughts. For example, a person could think of a question, and an appropriate web page could open as a 3D image. People could make payments by using a neural implant or a microchip in their fingertips. All devices would continue to be connected to the Web, but they could be controlled by humans with their thoughts or implants.

Web 5.0 could also see the emergence of intelligent virtual assistants that predict your needs from your behaviors without requiring many cues. Web 5.0 will also focus on the individual users, perhaps by enabling a website to present a different experience for each individual who interacts with it.

The Inrupt Project: A New Direction for Web Evolution

As of August 2020, the Web was well into version Web 3.0, and technologies were being developed to lead us into Web 4.0. However, in 2018 Berners-Lee had launched his Inrupt project (**www.inrupt.com**), disrupting business as usual on today's Web, regardless of the version. That is, while the Web will continue to evolve as advanced technologies such as artificial intelligence emerge, Berners-Lee is developing a new model for Web evolution.

Berners-Lee and other researchers designed Inrupt to decentralize the Web and take back power from platforms that have profited from centralizing it. As we have noted in previous chapters, the "bargain" with platforms such as Google and Amazon allows users to access the platforms' services in exchange for users' data. Inrupt is designed to redirect the balance of power from Web platforms to Web users.

Inrupt is the first major commercial venture that utilizes Solid, a decentralized web platform built by Berners-Lee and other researchers at MIT (**www.mit.edu**). Inrupt differs from current versions of the Web in that all data that users access, create, or upload exist within each user's Solid pod. Each user will have a Solid identity and a Solid pod; that is, his or her personal online data store. The pods provide users with control over their applications and data on the Web.

For example, the MIT team has created a decentralized version of Alexa, Amazon's digital assistant, called Charlie. In contrast to Alexa, Charlie users own all of their data. As a result, users could trust Charlie with information such as health records, children's school events, and financial records. For a list of Solid Inrupt apps, see **https://inrupt.com/solidApps/solid-app-listing/**.

With Inrupt, users can allow access to particular elements of their data for particular services as they see fit and move their data from app to app instead of surrendering it. Inrupt could also use blockchain technology (see Chapter 7), which offers a means of independently verified personal identity. This verification respects privacy better than the accounts that users maintain on various platforms.

Blockchain technology also enables users to make micropayments in return for particular online services or content. Further, if users voluntarily allow platforms to use elements of their data, the platforms can make micropayments to users.

Sources: Compiled from "5 Main Features of Web 3.0," *Expert System*, April 30, 2020; J. Zaino, "Semantic Web and Semantic Technology Trends in 2020," *Dataversity*, December 17, 2019; K. Spisak, "Eras of the Web—Web 0.0 through Web 5.0," *Business 2 Community*, September 13, 2019; K. Orphanides, "How Tim Berners-Lee Inrupt Project Plans to Fix the Web," *Wired*, February 15, 2019; J. Harris, "Together We Can Thwart the Big-Tech Data Grab. Here's How," *The Guardian*, January 7, 2019; K. Brooker, "Exclusive: Tim Berners-Lee Tells Us His Radical New Plan to Upend the World Wide Web," *Fast Company*, September 29, 2018; C. Smith, "Evolution of the World Wide Web from Web 1.0 to Web 5.0," *Geekswitdhblogs.net*, April 9, 2018; "What Is Web 4.0?" *Pandora FMS*, March 5, 2018; "The Symbiosis between Humans and Machines Is Our Best Hope for the Future," *Webit News*, June 23, 2017; D. Benito, M. Peris-Ortiz, et al., "Web 5.0: The Future of Emotional Competencies in Higher Education," *Global Business Perspectives*, May 7, 2013; **www.inrupt.com**, accessed July 21, 2020.

Questions

1. Trace the evolution of the Web for you personally along these dimensions: (1) ease of use, (2) overall usefulness, and (3) privacy concerns.

2. Would you use Inrupt, if it were available? Why or why not? Support your answer.

1. Describe the various ways that you can connect to the Internet.
2. Identify each part of an Internet address.
3. Describe the difference between the Internet and the World Wide Web.
4. What are the functions of browsers?

6.4 Network Applications: Discovery

Now that you have a working knowledge of what networks are and how you can access them, the key question is: How do businesses use networks to improve their operations? In the next four sections of this chapter, we explore four network applications: discovery, communication, collaboration, and education. These applications, however, are merely a sampling of the many network applications that are currently available to users. Even if these applications formed an exhaustive list today, they would not do so tomorrow, when inevitably something new will be developed. Furthermore, placing network applications in categories is difficult because there will always be borderline cases. For example, telecommuting combines communication and collaboration.

The Internet enables users to access, or *discover information*, located in databases all over the world. By browsing and searching data sources on the Web, users can apply the Internet's discovery capability to areas ranging from education to government services to entertainment to commerce. Although having access to all this information is a great benefit, it is critically important to realize that there is no quality assurance for information on the Web. The Web is truly democratic in that *anyone* can post information to it. Therefore, the fundamental rule about information on the Web is "User beware!"

Think about discovery in 1960. How did you find information? You probably had to go to the library to check out a physical book. Contrast that process with how you would discover that information today. In fact, the overall trends in discovery have been:

- In the past, you had to go to the information (the library). Today, the information comes to you through the Internet.
- In the past, only one person at a time could have the information (the book he or she checked out of the library). Today, the information is available to multiple users at the same time.
- In the past, you may not have been able to access the information you needed; for example, if the book was checked out. Today, the information is available to everyone simultaneously.
- In the past, you may have had to have your book translated if it were written in a different language. Today, automatic translation software tools are improving very rapidly.

However, there is a downside to the process of discovery. In June 2019 a crash outside Denver, Colorado, blocked the main access road to the Denver International Airport. Google Maps suggested a detour to many of the drivers trying to reach the airport.

The detour led some 100 drivers to a narrow dirt road near the airport. Unfortunately, the road ended up in a muddy, empty, privately owned field. Some cars in the front of the line became stuck in the mud. The narrow road only allowed passage of one car at a time, so cars at the back of the line had to turn around, one at a time, to untangle the mess.

Google's response? "While we always work to provide the best directions, issues can arise due to unforeseen circumstances."

Moral of the story: don't follow discovery on the Web blindly!

The Web's major strength—the vast stores of information it contains—also presents a major challenge. The amount of information on the Web can be overwhelming, and it doubles approximately each year. As a result, navigating through the Web and gaining access to necessary information are becoming more and more difficult. To accomplish these tasks, people are increasingly using search engines, directories, and portals.

Search Engines and Metasearch Engines

A **search engine** is a computer program that searches for specific information by keywords and then reports the results. A search engine maintains an index of billions of web pages. It uses that index to find pages that match a set of user-specified keywords. Such indexes are created and updated by *webcrawlers*, which are computer programs that browse the Web and create a copy of all visited pages. Search engines then index these pages to provide fast searches.

In mid-2020, four search engines accounted for almost all searches in the United States. They are, in order, Google (**www.google.com**), Bing (**www.bing.com**), Yahoo (**www.yahoo.com**), and DuckDuckGo (**www.duckduckgo.com**). The leading search engine in China is Baidu (**www.baidu.com**), which claims approximately 75 percent of the Chinese market.

Visual search uses real-world images (e.g., screenshots, Internet images, or photographs) as the basis for online searches. Modern visual search technology uses artificial intelligence (see Chapter 14) to understand the content and context of these images and return a list of related results. Approximately three-quarters of U.S. Internet users search for visual content prior to making a purchase. Leading visual search apps include Google Lens, Bing Visual Search, Amazon Camera Search, Pinterest Lens, and eBay Image Search.

You can also use a metasearch engine. **Metasearch engines** search several engines at once and then integrate the findings to answer users' queries. Examples are Metacrawler (**www.metacrawler.com**), Mamma (**www.mamma.com**), KartOO (**www.kartoo.com**), and Dogpile (**www.dogpile.com**).

Publication of Material in Foreign Languages

The World Bank (**www.worldbank.org**) estimates that 80 percent of online content is available in only 1 of 10 languages: English, Chinese, Spanish, Japanese, Arabic, Portuguese, German, French, Russian, and Korean. Roughly 3 billion people speak one of these as their first language. However, more than 50 percent of all online content is written in English, which is understood by only 21 percent of the world's population. Consider India, whose citizens speak roughly 425 languages and dialects. Industry analysts estimate that less than 0.1 percent of all Web content is composed in Hindi, the first language of approximately 260 million people.

So not only is there a huge amount of information on the Internet, but it is also written in many languages. How, then, do you access this information? The answer is that you use an *automatic translation* of web pages. Such translation is available to and from all major languages, and its quality is improving over time.

Companies invest resources to make their websites accessible in multiple languages as a result of the global nature of the business environment. That is, multilingual websites are now a competitive necessity. When companies are disseminating information around the world, getting that information correct is essential. It is not enough for companies to translate Web content. They must also localize that content and be sensitive to the needs of the people in local markets.

At 20 cents or more per word, translation services are expensive. Companies supporting 10 languages can spend $200,000 annually to localize information and another $50,000 to maintain their websites. Translation budgets for major multinational companies can total millions of dollars.

Some major translation products are Microsoft's Translator app (**https://translator.microsoft.com**), Google (**https://translate.google.com**) (see **Figure 6.9**), and Skype Translator (**https://www.skype.com/en/features/skype-translator/**), as well as products and services available at Trados (**www.sdltrados.com**) and Systran S.A. (**www.systransoft.com**).

In September 2016, Google announced its new translation service, which is based on deep learning (see Technology Guide 4). In a competition that compared the new translation system with human translators, the system came very close to matching the fluency of humans for some languages, such as translating between English and Spanish and between English and French. Google is expanding the system to multiple languages.

In December 2016, Microsoft launched its Translator app. With spoken conversation, the app can accommodate groups of speakers and nine languages: Arabic, Mandarin Chinese, Spanish, English, French, German, Russian, Portuguese, and Italian.

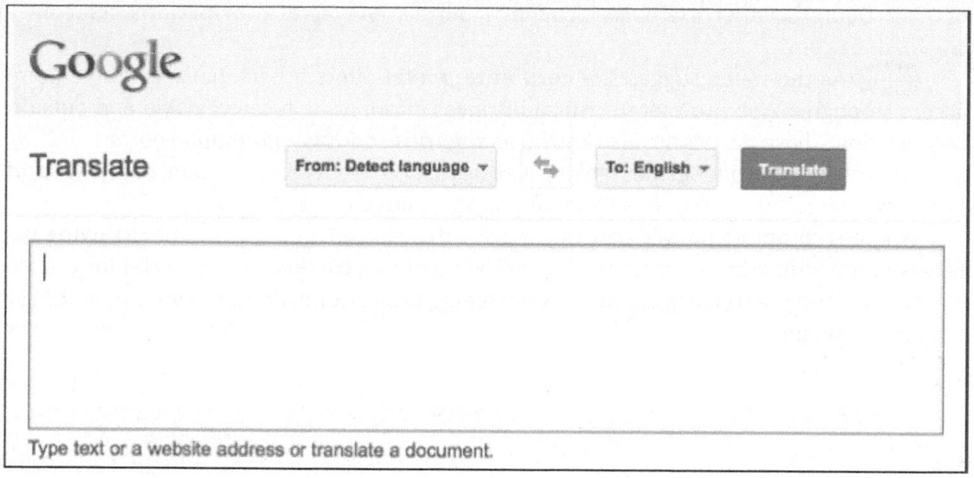

Source: Google LLC

FIGURE 6.9 **Google Translate. (Google and the Google logo are registered trademarks of Google Inc., used with permission).**

Portals

Most organizations and their managers encounter information overload. Information is scattered across numerous documents, e-mail messages, and databases at multiple locations and in multiple systems. Finding relevant and accurate information is often time consuming and may require users to access multiple systems.

MIS One solution to this problem is to use *portals*. A **portal** is a Web-based, personalized gateway to information and knowledge that provides relevant information from different IT systems and the Internet using advanced search and indexing techniques. After reading the next section, you will be able to distinguish among four types of portals: commercial, affinity, corporate, and industrywide. The four types of portals are differentiated by the audiences they serve.

A **commercial (public) portal** is the most popular type of portal on the Internet. It is intended for broad and diverse audiences, and it offers routine content, some of it in real time (e.g., a stock ticker). Examples are Lycos (**www.lycos.com**) and Microsoft Network (**www.msn.com**).

MKT In contrast, an **affinity portal** offers a single point of entry to an entire community of affiliated interests, such as a hobby group or a political party. Your university most likely has an affinity portal for its alumni. **Figure 6.10** displays the affinity portal for the University

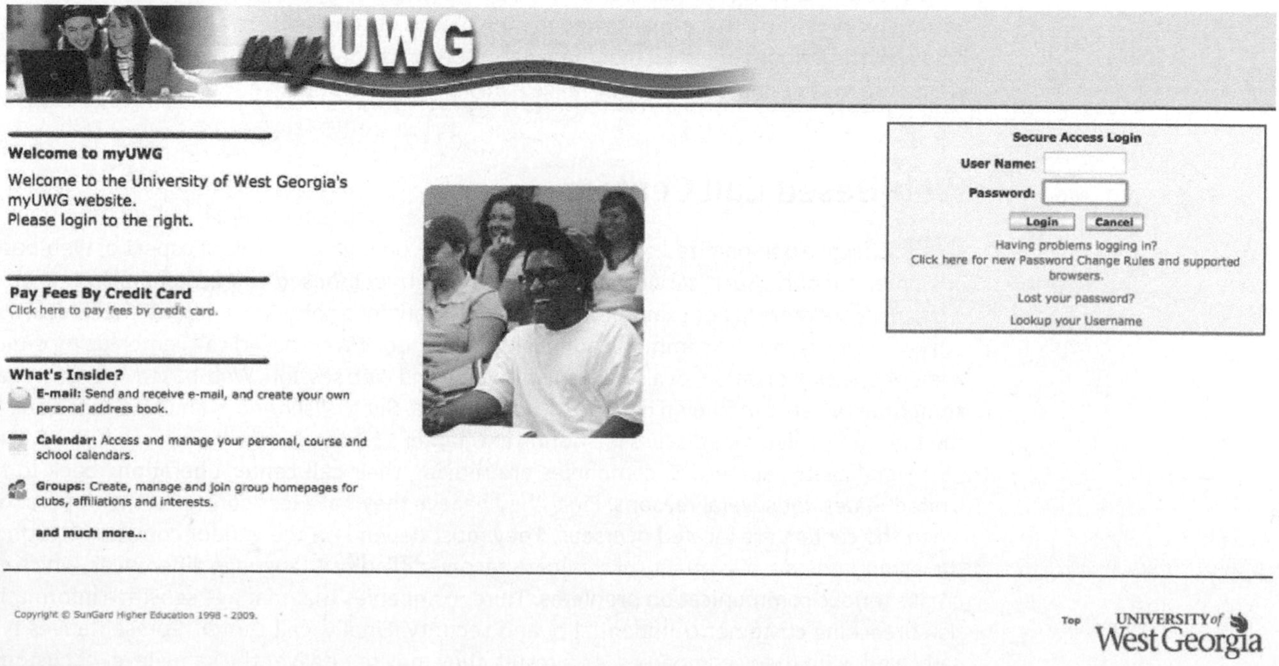

Source: University of West Georgia

FIGURE 6.10 **University of West Georgia affinity portal. (Courtesy of the University of West Georgia).**

of West Georgia. Other examples of affinity portals are **www.informationweek.com** and **www.zdnet.com**.

MIS As the name suggests, a **corporate portal** offers a personalized, single point of access through a Web browser to critical business information located inside and outside an organization. These portals are also known as *enterprise portals*, *information portals*, and *enterprise information portals*. Besides making it easier to find needed information, corporate portals offer customers and employees self-service opportunities.

Whereas corporate portals are associated with a single company, an **industrywide** portal serves entire industries. An example is TruckNet (**https://trucknet.io**), a portal for the trucking industry and the trucking community, including professional drivers, owner/operators, and trucking companies.

Before you go on...

1. Differentiate between search engines and metasearch engines.
2. What are some reasons why publication of material in a number of languages is so important?
3. Discuss the various reasons why portals are useful.

6.5 Network Applications: Communication

The second major category of network applications is communication. There are many types of communication technologies, including e-mail, call centers, chat rooms, and voice. Furthermore, we discuss an interesting application of communication: telecommuting. (Note: You will read about other types of communication—blogging and microblogging—in Chapter 9.)

Electronic Mail

Electronic mail (e-mail) is the largest-volume application running over the Internet. Studies have found that almost all companies conduct business transactions through e-mail, and the vast majority confirm that e-mail is tied to their means of generating revenue. At the same time, however, the amount of e-mail that managers receive has become overwhelming. The problem is that too much e-mail can actually make a business less productive.

Web-Based Call Centers

MKT Effective personalized customer contact is becoming an important aspect of Web-based customer support. Such service is provided through *Web-based call centers*, also known as *customer care centers*. For example, if you need to contact a software vendor for technical support, you will usually be communicating with the vendor's Web-based call center, using e-mail, a telephone conversation, or a simultaneous voice and Web session. Web-based call centers are sometimes located in foreign countries such as India. Such *offshoring* is an important issue for the U.S. companies. (We discuss offshoring in Chapter 13.)

Significantly, some U.S. companies are moving their call center operations back to the United States, for several reasons. First, they believe they have less control of their operations when the centers are located overseas. They must depend on the vendor company to uphold their standards, such as quality of service. A second difficulty is language differences, which can create serious communication problems. Third, companies that manage sensitive information risk breaching customer confidentiality and security. Finally, call center representatives typically work with many companies. As a result, they may not deliver the same level of customer services that each company requires.

Electronic Chat Rooms

Electronic chat refers to an arrangement in which participants exchange conversational messages in real time in a *chat room*. Chat programs allow you to send messages to people who are connected to the same channel of communication at the same time as you are. Anyone can join in the conversation. Messages are displayed on your screen as they arrive.

There are two major types of chat programs. The first type is Web based, which allows you to send messages to Internet users by using a Web browser and visiting a Web chat site. The second type is e-mail based (text only). It is called *Internet Relay Chat* (IRC). A business can use IRC to interact with customers, provide online experts for answers to questions, and so on.

Voice Communication

The plain old telephone service (POTS) has been largely replaced by Internet telephony. With **Internet telephony**, also known as **Voice-over-Internet Protocol** or **VoIP**, phone calls are treated as just another kind of data. That is, your analog voice signals are digitized, sectioned into packets, and then sent over the Internet.

Consider Skype (**www.skype.com**; now owned by Microsoft), which provides several VoIP services for free: voice and video calls to users who also have Skype, calls between Skype and landline and mobile phone numbers; wireless hotspot network access; instant messaging, text messaging, voice mail, one-to-one and group chats, and conference calls.

Unified Communications

In the past, organizational networks for wired and wireless data, voice communications, and videoconferencing operated independently, and the IT department managed each network separately. This arrangement increased costs and reduced productivity.

Unified communications (UC) simplifies and integrates all forms of communications—voice, voice mail, fax, chat, e-mail, instant messaging, short message service, presence (location) services, and videoconferencing—on a common hardware and software platform. *Presence services* enable users to know where their intended recipients are and if they are available, in real time.

UC unifies all forms of human and computer communications into a common user experience. For example, UC allows an individual to receive a voice mail message and then read it in his or her e-mail inbox. In another example, UC enables users to seamlessly collaborate with another person on a project, regardless of where the user is located. One user could quickly locate the other user by accessing an interactive directory, determining whether that user is available, engaging in a text messaging session, and then escalating the session to a voice call or even a video call, all in real time.

Telecommuting

Knowledge workers are being called the distributed workforce, or "digital nomads." This group of highly prized workers is now able to work anywhere and anytime, a process called **telecommuting**. Distributed workers are those who have no permanent office at their companies, preferring to work in home offices, in airport lounges or client conference rooms, or even on a high school stadium bleacher. The growth of the distributed workforce is driven by globalization, extremely long commutes to work, ubiquitous broadband communications links (wireline and wireless), and powerful computing devices.

HRM Telecommuting offers a number of potential advantages for employees, employers, and society. For employees, the benefits include reduced stress and improved family life. Telecommuting also offers employment opportunities for housebound people such as single parents and persons with disabilities. Benefits for employers include increased productivity, the ability to retain skilled employees, and the ability to attract employees who do not live within commuting distance.

HRM However, telecommuting also has some potential disadvantages. For employees, the major disadvantages are increased feelings of isolation, possible loss of fringe benefits, lower pay (in some cases), no workplace visibility, lack of socialization, and the potential for slower promotions. In a 2013 study, researchers at Stanford University found that telecommuting employees are 50 percent less likely to receive a promotion than onsite workers. The researchers concluded that a lack of "face time" with bosses caused careers to stall.

Another problem is that telecommuting employees also often have difficulties "training" their families to understand that they are at work even though they are physically at home. Families have to understand that they should not disturb the telecommuter for anything that they would not disturb him or her about in a "real" office. The major disadvantages to employers are difficulties in supervising work and potential data security problems.

Before you go on...

1. Discuss the advantages and disadvantages of e-mail.
2. Why are many companies bringing their call centers back to the United States?
3. Describe Voice-over-Internet Protocol.
4. What are the advantages and disadvantages of telecommuting to you as an individual?

6.6　Network Applications: Collaboration

The third major category of network applications is collaboration. **Collaboration** refers to efforts by two or more entities—that is, individuals, teams, groups, or organizations—who work together to accomplish certain tasks. The term *workgroup* refers specifically to two or more individuals who act together to perform a task.

Workflow is the movement of information as it progresses through the sequence of steps that make up an organization's work procedures. Workflow management makes it possible to pass documents, information, and tasks from one participant to another in a way that is governed by the organization's rules or procedures. Workflow systems are tools for automating business processes.

If group members are working in different locations, they constitute a **virtual group (team)**. Virtual groups conduct *virtual meetings*—that is, they "meet" electronically. **Virtual collaboration** (or *e-collaboration*) refers to the use of digital technologies that enable organizations or individuals who are geographically dispersed to collaboratively plan, design, develop, manage, and research products, services, and innovative applications. Organizational employees frequently collaborate virtually with one another. Some organizations collaborate virtually with customers, suppliers, and other business partners to become more productive and competitive.

Collaboration can be *synchronous*, meaning that all team members meet at the same time. Teams may also collaborate *asynchronously* when team members cannot meet at the same time. Virtual teams, whose members are located throughout the world, typically must collaborate asynchronously.

Although a variety of software products are available to support all types of collaboration, many organizations feel that too many software tools are being used in collaborative efforts. These firms want a single place to know what was shared, who shared it with whom, and when. Firms also want smarter collaboration tools that are capable of anticipating workers' needs.

Collaborative software products include Google Drive (**http://drive.google.com**), Microsoft Office 365 Teams (**www.microsoft.com/en-us/microsoft-teams/group-chat-software**), Jive (**www.jivesoftware.com**), Glip (**https://glip.com**), Slack (**www.slack.com**), Atlassian (**www.atlassian.com**), and Facebook's Workplace (**www.workplace.com**), as well as many others. In general, these products provide online collaboration capabilities, workgroup e-mail, distributed databases, electronic text editing, document management, workflow capabilities, instant virtual meetings, application sharing, instant messaging, consensus building, voting, ranking, and various application-development tools.

Two of these tools use analytics for more effective collaboration. IBM's Verse combines e-mail, social media, calendars, and file sharing with analytics in one software package designed to overhaul e-mail and increase productivity for organizations. Microsoft's Delve for Office 365 uses analytics to display information that is most relevant for each user.

Consider multinational banking and financial services company BNY Mellon (**www .bnymellon.com**). The bank uses a proprietary, in-house-developed enterprise social networking tool called MySource Social to share ideas and expertise. The social network is integrated with BNY Mellon's communication and collaboration tools, such as e-mail, calendar, and instant messaging systems. MySource Social is an intranet site within which users can explore business partner groups featuring blogs and information from executives, special-interest groups, and ad hoc groups, such as those created for project teams. More than 90 percent of the 55,000 BNY Mellon employees worldwide have accessed the site in some way, and 40 percent are hands-on participants.

Collaboration is so important that companies are using information technology to enable the process as much as possible. IT's About Business 6.3 explores how Rolls-Royce collaborates with its customers.

IT's About Business 6.3

`MIS` `POM` `MKT` Rolls-Royce Aerospace Collaborates with Its Airline Customers

Rolls-Royce Aerospace (RR; **www.rolls-royce.com**), a global manufacturer of jet engines, is collaborating closely with the world's largest airlines. As with any industry that involves a complex supply chain and comprehensive regulations, managing relationships among business partners is complicated, yet critical.

In the early 2000s, RR developed a new business model, which it called TotalCare®. The new model focused on optimal overall outcomes for the manufacturer and its airline customers. Optimal outcomes for RR included increased engine reliability, availability, and efficiency, coupled with lower total lifetime cost. Desirable outcomes for its customers included optimized fleet management, maintenance operations, and repair and overhaul operations. That is, TotalCare® was not just about selling engines. Rather, it involved collaborating with customers to achieve optimal outcomes for every organization.

Because RR's jet engines are so complex, the company needed access to as much data as possible to obtain full visibility and feedback on the performance of these engines. As a result, RR requested that the airlines share their data on engine performance in their fleets for mutual benefit.

The airlines, however, did not want to simply give away their data without first understanding how RR would use it. Therefore, RR demonstrated that it would add value to the airlines' data by creating digital twins of its engines. RR used a sample of airline data in experiments with its digital twin technology. A *digital twin* is a complete virtual software model of a physical object, for example, a Rolls-Royce engine. The digital twin enables RR engineers to virtually model different scenarios to improve the design of their engines. The engineers can study and predict the physical behaviors that an engine would exhibit under extreme conditions. In one test, the engineers replicated the highly unlikely event of an engine losing one of its large turbine fan blades. They were able to map out the exact effect that such an event would have on the aircraft's engine, wing, and fuselage.

When the airlines saw how the digital twin technology enabled RR to enhance engine reliability and availability while reducing maintenance, they began to share their data with the manufacturer. RR analyzes the airlines' data with its digital twins and then shares the results with the airline, creating a two-way exchange of information that benefits both parties.

RR pays for all of the sharing technological infrastructure and offers it completely free to the airlines. In essence, RR transfers cost uncertainty from the airlines to the manufacturer. RR emphasizes that this collaboration is not a revenue opportunity, meaning that it is the collaboration itself that holds true value for the manufacturer.

The August 2020 version of TotalCare® is Roll-Royce's IntelligentEngine project. This project encompasses the physical engine, the services that accompany that engine, and a wide variety of sensors in that engine. IntelligentEngine enables RR to monitor, map, and virtualize the engine through digital twins in order to model and forecast costs, provide predictive maintenance, and ultimately minimize risk for both RR and the airlines. Specifically, RR can measure and reduce the maintenance costs required to deliver optimal reliability and availability.

As a result of the IntelligentEngine project, RR's engines are increasingly connected, contextually aware, and comprehending. Let's look at each characteristic.

Connected. RR is taking engine health management (EHM) to new levels of connectivity. EHM describes the transfer of data from an engine to an RR operational center on the ground that records, monitors, and analyzes the data to improve the engine's availability and reliability.

The latest version of EHM is capable of measuring thousands of engine performance parameters and monitoring many parts of each engine. Engines can now respond to requests from an operational center to focus on one particular part or parameter, sending back data specifically tailored to that request.

EHM helps RR predict when parts need maintenance or replacement, rather than responding only after they have failed. For instance, if an aircraft is on the ground and unable to start, then RR's engineering teams at Rolls-Royce Availability Centers request data relating specifically to starting issues. The engine responds by transmitting data relating specifically to its past starts. RR's engineering teams then utilize those data to find a solution much more quickly.

Contextually aware. RR has pioneered research into how atmospheric conditions can affect engine performance. Specifically, Rory Clarkson, a Rolls-Royce Associate Fellow, created a new software application that helps airlines plan flights more effectively when ash from volcanic eruptions is in the air.

Clarkson examined the effects of ash on engine performance following the Eyjafjallajökull volcanic eruption in Iceland in 2010. This eruption grounded flights across Europe, affected roughly 10 million travelers, and cost the global economy approximately $7 billion. Collaborating with the United Kingdom's Met Office (the country's national weather service) and RR's airline customers, Clarkson analyzed the data and identified levels of engine tolerance to ash. He enabled the airlines to make better judgments about flight operations, reducing ash-related "no-fly" zones without compromising safety.

Comprehending. RR has continued its environmental research to better understand how humidity impacts engine turbine gas temperatures (TGT) in order to more accurately predict the life and required maintenance of engine parts. RR has found that humidity does affect TGT, making an engine appear to need maintenance earlier than is actually necessary. RR developed a new software application that uses humidity data for every major airport serviced by their customer airlines. The airlines were then able to adjust their maintenance schedules to reflect the impact of humidity on TGT data, resulting in increased availability of aircraft.

The COVID-19 pandemic severely impacted the airline industry. As the industry recovers from this unprecedented period of uncertainty, it will become even more crucial for them to maximize the efficiency and availability of their aircraft and to optimize their maintenance procedures to meet changing operating schedules. Data, digital technologies, and collaboration will be vital to achieving these outcomes. With the benefit of long experience in these areas, Rolls-Royce is well positioned as air travel recovers.

And the bottom line? In 2000, Rolls-Royce engines powered about 5 percent of the wide body aircraft market. By 2020, the manufacturer powered more than 50 percent of that market.

Sources: Compiled from N. Ward, "The Blue Data Thread that Connects Rolls-Royce to Its Customers and Improves Business Outcomes," *Diginomica*, June 16, 2020; C. Saran, "Rolls-Royce Uses Digital Twins in Power Systems Customer 4.0 Strategy," *Computer Weekly*, May 15, 2020; M. Ambasna-Jones, "Fly by Data: How Service Models Drive Data Collaboration in Aerospace," *Computer Weekly*, December 27, 2019; "Rolls-Royce IntelligentEngine Vision Makes Rapid Progress," *Aviation Pros*, July 26, 2018; "Rolls-Royce IntelligentEngine Vision Makes Rapid Progress," *Rolls-Royce Press Release*, July 16, 2018; O. Pickup, "What Is a Digital Twin and How Does It Keep Rolls-Royce Machines Safe?" *The Telegraph*, April 3, 2018; E. Biba, "The Jet Engines with 'Digital Twins'," *BBC*, February 14, 2017; "Power by the Hour," *Rolls-Royce Case Study*, 2017; S. Robinson, "Both Promise, Issues Abound when Supply Chain Partners Share the Cloud," *TechTarget*, October 12, 2016; **www.rolls-royce.com**, accessed July 24, 2020.

Questions

1. Describe the change in Rolls-Royce's business model from 2000 through 2020.

2. Discuss the impact of information technologies on the change in Rolls-Royce's business model.

3. Refer to Chapter 2. Would you consider Rolls-Royce's digital twins and IntelligentEngine to be strategic systems to the manufacturer? Why or why not? Support your answer.

Crowdsourcing

One type of collaboration is **crowdsourcing**, in which an organization outsources a task to an undefined, generally large group of people in the form of an open call. Crowdsourcing provides many potential benefits to organizations. First, crowds can explore problems—and often resolve them—at relatively low cost, and often very quickly. Second, the organization can tap a wider range of talent than might be present among its employees. Third, by listening to the crowd, organizations gain firsthand insight into their customers' desires. Finally, crowdsourcing taps into the global world of ideas, helping companies work through a rapid design process. Let's look at some examples of crowdsourcing.

- **MIS** Crowdsourcing help desks: IT help desks are a necessary service on college campuses because students depend on their computers and Internet access to complete their schoolwork and attend class online. At Indiana University at Bloomington, IT help desks use crowdsourcing to alleviate the cost and pressure of having to answer so many calls. Students and professors post their IT problems on an online forum, where other students and amateur IT experts answer them.

- **MKT** Recruitment: Champlain College in Vermont developed a Champlain For Reel program, inviting students to share YouTube videos that recounted their experiences at the school and the ways they benefited from their time there. The YouTube channel serves to recruit prospective students, and it even updates alumni on campus and community events.

- Scitable (**www.nature.com/scitable**) combines social networking and academic collaboration. Through crowdsourcing, students, professors, and scientists discuss problems, find solutions, and swap resources and journals. Scitable is a free site that lets each individual user turn to crowdsourcing for answers even while helping others.

- Violence broke out after the 2007 Kenyan elections. Within days, developers built a platform, Ushahidi (**www.ushahidi.com**), that crowdsourced 40,000 verified, first-hand reports of the violence via short-message service (SMS). The platform then sent alerts back to locals and to viewers around the world. By 2020, Ushahidi had evolved into an open-source, crisis-mapping platform accessible to anyone. To follow crises, Ushahidi analyzes millions of Tweets, hundreds of thousands of news articles, and geotagged, time-stamped data from a vast number of sources. Ushahidi has been used in over 150 countries, reaching a total of 20 million people.

Although crowdsourcing has numerous success stories, there are many questions and concerns about this system, including the following:

- Should the crowd be limited to experts? If so, then how would a company go about implementing this policy?

- How accurate is the content created by the nonexperts in the crowd? How is accuracy maintained?

- How is crowd-created content being updated? How can companies be certain the content is relevant?

- The crowd may submit too many ideas, with most of them being worthless. In this scenario, evaluating all of these ideas can be prohibitively expensive. For example, during the 2010 BP oil spill in the Gulf of Mexico, crowds submitted more than 20,000 suggestions on how to stem the flow of oil. The problem was very technical, so there were many poor suggestions. Nevertheless, despite the fact that BP was under severe time constraints, the company had to evaluate all of the ideas.

- Content contributors may violate copyrights, either intentionally or unintentionally.

- The quality of content (and therefore subsequent decisions) depends on the composition of the crowd. The best decisions may come if the crowd is made up of people with diverse opinions and ideas. In many cases, however, companies do not know the makeup of the crowd in advance.

Teleconferencing and Video Conferencing

Teleconferencing is the use of electronic communication technology that enables two or more people at different locations to hold a conference. There are several types of teleconferencing. The oldest and simplest is a telephone conference call, during which several people talk to one another from multiple locations. The biggest disadvantage of conference calls is that participants cannot communicate face-to-face, nor can they view graphs, charts, and pictures at other locations.

To overcome these shortcomings, organizations are increasingly turning to video teleconferencing, or videoconferencing. In a **videoconference**, participants in one location can see participants, documents, and presentations at other locations. The latest version of videoconferencing, called *telepresence*, enables participants to seamlessly share data, voice, pictures, graphics, and animation by electronic means. Conferees can also transmit data along with voice and video, which allows them to work together on documents and to exchange computer files.

Telepresence systems range from on-premise, high-end systems to cloud-based systems. (We discuss on-premise computing and cloud computing in Technology Guide 3.) On-premise, high-end systems are expensive and require dedicated rooms with large high-definition screens to show people sitting around conference tables (see **Figure 6.11**). These systems have advanced audio capabilities that let everyone talk at once without canceling out any voices. These systems also require technical staff to operate and maintain. An example of a high-end system is Cisco's TelePresence system (**www.cisco.com**).

Having dedicated rooms where telepresence meetings take place is not particularly useful when so many employees work remotely. As a result, companies such as Fuze (**www.fuze.com**) and BlueJeans Network (**www.bluejeans.com**) offer telepresence systems that utilize cloud

FIGURE 6.11   **Telepresence system.**

computing. (Verizon purchased BlueJeans in April 2020.) The cloud delivery model enables Fuze and BlueJeans to provide systems that are less expensive, more flexible, and require fewer in-house technical staff to operate and maintain. Fuze and BlueJeans can also deliver their telepresence systems to any device, including smartphones, tablets, and laptop and desktop computers.

Before you go on...

1. Describe virtual collaboration and why it is important to you.
2. Define crowdsourcing, and provide two examples of crowdsourcing not mentioned in this section.
3. Identify the business conditions that have made videoconferencing more important.

6.7   Network Applications: Educational

The fourth major category of network applications consists of education applications. In this section, we discuss e-learning, distance learning, and virtual universities.

E-Learning and Distance Learning

E-learning and **distance learning** are not the same thing, but they do overlap. E-learning refers to learning supported by the Web. It can take place inside classrooms as a support to conventional teaching, such as when students work on the Web during class. It also can take place in virtual classrooms, in which all coursework is completed online and classes do not meet face-to-face. In these cases, e-learning is a part of distance learning. Distance learning (DL) refers to any learning situation in which teachers and students do not meet face-to-face.

As a result of the Covid pandemic, distance education became a critical necessity in March 2020. Distance education increased dramatically in both K-12 and university classes in a matter of days and weeks.

According to the National Center for Education Statistics (NCES; **http://nces.ed.gov**), during the 2017–2018 school year, approximately 21 percent of K-12 schools offered at least one course entirely online. By April 2020, almost all K-12 schools had moved online and were employing distance education.

The NCES also noted that prior to the Covid pandemic, in 2018 35 percent of college students were enrolled in at least one online class. By April 2020, 98 percent of colleges and universities had deployed distance education initiatives, moving the majority of their classes online.

Today, the Web provides a multimedia interactive environment for self-study. Web-enabled systems make knowledge accessible to those who need it, when they need it, anytime, anywhere. For this reason, e-learning and DL can be useful for both formal education and corporate training.

There are many benefits of e-learning. For example, online materials can deliver very current content that is of high quality (created by content experts) and consistent (presented the same way every time). It also gives students the flexibility to learn at any place, at any time, and at their own pace. In corporate training centers that use e-learning, learning time generally is shorter, which means that more people can be trained within a given time frame. This system reduces training costs and eliminates the expense of renting facility space.

Despite these benefits, e-learning has some drawbacks. For one, students must be computer literate. Also, they may miss the face-to-face interaction with instructors and fellow students. In addition, accurately assessing students' work can also be problematic because instructors really do not know who completed the assignments.

E-learning does not usually replace the classroom setting. Rather, it enhances it by taking advantage of new content and delivery technologies. Advanced e-learning support environments, such as Blackboard (**www.blackboard.com**) or Canvas (**www.instructure.com**), add value to traditional learning in higher education.

A new form of distance learning has recently appeared, called *massive open online courses* or *MOOCs*. MOOCs are a tool for democratizing higher education. Several factors have contributed to the growth of MOOCs, including improved technology and the rapidly increasing costs of traditional universities. MOOCs are highly automated, complete with computer-graded assignments and exams.

MOOCs have not yet proved that they can effectively teach the thousands of students who enroll in them. They also do not provide revenues for universities. Furthermore, MOOCs can register a mixture of, for example, high school students, retirees, faculty, enrolled students, and working professionals. Designing a course that adequately meets the needs of such a diverse student population is quite challenging. Finally, although initial registrations for a MOOC might exceed 100,000 students, completion rates in any one MOOC tend to be less than 10 percent of that number. Nevertheless, despite these issues, hundreds of thousands of students around the world who lack access to universities are using MOOCs to acquire sophisticated skills and high-paying jobs without having to pay tuition or obtain a college degree.

In 2020, the world's top providers of MOOCs were:

- Coursera (U.S.), with 23 million registered users and 2329 courses
- edX (U.S.), with 10 million registered users and 1319 courses
- XuetangX (China), with 6 million users and 380 courses
- FutureLearn (U.K.), with 5.3 million users and 485 courses
- Udacity (U.S.), with 4 million users and 172 courses

Virtual Universities

Virtual universities are online universities in which students take classes on the Internet either at home or in an offsite location. A large number of existing universities offer online education of some form. Some universities, such as the University of Phoenix (**www.phoenix.edu**), Southern New Hampshire University (**www.snhu.edu**), California Virtual Campus (**www.cvc.edu**), and the University of Maryland (**www.umgc.edu**), offer thousands of courses and dozens of degrees to students worldwide, all of them online. Other universities offer limited online courses and degrees, but they employ innovative teaching methods and multimedia support in the traditional classroom.

Before you go on...

1. Describe the differences between e-learning and distance learning.
2. What are virtual universities? Would you be willing to attend a virtual university? Why or why not?

What's in IT for me?

ACCT For the Accounting Major

Accounting personnel use corporate intranets and portals to consolidate transaction data from legacy systems to provide an overall view of internal projects. This view contains the current costs charged to each project, the number of hours spent on each project by individual employees, and an analysis of how actual costs compare with projected costs. Finally, accounting personnel use Internet access to government and professional websites to stay informed on legal and other changes affecting their profession.

FIN For the Finance Major

Corporate intranets and portals can provide a model to evaluate the risks of a project or an investment. Financial analysts use two types of data in the model: historical transaction data from corporate databases through the intranet and industry data obtained through the Internet. Financial services firms can also use the Web for marketing and to provide services.

MKT For the Marketing Major

Marketing managers use corporate intranets and portals to coordinate the activities of the sales force. Sales personnel access corporate portals through the intranet to discover updates on pricing, promotion, rebates, customer information, and information about competitors. Sales staff can also download and customize presentations for their customers. The Internet, particularly the Web, opens a completely new marketing channel for many industries. Just how advertising, purchasing, and information dispensation should occur appears to vary from industry to industry, product to product, and service to service.

POM For the Production/Operations Management Major

Companies are using intranets and portals to speed product development by providing the development team with three-dimensional models and animation. All team members can access the models for to explore ideas more quickly and to enhance feedback. Corporate portals, accessed through intranets, enable managers to carefully supervise their inventories as well as real-time production on assembly lines. Extranets are also proving valuable as communication formats for joint research and design efforts among companies. The Internet is also a great source of cutting-edge information for POM managers.

HRM For the Human Resources Management Major

Human resources personnel use portals and intranets to publish corporate policy manuals, job postings, company telephone directories, and training classes. Many companies deliver online training obtained from the Internet to employees through their intranets. Human resources departments use intranets to offer employees health care, savings, and benefit plans, as well as the opportunity to take competency tests online. The Internet supports worldwide recruiting efforts; it can also be the communications platform for supporting geographically dispersed work teams.

MIS For the MIS Major

As important as the networking technology infrastructure is, it is invisible to users (unless something goes wrong). The MIS function is responsible for keeping all organizational networks up and running all the time. MIS personnel, therefore, provide all users with an "eye to the world" and the ability to compute, communicate, and collaborate any time, anywhere. For example, organizations have access to experts at remote locations without having to duplicate that expertise in multiple areas of the firm. Virtual teaming allows experts physically located in different cities to collaborate on projects as though they were in the same office.

Summary

6.1 Compare and contrast the two major types of networks.

The two major types of networks are local area networks (LANs) and wide area networks (WANs). LANs encompass a limited geographical area and are usually composed of one communications medium. In contrast, WANs encompass a broad geographical area and are usually composed of multiple communications media.

6.2 Describe the wireline communications media and channels.

Twisted-pair wire, the most prevalent form of communications wiring, consists of strands of copper wire twisted in pairs. It is relatively inexpensive to purchase, widely available, and easy to work with. However, it is relatively slow for transmitting data, subject to interference from other electrical sources, and can be easily tapped by unintended recipients.

Coaxial cable consists of insulated copper wire. It is much less susceptible to electrical interference than is twisted-pair wire and it can carry much more data. However, coaxial cable is more expensive and more difficult to work with than twisted-pair wire. It is also somewhat inflexible.

Fiber-optic cables consist of thousands of very thin filaments of glass fibers that transmit information by way of pulses of light generated by lasers. Fiber-optic cables are significantly smaller and lighter than traditional cable media. They can also transmit far more data, and they provide greater security from interference and tapping. Fiber-optic cable is often used as the backbone for a network, whereas twisted-pair wire and coaxial cable connect the backbone to individual devices on the network.

6.3 Describe the most common methods for accessing the Internet.

Common methods for connecting to the Internet include dial-up, DSL, cable modem, satellite, wireless, and fiber to the home.

6.4 Explain the impact that discovery network applications have had on business and everyday life.

Discovery involves browsing and information retrieval and provides users the ability to view information in databases, download it, and process it. Discovery tools include search engines, directories, and portals. Discovery tools enable business users to efficiently find needed information.

6.5 Explain the impact that communication network applications have had on business and everyday life.

Networks provide fast, inexpensive *communications*, through e-mail, call centers, chat rooms, voice communications, and blogs. Communications tools provide business users with a seamless interface among team members, colleagues, business partners, and customers.

Telecommuting is the process whereby knowledge workers are able to work anywhere and any time. Telecommuting provides flexibility for employees, with many benefits and some drawbacks.

6.6 Explain the impact that collaboration network applications have had on business and everyday life.

Collaboration refers to mutual efforts by two or more entities (individuals, groups, or companies) that work together to accomplish tasks. Collaboration is enabled by workflow systems. Collaboration tools enable business users to collaborate with colleagues, business partners, and customers.

6.7 Explain the impact that educational network applications have had on business and everyday life.

E-learning refers to learning supported by the web. Distance learning refers to any learning situation in which teachers and students do not meet face-to-face. E-learning provides tools for business users to facilitate their lifelong learning aspirations.

Virtual universities are online universities in which students take classes on the Internet at home or an offsite location. Virtual universities make it possible for students to obtain degrees while working full-time, thus increasing their value to their firms.

Chapter Glossary

affinity portal A website that offers a single point of entry to an entire community of affiliated interests.

backbone networks High-speed central networks to which multiple smaller networks (e.g., LANs and smaller WANs) connect.

bandwidth The transmission capacity of a network, stated in bits per second.

broadband The transmission capacity of a communications medium that is faster than 25 Mbps.

broadcast media (also called wireless media) Communications channels that use electromagnetic media (the "airwaves") to transmit data.

browsers Software applications through which users primarily access the Web.

cable media (also called wireline media) Communications channels that use physical wires or cables to transmit data and information.

client/server computing Form of distributed processing in which some machines (servers) perform computing functions for end-user PCs (clients).

clients Computers, such as users' personal computers, that use any of the services provided by servers.

coaxial cable Insulated copper wire; used to carry high-speed data traffic and television signals.

collaboration Mutual efforts by two or more individuals who perform activities to accomplish certain tasks.

commercial (public) portal A website that offers fairly routine content for diverse audiences. It offers customization only at the user interface.

communications channel Pathway for communicating data from one location to another.

computer network A system that connects computers and other devices through communications media so that data and information can be transmitted among them.

corporate portal A website that provides a single point of access to critical business information located both inside and outside an organization.

crowdsourcing A process in which an organization outsources a task to an undefined, generally large group of people in the form of an open call.

distance learning (DL) Learning situations in which teachers and students do not meet face-to-face.

distributed processing Network architecture that divides processing work between or among two or more computers that are linked together in a network.

domain name system (DNS) The system administered by the Internet Corporation for Assigned Names (ICANN) that assigns names to each site on the Internet.

domain names The name assigned to an Internet site, which consists of multiple parts, separated by dots, that are translated from right to left.

e-learning Learning supported by the Web; can be performed inside traditional classrooms or in virtual classrooms.

enterprise network An organization's network, which is composed of interconnected multiple LANs and WANs.

Ethernet A common local area network protocol.

extranet A network that connects parts of the intranets of different organizations.

fiber-optic cable A communications medium consisting of thousands of very thin filaments of glass fibers, surrounded by cladding, that transmit information through pulses of light generated by lasers.

file server (also called network server) A computer that contains various software and data files for a local area network as well as the network operating system.

hyperlink A connection from a hypertext file or document to another location or file, typically activated by clicking on a highlighted word or image on the screen or by touching the screen.

hypertext Text displayed on a computer display with references, called hyperlinks, to other text that the reader can immediately access.

Hypertext Transport Protocol (HTTP) The communications standard used to transfer pages across the WWW portion of the Internet; it defines how messages are formulated and transmitted.

industrywide portal A Web-based gateway to information and knowledge for an entire industry.

Internet (the Net) A massive global WAN that connects approximately 1 million organizational computer networks in more than 200 countries on all continents.

Internet backbone The primary network connections and telecommunications lines that link the computers and organizational nodes of the Internet.

Internet Protocol (IP) A set of rules responsible for disassembling, delivering, and reassembling packets over the Internet.

Internet Protocol (IP) address An assigned address that uniquely identifies a computer on the Internet.

Internet service provider (ISP) A company that provides Internet connections for a fee.

Internet telephony (Voice-over-Internet Protocol, or VoIP) The use of the Internet as the transmission medium for telephone calls.

Internet2 A new, faster telecommunications network that deploys advanced network applications such as remote medical diagnosis, digital libraries, distance education, online simulation, and virtual laboratories.

intranet A private network that uses Internet software and TCP/IP protocols.

local area network (LAN) A network that connects communications devices in a limited geographic region, such as a building, so that every user device on the network can communicate with every other device.

metasearch engine A computer program that searches several engines at once and integrates the findings of the various search engines to answer queries posted by users.

network access points (NAPs) Computers that act as exchange points for Internet traffic and determine how traffic is routed.

network server See **file server**.

packet switching The transmission technology that divides blocks of text into packets.

peer-to-peer (P2P) processing A type of client/server distributed processing that allows two or more computers to pool their resources, making each computer both a client and a server.

portal A Web-based personalized gateway to information and knowledge that provides information from disparate information systems and the Internet, using advanced searching and indexing techniques.

protocol The set of rules and procedures that govern transmission across a network.

router A communications processor that routes messages from a LAN to the Internet, across several connected LANs, or across a wide area network such as the Internet.

search engine A computer program that searches for specific information by keywords and reports the results.

servers Computers that provide access to various network services, such as printing, data, and communications.

telecommuting A work arrangement whereby employees work at home, at the customer's premises, in special workplaces, or while traveling, usually using a computer linked to their place of employment.

teleconferencing The use of electronic communication that allows two or more people at different locations to have a simultaneous conference.

Transmission Control Protocol/Internet Protocol (TCP/IP) A file transfer protocol that can send large files of information across sometimes unreliable networks with the assurance that the data will arrive uncorrupted.

twisted-pair wire A communications medium consisting of strands of copper wire twisted together in pairs.

unified communications Common hardware and software platform that simplifies and integrates all forms of communications—voice, e-mail, instant messaging, location, and videoconferencing—across an organization.

uniform resource locator (URL) The set of letters that identifies the address of a specific resource on the Web.

videoconference A virtual meeting in which participants in one location can see and hear participants at other locations and can share data and graphics by electronic means.

virtual collaboration The use of digital technologies that enable organizations or individuals to collaboratively plan, design, develop, manage, and research products, services, and innovative information systems and electronic commerce applications.

virtual group (team) A workgroup whose members are in different locations and who meet electronically.

virtual universities Online universities in which students take classes on the Internet at home or at an offsite location.

Voice-over-Internet Protocol (VoIP) See **Internet telephony.**

website Collectively, all the web pages of a particular company or individual.

wide area network (WAN) A network, generally provided by common carriers, that covers a wide geographical area.

wireless media See **broadcast media.**

wireline media See **cable media.**

workflow The movement of information as it flows through the sequence of steps that make up an organization's work procedures.

World Wide Web (the Web or WWW) A system of universally accepted standards for storing, retrieving, formatting, and displaying information through a client/server architecture; it uses the transport functions of the Internet.

Discussion Questions

1. What are the implications of having fiber-optic cable to everyone's home?

2. What are the implications of BitTorrent for the music industry? For the motion picture industry?

3. Discuss the pros and cons of P2P networks.

4. Should the Internet be regulated? If so, by whom?

5. Discuss the pros and cons of delivering this book over the Internet.

6. Explain how the Internet works. Assume you are talking with someone who has no knowledge of information technology (in other words, keep it very simple).

7. How are the network applications of communication and collaboration related? Do communication tools also support collaboration? Give examples.

8. Search online for the article from *The Atlantic:* "Is Google Making Us Stupid?" *Is* Google making us stupid? Support your answer.

9. Should businesses monitor network usage? Do see a problem with employees using company-purchased bandwidth for personal use? Please explain your answer.

Problem-Solving Activities

1. Calculate how much bandwidth you consume when using the Internet every day. How many e-mails do you send daily and what is the size of each? (Your e-mail program may have e-mail file size information.) How many music and video clips do you download (or upload) daily and what is the size of each? If you view YouTube often, surf the web to find out the size of a typical YouTube file. Add up the number of e-mail, audio, and video files you transmit or receive on a typical day. When you have calculated your daily Internet usage, determine if you are a "normal" Internet user or a "power" Internet user.

2. Access several P2P applications, such as SETI@home. Describe the purpose of each application and indicate which ones you would like to join.

3. Access **http://ipv6.com** and learn more about the advantages of IPv6.

4. Access **www.icann.org** and learn more about this important organization.

5. Set up your own website using your name for the domain name (e.g., KellyRainer).

   a. Explain the process for registering a domain.

   b. Which top-level domain will you use and why?

6. Access **www.icann.org** and obtain the name of an agency or company that can register a domain for the TLD that you selected. What is the name of that agency or company?

7. Access the website for that agency or company (in question 6) to learn the process that you must use. How much will it initially cost to register your domain name? How much will it cost to maintain that name in the future?

8. *Network neutrality* is an operating model under which Internet service providers (ISPs) must allow customers equal access to content and applications, regardless of the source or nature of the content. That is, Internet backbone carriers must treat all Web traffic equally rather than charge different rates based on the user, content, site, platform, or application.

On December 14, 2017, the Federal Communications Commission (**www.fcc.gov**) voted to eliminate network neutrality regulations. The elimination of network neutrality regulations took place on June 11, 2018.

- Why are telecommunications and cable companies (the Internet service providers) against network neutrality?
- Why are technology companies in favor of keeping network neutrality?
- What are fast lanes and slow lanes? What impacts could fast and slow lanes have on businesses and consumers?
- How could the end of network neutrality impact consumers?

- What is the practice of zero-rating?
- What is the relationship between the end of network neutrality and potential censorship?
- What is the relationship between network neutrality and innovation?
- Would entrepreneurs be in favor of, or opposed to, network neutrality?

9. From your own experience or from the vendor's information, list the major capabilities of IBM Notes. Do the same for Microsoft Exchange. Compare and contrast the products. Explain how the products can be used to support knowledge workers and managers.

10. Visit the websites of companies that manufacture telepresence products for the Internet. Prepare a report. Differentiate between telepresence products and videoconferencing products.

11. Access the website of your university. Does the website provide high-quality information (the right amount, clear, accurate, etc.)? Do you think a high-school student who is thinking of attending your university would feel the same way as you?

12. Access the website of the Recording Industry Association of America (**www.riaa.com**). Discuss what you find there regarding copyright infringement (i.e., downloading music files). How do you feel about the RIAA's efforts to stop music downloads? Debate this issue from your point of view and from the RIAA's point of view.

13. Research the companies involved in Internet telephony (Voice-over IP). Compare their offerings as to price, necessary technologies, ease of installation, and so on. Which company is the most attractive to you? Which company might be the most attractive for a large company?

14. Access various search engines other than Google. Search for the same terms on several of the alternative search engines and on Google. Compare the results on breadth (number of results found) and precision (results are what you were looking for).

15. Second Life (**www.secondlife.com**) is a three-dimensional, online world built and owned by its residents. Residents of Second Life are avatars who have been created by real people. Access Second Life, learn about it, and create your own avatar to explore this world. Learn about the thousands of people who are making "real-world" money from operations in Second Life.

16. Access Microsoft's Bing translator (**www.bing.com/translator**) or Google (**http://google.translate.com**) translation pages. Type in a paragraph in English and select, for example, English-to-French. When you see the translated paragraph in French, copy it into the text box, and select French-to-English. Is the paragraph that you first entered the same as the one you are looking at now? Why or why not? Support your answer.

Closing Case

MIS Internet Shutdowns

In most cases, governments want to control the Internet to control the political narrative. They view the Internet as a threat because it disrupts their control of information. They believe that social media, for instance, enables individuals and groups to produce and circulate alternative political narratives. The United Nations has explicitly defined government-led Internet shutdowns and censorship as human rights violations.

Governments adopt three general approaches to controlling citizens' access to the Internet. First, and most serious, is to completely block access to the Internet on all platforms. This approach incurs significant social, economic, and political costs. The financial costs can run into millions of dollars for each day that the Internet is blocked. A Deloitte report estimated that a highly connected country would lose on average $24 million per day per 10 million population, a medium-connected country would lose $7 million, and a low-connected country would lose $0.6 million.

The second method by which governments restrict Internet access is by blocking content, typically by restricting access to particular websites or applications. This strategy is the most common, and it usually targets social media platforms. Governments generally adopt this strategy because these sites have become platforms for various forms of political expression that many governments, especially those with authoritarian tendencies, consider subversive.

For instance, in January 2019 Zimbabwe's government blocked social media following demonstrations over an increase in fuel prices. The state argued that the ban was necessary because the platforms were being "used to coordinate the violence."

The third strategy, usually carried out secretly, is *bandwidth throttling*. In this method, the government forces telecommunications operators or ISPs to lower the quality of their cell signals or Internet speed. This process makes the Internet and phones too slow to use. Throttling can also target certain online destinations such as social media sites.

There are numerous examples of governments attempting to control the Internet by employing these methods. We consider several instances here.

India

On August 5, 2019, India announced that it was removing the autonomy of its only Muslim-majority state, Jammu and Kashmir. The state had been autonomous since the 1940s. India planned to divide the state in half, with each piece becoming a federal protectorate.

India immediately shut down the Internet and mobile communications in the state, and banned social media sites. In March 2020 India restored slow-speed Internet access in the state after seven months of blackout, allowed 2G (second generation wireless communications; see Chapter 8) cellular communications, and revoked its ban on social media sites. With only 2G available, Internet and cellular communications were so slow that physicians in the region could not download material related to treating COVID-19 patients, nor could they disseminate the latest news on how to slow the spread of the new coronavirus.

On December 11, 2019, the Indian government approved the Citizenship Amendment Bill, which created a path for citizenship non-Muslim immigrants from Afghanistan, Pakistan, and Bangladesh, but not for India's Muslim minority. The next day, the government shut down the Internet in the state of Assam after citizens protested the controversial bill. As the protests spread, the government shut down the Internet in other states, including New Delhi. The government restored Internet service in about one week, although protests continued.

Iran

The Iranian government has been deploying a centralized national Internet for some time. The effort has enabled it to provide its citizens with Internet services while monitoring all content on the network and limiting information from external sources. Essentially, the government has assumed increasing control over both public and private connectivity in the name of national security.

In mid-November 2019 the Iranian government unexpectedly announced its decision to ration gasoline, causing prices to rapidly increase by at least 50 percent. International observers viewed the move as part of an larger strategy to mitigate the effects of U.S. sanctions on Iran's economy.

When large-scale demonstrations erupted in response to these actions, the government almost immediately began to shut off the Internet for its citizens. Iran's largest mobile network operators went offline as well. It took Iranian authorities about 24 hours to completely block the nation's inbound and outbound Internet traffic. The government wanted to suppress the protests and prevent people outside Iran from paying attention to the unrest. The shutdown lasted one week.

One unfortunate result of the shutdown was that Iranians in the United States were unable to contact friends and family members in that country. A few people were able to use Skype credits to call landlines inside Iran to get in touch with their loved ones.

Myanmar

The National League for Democracy (NLD) won a landslide victory in the November 8, 2020 elections in Myanmar (formerly Burma). In a coup, the country's generals refused to recognize the results, claiming fraud. Thousands of citizens denounced the takeover and demanded the release of the country's elected leader Aung San Suu Kyi. In response to the protests, on February 6, 2021 the military junta began shutting down Internet access overnight throughout the country. On April 6, 2021 the junta shut down Myanmar's wireless Internet services. As a result, the only Internet access in the country was over fiber optic cable, which was operating at drastically reduced speeds.

A coalition of civil society organizations appealed to Internet providers and mobile networks to challenge the junta's orders blocking Internet access. The coalition noted that these companies were essentially legitimizing the military takeover. As of May 1, 2021 the junta had not responded to requests for comment.

Bangladesh

In September 2019, Bangladesh imposed an Internet shutdown at camps for Rohingya refugees who had fled persecution in Myanmar. This action impeded humanitarian groups from addressing the COVID-19 threat. As of August 2020, the blackout remained in place, and it continued to jeopardize the health of the 900,000 refugees in the camps as well as the Bangladeshi host communities.

Results

Even though Internet shutdowns continue, there is little evidence that they actually work. Let's consider three reasons why they are not effective.

- Shutdowns often encourage dissent and responses that many governments consider subversive. They can create camaraderie among citizens that can turn into an even more powerful protest movement. One observer noted that an Internet blackout just drives people into the streets.

- Governments damage their economies when they shut down Internet applications and services. Government-led Internet shutdowns cost the global economy $8 billion in 2019.

- Due to the fast-moving nature of the COVID-19 pandemic, an Internet blackout seriously obstructs citizens' ability to access the most reliable details on recent infection counts, social distancing measures imposed in their area, current medical information, and corrections to circulating misinformation. Blackouts also hinder the public's ability to communicate with others and to call wirelessly for medical assistance. The bottom line is that Internet shutdowns cause tangible, physical harm.

Sources: Compiled from S. Faleiro, "How India Became the World's Leader in Internet Shutdowns," *MIT Technology Review*, August 19, 2020; J. Sherman, "This Is No Time for an Internet Blackout," *Slate*, April 20, 2020; "Blocked Websites, Internet Shutdown, and Media Arrests Undermine Free Speech in Myanmar," *Global Voices*, April 6, 2020; "How Internet Shutdowns Have Affected the Lives of Millions of Ethiopians," *The Conversation*, April 2, 2020; "End Internet Shutdowns to Manage COVID-19," *Human Rights Watch*, March 31, 2020; "India Restores Internet in Kashmir after 7 Months of Blackout," *Aljazeera*, March 5, 2020; V. Tangermann, "Governments Shut Down the Internet Hundreds of Times in 2019," *Futurism*, February 26, 2020; M. Singh, "India's Top Court Rules Indefinite Internet Shutdown in Kashmir Unwarranted and Amounts to Abuse of Power," *TechCrunch*, January 10, 2020; C. Taylor, "Government-Led Internet Shutdowns Cost the Global Economy $8 Billion in 2019, Research Shows," *CNBC,* January 8, 2020; J. Sherman, "Democracies Can Become Digital Dictators," *Wired*, January 5, 2020; A. Ghoshal, "Indian Government Orders Mobile Internet to Be Suspended in the Capital, Says Airtel," *TheNextWeb*, December 19, 2019; "India Has Once Again Shut Down the Internet to Control Protesters," *MIT Technology Review*, December 12, 2019; M. Kadivar, "Iran Shut Down the Internet to Stop Protests. But for How Long?" *Washington Post*, November 27, 2019; E. Khatami, "Iranian Americans Struggle to Reach Family Amid Internet Blackout," *Wired*, November 20, 2019; "Iran Has Shut Off Internet Access for Its Citizens Amid Fuel Price Protests," *MIT Technology Review*, November 18, 2019; L. Newman, "How the Iranian Government Shut off the Internet," *Wired*, November 17, 2019; J. Gettleman, "In Kashmir, Growing Anger and Misery," *New York Times*, September 30, 2019; D. Flamini, "The Scary Trend of Internet Shutdowns," *Poynter.org*, August 1, 2019; "Shutting Down the Internet Doesn't Work—But Governments Keep Doing It," *The Conversation*, February 19, 2019; "Myanmar Shuts Down Internet in Bid to Stifle Protest," *People's World*, April 6, 2021; R. Ratcliffe, "Myanmar Coup: Military Expands Internet Shutdown," *The Guardian*, April 2, 2021; "Myanmar Generals Shut Down Internet as Thousands Protest Coup," *Reuters*, February 6, 2021.

Questions

1. Of the three methods that governments are using to control Internet access, which is the most effective at controlling internet usage?

2. Of the three methods that governments are using to control Internet access, which is the least effective?

3. Is Internet access a fundamental human right? Why or why not? Support your answer. Be sure to include in your answer what your day would look like without Internet access of any kind.

CHAPTER 7

E-Business and E-Commerce

Opening Case

MIS **POM** **MKT** **Brick-and-Mortar Retailers Fight the Amazon Effect**

The increase in electronic commerce sales has been remarkable, and it accelerated in 2020 as a result of the coronavirus pandemic. In 2019, e-commerce sales accounted for only 16 percent of overall retail sales. However, those sales were growing roughly five times faster than sales at traditional stores. In 2019, more than 9,000 brick-and-mortar stores closed, a 60 percent increase from the previous year.

The *Amazon Effect* refers to the disruption of traditional brick-and-mortar retailers by electronic commerce. Despite the seriousness of Amazon's impact, references to the death of physical, brick-and-mortar commerce seem to have been premature. As we see in this case, Costco (**www.costco.com**) and Best Buy (**www.bestbuy.com**) are thriving in the face of intense competition from electronic commerce. Let's take a closer look at what each company is doing to achieve outstanding results.

Costco

Strategy. Founded in 1983, Costco's goal is to reduce operating costs where possible and pass along the savings to its customers and employees. In essence, Costco prioritizes the interests of its customers and employees over those of its shareholders. As of August 2020,

Costco was one of the world's largest retailers, with 785 locations and 214,000 employees.

The retailer's huge purchasing power enables it to negotiate deep discounts with vendors. Costco then passes along these savings to its shoppers. According to the company's 2019 Annual Report, the markup on a typical item in the store is only 11 percent, compared to the 25–50 percent markup in other retail outlets. In fact, Costco's prices are so low that the company just barely breaks even on its merchandise sales.

Since 1990, the percentage of corporate profits in the United States going to stockholders has increased from 50 percent to 86 percent, resulting in higher prices for customers and low wages for employees. Not surprisingly, then, since Costco went public in December 1985, investors have complained that the chain should increase margins and prices for goods and reduce benefits for its employees. Costco's leadership, however, has resisted those demands, and the value of its stock has increased by almost 400 percent since 2000.

So, how does Costco make money? Costco's sells annual memberships—$60 for "Gold Star" and $120 for "Executive"—which people pay because they believe that having access to Costco's economies of scale and bulk quantities justifies the upfront cost. In 2019, Costco had 98 million members, 90 percent of whom renew each year. The majority of Costco's members are affluent (more than $100,000 annual income) and college educated. Membership fees in 2019 totaled $3.35 billion.

POM *Supply chain*. Conventional wisdom in retailing is that excess choice is good because shoppers want to be able to choose from many varieties and brands. Costco, however, limits brand selection and stocks massive volumes of fewer products. Costco adopted this strategy because it realizes that it makes more financial sense for a shopper to spend $400 once per month than $100 in four trips. The process saves customers time and money by eliminating multiple trips while reducing Costco's costs at the same time.

Costco's average store stocks only 3,700 *stock keeping units* (SKUs), less than 10 percent of the 40,000 to 50,000 items found in most supermarkets. Often, Costco provides only one or two brands in a given category.

Analysts note that Costco knows their customers very well, and that knowledge enables the chain to limit choices to items that their customers most likely want. With its retail process, Costco solves the "paradox of choice"—a problem that consumers face when too many options cause them stress and delay their decision making.

The company has an economic incentive to stock fewer items. Fewer selections require less labor. In retail operations, every person who touches an item—receiving, stocking, organizing, rearranging—incurs costs. Costco's supply chain is designed to minimize contact. Items are taken from trucks and driven directly to the aisles on forklifts, where they sit on giant pallets, ready for customers.

Costco is very careful about the vendors it selects. When the chain finds a product that it likes, it works closely with the vendor and its factories to both reduce the price of an item and increase its quality.

One Costco buyer found a toy he liked that retailed for $100. Costco had the option of buying each unit for $50 wholesale and selling it for $60, but that did not satisfy the chain. Instead, Costco worked with the vendor to redesign the toy, analyzing every part of the process for ways to cut costs. In the end, Costco convinced the vendor to reduce the price by 50 percent, and they sold it for $30. Costco's profit margin of $30 per toy was the same as what the company would have made at the $60 price point.

HRM *Human resources*. Retail workers are among America's lowest-paid employees. They rarely receive full benefits, and their employers often view them as expendable. Turnover rates in the retail industry approach 65 percent.

Costco realizes that it is more cost effective to retain happy employees and pay them a livable wage than it is to have to manage high employee turnover. As of August 2020, the average pay for Costco employees was between $14 and $15 per hour. Costco provides excellent benefits for its employees, including health care, 401K contributions, and paid time off. The result is that Costco has an amazingly high employee retention rate of 94 percent.

MKT *Electronic commerce*. Traditionally, when Costco's leadership was asked about the chain's e-commerce strategy, they would reply that they wanted to do "everything possible" to get customers into the stores. Costco realizes that its website is a useful channel to reach and satisfy its members. For example, the retailer relies on its website to drive more of what the chain calls "white-good sales"—bulky home appliances like refrigerators, washers, and dryers. In 2016, Costco sold about $50 million in white goods. Three years later that number had increased to $700 million.

Since 2018, Costco customers can order online from all Costco store. The retailer has been adding lockers to its stores to make the buy online and then pick up in-store process—called *click-and-collect*—more efficient. In addition, Costco has added self-checkout areas to 250 of its stores.

Like Walmart, Costco generates more than half of its revenue from groceries. Therefore, the chain has partnered with Instacart to offer same-day grocery delivery to shoppers near Costco locations and free two-day delivery on nonperishable items with a $75 minimum purchase to a larger part of the country.

Costco's app. In 2019, Costco added new features to its mobile app such as pharmacy order management, a photo-ordering center, easier shopping during member savings events through a "$ Savings" function, and the addition of various push and pick-up notifications. It has also started to make more products from popular national brands available on its website.

Results. Costco's e-commerce sales increased by 66 percent during the first half of 2020, largely due to the COVID-19 pandemic. The retailer reported a revenue for 2020 of $167 billion (10 percent increase over 2019) and a net income of $4 billion (10 percent increase over 2019).

Best Buy

In 2012, *Forbes* announced that Best Buy was "going out of business." Since that time, the retailer has defied expectations by focusing on what it could offer that online commerce could not: engaging physical stores, knowledgeable staff, and a Geek Squad who will install and synchronize electronics in your home.

Best Buy stores and staff. The success of Best Buy suggests that customers still value the physical experience of stores. However, these stores must offer a vibrant experience combined with integrated services that customers need and value and cannot be easily duplicated online. Best Buy stores are welcoming, and they allow customers to touch, use, and experiment with electronic devices. They also have knowledgeable staff members who are passionate about what they explain and demonstrate.

Best Buy also implemented an In-Home Advisor program. Through this initiative, Best Buy sends consultants to customers' homes to offer advice and assist with purchasing decisions. Best Buy encourages advisors to establish long-term relationships with customers, rather than simply trying to close a one-time sale. In-home advisors do not need to track weekly metrics—for example, number of customers visited and sales closed—and they are paid an annual salary rather than an hourly wage. House calls are free and can last up to 90 minutes. Best Buy instructs its advisors to "be comfortable not closing a deal by day's end."

The Geek Squad. Best Buy has identified the customer pain point in shopping for electronics; namely, installing, synchronizing, and integrating devices without having to waste time dealing with technical customer service. To accomplish this mission, Best Buy can send its Geek Squad to help set up those systems in customers' homes or offices and recommend other products and services.

HRM *Human resources*. In 2012, Best Buy CEO Hubert Joly visited many Best Buy stores and even worked at one store for a week. After speaking directly to employees he:

- Fixed broken systems, such as an internal search engine that provided poor data about which products were in stock

- Restored the employee discount program for purchasing products

- Invested heavily in regular employee training

His initiatives worked. In August 2020, workplace review website Glassdoor stated that 80 percent of employees would recommend working at Best Buy to a friend.

MKT *Strategy*. Best Buy turned showrooming into a competitive advantage. *Showrooming* refers to the practice in which customers enter a store to test products and then purchase them online from competitors. Joly used that practice to Best Buy's advantage by instituting a price-matching system. The strategy took advantage of the fact that customers want to see expensive items such as big-screen televisions and smartphones before they make a purchase. If the store was willing to price-match, then why not buy then and there?

Best Buy also partnered with large electronics companies such as Apple and Samsung to feature their products. These companies rent square footage within a Best Buy location to highlight all of their products together in a branded space. This arrangement gave Best Buy a new revenue stream.

Joly and his team also made changes that allowed stores to serve as mini-warehouses for online customers. This process enabled customers to order a product online and then choose whether to pick it up at a store (click-and-collect) or have it shipped to them.

Results. For the second quarter of 2020, which ended August 1, 2020, Best Buy reported domestic e-commerce revenue of $4.85 billion, an increase of 242 percent over the same quarter of 2019. Best Buy's net income for the quarter was $432 million, an increase of 81 percent over 2019.

A final note: other traditional brick-and-mortar retailers are also having success competing with the Amazon Effect. Notable examples are Target (**www.target.com**) and Tractor Supply (**www.tractorsupply.com**).

Sources: Compiled from J. Bowman, "Walmart Just Did Something that Amazon, Home Depot, and Target Couldn't," *The Motley Fool*, May 20, 2020; "Costco Earnings Hurt by Purchase Limits; eCommerce Sales Spike," *PYMNTS.com*, April 10, 2020; F. Ali, "A Decade in Review: Ecommerce Sales Vs. Retail Sales 2007–2019," *Digital Commerce 360*, March 3, 2020; Z. Karabell, "Best Buy Bucks the Trend That's Crushing Other Retailers," *Wired*, December 11, 2019; Z. Crockett, "How Costco Gained a Cult Followingby Breaking Every Rule of Retail," *The Hustle*, June 30, 2019; A. Hensel,

"'There Are Some Real Sales to Be Had There': Costco Is Finally Figuring out Its E-commerce Strategy," *Digiday*, June 3, 2019; D. Kalogeropoulos, "How Costco Crushed It in 2018," *The Motley Fool*, April 19, 2019; J. Bariso, "Amazon Almost Killed Best Buy. Then, Best Buy Did Something Completely Brilliant," *Inc.com*, March 4, 2019; J. Grill-Goodman, "Costco's Plans for Its E-Commerce Operations in 2019," *Retail Information Systems*, March 11, 2019; S. Berfield and M. Boyle, "Best Buy Should Be Dead, but It's Thriving in the Age of Amazon," *Bloomberg BusinessWeek*, July 19, 2018; M. Segarra, "Were Retail Jobs Always Low Wage, with Few Benefits?" *Marketplace*, February 9, 2018; J. Fox, "How Shareholders Are Ruining American Business," *The Atlantic*, July/August 2013, L. Downes, "Why Best Buy Is Going Out of Business…Gradually," *Forbes*, January 2, 2012; **www.costco.com**, **www.bestbuy.com**, accessed August 4, 2020.

Questions

1. Describe the nontechnological initiatives that traditional brick-and-mortar companies are employing to compete against Amazon and other electronic retailers.

2. Describe the technological initiatives that traditional brick-and-mortar companies are employing to compete against Amazon and other electronic retailers.

3. Given your answers to the first two questions, which iniatives are more effective: nontechnological or technological? Provide specific examples from this case to support your answer.

Introduction

Electronic commerce (**EC** or **e-commerce**) is the process of buying, selling, transferring, or exchanging products, services, or information through computer networks, including the Internet. E-commerce is transforming all of the business functional areas as well as their fundamental tasks, from advertising to paying bills. Its impact is so pervasive that it is affecting every modern organization. Regardless of where you land a job, your organization will be practicing electronic commerce.

Electronic commerce influences organizations in many significant ways. First, it increases an organization's *reach*: the number of potential customers to whom the company can market its products. In fact, e-commerce provides unparalleled opportunities for companies to expand worldwide at a small cost, to increase market share, and to reduce costs. By utilizing electronic commerce, many small businesses can now operate and compete in market spaces that were formerly dominated by larger companies.

Another major impact of electronic commerce has been to remove many of the barriers that previously impeded entrepreneurs seeking to start their own businesses. E-commerce offers amazing opportunities for you to open your own business.

As illustrated in the opening case, electronic commerce is also fundamentally transforming the nature of competition through the development of new online companies, new business models, and the diversity of EC-related products and services. Recall your study of competitive strategies in Chapter 2, particularly the impact of the Internet on Porter's five forces. You learned that the Internet can both endanger and enhance a company's position in a given industry.

It is important for you to have a working knowledge of electronic commerce because your organization almost certainly will be employing e-commerce applications that will affect its strategy and business model. This knowledge will make you more valuable to your organization, and it will enable you to quickly contribute to the e-commerce applications employed in your functional area. As you read "What's in IT for Me?" at the end of the chapter, envision yourself performing the activities discussed in your functional area.

Going further, you may decide to become an entrepreneur and start your own business. If you start your own business, it is even more essential for you to understand electronic commerce, because e-commerce, with its broad reach, will more than likely be critical for your business to survive and thrive. On the other hand, giant, well-known electronic commerce companies use the Internet to compete all over the world.

In this chapter, you will discover the major applications of e-business, and you will be able to identify the services necessary for its support. You will then study the major types of electronic commerce: business-to-consumer (B2C), business-to-business (B2B), consumer-to-consumer (C2C), business-to-employee (B2E), and government-to-citizen (G2C). You will conclude by examining several legal and ethical issues that impact e-commerce.

As you learn about electronic commerce in this chapter, note that e-commerce can be performed wirelessly, as you will see in our discussion of mobile commerce in Chapter 8. E-commerce also has many social aspects, as you will see in our discussion of social commerce in Chapter 8. Finally, e-commerce can now be performed with texting and messaging, as you will see in IT's About Business 7.1.

7.1 Overview of E-Business and E-Commerce

Just how important is electronic commerce? Consider these statistics. Industry analysts estimated that U.S. retail sales in 2019 totaled approximately $5.5 trillion. Electronic commerce accounted for 9 percent of these sales, for a total of $602 billion. Significantly, e-commerce increased 14 percent in 2019 over 2018. The increase in e-commerce has placed significant pressure on the retail industry. According to industry analysts, approximately 9,300 brick-and-mortar stores closed in 2019. In the first six months of 2020, analysts reported an additional 6,000 stores had closed, largely as a result of the COVID-19 pandemic.

This section examines the basics of e-business and e-commerce. First, we define these two concepts. You then become familiar with pure and partial electronic commerce and examine the various types of electronic commerce. Next, you focus on e-commerce mechanisms, which are the ways that businesses and people buy and sell over the Internet. You conclude this section by considering the benefits and limitations of e-commerce.

Author Lecture Videos are available exclusively in *WileyPLUS.*
Apply the Concept activities are available in the Appendix and in *WileyPLUS.*

Definitions and Concepts

Recall that electronic commerce describes the process of buying, selling, transferring, or exchanging products, services, or information through computer networks, including the Internet. **Electronic business (e-business)** is a somewhat broader concept. In addition to the buying and selling of goods and services, e-business refers to servicing customers, collaborating with business partners, and performing electronic transactions within an organization.

Electronic commerce can take several forms, depending on the degree of digitization involved. The *degree of digitization* is the extent to which the commerce has been transformed from physical to digital. This concept can relate to both the product or service being sold and the delivery agent or intermediary. In other words, the product can be either physical or digital, and the delivery agent can also be either physical or digital.

In traditional commerce, both dimensions are physical. Purely physical organizations are referred to as **brick-and-mortar organizations**. (You may also see the term *bricks-and-mortar*.) In contrast, in *pure EC* all dimensions are digital. Companies engaged only in EC are considered **virtual** (or **pure-play**) **organizations**. All other combinations that include a mix of digital and physical dimensions are considered *partial* EC (but not pure EC). **Clicks-and-mortar organizations** conduct some e-commerce activities, yet their primary business is carried out in the physical world. A common alternative to the term *clicks-and-mortar* is *clicks-and-bricks*. You will encounter both terms. Clicks-and-mortar organizations are examples of partial EC. E-commerce is now so well established that people generally expect companies to offer this service in some form.

Purchasing a shirt at Walmart Online or a book from Amazon.com is an example of partial EC because the merchandise, although bought and paid for digitally, is physically delivered by, for example, FedEx, UPS, or the U.S. Postal Service. In contrast, buying an e-book from Amazon.com or a software product from **Buy.com** constitutes pure EC because the product itself as well as its delivery, payment, and transfer are entirely digital. We use the term *electronic commerce* to denote both pure and partial EC.

There are a large number of e-commerce business models. **Table 7.1** describes several of these models.

Types of E-Commerce

E-commerce can be conducted between and among various parties. In this section, you will identify seven common types of e-commerce, and you will learn about three of them—C2C, B2E, and e-government—in detail. We discuss B2C and B2B in separate sections because they are very complex. We discuss mobile commerce in Chapter 8 and social commerce in Chapter 9.

- *Business-to-consumer electronic commerce (B2C)*: In B2C, the sellers are organizations, and the buyers are individuals. You will learn about B2C electronic commerce in Section 7.2.

- *Business-to-business electronic commerce (B2B)*: In B2B transactions, both the sellers and the buyers are business organizations. B2B comprises the vast majority of EC volume. You will learn more about B2B electronic commerce in Section 7.3. Look back to Figure 1.5 for an illustration of B2B electronic commerce.

- *Consumer-to-consumer electronic commerce (C2C)*: In C2C (also called customer-to-customer), an individual sells products or services to other individuals. The major strategies for conducting C2C on the Internet are auctions and classified ads. Most auctions are conducted by C2C intermediaries such as eBay (**www.ebay.com**). For another example, let's take a look at Directly Software (**www.directly.com**).

    MKT Many companies use Directly to facilitate the resolution of customer questions and complaints by knowledgeable customers themselves. Directly clients first enroll a group of knowledgeable customers, called answerers. Some client companies test their customers' writing skills and product knowledge before asking them to participate and become answerers. Directly's software has an artificial intelligence component that matches answerers with questions that it thinks they will be able to answer well, sending customer queries to them via the Directly app.

    HRM Directly answerers have *gig jobs*, similar to Amazon's Mechanical Turk and Uber. A gig job is one in which an organization contracts with independent workers for short-term engagements where the worker is paid for each engagement. Directly pays answerers 70 percent of the fee for each customer query they resolve. Answerers have reputation scores; those with higher scores receive more questions and may be asked to contribute to collections of stock answers to common questions (known as frequently asked questions or FAQs).

    Reputation scores, the flexibility of the work, and Directly's artificial intelligence component provide the startup with competitive advantage over rivals such as InSided (**www.insided.com**) and IAdvize (**www.iadvize.com**) in the $4.3 billion customer self-service software market. An average Directly representative makes about $200 per week and the top 5 percent earn more than $2,000 per week. Directly has experienced very rapid growth. Let's look at how game maker Kixeye uses Directly.

    MKT Kixeye (**www.kixeye.com**) receives approximately 40,000 customer support requests per month. About 40 percent of them go to Kixeye answerers via Directly. Kixeye says that while Directly's costs are comparable to those of overseas contractors, the startup delivers better results. Since replacing an Indian outsourcing firm with Kixeye answerers and Directly, the average response time for players' questions has decreased from 12 hours to 10 minutes, and customer satisfaction has risen by 50 percent.

- *Business-to-employee (B2E)*: In B2E, an organization uses EC internally to provide information and services to its employees. For example, companies allow employees to manage their benefits and to take training classes electronically. Employees can also buy discounted insurance, travel packages, and tickets to events on the corporate intranet. They can also order supplies and materials electronically. Finally, many companies have electronic corporate stores that sell the company's products to its employees, usually at a discount.

- *E-government*: E-government is the use of Internet technology in general and e-commerce in particular to deliver information and public services to citizens (called *government-to-citizen*, or *G2C EC*) and to business partners and suppliers (called *government-to-business*, or *G2B EC*). G2B EC is much like B2B EC, usually with an overlay of government procurement regulations. That is, G2B EC and B2B EC are conceptually similar. However, the functions of G2C EC are different from anything that exists in the private sector (e.g., B2C EC).

    E-government is also an efficient way of conducting business transactions with citizens and businesses and within the governments themselves. E-government makes government more efficient and effective, especially in the delivery of public services. An example of G2C electronic commerce is electronic benefits transfer, in which governments transfer benefits, such as Social Security and pension payments, directly to recipients' bank accounts.

- *Mobile commerce (m-commerce)*: The term *m-commerce* refers to e-commerce that is conducted entirely in a wireless environment. An example is using cell phones to shop over the Internet.

- *Social commerce*: Social commerce refers to the delivery of electronic commerce activities and transactions through social computing.

- *Conversational commerce*: Conversational commerce is a type of electronic commerce using natural language processing (see Chapter 14) to engage in various means of conversation, such as online chat with messaging apps, chatbots on messenging apps or websites, and voice assistants. We address chatbots in detail in IT's About Business 7.1 and take a closer look at messaging apps here.

IT's About Business 7.1

`MIS` `MKT` Chatbots

Chatbots, also known as *bots*, are interactive software programs that can conduct conversations with customers or other bots. Chatbots provide chatting experiences with human-like conversational and natural language abilities. There are two types of chatbot. The most common are those based on predetermined programmed responses. These chatbots are the easiest and cheapest to build. For example, simple chatbots could provide answers to an organization's frequently asked questions.

The other type consist of intelligent chatbots that can form natural sentences and understand humans. They function within boundaries that are constantly being expanded with artificial intelligence techniques such as machine learning. Chatbots can take the form of voice-controlled assistants such as Apple Siri, Amazon Alexa, Google Meena, and Microsoft Cortana as well as customer service representatives on the websites of many organizations.

These chatbots understand context, including what the user has asked or said previously; when, where, and how the user asked the question; and so on. Considering context also enables chatbots to understand and respond to different and unexpected inputs from users.

Intelligent chatbots become familiar with their users over time. For example, they learn the best times to get in touch with their users, and they proactively contact the users based on this knowledge. These chatbots remember users' preferences, which enables them to provide a truly personalized experience for each user.

Many organizations use chatbots to interact with customers. Well-known examples are Starbucks, Lyft, Fandango, Spotify, Whole Foods, Sephora, Mastercard, Staples, *Wall Street Journal*, and Pizza Hut. Let's look at some examples in more detail.

- In India, Digibank (**www.dbs.com/digibank/in**) is available to its customers only through mobile. The bank communicates using its *digibot* that can answer thousands of questions that customers send through chat.

- The Royal Bank of Scotland (RBS; **www.natwestgroup.com**) is using a bot called "Luvo" to provide basic customer service. The bank adopted Luvo to relieve staff from having to deal with easily answered questions so they can spend their time on more complex and value-added issues. Luvo can understand human language, so customers can describe what they are looking for instead of just choosing from standard options.

- Air France–KLM has deployed BlueBot, an adaptive, intelligent chatbot that lives on Facebook Messenger, where it helps travelers find and book flights, as well as remind them to check in. The bot is integrated with the airline's Salesforce CRM system so that employees can easily take over a conversation when the bot does not know how to respond to a question. Since the airline deployed BlueBot, the bot has managed 1.4 million queries and is responsible for 15 percent of all passenger boarding passes. Other airlines also employ chatbots, such as Air New Zealand's Oscar and Lufthansa's Mildred.

- Taco Bell (**www.tacobell.com**) developed the TacoBot, which processes orders at the chain's locations. The TacoBot understands and manages orders. It also stores customers' order histories and makes recommendations based on the time of day.

- Bots are helping organizations in their recruitment efforts. In the early stages of the process, bots can examine hundreds of résumés to screen candidates. Next, bots can manage the communications with candidates to request more information or to schedule interviews. Bots then hand off candidates who have met basic criteria so human recruiters can decide which ones to call for an interview. For example, Mya from Mya Systems (**https://mya.com**) is always enthusiastic and patient, uses natural language processing to make sense of an applicant's typed questions, and responds with accurate, realistic answers.

Many organizations use chatbots internally. Consider the case of the online retailer Overstock (**www.overstock.com**). Overstock's chatbot, called Mila, automates the simple but time-consuming process of requesting sick leave. Previously, on any given day, dozens of employees in the company's call center in Salt Lake City could become ill. When that happened, clerks manually checked the messages and alerted the employee's manager. The manager would then find a substitute for the ill employee.

Now, if workers are not feeling well, they notify Mila. The bot then sends a message to the person's manager. As a result, Overstock can replace ill employees much more quickly, thus saving the company money. In addition, Mila provides other employee self-serve functions such as requesting holidays and updating their schedules, which formerly required interacting with a human.

Another example is the bot DoNotPay. Hiring a lawyer to appeal a parking ticket is time consuming and expensive. However, with the help of DoNotPay, developed by 19-year-old British programmer Joshua Browder, the appeal now costs nothing. Since the bot was launched in late 2015, it has successfully appealed hundreds of thousands of parking tickets in cities around the world. In addition, by 2017 the bot was helping refugees fill out immigration applications to the United States and Canada, and it was offering assistance for asylum seekers in the United Kingdom. By July 2019 DoNotPay was advertising that people can use the bot to sue anyone. DoNotPay focuses on suing corporations and helping people navigate bureaucracies.

Chatbots have become extremely valuable during the COVID-19 pandemic. Here we look at two examples: government agencies and food delivery.

Government agencies. When the pandemic struck the state of New York, Governor Andrew Cuomo ordered all government staff to be reduced by 50 percent. As a result, many agencies had to downsize the number of call center employees. At the same time, calls were increasing as residents began to seek reliable COVID-19-related guidance and medical information.

Many agencies quickly deployed chatbots to address callers' most common questions, such as how to identify symptoms and how to get tested. The bots were able to expand the range of their responses as they analyzed additional queries.

The chatbots are popular with a range of organizations. For example, the city of Austin, Texas, and the Czech Ministry of Health use them to provide information related to COVID-19. The Oklahoma Employment Security Commission uses its bot to help answer 60,000 daily calls related to unemployment claims. Children's Healthcare of Atlanta uses IBM's chatbot to help parents assess their children's symptoms.

Food delivery. Social distancing and stay-home orders have led to huge demand for grocery delivery services. In some large cities, people are having difficulty finding open delivery time slots. In response, developers have produced bots that automatically hunt for a free delivery slot, take it, and then complete the user's food order, giving users a much better chance of buying food before other people can take that slot.

Chatbots clearly provide myriad benefits to organizations and customers. However, developers must deal with the ethical issue of releasing a bot that can be abused. That is, some populations who are most at risk of COVID-19, such as elderly people, are the most likely to use food delivery services. These people are probably not going to be able to use bots to help them order food. Instead, these bots will likely disproportionately benefit people who possess the technical knowledge to utilize them.

Unfortunately, bots are also an excellent tool for scalping tickets because it is easy to teach them how to perform simple tasks such as signing up for ticket-sales websites. They also make the process anonymous, so the scalpers are not caught. With these bots, scalpers can purchase tickets for an enormously popular show such as *Hamilton* ahead of anyone else. This process causes ticket prices on the resale market to become artificially inflated.

To address this problem, Ticketmaster (**www.ticketmaster. com**) has developed a technology known as Verified Fan, which works by scanning users' purchase histories to determine whether they want to see a particular show themselves or, more likely, they are just a bot being used by a scalper to buy a large volume of tickets. Users who pass the screening, and therefore are not bots, are given access to an advanced ticket sale. Furthermore, the 2016 Better Online Ticket Sales (BOTS) Act, enforced by the Federal Trade Commission (**www.ftc.gov**) now outlaws these kinds of automated ticket-buying schemes.

Another problem is that resellers are using bots to purchase popular toys ahead of the holiday rush. They then resell the toys at inflated prices on eBay and Amazon. The bots continuously monitor retailer websites, order items, and fill out order and payment details much faster than a human can. When a human is needed—for example, to defeat a CAPTCHA system (see Chapter 4)—resellers farm out the task to remote workers via websites such as Amazon's Mechanical Turk. The resellers use thousands of Internet Protocol (IP) addresses and thousands of credit card credentials to avoid suspicion. Unfortunately, the BOTS Act does not yet apply to online retail.

Sources: Compiled from C. Schebella, "How AI-Powered Self-Service Helps Agencies during COVID-19," *GCN.com*, July 29, 2020; P. Kumar, "Boosting Customer Experience with AI-Powered Chatbots," *Enterprise Times*, July 28, 2020; K. Hao, "The Pandemic Is Emptying Call Centers. AI Chatbots Are Swooping In," *MIT Technology Review*, May 14, 2020; J. Cox, "People Are Making Bots to Snatch Whole Foods Delivery Order Time Slots," *Vice.com*, April 21, 2020; B. Popken, "The Best Cyber Monday Deals and How Bots Could Spoil the Shopping," *NBC News*, December 1, 2019; "Conversational AI and the Rise of the Chatbots," *Hewlett-Packard Enterprise*, May 10, 2018; "A.I. Helps Oscar the Chatbot Answer 75 Percent of Travel Questions," *Digital Trends*, April 4, 2018; R. Hollander, "Chatbots and Voice Assistants Are Gaining Traction in the Workplace," *Business Insider*, April 2, 2018; D. Essex, "Your Competitors Are Amassing Armies of Recruiting Chatbots," *TechTarget*, February 22, 2018; "Broadway Hit 'Hamilton' Has a Plan to Stop Bots from Buying up Tickets," *Futurism*, August 17, 2017; S. Perez, "HelloAva Launches a Chatbot for Personalized Skin Care Recommendations," *TechCrunch*, May 15, 2017; E. Cresci, "Chatbot that Overturned 160,000 Parking Fines Now Helping Refugees Claim Asylum," *The Guardian*, March 6, 2017; C. Waxer, "Get Ready for the Bot Revolution," *Computerworld*, October 17, 2016; O. Williams-Grut, "RBS Is Launching an A.I. Chatbot Called 'Luvo' to Help Customers," *Business Insider*, September 28, 2016; W. Knight, "The HR Person at Your Next Job May Actually Be a Bot," *MIT Technology Review*, August 3, 2016; S. Brewster, "Do Your Banking with a Chatbot," *MIT Technology Review*, May 17, 2016; "Chatbots to Take 'HR Role' at Overstock.com," *Gadgets Now Beta*, May 9, 2016; T. Peterson, "Inside the Making of Taco Bell's Artificially Intelligent, Drunk-Tolerant TacoBot," *Martech Today*, April 14, 2016; L. Garfield, "A 19-Year-Old Made a Free Robot Lawyer that Has Appealed $3 Million in Parking Tickets," *Business Insider*, February 18, 2016.

Questions

1. Discuss how the capabilities of chatbots are expanding through the use of machine learning. (Hint: see Chapter 14.)

2. Describe how your university could use a chatbot in its admissions process. Provide specific examples.

Messaging apps include Facebook Messenger (**www.messenger.com**), WhatsApp (**www.whatsapp.com**), Kik (**www.kik.com**), and WeChat (**www.wechat.com**). Customers can chat with company representatives, access customer support, ask questions, receive personalized recommendations, and click to purchase, all from within messaging apps. They have the options of interacting with a human representative, a chatbot, or a combination of the two. Facebook Messenger and WeChat are among the largest messaging apps in the world.

Some 1.3 billion individuals use Facebook Messenger. Facebook's objective is to drive Messenger users to the more than 15 million businesses with an official brand Facebook page. For example, to shop for a T-shirt on Facebook Messenger, users can send a text to Messenger to start a chat with the mobile shopping app Spring. The app will request information concerning the buyer's budget and then display several possible T-shirts. If the customer does not like any of these choices, then Spring will present more options.

Messenger also has a chatbot-building capability. In August 2020 there were approximately 300,000 bots on the app. These bots can process purchases without directing shoppers to a third party. To process transactions in Messenger, Facebook is collaborating with leading companies in the payments industry, including electronic payment leaders Stripe and PayPal Braintree, as well as credit card giants Visa, MasterCard, and American Express.

Some 1.1 billion people use WeChat, China's massive social media site. They can utilize bots on the app to chat with friends about an upcoming concert, purchase tickets to the event, book a restaurant, split the check, and call a taxi. In addition to the individual WeChat users, 10 million Chinese businesses have an account. In fact, for some firms the WeChat bot completely replaces an Internet site.

Each type of EC is executed in one or more business models. A **business model** is the method by which a company generates revenue to sustain itself. **Table 7.1** summarizes the major EC business models.

TABLE 7.1   E-Commerce Business Models

Online direct marketing	Manufacturers or retailers sell directly to customers. Very efficient for digital products and services. Can allow for product or service customization (**www.dell.com**).
Electronic tendering system	Businesses request quotes from suppliers. Uses B2B with a reverse auction mechanism.
Name-your-own-price	Customers decide how much they are willing to pay. An intermediary tries to match a provider (**www.priceline.com**).
Find-the-best-price	Customers specify a need; an intermediary compares providers and shows the lowest price. Customers must accept the offer in a short time, or they may lose the deal (**www.hotwire.com**).
Affiliate marketing	Vendors ask partners to place logos (or banners) on partner's site. If customers click on a logo, go to a vendor's site, and make a purchase, then the vendor pays commissions to the partners.
Viral marketing	Recipients of your marketing notices send information about your product to their friends.
Group purchasing (e-coops)	Small buyers aggregate demand to create a large volume; the group then conducts tendering or negotiates a low price.
Online auctions	Companies run auctions of various types on the Internet. Very popular in C2C, but gaining ground in other types of EC as well (**www.ebay.com**).
Product customization	Customers use the Internet to self-configure products or services. Sellers then price them and fulfill them quickly (*build-to-order*)(**www.jaguar.com**).
Electronic marketplaces and exchanges	Transactions are conducted efficiently (more information to buyers and sellers; lower transaction costs) in electronic marketplaces (private or public).
Bartering online	Intermediary administers online exchange of surplus products or company receives "points" for its contribution, which it can use to purchase other needed items (**https://bbubarter.com**).
Deep discounters	Company offers deep price discounts. Appeals to customers who consider only price in their purchasing decisions.
Membership	Only members can use the services provided, including access to certain information, conducting trades, and so on.

Major E-Commerce Mechanisms

MKT Businesses and customers can buy and sell on the Internet through a number of mechanisms, including electronic catalogs and electronic auctions. Businesses and customers use electronic payment mechanisms to digitally pay for goods and services.

Catalogs have been printed on paper for generations. Today, they are also available over the Internet. *Electronic catalogs* consist of a product database, a directory and search capabilities, and a presentation function. They are the backbone of most e-commerce sites.

An **auction** is a competitive buying and selling process in which prices are determined dynamically by competitive bidding. Electronic auctions (e-auctions) generally increase revenues for sellers by broadening the customer base and shortening the cycle time of the auction. Buyers generally benefit from e-auctions because they can bargain for lower prices. They also do not have to travel to an auction at a physical location.

The Internet provides an efficient infrastructure for conducting auctions at lower administrative costs and with a greater number of involved sellers and buyers. Both individual consumers and corporations can participate in auctions.

There are two major types of auctions: forward and reverse. In **forward auctions**, sellers solicit bids from many potential buyers. Usually, sellers place items at sites for auction, and buyers bid continuously for them. The highest bidder wins the items. Both sellers and buyers can be either individuals or businesses. The popular auction site eBay.com is a forward auction site.

In **reverse auctions**, one buyer, usually an organization, wants to purchase a product or a service. The buyer posts a request for a quotation (RFQ) on its website or on a third-party site. The RFQ provides detailed information on the desired purchase. Interested suppliers study the RFQ and then submit bids electronically. Everything else being equal, the lowest-price bidder wins the auction. The reverse auction is the most common auction model for large purchases (in regard to either quantities or price). Governments and large corporations frequently use this approach, which may provide considerable savings for the buyer.

Auctions can be conducted from the seller's site, the buyer's site, or a third party's site. For example, eBay, the best-known third-party site, offers hundreds of thousands of different items in several types of auctions. Overall, more than 300 major companies, including Amazon.com and Dellauction.com, sponsor online auctions.

An *electronic storefront* is a website that represents a single store. An *electronic mall*, also known as a *cybermall* or an *e-mall,* is a collection of individual shops consolidated under one Internet address. Electronic storefronts and electronic malls are closely associated with B2C electronic commerce. You will study each one in more detail in Section 7.2.

An **electronic marketplace** (*e-marketplace*) is a central, virtual market space on the web where many buyers and many sellers can conduct e-commerce and e-business activities. Electronic marketplaces are associated with B2B electronic commerce. You will learn about electronic marketplaces in Section 7.3.

Electronic Payment Mechanisms

MIS **ACCT** Implementing EC typically requires electronic payments. **Electronic payment mechanisms** enable buyers to pay for goods and services electronically, rather than writing a check or using cash. Payments are an integral part of doing business, whether in the traditional manner or online. Traditional payment systems have typically involved cash or checks.

In most cases, traditional payment systems are not effective for EC, especially for B2B. Cash cannot be used because there is no face-to-face contact between buyer and seller. Not everyone accepts credit cards or checks, and some buyers do not have credit cards or checking accounts. Finally, contrary to what many people believe, it may be *less* secure for the buyer to use the telephone or mail to arrange or send payments, especially from another country, than to complete a secured transaction on a computer. For all of these reasons, a better method is needed to pay for goods and services in cyberspace. This method is electronic payment systems. Let's take a closer look at electronic checks, electronic cards, and digital, online payments. We discuss the blockchain and various cryptocurrencies such as Bitcoin later in this chapter, and then discuss digital wallets in Chapter 8.

ACCT **Electronic Checks.** *Electronic checks (e-checks),* which are used primarily in B2B, are similar to regular paper checks. A customer who wishes to use e-checks must first establish a checking account with a bank. Then, when the customer buys a product or a service, he or she e-mails an encrypted electronic check to the seller. The seller deposits the check in a bank account, and the funds are transferred from the buyer's account into the seller's account.

Like regular checks, e-checks carry a signature (in digital form) that can be verified (see **www.authorize.net**). Properly signed and endorsed e-checks are exchanged between financial institutions through electronic clearinghouses.

FIN **ACCT** **Electronic Cards.** There are a variety of electronic cards, and they are used for different purposes. The most common types are electronic credit cards, purchasing cards, stored-value money cards, and smart cards.

Electronic credit cards allow customers to charge online payments to their credit card account. These cards are used primarily in B2C and in shopping by small-to-medium enterprises (SMEs). Here is how e-credit cards work (see **Figure 7.1**).

1. When you purchase a book from Amazon, for example, your credit card information and purchase amount are encrypted in your browser. This procedure ensures the information is safe while it is "traveling" on the Internet to Amazon.

2. When your information arrives at Amazon, it is not opened. Rather, it is transferred automatically (in encrypted form) to a *clearinghouse*, where it is decrypted for verification and authorization.

3. The clearinghouse asks the bank that issued you your credit card (the card issuer bank) to verify your credit card information.

4. Your card issuer bank verifies your credit card information and reports this to the clearinghouse.

5. The clearinghouse reports the result of the verification of your credit card to Amazon.

6. Amazon reports a successful purchase and amount to you.

7. Your card issuer bank sends funds in the amount of the purchase to Amazon's bank.

8. Your card issuer bank notifies you (either electronically or in your monthly statement) of the debit on your credit card.

9. Amazon's bank notifies Amazon of the funds credited to its account.

Purchasing cards are the B2B equivalent of electronic credit cards (see **Figure 7.2**). In some countries, purchasing cards are the primary form of payment between companies. Unlike credit cards, where credit is provided for 30 days (for free) before payment is made to the merchant, payments made with purchasing cards are settled within a week.

Stored-value money cards allow you to store a fixed amount of prepaid money and then spend it as necessary. Each time you use the card, the amount is reduced by the amount you spent. **Figure 7.3** illustrates a New York City MetroCard (for the subway and bus).

Finally, *EMV smart cards* contain a chip that can store a large amount of information as well as on a magnetic stripe for backward compatibility (see **Figure 7.4**). EMV stands for Europay, MasterCard, and Visa, the three companies that originally created the standard. EMV is a technical standard for smart payment cards. EMV cards can be physically swiped through a reader, inserted into a reader, or read over a short distance using near-field communications.

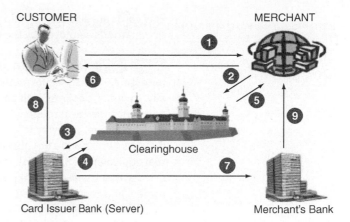

FIGURE 7.1 **How e-credit cards work. (The numbers 1–9 indicate the sequence of activities.)**

MIKE CLARKE/AFP/Getty Images

FIGURE 7.2 **Example of a purchasing card.**

Clarence Holmes Photography/ Alamy Stock Photo

FIGURE 7.3 **The New York City MetroCard.**

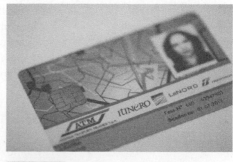

MARKA/Alamy Stock Photo

FIGURE 7.4 **Smart cards are frequently multipurpose.**

EMV cards are also called "chip and PIN" or "chip and signature" depending on the authentication methods employed by the card issuer.

ACCT MIS Digital, Online Payments.   The rapid growth of electronic commerce necessitated a fast, secure method for customers to pay online using their credit cards. Traditionally, to process online credit card payments, merchants set up Internet merchant accounts and payment gateway accounts. The merchants obtained their merchant accounts through a bank.

A payment gateway is an application that authorizes payments for e-businesses, online retailers, bricks-and-clicks businesses, or traditional brick-and-mortar businesses. It is the virtual equivalent of a physical point of sale terminal located in retail outlets.

Payment gateways link, on one hand, to credit card accounts belonging to online customers and to Internet merchant accounts on the other. Payment gateways interact with the card issuer's bank to authorize the credit card in real time when a purchase is made. The funds received flow into the merchant account.

The leading providers of payment gateway accounts are PayPal (**www.paypal.com**), Authorize.net (**www.authorize.net**), Cybersource (**www.cybersource.com**), and Verisign (**www.verisign.com**). These providers help merchants set up merchant accounts and payment gateways in one convenient package. Let's look at how Stripe is disrupting the payments industry.

FIN MIS   Founded in 2011, Stripe (**https://stripe.com**) is an electronic payment software solution in the financial technology (Fintech) industry whose goal is to transform e-payment systems. Stripe allows individuals and businesses to accept payments over the Internet. Stripe focuses on providing the technical, fraud prevention, and banking infrastructure required to operate online payment systems.

Using Stripe, merchants can integrate payment processing into their websites without having to register and maintain a merchant account. For online credit card transactions, merchants create a Stripe account and insert a few lines of JavaScript into their website's source code. When shoppers provide their credit card information, it's collected directly by Stripe's servers, so merchants do not need to handle sensitive data. Stripe processes the transaction, scans for signs of fraud, and charges a fee of 2.9 percent plus 30 cents per transaction. Stripe deposits the funds from the sale into the vendor's bank account a week later.

In the fall of 2018, Stripe moved into brick-and-mortar retail when the firm deployed a new product called Stripe Terminal. Terminal is Stripe's payments solution for fast-growing Internet businesses that sell products and services in person as well as online. For example, digital-first brands such as Warby Parker (eyeglasses; **www.warbyparker.com**) and Glossier (skin care and beauty products; **www.glossier.com**) use Terminal for in-person payments.

One of Stripe's main competitors is Adyen (**www.adyen.com**), a European service. Adyen offers merchants the ability to use one payment solution to globally track all online and brick-and-mortar sales.

Stripe says that it is targeting different customers than Adyen. Specifically, Stripe targets fast-growing, digital-first companies that have only recently begun expanding into physical retail. Ayden, however, targets large traditional brands such as L'Oréal and Burberry, although it does business with large Internet platforms such as eBay and Etsy.

Stripe also believes its technology differentiates it from Adyen. The firm states that Stripe Terminal will make it easy for stores to customize what shoppers see on the checkout screen, whether that is a discount offer or other messaging. Merchants will also be able to manage and send updates to all of their checkout equipment from one online account. Pricing for Stripe Terminal begins at a 2.7 percent fee, plus 5 cents for each transaction.

Beyond consumer product businesses, Stripe Terminal also targets business-to-business software platforms whose own customers operate brick-and-mortar chains. For instance, Mindbody (**www.mindbodyonline.com**), which makes software for wellness businesses like yoga studios and spas, is a Stripe customer.

Benefits and Limitations of E-Commerce

Few innovations in human history have provided as many benefits to organizations, individuals, and society as e-commerce has. E-commerce benefits organizations by making national and international markets more accessible and by lowering the costs of processing, distributing, and retrieving information. Customers benefit by being able to access a vast number of products and services around the clock. The major benefit to society is the ability to easily and conveniently deliver information, services, and products to people in cities, rural areas, and developing countries.

Despite all these benefits, EC has some limitations, both technological and nontechnological, that have restricted its growth and acceptance. One major technological limitation is the lack of universally accepted security standards. Also, in less-developed countries, telecommunications bandwidth is often insufficient, and accessing the Web is expensive. The remaining nontechnological limitation is the perception that EC is nonsecure.

Before you go on...

1. Define e-commerce and distinguish it from e-business.
2. Differentiate among B2C, B2B, C2C, and B2E electronic commerce.
3. Define e-government.
4. Discuss forward and reverse auctions.
5. Discuss the various online payment mechanisms.
6. Identify some benefits and limitations of e-commerce.

7.2 Business-to-Consumer (B2C) Electronic Commerce

B2B EC is much larger than B2C EC by volume, but B2C EC is more complex. The reason is that B2C involves a large number of buyers making millions of diverse transactions per day from a relatively small number of sellers. As an illustration, consider Amazon, an online retailer that offers thousands of products to its customers. Each customer purchase is relatively small, but Amazon must manage every transaction as if that customer were its most important one. The company needs to process each order quickly and efficiently, and ship the products to the customer in a timely manner. It also has to manage returns. Multiply this simple example by millions, and you get an idea of how complex B2C EC can be.

Overall, B2B complexities tend to be more business related, whereas B2C complexities tend to be more technical and volume related. As you noted in the previous section of this chapter, one of the complexities of B2C involves digital, online payments.

This section addresses the primary issues in B2C EC. We begin by studying the two basic mechanisms that customers utilize to access companies on the Web: electronic storefronts and electronic malls. In addition to purchasing products over the Web, customers access online services, such as banking, securities trading, job searching, and travel. Companies engaged in B2C EC must "get the word out" to prospective customers, so we turn our attention to online advertising. Finally, the complexity of B2C EC creates two major challenges for sellers: channel conflict and order fulfillment, which we examine in detail.

Author Lecture Videos are available exclusively in *WileyPLUS*.
Apply the Concept activities are available in the Appendix and in *WileyPLUS*.

Electronic Storefronts and Malls

For several generations, home shopping from catalogs, and later from television shopping channels, has attracted millions of customers. **Electronic retailing (e-tailing)** is the direct sale of products and services through electronic storefronts or electronic malls, usually designed around an electronic catalog format and auctions.

E-commerce enables you to buy from anywhere, at any time. EC offers a wide variety of products and services, including unique items, often at lower prices. The name given to selling unique items is "the long tail." The *long tail* describes the retailing strategy of selling a large number of unique items in small quantities.

Shoppers can also gain access to very detailed supplementary product information. They can also easily locate and compare competitors' products and prices. Finally, buyers can find hundreds of thousands of sellers. Two popular online shopping mechanisms are electronic storefronts and electronic malls.

As we saw earlier in the chapter, an **electronic storefront** is a website that represents a single store. Each storefront has a unique uniform resource locator (URL), or Internet address, at which buyers can place orders.

An **electronic mall**, also known as a *cybermall*, or an *e-mall*, is a collection of individual shops grouped under a single Internet address. Electronic malls may include thousands of vendors. For example, Microsoft Bing shopping, (**www.bing.com/shop**) includes tens of thousands of products from thousands of vendors, as does Amazon (**www.amazon.com**).

Online Service Industries

In addition to purchasing products, customers access needed services on the Web. Selling books, toys, computers, and most other products on the Internet can reduce vendors' selling costs by 20 to 40 percent. Further reduction is difficult to achieve because the products must be delivered physically. Only a few products, such as software and music, can be digitized and then delivered online for additional savings. In contrast, services such as buying an airline ticket and purchasing stocks or insurance can be delivered entirely through e-commerce, often with considerable cost reduction.

One of the most pressing EC issues relating to online services (as well as in marketing tangible products) is **disintermediation**. Intermediaries, also known as *middlemen*, have two functions: (1) they provide information, and (2) they perform value-added services such as consulting. The first function can be fully automated and most likely will be assumed by e-marketplaces and portals that provide information for free. When this development occurs, the intermediaries who perform only (or primarily) this function are likely to be eliminated. The process whereby intermediaries are eliminated is called *disintermediation.*

In contrast to simply providing information, performing value-added services requires expertise. Unlike the information function, then, this function can be only partially automated. Intermediaries who provide value-added services are thriving. The Web helps these employees in two situations: (1) when the number of participants is enormous, as with job searches, and (2) when the information that must be exchanged is complex.

In this section, you will examine some leading online service industries: banking, trading of securities (stocks, bonds), job matching, travel services, and advertising.

FIN **MIS** **Financial Technology (Fintech).**   Traditional banks have massive, entrenched, and inefficient legacy infrastructures: brick-and-mortar buildings and information technology infrastructures. These legacy infrastructures make it difficult for traditional banks to upgrade their systems or to be agile and flexible. Furthermore, their infrastructures are making banks' customer experience outdated. Customers now expect their financial experiences to be mobile, personalized, customizable, and accessible.

Responding to customer expectations, **Fintech** is an industry composed of companies that use technology to compete in the marketplace with traditional financial institutions and intermediaries in the delivery of financial services, which include banking, insurance, real estate, and investing. (Fintech is also a blanket term for disruptive technologies that are affecting the financial services industry.) Let's take a closer look at the many services that Fintech companies are offering.

FIN **Lending.**   An alternative source of financing, person-to-person (P2P) lending platforms use machine learning technologies and algorithms to save individuals and businesses time and money and help them access a line of credit. P2P lending platforms provide borrowers with an easy, fast, simple, and lower-cost service that most traditional banks cannot match. The leading companies in this area are Lending Tree (**www.lendingtree.com**), Lending Club (**www.lendingclub.com**), Prosper (**www.prosper.com**), and Zopa (**www.zopa.com**).

FIN **Trading and Investing.**   New automated financial advisors and wealth management services are making an impact on the industry. *Robo-advisors* create relatively straightforward asset allocation portfolios based on customers' ages and risk tolerance. Basically, they tell clients what percentage of stocks, bonds, and cash they shoud have. They then monitor the portfolio and reallocate funds as needed. *Robo-analysts* use sophisticated algorithms to make trading and investing a more automated online experience. Often in conjunction with human advisors, these platforms provide savings to users and offer financial research and planning services that are normally reserved for wealthy investors. They are also enabling users with small amounts of capital to begin investing. The leading companies in this area are Wealthfront (**www.wealthfront.com**), Betterment (**www.betterment.com**), motif (**www.motifinvesting .com**), etoro (**www.etoro.com**), and Robinhood (**www.robinhood.com**).

FIN **ACCT** **Personal Finance.**   Fintech companies are trying to make personal finance more transparent and more affordable. Mobile apps and online platforms are now helping individuals and businesses develop a budget, find a loan, file their taxes, and invest. These platforms are also using technology to track daily expenditures and to help users analyze their financial status in real time. Leading companies in this area are Acorns (**www.acorns.com**), Learnvest (**www.learnvest.com**), Mint (**www.mint.com**), Nerdwallet (**www.nerdwallet.com**), and Billguard (**www.crunchbase.com/organizations/billguard**).

FIN **Funding.**   Equity and crowdfunding platforms provide alternate sources of investment for individuals who want to start a business. Online crowdfunding platforms raise money from a large number of individuals who collectively fund projects that typically would not attract funding from traditional banks and venture capital firms. The leading companies in this area are Kickstarter (**www.kickstarter.com**), indiegogo (**www.indiegogo.com**), and gofundme (**www.gofundme.com**).

FIN **Currency Exchange and Remittances.**   Transferring and exchanging money internationally can be a time-consuming and expensive process. Fintech companies are developing innovative platforms that make this process simpler, faster, and less expensive. These companies range from P2P currency exchanges that reduce the costs of exchanging currencies to mobile phone–based money transfers and remittance platforms that provide a cost-effective method for people to transfer small amounts of money overseas. The leading companies in this area are Wise (**www.wise.com**), Xoom (**www.xoom.com**), WeSwap (**www.weswap .com**), WorldRemit (**www.worldremit.com**), and mPesa (**www.worldremit.com/en/**).

FIN **Mobile Banking.**   Mobile banking refers to the service that banks and other financial institutions provide to their customers that enables them to conduct a range of transactions by using an app on their mobile devices. The apps allow customers to remotely access and transact with their accounts. In the United States, approximately 72 percent of consumers use digital channels to open checking accounts.

FIN **Internet Banking (also called e-banking or online banking).**   Internet banking is closely related to mobile banking. However, instead of using an app, customers use the Internet. All of the transactions are conducted through the website of the financial institution. Several Internet-only banks have emerged including Ally (**www.ally.com**), TIAA Bank (**www.tiaabank.com**), and Axos Bank (**www.axosbank.com/Personal**).

FIN **ACCT** **Payments.**   Casual payments that people make every day, such as $75 for domestic help or $40 to split a lunch check with friends, have long been a problem for the U.S. banking system. Today, new payment technologies are changing the ways that consumers bank, transfer money, and pay for goods and services.

With P2P services, consumers link a bank account, credit card, or debit card to a smartphone app and can then send money to anyone else with only the recipient's e-mail address or phone number. In the near future, many consumers will not carry a physical wallet filled with cash and credit cards, but only use a smartphone. The leading companies in this area are Venmo (**http://venmo.com**; subsidiary of PayPal), PayPal (**www.paypal.com**), Square (**https://squareup.com**), Apple Pay (**www.apple.com/apple-pay**), Google Pay (**https:// payments.google.com**), and Facebook Messenger (**www.messenger.com**).

In June 2017, more than 30 major banks, including Bank of America, Citibank, JPMorgan Chase, and Wells Fargo, teamed up to introduce Zelle (**www.zellepay.com**), a digital payments network that allows consumers to send money instantly through participating banks' mobile apps. Consumers who utilize this network do not have to download a separate app.

ACCT **MIS** **Blockchain.** A *ledger* records a business's summarized financial information as debits and credits and displays their current balances. A blockchain is a decentralized, distributed, encrypted, secure, anonymous, tamper-proof, unchangeable, and often public digital ledger (a database, if you will) consisting of transactions bundled into *blocks*. Blocks contain details such as transaction timestamps and a link to the previous block. These links form the blockchain.

The blockchain records transactions across many computers so that blocks cannot be altered retroactively without the alteration of all subsequent blocks. This process allows all participants to independently verify and audit transactions. We now take a closer look at how blockchains function.

Nodes are the computers that support a blockchain network and keep it operating smoothly. Nodes are operated by individuals or groups of people who contribute money toward buying powerful computer systems. There are two types of nodes: full nodes and lightweight nodes. *Full nodes* keep a complete copy of the blockchain ledger, which is a record of every single transaction that has ever occurred. *Lightweight nodes* only download a fraction of the blockchain. Lightweight nodes are used by most people as a Bitcoin wallet for Bitcoin transactions.

A *miner* is a type of node that creates blocks in the blockchain. Miners bundle pending transactions into a block, verify that block, and add it to the blockchain.

To be able to add a block to the blockchain, a miner must compete to be the first to complete the Proof-of-Work (PoW) mining algorithm. Miners append a nonce, which is a random whole number, to the hashed contents of the block. (Note: The contents of the block are hashed when they are encrypted by a mathematical formula.) With the nonce appended to the block, miners rehash the contents to try to produce a hash value lower than or equal to the value set by the network. A *hash value* is a series of numbers and letters that is generated by the hash function. Miners keep trying different nonces until they obtain the correct hash value.

The miner who finds the correct hash value broadcasts the correct solution to the network. Receiving nodes validate the transactions in the block and accept it only if all are valid. Once a majority of nodes agree that all transactions in the recent past are unique (i.e., not double spent), the transactions in the block are cryptographically sealed into the block. Each new block is linked to previously sealed blocks to create a chain of accepted history, thereby preserving a verified record of every transaction.

The new block is then added to the blockchain and the winning miner receives 12.5 Bitcoin by the blockchain for its success. The winning miner also receives all of the fees from Bitcoin transactions that were included in that block.

The central problem in electronic cash is called *double spend*. Because electronic money consists of data, nothing stops a currency holder from trying to spend it twice.

Blockchain technology allows for the tracking of digital assets so that they can be verified as authentic and cannot be copied without permission. This capability makes blockchain ideal for financial transactions but also for other kinds of digital content such as contracts, and verified assets such as property deeds and election votes.

Blockchain technology does present problems, with the most significant being hacking. For instance, in 2019 an attacker gained control of more than half of Ethereum Classic (a cryptocurrency exchange) and was rewriting its transaction history. This attack is called a 51-percent attack. Between 2017 and 2019, industry analysts note that hackers had stolen nearly $2 billion in cryptocurrency, mostly from exchanges, and that is just what had been publicly revealed.

Another problem is that some blockchains allow for anonymity. As a result, cybercriminals use these blockchains for illegal purposes. Recall ransomware (see Chapter 4) where attackers typically require ransoms to be paid in cryptocurrency.

There are a variety of uses for blockchain technology. The most well-known is cryptocurrencies. We look at Bitcoin next and then examine other applications.

MIS **Bitcoin.** Blockchain is not Bitcoin but is the technology underlying Bitcoin. Bitcoin is the digital token and blockchain is the ledger to keep track of who owns the digital tokens.

Bitcoin is a decentralized cryptocurrency, which is a digital form of currency that uses blockchain and cryptography for validation. The blockchain records every bitcoin and every transaction related to it.

The Bitcoin network is a peer-to-peer payment network that operates with encryption. Users send and receive Bitcoins, units of digital currency, by sending digitally signed messages to the network using Bitcoin cryptocurrency wallet software.

Let's look at an example of a simple Bitcoin transaction. Jim wants to send one Bitcoin to Sally.

Jim and Sally both have Bitcoin wallets. Each wallet contains two pieces of information. One is the public key, which is that person's Bitcoin address. The other is the private key, which is that person's Bitcoin password.

If someone loses their private key, they lose access to their Bitcoin wallet and their Bitcoin. No centralized entity exists that can recover private keys. In fact, if someone else has your private key, they can take your Bitcoin.

Sally sends Jim her public key. Jim opens his Bitcoin wallet, enters the instruction to send one Bitcoin to Sally's public address, and enters his private key to authorize the transaction. The Bitcoin network examines the proposed transaction. It checks to see that Jim has enough Bitcoin in his account and if the address Sally provided is valid.

After Jim and Sally's transaction passes these two tests, miners bundle it with other pending transactions into a block. The winning miner verifies the block and after consensus is reached, adds it to the blockchain. The blockchain processes the transaction and updates the database. Jim's balance is decreased by one Bitcoin and Sally's is credited by one Bitcoin.

POM Energy Grid. Power companies manage and control modern electrical grids. The power companies, as trusted intermediaries between producers and consumers, buy and sell power at the prices they set because they control the infrastructure.

However, rapid improvements in renewable energy sources and batteries are leading to innovations like microgrids in communities. A *microgrid* is a self-sufficient energy system that serves a discrete area, such as a college campus or a neighborhood. For instance, if homeowners generate more power than they need, they can sell the excess power to neighbors or businesses at market value. The peer-to-peer process of selling and buying energy can operate with blockchain technology, saving money because there is no intermediary in each transaction. The process also saves energy by keeping it local, because the farther that energy travels, the more that is wasted.

MKT POM Digital Content Creators. A major problem in the digital content space today is the lack of transparency regarding royalty payments and rights management. For the creators of digital content and virtual property, blockchain means enforceable copyrights, transparency around royalty payments, and payments made securely without an intermediary. Blockchain technology can provide evidence of ownership of content in both digital media and music. Further, with smart contracts on the blockchain, copyright becomes more enforceable. A *smart contract* is a self-executing contract with the terms of agreement between buyer and seller directly written into the software. The software and the agreements in the contract exist on a blockchain network.

Blockchains could eliminate the middlemen and enable musicians and other digital content creators to get paid directly by their audience. As the market shifts to blockchain over time, consumers could see lower prices for content, while content creators could see increased returns.

ACCT The Music Industry. The digitization of the music industry and the rise of streaming services such as iTunes, Spotify, and Pandora have transformed the way people buy and listen to music. As the industry has transitioned into a streaming model, issues with rights management, copyright enforcement, and royalty payments have led to new challenges that will force the music industry to rethink how payments are made to artists and creators.

For example, royalty payments are often difficult to calculate when there are multiple collaborators on a single track. Record companies, publishers, and streaming service providers also operate with siloed databases, making it difficult to keep track of music rights and who is owed what money.

With blockchain, each song file can have its royalty and licensing rights contained in the file. Each download can automatically trigger micropayments to the artist and he or she can get paid first instead of last.

Artist Imogen Heap was among the first musicians to start experiments with blockchain. In 2015, she used the Ethereum blockchain-based Ujo platform to launch the song "Tiny Human" for $0.60 per download. Heap has also founded her own blockchain-based offering, Mycelia, that aims to give artists more control over how their music is sold and circulated.

ACCT Journalism.   Similar to the music industry, blockchain-verified micropayments could change the revenue system for journalism. Stories could have their rights embedded in each file and readers could be charged a small amount of Bitcoin for each piece of content that they actually consumed. Specifically, accessing an article would automatically send a micropayment to a smart contract that has been originally coded to transparently pay all of the parties involved in the creation and publication of that article with the appropriate payment percentages. The result could be that readers think about which material is worth consuming, leading to the best journalism being funded.

POM Supply Chains.   Blockchain technology could help track and monitor raw materials as they pass through supply chains, adding transparency and the ability to trace materials to their source. In logistics, blockchain could help keep track of each stage of a transport container's journey from point to point, creating a clear record of who authorized its movement, who moved it, and when.

- Diamond conglomerate De Beers has deployed its blockchain-backed platform, Tracr, to track diamonds throughout their journey from mines to stores. With Tracr, diamonds are given a Global Diamond ID that records carat, color, clarity, and other attributes. The ID number is used to track the diamond through the supply chain.

  A company called Everledger (**www.everledger.io**) combines blockchain technology with machine learning, the Internet of Things, and nanotechnology to create a digital twin of each diamond. This process ensures traceability of each diamond in a secure, unchangeable, and private platform. The unique identity of each diamond enables stakeholders to buy and sell with confidence and establishes trust all along the supply chain, from mine to customer.

- According to the World Health Organization, 400,000 people die each year from contaminated food. IBM said that many of the critical issues affecting food safety, such as cross-contamination, the spread of food-borne illness, unnecessary waste, and the cost of recalls, are magnified by a lack of transparency and traceability along the supply chain, encompassing growers, suppliers, processors, distributors, retailers, regulators, and consumers. As a result, it can take weeks to identify the precise point of contamination, causing further illness, lost revenue, and wasted product.

  Walmart, Wegmans, Nestle, and four other major food providers joined with IBM to create the IBM Food Trust Network. Before this network was created, it would take Walmart at least seven days to catch an E-coli outbreak. With blockchain and the IBM network, it now takes Walmart 2.2 seconds to trace any of their food products back to the exact farm of origin. In another example, one major fast food retailer uses blockchain to track the temperature of meat in near real time as it moves along the supply chain from farm to restaurant.

FIN Online Securities Trading.   Millions of Americans use computers to trade stocks, bonds, and other financial instruments. In fact, several well-known securities companies, including E*Trade, Ameritrade, and Charles Schwab, offer only online trading because it is cheaper than a full-service or discount broker. On the Web, investors can find a considerable amount of information regarding specific companies or mutual funds in which to invest (e.g., **www.cnn.com/business** and **www.bloomberg.com**).

HRM The Online Job Market.   Job seekers use online job market sites such as **www.monster.com**, **www.simplyhired.com**, and **www.linkedin.com** to help them find available positions. In many countries (including the United States), governments must advertise job openings on the Internet. (See our discussion on LinkedIn and "how to find a job" in Chapter 9.)

MKT **Travel Services.**   The Internet is an ideal place to plan, explore, and arrange almost any trip economically. Online travel services allow you to purchase airline tickets, reserve hotel rooms, and rent cars. Most sites also offer a fare-tracker feature that sends e-mail messages about low-cost flights. Examples of comprehensive online travel services are **www.expedia.com**, **www.travelocity.com**, and **www.orbitz.com**. Online services are also provided by all major airline vacation services, large conventional travel agencies, car rental agencies, hotels (e.g., **www.hotels.com**), and tour companies. In a variation of this process, **www.priceline.com** allows you to set a price you are willing to pay for an airline ticket or hotel accommodations. It then attempts to find a vendor that will match your price.

One costly problem that e-commerce can cause is "mistake fares" in the airline industry. For example, in January 2019 Cathay Pacific (**www.cathaypacific.com**) offered business class flights from Vietnam to several U.S. cities for $675. This price was incorrect; the actual price would have been about $4,000. The U.S. Department of Transportation no longer requires airlines to honor mistake fares, but Cathay honored the tickets purchased before the airline fixed the erroneous price.

MKT **Online Advertising.**   *Advertising* is the practice of disseminating information to attempt to influence a buyer–seller transaction. Traditional advertising on TV or in newspapers involves impersonal, one-way mass communication. In contrast, direct response marketing, or telemarketing, contacts individuals by direct mail or telephone and requires them to respond in order to make a purchase. The direct response approach personalizes advertising and marketing. At the same time, however, it can be expensive, slow, and ineffective. It can also be extremely annoying to the consumer.

Online advertising has redefined the advertising process, making it media rich, dynamic, and interactive. It improves on traditional forms of advertising in a number of ways. First, online ads can be updated any time at minimal cost and therefore can be kept current. These ads can also reach very large numbers of potential buyers all over the world. Furthermore, they are generally cheaper than radio, television, and print ads. Finally, online ads can be interactive and targeted to specific interest groups or individuals.

Online advertising is responsible in large part for the profit margins of content creators, and it plays a critical role in keeping online content free. In 2020, online advertising spending worldwide totaled $336 billion. Also that year, online advertising spending in the United States ($151 billion) exceeded spending on traditional advertising ($107 billion).

The predominant business model for content creators, as well as platforms such as Google and Facebook, has always involved the income from online advertising. Advertising is sold based on *impressions*, or the number of times that people view an ad. Consequently, content creators are placing more—and more intrusive—ads on each web page, thus irritating users even more. Such ads include banners, pop-up ads, pop-under ads, and e-mail. Although cost effective, e-mail advertising is often misused, causing consumers to receive a flood of unsolicited e-mail, or *spam*. **Spamming** is the indiscriminate distribution of electronic ads without the permission of the recipient. Unfortunately, spamming is becoming worse over time.

Today, online advertising is facing a crisis because content creators have been placing more and more intrusive ads. As a result, users have become irritated with videos that automatically start playing when they load a web page and full-screen takeovers that force them to find and then click on a tiny "x" before they can read the content that they wanted in the first place. They are also concerned with cookies that track every web page they visit and every click they make, thus enabling advertisers to target them with increasing frequency and precision. IT's About Business 7.2 discusses the problems associated with behavioral advertising, a type of online advertising.

MIS **MKT** As a result of these problems with online advertising, many Web users are employing ad-blocking software – called *ad blockers* – to prevent online advertising. According to the Global Ad-Blocking Behavior Report by GlobalWebindex (**www.globalwebindex.com**), approximately 47 percent of users worldwide used an ad blocker in 2020. Industry analysts estimate that the global revenue loss to content creators in 2020 ranged from $16 billion to $78 billion, depending on how actively the content creators adopted ad blocking countermeasures. There are several types of ad blockers:

- Ad blockers that will stop almost every ad and tracker; for example, Privacy Badger (**www.privacybadger.org**), which is operated by the nonprofit Electronic Frontier Foundation.

- Ad blockers that are for-profit businesses. The most popular ad blocker is Adblock Plus (**https://adblockplus.org**), with more than 100 million users worldwide. The tool blocks ads, banners, pop-ups, and video ads, and stops tracking services.

- Ad blockers that collect data. Ghostery (**www.ghostery.com**) monitors Web servers that are being accessed from a particular web page and matches them with its library of known trackers. Ghostery then shows that tracker to users.

- Ad blockers that use the freemium model. Blockers such as Disconnect (**https://disconnect.me**) and 1Blocker (**https://1blocker.com**) are free apps for mobile users, who then have to pay if they want to use features such as being able to simultaneously block more than one ad or tracker.

- Ad blockers that are a function of operating systems. For example, Google Chrome will block ads from sites that engage in particularly annoying behavior. Apple's latest operating systems enable owners of Apple devices to download Web browser extensions that block ads. Brave (**https://brave.com**) is a free, open-source Web browser that blocks ads and website trackers.

Not surprisingly, content creators are fighting back against ad-blocking software. For example, about 30 percent of the Internet's top 10,000 websites use software designed to subvert browser-level ad blocking. In addition, they have begun using ad-block detectors. This type of software tool looks for ad blockers and then asks the user to disable them. It might even deny access to content until they do.

It is very important to realize that all of the "free" content on the Web must be paid for in some manner. If online ads are no longer viable, then content on the Web will be displayed only behind paywalls. That is, users will have to pay (e.g., subscriptions) to view content. And the results? The battles between content creators and ad blockers continue.

IT's About Business 7.2

MIS MKT Behavioral versus Contextual Advertising

In the 1990s and early 2000s, digital display advertising—banner ads, pop-ups, and others—was the digital form of print advertising. Brands that employed digital display advertising would buy space directly from a website. Today, that process is increasingly rare, largely because technology platforms are using behavioral advertising, also called programmatic or targeted advertising.

As we discussed in IT's About Business 3.1, there are two major types of digital advertising: behavioral and contextual. In *behavioral advertising*, ads target specific types of users based on vast amounts of data such as gender, age, location, browsing history, and numerous other variables. In *contextual advertising*, ads target specific publications or content and are displayed to users based on content users access or searches they make.

Recall that in behavioral advertising, consumers and technology companies such as Google, Facebook, and Amazon—called *ad tech companies*—enter into a contract in which the companies provide free services in return for the use of consumers' data. Content publishers and website and app developers then utilize these data to monetize their products, and advertisers use them to reach their audiences.

Behavioral advertisers target users based on detailed and persistent third-party, cross-site user behavior tracking. That is, behavioral advertisers do not choose the website or app where their ads will run. Instead, they bid to display their ads to users who fit certain profiles.

The mechanism underlying behavioral advertising is very complex. The process involves a series of real-time auctions managed by other technology companies. Here is how the process works:

- *Sell-side*. Every time a page or an app running behavioral ads is loaded, the publisher sends its available ad space, along with whatever information it has about the user loading the page, to its ad server. (Google operates the most popular ad server.)

- The ad server sends out a bid request to advertisers who want to target that type of user.

- *Buy-side*. Brands place their ads into an ad-buying platform, along with their target audience and how much they are willing to pay. (Google also owns the largest buying-side platform.)

- The ad-buying platform sends that bid to the ad exchange, where it competes against other bids for the target audience. The winning bid then competes against all of the winners from all of the other ad exchanges. Finally, the ad from the winner of winners appears on the publisher's website.

The debate over the value of behavioral advertising is intensifying. Ad tech companies maintain that behavioral advertising is better for all participants: users prefer more relevant ads, advertisers prefer being able to reach potential customers more precisely, and publishers receive more money for ads that produce higher click-through rates. A *click-through rate*, or *click rate*, is the ratio of users who click on a specific link to the number of total users who view a page, an e-mail, or an advertisement. Click rates essentially measure the success of advertisements.

However, a growing body of evidence calls each of these premises into question. Further, governments and the public around the world are worrying about the ethical and privacy implications of the vast amounts of user data that ad tech companies are collecting and analyzing.

Let's take a look at an example that contradicts the economic benefits of behavioral advertising as asserted by ad tech companies. Our example also showcases the privacy implications of behavioral advertising.

In May 2018 the European Union's privacy law, the General Data Protection Regulation (GDPR), went into effect. Immediately, the Dutch public broadcaster Nederlandse Publieke Omroep (NPO, **www.npo.nl**) decided that visitors to any of its websites would be prompted to opt in or out of cookies, the tracking technology that enables ads to target users based on their online behavior and other data. Most companies assume that visitors who skip a privacy notice tacitly opt in, allowing themselves to be tracked. In contrast, NPO decided to opt out any visitor who did not make a choice on the consent screen. Significantly, 90 percent of the people visiting NPO websites opted out. In essence, NPO eliminated the use of cookies on its websites.

Like many publishers, NPO had been using Google Ad manager to sell its ad space. Therefore, when NPO eliminated cookies, it needed an alternative platform that did not track users, an option that Google does not offer. NPO's advertising sales company, Ster, created NPO's new platform.

Automation is key to the system. Whenever a user visits an NPO page, the system produces an automatic signal that goes out to advertisers inviting them to bid on whether or not the user sees their ad. With Google and most other ad servers, advertisers bid on the users. With Ster's new ad server, advertisers do not receive any information on the user. Instead, they receive information about what the user is viewing. Content is tagged based on content. Rather than targeting a certain type of customer, advertisers target customers who are reading a certain type of article or watching a certain type of video.

This approach is called *contextual advertising*. Prior to being able to microtarget customers by analyzing their behavior, companies had buy ads in publications whose audience probably included customers they were trying to reach. Today, technology has enabled contextual targeting to become much more precise and to operate on the level of a web page, rather than the publication itself.

Advertisers on NPO pay to have their advertisements affiliated with specific content. However, they can also choose to advertise on any 1 of 23 customer interest channels based on what users read or watch. The software scrapes subtitles to tag video. Channels include sport and fitness, love and dating, and politics and policy.

In 2019, Ster ran an experiment with 10 advertisers to compare the performance of ads shown to users who opted in or opted out of being tracked. Contextual ads performed as well as or better than microtargeted ads on *conversions.* This important metric measures the share of people who took the action that the advertiser wanted, whether it was adding an item to their shopping cart or signing up for a subscription or credit card. The new platform demonstrated that advertisers were still willing to buy ads that were not targeted based on user behavior.

The new ad server was working so well that in January 2020 NPO no longer asked visitors to its websites to opt in or opt out. The company simply does not track anyone. In January and February 2020 NPO announced that its digital ad revenue was up 62 percent and 79 percent, respectively, compared to the same months in 2019.

Industry observers analyzed NPO's data and found that even its smallest subsidiaries were making much more money after the company abandoned cookies. For example, Omroep MAX, an NPO publication targeted at people older than 50, is only the 4,539 ranked site in the Netherlands, according to data from the traffic measurement site SimilarWeb. Yet its revenue increased by 92 percent in 2019 compared to 2018.

How has NPO become so successful without tracking its visitors? The explanation is simple. Because NPO no longer relies on behavioral advertising, the company now keeps all of the money that advertisers spend rather than giving a large percentage to companies that operate the auctions. A report by the Incorporated Society of British Advertisers found that half the money spent by advertisers was going to various ad technology companies before any of the money reached the publishers running the ads.

Ad technology middlemen have largely become obsolete since contextual ad servers no longer rely on tracking. The money flows from advertisers to publishers, with just a small fee to the company that operates the ad server. In fact, one of the primary reasons why many organizations within the journalism industry have experienced major layoffs and been forced to declare bankruptcy is because advertising has been diverted to companies that specialize in using data to track people online.

A study by Google concluded that disabling cookies reduced publisher revenue by more than 50 percent. Research by an independent team of economists, however, asserted that the reduction would be only 4 percent, meaning that Google exaggerated the effect to discourage sites from disabling cookies. In sharp contrast, NPO found that ads served to users who opted out of cookies brought in as much or more money compared to ads served to users who opted in.

Although the GDPR is not a factor in the United States, there are signs that the country is moving in the same direction as the European Union: the increasing demand for privacy from users and lawmakers, the growing use of privacy tools that block ads and trackers, and Google's joining Safari and Firefox in blocking third-party trackers. As of August 2020 Safari and Firefox were already blocking third-party trackers by default, while Google was planning to phase out the trackers by 2022.

Companies in the behavioral advertising sector are developing methods to facilitate microtargeting in a post-cookie world. Some media companies, notably the *New York Times* and Condé Nast, are experimenting with a hybrid method, eliminating third-party cookies while allowing advertisers to target users based on data gathered by the publisher. This hybrid system can work only if the publisher has millions of logged-in subscribers.

If contextual advertising wins out, then the future of digital publishing could be one in which money shifts back to the organizations that develop the articles people are most interested in reading and the videos they are most interested in watching. If advertisers have to pay to appear in a certain context rather than to target a certain user, then the advantages will accrue to publishers with the highest-quality content.

Sources: Compiled from G. Edelman, "Can Killing Cookies Save Journalism?" *Wired*, August 5, 2020; T. Romm, "Amazon, Apple, Facebook and Google Grilled on Capital Hill over Their Market Power," *Washington Post*, July 29, 2020; G. Edelman, "Follow the Money: How Digital Ads Subsidize the Worst of the Web," *Wired*, July 28, 2020; N. Bose, "GOP Senator Wants to Tie Internet Firms' Liability Immunity to Curb on Behavioral Ads," *Insurance Journal*, July 28, 2020; A. Webb, "This Is the Way the Cookies Crumble," *Bloomberg Businessweek*, July 20, 2020; G. Edelman, "Why Don't We Just Ban Targeted Advertising?" *Wired*, March 22, 2020; K. Rahman and Z. Teachout, "From Private Bads to Public Goods: Adapting Public Utility Regulation for Informational Infrastructure," *Knight Institute Columbia University*, February 4, 2020; A. Cuthbertson, "Google Finally Getting Rid of Third-Party Cookies in Chrome," *Independent*, January 15, 2020; T. Gillespie, "We Need to Fix Online Advertising. All of It," *Slate*, November 15, 2019; D. Ravichandran and N. Korula, "Effect of Disabling Third-Party Cookies on Publisher Revenue," *Google White Paper*, August 27, 2019; V. Marotta, V. Abhishek, and A. Acquisti, "Online Tracking and Publishers' Revenues: An Empirical Analysis," *Workshop on the Economics of Information Security*, June 2019; H. Shaban, "Digital Advertising to Surpass Print, TV for the First Time, Report Says," *Washington Post*, February 20, 2019; J. Davies, "After GDPR, the New York Times Cut Off Ad Exchanges in Europe—and Kept Growing Ad Revenue," *Digiday*, January 16, 2019; J. Vanian, "Amazon Is Now the 3rd Largest Digital Ad Platform in the U.S.," *Fortune*, September 19, 2018.

Questions

1. Refute each of the claims that the ad tech companies make regarding the effectiveness of behavioral advertising. Use specific examples in your answers.

2. What problems could users encounter if companies could not use cookies at all? That is, if companies could not use behavioral advertising?

Issues in E-Tailing

Despite e-tailing's increasing popularity, many e-tailers continue to face serious issues that can restrict their growth. Three significant issues are channel conflict, order fulfillment, and personalized pricing.

MKT POM Channel Conflict.   Clicks-and-mortar companies may face a conflict with their regular distributors when they sell directly to customers online. This situation, known as **channel conflict**, can alienate distributors. Channel conflict has forced some companies to avoid direct online sales. For example, Walmart, Lowe's, and Home Depot would rather have customers come to their stores. Therefore, although all three companies maintain e-commerce websites, their sites place more emphasis on providing information—products, prices, specials, and store locations—than on online sales.

Channel conflict can arise in areas such as pricing and resource allocation—for example, how much money to spend on advertising. Another potential source of conflict involves the logistics services provided by the offline activities to the online activities. For example, how should a company handle returns of items purchased online? Some companies have completely separated the "clicks" (the online portion of the organization) from the "mortar" or "bricks" (the traditional bricks-and-mortar part of the organization). However, this approach can increase expenses, reduce the synergy between the two organizational channels, and alienate customers. As a result, many companies are integrating their online and offline channels, a process known as **multichanneling**.

Multichanneling has created the opportunity for showrooming. *Showrooming* occurs when shoppers visit a brick-and-mortar store to examine a product in person. They then conduct research about the product on their smartphones. Often, they then often purchase the product from the website of a competitor of the store they are visiting. Showrooming is causing problems for brick-and-mortar retailers, such as Target, Best Buy, and others. At the same time, showrooming benefits Amazon, eBay, and other online retailers.

POM Order Fulfillment.   The second major issue confronting e-commerce is *order fulfillment*, which can create problems for e-tailers. Anytime a company sells directly to customers, it is involved in various order-fulfillment activities. It must perform the following activities: quickly find the products to be shipped; pack them; arrange for the packages to be delivered speedily to the customer's door; collect the money from every customer, either in advance, by COD, or by individual bill; and handle the return of unwanted or defective products.

It is very difficult to accomplish these activities both effectively and efficiently in B2C, because a company has to ship small packages to many customers and do it quickly. For this reason, companies involved in B2C activities can experience difficulties in their supply chains.

In addition to providing customers with the products they ordered and doing it on time, order fulfillment provides all related customer services. For example, the customer must receive assembly and operation instructions for a new appliance. If the customer is unhappy with a product, the company must also arrange for an exchange or a return.

MKT Personalized Pricing.   The third major issue in e-commerce is personalized pricing. In the relationship between buyers and sellers, price has traditionally been a meeting point. The practice of setting a fixed price for a good or service, which appeared in the 1860s, eliminated haggling. Each party surrendered something in this relationship. Buyers were forced to accept, or not accept, the fixed price on the price tag. In return, retailers gave up the ability to exploit customers' varying willingness to pay more for a particular good or service. That is, retailers surrendered the ability to make more profit.

Today, consumers are accustomed to *standardized pricing*, which means that when a product is sold through multiple channels, the cost should not vary by more than the difference in shipping, taxation, and distribution costs. If the price is higher for a product at a certain retailer, then customers can easily use the Internet to compare prices and features among a huge number of retailers to purchase that product from another retailer, a process known as showrooming. There is even a website, **www.camelcamelcamel.com**, that tracks Amazon prices for specific products and alerts consumers when a price drops below a preset threshold.

In theory, charging all consumers the same price is ineffective for merchants, because some customers would have been willing to pay more, and others who opted not to buy would have bought at a lower price. Economic theory states that personalized pricing can save companies this lost revenue.

Personalized pricing is the practice of pricing items at a point determined by a particular customer's perceived ability to pay. The optimal outcome of personalized pricing *for the merchant* is maximizing the price that each customer will pay. Merchants are now able to approximate the maximum price that each customer will pay. How do merchants do this?

They analyze the data that consumers generate when they place items in shopping carts; swipe their rewards cards at store registers; "like" something on Facebook; provide ratings, reviews, and recommendations; and perform many other actions. They also virtually assess each customer who visits their website. Specifically, when a customer accesses a retailer's site, the merchant may know where the customer is located based on his or her Internet Protocol address. Merchants also may know the customer's ZIP code. In that case, they can determine the customer's socioeconomic status based on data from the most recent federal census.

As a result of analyzing this Big Data, retailers are developing increasingly sophisticated personalized pricing algorithms. That is, retailers can find the optimal, profit-maximizing price of a good or a service for a particular customer. As a result, prices can fluctuate hour-to-hour and even minute-to-minute. For example, the price of a can of soda in a vending machine can now vary with the outside temperature.

When merchants combine these data with cookies (see Chapter 4), they can learn a significant amount about individual customers. Based on these data, merchants can predict which products a customer is interested in purchasing, when he or she is likely to purchase them, and, critically, the price he or she would be willing to pay. That is, a merchant can estimate a customer's *reservation price*—the maximum amount they would be willing to pay for a specific product, before they had "reservations" about buying it—and then charge them that amount.

Furthermore, with e-commerce, merchants can easily adjust prices for different customers simply by changing them in the system in real time. They therefore avoid the expense of physically changing the prices on thousands of products.

For example, Delta Airlines (**www.delta.com**) uses personalized pricing to raise ticket prices for frequent flyers. The rationale is that these customers probably have to travel frequently, usually for business. They therefore are willing (however unenthusiastically) to pay more than infrequent travelers.

Companies such as Wiser (**www.wiser.com**), Dunnhumby (**www.dunnhumby.com**), and Blue Yonder (**www.blueyonder.com**; now owned by JDA Software) offer personalized pricing solutions to retailers. Blue Yonder claims it can optimize prices not only according to the region but also according to the channel in which the customer is interacting with the retailer.

Most companies hesitate to utilize personalized pricing because it remains to be seen whether consumers will accept the practice. Typically, when consumers hear about the practice, they react negatively, and companies employing the practice experience customer dissatisfaction.

A valuable source of data for companies in personalizing prices is what competitors are charging. Brick-and-mortar retailers can send mystery shoppers to their competitors' stores to note prices, but online merchants use software to scan rival websites and collect data, a process called scraping that is carried out by software called scraping bots.

Large companies have internal teams dedicated to scraping, whereas smaller companies use retail price optimization firms such as Competera (**https://competera.net**) and Price2Spy (**www.price2spy.com**). These firms scrape pricing data from websites and use machine-learning algorithms to help their customers decide how much to charge for different products.

Retailers want to see rivals' prices but they also want to prevent rivals from spying on them. Retailers also want to protect intellectual property like product photos and descriptions, which can be scraped and reused by competitors. So, many retailers show different prices to people than to scraping bots. The question is: How do retailers detect bots?

If a website visitor makes hundreds of requests per minute, it is probably a bot. Another method is to look for human behavior. Specifically, when humans tap a button on their phones, they move the phone very slightly. This movement can be detected by the phone's accelerometer and gyroscope. These movements predict that the site visitor is a human and the absence of such movements predicts that the user is probably a bot.

Keep in mind that retailers must allow some, but not all, bots to scrape a website. If websites blocked bots entirely, then they would not show up on search results. Furthermore, retailers generally want their pricing and items to appear on shopping comparison websites such as Google and Price Grabber (**www.pricegrabber.com**).

Before you go on...

1. Describe electronic storefronts and malls.
2. Discuss various types of online services, such as securities trading, job searches, travel services, and so on.
3. Discuss online advertising, its methods, and its benefits.
4. Identify the major issues related to e-tailing.
5. What are spamming, permission marketing, and viral marketing?

7.3 Business-to-Business (B2B) Electronic Commerce

In *business-to-business* (*B2B*) e-commerce, the buyers and sellers are business organizations. B2B comprises about 85 percent of EC volume. It covers a broad spectrum of applications that enable an enterprise to form electronic relationships with its distributors, resellers, suppliers, customers, and other partners. B2B applications use any of several business models. The major models are sell-side marketplaces, buy-side marketplaces, and electronic exchanges.

Sell-Side Marketplaces

In the **sell-side marketplace** model, organizations sell their products or services to other organizations electronically from their own private e-marketplace website or from a third-party website. This model is similar to the B2C model in which the buyer is expected to come to the seller's site, view catalogs, and place an order. In the B2B sell-side marketplace, however, the buyer is an organization.

The key mechanisms in the sell-side model are forward auctions and electronic catalogs that can be customized for each large buyer. Sellers such as Dell Computer (**www.dellrefurbished.com**) use auctions extensively. In addition to conducting auctions from their own websites, organizations can use third-party auction sites like eBay to liquidate items. Companies such as Ariba (**www.ariba.com**) help organizations to auction old assets and inventories.

The sell-side model is used by hundreds of thousands of companies. The seller can be either a manufacturer (e.g., Dell or IBM), a distributor (e.g., **www.avnet.com**), or a retailer (e.g., **www.bigboxx.com**). The seller uses EC to increase sales, reduce selling and advertising expenditures, increase delivery speed, and lower administrative costs. The sell-side model is especially suitable to customization. Many companies allow their customers to configure their orders online. For example, at Dell (**www.dell.com**), you can determine the exact type of computer that you want. You can choose the type of chip, the size of the hard drive, the type of monitor, and so on. Similarly, the Jaguar website (**www.jaguar.com**) allows you to customize the Jaguar you want. Self-customization greatly reduces any misunderstandings concerning what customers want, and it encourages businesses to fill orders more quickly.

Buy-Side Marketplaces

POM *Procurement* is the overarching function that describes the activities and processes needed to acquire goods and services. Distinct from purchasing, procurement involves the activities necessary to establish requirements, sourcing activities such as market research and vendor evaluation, and negotiation of contracts. *Purchasing* refers to the process of ordering and receiving goods and services. It is a subset of the procurement process.

The **buy-side marketplace** is a model in which organizations attempt to procure needed products or services from other organizations electronically. A major method of procuring goods and services in the buy-side model is the reverse auction.

The buy-side model uses EC technology to streamline the procurement process. The goal is to reduce both the costs of items procured and the administrative expenses involved in procuring them. EC technology can also shorten the procurement cycle time.

Procurement by using electronic support is referred to as **e-procurement.** E-procurement uses reverse auctions, particularly group purchasing. In **group purchasing**, multiple buyers combine their orders so that they constitute a large volume and therefore attract more seller attention. When buyers place their combined orders on a reverse auction, they can also negotiate a volume discount. Typically, the orders of small buyers are aggregated by a third-party vendor.

Electronic Exchanges

Private exchanges have one buyer and many sellers. Electronic marketplaces (e-marketplaces), called **public exchanges** or just **exchanges**, are independently owned by a third party, and they connect many sellers with many buyers. Public exchanges are open to all business organizations. Public exchange managers provide all of the necessary information systems to the participants. Thus, buyers and sellers merely have to "plug in" in order to trade. B2B public exchanges are often the initial point of contacts between business partners. Once the partners make contact, they may move to a private exchange or to private trading rooms provided by many public exchanges to conduct their subsequent trading activities.

Electronic exchanges deal in both direct and indirect materials. *Direct materials* are inputs to the manufacturing process, such as safety glass used in automobile windshields and windows. *Indirect materials* are items, such as office supplies, that are needed for maintenance, operations, and repairs (MRO).

There are three basic types of public exchanges: vertical, horizontal, and functional. All three types offer diversified support services, ranging from payments to logistics.

Vertical exchanges connect buyers and sellers in a given industry. Examples of vertical exchanges are **www.plasticsnet.com** in the plastics industry and **www.papersite.com** in the paper industry. Vertical e-marketplaces offer services that are particularly suited to the community they serve. Vertical exchanges are frequently owned and managed by a *consortium*, a term for a group of major players in an industry. For example, Marriott and Hyatt own a procurement consortium for the hotel industry, and Chevron owns an energy e-marketplace.

Horizontal exchanges connect buyers and sellers across many industries. They are used primarily for MRO materials. Examples of horizontal exchanges are TradersCity (**www.traderscity.com**), Globalsources (**www.globalsources.com**), and Alibaba (**www.alibaba.com**).

HRM Finally, in *functional exchanges*, needed services such as temporary help or extra office space are traded on an "as-needed" basis. For example, in April 2020 a group of chief human resources officers (CHROs) led by Accenture launched a new functional exchange, called People + Work, to connect companies laying off employees due to the COVID-19 pandemic with companies looking to fill positions. The platform gathers non-confidential workforce information by location, experience, and current job title. It gives organizations with open positions a view into the people available to fill those jobs. There is no cost for employers to submit information or to search for potential employees.

We have looked closely at B2B electronic commerce in this section. IT's About Business 7.3 examines Amazon's B2B business.

IT's About Business 7.3

POM **MKT** **MIS** **Amazon's B2B Marketplace**

Amazon Business (**https://business.amazon.com**) is Amazon's e-commerce website that caters to the wholesale and distribution business-to-business (B2B) sector. The site does for commercial customers what Amazon.com does for individuals (B2C).

Amazon's B2B efforts began with AmazonSupply, which debuted in 2012 offering 500,000 products. Within 2 years, the inventory expanded to more than 2.25 million items including tools, renovation materials, cleaning supplies, steel pipes, and a host of other products.

In 2015, Amazon created Amazon Business, incorporating what had previously been AmazonSupply. Amazon Business uses a hybrid business model, selling products directly from its own warehouses along with those from third-party vendors. The outside vendors, which are required to compete with Amazon products, receive a commission of between 6 and 15 percent of the sales price, depending on the type of product and the size of the order.

By August 2020, more than 1 million Amazon Business customers, who are eligible to buy and sell if they have a tax ID number, could access hundreds of millions of products from more than 5 million sellers. In addition, they could obtain bulk discounts, set up a corporate credit line, and receive free two-day shipping on orders that exceeded $49. Clients could also discuss product specifications with manufacturer representatives. This process is necessary for sales of complex technical products.

In 2019, Amazon Business totaled approximately $16 billion in revenue, an increase of 60 percent over the previous year. That same year, Amazon Business accounted for about 6 percent of all Amazon revenue, compared with 4.4 percent in 2018. In 2019 Amazon Business served 55 Fortune 100 companies, more than 50 of the 100 largest hospitals, 40 of the local governments serving the 100 largest populations, and 80 percent of the largest educational institutions.

Amazon Business emphasizes corporate *tail spend*, which is the 20 percent of business supply spend that is not related to core corporate functions and is not ordered from the same set of suppliers on a regular basis. Tail spend typically involves general office needs such as printer paper, bottled water, paper towels, break room supplies, IT cables, and many other products. In one rather unique example of tail spend, a large industrial company needed a small fleet of yellow tricycles so that personnel could more easily move around the plant.

Amazon Business offers many benefits to both vendors and customers. For example:

- The site lists products, along with any accompanying quality certifications such as ISO 9000.
- Amazon Business account holders can qualify for unique offers that are unavailable to individuals utilizing Amazon.com.

This feature helps vendors comply with regulations that prohibit them from selling certain products, such as high-tech health care equipment, directly to consumers.

- Customers can search for items by both manufacturer and distributor part number.
- The site offers demonstration videos and hosts downloadable computer-aided design (CAD) drawings.

Amazon Business also offers benefits for buyers. For example:

- Multiple buyers from within the same organization can create business accounts and share payment methods and shipping addresses.
- Multiple sellers can display promotions on a single product page, making it easier to compare pricing and vendor ratings from Amazon.
- Buyers can view other buyers' product reviews.
- Amazon Business integrates with buyers' procurement systems, enabling them to put Amazon on their procurement software's list of authorized sellers.
- Amazon Business provides an analytics dashboard that enables businesses to view purchasing activity at the individual, purchasing group, and type of spend levels. These insights also enable customers to adhere to compliance policies.
- Amazon Business has a seller credential program that allows third-party sellers to feature and display 1 or more of 18 nationally recognized diversity, ownership, and quality credentials. These credentials include small, minority-owned, women-owned, and veteran-owned businesses. This program provides customers with additional information on which to base their purchasing decisions.
- Amazon Business focuses on fighting counterfeit sales. Amazon's systems automatically and continuously scan data related to selling partners, products, brands, and offers to detect activity that could indicate that products are counterfeit. Amazon removes suspected counterfeit items and permanently bans counterfeiters from selling on its website. Amazon thoroughly investigates all authenticity claims, and it encourages owners to report any counterfeiting concerns.

Wholesalers are taking Amazon's threat seriously. The wholesale industry in the United States is approximately twice the size of the retail industry. In 2019, wholesale sales totaled more than $10 trillion, compared with $5.3 trillion for retail sales. Although the wholesale industry is larger than retail, the companies themselves tend to be smaller. The majority of America's 35,000 wholesalers and distributors are regional, family-run businesses. Typical yearly sales are less than $50 million, and only 160 of these businesses—less than 0.5 percent—report annual sales exceeding $1 billion.

In contrast, Amazon reported $281 billion in revenue in 2019, selling goods in both the B2C and B2B marketplaces. The average wholesaler offers approximately 50,000 products online, compared to Amazon Business's hundreds of millions of products.

Amazon Business is competitive even in niche markets. Take scientific equipment as an example. Items such as centrifuges and Bunsen burners are usually offered only by specialty distributors. However, customers can purchase one with the click of a mouse through Amazon Business. Few specialty distributors can compete with Amazon's huge product list, easy-to-use website, two-day delivery, physical infrastructure (fulfillment centers in the United States), and information technology infrastructure (e.g., Amazon Web Services).

To acquire and maintain competitive advantage, Amazon Business keeps specialty items in inventory that frequently do not sell quickly in order to avoid stockouts that plague other distributors. Industry analysts estimate that Amazon has on hand more than half the inventory that it offers on its website at any point.

B2B has very small margins, typically 2 to 4 percent. Amazon's size enables it to make money through high volumes. It achieves these high volumes through—what else?—beating competitors' prices by about 25 percent on common products, according to a Boston Consulting Group (**www.bcg.com**) report.

Despite its success, Amazon Business does have competition. Consider W.W. Grainger (**www.grainger.com**), in business since 1927, which captures about 6 percent of the entire U.S. B2B market. The company, which sells tools for maintenance and repair, now operates about 600 regional sales locations and 33 warehouses. The company recorded $11.5 billion in total revenue in 2019. Approximately 60 percent of that revenue was generated via its e-commerce channels. Grainger's CEO expects electronic commerce to eventually account for 80 percent of the company's sales.

One area that Amazon Business may not be able to penetrate is the close partnerships that some distributors have developed with their institutional clients. For example, medical supplier Cardinal Health (**www.cardinalhealth.com**) has taken control of the entire supply chain at the Nebraska Medical Center. Cardinal handles everything from truck to patient. It orders products from suppliers, tracks product distribution, handles loading dock workers, and deals with supplier invoicing.

The challenge confronting the nation's 35,000 wholesalers and distributors is to compete with Amazon Business. Industry analysts identify two possibilities:

1. Provide value-added, personalized services to customers. For example, Valin Corporation (**www.valin.com**) has specialized in the oil and gas sector, dispatching engineers to oilfields to help deploy the company's products that manage output at surface oil wells.

2. Go into areas that Amazon may not be interested in, such as specialized business environments. For example, will Amazon want to sell oxygen tanks or soda pumps? Furthermore, Amazon might not want to manage products that are dangerous or exotic—such as dentists' chairs—or that require specialists.

Sources: Compiled from M. Brohan, "Amazon Business Grows Faster than Amazon Itself," *Digital Commerce 360*, January 31, 2020; P. Lucas, "The Ins and Outs of Selling on Amazon Business," *Digital Commerce 360*, April 1, 2019; A. Moazed and N. Johnson, "Amazon Business Is a Top B2B Distributor—Now What?" *Modern Distribution Management*, June 25, 2018; A. Moazed and N. Johnson, "Amazon's B2B Marketplace Advantage," *Modern Distribution Management*, June 28, 2018; P. Demery, "Q&A: Inside Amazon Business with Martin Rohde," *Digital Commerce 360*, May 2, 2018; "Why Amazon Business Targets B2B eCommerce's 'Tail Spend'," *PYMNTS.com*, May 1, 2018; D. Davis, "Amazon Business Helps Buyers Beat Their Negotiated Supplier Prices," *B2B E-Commerce World*, June 7, 2016; P. Demery, "Amazon's Billion-Dollar B2B Portal Is Growing Rapidly," *B2B E-Commerce World*, May 4, 2016; E. Smith, "Can Amazon 'Uber' Distributors?" *Modern Distribution Management*, June 17, 2015; E. Smith, "Recommended Reading: Amazon Business Open to Distributors," *Modern Distribution Management*, June 9, 2015; E. Smith, "Amazon Reinvents B2B Model," *Modern Distribution Management*, April 29, 2015; S. Soper, "Amazon Business Aims for $1 Trillion Corporate-Spending Market," *Bloomberg-Business*, April 28, 2015; C. O'Connor, "Amazon Launches Amazon Business Marketplace, Will Close AmazonSupply," *Forbes*, April 28, 2015; C. O'Connor, "Amazon's Wholesale Slaughter: Jeff Bezos' $8 Trillion B2B Bet," *Forbes*, May 7, 2014; **https://business.amazon.com**, **www.grainger.com**, accessed August 5, 2020.

Questions

1. Consider Tulsa Community College (**www.tulsacc.edu**), which is using Amazon Business to order test tubes, basketballs, office supplies, and other goods instead of having employees buy them from local retailers or specialty sellers. The daily needs of the college's 15,000 students translate into about $10,000 of orders per month.

   a) What is the impact of Amazon Business on local wholesalers and retailers in Tulsa?

   b) How could local businesses in Tulsa compete with Amazon Business?

2. Provide other methods for wholesalers to compete with Amazon Business.

Before you go on...

1. Briefly differentiate between the sell-side marketplace and the buy-side marketplace.
2. Briefly differentiate among vertical exchanges, horizontal exchanges, and functional exchanges.

7.4 Ethical and Legal Issues in E-Business

Author Lecture Videos are
available exclusively in
WileyPLUS.
Apply the Concept activities
are available in the Appendix
and in *WileyPLUS*.

Technological innovation often forces a society to reexamine and modify its ethical standards. In many cases, the new standards are incorporated into law. In this section, you will learn about two important ethical considerations—privacy and job loss—as well as various legal issues arising from the practice of e-business.

Ethical Issues

Many of the ethical and global issues related to IT also apply to e-business. Here you will learn about two basic issues: privacy and job loss.

By making it easier to store and transfer personal information, e-business presents some threats to privacy. To begin with, most electronic payment systems know who the buyers are. It may be necessary, then, to protect the buyers' identities. Businesses frequently use encryption to provide this protection.

Another major privacy issue is tracking. For example, individuals' activities on the Internet can be tracked by cookies (discussed in Chapter 4). Cookies store your tracking history on your personal computer's hard drive, and anytime you revisit a certain website, the server recognizes the cookie. In response, antivirus software packages routinely search for potentially harmful cookies.

In addition to compromising individual privacy, the use of EC may eliminate the need for some of a company's employees, as well as brokers and agents. The manner in which these unneeded workers, especially employees, are treated can raise ethical issues. How should the company handle the layoffs? Should companies be required to retrain employees for new positions? If not, how should the company compensate or otherwise assist the displaced workers?

Another interesting ethical/legal question involves national governments. What if a government limited electronic commerce from foreign companies to favor local companies? IT's About Business 7.4 discusses this question.

IT's About Business 7.4

MIS   Amazon and Flipkart Experience Problems in India

In India, millions of small businesses dominate retailing. For this reason, many people identified the country as a prime location for Amazon and Flipkart, an Indian e-commerce company in which Walmart invested $16 billion for a majority stake in 2018.

The two companies' economies of scale, coupled with partners who could supply exclusive goods at lower prices, seemed certain to provide them with a competitive advantage over local retailers. Significantly, however, Walmart's and Amazon's strategies have been controversial in a country dominated by small neighborhood stores in which large retail operations account for only about 10 percent of retail sales. Perhaps not surprisinly, then, the Indian government slowed the companies' plans. On February 1, 2019, it tightened e-commerce regulations, forcing changes in the way Amazon and Flipkart operate. Because they are foreign-owned businesses, the government prohibited them from making exclusive arrangements with sellers, offering deep discounts, or holding any business interest in online merchants that sell goods on their websites.

These measures forced both Amazon and Walmart to revise their strategies in several ways. First, both companies had accumulated vast inventories of products from companies in which they had business interests. They requested a four- to six-month extension to sell those products. The Indian government denied their requests.

Second, Amazon and Flipkart removed from their Indian platforms thousands of products from vendors in which they had equity stakes. In fact, the new rules caused the two companies, which together account for 70 percent of India's online retail market, to remove thousands of products from their virtual shelves.

Shoppers quickly began to feel the impact of the changes. On February 1, 2019, many items were blanked out on both companies' websites, and customers were greeted with alerts identifying many products that were no longer available. Consumers used social media to express their frustrations.

Third, Amazon's plans to expand into food retailing might also be in jeopardy. In 2017 the government approved an Amazon proposal to invest $500 million in a separate online grocery venture. However, the rules banning Amazon's site from selling products from companies in which it owns a stake could block the e-tailer from proceeding. Amazon has asked the government to clarify.

Fourth, merchants who had signed partnership agreements with Amazon and Walmart were unable to sell on the companies' platforms. Both retailers had to draw up new contracts with thousands of merchants and brands, deleting wording such as "exclusive." They also began to develop India-specific private labels, which the government allows.

Fifth, Amazon and Flipkart had to cut back on cash-back deals and discounts. These incentives have been a particular sore point with smaller retailers, who have accused the two companies of predatory pricing practices.

Finally, the two companies had to prepare for added competition from physical retailers and well-funded local rivals such as the conglomerate Reliance Industries (**www.ril.com**), India's largest private company. Significantly, Reliance, the primary beneficiary from the crackdown, owns the country's largest brick-and-mortar retail chain.

Reliance had entered the B2B space with millions of small sellers marketing their products on an online platform that Reliance had created on its Jio wireless service. In the B2C space, Reliance has nearly 300 million Jio Telecom subscribers, who can access financial, educational, entertainment, and retail services on their phone's Jio app. Analysts estimate that Reliance will become India's largest omnichannel retailer by 2021.

On April 26, 2020, Reliance Retail launched JioMart, an online grocery service, in hundreds of its grocery stores in several Indian cities. Reliance immediately experienced fulfilment problems. For example, the retailer took grocery orders on Facebook's WhatsApp and fulfilled them through local stores. Due to the COVID-19 pandemic, Reliance had to stop taking orders due to a lack of delivery personnel. In addition, consumers complained of bad packaging, rotten vegetables, order cancellations, higher prices, delayed deliveries, and an overall poor customer service experience.

Perhaps due to JioMart's poor performance, in June 2020 Amazon India expanded its Pantry grocery delivery service to more than 200 cities and towns. The e-tailer also guaranteed the lowest prices, and it promised deliveries within two days from its fulfilment centers.

Meanwhile, Walmart's subsidiary Flipkart was operating in 26 Indian cities and was trying to expand its business via FarmerMart. Through FarmerMart, Flipkart planned to sell locally produced food items as well as packaged products with the help of local Indian farmers. Unfortunately, India's commerce ministry denied Flipkart a license to enter the food retail business, citing regulatory issues. Flipkart planned to reapply for the license.

The situation in India is troublesome for Amazon and Walmart. Amazon has had relatively poor results in China, so it regards India as its best opportunity for international expansion. Walmart has also been counting on India to propel international growth. Since 2018, the retailer has scaled back its holdings in Britain and Brazil to place the majority of its overseas investments in India and China. Both companies must deal with these uncertainties just as the slowing global economy resulting from the COVID-19 pandemic threatens to curtail consumer spending in many of its markets.

Besides the online retailers that operate broad shopping portals, the Indian government's regulations could impact e-commerce firms in areas such as furniture retailing, food delivery, and hotel reservation aggregation. Some of the startups in those sectors maintain other business ties with companies whose products and services they sell—arrangements that the new rules forbid. Meanwhile, the government's e-commerce rules did not change when Prime Minister Narendra Modi was re-elected for another five-year term in May 2019.

Sources: Compiled from I. Mehta, "Amazon and Flipkart Might Have to Give Their Source Code to the Indian Government," *TheNextWeb*, July 6, 2020; H. Chauhan, "Amazon and Walmart's Biggest Indian Rival Finds out Grocery Is Difficult Business," *The Motley Fool*, June 17, 2020; "India's COVID-19 Restrictions Hinder Amazon, Flipkart Delivery," *PYMNTS.com*, March 27, 2020; M. Toh, "Flipkart Shuts Down and Amazon Limits Orders for 1.3 Billion Indians under Lockdown," *CNN Business*, March 25, 2020; S. Rai and M. Boyle, "India's E-Commerce Crackdown," *Bloomberg BusinessWeek*, February 11, 2019; S. Choudhury, "If You Hold Amazon Shares, Here's What You Need to Know about India's E-Commerce Law," *CNBC*, February 5, 2019; C. Adams, "Products Yanked from Amazon in India to Comply with New E-Commerce Rules," *Wall Street Journal*, February 1, 2019; J. Vincent, "Amazon and Walmart Hit Hard after New E-Commerce Rules in India Restrict Sales," *The Verge*, February 1, 2019; S. Findlay and A. Kazmin, "India's Ecommerce Law Forces Amazon and Flipkart to Pull Products," *Financial Times*, February 1, 2019; S. Phartiyal, "Walmart, Amazon Scrambling to Comply with India's New E-Commerce Rules," *Reuters*, January 31, 2019; J. Russell, "New E-Commerce Restrictions in India Just Ruined Christmas for Amazon and Walmart," *TechCrunch*, December 27, 2018; **www.amazon.in**, **www.flipkart.com**, accessed August 5, 2020.

Questions

1. Refer back to Chapter 3. Are the Indian government's actions placing strict regulations on foreign electronic commerce companies ethical? Why or why not?

2. Describe the ways in which foreign electronic companies responded to the Indian government's new regulations. Can you think of any other strategies these companies could employ?

Legal and Ethical Issues Specific to E-Commerce

Many legal issues are related specifically to e-commerce. A business environment in which buyers and sellers do not know one another and cannot even see one another creates opportunities for dishonest people to commit fraud and other crimes. These illegal actions range from creating a virtual bank that disappeared along with the investors' deposits to manipulating stock prices on the Internet. Unfortunately, fraudulent activities on the Internet are increasing.

Fraud on the Internet.   Internet fraud has grown even faster than Internet use itself. In one case, stock promoters falsely spread positive rumors about the prospects of the companies they touted in order to boost the stock price. In other cases, the information provided might have been true, but the promoters did not disclose that they were paid to talk up the companies. Stock promoters specifically target small investors who are lured by the promise of fast profits.

Stocks are only one of many areas in which swindlers are active. Auctions are especially conducive to fraud, by both sellers and buyers. Other types of fraud include selling bogus investments, setting up phantom business opportunities, and fraudulent affiliate marketing.

MIS **MKT**   **Fraudulent Affiliate Marketing.**   *Affiliate marketing* involves a merchant paying a commission to other online entities, known as affiliates, for referring new business to the merchant's website. Affiliates are paid only when their marketing efforts actually result in a transaction, such as a customer registration, a completed lead form, a new free trial user, a new newsletter subscriber, or product sale.

Affiliates do promote legitimate businesses, such as Amazon.com and eBay, but they are also behind many of the misleading and fraudulent ads that appear on Facebook, Instagram, Twitter, Google, and the rest of the Internet. *Affiliate fraud* refers to false or unscrupulous activity conducted to generate commissions from an affiliate marketing program. Consider the following example.

A manufacturer of a fake nutritional supplement wants to sell it and does not care how the sales actually take place. The vendor approaches an affiliate network and offers to pay a commission per customer sign-up. The network spreads the word to affiliates, who design often misleading ads and pay to place them on various websites in hopes of earning commissions. The affiliates take the risk, paying to run ads without knowing if they will work. However, if even a small percentage of the people who see the ads become buyers, the profits could be substantial.

Affiliates once had to guess what kind of person might fall for their ads, targeting users by age, geography, or interests. Today, Facebook's analytics tools perform the targeting for them automatically.

Facebook tracks who clicks on ads as well as who buys the product, then starts targeting others whom its algorithms predict should be shown the ads because they are likely to buy. Affiliates typically lose money for a few days as Facebook gathers data through trial and error, and then their sales rapidly increase.

A software program called Voluum enables affiliates to track their campaigns and defeat the ad networks' defenses. The software can track marketing campaigns across multiple platforms, such as Facebook, Google, Twitter, and other websites. Voluum enables affiliates to tailor the content they deliver according to a number of factors, including the location or IP address associated with a user. The feature is useful for ad targeting—for example, showing Spanish speakers a message in their native language.

Facebook must police a $40 billion annual ad platform that malicious players are constantly trying to subvert. Facebook reviewers examine ads that users or Facebook algorithms have flagged as questionable and ban accounts that break the rules. However, Voluum makes it easy for affiliates to identify the addresses of Facebook's ad reviewers and program campaigns to show them, and only them, legitimate content. This process is called *cloaking*. Interestingly, Google has banned Voluum based on cloaking concerns but not Facebook.

Affiliates who are caught and banned can easily circumvent this problem. They simply open new Facebook accounts under different names. Some affiliates buy clean profiles from "farmers." Others rent accounts from strangers or make deals with underhanded advertising agencies to find other solutions.

The U.S. Federal Trade Commission (FTC; **www.ftc.gov**) regularly publishes examples of scams that are most likely to be spread by e-mail or to be found on the Web. Let's look at some ways in which consumers and sellers can protect themselves from online fraud.

Tips for safe electronic shopping:

- Look for reliable brand names at sites such as Walmart Online, Disney Online, and Amazon. Before purchasing, make sure that the site is authentic by entering the site directly and not from an unverified link.

- Search any unfamiliar selling site for the company's address and phone and fax numbers. Call and quiz the employees about the seller.

- Check out the vendor with the local Chamber of Commerce or Better Business Bureau (**www.bbbonline.org**). Look for seals of authenticity such as TRUSTe.

- Investigate how secure the seller's site is by examining the security procedures and by reading the posted privacy policy.

- Examine the money-back guarantees, warranties, and service agreements.
- Compare prices with those in regular stores. Too-low prices are too good to be true and some catch is probably involved.
- Ask friends what they know. Find testimonials and endorsements on community websites and well-known bulletin boards.
- Find out what your rights are in case of a dispute. Consult consumer protection agencies and the National Consumer League's Fraud Center (**www.fraud.org**).
- Check Consumerworld (**www.consumerworld.org**) for a collection of useful resources.
- For many types of products, **www.resellerratings.com** is a useful resource.

Domain Names.

Another legal issue is competition over domain names. Domain names are assigned by central nonprofit organizations that check for conflicts and possible infringement of trademarks. Obviously, companies that sell goods and services over the Internet want customers to be able to find them easily. In general, the closer the domain name matches the company's name, the easier the company is to locate.

A domain name is considered legal when the person or business who owns the name has operated a legitimate business under that name for some time. Companies such as Christian Dior, Nike, Deutsche Bank, and even Microsoft have had to fight or pay to acquire the domain name that corresponds to their company's name. Consider the case of Delta Air Lines. Delta originally could not obtain the Internet domain name delta.com because Delta Faucet had already purchased it. Delta Faucet had been in business under that name since 1954, so it had a legitimate business interest in using the domain name. Delta Air Lines had to settle for delta-airlines.com until it bought the domain name from Delta Faucet. Delta Faucet is now at deltafaucet.com.

Cybersquatting.

Cybersquatting refers to the practice of registering or using domain names for the purpose of profiting from the goodwill or the trademark that belongs to someone else. The Anti-Cybersquatting Consumer Protection Act (1999) permits trademark owners in the United States to sue for damages in such cases.

However, some practices that could be considered cybersquatting are not illegal, although they may well be unethical. Perhaps the more common of these practices is "domain tasting." Domain tasting lets registrars profit from the complex money trail of pay-per-click advertising. The practice can be traced back to the policies of the organization responsible for regulating web names, the Internet Corporation for Assigned Names and Numbers (ICANN) (**www.icann .org**). In 2000, ICANN established the five-day "Add Grace Period" during which a company or person can claim a domain name and then return it for a full refund of the registry fee. ICANN implemented this policy to allow someone who mistyped a domain to return it without cost. In some cases, companies engage in cybersquatting by registering domain names that are very similar to their competitors' domain names in order to generate traffic from people who misspell Web addresses.

Domain tasters exploit this policy by claiming Internet domains for five days at no cost. These domain names frequently resemble those of prominent companies and organizations. The tasters then jam these domains full of advertisements that come from Yahoo! and Google. Because this process involves zero risk and 100 percent profit margins, domain tasters register millions of domain names every day—some of them over and over again. Experts estimate that registrants ultimately purchase less than 2 percent of the sites they sample. In the vast majority of cases, they use the domain names for only a few days to generate quick profits.

FIN ACCT Taxes and Other Fees.

In offline sales, most states and localities tax business transactions that are conducted within their jurisdiction. The most obvious example is sales taxes. Federal, state, and local authorities are working on taxation policy for e-businesses. This problem is particularly complex for interstate and international e-commerce. For example, some people claim that the state in which the *seller* is located deserves the entire sales tax (in some countries, it is a value-added tax (VAT)). Others contend that the state in which the *server* is located should also receive some of the tax revenues.

In addition to the sales tax, there is a question about where—and in some cases, whether—electronic sellers should pay business license taxes, franchise fees, gross receipts taxes, excise taxes, privilege taxes, and utility taxes. Furthermore, how should tax collection be controlled? Legislative efforts to impose taxes on e-commerce are opposed by an organization named the Internet Freedom Fighters.

Even before electronic commerce over the Internet emerged, the basic law in the United States was that as long as a retailer did not have a physical presence in the state where the consumer was shopping, that retailer did not have to collect a sales tax. Shoppers were supposed to track such purchases and then pay the taxes owed in their annual tax filings. Few people, however, did this or were even aware of their obligation. The result was that online retailers were able to undercut the prices of their non-Internet (e.g., brick-and-mortar stores) competitors for years.

In December 2013, the U.S. Supreme Court declined to get involved in state efforts to force Web retailers such as Amazon to collect sales tax from customers even in places where the companies do not have a physical presence. In light of the court's decision to stay out of the issue, in July 2019 45 states and the District of Columbia had passed legislation requiring online retailers to collect sales taxes from their customers. (Alaska, Delaware, Montana, New Hampshire, and Oregon do not have state sales taxes.)

Copyright. Recall from Chapter 4 that intellectual property is protected by copyright laws and cannot be used freely. This point is significant because many people mistakenly believe that once they purchase a piece of software, they have the right to share it with others. In fact, what they have bought is the right to *use* the software, not the right to *distribute* it. That right remains with the copyright holder. Similarly, copying material from websites without permission is a violation of copyright laws. Protecting intellectual property rights in e-commerce is extremely difficult, however, because it involves hundreds of millions of people in 200 countries with differing copyright laws who have access to billions of web pages.

Before you go on...

1. List and explain some ethical issues in EC.
2. Discuss the major legal issues associated with EC.
3. Describe buyer protection and seller protection in EC.

What's in IT for me?

ACCT For the Accounting Major

Accounting personnel are involved in several EC activities. Designing the ordering system and its relationship with inventory management requires accounting attention. Billing and payments are also accounting activities, as are determining cost and profit allocation. Replacing paper documents with electronic ones will affect many of the accountant's tasks, especially the auditing of EC activities and systems. Finally, building a cost-benefit and cost-justification system to determine which products and services to take online and creating a chargeback system are critical to the success of EC.

FIN For the Finance Major

The worlds of banking, securities and commodities markets, and other financial services are being reengineered because of EC. Online securities trading and its supporting infrastructure are growing more rapidly than any other EC activity. Many innovations already in place are changing the rules of economic and financial incentives for financial analysts and managers. Online banking, for example, does not recognize national boundaries, and it may create a new framework for financing global trades. Public financial information is now accessible in seconds. These innovations will dramatically transform the manner in which finance personnel operate.

MKT For the Marketing Major

EC has brought about a major revolution in marketing and sales. Perhaps its most obvious feature is the transition from a physical to a virtual marketplace. Equally important, however, is the radical transformation to one-on-one advertising and sales and to customized and interactive marketing. Marketing channels are being combined, eliminated, or recreated. The EC revolution is creating new products and markets while significantly altering existing ones. Digitization of products and services also has implications for marketing and sales. The direct producer-to-consumer channel is expanding rapidly and is fundamentally redefining the nature of customer service. As the battle for customers intensifies, marketing and sales personnel are becoming the most critical success factor in many organizations. Online marketing can be a blessing to one company and a curse to another.

POM For the Production/Operations Management Major

EC is transforming the manufacturing system from product-push mass production to order-pull mass customization. This transformation requires a robust supply chain, information support, and reengineering of processes that involve suppliers and other business partners. Suppliers can use extranets to monitor and replenish inventories without having to constantly reorder. The Internet and intranets also help reduce cycle times. Many production/operations problems that have persisted for years, such as complex scheduling and excess inventories, are being solved rapidly with the use of Web technologies. Companies can now use external and internal networks to find and manage manufacturing operations in

other countries much more easily. Also, the Web is reengineering procurement by helping companies conduct electronic bids for parts and subassemblies, thus reducing costs. All in all, the job of the progressive production/operations manager is closely tied in with e-commerce.

HRM For the Human Resource Management Major

HR majors need to understand the new labor markets and the impacts of EC on old labor markets. Also, the HR department can use EC tools for such functions as procuring office supplies. Moreover, becoming knowledgeable about new government online initiatives and online training is critical. HR personnel must also become familiar with the major legal issues related to EC and employment.

MIS For the MIS Major

The MIS function is responsible for providing the information technology infrastructure necessary for electronic commerce to function. This infrastructure includes the company's networks, intranets, and extranets. The MIS function is also responsible for ensuring that e-commerce transactions are secure.

Summary

7.1 Describe the eight common types of electronic commerce.

In *business-to-consumer (B2C)* electronic commerce, the sellers are organizations and the buyers are individuals.

In *business-to-business (B2B)* electronic commerce, the sellers and the buyers are businesses.

In *consumer-to-consumer (C2C)* electronic commerce, an individual sells products or services to other individuals.

In *business-to-employee (B2E)* electronic commerce, an organization uses EC internally to provide information and services to its employees.

E-government is the use of Internet technology in general and e-commerce in particular to deliver information and public services to citizens (called government-to-citizen or G2C EC) and business partners and suppliers (called government-to-business or G2B EC).

Mobile commerce refers to e-commerce that is conducted entirely in a wireless environment.

Social commerce refers to the delivery of electronic commerce activities and transactions through social computing.

Conversational commerce refers to electronic commerce using messaging and chat apps to offer a daily choice, often personalized, of a meal, product, or service.

We leave the examples of each type to you.

7.2 Describe the various online services of business-to-consumer (B2C) commerce, along with specific examples of each.

Fintech is an industry composed of companies that use technology to compete in the marketplace with traditional financial institutions and intermediaries in the delivery of financial services, which include banking, insurance, real estate, and investing.

Online securities trading involves buying and selling securities over the Web.

Online job matching over the Web offers a promising environment for job seekers and for companies searching for hard-to-find employees. Thousands of companies and government agencies advertise available positions, accept résumés, and take applications on the Internet.

Online travel services allow you to purchase airline tickets, reserve hotel rooms, and rent cars. Most sites also offer a fare-tracker feature that sends you e-mail messages about low-cost flights. The Internet is an ideal place to economically plan, explore, and arrange almost any trip.

Online advertising over the Web makes the advertising process media-rich, dynamic, and interactive.

We leave the examples to you.

7.3 Describe the three business models for business-to-business electronic commerce.

In the *sell-side marketplace* model, organizations attempt to sell their products or services to other organizations electronically from their own private e-marketplace website or from a third-party website. Sellers such as Dell Computer (**www.dellrefurbished .com**) use sell-side auctions extensively. In addition to auctions from their own websites, organizations can use third-party auction sites, such as eBay, to liquidate items.

The *buy-side marketplace* is a model in which organizations attempt to buy needed products or services from other organizations electronically.

E-marketplaces, in which there are many sellers and many buyers, are called *public exchanges*, or just exchanges. Public exchanges are open to all business organizations. They are frequently owned and operated by a third party. There are three basic types of public exchanges: vertical, horizontal, and functional. *Vertical exchanges* connect buyers and sellers in a given industry. *Horizontal exchanges* connect buyers and sellers across many industries.

In *functional exchanges,* needed services such as temporary help or extra office space are traded on an as-needed basis.

7.4 Discuss the ethical and legal issues related to electronic commerce, along with examples.

E-business presents some threats to privacy. First, most electronic payment systems know who the buyers are. It may be necessary, then, to protect the buyers' identities with encryption. Another major privacy issue is tracking, through which individuals' activities on the Internet can be tracked by cookies.

The use of EC may eliminate the need for some of a company's employees, as well as brokers and agents. The manner in which these unneeded workers, especially employees, are treated can raise ethical issues. How should the company handle the layoffs? Should companies be required to retrain employees for new positions? If not, how should the company compensate or otherwise assist the displaced workers?

We leave the examples up to you.

Chapter Glossary

auction A competitive process in which either a seller solicits consecutive bids from buyers or a buyer solicits bids from sellers, and prices are determined dynamically by competitive bidding.

brick-and-mortar organizations Organizations in which the product, the process, and the delivery agent are all physical.

business model The method by which a company generates revenue to sustain itself.

buy-side marketplace B2B model in which organizations buy needed products or services from other organizations electronically, often through a reverse auction.

channel conflict The alienation of existing distributors when a company decides to sell to customers directly online.

chatbots (also known as *bots*) Interactive software programs that can conduct simple conversations with customers or other bots.

clicks-and-mortar organizations Organizations that do business in both the physical and digital dimensions.

disintermediation Elimination of intermediaries in electronic commerce.

electronic business (e-business) A broader definition of electronic commerce, including buying and selling of goods and services, and servicing customers, collaborating with business partners, conducting e-learning, and conducting electronic transactions within an organization.

electronic commerce (EC or e-commerce) The process of buying, selling, transferring, or exchanging products, services, or information through computer networks, including the Internet.

electronic mall A collection of individual shops under one Internet address; also known as a *cybermall* or an *e-mall*.

electronic marketplace A virtual market space on the Web where many buyers and many sellers conduct electronic business activities.

electronic payment mechanisms Computer-based systems that allow customers to pay for goods and services electronically, rather than writing a check or using cash.

electronic retailing (e-tailing) The direct sale of products and services through storefronts or electronic malls, usually designed around an electronic catalog format and auctions.

electronic storefront The website of a single company, with its own Internet address, at which orders can be placed.

e-procurement Purchasing by using electronic support.

exchanges (see **public exchanges**)

Fintech An industry composed of companies that use technology to compete in the marketplace with traditional financial institutions and intermediaries in the delivery of financial services, which include banking, insurance, real estate, and investing.

forward auctions Auctions that sellers use as a selling channel to many potential buyers; the highest bidder wins the items.

group purchasing The aggregation of purchasing orders from many buyers so that a volume discount can be obtained.

multichanneling A process in which a company integrates its online and offline channels.

public exchanges (or exchanges) Electronic marketplaces in which there are many sellers and many buyers, and entry is open to all; frequently owned and operated by a third party.

reverse auctions Auctions in which one buyer, usually an organization, seeks to buy a product or a service, and suppliers submit bids; the lowest bidder wins.

sell-side marketplace B2B model in which organizations sell to other organizations from their own private e-marketplace or from a third-party site.

spamming Indiscriminate distribution of e-mail without the recipient's permission.

virtual (or pure play) organizations Organizations in which the product, the process, and the delivery agent are all digital.

Discussion Questions

1. Discuss the major limitations of e-commerce. Which of these limitations are likely to disappear? Why?

2. Discuss the reasons for having multiple EC business models.

3. Distinguish between business-to-business forward auctions and buyers' bids for RFQs.

4. Discuss the benefits to sellers and buyers of a B2B exchange.

5. What are the major benefits of G2C electronic commerce?

6. Discuss the various ways to pay online in B2C. Which method(s) would you prefer and why?

7. Why is order fulfillment in B2C considered difficult?

8. Discuss the reasons for EC failures.

9. Should Mr. Coffee sell coffeemakers online? Hint: Take a look at the discussion of channel conflict in this chapter.

10. In some cases, individuals engage in cybersquatting so that they can sell the domain names to companies expensively. In other cases, companies engage in cybersquatting by registering domain names that are very similar to their competitors' domain names in order to generate traffic from people who misspell Web addresses. Discuss each practice in regard to its ethical nature and legality. Is there a difference between the two practices? Support your answer.

11. Do you think information technology has made it easier to do business? Or has it only raised the bar on what is required to be able to do business in the twenty-first century? Support your answer with specific examples.

12. With the rise of electronic commerce, what do you think will happen to those without computer skills, Internet access, computers, smartphones, and so on? Will they be able to survive and advance by hard work?

Problem-Solving Activities

1. Assume you are interested in buying a car. You can find information about cars at numerous websites. Access five websites for information about new and used cars, financing, and insurance. Decide which car you want to buy. Configure your car by going to the car manufacturer's website. Finally, try to find the car from **www.autobytel.com**. What information is most supportive of your decision-making process? Write a report about your experience.

2. Compare the various electronic payment methods. Specifically, collect information from the vendors cited in this chapter and find additional vendors using Google. Pay attention to security level, speed, cost, and convenience.

3. Conduct a study on selling diamonds and gems online. Access such sites as **www.bluenile.com**, **www.jtv.com**, **www.tiffany.com**, and **www.jewleryexchange.com**.

   a. What features do these sites use to educate buyers about gemstones?

   b. How do these sites attract buyers?

   c. How do these sites increase customers' trust in online purchasing?

   d. What customer service features do these sites provide?

4. Access **www.nacha.org**. What is NACHA? What is its role? What is the ACH? Who are the key participants in an ACH e-payment? Describe the "pilot" projects currently under way at ACH.

5. Access **www.espn.com**. Identify at least five different ways the site generates revenue.

6. Access **www.queendom.com**. Examine its offerings and try some of them. What type of electronic commerce is this? How does this website generate revenue?

7. Access **www.ediets.com**. Prepare a list of all the services the company provides. Identify its revenue model.

8. Access **www.theknot.com**. Identify the site's revenue sources.

9. Access **www.mint.com**. Identify the site's revenue model. What are the risks of giving this website your credit and debit card numbers, as well as your bank account number?

10. Enter **www.alibaba.com**. Identify the site's capabilities. Look at the site's private trading room. Write a report. How can such a site help a person who is making a purchase?

11. Enter **www.grubhub.com**. Explore the site. Why is the site so successful? Could you start a competing site? Why or why not?

12. Enter **www.dell.com**, go to "Desktops," and configure a system. Register to "My Cart" (no obligation). What calculators are used there? What are the advantages of this process as compared with buying a computer in a physical store? What are the disadvantages?

13. Enter **www.chime.com** and **www.ally.com** to identify their services. Prepare a report.

14. Access various travel sites such as **www.travelocity.com**, **www.orbitz.com**, **www.expedia.com**, **www.kayak.com**. Compare these websites for ease of use and usefulness. Note differences among the sites. If you ask each site for the itinerary, which one gives you the best information and the best deals?

Closing Case

MIS MKT The Story of Shopify

As we have noted previously (see this chapter's opening case), traditional brick-and-mortar retailers are being seriously challenged by electronic commerce. In addition, industry sectors that had resisted the shift from physical retail to online retail are now making the transition, largely as a result of the COVID-19 pandemic. For instance, physicians and therapists are offering telemedicine appointments, fitness providers are offering remote sessions, and schools and universities have moved classes online.

The transition from physical to digital is also creating problems in the labor force. Specifically, people who can work online are doing so, while workers who depend on face-to-face contact are suffering. This problem stands out in the retail industry, one of the largest employment sectors in the United States, with nearly 16 million workers in February 2020. As state and local authorities ordered nonessential businesses to close to slow the spread of the new coronavirus, unemployment in the retail industry soared.

As foot traffic rapidly declined at traditional retail stores, it was imperative for these stores to move into electronic commerce by creating online stores. Enter Shopify (**www.shopify.com**), a software-as-a-service (SaaS; see Technology Guide 3) platform founded in 2006 that enables merchants to quickly and cheaply set up an online store and sell their products.

Shopify offers a suite of services including payments, marketing, shipping, inventory levels, and customer relationship management tools to simplify the process of setting up and operating an online store. Shopify's mission is to "make commerce better for everyone, so businesses can focus on what they do best: building and selling their products." A $29 monthly fee buys a virtual shop and all of the functions necessary to operate it.

Shopify began as a simple tool for businesses to set up a home page. Traditionally, merchants used different applications to manage different channels to reach their customers. Shopify integrated all of these applications into a single platform. The idea is that no matter where or how a merchant sells, all sales activities feed into one centralized back office where merchants can see and operate the entirety of their businesses.

As just one example, in early April 2020, Heinz (**www.krafthein zcompany.com**) decided to open its first-ever online store. Within days, Shopify helped the well-known food brand establish a website selling its products for home delivery across the United Kingdom. The virtual shop performed so well that Heinz quickly expanded to offer its trademark condiments and baby food.

Very early in the coronavirus crisis, Tobi Lutke, Shopify's CEO and founder, instructed his staff to "delete all our existing plans and re-derive them from this new reality." Over the next three days, employees dropped their usual jobs and focused on identifying what small businesses needed the most to survive.

In subsequent weeks, Shopify rapidly deployed features to help merchants set up curbside pickup and local delivery. The firm also announced new partnerships with Facebook and Pinterest to expand social media as a shopping tool.

Shopify's huge scale indicates that an entire industry has grown up around the platform. For instance, smaller technology companies are selling software tools and templates that enhance the customer experience. One firm, for example, has developed an app that automatically converts prices into the local currency of the person browsing, thereby increasing the chances that the customer will make a purchase.

Shopify has visibility across all of its merchant customers on which products and services are trending and which apps are leading to sales. Shopify analyzes these vast amounts of data to help businesses increase their odds of making an online sale.

Shopify does face competition, notably from Amazon, but also from Austin, Texas–based BigCommerce (**www.bigcommerce.com**). BigCommerce CEO Brent Bellm stated that his company and Shopify lead the market in electronic commerce software-as-a-service, but the two firms have different strategies. Shopify's platform provides the full spectrum of software that companies need to set up their online operations. In contrast, BigCommerce offers a software platform that works with third-party software. Bellm contended that Shopify might be a better option for companies with no existing e-commerce offering, but that BigCommerce is a better choice for established companies.

In the United States, the world's largest e-commerce market after China, any purchase not made on Amazon.com is probably made through a website powered by Shopify. The company had the second-largest share of online retail sales in the United States in 2019 (passing eBay). Globally, Shopify powers more than 1 million merchants across 175 countries. In total, Shopify helped sell $61 billion of goods in 2019.

One reason for Shopify's success is the difference between this company and its major competitors, Amazon and eBay. Amazon and eBay are large enough to dictate how sellers must operate on their platforms. Merchants have no option other than to follow the platforms' stringent rules and lack of options. In contrast, Shopify enables merchants to custom-build their online stores. Shopify's tools allow merchants to manage an e-commerce operation on their own websites rather than rely on Amazon or eBay's platform.

New stores created on the Shopify platform increased 71 percent for the second quarter of 2020, compared with the first quarter. The shift to electronic commerce, due largely to the COVID-19 pandemic, drove this increase. Gross merchant volume totaled $30 billion, an increase of 119 percent in the second quarter of 2020 compared to the same period in 2019. *Gross merchant volume* is the amount of goods that merchants sold who had their stores on Shopify's platform.

Shopify's financials also looked healthy for the second quarter of 2020. Total revenue was $714 million, a 97 percent increase over the same period in 2019. Net income for the second quarter of 2020 was $36 million, compared with a net loss of $28 million for the same quarter in 2019.

A caveat: the rapid increase in the number of stores on Shopify's platform, the increase in gross merchant volume, and the platform's sound financials are due, at least in part, to the COVID-19 pandemic. It remains to be seen what Shopify's performance will look like after the pandemic begins to come under control.

Sources: Compiled from J. Brumley, "Forget Amazon: eBay now Has a Shopify Problem," *The Motley Fool*, August 5, 2020; E. Bary, "Shopify Stock Surges toward Record High as Pandemic Drives Booming E-Commerce Growth," *MarketWatch*, July 29, 2020; "Shopify Announces Second-Quarter 2020 Financial Results," *Business Wire*, July 29, 2020; D. Balji, "Shopify Sales Double as Merchants Forced into Online Future," *Yahoo! Finance*, July 29, 2020; D. Freedman, "Shopify Saved Main Street: Next Stop: Taking on Amazon," *marker.medium.com*, July 22, 2020; "Mastercard Research

Shows Surge in Digital Payments as E-Commerce Reaches New Heights around the World," *Business Wire*, June 18, 2020; J. Koetsier, "COVID-19 Accelerated E-Commerce Growth '4 to 6 Years'," *Forbes*, June 12, 2020; N. Pearson and D. Balji, "Shopify Is Enjoying a Big Moment and Hoping It Will Last," *Bloomberg BusinessWeek*, June 9, 2020; G. Khusainova, "Shopify Has a Plan for E-Commerce Domination and It Just Might Work," *Forbes*, May 21, 2020; "Shopify Unveils Its Consumer App: Shop," *Shopify.com*, April 28, 2020; L. Columbus, "How COVID-19 Is Transforming E-Commerce," *Forbes*, April 28, 2020; C. Schoenauer, "Buying Behavior after COVID-19: E-Commerce Boom Will Remain," *The Future of Commerce*, April 27, 2020; "Consumer Spend Is Shifting to Ecommerce: The Untold COVID-19 Story," *eMarketer*, April 24, 2020; D. Bosa, "Canadian Tech Rises again as Shopify Becomes the Second-Most Valuable Company in Canada," *CNBC*, April 23, 2020; K. Bakx, "Shop Owners Frantically Launch Online Stores to Stay Open during Pandemic," *CBC News*, April 20, 2020; H. Torry, "Coronavirus Pandemic Widens Divide between Online, Traditional Businesses," *Wall Street Journal*, April 1, 2020; **www.shopify.com**, accessed July 30, 2020.

Questions

1. Describe the various services that Shopify provides to merchants. Why wouldn't merchants develop these services themselves?

2. Discuss why and how the COVID-19 pandemic gave Shopify such a huge boost. How will Shopify's success be affected as the pandemic recedes?

CHAPTER 8

Wireless, Mobile Computing, and Mobile Commerce

Opening Case

MIS Hong Kong Pro-Democracy Protesters Turn to Technology

Hong Kong is a special administrative region of China, with an independent judiciary and a much broader range of freedoms than other Chinese citizens enjoy. The primary reason for this greater freedom is that Hong Kong was a British colony until 1997, when Britain turned over the territory to China. In turn, China agreed to respect the basic rights of Hong Kong citizens. However, in recent years, Chinese government policies have threatened democracy in Hong Kong. These actions have been met with large-scale protests.

In 2014 a series of street protests occurred from late September through mid-December. The protests were referred to as the Umbrella Movement because the protesters used umbrellas as a tool for passive resistance to the Hong Kong police's use of pepper spray to disperse crowds. The protests broke out in response to the Chinese government's decision regarding proposed reforms to the Hong Kong electoral system. Hong Kong citizens saw the decision as essentially enabling the Chinese Communist Party to prescreen candidates for the position of chief executive of Hong Kong.

Further protests erupted after the Hong Kong government proposed the Fugitive Offenders Amendment Bill in February 2019. The bill—which was subsequently withdrawn—would have empowered the government to extradite suspects to mainland China for prosecution. Hong Kong residents were concerned that they would be exposed to the legal system of mainland China, thereby undermining Hong Kong's autonomy and infringing on citizens' civil liberties.

The difference between the 2014 protests and the 2019–2020 protests was striking. In 2014, pro-democracy protesters relied on communication methods such as Facebook or writing articles in newspapers. In contrast, in the 2019–2020 protests, Hong Kong citizens used technology resources that made it easier and safer for them to communicate and collaborate. These technologies include mesh networks, encrypted messaging apps, a Reddit-like forum, online anonymity measures, a return to cash, and physical destruction of surveillance equipment.

Bridgefy. Bridgefy (**https://bridgefy.me**) is a software company that develops mesh-networking technology for mobile apps. In a *mesh network* users connect directly and cooperate with each other in receiving and sending messages.

Based on Bluetooth, the Bridgefy messaging app works the same way regardless of Internet access. Bridgefy built the app because a lack of communication can be critical in many places and situations. Prior to the Hong Kong protests, most users downloaded the app before going to a large music or sporting event. As of August 2020 people around the world were downloading the app for two reasons: authorities are increasingly limiting Internet access (refer to the closing case in Chapter 6), and it is a safe medium for people to communicate with little risk that the authorities will read their messages.

With Bridgefy, users can chat privately with contacts and broadcast to anyone within range, regardless of whether or not these individuals are contacts. It is possible to chat with people who are far apart because messages will hop via other Bridgefy users' phones until they reach the intended recipient.

Messaging apps. Craig Choy, a lawyer from Hong Kong–based attorney who focuses on privacy and data-protection laws, published a manual for pro-democracy citizens on how to use encrypted apps following the Umbrella Movement in 2014. An updated version of the manual was distributed to demonstrators. Choy specifically highlighted Telegram (**www.telegram.org**) and Signal (**www.signal.org**), which are messaging apps that offer end-to-end encryption.

Telegram did pose a problem to the protesters. When they used the app, protesters knew that setting their phone privacy to "My Contacts" would enable their contacts to see their number. To address this problem, activists had been instructing users to set their phones to "Nobody," believing that this procedure would hide their phone numbers in public groups. However, Hong Kong analysts discovered that was not the case. In fact, the Telegram app could have exposed the telephone numbers of everyone in a contact list to the authorities. In addition, the Chinese government has launched distributed denial-of-service (DDoS, discussed in Chapter 4) cyberattacks against Telegram in an effort to disrupt its service.

In response, people began to leave high-risk public Telegram groups, which made coordinating future demonstrations and actions more difficult. Activists began to advise one another to switch to burner phones. *Burner phones* are prepaid mobile phones that are replaced frequently.

The LIHKG forum. Another technology heavily used by protesters is the LIHKG forum, which is similar to Reddit in the United States. Many activists use the platform to discuss political ideas. The forum also contains many discussions about what pro-democracy citizens should do next. LIHKG users can then vote on what their favorite ideas are or what their next actions should be.

LIHKG is a major contributor to the concept of the *leaderless protest*. Leaderless protests do have a common goal. However, they are decentralized, grassroots, often spontaneous demonstrations without a clear leader and without a command-and-control governing structure. Significantly, the Chinese government is actively seeking out and imprisoning chat-group administrators as well as influential chat contributors.

Online anonymity. Online anonymity (and physical anonymity) are critical because Hong Kong's Public Order Ordinance imposes sweeping restriction on the right to assembly with the stated goal of maintaining "public order." In fact, government retaliation against protesters is quite severe. Protesters are at risk of losing their livelihoods. Some people have been fired from their jobs because their online activity was reported or they were identified at a demonstration.

Online anonymity is facilitated by having many facilitators of the protest movement. Further, citizens can organize themselves without revealing their identities. For anonymity, many protesters wear masks, goggles, and helmets, and they carry umbrellas. The idea is to remain anonymous for closed-circuit television (CCTV) cameras and helicopters, both of which the authorities use for surveillance.

Apple's AirDrop app is especially helpful on the front lines of a protest because users can access instant news about places that are safe and those that are not. The app enables protestors to send text, pictures, and information through Bluetooth to spread news to people who otherwise might not receive it through other communication channels. For example, demonstrators can learn where the next demonstration will be held and where to retreat after being tear-gassed.

Further, AirDrop enables users to send files anonymously, as devices are identified by their user-defined name. Though AirDrop is by default restricted to a user's contacts list, the user can configure that feature to allow connections with all nearby devices.

A return to cash. Instead of swiping through turnstiles with their prepaid rechargeable smart cards, activists are using cash-only ticketing machines. Local Hong Kong residents typically do not use ticketing machines because almost everyone has the Octopus card, which they use to pay for everything from transportation to meals and groceries. Purchasing a physical ticket not only takes time, but it costs more than the equivalent trip paid for with the Octopus card.

Activists were afraid that the authorities would trace their card data back to them and use those data as proof that they attended a protest. Each Octopus card contains a chip that stores its outstanding balance and transaction records, and each card has a serial number for identification. The cards can be linked to a credit card to automatically add funds when balances are low, making the cards even easier to trace to their owners. As police officers note, the Octopus card is like a GPS system because it can locate where and when the holder uses it.

Physical destruction of surveillance equipment. Protesters also targeted smart lampposts, which are equipped with sensors, cameras, and Internet connections. The government had given assurances that the lampposts would be used only for beneficial purposes, such as monitoring air quality and assisting with traffic control. They would not be used to collect facial or other personal data. The demonstrators did not believe the government. They used hand saws and ropes to take down several lampposts.

A problematic response from Apple. Critics in Hong Kong accused Apple of bowing to Chinese pressure after it removed HKMap.live from its App Store. HKMap is an app that uses crowdsourcing to reveal the locations of police and demonstrators. Apple defended its decision by claiming it had learned that the app "had been used in ways that endanger law enforcement and residents in Hong Kong." Apple further stated that the app displayed police locations and that it had been used to target and ambush police, threaten public safety, and victimize residents in areas where criminals knew there was no law enforcement. Pro-democracy demonstrators countered that the app's removal put protesters in a much more dangerous position.

Sources: Compiled from A. Ramzy and M. Ives, "Hong Kong Protests, One Year Later," *New York Times*, July 24, 2020; "New Security Law Sparks Protests in Hong Kong," *CNN*, July 2, 2020; Z. Tufekci, "In Hong Kong, Which Side Is Technology On?" *Wired*, October 22, 2019; C. Thorbecke, "How Tech Has Fueled a 'Leaderless Protest' in Hong Kong," *ABC News*, October 12, 2019; S. Byford, "Apple Removes App Used in Hong Kong Protests after Pressure from China," *The Verge*, October 10, 2019; "Hong Kong Protests: What Is the 'Umbrella Movement'?" *BBC*, September 28, 2019; J. Koetsier, "Hong Kong Protesters Using Mesh Messaging App China Can't Block: Usage Up 3685%," *Forbes*, September 2, 2019; S. Fussell, "Why Hong Kongers Are Toppling Lampposts," *The Atlantic*, August 30, 2019; J. Dujmovic, "Hong Kong Protesters Use Technology to Their Advantage,"

Market Watch, August 30, 2019; C. Cimpanu, "Hong Kong Protesters Warn of Telegram Feature that Can Disclose Their Identities," *ZDNet*, August 23, 2019; S. Banjo, "Hong Kong Protests Drive Surge in Telegram Chat App," *Bloomberg*, August 15, 2019; J. Griffiths, B. Westcott, and H. Regan, "Thousands of Protesters Shut Down Hong Kong Airport as Beijing Condemns 'Terrorism'," *CNN*, August 12, 2019; M. Hui, "Why Hong Kong's Protesters Were Afraid to Use Their Metro Cards," *Quartz*, June 13, 2019; P. Mozur and A. Stevenson, "Chinese Cyberattack Hits Telegram, App Used by Hong Kong Protesters," *New York Times*, June 13, 2019.

Questions

1. Describe the various technologies that Hong Kong activists use to protect themselves from the Chinese government.
2. Refer to Chapter 3, and discuss the ethicality and legality of Apple's actions regarding the HKMap app. In your opinion, was Apple justified in removing the app from its App Store? Why or why not? In your opinion, was Apple's stated justification the real reason the company removed the app? Why or why not?

Introduction

The traditional working environment that required users to sit at a wired computer is ineffective and inefficient. The solution was to build computers that are small enough to carry or wear and that can communicate through wireless networks. That is, your computing device now comes with you.

The ability to communicate anytime and anywhere provides organizations with a strategic advantage by increasing productivity and speed and improving customer service. We use the term **wireless** to describe telecommunications in which electromagnetic waves, rather than some form of wire or cable, carry the signal between communicating devices such as computers, smartphones, and iPads.

Before you continue, it is important to distinguish between the terms *wireless* and *mobile*—they can mean different things. The term *wireless* means exactly what it says: without wires. In contrast, *mobile* refers to something that changes its location over time. Some wireless networks, such as MiFi (discussed later in this chapter), are also mobile. Others, however, are fixed. For example, microwave towers form fixed wireless networks.

Wireless technologies enable individuals and organizations to conduct mobile computing, mobile commerce, and the Internet of Things. We define these terms here, and then we discuss each one in detail later in the chapter.

Mobile computing refers to a real-time, wireless connection between a mobile device and other computing environments, such as the Internet or an intranet. *Mobile commerce*—also known as *m-commerce*—refers to e-commerce (EC) transactions (see Chapter 7) conducted with a mobile device. The *Internet of Things* means that virtually every object contains embedded sensors and has processing power with either wireless or wired connections to a global network.

Wireless technologies and mobile commerce are spreading rapidly, replacing or supplementing wired computing. Cisco (**www.cisco.com**) predicts that the volume of mobile Web traffic will continue to increase rapidly over the next decade.

Almost all (if not all) organizations use wireless computing. Therefore, when you begin your career, you will likely be assigned a company smartphone and a wirelessly enabled computer. Clearly, then, it is important for you to learn about wireless computing not only because you will be using wireless applications but also because wireless computing will be important to your organization. In your job, you will be involved with customers who conduct wireless transactions, with analyzing and developing mobile commerce applications, and with wireless security. And the list goes on.

Simply put, an understanding of wireless technology and mobile commerce applications will make you more valuable to your organization. When you look at "What's in IT for Me?" at the end of the chapter, envision yourself performing the activities discussed in your functional area. For those of you who are inclined to be entrepreneurs, an understanding of wireless technology can also help you start and grow your own business.

The wireless infrastructure upon which mobile computing is built is reshaping the entire IT field. The technologies, applications, and limitations of mobile computing and mobile commerce are the focus of this chapter. You begin the chapter by learning about wireless devices, wireless transmission media, and wireless security. You continue by examining wireless computer networks and wireless Internet access. You then look at mobile computing and mobile commerce, which are made possible by wireless technologies. Next, you turn your attention to the Internet of Things.

8.1 Wireless Technologies

Wireless technologies include both wireless devices, such as smartphones, and wireless transmission media, such as microwave, satellite, and radio. These technologies are fundamentally changing the ways organizations operate.

Individuals are finding wireless devices convenient and productive to use, for several reasons. First, people can make productive use of time that was formerly wasted—for example, while commuting to work on public transportation. Second, because people can take these devices with them, their work locations are becoming much more flexible. Third, wireless technology enables people to schedule their working time around personal and professional obligations.

Author Lecture Videos are available exclusively in *WileyPLUS*.
Apply the Concept activities are available in the Appendix and in *WileyPLUS*.

Wireless Devices

Wireless devices provide three major advantages to users:

1. They are small enough to easily carry or wear.
2. They have sufficient computing power to perform productive tasks.
3. They can communicate wirelessly with the Internet and other devices.

Modern smartphones exhibit a process called *dematerialization*. Essentially, dematerialization occurs when the functions of many physical devices are included in one other physical device. Consider that your smartphone includes the functions of digital cameras for images and video, radios, televisions, Internet access through Web browsers, recording studios, editing suites, movie theaters, GPS navigators, word processors, spreadsheets, stereos, flashlights, board games, card games, video games, an entire range of medical devices, maps, atlases, encyclopedias, dictionaries, translators, textbooks, watches, alarm clocks, books, calculators, address books, credit card swipers, magnifying glasses, money and credit cards, car keys, hotel keys, cellular telephony, Wi-Fi, e-mail access, text messaging, a full QWERTY keyboard, and many, many other things. **Figure 8.1** illustrates the process of dematerialization with smartphones.

Our smartphones have come a long, long way in a short period of time. Compare these smartphone capabilities (as of August 2020):

- Apple's first iPhone (2007) had a 3.5-inch screen, a 2-megapixel camera, 16 gigabytes of storage, and it did not support third-party apps.
- The Apple iPhone 11 Pro (2019) has a 5.85-inch screen, three 12-megapixel cameras (wide angle, ultra-wide angle, and telephoto), up to 512 gigabytes of storage, provides biometrics for security, and supports a vast array of apps.

One downside of smartphones is that people can use them to copy and pass on confidential information. For example, if you were an executive at Intel, would you want workers snapping pictures of their colleagues with your secret new technology in the background? After all, one of the functions of a smartphone is that of a digital camera that can transmit wirelessly. New jamming devices are being developed to counter the threat. Some companies, such as Samsung (**www.samsung.com**), have recognized the danger and have banned these devices from their premises altogether.

Another downside of smartphones consists of scam calls. According to First Orion (**www.firstorion.com**), a company that provides call management and protection for wireless carriers, approximately 40 percent of U.S. mobile traffic consisted of scam calls in the first half of 2019.

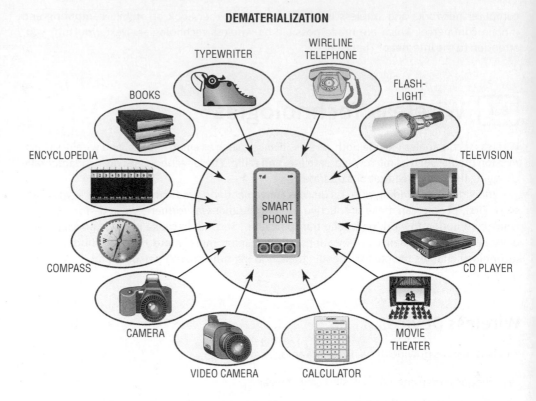

FIGURE 8.1 Dematerialization with smartphones.

In July 2019 the Federal Communications Commission passed a provision that forces network operators to implement SHAKEN/STIR, the new industry standard for verifying the source of phone calls. Carriers have until 2020 to implement SHAKEN/STIR. As of August 2020 here is what the major wireless carriers were doing about spam calls.

- Verizon (**www.verizon.com**) offers free tools to its mobile and home customers. For mobile, Call Filter is a free app that screens and automatically blocks incoming spam calls based on risk level and allows customers to report spam.
- T-Mobile (**www.t-mobile.com**) offers Scam Shield to every customer, which provides free scam identification and blocking.
- AT&T (**www.att.com**) Call Protect is a free service that automatically provides screen alerts for spam calls and blocks them.

Regardless of any disadvantages, however, cell phones, and particularly smartphones, have had a far greater impact on human society than most of us realize. On the other hand, smartphones can be used illegally, as you see in IT's About Business 8.1.

IT's About Business 8.1

MIS Phone Farming

A *phone farm* is a setup where people attempt to make money by faking human engagement with online content such as advertisements, video game trailers, celebrity gossip shows, sports, and programs from companies such as Netflix. A human is not actually performing these actions, but the targeted companies do not know that. Phone farmers can operate anywhere in the world. They sometimes buy dozens, hundreds, or thousands of phones in order to generate revenue.

Phone farmers take advantage of a marketing strategy called *incentivized traffic*. In this strategy, app developers publish advertisements or other online content that companies want to get customer attention on and pay that audience to watch or interact with the content. The advertisers find incentivized traffic to be an effective way to increase their brand's visibility.

Incentivized traffic is legitimate if a human is actually performing the actions. It is not illegal for people to be compensated for watching an advertisement or a movie trailer in an app. For example, in 2018, NBCUniversal (**www.nbcuniversal.com**) launched an app called WatchBack, which gave users a chance to win $100 in exchange for watching television shows. The objective was to attract new fans for the network's programming.

Another app, PerkTV, is a rewards app for mobile devices. PerkTV rewards users for watching trailers for apps, video games, and movies by awarding them points that they can exchange for more valuable goods.

In contrast, phone farming is illegal because, rather than actually performing these actions, the farmers use multiple phones and often automate the process to give the false impression that a human is watching the ads in order to generate income. Phone farms operate the phones on a 24/7/365 basis, with each phone collecting a fraction of a penny for each action it takes. These actions include advertisement views, clicks, registrations, installs, and other types of engagement to create the illusion of legitimate human activity.

There are startup costs associated with setting up a phone farm because the process is more complicated than simply purchasing phones, installing software, and making small amounts of money. Phone farmers may start with their own devices, or they can purchase used phones from eBay or Amazon. The most profitable phone-farming apps are constantly changing as some developers crack down on people using multiple devices at once. Developers also make changes to apps so that they require intervention by an actual person.

Phone farmers download apps that pay the most money for each action. As of August 2020 the top-rated phone-farming apps were Swagbucks, AppLike, Google Rewards, Lucktastic, Inbox-Dollars, and Nielsen. Phone farmers jump among different apps because some apps are better for generating money than others, though the various apps function more or less identically.

Phone farmers must monitor the phones closely, a labor-intensive process. This monitoring includes phone farmers occasionally clicking pop-ups on their screens to confirm that they are still watching the advertisements. Some farmers go beyond simply operating multiple phones at the same time and use software that simulates activity, including clicks and finger movements on their phones.

Some farmers use an app called FRep, or Finger Replayer, to loop a virtual finger's movement across the phone's screen and trick the app. Others use Automagic, which allows consumers to automate a series of commands or actions on an Android phone. Additional cash-generating techniques include outsourcing Google CAPTCHAs so that someone else can complete them for a small fee and/or routing their phone's activity through multiple IP addresses to circumvent the apps' anti-fraud mechanisms. In addition, there are invitation-only chat rooms where phone farmers discuss strategies to automate their devices to generate money with no interaction at all. These methods violate the app's terms of use.

Many advertisers do not like having their advertisements "watched" by software on phone farms, and they employ companies to help them combat this practice. For example, the anti-ad fraud company DoubleVerify (**www.doubleverify.com**) collaborates with Facebook and other partners to determine whether traffic from advertisements is coming from genuine, human viewers.

TV-TWO (**www.tv-two.com**) is an app that allows users to view content in exchange for cryptocurrency. The app takes several steps to ensure that the people using its app are actually watching the advertisements. TV-TWO only allows users to watch their app on a single phone or television. It works with another company called AppsFlyer (**www.appsflyer.com**) to weed out fraudulent viewers.

Some phone farmers report that they have made hundreds of dollars per month from passively running apps on their phones. Others claim that they make only "beer money."

Why do people pursue this illegal activity? Some phone farmers assert that they set up their farms because they were disabled and living on a fixed income. Others claim they needed money to buy food or to pay for childcare. Still others explain that it was easier than driving for Uber or delivering food for GrubHub.

Sources: Compiled from "Phone Farming: Can You Still Make Passive Income with It?" *Beermoney*, June 28, 2020; "Click Farms: What Are They & What Are They For?" *ClickCease*, April 16, 2020; S. Carr, "What Is a Click Farm? The Quick Way to Thousands of Likes," *PPC Protect*, September 11, 2019; "Americans Are Setting Up Hobby 'Phone Farms'…But Elsewhere, It's Big Business," *The Hustle*, August 2, 2019; J. Cox, "America's DIY Phone Farmers," *Vice.com*, August 1, 2019; K. Hu, "What Are Click Farms? A Shadowy Internet Industry Is Booming in China," *Yahoo! Finance*, July 20, 2019; T. Spangler, "NBCU Launches WatchBack App, Offering Users Who Sample New Shows a Chance to Win Rewards," *Variety*, October 5, 2018; L. Matsakis, "Look at This Massive Click Fraud Farm that Was Just Busted in Thailand," *Vice.com*, June 12, 2017; B. Jolly, "The Bizarre 'Click Farm' of 10,000 Phones that Give FAKE 'Likes' to Our Most-Loved Apps," *The Mirror*, May 15, 2017; "Inside a Chinese Phone Farm," *Beermoney*, May 12, 2017.

Questions

1. All technologies are double-edged swords; that is, they have advantages and disadvantages. Explain how this statement relates to smartphones. Provide another example of how smartphones can cause problems.

2. Refer to Chapter 3. Discuss the ethicality and legality of phone farming.

Wireless Transmission Media

Wireless media, or broadcast media, transmit signals without wires. The major types of wireless media are microwave, satellite, and radio. **Table 8.1** lists the advantages and disadvantages of each type.

Microwave.   **Microwave transmission** systems transmit data through electromagnetic waves. These systems are used for high-volume, long-distance, line-of-sight communication. *Line-of-sight* means that the transmitter and receiver are in view of each other. This requirement creates problems because the Earth's surface is curved. For this reason, microwave towers usually cannot be spaced more than 30 miles apart.

TABLE 8.1 **Advantages and Disadvantages of Wireless Media**

Channel	Advantages	Disadvantages
Microwave	High bandwidth Relatively inexpensive	Must have unobstructed line of sight Susceptible to environmental interference
Satellite	High bandwidth Large coverage area	Expensive Must have unobstructed line of sight Signals experience propagation delay Must use encryption for security
Radio	High bandwidth Signals pass through walls Inexpensive and easy to install	Creates electrical interference problems Susceptible to snooping unless encrypted

Clearly, then, microwave transmissions offer only a limited solution to data communications needs, especially over very long distances. Microwave transmissions are also susceptible to environmental interference during severe weather such as heavy rain and snowstorms. Although long-distance microwave data communications systems are still widely used, they are being replaced by satellite communications systems.

Satellite.   **Satellite transmission** systems make use of communication satellites. Currently, there are three types of satellites circling Earth: geostationary-earth-orbit (GEO), medium-earth-orbit (MEO), and low-earth-orbit (LEO). Each type has a different orbit, with GEO being farthest from Earth and LEO being the closest. In this section, you examine the three types of satellites and then discuss three satellite applications: global positioning systems, Internet transmission through satellites, and commercial imaging. **Table 8.2** compares and contrasts the three types of satellites.

As with microwave transmission, satellites must receive and transmit data through line of sight. However, the enormous *footprint*—the area of Earth's surface reached by a satellite's

TABLE 8.2 **Three Basic Types of Telecommunications Satellites**

Type	Characteristics	Orbit	Number	Use
GEO	Satellites stationary relative to point on Earth Few satellites needed for global coverage Transmission delay (approximately 0.25 second) Most expensive to build and launch Longest orbital life (many years)	22,300 miles	8	TV signal
MEO	Satellites move relative to point on Earth Moderate number needed for global coverage Requires medium-powered transmitters Negligible transmission delay Less expensive to build and launch Moderate orbital life (6 to 12 years)	6,434 miles	10 to 12	GPS
LEO	Satellites move rapidly relative to point on Earth Large number needed for global coverage Requires only low-power transmitters Negligible transmission delay Least expensive to build and launch Shortest orbital life (as low as 5 years)	400 to 700 miles	Many	Telephone

transmission—overcomes the limitations of microwave data relay stations. That is, satellites use *broadcast* transmission, which sends signals to many receivers at one time. So, even though satellites are line-of-sight, like microwave, they are high enough for broadcast transmission, thus overcoming the limitations of microwave.

The most basic rule governing footprint size is simple: the higher a satellite orbits, the larger its footprint. Thus, medium-earth-orbit satellites have a smaller footprint than geostationary satellites, and low-earth-orbit satellites have the smallest footprint of all. **Figure 8.2** compares the footprints of the three types of satellites.

Types of Orbits.   *Geostationary-earth-orbit satellites* orbit 22,300 miles directly above the equator. These satellites maintain a fixed position above Earth's surface because, at their altitude, their orbital period matches the 24-hour rotational period of Earth. For this reason, receivers on Earth do not have to track GEO satellites. GEO satellites are excellent for sending television programs to cable operators and for broadcasting directly to homes.

One major limitation of GEO satellites is that their transmissions take a quarter of a second to send and return. This brief pause, one kind of *propagation delay*, makes two-way telephone conversations difficult. Also, GEO satellites are large and expensive, and they require substantial amounts of power to launch. As you will see in IT's About Business 8.2, Skylo Technologies has developed an innovative use of geostationary satellites.

Medium-earth-orbit satellites are located about 6,000 miles above Earth's surface. MEO orbits require more satellites to cover Earth than GEO orbits because MEO footprints are smaller. MEO satellites have two advantages over GEO satellites: they are less expensive and they do not have an appreciable propagation delay. However, because MEO satellites move with respect to a point on Earth's surface, receivers must track these satellites. (Think of a satellite dish slowly turning to remain oriented to a MEO satellite.)

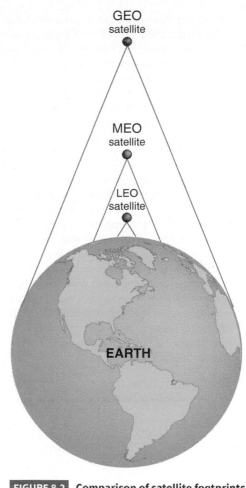

FIGURE 8.2   **Comparison of satellite footprints.**

IT's About Business 8.2

MIS Skylo Technologies

People living on islands, vacationing on cruise ships, and/or hiking in the mountains have relied on satellite communications for many years. Typically, the equipment necessary to operate these systems is expensive and requires large antennas that must be manually pointed in particular directions to access specific satellites. For years, companies have been trying to create global wireless networks that can connect all objects and people to the Internet, reaching places that do not have cell towers or fiber-optic cables.

Skylo Technologies (**www.skylo.tech**) is a company that provides Internet of Things connectivity to machines, sensors, and devices. It is the world's first company to leverage the cellular Narrowband Internet of Things (NB-IoT) protocol via satellite, making it possible to connect billions of sensors on objects and machines in remote areas. This protocol belongs to the category of low-power wide area networks, connecting devices that require small amounts of data, low bandwidth, and long battery life.

In August 2020 Skylo and Sony Semiconductor Israel formed a partnership to develop cellular chips that can connect via geostationary satellites by using the NB-IoT protocol. The two firms will be the first to deploy these chips with 5G networks.

On January 21, 2020, Skylo unveiled its small but powerful antenna that can connect to expensive satellite-based Internet

services and relay their signals to hundreds of other devices. The Skylo satellite terminal (its antenna), called the Skylo Hub, is about the size of a dinner plate. It uses software to lock on to existing geostationary satellites, which enables it to transmit data to nearby devices via Wi-Fi or Bluetooth. Skylo designed its Hub using off-the-shelf (existing) components to drastically reduce the cost while making the sensor and device more compatible.

Skylo requires customers to buy the antenna, which costs less than $100, and then pay for Skylo's service, which starts at $1 per month for a limited amount of data. The antenna is designed so that customers can install it themselves; for example, by attaching it to the roof of a boat or truck.

Significantly, Skylo is not trying to deliver high-speed Internet to homes or buildings. Rather, the startup is focusing on logistics applications. For example, the firm is more interested in enabling boats at sea or truckers on rural routes to send and receive data cheaply.

Skylo has tested its system extensively in India. Trucking companies are using the system to track their fleets and to make pickup routes more efficient. In addition, Indian fishermen have deployed the system to receive weather updates and help with auctions for their catches. Industry analysts note that there are 300,000 fishing boats in India, and they are away at sea for at least seven days at a time. The fishermen want to know which fish are in demand at which markets and where to go if a typhoon is approaching.

Other Indian customers include small farmers who use the system to coordinate tractor rentals during busy harvest seasons. Other farmers track the temperatures of animal vaccines and bull semen in transit to confirm that these expensive shipments stay within the necessary temperature range to remain viable.

Indian Railways (**http://indianrail.gov.in**) has tested Skylo's system on its passenger cars and freight cars. A company spokesperson noted that India is a huge country with many communications dead zones where connections can be lost for up to an hour. Skylo enables passenger and freight cars in these areas to report their location, speed, and direction, as well as maintenance concerns such as a bearing on a wheel that is overheating.

Skylo contends that its system performs more efficiently, effectively, and inexpensively than competitors, which include KORE Wireless Group, Starhome Mach, and Network Innovations. Skylo CEO Parthsarathi Trivedi asserts that this type of inexpensive connection will open up new markets for unconnected and underserved people. He further claims that Skylo will remain cheaper than its competitors by using existing satellites rather than launching its own satellites to build out infrastructure. Finally, he contends that competitors cannot match Skylo's antenna technology.

Sources: Compiled from D. Werner, "Skylo Forms Partnership with Sony Semiconductor Israel," *Space News*, August 18, 2020; D. Braue, "Satellite IoT Helps Remote Farmers," *Information Age*, July 23, 2020; "Heard of Skylo? It's Bringing Satellite Internet to Remote Areas," *The Quint*, April 4, 2020; A. Baker, "How Skylo Is Making It Easier to Connect to IoT Sensors," *Pulse 2.0*, February 10, 2020; A. Vance, "Cheap Internet, Anywhere," *Bloomberg Businessweek*, January 27, 2020; "Skylo One to Watch for Satellite IoT," *Advanced Television*, January 23, 2020; D. Werner, "Startup Skylo Seeks to Connect Millions of Devices, Vehicles, Vessels via Satellite," *Space News*, January 21, 2020; "Indian Railways Aims Big Transformation with Automation," *Construction Week Online*, January 9, 2020; "Indian Railways Is Aiming to Change the Way You Travel," *The Asian Age*, January 8, 2020; **www.skylo.tech**, accessed August 19, 2020.

Questions

1. Why is satellite connectivity so important to Internet of Things networks?

2. Why did Skylo choose geostationary satellites for its connectivity? Describe potential problems that could arise from this strategy.

3. Describe the ways that Skylo keeps the costs down for its service. Refer to Chapter 2. Do these methods constitute a competitive advantage for Skylo? Why or why not?

Low-earth-orbit satellites are located 400 to 700 miles above Earth's surface. Because LEO satellites are much closer to Earth, they have little, if any, propagation delay. Like MEO satellites, however, LEO satellites move with respect to a point on Earth's surface and therefore must be tracked by receivers. Tracking LEO satellites is more difficult than tracking MEO satellites because LEO satellites move much more quickly relative to a point on Earth.

Unlike GEO and MEO satellites, LEO satellites can pick up signals from weak transmitters. This feature makes it possible for satellite telephones to operate through LEO satellites, because they can operate with less power using smaller batteries. Another advantage of LEO satellites is that they consume less power and cost less to launch.

At the same time, however, the footprints of LEO satellites are small, which means that many satellites are needed to cover the planet. For this reason, a single organization often produces multiple LEO satellites, known as *LEO constellations*. Many companies have deployed LEO constellations to provide global voice and data communications. Two of the oldest are Iridium (**www.iridium.com**) and Globalstar (**www.globalstar.com**).

Global Positioning Systems. The **global positioning system (GPS)** is a wireless system that uses satellites to enable users to determine their position anywhere on Earth. GPS is supported by MEO satellites that are shared worldwide.

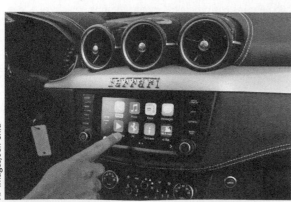

All GPS satellites have an extremely accurate clock. The exact position of each satellite is always known because the satellite continuously broadcasts its position along with a time signal. By using the known speed of the signals and the distance from three satellites (for two-dimensional location) or four satellites (for three-dimensional location), it is possible to find the location of any receiving station or user within a range of 2 meters (approximately 6 feet). GPS software can also convert the user's latitude and longitude to an electronic map.

Most of you are probably familiar with GPS in automobiles, which "talks" to drivers when giving directions. **Figure 8.3** illustrates a driver obtaining GPS information in a car.

Commercial use of GPS for activities such as navigating, mapping, and surveying has become widespread, particularly in remote areas. Cell phones in the United States now must have a GPS embedded in

AP Images/Jeff Chiu

FIGURE 8.3 **Drivers can obtain GPS information from their automobile.**

them so that the location of a person making an emergency call—for example, 911, known as *wireless 911*—can be detected immediately.

As of August 2020 three additional GPS system were fully operational. The Russian GPS, *GLONASS*, launched its 24th and final GPS satellite on March 16, 2020, and became fully operational.

On December 27, 2018, China's BeiDou GPS system began providing global services. China launched the 35th and final satellite into orbit on June 23, 2020.

The European Union GPS is called *Galileo*. In 2019 Galileo reached full operational capability and the complete 30-satellite Galileo system is expected to be complete by the end of 2020.

It is almost impossible to overstate how much the world's economy depends on the GPS system. There are some 2 billion GPS receivers in use around the world, and that number is expected to increase to 7 billion by 2022. In fact, a study by research firm RTI International (**www.rti.org**) estimated that the loss of GPS service globally would cost private sector organizations approximately $1 billion per day.

The telecommunications industry, banks, airlines, electric utilities, cloud computing businesses, television networks, emergency services, and the military require constantly precise GPS timing. In fact, the U.S. Department of Homeland Security has designed 16 sectors of infrastructure as critical, and 14 of them depend on GPS.

Prior to 2020, GPS technology could provide locations that were accurate to within about 1 meter. On December 23, 2018, the United States launched the first next-generation GPS III satellite. GPS III satellites provide better positioning accuracy because each carries a new atomic clock and each has increased transmitter power. As a result, GPS reception is more accurate and more reliable, even indoors and in dense urban areas. Further, GPS signals are more resistant to jamming.

NASA is working on developing international compatibility and interoperability for GPS satellites. A United Nations committee is proposing a common set of definitions for GPS signals from the United States, Europe, Russia, China, Japan, and India. When finished, GPS receivers will be able to access all GPS satellites, which in turn will lead to positioning within inches.

The most immediate threat to the GPS system is jamming signals, which does not have to be by a foreign adversary. For example, in 2013 flights at Newark airport were interrupted when truckers, trying to confuse the GPS receivers their companies use to track them, used commercially available GPS jammers on the New Jersey turnpike.

In 2017 Russia was jamming GPS signals in an effort to protect Khmeimim Air Base, one of its most important military bases in Syria. The jamming caused problems as far away as Israel and Cyprus.

Europe's Galileo satellite navigation system was out of service for one week beginning on July 11, 2019. The incident took down all of the system's timing and navigation features other than Search and Rescue, which helps people in remote areas.

Navigation systems that relied on Galileo could not function. However, these systems were able to seamlessly transition to the United States GPS system rather than taking flawed data and using it to calculate inaccurate positions and routes. The lengthy outage is a serious reminder of the modern world's reliance on GPS systems

Internet over Satellite.   In many regions of the world, Internet over satellite (IoS) is the only option available for Internet connections because installing cables is either too expensive or physically impossible. IoS enables users to access the Internet from GEO satellites on a dish mounted on the side of their homes. Although IoS makes the Internet available to many people who otherwise could not access it, it has its drawbacks. Not only do GEO satellite transmissions involve a propagation delay, but they can also be disrupted by environmental influences such as thunderstorms. Many companies are entering this market.

- OneWeb (**http://oneweb.world**) has deployed a LEO constellation to bring Internet access to all corners of the globe. The firm is targeting rural markets, emerging markets, and in-flight Internet services on airlines. As of March 2020, OneWeb had launched 74 satellites and was planning for 650 satellites in total.

- SpaceX's (**www.spacex.com**) LEO constellation, Starlink, provides long-distance Internet traffic for people in sparsely populated areas. As of August 2020, SpaceX had launched 655 satellites. The company is planning for 12,000 satellites in total.

- In April 2019, Amazon announced plans for its LEO constellation, called Project Kuiper, which will consist of 3,236 satellites.

Commercial Imaging. Another satellite application is commercial images from orbit, using very small satellites, called *nanosatellites*. Several companies are involved in launching nanosatellites for scientific and commercial purposes. Let's look at some of these companies here.

- Planet Labs (Planet; **www.planet.com**) takes pictures of the Earth more frequently than traditional satellites and at a small fraction of the cost. The company's LEO constellation, called Dove, helps entire industries obtain images anywhere on the earth. Planet can also capture video that can be used to develop three-dimensional models of any area that is imaged.

  By August 2018 Planet was able to image every location on the entire planet every day. Planet has deployed a platform, Queryable Earth, that customers can use to track, planes, ships, roads, buildings, and forests worldwide.

  A farm software business in the agriculture division of DowDuPont (**www.dupont .com**), called Granular (**http://granular.ag**), uses Planet's satellites to access daily images of the Earth, as well as some of Planet's six-year archive of images. Granular analyzes the images to provide information to farmers. For example, farmers use Granular's analyses to develop crop and field plans, delegate duties to employees, track inventory, and predict yield and revenue.

- **FIN** The World Bank (**www.worldbank.org**) monitors high-risk urban development by integrating satellite imaging data from NASA's Landsat satellites and the European Space Agency's Sentinel satellites with census data.

- **POM** Spire's (**www.spire.com**) LEO constellation locates objects. For example, more than 250,000 ships broadcast an automatic identification signal. Spire satellites pick up these signals and provide frequent updates of the ships' positions without the vessels having to use expensive dedicated satellite communications.

- **POM** Ursa Space Systems (**www.ursaspace.com**) analyzes satellite imaging data to estimate the amount of oil in 10,000 oil storage tanks worldwide by focusing on the heights of the lids to measure fluctuation in the oil levels of the tanks. The company estimates oil stockpiles and oil demand.

- **POM** Orbital Insight (**www.orbitalinsight.com**) also has an oil storage tracker and performs daily automobile counts for 80 U.S. retailers.

- **POM** EarthCast Technologies (**www.earthcastdemo.com**) provides in-flight forecasts to pilots. Pilots have long had access to basic weather information for their departure and arrival airports, but EarthCast gives them the ability to map out conditions along a particular flight path.

- Iceye Oy (**www.iceye.com**) is planning to launch a constellation of 18 satellites that will allow it to capture images of almost any spot on Earth every three hours.

- **POM** SpaceKnow (**www.spaceknow.com**) uses image data from about 200 public and private satellites to track everything from planes at airports, to shipping containers in ports, to cars at amusement parks. The company's clients are particularly interested in infrastructure development; for example, whether there are new mines in the cobalt-rich Democratic Republic of Congo, which could impact that mineral's prices.

- Imazon (**www.imazon.org.br**) uses image data from the European Space Agency's Sentinel satellites to police the deforestation of the Amazonian basin in Brazil. The organization focuses on providing data to local governments in the region through its "green municipalities" program, which trains officials to identify deforestation.

- **POM** Indigo Ag Inc. (**www.indigoag.com**) analyzes image data from NASA and European Space Agency satellites to track global crops, such as wheat, rice, and others.

- Global Fishing Watch (GFW; **www.globalfishingwatch.org**) analyzes satellite ship-tracking image data to help identify where and when vessels are fishing illegally. The organization was jointly founded by three companies: SkyTruth (**www.skytruth.org**), which uses satellites to monitor natural resource extraction and promote environmental protection; Oceana (**www.oceana.org**), an international ocean conservation organization; and Google, which provides data analytics.

  In August 2020 the flying squid population near North Korea collapsed. GFW tracked the source to a large group of untracked, so-called "dark" fishing vessels that were leaving

Chinese ports to fish illegally off the North Korean coast. The illegal fishing has serious consequences for North Korean fishermen, who must move north, fishing illegally off the coast of Russia.

Radio.   **Radio transmission** uses radio wave frequencies to send data directly between transmitters and receivers. Radio transmission has several advantages. First, radio waves travel easily through normal office walls. Second, radio devices are fairly inexpensive and easy to install. Third, radio waves can transmit data at high speeds. For these reasons, radio increasingly is being used to connect computers to both peripheral equipment and local area networks (LANs; discussed in Chapter 6). (Note: Wi-Fi and cellular also use radio frequency waves.)

As with other technologies, however, radio transmission has its drawbacks. First, radio media can create electrical interference problems. Also, radio transmissions are susceptible to snooping by anyone who has similar equipment that operates on the same frequency.

Another problem with radio transmission is that when you travel too far away from the source station, the signal breaks up and fades into static. Most radio signals can travel only 30 to 40 miles from their source. However, **satellite radio** overcomes this problem. Satellite radio, or *digital radio*, offers uninterrupted, near CD-quality transmission that is beamed to your radio, either at home or in your car, from space. In addition, satellite radio offers a broad spectrum of stations, including many types of music, news, and talk. Sirius XM (**www .siriusxm.com**) is a leading satellite radio company whose listeners subscribe to its service for a monthly fee.

Internet Blimps.   Altaeros (**www.altaeros.com**) makes the SuperTower, which is a tethered blimp that floats at about 800 feet altitude. Each blimp acts like a regular cell tower but with a footprint of up to 4,000 square miles. Altaeros claims that one SuperTower will replace 15 land-based cell towers and cut the cost of delivering wireless service by 60 percent. In 2019, the company completed a field test in New Hampshire and was looking for customers.

Wireless Security

Clearly, wireless networks provide numerous benefits for businesses. However, they also present a huge challenge to management—namely, their inherent lack of security. Wireless is a broadcast medium, and transmissions can be intercepted by anyone who is close enough and has access to the appropriate equipment. There are four major threats to wireless networks: rogue access points, war driving, eavesdropping, and radio frequency jamming.

A *rogue access point* is an unauthorized access point into a wireless network. The rogue could be someone in your organization who sets up an access point meaning no harm but fails to inform the IT department. In more serious cases, the rogue is an "evil twin"—someone who wishes to access a wireless network for malicious purposes.

In an *evil twin attack*, the attacker is in the vicinity with a Wi-Fi-enabled computer and a separate connection to the Internet. Using a *hotspotter*—a device that detects wireless networks and provides information on them—the attacker simulates a wireless access point with the same wireless network name, or SSID, as the one that authorized users expect. If the signal is strong enough, then users will connect to the attacker's system instead of the real access point. The attacker can then serve them a web page asking for them to provide confidential information such as usernames, passwords, and account numbers. In other cases, the attacker simply captures wireless transmissions. These attacks are more effective with public hotspots (e.g., McDonald's and Starbucks) than with corporate networks.

War driving is the act of locating WLANs while driving (or walking) around a city or elsewhere. To war drive or walk, you simply need a Wi-Fi detector and a wirelessly enabled computer. If a WLAN has a range that extends beyond the building in which it is located, then an unauthorized user might be able to intrude into the network. The intruder can then obtain a free Internet connection and possibly gain access to important data and other resources.

Eavesdropping refers to efforts by unauthorized users to access data that are traveling over wireless networks. Finally, in *radio frequency* (*RF*) *jamming*, a person or a device intentionally or unintentionally interferes with your wireless network transmissions.

To protect wireless networks, we encrypt our transmissions. Developed by the Wi-Fi Alliance, WPA2 is a type of encryption used to secure the vast majority of Wi-Fi networks. A WPA2 network provides unique encryption keys for each wireless client that connects to it. WPA3 is the latest implementation of WPA2.

Before you go on...

1. Describe the most common types of wireless devices.
2. Describe the various types of transmission media.
3. Describe four threats to the security of wireless transmissions.

8.2 Wireless Computer Networks and Internet Access

You have learned about various wireless devices and how these devices transmit wireless signals. These devices typically form wireless computer networks, and they provide wireless Internet access. In this section, you will study wireless networks, which we organize by their effective distance: short range, medium range, and wide area.

Short-Range Wireless Networks

Short-range wireless networks simplify the task of connecting one device to another. They also eliminate wires, and they enable users to move around while they use their devices. In general, short-range wireless networks have a range of 100 feet or less. In this section, you consider three basic short-range networks: Bluetooth, ultra-wideband (UWB), and near-field communications (NFC).

Bluetooth.   Bluetooth (www.bluetooth.com) is an industry specification used to create small personal area networks. A **personal area network** is a computer network used for communication among computer devices (e.g., telephones, personal digital assistants, smartphones) located close to one person. Bluetooth uses low-power, radio-based communication. Bluetooth 5.2 can transmit up to approximately 50 megabits per second (Mbps) up to 400 meters (roughly 1300 feet). These characteristics mean that Bluetooth 5 will be important for Internet of Things (discussed in Section 8.4) applications.

Common applications for Bluetooth are wireless handsets for cell phones and portable music players. Advantages of Bluetooth include low power consumption and the fact that it uses radio waves that are emitted in all directions from a transmitter. For this reason, you do not have to point one Bluetooth device at another to create a connection.

Bluetooth low energy, marketed as *Bluetooth Smart*, enables applications in the health care, fitness, security, and home entertainment industries. Compared to "classic" Bluetooth, Bluetooth Smart is less expensive and consumes less power, although it has a similar communication range. Bluetooth Smart is fueling the "wearables" (wearable computer) development and adoption.

Ultra-Wideband.   Ultra-wideband (UWB) is a high-bandwidth wireless technology with transmission speeds in excess of 100 Mbps. Let's take a closer look at Humatics (www .humatics.com), a leading company in UWB technologies. The firm offers several microlocation systems that use UWB technology, including the Humatics Rail Navigation System and the Milo Microlocation System.

The Rail Navigation System enables modern train systems to provide secure, reliable service for their riders. This system uses UWB sensors installed along tracks that continuously communicate with UWB sensors on trains. The sensors capture accurate, real-time location and speed data which seamlessly integrate with each train's control system. The Metropolitan Transportation Authority in New York City has successfully piloted the Rail Navigation System in part of the city's subway system.

The Milo System uses sensors embedded within products, equipment, or robots to provide real-time, reliable, ultra-precise (less than one millimeter) location data so that organizations know exactly where objects and equipment are and where they are going. For example, companies are using the Milo system to precisely control the movements of not only industrial robot arms, but also the movements of cobots.

Other interesting ultra-wideband applications include:

- Mobile robotics: Enable robots to navigate autonomously indoors and in other GPS-denied environments and to guide drones as they fly
- **POM** Heavy equipment industries such as manufacturing and mining: Precisely position the arm of a crane and track forklifts moving indoors and outdoors
- Defense and security: Low false alarm rate, wireless perimeter fences, and indoor mapping and through-wall surveillance

Near-Field Communication.   **Near-field communication (NFC)** has the smallest range of any short-range wireless network. It is designed to be embedded in mobile devices such as cell phones and credit cards. For example, using NFC, you can wave your device or card within a few centimeters of POS terminals to pay for items. NFC can also be used with mobile wallets (discussed in Section 8.3).

Medium-Range Wireless Networks

Medium-range wireless networks are the familiar **wireless local area networks (WLANs)**. The most common type of medium-range wireless network is **Wireless Fidelity**, or Wi-Fi. WLANs are useful in a variety of settings, some of which may be challenging.

Wireless Fidelity is a medium-range WLAN, which is a wired LAN but without the cables. In a typical configuration, a transmitter with an antenna, called a **wireless access point** (see **Figure 8.4**), connects to a wired LAN or to satellite dishes that provide an Internet connection. A wireless access point provides service to a number of users within a small geographical perimeter (up to approximately 300 feet), known as a **hotspot**. Multiple wireless access points are needed to support a larger number of users across a larger geographical area. To communicate wirelessly, mobile devices, such as laptop PCs, typically have a built-in wireless network interface capability.

Wi-Fi provides fast and easy Internet or intranet broadband access from public hotspots located at airports, hotels, Internet cafés, universities, conference centers, offices, and homes. Users can access the Internet while walking across a campus, to their office, or through their homes. Users can also access Wi-Fi with their laptops, desktops, or PDAs by adding a wireless network card. Most PC and laptop manufacturers incorporate these cards into their products.

The Institute of Electrical and Electronics Engineers (IEEE) has established a set of standards for wireless computer networks. The IEEE standard for Wi-Fi is the 802.11 family.

Wi-Fi 4 (802.11n) was deployed in 2009 and Wi-Fi 5 (802.11ac) in 2013. Deployed in 2019, Wi-Fi 6 (802.11ax) replaces both previous standards. Wi-Fi 6 advantages include faster speeds (eventually up to 10 gigabits per second), lower latency (delay in transmissions), much better battery life, improved security, and support for multi-user environments. As a result of these improvements, Wi-Fi 6 will be beneficial for Internet of Things applications.

Roman Samokhin/Shutterstock.com

FIGURE 8.4   **Wireless access point.**

The major benefits of Wi-Fi are its low cost and its ability to provide simple Internet access. It is the greatest facilitator of wireless Internet—that is, the ability to connect to the Internet wirelessly.

Corporations are integrating Wi-Fi into their strategies. For example, Starbucks, McDonald's, Panera, and Barnes & Noble offer customers Wi-Fi in many of their stores, primarily for Internet access. To illustrate the value of Wi-Fi, consider Bluetown's construction of Wi-Fi towers in remote areas of the world, as shown in IT's About Business 8.3.

IT's About Business 8.3

MIS Connecting Africans with Wi-Fi

The International Telecommunication Union (ITU; **www.itu.int**) is a United Nations agency that is responsible for issues that concern information and communication technologies. At the end of 2019, the ITU estimated that 54 percent of the global population had Internet access. Africa lagged behind other continents, except for Antarctica.

However, Africa has seen rapid growth in the percentage of its people who are online, from 2 percent in 2005 to almost 40 percent in the first quarter of 2020. In an attempt to connect the remainder of its population, the African Union (**www.au.int**), along with the World Bank, launched Moonshot Africa, an initiative to double broadband access on the continent by 2021 and make it universal by 2030. The African Union is a continental body consisting of the 55 member nations.

Connecting Africans via broadband access is a huge challenge. Africans who are offline are typically impoverished and tend to live in rural areas that lack any communications infrastructure. Telecommunications companies do not invest in these areas because capital expenditures are high and population density is low, a combination that seriously limits potential revenue.

However, the Danish company Bluetown (**www.bluetown. com**) has devised an innovative strategy to reach this underserved market. Company engineers construct Wi-Fi towers with microwave antennas, powered by solar panels. The company then connects these systems to the closest fiber-optic cables. Since 2014 Bluetown has brought nearly 1,000 villages in Tanzania, Ghana, Rwanda, and Mozambique online.

The installations cost one-tenth as much as a standard 3G base station, and they operate on free, unlicensed communications bands such as television white space. *Television white space* refers to unused TV channels situated between active channels. The company does not earn a great deal of profit from selling data, so it increases revenue by selling content distribution services to local organizations via a local cloud computing infrastructure. Specifically, it provides articles and videos about agriculture, education, and health care, all of which are free to users. These topics are critical to rural villagers.

Agriculture. In Africa, where agriculture employs approximately 65 percent of the labor force, people can benefit greatly from online connectivity. For example, Internet access can help educate farmers regarding better agricultural practices, enable transparency into market prices for crops, and expand access to financial services such as credit. In some areas, farmers' income has increased by 40 percent.

Education. The Internet offers opportunities for people who otherwise cannot afford or access quality classroom-based learning. Internet access opens up the world of online, distance education for underserved areas and for people who are challenged by geographical circumstances. Significantly, women who historically have been unable to access educational opportunities may now be able to do so.

Health care. Internet access opens up opportunities for services such as remote diagnosis and prevention education. In addition, it can provide e-learning and remote training to address the serious shortage of health workers in Africa.

The village of Sagara B is located in the Dodoma region of central Tanzania. Its population is less than 5,000, and it had never had an Internet connection until 2015. The system created a half-mile-wide Wi-Fi hot spot with download speeds up to 10 megabits per second (Mbps), fast enough to stream Netflix. Villagers rented smartphones from Bluetown and paid 50 cents per gigabyte for the data they used. This fee, just over 1 percent of average monthly income, was highly affordable.

The villagers' lives changed substantially. Approximately 250 villagers rented smartphones from Bluetown, including a tailor who used WhatsApp to communicate with clients, saving him multiple trips to the nearest city, and a teacher who depended on YouTube to check his English pronunciation. The system does have its critics, however. One woman complained that her husband spent too much time on Facebook and her daughters did not help as much with the housework anymore.

Unfortunately, Bluetown could not build its systems in other areas of Tanzania due to a difficult regulatory environment. Early in 2019, the company handed over its operations at nine sites to Mobiwire Tanzania. Bluetown then began to focus on India, where, by early 2020, it had connected more than 750 villages, and on Ghana, where it partnered with Microsoft to bring Internet access to 800,000 rural, underserved villagers.

Sources: Compiled from A. Bisoee, "Free Wi-Fi Rolls at 7 Spots in Jamshedpur," *The Telegraph*, May 2, 2020; H. Ghanem, "Shooting for the Moon: An Agenda to Bridge Africa's Digital Divide," *The Brookings Institution*, February 7, 2020; "Research Consensus: High Speed Internet Empowers Rural Renaissance," *Sparklight Business*, 2020; L. Mallonee, "A Remote Tanzanian Village Logs onto the Internet," *Wired*, December 8, 2019; "New ITU Data Reveal Growing Internet Uptake but a Widening Digital Gender Divide," *ITU Press Release*, November 5, 2019; "All Africa Digital Economy Moonshot," *The World Bank*, April 12, 2019; "Bluetown Announces Partnership with Microsoft to Close the Digital Divide," *Business Wire*, January 9, 2019; S. Crawford, "Microsoft Is Hustling Us with 'White Spaces'," *Wired*, July 26, 2017; F. Nyalandu, R. Rabana, and L. Uppink, "5 Ways Universal Internet Access Could Transform Africa," *World Economic Forum*, May 6, 2016; **www.bluetown.com**, accessed August 19, 2020.

Questions

1. Discuss the numerous benefits that Internet access provides to underserved people around the world.

2. Why would a government hinder Bluetown's efforts to provide affordable Internet access to its rural citizens?

Wi-Fi Direct.   Until late 2010, Wi-Fi could operate only if the hotspot contained a wireless antenna. Because of this limitation, organizations have typically used Wi-Fi for communications of up to about 800 feet. For shorter, peer-to-peer connections, they have used Bluetooth.

This situation changed following the introduction of a new iteration of Wi-Fi known as Wi-Fi Direct. *Wi-Fi Direct* enables peer-to-peer communications so devices can connect directly. It enables users to transfer content among devices without having to rely on a wireless antenna. Devices with Wi-Fi Direct can broadcast their availability to other devices just as Bluetooth can. Finally, Wi-Fi Direct is compatible with the more than 1 billion Wi-Fi devices currently in use.

Wi-Fi Direct will probably challenge the dominance of Bluetooth in the area of device-to-device networking. It offers a similar type of connectivity but with greater range and much faster data transfer.

MiFi.   *MiFi* is a small, portable wireless device that provides users with a permanent Wi-Fi hotspot wherever they go. Thus, users are always connected to the Internet. The range of the MiFi device is about 10 meters (roughly 30 feet). Developed by Novatel, the MiFi device is also called an *intelligent mobile hotspot*. Accessing Wi-Fi through the MiFi device allows up to five persons to be connected at the same time, sharing the same connection. MiFi also allows users to use Voice-over-Internet-Protocol technology (discussed in Chapter 6) to make free (or inexpensive) calls, both locally and internationally.

MiFi provides broadband Internet connectivity at any location that offers 3G cellular network coverage. One drawback is that MiFi is expensive both to acquire and to use.

Li-Fi.   *Light Fidelity* (Li-Fi) is a technology for wireless communication among devices using light to transmit data and position. Li-Fi is a visible communications system that can transmit data at high speeds over the visible light spectrum, ultraviolet, and infrared radiation.

In terms of users, Li-Fi is similar to Wi-Fi. The key difference is that Wi-Fi uses electromagnetic waves at radio frequencies to transmit data. Using light to transmit data allows Li-Fi to offer several advantages over Wi-Fi:

- Li-Fi provides far greater bandwidth capacity.
- Li-Fi provides very high peak data transmission rates (theoretically up to 200 Gbps).
- Li-Fi enables communications among 100 times more devices on the Internet of Things.
- Li-Fi provides enhanced security for wireless communications due to reduced interception of signals.
- Li-Fi is more effective in areas susceptible to electromagnetic interference, such as aircraft cabins and hospitals.

Super Wi-Fi.   The term *Super Wi-Fi* was coined by the U.S. Federal Communications Commission (FCC) to describe a wireless network proposal that creates long-distance wireless Internet connections. (Despite the name, Super Wi-Fi is *not* based on Wi-Fi technology.) Super Wi-Fi uses the lower-frequency "white spaces" between broadcast TV channels. These frequencies enable the signal to travel farther and penetrate walls better than normal Wi-Fi frequencies. Super Wi-Fi is already in use in Houston, Texas; Wilmington, North Carolina; and the University of West Virginia. The technology could eventually bring broadband wireless Internet access to rural areas.

Wide-Area Wireless Networks

Wide-area wireless networks connect users to the Internet over a geographically dispersed territory. These networks typically operate over the licensed spectrum—that is, they use portions of the wireless spectrum that are regulated by the government. In contrast, Bluetooth, Wi-Fi, and Super Wi-Fi operate over the unlicensed spectrum and are therefore more prone to interference and security problems. In general, wide-area wireless network technologies fall into two categories: cellular radio and wireless broadband.

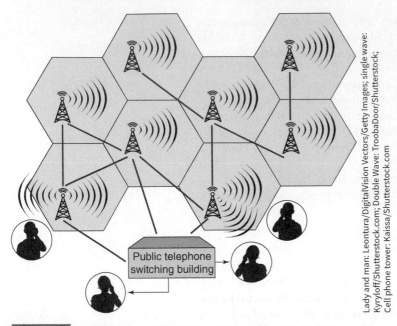

Lady and man: Leontura/DigitalVision Vectors/Getty Images; single wave: Kyryloff/Shutterstock.com; Double Wave: TroobaDoor/Shutterstock; Cell phone tower: Kaissa/Shutterstock.com

FIGURE 8.5   **A cellular network and the public switched telephone system.**

Sources: Image Source; © Engine **Images-Fotolia.com**; © AP/Wide World Photos

Cellular Radio.   **Cellular telephones (cell phones)** provide two-way radio communications over a cellular network of base stations with seamless handoffs. Cellular telephones differ from cordless telephones, which offer telephone service only within a limited range through a single base station attached to a fixed landline—for example, within a home or an office.

The cell phone communicates with radio antennas, or towers, placed within adjacent geographic areas called *cells* (see **Figure 8.5**). A telephone message is transmitted to the local cell—that is, the antenna—by the cell phone and is then passed from cell to cell until it reaches the cell of its destination. At this final cell, the message either is transmitted to the receiving cell phone or it is transferred to the public switched telephone system to be transmitted to a wireline telephone. This is why you can use a cell phone to call other cell phones as well as standard wireline phones.

Cellular technology is quickly evolving, moving toward higher transmission speeds, richer features, and lower latencies (delays). This rapid evolution is necessary because more people are using mobile phones and tablets and data traffic is exploding. Cellular technology has progressed through a number of stages:

- *First generation* (*1G*) cellular networks, introduced in 1982, used analog signals and had low bandwidth (capacity).
- *Second generation* (*2G*) networks, introduced in 1992, used digital signals primarily for voice communication and provided data communication up to 10 kilobits per second (Kbps).
- *2.5G* used digital signals and provided voice and data communication up to 144 Kbps.
- *Third generation* (*3G*) networks, introduced in 2001, used digital signals and could transmit voice and data up to 384 Kbps when the device was moving at a walking pace, 128 Kbps when it was moving in a car, and up to 2 Mbps when it was in a fixed location. 3G supported video, Web browsing, and instant messaging.
- *Fourth generation* (*4G*) networks, introduced in 2012, are not one defined technology or standard. The International Telecommunications Union (ITU) has specified speed requirements for 4G: 100 Mbps (million bits per second) for high-mobility communications such as cars and trains and 1 Gbps (billion bits per second) for low-mobility communications such as pedestrians. 4G systems provide a secure mobile broadband system to all types of mobile devices. See IT's Personal for more information.

  Long-term evolution (*LTE*) is a wireless broadband technology designed to support roaming Internet access through smartphones and handheld devices. LTE is approximately 10 times faster than 3G networks.

  XLTE (advanced LTE) is designed to handle network congestion when too many people in one area try to access an LTE network. XLTE is designed to provide access for all users with no decrease in bandwidth.

- *Fifth generation* (*5G*) is the latest cellular standard. After an early experiment at the 2018 Winter Olympics, 5G began more widespread deployment in 2019. We discuss 5G in detail in the next section.

Fifth-generation (5G) cellular networks.   By October 2020, some 14,000 cities in 99 countries had commercial 5G networks deployed, according to a market survey by mobile phone performance testing firm Ookla (**www.ookla.com**). The survey defined a deployment as when a provider had some level of 5G presence in a city. Countries with the most 5G deployments included the United States, Germany, Austria, the Netherlands, and

Switzerland. Interestingly, as of January 2021, PwC reported that U.S. mobile operators had collectively covered 75 percent of the country.

Research firm Gartner reported sales of 221 million 5G mobile phones in 2020, increasing to 489 million in 2021. By the end of 2021, Gartner estimates that 5G phones will represent 14 percent of the total number of the 3.8 billion smartphones in the world.

There are two types of 5G: millimeter wave and standard. AT&T and Verizon say that their 5G networks will consist mostly of standard 5G with small amounts of millimeter wave.

With *millimeter wave*, carriers can transmit data at very high speeds with extremely low latency. You could download an entire movie in a few seconds. The problem is that these signals travel shorter distances and have trouble penetrating obstacles such as walls. As a result, Verizon and AT&T are focusing on deployments of millimeter wave in large spaces such as sports stadiums and outdoor amphitheaters.

With *standard 5G*, speeds are only slightly faster than current 4G networks. The main benefit of standard 5G will be a reduction in latency. 5G technology has some interesting applications. We look at two of them here.

HRM *Augmented reality (AR) and virtual reality (VR)*. Companies have long trained new staff members in person with hard-copy materials and videos. With many firms experiencing high worker turnover rates, the high investment in training can lead to a loss in productivity over time as workers cycle through.

5G enables new ways to train employees with AR and VR. AR and VR can show step-by-step training procedures in real time. Trainees perform actions and can see with no delay if they need to change what they are doing. Companies will have shorter initial training times, increased procedural accuracy, more efficient switching between jobs, increased customization, reduced accidents, and increased performance monitoring.

Sports. In September 2019, the DFL Deutsche Fußball Liga (German Football (Soccer) League) and Vodafone activated the 5G infrastructure in the Volkswagen Arena for the home match of VfL Wolfsburg versus TSG 1899 Hoffenheim. With a 5G app, spectators at the stadium received, among other things, match statistics and data on individual players directly on their smartphones. For example, fans could see how quickly a player runs up to the rival team's goal and how successful his previous shots on goal were.

5G supports communication among objects as well as among people. In fact, the key advantage of 5G is that it enables machine-to-machine communications. That is, 5G is a necessary component of the Internet of Things (IoT). We discuss the IoT in Section 8.4. Keep in mind that all IoT applications will use, and be enhanced by, 5G technologies.

Wireless Broadband, or WiMAX.   Worldwide Interoperability for Microwave Access, popularly known as WiMAX, is the name for IEEE Standard 802.16. WiMAX has a wireless access range of up to 31 miles, compared to 300 feet for Wi-Fi. WiMAX also has a data transfer rate of up to 75 Mbps. It is a secure system, and it offers features such as voice and video. WiMAX antennas can transmit broadband Internet connections to antennas on homes and businesses located miles away. For this reason, WiMAX can provide long-distance broadband wireless access to rural areas and other locations that are not currently being served.

Consider this example of the use of WiMAX. On April 1, 2015, a fire broke out in the underground electrical cable ducts in a tunnel under a major highway in London. The fire burned for 36 hours and caused major disruptions to broadband service in the area. With fiber optic, broadband access to the Internet not available, businesses turned to WiMAX from the telecommunications company Luminet (**http://luminet.co.uk**). One business owner noted that Luminet helped his company get its main office back online in less than 24 hours. Furthermore, Luminet's broadband service helped the company quickly move its staff back from its disaster recovery site.

It's Personal: Wireless and Mobile

What the GSM3GHSDPA+4GLTE?   This chapter explains the many mobile platforms that are available to you as a consumer. Specifically, it discusses cellular, Bluetooth,

Wi-Fi, satellite, and other wireless options. Within the cellular area, however, things get confusing because telecommunications companies use so many acronyms. Have you ever wondered if Verizon 3G was equivalent to AT&T 3G? What about 4G and 4G LTE? Of course, most people assume that 4G is faster than 3G, but by how much?

To appreciate this confusion, consider that when Apple released one update to its mobile operating system (iOS), AT&T suddenly began to display 4G rather than 3G on the iPhone—despite the fact that the phone had not been upgraded! Pretty nice, right? Wrong. In this instance, the "upgrade" simply consisted of a new terminology for the existing technology. The speed of the 3G/4G network had *not* changed. (Note: AT&T "4G LTE" is a different technology that does offer significantly higher speeds than AT&T 3G or 4G.)

Actual connection speeds are described in bit rates, meaning how many bits (1s or 0s) a device can transmit in 1 second. For example, a speed listed as 1.5 Mbps translates to 1.5 million bits per second. That sounds like a tremendous rate. Knowing the bits per second, however, is only part of understanding the actual speed. In reality, connection speed is not the same as *throughput*, which is the amount of bandwidth actually available for you to use. Throughput will always be less than the connection speed.

To understand this point, consider how your car operates. It is probably capable of driving more than 100 mph. However, you are "throttled down" by various speed limits, so you never reach this potential speed. Your actual speed varies, depending on the route you take, the speed limits imposed along that route, the weather, the amount of traffic, and many other factors. In the same way, even though AT&T, Verizon, Sprint, and other companies boast incredible wireless speeds ("Up to 20 Mbps!"), they will always say "up to" because they know that you will never actually download a file at that rate.

The best method for determining the actual speeds of the various networks is to go to your local wireless store and run a speed test using the demo model they have on display. This test will give you firsthand experience of the actual throughput speed you can expect from their network. The result is much more realistic than terms such as 3G, 4G, and 4G LTE.

Here is how to perform the test. First, make certain the unit is connected only to a cellular network (not Wi-Fi). Then go to **http://speedtest.net**, and click "Begin Test." I ran this test from my iPhone 4S on AT&T's 4G (not 4G LTE) network. My download speed was 3.80 Mbps, and my upload speed was 1.71 Mbps. These numbers are more informative than any name they are given (3G, 4G, etc.) because they indicate exactly what I can expect from my wireless connection. Run this test at competing stores (AT&T, Verizon, Sprint, T-Mobile, etc.), and you will have real data to compare. As names change, you can always run a test to find the facts.

Before you go on...

1. What is Bluetooth? What is a WLAN?
2. Describe Wi-Fi, cellular service, and WiMAX.

8.3 Mobile Computing and Mobile Commerce

Author Lecture Videos are available exclusively in *WileyPLUS*.
Apply the Concept activities are available in the Appendix and in *WileyPLUS*.

In the traditional computing environment, users come to a computer, which is connected with wires to other computers and to networks. Because these networks need to be linked by wires, it is difficult or even impossible for people on the move to use them. In particular, salespeople, repair people, service employees, law enforcement agents, and utility workers can be more effective if they can use IT while in the field or in transit. Mobile computing was designed for workers who travel outside the boundaries of their organizations as well as for anyone traveling outside his or her home.

Mobile computing refers to a real-time connection between a mobile device and other computing environments, such as the Internet or an intranet. This innovation is revolutionizing how people use computers. It is spreading at work and at home; in education, health care, and entertainment; and in many other areas.

Mobile computing has two major characteristics that differentiate it from other forms of computing: mobility and broad reach. *Mobility* means that users carry a device with them and can initiate a real-time contact with other systems from wherever they happen to be. *Broad reach* refers to the fact that when users carry an open mobile device, they can be reached instantly, even across great distances.

Mobility and broad reach create five value-added attributes that break the barriers of geography and time: ubiquity, convenience, instant connectivity, personalization, and localization of products and services. A mobile device can provide information and communication regardless of the user's location (*ubiquity*). With an Internet-enabled mobile device, users can access the Web, intranets, and other mobile devices quickly and easily, without booting up a PC or placing a call through a modem (*convenience* and *instant connectivity*). A company can customize information and send it to individual consumers as a short message service (SMS) (*customization*). Further, knowing a user's physical location helps a company advertise its products and services (*localization*). Mobile computing provides the foundation for mobile commerce (m-commerce), to which we now turn.

Mobile Commerce

Besides affecting our everyday lives, mobile computing is also transforming the ways organizations conduct business by enabling businesses and individuals to engage in mobile commerce. As you saw at the beginning of this chapter, **mobile commerce** (or *m-commerce*) refers to electronic commerce (EC) transactions that are conducted in a wireless environment, especially on the Internet. Like regular EC applications, m-commerce can be transacted on the Internet, private communication lines, smart cards, and other infrastructures. M-commerce creates opportunities for businesses to deliver new services to existing customers and to attract new customers. The development of m-commerce is driven by the widespread availability of mobile devices, the declining prices of such devices, and rapidly improving wireless bandwidth.

Mobile computing and m-commerce include many applications, which result from the capabilities of various technologies. You will examine these applications and their impact on business activities in the next section.

Mobile Commerce Applications

Mobile commerce applications are many and varied. The most popular applications include location-based applications, financial services, intrabusiness applications, accessing information, and telemetry. The rest of this section examines these various applications and their effects on the ways people live and do business.

FIN **Financial Services.**   Mobile financial applications include banking, wireless payments and micropayments, money transfers, mobile wallets, and bill payment services. The bottom line for mobile financial applications is to make it more convenient for customers to transact business regardless of where they are or what time it is.

Web shoppers have historically preferred to pay with credit cards. Because credit card companies typically charge fees on transactions, however, credit cards are an inefficient way to make very small purchases. The growth of relatively inexpensive digital content, such as music (e.g., iTunes), ringtones, and downloadable games, is driving the growth of *micropayments*—that is, very small purchase amounts, usually less than $10—as merchants seek to avoid paying credit card fees on small transactions.

A **mobile wallet**, also called a *digital wallet*, is an app that people use to make financial transactions. These apps can be downloaded on users' desktops or on their smartphones.

When the app is on a smartphone, it becomes a mobile wallet. Mobile wallets replace the need to carry physical credit and debit cards, gift cards, and loyalty cards, as well as boarding passes and other forms of identification. Mobile wallets may also store insurance and loyalty cards, drivers' licenses, ID cards, website passwords, and login information. Furthermore, mobile wallets eliminate having to enter shipping, billing, and credit card data each time a user makes a purchase at a website. The data are encrypted in the user's phone, tablet, or computer, and the wallet contains a digital certificate that identifies the authorized cardholder.

FIN   To use a mobile wallet, consumers wave their phones a few inches above a payment terminal instead of swiping a plastic card. This process uses near-field communication. There are a number of mobile wallets and payment apps from which to choose.

- *Google Wallet* is a mobile wallet that uses near-field communications to allow its users to store debit cards, credit cards, loyalty cards, and gift cards on their smartphones. With Google Wallet, users launch an app and then type in a PIN so Google can access their stored card credentials. Google Wallet also provides a peer-to-peer payment system that can send money to a real, physical Google Wallet card.

- *Google Pay* (a different app from Google Wallet) allows users to tap and pay in stores and use and redeem loyalty cards, gift cards, and offers in stores.

- *Starbucks mobile pay app* launched before the other three top payments apps—Apple Pay, Google Pay, and Samsung Pay. The app lets users pay with their phones and earn credits toward future purchases. The Starbucks app is available on both iOS and Android, whereas Apple Pay, Google Pay, and Samsung Pay users are restricted by the type of phone they have.

- *Samsung Pay* is a mobile payment app and digital wallet that lets users make payments using compatible phones. The service supports contactless payments using near-field communications and also supports magnetic stripe–only payment terminals. In countries like India, the service supports bill payments.

- *MasterCard's Contactless*, *American Express's ExpressPay*, and *Visa's PayWave* are EMV-compatible, contactless payment features. EMV—which stands for Europay, MasterCard, and Visa, the three companies that originally created the standard—is a technical standard for smart payment cards. EMV cards are smart cards that store their data on chips rather than on magnetic stripes. They can be either contact cards that must be physically inserted into a reader or contactless cards that can be read over a short distance using radio-frequency identification (RFID) technology. (We discuss RFID in Section 8.4.) EMV cards are also called chip-and-pin cards.

- *Apple Pay* is a mobile wallet that uses near-field communications to enable users to make payments using various Apple devices. Apple Pay does not require Apple-specific contactless payment terminals; rather, it will work with Visa's PayWave, Mastercard's PayPass, and American Express's ExpressPay terminals. The wallet is similar to other wallets with the addition of two-factor authentication. Users hold their authenticated Apple device to the point-of-sale system. iPhone users authenticate by holding their fingerprint to the phone's Touch ID sensor, and Apple Watch users authenticate by double-clicking a button on the device.

- *Amazon Pay* is a service that lets customer use the payment methods already associated with their Amazon accounts to make payment for goods and services on third-party websites. Amazon Pay Places allows users to order ahead and pay for goods in-store via the Amazon app.

- *Alipay Wallet* (**https://intl.alipay.com**) is a mobile and online payment platform from the Ant Financial Services Group, an affiliate company of the Chinese Alibaba Group (**www .alibabagroup.com**). Alipay provides numerous payment services. The platform operates with Visa and MasterCard to provide payment services for Taobao (a Chinese online shopping website) and Tmall (a Chinese-language website for B2C online retail spun off from Taobao), as well as almost 500,000 online and local Chinese businesses.

  Users can employ the app to pay for local in-store purchases, credit card bills, bank account management, person-to-person money transfers, train tickets, food orders, ride hailing, taxi fees, water and electricity utility bills, cable television fees, tuition fees, and traffic fines.

- *WeChat* (**https://web.wechat.com**) is a Chinese messaging, social media, and mobile payment app developed by Tencent (**www.tencent.com**). WeChat Pay is a digital wallet service incorporated into WeChat. Users who have provided bank account information can use the app to pay bills, order goods and services, transfer money to other users, and pay in stores.

- *Huawei Pay*: Huawei (**www.huawei.com**), the Chinese mobile phone manufacturer, partnered with UnionPay, China's state-operated card network, to launch the Huawei Pay mobile wallet in September 2016. The wallet uses NFC and biometrics to make in-store payment through Huawei phones.

- *Peru Digital Payments*, a company owned and operated by that country's leading financial institutions, launched Bim in 2016. Bim is a mobile payment program that consolidates all of their online customer interfaces in a single system. The software is the first of its kind. Although there are 255 mobile money programs in 89 countries, no other program includes all of a country's banks. Furthermore, all three major Peruvian wireless carriers will offer users access to Bim.

The stakes in this competition are enormous because the small fees generated every time consumers swipe their cards add up to tens of billions of dollars annually in the United States alone. The potential for large revenue streams is real because mobile wallets have clear advantages. For example: Which are you more likely to have with you at any given moment—your phone or your physical wallet? Also, keep in mind that if you lose your phone, it can be located on a map and remotely deactivated. Plus, your phone can be password protected. Your physical wallet, however, cannot perform these functions.

Location-Based Applications and Services.   M-commerce B2C applications include location-based services and location-based applications. Location-based mobile commerce is called **location-based commerce** (or L-commerce).

Location-based services provide information that is specific to a given location. For example, a mobile user can (1) request the nearest business or service, such as an ATM or a restaurant; (2) receive alerts, such as a warning of a traffic jam or an accident; and (3) locate a friend. Wireless carriers can provide location-based services such as locating taxis, service personnel, doctors, and rental equipment; scheduling fleets; tracking objects such as packages and train boxcars; finding information such as navigation, weather, traffic, and room schedules; targeting advertising; and automating airport check-ins.

MKT Consider, for example, how location-based advertising can make the marketing process more productive. Marketers can use this technology to integrate the current locations and preferences of mobile users. They can then send user-specific advertising messages concerning nearby shops, malls, and restaurants to consumers' wireless devices.

MKT Mobile Advertising.   *Mobile advertising* is a form of advertising through cell phones, smartphones, or other mobile devices. Analysts estimate that mobile advertising revenue will reach approximately $7 billion by 2020.

Intrabusiness Applications.   Although business-to-consumer (B2C) m-commerce receives considerable publicity, most of today's m-commerce applications actually are used *within* organizations. In this section you will see how companies use mobile computing to support their employees.

POM Mobile devices are increasingly becoming an integral part of workflow applications. For example, companies can use non-voice mobile services to assist in dispatch functions—that is, to assign jobs to mobile employees, along with detailed information about the job. Target areas for mobile delivery and dispatch services include transportation (delivery of food, oil, newspapers, cargo; courier services; tow trucks; taxis), utilities (gas, electricity, phone, water); field service (computers, office equipment, home repair); health care (visiting nurses, doctors, social services); and security (patrols, alarm installation).

Accessing Information.   Another vital function of mobile technology is helping users obtain and use information. Two types of technologies—mobile portals and voice portals—are designed to aggregate and deliver content in a form that will work within the limited space available on mobile devices.

A **mobile portal** aggregates and provides content and services for mobile users. These services include news, sports, and e-mail; entertainment, travel, and restaurant information; community services; and stock trading. Major players around the world are i-mode from NTT DoCoMo, Vodafone, O2, T-Mobile, Yahoo!, AOL, and MSN.

A **voice portal** is a website with an audio interface. Voice portals are not websites in the normal sense because they can also be accessed through a standard phone or a cell phone. A phone number connects you to a website on which you can request information verbally. The system finds the information, translates it into a computer-generated voice reply, and tells you what you want to know. Most airlines use voice portals to provide real-time information on flight status.

Another example of a voice portal is the voice-activated 511 travel-information line developed by **Tellme.com**. This technology helps callers inquire about weather, local restaurants, current traffic, and other valuable information.

POM **Telemetry Applications.**   **Telemetry** refers to the wireless transmission and receipt of data gathered from remote sensors. Telemetry has numerous mobile computing applications. For example, technicians can use telemetry to identify maintenance problems in equipment, and doctors can monitor patients and control medical equipment from a distance. Car manufacturers use telemetry applications for remote vehicle diagnosis and preventive maintenance. For example, drivers of many General Motors cars use its OnStar system (**www.onstar.com**) in numerous ways.

An interesting telemetry application for individuals is an iPhone app called Find My iPhone. Find My iPhone is a part of the Apple iCloud (**www.apple.com/icloud**). This app provides several very helpful telemetry functions. If you lose your iPhone, for example, it offers two ways to find its approximate location on a map. First, you can sign in to the Apple iCloud from any computer. Second, you can use the Find My iPhone app on another iPhone, iPad, or iPod Touch.

If you remember where you left your iPhone, you can write a message and display it on your iPhone's screen. The message might say, "Left my iPhone. Please call me at 301-555-1211." Your message appears on your iPhone, even if the screen is locked. And if the map indicates that your iPhone is nearby—perhaps in your office under a pile of papers—you can tell Find My iPhone to play a sound that overrides the volume or silent setting.

If you left your iPhone in a public place, you may want to protect its contents. You can remotely set a four-digit passcode lock to prevent people from using your iPhone, accessing your personal information, or tampering with your settings. Going further, you can initiate a remote wipe (erase all contents) to restore your iPhone to its factory settings. If you eventually find your phone, then you can connect it to your computer and use iTunes to restore the data from your most recent backup.

If you have lost your iPhone and you do not have access to a computer, you can download the Find My iPhone app to a friend's iPhone, iPad, or iPod Touch and then sign in to access all the Find My iPhone features.

Before you go on...

1. What are the major drivers of mobile computing?
2. Describe mobile portals and voice portals.
3. Describe wireless financial services.
4. Discuss some of the major intrabusiness wireless applications.

8.4 The Internet of Things

The **Internet of Things (IoT)** refers to the billions of animate (living) and inanimate objects that are equipped with embedded sensors and connected wirelessly to the Internet. Each object has a unique identity (i.e., its own IP address) and is able to send and receive data over the Internet without human interaction. Because the IoT generates huge amounts of data, it is a significant driver of analytics (see Chapter 12) and machine learning systems (see Chapter 14).

There are two types of IoT: consumer IoT and industrial IoT. *Consumer IoT* devices range from smartwatches, smartphones, wearable devices, smart home speakers, lightbulbs, electrical outlets, thermostats, door locks, doorbells, appliances, and other smart home products. For consumers, the smart home is where they most likely come into contact with the consumer IoT.

The *Industrial Internet of Things (IIoT)*, also called the fourth industrial revolution, Industry 4.0, or machine-to-machine (M2M), all refer to the use of IoT technology in a business setting. The basic concept for the IIoT is to use a combination of sensors, wireless networks, Big Data, AI, and analytics to measure and optimize industrial processes. The IIoT refers to the billions of industrial devices—anything from machines in a factory to the engines on an airplane—that are equipped with sensors, connected to wireless networks, and gather and share data.

Security and privacy are two of the biggest problems with the IoT. Privacy is critically important because sensors are collecting our extremely sensitive data—for example, what you say in your own home or your personal medical data.

The IoT's security track record has been extremely poor. Many IoT devices are small and inexpensive and do not contain the necessary built-in security features to counter threats. Even worse, the majority of IoT transmissions are not encrypted. Therefore, these devices are permanently at risk.

Hackers are now targeting IoT devices because their inherent lack of security makes them easy to compromise and become part of botnets. In 2016, attackers used the Mirai worm to compromise hundreds of thousands of IoT devices to form a massive botnet. They then used their botnet to conduct distributed denial-of-service attacks to take down major websites.

Connecting industrial machinery into IIoT networks increases the risk of hackers attacking these devices. Industrial espionage or a destructive SCADA attack (see Chapter 4) are potential risks.

Three technologies have been essential factors in the rapid deployment of the IoT: IPv6 (discussed in Chapter 6), which created a vast number of IP addresses; 5G technologies, which provide a vastly improved communications infrastructure for the IoT; and wireless sensors.

A **wireless sensor** is an autonomous device that monitors its own condition as well as physical and environmental conditions around it, such as temperature, sound, pressure, vibration, and movement. Sensors can also control physical systems, such as opening and closing a valve and adjusting the fuel mixture in your car (see SCADA systems in Chapter 4).

Wireless sensors contain processing, storage, and radio-frequency antennae for sending and receiving messages. Each sensor "wakes up" or activates for a fraction of a second when it has data to transmit. It then relays those data to its nearest neighbor. So, rather than every sensor transmitting its data to a remote computer, the data travel from sensor to sensor until they reach a central computer, where they are stored and analyzed. An advantage of this process is that if one sensor fails, then another one can pick up the data. This process is efficient and reliable, and it extends the battery life of the sensor.

Radio-frequency identification tags are one type of wireless sensor. **Radio-frequency identification (RFID)** technology allows manufacturers to attach tags containing antennae and computer chips on products. The tags contain enough data to uniquely identify each item. As RFID tags are decreasing in size and cost, they are replacing bar codes and QR codes.

Bar codes are cheap but do not provide as much data as an RFID chip. Quick response (QR) codes were also developed to replace bar codes. A *QR code* is a two-dimensional code, readable by dedicated QR readers and camera phones. QR codes store much more information

Author Lecture Videos are available exclusively in *WileyPLUS*.
Apply the Concept activities are available in the Appendix and in *WileyPLUS*.

QR code

iStock.com/Oehoeboeroe

RFID tag

iStock.com/ra-photos

Barcode

Stoked/Stockbyte/Media Bakery

FIGURE 8.6 **Barcodes, RFID tags, and QR codes.**

Ecken, Dominique/Keystone Pressedienst/Zuma Press

FIGURE 8.7 **Small RFID reader and RFID tag.**

Source: © Ecken, Dominique/Keystone Pressedienst/Zuma Press

than bar codes because they store information horizontally and vertically. **Figure 8.6** illustrates bar codes, QR codes, and an RFID tag. **Figure 8.7** shows a small RFID reader and RFID tag.

There are numerous examples of how the Internet of Things is being deployed. We discuss just a few of them here.

The smart home. In a *smart home*, your home computer, television, lighting and heating controls, smart speakers, home security systems (including smart window and door locks), thermostats, and appliances have embedded sensors and can communicate with one another through a home network. You control these networked objects through your smartphone, television, home computer, and even your automobile. Appropriate service providers and homeowners can access the devices for which they are authorized. Smart home technology can be applied to any building, turning it into a smart building.

POM *Smart stores.* A smart store is a brick-and-mortar retail establishment that has deployed smart shelves and smart products. Smart shelves contain embedded weight sensors that automatically keep track of inventory. Smart products have embedded sensors such as RFID tags that uniquely identify each item. Smart stores also use cameras to track shoppers and products. A current example of smart store is Amazon Go, the cashierless checkout grocery store. Some smart stores have deployed smart mirrors, where customers can virtually try on as many pieces of clothing as they want without needing a fitting room.

POM *Smart cities.* A smart city is an urban area that uses a variety of IoT sensors to analyze data collected from citizens, devices (e.g., smart streetlight, traffic signals, environmental monitoring sensors, surveillance cameras), buildings, and other assets. City employees use the insights to manage assets, resources, and services efficiently to improve city operations. Examples of these operations include monitoring and managing traffic and transportation systems, power plants, utilities, water supply networks, waste systems, crime detection and prevention, libraries, hospitals, and other community services.

Automotive. Modern cars have many sensors that monitor functions such as engine operation, tire pressure, fluid levels, and many others. Cars can warn drivers of impending mechanical or other problems and automatically summon roadside assistance or emergency services when necessary. Furthermore, sensors provide advanced driver assistance such as automatic parking, monitoring blind spots, detecting driver drowsiness, forward collision warning, and many other functions.

The next evolution in the automotive space is autonomous vehicles. These vehicles must communicate with one another instantaneously many times per second to avoid collisions and operate correctly. 5G's high-bandwidth transmission speed, low latency, low battery consumption, high reliability, and ability to support huge numbers of connected devices are all critically important characteristics that will help to make autonomous vehicles a viable technology.

POM *Smart factories.* A smart factory is a flexible system that optimizes performance across an interconnected network of automated machines, robots, and humans. It can adapt to, and learn from, new conditions in real or near-real time and autonomously operate entire production processes. A network of IoT sensors monitors equipment and flags potential and current issues. For example, sensors using AI may recognize sounds or note other conditions that signal a problem with equipment. These sensors can reduce human site inspections, improve site inspection productivity as problem areas are predicted, reduce safety risks on the production floor, and increase productivity.

POM *Digital twins.* A digital twin is a virtual (digital) representation of a real-world (physical) product or service. With physical entities, such as engines, modeled in software and analyzing real-time sensor data, engineers can find potential problems before they actually occur as well as perform simulations to optimize performance. See IT's About Business 6.3.

Consider the Siemens Internet of Trains project, which has enabled the manufacturer to move from only selling trains to offering a guarantee that its trains will arrive on time. In this project, Siemens embedded sensors in trains and railroad tracks in select locations in Spain, Russia, and Thailand. The firm then used that data to train machine-learning models (the digital twin) to discover signs that tracks or trains may be having problems. Having detailed insights into which parts of the rail network are most likely to fail and when has allowed repairs to be targeted where they are most needed, a process called predictive maintenance. That process, in turn, has enabled Siemens to start selling what it calls *outcome as a service*, which is a guarantee that trains will arrive on time close to 100 percent of the time.

One of the first companies to integrate IoT sensor data with machine learning models was ThyssenKrupp, which operates 1.1 million elevators worldwide and has been feeding data collected by sensors in its elevators into machine-learning models (the digital twin) for years. These models provide real-time updates on the status of elevators and predict which are likely to fail and when, allowing the company to perform preventive maintenance where it is needed. This process reduces elevator outages and saves money on unnecessary servicing.

POM *Supply chain management.* The IoT can make a company's supply chain much more transparent. A company can now track, in real time, the movement of raw materials and parts through the manufacturing process to finished products delivered to the customer. Sensors in fleet vehicles (e.g., trucks) can monitor the condition of sensitive consignments (e.g., the temperature of perishable food). They can also trigger automatic security alerts if a container is opened unexpectedly.

POM *Energy management.* Sensors can be integrated into all forms of energy-consuming devices, for example, switches, power outlets, lightbulbs, and televisions. They will be able to communicate directly with utility companies through smart meters to balance power generation and energy usage. Another valuable application of sensors is to use them in smart electrical meters, thereby forming a *smart grid*.

POM *Transportation.* Sensors placed on complex transportation machines such as jet engines and locomotives can provide critical information on their operations. Consider General Electric (GE; **www.ge.com**), which embeds "intelligence" in the form of 250 sensors in each of its giant locomotives. The sensors produce 9 million data points every hour. How can these sensors improve the performance of such a huge machine?

One of the biggest problems on locomotives is faulty bearings. If a bearing fails, then an axle might freeze, leaving a train marooned on the tracks. To avoid this type of scenario, GE embeds one sensor inside each locomotive's gear case that transmits data on oil levels and contaminants. By examining these data, GE can predict the conditions that cause bearings to fail and axles to freeze. GE data analysts claim that sensors that predict part failures before they occur translate into billions of dollars of savings for GE's rail customers.

Health care. In a hospital in Gujarat, India, a patient had a tiny balloon inserted into a blood vessel in his heart. He then had a stent placed in the vessel to keep in wide open. While performing these two procedures, the surgeon was 20 miles away. The surgeon used augmented reality, high-definition video, and real-time data readings from medical sensors. The surgeon received precise three-dimensional data from X-rays sent to his augmented reality headset, which he used to control the remote robotic surgical tool. This process is called *telesurgery*.

Many patients reside and receive care outside traditional hospitals and clinics, such as assisted living facilities or their homes. Patients with non-life-threatening conditions can either wear sensors or have them implanted—for example, to monitor blood pressure or glucose levels. These sensors are monitored by medical staff. In many cases, the patients can be shown how to interpret the sensor data themselves. Also, consumer-oriented sensors such as the Fitbit and Apple iWatch can monitor patients' activity levels and overall health.

POM *Agriculture.* Sensors monitor, in real time, air temperature, humidity, soil temperature, soil moisture, leaf wetness, atmospheric pressure, solar radiation, trunk/stem/fruit diameter, wind speed and direction, and rainfall. The data from these sensors are used in precision agriculture. *Precision agriculture* is a farming technique based on observing, measuring, and responding to inter- and intra-field variability in crops. IT's About Business 8.4 illustrates how Fruition Sciences uses the IoT in vineyards.

IT's About Business 8.4

MIS **POM** The Internet of Things in the Vineyard

Today, vineyard workers place handheld scanners about the size of a flashlight up to bunches of grapes. Beams of shortwave light from the devices interact with molecules of *anthocyanins*, water-soluble pigments that give the grapes their color. As the light resonates with these pigments, it indicates a grape's ripeness. The grapes literally glow, and the higher the intensity of the glow, the riper the grapes. This scientific effort, which helps determine the best moment to harvest each bunch of grapes, is already in use at some of the world's finest vineyards, including Château Latour in Bordeaux, France, and Ovid in Napa Valley, California.

This weekly process starts as the fruit begins to ripen, and readings are recorded in a central server. There, machine-learning algorithms compare the readings with historical and theoretical data, answering questions such as: Is a given bunch riper now, meaning that it has higher levels of anthocyanins, or is it past peak, with lower levels? How does this bunch's current readings compare with the bunch's readings from the previous week? To improve a particular vintage, a vintner can use these data to ensure that only the vines currently producing the best grapes—called *grand cru*—are picked and crushed together.

Fruition Sciences (**www.fruitionsciences.com**) makes the scanner. It calls the process of collecting and analyzing data from the grapes 360viti. Fruition measures a broad range of key performance indicators for each vineyard. The company's overall goals are better wine and lower costs, both environmental and economic. To understand how Fruition is attempting to achieve these goals, let's focus on one aspect of viticulture (grape farming): water utilization.

Reducing costs is often related to water, a precious resource and major expense in drought-prone California. Fruition has changed vintners' thinking about when to water a vine. For instance, it is incorrect to simply assume that a wilting, droopy plant is thirsty. The plant could just be adjusting to the lack of moisture in the air. In fact, as the firm's data have demonstrated, watering plants that look this way can cause problems. If winemakers water plants based on their appearance, then these plants could become dependent on irrigation.

By analyzing data from its sensors, Fruition claims that it can reduce water usage per acre by 1.3 million gallons—the equivalent of two Olympic-sized swimming pools—per year. One Napa Valley vineyard using Fruition's service changed from watering every three days to watering only once every three weeks.

The service starts at $10,000 per year, and it does not rely only on the device. The firm's viticulture program features other technologies aimed at improving winemaking, each of which is customized to the vineyard's location. These technologies can include installing sensors in key locations and measuring wind speed, light, or atmospheric changes.

As one example, a winemaker can use a laser scanner in the winter after the leaves have fallen to measure the size and strengths of shoots from each plant. The winemaker can then cross-reference these data with past atmospheric readings to identify the long-term impact of weather changes on growth.

Sources: Compiled from M. Media, "Mechanizing Vineyard Canopy Management," *American Vineyard*, July 21, 2020; "Technology-Driven Vineyard Management Solutions—Process2Wine," *Wine Industry Advisor*, May 17, 2020; K. Prengaman, "Irrigation Insights," *Good Fruit Grower*, April 9, 2020; M. Galante, "How Technology Is Helping Vineyards Crop Up in New Areas," *Dimensional Insight*, March 3, 2020; "The Vintage Report Launches Series Analyzing 2019 Growing Season and Celebrates Its Tenth Year Anniversary," *Wine Industry Advisor*, January 17, 2020; T. Rieger, "The Latest in Vineyard Sensor Technology," *Wine Business*, December 29, 2019; "Wine's Magic Wand," *Bloomberg Businessweek*, September 30, 2019; D. Robinson, "Technology in the Wine Industry: How IoT Is Transforming Vineyards," *NS Agriculture*, September 20, 2019; M. Kettmann, "Top Innovations in the Vineyard," *Wine Enthusiast*, April 1, 2019; "Why the Internet of Things Will Lead to the Internet of Wines," *Future Wine Expo*, February 26, 2019; "Why to Implement IoT in the Vineyard?" *eVineyard*, August, 23, 2018; A. Solana, "Internet of Wines: How This Vineyard's Smart Sensors Improve the Vintage in Your Glass," *ZDNet*, May 2, 2018; **www.fruitionsciences.com**, accessed August 20, 2020.

Questions

1. Describe the advantages that the IoT provides vintners.
2. Describe problems that the IoT might cause vintners.

POM *Animal husbandry.* Dairy cattle are largely "produced" by artificial insemination but only if the procedure occurs when a cow is in estrus. Cows are only in estrus about once every 21 days and estrus lasts only 12 to 18 hours. Unfortunately, estrus usually occurs between 10:00 p.m. PM and 8:00 a.m., when farmers are sleeping. Further, estrus is difficult to predict as it relies on farmers' experience. In fact, farmers only get it right statistically about 55 percent of the time.

Japanese dairy farmers wanted to know how to increase their percentage of successful artificial inseminations and they turned to data scientists at Fujitsu. To gather data, the scientists inserted sensors into the cows' first stomach, which measured the number of steps a cow takes. After data collection, the scientists found that the onset of estrus could be detected because the cows took significantly more steps (measured by the sensor). When the number of steps for a particular cow increased in that manner, estrus began 16 hours later.

Significantly, if artificial insemination took place in the first 2 hours of estrus, there was a much higher probability of producing a female. If the procedure took place later in estrus, there was a higher probability of producing a male. Furthermore, the scientists claimed that, using the number of steps a cow takes, it is possible to detect as many as ten different diseases!

Using this application of the Internet of Things, Japanese farmers were able to significantly increase their herd size and the health of their cows.

Hospitality. The Royal Park Hotel in Detroit, Michigan, has integrated smart hotel technology to improve its guests' experience. The hotel first installed 160 wireless access points, one in each of the 143 guest rooms, and others across the property. The access points in each guest room contain an IoT module with a unique address.

The first application involved smart room locks. After a guest makes a reservation, that guest's phone or smart device can access their room once they arrive during the period of time that the reservation is valid. The connected locks enable management to monitor when doors are open or closed, locked or unlocked. If a guest has a reservation for a room and is also renting a meeting room, the app will provide seamless access to both.

Smart locks provide increased security for guests. If someone attempts to open a door with a device that is not associated with it, the smart lock will notify management through a "wandering intruder" feather. The key on the intruder's app will not work. With mapping capabilities, the IoT system will alert management of the intruder's location so security staff can investigate.

The hotel's IoT system also provides increased security for staff members. Wireless beacons on staff lanyards send alerts when pushed, notifying managers and security staff of the employee's exact location and that a potential situation could be occurring.

The hotel added beacons to carts, trays, and other hotel equipment such as rollaway beds. This process helps manage inventory in storage, hallways, and guest rooms, as well as notify staff when items, such as food carts or trays, should be picked up. A geofencing feature also alerts management when assets leave the property.

The hotel's lighting and HVAC (heating, ventilation, and air conditioning) systems are connected via the IoT. Therefore, each room has a smart thermometer to monitor room temperatures and the room can be "put to sleep" when there are no occupants in it. This process saves energy and lowers the carbon footprint of the hotel.

Before you go on...

1. Define the Internet of Things and RFID.

2. Provide two examples (other than those mentioned in this section) of how the Internet of Things benefits organizations (public sector, private sector, for-profit, or not-for-profit).

3. Provide two specific business uses of RFID technology.

What's in IT for me?

ACCT For the Accounting Major

Wireless applications help accountants count and audit inventory. They also expedite the flow of information for cost control. Price management, inventory control, and other accounting-related activities can be improved with the use of wireless technologies.

FIN For the Finance Major

Wireless services can provide banks and other financial institutions with a competitive advantage. For example, wireless electronic payments, including micropayments, are more convenient (anywhere, anytime) than traditional means of payment, and they are less expensive. Electronic bill payment from mobile devices is becoming more popular, increasing security and accuracy, expediting cycle time, and reducing processing costs.

MKT For the Marketing Major

Imagine a whole new world of marketing, advertising, and selling, with the potential to increase sales dramatically. Such is the promise of mobile computing. Of special interest for marketers are location-based advertising as well as the new opportunities resulting from the Internet of Things and RFID. Finally, wireless technology also provides new opportunities in sales force automation (SFA), enabling faster and better communications with both customers (CRM) and corporate services.

POM For the Production/Operations Management Major

Wireless technologies offer many opportunities to support mobile employees of all kinds. Wearable computers enable offsite employees and repair personnel working in the field to service customers faster, better, and less expensively. Wireless devices can also increase productivity within factories by enhancing communication and collaboration as well as managerial planning and control. Mobile computing technologies can also improve safety by providing quicker warning signs and instant messaging to isolated employees.

HRM For the Human Resource Management Major

Mobile computing can improve HR training and extend it to any place at any time. Payroll notices can be delivered as SMSs. Wireless

devices can also make it even more convenient for employees to select their own benefits and update their personal data.

MIS For the MIS Major

MIS personnel provide the wireless infrastructure that enables all organizational employees to compute and communicate anytime, anywhere. This convenience provides exciting, creative, new applications for organizations to reduce expenses and improve the efficiency and effectiveness of operations (e.g., to achieve transparency in supply chains). Unfortunately, as you read earlier, wireless applications are inherently insecure. This lack of security is a serious problem with which MIS personnel must contend.

Summary

8.1 Identify advantages and disadvantages of each of the three main types of wireless transmission media.

Microwave transmission systems are used for high-volume, long-distance, line-of-sight communication. One advantage is the high volume. A disadvantage is that microwave transmissions are susceptible to environmental interference during severe weather such as heavy rain and snowstorms.

Satellite transmission systems make use of communication satellites, and they receive and transmit data through line-of-sight. One advantage is that the enormous footprint—the area of Earth's surface reached by a satellite's transmission—overcomes the limitations of microwave data relay stations. Like microwaves, satellite transmissions are susceptible to environmental interference during severe weather.

Radio transmission systems use radio-wave frequencies to send data directly between transmitters and receivers. An advantage is that radio waves travel easily through normal office walls. A disadvantage is that radio transmissions are susceptible to snooping by anyone who has similar equipment that operates on the same frequency.

8.2 Explain how businesses can use short-range, medium-range, and long-range wireless networks, respectively.

Short-range wireless networks simplify the task of connecting one device to another, eliminating wires, and enabling people to move around while they use the devices. In general, short-range wireless networks have a range of 100 feet or less. Short-range wireless networks include Bluetooth, ultra-wideband, and near-field communications. A business application of ultra-wideband is the PLUS Real-Time Location System from Time Domain. Using PLUS, an organization can locate multiple people and assets simultaneously.

Medium-range wireless networks include Wi-Fi networks. *Wi-Fi* provides fast and easy Internet or intranet broadband access from public hotspots located at airports, hotels, Internet cafés, universities, conference centers, offices, and homes.

Wide-area wireless networks connect users to the Internet over geographically dispersed territory. They include cellular telephones and wireless broadband. *Cellular telephones* provide two-way radio communications over a cellular network of base stations with seamless handoffs. *Wireless broadband* has a wireless access range of up to 31 miles and a data transfer rate of up to 75 Mbps. WiMAX can provide long-distance broadband wireless access to rural areas and remote business locations.

8.3 Provide a specific example of how each of the five major m-commerce applications can benefit a business.

Location-based services provide information specific to a location. For example, a mobile user can (1) request the nearest business or service, such as an ATM or restaurant, (2) receive alerts, such as a warning of a traffic jam or an accident, and (3) find a friend. With *location-based advertising*, marketers can integrate the current locations and preferences of mobile users. They can then send user-specific advertising messages about nearby shops, malls, and restaurants to wireless devices.

Mobile financial applications include banking, wireless payments and micropayments, money transfers, wireless wallets, and bill payment services. The bottom line for mobile financial applications is to make it more convenient for customers to transact business regardless of where they are or what time it is.

Intrabusiness applications consist of m-commerce applications that are used *within* organizations. Companies can use non-voice mobile services to assist in dispatch functions—that is, to assign jobs to mobile employees, along with detailed information about the job.

When it comes to *accessing information*, mobile portals and voice portals are designed to aggregate and deliver content in a form that will work within the limited space available on mobile devices. These portals provide information anywhere and anytime to users.

Telemetry is the wireless transmission and receipt of data gathered from remote sensors. Company technicians can use telemetry to identify maintenance problems in equipment. Car manufacturers use telemetry applications for remote vehicle diagnosis and preventive maintenance.

8.4 Describe the Internet of Things, along with examples of how various organizations can use the Internet of Things.

The Internet of Things (IoT) is a system in which any object, natural or manmade, has a unique identity (using IPv6) and the ability to send and receive information over a network (i.e., the Internet) without human interaction.

We leave the examples of various uses of the IoT up to the student.

Chapter Glossary

Bluetooth Chip technology that enables short-range connection (data and voice) between wireless devices.

cellular telephones (cell phones) Phones that provide two-way radio communications over a cellular network of base stations with seamless handoffs.

global positioning system (GPS) A wireless system that uses satellites to enable users to determine their position anywhere on Earth.

hotspot A small geographical perimeter within which a wireless access point provides service to a number of users.

Internet of Things (IoT) A scenario in which objects, animals, and people are provided with unique identifiers and the ability to automatically transfer data over a network without requiring human-to-human or human-to-computer interaction.

location-based commerce (L-commerce) Mobile commerce transactions targeted to individuals in specific locations, at specific times.

microwave transmission A wireless system that uses microwaves for high-volume, long-distance, point-to-point communication.

mobile commerce (or m-commerce) Electronic commerce transactions that are conducted with a mobile device.

mobile computing A real-time connection between a mobile device and other computing environments, such as the Internet or an intranet.

mobile portal A portal that aggregates and provides content and services for mobile users.

mobile wallet (m-wallet) A technology that allows users to make purchases with a single click from their mobile devices.

near-field communication (NFC) The smallest of the short-range wireless networks that is designed to be embedded in mobile devices like cell phones and credit cards.

personal area network A computer network used for communication among computer devices close to one person.

propagation delay Any delay in communications from signal transmission time through a physical medium.

radio-frequency identification (RFID) technology A wireless technology that allows manufacturers to attach tags with antennae and computer chips on goods and then track their movement through radio signals.

radio transmission Uses radio-wave frequencies to send data directly between transmitters and receivers.

satellite radio (or digital radio) A wireless system that offers uninterrupted, near CD-quality sound that is beamed to your radio from satellites.

satellite transmission A wireless transmission system that uses satellites for broadcast communications.

telemetry The wireless transmission and receipt of data gathered from remote sensors.

ultra-wideband (UWB) A high-bandwidth wireless technology with transmission speeds in excess of 100 Mbps that can be used for applications such as streaming multimedia from, say, a personal computer to a television.

voice portal A website with an audio interface.

wireless Telecommunications in which electromagnetic waves carry the signal between communicating devices.

wireless access point An antenna connecting a mobile device to a wired local area network.

Wireless Fidelity (Wi-Fi) A set of standards for wireless local area networks based on the IEEE 802.11 standard.

wireless local area network (WLAN) A computer network in a limited geographical area that uses wireless transmission for communication.

wireless sensor An autonomous device that monitors its own condition as well as physical and environmental conditions around it, such as temperature, sound, pressure, vibration, and movement.

Discussion Questions

1. Given that you can lose a cell phone as easily as a wallet, which do you feel is a more secure way of carrying your personal data? Support your answer.

2. If mobile computing is the next wave of technology, would you ever feel comfortable with handing a waiter or waitress your cell phone to make a payment at a restaurant the way you currently hand over your credit or debit card? Why or why not?

3. What happens if you lose your NFC-enabled smartphone or it is stolen? How do you protect your personal information?

4. In your opinion, is the mobile (or digital) wallet a good idea? Why or why not?

5. Discuss how m-commerce can expand the reach of e-business.

6. Discuss how mobile computing can solve some of the problems of the digital divide.

7. Explain the benefits that wireless commerce provides to consumers and the benefits that wireless commerce provides to merchants.

8. Discuss the ways in which Wi-Fi is being used to support mobile computing and m-commerce. Describe the ways in which Wi-Fi is affecting the use of cellular phones for m-commerce.

9. You can use location-based tools to help you find your car or the closest gas station. However, some people see location-based tools as an invasion of privacy. Discuss the pros and cons of location-based tools.

10. Discuss the benefits of telemetry in health care for everyone during the COVID-19 pandemic.

11. Discuss how wireless devices can help people with disabilities.

12. Which of the applications of the Internet of Things do you think are likely to gain the greatest market acceptance over the next few years? Why?

Problem-Solving Activities

1. Investigate commercial applications of voice portals. Visit several vendors, for example, Microsoft and Nuance. What capabilities and applications do these vendors offer?

2. Examine how new data-capture devices such as RFID tags help organizations accurately identify and segment their customers for activities such as targeted marketing. Browse the Web and develop five potential new applications not listed in this chapter for RFID technology. What issues would arise if a country's laws mandated that such devices be embedded in everyone's body as a national identification system?

3. Investigate commercial uses of GPS. Start with **www.neigps.com**. Can some of the consumer-oriented products be used in industry? Prepare a report on your findings.

4. Access **www.bluetooth.com**. Examine the types of products being enhanced with Bluetooth technology. Present two of these products to the class and explain how they are enhanced by Bluetooth technology.

5. Explore **www.nokia.com**. Prepare a summary of the types of mobile services and applications Nokia currently supports and plans to support in the future.

6. Enter **www.ibm.com**. Search for "wireless e-business." Research the resulting stories to determine the types of wireless capabilities and applications IBM's software and hardware support. Describe some of the ways these applications have helped specific businesses and industries.

7. Enter **www.onstar.com**. What types of *fleet* services does OnStar provide? Are these any different from the services OnStar provides to individual car owners? (Play the movie.)

Closing Case

MIS   The Internet of Wild Things

The Internet of Things (IoT) can serve as a valuable tool in the planet-wide fight against biodiversity loss and global warming. IoT devices can monitor what remains of the natural world, supported by nanosatellites dedicated to wide-area IoT connectivity. Critical IoT technologies in this battle include edge analytics, IoT-streaming analytics, supervised and unsupervised machine learning, and low-power wide area networks. The two critical components of earth's biosphere are flora (plant life) and fauna (animal life). We examine both components below.

Flora

In August 2019 wildfires—many started deliberately—consumed large areas of the Amazon rainforest. Wildfires reduce the release of oxygen into Earth's atmosphere, increase the amounts of greenhouse gases in the atmosphere, and cause a loss of habitat for indigenous peoples and wildlife. Unfortunately, as of August 2020, illegal fires continued to burn in the Amazonian basin.

In addition, forests in Indonesian Borneo and Sumatra began burning in September 2019. As of October 2020, the fires continued. Humans are widely suspected, as palm oil planters clear the jungle for their crop. Similarly, beginning in September 2019 and continuing until mid-March 2020, massive bushfires raged in eastern Australia until they were finally extinguished by monsoon rains.

Wildfires are also occurring the far North, particularly northern Russia, with increasing frequency and intensity. From January until August 2020, fires in the Arctic emitted 240 megatons of carbon dioxide, a new record exceeding the previous record set in 2019.

Rainforest Connection (RFCx; **www.rfcx.org**), a nonprofit technology startup, has developed an early-warning system that is based on repurposed Android smartphones, installed in forest canopies, and powered by solar panels. RFCx personnel strip the phones down to a bare minimum of functions and then install an extra microphone along with specialized listening software.

RFCx employees designed the solar panels to accomodate momentary spots of direct sunlight in the forest canopy, called *sunflecks*. The result was seven petal-shaped panels, spaced to the average diameter of a sunfleck. These devices listen for suspicious activity such as chain saws and vehicle engines and then alert the authorities in near real time. Surprisingly, many rainforest areas, particularly at the vulnerable edges, have sufficient mobile phone coverage to make this project feasible.

Subsequent developments have moved the analysis of the audio captured by these devices to the cloud, where Google's TensorFlow machine-learning framework identifies sounds of illegal activity and adjusts audio alerts to minimize the number of false positives. A false positive in this case means that an alert sounds when no illegal activity is occurring.

RFCx has projects in northern Brazil, Ecuador, Peru, Romania, Costa Rica, and South Africa. In addition to detecting illegal deforestation, RFCx devices are learning to recognize normal sounds made by wildlife—called *bio-acoustic monitoring*—and the sounds related to poaching.

Global Forest Watch (GFW; **www.globalforestwatch.org**) is an open-source Web application that monitors global forests in near real time. GFW integrates several data sources into an interactive environmental early-warning system. These sources include deforestation alerts from the University of Maryland's Global Land Analysis and Discovery lab, Visible Infrared Imaging Radiometer Suite (VIIRS) fire alerts from infrared sensors on NASA weather satellites, and data from NASA's Landsat satellites.

Since 1972, Landsat satellites have been collecting high-resolution images of the Earth's surface to aid decision making on land-use practices. Landsat 9 is scheduled to launch in late 2020. Using Landsat data, GFW has documented severe rainforest loss in Brazil and Indonesia, as well as less severe loss in other areas.

Fauna

Instant Detect. The Zoological Society of London (ZSL; **www.zsl.org**) is an international conservation charity. One of ZSL's current technology projects is Instant Detect, a monitoring system that combines sensors, cameras, low-power radio networks, and satellite technology to capture and transmit real-time information on wildlife and human activity anywhere in the world. The goal is to remotely monitor wildlife behavior and habitat changes and provide timely warnings of illegal poaching activity.

In 2014 the ZSL deployed Instant Detect 1.0 (ID 1.0). This technology used cameras and metal-detecting sensors to identify poachers in protected areas, sending images or alerts to base stations. From there, data were transmitted via the Iridium satellite network to authorities, alerting them in near real time to detected threats.

In 2020 the ZSL began deploying ID 2.0. Enhancements over ID 1.0 include improved cameras for clearer images, an increased number of sensors that can connect to a base station, and cloud-based data and alert management. ID 2.0 uses a low-power wide area network for wireless communication among cameras, smart sensors, and the base station. Transmissions can travel 10 kilometers when sending small packets of data through scrub bush and up to 1 kilometer when sending through dense rainforest. The base station can receive data from up to eight devices simultaneously, and it can queue transmissions if this number is exceeded.

ID 2.0 devices send daily reports on battery and memory status, signal strength, and image/sensor event frequency. Although cost considerations ruled out GPS tracking, if a device is moved—as a result of human or animal activity, for example—a tamper alarm triggers an alert. The ID 2.0 devices are designed to "sleep" whenever possible, and they can be powered by both internal batteries and solar-powered batteries.

The ID 2.0 5-megapixel camera can deliver wide-angle or zoomed fields of view. The camera has image recognition software that determines whether captured images should be transmitted. A cloud-based interface supports image and alert management as well as remote management of devices in the field.

TrailGuard AI is another camera-based anti-poaching system with satellite connectivity, developed by Washington, D.C.–based nonprofit RESOLVE. To reduce false-positive threat alerts from its first-generation cameras, TrailGuard added machine learning to its second-generation camera, enabling it to determine when a person or a vehicle is present, rather than something harmless like an animal. The camera can perform in the field for up to 18 months on battery power.

Near-real-time alerting is achieved by transmitting images over cellular or satellite connections, depending on which connections are available in the particular protected area. British telecommunications company Inmarsat (**www.inmarsat.com**) provides satellite connectivity for TrailGuard.

Wildlife poaching in Africa is at epidemic levels. However, despite the efforts of dedicated rangers, they often find out about poaching only after it has occurred due to the large park boundaries and rough terrain.

With TrailGuard AI, ranger teams are able to respond rapidly, intercepting poachers before they place snares or shoot wildlife. The first-generation (non-AI version) of TrailGuard detected 50 intruders, leading to the arrests of 30 poachers representing 20 poaching gangs. Authorities seized more than 1,000 kilograms (2,200 pounds) of bushmeat in addition to motorcycles, snares, weapons, and other materials. The first 300 second-generation TrailGuard AI units were shipped to parks in Africa in early 2020 Authorities are anticipating even better results than they experienced with first-generation units.

The ICARUS Initiative—short for International Cooperation for Animal Research Using Space—is an international effort to track the migratory patterns of small flying animals using satellite communications. The project began in 2002. The system was finally installed on the International Space Station in August 2018 and switched on in July 2019.

The solar-powered ICARUS trackers—called *bio-loggers*—include GPS and communications capabilities. They are the size of two fingernails and weigh less than 3 grams (about one-tenth of an ounce). Significantly, ICARUS scientists contend they will have 1-gram trackers in 2021. The project is placing the trackers on an array of animal and insect species such as locusts, songbirds, and baby tortoises. In addition to location, the trackers will collect data on external conditions such as weather data.

The sensors are powerful enough to transmit data to the International Space Station. They can last for an animal's lifetime, can store up to 500 megabytes of data, and can even be reused.

Sources: Compiled from A. Freedman and L. Tierney, "Record Arctic Blazes May Herald New 'Fire Regime' Decades Sooner than Expected," *Washington Post*, August 14, 2020; L. Kimbrough, "More than 260 Major, Mostly Illegal Amazon Fires Detected since Late May," *Mongabay*, August 13, 2020; "New ICARUS Tracking System Helps Scientists Unlock the Mysteries of Migration," *Public Radio International*, August 3, 2020; J. Robbins, "With an Internet of Animals, Scientists Aim to Track and Save Wildlife," *New York Times*, June 9, 2020; H. Jong, "Forest Fires in Indonesia Set to Add Toxic Haze to COVID-19 Woes," *Mongabay*, April 23, 2020; "How IoT Could End Deforestation," *Inside Big Data*, May 20, 2020; "How the Internet of Things Is Saving Endangered Species," *NEC.com*, February 28, 2020; C. McLellan, "The Internet of Wild Things," *TechRepublic*, February 18, 2020; L. Cox, "Rain Deluge in Eastern Australia Set to Extinguish NSW Bushfires This Week," *The Guardian*, February 10, 2020; S. Chandler, "How the Internet of Things Will Help Fight Climate Change," *Forbes*, November 9, 2019; R. Hughes, "Amazon Fires: What's the Latest in Brazil?" *BBC News*, October 12, 2019.

Questions

1. Propose additional applications of the living Internet of Things as sensors continue to decrease in size and cost and increase in capabilities.

2. Oceans cover approximately 70 percent of the Earth's surface. Research underwater sensors. Can sensors be placed on fish, whales, and dolphins? Why or why not? Would it be important to monitor fish, whales, and dolphins? Why or why not?

CHAPTER 9

Social Computing

CHAPTER OUTLINE	LEARNING OBJECTIVES
9.1 Web 2.0	9.1 Describe six Web 2.0 tools and two major types of Web 2.0 sites.
9.2 Fundamentals of Social Computing in Business	9.2 Describe the benefits and risks of social commerce to companies.
9.3 Social Computing in Business: Shopping	9.3 Identify the methods used for shopping socially.
9.4 Social Computing in Business: Marketing	9.4 Discuss innovative ways to use social networking sites for advertising and market research.
9.5 Social Computing in Business: Customer Relationship Management	9.5 Describe how social computing improves customer service.
9.6 Social Computing in Business: Human Resource Management	9.6 Discuss different ways human resource managers make use of social computing.

Opening Case

MIS MKT Fake Reviews on Amazon

Amazon Marketplace, the etailer's third-party platform, had more than 5 million sellers and $175 billion in sales in 2019. *Third-party sellers* are independent vendors who offer a variety of merchandise through Amazon's website. These vendors depend on, and pay fees for, Amazon's logistics infrastructure, which encompasses its warehouses, shipping network, financial systems, and access to millions of global customers. With each seller paying $40 per month, the marketplace generates almost $3 billion in annual subscription revenue. In addition, the platform takes a varying percentage of sales, typically depending on each seller's volume.

There are two types of sellers on Amazon Marketplace; resellers and private label sellers. As the name suggests, *resellers* search for products they can buy and resell for a higher price on Amazon; for example, books purchased from libraries. They also browse local stores with a barcode scanner and a smartphone. They scan the barcodes of products in the stores. They then use smartphone apps to compare store prices with the prices of those products on Amazon. That way,

they find products they can resell for a profit. Resellers are also called *scanner monkeys*.

Private label sellers create their own brand, which provides them with their own product listing. An Amazon *product listing* is the product page for each of the items sold on Amazon. It contains information entered when a product is listed, including its title, images, description, and price. In this way, private label sellers do not have to compete with many other sellers on the same product page because each seller has his or her own page.

Some private label sellers create original products and operate traditional businesses on Amazon Marketplace. Others may simply put their logo on trending goods sourced from China.

About 70 percent of searches on Amazon are for generic products, such as "running shoes," rather than brands. In fact, Amazon has made it so easy to buy products that customers often purchase the first item with Prime shipping that they see. Amazon Marketplace offers 600 million products on the platform, but the number of high-search slots and Amazon Best Seller badges is limited. In 2019, for example, only about 20,000 sellers had more than $1 million in annual sales. As a result, search placement is all-important, and sellers compete ferociously for the highest placement on Amazon's search engine.

All sellers compete on price and a range of other metrics, most of which relate to customer satisfaction, to "win the Buy Box." Sellers have a common joke: "Where is the best place to bury a dead body? On the 10th page of Amazon's search results because no one ever goes there."

The competition is so fierce that sellers impersonate, copy, deceive, threaten, and sabotage their competitors. They even bribe Amazon employees for information on their rivals. For instance, in September 2018 the *Wall Street Journal* reported that Amazon was investigating employees in the United States and China for leaking internal data to sellers in exchange for bribes.

Sellers will sometimes buy Google ads for their competitors for unrelated products, such as a dog food ad linking to a shampoo listing. This fraudulent ad causes the rate of clicks converting to sales—called the product's *conversion rate*—to decrease. When this occurs, Amazon's algorithm will automatically lower the product in the search results.

Another fraudulent tactic involves fake reviews. Amazon prefers to think of its marketplace as a site where the best products get the best reviews by virtue of quality and honest consumer feedback. Unfortunately, the fake Amazon review economy continues to be a thriving market, encompassing underground forums such as "How to Game the Rankings!" tutorials and websites such as amazonverifiedreviews.com (now defunct).

However, Facebook presents an even larger problem regarding fake reviews. In a two-week period in mid-2020, researchers identified more than 150 private Facebook groups where sellers openly exchanged free products and commissions for 5-star reviews. Here is how the process generally operates:

- A seller posts an item to the Facebook group's discussion board with a message such as, "FREE. refund + $5 commission for 5 STAR. PM (private message) for details."
- An interested buyer sends the seller a private message.
- The seller directs the buyer to the product on Amazon using keywords.
- The buyer purchases the product and leaves a 5-star review.
- The seller sends the buyer a refund via PayPal, plus a commission (usually in the form of a $5 to $10 gift card).

The sellers hope that taking a short-term loss will pay off when their products have accumulated a sizeable number of positive reviews and a more favorable position in Amazon's rankings.

As a result of the sheer size of Amazon Marketplace—$120 billion in sales in 2019—and the competition among sellers, Amazon has instituted an extremely complicated set of rules and penalties to govern the platform. Judgments are severe. Let's take a closer look at one seller's experience with Amazon Marketplace.

One morning, John Stevens saw that the hunting gear that he was selling on Amazon had received 19 5-star reviews overnight. Ordinarily, he would have been very happy. However, these reviews were strange. His gear normally received about one review per day. Further, the new reviews actually referred to different hunting gear, not his.

As a precaution, Stevens reported the reviews to Amazon. Most of the reviews disappeared a few days later, and he did not worry further. Two weeks later, however, he received an email from Amazon claiming that he had manipulated product reviews on the platform. The email further stated that he could no longer sell on Amazon.com.

Amazon immediately froze the funds in Stevens's account and removed his listings from the site. Stevens clicked on the button at the bottom of Amazon's suspension email that read "appeal decision."

The process of appealing Amazon's decision and getting his store back on the site would turn out to be lengthy and complicated—and exasperating.

Humans probably read Stevens's appeal, but they are part of a highly automated bureaucracy, according to former Amazon employees. An algorithm identifies questionable seller behavior and performance based on a range of metrics—customer complaints, number of returns, certain key words used in reviews, and many other variables. The algorithm sends those sellers to Performance team members based in India, Costa Rica, and other locations around the world. These workers choose among several prewritten messages to send to sellers. The workers may see what the actual problem was in the listing or in the key item missing from an appeal, but they cannot be more specific than the prewritten forms allow.

Amazon's Performance team handles suspension appeals. The team has no phone number, and there is no one at Amazon from whom sellers can seek clarification. The only way to interact with the Performance team is to file an appeal. Significantly, if Amazon rejects an appeal, sellers often have no idea why. Sellers can call another Amazon department, Seller Support, but those employees cannot provide information about the Performance team, and they can offer only generic advice as to what the seller might have done wrong.

Performance team members' incentives favor rejecting appeals. Members must process approximately one claim every four minutes. Further, reinstating a seller who later is suspended again counts against the member. When team members fall behind their quota, they will often simply send requests to the seller for more information.

As a result, Stevens hired Susan Jones, a consultant who helps sellers navigate both the complex rules by which Amazon governs Marketplace and the complex appeals process itself. He selected Jones because she had assisted other sellers who had experienced similar issues with Amazon.

Jones had bad news for Stevens. The only way back from suspension is to "confess and repent," even if he did not think he had done anything wrong. The core of the appeal of an Amazon suspension is a plan of action, which is an explanation of how the seller will correct the problems that led to the suspension. Therefore, for a seller to make things right, he or she must admit to having done something wrong.

Stevens and Jones looked for something to confess to. In his appeal, Stevens admitted to providing discounts for reviews before Amazon banned the practice. He further conceded that he had sent customers emails about pricing on his products that Amazon's algorithm might have mistaken for bribes.

Stevens submitted his appeal after confessing to everything that could possibly be considered review manipulation. Several days later, Amazon rejected his appeal. Amazon will not consider the same appeal twice, so now Stevens had to find another infraction to confess to. Unable to think of anything else, he and Jones decided to email Amazon CEO Jeff Bezos as a last resort. His email was never answered. However, after he had sent it, a fellow Amazon seller gave him the name of a person "high up" in the company. Stevens emailed that person, and shortly afterward his account was reinstated, with no explanation as to why. In all, Stevens estimates that his suspension cost him more than $100,000 in sales.

What really happened to Stevens? A competitor had framed him, accusing him of buying 5-star reviews. As Amazon has escalated its war on fake reviews, sellers have realized that the most effective tactic is not buying fake reviews for themselves but instead buying them for their competitors. In fact, the more obviously fraudulent the review, the better. The crook wants glowing 5-star reviews, preferably in broken English, about unrelated products. If Amazon suspends the crook's competitor, then the scam artist can move up a place in Amazon's search results while the competitor must fight Amazon's suspension.

Many sellers cannot even figure out what Amazon is accusing them of. For example, another of Jones's clients had a listing on Amazon Marketplace for a wood picture frame. Amazon deemed the frame unsafe, removed the listing, and suspended the seller. It turned out that the problem was a single customer review that mentioned getting a splinter from the frame. (The customer actually gave the frame 5 stars.) Amazon reinstated the seller when he promised to add "wear gloves while installing" to his listing.

In fairness to Amazon, many of their suspensions are justified. The company's easily accessible global market attracts counterfeiters, money launderers, and fencers of stolen goods. To its credit, Amazon has sued more than 1,000 third-party fake review sites. The company is quick to act when links to fraudulent products come to light.

Fortunately, there are online tools that users can access to qualify product reviews. Companies such as Fakespot (**www.fakespot.com**) and ReviewMeta (**www.reviewmeta.com**) offer analytic tools that analyze and sort product reviews on Amazon, eBay, and other online shopping sites. Users simply copy the product's link into the analytic tool search engine to obtain the quality rating on the product's reviews.

Illustrating the points raised in this case, on September 18, 2020, the U.S. Department of Justice (**www.justice.gov**) released an indictment, asserting that a group of e-commerce consultants and former Amazon employees bribed Amazon workers to gain access to the retailers' most sensitive secrets. Two of the defendants are former employees who worked in seller support positions in India and now operate their own consulting businesses. The indictment suggested that the investigation was continuing to search for other perpetrators.

The group allegedly stole terabytes of confidential company data and devised methods to rig the system so some merchants would receive more business while their competitors were forced to close. Some of the suspects had products that Amazon had removed for safety reasons placed back on the site. The group purportedly stole more than $100 million from Amazon and its customers.

For a few hundred dollars, some merchants could bribe an Amazon insider to erase negative customer reviews about their products. Further, $5,000 would buy a takedown, in which company consultants conspired to eliminate a competitor from the site by buying its products and leaving negative feedback that they knew would trigger a suspension of the product.

Amazon's response stated that it is cooperating with the investigation and that it has systems in place to detect suspicious behavior by sellers and employees, as well as teams that investigate and stop prohibited activity. Amazon also said that it invests hundreds of millions of dollars per year to ensure that products are safe and compliant.

Sources: Compiled from S. Soper and I. Lee, "Amazon's Secrets Are up for Sale," *Bloomberg Businessweek*, September 28, 2020; E. Tolin, "Online Shopping Tip: How to Spot Fake Reviews," *Komando*, August 27, 2020; D. Lee and H. Murphy, "Facebook Groups Trading Fake Amazon Reviews Remain Rampant," *Financial Times*, August 12, 2020; "What to Do if Your Amazon Account Gets Suspended," *RepricerExpress*, July 1, 2020; G. Sterling, "Fake Reviews Problem Is Much Worse than People Know," *Search Engine Land*, April 22, 2020; "How to Sell on Amazon in 2020: Understanding Amazon Policies, Regulations, and Guidelines," *SellerEngine*, April 17, 2020; G. Sterling, "Consumers More Invested in Reviews, but Also More Skeptical of Authenticity," *Search Engine Land*, December 11, 2019; Z. Crockett, "5-Star Phonies: Inside the Fake Amazon Review Complex," *The Hustle*, April 13, 2019; R. Khan, "From Fake Reviews to Unvetted Sellers: Here's Why Amazon Marketplace Needs More Oversight," *Forbes*, April 1, 2019; G. Sterling, "FTC Busts Amazon Seller for Buying Reviews," *Search Engine Land*, February 27, 2019; N. Statt, "Fake Amazon Reviews Draw Fraud Charges in Groundbreaking FTC Case," *The Verge*, February 26, 2019; G. Sterling, "Study Finds 61 Percent of Electronics Reviews on Amazon Are 'Fake'," *Search Engine Land*, December 19, 2018; J. Dzieza, "Prime and Punishment," *The Verge*, December 19, 2018; J. Emont, L. Stevens, and R. McMillan, "Amazon Investigates Employees Leaking Data for Bribes," *Wall Street Journal*, September 16, 2018; M. Weinstein, "18 Big Mistakes New Amazon Sellers Can't Afford to Make," *Tinuiti*, August 24, 2018; "Amazon Sues 1,000 'Fake Reviewers'," *The Guardian*, October 18, 2015.

Questions

1. Reviews typically consist of five rankings, from 5-stars (outstanding) to 1-star (poor). Which ranking do you trust the most? Why? Which ranking do you trust the least? Why?

2. What could Amazon do to govern Amazon Marketplace more efficiently and effectively? What are the possible impacts of poor governance on buyers? On sellers?

3. Is it even possible for Amazon to govern such a vast, dynamic entity such as Marketplace? Why or why not?

Introduction

Humans are social beings. Therefore, human behavior is innately social. Humans typically orient their behavior around other members of their community. As a result, people are sensitive to the behavior of people around them, and their decisions are generally influenced by their social context.

Traditional information systems support organizational activities and business processes, and they concentrate on cost reductions and productivity increases. A variation of this traditional model, **social computing**, is a type of IT that combines social behavior and information systems to create value. Social computing focuses on improving collaboration and interaction among people and on encouraging user-generated content.

Significantly, in social computing, social information is not anonymous. Rather, it is important precisely because it is linked to particular individuals, who in turn are linked to their own networks of individuals.

Social computing makes socially produced information available to everyone. This information may be provided directly, as when users rate a movie (e.g., at Rotten Tomatoes), or indirectly (as with Google's PageRank algorithm, which sequences search results).

In social computing, users, rather than organizations, produce, control, use, and manage content via interactive communications and collaboration. As a result, social computing is transforming power relationships within organizations (see this chapter's opening case). Employees and customers are empowered by their ability to use social computing to organize themselves. Thus, social computing can influence people in positions of power to listen to the concerns and issues of "ordinary people." Organizational customers and employees are joining this social computing phenomenon, with serious consequences for most organizations.

Significantly, most governments and companies in modern developed societies are not prepared for the new social power of ordinary people. Today, managers, executives, and government officials can no longer control the conversation around policies, products, and other issues.

In the new world of business and government, organizational leaders will have to demonstrate authenticity, even-handedness, transparency, good faith, and humility. If they do not, then customers and employees may distrust them, to potentially disastrous effects. For example, customers who do not like a product or service can quickly broadcast their disapproval. Another example is that prospective employees do not have to take their employers at their word for what life is like at their companies—they can find out from people who already work there. A final example is that employees now have many more options to start their own companies, which could compete with their former employers.

As you see from these examples, the world is becoming more democratic and reflective of the will of ordinary people, enabled by the power of social computing. On the one hand, social power can help keep a company vital and can enable customers and employee activists to become a source of creativity, innovation, and new ideas that will move a company forward. On the other hand, companies that show insensitivity toward customers or employees quickly find themselves on a downward slide.

For instance, Kenneth Cole came under fire for suggesting on Twitter that news of its spring collection led to riots in Egypt, and American Apparel was blasted online for offering a Hurricane Sandy sale. Lesson to be learned: if companies want to win the favor and loyalty of customers, they should refrain from making comments that may suggest that they were trying to profit from other people's misery.

Social computing is exploding worldwide, with China having the world's most active social media population. In one McKinsey survey, 91 percent of Chinese respondents reported that they had visited a social media site in the previous six months, compared with 70 percent in South Korea, 67 percent in the United States, and 30 percent in Japan. Interestingly, the survey found that social media has a greater influence on purchasing decisions for Chinese consumers than for consumers anywhere else in the world.

In particular, messaging app usage is increasing dramatically, with certain apps dominating specific areas of the world. Let's look at the most popular messaging apps.

- With more than 2 billion users, *WhatsApp* (**www.whatsapp.com**, owned by Facebook) is the most widely used messaging app in many parts of the world, including much of South America, much of southern and central Africa, Great Britain, Spain, Germany, India, Mexico, southeast Asia, and Russia.

- *Facebook Messenger* (**www.messenger.com**) has more than 1.3 billion users globally. Messenger is the leading app in the United States, Australia, and northern Africa.

- Messaging app *WeChat* (**www.wechat.com**) dominates the Chinese market with more than 1 billion users.

- With almost 1 billion users, *Viber* (**www.viber.com**) is the leading app in countries such as Kyrgyzstan, Ukraine, Belarus, Armenia, Azerbaijan, and Bosnia–Herzegovina.

- *Moya Messenger* (**www.moya.app**), developed in South Africa, enables users to communicate without incurring data costs, provided that they do not send any attachments and are willing to be exposed to advertising. Moya uses are warned in advance if they will incur mobile data costs or need to switch to a Wi-Fi network.

Organizations today are using social computing in a variety of innovative ways, including marketing, production, customer relationship management, and human resource management. In fact, so many organizations are competing to use social computing in as many new ways as possible that an inclusive term for the use of social computing in business has emerged: *social commerce*. Because social computing is facilitated by Web 2.0 tools and sites, you begin this chapter by examining these technologies. You then turn your attention to a diverse number of social commerce activities, including shopping, advertising, market research, customer relationship management, and human resource management.

When you complete this chapter, you will have a thorough understanding of social computing and the ways in which modern organizations use this technology. You will be familiar with the advantages and disadvantages of social computing as well as the risks and rewards it can bring to your organization. For example, most of you already have pages on social networking sites, so you are familiar with the positive and negative features of these sites. This chapter will enable you to apply this knowledge to your organization's efforts in the social computing arena. You will be in a position to contribute to your organization's policies on social computing. You will also be able to help your organization create a strategy to utilize social computing. Finally, social computing offers incredible opportunities for entrepreneurs who want to start their own businesses.

9.1 | Web 2.0

Author Lecture Videos are available exclusively in *WileyPLUS*.
Apply the Concept activities are available in the Appendix and in *WileyPLUS*.

The World Wide Web, which you learned about in Chapter 6, first appeared in 1990. Web 1.0 was the first generation of the Web. We did not use this term in Chapter 6 because there was no need to say "Web 1.0" until Web 2.0 emerged.

The key developments of Web 1.0 were the creation of websites and the commercialization of the Web. Users typically had minimal interaction with Web 1.0 sites. Rather, they passively received information from those sites.

Web 2.0 is a popular term that has proved difficult to define. According to Tim O'Reilly, a noted blogger, **Web 2.0** is a loose collection of information technologies and applications, plus the websites that use them. These websites enrich the user experience by encouraging user participation, social interaction, and collaboration. Unlike Web 1.0 sites, Web 2.0 sites are not so much online places to visit as Web locations that facilitate information sharing, user-centered design, and collaboration. Web 2.0 sites often harness collective intelligence (e.g., wikis); deliver functionality as services, rather than packaged software (e.g., Web services); and feature remixable applications and data (e.g., mashups).

In the following sections, we discuss five Web 2.0 information technology tools: tagging, Really Simple Syndication, blogs, microblogs, and wikis. We then turn our attention to the two major types of Web 2.0 sites: social networking sites and mashups.

Tagging

A **tag** is a key word or term that describes a piece of information, for example, a blog, a picture, an article, or a video clip. Users typically choose tags that are meaningful to them. Tagging allows users to place information in multiple, overlapping associations rather than in rigid categories. For example, a photo of a car might be tagged with "Corvette," "sports car," and "Chevrolet." Tagging is the basis of *folksonomies*, which are user-generated classifications that use tags to categorize and retrieve Web pages, photos, videos, and other Web content.

One specific form of tagging, known as *geotagging*, refers to tagging information on maps. For example, Google Maps allows users to add pictures and information, such as restaurant or hotel ratings, to maps. Therefore, when users access Google Maps, their experience is enriched because they can see pictures of attractions, reviews, and things to do, posted by everyone, and all related to the map location they are viewing.

Really Simple Syndication

Really Simple Syndication (RSS) is a Web 2.0 feature that allows you to receive the information you want (customized information), when you want it, without having to surf thousands of websites. RSS allows anyone to syndicate (publish) his or her blog, or any other content, to any-one who has an interest in subscribing to it. When changes to the content are made, subscribers receive a notification of the changes and an idea of what the new content contains. Subscribers can then click on a link that will take them to the full text of the new content.

For example, CNN.com provides RSS feeds for each of its main topic areas, such as world news, sports news, technology news, and entertainment news. NBC uses RSS feeds to allow viewers to download the most current version of shows such as *Meet the Press* and *NBC Nightly News*. **Figure 9.1** illustrates how to search an RSS and locate RSS feeds.

To use RSS, you can utilize a special newsreader that displays RSS content feeds from the websites you select. Many such readers are available, several of them for free (see Feedspot; **www.feedspot.com**). In addition, most browsers have built-in RSS readers. For an excellent RSS tutorial, visit **www.mnot.net/rss/tutorial**.

Blogs

A **weblog** (**blog** for short) is a personal website, open to the public, in which the site creator expresses his or her feelings or opinions via a series of chronological entries. *Bloggers*—people who create and maintain blogs—write stories, convey news, and provide links to other articles and websites that are of interest to them. The simplest method of creating a blog is to sign up with a blogging service provider, such as **www.blogger.com** (now owned by Google), **www.xanga.com**, or **https://movabletype.com**. The **blogosphere** is the term for the millions of blogs on the Web.

MKT Many companies listen to consumers in the blogosphere who express their views on the companies' products. Marketers refer to these views as *consumer-generated media*. For example, Nielsen (**www.nielsen.com**) "mines" the blogosphere to provide information for its clients in several areas. Nielsen helps clients find ways to serve potential markets, ranging from broad-based to niche markets. The company also helps clients detect false rumors before these rumors appear in the mainstream media, and it gauges the potency of a marketing push or the popularity of a new product.

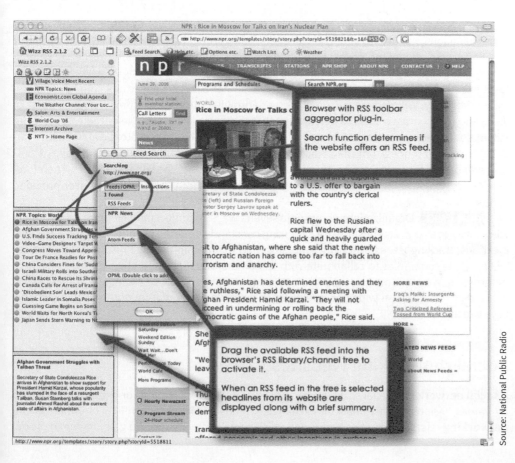

Source: National Public Radio

FIGURE 9.1 **The website of National Public Radio (NPR) with RSS toolbar aggregator and search function.**

Blogs often provide incredibly useful information, often before the information becomes available in traditional media outlets (e.g., television, newspapers). Although blogs can be very useful, they also have shortcomings. Perhaps the primary value of blogs is their ability to bring current, breaking news to the public in the fastest time possible. Unfortunately, in doing so, bloggers sometimes cut corners, and their blogs can be inaccurate. Regardless of their various problems, however, blogs have transformed the ways in which people gather and consume information.

Microblogging

Microblogging is a form of blogging that allows users to write short messages (or capture an image or embedded video) and publish them. These messages can be submitted via text messaging from mobile phones, instant messaging, e-mail, or simply over the Web. The content of a microblog differs from that of a blog because of the limited space per message (usually up to 140 characters). A popular microblogging service is Twitter.

Twitter (**www.twitter.com**) is a free microblogging service that allows its users to send messages and read other users' messages and updates, known as **Tweets**. Tweets are displayed on the user's profile page and delivered to other users who have signed up to receive them.

MKT Twitter is becoming a very useful business tool. It allows companies to quickly share information with people interested in their products, thereby creating deeper relationships with their customers. Businesses also use Twitter to gather real-time market intelligence and customer feedback. As an individual user, you can use Twitter to inform companies about your experiences with their business, offer product ideas, and learn about great offers.

Microblogging is very popular in China, with Weibo (**www.weibo.com**) being the most popular microblogging service in that country. Weibo has over 200 million monthly active members.

Wikis

A **wiki** is a website made up entirely of content posted by users. Wikis have an "edit" link on each page that allows any user to add, change, or delete material, thus fostering easy collaboration.

Wikis take advantage of the combined input of many individuals. Consider Wikipedia (**www.wikipedia.org**), an online encyclopedia that is the largest existing wiki. Wikipedia contains over five million articles in English (as of November 2016), which attract some 500 million views every day. Wikipedia relies on volunteer administrators who enforce a neutral point of view, and it encourages users to delete copy that displays a clear bias. Nevertheless, there are still major debates over the reliability of Wikipedia articles. Many educators will not allow students to cite references from Wikipedia because Wikipedia content is of uncertain origin. Moreover, Wikipedia does not provide any quality assessment or fact checking by experts. Therefore, academics and other professionals have major concerns about the accuracy of user-provided content.

POM MKT Organizations use wikis in several ways. In project management, for example, wikis provide a central repository for capturing constantly updated product features and specifications, tracking issues, resolving problems, and maintaining project histories. In addition, wikis enable companies to collaborate with customers, suppliers, and other business partners on projects. Wikis are also valuable in knowledge management. For example, companies use wikis to keep enterprise-wide documents, such as guidelines and frequently asked questions, accurate and current.

Social Networking Websites

A **social network** is a social structure composed of individuals, groups, or organizations linked by values, visions, ideas, financial exchange, friendship, kinship, conflict, or trade. **Social networking** refers to activities performed using social software tools (e.g., blogging) or social networking features (e.g., media sharing). Social networking allows convenient connections to those of similar interest.

A social network can be described as a map of all relevant links or connections among the network's members. For each individual member that map is his or her **social graph**. Mark Zuckerberg of Facebook originally coined this term to refer to the social network of relationships among Facebook users. The idea was that Facebook would take advantage of relationships among individuals to offer a richer online experience.

Social networks can also be used to determine the social capital of individual participants. **Social capital** refers to the number of connections a person has within and between social networks.

Participants congregate on *social networking websites*, where they can create their own profile page for free and on which they can write blogs and wikis; post pictures, videos, or music; share ideas; and link to other Web locations they find interesting. Social networkers chat using instant messaging and Twitter, and they tag posted content with their own key words, making content searchable and facilitating interactions and transactions. Social network members converse, collaborate, and share opinions, experiences, knowledge, insights, and perceptions with one another. They also use these websites to find like-minded people online, either to pursue an interest or a goal or just to establish a sense of community among people who may never meet in the real world.

Participants who post on social networking sites tend to reveal a great deal of personal information. As a result, if they are not careful, their information could be stolen.

Table 9.1 displays the variety of online social networking platforms. Social networking websites allow users to upload their content to the Web in the form of text, voice, images, and videos.

These social networking sites collect a massive amount of data, some of it uploaded by their users and some generated from monitoring user activity on the sites. The vast amount of data gathered by social networks has led to well-documented problems, which became prominent with the Facebook–Cambridge Analytica scandal.

TABLE 9.1   Categories of Social Networking Websites

Socially oriented: Socially focused public sites, open to anyone:
- Facebook (**www.facebook.com**)
- Instagram (**www.instagram.com**)
- Hi5 (**www.hi5.com**)

Professional networking: Focused on networking for business professionals:
- LinkedIn (**www.linkedin.com**)

Media sharing:
- *Netcasting* includes podcasting (audio) and videocasting (audio and video). For example, educational institutions use netcasts to provide students with access to lectures, lab demonstrations, and sports events. In 2007, Apple launched iTunes U, which offers free content provided by major U.S. universities such as Stanford and MIT.
- Web 2.0 media sites allow people to come together and share user-generated digital media, such as pictures, audio, and video.
- Video (Amazon Video on Demand, YouTube, Hulu, Facebook)
- Music (Amazon MP3, Last.fm, Rhapsody, Pandora, Facebook, iTunes)
- Photographs (Photobucket, Flickr, Shutterfly, Picasa, Facebook)

Communication:
- Blogs: Blogger, LiveJournal, TypePad, WordPress, Vox, Xanga
- Microblogging/Presence applications: Twitter, Tumblr, Yammer

Collaboration: Wikis (Wikimedia, PBworks, Wetpaint)

(continued)

TABLE 9.1   Categories of Social Networking Websites *(continued)*

Social bookmarking (or *social tagging*): Focused on helping users store, organize, search, and manage bookmarks of web pages:
- Mendeley (**www.mendeley.com**)
- Mix (**https://mix.com**)
- EndNote (**www.endnote.com**)

Social news: Focused on user-posted news stories that are ranked by popularity based on user voting:
- Digg (**www.digg.com**)
- Chime (**https://aws.amazon.com/chime**)
- Reddit (**www.reddit.com**)

Events: Focused on alerts for relevant events, people you know nearby, etc.:
- Eventful (**www.audacy.com/eventful**)
- Meetup (**www.meetup.com**)
- Foursquare (**www.foursquare.com**)

Virtual meeting place: Sites that are essentially three-dimensional worlds, built and owned by the residents (the users):
- Second Life (**www.secondlife.com**)

Discovery:
- Foursquare (**www.foursquare.com**) helps its members discover and share information about businesses and attractions around them.

Online marketplaces for microjobs: For example, TaskRabbit (**www.taskrabbit.com**) enables people to farm out chores to a growing number of temporary personal assistants. Thousands of unemployed and underemployed workers use these sites. The part-time or full-time tasks are especially popular with stay-at-home moms, retirees, and students. Workers choose their jobs and negotiate their rates.

Problems with Social Networks: Fake News, Deepfakes, Bots, Cyborgs, and Trolls

Recall our discussions of how social media platforms make money: they offer free services in exchange for users' data. They then analyze the data in order to target advertisements to each user. The more data they collect, the more accurate their targeting, the more likely that visitors will click on an ad, the higher the rates that advertisers will pay the platforms, and the more money the platforms will make.

The platforms pay the most attention to two metrics: the number of unique visitors to their websites and the length of time that each visitor spends on the sites. The more visitors to the site and the longer the time they spend on the site, the more money the platform can charge the advertising companies.

To attract more users, platforms offer a wide array of free services. For example, consider the large number of free services that Facebook and Google provide.

Engagement is the process of keeping users on websites as long as possible. Platforms program their algorithms to push (emphasize) content that results in high engagement. Not surprisingly, this content is often sensationalized. Consider the phrase, "If it bleeds, it leads." This phrase means that the more sensational the content, the greater number of people who will read it or watch it. For instance, if a large passenger airliner crashes, the news rapidly spreads globally on news networks, on social media, and in print. In contrast, we do not see content covering the fact that Atlanta Hartsfield International Airport handled 2,500 flights successfully and safely on a particular day.

There are three serious issues associated with social media platforms. First, they allow almost anyone to publish almost any content. Unfortunately, content on these platforms can consist of false information such as fake news and deepfakes. Second, the platforms employ psychological measures to keep visitors on the sites longer. Third, various third-party entities such as marketing agencies, governments, political parties, and publicity managers employ various means in conjunction with social media platforms to spread their messages, both true and false. Let's take a closer look at each of these issues.

False information.
There are two kinds of *fake news*: content that is entirely untrue and content that has some truth but is not totally accurate. Unfortunately, it can be difficult for readers to identify fake content. Fortunately, however, there are strategies that you can use to identify fake news.

- Consider the source of the content. Who or what organization is responsible for the content? Is there even a source listed? If so, then can you check these sources to determine whether they are legitimate?
- Read beyond the headline. If a piece of content has a provocative headline, then read the entire piece before you decide whether to believe it or to pass it along.
- Check the date. Some content is not completely fake, but it distorts real events. Fake news can claim that something that happened in the past is actually a current event.
- Check the facts. Access FactCheck.org (**www.factcheck.org**), Snopes.com (**www.snopes .com**), the *Washington Post* Fact Checker (**www.washingtonpost.com/news/fact-checker**), and PolitiFact.com (**www.politifact.com**). It is likely that at least one of these sites has already fact-checked the latest viral content that appears in your news feed.

Deepfakes are videos that have been digitally created with artificial intelligence to make it appear something happened that did not. They are an emerging threat because improvements in video-editing software make it possible for bad actors to create increasingly realistic footage of, for example, former U.S. President Barack Obama delivering a speech he never made, in a place he never visited. Deepfakes are expensive and difficult to create. However, advancing technologies are making them easier, faster, and less expensive to create.

In contrast, *shallowfakes*—also called *cheapfakes*—are videos that have been altered with more basic techniques, such as slowing down or speeding up footage or cutting and splicing it. Because shallowfakes are easy and inexpensive to create, they are dangerous as well.

An example of a shallowfake is the altered May 2019 video of Speaker Nancy Pelosi speaking at a conference. The video appeared to have sections cut out and having been slowed down to make her speech sound continually garbled. The video had more than 2.5 million views on Facebook. Significantly, the social platform did not take down the video, despite its fact-checkers flagging it as "partly false."

Psychological measures.
Remember that a primary function of social media platforms is to hold visitors' attention as long as possible. To accomplish this goal, the sites employ the infinite scroll and randomly scheduled rewards.

Infinite scroll is a design technique that loads content continuously as the user scrolls down the page, eliminating the need to keep clicking to load additional content. *Doomscrolling* refers specifically to an infinite scroll of bad news.

Randomly scheduled rewards is a strategy in which the platforms give visitors a "reward" at irregular intervals because someone liked a post or a photo that they uploaded, or sent them a text, or retweeted one of their tweets, or any number of other actions. When a visitor receives a reward, his or her brain releases a neurotransmitter called dopamine. Dopamine creates feelings of pleasure which motivates a visitor to repeat behaviors such as continuing to click on links or continuing to scroll on social media platforms. The irregularity and unpredictably of the rewards are what makes these platforms so addictive.

Third-party entities.
A variety of entities use an assortment of methods to spread their agendas around the world via social media. These methods include social bots, cyborgs, and troll factories.

Social bots are a type of chatbot (see Chapter 7) that automatically produce content on social media. This content can be either in support of or in opposition to campaigns, brands, politicians, and issues. For example, social bots can be programmed to leave supportive comments on a politician's Facebook page, target journalists with a number of angry Tweets, or engage with a post to artificially inflate its popularity. Social bots are typically programmed to conceal that they are bots so that they appear to be humans.

Some social bots are programmed to follow people, resulting in millions of *fake followers* for Internet influencers, politicians, and the platforms themselves. For example, researchers contend that bot software automatically operates nearly 50 million Twitter accounts. On Facebook, social bots are used to automate group pages and spread political advertisements.

Marketing agencies, governments, political parties, publicity managers, and other entities pay humans to create hundreds of fake accounts, operated by bots, that disseminate ambiguous or false information to influence and manipulate public opinion on social media, especially Facebook and Twitter. The humans and the bots they create are called *cyborgs*. Although it is not ethical or legal to use cyborgs to manipulate public opinion, the practice is widespread around the world.

A *troll* is a person who intentionally initiates online conflict or offends other users to distract or create divisions by posting inflammatory or off-topic posts in an online community or on a social media platform. The goal is to provoke others and derail discussions. A *troll farm* is a group of Internet trolls who interfere with the political process in various countries. One study revealed that 30 governments worldwide paid trolls in troll farms to spread propaganda and attack critics.

A combination of social bots, cyborgs, and trolls are very effective at manipulating public discussion on social media. Here is how the process works:

- Any one, or combination, of social bots, cyborgs, or trolls begins the conversation, seeding new ideas and driving discussion in online communities.
- Another type of social bot called amplifier bots escalate the importance of the new ideas by repurposing, retweeting, and republishing them.
- Yet another type of social bot, approval bots engage with specific Tweets or comments, "liking," "retweeting," or "replying" to make the ideas appear more credible and legitimate.
- Along with the first three functions, in hotly contested topic areas other social bots harass and attack individuals and organizations in an attempt to push them out of the conversation.

In the most successful bot- and cyborg-aided campaigns, real human social media users are influenced to the point that they willingly participate in sharing fake or inflammatory content with their own social groups. This process often leads to mainstream media coverage, which provides additional legitimacy to the ideas even when the media coverage is intended to debunk false or misleading information. For an excellent example of social media influence on political campaigns, see the impact of WhatsApp on the 2019 Indian general elections in this chapter's closing case.

Enterprise Social Networks

MIS Business-oriented social networks can be public, such as LinkedIn.com. As such, they are owned and managed by an independent company.

However, an increasing number of companies have created in-house, private social networks for their employees, former employees, business partners, and/or customers. Such networks are "behind the firewall" and are often referred to as *corporate social networks*. Employees utilize these networks to create connections that allow them to establish virtual teams, bring new employees up to speed, improve collaboration, and increase employee retention by creating a sense of community. Employees are able to interact with their coworkers on a level that is typically absent in large organizations or in situations where people work remotely.

Corporate social networks are used for many processes, including:

- Networking and community building, both inside and outside an organization
- *Social collaboration*: Collaborative work and problem-solving using wikis, blogs, instant messaging, collaborative office, and other special-purpose Web-based collaboration platforms

- *Social publishing*: Employees and others creating, either individually or collaboratively, and posting content—photos, videos, presentation slides, and documents—into a member's or a community's accessible-content repository such as YouTube, Flickr, and SlideShare
- Social views and feedback
- *Social intelligence and social analytics*: Monitoring, analyzing, and interpreting conversations, interactions, and associations among people, topics, and ideas to gain insights. Social intelligence is useful for examining relationships and work patterns of individuals and groups and for discovering people and expertise.

Mashups

A **mashup** is a website that takes different content from a number of other websites and mixes them together to create a new kind of content. The launch of Google Maps is credited with providing the start of mashups. A user can take a map from Google, add his or her data, and then display a map mashup on his or her website that plots crime scenes, cars for sale, or anything else (see **Figure 9.2**). There are many examples of mashups (for a complete list of mashups, see **www.programmableweb.com**):

- Craigslist developed a dynamic map of all available apartments in the United States that are listed on their website (**www.housingmaps.com**).
- Everyblock.com is a mashup of Web services that integrates content from newspapers, blogs, and government databases to inform citizens of cities such as Chicago, New York, and Seattle about what is happening in their neighborhoods. This information includes criminal activities, restaurant inspections, and local photos posted on Flickr.

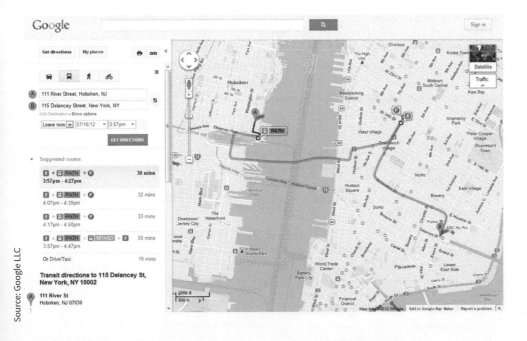

Source: Google LLC

FIGURE 9.2 **Google Maps** (**www.google.com/maps**) **is a classic example of a mashup. In this case, Google Maps is pulling in information from public transportation websites to provide the customer with transit directions.**

Before you go on...

1. Differentiate between blogs and wikis.
2. Differentiate between social networking websites and corporate social networks.

9.2 Fundamentals of Social Computing in Business

Social computing in business, or **social commerce**, refers to the delivery of electronic commerce activities and transactions through social computing. Social commerce also supports social interactions and user contributions, allowing customers to participate actively in the marketing and selling of products and services in online marketplaces and communities. With social commerce, individuals can collaborate online, obtain advice from trusted individuals, and find and purchase goods and services. A few examples of social commerce include:

- **POM** Disney allows people to book tickets on Facebook without leaving the social network.
- **MKT** PepsiCo provides a live notification when its customers are close to physical stores (grocery, restaurants, gas stations) that sell Pepsi products. The company then uses Foursquare to send them coupons and discount information.
- **MKT** Mountain Dew attracts video game lovers and sports enthusiasts via Dewmocracy contests. The company also encourages the most dedicated community members to contribute ideas on company products.
- **MKT** Levi's advertises on Facebook by enabling consumers to populate a "shopping cart" based on what their friends think they would like.

Benefits and Risks of Social Commerce

Social commerce offers numerous benefits to both customers and vendors, as described in **Table 9.2**. IT's About Business 9.1 illustrates one unexpected benefit of social commerce, which was that it helped Thailand merchants during the COVID-19 pandemic.

Despite all of its benefits, social commerce does involve risks. It is problematic, for example, to advertise a product, brand, or company on social computing websites where content is user generated and is not edited or filtered. Companies that employ this strategy must be willing to accept negative reviews and feedback. Of course, negative feedback can be some of the most valuable information that a company receives, if it utilizes this information properly.

TABLE 9.2   Potential Benefits of Social Commerce

Benefits to Customers
- Better and faster vendor responses to complaints, because customers can air their complaints in public (on Twitter, Facebook, YouTube)
- Customers can assist other customers (e.g., in online forums)
- Customers' expectations can be met more fully and quickly
- Customers can easily search, link, chat, and buy while staying on a social network's page

Benefits to Businesses
- Can test new products and ideas quickly and inexpensively
- Learn a lot about their customers
- Identify problems quickly and alleviate customer anger
- Learn about customers' experiences via rapid feedback
- Increase sales when customers discuss products positively on social networking sites
- Create more effective marketing campaigns and brand awareness
- Use low-cost user-generated content, for example, in marketing campaigns
- Obtain free advertising through viral marketing
- Identify and reward influential brand advocates

IT's About Business 9.1

MIS **POM** **MKT** **Social Commerce Helps Thailand Deal with COVID-19**

Despite an influx of foreign visitors early in 2020 from countries severely impacted by COVID-19, at the end of July, Thailand had recorded fewer than 3500 cases and 60 deaths. Further, at that time Thailand had reported no cases of local transmission for seven weeks.

Despite Thailand's outstanding management of COVID-19, however, the pandemic almost emptied Bangkok's huge open-air Chatuchak market. Some local residents still visit the market for essentials, but the well-known shopping complex was largely deserted. One small retailer in Thailand noted that operating a physical store was not viable until a vaccine had been developed and "there's no fear of going out."

Despite these difficult circumstances, the small brick-and-mortar retailers did not give up. Instead, they turned to e-marketplaces, social commerce, and online websites to sell their products.

E-marketplaces. An *e-marketplace*—also known as an *online marketplace*—is a type of e-commerce site that allows users to register and sell items for a fee. Essentially, the marketplace operator processes consumer transactions, and the participating merchants deliver the products. In general, because e-marketplaces aggregate products from a wide variety of merchants, these platforms offer more product choices with higher availability than do vendor-specific online retail stores.

The leading e-marketplaces in Thailand are Shopee (**www.shopee.co.th**) and Lazada (**www.lazada.co.th**). Let's take a closer look at Lazada's actions during the COVID-19 pandemic.

Lazada offered incentives to attract 50,000 brick-and-mortar small and medium-sized enterprises (SMEs) to the platform to assist them during the pandemic. Lazada charged no registration and commission fees, and merchants were able to open their online shops in less than 5 minutes. Lazada added 26,000 new merchants to its platform in March 2020 alone. As of August 2020, the platform hosted approximately 400,000 merchants.

Brands' websites. The e-marketplaces also accommodated the direct-to-consumer (DTC) strategy, where brands seek to reach buyers directly. They helped the brands set up their official branded shops within the e-marketplaces. Shopee deployed ShopeeMall and Lazada launched LazMall.

Social commerce. Thailand has become the global leader in social commerce, according to a report by the Boston Consulting Group (**www.bcg.com**). Up to 40 percent of Thais reported that they had shopped through social commerce platforms, the highest proportion in the world.

Facebook is the social media platform of choice in Thailand, where 50 million Thais (73 percent of the population) use the platform. Further, 11 million Thais (16 percent of the population) use Instagram.

Merchants are using these platforms to sell their goods. In fact, so many small vendors moved onto them that Thailand is now Southeast Asia's largest market for social commerce transactions. Some fishermen are even selling their daily catch from the Andaman Sea on the platforms.

For example, Lalilladar Sirisukamon, whose Rock Me jewelry (**www.rockmejewelry.com**) sells pineapple-shaped rings and tropical-motif pendants, established her first outlet at Chatuchak

in 2013. When COVID-19 hit Thailand and sales plummeted, she moved her operation online. She notes that the Chatuchak market had the poorest sanitation and cleanliness standards, so she moved to Facebook to make money to pay her employees.

Much of the social commerce activity in Thailand is *conversational commerce*, in which buying and selling take place in chatrooms, messaging apps such as Line (**http://line.me**) and WhatsApp, and platforms such as Facebook. Line leads the conversational commerce market in Thailand, followed by Facebook Messenger and WhatsApp.

Facebook and Line are providing convenient shopping through their platforms, including payment channels. Facebook provides Facebook Pay services, and Line offers its Line Pay digital wallet. Facebook Shops and Line MyShop allow merchants to set up online stores within their main apps. This arrangement demonstrates how social platforms are competing with e-marketplaces.

Conversational commerce is particularly useful for very small retailers because it enables them to connect quickly and directly with consumers and to offer personalized service with minimal upfront investment. One industry analyst noted that retailers simply need to know how to take a nice picture, post it online, and set a price for the product.

One disadvantage of using social media platforms to transact business is that not all of these platforms have payment systems. Money is typically transferred directly, via bank transfer or cash upon delivery. Essentially, the system relies on mutual trust. However, in much of Southeast Asia where cash payments are still common, those two methods work well.

The potential for growth is enormous. In terms of gross merchandise value, Thailand's total Internet economy, including e-commerce, was worth $16 billion in 2019 and is expected to grow to $50 billion by 2025.

Sources: Compiled from "Pandemic Has Online Sellers Leaning on Cloud," *Bangkok Post*, August 26, 2020; F. Chu, "The Future of E-Commerce Is Social Media," *Smart Brief*, August 3, 2020; "The Top Social Commerce Platforms in Southeast Asia," *J&T Express*, July 21, 2020; N. Chuwiruch and I. Sayson, "Without Tourists, Asia's Vendors Turn to Facebook," *Bloomberg BusinessWeek*, July 20, 2020; H. Beech, "No One Knows What Thailand Is Doing Right, but So Far It's Working," *New York Times*, July 16, 2020; "2020 Online Trade Set to hit B220bn," *Bangkok Post*, May 21, 2020; "Social Commerce New Key to Survival," *Bangkok Post*, May 8, 2020; "Lazada: Pandemic Making E-Commerce Mainstream," *Bangkok Post*, April 17, 2020; "E-Commerce Set to Build on Successes," *Bangkok Post*, January 27, 2020; "E-Commerce Players Eye New Income, Profitability," *Bangkok Post*, January 13, 2020; "Thais Setting the Pace for Social Commerce," *Bangkok Post*, November 28, 2019; S. Abudheen, "Southeast Asia Emerges as Leader in Conversational Commerce; Thailand, Vietnam Most Advanced in Adoption," *e27*, October 31, 2019; J. Rajeck, "Is Social Commerce Finally Taking off in Southeast Asia?" *Econsultancy*, October 29, 2019.

Questions

1. Discuss the competition between e-marketplaces and social commerce platforms in Thailand.

2. Discuss the common, overlapping functions that e-marketplaces and social commerce platforms demonstrate in this case.

Companies that engage in social computing are always concerned with negative posts. For example, when a company creates a Facebook business page, by default the site allows other members of the website—potentially including disgruntled customers or unethical competitors—to post notes on the firm's Facebook page and to comment on what the firm has posted.

Going further, if the company turns off the feature that lets other users write on its page, people may wonder what the company is afraid of. The company will also be eliminating its opportunity to engage in customer conversations, particularly conversations that could market the firm's products and services better than the company could do itself. Similarly, the company could delete posts. However, that policy only encourages the post author to scream even louder about being censored.

Another risk is the 20–80 rule of thumb, which posits that a minority of individuals (20 percent) contribute most of the content (80 percent) to blogs, wikis, social computing websites, and so on. For example, in an analysis of thousands of submissions to the news voting site Digg over a three-week time frame, the *Wall Street Journal* reported that roughly 33 percent of the stories that made it to Digg's homepage were submitted by 30 contributors (out of 900,000 registered members).

Other risks of social computing include:

- Information security concerns
- Invasion of privacy
- Violation of intellectual property and copyright
- Employees' reluctance to participate
- Data leakage of personal information or corporate strategic information
- Poor or biased quality of users' generated content
- Cyberbullying/cyberstalking and employee harassment

MKT Consider Rosetta Stone (**www.rosettastone.com**), which produces software for language translation. To obtain the maximum possible mileage out of social computing and limit the firm's risks on social media, Rosetta Stone implemented a strategy to control its customer interaction on Facebook. The strategy involves both human intervention and software to help monitor the firm's Facebook presence. Specifically, the software helps to monitor Wall posts and respond to them constructively.

A new business model has emerged, enabled by social computing and environmental concerns. This business model is called *collaborative consumption.*

Collaborative Consumption

Collaborative consumption is an economic model based on sharing, swapping, trading, or renting products and services, enabling access over ownership. The premise of collaborative consumption is that having access to goods and services is more important than owning them. This new model is transforming social, economic, and environmental practices.

Collaborative consumption is a broad term that includes many practices, such as collaborative production, crowdfunding, peer-to-peer lending, and others. In collaborative production, users sell the extra power generated from their solar panels back to the utility company's grid to help power someone else's home. Crowdfunding is the practice of funding a project by raising money from a large number of people, typically via the Internet. Peer-to-peer lending is the practice of lending money to unrelated individuals without using a traditional financial institution such as a bank.

Collaborative consumption is a very old concept. We have been bartering and cooperating throughout human history. If we did not have money, we traded time, meals, favors, or personal belongings, and many cultures today do the same. On the Web, the peer-to-peer model started with eBay (**www.ebay.com**) in 1995. Then Craigslist (**www.craigslist.com**) began in the late 1990s, followed by Zipcar (**www.zipcar.com**) in 2000, and Airbnb (**www.airbnb.com**) in 2007.

Trust is the greatest concern of this new economic model. Sharing works well only when the participants' reputations are involved. Most sharing platforms try to address this issue by creating a self-policing community. Almost all platforms require profiles of both parties, and they feature community rating systems.

Startups such as TrustCloud (**http://trustcloud.com**) are trying to become the portable reputation system of this new economy. The company has developed an algorithm that collects (if you choose to opt in) your online "data exhaust"—the trail you leave as you engage with others on Facebook, LinkedIn, Twitter, commentary-filled sites like TripAdvisor, and others. It then calculates your reliability, consistency, and responsiveness. The result is a contextual badge that you carry to any website, a trust rating similar to the credit rating you have in the "offline" world.

Collaborative consumption does have advantages. Participants cite advantages that include self-management, variety, and the flexibility that comes from being able to set one's own schedules. The model can be beneficial for part-time workers, young people such as students, the unemployed, stay-at-home parents, and retired persons. The model allows people to share their underused assets and earn income.

For example, over half of Airbnb hosts in San Francisco said that the service helps them pay their rent, and the average RelayRides member makes an extra $250 per month. PricewaterhouseCoopers estimates that the sharing economy (i.e., collaborative consumption) will reach $355 billion globally by 2025.

Collaborative consumption has positive environmental impacts. As our population grows, we are using valuable resources—water, food, oil—in a way that is not sustainable. The new model helps us to utilize our natural resources more wisely by sharing, not owning.

On the other hand, collaborative consumption does have disadvantages. Law and regulatory agencies are trying to keep abreast of the rapidly growing companies in this economy. Consider these examples:

- Without a permit, residents in San Francisco are prohibited from renting for under 30 days (although the practice still occurs).

- New York City passed an "illegal hotel law" in 2010 that prevents people from subletting apartments for less than 29 days, which is preventing Airbnb from expanding its market in the city.

- Uber and Lyft often function as taxi companies, but do not have to follow worker regulations or laws that apply to existing taxi companies because the services consider their employees to be independent contractors rather than employees.

People working for collaborative consumption services often work seven-day weeks, performing a series of one-off tasks. They have little recourse when the services for which they work change their business models or pay rates. To reduce the risks, workers typically sign up for multiple services. Another disadvantage is that the pay may be less than expected when participants factor in the time spent, expenses, insurance costs, and taxes on self-employment earnings.

Participants have no basic employee benefits or protections. As independent contractors, they do not quality for employee benefits such as health insurance, disability insurance, payroll deductions for Social Security, retirement savings plans, or unemployment benefits. They do not have the right to organize into a union, meaning that they do not have access to union-based collective bargaining processes. They also do not have the right to due process should a service remove them from its platform.

In April 2016, Uber reached a settlement in two class action lawsuits that require the company to pay as much as $100 million to the drivers represented in the cases, but will allow Uber to continue to categorize its drivers as contractors, not employees. To work more effectively with its drivers, Uber has a new driver deactivation policy in place and the company has agreed not to deactivate drivers who decline trips regularly.

There are numerous, diverse companies in the collaborative consumption market including:

- Uber (**www.uber.com**) operates the Uber mobile app, which allows consumers with smartphones to submit a trip request that is sent to Uber drivers who use their own cars.

- Airbnb (**www.airbnb.com**) is a website for people to list, find, and rent lodgings.
- Zipcar (**www.zipcar.com**) and Turo (**http://turo.com**) are car-sharing services.
- Skillshare (**www.skillshare.com**) provides access to top-class tutors very cheaply.
- Tradesy (**www.tradesy.com**) lets users sell and buy used clothes from well-known brands. The service takes 9 percent of profits.
- Bla Bla Car (**www.blablacar.com**) lets you rent out extra seats in your car when you go on a trip.
- Olio (**www.olioex.com**) is an app where users can find leftover food to share. This service is important in the United States, where we waste some 30 percent of our food.
- Marriott International (**www.marriott.com**) offers meeting spaces on LiquidSpace (**https://liquidspace.com**). LiquidSpace is an online marketplace that allows people to rent office space by the hour or the day. Hundreds of Marriott hotels now list meeting spaces, and the program has expanded the company's reach by attracting local businesspeople from surrounding areas.
- FLOOW2 (**www.floow2.com**), based in the Netherlands, calls itself a "business-to-business sharing marketplace where companies and institutions can share equipment, as well as the skills and knowledge of personnel." The company lists more than 25,000 types of equipment and services in industries such as construction, agriculture, transportation, real estate, and health care.

Companies are engaged in many types of social commerce activities, including shopping, advertising, market research, customer relationship management, and human resource management. In the next sections of this chapter, you will learn about each social commerce activity.

Before you go on...

1. Briefly describe the benefits of social commerce to customers.
2. Briefly describe the risks of social commerce to businesses.
3. What are the benefits of collaborative consumption to customers?
4. What are the benefits and risks of collaborative consumption to participants (i.e., workers)?

9.3 Social Computing in Business: Shopping

Author Lecture Videos are available exclusively in *WileyPLUS*.
Apply the Concept activities are available in the Appendix and in *WileyPLUS*.

Social shopping is a method of electronic commerce that takes all of the key aspects of social networks—friends, groups, voting, comments, discussions, reviews, and others—and focuses them on shopping. Social shopping helps shoppers connect with one another based on taste, location, age, gender, and other selected attributes.

The nature of shopping is changing, especially shopping for brand-name clothes and related items. For example, popular brands such as Gap, Shopbop, InStyle, and Lisa Klein are joining communities on Stylehive (**www.stylehive.com**) to help promote the season's latest fashion collections. Shoppers are using sites like ThisNext (**www.thisnext.com**) to create profiles and blogs about their favorite products in social communities. Shoppers can tag each item, so that all items become searchable. Moreover, searching within these websites can yield results targeted specifically to individual customers.

There are several methods to shop socially. You will learn about each of them in the next section. As you see in IT's About Business 9.2, Poshmark has applied an interesting business model to social shopping.

IT's About Business 9.2

MIS MKT The Story of Poshmark

Most electronic commerce companies, including Amazon, rely on *search-based shopping*. That is, visitors enter a term in the search bar relating to a product they want to buy and shop for products based on the results of their search. However, that is not the way many people shop for clothes in the real world. Instead, they browse stores and ask their friends about the clothes they are wearing. Reflecting this reality, one shopping app—Poshmark—relies on social shopping.

Social shopping—also called *discovery-based social shopping*—is a type of commerce in which shoppers' friends become involved in the shopping experience. Social shopping attempts to use technology to mimic the social interactions that take place in physical malls and stores, typically via social networks. The process provides merchants with the opportunity to enhance the retail experience for shoppers by helping them and their friends discover new products. The process also enables consumers to promote a brand in social networks, which can lead to increased sales based on word-of-mouth referrals.

The demand for discount clothing is significant. According to the National Retail Federation (**www.nrf.com**), some 90 percent of brick-and-mortar shoppers purchase clothing from discount stores. Further, the majority of those shoppers are looking for deals on clothing.

Founded in 2011, Poshmark (**www.poshmark.com**) is a social shopping app. Poshmark's philosophy is to introduce people to new fashion through other people, not brands. Therefore, the company has focused on individual buyers and sellers.

Poshmark has built a social network that is based not on people whom their users know but on people whose taste in clothes their users like. As of August 2020, the company had 60 million members, 8 million of whom were also sellers. The members are a combination of influencers and friends.

The platform's model is known as *digital consignment*, where people sell their items online. Poshmark started as a way for women to make money selling extra items from their closets—essentially an eBay for clothing. Whereas other companies in this space—for example, The RealReal (**www.therealreal.com**) and ThredUp (**www.thredup.com**)—handle the pricing and selling of items, Poshmark allows individuals to do the selling themselves.

With digital consignment, Poshmark does not maintain any inventory. Rather, its members sell directly to one another. The app has created a number of small-scale entrepreneurs who have built businesses around selling on the platform, whether as professional resellers or as people who have designed and launched their own clothing labels. Poshmark takes a 20 percent cut from each sale.

On the website and the app, members follow one another and share listings they believe their followers will find interesting. People follow one another's virtual closets full of clothes for sale, and they share items they find interesting. These clothes are often pre-worn items with a mix of boutique items the sellers have purchased wholesale. Daily "posh parties" within the app let people browse a certain theme, such as prom dresses and athletic wear. Each listing has a comment section for anyone to ask questions about items for sale.

In 2019 Poshmark paid out $2 billion to its sellers, just over 1 year after passing the $1 billion mark. Poshmark's members can look over 30 million secondhand listings on the platform. In 2019 the platform opened a new home goods segment. In addition, it expanded internationally into Canada, where more than 300,000 users joined the platform between May and October 2019.

Buyers and sellers can chat with one another via Poshmark, and they spend on average between 23 and 27 minutes on the app. In this way, the platform helps to create and nurture interpersonal relationships, a process that helps to organically grow the kind of community that other retailers would like to develop. Organic growth means that Poshmark expands more from word-of-mouth from its members than through advertising.

One entrepreneur from Texas began selling her used clothes on the app in December 2012. After running through her own closet, she started buying clothes wholesale and reselling them. She then launched her own clothing brand and started selling to other Poshmark sellers through the company's wholesale market. After six years, she became the first seller on Poshmark to achieve $1 million in total sales. She then opened her first brick-and-mortar store.

Poshmark now sells new clothes, complete with its own wholesale market and fashion entrepreneurs who are selling their own clothing lines on the platform. The company is planning to expand into menswear, children's clothing, plus sizes, makeup, home decor, and luxury goods. Approximately 20 percent of the platform's users are male.

In April 2020 Poshmark announced that it was adding a video feature to its fashion marketplace. The social network wants to offer a more real-world experience to shoppers. The company is hoping that video will increase engagement and sales among its members and create a closer connection among buyers and sellers. The app's sellers can post live 15-second videos or upload footage from their phones that links directly to the items they are selling. This new feature enables sellers to show off the ways they styled an outfit they are selling or to provide the backstory on how they acquired a particular item. The video content will disappear after 48 hours.

Sources: Compiled from "The Ultimate Guides to Using Popular Platforms like Amazon, Depop, and eBay to Start Your Own Online Business, Sell to a Massive Audience, and Make Big Money," *Business Insider*, August 20, 2020; H. Koss, "Social Commerce Is Replacing the Shopping Mall," *Builtin.com*, August 14, 2020; S. Stein, "Can Macy's Compete against Poshmark, Instagram and Amazon with Shoppable Content and Social Selling?" *Forbes*, August 7, 2020; "Social Shopping Emerges as Hottest Digital 3.0 Trend," *PYMNTS*, August 4, 2020; J. Schiffer, "Secondhand Shoppers Worry about Their Favorite Local Spots," *New York Times*, July 29, 2020; J. Gallagher, "Unemployed? Try Reselling Clothes on eBay or Poshmark," *Wall Street Journal*, May 27, 2020; L. Debter, "Fashion Reseller Poshmark Fast Tracks Video Feature, Targeting Shoppers Stuck at Home," *Forbes*, April 29, 2020; T. Rock-Morris, "Poshmark: Over Half of Consumers Would Buy through Social Media," *Retail Dive*, March 2, 2020; "Poshmark's Social Commerce Report Finds Social Shopping and Resale Are Driving Retail's Biggest Shifts," *PR Newswire*, February 25, 2020; C. Hernandez, "Couple Pays College Tuition in Full Thanks to Fashion Resale App," *ABC News*, February 6, 2020; K. Richards, "Poshmark Is Leaning into Sneakers to Grow Its Men's Business," *Glossy*, February 3, 2020; H. LeSavage, "Poshmark Has Surpassed $2 Billion in Revenue Paid to Its Sellers," *Morning Brew*, September 27, 2019; L. Baker, "Fashion Retail Site Poshmark to Delay IPO until 2020," *Bloomberg*, September 3, 2019; S. Edelson, "Secondhand E-Commerce Sites See a Silver lining," *Forbes*, June 23, 2019; B. Carson, "Social Shopping," *Forbes*, December 31, 2018; **www.poshmark.com**, accessed August 22, 2020.

Questions

1. What is the difference between search-based shopping and discovery-based social shopping?

2. If you were Jeff Bezos (CEO of Amazon), what features might you add to your platform to compete with Poshmark?

3. In your opinion, does Poshmark have a strategic advantage over ThredUp and The RealReal? Provide examples to support your answer.

Ratings, Reviews, and Recommendations

Prior to making a purchase, customers typically collect information such as what brand to buy, from which vendor, and at what price. Online customers obtain this information via shopping aids such as comparison agents and websites. Today, customers also use social networking to guide their purchase decisions. They are increasingly utilizing ratings, reviews, and recommendations from friends, fans, followers, and experienced customers. Significantly, this chapter's opening case illustrates how common fake reviews are and how careful we must all be when considering reviews about a product or a service.

Ratings, *reviews*, and *recommendations* are usually available in social shopping. In addition to seeing what is already posted, shoppers have an opportunity to contribute their own ratings and reviews and to discuss ratings and reviews posted by other shoppers (see **Figure 9.3**). The ratings and reviews come from the following sources:

- *Customer ratings and reviews*: Integrated into the vendor's web page, a social network page, a customer review site, or in customer feeds (e.g., Amazon, iTunes, Buzzillions, Epinions)
- *Expert ratings and reviews*: Views from an independent authority (e.g., Metacritic)
- *Sponsored reviews*: Paid-for reviews (e.g., SponsoredReviews, PayPerPost)
- *Conversational marketing*: Individuals converse via e-mail, blog, live chat, discussion groups, and tweets. Monitoring these conversations yields rich data for market research and customer service

MKT As one example, Maui Jim (**www.mauijim.com**), the sunglasses company, employed favorable word-of-mouth marketing as a key sales driver. The company uses Bazaarvoice's Ratings & Reviews to allow customers to contribute five-point ratings and authentic product reviews on the company's entire line of sunglasses and accessories. In effect, Maui Jim extended customers' word-of-mouth reviews across the Web.

Maui Jim encourages its customers to share their candid opinions on the style, fit, and performance of all of its sunglasses models. To accomplish this goal, the company integrates customer reviews into its website's search function to ensure that shoppers who are interested in a particular product will see that product's rating in the search results. Customer response to this rating system has been overwhelmingly positive.

Social recommendation websites such as Zinrelo (**www.zinrelo.com**), and Upserve (**www.upserve.com**), and Yelp (**www.yelp.com**) encourage conversations about purchases. The product recommendations are submitted by users' friends and acquaintances and arguably are more trustworthy than reviews posted by strangers.

FIGURE 9.3 Yelp (www.yelp.com) users submit reviews of local business within a local metropolitan area. Some communities have pages that feature a Review of the Day.

NetPhotos/Alamy Stock Photo

ThisNext (**www.thisnext.com**) is a website where people recommend their favorite products to others. The site blends two powerful elements of real-world shopping: word-of-mouth recommendations from trusted sources and the ability to browse products in a way that naturally leads to discovery.

We must be careful when our search results reflect only our thinking on a subject. This process forms a filter bubble (coined by Eli Pariser). A *filter bubble* is a result of a personalized search where a website algorithm predicts (e.g., makes recommendations) what information or product a user would like based on user location and past searches on the website. As a result, users receive only information that reinforces their past choices and reflects their viewpoints.

Examples of such website algorithms include Google Personalized Search results, Amazon's A9 search engine, and Facebook's personalized news stream. For example, if you search Amazon only for books in the science fiction category, you may miss out on outstanding books in other genres because Amazon will mainly recommend books in the science fiction genre.

In another example, one user who searched Google for "BP" received investment news for British Petroleum. Another user searched for that exact term and received information about the Deepwater Horizon oil spill.

Group Shopping

Group shopping websites such as Groupon (**www.groupon.com**) and LivingSocial (**www.livingsocial.com**, see **Figure 9.4**) offer major discounts or special deals during a short time frame. Group buying is closely associated with special deals (flash sales).

People who sign up with LivingSocial receive e-mails that offer deals at, for example, a restaurant, a spa, or an event in a given city. They can click on either "Today's Deal" or "Past Deal" (some past deals can still be active). They can also click on an icon and receive the deal the next day. Customers who purchase a deal receive a unique link to share with their friends. If a customer convinces three or more people to buy that specific deal using his or her link, then the customer's deal is free.

Individuals can also shop together virtually in real time. In this process, shoppers log on to a website and then contact their friends and family. Everyone then shops online at the same time. Some real-time shopping providers, such as DoTogether (**www.dotogether.com**) and Wet Seal (**www.wetseal.com**), have integrated their shopping service directly into Facebook. Customers log in to Facebook, install the firm's app, and then invite their friends to join them on a virtual retail shopping experience.

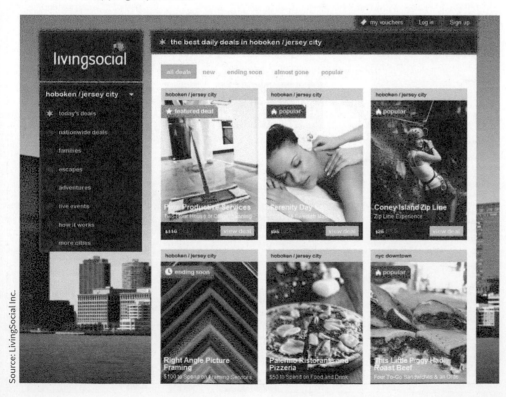

Source: LivingSocial Inc.

FIGURE 9.4 LivingSocial (www.livingsocial.com) is a popular example of a group shopping website.

Shopping Communities and Clubs

MKT Shopping clubs host sales for their members that last just a few days and usually feature luxury brands at heavily discounted prices. Club organizers host three to seven sales per day, usually via e-mail messages that entice club members to shop at more than 70 percent off retail—but quickly, before supplies run out.

Luxury brands effectively partner with online shopping clubs to dispose of special-run, sample, overstock, or liquidation goods. These clubs are rather exclusive, which prevents the brands' images from being diminished. Examples are Beyond the Rack (**www.beyondtherack.com**), Gilt Groupe (**www.gilt.com**), Rue La La (**www.ruelala.com**), and One King's Lane (**www.onekingslane.com**).

Kaboodle (**www.kaboodle.com**) is another example of a shopping community. Kaboodle is a free service that lets users collect information from the Web and store it on a Kaboodle list that they can share with other shoppers. Kaboodle simplifies shopping by making it easier for people to find items they want in a catalog and by allowing users to share recommendations with one another using Kaboodle lists and groups. People can also use Kaboodle lists for planning vacations, sharing research for work and school, sharing favorite bands with friends, and basically everything else they might want to collect and share information about.

Social Marketplaces and Direct Sales

MKT **Social marketplaces** act as online intermediaries that harness the power of social networks for introducing, buying, and selling products and services. A social marketplace helps members market their own creations (see Etsy in **Figure 9.5**). Other examples are as follows:

- Craigslist (**www.craigslist.com**) provides online classifieds in addition to supporting social activities such as meetings and events.
- Fotolia (**www.fotolia.com**) is a social marketplace for the community of creative people who enjoy sharing, learning, and expressing themselves through images, forums, and blogs; members provide royalty-free stock images that other individuals and professionals can legally buy and share.
- Flipsy (**www.flipsy.com**) can be used by anyone to list, buy, and sell books, music, movies, and games.

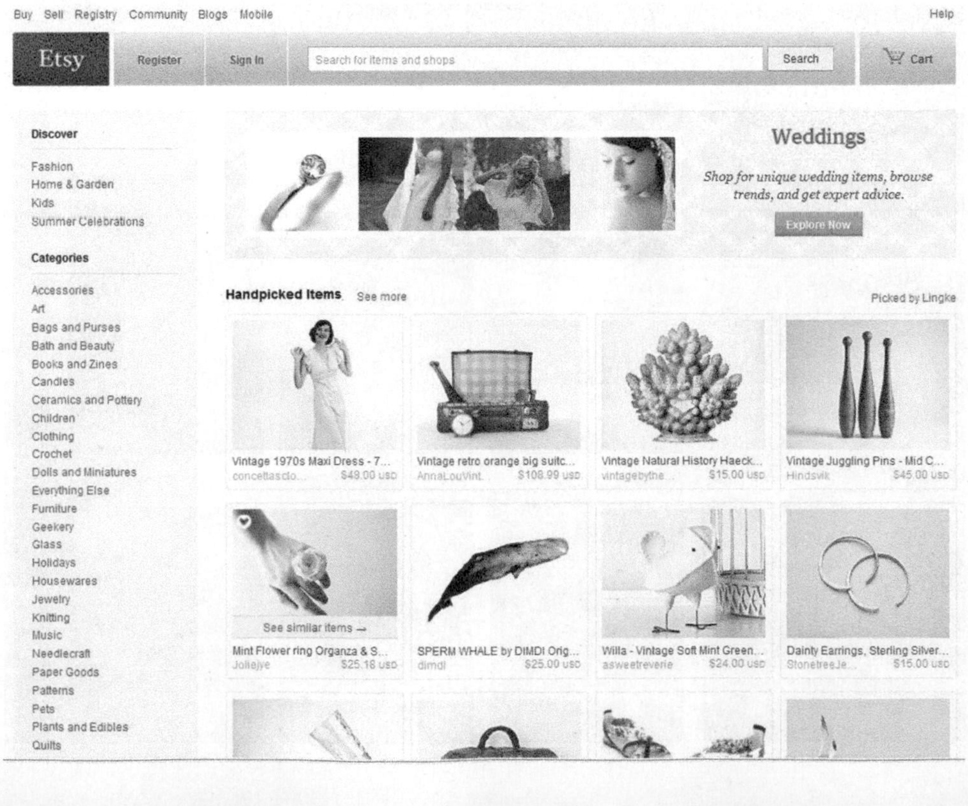

FIGURE 9.5 Etsy (www.etsy.com) is a social marketplace for all handmade or vintage items.

Source: Etsy, Inc.

1. Prior to making a purchase, why are ratings, reviews, and recommendations so important to potential customers?
2. Define collaborative consumption, and describe how collaborative consumption is a "green" phenomenon.

9.4 Social Computing in Business: Marketing

MKT *Marketing* can be defined as the process of building profitable customer relationships by creating value for customers and capturing value in return. There are many components to a marketing campaign, including (1) define your target audience; (2) develop your message (i.e., how you will solve their problem); (3) decide on how you will deliver your message (e.g., e-mail, snail mail, Web advertising, social networks); and (4) follow up. IT's About Business 9.3 shows how farmers are using YouTube to educate the public about farming operations and, in the process, develop another source of income.

Author Lecture Videos are available exclusively in *WileyPLUS.*
Apply the Concept activities are available in the Appendix and in *WileyPLUS.*

IT's About Business 9.3

MIS **POM** **Farmers Develop Another Source of Income**

Although modern farmers have benefitted from many technological developments, the weather still dictates much of the success or failure of a farm's crops. The cost of farming inputs, which include seeds, fertilizer, labor, equipment, and professional veterinary services, is rising, and many farmers must manage debt on their farms. Many farmers have also been hurt by U.S. trade differences with China.

In contrast, YouTube paints a somewhat rosier picture. There, farming can seem more like an aspirational lifestyle choice than a precarious livelihood. YouTube is home to influencers from a myriad of professional and cultural persuasions, and farming is no exception.

In fact, agricultural content on YouTube is increasing. Content creators uploaded 60 percent more farming-related videos to YouTube in 2020 than they did in 2019. Further, views of farming content increased by 70 percent in 2020 over 2019.

According to the U.S. Census Bureau, 80 percent of Americans live in urban areas. Many of these individuals claim they want to live in a rural area. Meeting this desire, new farming content creators are specifically documenting what it is like to farm after, or while, living in a city or working in a corporate job. Farming content can serve as a how-to guide to an alternate way of living. Farming YouTube content offers the chance to experience a way of life that is often idealized but is practically inaccessible to most people.

Some of the most popular farming videos involve livestock. However, the enduring appeal of animals can make some situations complex for farmers to navigate. As we have noted, farmers want to show the reality of what farming is actually about. This process often means teaching people where their food comes from, including butchering animals. YouTube's Community Guidelines prohibit videos containing violent or graphic content. However, farmers do show aspects of their work that are messy and potentially uncomfortable.

Let's look at several examples of farmers who have developed large social media followings and are earning notable income.

One South Dakota farmer, Cole Sonne, and his father made a 12-minute video for YouTube demonstrating to their fans how they moved large grass and alfalfa bales from one area of their farm to another. The video was viewed more than 100,000 times between July and November 2019. Sonne then started a YouTube channel dedicated to the farm, which has amassed more than 30,000 followers. He earns roughly $650 per month from YouTube advertisements.

Morgan Gold, who started Gold Shaw Farm (**www.gold shawfarm.com**) in Vermont with his wife, Allison Ebrahimi-Gold, in 2016, began his YouTube channel about the same time. By 2020 he had more than 20,000 followers and was generating between $2,500 and $4,000 per month. He has not reached the point where YouTube income will support him and his family. In fact, he still has his full-time job as a marketing executive for an insurance company.

After trying to take a month off in early 2020, Gold quickly learned that any gap in his YouTube publication schedule resulted in a steep decline in his audience. He also learned, through trial and error, what works with his audience and what does not. For instance, mounting a GoPro camera on his sheepdog did not work. In contrast, slow drone footage of the sun rising or setting over his 150 acres definitely works.

Few videos captivate audiences, though, as much as real-life setbacks. Gold realized this fact when a mink broke into his duck hutch and killed all of his ducks. His next videos featured night-vision footage of the mink among his ducks, increasing his audience to almost 100,000 viewers.

Gold's YouTube channel has been successful enough to help shape his business strategy on his farm. He is rethinking his farm products because he became aware that he has a broad, diverse audience who do not live close by. He is considering new products, such as charcuterie, that could be easily shipped to fans in other states. Charcuterie is the preparation of cured meats such as pork, ham, bacon, and sausage.

MN Millennial Farmer (**www.mnmillennialfarmer.com**), Zach Johnson, is from Minnesota. He grows corn and soybeans on the family farm, which was founded by his great-great-grandfather in 1876. Johnson's biggest paycheck comes from his YouTube channel, which has 400,000 followers and earns him about 5 times more money than his crops do.

In April 2016, Johnson launched his first few videos on YouTube, capturing the ups and downs of farming as well as issues he experienced while planting corn. It was not until the fall of 2017 that he realized that people cared about what he had to say.

Once the videos began attracting viewers, Johnson signed up his YouTube channel for a Google Adsense account, which matches ads to a user's site based on their content and visitors. Shortly after, he saw that a single video earned him $92, and he became even more enthusiastic. His "Gearing up for Harvest!" video was his first to hit 100,000 views on YouTube (in 3–4 days), and his "Tractor Stuck in the MUD" video collected more than 1.6 million views in just a few months. By August 2020, Johnson's YouTube channel had received more than 70 million views. He had 572,000 subscribers to his channel and had uploaded 319 videos.

The MN Millennial Farmer brand now includes YouTube videos, public speaking engagements, farm tours, merchandise, and the "Off the Husk" podcast, which is backed by Farmers Business Network, his biggest sponsor. The majority of his brand income comes from two main sources on YouTube: ads and sponsors. Advertisements are a part of Google Adsense, and they can appear before, after, or in the middle of a video. Sponsorships or brand deals include paid product endorsements that appear within a video's content.

Fortunately for Johnson, his videos can last 15 to 20 minutes or longer. Brands find more value in long-form content because this type of content is more likely to engage audiences. Analysts estimate that Johnson earns between $2,500 and $5,000 per month from YouTube ads alone.

The sponsors that support Johnson's content also earn him additional revenue. In addition to Farmers Business Network, his sponsors include or have included John Deere, WD-40, J&M Manufacturing, Walls Clothing, Dakota Micro, and others. Analysts estimate that sponsors could earn Johnson between $5,000 and $15,000 per branded post.

Johnson's online merchandise store sells branded T-shirts, caps, and hooded sweatshirts. Analysts estimate that the brand could sell between 1,000 and 2,000 units per month, earning between $3,000 and $6,000.

Unlike many influencers, Zach and his wife have not employed a marketing agency to help grow their brand. Instead, most advertisers come to them directly. The couple then decides which opportunities to take based on time availability and quality control.

Advertising revenue from YouTube can be problematic. One farmer claimed that he was hurt by policy changes the platform made in 2017 that resulted in many channels being blocked form earning ad revenue. The Adpocalypse, as it came to be known, occurred after a series of media reports revealed that prominent advertisers were showing up next to videos containing hate speech and extremist content. YouTube's policy changes impacted many content creators on the platform.

The farmer stated that his income was cut in half after the changes. He still uploads content to YouTube, but he now operates an independent membership website where people pay a subscription to view his videos. He is also unhappy that the most successful farming videos have outrageous titles and thumbnail images but often do not provide any practical information about growing food to viewers.

Amy Fewell, the founder of Homesteaders of America, stated that the number of farmers who earn substantial income from YouTube is steadily increasing. By August 2020 they numbered about 50.

Sources: Compiled from E. Barry, "In a Wistful Age, Farmers Find a New Angle: Chore TV," *New York Times*, August 7, 2020; N. Nittle, "Can YouTube Give Farmers a Financial Boost?" *Civil Eats*, February 25, 2020; P. Martineau, "The Wired Guide to Influencers," *Wired*, December 6, 2019; L. Matsakis, "On Farming YouTube, Emu Eggs and Hay Bales Find Loyal Fans," *Wired*, December 18, 2019; E. Gravier, "This Millenial Farmer Makes 5 Times More Money from His YouTube Channel than His Crops—Here's How," *CNBC*, November 27, 2019; A. Rappeport, "Farmers' Frustration with Trump Grows as U.S. Escalates China Fight," *New York Times*, August 27, 2019; L. Mulvany, "The Changing Face of Farms: Women Step in as U.S. Growers Age," *Bloomberg*, April 11, 2019; C. Ingraham, "Americans Say There's Not Much Appeal to Big-City Living. Why Do so Many of Us Live There?" *Washington Post*, December 18, 2018; Y. Liu, "The Chinese Farmer Who Live-Streamed Her Life and Made a Fortune," *The New Yorker*, October 29, 2018; H. Kaur, "Why China Is Moving Millions to Cities," *CNN*, June 15, 2018; R. Dunphy, "Can YouTube Survive the Adpocalypse?" *New York Magazine*, December 28, 2017.

Questions

1. Describe how farmers are using YouTube in their marketing efforts.
2. Describe how farmers generate income from YouTube.

Advertising

MKT **Social advertising** refers to advertising formats that make use of the social context of the user viewing the ad. Social advertising is the first form of advertising to leverage forms of social influence such as peer pressure and friend recommendations and likes.

Many experts believe advertising is the solution to the challenge of making money from social networking sites and social commerce sites. Advertisers have long noted the large number of visitors on social networks and the amount of time they spend there. As a result, they are willing to pay to place ads and run promotions on social networks. Advertisers now post ads on all major social networking websites.

Most ads in social commerce consist of branded content paid for by advertisers. These ads belong to two major categories: *social advertisements* (or *social ads*) and *social apps*. Social advertisements are ads placed in paid-for media space on social media networks. Social apps are branded online applications that support social interactions and user contributions (e.g., Nike+).

Viral marketing—that is, word-of-mouth advertising—lends itself especially well to social networking. For example, Stormhoek Vineyards (**www.stormhoek.com**) initiated a marketing campaign by offering bloggers a free bottle of wine. Within six months, roughly 100 of these bloggers had posted voluntary comments—the majority of them positive—about the wine on their blogs. In turn these comments were read by other bloggers.

There are other innovative methods to advertise in social media. Consider the following:

- Use a company Facebook page, including a store that attracts fans and lets them "meet" other customers. Then, advertise in your Facebook store.
- Tweet business success stories to your customers.
- Integrate ads into YouTube videos.
- Use native advertising. *Native advertising* is a sales pitch that fits into the flow of the information being shown. Many publishers view native advertising as risky because it has the potential to erode the public's trust.

Market Research

MKT Traditionally, marketing professionals used demographics compiled by market research firms as one of their primary tools to identify and target potential customers. Obtaining this information was time-consuming and costly because marketing professionals had to ask potential customers to provide it. Today, however, members of social networks provide this information voluntarily on their pages! (Think about all the information that you provide on your favorite social networking websites.) Because of the open nature of social networking, merchants can easily find their customers, see what they do online, and learn who their friends are.

This information provides a new opportunity to assess markets in near real time. Word-of-mouth has always been one of the most powerful marketing methods—more often than not, people use products that their friends like and recommend. Social media sites can provide this type of data for numerous products and services.

Companies are utilizing social computing tools to obtain feedback from customers. This trend is referred to as *conversational marketing*. These tools enable customers to supply feedback via blogs, wikis, online forums, and social networking sites. Again, customers are providing much of this feedback to companies voluntarily and free. Social computing not only generates faster and cheaper results than traditional focus groups but also fosters closer customer relationships.

Retailers are aware that customers, especially younger ones, not only want to be heard but also want to know whether other customers agree with them. Consequently, retailers are increasingly opening up their websites to customers, allowing them to post product reviews, ratings, and, in some cases, photos and videos.

As a result of this strategy, customer reviews are emerging as prime locations for online shoppers to visit. Approximately half of consumers consult reviews before making an online purchase, and almost two-thirds are more likely to purchase from a site that offers ratings and reviews.

Using social computing for market research is not restricted to businesses. Customers also enjoy the capabilities that social computing offers when they are shopping.

Conducting Market Research Using Social Networks

MKT Customer sentiment expressed on Twitter, Facebook, and similar sites represents an incredibly valuable source of information for companies. Customer activities on social networking sites generate huge amounts of data that must be analyzed, so that management can conduct better marketing campaigns and improve their product design and their service offerings. The monitoring, collection, and analysis of socially generated data, and the resultant strategic decisions are combined in a process known as **social intelligence** (also called *social listening*).

MKT An example of social intelligence comes from TOMS Shoes (**www.toms.com**). The retailer used social intelligence to analyze conversations. During the research, TOMS discovered a high number of conversations around My Little Pony. This finding meant that people who were interested in, or discussing, TOMS were also highly interested in My Little Pony. Moving quickly, TOMS created a brand new "My Little Pony" themed shoe. The new product sold out within 48 hours.

With the increase in awareness around high sodium intake, fast food customers were showing hesitance about some foods. Wendy's (**www.wendys.com**) wanted to keep the favorability toward their french fries at a high level. Through social intelligence, Wendy's discovered that "sea salt" was mentioned much more positively than salt or sodium. The chain added sea salt into the marketing and advertising for their french fries, which helped improve their sales.

Luxury automobile brands such as BMW (**www.bmw.com**) are interested in which vehicle features that drivers like the most. The automaker measured sentiment levels to understand how consumers felt with new features of its cars. With social intelligence, BMW found that their new laser-guided headlights had high conversation volume and favorability levels. The firm began to emphasize the headlights in their advertising as an exciting new feature.

Social networks provide excellent sources of valuable information for market research. In this section you will see illustrative examples of how to use Facebook, Twitter, and LinkedIn for market research.

Using Facebook for Market Research.
There are several ways to use Facebook for market research. Consider the following examples:

- Obtain feedback from your Facebook fans (and their friends if possible) on advertising campaigns, market research, and so on. It is the equivalent of holding a free focus group.

- Test-market your messages. Provide two or three options, and ask fans which one they prefer and why.

- Use Facebook for survey invitations (i.e., to recruit participants). Essentially, turn Facebook into a giant panel, and ask users to participate in a survey. Facebook offers a self-service model for displaying ads, which can function as invitations to take a survey. Facebook also allows you to target your audience very specifically based on traditional demographic criteria such as age and gender.

Using Twitter for Market Research.
Your customers, your prospects, and industry thought leaders all use Twitter, making it a rich source of instantly updated information. Consider the following examples:

- Visit Twitter Search (**www.twitter.com/search**). Enter a company's Twitter name. Not only can you follow what the company is saying, you can also follow what everyone is saying to them. Monitoring replies to your competitors and their employees will help you develop your own Twitter strategy by enabling you to observe (a) what your competitors are doing and, more important, (b) what people think about them. You can also follow the company's response to this feedback.

- Take advantage of the tools that enable you to find people in the industries in which they operate. Use search.twitter.com to monitor industry-specific keywords. Check out Twellow (**www.twellow.com**). This site automatically categorizes a Twitter user into one to three industries based on that person's bio and tweets.

- Do you want to know what topic is on most people's minds today? If so, then review the chart on TweetStats (**www.tweetstats.com**). It will show you the most frequently used words in all of Tweetdom, so you can be a part of those conversations.
- An increasing number of companies are utilizing Twitter to solicit information from customers and to interact with them. Examples are Dell (connecting with customers), JetBlue (learning about customers), Teusner Wines (gathering feedback, sharing information), and Pepsi (rapid response time in dealing with complaints).

Using LinkedIn for Market Research.   Post a question (e.g., solicit advice) regarding the topic or issue you are interested in. You may obtain a better result if you go to a specific LinkedIn group.

Before you go on...

1. Is social advertising more effective than advertising without a social component? Why or why not?
2. Describe how marketing professionals use social networks to perform marketing research.

9.5 Social Computing in Business: Customer Relationship Management

The customer service profession has undergone a significant transformation, both in the ways that customer service professionals conduct business and in the ways that customers adapt to interacting with companies in a newly connected environment. Social computing has vastly altered both the expectations of customers and the capabilities of corporations in the area of customer relationship management. (We discuss customer relationship management in detail in Chapter 11.)

Author Lecture Videos are available exclusively in *WileyPLUS*.
Apply the Concept activities are available in the Appendix and in *WileyPLUS*.

Customers are now incredibly empowered. Companies are closely monitoring social computing not only because they are mindful of the negative comments posted by social network members but also because they perceive an opportunity to involve customers proactively to reduce problems through improved customer service.

Consider this example. Papa John's Pizza fired a cashier at one of its New York restaurants and apologized to an Asian-American customer for a receipt that identified her as "lady chinky eyes." Minhee Cho, a communications manager at the nonprofit investigative journalism group ProPublica, posted a photo of the receipt on her Twitter account, and it was viewed almost 200,000 times in a single day. John Schnatter, chairman and CEO of Papa John's, immediately posted an apology on Facebook. In his apology, he asserted that he had apologized personally to Ms. Cho as well.

Empowered customers know how to use the wisdom and power of crowds and communities to their benefit. These customers choose how they interact with companies and brands, and they have elevated expectations concerning their experiences with a company. They are actively involved with businesses, not just as purchasers but also as advocates and influencers. As a result, businesses must respond to customers quickly and appropriately. Fortunately, social computing provides many opportunities for businesses to do just that, thereby offering them the opportunity to turn disgruntled customers into champions for the firm.

Before you go on...

1. Discuss why social computing is so important in customer relationship management.
2. Describe how social computing improves customer service.

9.6 Social Computing in Business: Human Resource Management

HRM Human resource (HR) departments in many organizations use social computing applications outside their organizations (recruiting) and inside their organizations (employee development). For example, Deloitte Touche Tohmatsu (**www.deloitte.com**) created a social network to assist its HR managers in downsizing and regrouping teams.

Recruiting

HRM Both recruiters and job seekers are moving to online social networks as recruiting platforms. Enterprise recruiters are scanning online social networks, blogs, and other social resources to identify and find information about potential employees. If job seekers are online and active, there is a good chance that they will be seen by recruiters. In addition, on social networks there are many passive job seekers—people who are employed but would take a better job if one appeared. So, it is important that both active and passive job seekers maintain online profiles that accurately reflect their background and skills. Closing Case 1 takes a look at the rewards and the difficulties inherent in the online recruiting process. It also provides some tips to assist you in a job search.

One HR director uses the HR social media management software Bullhorn Reach (**www.bullhorn.com**), which allows her to post jobs to eight different social networks simultaneously. Bullhorn Reach also enables her to analyze metrics that measure the effectiveness of her social recruiting efforts.

Onboarding

HRM *Onboarding* is how new employees acquire the necessary knowledge, skills, and behaviors to become effective members of the organization. Through the use of social media, new hires can learn what to expect in their first few days on the job and find answers to common questions. Because they are available inside the company's firewall, these social communities can provide detailed information about corporate policies, as well as giving employees the opportunity to complete necessary forms online. These communities also provide introductory training, such as workplace safety information and how to use enterprise applications.

Employee Development

HRM Human resource managers know that the best strategy to enable, encourage, and promote employee development is to build relationships with employees. To this end, a number of HR professionals are using enterprise social tools such as Chatter (**www.salesforce.com/chatter**), Yammer (**www.yammer.com**), and Tibbr (**www.tibbr.com**) to tap in to the wisdom of every employee. These tools help connect employees to work efficiently across organizations and to collaborate on sales opportunities, campaigns, and projects. They help companies simplify workflows and capture new ideas. They enable HR managers to find subject matter experts within the organization, recommending relevant people for every project team, sales team, and other functions.

As HR managers learn more about employees' skills, expertise, and passions through such tools, they can better motivate them, thereby helping them become more engaged and excited about their work. Employees can then be better rewarded for their expertise.

Another area of employee development is training. A large percentage of the time and expense of employee education and learning management can be minimized by utilizing e-learning and interactive social learning tools. These tools help create connections among learners, instructors, and information. Companies find that these tools facilitate knowledge transfer within departments and across teams. Examples of these tools are Moodle (**http://moodle.com**), Joomla (**www.joomla.org**), and Bloomfire (**www.bloomfire.com**).

In 2015, LinkedIn acquired Lynda.com (**www.lynda.com**), an online education company offering thousands of video courses in software, creative, and business skills. The company produces video tutorials taught by industry experts. Members of Lynda have unlimited access to watch the videos.

With this acquisition, LinkedIn plans to incorporate job certifications and training into its offerings. One LinkedIn executive noted that a LinkedIn user could be looking for a job, immediately see the skills necessary for that job, and then be prompted to take the relevant and accredited course on Lynda that will help him or her acquire those skills and land the job.

Finding a Job

The other side of organizational recruiting are those people looking for jobs. Let's say you want to find a job. Like the majority of job hunters, you will probably conduct at least part of your search online because the vast majority of entry-level positions in the United States are now listed only online. Job sites are the fastest, least expensive, and most efficient method to connect employers with potential employees.

Today, job searchers use traditional job sites and social networks such as LinkedIn. Applicants like you have helped LinkedIn raise its market share in job searches from 4.7 percent in 2010 to more than 12 percent by early 2015.

To find a job, your best bet is to begin with LinkedIn (**www.linkedin.com**), which has roughly 165 million members. You should definitely have a profile on LinkedIn, which, by the way, is free. (See the bulleted list that follows for mistakes to avoid on your LinkedIn profile.)

LinkedIn's success comes from its ability to accurately identify its market segment. The company's automated approach does not lend itself well to the upper tier of the job market—for example, CEO searches—where traditional face-to-face searches continue to be the preferred strategy. At the other end of the spectrum—that is, low-paying, low-skill jobs such as cashiers and truck drivers—job boards provide faster results. LinkedIn targets the vast sweet spot between these two extremes, helping to fill high-skill jobs that pay anywhere from $50,000 to $250,000 or more per year. This is the spot you will likely occupy when you graduate.

A number of job-search companies are competing with LinkedIn. These companies are trying to create better-targeted matching systems that leverage social networking functionality. These companies include Monster (**www.monster.com**), Simply Hired (**www.simplyhired.com**), Career Builder (**www.careerbuilder.com**), Indeed (**www.indeed.com**), Jobvite (**www.jobvite.com**), Dice Open Web (**www.dice.com**), and many others.

The most important secret to making online job search sites work for you is to use them carefully. Job coaches advise you to spend 80 percent of your day networking and directly contacting the people in charge of jobs you want. Devote another 10 percent to headhunters. Spend only the remaining 10 percent of your time online.

Here is how to make your time online count. To start with, as you saw above, you should have a profile on LinkedIn. The following list shows you the mistakes NOT to make on your LinkedIn profile.

- Do have a current, professional picture. (No dogs, no spouses, no babies, etc.)
- Do make certain your LinkedIn Status is correct and current.
- Do join groups related to your field of study or even to your personal interests.
- Do list an accurate skill set. Do not embellish.
- Do not use the standard connection request. Do some research on that person and tailor your connection request to that person.
- Do not neglect LinkedIn's privacy settings. When you have a job and are looking for another one, you will want to be discreet. You can set your privacy settings so that your boss does not see that you are looking for opportunities.
- Do not skip the Summary. The Summary is a concise way of selling yourself. Write it in the first person.
- Do not eliminate past jobs or volunteer work.
- Do not say you have worked with someone when you have not.

Next, access the job sites such as those listed above. These sites list millions of jobs and they make it easy to narrow your search using filters. These filters include title, company name, location, and many others. Indeed allows you to search within a specific salary range. Simply-Hired lets you sort for friendly, socially responsible, and even dog-friendly workplaces.

These sites have advanced search options. Try plugging in the name of a company you might want to work for or an advanced degree that qualifies you for specialized work. For example, you could enter "CFA" if you are a certified financial analyst or "LEED" if you are a building engineer with expertise in environmental efficiency.

SimplyHired has a useful tool called "Who do I know?" If you have a LinkedIn profile, then this tool will instantly display your LinkedIn contacts with connections to various job listings. "Who do I know?" also syncs with Facebook.

One more trick to using the aggregators: configure them to deliver listings to your inbox. Set up an e-mail alert that delivers new job postings to you every day.

You should also search for niche sites that are specific to your field. For technology-related jobs, for instance, Dice (**www.dice.com**) has a strong reputation. For nonprofit jobs, try Idealist (**www.idealist.org**). For government jobs, the U.S. government's site is an excellent resource: **www.usajobs.gov**.

One more great online resource is Craigslist (**www.craigslist.com**). It is one site the aggregators do not tap. Craigslist focuses on local listings, and it is especially useful for entry-level jobs and internships.

Beyond locating listings for specific jobs, career coaches contend that job sites can be a resource for keywords and phrases that you can pull from job descriptions and include in your résumé, cover letters, and e-mails. Use the language from a job description in your cover letter.

Websites like Vault (**www.vault.com**), Monster, and CareerBuilder provide some helpful career tips. Vault, in particular, offers very useful career guides.

The bottom line: it is critical to extend most of your efforts *beyond* an online search.

Before you go on...

1. Explain why LinkedIn has become so important in the recruiting process.
2. If you are looking for a job, what is the major problem with restricting your search to social networks?

What's in IT for me?

ACCT For the Accounting Major

Audit teams use social networking technologies internally to stay in touch with team members who are working on multiple projects. These technologies serve as a common channel of communications. For example, an audit team manager can create a group, include his or her team members as subscribers, and then push information regarding projects to all members at once. Externally, these technologies are useful in interfacing with clients and other third parties for whom the firm and its staff provide services.

FIN For the Finance Major

Many of the popular social networking sites have users who subscribe to finance-oriented subgroups. Among these groups are finance professionals who collaborate and share knowledge as well as nonfinancial professionals who are potential clients.

MKT For the Marketing Major

Social computing tools and applications enable marketing professionals to become closer to their customers in a variety of ways, including blogs, wikis, ratings, and recommendations. Marketing professionals now receive almost real-time feedback on products.

POM For the Production/Operations Management Major

Social computing tools and applications enable production personnel to "enlist" business partners and customers in product development activities.

HRM For the Human Resource Management Major

Social networks offer tremendous benefits to human resource professionals. HR personnel can perform a great deal of their recruiting activities by accessing such sites as LinkedIn. They can also check out potential new hires by accessing a large number of social networking sites. Internally, HR personnel can utilize private, internal social networks for employee expertise and experience in order to find the best person for a position or project team.

MIS For the MIS Major

The MIS department is responsible for two aspects of social computing usage: (1) monitoring employee usage of social computing applications while at work, both time and content, and (2) developing private, internal social networks for company employees and then monitoring the content of these networks.

Summary

9.1 Describe five Web 2.0 tools and two major types of Web 2.0 sites.

A *tag* is a keyword or term that describes a piece of information (e.g., a blog, a picture, an article, or a video clip).

Really Simple Syndication allows you to receive the information you want (customized information), when you want it, without having to surf thousands of websites.

A *weblog* (*blog* for short) is a personal website, open to the public, in which the site creator expresses his or her feelings or opinions with a series of chronological entries.

Microblogging is a form of blogging that allows users to write short messages (or capture an image or embedded video) and publish them.

A *wiki* is a website on which anyone can post material and make changes to already posted material. Wikis foster easy collaboration and harness the collective intelligence of Internet users.

Social networking websites allow users to upload their content to the Web in the form of text (e.g., blogs), voice (e.g., podcasts), images, and videos (e.g., videocasts).

A *mashup* is a website that takes different content from a number of other websites and mixes them together to create a new kind of content.

9.2 Describe the benefits and risks of social commerce to companies.

Social commerce refers to the delivery of electronic commerce activities and transactions through social computing.

Benefits of social commerce to customers include the following: better and faster vendors' response to complaints; customers can assist other customers; customers' expectations can be met more fully and quickly; customers can easily search, link, chat, and buy while staying in the social network's page.

Benefits of social commerce to vendors include the following: can test new products and ideas quickly and inexpensively; learn much about their customers; identify problems quickly and alleviate anger; learn from customers' experiences with rapid feedback; increase sales when customers discuss products positively on social networking site; create better marketing campaigns and brand awareness; use low-cost user-generated content, for example, in marketing campaigns; get free advertising through viral marketing; identify influential brand advocates and reward them.

Risks of social computing include information security concerns; invasion of privacy; violation of intellectual property and copyright; employees' reluctance to participate; data leakage of personal information or corporate strategic information; poor or biased quality of users' generated content; cyberbullying or cyberstalking and employee harassment.

9.3 Identify the methods used for shopping socially.

Social shopping is a method of electronic commerce that takes all of the key aspects of social networks—friends, groups, voting, comments, discussions, reviews, and others—and focuses them on shopping.

Methods for shopping socially include what other shoppers say, group shopping, shopping communities and clubs, social marketplaces and direct sales, and peer-to-peer shopping.

9.4 Discuss innovative ways to use social networking sites for advertising and market research.

Social advertising represents advertising formats that employ the social context of the user viewing the ad.

Innovative ways to advertise in social media include the following: create a company Facebook page; Tweet business success stories to your customers; integrate ads into YouTube videos; add a Facebook "Like" button with its sponsored story to your product; use sponsored stories.

- *Using Facebook for market research*: Get feedback from your Facebook fans (and their friends if possible) on advertising campaigns, market research, etc.; test-market your messages; use Facebook for survey invitations.

- *Using Twitter for market research*: Use Twitter Search; use Twellow; look at the chart on TweetStats.

- *Using LinkedIn for market research*: Post a question (e.g., solicit advice) regarding the topic or issue you are interested in.

9.5 Describe how social computing improves customer service.

Customers are now incredibly empowered. Companies are closely monitoring social computing not only because they are mindful of the negative comments posted by social network members but also because they see an opportunity to involve customers proactively to reduce problems by improved customer service.

Empowered customers know how to use the wisdom and power of crowds and communities to their benefit. These customers choose how they interact with companies and brands, and they have elevated expectations. They are actively involved with businesses, not just as purchasers but also as advocates and influencers. As a result, businesses must respond to customers quickly and accurately. Fortunately, social computing provides many opportunities for businesses to do just that, thereby giving businesses the opportunity to turn disgruntled customers into champions for the firm.

9.6 Discuss different ways in which human resource managers make use of social computing.

- *Recruiting*: Both recruiters and job seekers are moving to online social networks as new recruiting platforms. Enterprise recruiters are scanning online social networks, blogs, and other social resources to identify and find information about potential employees. If job seekers are online and active, there is a good chance that they will be seen by recruiters. In addition, on social networks there are many passive job seekers—people who are employed but would take a better job if it appeared. So, it is important that both active and passive job seekers maintain profiles online that truly reflect them.

- *Onboarding*: The use of social media to help new employees acquire the necessary knowledge, skills, and behaviors to become effective members of the organization.

- *Employee development*: HR managers are using social tools to build relationships with employees. As HR managers learn more about employees, they can help them become more engaged and excited about their work.

Chapter Glossary

blog (weblog)   A personal website, open to the public, in which the site creator expresses his or her feelings or opinions with a series of chronological entries.

blogosphere   The term for the millions of blogs on the Web.

collaborative consumption   An economic model based on sharing, swapping, trading, or renting products and services, enabling access over ownership.

mashup   A website that takes different content from a number of other websites and mixes them together to create a new kind of content.

microblogging   A form of blogging that allows users to write short messages (or capture an image or embedded video) and publish them.

Really Simple Syndication (RSS)   A technology that allows users to receive the information they want, when they want it, without having to surf thousands of websites.

social advertising   Advertising formats that make use of the social context of the user viewing the ad.

social capital   The number of connections a person has within and between social networks.

social commerce   The delivery of electronic commerce activities and transactions through social computing.

social computing   A type of information technology that combines social behavior and information systems to create value.

social graph   A map of all relevant links or connections for one member of a social network.

social intelligence   The monitoring, collection, and analysis of socially generated data and the resultant strategic decisions.

social marketplaces   websites that act as online intermediaries that harness the power of social networks for introducing, buying, and selling products and services.

social network   A social structure composed of individuals, groups, or organizations linked by values, visions, ideas, financial exchange, friendship, kinship, conflict, or trade.

social networking   Activities performed using social software tools (e.g., blogging) or social networking features (e.g., media sharing).

social shopping   A method of electronic commerce that takes all of the key aspects of social networks (friends, groups, voting, comments, discussions, reviews, etc.) and focuses them on shopping.

tag   A keyword or term that describes a piece of information.

Tweet   Messages and updates posted by users on Twitter.

Twitter   A free microblogging service that allows its users to send messages and read other users' messages and updates.

Web 2.0   A loose collection of information technologies and applications, plus the websites that use them.

wiki   A website on which anyone can post material and make changes to other material.

Discussion Questions

1. How would you describe Web 2.0 to someone who has not taken a course in information systems?

2. If you were the CEO of a company, would you pay attention to blogs about your company? Why or why not? If yes, would you consider some blogs to be more important or more reliable than are others? If so, which ones? How would you find blogs relating to your company?

3. Do you have a page on a social networking website? If yes, why? If no, what is keeping you from creating one? Is there any content that you definitely would not post on such a page?

4. How can an organization best employ social computing technologies and applications to benefit its business processes?

5. What factors might cause an individual, an employee, or a company to be cautious in the use of social networks?

6. Why are advertisers so interested in social networks?

7. What sorts of restrictions or guidelines should firms place on the use of social networks by employees? Are social computing sites a threat to security? Can they tarnish a firm's reputation? If so, how? Can they enhance a firm's reputation? If so, how?

8. Why are marketers so interested in social networks?

9. Why are human resource managers so interested in social networks?

Problem-Solving Activities

1. Enter **www.programmableweb.com** and study the various services that the website offers. Learn how to create mashups and then propose a mashup of your own. Present your mashup to the class.

2. Go to Amazon's Mechanical Turk website (**www.mturk.com**). View the available Human Intelligence Tasks (HITs). Are there any HITs that you would be interested in to make some extra money? Why or why not?

3. Access Pandora (**www.pandora.com**). Why is Pandora a social networking site?

4. Access ChatRoulette (**www.chatroulette.com**). What is interesting about this social networking site?

5. Using a search engine, look up the following:
   - *Most popular or most visited blogs.* Pick two and follow some of the posts. Why do you think these blogs are popular?
   - *Top10Best Blogsites* (**www.top10best-blogsites.com**). Pick two and consider why they might be the "best blogs."

6. Research how to be a successful blogger. What does it take to be a successful blogger? What time commitment might be needed? How frequently do successful bloggers post?

Closing Case

MIS WhatsApp Creates Problems in India

WhatsApp Messenger (WhatsApp; **www.whatsapp.com**) is a messaging platform owned by Facebook. The app allows users to send text and voice messages; make voice and video calls; and share images, documents, user locations, and other media. WhatsApp provides end-to-end encryption, which means that only the sender and recipient can read what is sent. No one else, including WhatsApp, can read the message. This system makes it technically impossible to narrow down extensive forwarded messages to one source.

WhatsApp allows group chats to be private or public. The private chats require the group administrator to add new members. As a result, these groups are more difficult to join. In contrast, users can join public groups via invitation links that can be shared with anyone or that are available on the Internet.

By August 2020, WhatsApp had 2 billion users around the world, and was available in more than 180 countries in 60 languages. WhatsApp launched in India in November 2009. By August 2020, the app had 400 million users there, more than any other country. Further, 80 percent of Indian smartphone users were on WhatsApp.

The platform has transformed daily life for Indian users. The app's simple design makes it very easy to use, even for people who are buying a phone for the first time. WhatsApp typically functions without problems, even in parts of rural India where connectivity is limited and websites take time to load.

WhatsApp has developed into much more than a way to stay in touch with friends and family. Magazines use the app to distribute news, shops use it to sell goods, and political parties send out tremendous amounts of promotional material, both verified and fake.

In India, WhatsApp's ease of use and low-cost phones have enabled fake news to spread very quickly to vast numbers of people. Specifically, the launch of the $43 JioPhone 2 in July 2018 enabled many people who were coming online for the first time to access WhatsApp. These users call their new phones "WhatsApp phones." To them, WhatsApp *is* the Internet. Because they are new to the technology, they are particularly vulnerable to the kind of online manipulation that people more familiar with the Internet would detect.

WhatsApp has become a clearinghouse for fake news. Research by BBC News revealed that the app can sometimes mobilize groups into acts of violence. Rumors and misinformation that spread quickly through the app led to a series of lynchings in India in 2017 and 2018 that left 46 people dead and 43 others injured.

In a horrific example, on July 1, 2018, in the village of Rainpada, a mob beat five men to death. According to authorities, the victims were members of a Nath Panthi Davari Gosavi tribe, a nomadic group from India's Maharashtra state. They had come to Rainpada to attend a Sunday market. While they ate lunch together, they gave a cookie to a young girl.

The men's interaction with the girl attracted attention. A crowd gathered, asking the men questions. The confrontation grew and the men were taken to the village office for their safety. In less than an hour, a mob gathered in front of the office, stormed it, and beat the men to death before police could arrive from a town some 25 miles away.

For about a week before the men arrived in the village, rumors were circulating on WhatsApp warning about strangers in the area entering villages to kidnap young children. A video on WhatsApp displayed a sequence of photos of lifeless children. A voiceover warned parents to be watchful for child snatchers. In fact, the images were of children who were killed in Syria during a chemical attack in 2013. The video was real, but it was placed out of context on WhatsApp. Significantly, the majority of videos and photos are not altered using Photoshop or sophisticated video-editing software. Rather, most are simply cut, copied, placed out of context, or presented as new when in fact they are years old.

The police arrested a total of 35 people after the incident, whom they identified from numerous videos of the riot captured by bystanders on their phones. All of them denied taking part in the violence. The alleged perpetrators were set to face trial for murder in November 2019. As of October 2020, the case had not been resolved.

The Indian government placed much of the blame for the killings on WhatsApp. In response, Facebook implemented several changes in the platform.

- The company established a forwarding limit for messages. Users are able to forward messages to only five chats at once.
- WhatsApp removed the feature that enabled Indian users to quickly forward video and photos.
- The app marks messages that are being extensively circulated as "Frequently Forwarded."
- Facebook has been actively banning accounts (more than 2 million per month).
- Facebook is training its machine learning algorithms to detect profiles that send out an abnormally high volume of messages immediately after a user signs up.
- WhatsApp has a "search the Web" feature to help identify fake forwarded messages. This feature provides a simple way to search messages that have been forwarded many times that may help people find news results or other sources of information about the content that they have received. With this feature, users see a magnifying glass button next to a forwarded message. When they click on this button, they are taken to Google search and shown results of whether the message is fake or true.
- Facebook has hired seven small fact-checking firms to restore some of its credibility among Indian users. One of these firms, Boom Live (**www.boomlive.in**), has 11 employees that analyze news in 10 of India's 23 official languages. A Facebook spokesperson asserted that fact checking is part of the platform's strategy to fight fake news. This effort includes extensive work to remove fake accounts, to cut off incentives to financially motivated bad actors who spread misinformation, and to promote news literacy. Unfortunately, these firms are not nearly enough to accomplish the vast scope of these missions.

Boom does have some advantages, including access to internal Facebook software that alerts the teams to posts that it finds suspiciously popular (widely forwarded). The fact checkers also examine lists of complaints they have received from users about questionable forwarded WhatsApp messages. The team spends much of its time working to verify or debunk a list of questionable Facebook posts and WhatsApp forwards.

As one discouraging, but all too typical, example, the Boom team spent a great deal of time building a case to persuade Facebook to take down the page for Postcard News, known for its alleged stream of fake news. Hours after Facebook took down the page, a fan page appeared that resumed sharing Postcard videos with the page's millions of followers.

Another example: Congress Party leader Rahul Gandhi announced plans to stand for election. A viral photo from one of his speeches mislabeled flags in the photo as the national flag of Pakistan. The implication was that sympathizers with Pakistan, India's bitter rival, supported Gandhi.

Facebook also implemented some low-technology measures.

- WhatsApp ran print ads in newspapers in 11 languages to educate users, and radio and television programs did the same thing. The app also launched a digital literacy education course.
- Facebook has organized roadside skits to spread awareness of the consequences of forwarding unverified messages.
- The company ran a nationwide ad campaign asking users to "Spread joy, not rumors."
- Facebook has commissioned several research initiatives, grants, workshops, and digital literacy programs.

Not only did WhatsApp contribute to a series of killings across India, but the platform was a key campaign tool used widely by both the ruling Bharatiya Janata Party (BJP) and the opposition Congress Party in the runup to the May 2019 general election. (The BJP won a landslide victory.) Both parties accused each other of creating and spreading fake news while denying they were doing so themselves.

Let's consider some examples of social media manipulation in the Indian elections. One Facebook user shared a recording of a call in which the BJP head, Amit Shah, is allegedly heard saying, "We agree that for election, we need a war." The fake post, meant to show the BJP indulging in warmongering for electoral gains, had used spliced audio from older interviews. It was seen by 2.5 million viewers before being taken down.

On the other hand, a message spread via WhatsApp portrayed the opposition Congress Party as soft on militancy. It claimed that a party leader had promised money to free "terrorists" from prison if voted to power. It was later flagged as false.

Other posts have been debunked. One claimed that Prime Minister Narendra Modi topped the list of 50 most honest politicians. Another showed a photoshopped image of Priyanka Gandhi Vadra of the Congress Party wearing a cross intended to show her as a non-Hindu in an extremely polarized election campaign.

Final thoughts: The Indian government has repeatedly asked WhatsApp for the ability to stop and trace problematic messages, a demand that would bypass the encrypted security that is central to the app's popularity. Specifically, the government urged WhatsApp to take measures that could prevent the proliferation of fake news. WhatsApp responded that the platform was working to educate people on how to use the app safely and how to prevent its misuse through a variety of measures discussed above. However, WhatsApp refused to modify its strict policies regarding encryption and privacy.

WhatsApp and the Indian government remain at an impasse over how to trace problematic messages that have caused real-world harm. The question that the government wants answered is simple: Who started the rumor?

A spokesperson for WhatsApp stated that creating and storing a permanent record for every message for the purpose of future government surveillance would change the very premise of WhatsApp, which is to provide for private communication. The government responded that it did not want to decrypt messages, but it still wanted access to the "location and identification" of the senders of messages that lead to violence.

Indian law enforcement officials support the government's view that WhatsApp should make its messages traceable. They assert that their hands are tied in investigations that involve WhatsApp's encrypted messages.

None of Facebook's actions brought about the fundamental changes necessary to combat the platform's misinformation problems in India and WhatsApp will not provide the government with what it demands. Further, Facebook has largely overlooked and underestimated the impact that WhatsApp has had in India.

Critics of Facebook and WhatsApp assert that the steps taken by the platforms to curb fake news do not even begin to address the problem because false sites and posts spread faster than they can be taken down. They also ask how many people actually look at fact-checking sites. They contend that people have *confirmation bias*, meaning that if a post or video agrees with what they think, they tend to believe that it is true without checking its veracity.

Sources: Compiled from "WhatsApp Brings a New Feature to Help Users Spot Fake Forwarded Messages," *The Indian Express*, August 5, 2020; M. Singh, "WhatsApp Reaches 400 Million Users in India, Its Biggest Market," *TechCrunch*, July 26, 2020; A. Mitra, "Why Do WhatsApp Users End Up Spreading Misinformation in India?" *Forbes*, June 29, 2020; "An Indian Politician Is Using Deepfake Technology to Win New Voters," *MIT Technology Review*, February 19, 2020; A. Rao, "How Did Social Media Impact India's 2019 General Election?" *Economic and Political Weekly*, December 27, 2019; S. Modak, "Dhule Lynching: 35 Set to Face Trial for Murder," *The Indian Express*, November 23, 2019; "Why India Wants to Track WhatsApp Messages," *BBC News*, October 30, 2019; "WhatsApp Was Extensively Exploited During 2019 Elections in India," *Forbes India*, October 1, 2019; S. Agarwal, "WhatsApp Has 400 Million Users in India, but No Fix for Its Fake News Problem," *Digital Trends*, August 12, 2019; B. Dale and C. Jeavans, "India General Election 2019: What Happened?" *BBC News*, May 24, 2019; S. Rai, "How 11 People Are Trying to Stop Fake News in the World's Largest Election," *Bloomberg*, April 21, 2019; V. Goel and S. Frenkel, "In India Election, False Posts and Hate Speech Flummox Facebook," *New York Times*, April 1, 2019; S. Phartiyal and A. Kalra, "Indian Political Parties Abuse WhatsApp Service Ahead of Election," *Reuters*, February 6, 2019; "WhatsApp Forwards Restricted to Just Five Chats, Globally," *The Indian Express*, January 25, 2019; T. McLaughlin, "How WhatsApp Fuels Fake News and Violence in India," *Wired*, December 12, 2018; S. Chakrabarti, "Duty, Identity, Credibility: Fake News and the Ordinary Citizen in India," *BBC News*, November 2, 2018; S. Agarwal, "Not Seeking Decryption, but Location, Identity of Those Sending Provocative Messages," *The Economic Times*, November 1, 2018; J. Russell, "WhatsApp Hires 'Grievance Officer' to help Combat False Information in India," *TechCrunch*, September 24, 2018.

Questions

1. Should WhatsApp provide the Indian government the information it demands (who started the rumor) if authorities have proper warrants? Why or why not?

2. Is it even possible for WhatsApp and Facebook to fact-check user-generated content? Why or why not?

3. If social media platforms are not able to fact-check user-generated content, then speculate on the future of these platforms.

CHAPTER 10

Information Systems within the Organization

CHAPTER OUTLINE	LEARNING OBJECTIVES
10.1 Transaction Processing Systems	**10.1** Explain the purpose of transaction processing systems.
10.2 Functional Area Information Systems	**10.2** Explain the types of support that information systems can provide for each functional area of the organization.
10.3 Enterprise Resource Planning (ERP) Systems	**10.3** Identify advantages and drawbacks to businesses implementing an enterprise resource planning (ERP) system.
10.4 ERP Support for Business Processes	**10.4** Describe the three main business processes supported by ERP systems.

Opening Case

POM Spinning the Wheels of Bicycle Inventory

Inventory control is critically important to all businesses and industries. Although modern inventory management systems help with manage inventory, the process can still be cumbersome. In fact, some organizations still conduct inventory control by manually checking items one at a time.

To manage inventory, modern manufacturers have implemented just-in-time inventory (JIT) systems. JIT systems align raw material orders from suppliers directly with production schedules. Modern organizations have a good understanding of the volatility in supply-and-demand forecasts, which allows the JIT inventory model to work.

However, when the COVID-19 pandemic struck, previously used forecasting models were no longer valid. COVID-19 impacted all industries. The bicycle industry, in particular, expected a significant loss of revenue because the pandemic sent the public into lockdown.

As authorities discouraged the use of buses and subways, the population began looking for alternative means of transportation. The result? Hundreds of thousands of Americans resorted to one of the most basic forms of pleasure and mobility: the bicycle. And an industry that expected a bust experienced a boom!

In March 2020, nationwide sales of bicycles, equipment, and repair services increased dramatically compared to the same period in 2019. That month, sales of commuter and fitness bikes increased 66 percent, leisure bikes 121 percent, children's bikes 59 percent, and electric bikes 85 percent. The bicycle industry was indeed experiencing a boom until the minimal JIT inventory ran out.

According to Chris Rogers, a supply chain analyst at S&P Global Market Intelligence, the industry was already low on inventory. The 2018 tariffs that President Trump ordered on goods produced in China had slowed imported parts, and nearly all bike parts are manufactured in China.

The bicycle industry's record low inventory levels meant that there were almost 25 percent fewer bikes in the United States than in previous years. The industry as a whole had already been trying to meet their traditional demand with limited inventory. Due to the global COVID-19 shutdown, factories were not able to manufacture parts. And even when some manufacturers were able to resume operations, there was an ongoing threat of a COVID-19 interruption.

One solution for the bicycle industry was to double its capacity to meet demand. However, this option was not viable because post-pandemic demand would likely drop. This decrease would result in idle factories and excess capacity. The industry needed robust inventory management systems to weather this storm. Supply chain logistics suddenly became a significant challenge.

Trek (**www.trekbikes.com/us/en_us**), a bicycle manufacturer based in Waterloo, Wisconsin, was positioned to handle this fluctuating demand. Strategically, Trek kept 60 days of stock on hand rather than minimizing levels with the goal of JIT inventory. This decision allowed the firm to sell bicycles far into the pandemic when many other manufacturers ran out of stock.

In early 2020, Trek executives monitored daily global sales. In March, they began to see an increase in sales. By analyzing data from point-of-sale systems, Trek's forecasting group predicted the increase in global orders. At first, executives thought the increase was an anomaly. As the increase in sales continued, they realized what was happening and immediately reacted. While other bicycle manufacturers canceled orders submitted in the pre-COVID environment, Trek began increasing them.

The executives knew that Trek could not rely on a single provider for parts, so they analyzed the firm's supply chain. They examined their suppliers' capabilities and began doubling component orders.

Yutaka Taniyama, vice president of sales of bicycle components at Shimano (**www.shimano.com**), heard from Trek as early as April. Shimano supplies shifters, drivetrains, and many other cycling parts to bicycle manufacturers. Shimano had been experiencing difficulties due to the COVID-19 pandemic, with most of their customers canceling orders.

When Taniyama received the order increases from Trek, he contacted the manufacturer for clarification. Trek executives explained what their demand forecasts were indicating. In response, Shimano, which operates on a first-come, first-served basis with its clients, directed its excess capacity to Trek.

The results were significant. Trek, which is a privately held company, does not disclose sales numbers. But the company has reported that, despite the supply chain problems brought on by U.S. tariffs and the global COVID-19 pandemic, it has sold more than double the usual amount of bikes that they would in any given year. The sales increase resulted in part from the data provided by their internal information systems. We say in part because Trek executives were able to use the data and the analyses from the firm's forecasting group to make quick, correct decisions to get ahead of the global shortage of bicycle components.

And the bottom line? Trek's quick, information-based actions illustrate the value of agile, flexible, adaptable information systems.

Sources: Compiled from C. Goldbaum, "Thinking of Buying a Bike? Get Ready for a Very Long Wait," *New York Times*, May 18, 2020; M. Cerullo, "A Vicious Cycle: Bike Sales Soar, Causing Shortages and 'Panic Buying'," *CBS News Moneywatch*, May 21, 2020; L. Kaner, "Inside the Company Trying to Solve the Global Bicycle Shortage," *Marker*, August 4, 2020; O. Schatterman, D. Woodhouse, and J. Terino, "Supply Chain Lessons from Covid-19: Time to Refocus on Resilience," *Bain Company*, April 27, 2020; M. Arthurs-Brennan, "How Is the Coronavirus Crisis Affecting the Bike Industry?" *Cycling Weekly*, March 18, 2020; S. Ben-Achour, "Bike Shortage Is a Tale of Changed Lives and Disrupted Supply Chains," *Marketplace.org*, August 20, 2020; E. Davies, "What Do Bikes and Toilet Paper Have in Common? Both Are Flying out of Stores Amid the Coronavirus Pandemic," *Washington Post*, May 15, 2020; E. Frauenheim, "How Trek Bicycles Has Kept a Great Culture Rolling in a Fast-Moving 2020," *Fortune*, November 23, 2020; R. Annis, "Bike Shortages Will Likely Last Until Next Year, and Possibly into 2022," *Bicycling*, November 6, 2020; http://www.trekbikes.com/us/en_US, accessed December 12, 2020.

Questions

1. How did information management help Trek navigate the global bicycle-part supply shortage caused by the COVID-19 pandemic?

2. It took both policy (60-days inventory) and procedure (information management) for Trek to survive. Discuss the ways these two work together to support effective business operations.

Introduction

The opening case illustrates the integral part that an information system (IS) plays in an organization's success, particularly in times of great uncertainty such as the COVID pandemic. As you noted in the case, without information systems, effective inventory control could not exist. ISs are everywhere, and they affect organizations in countless ways. Although ISs are frequently discussed within the context of large organizational settings, the chapter opening case illustrates how ISs play a critical role in small organizations.

It is important to note that "systems within organizations" do not have to be owned by the organization itself. Instead, organizations can deploy very productive ISs that are owned by an external vendor. The key point here is that "systems within an organization" are intended to support internal processes, regardless of who actually owns the systems.

It is important for you to have a working knowledge of ISs within your organization for a variety of reasons. First, your job will require you to access corporate data that are supplied primarily by your firm's transaction processing systems and enterprise resource planning systems. Second, you will have a great deal of input into the format and content of the reports that you receive from these systems. Third, you will use the information contained in these reports to perform your job more productively.

This chapter will teach you about the various information systems that modern organizations use. We begin by considering transaction processing systems, the most fundamental organizational information systems. We continue with the functional area management information systems, and we conclude with enterprise resource planning systems.

10.1 Transaction Processing Systems

Millions (sometimes billions) of transactions occur in large organizations every day. A **transaction** is any business event that generates data worthy of being captured and stored in a database. Examples of transactions are a product manufactured, a service sold, a person hired, and a payroll check generated. In another example, when you are checking out of Walmart, each time the cashier swipes an item across the bar code reader, that is one transaction.

A **transaction processing system (TPS)** supports the monitoring, collection, storage, and processing of data from the organization's basic business transactions, each of which generates data. The TPS collects data continuously, typically in *real time*—that is, as soon as the data are generated—and it provides the input data for the corporate databases. TPSs are critical to the success of any enterprise because they support core operations.

In the modern business world, TPSs are inputs for the functional area information systems and business intelligence systems, as well as business operations such as customer relationship management, knowledge management, and e-commerce. TPSs have to efficiently handle both high volumes of data and large variations in those volumes (e.g., during periods of peak processing). They must also avoid errors and downtime, record results accurately and securely, and maintain privacy and security. **Figure 10.1** illustrates how TPSs manage data. Consider these examples of how TPSs handle the complexities of transactional data:

- When more than one person or application program can access the database at the same time, the database has to be protected from errors resulting from overlapping updates. The most common error is losing the results of one of the updates.

- When processing a transaction involves more than one computer, the database and all users must be protected against inconsistencies arising from a failure of any component at any time. For example, an error that occurs at some point in an ATM withdrawal can enable a customer to receive cash, although the bank's computer indicates that he or she did not. (Conversely, a customer might not receive cash, although the bank's computer indicates that he or she did.)

- **ACCT** It must be possible to reverse a transaction in its entirety if it turns out to have been entered in error. It is also necessary to reverse a transaction when a customer returns a purchased item. For example, if you return a sweater that you have purchased, then the store must credit your credit card for the amount of the purchase, refund your cash, or offer you an in-store credit to purchase another item. The store must also update its inventory.

- **ACCT** It is frequently important to preserve an audit trail. In fact, for certain transactions an audit trail may be legally required.

These and similar issues explain why organizations spend millions of dollars on expensive mainframe computers. In today's business environment, firms must have the dependability, reliability, and processing capacity of these computers to handle their transaction processing loads.

Regardless of the specific data processed by a TPS, the actual process tends to be standard, whether it occurs in a manufacturing firm, a service firm, or a government organization. As the first step in this procedure, people or sensors collect data, which are entered into the computer through any input device. Generally speaking, organizations try to automate the TPS data entry

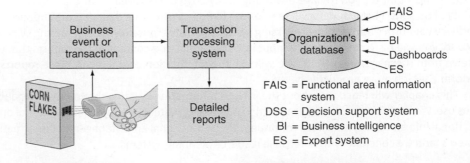

FIGURE 10.1 How transaction processing systems manage data.

as much as possible because of the large volume involved, a process called *source data automation* (discussed in Technology Guide 1).

Next, the system processes data in one of two basic ways: batch processing and online processing. In **batch processing**, the firm collects data from transactions as they occur, placing them in groups, or *batches.* The system then prepares and processes the batches periodically (say, every night).

In **online transaction processing (OLTP)**, business transactions are processed online as soon as they occur. For example, when you pay for an item at a store, the system records the sale by reducing the inventory on hand by one unit, increasing sales figures for the item by one unit, and increasing the store's cash position by the amount you paid. The system performs these tasks in real time by means of online technologies.

Before you go on...

1. Define TPS.
2. List the key functions of a TPS.

10.2 Functional Area Information Systems

Each department or functional area within an organization has its own collection of application programs, or information systems. Each of these **functional area information systems (FAIS)** supports a particular functional area in the organization by increasing each area's internal efficiency and effectiveness. FAISs often convey information in a variety of reports, which you will see later in this chapter. Examples of FAISs are accounting IS, finance IS, production/operations management (POM) IS, marketing IS, and human resources IS.

As illustrated in Figure 10.1, the FAIS access data from the corporate databases. The following sections discuss the support that FAISs provide for these functional areas.

Author Lecture Videos are available exclusively in *WileyPLUS*.
Apply the Concept activities are available in the Appendix and in *WileyPLUS*.

ACCT FIN Information Systems for Accounting and Finance

A primary mission of the accounting and finance functional areas is to manage money flows into, within, and out of organizations. This mission is very broad because money is involved in all organizational functions. Therefore, accounting and finance information systems are very diverse and comprehensive. In this section, you focus on certain selected activities of the accounting and finance functional area. IT's About Business 10.1 discusses Fintech and its impact on internal (and external) information systems.

Financial Planning and Budgeting.   Appropriate management of financial assets is a major task in financial planning and budgeting. Managers must plan for both acquiring and using resources. For example:

- *Financial and economic forecasting*: Knowledge about the availability and cost of money is a key ingredient for successful financial planning. Cash flow projections are particularly important because they inform organizations what funds they need, when they need them, and how they will acquire them.

  Funds for operating organizations come from multiple sources, including stockholders' investments, bond sales, bank loans, sales of products and services, and income from investments. Decisions concerning funding for ongoing operations and for capital investment can be supported by decision support systems and business analytics applications (discussed in Chapter 12). Numerous software packages for conducting economic and financial forecasting are also available. Many of these packages can be downloaded from the Internet, some of them free.

- *Budgeting*: An essential component of the accounting and finance function is the annual budget, which allocates the organization's financial resources among participants and activities. The budget allows management to distribute resources in the way that best supports the organization's mission and goals.

  Several software packages are available to support budget preparation and control and to facilitate communication among participants in the budget process. These packages can reduce the time involved in the budget process. Furthermore, they can automatically monitor exceptions for patterns and trends.

IT's About Business 10.1

FIN **Small Fintech Banks Know the Show Must Go On**

In April 2020, the United States government announced the Paycheck Protection Program (PPP) in response to the COVID-19 pandemic. Large and small businesses went to their traditional banks to apply for and obtain these funds to survive the challenges brought on by the pandemic. However, traditional banks prioritized their large customers over their smaller customers, who typically consisted of small-businesses and self-employed people.

The banks' decisions were strategic. They had worked for years to develop strong relationships with large customers, and those relationships needed to continue during this challenging time. Taking care of large customers meant that smaller customers fell by the wayside. Despite the fact that small businesses also had employees, the banks' prioritization created a divide between who could and could not access the government's PPP funds.

At this point, Fintech came to the rescue. As you saw in Chapter 7, Fintech is an industry composed of companies that use technology (e.g., apps on mobile devices, cloud computing, and others) to compete in the marketplace with traditional financial institutions and intermediaries in the delivery of financial services, which include banking, insurance, real estate, and investing.

Consider banking. Startup banks typically consider the opportunities offered by Fintech and then develop procedures for these opportunities rather than trying to integrate Fintech with current procedures. As a result, when PPP funds became available, agile startup banks could manage the challenges involved with providing PPP funds faster than large banks that had to contend with legacy infrastructures.

Let's take a closer look at Dominick Pietrzak, one of many small-business owners who struggled to make ends meet during the COVID-19 pandemic. Pietrzak owns a film production company in Brooklyn, New York, and is the only full-time employee.

He first tried to apply for PPP funds through his bank, Capital One, but it did not accept PPP applications. In fact, Capital One's PPP application system did not become operational until the first round of PPP money was gone.

The fact that Capital One did not deploy its PPP application system in a timely fashion turned out to be a blessing in disguise for Pietrzak. His bookkeeping company, Bench (**www.bench.co**),

invited him to apply for PPP funds through them. Bench's primary service is to help entrepreneurs by taking care of all bookkeeping and providing monthly financial statements while also connecting them with potential funding sources. Since its founding in 2013, Bench has served more than 500 small businesses and helped them obtain over $50 million in funding.

Bench connected Pietrzak to Fundera (**www.fundera.com**), a free marketplace that allows firms to compare lenders. A Fundera lending specialist matched Pietrzak with Cross River Bank (**www.crossriver.com**) and helped him fill out an application for PPP funds via the bank. Pietrzak signed closing documents from the bank and two days later the PPP funds were in his bank account.

Pietrzak's story illustrates the power of Fintech. He received the kind of service and financial support in the early days of the PPP program that many other large and small businesses did not receive. Further, his support came from two Fintech companies and a bank specializing in Fintech services rather than from larger, traditional banks.

Sources: Compiled from A. Sraders, "What Is Fintech? Uses and Examples in 2020," *TheStreet*, February 11, 2020; S. Walden, "What Is Fintech And How Does It Affect How I Bank?" *Forbes*, August 3, 2020; P. Sullivan, "What Are Fintechs and How Can They Help Small Business?" *New York Times*, June 10, 2020; E. Zimmerman, "The Evolution of Fintech," *DealBook*, April 6, 2016; T. Tse, A. Cosentino, and M. Esposito, "Financial Inclusion: 'Finteching' the Underbanked," *MIT Technology Review*, May 6, 2020; M. Gorman, "Why FinTechs Are Declaring Victory in PPP Loans," *Forbes*, August 13, 2020; R. Shevlin, "The Future of Fintech: The New Normal After The Covid-19 Crisis," *Forbes*, May 26, 2020; A. Sraders, "Does Robinhood Make Money?" *TheStreet*, February 10, 2019; B. O'Connell, "What is a Robo Advisor and How Do You Choose One?" *TheStreet*, July 11, 2018; http://bench.co accessed December 3, 2020.

Questions

1. How has the growth in the high-speed, wireless, smartphone market impacted Fintech companies? In particular, how will the growth in 5G wireless communications impact Fintech companies?

2. In what ways does Fintech allow startups to compete with long-established banks?

Managing Financial Transactions. Many accounting and finance software packages are integrated with other functional areas. For example, Sage 50cloud Accounting by Sage (**www.sage.com/en-us/products/sage-50cloud/**) offers a sales ledger, a purchase ledger, a cash book, sales order processing, invoicing, stock control, a fixed assets register, and more.

Companies involved in electronic commerce need to access customers' financial data (e.g., credit line), inventory levels, and manufacturing databases (to determine available capacity and place orders). For example, Microsoft Dynamics GP (formerly Great Plains Software) offers 50 modules that meet the most common financial, project, distribution, manufacturing, and e-business needs.

Organizations, business processes, and business activities operate with, and manage, financial transactions. Consider these examples:

- *Global stock exchanges*: Financial markets operate in global, 24/7/365, distributed electronic stock exchanges that use the Internet both to buy and sell stocks and to broadcast real-time stock prices.

- *Managing multiple currencies*: Global trade involves financial transactions that are carried out in different currencies. The conversion ratios of these currencies are constantly in flux. Financial and accounting systems use financial data from different countries, and they convert the currencies from and to any other currency in seconds. Reports based on these data, which formerly required several days to generate, can now be produced in only seconds. In addition to currency conversions, these systems manage multiple languages.

- *Virtual close*: Companies traditionally closed their books (accounting records) quarterly, usually to meet regulatory requirements. Today, many companies want to be able to close their books at any time, on very short notice. Information systems make it possible to close the books quickly in what is called a *virtual close*. This process provides almost real-time information on the organization's financial health.

- *Expense management automation*: Expense management automation (EMA) refers to systems that automate the data entry and processing of travel and entertainment expenses. EMA systems are Web-based applications that enable companies to quickly and consistently collect expense information, enforce company policies and contracts, and reduce unplanned purchases as well as airline and hotel expenses. They also allow companies to reimburse their employees more quickly because expense approvals are not delayed by poor documentation.

Investment Management.   Organizations invest large amounts of money in stocks, bonds, real estate, and other assets. Managing these investments is a complex task for several reasons. First, organizations have literally thousands of investment alternatives dispersed throughout the world to choose from. These investments are also subject to complex regulations and tax laws, which vary from one location to another.

Investment decisions require managers to evaluate financial and economic reports provided by diverse institutions, including federal and state agencies, universities, research institutions, and financial services firms. Thousands of websites also provide financial data, many of them free.

To monitor, interpret, and analyze the huge amounts of online financial data, financial analysts employ two major types of IT tools: Internet search engines and business intelligence and decision support software.

Control and Auditing.   One major reason why organizations go out of business is their inability to forecast or secure a sufficient cash flow. Underestimating expenses, overspending, engaging in fraud, and mismanaging financial statements can lead to disaster. Consequently, it is essential that organizations effectively control their finances and financial statements. Let's examine some of the most common forms of financial control.

- *Budgetary control*: After an organization has finalized its annual budget, it divides those monies into monthly allocations. Managers at various levels monitor departmental expenditures and compare them against the budget and the operational progress of corporate plans.

- *Auditing*: Auditing has two basic purposes: (1) to monitor how the organization's monies are being spent and (2) to assess the organization's financial health. *Internal audits* are performed by the organization's accounting and finance personnel. These employees also prepare for periodic *external audits* by outside CPA firms.

- *Financial ratio analysis*: Another major accounting and finance function is to monitor the company's financial health by assessing a set of financial ratios, including liquidity ratios (the availability of cash to pay debt), activity ratios (how quickly a firm converts noncash assets to cash assets), debt ratios (measure the firm's ability to repay long-term debt), and profitability ratios (measure the firm's use of its assets and control of its expenses to generate an acceptable rate of return).

MKT Information Systems for Marketing

It is impossible to overestimate the importance of customers to any organization. Therefore, any successful organization must understand its customers' needs and wants and then develop its marketing and advertising strategies around them. Information systems provide numerous types of support to the marketing function. Customer-centric organizations are so important that we cover this topic in detail in Chapter 11.

POM Information Systems for Production/Operations Management

The production/operations management (POM) function in an organization is responsible for the processes that transform inputs into useful outputs as well as for the overall operation of the business. The POM function is responsible for managing the organization's supply chain. Because supply chain management is vital to the success of modern organizations, we address this topic in detail in Chapter 11. Because of the breadth and variety of POM functions, we discuss only four here: in-house logistics and materials management, planning production and operation, computer-integrated manufacturing (CIM), and product life cycle management (PLM).

In-House Logistics and Materials Management.
Logistics management deals with ordering, purchasing, inbound logistics (receiving), and outbound logistics (shipping) activities. Related activities include inventory management and quality control.

Inventory Management.
As the name suggests, inventory management determines how much inventory an organization should maintain. Both excessive inventory and insufficient inventory create problems. Overstocking can be expensive because of storage costs and the costs of spoilage and obsolescence. However, keeping insufficient inventory is also expensive because of last-minute orders and lost sales.

Operations personnel make two basic decisions: when to order and how much to order. Inventory models, such as the economic order quantity (EOQ) model, support these decisions. A large number of commercial inventory software packages are available that automate the application of these models.

Many large companies allow their suppliers to monitor their inventory levels and ship products as they are needed. This strategy, called *vendor-managed inventory (VMI)*, eliminates the need for the company to submit purchasing orders. We discuss VMI in Chapter 11.

Quality Control.
Quality control systems used by manufacturing units provide information about the quality of incoming material and parts, as well as the quality of in-process semifinished and finished products. These systems record the results of all inspections and then compare these results with established metrics. They also generate periodic reports that contain information about quality—for example, the percentage of products that contain defects or that need to be reworked. Quality control data, collected by Web-based sensors, can be interpreted in real time. Alternatively, they can be stored in a database for future analysis.

Planning Production and Operations.
In many firms, POM planning is supported by IT. POM planning has evolved from material requirements planning (MRP) to manufacturing resource planning (MRP II), to enterprise resource planning (ERP). We briefly discuss MRP and MRP II here, and we examine ERP in detail later in this chapter.

Inventory systems that use an EOQ approach are designed for items for which demand is completely independent—for example, the number of identical personal computers a computer manufacturer will sell. In manufacturing operations, however, the demand for some items is interdependent. Consider, for example, a company that makes three types of chairs, all of which use the same screws and bolts. In this case, the demand for screws and bolts depends on the total demand for all three types of chairs and their shipment schedules. The planning process that integrates production, purchasing, and inventory management of interdependent items is called *material requirements planning (MRP)*.

MRP deals only with production scheduling and inventories. More complex planning also involves allocating related resources, such as money and labor. For these cases, more complex, integrated software, called *manufacturing resource planning (MRP II)*, is available. MRP II integrates a firm's production, inventory management, purchasing, financing, and labor activities. Thus, MRP II adds functions to a regular MRP system. In fact, MRP II has evolved into *enterprise resource planning (ERP)*.

Computer-Integrated Manufacturing.

Computer-integrated manufacturing (CIM) (also called *digital manufacturing*) is an approach that integrates various automated factory systems. CIM has three basic goals: (1) to simplify all manufacturing technologies and techniques, (2) to automate as many of the manufacturing processes as possible, and (3) to integrate and coordinate all aspects of design, manufacturing, and related functions through computer systems.

Product Life Cycle Management.

Even within a single organization, designing and developing new products can be expensive and time consuming. When multiple organizations are involved, the process can become very complex. *Product life cycle management (PLM)* is a business strategy that enables manufacturers to share product-related data that support product design and development and supply chain operations. PLM applies Web-based collaborative technologies to product development. By integrating formerly disparate functions, such as a manufacturing process and the logistics that support it, PLM enables these functions to collaborate, essentially forming a single team that manages the product from its inception through its completion, as shown in **Figure 10.2**.

(HRM) Information Systems for Human Resource Management

Initial human resource information system (HRIS) applications dealt primarily with transaction processing systems such as managing benefits and keeping records of vacation days. As organizational systems have moved to intranets and the Web, so have HRIS applications.

Many HRIS applications are delivered through an HR portal. (See our discussion of LinkedIn in Chapter 9.) For example, numerous organizations use their Web portals to advertise job openings and to conduct online hiring and training. In this section, you consider how organizations are using IT to perform some key HR functions: recruitment, HR maintenance and development, and HR planning and management.

Recruitment.

Recruitment involves finding potential employees, evaluating them, and deciding which ones to hire. Some companies are flooded with viable applicants; others have difficulty finding the right people. IT can be helpful in both cases. IT can also assist in related activities such as testing and screening job applicants.

With millions of résumés available online (in particular, LinkedIn), it is not surprising that companies are trying to find appropriate candidates on the Web, usually with the help of specialized search engines. Companies also advertise hundreds of thousands of jobs on the Web. Online recruiting can reach more candidates, which may bring in better applicants. The costs of online recruitment are also usually lower than traditional recruiting methods such as advertising in newspapers or in trade journals.

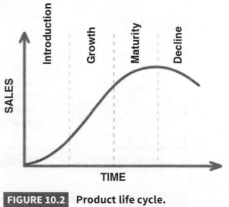

FIGURE 10.2 Product life cycle.

Human Resources Development.

After employees are recruited, they become part of the corporate human resources pool, which means they must be evaluated and developed. IT provides support for these activities. Throughout their career, they have access to various internal resources, and IT helps to manage their access levels.

Most employees are periodically evaluated by their immediate supervisors. In some organizations, peers or subordinates also evaluate other employees. Evaluations are typically digitized, and they are used to support many decisions, ranging from rewards to transfers to layoffs.

IT also plays an important role in training and retraining. Some of the most innovative developments are taking place in the areas of intelligent computer-aided instruction and the application of multimedia support for instructional activities. For example, companies conduct much of their corporate training over their intranet or on the Web.

Human Resources Planning and Management.

Managing human resources in large organizations requires extensive planning and detailed strategy. IT support is particularly valuable in the following three areas:

1. *Payroll and employees' records*: The HR department is responsible for payroll preparation. This process is typically automated, meaning that paychecks are printed or money is transferred electronically into employees' bank accounts.

2. *Benefits administration*: In return for their work contributions to their organizations, employees receive wages, bonuses, and various benefits. These benefits include health care and dental care, pension contributions (in a decreasing number of organizations), 401(k) contributions, wellness centers, and child care centers.

   Managing benefits is a complex task because organizations typically offer multiple options, allowing employees to choose and trade off their benefits. In many organizations, employees can access the company portal to self-register for specific benefits.

3. *Employee relationship management*: In their efforts to better manage employees, companies are developing *employee relationship management* (ERM) applications, for example, a call center for employees to discuss problems.

Table 10.1 provides an overview of the activities that the FAIS support. **Figure 10.3** identifies many of the information systems that support these five functional areas.

Profitability Planning	Financial Planning	Employment Planning, Outsourcing	Product Life Cycle Management	Sales Forecasting, Advertising Planning	**STRATEGIC**
Auditing, Budgeting	Investment Management	Benefits Administration, Performance Evaluation	Quality Control, Inventory Management	Customer Relations, Sales Force Automation	**TACTICAL**
Payroll, Accounts Payable, Accounts Receivable	Manage Cash, Manage Financial Transactions	Maintain Employee Records	Order Fulfillment, Order Processing	Set Pricing, Profile Customers	**OPERATIONAL**
ACCOUNTING	**FINANCE**	**HUMAN RESOURCES**	**PRODUCTION/ OPERATIONS**	**MARKETING**	

FIGURE 10.3   **Examples of information systems supporting the functional areas.**

TABLE 10.1	Activities Supported by Functional Area Information Systems

`ACCT` `FIN` Accounting and Finance

Financial planning and cost of money

Budgeting—allocates financial resources among participants and activities

Capital budgeting—financing of asset acquisitions

Managing financial transactions

Handling multiple currencies

Virtual close—the ability to close the books at any time on short notice

Investment management—managing organizational investments in stocks, bonds, real estate, and other investment vehicles

Budgetary control—monitoring expenditures and comparing them against the budget

Auditing—ensuring the accuracy of the organization's financial transactions and assessing the condition of the organization's financial health

Payroll

`MKT` Marketing and Sales

Customer relations—knowing who customers are and treating them appropriately

Customer profiles and preferences

Salesforce automation—using software to automate the business tasks of sales, thereby improving the productivity of salespeople

`POM` Production/Operations and Logistics

Inventory management—when to order new inventory, how much inventory to order, and how much inventory to keep in stock

Quality control—controlling for defects in incoming materials and goods produced

Materials requirements planning (MRP)—planning process that integrates production, purchasing, and inventory management of interdependent items

Manufacturing resource planning (MRP II)—planning process that integrates an enterprise's production, inventory management, purchasing, financing, and labor activities

Just-in-time systems (JIT)—a principle of production and inventory control in which materials and parts arrive precisely when and where needed for production

Computer-integrated manufacturing—a manufacturing approach that integrates several computerized systems, such as computer-assisted design (CAD), computer-assisted manufacturing (CAM), MRP, and JIT

Product life cycle management—business strategy that enables manufacturers to collaborate on product design and development efforts, using the Web

`HRM` Human Resource Management

Recruitment—finding employees, testing them, and deciding which ones to hire

Performance evaluation—periodic evaluation by superiors

Training

Employee records

Benefits administration—retirement, disability, unemployment, and so on

Reports

All information systems produce reports: transaction processing systems, functional area information systems, ERP systems, customer relationship management systems, business intelligence systems, and so on. We discuss reports here because they are so closely associated with FAIS and ERP systems. These reports generally fall into three categories: routine, ad hoc (on-demand), and exception.

Routine reports are produced at scheduled intervals. They range from hourly quality control reports to daily reports on absenteeism rates. Although routine reports are extremely valuable to an organization, managers frequently need special information that is not included in these reports. At other times, they need the information that is normally included in routine reports, but at different times ("I need the report today, for the last three days, not for one week").

Such out-of-the routine reports are called **ad hoc (on-demand) reports.** Ad hoc reports can also include requests for the following types of information:

- **Drill-down reports** display a greater level of detail. For example, a manager might examine sales by region and decide to "drill down" by focusing specifically on sales by store and then by salesperson.
- **Key indicator reports** summarize the performance of critical activities. For example, a chief financial officer might want to monitor cash flow and cash on hand.
- **Comparative reports** compare, for example, the performances of different business units or of a single unit during different times.

Some managers prefer exception reports. **Exception reports** include only information that falls outside certain threshold standards. To implement *management by exception*, management first establishes performance standards. The company then creates systems to monitor performance (through the incoming data about business transactions such as expenditures), to compare actual performance to the standards, and to identify exceptions to the standards. The system alerts managers to the exceptions through exception reports.

MKT Let's use sales as an example. First, management establishes sales quotas. The company then implements a FAIS that collects and analyzes all of the sales data. An exception report would identify only those cases in which sales fell outside an established threshold—for example, more than 20 percent short of the quota. It would *not* report expenditures that fell *within* the accepted range of standards. By leaving out all "acceptable" performances, exception reports save managers time, thus helping them focus on problem areas.

Before you go on...

1. Define a functional area information system and list its major characteristics.
2. How do information systems benefit the finance and accounting functional area?
3. Explain how POM personnel use information systems to perform their jobs more effectively and efficiently.
4. What are the most important HRIS applications?
5. Compare and contrast the three basic types of reports.

10.3 Enterprise Resource Planning Systems

Author Lecture Videos are available exclusively in *WileyPLUS*.
Apply the Concept activities are available in the Appendix and in *WileyPLUS*.

Historically, functional area information systems were developed independent of one another, resulting in *information silos.* These silos did not communicate well with one another, and this lack of communication and integration made organizations less efficient. This inefficiency was particularly evident in business processes that involve more than one functional area, such as procurement and fulfillment.

Enterprise resource planning (ERP) systems are designed to correct a lack of communication among the FAISs. ERP systems resolve this problem by tightly integrating the FAIS through a common database. For this reason, experts credit ERP systems with greatly increasing organizational productivity. ERP systems adopt a business process view of the overall organization to integrate the planning, management, and use of all of an organization's resources, employing a common software platform and database.

The major objectives of ERP systems are: tightly integrate the functional areas of the organization and enable information to flow seamlessly across them. Tight integration means that changes in one functional area are immediately reflected in all other pertinent functional areas. In essence, ERP systems provide the information necessary to control the business processes of the organization.

It is important to understand that ERP systems are an evolution of FAIS. That is, ERP systems have much the same functionality as FAIS, and they produce the same reports.

Although some companies have developed their own ERP systems, most organizations use commercially available ERP software. The leading ERP software vendor is SAP (**www.sap.com**). Other major vendors include Oracle (**www.oracle.com**).

ERP II Systems

ERP systems were originally deployed to facilitate business processes associated with manufacturing, such as raw materials management, inventory control, order entry, and distribution. However, these early ERP systems did not extend to other functional areas, such as sales and marketing. They also did not include any customer relationship management (CRM) capabilities that enable organizations to capture customer-specific information. Finally, they did not provide Web-enabled customer service or order fulfillment.

Over time, ERP systems evolved to include administrative, sales, marketing, and human resources processes. Companies now employ an enterprise-wide approach to ERP that uses the Web and connects all facets of the value chain. (You might want to review our discussion of value chains in Chapter 2.) These systems are called ERP II.

ERP II systems are interorganizational ERP systems that provide Web-enabled links among a company's key business systems—such as inventory and production—and its customers, suppliers, distributors, and other relevant parties. These links integrate internal-facing ERP applications with the external-focused applications of supply chain management and customer relationship management. **Figure 10.4** illustrates the organization and functions of an ERP II system.

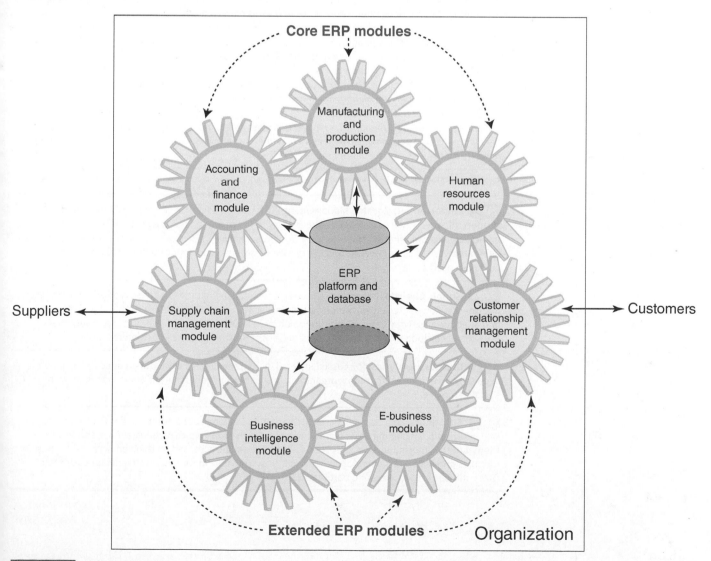

FIGURE 10.4 ERP II system.

The various functions of ERP II systems are now delivered as e-business suites. The major ERP vendors have developed modular, Web-enabled software suites that integrate ERP, customer relationship management, supply chain management, procurement, decision support, enterprise portals, and other business applications and functions. Examples are Oracle's e-Business Suite and SAP's mySAP. The goal of these systems is to enable companies to execute most of their business processes using a single Web-enabled system of integrated software rather than a variety of separate e-business applications.

ERP II systems include a variety of modules that are divided into core ERP modules—financial management, operations management, and human resource management—and extended ERP modules—customer relationship management, supply chain management, business intelligence, and e-business. If a system does not have the core ERP modules, then it is not a legitimate ERP system. The extended ERP modules, in contrast, are optional. **Table 10.2** describes each of these modules.

TABLE 10.2   ERP Modules

Core ERP Modules

`ACCT` `FIN` **Financial Management.** These modules support accounting, financial reporting, performance management, and corporate governance. They manage accounting data and financial processes such as general ledger, accounts payable, accounts receivable, fixed assets, cash management and forecasting, product-cost accounting, cost-center accounting, asset accounting, tax accounting, credit management, budgeting, and asset management.

`POM` **Operations Management.** These modules manage the various aspects of production planning and execution such as demand forecasting, procurement, inventory management, materials purchasing, shipping, production planning, production scheduling, materials requirements planning, quality control, distribution, transportation, and plant and equipment maintenance.

`HRM` **Human Resource Management.** These modules support personnel administration (including workforce planning, employee recruitment, assignment tracking, personnel planning and development, and performance management and reviews), time accounting, payroll, compensation, benefits accounting, and regulatory requirements.

Extended ERP Modules

`MKT` **Customer Relationship Management.** (Discussed in detail in Chapter 11.) These modules support all aspects of a customer's relationship with the organization. They help the organization to increase customer loyalty and retention, and thus improve its profitability. They also provide an integrated view of customer data and interactions, helping organizations to be more responsive to customer needs.

`POM` **Supply Chain Management.** (Discussed in detail in Chapter 11.) These modules manage the information flows between and among stages in a supply chain to maximize supply chain efficiency and effectiveness. They help organizations plan, schedule, control, and optimize the supply chain from the acquisition of raw materials to the receipt of finished goods by customers.

`MIS` **Business Analytics.** (Discussed in detail in Chapter 12.) These modules collect information used throughout the organization, organize it, and apply analytical tools to assist managers with decision making.

`MIS` **E-Business.** (Discussed in detail in Chapter 7.) Customers and suppliers demand access to ERP information, including order status, inventory levels, and invoice reconciliation. Furthermore, they want this information in a simplified format that can be accessed on the Web. As a result, these modules provide two channels of access into ERP system information—one channel for customers (B2C) and one for suppliers and partners (B2B).

Benefits and Limitations of ERP Systems

ERP systems can generate significant business benefits for an organization. The major benefits fall into the following three categories:

1. *Organizational flexibility and agility*: As you have seen, ERP systems break down many former departmental and functional silos of business processes, information systems, and information resources. In this way, they make organizations more flexible, agile, and adaptive. The organizations can therefore respond quickly to changing business conditions and capitalize on new business opportunities.

2. *Decision support*: ERP systems provide essential information on business performance across functional areas. This information significantly improves managers' ability to make better, more timely decisions.

3. *Quality and efficiency*: ERP systems integrate and improve an organization's business processes, generating significant improvements in the quality of production, distribution, and customer service.

Despite all of their benefits, however, ERP systems do have drawbacks. The major limitations of ERP implementations include the following:

- The business processes in ERP software are often predefined by the best practices that the ERP vendor has developed. *Best practices* are the most successful solutions or problem-solving methods for achieving a business objective. As a result, companies may need to change their existing business processes to fit the predefined business processes incorporated into the ERP software. For companies with well-established procedures, this requirement can create serious problems, especially if employees do not want to abandon their old ways of working and resist the changes.

- At the same time, however, an ERP implementation can provide an opportunity to improve and in some cases completely redesign inefficient, ineffective, or outdated procedures. In fact, many companies benefit from implementing best practices for their accounting, finance, and human resource processes, as well as other support activities that companies do not consider a source of competitive advantage.

  Recall from Chapter 2, however, that different companies organize their value chains in different configurations to transform inputs into valuable outputs and achieve competitive advantages. Therefore, although the vendor's best practices, by definition, are appropriate for most organizations, they might not be the "best" one for your company if they change those processes that give you a competitive advantage.

- ERP systems can be extremely complex, expensive, and time consuming to implement. (We discuss the implementation of ERP systems in detail in the next section.) In fact, the costs and risks of failure in implementing a new ERP system are substantial. Quite a few companies have experienced costly ERP implementation failures. Specifically, they have suffered losses in revenue, profits, and market share when core business processes and information systems failed or did not work properly. In many cases, orders and shipments were lost, inventory changes were not recorded correctly, and unreliable inventory levels caused major stock outs. Companies such as Hershey Foods, Nike, A-DEC, and Connecticut General sustained losses in amounts up to hundreds of millions of dollars. In the case of FoxMeyer Drugs, a $5 billion pharmaceutical wholesaler, the ERP implementation was so poorly executed that the company had to file for bankruptcy protection.

In almost every ERP implementation failure, the company's business managers and IT professionals underestimated the complexity of the planning, development, and training that were required to prepare for a new ERP system that would fundamentally transform their business processes and information systems. The following are the major causes of ERP implementation failure:

- Failure to involve affected employees in the planning and development phases and in change management processes
- Trying to accomplish too much too fast in the conversion process
- Insufficient training in the new work tasks required by the ERP system
- Failure to perform proper data conversion and testing for the new system

Implementing ERP Systems

Companies can implement ERP systems by using either on-premise software or software-as-a-service (SaaS). We differentiate between these two methods in detail in Technology Guide 3.

On-Premise ERP Implementation. Depending on the types of value chain processes managed by the ERP system and a company's specific value chain, there are three strategic approaches to implementing an on-premise ERP system:

1. *The vanilla approach*: In this approach, a company implements a standard ERP package using the package's built-in configuration options. When the system is implemented in this way, it will deviate only minimally from the package's standardized settings. The vanilla approach can enable the company to perform the implementation more quickly. However, the extent to which the software is adapted to the organization's specific processes is limited. Fortunately, a vanilla implementation provides general functions that can support the firm's common business processes with relative ease, even if they are not a perfect fit for those processes.

2. *The custom approach*: In this approach, a company implements a more customized ERP system by developing new ERP functions designed specifically for that firm. Decisions concerning the ERP's degree of customization are specific to each organization. To use the custom approach, the organization must carefully analyze its existing business processes to develop a system that conforms to the organization's particular characteristics and processes. Customization is also expensive and risky because computer code must be written and updated every time a new version of the ERP software is released. Going further, if the customization does not perfectly match the organization's needs, then the system can be very difficult to use.

3. *The best-of-breed approach*: This approach combines the benefits of the vanilla and customized systems while avoiding the extensive costs and risks associated with complete customization. Companies that adopt this approach mix and match core ERP modules as well as other extended ERP modules from different software providers to best fit their unique internal processes and value chains. Thus, a company may choose several core ERP modules from an established vendor to take advantage of industry best practices—for example, for financial management and human resource management. At the same time, it may also choose specialized software to support its unique business processes—for example, for manufacturing, warehousing, and distribution. Sometimes companies arrive at the best-of-breed approach the hard way. For example, Dell wasted millions of dollars trying to customize an integrated ERP system from a major vendor to match its unique processes before it realized that a smaller, more flexible system that integrated well with other corporate applications was the answer.

Software-as-a-Service ERP Implementation. Companies can acquire ERP systems without having to buy a complete software solution (i.e., on-premise ERP implementation). Many organizations are using software-as-a-service (SaaS) (discussed in Chapter 13 and Technology Guide 3) to acquire cloud-based ERP systems. (We discuss cloud computing in Technology Guide 3).

In this business model, the company rents the software from an ERP vendor who offers its products over the Internet using the SaaS model. The ERP cloud vendor manages software updates and is responsible for the system's security and availability.

Cloud-based ERP systems can be a perfect fit for some companies. For example, companies that cannot afford to make large investments in IT, yet already have relatively structured business processes that need to be tightly integrated, might benefit from cloud computing.

The relationship between the company and the cloud vendor is regulated by contracts and by service level agreements (SLAs). The SLAs define the characteristics and quality of service; for example, a guaranteed uptime, or the percentage of time that the system is available. Cloud vendors that fail to meet these conditions can face penalties.

The decision about whether to use on-premise ERP or SaaS ERP is specific to each organization, and it depends on how the organization evaluates a series of advantages and disadvantages. The following are the three major advantages of using a cloud-based ERP system.

1. The system can be used from any location that has Internet access. Consequently, users can work from any location using online shared and centralized resources (data and databases). Users access the ERP system through a secure virtual private network (VPN) connection (discussed in Chapter 4) with the provider.

2. Companies using cloud-based ERP avoid the initial hardware and software expenses that are typical of on-premise implementations. For example, to run SAP on-premise, a company must purchase SAP software as well as a license to use SAP. The magnitude of this investment can hinder small- to medium-sized enterprises (SMEs) from adopting ERP.

3. Cloud-based ERP solutions are scalable, meaning it is possible to extend ERP support to new business processes and new business partners (e.g., suppliers) by purchasing new ERP modules.

There are also disadvantages to adopting cloud-based ERP systems that a company must carefully evaluate. The following are the three major disadvantages of using a cloud-based ERP system.

1. It is not clear whether cloud-based ERP systems are more secure than on-premise systems. In fact, a survey conducted by North Bridge Venture Partners indicated that security was the primary reason why organizations did not adopt cloud-based ERP.

2. Companies that adopt cloud-based ERP systems sacrifice their control over a strategic IT resource. For this reason, some companies prefer to implement an on-premise ERP system, using a strong in-house IT department that can directly manage the system.

3. A direct consequence of the lack of control over IT resources occurs when the ERP system experiences problems; for example, if some ERP functions are temporarily slow or are not available. In such cases, having an internal IT department that can solve problems immediately rather than dealing with the cloud vendor's system support can speed up the system recovery process.

    This situation is particularly important for technology-intensive companies. In such companies, IT is crucial to conduct any kind of business with customers. Examples are e-commerce companies, banks, and government organizations that manage emergencies or situations that might involve individual and national security (e.g., health care organizations, police, the homeland security department, antiterrorism units, and others).

Finally, slow or unavailable software from a cloud-based ERP vendor creates business continuity problems for the client. (We discuss business continuity in Chapter 4.) That is, a sudden system problem or failure makes it impossible for the firm to operate. Companies lose money when they lose business continuity because customers cannot be serviced and employees cannot do their jobs. A loss of business continuity also damages the company's reputation because customers lose trust in the firm.

Enterprise Application Integration

For some organizations, integrated ERP systems are not appropriate. This situation is particularly true for companies that find the process of converting from their existing system too difficult or time consuming.

Such companies, however, may still have isolated information systems that need to be connected with one another. To accomplish this task, these companies can use enterprise application integration. An **enterprise application integration (EAI) system** integrates existing systems by providing software, called *middleware*, that connects multiple applications. In essence, the EAI system allows existing applications to communicate and share data, thereby enabling organizations to existing applications while eliminating many of the problems caused by isolated information systems. EAI systems also support implementation of best-of-breed ERP solutions by connecting software modules from different vendors.

Before you go on...

1. Define ERP and describe its functions.
2. What are ERP II systems?
3. Differentiate between core ERP modules and extended ERP modules.
4. List some drawbacks of ERP software.
5. Highlight the differences between ERP configuration, customization, and best-of-breed implementation strategies.

10.4   ERP Support for Business Processes

ERP systems effectively support a number of standard business processes. In particular, ERP systems manage end-to-end, cross-departmental processes. A **cross-departmental process** is one that (1) originates in one department and ends in a different department or (2) originates and ends in the same department but involves other departments.

The Procurement, Fulfillment, and Production Processes

The following are the three prominent examples of cross-departmental processes:

1. The *procurement process*, which originates in the warehouse department (need to buy) and ends in the accounting department (send payment)
2. The *fulfillment process*, which originates in the sales department (customer request to buy) and ends in the accounting department (receive payment)
3. The *production process*, which originates and ends in the warehouse department (need to produce and reception of finished goods) but involves the production department as well

These three processes are examined in more detail In the following sections, focusing on the steps that are specific to each one.

POM ACCT   The Procurement Process.   The **procurement process** originates when a company needs to acquire goods or services from external sources, and it concludes when the company receives and pays for them. Let's consider a procurement process in which the company needs to acquire physical goods (see **Figure 10.5**). This process involves three main departments—Warehouse, Purchasing, and Accounting—and it consists of the following steps:

1. The process originates in the warehouse department, which generates a purchase requisition to buy the needed products.
2. The warehouse forwards the requisition to the purchasing department, which creates a purchase order (PO) and forwards it to a vendor. Generally, companies can choose from

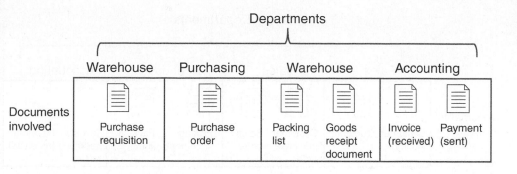

a number of vendors, and they select the one that best meets their requirements in regard to convenience, speed, reliability, and other characteristics.

3. After the company places the order, it receives the goods in its warehouse department, where someone physically checks the delivery to make certain that it corresponds to what the company ordered. He or she performs this task by comparing a packing list attached to the shipment against the PO.

4. If the shipment matches the order, then the warehouse issues a goods receipt document.

5. At the same time or shortly thereafter, the accounting department receives an invoice from the vendor. Accounting then checks that the PO, the goods receipt document, and the invoice match. This process is called the *three-way-match*.

6. After Accounting verifies the match, it processes the payment and sends it to the vendor.

The Order Fulfillment Process.

In contrast to procurement, in which the company purchases goods from a vendor, in the **order fulfillment process**, also known as the *order-to-cash process*, the company sells goods to a customer. Fulfillment originates when the company receives a customer order, and it concludes when the company receives a payment from the customer.

The fulfillment process can follow two basic strategies: sell-from-stock and configure-to-order. *Sell-from-stock* involves fulfilling customer orders directly using goods that are in the warehouse (stock). These goods are standard, meaning that the company does not customize them for buyers. In contrast, in *configure-to-order*, the company customizes the product in response to a customer request.

MKT POM ACCT A fulfillment process involves three main departments: Sales, Warehouse, and Accounting. This process includes the following steps:

1. The sales department receives a customer inquiry, which essentially is a request for information concerning the availability and price of a specific good. (We restrict our discussion here to fulfilling a customer order for physical goods rather than services.)

2. After Sales receives the inquiry, it issues a quotation that indicates availability and price.

3. If the customer agrees to the price and terms, then Sales creates a customer purchase order (PO) and a sales order.

4. Sales forwards the sales order to the warehouse. The sales order is an interdepartmental document that helps the company keep track of the internal processes that are involved in fulfilling a specific customer order. It also provides details of the quantity, price, and other characteristics of the product.

5. The warehouse prepares the shipment and produces two other internal documents: the picking document, which it uses to remove goods from the warehouse, and the packing list, which accompanies the shipment and provides details about the delivery.

6. At the same time, Accounting issues an invoice for the customer.

7. The process concludes when Accounting receives a payment that is consistent with the invoice.

FIGURE 10.6 Departments
and documents flow in the
fulfillment process.

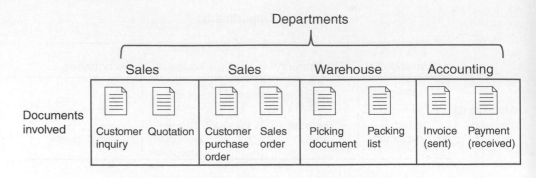

Figure 10.6 shows the fulfillment process. Note that it applies to both sell-from-stock and configure-to-order because the basic steps are the same for both strategies.

POM The Production Process.   The **production process** does not occur in all companies because not all companies produce physical goods. In fact, many businesses limit their activities to buying (procurement) and selling products (e.g., retailers).

The production process can follow two different strategies: make-to-stock and make-to-order. (See the discussion of the pull model and the push model in Chapter 11.) *Make-to-stock* occurs when the company produces goods to create or increase an *inventory*; that is, finished products that are stored in the warehouse and are available for sales. In contrast, *make-to-order* occurs when production is generated by a specific customer order.

Manufacturing companies that produce their own goods manage their interdepartmental production process across the production and warehouse departments. The production process involves the following steps:

1. The warehouse issues a planned order when the company needs to produce a finished product, either because the warehouse has insufficient inventory or because the customer placed a specific order for goods that are not currently in stock.

2. Once the planned order reaches Production, the production controller authorizes the order and issues a production order, which is a written authorization to start the production of a certain amount of a specific product.

3. To assemble a finished product, Production requires a number of materials (or parts). To acquire these materials, Production generates a material withdrawal slip, which lists all of the needed parts, and forwards it to the warehouse.

4. If the parts are available in the warehouse, then the warehouse delivers them to Production. If the parts are not available, then the company must purchase them through the procurement process.

5. After Production has created the products, it updates the production order specifying that, as planned, a specific number of units of product now can be shipped to the warehouse.

6. As soon as the warehouse receives the finished goods, it issues a goods receipt document that certifies how many units of a product it received that are available for sales.

This overview of the production process is a highly simplified one. In reality, the process is very complex, and it frequently involves additional steps. ERP systems also collect a number of other documents and pieces of information such as the bill of materials (a list of all materials needed to assemble a finished product), the list of work centers (locations where the production takes place), and the product routing (production steps). All of these topics require an in-depth analysis of the production process and are therefore beyond the scope of our discussion here. **Figure 10.7** illustrates the production processes.

A number of events can occur that create exceptions or deviations in the procurement, fulfillment, and production processes. Deviations may include the following:

- A delay in the receipt of products
- Issues related to an unsuccessful three-way-match regarding a shipment and its associated invoice (procurement)

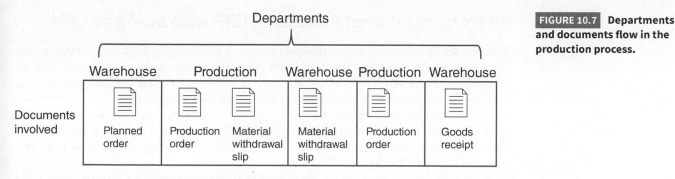

FIGURE 10.7 **Departments and documents flow in the production process.**

- Rejection of a quotation
- A delay in a shipment
- A mistake in preparing the shipment or in invoicing the customer (fulfillment)
- Overproduction of a product
- Reception of parts that cannot be used in the production process
- Unavailability of certain parts from a supplier

Companies use ERP systems to manage procurement, fulfillment, and production because these systems track all of the events that occur within each process. Furthermore, the system stores all of the documents created in each step of each process in a centralized database, where they are available as needed in real time. Any exceptions or mistakes made during one or more interdepartmental processes are handled right away by simply querying the ERP system and retrieving a specific document or piece of information that needs to be revised or examined more carefully. Therefore, it is important to follow each step in each process and to register the corresponding document into the ERP system.

Figure 10.8 portrays the three cross-functional business processes we just discussed. It specifically highlights the integration of the three processes, which is made possible by ERP systems.

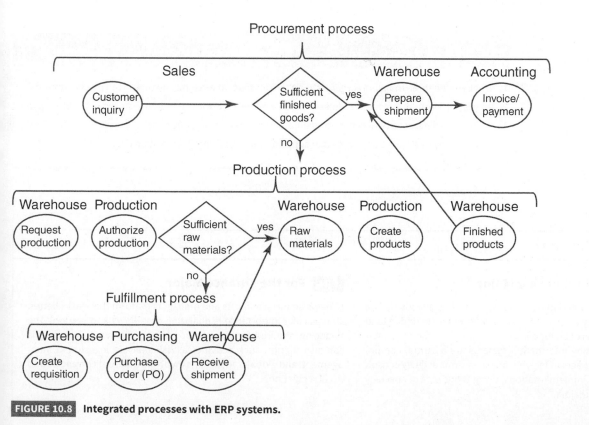

FIGURE 10.8   **Integrated processes with ERP systems.**

Interorganizational Processes: ERP with SCM and CRM

Although the procurement and the fulfillment processes involve suppliers and customers, they are considered (together with the production process) intraorganizational processes because they originate and conclude within the company. However, ERP systems can also manage processes that originate in one company and conclude in another company. These processes are called *interorganizational processes*, and they typically involve supply chain management (SCM) and customer relationship management (CRM) systems. (You can find a more detailed description of CRM and SCM in Chapter 11). Here, we focus on the integration of these processes within a firm's industry value chain.

SCM and CRM processes help multiple firms in an industry coordinate activities such as the production-to-sale of goods and services. Let's consider a chain of grocery stores whose supply chain must properly manage perishable goods. On the one hand, store managers need to stock only the amount of perishable products that they are reasonably sure they will sell before the products' expiration dates. On the other hand, they do not want to run out of stock of any products that customers need.

ERP SCM systems have the capability to place automatic requests to buy fresh perishable products from suppliers in real time. That is, as each perishable product is purchased, the system captures data on that purchase, adjusts store inventory levels, and transmits these data to the grocery chain's warehouse as well as the products' vendors. The system executes this process by connecting the point-of-sale barcode scanning system with the warehouse and accounting departments, as well as with the vendors' systems. SCM systems also use historical data to predict when fresh products need to be ordered before the store's supply becomes too low.

ERP CRM systems also benefit businesses by generating forecasting analyses of product consumption based on critical variables such as geographical area, season, day of the week, and type of customer. These analyses help grocery stores coordinate their supply chains to meet customer needs for perishable products. Going further, CRM systems identify particular customer needs and then use this information to suggest specific product campaigns. These campaigns can transform a potential demand into sales opportunities and convert sales opportunities into sales quotations and sales orders. This process is called the *demand-to-order* process.

Before you go on...

1. What are the three main intraorganizational processes that are typically supported by ERP systems?
2. Why is it important that all steps in each process generate a document that is stored in the ERP system?
3. What is the difference between intraorganizational and interorganizational processes?
4. What are the two main ES systems that support interorganizational processes?

What's in IT for me?

ACCT For the Accounting Major

Understanding the functions and outputs of TPSs effectively is a major concern of any accountant. It is also necessary to understand the various activities of all functional areas and how they are interconnected. Accounting information systems are a central component in any ERP package. In fact, all large CPA firms actively consult with clients on ERP implementations, using thousands of specially trained accounting majors.

FIN For the Finance Major

IT helps financial analysts and managers perform their tasks better. Of particular importance is analyzing cash flows and securing the financing required for smooth operations. Financial applications can also support such activities as risk analysis, investment management, and global transactions involving different currencies and fiscal regulations.

Finance activities and modeling are key components of ERP systems. Flows of funds (payments), at the core of most supply chains, must be executed efficiently and effectively. Financial arrangements are especially important along global supply chains, where currency conventions and financial regulations must be considered.

MKT For the Marketing Major

Marketing and sales expenses are usually targets in a cost-reduction program. Also, sales force automation improves not only sales-peoples' productivity (and thus reduces costs) but also customer service.

POM For the Production/Operations Management Major

Managing production tasks, materials handling, and inventories in short time intervals, at a low cost, and with high quality is critical for competitiveness. These activities can be achieved only if they are properly supported by IT. IT can also greatly enhance interaction with other functional areas, especially sales. Collaboration in design, manufacturing, and logistics requires knowledge of how modern information systems can be connected.

HRM For the Human Resource Management Major

Human resources managers can increase their efficiency and effectiveness by using IT for some of their routine functions. Human resources personnel need to understand how information flows between the HR department and the other functional areas. Finally, the integration of functional areas through ERP systems has a major impact on skill requirements and scarcity of employees, which are related to the tasks performed by the HRM department.

MIS For the MIS Major

The MIS function is responsible for the most fundamental information systems in organizations: the transaction processing systems. The TPSs provide the data for the databases. In turn, all other information systems use these data. MIS personnel develop applications that support all levels of the organization (from clerical to executive) and all functional areas. The applications also enable the firm to do business with its partners.

Summary

10.1 Explain the purpose of transaction processing systems.

TPSs monitor, store, collect, and process data generated from all business transactions. These data provide the inputs into the organization's database.

10.2 Explain the types of support that information systems can provide for each functional area of the organization.

The major business functional areas are production/operations management, marketing, accounting/finance, and human resources management. Table 10.1 provides an overview of the many activities in each functional area supported by FAIS.

10.3 Identify advantages and drawbacks to businesses of implementing an ERP system.

Enterprise resource planning (ERP) systems integrate the planning, management, and use of all of the organization's resources. The major objective of ERP systems is to tightly integrate the functional areas of the organization. This integration enables information to flow seamlessly across the various functional areas.
    The following are the major benefits of ERP systems.

- Because ERP systems integrate organizational resources, they make organizations more flexible, agile, and adaptive. The organizations can therefore react quickly to changing business conditions and capitalize on new business opportunities.
- ERP systems provide essential information on business performance across functional areas. This information significantly improves managers' ability to make better, more timely decisions.

- ERP systems integrate organizational resources, resulting in significant improvements in the quality of customer service, production, and distribution.

    The following are the major drawbacks of ERP systems.

- The business processes in ERP software are often predefined by the best practices that the ERP vendor has developed. As a result, companies may need to change existing business processes to fit the predefined business processes of the software. For companies with well-established procedures, this requirement can be a huge problem.
- ERP systems can be extremely complex, expensive, and time consuming to implement. In fact, the costs and risks of failure in implementing a new ERP system are substantial.

10.4 Describe the three main business processes supported by ERP systems.

The *procurement process*, which originates in the warehouse department (need to buy) and ends in the accounting department (send payment).

The *fulfillment process* that originates in the sales department (customer request to buy) and ends in the accounting department (receive payment).

The *production process* that originates and ends in the warehouse department (need to produce and reception of finished goods), but involves the production department as well.

We leave the details of the steps in each of these processes up to you.

Chapter Glossary

ad hoc (on-demand) reports   Nonroutine reports that often contain special information that is not included in routine reports.

batch processing   Transaction processing system (TPS) that processes data in batches at fixed periodic intervals.

comparative reports   Reports that compare performances of different business units or times.

computer-integrated manufacturing (CIM)   An information system that integrates various automated factory systems; also called *digital manufacturing.*

cross-departmental process   A business process that originates in one department and ends in another department or originates and ends in the same department while involving other departments.

drill-down reports   Reports that show a greater level of details than is included in routine reports.

enterprise application integration (EAI) system   A system that integrates existing systems by providing layers of software that connect applications together.

enterprise resource planning (ERP) systems   Information systems that take a business process view of the overall organization to integrate the planning, management, and use of all of an organization's resources, employing a common software platform and database.

ERP II systems   Interorganizational ERP systems that provide Web-enabled links among key business systems (e.g., inventory and production) of a company and its customers, suppliers, distributors, and others.

exception reports   Reports that include only information that exceeds certain threshold standards.

functional area information systems (FAIS)   Systems that provide information to managers (usually mid-level) in the functional areas to better support managerial tasks of planning, organizing, and controlling operations.

key indicator reports   Reports that summarize the performance of critical activities.

online transaction processing (OLTP)   Transaction processing system (TPS) that processes

data after transactions occur, frequently in real time.

order fulfillment process   A cross-functional business process that originates when the company receives a customer order, and it concludes when it receives a payment from the customer.

procurement process   A cross-functional business process that originates when a company needs to acquire goods or services from external sources, and it concludes when the company receives and pays for them.

production process   A cross-functional business process in which a company produces physical goods.

routine reports   Reports produced at scheduled intervals.

transaction   Any business event that generates data worth capturing and storing in a database.

transaction processing system (TPS)   Information system that supports the monitoring, collection, storage, and processing of data from the organization's basic business transactions, each of which generates data.

Discussion Questions

1. Why is it logical to organize IT applications by functional areas?

2. Describe the role of a TPS in a service organization.

3. Describe the relationship between TPS and FAIS.

4. Discuss how IT facilitates the budgeting process.

5. How can the Internet support investment decisions?

6. Describe the benefits of integrated accounting software packages.

7. Discuss the role that IT plays in support of auditing.

8. Investigate the role of the Web in human resources management.

9. What is the relationship between information silos and enterprise resource planning?

Problem-Solving Activities

1. Finding a job on the Internet is challenging, as there are almost too many places to look. Visit the following sites: **www.careerbuilder.com**, **www.craigslist.org**, **www.linkedin.com**, **www.jobcentral.com**, and **www.monster.com**. What does each of these sites provide you with as a job seeker?

2. Enter **www.sas.com** and access *revenue optimization*. Explain how the software helps in optimizing prices.

3. Enter **www.eleapsoftware.com** and review the product that helps with online training (training systems). What are the most attractive features of this product?

4. Examine the capabilities of the following (and similar) financial software packages: Financial Analyzer (from Oracle) and CFO Vision (from SAS Institute). Prepare a report comparing the capabilities of the software packages.

5. Surf the Net and find free accounting software. (Try **www.cnet.com** and **www.tucows.com**.) Download the software and try it. Compare the ease of use and usefulness of each software package.

6. Examine the capabilities of the following financial software packages: Financial Analyzer (from **www.oracle.com**) and Financial Management (from **www.sas.com**). Prepare a report comparing the capabilities of the software packages.

7. Find Simply Accounting Basic from Sage Software (**http://www.sage.com/us/sage-50-accounting**). Why is this product recommended for small businesses?

8. Enter **www.cornerstoneondemand.com** and **www.sap.com**. Examine their software products and compare them.

Closing Case

MIS Western Digital Acquires Companies and Merges Systems

The Business Problem

Western Digital (WD; www.westerndigital.com) is an American computer hard disk drive manufacturer and data storage company. It designs, manufactures, and sells data technology products, including storage devices, data center systems, and cloud storage services. In 2011 WD began a series of acquisitions to expand their products across the data storage sector.

The firm first acquired Hitachi Global Storage Technology (HGST) for $4.3 billion. Initially, Chinese government regulators mandated that Western Digital and HGST operate as two separate companies. However, in 2015, the Chinese government lifted the restrictions, and WD folded HGST into the WD brand. WD then acquired SanDisk in 2015 for $19 billion and began formalizing plans to create one entity from the former three under the parent name of Western Digital.

WD planned the integration of the three companies in three phases. First, they would consolidate the communication and collaboration tools within their organizations. This consolidation meant moving to a single platform for office tools, cloud storage, and online meeting capabilities. Second, they would integrate internal information systems through a single enterprise resource planning (ERP) system. Finally, they would move the company to uniform, standard reports. This case focuses on the second part of this transition: integrating the three internal information systems into a single ERP.

Typically, when one business acquires another, a natural order emerges for the integration of systems. If a larger company acquires a smaller one, it is standard to default to the larger company's systems. If two companies are similar in size, information systems personnel test each firm's systems and determine which one is best. However, Western Digital was trying to integrate three similar-sized companies and there was no clear path forward for systems integration

Each of the three companies had a different legacy, on-premise ERP system. WD could have chosen one of the three ERP systems and begun a 3- to 5-year process to migrate the other two systems into the one selected.

Fortunately, WD was beginning its integration process in 2016 when many ERP systems were becoming available as services in the cloud. As a result, WD decided to move to the cloud.

The IT Solution

In fact, WD had to integrate more than 3,000 applications from the equivalent of three Fortune 500 companies in a single technology platform and ERP system. As soon as WD decided to implement a cloud ERP solution, the project team began investigating the three firms' systems for similarities and differences. They quickly discovered that the three companies managed data differently. All three lacked mature data standards across systems and functional areas, resulting in significant data quality and interoperability issues.

It became apparent that the migration would require more than systems upgrades. It would also be necessary to streamline business processes and data management.

WD considered many providers but chose to implement the Oracle ERP Cloud. WD hoped to create consistency in several operations across the following:

- Cost center management
- Information technology
- Human resource management
- Payroll processing
- Streamlined systems for forecasting business analytics and forecasts
- Workforce planning
- Comprehensive dashboards and automated reporting
- Improved customer relationship analysis

WD seriously underestimated the cost and time for the migration process. The process cost $40 million more than the estimate and took more than one year longer than the estimate to complete.

Sadly, this kind of estimation error is not uncommon. Unforeseen process integration—particularly data migration—can add costs and complexities to companies merging or migrating technologies. Despite the potential difficulties, WD proceeded with its ERP migration because the company really had no other choice. WD simply could not continue to operate with three independent and non-communicating systems.

The Results

The ERP upgrade had a direct impact on process improvements. Tasks that took 17 or 18 steps before the ERP implementation now required only four or five steps.

Further, the implementation of a cloud-based ERP solution meant that WD benefited from seamless and continuous upgrades. Upgrades no longer required system downtime that upgrades to locally hosted systems require. WD deployed the first phase of the ERP migration in July 2017. Since that time, the company has successfully implemented another nine system upgrades. Significantly, WD has completed each upgrade during a typical working day with minimal interruption to business operations.

Sources: Compiled from J. Fruhlinger, T. Wailgum, and P. Sayer, "16 Famous ERP Disasters, Dustups and Disappointments," *CIO*, March 20, 2020; J. Young, "Case Studies of Successful Enterprise Resource Planning," *Investopedia*, June 14, 2020; P. Sayer, "Inside Western Digital's Massive Cloud ERP Migration," *CIO*, November 30, 2018; L. Lawson, "ERP Integration: An Overlooked Challenge During Merger & Acquisition," *ITBusinessEdge*, March 2, 2015; N. Eide, "Western Digital's Roadmap to Merging 3 Distinct Technology Stacks," *CIODIVE*, August 8, 2019; P. Tayal, "Challenges for the Western Digital–SanDisk Merger," *Market Realist*, March 2016; www.westerndigital.com, accessed December 12, 2020.

Questions

1. Why do you think so many ERP implementations fail? Why is it so difficult to integrate multiple ERPs?

2. What do you see as the major advantages for WD of moving all three companies to a single platform?

CHAPTER 11

Customer Relationship Management and Supply Chain Management

CHAPTER OUTLINE	LEARNING OBJECTIVES
11.1 Defining Customer Relationship Management	11.1 Identify the primary functions of both customer relationship management (CRM) and collaborative CRM strategies.
11.2 Operational Customer Relationship Management	11.2 Discuss how businesses might use applications of each of the two major components of operational CRM systems.
11.3 Other Types of Customer Relationship Management Systems	11.3 Explain the advantages and disadvantages of mobile CRM systems, on-demand CRM systems, open-source CRM systems, social CRM systems, and real-time CRM systems.
11.4 Supply Chains	11.4 Describe the three components and the three flows of a supply chain.
11.5 Supply Chain Management	11.5 Identify popular strategies to solve the multiple challenges of supply chains.
11.6 Information Technology Support for Supply Chain Management	11.6 Explain the utility of each of the three major technologies that support supply chain management.

Opening Case

MIS **POM** **Digital Freight Brokers**

Historically, freight pricing has been complex and unclear. As a result, brokers were able to create a bigger spread. The *spread* is the difference between what brokers charge shippers and what they pay truckers, typically about 16 percent.

Since trucking was deregulated in the 1980s, roughly 18,000 digital freight brokerages have emerged, largely due to the potential for technology to transform the previously paper-based industry. Digital brokerages use apps, websites, and algorithms to match loads from shippers with trucks from carriers. The brokers use the algorithms to set prices based on a number of variables including supply, demand, time of day, and weather. Carriers need to make $1.70 per loaded mile to break even. Further, they lose money if their truckers drive empty, as they do for more than 50 billion miles every year.

Significantly, the digital freight brokerage industry has become highly fragmented. The largest company, publicly traded C. H. Robinson (**www.chrobinson.com**), claims less than 3 percent of the market.

Some shippers—for example, Walmart—have their own fleets of trucks, which are driven by their employees. However, these shippers are the exceptions. Most trucking is performed by contractors. The vast majority of contractors are small operators who must keep their trailers full to cover the financing on their trucks.

Founded in 2013, Transfix (**www.transfix.io**), an online freight marketplace, uses algorithms and machine learning to provide full-load shippers with better prices and truck owners with more efficient routes. The more efficient the route, the less truckers need to drive with empty loads.

In 2010, Transfix launched on a shoestring. The startup picked up a shipment of books from a printer in Indianapolis, Indiana, and took them to a warehouse in New Jersey for $1,700 per load a few times a week, despite having no software developed for its app. In fact, Transfix did not deploy the first version of its app until January 2014.

To entice truck owners to sign up for the Transfix app, founder and CEO Drew McElroy visited truck stops and attended the annual Truckers Jamboree at the Iowa 80 Truckstop. He offered drivers pork chops and beer if they would download the app. One year the startup set up a tank for a game of dunk-a-broker, a lighthearted way to make fun of the truckers' distrust of brokers.

Transfix deployed a dedicated smartphone app that allows shippers to request available drivers on an on-demand basis. Shippers make requests to the firm's online brokerage system, designating pickup and delivery locations, dates, times, product description details, and driver instructions. Shippers' orders are routed to the dispatch page, where truckers place offers for the shipments. Truckers can enter either a set amount or an amount per mile. The system optimizes the match between shippers and truckers.

Transfix's pricing algorithm produces a shipping rate by relying on data from thousands of variables, including historical shipments, loading times, and weather forecasts. The company takes the risk that occasionally its rate will fall below the break-even point, and it uses each new data point about cost to improve the algorithm. Its matching algorithm, meanwhile, forecasts which truckers are most likely to want a shipment based on their current location, stated preferences, and historical driving patterns. Transfix pays the majority of its gross revenue to the truckers. The company's mission is to help shippers manage their logistics while also enabling truckers to make more money by reducing the time they travel empty.

McElroy believes he can increase truckers' take-home pay by routing the truckers more efficiently. For shippers, the advantage is a better, more reliable price. McElroy further contends that Transfix may ultimately be able to use its technology to cut the 16 percent spread in half.

Transfix's app also offers real-time tracking, which enables shippers to better plan loading and unloading schedules and occasionally to detect fraud. In one instance, Transfix's data indicated that a truck filled with aluminum ingots had gone off course. The truck ended up stopped at the side of the road in a high-crime neighborhood for several hours, a red flag indicating a driver-enabled hijacking. Transfix notified the authorities, who found the truck. Unfortunately, the ingots had already been stolen.

Transfix's tracking data also help shippers to prepare warehouses and workers to increase the efficiency of a truck's arrival. For example, the shipper knows the precise time a truck is arriving and can dynamically schedule it to pull up to Door 3 of the loading dock, for example, instead of Door 5.

In April 2020, Transfix launched a new feature called the Core Carrier Program, which targets "exceptional carriers" that have shown reliability and strong performance in moving freight with the company. The key metrics that determine which carriers receive an invitation to participate in the program include high load volume and consistently strong on-time pickup and delivery. Transfix maintains that the new program offers various benefits for carriers such as increased freight volume, early access to consistent loads, a dedicated carrier account manager, and 24/7 support.

Transfix deployed a pricing tool called TrueRate to its shippers. The firm uses its own predictive pricing algorithms to guarantee shipping rates up to one year in advance. Using a machine-learning model that factors in demand, weather, and fuel prices, among other variables, Transfix enables shippers to price routes in advance. The difference between Transfix's model and other digital freight brokerages that provide predictive pricing is that Transfix guarantees that its load will be covered by carriers, regardless of the conditions that exist when the load is transported.

Sources: Compiled from C. White, "Brokers Using Digital Freight Matching Win More Freight and Satisfied Shippers," *Freight Waves*, August 31, 2020; "Freight Broker Software Market May Set New Growth Story," *Digital Journal*, August 25, 2020; S. Beckwith, "16 Transportation Metrics that Matter," *Inbound Logistics*, August 17, 2020; B. Straight, "Technology Is Changing the Way Freight Brokerages Operate," *Freight Waves*, August 7, 2020; L. Shen, "U.S. Small Trucking Companies Need Federal Support: Transfix," *JOC.com*, June 17, 2020; C. Hawes, "Transfix Lays off 10% of Its Staff," *Freight Waves*, April 29, 2020; B. Ames, "Transfix Offers Increased Freight Volume to Top Performing Carriers," *DC Velocity*, April 22, 2020; J. Berman, "New 'Core Carrier Program' from Transfix Focuses on Strategic Partnership for Exceptional Carriers, *Logistics Management*, April 21, 2020; E. Johnson, "Transfix Looks to the Future with Guaranteed Rate Product," *JOC.com*, February 18, 2020; A. Feldman, "18-Wheelers at App Speed," *Forbes*, December 31, 2018; **www.transfix.io**, accessed September 3, 2020.

Questions

1. Compare Transfix with Uber, Lyft, and Airbnb. Discuss similarities and differences in their business models.

2. What impacts has the COVID-19 pandemic had on the emergence of digital freight brokerages and their continuing importance?

Introduction

In Chapter 10, you learned about information systems that support activities within the organization. In this chapter, you study information systems that support activities that extend outside the organization to customers and suppliers. The first half of this chapter addresses customer relationship management (CRM) systems and the second half addresses supply chain management systems (SCM).

Organizations are emphasizing a customer-centric approach to their business practices because they realize that long-term customer relationships provide sustainable value that extends beyond an individual business transaction. Organizations are also integrating their strategy and operations with supply chain partners because tight integration along the supply chain also leads to sustainable business value. Significantly, customer relationship management and supply chain management are critically important for all enterprises, regardless of size.

The chapter opening case points out how important data are to the customer-centric approach to business. Businesses are now able to discover when customers are having trouble with their site before the customers even complain. This type of data analysis is crucial to helping organizations understand customer problems and implement timely solutions.

Supply chain management (SCM) is equally important for organizations to successfully compete in the marketplace. Today, supply chain management is an integral part of all organizations and can improve customer service and reduce operating costs. Let's look at these two areas in more detail.

- **POM** *Improve the fulfillment process.* Customers expect to receive the correct products as quickly as possible. Therefore, products must be on hand in the correct locations. Furthermore, follow-up support after a sale must effective and efficient.

- **FIN** *Reduce operating costs.* For example, retailers depend on their supply chains to quickly distribute expensive products so that they will not have the inventory carrying costs for costly, depreciating products.

Delays in production are costly. Supply chains must ensure the reliable delivery of materials to assembly plants to avoid expensive delays in manufacturing.

At this point, you might be asking yourself: Why should *I* learn about CRM and SCM? The answer, as you will see in this chapter, is that customers and suppliers are supremely important to *all* organizations. Regardless of your job, you will have an impact, directly or indirectly, on managing your firm's customer relationships and its supply chain. When you read the What's in IT for Me? section at the end of this chapter, you will learn about opportunities to make immediate contributions on your first job. Therefore, it is essential that you acquire a working knowledge of CRM, CRM systems, supply chains, SCM, and SCM systems.

11.1 Defining Customer Relationship Management

Author Lecture Videos are available exclusively in *WileyPLUS*.
Apply the Concept activities are available in the Appendix and in *WileyPLUS*.

Before the supermarket, the mall, and the automobile, people purchased goods at their neighborhood store. The owners and employees recognized customers by name and knew their preferences and wants. For their part, customers remained loyal to the store and made repeated purchases. Over time, however, this personal customer relationship became impersonal as people moved from farms and small towns to cities, consumers became mobile, and supermarkets and department stores achieved economies of scale through mass marketing. Although prices were lower and products were more uniform in quality, the relationship with customers became nameless and impersonal.

The customer relationship has become even more impersonal with the rapid growth of the Internet and the World Wide Web. In today's hypercompetitive marketplace, customers are increasingly powerful; if they are dissatisfied with a product or a service from one organization, a competitor is often just one mouse click away. Furthermore, as more and more customers shop on the Web, an enterprise does not even have the opportunity to make a good first impression *in person*.

Customer relationship management returns to personal marketing. That is, rather than market to a mass of people or companies, businesses market to each customer individually. By employing this approach, businesses can use information about each customer—for example, previous purchases, needs, and wants—to create highly individualized offers that customers are more likely to accept. The CRM approach is designed to achieve *customer intimacy*.

Customer relationship management is a customer-focused and customer-driven organizational strategy. That is, organizations concentrate on assessing customers' requirements for products and services and then provide a high-quality, responsive customer experience. CRM is not a process or a technology per se; rather, it is a customer-centric way of thinking and acting. The focus of modern organizations has shifted from conducting business transactions to managing customer relationships. In general, organizations recognize that customers are the core of a successful enterprise, and the success of the enterprise depends on effectively managing relationships with them.

The CRM approach is enabled by information technology in the form of various systems and applications. However, CRM is not only about the software. Sometimes the problem with managing relationships is simply a lack of time or information. Old systems may contain the needed information, but this information may take too long to access and may not be usable across a variety of applications or devices. The result is that companies have less time to spend with their customers.

In contrast, modern CRM strategies and systems build sustainable long-term customer relationships that create value for the company as well as for the customer. That is, CRM helps companies acquire new customers and retain and expand their relationships with profitable existing customers. Retaining customers is particularly important because repeat customers are the largest generator of revenue for an enterprise. Also, organizations have long understood that winning back a customer who has switched to a competitor is vastly more expensive than keeping that customer satisfied in the first place.

Figure 11.1 depicts the CRM process. The process begins with marketing efforts, through which the organization solicits prospects from a target population of potential customers. A certain number of these prospects will make a purchase and thus become customers. A certain number of these customers will become repeat customers. The organization then segments its repeat customers into low- and high-value repeat customers. An organization's overall goal is

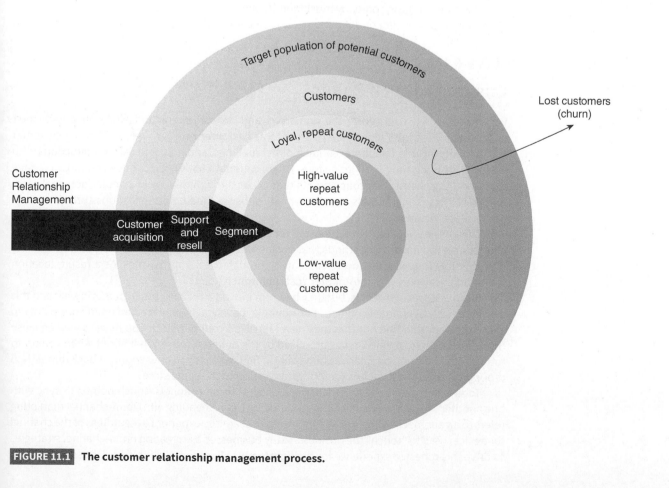

FIGURE 11.1   **The customer relationship management process.**

to maximize the *lifetime value* of a customer, which is that customer's potential revenue stream over a number of years.

Over time all organizations inevitably lose a certain percentage of customers, a process called *customer churn.* The optimal result of the organization's CRM efforts is to maximize the number of high-value repeat customers while minimizing customer churn.

CRM is a fundamentally simple concept: treat different customers differently because their needs differ and their value to the company may also differ. A successful CRM strategy not only improves customer satisfaction but also makes the company's sales and service employees more productive, which in turn generates increased profits. Researchers at the National Quality Research Center at the University of Michigan discovered that a 1 percent increase in customer satisfaction can lead to as much as a 300 percent increase in a company's *market capitalization*, defined as the number of shares of the company's stock outstanding multiplied by the price per share of the stock. Put simply, a minor increase in customer satisfaction can generate a major increase in a company's overall value.

Up to this point, you have been looking at an organization's CRM strategy. It is important to distinguish between a CRM *strategy* and CRM *systems.* Basically, CRM systems are information systems designed to support an organization's CRM strategy. For organizations to pursue excellent relationships with their customers, they need to employ CRM systems that provide the infrastructure needed to support those relationships. Because customer service and support are essential to a successful business, organizations must place a great deal of emphasis on both their CRM strategy and their CRM systems.

Broadly speaking, CRM systems lie along a continuum, from *low-end CRM systems*—designed for enterprises with many small customers—to *high-end CRM systems*—for enterprises with a few large customers. An example of a low-end system is Amazon, which uses its CRM system to recommend products to returning customers. An example of a high-end system is Boeing, which, for example, uses its CRM system to coordinate staff activities in a campaign to sell its new 787 aircraft to Delta Airlines. As you study the cases and examples in this chapter, consider where on the continuum a particular CRM system would fall.

Although CRM varies according to circumstances, all successful CRM policies share two basic elements: (1) the company must identify the many types of customer touch points, and (2) it needs to consolidate data about each customer. Let's examine these two elements in more detail.

Customer Touch Points

Organizations must recognize the numerous and diverse interactions they have with their customers. These interactions are referred to as **customer touch points**. Traditional customer touch points include telephone contact, direct mailings, and actual physical interactions with customers during their visits to a store. Organizational CRM systems, however, must manage many additional customer touch points that occur through the use of popular personal technologies. These touch points include e-mail, websites, and communications through smartphones (see **Figure 11.2**).

The business–customer relationship is constantly evolving. As personal technology usage changes, so too must the methods that businesses use to interface with their customers. It is now possible to physically locate customers through their smartphones. As a result, location information can now provide another customer touch point.

Businesses recognize this, but they have not moved all of their touch points in sync and this has led to several channel conflicts. For example, have you ever placed an online order only to get to the store and find out that they never received your order? Or you have to wait because they didn't prepare it when it was promised by the online system? What about when you try to return something you purchased online only to find out that you have to ship it back rather than dropping it off at the local brick-and-mortar version of the same store?

Today, effective marketing makes use of all of these channels (touch points) in sync with one another. We call this omni-channel marketing (*omni* meaning all). Omni-channel marketing refers to an approach to customers that creates a seamless experience regardless of the channel (or device) used to "touch" the business. Many businesses are creating omni-channel strategies to drive this cohesive experience for their customers. To accomplish this goal, businesses must

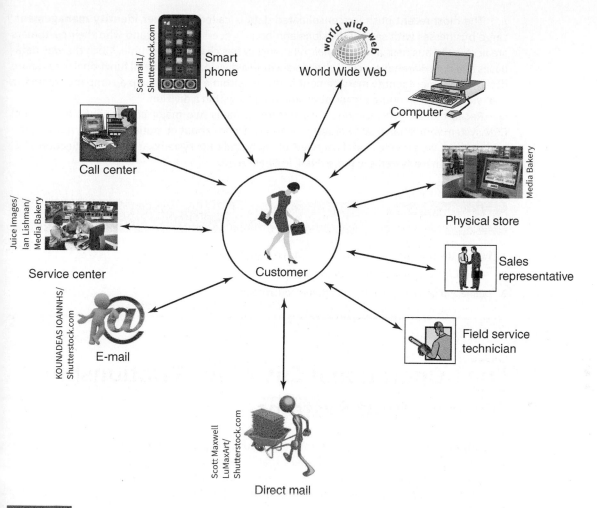

FIGURE 11.2 **Customer touch points.**

utilize information systems (specifically CRM) because the need for data consistency across channels is more apparent now than ever.

Data Consolidation

MIS Data consolidation is also critical to an organization's CRM efforts. The organization's CRM systems must manage customer data effectively. In the past, customer data were stored in isolated systems (or silos) located in different functional areas across the business—for example, in separate databases in the finance, sales, logistics, and marketing departments. Consequently, data for individual customers were difficult to share across the various functional areas.

As you saw in Chapter 5, modern interconnected systems built around a data warehouse now make all customer-related data available to every unit of the business. This complete data set on each customer is called a *360° view* of that customer. By accessing this view, a company can enhance its relationship with its customers and ultimately make more productive and profitable decisions.

Data consolidation and the 360° view of the customer enable the organization's functional areas to readily share information about customers. This information sharing leads to collaborative CRM. **Collaborative CRM systems** provide effective and efficient interactive communication with the customer throughout the entire organization. That is, they integrate communications between the organization and its customers in all aspects of marketing, sales, and customer support. Collaborative CRM systems also enable customers to provide direct feedback to the organization. As you read in Chapter 9, social media applications such as social networks, blogs, microblogs, and wikis are very important to companies that value customer input into their product and service offerings, as well as into new product development.

The most recent push for consolidated data is called **customer identity management**. Large businesses with several divisions and brands need to understand who their customers are across the business and how their relationship has changed over time. Much the way databases and data warehouses centralize data within a division (meaning all functional areas share data), a customer identity management platform within a CRM will help a company create the 360° view across an entire organization and not just within a division.

Recall that an organization's CRM system contains two major components: operational CRM systems and analytical CRM systems. You will learn about operational CRM systems in the next section. We provide a brief overview of analytical CRM systems at the end of Section 11.2, and discuss these systems in more detail in Chapter 12.

Before you go on...

1. What is the definition of customer relationship management?
2. Why is CRM so important to an organization?
3. Define and provide examples of customer touch points.

11.2 Operational Customer Relationship Management Systems

Author Lecture Videos are available exclusively in *WileyPLUS*.
Apply the Concept activities are available in the Appendix and in *WileyPLUS*.

Operational CRM systems support front-office business processes. **Front-office processes** are those that directly interact with customers; that is, sales, marketing, and service. The two major components of operational CRM systems are customer-facing applications and customer-touching applications (discussed further on). Operational CRM systems provide the following benefits:

- Efficient, personalized marketing, sales, and service
- A 360° view of each customer
- The ability of sales and service employees to access a complete history of customer interaction with the organization, regardless of the touch point

An example of an operational CRM system involves Caterpillar, Inc. (**www.cat.com**), an international manufacturer of industrial equipment. Caterpillar uses its CRM tools to accomplish the following objectives:

- Improve sales and account management by optimizing the information shared by multiple employees and by streamlining existing processes (e.g., taking orders using mobile devices)
- Form individualized relationships with customers, with the aim of improving customer satisfaction and maximizing profits
- Identify the most profitable customers and provide them with the highest level of service
- Provide employees with the information and processes necessary to know their customers
- Understand and identify customer needs, and effectively build relationships among the company, its customer base, and its distribution partners

Customer-Facing Applications

In **customer-facing CRM applications**, an organization's sales, field service, and customer interaction center representatives interact directly with customers. These applications include customer service and support, sales force automation, marketing, and campaign management.

MKT ### Customer Service and Support.   Customer service and support refers to systems that automate service requests, complaints, product returns, and requests for information. Today, organizations have implemented **customer interaction centers (CIC)**, in which organizational representatives use multiple channels such as the Web, telephone, fax, and face-to-face interactions to communicate with customers.

One of the best-known customer interaction centers is the *call center*, a centralized office set up to receive and transmit a large volume of requests by telephone. Call centers enable companies to respond to a large variety of questions, including product support and complaints.

MIS ### Sales Force Automation.   **Sales force automation (SFA)** is the component of an operational CRM system that automatically records all of the components in a sales transaction process. SFA systems include a *contact management system*, which tracks all communications between the company and the customer, the purpose of each communication, and any necessary follow-up. This system eliminates duplicated contacts and redundancy, which in turn reduces the risk of irritating customers. SFA also includes a *sales lead tracking system*, which lists potential customers or customers who have purchased related products; that is, products similar to those that the salesperson is trying to sell to the customer.

Other elements of an SFA system can include a *sales forecasting system*, which is a mathematical technique for estimating future sales, and a *product knowledge system*, which is a comprehensive source of information regarding products and services. More-developed SFA systems also have online product-building features, called *configurators*, that enable customers to model the product to meet their specific needs. For example, you can customize your own running shoe at Nike By You (**www.nike.com/nike-by-you**). Finally, many current SFA systems enable salespeople in the field to connect remotely with customers and the home office through Web-based interfaces on their smartphones.

MKT ### Marketing.   Thus far, you have focused primarily on how sales and customer service personnel can benefit from CRM systems. However, CRM systems have many important applications for an organization's marketing department as well. For example, they enable marketers to identify and target their best customers, to manage marketing campaigns, and to generate quality leads for sales teams. CRM marketing applications can also sift through volumes of customer data—a process known as *data mining* (discussed in Chapter 12)—to develop a *purchasing profile*; that is, a snapshot of a consumer's buying habits that may lead to additional sales through cross-selling, upselling, and bundling.

Cross-selling is the marketing of additional related products to customers based on a previous purchase. This sales approach has been used very successfully by banks. For example, if you have a checking and savings account at your bank, then a bank officer will recommend other products for you, such as certificates of deposit (CDs) or other types of investments.

Upselling is a strategy in which the salesperson provides customers with the opportunity to purchase related products or services of greater value in place of, or along with, the consumer's initial product or service selection. For example, if a customer goes into an electronics store to buy a new television, a salesperson may show him a pricey 1080i HD LED television placed next to a less expensive LCD television in the hope of selling the more expensive set (assuming that the customer is willing to pay more for a sharper picture). Other common examples of upselling are warranties on electronics merchandise and the purchase of a car wash after buying gas at a gas station.

Finally, *bundling* is a form of cross-selling in which a business sells a group of products or services together at a lower price than their combined individual prices. For example, your cable company might bundle cable TV, broadband Internet access, and telephone service at a lower price than you would pay for each service separately.

MKT ### Campaign Management.   *Campaign management applications* help organizations plan campaigns that send the right messages to the right people through the right channels. Organizations manage their campaigns very carefully to avoid targeting people who have opted out of receiving marketing communications. Furthermore, companies use these applications to personalize individual messages for each particular customer.

Customer-Touching Applications

Corporations have used manual CRM systems for many years. In the mid-1990s, for example, organizations began to use the Internet, the Web, and other electronic touch points (e.g., e-mail, point-of-sale terminals) to manage customer relationships. In contrast with customer-facing applications, through which customers deal with a company representative, customers who use these technologies interact directly with the applications themselves. For this reason, these applications are called **customer-touching CRM applications** or **electronic CRM (e-CRM) applications**. Customers typically can use these applications to help themselves. There are many types of e-CRM applications. Let's examine some of the major ones.

Search and Comparison Capabilities.   It is often difficult for customers to find what they want from the vast array of products and services available on the Web. To assist customers, many online stores and malls offer search and comparison capabilities, as do independent comparison websites (see **www.mysimon.com**).

Technical and Other Information and Services.   Many organizations offer personalized experiences to induce customers to make purchases or to remain loyal. For example, websites often allow customers to download product manuals. One example is General Electric's website (**www.ge.com**), which provides detailed technical and maintenance information and sells replacement parts to customers who need to repair outdated home appliances. Another example is Goodyear's website (**www.goodyear.com**), which provides information about tires and their use.

Customized Products and Services.   Another customer-touching service that many online vendors use is mass customization, a process through which customers can configure their own products. For example, Dell (**www.dell.com**) allows customers to configure their own computer systems. The Gap (**www.gap.com**) enables customers to "mix and match" an entire wardrobe. Websites such as Hitsquad (**www.hitsquad.com**) and Apple's iTunes (**www.apple.com/itunes**) allow customers to pick individual music titles from a library and customize a CD, a feature that traditional music stores do not offer.

Customers now also view account balances or check the shipping status of orders at any time from their computers or smartphones. If you order books from Amazon, for example, you can look up the anticipated arrival date. Many other companies, including FedEx and UPS, provide similar services (see **www.fedex.com** and **www.ups.com**).

Personalized Web Pages.   Many organizations permit their customers to create personalized web pages. Customers use these pages to record purchases and preferences, as well as problems and requests. For example, American Airlines generates personalized web pages for each of its registered travel-planning customers.

FAQs.   Frequently asked questions (FAQs) are a simple tool for answering repetitive customer queries. Customers may find the information they need by using this tool, thereby eliminating the need to communicate with an actual person.

E-mail and Automated Response.   The most popular tool for customer service is e-mail. Inexpensive and fast, companies use e-mail not only to answer customer inquiries but also to disseminate information, send alerts and product information, and conduct correspondence on any topic.

Loyalty Programs.   Loyalty programs recognize customers who repeatedly use a vendor's products or services. Loyalty programs are appropriate when two conditions are met: a high frequency of repeat purchases, and limited product customization for each customer.

Although loyalty programs are frequently referred to as "rewards programs," their actual purpose is not to reward *past* behavior, but rather to influence *future* behavior. Significantly, the most profitable customers are not necessarily those whose behavior can be most easily influenced. As one example, most major U.S. airlines provide some "elite" benefits to anyone who flies 25,000 miles with them and their partners over the course of a year. Customers who fly first class pay much more for a given flight than those who fly in economy class.

Nevertheless, these customers reach elite status only 1.5 to 2 times faster than economy-class passengers. Why is this true? The reason is that, although first-class passengers are far more profitable than discount seekers, they also are less influenced by loyalty programs. Discount fly-ers respond much more enthusiastically to the benefits of frequent flyer programs. Therefore, air-lines award more benefits to discount flyers than to first-class flyers (relative to their spending).

The airlines' frequent flyer programs are probably the best-known loyalty programs. Other pop-ular loyalty programs are casino players' clubs, which reward frequent players, and supermarkets, which reward frequent shoppers. Loyalty programs use a database or data warehouse to maintain a record of the points (or miles) a customer has accrued and the rewards to which he or she is enti-tled. The programs then use analytical tools to mine the data and learn about customer behavior.

Analytical CRM Systems

Analytical CRM systems provide business intelligence by analyzing customer behavior and perceptions. (We discuss analytics in detail in Chapter 12.) For example, analytical CRM systems typically provide information concerning customer requests and transactions, as well as cus-tomer responses to the organization's marketing, sales, and service initiatives. These systems also create statistical models of customer behavior and the value of customer relationships over time, as well as forecasts about acquiring, retaining, and losing customers.

Important technologies in analytical CRM systems include data warehouses, data mining, decision support, and other business intelligence technologies. After these systems have com-pleted their various analyses, they supply information to the organization in the form of reports and digital dashboards.

Analytical CRM systems analyze customer data for a variety of purposes, including:

- Designing and executing targeted marketing campaigns
- Increasing customer acquisition, cross-selling, and upselling
- Providing input into decisions relating to products and services (e.g., pricing and product development)
- Providing financial forecasting and customer profitability analysis

Figure 11.3 illustrates the relationship between operational CRM systems and analytical CRM systems.

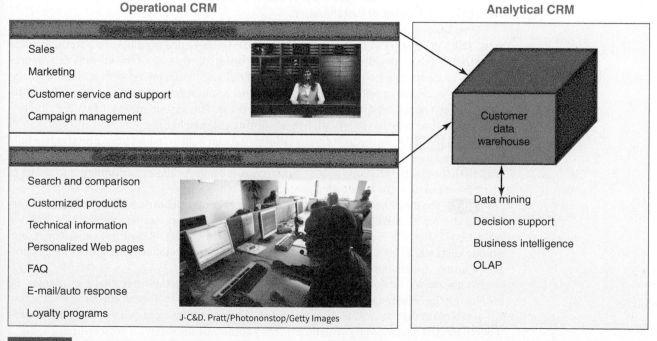

FIGURE 11.3 The relationship between operational CRM and analytical CRM.

Before you go on...

1. Differentiate between customer-facing applications and customer-touching applications.
2. Provide examples of cross-selling, upselling, and bundling (other than the examples presented in the text).

11.3 Other Types of Customer Relationship Management Systems

Now that you have examined operational and analytical CRM systems, let's shift our focus to other types of CRM systems. Five exciting developments in this area are on-demand CRM systems, mobile CRM systems, open-source CRM systems, social CRM, and real-time CRM.

On-Demand CRM Systems

Customer relationship management systems may be implemented as either *on-premise* or *on-demand*. Traditionally, organizations used on-premise CRM systems, meaning that they purchased the systems from a vendor and then installed them on site. This arrangement was expensive, time consuming, and inflexible. Some organizations, particularly smaller ones, could not justify the costs of these systems.

On-demand CRM systems became a solution for the drawbacks of on-premise CRM systems. An **on-demand CRM system** is one that is hosted by an external vendor in the vendor's data center. This arrangement spares the organization the costs associated with purchasing the system. Because the vendor creates and maintains the system, the organization's employees also need to know how to access it and use it. The concept of on-demand is also known as *utility computing* or *software-as-a-service* (SaaS) (see Technology Guide 3).

Salesforce (**www.salesforce.com**) is the best-known on-demand CRM vendor. The company's goal is to provide a new business model that allows companies to rent the CRM software instead of buying it. The secret to their success is that CRM has common requirements applicable to many customers. Consequently, Salesforce's product meets the demands of its customers without a great deal of customization.

One Salesforce customer is Babson College (**www.babson.edu**) in Wellesley, Massachusetts. Babson's goal is to deliver the best applicant experience possible. To accomplish this mission, the school decided to use Salesforce to bring together all of the information on prospective students in a single location. All personnel who are involved with admissions have immediate access to candidate contact information, applications, and reports that indicate the status of each applicant within the enrollment process. This system makes it easy for administrators to deliver valuable information to applicants at the right time.

POM **MKT** Using the Salesforce platform, Babson built an admissions portal with a fully personalized user experience for prospective students. The portal consolidates all of the information that potential students need. Furthermore, it displays different information to students at different points in the application process.

MKT The Bespoke Collection (**www.bespokecollection.com**) is a wine producer and lifestyle brand based in Yountville, California. The company comprises two wine labels and two art galleries. The firm is noted for its commitment to fine wines, elegant art experiences, and unique customer experiences. Bespoke builds deep customer relationships with its loyalty programs and memberships.

As Bespoke's customer base grew, managing customer data became a challenge. By employing the Salesforce CRM, the company was able to offer their customers the kind of personal attention that defined their organization. As just one example, when a customer makes a purchase, the next morning at 10:00 a.m. they automatically receive a personalized e-mail.

Salesforce enables Bespoke to concentrate on relationship-based rather than transaction-based sales. The company was able to increase customer retention, customer satisfaction, referrals, and order value.

Despite their benefits, on-demand CRM systems have potential problems. First, the vendor could prove to be unreliable, in which case the client company would have no CRM functionality at all. Second, hosted software is difficult or impossible to modify, and only the vendor can upgrade it. Third, vendor-hosted CRM software may be difficult to integrate with the organization's existing software. Finally, giving strategic customer data to vendors always carries security and privacy risks.

Mobile CRM Systems

A **mobile CRM** system is an interactive system that enables an organization to conduct communications related to sales, marketing, and customer service activities through a mobile medium for the purpose of building and maintaining relationships with its customers. Mobile CRM systems involve interacting directly with consumers through portable devices such as smartphones. Mobile CRM systems help to create personalized customer relationships that may be accessed anywhere and at any time. In fact, the opportunities offered by mobile marketing are so rich that many companies are employing mobile CRM systems in their marketing activities. An excellent example of a mobile CRM system is Walt Disney's Magic Band.

Open-Source CRM Systems

As explained in Technology Guide 2, the source code for open-source software is available at no cost. **Open-source CRM systems**, therefore, are CRM systems whose source code is available to developers and users.

Open-source CRM systems provide the same features or functions as other CRM software, and they may be implemented either on-premise or on-demand. Leading open-source CRM vendors include SugarCRM (**www.sugarcrm.com**), Concursive (**www.concursive.com**), and Vtiger (**www.vtiger.com**). Let's look at an example.

MKT Larsen Jewellery (**www.larsenjewellery.com.au**), founded by Lars Larsen, is an Australian jeweler. He has created a niche in custom-made fine jewelry, focusing on special experiences, lifetime customer relationships, and personal service.

Interestingly, Larsen operates as a face-to-face retailer without a traditional store. He has established studio workshops where customers work with jewelers to participate in the creation of their own unique pieces of jewelry.

Traditionally, Larsen recorded and managed its customer information entirely on paper, including customer inquiries, payments, production, and servicing. This process worked when the firm had a low volume of high-value sales. However, Larsen wanted to expand his locations, which meant that manual processes would no longer be feasible.

Because all customer details were maintained manually, capturing, finding, and using this data took time. Larsen needed to keep all customer information such as contact details, purchases, and design sketches in an easily accessible central repository.

Larsen also could not effectively analyze manual data. He wanted to know how many of the people who visited his studios actually became customers. He also wanted to understand the products and experiences that people were interested in so he could shape his strategy and marketing efforts accordingly.

In addition to transitioning away from manual processes, Larsen had to contend with pressure from online jewelers. These firms operate high-volume, low-margin businesses, which impact customer attitudes and lower their price expectations.

While Larsen does offer value for the money, the brand is not the cheapest. Larsen's value is based on personal service with customers helping to create their own jewelry and then returning regularly to have their jewelry cleaned and maintained.

Larsen had three problems. First, brands that focus on value rather than price must set themselves apart through service and customer experience. Second, the firm had to automate its business processes. Third, with plans to open branches around Australia, Larsen needed to ensure that the business had efficient and repeatable processes. As a result, Larsen needed a CRM package that would help the jeweler solve these problems.

Larsen chose SugarCRM (**www.sugarcrm.com**). The CRM software, enhanced with Flexidocs, lets staff easily capture information and use it to enhance the customer experience. Customer details are all in one place, along with their jewelry certificates, payment histories, and service records. Flexidocs (**www.flexidocs.co**) allows users to generate documents with a single click using data from CRM systems. Firms can then e-mail the documents to customers, ready for electronic signing.

Larsen implemented SugarCRM over a six-month period. The jeweler first deployed the package in its Sydney branch so problems could be worked out before extending it to Melbourne.

The benefits became clear very quickly. SugarCRM provided Larsen with checks, balances, and automated prompts to ensure that the company's processes became more efficient and human errors were minimized. The package also provided a central repository for all customer information that makes it easy for users to access for analysis.

The benefits of open-source CRM systems include favorable pricing and a wide variety of applications. These systems are also easy to customize. This is an attractive feature for organizations that need CRM software that is designed for their specific needs. Finally, updates and bug (software error) fixes for open-source CRM systems are rapidly distributed, and extensive support information is available free of charge.

Like all software, however, open-source CRM systems have certain risks. The most serious risk involves quality control. Because open-source CRM systems are created by a large community of unpaid developers, there is sometimes no central authority responsible for overseeing the quality of the product. (We discuss open-source software in Technology Guide 2). Furthermore, for best results, companies must have the same IT platform in place as the one on which the open-source CRM system was developed.

Social CRM

Social CRM is the use of social media technology and services to enable organizations to engage their customers in a collaborative conversation in order to provide mutually beneficial value in a trusted and transparent manner. Social CRM is the company's response to the customers' ownership of this two-way conversation. In social CRM, organizations monitor services such as Facebook, Twitter, and LinkedIn (among many others) for relevant mentions of their products, services, and brand, and they respond accordingly.

MKT *Example*. When organic tea brand Steaz (**www.steaz.com**) began posting on Facebook and Twitter about the importance of teas being organic, consumers paid attention and sales doubled. When Steaz offered downloadable coupons on the two social media sites, in one hour 250,000 coupons were downloaded and 2,830 tweets about the offer were recorded.

MKT *Example*. General Motors (**www.gm.com**) launched Fastlane, one of the first blogs personally written by senior executives. Customer feedback through the blog save the company $180,000 per year versus traditional focus group research. The blog also generated enormous goodwill from company executives responding to consumers.

MKT *Example*. H&R Block (**www.hrblock.com**) used Facebook and Twitter to provide immediate access to a tax professional in the tax preparation firm's Get It Right social media campaign. The effort resulted in 1.5 million unique visitors and answered 1 million questions for a 15 percent increase in business versus the prior year.

Social media are also providing methods that customers are using to obtain faster, better customer service. Morton's Steakhouse certainly put social media to good use in surprising a customer.

MKT A corporate manager was in meetings all day, and he had to take a later flight home that caused him to miss his dinner. So, he jokingly tweeted Morton's Steakhouse (**www.mortons.com**) and requested that the restaurant show up with a steak when he landed.

Morton's saw the Tweet, discovered that the tweeter was a frequent customer (and frequent tweeter—he had 100,000 Twitter followers), pulled data on what he typically ordered, identified the flight he was on, and then sent a delivery person to Newark Airport (New Jersey) to serve him his dinner. When he got to the reception lobby at the airport, he noticed a man in a tuxedo holding a card with his name. The man was also carrying a bag that contained a Porterhouse steak, shrimp, potatoes, bread, two napkins, and silverware.

The nearest Morton's restaurant was 24 miles from the airport, and the manager's flight took only two hours. This scenario says a lot about both Morton's customer service and the speed of social media. Admittedly, the entire scenario was a publicity stunt that went explosively viral over the Internet. This is not the point, however. The questions that businesses should be asking themselves are: Would your company even consider doing something like this? If not, why not?

Real-Time CRM

Organizations are implementing real-time customer relationship management to provide a superior level of customer satisfaction for today's always-on, always-connected, more knowledgeable, and less loyal customers. **Real-time CRM systems** help organizations to respond to customer product searches, requests, complaints, comments, ratings, reviews, and recommendations in near real-time, 24/7/365. Southwest Airlines provides an excellent example of real-time CRM.

POM **MKT** A passenger was in her seat on a Southwest Airlines flight about to take off when the plane turned back to the gate. A flight attendant asked her to get off the plane. When she checked with the Southwest agent at the desk inside the terminal, he told her that her son was in a coma after suffering a head injury and to call her husband.

Even before she had disembarked, Southwest had rebooked her on the next nonstop flight to her son's city—free of charge. The airline offered her a private waiting area, rerouted her luggage, allowed her to board first, and packed a lunch for her. Moreover, the airline delivered her luggage to where she was going to stay and called her to ask about her son. The woman said that her son was recovering and that she could not be more grateful for the way she was treated.

Southwest Airlines went above and beyond their responsibilities after they learned of the son's accident. Details were not available about how the airline learned of the son's accident, but it is clear that Southwest brought customer relationship management to a new level.

Before you go on...

1. Describe on-demand CRM.
2. Describe mobile CRM.
3. Describe open-source CRM.
4. Describe social CRM.
5. Describe real-time CRM.

11.4 | Supply Chains

Modern organizations are increasingly concentrating on their core competencies and on becoming more flexible and agile. To accomplish these objectives, they rely on other companies rather than on companies they own to supply the goods and services they need. Organizations recognize that these suppliers can perform these activities more efficiently and effectively than they can. This trend toward relying on an increasing number of suppliers has led to the concept of supply chains. A **supply chain** is the flow of materials, information, money, and services from raw material suppliers, through factories and warehouses, to the end customers. A supply chain also includes the *organizations* and *processes* that create and deliver products, information, and services to the end customers.

Supply chains enhance trust and collaboration among supply chain partners, thus improving supply chain visibility and inventory velocity. **Supply chain visibility** refers to the ability of

Author Lecture Videos are available exclusively in *WileyPLUS.*
Apply the Concept activities are available in the Appendix and in *WileyPLUS.*

all organizations within a supply chain to access or view relevant data on purchased materials as these materials move through their suppliers' production processes and transportation networks to their receiving docks. Organizations can also access or view relevant data on outbound goods as they are manufactured, assembled, or stored in inventory and then shipped through their transportation networks to their customers' receiving docks. The more quickly a company can deliver products and services after receiving the materials required to make them—that is, the higher the *inventory velocity*—the more satisfied the company's customers will be. In addition, supply chain visibility promotes quick responses to problems or changes along the supply chain by enabling companies to shift products to where they are needed.

Supply chain information has historically been obtained by manual, labor-based tracking and monitoring, but is now increasingly being generated by sensors, RFID tags, meters, GPS, and other devices and systems. How does this transformation affect supply chain managers? For one thing, they now have real-time information on all products moving through their supply chains. Supply chains will therefore rely less on labor-based tracking and monitoring, because the new technology will allow shipping containers, trucks, products, and parts to report on their own status. The overall result is a vast improvement in supply chain visibility.

Supply chains are a vital component of the overall strategies of many modern organizations. To use supply chains efficiently, a business must be tightly integrated with its suppliers, business partners, distributors, and customers. A critical component of this integration is the use of information systems to facilitate the exchange of information among the participants in the supply chain.

The Structure and Components of Supply Chains

POM The term *supply chain* comes from a picture of how the partnering organizations are linked. **Figure 11.4** illustrates a typical supply chain. (Recall that Figure 1.5 also illustrated a supply chain, in a slightly different way.) Note that the supply chain involves three segments:

1. *Upstream*, where sourcing or procurement from external suppliers occurs.

   In this segment, supply chain managers select suppliers to deliver the goods and services the company needs to produce its product or service. Furthermore, SC managers develop the pricing, delivery, and payment processes between a company and its suppliers. Included here are processes for managing inventory, receiving and verifying shipments, transferring goods to manufacturing facilities, and authorizing payments to suppliers.

2. *Internal*, where packaging, assembly, or manufacturing takes place.

   SC managers schedule the activities necessary for production, testing, packaging, and preparing goods for delivery. They also monitor quality levels, production output, and worker productivity.

3. *Downstream*, where distribution takes place, frequently by external distributors.

   In this segment, SC managers coordinate the receipt of orders from customers, develop a network of warehouses, select carriers to deliver products to customers, and implement invoicing systems to receive payments from customers.

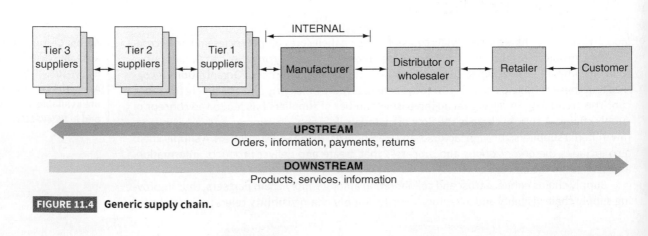

FIGURE 11.4 Generic supply chain.

The flow of information and goods can be bidirectional. For example, damaged or unwanted products can be returned, a process known as *reverse flows* or *reverse logistics.* In the retail clothing industry, for example, reverse logistics involves clothing that customers return, either because the item had defects or because the customer did not like the item.

Tiers of Suppliers.   Figure 11.4 shows several tiers of suppliers. As the diagram indicates, a supplier may have one or more subsuppliers, a subsupplier may have its own subsupplier(s), and so on. For an automobile manufacturer, for example, Tier 3 suppliers produce basic products such as glass, plastic, and rubber; Tier 2 suppliers use these inputs to make windshields, tires, and plastic moldings; and Tier 1 suppliers produce integrated components such as dashboards and seat assemblies.

The Flows in the Supply Chain.   There are typically three flows in the supply chain: material, information, and financial. *Material flows* are the physical products, raw materials, supplies, and so forth that flow along the chain. Material flows also include the reverse flows discussed earlier. A supply chain thus involves a *product life cycle* approach, from "dirt to dust."

Information flows consist of data related to demand, shipments, orders, returns, and schedules, as well as changes in any of these data. Finally, *financial flows* involve money transfers, payments, credit card information and authorization, payment schedules, e-payments, and credit-related data.

Significantly, different supply chains have different numbers and types of flows. For example, in service industries, there may be no physical flow of materials, but there is frequently a flow of information, often in the form of documents (physical or electronic copies). For example, the digitization of software, music, and other content can create a supply chain without any physical flow. Notice, however, that in such a case there are two types of information flows: one that replaces materials flow (digitized software), and another that provides the supporting information (orders, billing, and so on). To manage the supply chain, an organization must coordinate all three flows among all of the parties involved in the chain, a topic we turn to next.

Before you go on...

1. What is a supply chain?
2. Describe the three segments of a supply chain.
3. Describe the flows in a supply chain.

11.5 Supply Chain Management

The function of **supply chain management (SCM)** is to improve the processes a company uses to acquire the raw materials it needs to produce a product or service and then deliver that product or service to its customers. That is, supply chain management is the process of planning, organizing, and optimizing the various activities performed along the supply chain. There are five basic components of SCM:

1. *Plan*: Planning is the strategic component of SCM. Organizations must have a strategy for managing all the resources that are involved in meeting customer demand for their product or service. Planning involves developing a set of metrics (measurable deliverables) to monitor the organization's supply chain to ensure that it is efficient and it delivers high quality and value to customers for the lowest cost.

2. *Source*: In the sourcing component, organizations choose suppliers to deliver the goods and services they need to create their product or service. Supply chain managers develop pricing, delivery, and payment processes with suppliers, and they create metrics to

Author Lecture Videos are available exclusively in *WileyPLUS.*
Apply the Concept activities are available in the Appendix and in *WileyPLUS.*

monitor and improve their relationships with their suppliers. They also develop processes for managing their goods and services inventory, including receiving and verifying shipments, transferring the shipped materials to manufacturing facilities, and authorizing supplier payments.

3. *Make*: This is the manufacturing component. Supply chain managers schedule the activities necessary for production, testing, packaging, and preparation for delivery. This component is the most metric-intensive part of the supply chain, in which organizations measure quality levels, production output, and worker productivity.

4. *Deliver*: This component, often referred to as logistics, is in which organizations coordinate the receipt of customer orders, develop a network of warehouses, select carriers to transport their products to their customers, and create an invoicing system to receive payments.

5. *Return*: Supply chain managers must create a responsive and flexible network for receiving defective, returned, or excess products back from their customers, as well as for supporting customers who have problems with delivered products.

Like other functional areas, SCM uses information systems. The goal of SCM systems is to reduce the problems, or friction, along the supply chain. Friction can increase time, costs, and inventories and decrease customer satisfaction. SCM systems, therefore, reduce uncertainty and risks by decreasing inventory levels and cycle time while improving business processes and customer service. These benefits make the organization more profitable and competitive.

Various circumstances can cause problems with global supply chains, including hurricanes, tornados, and other weather events. However, the COVID-19 pandemic has had a far greater impact than these other phenomena. The pandemic was totally unforeseen, it had global impacts, and it did not give supply chain planners much time to react. IT's About Business 11.1 illustrates one possible solution to the fragility of the global food supply chain for the United States.

IT's About Business 11.1

MIS **POM** **U.S. Global Food Supply Chain Proves to be Fragile**

The COVID-19 pandemic forced restaurants, hotels, and schools to close, leaving some farmers with no buyers for more than half their crops and milk. As a result, U.S. producers had to bury crops, plow edible produce into fields, and dump millions of gallons of milk. The amount of waste is staggering. The nation's largest dairy cooperative, Dairy Farmers of America, estimated that farmers were dumping almost 4 million gallons of milk each day. A single chicken processor had to smash 750,000 unhatched eggs every week.

Many farmers donated part of their surplus to food banks and Meals on Wheels programs, which have been overwhelmed with demand. Unfortunately, charities can accept only so much perishable food because they have limited refrigerator space. Further, charities had fewer volunteers due to the pandemic, making it difficult to manage increased supplies of food.

The pandemic has highlighted the fragility of international supply chains, especially the U.S. global food supply chain. In addition to the pandemic, changing regional weather patterns related to global warming are altering food production in critical areas. For instance, the United States grows or imports almost all of its fruits and vegetables in areas that are undergoing severe drought, such as California and Mexico. In fact, produce imports from Mexico to the United States have nearly tripled since 2010.

Clearly, the United States must take measures to help ensure the security of the nation's food supply chain. One method to accomplish this goal is vertical farms, which shorten food supply chains and do not depend on the weather.

Vertical farming is the practice of growing crops in vertically stacked layers in controlled environments. The practice uses techniques such as hydroponics and aeroponics. *Hydroponics* is a method of growing plants without soil by using nutrient solutions in water. *Aeroponics* is a method of growing plants without soil by using nutrients in a mist. Significantly, hydroponics is about 70 percent more efficient than classic agriculture, and aeroponics is 70 percent more efficient than hydroponics.

Vertical farms provide many advantages over classic agriculture.

- The largest benefit is reliable, year-round, 24/7/365 crop production that is not dependent on the weather. This benefit enables commercial growers to commit to the delivery schedules of their customers.

- Whereas traditional farms need fertile, arable land, vertical farms can be constructed in any climate or location. Further, compared to traditional farms, vertical farms achieve much higher productivity on a smaller land area. Depending on which crop is grown, 1 acre of vertical farm can consistently produce the equivalent of 10–20 soil-based acres.

- Vertical farms using hydroponics use about 5–7 percent of the amount of water used in traditional farms; farms using aeroponics use even less.

- Vertical farms are environmentally sound, using far less fossil fuels—which traditional farms need for farming equipment—as well as far less (if any) pesticides and herbicides. Further, because vertical farms can be located anywhere, they also reduce transportation costs, which in turn reduces carbon dioxide emissions.

- Vertical farms require much less manual labor for year-round production than traditional farms. Further, working conditions are safer because vertical farms do not utilize heavy machinery and chemicals.

The cost of new technologies has decreased enough to enable cost-effective implementation in large vertical farms. For example, the once high costs associated with wind, solar, and lithium batteries have decreased substantially, enabling more and more farmers to adopt and invest in these sustainable technologies. Vertical farming operations also use robots, sensors, and machine-learning algorithms to optimize production processes.

Let's look at an example of a large vertical farm. In June 2020 Kentucky governor Andy Beshear signed an international agreement involving future plans for his state's agricultural technology (agtech) industry. *Agricultural technology* is the use of technology in agriculture, horticulture, and aquaculture to improve yield, efficiency, and profitability while decreasing environmental costs.

An early implementer of Kentucky's plan is AppHarvest (**www.appharvest.com**), a startup that is building North America's largest vertical farm in Eastern Kentucky. AppHarvest's 2.76-million-square-foot farm opened in Morehead, Kentucky, in late 2020. AppHarvest's ultimate goal is to bring outdoor agriculture indoors as a critical step toward achieving food security in the region.

The primary logistical benefit behind choosing Eastern Kentucky as a new agricultural hub is location. Hubs in Kentucky can reach three-quarters of the U.S. population in a single day's drive. AppHarvest does not need to truck food for six to eight days to reach markets.

Vertical farms do have disadvantages. For indoor operations to compete with cheap, outdoor, inefficient, vast, and in many cases, dirty, agriculture, they must be able to compete on pricing as well. As of September 2020 vertical farms produced food that was more expensive than traditional agriculture. As a result, vertical farms competed on freshness and the fact that many consumers want to

know where their food comes from; that is, that their produce was not grown in some unknown field using unknown chemicals handled by unknown people and shipped for an unknown distance to sit on shelves for an unknown period of time. If consumers knew these variables, then they might be willing to pay a premium for the produce.

A second disadvantage is that it will be very difficult for vertical farms to scale up anywhere near the size of traditional farms. Constructing a vertical farm is expensive, and operating it is expensive as well. Of course, being able to produce crops 24/7/365 will offset some of the cost disadvantages.

Sources: Compiled from M. Dent, "Innovative Companies Changing the Face of Vertical Farming," *IDTechEx*, September 3, 2020; R. Adams, "The Future of Farming: Building an Agtech Center in the Heart of the Bluegrass State," *TechRepublic*, July 8, 2020; N. Kulish, "'Never Seen Anything Like It': Cars Line up for Miles at Food Banks," *New York Times*, May 6, 2020; K. Severson and D. Yaffe-Bellany, "Independent Restaurants Brace for the Unknown," *New York Times*, April 21, 2020; D. Yaffe-Bellany and M. Corkery, "Dumped Milk, Smashed Eggs, Plowed Vegetables: Food Waste of the Pandemic," *New York Times*, April 11, 2020; K. Severson, "The Farm-to-Table Connection Comes Undone," *New York Times*, April 9, 2020; A. Thompson, "Indoor Vertical Farm in Cincinnati Will Be Fully Automated," *NPR*, January 29, 2020; L. Kamping-Carder, "The Indoor Farmer Who Wants to Remake Appalachia's Agriculture," *Wall Street Journal*, August 15, 2019; C. Kenning, "When Coal Jobs Leave an Appalachian Town, What Happens to the Families Left Behind?" *USA Today*, July 31, 2019; P. Sisson, "Will Kentucky's 'Giga-Greenhouse' Revolutionize High-Tech Farming?" *Curbed*, June 28, 2019; T. Maddox, "Agriculture 4.0: How Digital Farming Is Revolutionizing the Future of Food," *TechRepublic*, December 12, 2018.

Questions

1. Discuss how vertical farms could increase the food security of the United States.

2. One food industry analyst stated, "Vertical farms will never be able to feed the United States." Do you agree with this statement? Why or why not? Support your answer.

POM Supply chains also lead to increased sales and profits. Consider Adidas (**www.adidas.com**), the leading sports shoe brand in Russia, with more than 1,200 stores in that country. As part of its strategy to optimize the customer experience, Adidas built the supply chain infrastructure needed to enable initiatives such as RFID chips (see Chapter 8), ship from store, click and collect, and endless aisle.

- *Ship from store*: Goods ordered online are delivered from a physical store.

- *Click and collect*: Customers buy products online and collect the products at a physical store or warehouse. By October 2018 some 70 percent of Adidas online sales were through click and collect.

- *Endless aisle*: Using in-store kiosks, customers can order products not in stock in their local store but available in another store. Products are then delivered using the ship from store process or click and collect process.

Russia is, physically, the largest country in the world. Shipping goods from one end of Russia to the other can take up to 15 days using traditional delivery systems. With its three supply chain initiatives, Adidas reduced delivery times and costs while increasing sales and profits. Here is the reason why. Consumers typically return 50 percent of the products they buy online if delivery is made within 24 hours. However, if delivery takes 3 days, consumers may return 70 percent of products. Therefore, because these three processes increase the speed of delivery, customers return fewer goods, which leads to higher completed sales and increased profits.

Significantly, SCM systems are a type of interorganizational information system. In an **interorganizational information system (IOS)**, information flows among two or more organizations. By connecting the IS of business partners, IOSs enable the partners to perform a number of tasks.

- Reduce the costs of routine business transactions
- Improve the quality of the information flow by reducing or eliminating errors
- Compress the cycle time involved in fulfilling business transactions
- Eliminate paper processing and its associated inefficiencies and costs
- Make the transfer and processing of information easier for users

The Push Model Versus the Pull Model

Many SCM systems employ the **push model**. In this model, also known as *make-to-stock*, the production process begins with a forecast, which is simply an educated guess as to customer demand. The forecast must predict which products customers will want and in what quantities. The company then produces the amount of products in the forecast, typically by using mass production, and sells, or "pushes," those products to consumers.

Unfortunately, these forecasts are often incorrect. Consider, for example, an automobile manufacturer that wants to produce a new car. Marketing managers conduct extensive research, including customer surveys and analyses of competitors' cars, and then provide the results to forecasters. If the forecasters' predictions are too high—that is, if they predict that customers will purchase a certain number of these new cars but actual demand falls below this amount—then the automaker has excess cars in inventory and will incur large carrying costs (the costs of storing unsold inventory). Furthermore, the company will probably have to sell the excess cars at a discount.

From the opposite perspective, if the forecasters' predictions are too low—that is, actual customer demand exceeds expectations—then the automaker probably will have to run extra shifts to meet the demand, thereby incurring substantial overtime costs. Furthermore, the company risks losing business to its competitors if the car that customers want is not available. Thus, using the push model in supply chain management can cause problems, as you will see in the next section.

To avoid the uncertainties associated with the push model, many companies now employ the pull model of supply chain management, using Web-enabled information flows. In the **pull model**, also known as *make-to-order*, the production process begins with a customer order. Therefore, companies make only what customers want, a process closely aligned with mass customization (discussed in Chapter 1).

POM A prominent example of a company that uses the pull model is Dell Computer. Dell's production process begins with a customer order. This order not only specifies the type of computer the customer wants but also alerts each Dell supplier as to the parts of the order for which that supplier is responsible. That way, Dell's suppliers ship only the parts that Dell needs to produce the computer.

Not all companies can use the pull model. Automobiles, for example, are far more complicated and more expensive to manufacture than computers, so automobile companies require longer lead times to produce new models. Automobile companies do use the pull model, but only for specific automobiles that some customers order (e.g., Rolls-Royce, Bentley, and other extremely expensive cars).

Problems Along the Supply Chain

As you saw earlier, friction can develop within a supply chain. One major consequence of friction is poor customer service. In some cases, supply chains do not deliver products or services when and where customers—either individuals or businesses—need them. In other cases, the supply chain provides poor quality products. Other problems associated with supply chain friction are high inventory costs and revenue loss.

The problems along the supply chain arise primarily from two sources: (1) uncertainties, and (2) the need to coordinate multiple activities, internal units, and business partners. A major source of supply chain uncertainties is the *demand forecast*. Demand for a product can be influenced by numerous factors such as competition, price, weather conditions, technological developments, overall economic conditions, and customers' general confidence. Another uncertainty is delivery times, which can be affected by numerous factors ranging from production machine failures to road construction and traffic jams. Quality problems in materials and parts can also create production delays, which also generate supply chain problems.

One major challenge that managers face in setting accurate inventory levels throughout the supply chain is known as the bullwhip effect. The **bullwhip effect** refers to erratic shifts in orders up and down the supply chain (see **Figure 11.5**). Basically, the variables that affect customer demand can become magnified when they are viewed through the eyes of managers at each link in the supply chain. If each distinct entity that makes ordering and inventory decisions places its interests above those of the chain, then stockpiling can occur at as many as seven or eight locations along the chain. Research has revealed that in some cases this type of hoarding has led to as much as a 100-day supply of inventory that is waiting "just in case," versus the 10- to 20-day supply manufacturers normally keep at hand. As you see in IT's About Business 11.2, Flexe's business model is able to assist organizations with demand forecast and with problems related to the bullwhip effect.

Solutions to Supply Chain Problems

Supply chain problems can be very costly. Therefore, organizations are motivated to find innovative solutions. During the oil crises of the 1970s, for example, Ryder Systems, a large trucking company, purchased a refinery to control the upstream part of the supply chain and to ensure it had sufficient gasoline for its trucks. Ryder's decision to purchase a refinery is an example of vertical integration. **Vertical integration** is a business strategy in which a company purchases its upstream suppliers to ensure that its essential supplies are available as soon as the company needs them. Ryder later sold the refinery because it could not manage a business it did not understand and because oil became more plentiful.

Ryder's decision to vertically integrate was not the best method for managing its supply chain. In the remainder of this section, you will look at some other possible solutions to supply chain problems, many of which are supported by IT.

Using Inventories to Solve Supply Chain Problems.   Undoubtedly, the most common solution to supply chain problems is *building inventories* as insurance against supply chain uncertainties. As you have learned, holding either too much or too

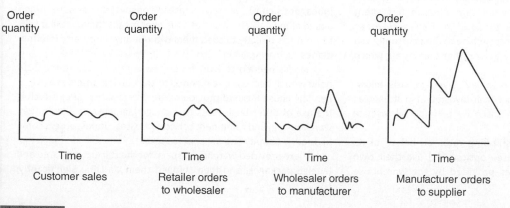

FIGURE 11.5   **The bullwhip effect.**

IT's About Business 11.2

POM   Flexe, the Airbnb of Warehousing

Online retailers, in particular Amazon, are rapidly adopting a supply chain strategy of opening geographically dispersed brick-and-mortar warehouses so that they can deliver orders to customers in one day or less. In fact, if a company wants to sell a product and deliver it the next day, they would need 16 warehouses spread across the country in order to reach 98 percent of the U.S. population. Consider Amazon, for example.

Amazon's strategy does have problems. The electronic commerce giant tends to insist that customers order through its website, which enables the firm to collect customers' data. Amazon is also likely to brand the packages with its own logo, which irritates startups that are striving to build their own brands. Finally, Amazon is expanding its third-party fulfillment services, where it manages storage and delivery for retailers that sell goods in its online marketplace. These problems have led to a growth in supply chain services aimed at retailers who might not want to ship their goods via Amazon.

Vacant U.S. warehouse space is extremely low because consumers are increasingly shopping online due in large part to the COVID-19 pandemic. As a result, merchants need warehouse space located close to their customers in order to provide rapid delivery. Flexe (**www.flexe.com**) is a Seattle startup that provides on-demand warehouse and fulfillment storage space. Flexe accesses an inventory of space that is tied up in long-term contracts but that may sit empty for months. For example, beverage and home improvement companies build warehouses with extra capacity for the summer, so they usually have leftover space. Similarly, Halloween costume wholesalers' warehouses empty out just as the Christmas shopping season arrives. Flexe manages this mismatch between supply and demand, taking an undisclosed commission on each transaction and paying part of its commission to the warehouse operator.

Flexe developed a software platform to facilitate the reliable supply-demand matching of warehouse space at transaction sizes that are too small to justify the attention of traditional warehouse operators. This strategy reflects successful start-ups in other areas: Uber developed its software platform for cars, Airbnb for lodging, Instacart (**www.instacart.com**) for direct-to-consumer groceries, and Transfix (**www.transfix.io**) for trucks (see this chapter's opening case).

Flexe connects more than 1000 warehouse operators—its partners—with businesses in need of storage space—its clients. With its partners, the firm has established broader geographic coverage than the delivery network that Amazon has spent decades and billions of dollars to develop. Flexe's coverage enables merchants to locate inventory close to their customers so they can deliver their products by truck rather than by air, which is more expensive.

Flexe offers storage services on a pay-as-you-go basis, allowing its clients to expand or contract their investment in storage as needed. Merchants book storage space via a simple-to-navigate website.

Flexe does not negotiate shipping rates on behalf of its clients. Instead, clients have three options: (1) use their own shipping contracts, (2) use rates provided by the warehouse operators who pick and pack their orders, or (3) use Flexe's rates with carriers. Flexe is particularly valuable to startups; these businesses do not know how much space they will need because it is difficult for them to predict their sales a year or two into the future.

Flexe offers online merchants overnight ground delivery to nearly everyone in the United States. This service is valuable to merchants who are looking for new ways to reach customers but who have few options that match Amazon's speed. It enables warehouse operators the option to charge more to pack and ship individual orders directly to shoppers' homes rather than to a store. Flexe notes that its customers can deliver goods to their customers as fast or faster than they can through Amazon Prime, at a competitive price. Furthermore, the delivery will arrive in their own branded boxes rather than in an Amazon box.

Flexe's appeal extends to brick-and-mortar retailers that are struggling to compete with Amazon online as well as to brands that are hesitant to work with such a giant retail competitor. Flexe targets manufacturers, brands, and retailers that want to compete with Amazon on delivery without giving up customer data. Flexe helps them to compete with Amazon on delivery without having to make huge investments in new facilities. Flexe's customers include Ace Hardware, Ralph Lauren, Staples, Walmart, and P&G. Other Flexe customers, Toms and Great Jones, provide interesting use cases for Flexe.

Toms. Shoe and apparel brand Toms (**www.toms.com**) uses Flexe to expand its holiday season pop-up stores beyond the reach of its West Coast distribution network. A *pop-up store* is a small, temporary location that companies use to build interest in their product or service and engage their customers. These stores are usually used for seasonal items such as Halloween costumes, Christmas gifts, Christmas trees, and fireworks. Flexe identified the best locations to help Toms serve three new markets. Tom plans its pop-up stores only a few weeks in advance, making it difficult to find warehouse space through traditional long-term leases.

Great Jones. In the past, a new company needed brick-and-mortar stores, a network of warehouses, print advertising, and cash registers. Today, a combination of Instagram (advertising), Shopify (e-commerce platform), and Flexe (warehousing) can provide most of the necessary support for the business. Therefore, many of the traditional fixed costs of starting a business and building a brand have decreased. As an example, let's take a look at Great Jones.

Maddy Moelis is the co-founder of Great Jones (**www.greatjonesgoods.com**), a new direct-to-consumer cookware brand aimed at millennials. *Direct-to-consumer* means that a retailer sells its products directly to customers without any third-party intermediaries such as Amazon.

Moelis needed to launch her new company before the 2019 holiday rush because she planned to start taking orders in November. She chose Flexe to provide *third-party logistics* (3PL), which is the use of other businesses to manage elements of distribution, warehousing, and fulfillment services. At Great Jones, orders come in through Shopify and are sent to Flexe.

Flexe provided warehouse space for the startup, prepared and labeled packages, and then shipped them via UPS. Significantly,

Flexe cost Moelis 10 to 15 percent less than other shipping and fulfillment options.

Flexe partnership with Google Merchant Center. Online shoppers abandon shopping carts nearly 70 percent of the time, largely due to high shipping fees and slow delivery times. With e-commerce demand accelerating due to COVID-19, retailers and brands face increased pressure to execute free and fast delivery promises.

Amazon has the advantage of being a shopping portal and having a logistics infrastructure. Therefore, when you shop for an item, Amazon informs the shopper on the shopping page how much the item costs, how long it will take to be delivered, and whether shipping is free. Google was not able to provide that information when consumers searched for items, because the search engine had no way of knowing which of its merchants had inventory or where the consumer lived.

To address this problem, Google created a link that enabled external platforms such as Flexe to connect to its Merchant Center. In July 2020 Flexe announced its integration with Google Merchant Center to promote free and fast shipping. This arrangement has enabled Google to compete with Amazon.

Now Google knows exactly where physical inventory is stored at the moment of the consumer's search. If that inventory is available within a one-day shipping window, then the ad result that the buyer sees will include a free and fast delivery promise alongside the product's price and rating. Shopper conversion rates with this added feature have increased by an average of 9 percent.

Significantly, Flexe built its marketplace without spending any money on physical facilities. As of September 2020, the firm had access to more than 1,000 warehouses in the United States and Canada, compared to Amazon's 110 fulfillment centers in North America. However, Flexe's total warehouse space is only about 20 percent of the space in Amazon's fulfillment centers. Flexe plans to continue to expand its geographical footprint by convincing warehouse operators that they can accommodate other businesses on short-term intervals without disrupting their own operations.

Sources: Compiled from "FLEXE Launches Integration with Google Merchant Center," *PR Newswire*, July 15, 2020; T. Soper, "Why This Supply Chain Startup Is Drawing Comparisons to Amazon Web Services and Airbnb," *Geekwire*, July 3, 2019; M. Kaplan, "5 On-Demand Warehousing, Fulfillment Providers," *Practical Ecommerce*, March 12, 2020; P. Sisson, "On-Demand Warehouses Power Today's Hip Consumer Brands," *Curbed*, May 24, 2019; T. Soper, "'Airbnb for Warehousing' Startup Flexe Raises $43M to Help Online Retailers Take on Amazon," *GeekWire*, May 7, 2019; K. Patrick, "Innovator of the Year: Flexe," *Supply Chain Dive*, December 4, 2017; S. Lacefield, "Going Direct: Manufacturers Set Their Sights on Direct-to-Consumer Delivery," *Supply Chain Quarterly*, July 4, 2017; K. O'Marah, "Uber Your Supply Chain," *Forbes*, May 18, 2017; R. Sarver, "Leveling the Playing Field in E-Commerce," *Medium*, May 11, 2017; S. Soper, "This Startup Is the Airbnb of Warehouses and Has Amazon in Its Sights," *Bloomberg*, May 11, 2017; J. Smith, "Flexe to Offer Next-Day Delivery for Online Retailers," *Wall Street Journal*, May 11, 2017; N. Levy, "FLEXE Launches Nationwide Next-Day Delivery Service to Help E-Commerce Companies Take on Amazon," *GeekWire*, May 11, 2017; M. O'Brien, "Flexe Offers Shippers Marketplace of Fulfillment Nodes," *Multichannel Merchant*, April 26, 2017; P. Lantrip, "On-Demand Storage Offers Seasonal Space Relief," *Memphis Daily News*, November 30, 2016; **www.flexe.com**, accessed September 1, 2020.

Questions

1. You are the CEO of Amazon. How would you compete with Flexe? Provide specific examples to support your answer.

2. Describe how information technology is essential to supporting Flexe's business model.

3. How does Flexe help retailers with demand forecast and bullwhip effect problems? Provide specific examples to support your answer.

---

little inventory can be very costly. Thus, companies make major attempts to optimize and control inventories.

One widely used strategy to minimize inventories is the **just-in-time (JIT)** inventory system. Essentially, JIT systems deliver the precise number of parts, called *work-in-process* inventory, to be assembled into a finished product at precisely the right time.

Although JIT offers many benefits, it has certain drawbacks as well. To begin with, suppliers are expected to respond instantaneously to requests. As a result, they have to carry more inventory than they otherwise would. In this sense, JIT does not *eliminate* excess inventory; rather, it simply *shifts* it from the customer to the supplier. This process can still reduce the overall inventory size if the supplier can spread the increased inventory over several customers. However, that is not always possible.

JIT also replaces a few large supply shipments with a large number of smaller ones. In terms of transportation, then, the process is less efficient.

Information Sharing.   Another common approach to solving supply chain problems, and especially to improving demand forecasts, is *sharing information* along the supply chain. Information sharing can be facilitated by electronic data interchange and extranets, topics you will learn about in the next section.

One notable example of information sharing occurs between large manufacturers and retailers. For example, Walmart provides Procter & Gamble (P&G) with access to daily sales information from every store for every item that P&G makes for Walmart. This access enables P&G to manage the *inventory replenishment* for Walmart's stores. By monitoring inventory levels, P&G knows when inventories fall below the threshold for each product at any Walmart store. These data trigger an immediate shipment.

Information sharing between Walmart and P&G is executed automatically. It is part of a vendor-managed inventory strategy. **Vendor-managed inventory (VMI)** occurs when the supplier, rather than the retailer, manages the entire inventory process for a particular product or group of products. Significantly, P&G has similar agreements with other major retailers. The benefit for P&G is accurate and timely information on consumer demand for its products. Thus, P&G can plan production more accurately, minimizing the bullwhip effect.

Before you go on...

1. Differentiate between the push model and the pull model.
2. Describe various problems that can occur along the supply chain.
3. Discuss possible solutions to problems along the supply chain.

11.6   Information Technology Support for Supply Chain Management

Clearly, SCM systems are essential to the successful operation of many businesses. As you have seen, these systems—and IOSs in general—rely on various forms of IT to resolve problems. Three technologies, in particular, provide support for IOSs and SCM systems: electronic data interchange, extranets, and Web services. You will learn about Web services in Technology Guide 3. In this section, you examine the other two technologies.

Electronic Data Interchange (EDI)

Electronic data interchange (EDI) is a communication standard that enables business partners to exchange routine documents, such as purchasing orders, electronically. EDI formats these documents according to agreed-upon standards (e.g., data formats). It then transmits messages over the Internet using a converter, called a *translator*.

EDI provides many benefits that are not available with a manual delivery system. To begin with, it minimizes data entry errors, because each entry is checked by the computer. The length of the message can also be shorter, and the messages are secured. EDI also reduces cycle time, increases productivity, enhances customer service, and minimizes paper usage and storage. **Figure 11.6** contrasts the process of fulfilling a purchase order with and without EDI.

EDI does have some disadvantages. Business processes must sometimes be restructured to fit EDI requirements. Also, there are many EDI standards in use today, so one company might have to use several standards to communicate with multiple business partners.

In today's world, in which every business has a broadband connection to the Internet and where multi-megabyte design files, product photographs, and PDF sales brochures are routinely e-mailed, the value of reducing a structured e-commerce message from a few thousand XML bytes to a few hundred EDI bytes is negligible. As a result, EDI is being replaced by XML-based Web services. (You will learn about XML in Technology Guide 3.)

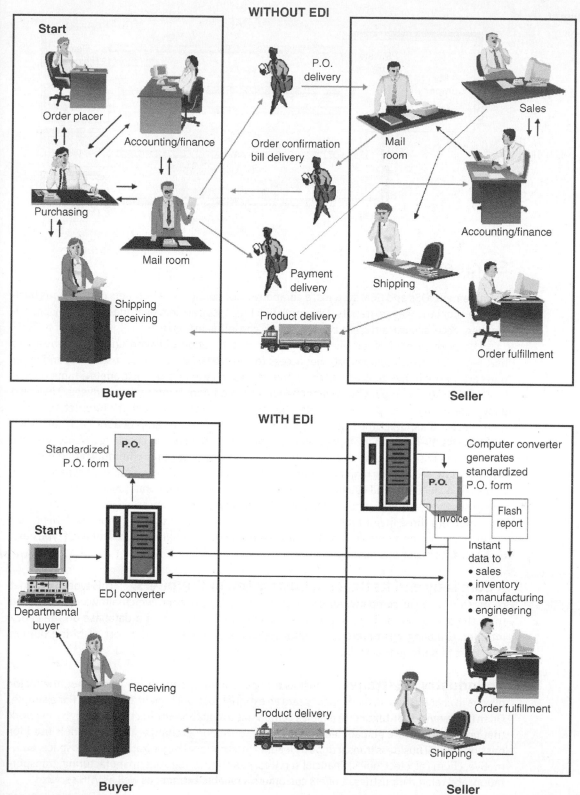

Drawn by E. Turban.

FIGURE 11.6 Comparing purchase order (PO) fulfillment with and without EDI.

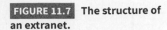**FIGURE 11.7** **The structure of an extranet.**

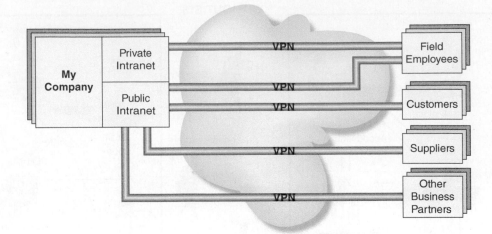

Extranets

To implement IOSs and SCM systems, a company must connect the intranets of its various business partners to create extranets. **Extranets** link business partners over the Internet by providing them access to certain areas of each other's corporate intranets (see **Figure 11.7**).

The primary goal of extranets is to foster collaboration between and among business partners. A business provides extranet access to selected B2B suppliers, customers, and other partners. These individuals access the extranet through the Internet. Extranets enable people located outside a company to collaborate with the company's internal employees. They also allow external business partners to enter the corporate intranet, through the Internet, to access data, place orders, check the status of those orders, communicate, and collaborate. Finally, they make it possible for partners to perform self-service activities such as checking inventory levels.

Extranets use virtual private network (VPN) technology to make communication over the Internet more secure. The major benefits of extranets are faster processes and information flow, improved order entry and customer service, lower costs (e.g., for communications, travel, and administrative overhead), and overall improved business effectiveness.

There are three major types of extranets. The type that a company chooses depends on the business partners involved and the purpose of the supply chain. We present each type next, along with its major business applications.

A Company and Its Dealers, Customers, or Suppliers.
This type of extranet centers on a single company. An example is the FedEx extranet, which allows customers to track the status of a delivery. Customers use the Internet to access a database on the FedEx intranet. Enabling customers to monitor deliveries saves FedEx the cost of hiring human operators to perform that task over the phone.

An Industry's Extranet.
Just as a single company can set up an extranet, the major players in an industry can team up to create an extranet that will benefit all of them. For example, OpenText (**www.opentext.com**) enables companies to collaborate effectively through a network that provides a secure global medium for B2B information exchange. This network is used for mission-critical business transactions by leading international organizations in aerospace, automotive, chemical, electronics, financial services, health care, logistics, manufacturing, transportation, and related industries. It offers customers a reliable extranet as well as VPN services.

Joint Ventures and Other Business Partnerships.
In this type of extranet, the partners in a joint venture use the extranet as a vehicle for communication and collaboration. An example is Bank of America's extranet for commercial loans. The partners involved in making these loans include a lender, a loan broker, an escrow company, and a title company. The extranet connects lenders, loan applicants, and the loan organizer, Bank of America. A similar case is Lending Tree (**www.lendingtree.com**), a company that provides mortgage quotes for homeowners and also sells mortgages online. Lending Tree uses an extranet for its business partners (e.g., the lenders).

Portals and Exchanges

As you saw in Chapter 6, corporate portals offer a single point of access through a web browser to critical business information in an organization. In the context of B2B supply chain management, these portals enable companies and their suppliers to collaborate very closely.

There are two basic types of corporate portals: procurement (sourcing) portals for a company's suppliers (upstream in the supply chain), and distribution portals for a company's customers (downstream in the supply chain). **Procurement portals** automate the business processes involved in purchasing or procuring products between a single buyer and multiple suppliers. For example, Boeing has deployed the Boeing Supplier Portal through which it conducts business with its suppliers. **Distribution portals** automate the business processes involved in selling or distributing products from a single supplier to multiple buyers. For example, Dell services its business customers through its distribution portal at **http://premier.dell.com**.

Emerging Technologies

Logistics experts predict that several technologies will significantly impact supply chains by 2025. IT's About Business 11.3 illustrates the impact of four of these technologies: robotics, drones, autonomous (driverless) vehicles, and three-dimensional (3D) printing.

IT's About Business 11.3

POM **MIS** **Emerging Technologies and Supply Chain Management**

Robotics. Increases in workers' wages enhance the competitive advantage of using robots rather than human labor. Robots will not form unions; take vacations or even breaks; become ill; or need medical plans, retirement plans, or unemployment benefits. Furthermore, robots can work in environmental conditions that are unsuitable for humans. For example, temperatures can be kept lower for robots, thereby saving energy, and robots can often work without lights.

There are a great variety of robots. In fact, you could classify drones and autonomous vehicles as robots. You are probably familiar with industrial robots, which are essentially giant arms used in manufacturing. Here we focus on robots that are used in logistic operations.

Automated delivery robots are revolutionizing local delivery services in cities. For example, Starship (**www.starship.xyz**) has released a robot that delivers meals and groceries to people in urban markets. The cost for each delivery is about $1. The 35-pound robot is essentially a medium-sized cooler on six wheels that moves at about 4 miles per hour. It has lights and a tall, bright orange flag to make it more visible to pedestrians on the sidewalk. A smartphone app unlocks the lid to access the insulated holding area and then automatically locks it back into place.

Goods-to-person robots help pick products for orders. The robots scan a grid on the warehouse floor that contains bar codes or QR codes, which provide the location relative to other robots, the location of the products to be picked, and the location to which the robot must take the products. Amazon Robotics (**www.amazonrobotics.com**), formerly Kiva Systems, manufactures and uses these mobile robotic fulfillment systems.

Telepresence robots are remote-controlled, wheeled devices that have wireless Internet connectivity. Typically, the robots have a display that provides video and audio capabilities. They are commonly used to stand in for tour guides, night watchmen, factory inspectors, and consultants. For example, BEAM robots from Suitable Tech (**https://suitabletech.com**) allow users to remotely consult on problems or repairs or to conduct a tour. Companies justify the costs of these robots by arguing that they lower travel costs.

Follow-me robots move with people in the picking operation. The human picker selects the products and places them in the robot's basket. The robot then delivers them to another human. These robots are an example of a *collaborative robot* or *cobot*. Locus Robotics (**www.locusrobotics.com**) and Fetch Robotics (**http://fetchrobotics.com**) offer follow-me robots.

Drones. A drone is an unmanned aerial vehicle. The first major impact of drones will be in customer delivery.

Experts maintain that drones will be valuable both in urban and rural areas. Current predictions are that 5 billion people will live in urban areas by 2030. Last-mile delivery will become increasingly difficult in these crowded areas. Rural locations are also problematic for delivery because it is not cost effective for ground vehicles to visit numerous isolated areas.

In August 2020 Amazon received federal approval to use drones to deliver packages, bringing the retailer closer to its goal of shortening delivery times to 30 minutes or less. UPS (**www.ups.com**) and FedEx (**www.fedex.com**) are also experimenting with drones that fly from their trucks to deliver parcels over the last few miles to customers. These trials typically are conducted in rural areas.

Drone startup Flirtey (**http://flirtey.com**) has successfully completed a number of deliveries in New Zealand. Drone operator Flytrex (**www.flytrex.com**) has carried out numerous successful deliveries in Iceland and is seeking authorization to expand operations to North America.

The second major impact of drones will involve warehouse and logistics functions. For example, Corvus Robotics (**www.corvus-robotics.com**) uses drones to track inventory in a warehouse. In this application, drones navigate the warehouse and perform a physical inventory by scanning barcodes or reading RFID tags (see Chapter 8).

Several companies are experimenting with image recognition technology to identify and track inventory. For example, Walmart is using drones to verify the inventory in one of its large distribution centers. The drones reportedly examine the entire inventory in a one-million-square-foot Walmart facility in one day, as opposed to the month that it takes for a team of humans.

BNSF Railway (**www.bnsf.com**) uses drones to inspect tracks, bridges, and rail yards. The company has 32,500 miles of track in its system, all of which must be inspected multiple times every week. Drones capture data with cameras and sensors to detect any changes in the tracks (even as small as one-quarter inch) that could cause safety problems. BNSF uses predictive analytics to examine the data from the drones to forecast potential problem areas.

Autonomous vehicles.   Driverless vehicles in the form of autonomous forklifts have been in use for some time. Here we consider driverless trucks, which use short- and longer-range radar and cameras to detect lanes, signs, and markings.

In August 2020, Waymo began testing its driverless fleet of trucks, consisting of 13 Peterbilt 18-wheelers complete with cameras, lidar, and on-board computer. The trucks all have a safety driver onboard. *Lidar* (light detection and ranging) is a method for measuring distances by illuminating the target with laser light and measuring the reflection with a sensor.

Driverless trucks offer several advantages including reduced labor costs, increased vehicle efficiency, and vastly improved safety. Let's look at these advantages more closely.

When companies deploy driverless trucks, it is possible that the Hours of Service (HoS) regulations can be relaxed. Under current regulations, trucks are only 45 percent utilized, because drivers can drive only 11 out of 24 hours. In contrast, some companies are planning to operate driverless truck fleets 24 hours per day at 45 miles per hour. At this speed, these trucks will use much less fuel than they would at 70 miles per hour. By operating 24 hours per day, the trucks can compensate for lower speeds and actually travel greater distances in one day.

Second, automated platooning software allows multiple trucks to autonomously follow one another in a closely bunched convoy. Only the lead truck has a driver, who monitors the group of trucks. By following one another closely, platooning trucks encounter less wind resistance, which increases their fuel efficiency. In July 2019, Peloton (**https://peloton-tech.com**) released its Automated Following System and began experiments with truck platoons.

In March 2020, automation company Locomation (**www.locomation.ai**) teamed up with Wilson Logistics (**www.wilsonlogistics.com**), a 48-state trucking and logistics company, to launch an automated platooning initiative. Unlike other platooning experiments, the Wilson trucks will be hauling standard commercial freight loads for customers.

Third, driverless trucks offer safety advantages. More than 90 percent of vehicle crashes are the result of human error. These crashes result in more than 30,000 deaths annually in the United States and 1.2 million deaths worldwide. Driverless trucks are intended to reduce or eliminate these accidents. Not only would this development save lives, but it would also lead to lower insurance rates.

Three-dimensional printing.   Beginning with an object represented in digital form, the 3D printing process applies material in layers in an additive manner. Global shipments of 3D printers approached 7 million units in 2020, a huge increase from the 450,000 units delivered in 2016.

3D printing is shortening or eliminating some supply chain applications. Consider the following examples.

- *Running shoes*: Nike, Adidas, and New Balance are experimenting with 3D printing soles designed specifically for the user. The customer runs on a treadmill that is equipped with sensors that create an accurate digital mapping of each foot. Using this mapping, the companies 3D print soles that precisely fit their customers' feet.

- *Rapid prototyping*: Many companies are rapidly developing 3D printing prototypes for new parts or products.

- *3D printing as a service*: UPS has about 100 stores with 3D printers, and it offers 3D printing as a service. Staples and Shapeways offer similar services.

- *Repair parts*: Manufacturers are beginning to 3D print repair parts on an as-needed basis. As one example, in December 2014, NASA sent a digital file of a wrench to the space station. The wrench was 3D printed on the space station.

- *Low-volume, high-value components*: General Electric (**www.ge.com**) Aeronautics uses 3D printing to manufacture fuel nozzles for jet airplane engines. Before the company implemented the 3D printing process, the nozzles consisted of more than 20 components. These components had to be sourced through an extensive supply chain and then welded together. Today, GE produces its fuel nozzles by 3D printing them in a single manufacturing process in one plant. Siginificantly, these nozzles are 25 percent lighter and 5 times more durable than the welded nozzles.

Sources: Compiled from C. Cushing, "Can Digital Technologies Make Supply Chains More Resilient?" *IoT Agenda*, September 3, 2020; A. Palmer, "Amazon Wins FAA Approval for Prime Air Drone Delivery Fleet," *CNBC*, August 31, 2020; V. Ramirez, "Waymo Just Started Testing Its Driverless Trucks in Texas," *Singularity Hub*, August 27, 2020; R. Bowman, "Drones, Driverless Trucks, and Robots: Dreams of a Final Mile," *Supply Chain Brain*, August 24, 2020; S. Sutner, "AI, Robotics Help Businesses Pivot Supply Chain during COVID-19," *TechTarget*, August 21, 2020; "Digital Technologies to Power the Supply Chain of the Future," *Supply and Demand Chain Executive*, August 20, 2020; D. Veisz, "Is 3D Printing the Missing Link in Your Supply Chain?" *Supply Chain*, August 9, 2020; "Wilson Logistics Signs on to Platooning Deal with Locomation," *Freight Waves*, March 10, 2020; V. Soneja, "Emerging Technology and Supply Chain: Breaking through the Hype," *Supply Chain Digital*, July 2, 2018; "Robot Makers Competing for Share in Warehouse Market," *MH&L News*, November 21, 2017; "The Top 5 Disruptive Trends in Self-Driving Cars, Delivery, Transportation, and Logistics," *Business Insider*, September 12, 2017; B. McCrea, "How Technology Will Impact the Supply Chain of the Future," *SourceToday*, July 25, 2017; A. Meola, "Shop Online and Get Your Items Delivered by a Drone Delivery Service: The Future Amazon and Domino's Have Envisioned for Us," *Business Insider*, July 18, 2017; "The Internet of Things in Supply Chain," *Veridiansol.com*, June 12, 2017; J. Potts, "How Driverless Trucks Will Change Supply Chain Strategy," *Inbound Logistics*, December 29, 2016; A. Meola, "How IoT Logistics Will Revolutionize Supply Chain Management," *Business Insider*, December 21, 2016; T. Gresham, "6 Technologies Guaranteed to Disrupt Your Supply Chain," *Inbound Logistics*, July 13, 2016.

Questions

1. Considering all of these technologies together, is it possible to eliminate supply chains altogether? Why or why not? Support your answer.

2. Discuss potential disadvantages of robotics, drones, driverless vehicles, and 3D printing.

Before you go on...

1. Define EDI, and list its major benefits and limitations.
2. Define an extranet, and explain its infrastructure.
3. List and briefly define the major types of extranets.
4. Differentiate between procurement portals and distribution portals.

What's in IT For me?

ACCT For the Accounting Major

Customer Relationship Management. CRM systems can help companies establish controls for financial reporting related to interactions with customers in order to support compliance with legislation. For example, Sarbanes–Oxley requires companies to establish and maintain an adequate set of controls for accurate financial reporting that can be audited by a third party. Other sections (302 and 401(b)) have implications for customer activities, including the requirements that sales figures reported for the prior year be correct. Section 409 requires companies to report material changes to financial conditions, such as the loss of a strategic customer or significant customer claims about product quality.

CRM systems can track document flow from a sales opportunity to a sales order, to an invoice, to an accounting document, thus enabling finance and accounting managers to monitor the entire flow. CRM systems that track sales quotes and orders can be used to incorporate process controls that identify questionable sales transactions. CRM systems can provide exception-alert capabilities to identify instances outside defined parameters that put companies at risk.

Supply Chain Management. The cost accountant will play an important role in developing and monitoring the financial accounting information associated with inventory and cost of goods sold. In a supply chain, much of the data for these accounting requirements will flow into the organization from various partners within the chain. It is up to the chief accountant, the comptroller or CFO, to prepare and review these data.

Going further, accounting rules and regulations and the cross-border transfer of data are critical for global trade. IOSs can facilitate such trade. Other issues that are important for accountants are taxation and government reports. Creating information systems that rely on EDI also requires the attention of accountants. Finally, detecting fraud in global settings (e.g., transfers of funds) can be facilitated by appropriate controls and auditing.

FIN For the Finance Major

Customer Relationship Management. CRM systems allow companies to track marketing expenses, collecting appropriate costs for each individual marketing campaign. These costs then can be matched to corporate initiatives and financial objectives, demonstrating the financial impact of the marketing campaign.

Pricing is another key area that impacts financial reporting. For example, what discounts are available? When can a price be overridden? Who approves discounts? CRM systems can put controls into place for these issues.

Supply Chain Management. In a supply chain, the finance major will be responsible for analyzing the data created and shared among supply chain partners. In many instances, the financial analyst will recommend actions to improve supply chain efficiencies and cash flow. This may benefit all of the partners in the chain. These recommendations will be based on financial models that incorporate key assumptions such as supply chain partner agreements for pricing. Through the use of extensive financial modeling, the financial analyst helps to manage liquidity in the supply chain.

Many finance-related issues exist in implementing IOSs. For one thing, establishing EDI and extranet relationships involves structuring payment agreements. Global supply chains may involve complex financial arrangements, which can have legal implications.

MKT For the Marketing Major

Customer Relationship Management. CRM systems are an integral part of every marketing professional's work activities. CRM systems contain the consolidated customer data that provides the foundation for making informed marketing decisions. Using these data, marketers develop well-timed and targeted sales campaigns with customized product mixes and established price points that enhance potential sales opportunities and therefore increase revenue. CRM systems also support the development of forecasting models for future sales to existing clients through the use of historical data captured from previous transactions.

Supply Chain Management. A tremendous amount of useful sales information can be derived from supply chain partners through the supporting information systems. For example, many of the customer support activities take place in the downstream portion of the supply chain. For the marketing manager, an understanding of how the downstream activities of the supply chain relate to prior chain operations is critical.

Furthermore, tremendous amounts of data are fed from the supply chain supporting information systems into the CRM systems that are used by marketers. The information and a complete understanding of its genesis are vital for mixed-model marketing programs.

POM For the Production/Operations Management Major

Customer Relationship Management. Production is heavily involved in the acquisition of raw materials, conversion, and distribution of finished goods. However, all of these activities are driven by sales. Increases or decreases in the demand for goods will increase or decrease a company's need for raw materials. Integral to a company's demand is forecasting future sales, an important feature of CRM systems. Sales forecasts are created from the historical data stored in CRM systems.

This information is critical to a production manager who is placing orders for manufacturing processes. Without an accurate future sales forecast, production managers can face inventory problems (discussed in detail in this chapter). The use of CRM systems for production and operational support is critical to efficiently managing the company's resources.

Supply Chain Management.   The production/operations management major plays an important role in the supply chain development process. In many organizations, the production/operations management staff may even lead the supply chain integration process because of their extensive knowledge of the organization's manufacturing components. Because the production/operations staff are in charge of procurement, production, materials control, and logistical handling, they must possess a comprehensive understanding of SCM techniques.

The downstream segment of supply chains is where marketing, distribution channels, and customer service are conducted. An understanding of how downstream activities are related to the other segments is critical. Supply chain problems can reduce customer satisfaction and negate marketing efforts. It is essential, then, that marketing professionals understand the nature of such problems and their solutions. Also, learning about CRM, its options, and its implementation is important for designing effective customer services and advertising.

As competition intensifies globally, finding new global markets becomes critical. IOSs provide an opportunity to improve marketing and sales. Understanding the capabilities of these technologies as well as their implementation issues will enable the marketing department to excel.

HRM For the Human Resources Major

Customer Relationship Management.   Companies trying to enhance their customer relationships must recognize that employees who interact with customers are critical to the success of CRM

strategies. Essentially, the success of CRM is based on the employees' desire and ability to promote the company and its CRM initiatives. In fact, research analysts have found that customer loyalty is based largely on employees' capabilities and their commitment to the company.

As a result, human resource managers know that a company that desires valued customer relationships needs valued relationships with its employees. Therefore, HR managers are implementing programs to increase employee satisfaction and are training employees to execute CRM strategies.

Supply Chain Management.   Supply chains require the employees of partners in the chain to interact effectively. These interactions are the responsibility of the human resources manager, who must be able to address supply chain issues that relate to staffing, job descriptions, job rotations, and accountability. All of these areas are complex within a supply chain, and they require the HR function to understand the relationships among partners as well as the movement of resources.

Preparing and training employees to work with business partners (frequently in foreign countries) requires knowledge about how IOSs operate. Sensitivity to cultural differences and extensive communication and collaboration can be facilitated with IT.

MIS For the MIS Major

Customer Relationship Management.   The IT function in the enterprise is responsible for the corporate databases and data warehouse, as well as the correctness and completeness of the data stored in them. That is, the IT department provides the data used in a 360° view of the customer. Furthermore, IT personnel provide the technologies underlying the customer interaction center.

Supply Chain Management.   The MIS staff will be instrumental in the design and support of information systems—both internal organizational and interorganizational—that will underpin the business processes that are part of the supply chain. In this capacity, the MIS staff must have a concise knowledge of the business, the systems, and the points of intersection between the two.

Summary

11.1 Identify the primary functions of both customer relationship management (CRM) and collaborative CRM.

Customer relationship management (CRM) is an organizational strategy that is customer focused and customer driven. That is, organizations concentrate on assessing customers' requirements for products and services and then on providing high-quality, responsive services. CRM functions include acquiring new customers, retaining existing customers, and growing relationships with existing customers.

Collaborative CRM is an organizational CRM strategy in which data consolidation and the 360° view of the customer enable the organization's functional areas to readily share information about customers. The functions of collaborative CRM include integrating communications between the organization and its customers in all aspects of

marketing, sales, and customer support processes, and enabling customers to provide direct feedback to the organization.

11.2 Describe how businesses might use applications of each of the two major components of operational CRM systems.

Operational CRM systems support the front-office business processes that interact directly with customers (i.e., sales, marketing, and service). The two major components of operational CRM systems are customer-facing applications and customer-touching applications.

Customer-facing CRM applications include customer service and support, sales force automation, marketing, and campaign management. *Customer-touching applications* include search and comparison capabilities, technical and other information and services, customized products and services, personalized web pages, FAQs, e-mail and automated response, and loyalty programs.

11.3 Explain the advantages and disadvantages of mobile CRM systems, on-demand CRM systems, open-source CRM systems, social CRM systems, and real-time CRM systems.

On-demand CRM systems are hosted by an external vendor in the vendor's data center. Advantages of on-demand CRM systems include lower costs and a need for employees to know only how to access and use the software. Drawbacks include possibly unreliable vendors, difficulty in modifying the software, and difficulty in integrating vendor-hosted CRM software with the organization's existing software.

Mobile CRM systems are interactive systems through which communications related to sales, marketing, and customer service activities are conducted through a mobile medium for the purpose of building and maintaining customer relationships between an organization and its customers. Advantages of mobile CRM systems include convenience for customers and the chance to build a truly personal relationship with customers. A drawback could be difficulty in maintaining customer expectations; that is, the company must be extremely responsive to customer needs in a mobile, near-real-time environment.

Open-source CRM systems are those whose source code is available to developers and users. The benefits of open-source CRM systems include favorable pricing, a wide variety of applications, easy customization, rapid updates and bug (software error) fixes, and extensive free support information. The major drawback of open-source CRM systems is quality control.

Social CRM is the use of social media technology and services to enable organizations to engage their customers in a collaborative conversation to provide mutually beneficial value in a trusted and transparent manner.

Real-time CRM means that organizations are able to respond to customer product searches, requests, complaints, comments, ratings, reviews, and recommendations in near real-time, 24/7/365.

11.4 Describe the three components and the three flows of a supply chain.

A *supply chain* is the flow of materials, information, money, and services from raw material suppliers, through factories and warehouses, to the end customers. A supply chain involves three segments: upstream, where sourcing or procurement from external suppliers occurs; internal, where packaging, assembly, or manufacturing takes place; and downstream, where distribution takes place, frequently by external distributors.

There are three flows in the supply chain: *material flows*, which are the physical products, raw materials, supplies, and so forth; *information flows*, which consist of data related to demand, shipments, orders, returns, and schedules, as well as changes in any of these data; and *financial flows*, which involve money transfers, payments, credit card information and authorization, payment schedules, e-payments, and credit-related data.

11.5 Identify popular strategies to solving different challenges of supply chains.

Two major challenges in setting accurate inventory levels throughout a supply chain are the *demand forecast* and the *bullwhip effect.* Demand for a product can be influenced by numerous factors such as competition, prices, weather conditions, technological developments, economic conditions, and customers' general confidence. The *bullwhip effect* refers to erratic shifts in orders up and down the supply chain.

The most common solution to supply chain problems is *building inventories* as insurance against SC uncertainties. Another solution is the *just-in-time* (JIT) inventory system, which delivers the precise number of parts, called *work-in-process inventory*, to be assembled into a finished product at precisely the right time. The third possible solution is *vendor-managed inventory* (VMI), which occurs when the vendor, rather than the retailer, manages the entire inventory process for a particular product or group of products.

11.6 Explain the utility of each of the three major technologies that support supply chain management.

Electronic data interchange (EDI) is a communication standard that enables the electronic transfer of routine documents, such as purchasing orders, between business partners.

Extranets are networks that link business partners over the Internet by providing them access to certain areas of each other's corporate intranets. The main goal of extranets is to foster collaboration among business partners.

Corporate portals offer a single point of access through a Web browser to critical business information in an organization. In the context of business-to-business supply chain management, these portals enable companies and their suppliers to collaborate very closely.

Chapter Glossary

analytical CRM system CRM system that analyzes customer behavior and perceptions in order to provide actionable business intelligence.

bullwhip effect Erratic shifts in orders up and down the supply chain.

collaborative CRM system A CRM system in which communications between the organization and its customers are integrated across all aspects of marketing, sales, and customer support processes.

customer-facing CRM applications Areas in which customers directly interact with the organization, including customer service and support, sales force automation, marketing, and campaign management.

customer interaction center (CIC) A CRM operation in which organizational representatives use multiple communication channels to interact with customers in functions such as inbound teleservice and outbound telesales.

customer identity management A marketing technology intended to complete a 360° view of a customer across an organization.

customer relationship management (CRM) A customer focused and customer-driven organizational strategy that concentrates on addressing customers' requirements for products and services, and then providing high-quality, responsive services.

customer-touching CRM applications (also called electronic CRM or e-CRM)   Applications and technologies with which customers interact and typically help themselves.

customer touch point   Any interaction between a customer and an organization.

distribution portals   Corporate portals that automate the business processes involved in selling or distributing products from a single supplier to multiple buyers.

electronic CRM (e-CRM)   See **customer-touching CRM applications**.

electronic data interchange (EDI)   A communication standard that enables business partners to transfer routine documents electronically.

extranets   Networks that link business partners over the Internet by providing them access to certain areas of each other's corporate intranets.

front-office processes   Those processes that directly interact with customers; that is, sales, marketing, and service.

interorganizational information system (IOS)   An information system that supports information flow among two or more organizations.

just-in-time (JIT)   An inventory system in which a supplier delivers the precise number of parts to be assembled into a finished product at precisely the right time.

loyalty program   Programs that offer rewards to customers to influence future behavior.

mobile CRM system   An interactive CRM system in which communications related to sales, marketing, and customer service activities are conducted through a mobile medium for the purpose of building and maintaining customer relationships between an organization and its customers.

on-demand CRM system   A CRM system that is hosted by an external vendor in the vendor's data center.

open-source CRM system   CRM software whose source code is available to developers and users.

operational CRM system   The component of CRM that supports the front-office business processes that directly interact with customers (i.e., sales, marketing, and service).

procurement portals   Corporate portals that automate the business processes involved in purchasing or procuring products between a single buyer and multiple suppliers.

pull model   A business model in which the production process begins with a customer order and companies make only what customers want, a process closely aligned with mass customization.

push model   A business model in which the production process begins with a forecast, which predicts the products that customers will want as well as the quantity of each product. The company then produces the amount of products in the forecast, typically by using mass production, and sells, or "pushes," those products to consumers.

real-time CRM system   A CRM system enabling organizations to respond to customer product searches, requests, complaints, comments, ratings, reviews, and recommendations in near real time, 24/7/365.

sales force automation (SFA)   The component of an operational CRM system that automatically records all the aspects in a sales transaction process.

social CRM   The use of social media technology and services to enable organizations to engage their customers in a collaborative conversation in order to provide mutually beneficial value in a trusted and transparent manner.

supply chain   The coordinated movement of *resources* from organizations through *conversion* to the end consumer.

supply chain management (SCM)   An activity in which the leadership of an organization provides extensive oversight for the partnerships and processes that compose the supply chain and leverages these relationships to provide an operational advantage.

supply chain visibility   The ability of all organizations in a supply chain to access or view relevant data on purchased materials as these materials move through their suppliers' production processes.

vendor-managed inventory (VMI)   An inventory strategy where the supplier monitors a vendor's inventory for a product or group of products and replenishes products when needed.

vertical integration   Strategy of integrating the upstream part of the supply chain with the internal part, typically by purchasing upstream suppliers, so as to ensure timely availability of supplies.

Discussion Questions

1. How do customer relationship management systems help organizations achieve customer intimacy?

2. What is the relationship between data consolidation and CRM systems?

3. Discuss the relationship between CRM and customer privacy.

4. Distinguish between operational CRM systems and analytical CRM systems.

5. Differentiate between customer-facing CRM applications and customer-touching CRM applications.

6. Explain why Web-based customer interaction centers are critical for successful CRM systems.

7. Why are companies so interested in e-CRM applications?

8. Discuss why it is difficult to justify CRM applications.

9. You are the CIO of a small company with a rapidly growing customer base. Which CRM system would you use: an on-premise CRM system, an on-demand CRM system, or an open-source CRM system? Remember that open-source CRM systems may be implemented either on-premise or on-demand. Discuss the pros and cons of each type of CRM system for your business.

10. List and explain the important components of a supply chain.

11. Explain how a supply chain approach may be part of a company's overall strategy.

12. Explain the important role that information systems play in supporting a supply chain strategy.

13. Would Rolls-Royce Motorcars (**www.rolls-roycemotorcars.com**) use a push model or a pull model in its supply chain? Support your answer.

14. Why is planning so important in supply chain management?

Problem-Solving Activities

1. Access **www.ups.com** and **www.fedex.com**. Examine some of the IT-supported customer services and tools provided by the two companies. Compare and contrast the customer support provided on the two companies' websites.

2. Enter **www.anntaylor.com**, **www.hermes.com**, and **www.tiffany.com**. Compare and contrast the customer service activities offered by these companies on their websites. Do you see marked similarities? Differences?

3. Access your university's website. Investigate how your university provides for customer relationship management. (*Hint:* First decide who your university's customers are.)

4. Access **www.sugarcrm.com**, and take the interactive tour. Prepare a report on SugarCRM's functionality to the class.

5. Enter **www.apics.org**, **www.cio.com**, **www.findarticles.com**, and **www.google.com**, and search for recent information on supply chain management.

6. Surf the Web to find a procurement (sourcing) portal, a distribution portal, and an exchange (other than the examples presented in this chapter). List the features they have in common and those features that are unique.

Closing Case

POM   Amazon's Global Supply Chain

Amazon is implementing a multiyear plan to develop a global shipping and logistics business, competing directly with UPS (**www.ups.com**), FedEx (**www.fedex.com**), and Chinese e-commerce leader Alibaba (**www.alibaba.com**). This plan includes developing and registering an ocean freight-forwarding business, leasing planes, and developing a parcel-delivery business.

Amazon is globally expanding its Fulfillment by Amazon (FBA) service, which provides storage, packing, and shipping for independent merchants who sell products through amazon.com. Amazon is the center of a logistics network that currently involves shippers such as FedEx and UPS as well as thousands of freight forwarders who handle international cargo and the associated paperwork. Amazon collects inventory from thousands of merchants around the world and purchases space on delivery vans, trucks, planes, trains, and ships at favorable rates to ship that inventory.

Amazon argues that its logistics business will open cross-border commerce to smaller merchants who otherwise would not have the time or money to manage the complexities of international commerce. In turn, Amazon shoppers will have access to many more products from merchants around the world.

Amazon's interest in developing a global logistics platform dates from 2012, when the e-commerce giant first allowed Chinese suppliers to sell goods in Amazon's online marketplace. In September 2020 more than 40 percent of Chinese e-commerce retailers sold on Amazon platforms. Sellers can ship products either directly to customers or to Amazon, which then packs and delivers the products on their behalf.

As noted above, Amazon's plan includes ocean freight forwarding, air cargo, and parcel delivery. Let's look at each of these options.

Freight Forwarding Business. Any parcel weighing more than 330 pounds qualifies as freight. Delivering freight across land, sea, or air from its source (e.g., a factory) to its destination (e.g., a retail store) can involve multiple vehicles owned by different companies. Shipping these parcels internationally is difficult and time consuming, particularly for small- and medium-sized companies that tend to sell on Amazon. Large brands and manufacturers have the necessary size to directly arrange and negotiate favorable rates for shipments. Other, smaller firms must use freight forwarders.

Freight forwarding is opaque and very inefficient. Many freight forwarders still conduct their business via phone, e-mail, paper manifests, or fax machine. Online portals where manufacturers can track their shipments are largely unknown. A *manifest* is a document listing the cargo, passengers, and crew of a ship, aircraft, or vehicle, for the use of customs and other officials.

Freight forwarders perform many functions. They negotiate the best shipping rates and the most efficient use of multiple modes of transport, including trucks, trains, planes, and ships. They prepare all of the accompanying paperwork, including customs documentation. When a problem arises, such as when a container is delayed at a port, freight forwarders are expected to have the necessary relationships with port personnel to get the container moving again.

Amazon's freight forwarding business, Amazon Maritime, can perform freight pickups, warehousing, and transportation and delivery of goods, as well as handle import and export services. As a freight forwarder between the United States and China, Amazon holds two licenses to act as a wholesaler for ocean container shipping, one from the United States Federal Maritime Commission as a non-vessel-owning common carrier, and the other from China.

Amazon faces stiff competition in the freight forwarding business. For example, freight forwarding startup Flexport (**www.flexport.com**) has indexed all of the available freight carriers into a searchable database, which shippers can use for free to organize and track shipments. Flexport simultaneously operates its own freight forwarding service that provides shippers with the shortest and least expensive option. Flexport uses analytics to optimize its recommendations based on the large amounts of data it collects from shippers who utilize its free software. By analyzing all of the routes, rates, speeds, and customs compliance data of shipments booked through its software, Flexport can identify the most efficient method to ship goods internationally. In 2019, Flexport worked with almost 10,000 clients and earned an estimated $860 million in revenue.

Air Cargo Business. Cargo planes are one of the latest tools that Amazon is utilizing to control and improve delivery. Amazon's air cargo business is called Amazon Air.

By September 2020, Amazon had leased 51 cargo planes from the Air Transport Services Group, with orders for 19 more. The retailer had two air hubs, one operating out of the Cincinnati/Northern Kentucky International Airport and the other at Fort Worth Alliance Airport. Amazon's planes do not airlift third-party packages.

As with freight forwarding, competition in the airlift industry is intense. Amazon utilizes its planes only six to seven hours per day, less than half that of FedEx Express and UPS Airlines planes. From its air hubs, Amazon reaches fewer than 30 markets, some of them not even on a daily schedule. In contrast, FedEx's planes touch 130 markets multiple times per day, with little overlap in capacity, frequency, or markets served.

Parcel Delivery Business. Amazon still depends on third parties such as FedEx, UPS, and the U.S. Postal Service for delivery and logistics services. These services represent some of Amazon's largest expenses, because delivering packages promptly is the core of Amazon's mission.

Seller Flex. To become less dependent on third-party logistics providers, Amazon launched Seller Flex, an on-demand local delivery service. Seller Flex is essentially Fulfillment by Amazon for merchants who are not using the program. The service enables Amazon to ship a wider assortment of products to customers in the Amazon Prime window. When one of Amazon's third-party partners ships a product that is part of the Seller Flex program, Amazon charges them a lower amount. Therefore, Seller Flex provides a negotiating tool for better rates with FedEx and UPS.

Independent contractors. In 2018, Amazon launched its Delivery Service Partners program aimed at building a network of independent delivery companies around the United States. Amazon CEO Jeff Bezos incentivized Amazon employees to quit their jobs and start their own Amazon delivery business by offering them $10,000 and the equivalent of three months' salary to participate.

Amazon uses its bargaining power to obtain good deals for couriers on vans and insurance, as well as offering them steady streams of packages. In return, couriers must pay for vehicles, gas, and insurance, as well as recruiting, hiring, and training drivers.

Amazon contractors often pay their drivers less than drivers for other companies earn, leading to high turnover. For example, UPS's union drivers earn up to $80,000 per year, excluding overtime, plus health care and pension benefits. Median annual pay for union postal workers is $57,000. Most FedEx contractors pay drivers about $40,000 per year, and some offer health insurance. In contrast, Amazon contractors pay drivers between $30,000 and $40,000 per year, excluding overtime.

Robots. In 2019, Amazon deployed its first robot delivery vehicles in residential neighborhoods in a Seattle suburb to deliver packages. The robots, called Amazon Scouts, are six-wheeled, battery-powered, and about the size of a cooler. After eight months of testing and thousands of successful deliveries, Amazon is using the Scouts in Irvine, California. The Scouts do not climb steps, they operate during daylight hours, and they are initially being chaperoned by a human employee to monitor their progress.

Integrating the three businesses. Amazon is utilizing information technology (IT) to integrate all areas of its global logistics business. For example, determining the most cost-effective shipping rate is essentially a question of data collection and analytics. Amazon performs both of these processes very effectively.

Using Amazon's IT, merchants will be able to book cargo space online, creating what Amazon calls one-click-ship for seamless international trade and shipping. That is, merchants will be able to claim cargo space online with a single click. Essentially, Amazon has the ability to develop a one-stop, one-click shipping portal that would vastly simplify the process for manufacturers while making it easier for them to track shipments. Eventually, Amazon could offer the service to any manufacturer, even those who do not sell on its platforms. More efficient logistics would also help Amazon to reduce various transaction costs, including booking fees and government filings.

Amazon faces international competition from Alibaba. Like Amazon, Alibaba is striving to dominate international electronic commerce. That market exceeded $1 trillion and 900 million shoppers in 2020, according to a report by consulting firm Accenture and AliResearch (**www.aliresearch.com**), Alibaba's research group.

As one example, Alibaba's OneTouch service has been helping Chinese manufacturers arrange air freight and customer clearances since 2010. Furthermore, in January 2017, Alibaba began booking space for its suppliers on Maersk container ships, joining an increasing number of e-commerce companies that are trying to bring greater efficiency and transparency to the business of arranging cargo shipments. Maersk Line (**www.maersk.com**) is the world's largest container shipping company by both fleet size and cargo capacity.

Executives at FedEx (**www.fedex.com**) and UPS (**www.ups.com**), as well as logistics industry analysts are skeptical about Amazon's plans. They contend that it will be extremely difficult and expensive to build an international delivery network to rival FedEx and UPS. Consider, for example, that FedEx has 650 planes, UPS has 269, and Amazon has only 51.

FedEx asserts that it is spending more than $5 billion annually on expansion and upgrades to its services, and UPS claims it is spending more than $2.5 billion in similar areas. Combined, the two companies have a total of roughly 4,000 hubs and other facilities to sort tens of millions of packages per day. They also operate almost 200,000 vehicles to deliver packages to doors.

Even with increasing investments, it appears likely that Amazon will have to continue to rely on UPS, FedEx, and the USPS for years to come. Furthermore, UPS, FedEx, and freight forwarder DSV claim to possess the logistics technologies that provide them with a competitive advantage over Amazon. It remains to be seen if Amazon can scale up its global logistics operations to a point where it can compete effectively with these giants.

Sources: Compiled from T. Soper, "Amazon Makes It Harder for Sellers to Avoid Its Shipping Service," *Bloomberg*, August 19, 2020; T. Soper, "Amazon Stops Working with Several Small Delivery Contractors, Forcing Companies to Lay Off Hundreds," *GeekWire*, February 14, 2020; J. Dzieza, "The Everything Town in the Middle of Nowhere," *The Verge*, November 14, 2019; P. Holley, "Amazon's Autonomous Robots Have Started Delivering Packages in a New Location: Southern California," *Washington Post*, August 12, 2019; S. Soper and T. Black, "Forget Drones, Amazon's Jeff Bezos Needs Lots of Delivery Humans," *Bloomberg Businessweek*, December 17, 2018; "Move over UPS Truck: Amazon Delivery Vans to Hit the Street," *U.S. News and World Report*, June 28, 2018; C. Wienberg, "Freight Forwarder DSV Says Technology Gives It Edge over Amazon," *Bloomberg News*, May 1, 2018; V. Rajamanickam, "Flexport Is Redefining the Trillion Dollar International Freight Forwarding Industry," *Freight Waves*, March 23, 2018; "Amazon Launches Service to Disrupt Shipping Industry," *Port Technology*, February 13, 2018; B. Rubin, "Amazon's New Delivery Program Shouldn't Hurt FexEx, UPS," *CNET*, February 9, 2018; L. Chang, "Amazon Is Ready to Do More of Its Own Delivery with Seller Flex," *Digital Trends*, October 5, 2017; R. Howells, "The 'Amazon Effect' on the Supply Chain," *Digitalist*, September 8, 2017; R. King, "Amazon Prime Air Cargo Planes Ready for Takeoff for Prime Day for the First Time," *Fortune*, July 10, 2017; "Amazon May Have Redesigned the Global Supply Chain Process," *Land Link Traffic Systems*, June 2, 2017; R. Coates, "The Amazon Effect and the Global Supply Chain," *Supply Chain Management Review*, May 30, 2017; "Amazon Continues to Expand Global Logistics Offering with New Air Service for Chinese Vendors," *Supply Chain Digest*, March 20, 2017; A. Minter, "Will Amazon Revolutionize Shipping?" *Bloomberg*, February 14, 2017; D. Benton, "Supply Chain 4.0: Adidas and Amazon Rewrite the Rules on Supply Chain Management," *Supply Chain Digital*, February 10, 2017; J. Del Rey, "Amazon Is Building a $1.5 Billion Hub for Its Own Cargo Airline," *Recode*, January 31, 2017; B. Steele, "Amazon Is Now Managing Its Own

Ocean Freight," *Engadget*, January 26, 2017; J. Constine, "The Unsexiest Trillion-Dollar Startup," *TechCrunch*, June 7, 2016; R. Lewis, "Amazon's Shipping Ambitions Are Larger than It's Letting on," *Forbes*, April 1, 2016; E. Weise, "Amazon Leases 20 Planes, Starts Air Freight Service," *USA Today*, March 9, 2016; D. Gilmore, "Amazon—The Most Audacious Logistics Plan in History?" *Supply Chain Digest*, February 18, 2016; S. Soper, "Amazon's Plan to Take on UPS and Alibaba," *Bloomberg BusinessWeek*, February 15–21, 2016; E. Schuman, "What Amazon Is Doing with Its Supply Chain Could Devastate the Competition," *Computerworld*, February 12, 2016; E. Weise, "Amazon's Chinese Shipping License Reflects Global Goals," *USA Today*, February 9, 2016; **www.amazon.com**, accessed September 5, 2020.

Questions

1. Perform a strengths, weaknesses, opportunities, and threats (SWOT) analysis of Amazon's entry into the global logistics business.

2. What are the disadvantages to Amazon of entering the global logistics business?

3. You are the CEO of FedEx or UPS. What strategies would you implement to compete with Amazon? Provide specific examples to support your answer.

CHAPTER 12

Business Analytics

CHAPTER OUTLINE	LEARNING OBJECTIVES
12.1 Managers and Decision Making	12.1 Use a decision-support framework to demonstrate how technology supports managerial decision making at each phase of the decision-making process.
12.2 The Business Analytics Process	12.2 Describe each phase of the business analytics process.
12.3 Descriptive Analytics	12.3 Provide a definition and a use case example for descriptive analytics.
12.4 Predictive Analytics	12.4 Provide a definition and a use case example for predictive analytics.
12.5 Prescriptive Analytics	12.5 Provide a definition and a use case example for prescriptive analytics.
12.6 Presentation Tools	12.6 Identify and discuss two examples of presentation tools.

Opening Case

MIS **Spotify**

Founded in 2006, Spotify (**www.spotify.com**) is a Swedish digital music streaming service that gives users access to millions of songs, podcasts, and videos from artists all over the world. Users can access content for free by signing up using an email address. The free version is supported with ads. Spotify Premium is a subscription service that does not offer ads.

Spotify has created algorithms to personalize the user's home screen and playlists (a collection of songs) on its feature, Discover Weekly. Updated every Monday, Discover Weekly sends each user a playlist of 30 songs that they have not previously heard. This feature finds songs from other people with similar preferences to the user that sound similar to the music the user likes.

Spotify designed its home screen to help users quickly find songs they will enjoy. An artificial intelligence system called Bandits for Recommendations as Treatments, or BaRT, controls the home screen and personalizes it for each user. BaRT creates shelves, or rows of

playlists, that follow themes such as "best of artists" as well as the order the playlists appear on the shelves.

BaRT creates shelves and playlists for individual users based on their previous listening activity. Just as important, BaRT must add new, fresh music so that users do not tire of listening to the same songs and genres all the time. Examples of song genres are rhythm and blues, jazz, and classical.

BaRT has two functions: exploit and explore. With *exploit*, BaRT utilizes the information it has obtained about users. The system analyzes users' music listening history, which songs they have skipped, what playlists they have created, and their physical locations. With *explore*, BaRT uses information about users across the rest of the world, such as playlists and artists that are similar to users' tastes but that they have not heard yet, the popularity of other artists, and many other variables.

Not only does BaRT exploit and explore, but it explains its choices to users. Each label for shelves such as "Jump back in" or "More of what you like" informs users why it is recommending those specific playlists. Spotify has found that explanation is critical to making users trust BaRT's recommendations.

Spotify measures success for BaRT based on whether users actually listen to the music on the shelves and, if they do, for how long. When a user listens to a song for more than 30 seconds, Spotify classifies that song as a correct recommendation. The longer a user listens to the recommended playlist or set of songs, the more accurate the recommendation. Listening to a song for less than 30 seconds is the equivalent of a thumbs down for that song on the user's Discover Weekly playlist.

The success of Spotify's recommendations arises directly from the fact that the platform tracks and records every action that users take. In fact, Spotify logs one terabyte of user data per day.

Initially, when new music was uploaded to Spotify, the platform had no system in place to recommend music if it had not been performed by a previously popular artist. *Collaborative filtering*, or the method of recommending music liked by people with similar musical interests, did not work when no one knew the artist in the first place. Spotify called this situation the "cold-start problem."

To resolve this problem, Spotify developed its *audio analysis algorithm*, which analyzed the audio itself. Spotify used the data from a huge number of audio analyses to train an algorithm to recognize different aspects of music that might be desirable to users. Some experiments identified aspects of songs that were as definitive as particular types of guitars. Other experiments applied more abstract aspects such as the genre of a song. The algorithm is now an important element of the Discover Weekly playlist, which is why users might see an artist being recommended that they have not yet heard.

Spotify uses recommendation algorithms, such as the ones that power the home screen and Discover Weekly, but it also employs others. For instance, automatic playlist continuation analyzes the songs in certain playlists and tries to predict the music that should come next, as if the person who created it had just kept adding music.

Spotify wanted to improve this feature, so the company issued a challenge to the global developer community. The challenge worked this way.

First, Spotify had to provide the participants with data to analyze. Therefore, the company released a "Million Playlist Dataset" of user-generated Spotify playlists that participants could use to analyze and understand the characteristics of what humans considered a good playlist.

Given a set of playlist features, participants' algorithms had to generate a list of recommended songs that could be added to that playlist, thereby "continuing" the playlist. By suggesting appropriate songs to add to a playlist, an accurate system would increase user engagement by extending listening past the end of existing playlists. The winner of the challenge was TD Bank Group's Layer 6, in collaboration with the faculty and students at the Vector Institute for Artificial Intelligence, a not-for-profit Canadian research company.

Spotify has also developed algorithms to detect covers of songs on the platform, which could play instead of the original version of the song that a user actually wanted to hear. A *cover* is a new performance or recording of a song by someone other than the original artist or composer. After the algorithm has been trained, it is able to distinguish covers from the original song with high accuracy, especially instrumental covers and live performances. Jazz has proved to be more difficult because it typically involves more improvisation by artists.

Spotify has also been developing an algorithm that aligns written lyrics with the moment in a song where the lyric is sung. This ability will help with the platform's Behind the Music feature that displays lyrics alongside popular songs. It will also create new opportunities for Spotify. For example, time-aligned lyrics can enrich the music listening experience by enabling karaoke, text-based song retrieval, and navigation within songs.

Spotify has analyzed data by tracking the listening patterns of millions of its users, including how many times someone streamed a specific artist or song per day and in which U.S. state they resided. Those data, coupled with users' self-reported gender and age, enabled Spotify to analyze whether music taste changes after someone moved to a different state, as well as how age impacts the kind of music a person listens to.

By studying the musical tastes of people in each state and then contrasting the group of people who have moved with the different overall trends, Spotify concluded that over a long period of time, location does influence musical taste, although not significantly. Regarding age, Spotify discovered that music that is popular with users from ages 10 to 20 is the music that they will predominantly listen to in the future, because their musical identity is shaped during these years.

Spotify continues to experiment with new ways to understand music and the reasons why people listen to one song or genre over another. While competitors such as Apple Music, Amazon Prime Music, and Google Music rely on a mix of paid humans and community-created playlists, Spotify's major competitive advantage is the level of customization and expansion of music knowledge the company offers its customers.

Available in 80 countries, Spotify has become the most popular global audio streaming subscription service. The company had almost 300 million users by July 2020, with 113 million of them being premium listeners. Spotify offers more than 50 million songs, 700,000 podcasts, and 3 billion playlists.

And the bottom line? Spotify reported 2019 revenue of $7.5 billion, a 21 percent increase over the previous year.

Sources: Compiled from A. Willings, "What Is Spotify and How Does It Work?" *Pocket-lint*, September 7, 2020; D. Kopf, "Is Spotify Killing the Top 40?" *Quartz*, September 5, 2020; S. Balanganur, "How Spotify's Algorithm Manages to Find Your Inner Groove," *Analytics India Magazine*, June 1, 2020; S. Nigam, "How Spotify Knows a Lot about You Using Machine Learning and AI," *Data Science Central*, November 25, 2019; D. Gershgorn, "How Spotify's Algorithm Knows Exactly What You Want to Listen to," *OneZero*, October 4, 2019; J. Porter, "Spotify Is First to 100 Million Paid Subscribers," *The Verge*, April 29, 2019; B. Lovejoy, "Spotify Now Has 100M Paid Subscribers, Double Apple Music's Last Reported Number," *9to5Mac*, April 29, 2019; K. Cooper, "How Spotify Does It: Using Data and AI to Know the Customer," *Customer Contact Week Digital*, April 1, 2019; "TD's Layer 6 Wins Spotify RecSys Challenge 2018," *TD Press Release*, July 26, 2018; T. Moynihan, "You're Probably Listening to Spotify Wrong. Be a Power User," *Wired*, February 19, 2016; I. Lunden, "Spotify Acquired Music Tech Company The Echo Nest in a $100 Million Deal," *TechCrunch*, March 7, 2014; **www.spotify.com**, accessed September 19, 2020.

Questions

1. What is Spotify's business problem? (Hint: There may be more than one.)
2. What types of data does Spotify collect? (Hint: Consider songs and users.)
3. Describe the descriptive analytics applications of Spotify's business model.
4. Describe the predictive analytics applications of Spotify's business model.

Introduction

The chapter's opening case illustrates the importance and far-reaching nature of business analytics applications. **Business analytics (BA)** is the process of developing actionable decisions or recommendations for actions based on insights generated from historical data. Business analytics examines data with a variety of tools; formulates descriptive, predictive, and prescriptive analytics models; and communicates these results to organizational decision makers. This definition distinguishes between business analytics and statistics. Essentially, the business analytics process uses statistical procedures to accomplish its goals.

Business analytics can answer questions such as: what happened, how many, how often, where is the problem, what actions are needed, why is this happening, what will happen if these trends continue, what will happen next, what is the best (or worst) that can happen, and what actions should the organization take to achieve various successful business outcomes.

There is also some confusion between the terms *business analytics* and *business intelligence*. **Business intelligence (BI)** has been defined as a broad category of applications, technologies, and processes for gathering, storing, accessing, and analyzing data to help business users make better decisions. Many experts argue that the terms should be used interchangeably. We agree and, for simplicity, we use the term *business analytics (BA)* throughout this chapter.

This chapter describes information systems (ISs) that support *decision making*. Essentially all organizational information systems support decision making (refer to Figure 1.4). Fundamental organizational ISs such as transaction processing systems, functional area information systems, and enterprise resource planning systems provide a variety of reports that help decision makers. This chapter focuses on business analytics systems, which provide critical support to the vast majority of organizational decision makers.

The chapter begins by reviewing the manager's job and the nature of modern managerial decisions. This discussion will help you to understand why managers need computerized support. The chapter then introduces the business analytics process and addresses each step in that process in turn.

It is impossible to overstate the importance of business analytics within modern organizations. Recall from Chapter 1 that the essential goal of information systems is to provide the right information to the right person, in the right amount, at the right time, in the right format. In essence, BA achieves this goal. Business analytics systems provide actionable business results that decision makers can act on in a timely fashion.

It is also impossible to overstate the importance of your input into the BA process within an organization, for several reasons. First, you will use your organization's BA applications, probably from your first day on the job, *regardless of your major field of study*. You will decide how you want to analyze the data by using analytics models and statistical tools. We refer to this process as *user-driven analysis*. You will use BA presentation applications such as dashboards to present your findings succinctly and understandably. You will work closely with your MIS department to ensure that these applications meet your needs.

In general, there are three types of analytics users: business users, business analysts, and data scientists. The *business user* accesses analytics applications to perform their jobs. The *business analyst* typically manages, cleans, abstracts, and aggregates data as well as conducts a range of analytical and statistical procedures on that data. The *data scientist* builds upon the core competencies of the business analyst with additional mathematics, modeling, algorithmic, programming, and machine-learning skills.

As we proceed from business users, to business analysts, to data scientists, technical skill requirements increase. For example, business users would typically be all majors (other than business analytics majors) who take the introductory course(s) in analytics in colleges of business. Business analysts typically major in business analytics in colleges of business and data scientists typically major in mathematics, statistics, or computer science.

Much of this chapter is concerned with large-scale BA applications. You should keep in mind, however, that smaller organizations, and even individual users, can implement small-scale BA applications as well.

After you finish this chapter, you will have a basic understanding of decision making, the BA process, and the incredibly broad range of BA applications that are employed in modern organizations. This knowledge will enable you to immediately and confidently provide input into your organization's BA processes and applications. Furthermore, this chapter will help you use your organization's BA applications to effectively analyze data and thus make better decisions. We hope that this chapter will help you "ask the next question." Enjoy!

12.1 Managers and Decision Making

Management is a process by which an organization achieves its goals through the use of resources (people, money, materials, and information). These resources are considered to be *inputs*. Achieving the organization's goals is the *output* of the process. Managers oversee this process in an attempt to optimize it. A manager's success is often measured by the ratio between the inputs and outputs for which he or she is responsible. This ratio is an indication of the organization's **productivity**.

Author Lecture Videos are available exclusively in *WileyPLUS*.
Apply the Concept activities are available in the Appendix and in *WileyPLUS*.

The Manager's Job and Decision Making

To appreciate how information systems support managers, you must first understand the manager's job. Managers do many things, depending on their position within the organization, the type and size of the organization, the organization's policies and culture, and the personalities of the managers themselves. Despite these variations, however, all managers perform three basic roles (Mintzberg, 1973):[1]

1. *Interpersonal roles:* figurehead, leader, liaison
2. *Informational roles:* monitor, disseminator, spokesperson, analyzer
3. *Decisional roles:* entrepreneur, disturbance handler, resource allocator, negotiator

Early information systems primarily supported the informational roles. In recent years, however, information systems have been developed that support all three roles. In this chapter you will focus on the support that IT can provide for decisional roles.

A **decision** refers to a choice among two or more alternatives that individuals and groups make. Decisions are diverse and are made continuously. Decision making is a systematic process. Economist Herbert Simon (1977)[2] described decision making as composed of three major phases: intelligence, design, and choice. Once the choice is made, the decision is implemented. **Figure 12.1** illustrates this process, highlighting the tasks that are in each phase. Note that there is a continuous flow of information from intelligence, to design, to choice (bold lines). At any phase, however, there may be a return to a previous phase (broken lines).

This model of decision making is quite general. Undoubtedly, you have made decisions in which you did not construct a model of the situation, validate your model with test data, or conduct a sensitivity analysis. The model we present here is intended to encompass *all* of the conditions that might occur when making a decision. For some decisions, some steps or phases may be minimal, implicit (understood), or completely absent.

The decision-making process starts with the *intelligence phase*, in which managers examine a situation and then identify and define the problem or opportunity. In the *design phase*, decision makers construct a model for addressing the situation. They perform this task by making assumptions that simplify reality and by expressing the relationships among all of the relevant variables. Managers then validate the model by using test data. Finally, decision makers set criteria for evaluating all of the potential solutions that are proposed. The *choice phase* involves selecting a solution or course of action that seems best suited to resolve the problem. This solution (the decision) is then implemented. Implementation is successful if the proposed solution solves the problem or seizes the opportunity. If the solution fails, then the process returns to the previous phases. Computer-based decision support assists managers in the decision-making process.

---

[1]Mintzberg, H. (1973) *The Nature of Managerial Work*, Harper & Row, New York.
[2]Simon, H. A. (1977) *The New Science of Management Decision*, Prentice-Hall, Englewood Cliffs, New Jersey.

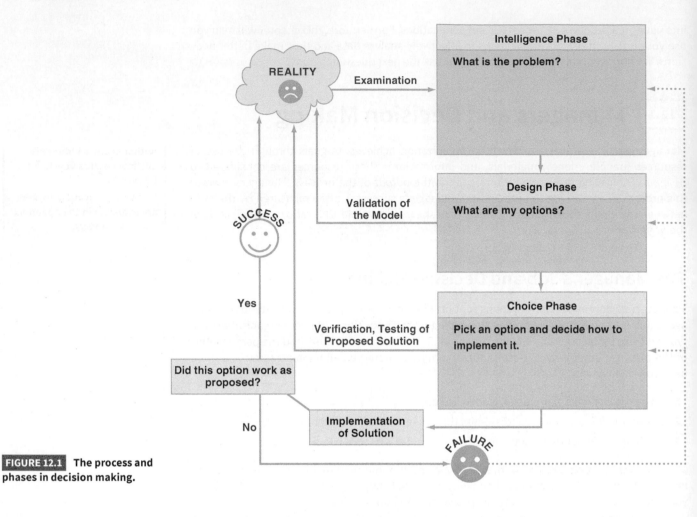

FIGURE 12.1   **The process and phases in decision making.**

Why Managers Need IT Support

Making good decisions is very difficult without solid information. Information is vital for each phase and activity in the decision-making process. Even when information is available, however, decision making is difficult because of the following trends:

- The *number of alternatives* is constantly *increasing* because of innovations in technology, improved communications, the development of global markets, and the use of the Internet and e-business. A key to good decision making is to explore and compare many relevant alternatives. The greater the number of alternatives, the more a decision maker needs computer-assisted searches and comparisons.

- Most decisions must be made *under time pressure*. It is often not possible to manually process information fast enough to be effective.

- Because of increased uncertainty in the decision environment, decisions are becoming more complex. It is usually necessary to *conduct a sophisticated analysis* to make a good decision.

- It is often necessary to rapidly access remote information, consult with experts, or conduct a group decision-making session, all without incurring major expenses. Decision makers, as well as the information they need to access, can be situated in different locations. Bringing everything together quickly and inexpensively represents a serious challenge.

These trends create major difficulties for decision makers. Fortunately, as you will see throughout this chapter, computerized decision support can be of enormous help. Next you will learn about two aspects of decision making that place our discussion of BA in context—problem structure and the nature of the decisions.

A Framework for Computerized Decision Analysis

To better understand business analytics, note that various types of decisions can be placed along two major dimensions: problem structure and the nature of the decision (Gorry and Scott Morton, 1971).[3] **Figure 12.2** provides an overview of decision making along these two dimensions.

Problem Structure.

The first dimension is *problem structure*, in which decision-making processes fall along a continuum ranging from highly structured to highly unstructured (see the left column in Figure 12.2). *Structured decisions* deal with routine and repetitive problems for which standard solutions exist, such as inventory control. In a structured decision, the first three phases of the decision process—intelligence, design, and choice—are laid out in a particular sequence, and the procedures for obtaining the best (or at least a good enough) solution are known. These types of decisions are candidates for decision automation.

At the other extreme of complexity are *unstructured decisions*. These decisions are intended to deal with "fuzzy" complex problems for which there are no cut-and-dried solutions. An unstructured decision is one in which there is no standardized procedure for carrying out any of the three phases. In making such a decision, human intuition and judgment often play an important role. Typical unstructured decisions include planning new service offerings, hiring an executive, and choosing a set of research and development (R&D) projects for the coming year. Although BA cannot make unstructured decisions, it can provide information that assists decision makers.

Located between structured and unstructured decisions are *semistructured* decisions, in which only some of the decision-process phases are structured. Semistructured decisions require a combination of standard solution procedures and individual judgment. Examples of semistructured decisions are evaluating employees, setting marketing budgets for consumer products, performing capital acquisition analysis, and trading bonds.

	Operational Control	Management Control	Strategic Planning	IS Support
Structured	Accounts receivable, order entry [1]	Budget analysis, short-term forecasting, personnel reports, make-or-buy analysis [2]	[3]	MIS, statistical models (management science, financial, etc.)
Semistructured	Production scheduling, inventory control [4]	Credit evaluation, budget preparation, plant layout, project scheduling, reward systems design [5]	Building a new plant, mergers and acquisitions, planning (product, quality assurance, compensation, etc.) [6]	Decision support systems, business intelligence
Unstructured	[7]	Negotiating, recruiting an executive, buying hardware, lobbying [8]	New technology development, product R&D, social responsibility planning [9]	Decision support systems, expert systems, enterprise resource planning, neural networks, business intelligence, Big Data

FIGURE 12.2 Decision-support framework.

[3]Gorry, G.A. and Scott Morton, M. (1971) "A Framework for Management Information Systems," *Sloan Management Review*, Fall, 21–36.

The Nature of Decisions.
The second dimension of decision support deals with the *nature of decisions.* All managerial decisions fall into one of three broad categories:

1. *Operational control:* Executing specific tasks efficiently and effectively
2. *Management control:* Acquiring and using resources efficiently in accomplishing organizational goals
3. *Strategic planning:* The long-range goals and policies for growth and resource allocation

These categories are displayed along the top row of Figure 12.2.

The Decision Matrix.
The three primary classes of problem structure and the three broad categories of the nature of decisions can be combined in a decision-support matrix that consists of nine cells, as diagrammed in Figure 12.2. Lower-level managers usually perform the tasks in cells 1, 2, and 4. The tasks in cells 3, 5, and 7 are usually the responsibility of middle managers and professional staff. Finally, the tasks in cells 6, 8, and 9 are generally carried out by senior executives.

Today, it is difficult to state that certain organizational information systems support certain cells in the decision matrix. The fact is that the increasing sophistication of ISs means that essentially any information system can be useful to any decision maker, regardless of their level or function in the organization. As you study this chapter, you will see that business analytics is applicable across all cells of the decision matrix.

Before you go on...

1. Describe the decision-making process proposed by Simon.

2. You are registering for classes next semester. Apply the decision-making process to your decision about how many and which courses to take. Is your decision structured, semistructured, or unstructured? Support your answer.

3. Consider your decision-making process when registering for classes next semester. Explain how information technology supports (or does not support) each phase of this process.

12.2 The Business Analytics Process

Author Lecture Videos are available exclusively in *WileyPLUS*.
Apply the Concept activities are available in the Appendix and in *WileyPLUS*.

As previously defined, *business analytics* is the process of developing actionable decisions or recommendations for actions based on insights generated from historical data. Business analytics encompasses not only applications, but also technologies and processes. It includes both "getting data in" (to a data mart or warehouse) and "getting data out" (through BA applications).

The use of BA in organizations varies considerably. In smaller organizations, BA may be limited to Excel spreadsheets. In larger ones, BA is enterprise-wide, and it includes a wide variety of applications. The importance of BA to organizations continues to grow, to the point where it is now a requirement for competing in the marketplace. That is, BA is a competitive necessity for organizations.

Although BA has become a common practice across organizations, not all organizations use BA in the same way. For example, some organizations employ only one or a few applications, whereas others use enterprise-wide BA. In general, there are three specific analytics targets that represent different levels of change. These targets differ in regard to their focus; scope; level of sponsorship, commitment, and required resources; technical architecture; impact on personnel and business processes; and benefits.

- *The development of one or a few related analytics applications.* This target is often a point solution for a departmental need, such as campaign management in marketing. Sponsorship, approval, funding, impacts, and benefits typically occur at the departmental level.

For this target, organizations usually create a data mart to store the necessary data. Organizations must be careful that the data mart—an "independent" application—does not become a "data silo" that stores data that are inconsistent with, and cannot be integrated with, data used elsewhere in the organization.

- *The development of infrastructure to support enterprise-wide analytics.* This target supports both current and future analytics needs. A crucial component of analytics at this level is an enterprise data warehouse. Because it is an enterprise-wide initiative, senior management often provides sponsorship, approval, and funding. The impacts and benefits are also felt throughout the organization.

  MKT **MIS** An example of this target is the 3M Corporation (**www.3m.com**). Historically, 3M's various divisions had operated independently, using separate decision-support platforms. Not only was this arrangement costly, it prevented 3M from integrating the data and presenting a "single face" to its customers. For example, sales representatives did not know whether or how business customers were interacting with other 3M divisions. The solution was to develop an enterprise data warehouse that enabled 3M to operate as an integrated company. As an added benefit, the costs of implementing this system were offset by savings resulting from the consolidation of the various platforms.

- *Support for organizational transformation.* With this target, a company uses business analytics to fundamentally transform the ways it competes in the marketplace. Business analytics supports a new business model, and it enables the business strategy. Because of the scope and importance of these changes, critical elements such as sponsorship, approval, and funding originate at the highest organizational levels. The impact on personnel and processes can be significant, and the benefits accrue across the organization.

  MKT Harrah's Entertainment (a brand of Caesars Entertainment; **www.caesars .com**) provides a good example of this analytics target. Harrah's developed a customer loyalty program known as Total Rewards. To implement the program, Harrah's created a data warehouse that integrated data from casino, hotel, and special event systems— for example, wine-tasting weekends—across all of the various customer touchpoints, such as slot machines, table games, and the Internet. Harrah's used these data to reward loyal customers and to reach out to them in personal and appealing ways, such as through promotional offers. These efforts helped the company to become a leader in the gaming industry.

Regardless of the scope of BA, all organizations employ a BA process, which **Figure 12.3** depicts. Let's look at each step of Figure 12.3 in turn, from left to right.

The Business Analytics Process

The entire BA process begins with a business problem, often called *pain points* by practicing managers. When organizations face business problems, they often turn to business analytics, through the process illustrated in Figure 12.3, to help solve those problems. Before we begin our discussion of the BA process, let's emphasize the importance of the technologies that underlie the entire process (see Figure 12.3). These technologies are all improving very rapidly.

MIS Microprocessors (or chips) are becoming increasingly powerful (see Technology Guide 1). In particular, graphics processing units (GPUs) are essential to neural networks, another underlying technology of the BA process. (We discuss neural networks in Chapter 14.)

Advances in digital storage capacity and access speed are driving the cost of storage down, meaning that organizations are able to store and analyze huge amounts of data. Transmission speed (bandwidth; see Chapter 6) in computer networks, particularly the Internet, is also rapidly increasing. As a result, decision makers are able to collaborate on difficult, time-sensitive decisions regardless of their locations. Other underlying technologies include machine learning and deep learning, which we discuss in Chapter 14.

Now let's examine the BA process in detail. To illustrate each step in the BA process, we look at Fandango as an example. The BA process begins with defining the business problem.

Define the business problem. The first, an arguably most important, issue that you will face in the BA process is to define the business problem that you want to address.

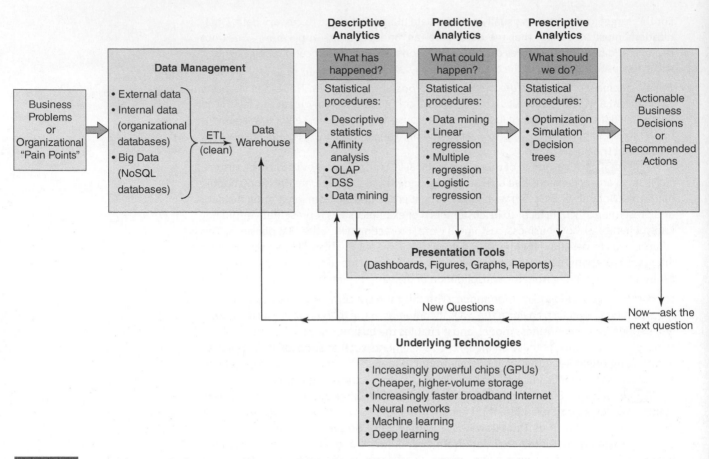

FIGURE 12.3   **The Business Analytics Process (drawn by Kelly Rainer, Bill Hardgrave, and Regina Halpin).**

Defining the business problem is not always easy, but these questions can provide you with guidance:

- What is the organization trying to accomplish?
- What are the organization's goals?
- What business process is the organization trying to improve? Recall that a *business process* (see Chapter 2) is an ongoing collection of related activities that create a product or service of value to the organization, its business partners, and its customers.
- How would improving this business process contribute to making the organization more successful?
- Other, more specific, questions include:
  - Why have profits decreased?
  - Which customers are moving to our competitors and why?
  - Why has demand for a particular product decreased and why?

Recall that we are using Fandango to illustrate each step in the BA process. Here we discuss Fandango's business problem. Fandango (**www.fandango.com**) is the leading online (website and mobile) ticket seller for movie theaters. The company sells millions of tickets to approximately 20,000 movie theaters across the United States. Customers can print their tickets at home with bar codes scanned at the theater or they can have their tickets printed out upon arrival at the theater. Fandango charges a premium over the ticket price to use its services but does enable people to procure tickets to popular movies without having to stand in long lines.

Because Fandango receives a premium for each movie ticket sold, the company's business problem is how to best target the movies that their customers most likely want to see, advertise those movies on Fandango's website, and offer promotions to those movies. In that way, customers will buy more tickets, increasing Fandango's revenue.

MIS **Data Management.**   After defining the business problem, we consider the data that we have for analysis. As we have noted, organizations are now able to analyze rapidly increasing amounts of data. As you learned in Chapter 5, these data can come from data streams. These streams include:

- *Point-of-sale (POS) data.* Organizations capture data from each customer purchase with their POS systems.
- *Clickstream data.* Clickstream data are those data that visitors and customers produce when they visit a website and click on hyperlinks (described in Chapter 6).
- *Social media data.* Social media data (also called social data) are the data collected from individuals' activity on social media websites. These data include shares, likes and dislikes, ratings, reviews, recommendations, comments, and many other examples.
- *Sensor data.* The Internet of Things (IoT; see Chapter 8) is a system in which any object, natural or manmade, contains internal or external wireless sensor(s) which communicate with each other without human interaction. Each sensor monitors and reports data on physical and environmental conditions around it, such as temperature, sound, pressure, vibration, and movement.

As noted in Chapter 5, these four data streams, together with data in organizational databases, comprise Big Data. We defined Big Data as diverse, high-volume, high-velocity information assets that require new forms of processing in order to enhance decision making, lead to insights, and optimize business processes. Essentially, Big Data is the heart of the analytics process.

At this point, organizations integrate and "clean" these data into data marts and data warehouses (see Chapter 5) through a process called *extract, transform, and load (ETL)*. The data in the data warehouse are now available to be analyzed by business users, business analysts, and data scientists.

MIS **Fandango.**   Recall that we are using Fandango to illustrate each step in the BA process. Here we discuss Fandango's data management. Fandango captures data about customers, movie theaters, ticket sales, and show times. For each customer, Fandango collects data on the movies they see, how often they go to movie theaters, their favorite movie genre, the day of the week they go to theaters, and many other variables. Fandango collects Big Data from its website (clickstream data), social media sites (social data), promotions, and other sources.

Descriptive Analytics, Predictive Analytics, and Prescriptive Analytics.
Organizations perform three types of analytics applications: descriptive analytics, predictive analytics, and prescriptive analytics. We discuss these analytics applications in Sections 12.3, 12.4, and 12.5 respectively.

At the end of Section 12.4, we present an example (with summarized data) that illustrates how a decision maker proceeds through the BA process. In our example, we address only descriptive analytics and predictive analytics. We do not include prescriptive analytics in this example because this type of analytics is not yet widespread in industry.

Presentation Tools.
All three types of analytics produce results, which must be communicated to decision makers in the organization. In general, data scientists perform these analyses. Many organizations have employees who "translate" the results of these analyses into business terms for the decision makers. These employees often use presentation tools in the form of dashboards to communicate the message visually. We discuss dashboards and other presentation tools in Section 12.6.

Ask the Next Question.
What is critically important about the analytics process is that once the results are obtained and presented, decision makers must be ready to "ask the next question." Everyone involved in the BA process must use his or her creativity and intuition

at this point. In addition, the results of the BA process will almost always lead to new, unanswered questions.

Business Analytics Tools

A variety of BA tools are available to analyze data. They include Excel, multidimensional analysis (also called online analytical processing, or OLAP), data mining, and decision-support systems. BA also employs numerous statistical procedures, which include descriptive statistics; affinity analysis; linear, multiple, and logistic regression; as well as many others.

Other than Excel, we discuss BA tools and statistical procedures in the context of the analytics application for which they are most appropriate. We discuss Excel here because it is the most popular and common BA tool. Furthermore, Excel incorporates the functionality of many of the other BA tools and statistical procedures. For example, analysts can use Excel to provide descriptive statistics and to perform regression analyses.

BA vendors typically design their software so that it interfaces with Excel. How does this process work? Essentially, users download plug-ins that add functionality—for example, the ability to list the top 10 percent of customers, based on purchases—to Excel. Excel then connects to the vendor's application server, which provides additional data analysis capabilities, which in turn connects to a backend database, a data mart, or a data warehouse. This arrangement gives Excel users the functionality and access to data that are typical of sophisticated BA products while allowing them to work with a familiar tool.

In the next three sections, we address descriptive analytics, predictive analytics, and prescriptive analytics respectively. Each section begins by defining the type of analytics, continues with a discussion of the BA tools and statistical procedures that are appropriate to that type of analytics, and closes with examples of that type of analytics.

Before you go on...

1. Describe the three business analytics targets.
2. Describe the business analytics process.

12.3 Descriptive Analytics

Author Lecture Videos are
available exclusively in
WileyPLUS.
Apply the Concept activities
are available in the Appendix
and in *WileyPLUS*.

Organizations must analyze huge amounts of raw data to make sense of them. This overall process is known as *data reduction*. Data reduction is the conversion of raw data into a smaller amount of more useful information. Descriptive, predictive, and prescriptive analytics are essentially steps in data reduction.

Descriptive analytics is the first step in data reduction. **Descriptive analytics** summarizes what has happened in the past and enables decision makers to learn from past behaviors. Organizations employ descriptive analytics to generate information such as total stock in inventory, average dollars spent per customer, and year-over-year change in sales. Common examples of descriptive analytics are reports that provide historical insights regarding an organization's production, financials, operations, sales, finance, inventory, and customers.

BA Tools in Descriptive Analytics

BA tools in descriptive analytics applications include online analytical processing, data mining, decision-support systems, and a variety of statistical procedures. Examples of such statistical procedures are descriptive statistics, affinity analysis, and many others (see Figure 12.3). We take a closer look at these tools here.

Online Analytical Processing.   Some BA applications include **online analytical processing (OLAP)**, also referred to as **multidimensional analysis** capabilities. OLAP involves "slicing and dicing" the data that are stored in a dimensional format, "drilling down" in the data to greater detail, and "rolling up" the data to greater summarization (less detail).

Consider our example from Chapter 5. Recall Figure 5.6, which illustrates the data cube. The product is on the x-axis, geography is on the y-axis, and time is on the z-axis. Now, suppose you want to know how many nuts the company sold in the West region in 2017. You would slice and dice the cube, using *nuts* as the specific measure for product, *West* as the measure for geography, and *2017* as the measure for time. The value or values that remain in the cell(s) after our slicing and dicing is (are) the answer to our question. As an example of drilling down, you might also want to know how many nuts were sold in January 2017. Alternatively, you might want to know how many nuts were sold from 2017 through 2019, which is an example of aggregation, also called "roll up."

Data Mining.   **Data mining** refers to the process of searching for valuable business information in a large database, data warehouse, or data mart. Data mining can perform two basic operations: (1) identifying previously unknown patterns and (2) predicting trends and behaviors. The first operation is a descriptive analytics application, and the second is a predictive analytics application.

In descriptive analytics, data mining can identify previously hidden patterns in an organization's data. For example, a descriptive analytics application can analyze retail sales data to discover seemingly unrelated products that people often purchase together. A classic example is beer and diapers (even though it is an urban legend). Data mining found that young men tend to buy beer and diapers at the same time when shopping at convenience stores. This type of analysis is called affinity analysis or market basket analysis.

POM **MKT** *Affinity analysis* is a data mining application that discovers co-occurrence relationships among activities performed by specific individuals or groups. In retail, affinity analysis is used to perform *market basket analysis*, in which retailers seek to understand the purchase behavior of customers. Retailers use this information for the purposes of cross-selling, up-selling, sales promotions, loyalty programs, store design (physical location of products), and discount offers. An example of cross-selling with market basket analysis is Amazon's use of "customers who bought book A might also like to buy book B."

In another example, market basket analysis could inform a retailer that customers often purchase shampoo and conditioner together. Therefore, putting both items on promotion at the same time would not create an increase in revenue, whereas a promotion involving just one of the items would likely drive sales of the other.

Decision-Support Systems.   **Decision-support systems (DSSs)** combine models and data to analyze semistructured problems and some unstructured problems that involve extensive user involvement. *Models* are simplified representations, or abstractions, of reality. Decision-support systems enable business managers and analysts to access data interactively, to manipulate these data, and to conduct appropriate analyses.

DSSs can enhance learning, and they can contribute to all levels of decision making. They also employ mathematical models. Finally, they have the related capabilities of sensitivity analysis, what-if analysis, and goal-seeking analysis, which you will learn about next. Keep in mind that these three types of analysis are useful for any type of decision-support application. Excel, for example, supports all three.

POM **MKT** To learn about DSSs and the three types of analysis, let's look at an example. Blue Nile (**www.bluenile.com**) is an online retailer of certified diamonds. The firm's website has a built-in decision-support system to help customers find the diamond that best meets their needs. Blue Nile's DSS provides an excellent example of sensitivity analysis, what-if analysis, and goal-seeking analysis.

Access the Blue Nile website, and click on "Diamonds" in the upper left corner. On the drop-down box, you will see "View all diamonds." Keep in mind that when you experiment with the Blue Nile DSS, the number of round diamonds available will vary from what we obtained when we accessed the DSS and performed the analyses. The reason is that the Blue Nile website is updated in near-real time as the company sells its diamonds.

There are many types of diamonds, but for this example click on "Round." You will see:

- The number of round diamonds available for sale, again in the upper left corner. When we accessed the Blue Nile DSS, the firm offered 112,333 round diamonds for sale.
- Five slide bars labeled: Price, Carat, Cut, Color, and Clarity. Each slide bar represents a variable in Blue Nile's DSS.
- A list of each diamond accompanied by a value for each of the five variables. This list constitutes the data—that is, all round diamonds available for sale—for your analyses.

Sensitivity Analysis. Sensitivity analysis examines how sensitive an output is to any change in an input while keeping other inputs constant. Sensitivity analysis is valuable because it enables the system to adapt to changing conditions and to the varying requirements of different decision-making situations. Let's perform *two sensitivity analyses* on the data:

- First, adjust the slide bars for the Carat variable, so that you will see only those round diamonds between 1.00 and 1.50 carats. Keep all of the other slide bars in their fully open position. In that way, you keep the other variables constant. Note that the number of round diamonds available decreases dramatically. When we followed this procedure, the number of round diamonds for sale dropped to 14,009.
- Second, adjust the slide bars for the Color variable, so that you will see only those round diamonds of D, E, and F color. Be sure to open the slide bars for Carat and to keep the other slide bars in their fully open position. When we followed this procedure, the number of round diamonds available for sale dropped to 58,993.

Comparing the results of these two sensitivity analyses, we can say that the number of round diamonds for sale is more sensitive to changes in Carat than to changes in Color, if we keep the other variables constant.

What-If Analysis. A model builder must make predictions and assumptions regarding the input data, many of which are based on the assessment of uncertain futures. The results depend on the accuracy of these assumptions, which can be highly subjective. *What-if analysis* attempts to predict the impact of changes in the assumptions—that is, the input data—on the proposed solution.

Let's perform a *what-if analysis* on the data. A young man's fiancée has decided that she would like her engagement ring to be between one and two carats, at least a Very Good cut, an F color or better, and a clarity of at least VVS2 (VVS2 means "two very, very small imperfections"). Adjust the slide bars for all four of the variables at the same time. When we followed this procedure, the number of round diamonds available for sale dropped to 3,830.

Goal-Seeking Analysis. *Goal-seeking analysis* represents a "backward" solution approach. Goal seeking attempts to calculate the value of the inputs necessary to achieve a desired level of output.

Let's perform a *goal-seeking analysis* on the data. When the young man in our example looked at the list of 3,830 diamonds (using the scroll bar on the right side of the list), he noticed that the prices ranged from $6,356 to $10,117. He told his fiancée that he had only $5,000 to invest in a diamond. They consequently opened up the slide bars for the Carat, Cut, Color, and Clarity variables and adjusted the slide bar for the Price variable to be between $4,500 and $5,000. When we followed this procedure, the number of round diamonds available for sale increased to 3,874.

The couple now had the problem of examining the list of diamonds to decide which combination of the four variables would be suitable. They did this by performing several what-if analyses:

- She decided that she really wanted a diamond between one and two carats. After adjusting the Carat slide bar, the number of round diamonds available dropped to 2,035.

- She then decided that she wanted a D, E, or F color. After adjusting the Color slide bar, the number of round diamonds available dropped to 424.

- Next, she chose a Cut that was at least Very Good. After adjusting the Cut slide bar, the number of round diamonds available dropped to 266.

- The couple noticed that all 266 diamonds had a Clarity variable of either SI1 (one small imperfection) or SI2 (two small imperfections). At this point they either could decide that this level of clarity is acceptable or they could perform additional what-if analyses on other variables.

Examples of Descriptive Analytics Applications

We present several examples of descriptive analytics in this section. Keep in mind that descriptive analytics applications often immediately suggest predictive analytics applications. Let's look at your class attendance, Fandango, and OptumRx.

MKT **Fandango.** Recall that we are using Fandango to illustrate each step in the BA process. Here we discuss examples of Fandango's descriptive analytics applications. Fandango analyzes the historical movie preferences of its customers and historical data from movie titles. Using these data, Fandango analysts investigate the total sales for different genres of movies; for example, comedy, drama, action, and others. Using a sample of moviegoers, the company calculates the average ticket sales for a week for each movie and each genre, the most popular movie, the distribution of customers among the movie genres and specific titles, the busiest hours of the day and most popular day of the week for each movie theater, and many other analyses. These descriptive analyses help Fandango set ticket prices, offer discounts for certain movies, certain show times, and certain days of the week, set budgets for promotions and advertising, and many other possible actions.

FIN **HRM** **OptumRx.** Pharmacy care service company OptumRx (**www.optumrx .com**) was analyzing a client company's prescription-drug claims when the firm noticed that the client's spending on acne medicine seemed high compared with other clients' spending on the medication. Analyzing the data, OptumRx found that employees had been prescribed newer brand-name acne drugs that were largely combinations of older generic medicines. OptumRx informed the client, a 60,000-employee company, who then began to require patients to begin treatment with the cheaper medicines and to use the more expensive medicines only if the others did not work. Within six months, the company had saved more than $70,000.

POM **HRM** In another case, OptumRx noted that at one of its client companies, drugs for attention deficit hyperactivity disorder (ADHD) were being overprescribed to adults. Some of these employees were using the drug to improve their performance at work. The firm's benefit manager formulated stricter rules concerning reimbursement for ADHD prescriptions and saved the 19,000-worker company $110,000.

HRM OptumRx also uses descriptive analytics to improve patient health. For instance, the company can analyze how frequently asthma sufferers are refilling their prescriptions to discover whether they are taking too many puffs on their inhalers. This could indicate that these employees require a different drug. Switching patients to more effective medicines is worthwhile even if these drugs are more expensive, because they can help reduce costly hospitalizations and visits to emergency rooms.

The emergence of technology for capturing, storing, and using real-time data (e.g., the Internet of Things, see Chapter 8) has enabled real-time BA users to employ analytics to analyze data in real time. Real-time BA also helps organizations to make decisions and to interact with customers in new, innovative ways. Real-time BA is closely related to descriptive analytics because the focus of decisions is real time rather than some point in the future. As you see in IT's About Business 12.1, Google Analytics provides real-time BA of clickstream data.

IT's About Business 12.1

MIS **MKT**   Google Analytics

Google Analytics is the leading Web analytics service, used by approximately 55 percent of all websites. The service is free, and it is a platform under the Google Marketing Platform. *Web analytics* is the collection and analysis of clickstream data to measure Web traffic, to assess and improve the performance of a website, and to perform market research. Google Analytics offers many benefits to organizations including:

- Automatic data collection: A company sets up its Google Analytics account and places computer code on its website. This code enables Google Analytics to immediately begin collecting data.

- Users can choose from many reports that Google has created, or build their own customized report using the drag-and-drop interface.

- Users can link their Google Ads account seamlessly with Google Analytics. *Google Ads* is an online advertising platform that is triggered every time a user performs a keyword search. Through auctions, advertisers bid to display advertisements, service offerings, product listings, and videos to users.

- Users can track internal site searches to reveal what goods and services potential customers are looking for after they arrive on the website. Users can also track the number of unique visitors to a website, the pages they view, the number of views per page, the length of time viewers spend per page, and many other variables. With these insights, users can make necessary changes or additions to their website navigation and their product and service offerings.

- Users can determine how visitors reached their websites. That is, which keywords did visitors employ to find the user's website?

- *Bounce rate* is the percentage of visitors who leave a website after visiting only one page. Google Analytics provides detailed reports of any pages on users' websites that experience a high bounce rate. These data enable users to identify the reasons for this problem and fix them.

- The Audience section of Google Analytics provides data about visitors to websites, including their age, gender, interests, devices, language used, and location (country and city).

- Users can see how much traffic to their websites is driven by social media platforms. Google Analytics also indicates the conversion rate of website visitors from each social platform. *Conversion rate* is the percentage of visitors who take a desired action, such as making a purchase. This information enables users to allocate their advertising budget efficiently across various social media platforms.

- Users can perform A/B testing without having to write any code. A/B testing is a user experience research method that compares two versions of, for instance, a website. The method compares user responses to each version to determine which version is more effective. For example, on version A of its website, a company places the buy button at the top right of a page. On version B, the company places the buy button at the bottom right of that page. The company analyzes the data from Web visitors to determine which version leads to the most purchases.

Let's look at how several companies use Google Analytics.

- General Electric (**www.ge.com**) tracks the country of origin for visitors to its website. This information provides GE with insights into market demand as well as strategies to improve its website to manage multiple languages and cultures.

- Twitter (**www.twitter.com**) views critical data such as how often visitors to the site end up Tweeting and how they navigate from link to link within the site.

- The *Financial Times* (**www.ft.com**) receives data about how visitors to the site interact with social features such as +1 buttons and like buttons and how "Tweetable" their news stores and content are.

- Barnes and Noble (**www.barnesandnoble.com**) learns how different author layouts, chapter snippets, and reviews impact the ways that visitors navigate content on the site. The bookseller also receives valuable data on the most viewed titles and the characteristics of visitors who purchased certain titles.

- The Four Seasons (**www.fourseasons.com**) gains insights into the travel patterns and habits of its guests and potential guests. Integrating these data into the company's strategy helps the hotelier to market to customers and to decide which other sites to partner with for advertising.

Sources: Compiled from D. Daily, "Google Analytics Should Be Your Company's Best Friend," *Inside Indiana Business*, September 21, 2020; M. Jones, "Using Google Analytics to Optimize Google Ads," *Practical Ecommerce*, September 13, 2020; "Popular Use Cases: Accessing Data from Your Google Analytics Account," *databox.com*, September 1, 2020; C. Christoff, "5 Tips for Learning about Your Audience with Google Analytics," *Business.com*, August 28, 2020; M. Jones, "Using Google Analytics to Track Site Changes," *Practical Ecommerce*, July 7, 2020; "Usage Statistics of Traffic Analysis Tools for Websites," *W3techs.com*, February 27, 2019; "What Is Google Analytics and How Does It Work?" *antevenio.com*, November 6, 2018; B. Su, "What Is Google Analytics, and Why Is It Important to My Business?" *Medium.com*, May 16, 2017; "5 Real Time Analytics Use Cases with Google Analytics," *segmentify.com*, February 18, 2017; https://analytics.google.com, accessed September 22, 2020.

Questions

1. Describe the descriptive analytics applications of Google Analytics.

2. Describe the predictive analytics applications of Google Analytics.

Before you go on...

1. Describe the purpose of descriptive analytics.

2. Discuss the BA tools that are commonly used in descriptive analytics.

Author Lecture Videos are available exclusively in *WileyPLUS*.
Apply the Concept activities are available in the Appendix and in *WileyPLUS*.

12.4 Predictive Analytics

Predictive analytics examines recent and historical data to detect patterns and predict future outcomes and trends. Predictive analytics provides estimates about the likelihood of a future outcome.

The purpose of predictive analytics is *not* to tell decision makers what will happen in the future. Predictive analytics can only forecast what *might* happen in the future, based on probabilities. Predictive analytics applications forecast customer behavior and purchasing patterns, identify trends in sales activities, and forecast demand for inputs from suppliers.

BA Tools in Predictive Analytics

Organizations use a variety of BA tools and statistical procedures in performing predictive analytics. The tools include data mining, and the statistical procedures include linear regression, multiple regression, and logistic regression. Recall that data mining can perform two basic operations: (1) identifying previously unknown patterns and (2) predicting trends and behaviors. The first operation is a descriptive analytics application, and the second is a predictive analytics application. There are many other tools and statistical procedures that are used in predictive analytics.

Examples of Predictive Analytics Applications

In this section we present numerous examples of predictive analytics. Keep in mind that descriptive analytics applications often immediately suggest predictive analytics applications. Let's continue with the examples of class attendance and Fandango.

Should I go to class?   If I go to class today, will my attendance positively impact my grade? Conversely, if I do not go to class today, will my absence negatively impact my grade?

MKT Fandango.   Recall that we are using Fandango to illustrate each step in the BA process. Here we discuss examples of Fandango's predictive analytics applications. How does the ticket seller know when to send e-mails to its members with discount offers for a specific movie on a specific day? Consider John Jones. Predictive analytics tools analyze terabytes of data to determine that although John likes science fiction movies, he has not seen the latest science fiction movie, which has been in theaters since the previous Friday. Consequently, Fandango could send him a discount offer for this movie.

In some cases, organizations experience problems with predictive analytics due to the types of data they need to analyze. Two organizations, Etsy and Liverpool Football Club, had to collect and analyze challenging data. IT's About Business 12.2 describes Etsy's success, and IT's About Business 12.3 describes the success of the Liverpool Football Club.

MKT Marketing Examples

- Using predictive analytics, organizations can employ targeted marketing, where firms classify customer demographics to predict which customers will respond to a mailing or buy a particular product. Further, firms can use data from past promotional mailings to identify those prospects who are most likely to respond favorably to future mailings.

- Predictive analytics drives the coupons you receive at the grocery cash register. United Kingdom grocery giant Tesco (**www.tesco.com**) predicts which discounts customers will redeem so it can better target more than 100 million personalized coupons annually at cash registers in 13 countries. This process increased coupon redemption rates by 360 percent over previous methods.

- Websites predict which ads you will click so they can instantly choose which ad to show you, a process that drives millions of dollars in new revenue.

- Wireless carriers predict how likely you are to cancel and defect to a competitor—a process called *churn*—possibly before you have decided to do so. These predictions are based on factors such as dropped calls, your phone usage, your billing information, and whether your contacts have already defected.

- Leading online dating companies Match (**www.match.com**), OkCupid (**www.okcupid.com**), and eHarmony (**www.eharmony.com**) predict which prospect on your screen will be the most compatible with you.

IT's About Business 12.2

MIS **MKT** Etsy

Founded in 2005, Etsy (**www.etsy.com**) is an e-commerce website that sells handmade or vintage items and craft supplies. These items encompass a wide range of categories including jewelry, bags, clothing, home decor and furniture, toys, and art, as well as craft supplies and tools. All vintage items must be at least 20 years old.

At Etsy, the search challenge is particularly difficult. The site's offerings are not mass-produced goods that can easily be categorized. Instead, 75 percent of the 60 million items that the company's almost 3 million merchants offer are handmade and therefore one of a kind. Consequently, if Etsy applied standard search technology to the vast number of products on the site, the results would be vague and disappointing.

To improve its search capability, Etsy had to display items that not only matched shoppers' search terms but also appealed to their particular aesthetic preferences. This type of search process would increase the chances that shoppers would like what they saw, a very desirable outcome for both Etsy and its buyers and sellers.

As a result, Etsy had to teach its search engine to understand style. *Style* is a difficult concept to define. Style is the way individuals express themselves through aesthetic choices. Style is also defined as any distinctive, and therefore recognizable, way in which an artifact is made.

When Etsy's analytics team concluded that they needed to qualify style, they did not have to start from scratch. The firm's merchandising groups already understood what was being sold, what people were buying, and what people were offering on the site. By analyzing merchandising data, these groups were able to quantify 43 styles of goods. Examples are romantic, geometric, celestial, minimal, tropical, and midcentury. After a year of work, Etsy trained a machine learning (ML) model to effectively define the styles of items on the site, based on both textual and visual cues.

Etsy's merchandisers had also carefully classified 130,000 products into one style or another. Those product placements were effective for the merchandising group, but they did not provide nearly enough data to train an ML algorithm. Consequently, the analytics team used the 43 styles as a framework, and they collected 3 million data points from one month of search queries to feed into their model.

Because sellers do not reliably convey a product's style in their descriptions, scanning text alone produced results from the ML model that were not accurate enough to satisfy shoppers. Similarly, standard approaches to image recognition produced inadequate search results from the ML model, because style is not only about color, patterns, or other visuals that are easy to categorize for a ML algorithm.

Etsy found a solution in a model that integrated text analysis with an approach to image recognition based on its 43 styles. This model enabled the algorithm to draw conclusions such as identifying a piece of art depicting a whale as being "nautical" in theme, regardless of whether its listing used that term. The model could then direct a shopper to other nautically themed products, even if they did not involve whales.

There was a reassuring indication that the ML algorithm was classifying products correctly. When Etsy graphed the sales of items whose styles the model had identified, the graphs made sense. For instance, products that the model had identified as being "tropical" peaked in the summer months. "Romantic" goods performed particularly well around Valentine's Day and other holidays associated with gift giving.

Etsy should be able to apply its algorithm to other aspects of the website in addition to search. In tests, the analytics team gave listed items their own style score, expressing the intensity with which the items matched a specific style. The company discovered that products that more closely show or demonstrate a particular style sell better than products that make less of a statement. Etsy is extending this finding to useful merchant tools. For instance, the company can help sellers determine whether their product has a strong style.

Etsy has learned many lessons during the process of developing its search algorithm. For example, even Etsy's huge amounts of data are not that big when it comes to developing ML models. The firm states that it collects data from 1 billion events per day. When you apply those data to more than 60 million items, the amount of data per item is rather small for ML algorithms. To handle its data, Etsy has migrated its data management to Google Cloud. This move has enabled the e-tailer to maintain a vast backlog of historical data without having to manage those data itself. These much larger data aggregations are extremely useful in developing the firm's ML algorithms.

The development process for the algorithm reinforced a concept that the company already knew: the emotional attachment that shoppers form with an item based on its aesthetics are core to Etsy's mission, which is to keep commerce human.

And the bottom line? By September 2020, Etsy was operating in 86 countries. In 2019, the company reported $5 billion in gross merchandise sales by their sellers. Etsy's percentage of these sales resulted in $818 million in revenue.

Sources: Compiled from S. Castellanos, "Etsy Accelerates AI Experimentation Thanks to Cloud," *Wall Street Journal*, February 19, 2020; S. Purohit, "Behind the Scenes: Machine Learning at Etsy," *Springboard*, February 12, 2020; H. McCracken, "How Etsy Taught Style to an Algorithm," *Fast Company*, July 11, 2019; S. Fedorenko, "Etsy Search Evolution: Etsy Uses Machine Learning to Boost Search-Based Purchases," *tamebay*, May 14, 2019; I. Steiner, "Can Etsy Fix Search with Machine Learning?" *eCommerce Bytes*, March 13, 2019; "Using Search Analytics to Understand Your Search Traffic," *Etsy Seller Handbook*, November 1, 2018; G. Taylor, "Get Predictive: The Keys to Achieving Data-Driven Personalization and Pricing," *Retail Touch Points*, April 11, 2017; N. Laskowski, "A Tale of Two Retailers Profiting from Big Data," *TechTarget*, January 7, 2015; A. Bednarz, "Etsy Gets Crafty with Big Data," *Network World*, February 25, 2013; **www.etsy.com**, accessed September 19, 2020.

Questions

1. Describe Etsy's business problem. (Keep in mind that there may be more than one.)
2. Describe the various types of data that Etsy collects.
3. Describe the descriptive analytics applications that Etsy employs.
4. Describe the predictive analytics applications that Etsy employs.

POM Production and Operations Management Examples

- Predictive analytics can enable organizations to determine correct inventory levels and distribution schedules among outlets.

- The difference between *preventive maintenance* and *predictive maintenance* is that preventive maintenance is scheduled at regular intervals, while predictive maintenance occurs as needed based on conditions of the asset. Because predictive maintenance occurs only when needed, it reduces labor and material costs.

  In 2015, ThyssenKrupp launched a predictive maintenance service based on data from sensors which measure a variety of operating conditions on the firm's 120,000 elevators around the world. Based on predictive analytics of the sensor data, if a condition falls outside normal limits the company dispatches an engineer. The goal is to get an engineer to the site before the elevator breaks down. Often when the engineer arrives, the system has already done much of the diagnostic work.

- Car maker BMW (**www.bmw.com**) is using predictive analytics to address vulnerabilities early in its production cycle. The manufacturer analyzes data from its global warranty, diagnostics, and repair units to optimize the design and production of new vehicles. By analyzing multiple data sources, BMW can find patterns that will help it to pinpoint potential design flaws.

- Tyson Foods (**www.tysonfoods.com**) is using predictive analytics to predict the potential of the coronavirus to impact its meat processing plants. The company's insights-as-a-service unit integrates COVID-19 testing data from counties where its plants are located, data about areas where Tyson employees live, and public data such as county population density and socioeconomic data to predict COVID-19 outbreaks in (and around) its plants.

FIN Finance Examples

- Banks use predictive analytics to forecast levels of bad loans, to predict credit card spending by new customers, to determine which kinds of customers will best respond to (and qualify for) new loan offers, and to forecast bankruptcy and other forms of default.

  Banks also use predictive analytics to detect fraudulent credit card transactions. Over time, a pattern emerges of the typical ways that you use your credit card, the amounts you spend, and so on. If a thief steals your card and uses it fraudulently, then that usage typically varies noticeably from your established pattern and the charges are denied.

- Financial services firms employ predictive analytics to produce credit scores. They use these scores to determine the probability that customers will make future credit payments on time.

- Retailers such as AAFES (stores on military bases) use Fraud Watch from SAP (**www.sap.com**) to combat fraud by employees in the company's 1,400 stores.

- Simpa Networks (**www.simpanetworks.com**) sells solar-as-a-service to poor households and small businesses in India. Simpa partnered with DataKind (**www.datakind.org**), whose data scientists analyzed Simpa's historical customer data to help Simpa assess the credit worthiness of potential customers.

HRM Human Resource Management Examples

- Credit Suisse (**www.credit-suisse.com**) uses predictive analytics to determine who might leave the company and why. Analysts provided this information anonymously to managers so that they could address the issues raised for all employees. In this way, no employee was singled out. This analysis reduced turnover risk factors and increased employee retention. The company saves approximately $70 million per year through reduced employee turnover.

- An engaged employee is one who is enthusiastic about his or her work and takes positive action to further the organization's goals. Shoe retailer Clarks (**www.clarksusa.com**) used predictive analytics to examine the relationship between employee engagement and the company's financial performance. The results indicated that every 1 percent improvement in engagement led to a 0.4 percent in business performance.

- United Kingdom based KPMG (**https://home.kpmg**) developed a proprietary system, Workplace Analytics, to implement retention solutions as soon as an employee is identified as considering leaving a firm. The system analyzes hundreds of behaviors such as email use, phone use, travel habits, commute times, and paid time off, while considering unemployment and opportunity in the surrounding geographic area, to provide individuals' retention scores. If that score changes, an employer can take appropriate actions to counter the likelihood that the individual will quit. For example, the employer can promote workplace flexibility, adjust workloads to prevent burnout, or offer perks.

IT's About Business 12.3

MIS HRM Analytics Helps Liverpool Football Club Succeed

Analytics has notably influenced the strategy and tactics of professional baseball and basketball associations in recent years. These sports analyze a huge number of variables to assess teams and players.

In contrast, soccer organizations have not paid much attention to analytics. However, that situation is beginning to change. Until recently, soccer organizations collected and analyzed data on who scored the goals, how many shots different players took, what percentage of the time each team controlled the ball, and many other metrics. However, these metrics have not been able to provide a clear explanation of what is happening on the field or why the winning team achieved victory.

Soccer is not composed of discrete events, such as baseball, and there are not dozens of scoring plays to analyze, as in basketball. Instead, much of the action in soccer seems impossible to quantify.

Further, pure chance can influence soccer outcomes to a much greater extent than in other sports. Goals are relatively rare. For instance, England's Premier League averages fewer than three per game. So, whether a ball goes into the net for a score or misses by a few inches has, on average, more of an effect upon the final result of a soccer game than whether, for instance, a potential home run in baseball lands foul or a National Football League field goal is wide to the right.

Consider just corner kicks in a soccer game. A ball deflected by a defensive player over the end line gives the opposition player a corner kick, which is a goal-scoring opportunity. In theory, therefore, corner kicks are a positive outcome, and having more of them than your opponents should be a successful strategy.

However, corner kicks are more helpful to some teams than others. Teams with players who are skilled at redirecting corner kicks work to create these kicks. Conversely, teams with players who have the talent to elude defenders and make shots on goal often avoid corner kicks.

And the results? Soccer executives assumed that the sport was unsuited to analytics, largely because much of the game involves probing and assessing, passing the ball from player to player while waiting for an opening. The executives felt that these actions could not easily be quantified and therefore were not suitable for analytics.

Despite the misgivings of soccer executives, the Chelsea Football Club (**www.chelseafc.com**) created the English Premier League's first analytics department in 2008. In 2012, the Arsenal Football Club (**www.arsenal.com**) bought a statistical analysis company, StatDNA. However, while executives saw the potential in analytics, the managers of the two clubs still did not see an advantage in applying data analysis to the sport. Further, as new metrics emerged concerning soccer, commentators and coaches were quick to repudiate them. Another premier league club ignored conventional wisdom about soccer analytics: Liverpool (**www.liverpoolfc.com**).

Between 1975 and 1990, Liverpool was a dominant soccer team. (Note: outside the United States, soccer is called football.) The club won 10 titles in England's top soccer division and won the European Cup four times in eight years. After 1990, however, the team's fortunes began to decline. By 2010 Liverpool had not won the Premier League in 20 years, and new owners purchased the team. In the first six seasons under the new ownership, Liverpool finished above sixth place only once. In 2012 Liverpool hired a new director of research, Ian Graham. The process took time, but Graham incorporated analytics into the club's decisions in two major areas: personnel and game analysis. Let's look closely at the club's analytics efforts.

Personnel. Graham's primary responsibility is helping Liverpool decide which players to acquire. He performs this process by feeding data on games into his analytics algorithms. Graham built a database to track the play of more than 100,000 players around the world. Based on these data he identified players Liverpool should try to acquire and then how the new players should be used.

Graham's model calculates each team's chance of scoring a goal before any given action by a player, such as a pass, a missed shot, or a slide tackle. The model then calculates what chance each team has immediately after that action. Using his model, Graham can quantify how much each player affected his team's chance of winning during the game.

For example, Graham recommended that Liverpool acquire Egyptian midfielder Mohamed Salah. The club paid about $41 million for him. Graham's analysis suggested that Salah would play particularly well with Roberto Firmino, a Liverpool striker. The next season, Salah broke the Premier League record by scoring 32 goals. The website Transfermarkt (**www.transfermarkt.us**), which tracks player valuations, estimated Salah's value at $173 million in 2019.

Graham also identified a left winger at Inter Milan named Philippe Coutinho. In 2013 Liverpool purchased Coutinho's rights for $16 million. Coutinho's excellent play contributed to Liverpool's revival (see below). In 2018, Barcelona paid Liverpool $170 million for Coutinho. Soon after, Liverpool spent more than $200 million for three new players who made crucial contributions during the 2019 season.

Game analysis. Graham and his team built a model that analyzes videos of entire games. The model assigns numerical scores to everything that happens to every player, even when the player does not touch the ball. Examples of these actions are a fullback running down the sideline, forcing a single defender to choose between two players to cover, and a striker getting into position to receive a pass directly in front of the goalkeeper, even if the pass goes over his head. The model also calculates possession value, team expected goals, player expected goals, and passing ability. Let's take a closer look at these variables.

Possession value. Expected goals are a good measure for the chances that a team creates and concedes, but they are recorded only when a team takes a shot. Possession value, in contrast, calculates the probability of a goal being scored at any point in a possession. For instance, a team with the ball right outside the opponent's box is much more dangerous than a team passing the ball in its own half of the field. Soccer analytics focuses on determining which actions lead to higher and lower value possessions, rather than simply time of possession.

Generally, soccer analytics adjusts for time of possession when analyzing defensive ability. A team with less possession time has more opportunities to make defensive plays, so measures of their actions are adjusted accordingly. Defensive metrics include passes per defensive action, where on the field a team chooses to put pressure on the ball, steals, slide tackles, and others.

Team expected goals. Not all shots on goal are equal. A shot closer to a goal is obviously more valuable than a shot farther from goal. That is, a short shot is more likely to result in a score than a long shot is.

Expected goals (xG) applies a number to the quality of a shot. A shot that has a 50 percent chance of scoring has an xG of 0.5. To calculate xG, analysts typically include data such as the distance from the goal, the angle to the goal, and what scenario the shot came from (e.g., a cross pass or a corner pass).

Adding up the xG of the shots a team takes produces their "xG for" or xGF. Adding up the xG of the shots the team allows its opponents generates the "xG against" (xGA). xGF minus xGA equals the "xG difference" or xGD.

Player expected goals. Clearly, players who take many high-quality shots tend to score more goals. As a result, many teams consider a player's ability to get shots from good locations to be almost as important as his ability to score goals.

Goalkeeper expected goals. For goalkeepers, xG relates to how difficult a save is. A goalkeeper's "goals saved above expected" measures shot-stopping ability; that is, how many more goals a keeper saved than an average keeper would have.

Passing ability. Soccer analytics can model the difficulty of a pass. Completing a pass into an opponent's box directly in front of its goalkeeper is much more difficult than completing a pass between two opponents in the center of the field. Passing scores measure which players are able to hit passes at rates above what would be expected.

Analytics can only incrementally influence Liverpool's outcomes in a positive direction, one recommendation at a time. Jurgen Klopp, the club's coach, also receives advice from other sources, so the tactics he chooses are a mix of data-driven and intuitive. Before each game, Graham and his team compile a packet of information for him, detailing the strengths and weaknesses of Liverpool and its opponent. Klopp decides how to utilize this information.

Further, analytics does not replace traditional scouting. Video analysis (the "eye" test) and traditional scouting remain important. Further, analytics must be tied closely to a knowledge and understanding of the game itself.

And the results? In the spring of 2019, Liverpool finished an amazingly successful season. The club lost only 1 of its 38 games in England's Premier League, yet it finished second. Manchester City, the defending champion, beat Liverpool by a single point on the last day of the season after winning every one of its league games since January. (In soccer, a victory counts as 3 points in the standings, and a draw counts as 1.) Liverpool set the record for most points in a season by a runner-up. Then, on June 1, 2019, Liverpool defeated a Premier League opponent, Tottenham Hotspur, in the finals of the European Champions League

Sources: Compiled from T. Bogert, "Soccer Analytics: Three Real-Life Examples that Show How Analysts Impact Their Clubs," *MLSoccer.com*, April 16, 2020; "What Impact Is Big Data Having on Soccer?" *Analytics Insight*, January 17, 2020; K. Draper, "Why Nerds Rule the N.B.A.," *New York Times*, November 27, 2019; R. Oster, "The Numbers Game: How Analytics Have Thrown a Curveball at the MLB Playoffs," *Digital Trends*, October 2, 2019; R. Kidd, "Soccer Clubs, Afraid of Missing Out, Are Joining the Data Revolution Before They're Ready," *Forbes*, June 16, 2019; S. McCaskill, "FA Accelerates Digital Transformation and Player Analysis Capabilities with the Cloud," *Forbes*, June 3, 2019; B. Schoenfeld, "How Data (and Some Breathtaking Soccer) Brought Liverpool to the Cusp of Glory," *The New York Times Magazine*, May 22, 2019; R. Smith, "Inside a Premier League Title Race in Which No One Dared to Blink," *New York Times*, May 12, 2019; R. Kidd, "Soccer's Moneyball Moment: How Enhanced Analytics Are Changing the Game," *Forbes*, November 19, 2018; K. Minkus, "Can Data Analytics Elevate Soccer's Profile in the U.S.?" *Dataconomy*, April 27, 2018; D. Kopf, "Data Analytics Have Made the NBA Unrecognizable," *Quartz*, October 18, 2017; J. McNicholas, "What Buying StatDNA Means for Arsenal and Their Moneyball Approach to Football," *Bleacher Report*, November 22, 2014; M. Lewis, *Moneyball: The Art of Winning an Unfair Game*, New York: W. W. Norton, 2003; **www.liverpoolfc.com**, accessed September 23, 2020.

Questions

1. Describe the descriptive analytics applications employed by Liverpool.

2. Describe the predictive analytics applications employed by Liverpool.

Insurance Examples

- Allstate Insurance (**www.allstate.com**) tripled the accuracy of predicting bodily injury liability from car crashes based on the characteristics of the insured vehicle. That is, the insurer adjusted the rates based on the vehicle. This process resulted in approximately $40 million in annual savings.

- Insurers use predictive analytics to forecast claim amounts and medical coverage costs, classify the most important elements that affect medical coverage, and predict which customers will buy new insurance policies.

Government Examples

- In his FiveThirtyEight blog (**https://fivethirtyeight.com**), Nate Silver famously analyzed polling and economic data to predict the results of the 2008 presidential election, calling 49 out of 50 states correctly. He then correctly predicted all 50 states in the 2012 presidential election. In contrast, Silver failed to correctly predict that Donald Trump would win the 2016 presidential election.

- Officials in some states are using predictive analytics to assess the risk that a convict will offend again.

Health Care Examples

- Health care organizations correlate demographics of patients with critical illnesses and develop more accurate insights on how to identify and treat symptoms and their causes. For example, Microsoft and Stanford University analyzed the search data of millions of users to successfully identify previously unreported side effects of certain medications.

- Stanford University data scientists used predictive analytics to diagnose breast cancer better than human physicians by discovering an innovative method that takes into account additional contributing factors in tissue samples.

Other Examples

- The National Weather Service (**www.weather.gov**) predicts weather with increasing accuracy and precision by analyzing a myriad of variables including past and present atmospheric conditions, location, temperature, air pressure, wind speed, and many others.

- Sentiment analysis is another type of predictive analysis. *Sentiment analysis* is the process of analyzing opinions expressed in a piece of text (e.g., a Tweet) or in a speech to determine whether the writer's or listener's attitude toward a particular topic, product, or service is positive, negative, or neutral. The output of sentiment analysis is a sentiment score, which can be positive or negative. Further, this score can also be any number between –1 and +1, indicating the degree of positivity or negativity.

Unintended Consequences of Predictive Analytics

Predictive analytics clearly provides organizations with numerous advantages. In fact, one could say that predictive analytics is critically important for an organization's success. However, predictive analytics applications can produce questionable, or even harmful, results for organizations. For example, we look at unintended consequences of predictive analytics for Target, Uber, and the Los Angeles Police Department.

MKT *Target.* Target identified 25 products that, when purchased together, indicate that a woman is likely pregnant. The value of these data was that Target could send coupons to the pregnant woman at a habit-forming period of her life. Unfortunately, Target's algorithms led to a public-relations problem.

A man walked into a Target outside Minneapolis, Minnesota, and demanded to see the manger. He had coupons that had been sent to his daughter, and he was quite angry. He told the manager that his daughter was a teenager, and he wanted to know if Target was trying to encourage her to become pregnant.

The manager did not know what the man was talking about. He noted that the mailer was addressed to the man's daughter and it contained advertisements for maternity clothing, nursery furniture, and pictures of smiling infants. The manager apologized and then called the man a few days later to apologize again. However, the father was embarrassed. He told the manager that his daughter was indeed pregnant and that he owed the manager an apology.

POM *Uber.* In December 2016, Uber's algorithm automatically raised rates (surge pricing) in Sydney, Australia, as people tried to get away from a downtown restaurant where an armed man was holding 17 people hostage. Three people, including the gunman, died. Uber later apologized for raising fares, which reportedly quadrupled, and then offered refunds.

Problems are most likely to arise when algorithms make things happen automatically, without human intervention or oversight. Uber is now working on a global policy to prevent price increases in times of disaster or emergency.

Example of Descriptive Analytics and Predictive Analytics

Let's consider the following example to demonstrate how descriptive and predictive analytics are used to bridge the gap between data management and actionable business decisions.

POM Weather data can be used to make predictions relating to certain business problems. Suppose you are the northeast district manager for the American Automobile Association (AAA; **www.aaa.com**), and your district covers multiple offices in several states. You need to create a work schedule for your employees, who receive and dispatch service calls. Your goal is to provide optimal coverage in your offices, reduce unnecessary salary expenses, and provide excellent customer service by reducing customers' wait time. Therefore, you decide to predict the number of service calls your offices receive per day during normal business hours based on the daily low temperature measured in degrees.

Data Management: To investigate this business problem, you collect data on service calls for the past year from the AAA locations within your district. You first "clean" the data by adjusting for outliers and missing values, resulting in a final sample of 3,219 service calls.

You are now ready to build a regression model using temperature as the independent variable to predict the number of customer service calls received in any given day; this is the dependent variable. You will use the results to predict how many employees should be available to receive and dispatch customer service calls.

Descriptive Analytics: For this example, the correlation between daily low temperature and the number of service calls was found to be –0.84, with an average of 48 service calls per day. The correlation is negative because as the temperature decreases, the data indicate that the number of service calls increases.

The square of this correlation, $R^2 = .71$, is the predictive power of the model. That is, the model, using low daily temperature, explains approximately 71 percent of the variation in the number of calls received each day. Therefore, 1 minus R^2 means that 29 percent of the variance in the dependent variable is due to extraneous or unexplained variables.

Predictive Analytics: The manager has decided to use linear regression for his predictive analysis. To do so, certain reasonable assumptions must be met:

- He must have at least 30 data points.
- The relationship between the independent and dependent variables must be linear. The linearity assumption can best be tested with scatter plots.
- Even thought the data are assumed to be normally distributed, he should check this assumption.

The sample size of 3,219 satisfies the first assumption. The manager then used Excel to test the second assumption, producing a scatterplot to determine if the plot of each ordered pair of data (independent variable, dependent variable) produced a linear pattern. The scatterplot for the data did exhibit a linear pattern. Therefore, linear regression is an acceptable statistical procedure for these data.

To check for normality, the manager calculated the correlation between the data and the normal scores of the data. If the value is near 1, then the sample dataset is likely to be normal. This dataset met the normality assumption.

Now that the three linear regression assumptions have been met, the next step is to define the linear regression model between these two variables using Excel or a similar statistical package. The linear regression model is:

Number of calls received = 124.79 − 1.5 × (daily low temperature)

These results indicate that for every one degree of increase in the daily low temperature, the predicted daily number of calls received will decrease by 1.5. That is, AAA will expect to receive fewer calls on warmer days and more calls on colder days. At a temperature of 0 degrees ($x = 0$), the expected number of calls will be approximately 125.

Actionable Business Decision: Based on the linear regression, the district manager is able to use the projected daily low temperature for up to 10 days in advance to predict how many service calls the offices will receive each day. (The Weather Channel provides reasonably accurate daily temperatures on a 10-day outlook.) Therefore, he can predict how many employees will be needed to manage the expected number of service calls in order to ensure low wait times for the customers.

Now, ask the next question: At this point, the manager can return to the data management stage with new input variables. For the AAA data in this example, it is feasible to consider another business problem with the appropriate inputs or to expand the analysis by considering other variables relevant to the business question in the example. For example, the manager might want to include the actual time of day, by hour, so that he could more accurately decide on staffing levels. He also might want to examine the location of his AAA branches as a variable. Adding these variables would require the use of new regression models.

You also want to recall that our example is for the northeast district, where temperatures are cooler than in some other regions of the country. Therefore, if we were to use data from the southwest, then we would have to perform the analyses again. Otherwise, if we used the northeast regression model for the southwest, what would be the result for a 100-degree day? The answer is that the number of calls received would be negative!

Our example proceeds from data management, to descriptive analytics, to predictive analytics (through a simple linear regression model). We address how the results of predictive analytics often lead to additional questions that include additional variables, which would require a multiple linear regression model.

From a statistical perspective, we might ask: Aren't there many different analytical approaches to solving the same problem? The answer is yes. But a more important question to ask is: Which one approach is the best? The answer to this question is—none! The best approach depends on the kind of data you are working with. And because data come in all shapes and sizes, there cannot be one best approach for all problems. Therefore, selecting the best model for the particular data is always an important exercise in data analytics.

Before you go on...

1. Describe the purpose of predictive analytics.
2. Discuss the BA tools that are commonly used in predictive analytics.

12.5 Prescriptive Analytics

Prescriptive analytics goes beyond descriptive and predictive models by recommending one or more courses of action and by identifying the likely outcome of each decision. Predictive analytics does not predict one possible future; rather, it suggests multiple future outcomes based on the decision maker's actions. Prescriptive analytics attempts to quantify the effect of future decisions in order to advise on possible outcomes before the decisions are actually made.

Some companies are successfully using prescriptive analytics to optimize production, scheduling, and inventory along the supply chain to ensure they deliver the right products at the right time so they can optimize the customer's experience.

Prescriptive analytics requires predictive analytics with two additional components: actionable data and a feedback system that tracks the outcome produced by the action taken. Because prescriptive analytics is able to predict the possible consequences based on different choices of action, it can also recommend the best course of action to achieve any prespecified outcome.

BA Tools in Prescriptive Analytics

Organizations use a variety of BA tools and statistical procedures to perform prescriptive analytics. Statistical procedures include optimization, simulation, and others. A discussion of these procedures is beyond the scope of this text.

Examples of Prescriptive Analytics Applications

We present numerous examples of prescriptive analytics in this section. Let's begin by returning once again to our examples of class attendance and Fandango.

Should I go to class?   Based on my predictive analytics results, I will set the alarm on my phone and check the transit bus schedule. If I decide to drive my car, I may have to get up earlier in order to find a parking place.

POM **Fandango.**   Recall that we are using Fandango to illustrate each step in the BA process. Here we discuss examples of Fandango's prescriptive analytics applications. Fandango uses prescriptive analytics so it can change ticket price offerings every hour. The company has identified the most desirable movie times by analyzing millions of show times instantaneously. The company then uses these data to set an optimal price for any given time, based on the supply of show times and the demand for movie tickets. This process maximizes profits. The data from each show indicate how much each ticket price contributes to profits.

MIS **Waymo (Google) Driverless Car.**   During every trip, the car makes multiple decisions about what to do based on predictions of future outcomes. For example, when approaching an intersection, the car must determine whether to go left, right, or straight ahead. Based on its destination, it makes a decision. Additionally, the car must anticipate what might be coming in regard to vehicular traffic, pedestrians, bicyclists, and so on. The car must also analyze the impact of a possible decision before it actually makes that decision.

POM **The Oil and Gas Industry.**   Companies in this industry analyze a variety of structured and unstructured data, including video, image, and sound data, to optimize hydraulic fracturing (fracking) operations. One prescriptive analytics application optimizes the materials and equipment necessary to pump oil out of the ground. It further optimizes scheduling, production, inventory, and supply chain design to ensure that the right products are delivered in the right amount to the right customers at the right time in the most efficient manner.

UPS provides an outstanding example of how an enterprise can employ all three analytics applications. IT's About Business 12.4 details how UPS has progressed from descriptive analytics, to predictive analytics, and finally to prescriptive analytics.

IT's About Business 12.4

POM United Parcel Service Uses Three Types of Analytics

The Problem

United Parcel Service (UPS; **www.ups.com**) is a global organization with 424,000 employees and nearly 100,000 vehicles. UPS drivers typically make between 120 and 175 "drops" per day. Between any two drops, drivers can take a number of possible paths. With 55,000 routes in the Unites States alone, the total number of possible routes is inconceivably vast. Clearly, it is in the best interest of UPS and its drivers to find the most efficient routes. Therefore, any tiny amount of efficiency that can be gained in daily operations yields significant improvements to the company's bottom line. Essentially, "little" things matter a great deal to UPS.

In addition, the rapid increase in electronic commerce has shifted an increasing number of UPS's delivery stops from retailers to residences. (We discuss e-commerce in Chapter 7.) In fact, half of UPS's total deliveries in 2018 were to residences. Historically, drivers would drop off multiple packages at a retailer. Today, they must make scattered stops to drop off packages at individual homes. This scenario involves more routes and is more time consuming.

UPS must also manage a low-margin business as well as a unionized workforce that is compensated at the high end of the industry scale. Significantly, rival FedEx (**www.fedex.com**) uses independent contractors for its ground network. Consequently, FedEx does not have the burden of expensive employee benefits packages. UPS also faces intense competition from Amazon with its low-cost package delivery service, called the Delivery Service Partner program.

UPS is deploying analytics applications to address the company's challenges. Since 2016, UPS has been collecting and analyzing some 1 billion data points per day across its facilities. By the end of 2020, numerous analytics projects were utilizing these data, grouped under the Enhanced Dynamic Global Execution (EDGE) program. EDGE is providing UPS with $200 million to $300 million in savings per year.

The Solution

For decades UPS has been using three types of analytics to produce efficiencies.

- Descriptive analytics asks, "Where are we today?"
- Predictive analytics asks, "With our current trajectory, where *will* we be tomorrow?"
- Prescriptive analytics asks, "Where *should* we be tomorrow?"

As UPS has moved from descriptive to predictive to prescriptive analytics, its data needs have increased, the skill set of its people has improved, and the business impact of analytics has increased. We consider these developments next.

Descriptive Analytics

DIADs. UPS implemented descriptive analytics in the 1990s when the company provided its drivers with hand-held computers, called Delivery Information Acquisition Devices (DIADs). The DIADs enabled UPS to capture detailed data that measured the company's current status. For example, the company measured driving variables in hundredths of a second. Their reasoning was that if they could reduce one mile per driver per day in the United States alone, that would add up to $50 million to the bottom line annually.

Package placement on delivery vans. In 2017, UPS began equipping its delivery trucks with Bluetooth receivers to reduce the number of incorrectly loaded packages. The receivers emit a loud beep if a worker puts a package into a vehicle that is not going to the package's destination. When workers enter the correct truck, a different beep confirms that they are in the right place. The system works by transmitting wireless signals between the Bluetooth receivers and the scanning devices that workers wear on their hips and hands to read the labels on UPS packages.

When UPS workers scan packages in the morning, the data update the service that the company has deployed to send customers progress emails about their shipments. Customers who have signed up for the free service then receive a message that their package will arrive that day, along with an estimated delivery time.

Routing outbound packages. Another project informs seasonal workers where to direct the outbound packages that UPS vehicles pick up throughout the day and bring to the company's sorting facilities. UPS hires nearly 100,000 of these workers from November through January. In the winter of 2018, UPS outfitted about 2,500 of these workers with scanning devices and $8 Bluetooth headphones that issue one-word directions, such as "Green," "Red," or "Blue." The colors correspond to specific conveyor belts, which then transport the packages to other parts of the building for further processing.

Undeliverable packages. UPS does make mistakes with some deliveries. In the past, UPS managers relied on historical data and radio conversations with drivers to estimate how many undeliverable packages they would need to handle each night. As a result, the company has a project that tells managers how many returned packages will arrive at their processing center and when. Now they can assemble the appropriate number of workers to reroute the packages.

Predictive Analytics

In 2003, UPS deployed its Package Flow Technologies system to provide predictive analytics. With this system, drivers started the day with a DIAD that detailed the packages they were to deliver and the order in which they were to deliver those packages. The DIAD became the drivers' assistant. The system enabled UPS to reduce total delivery driving globally by 85 million miles per year. That process saved the firm 8.5 million gallons of fuel, and it prevented 85,000 metric tons of carbon dioxide from entering the atmosphere.

However, drivers had to provide different services from the same vehicle—for example, deferred service and premium service. Some packages had to be delivered by 10:30 a.m., others had to be delivered by noon, and still others had to be delivered by 2:00 p.m. Drivers therefore had to decide how they were going to service those customers. With so many variables to consider, it was practically impossible for drivers to optimize their routes.

Prescriptive Analytics

UPS realized that it needed to take analytics to the next level. So, in mid-2012 the company began deploying its On-Road Integrated Optimization and Navigation (ORION) system. ORION reorganizes the drivers' routes based on today's customers, today's needs, and today's packages, and it designs deliveries in a very specific, optimized order. ORION takes into account UPS business rules, maps, what time drivers need to be at specific locations, and customer preferences. ORION can alter delivery routes dynamically based on changing weather conditions and accidents. The system can also examine the deliveries that still need to be completed and continue to optimize the remaining route.

At first, ORION used publicly available maps. However, these maps were not detailed enough. Therefore, UPS drew their own maps, which displayed features such as a customer's half-mile driveway or a back alley that saves time getting to a receiving dock. These were data points that ORION needed to optimize package delivery.

Unfortunately, analytics algorithms cannot anticipate every variable. For example, a business customer typically receives one package per day. If ORION knows that the package is not tied to a certain delivery time, then the algorithm might suggest dropping it off in the morning one day but in the afternoon the next day, depending on that day's tasks. That process might be the most efficient approach for UPS, but customers would not know when to expect deliveries. This can be a problem because customers typically do not like that amount of uncertainty.

When UPS drivers are on the road, they usually travel at speeds of 20 to 25 miles per hour. Therefore, every mile reduced equates to a savings of two to three minutes. By shortening routes by seven to eight miles per day, ORION enables UPS to deliver more packages.

ORION enhances UPS customer service with more efficient routing, and it enables UPS to offer innovative services and customized solutions. An example of this type of service is UPS My Choice, which is a free system that allows residential customers to decide "how, where, and when home deliveries occur." UPS's chatbot, called UPS Bot, is integrated with the UPS My Choice system, so customers are able to obtain information about their incoming packages and deliveries without providing a tracking number.

UPS Bot mimics human conversation and can respond to customer queries such as "Where is the nearest UPS location?" In addition, it can track packages and provide shipping rates. Customers can ask the bot questions through text or voice commands, mobile devices, social media channels, and virtual assistants such as Alexa and Google Assistant. UPS Bot is able to recognize these requests and take the appropriate steps to respond to them.

A recent UPS project, Network Planning Tool (NPT), optimizes the flow of packages in the UPS network from loading docks to sorting to the final destination. NPT enables UPS engineers to view activity at UPS facilities around the world and route shipments to the ones with the most capacity. NPT creates forecasts about package volume and weight based on an analysis of historical data.

NPT enables UPS to organize packages by destination and move them at the lowest possible cost while still meeting delivery dates. The tool helps engineers group all outbound packages into the smallest number of trailers or cargo planes. NPT can also schedule truck and plane trips so those drivers and pilots always pick up parcels on their return trips and therefore do not return home with empty vehicles.

NPT provides a single cloud-based platform where UPS engineers can view data and run simulations to help create their plans and schedules. NPT's algorithms understand the distribution of all of the packages in the UPS logistics system, and it can determine the best way to bypass a problematic facility while meeting deadlines and not overwhelming other UPS facilities.

The Results

In April 2016, UPS won the prestigious Edelman Prize for excellence in analytics and operations research for its ORION project. UPS completed the deployment of ORION at the end of 2016.

The results from ORION have been outstanding. UPS is realizing savings of between $300 and $400 million per year in driver productivity and fuel economy. Furthermore, with ORION,

UPS drivers have saved 100 million miles in driving, decreasing carbon emissions by 100,000 metric tons per year. ORION will generate further environmental benefits and cost reductions when UPS equips its vehicles outside the United States with this technology.

UPS continues to look into the future. As a major example, ORION provides a natural transition to driverless vehicles. The company need only integrate ORION with the software of autonomous delivery vehicles, and those vehicles will take optimal routes to get UPS personnel where they need to go to deliver packages.

Finally, UPS is testing the use of drone deliveries for some applications, including dropping essential supplies in Rwanda and demonstrating how medicines could be delivered to islands. In rural areas, where drones have the space to execute deliveries and the distance between stops makes efficient deliveries challenging, drones launched from the roofs of UPS trucks provide a solution to reduce costs and improve service. On October 1, 2019, UPS received the Federal Aviation Administration's first full approval for the company's drone airline, called UPS Flight Forward.

Sources: Compiled from "UPS Flight Forward Attains FAA's First Full Approval for Drone Airline," *UPS Press Release*, October 1, 2019; P. High, "UPS's Chief Information and Engineering Officer Champions Prescriptive Analytics," *Forbes*, July 15, 2019; E. Woyke, "How UPS Uses AI to Deliver Holiday Gifts in the Worst Storms," *MIT Technology Review*, November 21, 2018; N. Shields, "UPS Is Turning to Predictive Analytics," *Business Insider*, July 20, 2018; S. Schwartz, "UPS Working to Consolidate Data Points on Single Platform with Analytics, Machine Learning," *CIO Dive*, July 19, 2018; B. Marr, "The Brilliant Ways UPS Uses Artificial Intelligence, Machine Learning and Big Data," *Forbes*, June 15, 2018; S. Rosenbush, "UPS Expands Role of Predictive Analytics," *Wall Street Journal*, April 26, 2018; E. Woyke, "How UPS Delivers Faster Using $8 Headphones and Code that Decides When Dirty Trucks Get Cleaned," *MIT Technology Review*, February 16, 2018; "How UPS Delivers Predictive Analytics," *CIO*, September 28, 2016; T. Davenport, "Prescriptive Analytics Project Delivering Big Dividends at UPS," *DataInformed*, April 19, 2016; C. Powers, "How UPS Augments Its Drivers' Intuition with Predictive Analytics," *ASUG News*, June 9, 2015; E. Siegel, "Predictive Analytics Driving Results, ROI at UPS," *Data Informed*, June 1, 2015; E. Siegel, "Wise Practitioner—Predictive Analytics Interview Series: Jack Levis of UPS," *Predictive Analytics World*, April 28, 2015; J. Berman, "UPS Is Focused on the Future for Its ORION Technology," *Logistics Management*, March 3, 2015; S. Rosenbush and L. Stevens, "At UPS, the Algorithm Is the Driver," *Wall Street Journal*, February 16, 2015; J. Dix, "How UPS Uses Analytics to Drive Down Costs," *Network World*, December 1, 2014; K. Noyes, "The Shortest Distance Between Two Points? At UPS, It's Complicated," *Fortune*, July 25, 2014; www.ups.com, accessed September 13, 2020.

Questions

1. Explain how DIADs were a descriptive analytics solution for UPS.

2. Explain how the Package Flow Technologies system was a predictive analytics solution for UPS.

3. Explain how the ORION system was a prescriptive analytics solution for UPS.

4. Describe another potential application for the UPS ORION system. That is, what is the next question that UPS managers might ask of the ORION system?

5. Is UPS's Network Planning Tool a descriptive analytics application, a predictive analytics application, a prescriptive analytics application, or some combination? Support your answer with examples.

12.6   Presentation Tools

As you saw in Figure 12.3, organizations use presentation tools to display the results of analyses to users in visual formats such as charts, graphs, figures, and tables. This process, known as *data visualization*, makes the results more attractive and easier to understand. Organizations can present the results after they have performed descriptive analytics, predictive analytics, and prescriptive analytics. A variety of visualization methods and software packages that support decision making are available. Dashboards are the most common BA presentation tool. We discuss them next. We also consider geographic information systems, another valuable data visualization tool.

Dashboards

Dashboards evolved from executive information systems, which were designed specifically for the information needs of top executives. Today, however, many employees, business partners, and customers use digital dashboards.

A **dashboard** provides easy access to timely information and direct access to management reports. It is user friendly, it is supported by graphics, and, most important, it enables managers to examine exception reports and drill down into detailed data. **Table 12.1** summarizes the various capabilities that are common to many dashboards. Some of the capabilities discussed in this section have been incorporated into many BA products, as illustrated in **Figure 12.4**.

One outstanding example of a dashboard is Bloomberg LP (**www.bloomberg.com**), a privately held company that provides a subscription service that sells financial data, software to analyze these data, trading tools, and news (electronic, print, TV, and radio). All of this information is accessible through a color-coded Bloomberg keyboard that displays the desired information on a computer screen, either the user's screen or one that Bloomberg provides. Users can also set up their own computers to access the service without a Bloomberg keyboard. The

TABLE 12.1   The Capabilities of Dashboards

Capability	Description
Drill down	The ability to go to details, at several levels; it can be done by a series of menus or by clicking on a drillable portion of the screen.
Critical success factors (CSFs)	The factors most critical for the success of business. These can be organizational, industry, departmental, or for individual workers.
Key performance indicators (KPIs)	The specific measures of CSFs.
Status access	The latest data available on a KPI or some other metric, often in real time.
Trend analysis	Short-, medium-, and long-term trends of KPIs or metrics, which are projected using forecasting methods.
Exception reporting	Reports highlight deviations larger than defined thresholds. Reports may include only deviations.

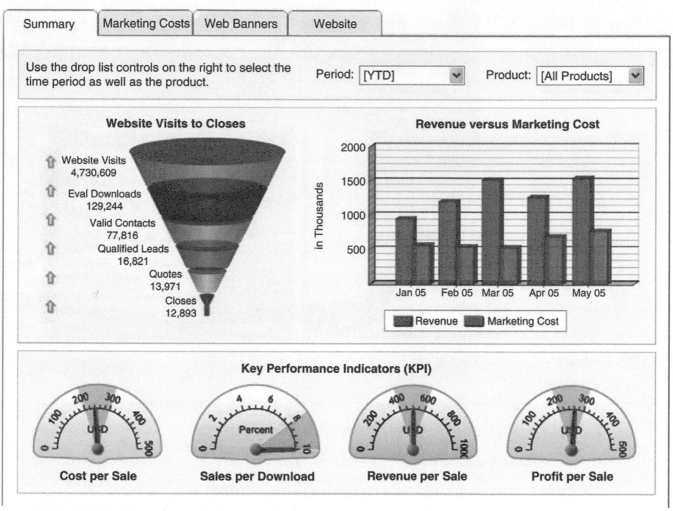

FIGURE 12.4   **Sample performance dashboard.**

subscription service plus the keyboard is called the Bloomberg Terminal. It is literally a do-it-yourself dashboard because users can customize their information feeds as well as the look and feel of those feeds (see **Figure 12.5**).

A unique and interesting application of dashboards to support the informational needs of executives is the Management Cockpit. Essentially, a Management Cockpit is a strategic management room containing an elaborate set of dashboards that enable top-level decision makers to pilot their businesses better. The goal is to create an environment that encourages more efficient management meetings and boosts team performance through effective communication. To help achieve this goal, the dashboard graphically displays KPIs and information relating to critical success factors on the walls of a meeting room called the *Management Cockpit Room* (see **Figure 12.6**). The cockpit-like arrangement of instrument panels and displays helps managers visualize how all of the different factors in the business interrelate.

Within the room, the four walls are designated by color: Black, Red, Blue, and White. The Black Wall displays the principal success factors and financial indicators. The Red Wall measures market performance. The Blue Wall projects the performance of internal processes and employees. Finally, the White Wall indicates the status of strategic projects. The Flight Deck, a six-screen, high-end PC, enables executives to drill down to detailed information. External information needed for competitive analyses can easily be imported into the room.

Board members and other executives hold meetings in the Management Cockpit Room. Managers also meet there with the comptroller to discuss current business issues. The Management Cockpit can implement various what-if scenarios for this purpose. It also provides a common basis for information and communication. Finally, it supports efforts to translate a corporate strategy into concrete activities by identifying performance indicators.

Carlos Osorio/Toronto Star/Zuma Press

FIGURE 12.5 **Bloomberg Terminal.**

Geographic Information Systems

A **geographic information system (GIS)** is a computer-based system for capturing, integrating, manipulating, and displaying data using digitized maps. Its most distinguishing characteristic is that every record or digital object has an identified geographical location. This process, called *geocoding*, enables users to generate information for planning, problem solving, and decision making. The graphical format also makes it easy for managers to visualize the data. There are countless applications of GISs to improve decision making in both the public and private sectors.

The Management Cockpit is a registered trademark of SAP, created by Professor Patrick M. Georges.

FIGURE 12.6 **Management Cockpit.**

POM As one example, Children's National Health System offers injury prevention advice to the community. Clinicians have found that using geospatial data helps them accomplish this mission. The health care center integrated its existing electronic health records system with GIS software from ESRI (**www.esri.com**) to display health data with geospatial coordinates. One of the integrated system's first projects focused on pediatric burn cases.

GIS mapping enabled the clinic to identify on a map the hotspots where injuries were occurring. That map allowed staff members to develop prevention programs tailored to the demographics of areas with high rates of injuries. For example, if the system identifies a cluster of children with burns in a particular neighborhood, then the staff will work with community groups to provide parents with Spanish translations of information about safety.

The new system has produced results. The clinic is seeing fewer burn patients overall and fewer patients requiring high-level burn care. Children's National Health System is now using its system to map concentrations of other medical conditions such as obesity and asthma.

Before you go on...

1. Discuss why presentation tools are so valuable in the business analytics process.
2. What is a dashboard? Why are dashboards so valuable to an organization's decision makers?

What's in IT for me?

ACCT For the Accounting Major

BA is used extensively in auditing to uncover irregularities. It also is used to uncover and prevent fraud. CPAs use BA for many of their duties, ranging from risk analysis to cost control.

FIN For the Finance Major

People have been using computers for decades to solve financial problems. Innovative BA applications have been created for activities such as making stock market decisions, refinancing bonds, assessing debt risks, analyzing financial conditions, predicting business failures, forecasting financial trends, and investing in global markets.

MKT For the Marketing Major

Marketing personnel utilize BA in many applications, from planning and executing marketing campaigns, to allocating advertising budgets, to evaluating alternative routings of salespeople. New marketing approaches such as targeted marketing and database marketing depend heavily on IT in general and on data warehouses and business intelligence applications in particular.

POM For the Production/Operations Management Major

BA supports complex operations and production decisions from inventory control, to production planning, to supply chain integration.

HRM For the Human Resources Management Major

Human resources personnel employ BA for many of their activities. For example, BA applications can find résumés of applicants posted on the Web and sort them to match needed skills and to support management succession planning.

MIS For the MIS Major

MIS provides the data infrastructure used in BA. MIS personnel are also involved in building, deploying, and supporting BA applications.

Summary

12.1 Use a decision-support framework to demonstrate how technology supports managerial decision making at each phase of the decision-making process.

When making a decision, either organizational or personal, the decision maker goes through a three-step process: intelligence, design, and choice. When the choice is made, the decision is implemented. In general, it is difficult to state which information systems support specific decision makers in an organization. Modern information systems, particularly business analytics systems, are available to support everyone in an organization.

12.2 Describe each phase of the business analytics process.

Business analytics is the process of developing actionable decisions or recommendations for actions based on insights generated from historical data. The phases in the business analytics process are shown in Figure 12.3 and include data management, descriptive analytics (with associated analytics tools and statistics procedures), predictive analytics (with associated analytics tools and statistical procedures), prescriptive analytics (with associated analytics tools and statistical procedures), and presentation tools. The results of the business analytics process are actionable business decisions.

12.3 Provide a definition and a use case example for descriptive analytics.

Descriptive analytics summarizes what has happened in the past and allows decision makers to learn from past behaviors. We leave the example to you.

12.4 Provide a definition and a use case example for predictive analytics.

Predictive analytics examines recent and historical data in order to detect patterns and predict future outcomes and trends. We leave the example to you.

12.5 Provide a definition and a use case example for prescriptive analytics.

Prescriptive analytics goes beyond descriptive and predictive models by recommending one or more courses of action and identifying the likely outcome of each decision. We leave the example to you.

12.6 Describe two examples of presentation tools.

A dashboard provides easy access to timely information and direct access to management reports. It is user friendly, it is supported by graphics, and, most important, it enables managers to examine exception reports and drill down into detailed data.

A geographic information system (GIS) is a computer-based system for capturing, integrating, manipulating, and displaying data using digitized maps. Its most distinguishing characteristic is that every record or digital object has an identified geographical location.

Chapter Glossary

business analytics (BA)   The process of developing actionable decisions or recommendations for actions based on insights generated from historical data.

business intelligence (BI)   A broad category of applications, technologies, and processes for gathering, storing, accessing, and analyzing data to help business users make more informed decisions.

dashboard   A business analytics presentation tool that provides rapid access to timely information and direct access to management reports.

data mining   The process of searching for valuable business information in a large database, data warehouse, or data mart.

decision   A choice that individuals and groups make among two or more alternatives.

decision-support systems (DSSs)   Business intelligence systems that combine models and data in an attempt to solve semistructured and some unstructured problems with extensive user involvement.

descriptive analytics   A type of business analytics that summarize what has happened in the past and allow decision makers to learn from past behaviors.

geographic information system (GIS)   A computer-based system for capturing, integrating, manipulating, and displaying data using digitized maps.

management   A process by which organizational goals are achieved through the use of resources.

multidimensional data analysis   See **online analytical processing (OLAP)**.

online analytical processing (OLAP) (or multidimensional data analysis)   A set of capabilities for "slicing and dicing" data using dimensions and measures associated with the data.

predictive analytics A type of business analytics that examines recent and historical data in order to detect patterns and predict future outcomes and trends.

prescriptive analytics A type of business analytics that recommend one or more courses of action and showing the likely outcome of each decision.

productivity The ratio between the inputs to a process and the outputs from that process.

Discussion Questions

1. Your company is considering opening a new factory in China. List several typical activities involved in each phase of the decision (intelligence, design, and choice).

2. Recall that a market basket analysis (a type of data mining) of convenience store purchases revealed that customers tended to buy beer and diapers at the same time when they shopped. Now that the analysis uncovered this relationship exists, provide a rationale for it. Note: you will have to decide what the next question is.

3. American Can Company announced that it was interested in acquiring a company in the health maintenance organization (HMO) field. Two decisions were involved in this act: (1) the decision to acquire an HMO, and (2) the decision of which HMO to acquire. How can the use of BA assist the company in this endeavor?

4. Discuss the strategic benefits of business analytics.

5. In early 2012, the *New York Times* reported the story of a Target data scientist who was able to predict if a customer was pregnant based on her pattern of previous purchases.

    a. Describe the business analytics models that the data scientist used.

    b. Refer to Chapter 3 and discuss the ethics of Target's analytics process.

    c. Research the story and note the unintended consequences of Target's analytics process.

6. Consider the admissions process at your university. Your university's admissions process involves the analysis of many variables to decide whom to admit to each year's freshman class. Contact your admissions office and gather information on the variables used in the admissions process. As you recall from applying at your university, typical variables would include high school attended, high school grade point average, standardized test scores such as ACT or SAT, and many others. (Do not be surprised if there are variables that your admissions office cannot provide.)

    a. Provide an example of how your admissions office uses descriptive analytics in the admissions process. Use the variables you have found in your example.

    b. Provide an example of how your admissions office uses predictive analytics in the admissions process. Use the variables you have found in your example.

    c. Provide an example of how your admissions office uses prescriptive analytics in the admissions process. Use the variables you have found in your example.

Problem-Solving Activities

1. Consider a large city, which has placed sensors in all its trash dumpsters. The sensors measure how full each dumpster is.

    a. Describe a descriptive analytics application using this sensor data.

    b. Describe a predictive analytics application using this sensor data.

    c. Describe a prescriptive analytics application using this sensor data.

2. Consider General Electric's latest-generation LEAP aircraft engine. Sensors in this engine measure vibration and several different temperatures (depending on the location of the sensor).

    a. Describe a descriptive analytics application using this sensor data.

    b. Describe a predictive analytics application using this sensor data.

    c. Describe a prescriptive analytics application using this sensor data.

3. You are a business analyst for a chain of grocery stores. You analyze retail sales data, perform a descriptive analytics application, and discover that bread and milk are the two products that are purchased together more often than any other pair of products.

    a. Describe a predictive analytics application using these data.

    b. Describe a prescriptive analytics application using these data.

4. Consider Rent the Runway (RTR; **www.renttherunway.com**). RTR buys designer dresses wholesale and rents them over the Web, charging only a fraction of the price of the dress. When RTR merchandisers decide whether to buy a new dress, they follow a list of 40 data points such as fabric, zippers, stitching, and shape to determine whether the dress will hold up to the rigors of multiple rentals. The longer the lifespan, the higher the return on capital. In mid-2017, RTR was averaging more than 30 turns (rentals) per dress.

With every dress it rents, RTR's analytics algorithms learn more about effective strategies to track the location of each item, forecast demand, select shipping methods, set prices, and control inventory. RTR's algorithms also examine customer reviews to learn which dresses women are renting for certain occasions. They then forecast demand to determine whether the prepaid shipping label that goes with a dress should require the customer to return the dress overnight or whether a three-day return, which costs less, is sufficient.

a. Describe a descriptive analytics application using this sensor data.

b. Describe a predictive analytics application using this sensor data.

c. Describe a prescriptive analytics application using this sensor data

Closing Case

POM MKT MIS Stitch Fix

Hundreds of customers enter traditional brick-and-mortar retail clothing stores every day. In most cases, however, the retailers do not learn much about them. Unless sales associates interact with them, those businesses will not know customers' pants sizes, purchase histories, or which products they are looking to buy. Furthermore, many customers do not have time to go into stores and look through hundreds of items of clothing to find something they like.

Enter Stitch Fix, a personal styling service. Launched in 2011, Stitch Fix (www.stitchfix.com) is an online retailer that initially marketed to busy working women. (Stitch Fix for Men launched in 2016 and Stitch Fix Kids in 2018.) The firm's service essentially shops for its clients, matching them with boutique-brand clothes, shoes, and accessories based on recommendations from its analytics algorithms and human stylists.

Rather than visit a store, Stitch Fix customers pay a $20 "styling fee" to receive a box of five personally selected items either on demand or by subscription at regular intervals. They try on the clothes at home, keep the items they want, and return those they do not want. Clients pay the full retail price of any clothes they keep, minus the $20 fee, which is applied as a credit. For the company to make a profit, customers must keep at least two of the five items in each shipment. To encourage purchases, Stitch Fix offers its customers a 25 percent discount if they keep all of the items in the box.

MKT Stitch Fix's business model is all about experience and relevance. The lines of clothing are not exclusive to Stitch Fix, and Stitch Fix does not price them lower than its competitors. Furthermore, the company does not try to ship faster than its competitors. Its strategy is simply to be more relevant and to understand its customers better than the competition does. Stitch Fix's increased relevance enables the company to address the problem of overabundance of products offered in stores and especially over the Internet. Specifically, CEO Katrina Lake noted that while the vastness of apparel available to consumers might seem appealing at first, customers eventually feel overwhelmed by so much choice.

The key concept of Stitch Fix is personalization. The firm's machine-learning algorithms are central to the company's business model, and they drive every business process, including selecting clothing, assigning human stylists, optimizing production and logistics, and designing new styles. Let's take a closer look at these processes.

MKT *Selecting clothing.* Essentially, selecting clothing involves predicting the likelihood that a particular client will like a certain piece of clothing. These predictions require data, so Stitch Fix gathers data from both its customers and its merchandise.

In contrast to traditional retailers, Stitch Fix knows that anyone who is willing to pay the $20 styling fee is probably willing to provide personal data to ensure an optimal experience. To promote this experience, the retailer collects more than 50 pieces of data from each customer such as personal characteristics including height, weight, and various sizes as well as links to customers' Pinterest, Twitter, and LinkedIn profiles. The firm's algorithms analyze a customer's data to predict how likely they are to keep a given item based on parameters that include the customer's style, occupation, age, ZIP code (which Stitch Fix uses to predict the weather in the customer's location), and many other data points. Stitch Fix has found that the weather is an important variable in predicting what people wear during different seasons.

Stitch Fix also uses images from social media and other sources to track emerging fashion trends and evolving customer preferences. With the client's permission, the company's data scientists augment data obtained from client questionnaires by scanning images on customers' Pinterest boards and other social media websites, analyzing them, and using the resulting insights to develop a deeper understanding of each customer's sense of style.

The second set of data involves the firm's merchandise. For any given item from the more than 1,000 brands that it carries, Stitch Fix gathers 100 to 150 data points, ranging from sleeve length to color. Algorithms then use both sets of data to match a client to the firm's best-suited merchandise.

Over time, the algorithms learn from the customers, based on feedback the customers provide. To gather feedback, the retailer captures customer comments in text boxes. Natural language processing algorithms analyze these comments to further refine the matching algorithms.

Matching the right stylist with the right customer. At Stitch Fix, human stylists finalize the clothing selections and even write personal notes describing how the client might accessorize the items for a particular occasion and how to pair them with other clothing in his or her closet. To match stylists with customers, Stitch Fix calculates a match score between each available stylist and each client who has requested a shipment. This score takes into account the history between the client and the stylist (if any) as well as the similarities between the client's preferences and those of the stylist.

One of Stitch Fix's stylists then reviews the data and chooses five items to include in a customer's "fix" (box of items). In addition, the company treats returns as valuable data points. Stitch Fix's stylists study the negative feedback in a customer's comments to better discern her or his style or an item's description.

POM *Optimize production and logistics.* One challenge that Stitch Fix faces is managing inventory while selling so many different pieces of clothing and pairs of shoes. A traditional retailer must largely guess how many pairs of jeans it will sell at the start of a season and then place an order. In contrast, Stitch Fix can be more reactive, thereby limiting its inventory risk. That is, Stitch Fix can order based on a customer order—the pull model—rather than order on the basis of a forecast—the push model.

The algorithms are a tremendous help in the ordering process. For instance, Stitch Fix can make predictions based on how many customers are buying pants and then instruct the manufacturers to produce particular styles, colors, or patterns when it places an order.

Algorithms calculate a cost function for each Stitch Fix warehouse based on data about its location relative to a client and how well the inventories in the various warehouses match the client's needs. In this way, algorithms reduce transportation costs.

Designing new styles. The fashion industry has been built around creative designers. At Stitch Fix, algorithms identify attributes of clothing that clients are likely to accept. The retailer then works with human designers to refine these attributes and ultimately offer new styles that are tailored for particular client segments who tend to be underserved by other brands.

In August 2017, Stitch Fix began to offer more than 100 new contemporary brands including Theory, Steven Alan, Todd Snyder, Kate Spade, and Rebecca Minkoff, with pieces ranging in price from $100 to $600. The company sourced these brands in response to customer requests for more well-known brand names and higher-quality fabrics, such as leather and cashmere. Providing these new brands enables the company to attract new customers who may have found the company's previous offerings too basic.

Based on data provided by its customers, Stitch Fix is able to offer exclusive styles. For example, Paige Denim has designed a petite line for Stitch Fix because the retailer already knows which customers might be interested based on data regarding size and price preferences that the company has collected. These targeted collections are one of the many benefits that Stitch Fix can offer brands, along with awareness, discovery, and matching for customers who may not be familiar with a certain label but have expressed interest in similar products. Stitch Fix has its own exclusive brand of children's clothing, Rumi + Ryder.

Stitch Fix does face stiff competition. MM. LaFleur (**www.mmlafleur .com**) for professional women, Dia & Co. (**www.dia.com**) for plus sizes, and Rocksbox (**www.rocksbox.com**), which sells only jewelry, are all operating in this space. In addition, Rent the Runway (**www .renttherunway.com**) has been rolling out its "Unlimited" subscription. Stitch Fix for Men competes directly with Trunk Club, owned by Nordstrom. (Interestingly, Trunk Club entered the women's category in 2016.) Instagram has enabled in-app checkout for its shoppable posts, and Pinterest offers shoppable pins and recommendations like a personal stylist.

Amazon offers a program called Prime Wardrobe that allows people to order clothing—from 3 to 15 items at a time—without actually buying it. Amazon also provides an AI-powered tool called StyleSnap that helps customers find clothes to buy. Users can take a picture or upload an image, and StyleSnap will use machine learning to "match the look in the photo" and find similar items for sale on Amazon.

Stitch Fix is one of the few major success stories in the subscription shopping marketplace. Just prior to the COVID-19 pandemic, the firm had more than 8,000 employees, and it operated five clothing warehouses across the United States. In June 2020 Stitch Fix announced that it would lay off 1,400 stylists based in California. However, the retailer planned to hire 2,000 stylists in lower-priced U.S. locations such as Dallas, Minneapolis, and Austin.

Stitch Fix continues to explore new opportunities. For example, the company's Style Pass is an invitation-only feature that costs $49, lasts for an entire year, and waives all of a member's styling fees for that year. Furthermore, the cost of the Style Pass is automatically deducted from the member's next Stitch Fix purchase.

Stitch Fix is now analyzing how multiple clothing items look together in outfits. In February 2020, the retailer launched a new feature, called Shop Your Looks, that suggests items that "go" with a piece of clothing previously purchased through Stitch Fix, rather than leaving that choice to their stylist.

To make Shop Your Looks work, the retailer turned to "outfit cards" that stylists create about each item that goes out in a client's box. Each card illustrates how a singular piece could be styled into a complete outfit, using data about a client's personal preferences.

To analyze the data from a huge number of cards, Stitch Fix built an "outfit picker" tool that asks Stitch Fix's stylists, as well as members of the merchandising and creative teams, to create outfits based on various prompts, such as "date night outfit" or "business meeting outfit." Each prompt starts with a single item and then mixes-and-matches items from Stitch Fix's inventory.

This growing database of complete outfits provided the data for a machine-learning model that uncovers patterns to predict which items go together. Several of the algorithmically generated outfits appear for each item a client purchases. Each outfit combination is personalized for each client. Stitch Fix updates these outfit options based on inventory, new data, and new styles. The options feed into Style Shuffle, an app where clients can vote yes or no on complete outfits, providing Stitch Fix with even more data to refine its models.

In June 2020 Stitch Fix launched its Direct Buy program. Here, customers who have not yet purchased an item from the retailer can fill out their style profile and shop on Stitch Fix as they would on a traditional e-commerce site.

How successful is Stitch Fix? For its 2019 fiscal year, Stitch Fix reported revenue of $1.6 billion, an increase of 29 percent over 2018, with net income of $37 million. As of September 2020, the retailer had 3.5 million clients and claimed that nearly 40 percent of them spend more than half of their annual apparel budget on its collections.

Sources: Compiled from J. Ballard, "Stitch Fix Is about to Turn on the Jets with Its Direct Buy Service," *The Motley Fool*, June 14, 2020; P. Wahba, "Stitch Fix's New Growth Strategy: Letting Non-Clients Shop Directly, Too," *Fortune*, June 8, 2020; L. Kolodny, "Stitch Fix Is Laying off 1,400 Employees in California, and Plans to Hire in Lower-Cost U.S. Cities," *CNBC*, June 1, 2020; D. Howland, "Stitch Fix Officially Launches 'Shop Your Looks,"

Retail Dive, February 13, 2020; A. Pardes, "Need Some Fashion Advice? Just Ask the Algorithm," *Wired*, September 12, 2019; P. Wahba, "Stitch Fix Is Testing New Ways to Generate Revenue," *Fortune*, July 15, 2019; J. Kowaleski, "Stitch Fix's Unbelievable Opportunity that No One Is Talking About," *Seeking Alpha*, June 19, 2019; J. Vincent, "Amazon Launches AI-Powered 'Shazam for Clothes' Fashion Search," *The Verge*, June 5, 2019; A. Pardes, "Instagram's New Shopping Feature Makes It a Digital Mall," *Wired*, March 19, 2019; "What Not to Wear: How Algorithms Are Taking the Uncertainty Out of Fashion," *Forbes*, July 17, 2018; T. Lien, "With Personalized Styling and Now Kids Clothing, Stitch Fix Looks to Avoid the Pitfalls of Subscription Boxes," *Los Angeles Times*, July 10, 2018; L. Varon, "Amazon Prime Wardrobe Won't Kill Subscription Boxes—Bad Strategies Will," *Internet Retailer*, June 21, 2018; Z. Stambor, "Amazon Answer to Stitch Fix Launches to All U.S. Prime Members," *Internet Retailer*, June 20, 2018; E. Winkler, "Is Stitch Fix the Netflix of Fashion?" *Wall Street Journal*, June 7, 2018; M. Lynley, "Stitch Fix Blows Out Wall Street's Expectations and Announces the Launch of Stitch Fix Kids," *TechCrunch*, June 7, 2018; B. Marr, "Stitch Fix: The Amazing Use Case of Using Artificial Intelligence in Fashion Retail," *Forbes*, May 25, 2018; L. Hirsch, "Stitch Fix Prices IPO of 8 Million Shares at $15, Below Expectations," *CNBC*, November 16, 2017; C. Fernandez, "Stitch Fix Introduces over 100 Contemporary Brands," *Business of Fashion*, August 22, 2017; N. Wingfield, "Amazon Will Let Customers Try on Clothes before Buying," *New York Times*, June 20, 2017; T. Lien, "Stitch Fix Founder Built One of the Few Successful E-Commerce Subscription Services," *Seattle Times*, June 19, 2017; M. Merced and K. Benner, "As Department Stores Close, Stitch Fix Expands Online," *New York Times*, May 10, 2017; S. Maheshwari, "Stitch Fix and the New Science behind What Women Want to Wear," *BuzzFeed*, September 24, 2014; **www.stitchfix.com**, accessed September 13, 2020.

Questions

1. Describe the descriptive analytics applications of Stitch Fix's business model.

2. Describe the predictive analytics applications of Stitch Fix's business model.

3. Which companies and industries are in danger of being disrupted by Stitch Fix? (Hint: will Stitch Fix change the way that women and men buy clothes?)

CHAPTER 13

Acquiring Information Systems and Applications

CHAPTER OUTLINE	LEARNING OBJECTIVES
13.1 Planning for and Justifying IT Applications	**13.1** Explain the different cost–benefit analyses that companies must take into account when they formulate an IT strategic plan.
13.2 Strategies for Acquiring IT Applications	**13.2** Discuss the four business decisions that companies must make when they acquire new applications.
13.3 Traditional Systems Development Life Cycle	**13.3** Enumerate the primary tasks and the importance of each of the six processes involved in the systems development life cycle.
13.4 Alternative Methods and Tools for Systems Development	**13.4** Describe alternative development methods and the tools that augment these methods.

Opening Case

MIS **Updating the Census After 230 Years**

The U.S. Constitution requires a census every ten years. The first census was completed in 1790 and the data collection technology remained relatively unchanged for the next 210 years.

The census determines each state's representation in Congress and guides the allocation of as much as $1.5 trillion a year in federal funds. Census data is also crucial to a broad array of research conducted by government agencies, academics, and businesses. These organizations rely on accurate demographic statistics to develop marketing plans, choose locations for factories or stores, as well as a vast array of other applications and projects.

The idea of a census sounds deceptively simple: count everybody in the country and count them in the right place. However, accomplishing a complete and accurate count of the estimated 330 million people living in about 140 million households in the United States is an enormous undertaking. The coronavirus pandemic complicated the 2020 census, largely because the Census Bureau (**www.census.gov**) lost many door-to-door workers (called enumerators) from fear of the virus.

In preparation for the 2010 census, the bureau tried to implement a handheld device for data collection, but ultimately scrapped the idea due to "mission creep" and missed deadlines. *Mission creep* is the gradual or incremental expansion of a project beyond its original scope and goals.

In 2020, it was time for the census to join the digital age. The goal of the 2020 census was to have as many people as possible respond via a website. There were several reasons for the digital transformation of the census. Since 2010, access to broadband Internet via smartphones had dramatically increased. Additionally, the coronavirus pandemic forced Americans to do more online shopping, increasing public trust in online systems. For people who did not respond on the website, enumerators (people hired to travel to specific household addresses for information gathering) would go door-to-door to complete the census.

The Census Bureau had many issues to address concerning the development or acquisition of a platform to safely, securely, and accurately count the U.S. population. Economically, what could they afford without public backlash? Technically, what could they (or their vendors) accomplish? Behaviorally, if they built a website, would users utilize it? Regardless of where the data was collected, could it be transmitted and stored securely to ensure the data's accuracy? All these questions had to be answered to provide an accurate, secure, and efficient count of the U.S. population in line with the U.S. Constitution.

Failure could lead to poorly secured data vulnerable to hackers who could manipulate demographic figures for various nefarious purposes. As just one example, bad actors could add or subtract Congressional seats allocated to states by altering their official population statistics.

One alternative was to develop the system in-house or (more accurately) continue developing a system in-house. The bureau already had a workable system for data collection, built by in-house staff. Starting in 2014, small teams had developed prototypes for online responses and mobile apps that seemed to work. The online response prototype, known as Primus, had been built at little cost beyond the half-dozen or so computer programmers' salaries. The bureau used Primus in several small, real-world surveys and the system seemed to work adequately.

However, after considering alternatives, in 2016 the Bureau chose to go with an outside contractor, Pegasystems (**www.pega.com**). The bureau said the firm's product, a "commercial off-the-shelf solution," would work with minimal alterations. Pegasystems would do what Primus and the in-house mobile apps could do, but cheaper, with an estimated price tag of $84.5 million, compared to the $127 million the bureau forecasted for completing the in-house system. Pegasystems would also supply other vital functions, such as transferring user responses to data storage. By 2019, the project faced serious reliability and security problems, and its projected cost had doubled to $167 million.

In 2018 attackers with Internet Protocol addresses from Russia hacked the Pegasystems-built website. Intruders bypassed a firewall and accessed restricted parts of the system. The incident did not result in system damage or stolen data, but it raised alarms among census security staff about the ability of the bureau to defend the system against more sophisticated cyberattacks.

After spending more than an estimated $167 million with Pegasystems, the bureau decided to deploy Primus, the in-house system. The change came just weeks before the decennial survey went live.

Concerns mounted among experts about both the cost and security of what was to be America's first online census.

The bureau did not shelve Pegasystems' iPhone app. Unfortunately, it appears that the bureau did not thoroughly test iPhone and the app in the field. For instance, the iPhone 8s that many of the more than 500,000 field workers received for inputting data did not have the battery life to last an eight-hour shift.

Enumerators reported frequent crashes, clunky functionality, and other problems with the app that made data collection slow and tedious. Additionally, the system would not share notes from one enumerator to another. Sometimes these notes refer to dangerous addresses where citizens have been unreceptive to being counted, or dog attacks have occurred.

The good news is that the 2020 Census process was completed with no reported hacks or lost data and no security breaches have been reported as of the end of 2020. The bad news is that the process of developing and choosing the census app was slow, expensive, and error prone, illustrating many of the problems associated with system upgrades.

Sources: Compiled from N. Brown, "Special Report: 2020 Census Plagued By Hacking Threats, Cost Overruns," *Reuters*, December 4, 2019; W. Carless, "Census Launches Online After Last-Minute Software Switch," *Revealnews.org*, March 11, 2020; N. Brown, "Census Says Switching Software for U.S. Population Count," *Reuters*, February 13, 2020; W. Carless and D. Rodriguez, "We've All Started Calling It 'The Senseless'," *Revealnews.org*, September 15, 2020; L. La, "Census 2020: Armed With The iPhone 8, Canvassers Are Going Modern," *Cnet.com*, August 4, 2020; C. Miller, "U.S. Census Bureau Teaming Up With Apple To Equip 500,000 Canvassers With iPhone 8," *9TO5Mac.com*, April 1, 2020; www.census.gov, accessed December 15, 2020.

Questions

1. Why did the U.S. Census Bureau first decide to use a vendor rather than its internal system?

2. Why did the bureau switch back to its internal system?

3. Why do you think the bureau deployed the Pegasystems iPhone app rather than using its internal Primus iPhone app?

Introduction

Competitive organizations move as quickly as they can to acquire new information technologies or modify existing ones when they need to improve efficiencies and gain strategic advantage. As you learned from the chapter opening case, problems and pitfalls can arise from the acquisition process.

Today, acquisition goes beyond building new systems in-house, and IT resources involve far more than software and hardware. As you saw in the chapter opening case, the old model in which firms built their own systems is being replaced with a broader perspective of IT resource acquisition that provides companies with a number of options. Now companies must decide which IT tasks will remain in-house, and even whether the entire IT resource should be provided and managed by outside organizations. Regardless of which approach an organization chooses, however, it must be able to manage IT projects adeptly.

In this chapter, you learn about the process of acquiring IT resources from a managerial perspective. This means from *your* perspective, because you will be closely involved in all aspects of acquiring information systems and applications in your organization. In fact, when we mention "users" in this chapter, we are talking about you. You also study the available options for acquiring IT resources and how to evaluate those options. Finally, you learn how organizations plan and justify the acquisition of new information systems.

13.1 Planning for and Justifying IT Applications

Organizations must analyze the need for applications and then justify each purchase in regard to costs and benefits. The need for information systems is usually related to organizational planning and to the analysis of its performance vis-à-vis its competitors. The cost–benefit justification must consider the wisdom of investing in a specific IT application versus spending the funds on alternative projects. This chapter focuses on the formal processes of large organizations. Smaller organizations employ fewer formal processes, or no processes at all. It is important to note, however, that even if a small organization does not have a formal process for planning and justifying IT applications, the steps of a formal process exist for a reason, and they have value. At the very least, decision makers in small organizations should consider each step when they are planning changes in their information systems.

When a company examines its needs and performance, it generates a prioritized list of both existing and potential IT applications, called the **application portfolio**. These are the applications that have to be added, or modified if they already exist.

Author Lecture Videos are available exclusively in *WileyPLUS*.
Apply the Concept activities are available in the Appendix and in *WileyPLUS*.

IT Planning

The planning process for new IT applications begins with an analysis of the *organizational strategic plan*, which is illustrated in **Figure 13.1**. The organization's strategic plan identifies the firm's overall mission, the goals that follow from that mission, and the broad steps required to reach these goals. The strategic planning process modifies the organization's objectives and resources to match its changing markets and opportunities.

The organizational strategic plan and the existing IT architecture provide the inputs in developing the IT strategic plan. The *IT architecture* delineates the way an organization should utilize its information resources to accomplish its mission. It encompasses both the technical and the managerial aspects of information resources. The technical aspects include hardware and operating systems, networking, data management systems, and applications software. The managerial aspects specify how the IT department will be managed, how the functional area managers will be involved, and how IT decisions will be made.

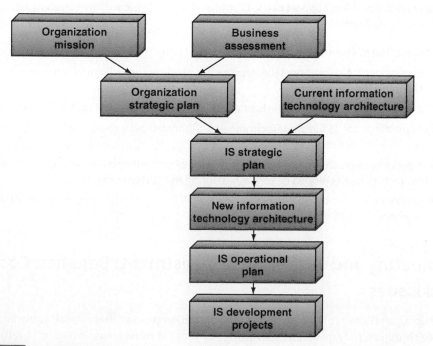

FIGURE 13.1 The information systems planning process.

The **IT strategic plan** is a set of long-range goals that describe the IT infrastructure and identify the major IT initiatives needed to achieve the organization's goals. The IT strategic plan must meet three objectives:

1. *It must be aligned with the organization's strategic plan.* This alignment is critical because the organization's information systems must support the organization's strategies. (Recall the discussion of organizational strategies and information systems in Chapter 2.)

    Consider the example of Nordstrom versus Walmart. An application that improves customer service at a small cost would be considered favorably at Nordstrom, but it would be rejected at Walmart. The reason is that the application would fit in favorably (i.e., align) with Nordstrom's service-at-any-cost strategy. However, it would not fit in well with Walmart's low-cost strategy. You see two department stores, same application, same cost and benefits—but different answers to the question, "Should we develop the application?"

2. *It must provide for an IT architecture that seamlessly networks users, applications, and databases.*

3. *It must efficiently allocate IS development resources among competing projects so that the projects can be completed on time and within budget and still have the required functionality.*

The existing IT architecture is a necessary input into the IT strategic plan because it acts as a constraint on future development efforts. It is not an absolute constraint, however, because the organization can change to a new IT architecture. Companies prefer to avoid this strategy, however, because it is expensive and time consuming.

Consider this example. You have a Mac (Apple) system, and you need a new software application. You search and find several such packages for both Mac and MS Windows. Unfortunately, the best package runs only on Windows. How much better would this package have to be for you to justify switching from Mac to Windows?

One critical component in developing and implementing the IT strategic plan is the **IT steering committee**. This committee, comprised of a group of managers and staff who represent the various organizational units, is created to establish IT priorities and to ensure that the MIS function is meeting the organization's needs. The committee's major tasks are to link corporate strategy with IT strategy, to approve the allocation of resources for the MIS function, and to establish performance measures for the MIS function and ensure they are met. The IT steering committee is important to you because it ensures that you get the information systems and applications that you need to do your job.

After a company has agreed on an IT strategic plan, it next develops the **IS operational plan**. This plan consists of a clear set of projects that the IS department and the functional area managers will execute in support of the IT strategic plan. A typical IS operational plan contains the following elements:

- *Mission:* The mission of the IS function (derived from the IT strategy).
- *IS environment:* A summary of the information needs of the individual functional areas and of the organization as a whole.
- *Objectives of the IS function:* The best current estimate of the goals of the IS function.
- *Constraints on the IS function:* Technological, financial, personnel, and other resource limitations on the IS function.
- *The application portfolio:* A prioritized inventory of present applications and a detailed plan of projects to be developed or continued during the current year.
- *Resource allocation and project management:* A listing of who is going to do what, how, and when.

Evaluating and Justifying IT Investment: Benefits, Costs, and Issues

Developing an IT plan is the first step in the acquisition process. Because all companies have limited resources, they must justify investing resources in some areas, including IT, rather than in others. Essentially, justifying IT investment involves calculating the costs, assessing the benefits (values), and comparing the two. This comparison is frequently referred to as cost–benefit analysis. Cost–benefit analysis is not a simple task.

Assessing the Costs.
Calculating the dollar value of IT investments is not as simple as it may seem. One of the major challenges that companies face is to allocate fixed costs among different IT projects. *Fixed costs* are those costs that remain the same regardless of any change in the company's activity level. Fixed IT costs include infrastructure costs and the costs associated with IT services and IT management. For example, the salary of the IT director is fixed, and adding one more application will not change it.

Another complication is that the costs of a system do not end when the system is installed. Rather, costs for maintaining, debugging, and improving the system can accumulate over many years. This is a critical point because organizations sometimes fail to anticipate these costs when they make the investment.

A dramatic example of unanticipated expenses was the Year 2000 (Y2K) reprogramming projects, which cost organizations worldwide billions of dollars. In the 1960s, computer memory was very expensive. To save money, programmers coded the "year" in the date field 19_ _, instead of _ _ _ _. With the "1" and the "9" hard-coded in the computer program, only the last two digits varied, so computer programs needed less memory. However, this process meant that when the year 2000 rolled around, computers would display the year as 1900. This programming technique could have caused serious problems with financial applications, insurance applications, and countless other apps.

Programmers who wanted to avoid the Y2K bug had two options: entirely rewrite the code or adopt a quick fix called windowing, which would treat all dates from 00 to 20 as from the 2000s rather than the 1900s. As estimated 80 percent of computers fixed in 1999 used the quicker, cheaper option. The theory was that these systems would no longer be in use in 2020, but many are still operational.

The Year 2020 bug (Y2020) is a lingering side effect of attempts to fix the Y2K, or millennium bug. Programmers chose 1920 to 2020 as the standard window because of the significance of the midpoint, 1970. Many programming languages and systems manage dates and times as seconds from 1970/01/01, also called Unix time.

As of January 1, 2020, the systems that used the quick fix have rolled back to 1920. Utility company bills have reportedly been produced with the erroneous date of 1920, while tens of thousands of parking meters in New York City have declined credit card transactions. Thousands of cash registers manufactured by Polish firm Novitus have been unable to print receipts due to a problem with the register's clock. *WWE 2K20*, a professional wrestling videogame, stopped working at midnight on January 1, 2020. Within 24 hours, the game's developers, 2K, issued a downloadable fix.

The Y2K and the Y2020 examples illustrate the point that database design choices tend to affect the organization for a long time. As the twenty-first century approached, no one was still using hardware or software from the 1960s (other than a few legacy applications). Database design choices made in the 1960s, however, were often still in effect decades after the companies implemented them.

Assessing the Benefits.
Evaluating the benefits of IT projects is typically even more complex than calculating their costs. Benefits may be more difficult to quantify, especially because many of them are intangible (for example, improved customer or partner relations and improved decision making). As an employee, you will probably be asked for input about the intangible benefits that an IS provides for you.

The fact that organizations use IT for multiple purposes further complicates benefit analysis. To obtain a return from an IT investment, the company must also implement the technology successfully. In reality, many systems are not implemented on time, within budget, or with all of the features originally envisioned for them. Also, the proposed system may be "cutting edge." In these cases, there may be no precedent for identifying the types of financial payback the company can expect.

Conducting the Cost–Benefit Analysis.   After a company has assessed the costs and benefits of IT investments, it must compare them. You have studied, or will study, cost–benefit analyses in more detail in your finance courses. The point is that real-world business problems do not come in neatly wrapped packages labeled "this is a finance problem" or "this is an IS problem." Rather, business problems span multiple functional areas.

There is no uniform strategy for conducting a cost–benefit analysis. Rather, an organization can perform this task in several ways. Here you see four common approaches: (1) net present value, (2) return on investment, (3) breakeven analysis, and (4) the business case approach.

1. Analysts use the *net present value (NPV)* method to convert future values of benefits to their present-value equivalent by "discounting" them at the organization's cost of funds. They can then compare the present value of the future benefits with the cost required to achieve those benefits to determine whether the benefits exceed the costs.

2. *Return on investment (ROI)* measures management's effectiveness in generating profits with its available assets. ROI is calculated by dividing the net income generated by a project by the average assets invested in the project. ROI is a percentage, and the higher the percentage return, the better.

3. *Breakeven analysis* determines the point at which the cumulative dollar value of the benefits from a project equals the investment made in the project.

4. In the *business case approach*, system developers write a business case to justify funding one or more specific applications or projects. IS professionals will be a major source of input when business cases are developed because these cases describe what you do, how you do it, and how a new system could better support you.

Before you go on...

1. What are some problems associated with assessing the costs of IT?
2. Why are the intangible benefits from IT so difficult to evaluate?
3. Describe the NPV, ROI, breakeven analysis, and business case approaches.

13.2 Strategies for Acquiring IT Applications

Author Lecture Videos are available exclusively in *WileyPLUS*.
Apply the Concept activities are available in the Appendix and in *WileyPLUS*.

After a company has justified an IT investment, it must then decide how to pursue it. As with cost–benefit analyses, there are several options for acquiring IT applications. To select the best option, companies must make a series of business decisions. The fundamental decisions are the following:

- *How much computer code does the company want to write?* A company can choose to use a totally prewritten application (write no computer code), customize a prewritten application (write some computer code), or custom write an entire application (write all new computer code).

- *How will the company pay for the application?* Once the company has decided how much computer code to write, it must decide how to pay for it. With prewritten applications or customized prewritten applications, companies can buy them or lease them. With totally custom applications, companies use internal funding.

- *Where will the application run?* The next decision is whether to run the application on the company's platform or on someone else's platform. In other words, the company can employ either a software-as-a-service vendor or an application service provider. (You will examine these options later in this chapter.)

- *Where will the application originate?* Prewritten applications can be open-source software or they can come from a vendor. The company may choose to customize prewritten open-source applications or prewritten proprietary applications from vendors. Furthermore, it may customize applications in-house, or it can outsource the customization. Finally, it can write totally custom applications in-house, or it can outsource this process.

In the following sections, you will find more details on the variety of options that companies looking to acquire applications can select from. A good rule of thumb is that an organization should consider all feasible acquisition methods in light of its business requirements. You will learn about the following acquisition methods:

- Purchase a prewritten application
- Customize a prewritten application
- Lease the application
- Use application service providers and software-as-a-service vendors
- Use open-source software
- Use outsourcing
- Employ continuous development
- Employ custom development

Purchase a Prewritten Application

Many commercial software packages contain the standard features required by IT applications. Therefore, purchasing an existing package can be a cost-effective and time-saving strategy compared with custom-developing the application in-house. Nevertheless, a company should carefully consider and plan the buy option to ensure that the selected package contains all of the features necessary to address the company's current and future needs. Otherwise, these packages can quickly become obsolete. Before a company can perform this process, it must decide which features a suitable package must include.

In reality, a single software package can rarely satisfy all of an organization's needs. For this reason, a company must sometimes purchase multiple packages to fulfill different needs. It then must integrate these packages with one another as well as with its existing software. Table 13.1 summarizes the advantages and limitations of the buy option.

TABLE 13.1   Advantages and Limitations of the Buy Option

Advantages
Many different types of off-the-shelf software are available.
The company can try out the software before purchasing it.
The company can save time by buying rather than building.
The company can know what it is getting before it invests in the product.
Purchased software may eliminate the need to hire personnel specifically dedicated to a project.

Disadvantages
Software may not exactly meet the company's needs.
Software may be difficult or impossible to modify, or it may require huge business process changes to implement.
The company will not have control over software improvements and new versions.
Purchased software can be difficult to integrate with existing systems.
Vendors may discontinue a product or go out of business.
The software is controlled by another company with its own priorities and business considerations.
The purchasing company lacks intimate knowledge about how and why the software functions as it does.

Customize a Prewritten Application

Customizing existing software is an especially attractive option if the software vendor allows the company to modify the application to meet its needs. However, this option may not be attractive in cases when customization is the *only* method of providing the necessary flexibility to address the company's needs. It is also not the best strategy when the software is either very expensive or likely to become obsolete in a short time. Furthermore, customizing a prewritten application can be extremely difficult, particularly for large, complex applications.

Lease the Application

Compared with the buy option and the option to develop applications in-house, the lease option can save a company both time and money. Of course, leased packages (like purchased packages) may not exactly fit the company's application requirements. However, as noted, vendor software generally includes the features that are most commonly needed by organizations in a given industry. Again, the company will decide which features are necessary.

Interested companies commonly apply the 80/20 rule when they evaluate vendor software. Put simply, if the software meets 80 percent of the company's needs, then the company should seriously consider modifying its business processes so that it can use the remaining 20 percent. Many times, this is a better long-term solution than modifying the vendor software. Otherwise, the company will have to customize the software every time the vendor releases an updated version.

Leasing can be especially attractive to small and medium-sized enterprises (SMEs) that cannot afford major investments in IT software. Large companies may also prefer to lease packages to test potential IT solutions before committing to major investments. A company that does not employ sufficient IT personnel with the appropriate skills for developing custom IT applications may also choose to lease instead of develop the software it needs in-house. Even those companies that employ in-house experts may not be able to afford the long wait for strategic applications to be developed in-house. Therefore, they lease (or buy) applications from external resources to establish a quicker presence in the market.

Leasing can be executed in one of three ways. The first way is to lease the application from a software developer, install it, and run it on the company's platform. The vendor can assist with the installation and will frequently offer to contract for the support and maintenance of the system. Many conventional applications are leased this way.

The other two options involve leasing an application and running it on the vendor's platform. Organizations can accomplish this process by using an application service provider or a software-as-a-service vendor.

Application Service Providers and Software-as-a-Service Vendors

An **application service provider (ASP)** is an agent or a vendor who assembles the software needed by enterprises and then packages it with services such as development, operations, and maintenance. The customer then accesses these applications through the Internet. **Figure 13.2** illustrates the operation of an ASP. Note that the ASP hosts both an application and a database for each customer.

Software-as-a-service (SaaS) is a method of delivering software in which a vendor hosts the applications and provides them as a service to customers over a network, typically the Internet. Customers do not own the software. Rather, they pay for using it. SaaS eliminates the need for customers to install and run the application on their own computers. Therefore, SaaS customers save the expense (money, time, IT staff) of buying, operating, and maintaining the

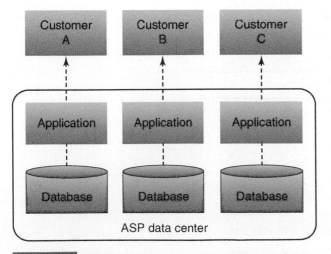

FIGURE 13.2 **Operation of an application service provider.**

software. For example, Salesforce (**www.salesforce.com**), a well-known SaaS provider for customer relationship management (CRM) software solutions, provides these advantages for its customers. **Figure 13.3** displays the operation of a SaaS vendor. Note that the vendor hosts an application that multiple customers can use. The vendor also hosts a database that is partitioned for each customer to protect the privacy and security of each customer's data.

At this point, companies have made the first three decisions and must now decide where to obtain the application. Recall that in general, for prewritten applications, companies can use open-source software or obtain the software from a vendor. For customized prewritten applications, they can customize open-source software or customize vendor software. For totally customized applications, they can write the software in-house, or they can outsource the process.

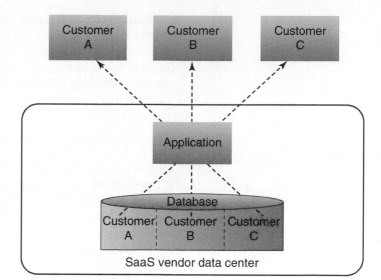

FIGURE 13.3 **Operation of a software-as-a-service vendor.**

Use Open-Source Software

Organizations obtain a license to implement an open-source software product and either use it as is, customize it, or develop applications with it. Unless the company is one of the few that want to tinker with their source code, open-source applications are basically the same as a proprietary application except for licensing, payment, and support. Open-source software is really an alternative source of applications rather than a conceptually different development option. (We discuss open-source software in Technology Guide 2.)

Outsourcing

Acquiring IT applications from outside contractors or external organizations is called **outsourcing**. Companies can use outsourcing in many situations. For example, they might want to experiment with new IT technologies without making a substantial up-front investment. They also might use outsourcing to obtain access to outside experts. One disadvantage of outsourcing is that companies must frequently place their valuable corporate data under the control of the outsourcing vendor.

Several types of vendors offer services for creating and operating IT systems, including e-commerce applications. Many software companies, from IBM to Oracle, offer a range of outsourcing services for developing, operating, and maintaining IT applications. IT outsourcers, such as EDS, offer a variety of services. Also, the large CPA companies and management consultants—for example, Accenture—offer outsourcing services.

For example, Philip Morris International (the non-U.S. operation of Philip Morris) outsourced its IT infrastructure management to Indian services firm Wipro. The companies concluded a five-year contract in which Wipro manages the tobacco company's applications and IT using Wipro's cloud-based management platform. (We discuss cloud computing in Technology Guide 3.) The contract is reported to be worth some $35 million.

Some companies outsource offshore, particularly in India and China. *Offshoring* can save money, but it includes risks as well. The risks depend on which services are being offshored. If a company is offshoring application development, then the major risk is poor communication between users and developers. In response to these risks, some companies are bringing outsourced jobs back in-house, a process called *reverse outsourcing*, or *insourcing*.

Continuous Development

Continuous application development automates and improves the process of software delivery. In essence, a software development project is not viewed as having a defined product, with development stopped when the product is implemented. Rather, a software development project is viewed as constantly changing in response to changing business conditions and in response to user acceptance.

Continuous application development is the process of steadily adding new computer code to a software project when the new computer code is written and tested. Each development team member submits new code when it is finished. Automated testing is performed on the code to ensure that it functions within the software project. Continuous code submission provides developers with immediate feedback from users and status updates for the software on which they are working.

Employ Custom Development

Another option is to custom build an application. Companies can either perform this operation in-house or outsource the process. Although custom development is usually more time consuming and costly than buying or leasing, it often produces a better fit with the organization's specific requirements.

The development process starts when the IT steering committee (discussed previously in this chapter), having received suggestions for a new system, decides it is worth exploring. These suggestions come from users (you in the near future). Understanding this process will help you obtain the systems that you need. Conversely, not understanding this process will reduce your chances, because other people who understand it better will make suggestions that use up available resources.

As the company goes through the development process, its mindset changes. In systems investigation (the first stage of the traditional systems development life cycle), the organization is trying to decide whether to build something. Everyone knows it may or may not be built. In the later stages of the development process, the organization is committed to building the application. Although a project can be canceled at any time, this change in attitude is still important.

The basic, backbone methodology for custom development is the systems development life cycle (SDLC), which you will read about in the next section. Section 14.4 examines the methodologies that complement the SDLC: prototyping, joint application development, integrated computer-assisted systems development tools, and rapid application development. You will also consider four other methodologies: agile development, end-user development, component-based development, and object-oriented development.

Before you go on...

1. Describe the four fundamental business decisions that organizations must make when they acquire information systems.
2. Discuss each of the seven development methods in this section with regard to the four business decisions that organizations must make.

13.3 Traditional Systems Development Life Cycle

The **systems development life cycle (SDLC)** is the traditional systems development method that organizations use for large-scale IT projects. The SDLC is a structured framework that consists of sequential processes by which information systems are developed. For our purposes (see **Figure 13.4**), we identify six processes, each of which consists of clearly defined tasks:

1. Systems investigation
2. Systems analysis
3. Systems design
4. Programming and testing
5. Implementation
6. Operation and maintenance

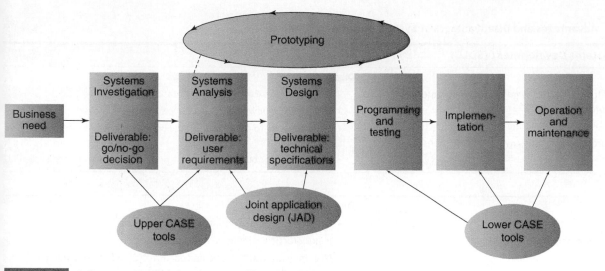

FIGURE 13.4   A six-stage systems development life cycle with supporting tools.

Alternative SDLC models contain more or fewer stages. The flow of tasks, however, remains largely the same. When problems occur in any phase of the SDLC, developers often must go back to previous phases.

Systems development projects produce desired results through team efforts. Development teams typically include users, systems analysts, programmers, and technical specialists. *Users* are employees from all functional areas and levels of the organization who interact with the system, either directly or indirectly. **Systems analysts** are IS professionals who specialize in analyzing and designing information systems. **Programmers** are IS professionals who either modify existing computer programs or write new programs to satisfy user requirements. **Technical specialists** are experts on a certain type of technology, such as databases or telecommunications. The **systems stakeholders** include everyone who is affected by changes in a company's information systems—for example, users and managers. All stakeholders are typically involved in systems development at various times and in varying degrees.

Figure 13.5 indicates that users have high involvement in the early stages of the SDLC, lower involvement in the programming and testing stage, and higher involvement in the later stages. **Table 13.2** discusses the advantages and disadvantages of the SDLC.

Systems Investigation

The initial stage in a traditional SDLC is systems investigation. Systems development professionals agree that the more time they invest in (1) understanding the business problem to be solved, (2) specifying the technical options for the systems, and (3) anticipating the problems they are likely to encounter during development, the greater the chances of success. For these reasons, **systems investigation** addresses *the business problem* (or business opportunity) by means of the feasibility study.

The primary task in the systems investigation stage is the feasibility study. Organizations have three basic solutions to any business problem relating to an information system: (1) do nothing and continue to use the existing system unchanged,

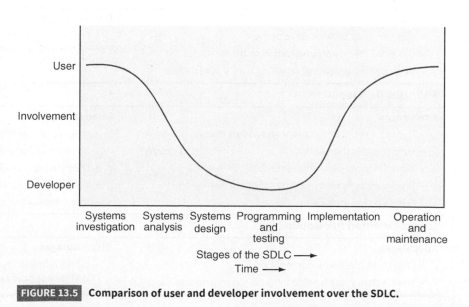

FIGURE 13.5   Comparison of user and developer involvement over the SDLC.

TABLE 13.2 Advantages and Disadvantages of System Acquisition Methods

Traditional Systems Development (SDLC)

Advantages	Disadvantages
• Forces staff to systematically go through every step in a structured process • Enforces quality by maintaining standards • Has lower probability of missing important issues in collecting user requirements	• May produce excessive documentation • Users may be unwilling or unable to study the approved specifications • Takes too long to progress from the original ideas to a working system • Users have trouble describing requirements for a proposed system

Prototyping

Advantages	Disadvantages
• Helps clarify user requirements • Helps verify the feasibility of the design • Promotes genuine user participation • Promotes close working relationship between systems developers and users • Works well for ill-defined problems • May produce part of the final system	• May encourage inadequate problem analysis • Is not practical with large number of users • User may not want to give up the prototype when the system is completed • May generate confusion about whether the system is complete and maintainable • System may be built quickly, which can result in lower quality

Joint Application Design

Advantages	Disadvantages
• Involves many users in the development process • Saves time • Generates greater user support for the new system • Improves the quality of the new system • The new system is easier to implement • The new system has lower training costs	• Difficult to get all users to attend the JAD meeting • The JAD approach is subject to all of the problems associated with any group meeting

Integrated Computer-Assisted Software Engineering

Advantages	Disadvantages
• Can produce systems with a longer effective operational life • Can produce systems that closely meet user requirements • Can speed up the development process • Can produce systems that are more flexible and adaptable to changing business conditions • Can produce excellent documentation	• Systems are often more expensive to build and maintain • The process requires more extensive and accurate definition of user requirements • It is difficult to customize the end product

Rapid Application Development

Advantages	Disadvantages
• Can speed up systems development • Users are intensively involved from the start • Improves the process of rewriting legacy applications	• Produces functional components of final systems, but not the final systems themselves

End-User Development

Advantages	Disadvantages
• Bypasses the IS department and avoids delays • User controls the application and can change it as needed • Directly meets user requirements • Promotes increased user acceptance of new system • Frees up IT resources	• May eventually require maintenance from IS department • Documentation may be inadequate • Leads to poor quality control • System may not have adequate interfaces to existing systems • May create lower-quality systems

Object-Oriented Development

Advantages	Disadvantages
• Objects model real-world entities • New systems may be able to reuse some computer code	• Works best with systems of more limited scope (i.e., with systems that do not have huge numbers of objects)

(2) modify or enhance the existing system, or (3) develop a new system. The **feasibility study** analyzes which of these three solutions best fits the particular business problem. It also provides a rough assessment of the project's technical, economic, and behavioral feasibility.

- *Technical feasibility* determines whether the company can develop or otherwise acquire the hardware, software, and communications components needed to solve the business problem. Technical feasibility also determines whether the organization can use its existing technology to achieve the project's performance objectives.
- *Economic feasibility* determines whether the project is an acceptable financial risk and, if so, whether the organization has the necessary time and money to successfully complete the project. You have already learned about the commonly used methods to determine economic feasibility: NPV, ROI, breakeven analysis, and the business case approach.
- *Behavioral feasibility* addresses the human issues of the systems development project. You will be heavily involved in this aspect of the feasibility study.

After the feasibility analysis is completed, a go/no-go decision is reached by the steering committee if there is one or by top management in the absence of a committee. The go/no-go decision does not depend solely on the feasibility analysis. Organizations often have more feasible projects than they can fund. Therefore, the firm must prioritize the feasible projects and pursue those with the highest priority. Unfunded feasible projects may not be presented to the IT department at all. These projects therefore contribute to the *hidden backlog*, which are projects that the IT department is not aware of.

If the decision is no-go, then the project is either put on the shelf until conditions are more favorable or it is discarded. If the decision is go, then the project proceeds, and the systems analysis phase begins.

Systems Analysis

Once a development project has the necessary approvals from all participants, the systems analysis stage begins. **Systems analysis** is the process whereby systems analysts examine the business problem that the organization plans to solve with an information system.

The primary purpose of the systems analysis stage is to gather information about the existing system to determine the requirements for an enhanced system or a new system. The end product of this stage, known as the *deliverable*, is a set of *system requirements*.

Arguably, the most difficult task in systems analysis is to identify the specific requirements that the system must satisfy. These requirements are often called *user requirements*, because users (meaning you) provide them. When the systems developers have accumulated the user requirements for the new system, they proceed to the systems design stage.

Systems Design

Systems design describes how the system will resolve the business problem. The deliverable of the systems design phase is the set of *technical system specifications*, which specify the following:

- System outputs, inputs, and user interfaces
- Hardware, software, databases, telecommunications, personnel, and procedures
- A blueprint of how these components are integrated

When the system specifications are approved by all participants, they are "frozen." That is, they should not be changed. Adding functions after the project has been initiated causes **scope creep**, in which the time frame and expenses associated with the project expand beyond the agreed-upon limits. Scope creep endangers both the project's budget and its schedule.

Because scope creep is expensive, successful project managers place controls on changes requested by users. These controls help to prevent runaway projects.

Programming and Testing

If the organization decides to construct the software in-house, then programming begins. **Programming** involves translating the design specifications into computer code. This process can be lengthy and time consuming, because writing computer code is as much an art as it is a science. Large-scale systems development projects can involve hundreds of computer programmers who are charged with creating hundreds of thousands of lines of computer code. These projects employ programming teams. The teams often include functional area users, who help the programmers focus on the business problem.

Thorough and continuous testing occurs throughout the programming stage. Testing is the process that assesses whether the computer code will produce the expected and desired results. It is also intended to detect errors, or bugs, in the computer code.

Implementation

Implementation (or *deployment*) is the process of converting from an old computer system to a new one. The conversion process involves organizational change. Only end users can manage organizational change, not the MIS department. The MIS department typically does not have enough credibility with the business users to manage the change process. Organizations use three major conversion strategies: direct, pilot, and phased.

In a **direct conversion**, the old system is cut off and the new system is turned on at a certain point in time. This type of conversion is the least expensive. It is also the riskiest because if the new system does not work as planned, there is no support from the old system. Because of these risks, few systems are implemented using direct conversion.

A **pilot conversion** introduces the new system in one part of the organization, such as in one plant or one functional area. The new system runs for a period of time and is then assessed. If the assessment confirms that the system is working properly, then the system is implemented in other parts of the organization.

A **phased conversion** introduces components of the new system, such as individual modules, in stages. Each module is assessed. If it works properly, then other modules are introduced until the entire new system is operational. Large organizations commonly combine the pilot and phased approaches. That is, they execute a phased conversion using a pilot group for each phase. A fourth strategy is *parallel conversion*, in which the old and new systems operate simultaneously for a time. This strategy is seldom used today. One reason is that parallel conversion is totally impractical when both the old and new systems are online. Imagine that you are completing an order on Amazon, only to be told, "Before your order can be entered here, you must provide all the same information again, in a different form, and on a different set of screens." The results would be disastrous for Amazon. Regardless of the type of implementation process that an organization uses, the new system may not work as advertised. In fact, the new system may cause more problems than the old system that it replaced.

Operation and Maintenance

After the new system is implemented, it will operate for a period of time, until (like the old system it replaced) it no longer meets its objectives. Once the new system's operations are stabilized, the company performs audits to assess the system's capabilities and to determine if it is being used correctly.

Systems require several types of maintenance. The first type is *debugging* the program, a process that continues throughout the life of the system. The second type is *updating* the system to accommodate changes in business conditions. An example is adjusting to new governmental regulations, such as changes in tax rates. These corrections and upgrades usually do not add any new functions. Instead, they simply help the system continue to achieve its objectives. In contrast, the third type of maintenance *adds new functions* to the existing system without disturbing its operation.

13.4 Alternative Methods and Tools for Systems Development

Alternative methods for systems development include joint application design, rapid application development, agile development, and end-user development.

Joint Application Design

Joint application design (JAD) is a group-based tool for collecting user requirements and creating system designs. It is most often used within the systems analysis and systems design stages of the SDLC. JAD involves a group meeting attended by the analysts and all of the users that can be conducted either in person or through the computer. During this meeting, all users jointly define and agree on the systems requirements. This process saves a tremendous amount of time. Table 13.2 lists the advantages and disadvantages of the JAD process.

Rapid Application Development

Rapid application development (RAD) is a systems development method that can combine JAD, prototyping, and integrated computer-assisted software engineering (ICASE) tools (discussed later in this section) to rapidly produce a high-quality system. In the first RAD stage, developers use JAD sessions to collect system requirements. This strategy ensures that users are intensively involved early on. The development process in RAD is iterative; that is, requirements, designs, and the system itself are developed and then undergo a series, or sequence, of improvements. RAD uses ICASE tools to quickly structure requirements and develop prototypes. As the prototypes are developed and refined, users review them in additional JAD sessions. RAD produces the functional components of a final system rather than prototypes. To understand how RAD functions and how it differs from SDLC, see **Figure 13.6**. Table 13.2 highlights the advantages and disadvantages of the RAD process.

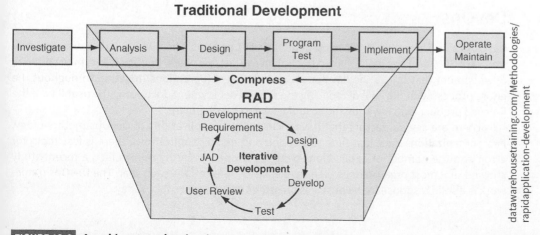

datawarehousetraining.com/Methodologies/rapidapplication-development

FIGURE 13.6   **A rapid prototyping development process versus SDLC.**

Agile Development

Agile development is a software development methodology that delivers functionality in rapid iterations, which are usually measured in weeks. To be successful, this methodology requires frequent communication, development, testing, and delivery. Agile development focuses on rapid development and frequent user contact to create software that addresses the needs of business users. This software does not have to include every possible feature the user will require. Rather, it must meet only the user's more important and immediate needs. It can be updated later to introduce additional functions as they become necessary. The core tenet of agile development is to do only what you have to do to be successful right now.

One type of agile development uses the *scrum approach.* A key principle of scrum is that during a project, users can change their minds about what they want and need. Scrum acknowledges that a development problem cannot be fully understood or defined from the start. Therefore, scrum focuses on maximizing the development team's ability to deliver iterations quickly and to respond effectively to additional user requirements as they emerge.

Scrum contains sets of practices and predefined roles. The primary roles are:

- *Scrum master:* Maintains the processes (typically replaces a project manager)
- *Product owner:* Represents the business users and any other stakeholders in the project
- *Team:* A cross-functional group of about seven people who perform the actual analysis, design, coding, implementation, testing, and so on

Scrum works this way: during each *sprint*—typically a two- to four-week period—the team creates a potentially shippable product increment, such as working and tested software. The set of features that goes into each sprint comes from the product backlog, which is a prioritized set of high-level work requirements to be completed.

The sprint planning meeting determines which backlog items will be addressed during a sprint. During this meeting, the product owner informs the team of the items in the product backlog that he or she wants to be completed. The team members then determine how many of these projects they can commit to during the next sprint, and they record this information in the sprint backlog.

During a sprint, no one is allowed to change the sprint backlog, which means that the requirements are frozen for the sprint. Each sprint must end on time. If the requirements are not completed for any reason, then they are left out and returned to the product backlog. After each sprint is completed, the team demonstrates how to use the software.

An interesting type of agile development is a methodology called *minimum viable product (MVP)* development. Applications developed using MVP methodology have just the required amount of functionality to operate successfully. On the other hand, MVP applications do not have so much functionality (that is, too many features) that the development process takes too long and cost too much.

DevOps

DevOps (a combination of "development" and "operations") is a practice that was first presented in 2009 and has really gained traction in the last few years. DevOps is a form of software development that brings the developers and the users (operations) together throughout the entire process with the goal of reducing the time to deployment, increasing the usability of the finished product, and lowering the cost of new app development.

There are several factors that have increased the applications of DevOps methodology. First, organizations have less time to develop and deploy applications, there is less room for error, and the number of applications being developed is on the rise. In fact, a recent study showed that most organizations plan to release 17 applications each year. The DevOps framework is a solid response to the business pressures organizations face today.

End-User Development

End-user development is an approach in which the organization's end users develop their own applications with little or no formal assistance from the IT department. Table 13.2 lists the advantages and disadvantages of end-user development. Sometimes this form of IT development or acquisition is called **Shadow IT** (also known as *Stealth IT* or *Rogue IT*). While the end-users bypassing the IT department might make it easier for them to adopt the tools that they want to work with, this process also bypasses the security measures that the IT department is trying to enforce. These shadow IT systems can open systems to vulnerabilities and create avenues for criminals to access private company and customer data. As an employee, it is important to carefully consider adopting something that has not been approved by your organization. If your Shadow IT creates a vulnerability that allows a breach, you will probably lose your job!

Tools for Systems Development

Several tools can be used with various systems development methods. These tools include prototyping, integrated computer-assisted software engineering, component-based development, and object-oriented development.

Design Thinking.

Design Thinking is a user-centered approach to application development. As you saw in the discussion of the SDLC, users' needs are considered at the very beginning of the process. And users are considered in all development methodologies. Unfortunately, development teams often move away from users' needs as they move toward the technical development of applications, integrations, implementations, and other considerations. Design Thinking is an approach that, when used in conjunction with other development methodologies, will keep the user's needs front and center, increasing the chances of a successful adoption of the project. There are five steps to the Design Thinking process.

Empathize: Empathy is the ability to see how a situation could feel to another person. Empathy does not mean you agree with the feeling, problem, or situation. Rather, you simply learn to see it as the other person does. In the design process, this helps designers and managers to set aside their own assumptions and feelings in order to see the situation as the person who will be the recipient of the final product. This is critical to successful IT projects and the reason why so many projects today include users in the entire process.

Define: In the Define stage, the problem is defined from the perspective of the user that the developers empathized with in the first stage. The problem is not stated in terms of systems, managerial goals, or corporate strategy. Rather, the focus is kept on the user and how the outcome of the project will change the way they accomplish their tasks.

Ideate: Brainstorming comes in many forms and methods. The important thing at this stage is that ideas are based on stages 1 and 2. Ideas are more likely to move the team toward a successful outcome when they are generated from a well-formed, empathy-based problem statement. There is no magic potion, except that all ideas have to stay aligned with the first two stages.

Prototype and Test: Stages 4 and 5 of Design Thinking can incorporate any of the development tools discussed below and any of the methods presented above. SDLC, RAD, JAD, and Agile all include users, but not to the extent or in the fashion of the design thinking process.

Design Thinking is presented here as a linear process, but in practice, it is very non-linear. The goal is to keep these considerations at the top of your mind during the entire project. For example, as you prototype and test a program, you will likely deepen your empathy for the users which can improve ideas and future iterations of the application.

Prototyping.

The **prototyping** approach defines an initial list of user requirements, builds a model of the system, and then refines the system in several iterations based on users' feedback. Developers do not try to obtain a complete set of user specifications for the system at the outset, and they do not plan to develop the system all at once. Instead, they quickly develop a smaller version of the system known as a **prototype**. A prototype can take two forms. In some cases, it contains only the components of the new system that are of most interest to the users. In other cases, it is a small-scale working model of the entire system.

Users make suggestions for improving the prototype based on their experiences with it. The developers then review the prototype with the users and use their suggestions to refine it. This process continues through several iterations until the users approve the system or it becomes apparent that the system cannot meet the users' needs. If the system is viable, then the developers can use the prototype to build the full system. One typical use of prototyping is to develop screens that a user will see and interact with. Table 13.2 describes the advantages and disadvantages of the prototyping approach.

A practical problem with prototyping is that a prototype usually looks more complete than it actually is. That is, it may not use the real database, it usually does not have the necessary error checking, and it almost never includes the necessary security features. Users who review a prototype that resembles the finished system may not recognize these problems. Consequently, they might have unrealistic expectations about how close the actual system is to completion.

Integrated Computer-Assisted Software Engineering Tools.

Computer-aided software engineering (CASE) refers to a group of tools that automate many of the tasks in the SDLC. The tools that are used to automate the early stages of the SDLC (systems investigation, analysis, and design) are called **upper CASE tools**. The tools used to automate later stages in the SDLC (programming, testing, operation, and maintenance) are called **lower CASE tools**. CASE tools that provide links between upper CASE and lower CASE tools are called **integrated CASE (ICASE) tools**. Table 13.2 lists the advantages and disadvantages of ICASE tools.

Component-Based Development.

Component-based development uses standard components to build applications. Components are reusable applications that generally have one specific function, such as a shopping cart, user authentication, or a catalog. Compared with other approaches, component-based development generally involves less programming and more assembly. Component-based development is closely linked with the idea of Web services and service-oriented architectures, which you will study in Technology Guide 3.

Many startup companies are pursuing the idea of component-based application development. One example is Ning (**www.ning.com**), which allows organizations to create, customize, and share their own social network.

Object-Oriented Development.

Object-oriented development is based on a different view of computer systems than the perception that characterizes traditional development approaches. Traditional approaches can produce a system that performs the original task but may not be suited for handling other tasks. This limitation applies even when these other tasks involve the same real-world entities. For example, a billing system will handle billing, but it probably cannot be adapted to handle mailings for the marketing department or to generate leads for the sales force. This is true even though the billing, marketing, and sales functions all use similar data, including customer names, addresses, and purchases. In contrast, an *object-oriented (OO) system* begins not with the task to be performed, but with the aspects of the real world that must be modeled to perform that task. Therefore, in our example, if the firm has a good model of its customers and its interactions with them, then it can use this model equally well for billings, mailings, and sales leads.

The development process for an object-oriented system begins with a feasibility study and an analysis of the existing system. Systems developers identify the *objects* in the new system—the fundamental elements in OO analysis and design. Each object represents a tangible, real-world entity such as a customer, bank account, student, or course. Objects have *properties*, or *data values*. For example, a customer has an identification number, a name, an address, an account number(s), and so on. Objects also contain the *operations* that can be performed on their properties. For example, operations that can be performed on the customer object may include obtain-account-balance, open-account, withdraw-funds, and so on. Operations are also referred to as *behaviors*.

This approach enables OO analysts to define all the relevant objects needed for the new system, including their properties and operations. The analysts then model how the objects interact to meet the objectives of the new system. In some cases, analysts can reuse existing objects from other applications (or from a library of objects) in the new system. This process saves the analysts the time they otherwise would spend coding these objects. In most cases, however, even with object reuse, some coding will be necessary to customize the objects and their interactions for the new system.

Containers.
Containers are a method of developing applications that run independently of the base operating system of the server. Containers allow application providers to develop, test, and deploy technology that will always run in practice exactly like it does in testing. This would allow software to be developed more rapidly. Primarily, they provide a level of portability that has brought about one of the biggest shifts in application development in years

To better understand containers, imagine that your vehicle is a container. You only interact with the environment inside the vehicle (the container). Your vehicle can travel on different types of terrain (platforms), but you do the same things inside (gas, brakes, lights, signals, etc.). The vehicle (container) has features built in to help manage the external environment (tires, shocks, windshield wipers, etc.). Containers have begun to revolutionize the speed of development because developers can focus on the container rather than the environments.

Application developers have always been plagued with platform challenges. (A platform is an underlying computer system on which application programs can run. On personal computers, Windows and Mac OS X are examples of platforms.) As one example, if a developer built an application in a Windows environment, then it might not run properly if it were deployed after a Windows update. In addition, it probably would not work in a Linux environment. Further, multiple versions of an application need to be developed to run on different environments, and they have to be continuously tested on platform updates.

One solution for this problem is to build and test applications on a virtual machine and then implement them on an identical virtual machine for customers. A *virtual machine* is a self-contained operating environment that behaves as if it were a separate physical computer. Building and testing on a virtual machine ensures that an application developed on one platform will run on a different platform. But what if you could develop an application that included its own environment and would run as it was developed regardless of the operating system on which it was deployed? That is exactly the idea behind a container.

Containers are not new; in fact, they have been tested since 2005. However, they were not widely embraced by mainstream IT leaders until 2014. The increased popularity of containers is largely due to Docker, an open-source project by Docker, Inc. (**www.docker.com**). Docker is a Linux-based product that enables applications to be developed and deployed in a container. Docker-created apps will run on any platform.

Low-Code Development Platform.
Low-Code Development Platforms (LCDPs) make use of visual interfaces to develop applications rather than traditional procedural hand-coding. LCDPs were first discussed as "no-code" but it was not practical because any integration with other existing systems relied on code. The amount of code necessary was reduced, but not removed, so the name "low-code" was adopted for this tool. This method allows for more rapid app development (because it reduces the amount of code that has to be written), and an expansion of those who can contribute to a project. LCDPs allow non-technical users to provide input and efforts into app development. LCDPs will help to extend end-user development by making it easier to produce new programs with less formal training.

Apple has introduced a new enterprise development platform with low-code/no-code capabilities. Their product, called Claris Connect, allows users with little to no programming experience stitch together apps by connecting components of popular online services such as Trello, Slack, DocuSign, and Box, among others. Claris Connect uses a drag-and-drop interface for users to create workflows. Similarly, on the consumer side, Apple has created an app called "Shortcuts" that is drag-and-drop development that also stitches together apps that are installed on users' devices. It creates automation, reminders, and triggers to create workflows across apps saving users time and effort. IT's About Business 13.1 presents an example of low-code development.

IT's About Business 13.1

MIS Hospitals Automate Workflow with Low-Code Systems

Historically, IT managers have focused on developing or acquiring individual monolithic systems that meet business needs. Monolithic refers to single comprehensive systems as the "end all be all" of IT solutions. Today, however, companies rarely have a single system but instead, rely on a collection of solutions.

This chapter presents many methods and models to guide this decision-making process for developing or acquiring any system. Business needs are defined, solutions identified, and then implemented. However, IT managers now realize there is a gap in their system implementations.

Business workflows commonly include multiple steps of copying and pasting data between apps or merely updating a transaction's status. For example, suppose that a sales rep completes a sale and receives a signed contract. Here are just a few of the steps that could take place in different systems.

1. DocuSign: Sales rep receives a signed contract through DocuSign (the firm's formal e-signature program).

2. Pipedrive: The account is updated in Pipedrive, the company's customer relationship management (CRM) tool.

3. Box: A business employee uploads the contract to Box (the firm's cloud storage provider).

4. Slack: A business employee communicates with the sales team via Slack to let them know the deal is closed. (Slack is a team communication and collaboration tool.)

In this illustration, one transaction triggers workflow interactions with several apps. Each app is a stand-alone system that serves specific purposes within the organization. However, they are all related through this one workflow!

It is a common problem that a typical workplace ends up demanding multiple tasks and workflows across a growing number of apps. Employees spend more and more time "between" apps, manually moving data around in repetitive, time-consuming workflows.

What if it were possible for a user to develop code for custom automation based on typical workflows within their business role? Some companies might embrace this opportunity while others might continue in their routine until they had no option but to find a better way to complete workflows.

For example, the Royal National Hospital for Rheumatic Diseases (RNHRD; **www.rnhrd.nhs.uk**) is known for continually trying to improve patient care. The COVID-19 pandemic caused them to rethink their workflow.

Part of their standard patient process was a paper-based survey completed at check-in. This procedure had two challenges. First, it required close contact between employees and patients

and required the movement of the physical documents through many hands, potentially spreading the virus. Second, the paper system was cumbersome and slow to analyze because it was not immediately machine readable. Doctors had to manually read surveys, look at past surveys, and mentally build an image of patient progress. The hospital needed to find a better way to automate this process and provide better care.

The RNHRD turned to Decent Group (**www.decentgroup.co.uk**) for a custom app that would collect and store the patient progress and care data. Decent Group is a partner with Claris Connect, an Apple subsidiary that provides a way for users to create workflows between software packages. Claris is a combination of IPaaS (Integration Platform as a Service) and a low-code solution intended to fill the manual gaps between existing IT solutions.

The goal of Decent Group was to simplify the way RHNRD tracks and reports patient progress and care. Working within the Claris platform, Decent created an app to accomplish this goal. The app was not stand-alone, but a collection of automated workflows between existing systems.

Today, patients use the app to complete the survey electronically before their appointments. The app pulls data from previous surveys, analyzes the data, assesses a patient's functional ability, and presents reports to doctors allowing them to measure progress over time. Patients receive reduced time of service and data privacy increases.

"Collecting information electronically makes tracking patient progress and care over time particularly simple," says Dr. Sengupta. "By automating the collection and scoring process, clinicians can quickly consult a patient's history, which assists in identifying changes since their last visit." For RNHRD, this automation successfully reduced contact to slow the spread of COVID-19 and increased the quality of service they offer to their customers.

Sources: Compiled from: J. Evans, "Apple's Claris Brings Digital Transformation To The Rest Of Us," *Computer World*, March 4, 2020; E. Rosenbaum, "An Apple Business You May Not Know That's Posed To Boom From Coronavirus Crisis," *CNBC*, May 1, 2020; I. Sacolick, "Public Clouds And Big Tech Target Low-Code Capabilities," *Reseller News*, November 24, 2020; S. Brooks, "Claris Connect Emerges Into The Light," *Enterprise Times*, March 3, 2020; A. Levitsky, "Claris CEO On How The Apple Subsidiary Is Going 'On The Offensive' Against Covid-19," *Silicon Valley Business Journal*, March 26, 2020; "UK healthcare providers use Claris Platform to organise and mobilise resources in record time," *Claris*, October 22, 2020.

Questions

1. What is the purpose of workflow automation?
2. What is meant by a "gap" between apps?
3. What are some advantages of a monolithic system?

You have studied many methods that can be used to acquire new systems. Table 13.2 provides an overview of the advantages and disadvantages of each of these methods.

Before you go on...

1. Describe the tools that augment the traditional SDLC.
2. Describe the alternate methods that can be used for systems development other than the SDLC.

What's in IT for me?

ACCT For the Accounting Major

Accounting personnel help perform cost–benefit analyses on proposed projects. They may also monitor ongoing project costs to keep them within budget. Accounting personnel undoubtedly will find themselves involved with systems development at various points throughout their careers.

FIN For the Finance Major

Finance personnel are frequently involved with the financial issues that accompany any large-scale systems development project (e.g., budgeting). They also are involved in cost–benefit and risk analyses. To perform these tasks, they need to stay abreast of the emerging techniques used to determine project costs and ROI. Finally, because they must manage vast amounts of information, finance departments are also common recipients of new systems.

MKT For the Marketing Major

In most organizations, marketing, like finance, involves massive amounts of data and information. Like finance, then, marketing is also a hotbed of systems development. Marketing personnel will increasingly find themselves participating in systems development teams. Such involvement increasingly means helping to develop systems, especially Web-based systems that reach out directly from the organization to its customers.

POM For the Production/Operations Management Major

Participation in development teams is a common role for production/operations people. Manufacturing is becoming increasingly computerized and integrated with other allied systems, from design to logistics to customer support. Production systems interface frequently with marketing, finance, and human resources. They may also be part of a larger enterprise-wide system. Also, many end users in POM either develop their own systems or collaborate with IT personnel on specific applications.

HRM For the Human Resources Management Major

The human resources department is closely involved with several aspects of the systems acquisitions process. Acquiring new systems may require hiring new employees, changing job descriptions, or terminating employees. Human resources staff perform all of these tasks. Furthermore, if the organization hires consultants for the development project, or outsources it, the human resources department may handle the contracts with these suppliers.

MIS For the MIS Major

Regardless of the approach that the organization adopts for acquiring new systems, the MIS department spearheads it. If the organization chooses either to buy or to lease the application, the MIS department leads in examining the offerings of the various vendors and in negotiating with the vendors. If the organization chooses to develop the application in-house, then the process falls to the MIS department. MIS analysts work closely with users to develop their information requirements. MIS programmers then write the computer code, test it, and implement the new system.

Summary

13.1 Discuss the different cost–benefit analyses that companies must take into account when formulating an IT strategic plan.

The four common approaches to cost–benefit analysis are the following.

1. *The net present value* method converts future values of benefits to their present-value equivalent by discounting them at the organization's cost of funds. They can then compare the present value of the future benefits with the cost required to achieve those benefits to determine whether the benefits exceed the costs.

2. *Return on investment* measures management's effectiveness in generating profits with its available assets. ROI is calculated by dividing net income attributable to a project by the average assets invested in the project. ROI is a percentage, and the higher the percentage return, the better.

3. *Breakeven analysis* determines the point at which the cumulative dollar value of the benefits from a project equals the investment made in the project.

4. In the *business case approach*, system developers write a business case to justify funding one or more specific applications or projects.

13.2 Discuss the four business decisions that companies must make when they acquire new applications.

- *How much computer code does the company want to write?* A company can choose to use a totally prewritten application (write no computer code), to customize a prewritten application (write some computer code), or to customize an entire application (write all new computer code).

- *How will the company pay for the application?* Once the company has decided how much computer code to write, it must decide how to pay for it. With prewritten applications or customized prewritten applications, companies can buy them or lease them. With totally custom applications, companies use internal funding.

- *Where will the application run?* Companies must decide where to run the application. The company may run the application on its own platform or run the application on someone else's platform (use either a software-as-a-service vendor or an application service provider).

- *Where will the application originate?* Prewritten applications can be open-source software or come from a vendor. Companies may choose to customize prewritten open-source applications or prewritten proprietary applications from vendors. Companies may customize applications in-house or outsource the customization. They also can write totally custom applications in-house or outsource this process.

13.3 Enumerate the primary tasks and the importance of each of the six processes involved in the systems development life cycle.

The six processes are the following:

1. *Systems investigation:* Addresses the business problem (or business opportunity) by means of the feasibility study. The main task in the systems investigation stage is the feasibility study.

2. *Systems analysis:* Examines the business problem that the organization plans to solve with an information system. Its main purpose is to gather information about the existing system to determine the requirements for the new system. The end product of this stage, known as the "deliverable," is a set of system requirements.

3. *Systems design:* Describes how the system will resolve the business problem. The deliverable is the set of technical system specifications.

4. *Programming and testing:* Programming translates the design specifications into computer code; testing checks to see whether the computer code will produce the expected and desired results and detects errors, or bugs, in the computer code. A deliverable is the new application.

5. *Implementation:* The process of converting from the old system to the new system through three major conversion strategies: direct, pilot, and phased. A deliverable is a properly working application.

6. *Operation and maintenance:* Types of maintenance include debugging, updating, and adding new functions when needed.

13.4 Describe alternative development methods and tools that augment development methods.

These are the *alternative methods:*

- *Joint application design* is a group-based tool for collecting user requirements and creating system designs.

- *Rapid application development* is a systems development method that can combine JAD, prototyping, and ICASE tools to rapidly produce a high-quality system.

- *Agile development* is a software development methodology that delivers functionality in rapid iterations, which are usually measured in weeks.

- *DevOps* is a software development methodology that includes employees from the IT *DEV*elopment group and the user *OP*erations group. The goal is to keep users involved in the entire development process.

- *End-user development* refers to an organization's end users developing their own applications with little or no formal assistance from the IT department.

These are the *tools:*

- *Design Thinking* directs developers to create a deep understanding of users' needs by empathizing with their needs and defining the problem from the user perspective. Ideas and prototypes are generated to address this problem. The testing phase reveals a deeper appreciation for the user, clarifying empathy, and directing future revisions to the project.

- The *prototyping* approach defines an initial list of user requirements, builds a model of the system, and then improves the system in several iterations based on users' feedback.

- *Integrated computer-aided software engineering* combines upper CASE tools (automate systems investigation, analysis, and design) and lower CASE tools (programming, testing, operation, and maintenance).

- *Component-based development* uses standard components to build applications. Components are reusable applications that generally have one specific function, such as a shopping cart, user authentication, or a catalog.

- *Object-oriented development* begins with the aspects of the real world that must be modeled to perform that task. Systems developers identify the objects in the new system. Each object represents a tangible, real-world entity such as a customer, bank account, student, or course. Objects have *properties*, or *data values.* Objects also contain the *operations* that can be performed on their properties.

Table 13.2 shows advantages and disadvantages of alternative methods and tools.

Chapter Glossary

agile development   A software development methodology that delivers functionality in rapid iterations, measured in weeks, requiring frequent communication, development, testing, and delivery.

application portfolio   The set of recommended applications resulting from the planning and justification process in application development.

application service provider (ASP)   An agent or vendor who assembles the software needed by enterprises and packages them with outsourced development, operations, maintenance, and other services.

component-based development   A software development methodology that uses standard components to build applications.

computer-aided software engineering (CASE)   Development approach that uses specialized tools to automate many of the tasks in the SDLC. Upper CASE tools automate the early stages of the SDLC and lower CASE tools automate the later stages.

containers   A method of developing applications that run independently of the base operating system of the server.

continuous application development   The process of steadily adding new computer code to a software project when the new computer code is written and tested.

direct conversion   Implementation process in which the old system is cut off and the new system is turned on at a certain point in time.

end-user development   Approach in which the organization's end users develop their own applications with little or no formal assistance from the IT department.

feasibility study   Investigation that gauges the probability of success of a proposed project and provides a rough assessment of the project's feasibility.

implementation   The process of converting from an old computer system to a new one.

integrated CASE (ICASE) tools   CASE tools that provide links between upper CASE and lower CASE tools.

IS operational plan   Consists of a clear set of projects that the IS department and the functional area managers will execute in support of the IT strategic plan.

IT steering committee   A committee composed of a group of managers and staff representing various organizational units that is set up to establish IT priorities and to ensure that the MIS function is meeting the needs of the enterprise.

IT strategic plan   A set of long-range goals that describe the IT infrastructure and major IT initiatives needed to achieve the goals of the organization.

joint application design (JAD)   A group-based tool for collecting user requirements and creating system designs.

lower CASE tools   Tools used to automate later stages in the SDLC (programming, testing, operation, and maintenance).

object-oriented development   A systems development methodology that begins with aspects of the real world that must be modeled to perform a task.

outsourcing   Use of outside contractors or external organizations to acquire IT services.

phased conversion   Implementation process that introduces components of the new system in stages, until the entire new system is operational.

pilot conversion   Implementation process that introduces the new system in one part of the organization on a trial basis. When the new system is working properly, it is introduced in other parts of the organization.

programmers   IS professionals who modify existing computer programs or write new computer programs to satisfy user requirements.

programming   The translation of a system's design specifications into computer code.

prototype   A small-scale working model of an entire system or a model that contains only the components of the new system that are of most interest to the users.

prototyping   An approach that defines an initial list of user requirements, builds a prototype system, and then improves the system in several iterations based on users' feedback.

rapid application development (RAD)   A development method that uses special tools and an iterative approach to rapidly produce a high-quality system.

scope creep   Adding functions to an information system after the project has begun.

shadow IT   Technology implemented by end-users without receiving proper approvals from the organizational IT department.

software-as-a-service (SaaS)   A method of delivering software in which a vendor hosts the applications and provides them as a service to customers over a network, typically the Internet.

systems analysis   The examination of the business problem that the organization plans to solve with an information system.

systems analysts   IS professionals who specialize in analyzing and designing information systems.

systems design   Describes how the new system will resolve the business problem.

systems development life cycle (SDLC)   Traditional structured framework, used for large IT projects, that consists of sequential processes by which information systems are developed.

systems investigation   The initial stage in the traditional SDLC that addresses the business problem (or business opportunity) by means of the feasibility study.

systems stakeholders   All people who are affected by changes in information systems.

technical specialists   Experts on a certain type of technology, such as databases or telecommunications.

upper CASE tools   Tools that are used to automate the early stages of the SDLC (systems investigation, analysis, and design).

Discussion Questions

1. Discuss the advantages of a lease option over a buy option.

2. Why is it important for all business managers to understand the issues of IT resource acquisition?

3. Why is it important for everyone in business organizations to have a basic understanding of the systems development process?

4. Should prototyping be used on every systems development project? Why or why not?

5. Discuss the various types of feasibility studies. Why are they all needed?

6. Discuss the issue of assessing intangible benefits and the proposed solutions.

7. Discuss the reasons why end-user–developed information systems can be of poor quality. What can be done to improve this situation?

Problem-Solving Activities

1. Access **www.ecommerceguide.com**. Find the product review area. Read reviews of three software payment solutions. Assess them as possible components.

2. Use an Internet search engine to obtain information on CASE and ICASE tools. Select several vendors and compare and contrast their offerings.

3. Access **www.ning.com**. Observe how the site provides components for you to use to build applications. Build a small application at the site.

4. Enter **www.ibm.com/software**. Find its WebSphere product. Read recent customers' success stories. What makes this software so popular?

5. Enter the websites of Gartner (**www.gartner.com**), 451 Research (**https://451research.com**), and CIO (**www.cio.com**). Search for recent material about ASPs and outsourcing, and prepare a report on your findings.

6. StoreFront (**www.storefront.net**) is a vendor of e-business software. At its site, the company provides demonstrations illustrating the types of storefronts that it can create for shoppers. The site also provides demonstrations of how the company's software is used to create a store.

a. Run the StoreFront demonstration to see how this is done.

b. What features does StoreFront provide?

c. Does StoreFront support smaller or larger stores?

d. What other products does StoreFront offer for creating online stores? What types of stores do these products support?

Closing Case

MIS **Etsy Improves Culture and Speeds Deployment with DevOps**

Etsy (**www.etsy.com**) is a global online marketplace for unique, vintage, unusual, or custom products. Etsy does not produce any goods. The firm provides a place for sellers and customers to find each other. As such, its website's functionality is key to its business model and to the success of the vendors that rely on Etsy to connect with customers.

At first, Etsy struggled with slow, difficult website updates that frequently caused the site to go down. Problematic website updates were a common issue for many businesses. The standard method of deploying updates was for the development team to provide new code and the operations team to test and deploy it to the website. There are many more steps to this process, often referred to as the waterfall or SDLC model. This method's slowness left users to work around known bugs and wait for fixes. It also required extensive system downtime to install updates. It was frustrating for visitors, and downtime impacted Etsy's millions of users who sold goods through the online marketplace. Even worse, Etsy ran the risk of driving customers and vendors to a competitor.

At the end of 2009, an idea emerged that would change Etsy's culture. Etsy wanted to move toward nearly constant updates with minimal downtime by increasing the communication and collaboration between the IT development team and the IT operations team. The old, siloed structure had unintentionally created an opportunity to blame other departments when there were problems. Removing the silos reminded both teams that they were all on the same team with the same goal.

There was no name for this model at the time, but the proposal made good business sense. While Etsy is a platform for others to sell goods, it was (and is) ultimately an IT organization. Essentially, Etsy had to deploy updates for their users in a timelier fashion.

Etsy took two critical actions to accomplish this goal. First, they broke down the work silos of the development and operations team. The IT development group became responsible for the development of new technologies. This group was responsible for Etsy's front-end (customer-facing) website, mobile apps, back-end financials, logistics, and other systems necessary for buyers and sellers to conduct transactions. The IT operations group was responsible for managing the hardware and software that maintained Etsy's customers' existing experience. Development focused on the future, while operations concentrated on the "now."

Second, they adopted and encouraged a team-wide, user-centric focus. This common goal brought developers and operations together on a common purpose—to provide their end users the best features and most robust functionality. For Etsy, there were two end users of their platform: sellers and buyers.

Etsy accomplished both goals with a new position they called *designated ops*. This role was tasked with increasing cross-team collaboration and communication while keeping the conversation focused on the user's experience with the platform.

Collaboration efforts focused on the end-user experience have become the hallmark of the DevOps movement. But the benefits of implementing a DevOps culture are not immediate. Instead, they become visible during operation. DevOps allows companies to deliver better software faster. This process, in turn, provides a competitive advantage because DevOps enables innovation and fast reactions to changing market requirements. Further, the consistency of uptime keeps buyers and sellers on the platform.

By 2020. Etsy transitioned from its waterfall model (discussed in this chapter as the SDLC), which had been producing four-hour full-site deployments twice weekly, to a more agile approach. Etsy can now safely and efficiently deploy code more than 80 times per day. Though Etsy has no DevOps group as such, its commitment to collaboration across teams has made the company a pioneer of the DevOps framework model.

As Etsy adopted this new methodology, the culture in the whole organization began to improve. Interdepartmental trust began to rise, and everyone focused on the common goal of providing the best platform for the user. Today, Etsy is known for its outstanding culture and strong DevOps practices. Their continuous delivery pipeline allows anyone—developers, information security officers, IT operations—to deploy updates as needed. In fact, their process is so safe that new engineers can deliver updates their very first day on the job.

Sources: Compiled from J. Dix, "How Etsy Makes Devops Work," *Network World*, February 19, 2015; A. Hawkins, "How Google, HP, and Etsy Succeed With DevOps," *Cloud Academy*, September 13, 2019; C. Null, "10 Companies Killing It At DevOps," *TechBeacon*, January 22, 2019; B. Dawson, "Realize Competitive Advantages with DevOps," *Techspective*, May 30, 2020; N. Forsgren, "High-Performance Continuous Delivery: 3 Technical Practices That Work," *TechBeacon*, January 23, 2019; M. Heusser, "6 Ways To Reduce Deployment Risk Without Adding Cost," *TechRepublic*, April 13, 2020; H. Shah, "The Role of DevOps in Custom Software Development," *DevOps.com*, December 5, 2019; **www.etsy.com**, accessed December 15, 2020.

Questions

1. Etsy facilitates the sales of unique goods on the Web. If they primarily support retail, why do they need such a strong culture of IT development?

2. As a buyer or seller, how long would you continue to use a platform that allowed bugs to remain on their website for multiple days or weeks? Why?

3. What were the two parts of the IT operation that Etsy "combined" by creating greater collaboration?

CHAPTER 14

Artificial Intelligence

CHAPTER OUTLINE	LEARNING OBJECTIVES
14.1 Introduction to Artificial Intelligence	14.1 Explain the potential value and the potential limitations of artificial intelligence.
14.2 Machine Learning and Deep Learning	14.2 Differentiate among supervised, semi-supervised, unsupervised, reinforcement, and deep learning.
14.3 Neural Networks	14.3 Describe the structure of a neural network and discuss how that structure contributes to the purpose of neural networks in machine learning.
14.4 Artificial Intelligence Applications	14.4 Provide use case examples of computer vision, natural language processing, robotics, image recognition, and intelligent agents.
14.5 Artificial Intelligence in the Functional Areas	14.5 Provide use case examples of artificial intelligence applications in accounting, finance, marketing, production and operations management, human resource management, and management information systems.
14.6 Appendix	14.6 Understand the process by which a neural network transforms data values from the input node to the output node, and then calculates the loss function to initiate the back propagation process.

Opening Case

MIS MKT POM Artificial Intelligence in Retail

There are literally millions of brands today, and shoppers can actually have too many choices. What customers really want are personalized product recommendations, shorter wait times, quicker order fulfillment, and frictionless checkout experiences. In fact, shoppers are used to Amazon's shopping experience, meaning that retailers must implement artificial intelligence applications to thrive, both in their physical stores and their online stores.

Physical Stores

In the store. Retailers today are leveraging machine learning (ML)–driven technologies to help customers throughout the shopping process. Let's look at several examples.

- Kroger's Edge technology, which stands for Enhanced Display for Grocery Environment, replaces paper price tags in their stores with smart product tags. Edge also provides video ads, nutritional information, and promotions on the digital displays.

- Amazon's Just Walk Out technology integrates machine learning with cameras and sensors in its Amazon Go cashierless stores. This technology automatically detects when products are taken from or returned to shelves. In addition, it keeps track of the items in a customer's virtual cart. When customers are finished shopping, they simply leave the store. Amazon then sends them a digital receipt and charges their Amazon accounts.

  Other physical stores can use Amazon's Dash Cart, which is a ML-powered shopping cart that allows shoppers to skip the checkout line. Shoppers use a QR code in the Amazon app that enables them to easily sign in and begin using the cart. The cart has a screen where shoppers can access their Alexa Shopping Lists to check off items and view their subtotals and coupon scanners, where shoppers can apply store coupons as they shop.

  The cart uses a combination of computer vision algorithms and sensors to identify items that shoppers put in their carts. When shoppers exit through the store's Amazon Dash Cart line, sensors automatically identify the cart, and their payment is processed using the credit card on their Amazon account.

- Founded in 1970, Sephora (**www.sephora.com**) is the number-one specialty beauty retailer in the world. The company operates 2,300 stores in 33 countries worldwide. Whereas other cosmetic companies rely on department store sales, Sephora offers its customers a number of technology options that allow them to personalize their shopping experience by trying on makeup virtually using virtual reality and matching their skin tone to a foundation with machine learning.

  Sephora Virtual Artist is the firm's virtual reality tool that allows customers to try on thousands of shades of lipstick, eyeshadow, false eyelashes, blush, concealer, and many other Sephora makeup products. The retailer also provides beauty tutorials so customers can learn how to achieve certain looks. To accompany Virtual Artist, Sephora has trained an ML system called Color Match that helps customers find the correct color shade for their skin tone via an uploaded photo.

  Finding the correct foundation color is one of the major beauty concerns of Sephora's customers. In response, the company trained a ML-driven, shade-matching system called Color IQ. The system is on a handheld device that provides a Color IQ number for each customer's skin tone. This number helps each customer search through thousands of lip colors, foundations, and concealer shades to choose products that are best suited for that customer's specific skin color and tone.

- Ubamarket (**http://ubamarket.com**) is a United Kingdom firm that makes a shopping app for customers' phones. The app enables customers to pay for items, make lists, and scan products for ingredients and allergens.

  The more that customers shop, the more the Ubamarket app knows about what kinds of products they like. The app becomes anticipatory over time, building a profile of how likely a shopper is to try a different brand or to buy chocolate just before Valentine's Day. The app can also make personalized offers to shoppers while they are in the store.

  More and more customers are adopting the app, due in part to the COVID-19 pandemic, which has made shoppers more reluctant to stand in lines. Ubamarket claims that in stores that utilize the app, the average contents of a basket have increased by 20 percent. In addition, customers who use the app are three times more likely to return to shop in that store than customers who do not use the app.

Monitoring customer satisfaction. ML systems such as facial recognition can detect customers' moods while they are shopping. Walmart has installed cameras at each checkout lane. If a customer looks annoyed, then a store representative will talk to them to resolve any potential problems.

Stock forecasting. Consider the partnership between Morrisons and Blue Yonder. Morrisons (**www.morrisons-corporate.com**) is the fourth-largest supermarket chain in the United Kingdom. Blue Yonder (**www.blueyonder.com**) is a leading digital fulfillment platform that provides supply chain, retailing planning, and store operations solutions. With the help of Blue Yonder's ML-based solutions, Morrisons improved stock forecasting in its 491 stores so dramatically that the chain was able to reduce out-of-stock items by 30 percent.

Online Stores

Product discovery. Product discovery is the first, and, arguably, the most important component of the shopping process. Retailers employ visual and voice search to help customers find what they are looking for.

ML-powered *visual search* systems enable customers to upload images and find similar products based on colors, shapes, and patterns. For example, American Eagle's (**www.ae.com**) ML-powered image recognition system uses visual search to help people find the same or similar clothes as the image they have uploaded. The system also suggests other items that would go well with the product they buy.

Neiman Marcus uses ML-based intelligent visual search in its Snap. Find. Shop. app. Customers "snap" pictures of their favorite items. The app then searches inventory to find similar products. Customers who use this app can shop more efficiently.

Walmart, Tesco, Kohl's, Costco, and many other companies use Google or Amazon ML-powered voice recognition technology and natural language processing to provide customers with simple and quick *voice search*. For instance, customers can ask Amazon's Alexa for a desired item and its delivery status without typing anything.

Alibaba (**www.alibaba.com**) is a Chinese multinational technology company that specializes in e-commerce. Alibaba's ML system chooses which items to display to customers when they visit the website and search for products. The system builds a customized page view for every visitor, displaying items they will be interested in. Significantly, the system also dynamically prices items based on its knowledge of the customer's past spending habits. By monitoring customer actions—whether they make a purchase, browse to a different item, or leave the site—the system learns in real time to make adjustments to these page views to increase the probability that the visit will end with the customer making a purchase. Alibaba's ML-powered chatbot, Dian Xiaomi, answers more than 350 million customer inquiries per day, successfully understanding more than 90 percent of them.

Alibaba has deployed automated content generation to make it easier to write descriptions for items it sells. Its ML-driven copywriter uses natural language processing algorithms to produce 20,000 lines of copy in one second. The copywriter creates multiple versions of advertisements and runs them through algorithms trained on customer behavior data. The system finds which combination of words is most likely to result in customers clicking on them. It then uses those words to create its copy.

Chatbots. ML-powered chatbots improve customer service by, among other features, improving search, sending notifications about new collections, and suggesting similar products. See IT's About Business 7.1.

Dynamic pricing. ML systems can help retailers set prices for their products, visualizing the likely outcomes of multiple pricing strategies. These systems can also help retailers predict the price of a product based on demand, seasonal trends, product characteristics, the release date of new models of the same item, and many other variables. A notable example of price forecasting is the travel industry. Retailers are adopting the strategy as well.

Product categorization. Love the Sales (**www.lovethesales.com**) is a fashion e-commerce aggregator that allows consumers to shop all sale items from multiple brands and retailers in a single online destination. The website uses ML systems to classify more than 1 million items from more than 500 brands and retailers. These systems tag items and sort them in different categories for customers.

Sources: Compiled from J. Wakefield, "How Artificial Intelligence May Be Making You Buy Things," *BBC News*, November 18, 2020; C. Levine, "Amazon Fresh Store Replacing North Jersey Fairway Market," *South Passaic Daily Voice*, November 7, 2020; J. Horwitz, "Hands-On: Amazon Fresh Grocery Stores Tease Brick-and-Mortar Retail's Future, *Venture Beat*, October 30, 2020; R. Saker, "The Impact of Artificial Intelligence in Retail," *Total Retail*, May 21, 2020; Z. Kerravala, "How AI Is Transforming Retail," *CIO*, April 17, 2020; S. Ravishankar, "Artificial Intelligence in Retail 2020,"

Vue.ai, February 27, 2020; R. Chuprina, "Artificial Intelligence for Retail in 2020: 12 Real-World Use Cases," *SPD Group*, December 20, 2019; K. Askew, "App Developer Ubamarket Wants to Bring Shoppers Back to the Supermarket," *Food Navigator*, August 13, 2019; A. Peterson, "How Artificial Intelligence Is Powering the Retail Experience," *The Store Front*, March 16, 2019; B. Morgan, "The 20 Best Examples of Using Artificial Intelligence for Retail Experiences," *Forbes*, March 4, 2019; D. Heaven, "The World's Most Prolific Writer Is a Chinese Algorithm," *BBC*, August 29, 2018.

Questions

1. What potential problems can arise from retailers implementing machine learning applications? Provide examples to support your answer.

2. Are ML applications more important to physical stores or online stores? Support your choice with examples.

14.1 Introduction to Artificial Intelligence

Artificial intelligence (AI) is a subfield of computer science that studies the thought processes of humans and recreates the effects of those processes through information systems. We define **artificial intelligence** as the theory and development of information systems that are capable of performing tasks that normally require human intelligence. That is, we define AI in terms of the tasks that humans perform, rather than how humans think.

This definition raises the question, "What is *intelligent behavior*?" The following capabilities are considered to be signs of intelligence: learning or understanding from experience, making sense of ambiguous or contradictory messages, and responding quickly and successfully to new situations.

The ultimate goal of AI is to build machines that mimic human intelligence. A widely used test to determine whether a computer exhibits intelligent behavior was designed by Alan Turing, a British AI pioneer. The *Turing test* proposes a scenario in which a man and a computer both pretend to be human, and a human interviewer has to identify which is real. Based on this standard, the intelligent systems exemplified in commercial AI products are far from exhibiting any significant intelligence.

We can better understand the potential value of AI by contrasting it with *natural (human) intelligence*. AI has several important commercial advantages over natural intelligence, but it also displays some limitations. The strengths and limitations are outlined in **Table 14.1**.

Before we proceed, it is important to distinguish between strong artificial intelligence and weak artificial intelligence. **Strong AI**—also known as *artificial general intelligence*—is *hypothetical* artificial intelligence that matches or exceeds human intelligence. In other words, it refers to the intelligence of a machine that could successfully perform any intellectual task that a human being can. Strong AI, therefore, could be considered to have consciousness or sentience. **Weak AI**—also called **narrow AI**—performs a useful and specific function that once required human intelligence to perform, and it does so at human levels or better. Common examples are character recognition, speech recognition, machine vision, robotics, data mining, medical informatics, and automated investing.

Today, systems that are labeled "artificial intelligence" are typically weak AI. However, weak AI is already powerful enough to make a dramatic difference in human life. Weak AI applications enhance human endeavors by complementing what people can do. For example, when you call your bank and talk to an automated voice, you are probably talking to a weak AI program. Researchers at universities and companies around the world are building weak AI applications that are rapidly becoming more capable.

Consider chess, which weak AI systems now play better than any human. In 1997, IBM's Deep Blue system beat the world chess champion, Garry Kasparov, for the first time. Since that time, chess-playing systems have become significantly more powerful.

In December 2017, Alphabet (Google's parent corporation) introduced AlphaZero, a deep reinforcement learning system (discussed later in this chapter). AlphaZero began with no

TABLE 14.1   The Capabilities of Natural Versus Artificial Intelligence

Capabilities	Natural Intelligence	Artificial Intelligence
Preservation of knowledge	Perishable from an organizational point of view	Permanent
Duplication and dissemination of knowledge in a computer	Difficult, expensive, time consuming	Easy, fast, and inexpensive
Total cost of knowledge	Can be erratic and inconsistent, incomplete at times	Consistent and thorough
Documentation of process and knowledge	Difficult, expensive	Fairly easy, inexpensive
Creativity	Can be very high	Low, uninspired
Use of sensory experiences	Direct and rich in possibilities	Must be interpreted first; limited
Recognizing patterns and relationships	Fast, easy to explain	Machine learning still not as good as people in most cases, but in some cases better than people
Reasoning	Making use of a wide context of experiences	Good only in narrow, focused, and stable domains

knowledge of chess beyond the basic rules of the game. It then played against itself millions of times and learned from its mistakes. In a matter of hours, AlphaZero became the world's best chess player.

Interestingly, the advent of AI did not diminish the performance of purely human chess players. Instead, the opposite occurred. Cheap, highly functional chess programs have inspired more people than ever to play chess. Further, the players have become better than ever. In fact, today there are more than twice as many grandmasters as there were when Deep Blue beat Kasparov.

Similar to chess players, physicians who are supported by AI will have an enhanced ability to spot cancer in medical images; speech recognition algorithms running on smartphones will bring the Internet to millions of illiterate people in developing countries; digital assistants will suggest promising hypotheses for academic research; and image classification algorithms will enable wearable computers to layer useful digital information onto people's views of the real, physical world.

Despite these impressive results, however, AI does present challenges. For example, consider the power that AI brings to national security agencies in both autocracies and democracies. The capacity to monitor billions of conversations and to pick out every citizen from the crowd by his or her voice or face poses serious threats to privacy and liberty. Also, many individuals could become unemployed when AI develops the capabilities to perform their jobs.

Weak AI has become so powerful that scientists from University College London (UCL; **www.ucl.ac.uk**) compiled a list of AI-enabled crimes based on academic papers, news stories, popular culture, and a discussion with several dozen experts.

- *AI-enabled crimes of high concern:* Deepfakes, driverless vehicles as a weapon, spear phishing and whaling, AI-controlled systems (see SCADA systems in Chapter 4), large-scale ransomware, and AI-authored fake news
- *AI-enabled crimes of moderate concern:* Misuse of military robots, autonomous attack drones, tricking facial recognition systems, manipulating financial or stock markets, and data poisoning. *Data poisoning* is an attack that tries to manipulate the training dataset of a machine learning system to control the predictive behavior of a trained model such that

the model will label malicious examples into a desired class (e.g., labeling spam e-mails as safe).

- *AI-enabled crimes of low concern:* AI-authored fake reviews, AI-assisted stalking, forgery of content such as art and music, and burglar bots. *Burglar bots* are very small robots that can enter a home through a letter slot or a pet door and then send information to the thief about what is inside the home and whether anyone is at home.

Several technological advancements have led to enhancements of artificial intelligence. We take a brief look at each of them here.

- *Advancements in chip technology:* AI systems employ graphics processing units (called GPU chips; discussed in Technology Guide 1), which were developed to meet the visual and parallel processing demands of video games. GPU chips facilitate parallel processing in neural networks, which are the primary information architecture of AI software. (We discuss neural networks later in this chapter.)
- *Big Data:* As we discussed in Chapter 5, Big Data consists of diverse, high-volume, high-velocity information assets that require new types of processing that enhance decision making, insight discovery, and process optimization. Big Data is now being used to train *deep learning* software. (We discuss deep learning later in this chapter.)
- *The Internet and cloud computing:* The Internet (discussed in Chapter 6) and cloud computing (discussed in Technology Guide 3) make Big Data available to AI systems, specifically neural networks, and provide the computational capacity needed for AI systems.
- *Improved algorithms:* An **algorithm** is a problem-solving method expressed as a finite sequence of steps. Researchers are rapidly improving the capabilities of AI algorithms. AI algorithms also run much faster on GPU chips.

Before you go on...

1. What is artificial intelligence?
2. Differentiate between artificial intelligence and human intelligence.
3. Differentiate between strong AI and weak AI.

14.2 # Machine Learning and Deep Learning

Machine learning (**ML**) is an application of artificial intelligence that provides systems with the ability to automatically learn and improve from experience without being explicitly programmed. Machine learning focuses on the development of computer programs that can access data and use those data to learn from themselves.

First we discuss how machine learning differs from traditional computer programming and expert systems. We then discuss problems inherent to developing ML systems. We close this section with a discussion of several types of machine learning: supervised, semi-supervised, unsupervised, and reinforcement.

Traditional Programming versus Machine Learning

Fundamentally, traditional programming is a structured combination of data and a computer algorithm (computer program) that produces answers. In supervised machine learning, developers train the system with labeled input data and the expected output results. After the system is trained, developers feed it with unlabeled input data and examine the accuracy of the output data. Let's look at an example of the difference between traditional programming and supervised machine learning.

Traditional programming.   Let's say that we want to know the product of two numbers. The first column is **a** and the second column is **b**. With traditional programming, we create an algorithm (computer code), or **c** = **a** x **b**. The results are 24, 15, and 18.

a	b	c = a × b
6	4	24
3	5	15
9	2	18

Supervised machine learning.   Let's use the same numbers as our example above as labeled input data to train a supervised machine learning system. We feed the system with these relationships:

6 and 4 are related to 24

3 and 5 are related to 15

We want to know how these numbers relate, so we let the system evaluate the relationships of known values and check its accuracy.

6 ? 4 = 24

3 ? 5 = 15

The system determines that the relationship between each pair is "multiply." If we say that the question mark is multiply and check our results, we find that they are correct.

So, if we then feed 9 and 2 into the system, it will tell us that the relationship is 9 x 2 = 18.

When the machine learning algorithm is trained on large amounts of labeled training data, it produces predictions for additional examples.

Expert Systems versus Machine Learning

Expert systems (ESs) are computer systems that attempt to mimic human experts by applying expertise in a specific domain. Essentially, an ES transfers expertise from a human domain expert (or other source) to the system. This knowledge is then stored in the system, typically in the form of IF-THEN rules. The more complex ESs are comprised of thousands of these rules.

ESs can make inferences and arrive at conclusions. Then, like a human expert, they offer advice or recommendations. Also like human experts, they can explain the logic behind the advice.

Expert systems do present problems. For instance, transferring domain expertise from human experts to the expert system can be difficult because humans cannot always explain *how* they know what they know. In addition, even if the domain experts can explain their entire reasoning process, automating that process might not be possible. The process might be either too complex or too vague, or it might require too many rules. Essentially, it is very difficult to program all the possible decision paths into an expert system.

There are significant differences between expert systems and machine learning systems. First, ESs require human experts to provide the knowledge for the system. In contrast, ML systems do not require human experts. Further, much like traditional programming, expert systems must be formally structured in the form of rules. By contrast, machine learning algorithms learn from ingesting vast amounts of data and by adjusting hyperparameters and parameters (discussed below).

Bias

Designers must consider the many types of bias when developing machine learning systems. The types of bias include underspecification, how developers approach a problem, and the data used to train the system.

Machine Learning Bias (also called Algorithm Bias)

Designers must consider the many types of bias when developing machine learning systems. The sources of bias include underspecification, how developers approach a problem, and the data used to train the system.

Underspecification.   The training process for a machine learning system can produce multiple models, all of which pass the testing phase. However, these models will differ in small, arbitrary ways, depending on things such as the random values given to the nodes in a neural network before training starts, the number of training runs, and others (see Section 14.3). Developers typically overlook these differences if they do not impact how a ML model performs on its test. Unfortunately, these differences can lead to huge variations in how the model performs in the real world. Essentially, even if a training process can produce a good model, it could still ultimately produce a poor model. The process will not know the difference, and neither will the developers, until the model is employed in the real world.

How developers approach a problem.   Let's look at a simple example that illustrates how you might frame a problem. Consider the following numbers: 4, 9, 3, 6, 11, and 5. What is the next number in this series? Your answer to this problem is a product of how you intuitively see the problem and how you frame it. If you think in arithmetic terms, you may try some combination of addition and subtraction based on a pattern that you think exists. If you are a statistician, you may try to perform regression on the numbers to determine what the next one would be. There are many possible approaches.

The "answer" here is that there is no right answer because we picked these numbers at random. The critical point is how you chose to approach the problem. Your approach reveals your bias as to how you would try to solve the problem.

This simple example illustrates an essential issue in the field of AI. How developers approach or frame a problem determines how they set up the process of building the AI system and, ultimately, how the algorithm learns and produces answers.

How data can bias a ML system.   The third type of bias comes from the data that are used to train the system. This bias, known as *data shift*, comes from a mismatch between the data used to train and test the system and the data the system actually encounters in the real world. For example, an ML system trained only with current customers might not be able to predict the behaviors of new customers who are not represented in the training data.

When trained on some data, ML will likely pick up the same biases that already exist in society. For instance, ML systems used for criminal risk assessment have been found to be biased against people of color.

As a result, machine learning raises many ethical questions. ML systems trained on datasets collected from biased samples can exhibit these biases when they used, a problem called *algorithmic bias*. For example, using job hiring data from a firm with biased hiring policies could cause an ML system to duplicate this bias by scoring job applicants accordingly. Clearly, collecting the data and documenting the algorithmic rules used by an ML system in a responsible manner is a critical component of developing ML systems.

False Positives

Another challenging problem when building AI systems or evaluating outputs is seeing conditions where none actually exist, which is called a false positive. A *false positive* is a result that indicates that a given condition exists when it in fact does not. An example of a false positive is convicting an innocent person, identifying an e-mail as spam when it is not, flagging a legitimate transaction as fraudulent, and many others.

Analyzing complex data sets can be difficult. However, by being aware of false positives, AI practitioners can assess data objectively and not be misled by apparent, but erroneous, conditions.

We now turn our attention to the various types of machine learning: supervised, semi-supervised, unsupervised, reinforcement, and deep. **Figure 14.1** provides a visual look at how these types differ.

The Types of Machine Learning

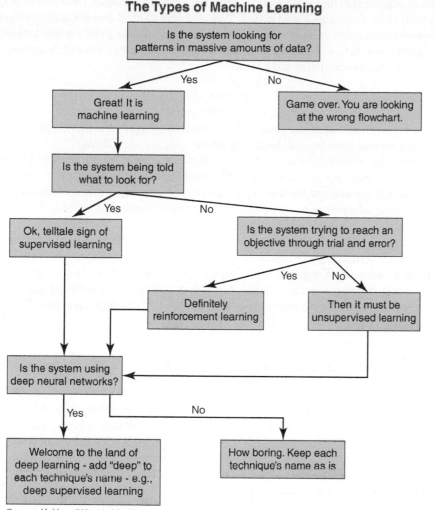

Source: K. Hao, "What is Machine Learning?" MIT Technology Review, November 17, 2018.

FIGURE 14.1   **The Types of Machine Learning**

Supervised Learning

As we discussed in the previous section, **supervised learning** is a type of machine learning in which the system is given labeled input data and the expected output results. Developers input massive amounts of data during the training phase as well as what output should be obtained from each specific input value. Developers then input unlabeled, never-been-seen data values to verify that the model is accurate.

Classification and regression analysis are important techniques for supervised learning. Classification algorithms are used when the outputs are restricted to a limited set of values; regression algorithms are used when the outputs can have any numerical value within a certain range.

Classification refers to a predictive modeling problem in which the system generates a class label for a given set of input data. There are four types of classification.

- *Binary classification* refers to classification problems that have only two class labels. Examples are e-mail spam detection (spam or not), churn prediction (churn or not), and conversion prediction (buy or not).

- *Multi-class classification* refers to classification problems with more than two class labels. Examples are news article categories, plant species classification, and optical character recognition.

- *Multi-label classification* refers to classification problems that have two or more class labels, where one or more class labels can be predicted from each example. Consider the example of photo classification, where a given photo may have multiple objects in the scene. The classification model may predict the presence of multiple known objects in the photo, such as an automobile, a person, a stop sign, and so on.

- *Imbalanced classification* refers to classification problems in which the number of classes in each class is unequally distributed. Typically, imbalanced classification problems are binary classification problems in which the majority of data points in the training data belong to one class and a minority to another class. Examples are fraud detection, outlier detection, and medical diagnostic tests.

Linear regression is a supervised machine learning algorithm in which the predicted output is continuous and has a constant slope. This algorithm is used to predict continuous variables such as sales or price, rather than classifying them into categories with a classification algorithm. There are two main types of linear regression: simple and multiple.

In *simple linear regression*, a single independent variable is used to predict the value of a dependent variable. For example, the Italian clothing company Benetton is examining its annual sales and the amount the firm is spending on advertising. Benetton uses simple linear regression, using advertising as the independent (predictor) variable to predict the dependent variable, sales.

In *multiple linear regression*, two or more independent variables are used to predict the value of a dependent variable. Suppose that Benetton wants to analyze the impact of product price, product advertising expense, store location, and season of the year on product sales. The firm would conduct a multiple linear regression, with price, advertising expense, store location, and season as the independent variables predicting the dependent variable, product sales.

Semi-supervised learning

Semi-supervised learning is a type of machine learning that combines a small amount of labeled data with a large amount of unlabeled data during training. For example, semi-supervised learning is an excellent text document classifier because it is very difficult to find a large amount of labeled text documents. The reason is that it is not efficient to have a human read through entire text documents to classify and label them. In this case, the algorithm learns from a small amount of labeled text documents while still being able to classify large amounts of unlabeled text documents in the training data.

Unsupervised Learning

Unsupervised learning is a type of machine learning that searches for previously undetected patterns in a data set with no pre-existing labels and with minimal human supervision. The best time to use unsupervised learning is when an organization does not have data on desired outcomes. An example is when the firm wants to determine a target market for an entirely new product that it has never before sold.

Cluster analysis is one of the primary techniques in unsupervised learning. Cluster analysis groups, or segments, data points to identify common characteristics. It then reacts based on whether each new piece of data exhibits these characteristics.

Example: Finding customer segments. Clustering is an unsupervised ML technique in which the goal is to find groups or clusters in input data. Developers use clustering to determine customer segments in marketing data using variables such as gender, location, age, education, income bracket, and many others.

Example: Feature selection. Assume that developers want to predict how capable an applicant is of repaying a loan from the perspective of a bank. The goal is to provide loans to applicants who can repay them. Banks analyze large amounts of data about each application to make these predictions, including the applicant's average monthly income, average monthly debt payments, credit history, age, and many other variables.

Because banks typically collect more data than they use in making loan decisions, not all of the variables are relevant for predicting an applicant's ability to repay a loan. For instance, does an applicant's age make any difference in deciding whether he or she can repay the loan? Is the applicant's gender important? For this reason, eliminating unnecessary variables is an essential part of training a ML system. In feature selection, developers try to eliminate a subset of the original set of features (variables).

Reinforcement Learning

Reinforcement learning is a type of machine learning in which the system learns to achieve a goal in an uncertain, potentially complex environment. In reinforcement learning, the system faces a game-like situation where it employs trial and error to find a solution to a problem. The developer awards penalties or rewards to the system for the actions it performs so that it will do what the developer wants. The system's goal is to maximize the total reward.

Although the designers set the reward policy—that is, the rules of the game—they give the model no hints or suggestions for how to solve the problem. The system must determine how to perform the task to maximize the reward, beginning with totally random trials and finishing with sophisticated tactics.

There are numerous examples of reinforcement learning applications. Some of these are:

- Recommendation systems
- Automated ad bidding and buying
- Dynamic resource allocation in wind farms, HVAC (heating and air conditioning) systems, and computer clusters in data centers
- Automated calibration of engines and other machines
- Robotic control
- Autonomous vehicles such as self-driving cars
- Supply chain optimization

Deep Learning

Deep learning is a subset of machine learning in which artificial neural networks learn from large amounts of data. When supervised, semi-supervised, unsupervised, and reinforcement learning systems use neural networks, we add the term *deep* to each one, resulting in deep supervised learning, deep semi-supervised learning, and so on.

Deep learning systems can solve complex problems even when they utilize a data set that is very diverse and unstructured. These systems can discover new patterns without being exposed to labeled historical or training data. Widely used examples of deep learning are automatic speech recognition, image recognition, natural language processing, customer relationship management, recommendation systems, and drug discovery.

IT's About Business 14.1

POM MKT HRM PepsiCo Uses AI

Food-and-beverage company, PepsiCo (**www.pepsico.com**), sells products in more than 200 countries and reported $67 billion in revenue in 2019. PepsiCo uses artificial intelligence throughout the organization.

POM The company has deployed a ML-powered, 6-wheeled mobile vending machine robot called Snackbot at the University of the Pacific (**www.pacific.edu**). The robot carries PepsiCo snacks and beverages from Hello Goodness, its healthy selection brand that includes SunChips, Baked Lay's, and bubbly sparkling water. The self-driving robots are a partnership between Robby Technologies (**www.robby.io**) and PepsiCo.

Students order their snacks from the Snackbot app and the robot will deliver to more than 50 spots across the campus without charging a delivery fee. The bots have a range of 20 miles on a single battery charge and can navigate at night, in rain, or over curbs thanks to onboard headlights and all-wheel drive capabilities.

POM The Frito-Lay (a subsidiary of PepsiCo; **www.fritolay. com**) manufacturing plant is using machine learning. One project uses lasers to "paint" chips. ML algorithms then listen to the sounds coming from the chip to determine its texture. The system automates the quality control process for Frito-Lay's chip production systems.

Another ML system uses computer vision to predict the weight of potatoes being processed. This system produces savings because the company did not have to spend $300,000 per production line for weighing potatoes. An additional use of computer vision is to assess the "percent peel" of a potato after it has gone through the peeling process. This project saves the company more than $1 million per year just in the United States.

HRM In Russia, PepsiCo human resource professionals needed to fill 250 jobs in a company in two months. PepsiCo used Robot Vera to phone and interview candidates for sales, driver, and factory positions. Russian startup Stafory developed Vera, which is capable of interviewing 1,500 candidates in 9 hours, a job that would take humans 9 weeks.

ML-based speech recognition software and ML tools from Amazon, Google, Microsoft, and Russian technology company Yandex allow Vera to make calls and screen candidates for open positions such as fork-lift operators, factory workers, and sales staff. Its software can scan resumés to determine if a potential candidate has the right experience for the position, can respond to yes and no answers, ask follow-up questions, and send out follow-up correspondence. It can also forward transcripts of a call to a human HR specialist for further review.

MKT **POM** PepsiCo was facing changes in consumer behavior toward healthier foods and drinks. As a result, the company asked BlackSwan Technologies (**www.blackswantechnologies.ai**) to analyze consumer conversations at scale to help PepsiCo develop product innovations. BlackSwan is an AI company whose product, Element, integrates Big Data and machine learning to address data acquisition, insight discovery, and predictions.

BlackSwan analyzed 157 million data points about beverages from tweets, restaurant menus, recipe blogs, cooking blogs, on-line message boards, and other sources. BlackSwan filtered out irrelevant content such as duplication, spam, advertising, and automated bots, leaving only useful consumer data. The company then applied ML-driven natural language processing analysis to understand and organize the data and make predictions about beverage trends.

The result was that PepsiCo launched a new range of eight flavored, zero-calorie, sweetener-free sparkling waters. Within 12 months, sales exceeded $100 million.

Sources: Compiled from S. Ciment, "How PepsiCo Is Tracking Consumer Preferences," *Business Insider*, October 16, 2020; "How PepsiCo Scours Restaurant Menus and Tweets for Consumer Trends," *The Best*

Food Recipe, October 15, 2020; I. Dulange, "PepsiCo Experiments with AI," *AI Daily*, April 6, 2019 B. Marr, "The Fascinating Ways PepsiCo Uses Artificial Intelligence and Machine Learning to Deliver Success," *Forbes*, April 5, 2019; A. Hanson, "New PepsiCo Solution Offers Tailored Insights to Retailer Partners," *Convenience Store News*, February 27, 2019; M. Kelly, "PepsiCo Is Rolling out a Fleet of Robots to Bring Snacks to College Students," *The Verge*, January 4, 2019; "PepsiCo's Hello Goodness Snackbot is off to College," *PR Newswire*, January 3, 2019; B. Goodwin, "PepsiCo Hires Robots to Interview Job Candidates," *Computer Weekly*, April 12, 2018; I. Khrennikov, "The Russian Robot That's Hiring Humans," *Bloomberg*, March 27, 2018; www.pepsico.com, accessed November 11, 2020.

Questions

Which type of machine learning applies to the following applications in this case? Support your answer for each application.

- The Snackbot robot;
- Frito-Lay using lasers to paint chips to determine texture;
- Frito-Lay using computer vision to determine percent peel of potatoes;
- PepsiCo using Robot Vera to fill 250 jobs;
- PepsiCo's use of BlackSwan Technologies to analyze consumer behavior.

Before you go on...

1. What is the difference between traditional computer programming and machine learning systems?
2. What is the difference between expert systems and machine learning systems?
3. Describe three types of bias that can negatively impact the development of machine learning systems.
4. Refer back to IT's About Business 3.3. Why are false positives so important in evaluating the output of machine learning systems in the case of facial recognition?
5. Differentiate between supervised learning, semi-supervised learning, unsupervised learning, reinforcement learning, and deep learning.

14.3 Neural Networks

An **artificial neural network**, also known as a **neural network (NN)**, is a set of *virtual neurons*, or *nodes*, that work in parallel to simulate the way the human brain works, although in a greatly simplified form. Improvements in algorithms and increasingly powerful computer chips and storage are enabling developers to create neural networks with billions of neurons. As a result, developers are training them to learn, recognize patterns, and make decisions in a humanlike way.

Neural networks consist of nodes, synapses (connections between nodes), weights, biases, and functions. A **node** in a neural network consists of software that has one or more weighted input connections, a bias function, an activation function, and one or more output connections.

The nodes are arranged in several layers: one input layer, one or more hidden layers, and one output layer (see **Figure 14.2**). The hidden layers are called "hidden" simply because they are located between the input and output layers. See **Figure 14.3** for an example of a generic neural network with one hidden layer. Note that a *deep neural network* contains multiple hidden layers.

Neural network developers choose the network's *hyperparameters*, which include the number of hidden layers, the number of nodes in each layer, the learning rate (how much the

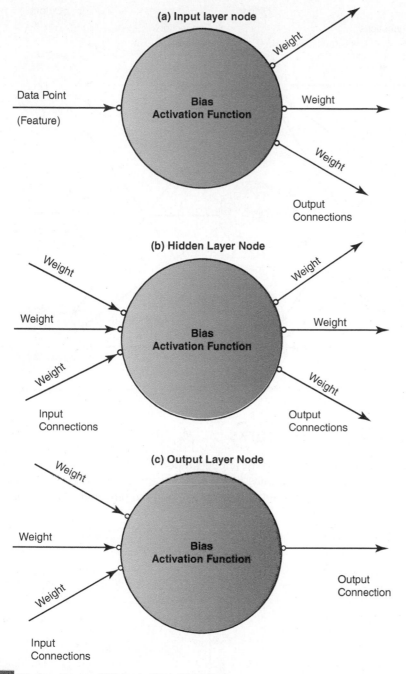

(a) Input layer node

Data Point

(Feature)

Bias
Activation Function

Weight

Weight

Weight

Output
Connections

(b) Hidden Layer Node

Weight

Weight

Weight

Bias
Activation Function

Weight

Weight

Weight

Input
Connections

Output
Connections

(c) Output Layer Node

Weight

Weight

Weight

Bias
Activation Function

Output
Connection

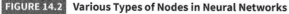

Input
Connections

FIGURE 14.2   **Various Types of Nodes in Neural Networks**

system is allowed to change the parameters after each training iteration), and the activation functions in each node.

The *activation functions (AFs)* that reside at each node define the output of that node given an input or a set of inputs. (See **Figure 14.4** for an example of an activation function). AFs are a critical component of neural network design, and their selection is crucial for efficient and accurate performance. There are dozens of activation functions available to developers. These functions process incoming data in different ways, and developers chose them to provide the best model for the data. The key is to match the correct activation function with the data and the desired output predictions. For example, some activation functions are better suited for binary classification, while others perform best with continuous data.

Weights and biases are examples of *parameters* in a neural network. For the first training iteration, developers set weights and biases to some neutral value, such as 0 or 0.5, depending on the particular application. In subsequent iterations, weights and biases are adjusted by the loss function of the network with the goal of minimizing system inaccuracies.

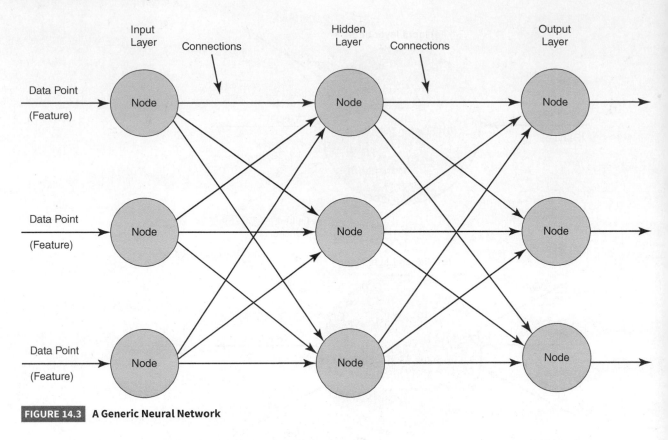

FIGURE 14.3 A Generic Neural Network

Training Neural Networks

NNs learn best from large data sets. Developers randomly separate the data into *training*, *validation*, and *test* data sets. Typically, developers use approximately 60 percent of the overall data set for training, 10 percent for validation, and the remaining 30 percent for testing.

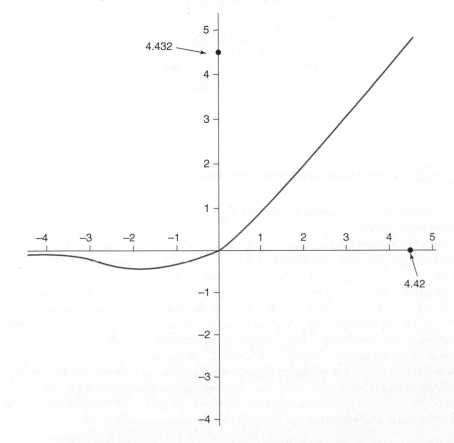

FIGURE 14.4 Swish Activation
Function

During training, developers use the validation data to evaluate how well the training process is progressing and to adjust the hyperparameters to better tune the network. When training is completed, developers use the test data to measure the performance of the NN to determine whether it is optimally trained and is a viable system that the organization can deploy.

During the learning or training process, developers feed the numeric values of the training data into the input layer of nodes. Developers feed one feature, or variable, into each input node. For example, if developers are training an NN to predict house values, they might use the house's square footage, its age, the zip code, and the number of bedrooms and bathrooms. Each of those five variables is a feature, and there will be an input node for each feature. Therefore, the input layer will consist of five nodes. Because the goal of the NN is to predict a home's value, the output layer will consist of a single node, the predicted price. The NN will consist of one or more hidden layers (a decision made by the developers), each of which has one or more nodes.

Input nodes apply the *bias* (a mathematical change) to the input data value, producing a new value. The input node then applies the *activation function* to this new value, producing another new value. The input node then sends this new value to the next layer of nodes; that is, the first hidden layer. Along the pathways to the next layer, additional adjustments, known as *weights*, are applied to the data values.

As the weight-adjusted data arrive at the hidden-layer node from previous nodes, they are summed and the hidden-layer node applies another bias and an activation function to the summed data, producing a new value. The node then sends this value along the pathways to the next layer of nodes. The process in which biases, activation functions, and weights change the data values continues through to the last layer of nodes, the output layer. In the nodes of the output layer, the data undergo their final adjustments from the bias and activation function, and a *loss function* compares the just-processed data to the expected output value.

The difference between the derived data value and the expected value—that is, the loss function—initiates the process of **back propagation**. In this process, the values of the weights of each pathway and the bias values of each node are slightly changed in anticipation that the next iteration of data flowing through the neural network will result in a smaller error, or loss, upon output. After the adjustments by back propagation, the next data values begin their journey through the NN.

This process—new data, vast numbers of slight adjustments, the systems adjustments by back propagation—continues over and over until the training data are exhausted. At this point—if the loss function reveals that there are little to no required adjustments—developers consider the NN to be trained.

This chapter's Appendix shows an example of how neural networks function. While this example is highly simplified, it provides a look into the steps that neural networks take to learn the patterns that may exist among the large amounts of data they process.

Neural Networks for Specific Applications

Recurrent Neural Networks (RNNs).   A recurrent neural network is designed to access previous data such as sequential data or time series data during iterations of input. RNNs are used in applications where the RNN's decision must be based on previous output such as moving a robotic arm, reading a sentence, predicting time series, and composing music.

Convolutional Neural Networks (CNNs).   A convolutional neural network is designed to separate areas of image inputs by extracting features to identify edges, curves, and color density and then recombine these inputs for classification and prediction. CNNs are highly effective for image and pattern recognition applications such as facial recognition, video analysis, natural language processing, drug discovery, and anomaly detection. Let's take a closer look at how CNNs process images.

Each layer of the CNN manages a different level of abstraction. To process an image, the first layer is fed with raw images. That layer notes aspects of the images such as the brightness and colors of individual pixels and how those properties are distributed across the image. The next layer takes the first layer's observations and places them into more abstract categories such as identifying edges, shadows, and so on. The next layer analyzes those edges and shadows, searching for combinations that signify features such as eyes, lips, and ears. The final layer combines these observations into a representation of a face.

To train a CNN to learn facial recognition, developers will input millions of images. Some images will contain faces, and some will not. Each image will be labeled by a human, for example, through Amazon's Mechanical Turk. The images act as inputs to the neural network, and the labels—"face" or "not face"—are the outputs. The network's task is to develop a statistical rule, operationalized through the weights between processors, that correlates inputs with correct outputs.

To accomplish this task, the network will search for those features that are common to the images that display faces. Once these correlations are strong enough—that is, the weights, or strength of the connections between processors, are high enough—the network will be able to reliably differentiate faces from not-faces in its training set. The next step is to feed the neural network with a fresh set of unlabeled images to determine whether the facial recognition algorithms that the network has developed actually function with the new data.

NNs can also make mistakes. For example, developers trained a CNN to differentiate between images of wolves and Husky dogs. The researchers trained the CNN with numerous examples of photographs, and the CNN eventually achieved an accuracy rate of about 90 percent. The researchers then examined the inner workings of the CNN, focusing on which features contributed to correct classifications. They found that the CNN had learned based on the backgrounds of the training images—wolves were generally photographed on snow, and the dogs were photographed on grass. Therefore, the CNN tended to misclassify a photograph of a dog on a snowy background as being a wolf and to misclassify a wolf standing on a grassy field as a dog. The excellent performance of the CNN was misleading, and the CNN was unreliable for the purpose for which it was trained.

Generative Adversarial Networks (GANs).   A **generative adversarial network** consists of two neural networks that compete with each other in a zero-sum game in an effort to segregate real data from synthetic data. GANs separate real data from noise. They perform well in applications where filling in missing or incomplete data may be required. For example, GANs are used for improving deep-space photography, for inpainting, and in other applications where completing missing digital data is required. (Note: *inpainting* is a conservation process where damaged, deteriorating, or missing pars of an artwork are filled in to present a complete image). GANs can also be used for creating deepfakes ranging from image manipulation to news embellishments.

Before you go on...

1. Describe the structure of a neural network.
2. Describe how a neural network operates. That is, describe how developers train neural networks.

14.4 Artificial Intelligence Applications

Author Lecture Videos are available exclusively in *WileyPLUS*.
Apply the Concept activities are available in the Appendix and in *WileyPLUS*.

The field of artificial intelligence has many applications. Note that these applications use machine learning, deep learning, and neural networks. In this section, we discuss computer vision, natural language processing, robotics, speech recognition, and intelligent agents. In Section 14.5, you will see numerous examples of these applications in use in all functional areas of organizations. These examples will emphasize how important artificial intelligence is to you, *regardless of your major*.

Computer Vision

Computer vision refers to the ability of information systems to identify objects, scenes, and activities in images. Computer vision has diverse applications, including medical imaging to improve predicting, diagnosing, and treating diseases; facial recognition; and autonomous vehicles. Let's take a closer look at examples of computer vision at Amazon, Descartes Labs, and eBay.

POM *Amazon.* Amazon has deployed an ML-based system in its fulfillment centers that enables workers to skip one manual item-scanning step per order. The system impacts Amazon's *stowing process*, which lets workers store items that have arrived from distributors and manufacturers anywhere on a warehouse's shelves, as long as each item's location is recorded in a computer so that it can be found again on the first try. This method requires workers to take an item out of a box, scan its bar code, place it on a shelf, and then scan the bar code on the shelf. The two scans provide the exact location of the item.

Computer vision enables workers to pick up an item, slide it under a scanner mounted nearby, and place it on a shelf. Amazon has trained the system to recognize where the worker places the item, and it records that location for future reference. The worker no longer has to scan the shelf. Eliminating this step improves efficiency. Given the hundreds of millions of items stored in its fulfillment centers, the system is providing large cost savings to Amazon.

POM *Descartes Labs.* Descartes Labs (**www.descarteslabs.com**), which uses artificial intelligence to analyze satellite imagery, launched its wildfire detector in the United States in July 2019. The company's system analyzes images that come in every five minutes from two U.S. government weather satellites.

The system uses several ML algorithms to determine whether a fire has begun. One algorithm examines spatial context, assessing whether the suspected fire is hotter than its surroundings. A second algorithm looks back in time to see what the area normally looks like when there is no fire. A third algorithm searches for areas that are unexpectedly hot compared to historical temperatures. Still another algorithm checks for the presence of smoke. Descartes claims that its system can detect a fire faster than firefighters or civilians. In fact, the company states that it can detect fires when they are only 10 acres in size.

MKT **POM** *eBay.* eBay's ML platform, Krylov, helps users locate items based on taking a picture of an object or an image. Users can take a photo of an item they are searching for and then upload the image to the eBay app. Within milliseconds, the platform presents items that match the image.

Natural Language Processing

Natural language processing refers to the ability of information systems to work with text the way that humans do. For example, these systems can extract the meaning from text, and they can generate text that is readable, stylistically natural, and grammatically correct.

Because context is critical, the practical applications of natural language processing typically address relatively narrow areas such as analyzing customer feedback about a particular product or service, automating discovery in civil litigation or government investigations (e-discovery), and automating the writing of formulaic stories on topics such as corporate earnings and sports. We take a closer look at two examples of natural language processing, Google and eBay.

Google. In November 2020, Google open-sourced an ML model called MT5 that the company claims can achieve state-of-the-art results on a range of English natural language processing tasks. Google trained the model on a dataset that covers 101 languages.

POM *eBay.* In addition to computer vision, eBay's ML platform, Krylov, provides ML-powered language translation services. The company has trained Krylov with vast amounts of data from its 1.4 billion listings for 183 million users in 190 markets.

Cross-border trade makes up nearly 60 percent of eBay's international revenue. Therefore, accurate, instantaneous translation is critical. eBay offered automatic translation prior to developing Krylov. However, the platform has significantly improved eBay's translation accuracy, which in turn has helped to increase the company's international sales by 11 percent.

Robotics

Integrating computer vision with tiny, high-performance sensors and actuators, a new generation of robots can work alongside people and flexibly perform multiple tasks in unpredictable environments. Examples are unmanned aerial vehicles; cooperative robots, called *cobots*, that share jobs with humans on the factory floor; robotic vacuum cleaners; and so on.

POM Amazon Robotics—formerly Kiva Systems, acquired by Amazon in March 201 is an excellent example of cobots working in distribution centers. Rather than human inventory pickers selecting items for order fulfilment, Amazon's cobots bring the items to a human who fills the orders. Section 14.7 provides additional examples of the use of robots.

Speech recognition

Speech recognition focuses on automatically and accurately transcribing human speech. This technology must manage diverse accents, dialects, and background noise. Furthermore, it must distinguish between homophones and work at the speed of natural speech. A *homophone* is a word that is pronounced the same as another word but differs in meaning; for example, "break" and "brake." Applications include medical dictation, hands-free writing, voice control of information systems, and telephone customer service applications. For example, popular voice-based digital assistants, such as Apple Siri, Microsoft Cortana, Google Assistant, Amazon Alexa, and Samsung Bixby, can understand our words, analyze our questions, and point us in the general direction of the right answer.

Intelligent Agents

The terms *chatbot* and intelligent agent are often used interchangeably. Further, both applications use various technologies to deliver an experience or service for a user. Chatbots communicate with a user when a predetermined action occurs, such as a user typing in a pop-up box or speaking to a device. The chatbot then compares keywords from the user to its stored knowledge base. Taking the most likely response, the chatbot delivers scripted information to the user. However, chatbots are typically do not learn from the interaction. Thus, they are not considered intelligent.

An **intelligent agent** is a software program that assists users, or acts on their behalf, in performing computer-related tasks. These agents are more advanced than chatbots. They do not simply provide answers from a knowledge base. Rather, they must be able to do something for a user, such as understand customer intent; provide personalized, accurate answers; and offer basic problem solving.

Today, there are many intelligent agents that are utilized for a wide variety of tasks. We take a closer look at two types of agents: information agents and monitoring and surveillance agents.

Information Agents. **Information agents** search for information and display it to users. Consider this example of an information agent at USAA.

MKT Insurance company USAA (**www.usaa.com**) uses IBM Watson as a customer-facing intelligent agent that enables its customers who are leaving military service to ask questions about, for example, college tuition reimbursement or changes to their health benefits. USAA executives note that the agent augments employees' expertise rather than replacing them. Watson helps shorten service calls, offers more context to incoming calls, and reduces the amount of paperwork around customer interactions.

Monitoring and Surveillance Agents. **Monitoring and surveillance agents,** also called **predictive agents**, constantly observe and report on some item of interest. There are many examples of predictive agents.

- **MIS** Allstate uses predictive agents to monitor its computer networks 24/7/365. These agents can predict a system crash 45 minutes before it happens and can detect electronic attacks to help prevent them.

- **MIS** Predictive agents can monitor Internet sites, discussion groups, and mailing lists for stock manipulations, insider trading, and rumors that might affect stock prices.

- **MIS** Predictive agents can search websites for updated information on topics of your choice, such as price changes on desired products (e.g., airline tickets).

Before you go on...

1. Describe the advantages of computer vision, natural language processing, and speech recognition.
2. What are cobots?
3. Discuss how you might use information agents and monitoring and surveillance agents.

14.5 Artificial Intelligence in the Functional Areas

ACCT AI in Accounting

Author Lecture Videos are available exclusively in *WileyPLUS*.
Apply the Concept activities are available in the Appendix and in *WileyPLUS*.

By the end of 2020, machine learning systems were performing routine functions, freeing accountants to focus on performing judgment-intensive tasks and communicating with clients. Machine learning requires huge amounts of data to provide accurate results. Not surprisingly, then, the largest accounting firms are leading the industry in developing ML applications. The Big Four are Ernst & Young (**www.ey.com**), PwC (**www.pwc.com**), Deloitte (**www.deloitte.com**), and KPMG (**www.kpmg.com**). Consider these examples:

- KPMG uses IBM Watson, an ML system, to help leasing companies comply with the IFRS 16 lease accounting standard.

- Argus, an ML tool developed by Deloitte, reviews documents for key accounting information. The tool works with many types of documents, including but not limited to: sales, leasing and derivatives contracts, employment agreements, invoices, client meeting minutes, legal letters, and financial statements. Deloitte has also deployed a service that monitors risk associated with ML algorithms. This service can help early adopters use machine learning tools with reduced fear of adverse effects.

- Suppose an accounting clerk is processing a transaction but is unsure whether to post the expense in this month's financials or the next month. Without an ML system, the clerk decides how to record that transaction. However, this decision might not be correct. If the entry is incorrect, it might go unchecked and uncorrected. This problem is one of the reasons why many companies are not confident in the accuracy of their most recent close and have had to reopen their books after close to correct errors.

    To help with such problems, Flexi (**www.flexi.com**), a provider of enterprise financial management software, has deployed an ML system that helps organizations avoid errors and accelerate the financial close process. Specifically, the system offers suggestions on how to correctly record transactions based on accounting rules.

Taxes.   ML systems use knowledge of the tax code to process clients' tax information through a set of rules and calculate the amount of taxes they owe. In 2017, for example, H&R Block (**www.hrblock.com**) incorporated IBM Watson to help deliver the best outcome for each unique tax situation.

Tax preparation involves massive volumes of data, encompassing thousands of pages of the federal tax code, as well as state tax codes and local tax codes, all of which impact a client's tax outcome. H&R Block and IBM trained Watson using data from the more than 750 million returns that H&R Block had filed since 1955. H&R Block tax experts then validated Watson's conclusions and first applied Watson to the thousands of client questions and topics discussed with clients during the return filing process.

H&R Block uses Watson to understand context, interpret client intent, and draw connections between clients' statements and relevant areas of their returns. H&R Block professionals can then identify additional areas of possible tax implications to maximize client refunds or reduce their tax liabilities. The client can also follow along with the tax preparation process on a dedicated client companion screen that highlights areas for deductions, making the preparation process more transparent and understandable.

Here is how the process works. A customer enters an H&R Block office and sits down in front of a screen. A tax professional begins the usual interview, asking about life events, potential deductions, and possible credits, entering data as the client watches the screen. Throughout the process, Watson references 600 million data points, the entire U.S. tax code, and state and local tax codes, to outline areas with potential savings. After the customer interview, Watson displays a chart of all possible deductions and credits. The tax professional then goes through the chart with the customer, explaining all the different ways to increase a refund or reduce liabilities.

Auditing. An *audit* is an independent examination of the financial information of organizations to determine whether their financial statements are accurate. Let's look at examples where organizations use ML systems in auditing and compliance.

- *Problem:* Most enterprises audit only a fraction of their invoices, meaning they could miss errors, fraud, and contract violations. Machine learning systems validate all invoices against contract terms and assign a risk score based on errors, anomalies, and noncompliance with contract terms.

    Requirement: Automatically audit all invoices and flag high-risk invoices for manual review.

    Solution: ML systems will enable auditors to examine 100 percent of companies' financial transactions. ML algorithms will process and review the data, recognize anomalies, and compile a list of outliers for auditors to check. Instead of spending most of their time checking data, auditors can focus specifically on the reasons behind a pattern or anomaly. If auditors can check every transaction, then their financial information will be more accurate, and they can provide better advice to their clients. ML systems automatically approve low-risk invoices so they can proceed to payment, and they flag high-risk invoices for manual review.

- *Problem:* Accounting teams typically audit invoices after they have been paid. As time passes, it can become increasingly difficult for companies to recover erroneous or fraudulent spend. Even if a company can eventually recover the spend, there is a cost to not having that cash on hand.

    Requirement: Streamline the audit process to ensure that review of all spend happens prior to payment.

    Solution: ML systems streamline the manual review process to efficiently audit all spend prior to payment.

- *Problem:* Procurement teams may spend large amounts of time negotiating contract terms only to have vendor invoices violate them. Contract violations may relate to payment terms, volume discounts, and pricing mismatches.

    Requirement: Make sense of all contract terms and validate invoices against them to ensure that the invoice adheres to the contract.

    Solution: ML systems integrate with contract management systems and repositories to extract all contract terms. ML systems use semantic analysis to make sense of those terms in business contexts. Further, they are trained to identify invoices whose details do not comply. *Semantic analysis* is the process of drawing meaning from text; it is related to natural language processing.

- *Problem:* With thousands of invoices being processed every month, it is very difficult to examine each one. Fake invoices, shell companies, and vendor impersonation are only some of the methods that criminals use to target companies.

    Requirement: Identify suspect fraud in invoices.

    Solution: ML systems review invoices in relation to data in contracts, business systems, online sources, and other invoices to identify suspected fraud.

- *Problem:* Companies could be paying the same bill twice—once via expense reimbursement and again via invoice. If invoice and expense automation systems do not communicate, then duplicate spend can go unnoticed.

    Requirement: Detect duplicate spend across both invoice and expense automation systems.

Solution: ML systems remember all of the invoice- and expense-based spend that they process, regardless of when the spend occurs and what the receipts and invoices look like. Therefore, ML systems ensure that companies do not pay the invoice when they have already reimbursed the employee for the same spend, or vice versa.

- *Problem:* Duplicate invoices can occur. In rare cases, vendors send duplicate invoices on purpose. In the majority of cases, however, they are a mistake. They can also be a case of fraud by an employee. Invoice automation systems can catch duplicates, generally when those invoices have the same invoice number. If a vendor is sending a separate monthly or quarterly summary invoice, then duplicates can be even more difficult to catch.

  Requirement: Identify all duplicate invoices, regardless of when they are received, how they are grouped, and whether they have the same invoice number.

  Solution: ML systems do not forget data that they have ingested. They catch duplicate invoices—even ones sent at different times, broken up into smaller pieces, or having different invoice numbers—by matching individual line items and other data, and flag them for review prior to payment.

- *Problem:* An organization's reputation can be damaged by its vendor associations. Therefore, firms should consider reputation risks and monetary penalties arising from vendor misconduct, such as violation of the Foreign Corrupt Practices Act, the United Kingdom Bribery Act, and payments to companies with which a board member has a relationship.

  Requirement: Limit your exposure to vendor misconduct such as regulatory violations and conflicts of interest.

  Solution: ML systems check the names of vendors, politically exposed employees, and board members and their associations against online databases, flagging high-risk organizations and people.

- *Problem:* Companies receive thousands of invoices every month, making keeping abreast of associated discount opportunities very difficult.

  Requirement: Validate invoice amounts against early payment contract terms, and flag those that do not include these savings.

  Solution: ML systems extract and understand contract terms related to early payment. When an invoice payment deadline approaches, these systems flag savings opportunities associated with early payments.

- *Problem:* A minor delay in a firm's invoice automation system can result in paying invoices twice. The system may hold the invoice because an approver is on vacation or the invoice failed a two-way match for a minor reason. A business partner who would like to have the invoice paid might intervene to get the invoice paid manually. Afterward, the system may clear the hold and process the invoice, meaning that the firm has double-paid. The vendor might not realize it, and the firm will not discover the problem until it has audited the spend.

  Requirement: Flag all duplicate invoices as high risk if they have already been paid, even if payment occurred outside the normal process.

  Solution: ML systems remember all invoices and their payments, and they are trained to search for duplicate spend regardless of when invoices are paid, by whom, and under what circumstances.

- *Problem:* Many vendors are required to maintain insurance policies that protect them and your company. How does your company ensure that those policies provide sufficient coverage?

  Requirement: Ensure that your vendors are properly insured and that all policies are current.

  Solution: ML systems extract and make sense of the various insurance requirements in a firm's contracts, as well as their expiration dates. This process validates that all required insurance policies are current and meet a firm's coverage criteria. It also alerts the firm when coverage limits are insufficient or certificates need to be updated.

- *Problem:* Most companies employ contractors in a variety of departments such as janitorial services, temporary workers, systems integrators, and consultants. Firms generally trust their contractors to bill them for the hours they actually work. But how can the firms verify that they were billed correctly?

  Requirement: Ensure that contractors are working the hours they claim in their invoices.

Solution: ML systems integrate with relevant business systems such as time tracking, card access, and e-mail and messaging. The systems build a profile of access and work activity for different types of contractors. When the system audits an invoice for a contractor who is inconsistent with the profile, it will flag the invoice as high-risk.

- *Problem:* A three-way match refers to the three components—purchase order, receipt of goods, and supplier invoice—that must match within agreed-upon tolerance levels to ensure a proper and timely payment. This method is limited to price and units across invoices, receipts, and purchase orders. As a business becomes more sophisticated, it needs to validate not just price and units, but also volume discounts, payment terms, delivery times, transport conditions, chain of custody, service level agreements, and whatever else is meaningful to the business, based on data from any of the business systems.

  Requirement: Automatically match data elements from any of your business systems.

  Solution: ML systems recognize the content of invoices and match those data with data from enterprise systems such as contract management and enterprise resource planning to ensure that transactions are accurate.

- *Problem:* Businesses might have to make a conscious choice to pay more to ensure quality and timeliness in a supply chain. At the same time, however, businesses might want the lowest price, or at least the market rate, for goods and services. It is important for a firm to know how much it is paying and what the market rate is when it renegotiates contracts or chooses future business partners.

  Requirement: Have visibility into what you pay for goods and services versus market rate.

  Solution: ML systems gather information from thousands of online sources to understand market pricing and other details for goods and services. When an invoice price exceeds a certain threshold over the market price, the system will flag the invoice for review. By keeping track of overcharges over time, the firm will have improved insights into what suppliers are doing. These insights empower the company to have stronger negotiations at a later time.

- *Problem:* When a company renegotiates a contract for volume discounts, it should review vendors' invoices to ensure that they follow agreed-upon terms.

  Requirement: Ensure that invoices reflect the volume discounts specified in your contracts.

  Solution: ML systems make sense of the volume discounts in the firm's contracts and keep track of the firm's purchase volume. When the system audits an invoice that does not comply with the price for the firm's current volume, it will flag it for review.

- *Problem:* A small percentage of vendors might try to cheat a company's system. For example, they can send the firm a stream of fraudulent invoices that fall just below the review threshold, break up large invoices into smaller amounts, or slowly add extras and surcharges to each new invoice in hopes that the company will not notice. These anomalies can go unnoticed in many business systems.

  Requirement: Firm must be alerted to suspicious invoice activity before they make payment.

  Solution: ML systems use a combination of computer vision and semantic analysis to build a profile of what "good" invoices look like and uncover unusual patterns that humans might not notice.

- *Problem:* Company employees are often bogged down with invoice reviews and contract checks, forcing them to waste time on outdated, manual processes. Employees are responsible for validating invoices and work under the assumption that the service the firm is being billed for was delivered.

  Requirement: Ensure that invoices are for the correct amounts, are being paid to the correct vendors, and match the negotiated contract terms. This process removes employees from manual approvals so they can focus on more important tasks.

  Solution: ML systems gather information from digital sensors such as an office key fob system and supplier contract terms, cross-matching them with invoices and enforcing compliance across the process. A *key fob* is a small, programmable device that provides access to a physical object. The device can be used to provide one-device, one-factor authentication to objects such as doors or automobiles.

FIN AI in Finance

Machine learning systems have been in use for years in the financial sector. Here we look at four areas where these systems are widely used: process automation, security, insurance and risk management, and algorithmic training.

Process Automation.   ML systems enable organizations to replace manual work, automate repetitive tasks, and increase productivity.

- *Chatbots*. ML-driven chatbots provide access to all of a customer's data. They communicate with customers to provide account information, send notifications to customers, track spending habits, provide credit scores, set and manage budgets, suggest how to save money, pay bills, and help them reset their passwords. Chatbots can also enable customer to search their account history for a specific transaction with a specific merchant, avoiding the hassle of searching their bank statements. The bots can also compute total amounts of credit and debt, a task that customers previously had to perform manually.

    Chatbots also assist in call centers. Organizations train the chatbots with data from previous customer interactions. The chatbots then interact directly with customers. If a chatbot cannot answer a query, it refers the customer to a human. For instance, Privatbank, a Ukrainian bank, has deployed chatbots across its mobile and Web platforms. The chatbots resolve general customer queries quickly, thereby enabling the bank to decrease the number of human assistants. Examples of chatbots are Bank of America's Erica, Capital One's Eno, Ally Bank's Ally Assist, USAA's Clinc, and HSBC's Amy.

    Robo-advisors are a special type of chatbot that analyze each customer's portfolio, risk tolerance, and previous investment decisions to offer advice to financial advisors on portfolio management and investment rebalancing decisions. For example, ForwardLane (**www.forwardlane.com**) provides advisors with personalized investment advice and quantitative modeling that used to be available only to extremely wealthy clients. The advisors can then pass along the information to their clients.

    Traditionally, human investment advisors have been responsible for managing financial portfolios. Today, financial institutions use ML to manage client portfolios and optimize clients' assets. Customers enter their present financial assets and goals. A robo-advisor then allocates the current assets across investment opportunities based on the customer's risk preferences and goals, taking into account real-time market dynamics.

- *Paperwork automation*. JPMorgan Chase & Co. (**www.jpmorganchase.com**) is a U.S. multinational investment bank and financial services company. The firm has implemented a ML system called Contract Intelligence (COiN) that leverages natural language processing and image recognition. COiN analyzes legal documents and extracts important data points and clauses. Before the bank deployed COiN in 2016, their lawyers spent 360,000 hours each year manually reviewing 12,000 commercial loan agreements. With COiN, the task is completed in seconds, saving huge amounts of time and expense

Security.   Banks are introducing ML systems into their fraud detection systems. The banks have two objectives: (a) to detect real incidents of fraud quickly and accurately and (b) to prevent false positives. Banks do not want to abolish existing fraud detection rules, many of which were implemented to comply with government regulations. Rather, they want to augment their existing systems with new ML systems. Consider the following examples.

- *Monitoring*. Banks use ML systems to monitor thousands of transaction variables for every account in real time. These systems examine each action that a cardholder takes and then determine whether an attempted activity is characteristic of that individual. Significantly, they identify fraudulent behavior with high accuracy in real time. When they identify suspicious account behavior, they can request additional identification from the customer to validate the transaction. Alternatively, they can block the transaction.

Consider rogue trading, which is a serious problem for banks around the world. Losses and fines since 2010 for the top 13 global banks have totaled more than $10 billion.

In an attempt to stop rogue trading, banks have deployed ML systems that attempt to predict which traders are likely to go rogue. They monitor traders and their communications. For example, they search for obvious phrases and key words such as "Let's take this conversation offline." They also monitor traders' credit scores, human resources reviews, court convictions, sizable divorce settlements, and many other variables to make their predictions more accurate.

These ML systems make it more difficult for a trader to make the kind of enormous bets that led to one-off losses of as much as $6 billion in JPMorgan Chase and Co.'s "London Whale" scandal. In April and May 2012, $2 billion in trading losses occurred at the firm, based on transactions booked through their London branch. Trader Bruno Iksil, nicknamed the London Whale, accumulated enormous credit default swap (CDS) positions in the market. A *credit default swap* is a financial contract that allows an investor to swap or offset his or her credit risk with that of another investor.

- *Finding false positives*. False positives, which are legitimate transactions that are wrongly rejected due to suspected fraud, account for more than $100 billion in annual losses for global retailers, in addition to lost customers. ML systems, such as Mastercard's Decision Intelligence technology, analyze various data points to identify fraudulent transactions that human analysts might miss, while improving real-time approval accuracy and decreasing false positives. Using ML to spot unusual patterns and improve general regulatory compliance workflows helps financial organizations to be more efficient and accurate in their processes.

    The Nasdaq stock market is an attractive target for criminals. As the world's largest stock exchange by volume, it must be constantly monitored for attempts to illicitly beat the system. These attempts can include manipulations to inflate a stock's closing price; rapidly buying and selling stocks to give the false impression that a lot of activity has occurred; and spoofing, which is placing a large buy or sell order with no intention of actually executing it to create artificially high demand.

    The legacy Nasdaq surveillance system issued around 1,000 alerts per day for human analysts to investigate. Only a fraction of those cases were subsequently confirmed as fraud, which resulted in heavy fines. A ML system is now helping to monitor Nasdaq, augmenting the existing system to flag any signs of market abuse. The ML system also works with human analysts to monitor more than 17.5 million trades per day.

    The ML system was trained to detect particular types of abuse by learning from historical examples. Every time it detects similar suspicious activity, it alerts a human analyst, who possesses the appropriate expertise. After investigating the case, the analyst enters the outcome back into the ML system. In that way, the system learns and becomes better at catching instances of attempted abuse.

- *Image recognition*. Using image recognition, Confirm.io automatically authenticates consumer identity documents. Similarly, Onfido's platform plugs into various publicly available databases to provide employers with rapid identity verification and background checks for issues such as driving and criminal records.

Insurance and Risk Management.
Consider usage-based insurance models, which are based on ML systems that utilize data from telematics and IoT sensors. The transformation from legacy fixed premium insurance models to modern pay-as-you-go models is the result of leveraging ML systems and driving data to more accurately profile driver and trip specifics in order to offer accurate micro-insurance premiums.

- *Client behavioral modeling*. Consider this hypothetical scenario from the near future. Suppose that a customer is driving a car on the highway on a long and tiring trip. The ML system in the car uses computer vision to note that his eyes are droopy. The system's sensors gather data that shows the way he is driving—for example, speed, handling, and braking—is different from the way he normally operates his car. The system then uses natural language processing over the car's speakers to tell him to park his car and get some rest. He resists, thinking that he does not need a break. The system tells him that after analyzing the number of hours that he has been driving, the speed at which the car is running, and his head movements, it feels that he must take at least a small break. On the automobile's digital screen, the system then offers to buy a coffee for him from the next coffee shop on the highway. He accepts the offer. In the near future, if he does not accept the offer, then the system will be able to slow the car and pull it gently off the highway

- *Claim settlement*. ML systems are also impacting claim settlement. By leveraging computer vision and natural language processing in ML systems, insurance assessors can gather real-time information related to accidents and settle claims faster.

  The system takes charge of the entire process, walking the customer through it, step-by-step, in a conversational format. It gathers all the information required for processing the claim, including videos or photos of the damage, and uploads that information into a database. Next, the system examines the application for fraud, searching for anomalies and noncompliant data. It then accesses the insurer's adjustment model, where it examines a range of values for payout. Finally, it calculates and proposes payout amounts, based on a payout predictor model it has been trained on.

- *Compliance issues, regulatory issues, and risk management*. ML-powered systems help lenders lower compliance and regulatory costs by providing robust credit scoring and lending applications. These applications help lenders achieve faster and more accurate risk assessment by factoring in the applicant's character and repayment capacity. For example, Underwrite.ai applies ML to provide lenders with dynamic models of credit risk. Significantly, these models outperform traditional approaches to lending.

  Banks use ML systems to stay in compliance and to identify fraud. For example, IPSoft's Amelia uses natural language processing to scan legal and regulatory text for compliance issues.

Algorithmic Trading. ML systems help to make better algorithmic trading decisions. ML algorithms monitor thousands of data sources in real time, including the news and trading results, to detect patterns that could force stock prices to go up or down. These systems can then act to sell, hold, or buy stocks according to its predictions.

ᴹᴷᵀ AI in Marketing

Improved lead scoring accuracy. Lead scoring helps enterprises rank prospective customers on a scale that represents their value to the firm. Improving lead scoring accuracy helps the company prioritize its lead generation strategies.

Marketing managers use ML systems to monitor customer behavior in order to obtain data for these calculations. For example, the systems track websites visited, e-mails opened, downloads, clicks, and many other variables. They also consider a customer's behavior on social media platforms, such as accounts they follow, posts they like and dislike, ads they engage with, and many other variables.

Easier to predict customer churn. *Customer churn*, also known as customer turnover, is the number of customers who ended their relationship with a business. The *churn rate* is the percentage of customers who leave a business within a specified period of time.

Companies want to know how customers engage with a product, service, or mobile app. Churn rates are an indicator of customer satisfaction with the firms' products and services. Firms need to be able to predict their churn rate in order to minimize it.

To predict churn rates, companies are using ML systems to monitor customer behavior. For example, they ask when the last time a customer signed into their profile on the firm's website, how long they stayed on the website, and when their last purchase was. The answers to such questions, and many others, can predict that a customer will end their relationship with this company. ML systems can analyze such customer behavior at huge scale, enabling firms to better predict that certain customers might leave.

Profitable dynamic pricing models.

A *dynamic pricing* strategy allows businesses to offer flexible prices for the product and services they offer. Essentially, this strategy helps companies segment prices based on customer choices. Dynamic pricing is common in the hospitality, travel, and entertainment industries. The retail industry is now employing ML systems to implement this strategy as well.

Dynamic pricing is related to *real-time pricing*, which occurs when the value of goods is based on specific market conditions. For example, purchasing an airline ticket depends on how far in advance the customer purchases it, the number of tickets already purchased on that particular flight, and the location of the seat on the aircraft. Another example of real-time pricing is surge pricing on Uber and Lyft.

ML systems make it easier for companies to implement and improve their dynamic pricing models by analyzing vast amounts of data. These data include historical prices for each service or product, customer demand, and external factors such as industry trends, seasonality, weather, and location. ML systems also analyze customer information such as search and/or booking history, demographic features, income, and many other variables.

Sentiment analysis.

Companies that implement e-commerce cannot have face-to-face relationships with their customers. As a result, it is difficult to understand how customers are feeling. For instance, with face-to-face conversations, you can make judgments based on facial expressions, tone, and body language. You can then use these judgments to determine whether the person with whom you are speaking is happy, satisfied, or excited.

Companies that employ e-commerce need to know how customers are feeling in order to respond properly. ML systems can help in this area by analyzing text to determine whether the sentiment expressed by customers is positive or negative, a process called *sentiment analysis*. ML systems read all digital communications and classify them as positive or negative. They then alert marketing managers, who can respond to negative comments and trends. ML systems can also identify happy and satisfied customers to help companies find social influencers and brand ambassadors.

Improve website experiments.

A/B testing is an excellent method to improve the features of a company's website, mobile app, and e-mail marketing content. *A/B testing* is the process of showing two versions of, for example, the same web page to different segments of website visitors at the same time and comparing which version drives more purchases or sign-ups. ML systems analyze the results of thousands of A/B tests every day. Companies then use these data to improve their content to increase visitor engagement.

Consider Google RankBrain, a ML-based search engine algorithm that helps Google learn from users' search results to provide more relevant search results in the future. For example, if two people search for the same term on Google at the same time, they are most likely to see different search results based on the results of Google's A/B testing.

Prioritize ad targeting and customer personalization.

ML systems are helping marketing managers target their ads more effectively. A company might produce excellent ads, but they will not be effective if the correct audiences are not viewing them. ML systems can help ensure that companies reach their target audience.

ML systems can also help personalize the customer experience. ML algorithms can predict which type of content will be the most popular with each unique visitor. ML systems can:

- Recommend content on a company's website based on users' history and preferences
- Remarket company's content across desktop, laptop, mobile, and social interfaces
- Personalize branded content in e-mails based on users' history across other channels
- Drive new, targeted users to relevant content

When Delta Faucet (**www.deltafaucet.com**) used ML systems to improve its website, it noted several benefits. For example, the company experienced a 50 percent increase in page views per visitor. Further, clicks on call-to-action (CTA) buttons quadrupled. A *call-to-action button* is a button on a website that users need to click in order to take the action the company wants them to take. A common example is the "buy" button. Finally, more than 33 percent of visitors viewed multiple pages in a single session. ML systems made it possible for Delta Faucet to run personalized, relevant, and targeted content tailored to visitors' personal preferences. Visitors were more engaged, and they stayed longer on the company's website.

Computer vision for product recognition.

ML systems help brands recognize their products in online images and videos. For instance, Miller Lite (**www.millerlite.com**) used a ML system to scan through user-generated content on social media. ML algorithms searched for images to find posts related to the brand. The systems tracked information about competing brands and influencers. In addition, it collected data about users who posted on social media about Miller Lite. The ML systems found 1.1 million posts associated with the brand, and they identified 575 Miller Lite promoters.

Clicktivated (**www.clicktivated.com**) uses machine learning to create interactive videos that advertise products. Consumers can tap or scroll over a product in a video and receive information about that product to the side of the video. This process contrasts with consumers having permanent ads at the bottom of a video or having to watch a few seconds of a commercial before a video will play, as many firms that advertise on YouTube and other streaming services require.

For instance, a consumer watching a workout video can hover over a shirt in the video, which would then bring up details about the product. These details could include the brand, the price, and a link to purchase it.

Relevant recommendation systems.

ML systems in the form of intelligent personalization software can identify user preferences as well as people who know them best. For example, if users have multiple profiles on their Netflix account, they know that each time they launch the platform, it asks "Who is watching"? Then it provides "recommendations for you" based on shows, movies, and documentaries the user have already watched. These recommendations improve the customer experience.

ML systems help marketing managers discover which types of products consumers want based on their browsing histories and shopping behaviors. Relevant product suggestions increase conversions.

Chatbots.

Live chat enjoys a very high customer satisfaction rating. In fact, industry analysts assert that more than 60 percent of customers are more likely to return to a website if it offers a live chat feature.

Chatbots can help firms improve their live chat feature because ML systems improve chatbots' capabilities. For example, these systems use sentiment analysis to judge the mood of a customer message. When paired with social media, ML systems can gather more information about customers to apply when a chatbot receives a new message. That is, ML systems enable chatbots to personalize the customer experience. As a result, chatbots keep customers on pages for longer periods of time. They also decrease wait times for customers because they can handle simple, routine queries without human assistance.

Improved audience insights.

With ML systems, companies can learn valuable information about their customers. This information provides more accurate data that firms can use to build more comprehensive, targeted customer profiles to increase customer engagement. For example, Affinio (**www.affinio.com**) helps companies discover various aspects of customer behavior, such as which customers are foodies, which ones watch a particular television show, and which ones have traveled to similar places.

Discover trends.

ML systems are capable of monitoring social media to inspire fresh product and content ideas that directly respond to customers' preferences. As one example, ice cream giant Ben & Jerry's (**www.benjerry.com**) launched a range of breakfast-flavored ice creams, including Fruit Loot, Frozen Flakes, and Cocoa Loco. The company introduced these products after it had employed ML systems to help its Insight division listen to what was being talked about in the public sphere. For instance, at least 50 songs within the public domain had mentioned "ice cream for breakfast" at one point. Discovering the popularity of this phrase across various platforms revealed the value of ML systems in identifying emerging trends.

Intelligent marketing campaigns.   AdGreetz (**www.adgreetz.com**) is a marketing services company that has developed a ML-based advertising platform that can quickly generate thousands or millions of personalized ads.

The first campaign that AdGreetz conducted for Flipkart, giant Indian e-commerce vendor, reached 200 million people across multiple social media platforms. The audience, spread across different regions of India, was extremely diverse, consisting of people who live in different cities, speak different languages, and have different motivations and different relationships with Flipkart.

To give the ads a more significant impact, AdGreetz and Flipkart created about a million *creatives*, or ad banners and other forms of created online advertising. Each creative targeted different groups based on data collected from social media and Flipkart's e-commerce platform. These ads varied dramatically, including different colors, voices, and languages, depending on the target audience. Flipkart has subsequently used AdGreetz to produce an additional 40 campaigns.

POM AI in Production/Operations Management

In the Factory.   The *smart factory* is a highly digitized operation that continuously collects and shares data through connected machines, devices, and production systems. Smart factories use Big Data analytics (see Chapter 12), the industrial Internet of Things (see Chapter 8), machine learning, and robotics.

- *Production*. Volkswagen (**www.volkswagen.com**) is using computer vision to increase its production by 30 percent by 2025. The automaker deployed its first application in its Porsche Leipzig plant. Workers attach several labels to each vehicle they produce. These labels contain vehicle information. Many of the labels contain country-specific information and are written in the customer's language. The computer vision system ensures that the labels are applied properly.

    At the Leipzig plant, an employee on the production line now scans the vehicle identification number (VIN) to ensure that the vehicle is identified correctly. The employee also takes photos of each label attached to each car. The computer vision app checks the images in real time to ensure that the labels have the correct content and are written in the appropriate language. This process saves several minutes per vehicle.

    Another application of computer vision comes from Volkswagen's Ingolstadt plant, where Audi uses it for quality testing. The system detects the smallest cracks on the vehicle as well as defects in vehicle components.

- *Quality control*. Quality control is critical because customers expect products with zero defects. Defects damage the reputation of the manufacturer and its brand.

    Industry analysts have noted that ML systems increase defect detection rates up to 90 percent. These systems can also check for defects on all products in a production process rather than simply examining samples.

- *Predictive maintenance*. Equipment maintenance is a critical feature of every asset-reliant production operation. Unplanned downtime is expensive. Predictive maintenance techniques help determine the condition of in-service equipment to estimate when maintenance should be performed. This approach saves money and time over routine or time-based preventive maintenance because maintenance is performed only when needed.

    ML-based predictive maintenance systems are trained with data from sensors on the equipment. These systems search for patterns and anomalies in various equipment. They can help to reduce costs, enhance predictability, and make certain that equipment is available when needed. As an additional benefit, they can increase the length of the remaining useful life (RUL) of equipment.

    Consider smart locomotives manufactured by General Electric (GE; **www.ge.com**). GE has equipped its locomotive with sensors and cameras that gather data for the locomotives' ML system. GE improved its speed and accuracy in detecting problems in these giant, complex machines, which in turn reduced locomotive failure by 25 percent.

- *Robotics*. Smart factories are deploying increasing numbers of robots, which are driven by ML systems. An excellent example is Amazon's Kiva robots in the firm's distribution centers.

In Transportation.

An *autonomous vehicle* (automobile, bus, tractor, combine, boat, forklift, etc.) is a vehicle capable of sensing its environment and moving safely with little or no human input. These vehicles are powered by ML systems.

An early application of autonomous vehicles is in public transportation. For instance, Olli is an autonomous electric shuttle bus that operates around the world.

Another application involves autonomous delivery robots. For instance, Nuro delivery robots are delivering groceries and pizza from Domino's. These vehicles are geofenced, meaning that they can operate only inside a predetermined virtual perimeter overlaid on a real-world geographic area.

Another transportation-related application of ML systems is to resolve traffic control and traffic optimization problems using traffic sensors and cameras. Consider Surtrac from Rapid Flow Technologies (**www.rapidflowtech.com**). Surtrac is an ML-based traffic optimization system that responds in real time to changing traffic conditions by optimizing traffic flows. The system coordinates traffic flows on complex grids, not just on main streets. Surtrac also optimizes for many modes of travel, keeping vehicles, cyclists, pedestrians, and public transportation moving and safe.

Surtrac was first tested in Pittsburgh with a network of nine traffic signals on the city's major roads. The system reduced travel time by 25 percent, wait times at signals by 40 percent, stops by 30 percent, and vehicle emissions by 20 percent.

Along Supply Chains.

AI in supply chains helps to deliver optimization capabilities required for more accurate capacity planning, improved productivity, higher quality, lower costs, and greater output, while promoting safer working conditions.

Supply chain optimization. ML systems contribute to solving complex constraint, cost, and delivery problems that companies face today. ML systems can provide supply chain managers with significant insights into how they can improve supply chain performance, anticipating anomalies in logistics costs and performance before they occur. Here are some of the ways in which ML systems help optimize supply chains.

- ML systems use data from Internet of Things sensors, telematics, intelligent transport systems, and traffic data.
- ML systems can improve the accuracy of demand forecasting.
- ML systems can reduce logistics costs by identifying patterns in track-and-trace data captured by IoT sensors. Track-and-trace apps provide real-time data on the location and status of items as they move through a supply chain.
- ML-based planning and optimization systems can reduce lost sales that result when products are not available. Further, these systems can reduce inventory along the supply chain.
- ML systems can optimize capacity utilization along the supply chain.
- ML systems can detect and act on inconsistent supplier quality levels and deliveries. These systems provide visibility into inbound deliveries and delays, and they enable firms to monitor the status of critical orders, including multicomponent orders, in near real time. They also alert companies when a late delivery will impact a customer order.

  When a supply chain disruption does occur, an ML system generates an alert and automatically brings together the right members of the supply chain team to resolve the issue. The system provides the team with the most relevant information, including insights into the orders that are being affected and the potential financial impacts. The system learns from each resolution, thereby improving its performance for the next disruption.

- ML systems use data from automated inspections to reduce the risk and the potential for fraud, while improving product and process quality. Inspectorio (**www.supplychain .inspectorio.com**), a ML company, is addressing the many problems that a lack of inspection and supply chain visibility creates. Because there can be a time lag to receive handwritten factory inspections, Inspectorio digitizes those inspections and uses machine learning that enables retailers to monitor their supply chains in real time. This process enables retailers to quickly find and address problems in quality and compliance.

- ML systems provide end-to-end supply chain visibility as well as predictive and prescriptive insights into supply chain operations.

- ML systems help companies find and stop privileged credential abuse, which is the leading cause of security breaches across global supply chains. By using the least privilege access approach (see Chapter 4), firms can minimize attacks. Firms know that if a privileged user has entered the correct credentials but the request comes from a risky context, then stronger verification is needed to permit access. Zero Trust Privilege is a framework for verifying who is requesting access, the context of the request, and the risk of the access environment (see O'Reilly Media; **www.oreilly.com**). Centrify (**www.centrify.com**) is a leader in this area.

Security.   There are numerous examples of organizations applying ML systems to various aspects of security.

- In 2020, Facebook took down almost 6 billion fake accounts. Criminals use such accounts to spread spam, phishing links, and malware.

  Facebook distinguishes between two types of fake accounts: user-misclassified accounts and violating accounts. User-misclassified accounts are personal profiles for businesses that are meant to be Pages. Facebook simply converts these accounts to Pages.

  Violating accounts are more serious. These are personal profiles that engage in nefarious activities and violate the platform's terms of service. These activities can include using a fake name, impersonating someone, contacting other people to harass them, and many others. Facebook wants to remove violating accounts as quickly as possible without involving legitimate accounts (false positives).

  Facebook uses hand-coded rules and ML to block a fake account either before it is created or before it becomes active. After a fake account has gone live, detection is more difficult. At this point, Facebook's ML system, called Deep Entity Classification (DEC), becomes involved.

  Facebook has trained DEC to differentiate fake and real users by their connection patterns across the network. The company calls these patterns *deep features*. They include average age or gender distribution of the user's friends, among thousands of others. In fact, Facebook uses more than 20,000 deep features to characterize each account, providing a snapshot of how each profile behaves.

  DEC can identify one of four types of fake profiles:

  - Illegitimate accounts that are not representative of the person
  - Compromised accounts of real users that attackers have taken over
  - Spammers who repeatedly send revenue-generating messages
  - Scammers who manipulate users into divulging personal information

  Since Facebook implemented DEC, it has limited the volume of fake accounts on the platform to roughly 5 percent of monthly active users. Unfortunately, Facebook has approximately 2.7 billion monthly active users, meaning that 135 million Facebook accounts are still fake!

- Amazon, which has long tried to eliminate counterfeit products from its site, is using machine learning to automatically monitor its website for fake items. The system uses data from Amazon sellers, which give Amazon their logos, trademarks, and other important data about their brands. Amazon's system then scans product listings every day searching for fake items before they are purchased.

  Previously, brands had to report counterfeit items to Amazon. In 2019, Amazon deployed ML-powered Project Zero, which allows brands to take down counterfeit items on their own without Amazon's help.

- In 2018, Walmart began using ML-powered computer vision from Irish startup Everseen (**www.everseen.com**) to deter theft and losses at its checkouts and self-checkouts in more than 1,000 of its stores. The system, called Missed Scan Detection, notifies attendants if an item moves past a scanner without being scanned, giving them a chance to correct the situation. Walmart maintains that *shrinkage rates*—the loss of goods to theft and accidents—have decreased at stores that employ the system.

  However, a group of Walmart employees who call themselves the Concerned Home Office Associates have claimed that the computer vision system often misidentifies innocuous behavior as theft (false positives) and often fails to stop actual instances of stealing. The group created a video that purports to show the technology failing to flag items that not being scanned in three Walmart stores. Their primary concern is false positives at self-checkouts, which frustrates customers and store associates and leads to longer checkout lines.

HRM AI in Human Resources

Recruiting.   Recruiting refers to the overall process of identifying, screening, and interviewing suitable candidates for available positions within an organization.

- *Candidate identification and screening.* Finding the right talent is a major problem for virtually all organizations. To assist with this process, AI companies are developing tools to scan résumés, online job profiles, and job queries much more quickly than humans can. These tools automate the candidate search process and move the best candidates to the top of the list.

  Consider DBS Bank (**www.dbs.com**). The DBS Talent Acquisition team created Jobs Intelligence Maestro (JIM), a virtual recruitment bot powered by artificial intelligence. The bank uses JIM to screen candidates applying to be wealth planning managers, a high-value job in the consumer bank.

  After DBS introduced JIM in 2018, the firm was able to shorten the screening time from 32 minutes per candidate to 8 minutes, improve the completion rate of job applications from 85 percent to 97 percent, and respond to 96 percent of all candidate queries through JIM. As a result, recruiters were able to spend more time personally sharing the culture and values of DBS with candidates.

  CareerBuilder (**www.careerbuilder.com**) is an employment website founded in 1995. In 2019 the company launched its Talent Discovery platform. CareerBuilder claims that the machine-learning tool finds potential employees faster and increases job applications. The company trained the tool with data that include 2.3 million job postings, 680 million unique profiles, 310 million unique résumés, 10 million job titles, and 1.3 billion skills.

  Talent Discovery provides a candidate appeal score that helps companies understand how effective a job posting will be at attracting candidates. It also offers recommendations to increase the posting's appeal. Further, it provides a map that displays similar competing jobs in a geographic area and the salaries those jobs are offering. Talent Discovery uses machine learning to help companies create job descriptions that are gender-neutral and tone-neutral to save time and help increase diversity.

- *Promoting diversity and inclusion.* Job descriptions can contain subtle messages about company culture, including its inclusiveness or lack thereof. An AI tool that helps identify problems with the language employed in job descriptions is Textio (**www.textio.com**). The tool analyzes writing for gender bias and other unintentional messages. It suggests alternative wording, serving as a writing coach on diversity and inclusion. Textio has a number of customers, including Expedia (**www.expedia.com**) and Zillow (**www.zillow.com**). Interestingly, Zillow has seen an 11 percent increase in female applicants since it began to use the tool.

- *Video interview analysis.* Because companies want to spend less time on the interviewing process, video interviewing software is becoming increasingly popular. For example, HireVue's video interviewing system employs voice and facial recognition technology, along with an ML ranking algorithm, to evaluate candidates.

Onboarding.   *Onboarding* is the process by which new employees acquire the knowledge, skills, and behaviors they need to become effective organizational members.

As companies strive to retain talented employees, mentoring is becoming increasingly important. Consider the AI-driven app Ellen from Next Play. Ellen helps to (a) connect mentees with mentors at their company, (b) expand the mentee's network within the company, and (c) foster a sense of belonging at the workplace. Ellen also nudges mentors and mentees to engage in high-quality conversations. According to Next Play, more than 90 percent of Ellen matches stay in contact beyond their first three mentor/mentee meetings.

IBM is creating a system that answers new employees' most pressing or job-critical questions to help get them up to speed quickly. The system offers training suggestions and provides the names, locations, and contact information for people the employee should connect with very early in their employment.

Career pathing.

AI technology is helping HR professionals in the role of career pathing to enhance employee satisfaction and retention, succession planning, workforce planning, and overall company productivity and profitability. AI systems can efficiently match employees to suitable next-step positions based on their profiles and experience. This process is similar to the way these systems align external candidates to recommended positions within the company.

There are limitations of career pathing ML systems. Along with these systems, employees must be motivated to acquire, apply, and refine their skills to make the most of ML-recommended career paths. Further, more senior employees must help the employee progress through mentorship, project-based work, and vertical and lateral moves. Finally, if an employee wants a complete career overhaul or change, AI systems are not independently creative enough to design an entirely unique career path.

Identifying employees who might be leaving the organization.

Veriato's (www.veriato.com) ML platform is designed to identify employees who might be considering leaving the organization. The tool tracks employee computer activity, such as e-mails, keystrokes, and Internet browsing, and stores the information for one month. It then analyzes these data to determine a baseline of normal activity patterns within the organization. Finally, it flags outliers by detecting changes in the overall tone of employees' communications, and it reports them to the employee's supervisor.

Monitoring employees.

Consider employee monitoring at Outback Steakhouse (www.outback.com). Casual dining chains are experimenting with surveillance technology designed to maximize employee efficiency and performance. One Outback location is testing a computer vision tool called Presto Vision (www.presto.com).

Presto Vision uses surveillance cameras that many restaurants already have installed. The system uses machine learning to analyze video footage of restaurant staff at work, particularly their interactions with guests. It provides metrics such as how often servers tend to their tables and how long it takes for food to come out of the kitchen and reach each table. At the end of a shift, managers receive an e-mail of the compiled statistics. They can then use these data to identify problems and determine whether servers, hostesses, and kitchen staff are adequately doing their jobs.

Presto Vision can also be used to correct employee performance in near real time. For instance, managers could be sent text messages when the number of people waiting for a table reaches a certain threshold. In another example, the system could detect when a guest's drink is almost empty and prompt servers to offer them a refill.

Significantly, Presto Vision's software does not identify individual diners, and it does not employ facial recognition technology. The company maintains that it does not collect any personal information and it deletes all video within three days of collection.

Such employee monitoring is a double-edged sword. Industry analysts note that workplace surveillance can have negative effects on employees, such as increased stress and lower job satisfaction.

Monitoring and improving employees' health.

Physically or mentally toxic work environments can negatively impact employees' health, resulting in organizational losses up to $300 billion annually. Analysts note further that 60 percent of working Americans experience chronic work-related stress.

To deal with these problems, many firms are asking their employees to opt in to company exercise and diet plans. For example, companies provide their employees with wearables such as the Fitbit and Apple Watch. In return, employees agree to share the data from their wearables with the company in return for a reduction in their health-care premiums. Let's look at how the National Football League (NFL; www.nfl.com) is using sensors to improve the health of players.

Research has highlighted the health risks associated with playing U.S. football. For example, in 2017 researchers from the Veterans Administration Boston Healthcare System and the Boston University School of Medicine published a study in the *Journal of the American Medical Association* that indicated that football players are at a high risk for developing long-term neurological conditions. The study, which did not include a control group, examined the brains of high school, college, and professional football players. Of the 111 NFL-level football players the researchers examined, all but 1 had some form of degenerative brain disease.

As a result, the NFL adopted Amazon Web Services (AWS; **http://aws.amazon.com**) and Amazon's machine learning products and services to better simulate and predict player injuries, with the goal of improving player health and safety. The partnership uses Next Gen Stats (**http://nextgenstats.nfl.com**), an existing NFL and AWS agreement that enables the NFL to capture and process data on its players.

Sensors on player equipment and the football itself capture real-time location, speed, and acceleration data of players and the football. The data are then fed into AWS data analytics and machine learning tools to provide fans, broadcasters, and NFL teams with live and on-screen statistics and predictions, such as expected catch rates and pass completion probabilities. Using those data, as well as data from other sources such as video footage, equipment choice, playing surfaces, player injury data, type of play (run or pass), type, frequency, and angle of impact, the speed the players are running, as well as environmental factors (temperature, rain, wind, etc.), the NFL and AWS partnership creates a digital twin of each player.

Typically used in manufacturing to predict machine outputs and potential breakdowns, a *digital twin* is a virtual, digital model of a machine or a person created from real-time and historical data. Using machine learning and predictive analytics, a digital twin can be placed in any number of virtual scenarios, enabling data scientists to see how the digital twin's real-life counterpart would react. These scenarios do not risk the health and safety of real players. Further, data collected from these scenarios provide insights into changes to game rules, player equipment, and other factors that could make football a safer game.

MIS AI in Management Information Systems

Organizational information technology groups use machine learning in many areas. We consider several examples here.

Security.   Organizations store vast amounts of customer, strategic, and other forms of data, which must be secured at all times. ML algorithms help identify potential threats and data breaches while also providing solutions to eliminate or mitigate such threats.

Server optimization.   Company servers frequently receive millions of requests per day. The servers, in turn, are required to open web pages requested by users. Servers can become unresponsive if the number of requests exceeds their processing capacity. ML algorithms can optimize server processing to help meet this demand. In a server farm, ML algorithms allocate user requests among multiple servers to optimally meet demand.

Service management.   IT service management encompasses the activities performed by an IT team to design, deliver, operate, and control information technology services offered to organizational users. ML systems can assist the IT service team in several ways.

- Chatbots can recognize, categorize, and prioritize underlying problems in employee requests. In live chat, chatbots can use natural language processing to answer common questions without human intervention.

- Service desk teams have different skill sets. Some are better at resolving different types of requests than others. ML algorithms can automatically send requests to appropriate employees.

- Many IT requests require humans to perform a complex set of steps to fulfill the requests. In the case of employee onboarding, ML algorithms learn from a historical database of requests that cover a range of actions taken based on the type of employment and the employee's role and department. The algorithms can suggest what types of hardware and software an employee needs as well as the amount of access to organizational applications the employee should receive.

- Based on the historical database of requests and current user behavior patterns, ML algorithms can forecast and fulfill users' requests.

Software development. · Software development is the process of conceiving, specifying, designing, programming, documenting, testing, and error correcting involved in creating and maintaining applications.

- *DevOps* is the combination of cultural philosophies, practices, and tools that increase an organization's ability to quickly develop and deliver applications. Key functions within DevOps projects include continuous integration and continuous delivery. *Continuous integration* is the practice of combining computer code from multiple contributors on a single software project. *Continuous delivery* refers to a situation in which a version of the final software package is always ready to be released but is not sent to production before the decision is made to release it. *DevOps bots*, which are still under development, will be ML-powered bots that assist in all stages of the software development process. Let's take a closer look at bots' potential contributions to the process.

  Requirements gathering. Gathering user requirements remains an art form. DevOps bots will listen in on stakeholder interviews. As stakeholders define their requirements, the bots could conduct a real-time sentiment analysis. They could then determine which requirements the stakeholders considered important and which ones they were uncertain about. The bots could also flag any requirement with a history of negative project outcomes, proactively alert the project manager, and suggest improvements and alternative approaches.

  Users often do not comprehend the risk and cost implications of requested features. The bots will make the DevOps process more transparent to these users. This feature would help business users make more informed choices, particularly if they have a limited software development budget.

  The bots will also make the users aware of the different cost/risk profiles of alternative technologies. For example, if a development team proposes to introduce NoSQL databases into the existing IT environment, stakeholders need to know the operational impact of adding this type of database and the financial return they might expect.

  In the end, the bots could provide a list of prioritized project requirements, risk elements, and technology alternatives. The technology alternative would be in the form of a *DevOps toolchain,* which is a set of tools that help in the development, delivery, and management of software applications. Finally, the bots could provide a list of development project resources, including the appropriate developer skills, business experience, and availability.

  Writing the code. If developers are writing new computer code, then ML algorithms could examine its structure and syntax to help programmers write better code, find and repair software errors, save time, and improve productivity.

  If the developers are working with legacy (existing) code, they might find that this code is poorly documented. If the code was not fully documented, then developers typically begin their improvement efforts somewhere in the legacy code without being certain of the proper entry point. DevOps bots should automatically document the legacy code as well as the code developed by the new team. The bots should also assist the developers in finding the right entry points for enhancing the legacy code.

  Software testing and quality assurance. Software developers use ML algorithms to automatically find and repair errors and other issues within applications during development cycles. For example, tools such as Bugspots can be used to ensure that all software bugs are eliminated without human intervention. Bugspots is a Python implementation of the bug prediction algorithm used at Google.

  Application deployment. Software versioning, a form of continuous deployment, is a strategy to categorize the unique states of computer software as it is developed and released. For example, Apple's iOS 14 is a version of Apple's mobile operating system. Software versioning is a critical component of application development and deployment. ML algorithms are useful in predicting problems that can occur in deployment.

AIOps. AIOps, the application of artificial intelligence to IT operations, gives IT professionals a real-time understanding of the issues that affect the availability and performance of the organization's information systems. AIOps learns from data sources such as traditional IT monitoring, logs, application and performance anomalies, and many others.

AIOps provides organizations with an overview across the entire IT environment—computation, network, storage, physical, virtual, and cloud. Specialized algorithms focus on specific tasks. For example, algorithms can pick out significant alerts from an event stream, identify correlations between alerts from different sources, assemble the correct team of human specialists to diagnose and resolve a situation, propose probable root causes and possible solutions based on past experiences, and learn from feedback to improve continuously over time.

Common uses of AIOps include:

- Predictive analytics to prevent system failure or disruption
- Event correlation and root cause analysis
- Optimization of infrastructure utilization
- Capacity planning and forecasting
- IT service management

Before you go on...

1. Look at the functional area that corresponds to your major.
    a. Discuss potential impacts of ML applications on your profession.
    b. Describe additional ML applications not discussed in the text.

14.6 | Appendix

Consider a neural network designed to predict salaries based on the GPA of graduating seniors. We have data from four recent graduates and will use three of them to train the NN (see below). We have an input node for the GPA, two nodes in the hidden layer and an output node for predicting salaries. The output salaries are in thousands of dollars. We randomly select 3.42, 2.63, and 4.00 as our training data and we use the 3.70 GPA to test our NN.

GPA	Starting Salary (000)
3.42	$78.250
2.63	$49.200
4.00	$83.250
3.70	$79.800

For simplicity in our NN, we use Google's Swish activation function for all nodes. See Figure 14.4. Keep in mind that today's NNs typically use the same activation function for each layer of nodes, Meaning that different layers can have different activation functions.

In **Figure 14.5**, the first GPA value, 3.42, enters the neural network at its input node. The input node bias (+1.00) shifts the GPA to 4.42 and the input node activation function shifts the 4.42 GPA to a value of 4.432. Look back to Figure 14.4, where you will see the Swish activation function shifting the value of 4.42 on the X-axis to the value of 4.432 on the Y-axis. The value of 4.432 now moves to the hidden layer nodes.

Along the way, the data value of 4.432 is shifted by the upper pathway weight ($w_1 = 3.43$) to 15.202 and the lower pathway weight ($w_2 = 0.875$) to 3.878. Note: for the upper pathway, 4.432 x 3.43 = 15.202. For the lower pathway, 4.432 x 0.875 = 3.878.

The upper pathway node bias ($b_1 = -1.27$) shifts the data value to 13.932 (15.202 − 1.27) while the lower pathway bias, ($b_2 = 1.12$) shifts the data value to 4.998 (3.878 + 1.12).

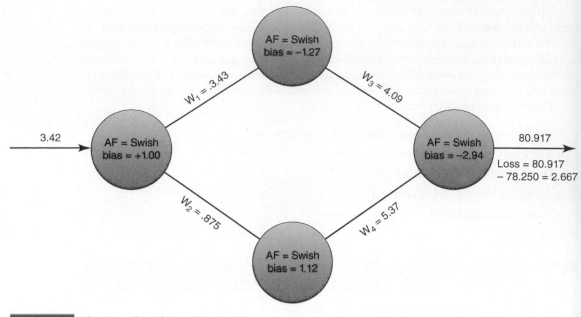

FIGURE 14.5 First Iteration of Neural Network

Then, the hidden layer activation functions model the respective values to 13.932 (upper pathway) and 5.005 (lower pathway).

Next, weights ($w_3 = 4.09$, upper; $w_4 = 5.37$, lower) shift the data values to 56.981 and 26.876. Note: for the upper pathway, 13.932 x 4.29 = 56.981. For the lower pathway, 5.005 x 5.37 = 26.876.

Those two values are summed (56.981 + 26.876) to yield a value of 83.857 and then the last bias, b_4 (−2.94), shifts the value to 80.917 (83.857 − 2.94 = 80.917). The output node activation function performs the final calculation and produces an output value of 80.917. The NN's loss function compares the output value, 80.917, to the input salary value associated with the 3.42 GPA, 78.250, and determines a difference, a loss value, of 2.667.

The loss function uses the difference of 2.667 to recalculate the weights and biases throughout the neural network in the back propagation process. These weights and biases will be applied during the second iteration. See **Figure 14.6**.

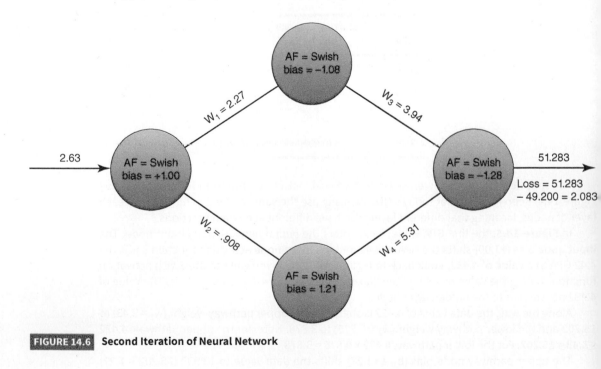

FIGURE 14.6 Second Iteration of Neural Network

The next GPA, 2.63, enters the neural network at the input node. The input node bias (+1.00) shifts the GPA to 3.63 and the input node activation function shifts the 3.63 GPA to a value of 3.657, which then moves to the hidden layer nodes.

Along the way, the data value of 3.657 is shifted by the upper pathway weight (w_1 = 2.27) to 8.300 and the lower pathway weight (w_2 = 0.908) to 3.320. Note: for the upper pathway, 3.657 x 2.27 = 8.300. For the lower pathway, 3.657 x 0.908 = 3.32.

The upper pathway node bias (b_1 = −1.08) shifts the data value to 7.220 (8.300 − 1.08) while the lower pathway bias, (b_2 = 1.21) shifts the data value to 4.530 (3.320 + 1.21).

Then, the hidden layer activation functions model the respective values to 7.221 (upper pathway) and 4.541 (lower pathway).

Next, weights (w_3 = 3.94, upper; w_4 = 5.31, lower) shift the data values to 28.451 and 24.112. Note: for the upper pathway, 7.221 x 3.94 = 28.451. For the lower pathway, 4.541 x 5.31 = 24.112).

Those two values are summed (28.451 + 24.112) to yield a value of 52.563 and then the last bias, b_4 (−1.28), shifts the value to 51.283 (52.563 − 1.28 = 51.283). The output node activation function performs the final calculation and produces an output value of 51.283. The NN's loss function compares the output value, 51.283, to the input salary value associated with the 2.63 GPA, 49.200, and determines a difference, a loss value, of 2.083.

The loss function uses that difference, 2.083, to recalculate the weights and biases throughout the neural network in the back propagation process. These weights and biases will be applied during the third iteration. See **Figure 14.7**.

The next GPA, 4.00, enters the neural network at the input node. The input node bias (+1.00) shifts the GPA to 5.00 and the input node activation function shifts the 5.00 GPA to a value of 5.007, which then moves to the hidden layer nodes.

Along the way, the data value of 5.007 is shifted by the upper pathway weight (w_1 = 2.22) to 11.115 and the lower pathway weight (w_2 = 1.17) to 5.858. Note: for the upper pathway, 5.007 x 2.22 = 11.115. For the lower pathway, 5.007 x 1.17 = 5.858.

The upper pathway node bias (b_1 = −0.42) shifts the data value to 10.695 (11.115 − 0.42) while the lower pathway bias, (b_2 = 1.32) shifts the data value to 7.178 (5.858 + 1.32).

Then, the hidden layer activation functions model the respective values to 10.695 (upper pathway) and 7.179 (lower pathway).

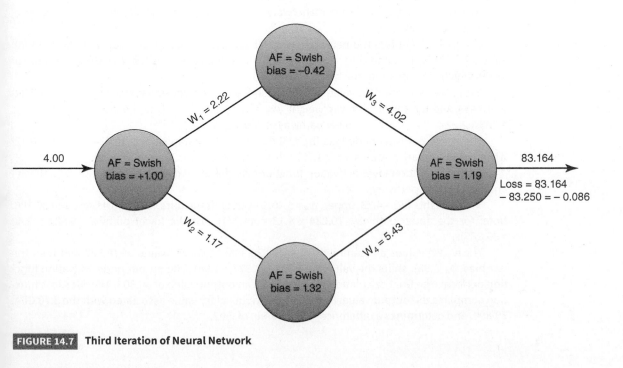

FIGURE 14.7   **Third Iteration of Neural Network**

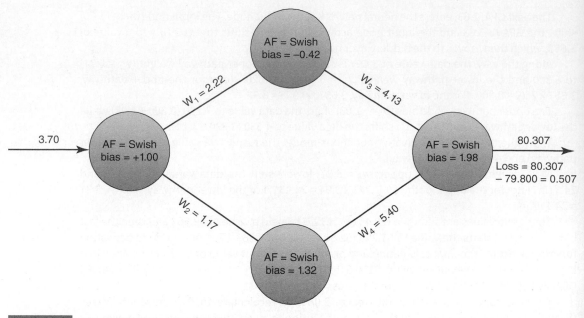

FIGURE 14.8 **Fourth Iteration of Neural Network**

Next, weights (w_3 = 4.02, upper; w_4 = 5.43, lower) shift the data values to 42.994 and 38.980. Note: for the upper pathway, 10.695 x 4.02 = 42.994. For the lower pathway, 7.179 x 5.43 = 38.980).

Those two values are summed (42.994 + 38.980) to yield a value of 81.974 and then the last bias, b_4 (1.19), shifts the value to 83.164 (81.974 + 1.19 = 83.164). The output node activation function performs the final calculation and produces an output value of 83.164. The NN's loss function compares the output value, 83.164, to the input salary value associated with the 4.00 GPA, 83.250, and determines a difference, a loss value, of −0.086.

The loss function uses that difference, −0.086, to recalculate the weights and biases throughout the neural network in the back propagation process. These weights and biases will be applied during the third iteration. See **Figure 14.8**.

Now we check to see if the neural network is performing accurately for test data. Therefore, we enter the GPA of 3.70.

The GPA 3.70 enters the neural network at the input node. The input node bias (+1.00) shifts the GPA to 4.70 and the input node activation function shifts the 4.70 GPA to a value of 4.709, which then moves to the hidden layer nodes.

Along the way, the data value of 4.709 is shifted by the upper pathway weight (w_1 = 2.22) to 10.454 and the lower pathway weight (w_2 = 1.17) to 5.510. Note: for the upper pathway, 4.709 x 2.22 = 10.454. For the lower pathway, 4.709 x 1.17 = 5.510.

The upper pathway node bias (b_1 = −0.42) shifts the data value to 10.034 (10.454 − 0.42) while the lower pathway bias, (b_2 = 1.32) shifts that value to 6.830 (5.510 + 1.32).

Then, the hidden layer activation functions model the values to 10.034 (upper pathway) and 6.831 (lower pathway).

Next, weights (w_3 = 4.13, upper; w_4 = 5.40, lower) shift the data values to 41.441 and 36.886. Note: for the upper pathway, 10.034 x 4.13 = 44.041). For the lower pathway, 6.831 x 5.40 = 36.886).

Those two values are summed (41.441 + 36.886) to yield a value of 78.327 and then the last bias, b_4 (1.98), shifts the value to 80.307 (78.327 + 1.98). The output node activation function performs the final calculation and produces an output value of 80.307. The NN's loss function compares the output value, 80.307, to the input salary value associated with the 3.70 GPA, 79.800, and determines a difference, a loss value, of .507.

Our neural network predicted a salary of 80.307, or $80,307. The actual salary of the individual who had the 3.70 GPA was $79,800. Our network is off by $507 (approximately 99.3 percent accurate), an excellent result.

As you see in this example, the neural network continually shifts the system's weights and biases based on the magnitude of the difference between the computed salary and the actual salary (the loss) in an effort to match the pattern between GPAs and starting salaries of graduates from the sample data. The shifts in these values are usually small and occur over thousands of input values and iterations of the neural network.

Our example is very simplified because it involves only three sample values for training. However, it should convey how a neural network is trained by this continual shifting of parameters. When the differences between computed and actual salaries minimize over large amounts of data, the system is said to be trained.

Now imagine entering millions of data points into hundreds of input nodes that feed more than a dozen hidden layers comprised of hundreds of nodes each, and outputting dozens of discrete, computed data points to be compared to the actual data values. Then imagine the thousands of adjustments to the weights and biases throughout the network to accommodate the next data inputs. This is how complex and sophisticated machine learning can be.

What's in IT for me?

The sections below provide a quick summary of artificial intelligent applications in each functional area of the organization. You will find detailed discussions of AI systems in the functional areas in Section 14.5.

ACCT For the Accounting Major

AI systems are used extensively in auditing to uncover irregularities. They are also used to uncover and prevent fraud. Today's CPAs use AI systems for many of their duties, ranging from risk analysis to cost control. Accounting personnel also use intelligent agents for mundane tasks such as managing accounts and monitoring employees' Internet use.

FIN For the Finance Major

People have been using computers for decades to solve financial problems. Innovative AI systems have been developed for activities such as making stock market decisions, refinancing bonds, assessing debt risks, analyzing financial conditions, predicting business failures, forecasting financial trends, and investing in global markets. AI systems can often facilitate the use of spreadsheets and other computerized systems used in finance. Finally, AI systems can help reduce fraud in credit cards, stocks, and other financial services.

MKT For the Marketing Major

Marketing personnel use AI systems in many applications, from allocating advertising budgets to evaluating alternative routings of salespeople. New marketing approaches such as targeted marketing and marketing transaction databases are heavily dependent on IT in general and on AI systems in particular. AI systems are especially useful for mining customer databases and predicting customer behavior. Successful AI applications appear in almost every area of marketing and sales, from analyzing the success of one-to-one advertising to supporting customer help desks. With customer service becoming increasingly important, the use of intelligent agents is critical for providing fast response.

POM For the Production/Operations Management Major

AI systems support complex operations and production decisions, from inventory to production planning. AI systems in the production/operations management field manage tasks ranging from diagnosing machine failures and prescribing repairs to complex production scheduling and inventory control. Some companies, such as DuPont and Kodak, have deployed hundreds of AI systems in the planning, organizing, and control of their operational systems.

HRM For the Human Resources Management Major

Human resources personnel employ AI systems for many applications. For example, recruiters use these systems to find applicants' resumes on the Web and sort them to match needed skills. HR managers also use AI systems to evaluate candidates (e.g., tests, interviews). HR personnel use AI systems to train and support employees in managing their fringe benefits and to predict employee job performance and future labor needs.

MIS For the MIS Major

The MIS function develops (or acquires) and maintains the organization's various AI systems, as well as the data and models that these systems use. MIS staffers also interact frequently with subject area experts to capture the expertise used in AI systems.

Summary

14.1 Explain the potential value and the potential limitations of artificial intelligence.

Table 14.1 differentiates between artificial and human intelligence on a number of characteristics.

14.2 Differentiate among supervised, semi-supervised, unsupervised, reinforcement, and deep learning.

Supervised learning is a type of machine learning in which the system is given labeled input data and the expected output results.

Semi-supervised learning is a type of machine learning that combines a small amount of labeled data with a large amount of unlabeled data during training.

Unsupervised learning is a type of machine learning that looks for previously undetected patterns in a data set with no pre-existing labels and with minimal human supervision.

Reinforcement learning is a type of machine learning in which the system learns to achieve a goal in an uncertain, potentially complex environment.

Deep learning is a subset of machine learning in which artificial neural networks learn from large amounts of data.

14.3 Describe the structure of a neural network, and discuss how that structure contributes to the purpose of neural networks in machine learning.

A neural network is a set of nodes, or virtual neurons, that work in parallel in an attempt to simulate the way the human brain works, although in a greatly simplified form. Neural networks consist of several layers of nodes, called the input layer, hidden layers, and the output layer. Current neural networks are able to simulate billions of neurons. In this way, developers can train a neural network to learn, recognize patterns, and make decisions in a humanlike way.

14.4 Provide use case examples (in addition to the ones in the text) of computer vision, natural language processing, robotics, image recognition, and intelligent agents.

We leave the additional examples to you. You can search the Web to find numerous examples of each machine learning application.

14.5 Provide use case examples (in addition to the ones in the text) of artificial intelligence applications in accounting, finance, marketing, production and operations management, human resource management, and management information systems.

We leave the additional examples to you. You can search the Web to find numerous examples of numerous examples of machine learning applications in each functional area.

14.6 Understand the process by which a neural network transforms data values from the input node to the output node, and then calculates the loss function to initiate the back propagation process.

Chapter Glossary

algorithm A problem-solving method expressed as a finite sequence of steps.

artificial intelligence (AI) A subfield of computer science concerned with studying the thought processes of humans and recreating the effects of those processes with machines such as computers.

computer vision The ability of information systems to identify objects, scenes, and activities in images.

convolutional neural network A type of neural network designed to separate areas of image inputs by extracting features to identify edges, curves, and color density and then recombine these inputs for classification and prediction.

deep learning A subset of machine learning where artificial neural networks learn from large amounts of data.

expert systems (ESs) Information systems that attempt to mimic human experts by applying expertise in a specific domain.

information agent A type of intelligent agent that searches for information and displays it to users.

intelligent agent A software program that assists you, or acts on your behalf, in performing repetitive, computer-related tasks.

machine learning systems The ability of information systems to accurately perform new, unseen tasks, built on known properties learned from training or historical data that are labeled.

monitoring and surveillance agents (or *predictive agents*) Intelligent agents that constantly observe and report on some item of interest.

narrow AI See **weak AI**.

natural language processing The ability of information systems to work with text the way that humans do.

neural network A set of virtual neurons, placed in layers, which work in parallel in an attempt to simulate the way the human brain works, although in a greatly simplified form.

node Software unit in a neural network that has one or more weighted connections, a transfer function that combines the inputs in some way, and an output connection.

predictive agents See **monitoring and surveillance agents**.

reinforcement learning A type of machine learning where the system learns to achieve a goal in an uncertain, potentially complex environment.

semi-supervised learning   A type of machine learning that combines a small amount of labeled data with a large amount of unlabeled data during training.

speech recognition   The ability of information systems to automatically and accurately transcribe human speech.

strong AI   Hypothetical artificial intelligence that matches or exceeds human intelligence and could perform any intellectual task that humans can.

supervised learning   A type of machine learning where the system is given labeled input data and the expected output results.

unsupervised learning   A type of machine learning that looks for previously undetected

patterns in a data set with no pre-existing labels and with a minimum of human supervision.

weak AI   (also called *narrow AI*) Performs a useful and specific function that once required human intelligence to perform and does so at human levels or better.

Discussion Questions

1. What are the pros and cons of facial recognition as a business policy? As a public policy?

2. Consider your health care provider's data.

- Who owns those data?
- Who profits from analyzing them?
- What are they used for?
- Provide an example of an ML system that uses your data.

3. You are a passenger in a rented, autonomous vehicle that hits a pedestrian. Who or what has the liability for the accident? Support your conclusions.

4. You are a passenger in an autonomous vehicle that you own. While you are riding in the vehicle and reading a report for a business meeting, your vehicle hits a pedestrian. Who or what has the liability for the accident? Support your conclusions.

5. Suppose that your insurance company decides to price your car insurance premium based on data about your driving habits collected by sensors in your car that the firm inputs into an ML system.

   a. Would you be in favor of this new process? Why or why not?

   b. Would the cost of your new policy be in your favor? Why or why not? For example, what if you were speeding?

6. Suppose that your health care company decides to price your insurance premiums based on data about your health (e.g., blood pressure, glucose in your blood) and health habits (eating, exercising, sleeping, etc.) obtained from Fitbit sensors, smart watches, and intelligent scales in your bathroom.

   a. Would you be in favor of this new process? Why or why not?

   b. Would the cost of your new policy be in your favor? Why or why not? For example, what if you were under stress at your job and your blood pressure increased?

Problem-Solving Activities

1. Which machine learning algorithm would you use to predict admittance to your university's freshman class? Describe your algorithm by including your input data and output data.

2. Which machine learning algorithm would you use to identify an image as a dog or a cat? Describe your algorithm by including your input data and output data.

3. Which machine learning algorithm would you use to predict the weather? Hint: first define what "predicting the weather" means. Describe your algorithm by including your input data and output data.

Closing Case

MIS **POM** **MKT**   AI at McDonald's

In recent years, fast-food sales have slowed across the United States as Americans turn to healthier alternatives. Although McDonald's (**www .mcdonalds.com**) has performed better than many of its competitors, the chain has lost customers and closed restaurants. Further, McDonald's financial performance has failed to meet analysts' expectations.

Making matters worse, due to the COVID-19 pandemic, by April 2020 some 97 percent of restaurants in the United States were not permitted to host in-person dining. That situation made drive-throughs vital to all fast-food chains. In fact, during the pandemic, drive-through customers accounted for roughly 70 percent of McDonald's sales.

As a result of these issues, McDonald's embarked on a digital transformation of its entire customer experience. The transformation encompasses self-service kiosk ordering, a mobile app, mobile payments, and ML-driven drive-through menus and ordering.

McDonald's began installing self-ordering kiosks in 2015. By the end of 2020, most of its U.S. locations had them. Also in 2015, McDonald's launched its mobile app. By 2020, more than 60 million people had downloaded it. The app has improved the speed and convenience of ordering. In addition, it generates data about users that McDonald's utilizes to make product recommendations and thus increase sales.

In March 2019, McDonald's acquired Dynamic Yield (**www .dynamicyield.com**), an Israeli AI startup with extensive expertise in personalization. Analyzing the massive amounts of data from the fast-food company's 70 million daily customers, augmented with environmental data from a variety of sources, Dynamic Yield customizes offerings in real time, taking the upselling approach ("Do you want fries with that?") that McDonald's employees have long used successfully.

McDonald's deployed Dynamic Yield's ML system on electronic ordering boards at its drive-through locations. The ML-powered menu boards dynamically change based on factors such as the user's existing order, the time of day, the current weather, traffic conditions around the store, nearby events, and how busy the restaurant is. As a result, McDonald's is able to deliver personalized offerings that not only have more appeal to the customer but are also easier on the kitchen during periods of peak activity.

Here is how the system works. When customers drive up to place their orders, they see a digital display with banner items and promotions. As they move up toward the ordering station, they eventually see the full menu. Prior to the ML system, both displays were largely static, other than the obvious changes such as rotating in new offers or changing from breakfast to lunch. With the new system, displays show customers other items that have been popular at that location, and they prompt customers with potential upsells.

In addition to enhanced customer satisfaction and increased sales, the system offers several benefits. For example, if the drive-through is moving slowly, then the menu can dynamically switch to show items that are simpler to prepare to help increase the speed of fulfilling orders. Conversely, the display could highlight more complex sandwiches during a slower period. McDonald's also links the predictive nature of customer demand to the stock levels in the restaurant and the kitchen.

McDonald's has also implemented Dynamic Yield's personalization functionality on its touchscreen self-ordering kiosks and its mobile app. The fast-food chain's goals are to increase customer satisfaction by reducing wait times and fulfilling orders more accurately as well as to increase efficiency and traffic flow. McDonald's plans to complete the deployment of the technology to all 14,000 U.S. restaurants and 22,000 international locations by 2023.

Going further, if customers are willing to identify themselves, McDonald's believes the ML system can be even more useful because the system can display their favorites. On a strictly opt-in basis, the company uses geofencing around each of its stores that alerts them when a mobile app customer is approaching. The restaurant then prepares their orders accordingly. Again through opt-in only, the company could extend that feature to customers' smartphones using beacons. Further, the system could also include license plate recognition to identify specific customers as they approach and adjust the digital menu based on their recent orders.

In September 2019, McDonald's purchased Apprente, a startup that develops ML-powered, voice-activated platforms that can process orders in multiple languages and accents. McDonald's is employing Apprente's technology rather than humans to take customer orders.

Apprente calls its technology sound-to-meaning rather than speech-to-text. Unlike other ML-powered voice tools, Apprente does not transcribe what the customer says and then infer meaning from the transcript. Rather, it works directly from speech signals to result. The company asserts that this process is more accurate for customer experience cases, particularly in noisy environments such as in restaurants and public areas. The approach also works well when customers use colloquial, poorly structured language, which could make speech recognition less accurate.

Sources: Compiled from J. Maze, "Inside McDonald's Digitally-Focused Future," *Restaurant Business*, November 10, 2020; B. Barrett, "The Future of McDonald's Is in the Drive-Thru Lane," *Wired*, November 9, 2020; J. Walker, "Fast Food Robots, Kiosks, and AI Use Cases from 6 Restaurant Giants," *Emerj*, November 22, 2019; M. Stern, "McDonald's AI Drive-Thrus May Be Too Smart for Their Own Good," *Forbes*, November 11, 2019; "How Fast Food Restaurants Can Use AI for Better Customer Service, *Restaurant Magic*, November 5, 2019; D. Yaffe-Bellany, "Would You Like Fries with That? McDonald's Already Knows the Answer," *New York Times*, November 4, 2019; B. Barrett, McDonald's Doubles Down on Tech with Voice AI Acquisition," *Wired*, September 10, 2019; S. Robinson, "McDonald's Orders up Customer Service Analytics, Shakes up Fast Food," *TechTarget*, May 17, 2019; D. Newman, "AI and Personalization Transforming an Unlikely Industry: Fast Food," *Forbes*, April 23, 2019; R. Carpenter, "How AI Can Solve Fast-Food Labor Problems," *QSR Magazine*, April 2019; T. Mogg, "McDonald's Uses A.I. to Tempt You into Extra Purchases at the Drive-Thru," *Digital Trends*, March 27, 2019; B. Barrett, "McDonald's Bites on Big Data with $300 Million Acquisition," *Wired*, March 25, 2019; E. Rensi, "McDonald's Says Goodbye to Cashiers, Hello Kiosks," *Forbes*, July 11, 2018; **www.mcdonalds.com**, accessed November 5, 2020.

Questions

1. Propose another machine learning application for McDonald's.

2. Discuss the potential problems that machine learning applications can pose for McDonald's.

Hardware

TECHNOLOGY GUIDE OUTLINE	LEARNING OBJECTIVES
TG 1.1 **Introduction to Hardware**	TG 1.1 Identify the major hardware components of a computer system.
TG 1.2 **Strategic Hardware Issues**	TG 1.2 Discuss strategic issues that link hardware design to business strategy.
TG 1.3 **Computer Hierarchy**	TG 1.3 Describe the various types of computers in the computer hierarchy.
TG 1.4 **Input and Output Technologies**	TG 1.4 Differentiate the various types of input and output technologies and their uses.
TG 1.5 **The Central Processing Unit**	TG 1.5 Describe the design and functioning of the central processing unit.

Introduction

As you begin this Technology Guide, you might be wondering, "Why do I have to know anything about hardware?" There are several reasons why you will benefit from understanding the basics of hardware. First, regardless of your major (and future functional area in an organization), you will be using different types of hardware throughout your career. Second, you will have input concerning the hardware that you will use. In this capacity, you will be required to answer many questions, such as these:

- Is my hardware performing adequately for my needs? If not, what types of problems am I experiencing?
- Do I need more functionality in my hardware, and if so, what functionality would be most helpful to me?

Third, you will have input into decisions when your functional area or organization upgrades or replaces its hardware. Some organizations will allocate the hardware budget to functional areas or departments. In such cases, you might be responsible for making hardware decisions (at least locally) yourself. MIS employees will act as advisors, but you will provide important input into such decisions.

TG 1.1 Introduction to Hardware

Recall from Chapter 1 that the term *hardware* refers to the physical equipment used for the input, processing, output, and storage activities of a computer system. Decisions about hardware focus on three interrelated factors: appropriateness for the task, speed, and cost. The incredibly rapid rate of innovation in the computer industry complicates hardware decisions because computer technologies become obsolete more quickly than other organizational technologies.

The overall trends in hardware are that it becomes smaller, faster, cheaper, and more powerful over time. In fact, these trends are so rapid that they make it difficult to know when to purchase (or upgrade) hardware. This difficulty lies in the fact that companies that delay hardware purchases will, more than likely, be able to buy more powerful hardware for the same amount of money in the future. It is important to note that this is a trade-off. An organization that delays purchasing computer hardware gives up the benefits of whatever it could buy today until the future purchase date arrives.

Hardware consists of the following:

- *Central processing unit (CPU):* Manipulates the data and controls the tasks performed by the other components
- *Primary storage:* Temporarily stores data and program instructions during processing
- *Secondary storage:* Stores data and programs for future use
- *Input technologies:* Accept data and instructions and convert them to a form that the computer can understand
- *Output technologies:* Present data and information in a form people can understand
- *Communication technologies:* Provide for the flow of data from external computer networks (e.g., the Internet and intranets) to the CPU, and from the CPU to computer networks

TG 1.2 Strategic Hardware Issues

For most businesspeople, the most important issues are what the hardware enables, how it is advancing, and how rapidly it is advancing. In many industries, exploiting computer hardware is a key to achieving competitive advantage. Successful hardware exploitation comes from thoughtful consideration of the following questions.

- How do organizations keep up with the rapid price reductions and performance advancements in hardware? For example, how often should an organization upgrade its computers and storage systems? Will upgrades increase personal and organizational productivity? How can organizations measure such increases?
- How should organizations determine the need for the new hardware infrastructures, such as cloud computing? (We discuss cloud computing in Technology Guide 3.)
- Portable computers and advanced communications technologies have enabled employees to work from home or from anywhere. Will these new work styles benefit employees and the organization? How do organizations manage such new work styles?
- How do organizations manage employees who use their own portable devices (e.g., tablets and smartphones) for both personal and work purposes? That is, how do organizations handle the bring-your-own-device (BYOD) phenomenon?

TG 1.3 Computer Hierarchy

The traditional standard for comparing classes of computers is their processing power. This section presents each class of computers from the most powerful to the least powerful. It describes both the computers and their roles in modern organizations.

Supercomputers

The term *supercomputer* does not refer to a specific technology. Rather, it indicates the fastest computers available at any given time. In mid-2017, the fastest supercomputers had speeds approaching 100 petaflops (1 petaflop is 1,000 trillion floating-point operations per second). A floating-point operation is an arithmetic operation that involves decimals.

Large organizations use supercomputers to execute computationally demanding tasks involving very large data sets, such as for military and scientific applications. In the business environment, for example, large banks use supercomputers to calculate the risks and returns of various investment strategies, and health-care organizations use them to analyze giant databases of patient data to determine optimal treatments for various diseases.

Mainframe Computers

Mainframes remain popular in large enterprises for extensive computing applications that are accessed by thousands of users at one time. Examples of mainframe applications are airline reservation systems, corporate payroll programs, website transaction processing systems (e.g., Amazon and eBay), and student grade calculation and reporting.

Today's mainframes perform at teraflop (trillions of floating-point operations per second) speeds and can handle millions of transactions per day. Mainframes can also provide a secure, robust environment in which to run strategic, mission-critical applications.

Microcomputers

Microcomputers—also called *micros, personal computers,* or *PCs*—are the smallest and least expensive category of general-purpose computers. It is important to point out that people frequently define a PC as a computer that uses the Microsoft Windows operating system. In fact, a variety of PCs are available, and many of them do not use Windows. One well-known example is the Apple Mac, which uses the Mac OS X operating system (discussed later in this Technology Guide).

Laptop computer

Laptop and Notebook Computers

Laptop computers (or **notebook computers**) are small, easily transportable, lightweight microcomputers that fit comfortably into a briefcase (**Figure TG 1.1**). They provide users with access to processing power and data outside an office environment.

For example, the Google Chromebook is a thin client laptop that runs Google's Chrome operating system. A **thin client** is a computer that does not offer the full functionality of a PC. A **fat client** is a computer that has the ability to perform many functions without a network connection. Thin clients are less complex than fat clients because they do not have locally installed software. When thin clients need to run an application, they access it from a server over a network rather than from a local disk drive.

A thin client would not have Microsoft Office installed on it. Thus, thin clients are easier and less expensive to operate and support than fat clients. The benefits of thin clients include fast application deployment; centralized management; lower cost of ownership; and easier installation, management, maintenance, and support. The main disadvantage of thin clients is that if the network fails, users can do very little on their computers. In contrast, if users have fat clients and the network fails, they can still perform some functions because they have software, such as Microsoft Office, installed on their computers.

Motorola Xoom tablet

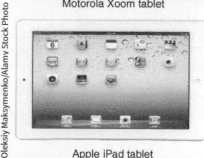
Apple iPad tablet

FIGURE TG 1.1 Laptop, notebook, and tablet computers.

IT's Personal: Purchasing a Computer

One day you will purchase a computer for yourself or your job. When that day comes, it will be important for you to know what to look for. Buying a computer can be very confusing if you just read the box. This Technology Guide has explained the major hardware components of a computer. There are more things you need to consider, however, when you purchase a computer. What do you plan to do with it? Where do you plan to use it? How long do you need service from it? Let's look at each question more closely.

- *What do you plan to do with your computer?* Consider that when you buy a vehicle, your plans for using the vehicle determine the type of vehicle you will purchase. The same rules apply to purchasing a computer. You need to consider what you currently do with a computer and what you may do before you replace the one under consideration. Although many people simply buy as much as they can afford, they may overpay because they do not consider what they need the computer for.

- *Where do you plan to use your computer?* If you plan to use it only at home at your desk, then a desktop model will be fine. In general, you can get more computer for your money in a desktop model as opposed to a laptop (i.e., you pay extra for mobility). However, if you think you may want to take the computer with you, then you will need some type of a laptop or tablet computer. When portability is a requirement, you will want to reconsider what you plan to use the computer for, because as computers become more portable (smaller), their functionality changes, and you want to make sure the computer will meet your needs.

- *How long do you need service from this computer?* Today, we anticipate that most of the devices we purchase will become outdated and need to be replaced in a few years. Therefore, the length of service is really more about warranty and the availability of repair services. In some cases, you should base your purchase decision on these issues rather than speed because they can extend the life of your computer.

Tablet Computers

A **tablet computer** (or *tablet*) is a complete computer contained entirely in a flat touch screen that users operate with a stylus, digital pen, fingertip, or soft (virtual) keyboard, instead of a physical keyboard or mouse. Examples of tablets include the Apple iPad Pro and the Microsoft Surface Pro 7.

Wearable Computers

Wearable computers are miniature computers that people wear under, with, or on top of their clothing. Key features of wearable computers are that there is constant interaction between the computer and the users and that the users can multitask, meaning they do not have to stop what they are doing to use the device. Examples of wearable computers are the Apple Watch (**www.apple.com/watch**), the Sony SmartWatch, Google Glass (**www.google.com/glass/start/**), and the Fitbit (**www.fitbit.com**) activity tracker.

TG 1.4 | Input and Output Technologies

Input Technologies

Author Lecture Videos are available exclusively in *WileyPLUS*.
Apply the Concept activities are available in the Appendix and in *WileyPLUS*.

Input technologies allow people and other technologies to enter data into a computer. The two main types of input devices are human data-entry devices and source-data automation devices. As their name implies, *human data-entry* devices require a certain amount of human effort to input data. Examples are keyboard, mouse, pointing stick, trackball, joystick, touchscreen, stylus, and voice recognition.

In contrast, *source-data automation* devices input data with minimal human intervention. These technologies speed up data collection, reduce errors, and gather data at the source of a transaction or other event. Bar code readers are an example of source-data automation.

An interesting type of human input is gesture-based input. **Gesture recognition** refers to technologies that enable computers to interpret human gestures. These technologies are an initial step in designing computers that can understand human body language. This process creates a richer interaction between machines and humans than has been possible with other input devices.

Gesture recognition enables humans to interact naturally with a computer without any intervening mechanical devices. With gesture-based technologies, the user can move the cursor by pointing a finger at a computer screen. These technologies could make conventional input devices (the mouse, keyboards, and touchscreens) redundant. Examples of gesture-based input devices are the Microsoft Kinect (**www.xbox.com/kinect**) and the Leap Motion Controller (**www.ultraleap.com**).

Common source-data automation input devices include magnetic stripe readers, point-of-sale terminals, bar code scanners, optical mark readers, magnetic ink character readers, sensors (see the Internet of Things in Chapter 8), and cameras.

Output Technologies

The output generated by a computer can be transmitted to the user through several output devices and media. These devices include monitors, printers, plotters, and voice.

Current output technologies include retinal scanning displays and heads-up displays. Retinal scanning displays project images directly onto a viewer's retina and are used in medicine, air traffic control, and controlling industrial machines. Heads-up displays are transparent and present data without requiring the user to look away from his or her usual viewpoint.

Augmented Reality, Virtual Reality, and Mixed Reality

Augmented reality (AR) is a live, direct, or indirect, view of a physical, real-world environment whose elements are augmented, or enhanced, by computer-generated sensory input such as sound, video, graphics, or GPS data via smartphones, tablets, heads-up displays, or smart glasses. Smart glasses include Google Glass Enterprise Edition 2 and Vuzix Blade (**www.vuzix.com**).

Virtual reality (VR) is a fully immersive experience that provides a realistic, three-dimensional, computer-generated environment replicating sight, touch, hearing, and in some cases, smell. Virtual reality brings the user into the virtual environment by removing outside stimuli via VR headsets.

VR is designed to reproduce a real environment or create an imaginary environment in which users can explore and interact. The user becomes a part of the virtual world and, while there, can manipulate objects or perform a series of actions. VR devices include Facebook's Oculus Quest 2 and Oculus Rift S (**www.oculus.com**), Sony's Playstation VR (**www.playstation.com**), Magic Leap One (**www.magicleap.com**), and HTC's Vive Cosmos (**www.vive.com**).

Mixed reality (MR) is an extension of augmented reality that allows physical and virtual elements to interact with one another in an environment. Because MR maintains a connection to the real world, it is not considered a fully immersive experience. In a MR environment, wherever users go and whatever they see wearing MR technology, the three-dimensional content that they encounter will react to them the same way as it would in the real world. For example, an object will move closer to users when they move closer to it. Also, users can turn an object using gestures.

Mixed reality technology integrates the virtual and physical worlds into one connected experience with the help of eye tracking, gesture recognition, and voice recognition technology through a headset or a pair of smart glasses and a pair of motion controllers. MR devices include Microsoft HoloLens 2 (**www.microsoft.com**), Lenovo Explorer (**www.lenovo.com**), Samsung Odyssey (**www.samsung.com**), Acer Windows Mixed Reality (**www.acer.com**), and Google Cardboard (**http://arvr.google.com/cardboard**).

In a look into the near future, Mojo Vision (**www.mojo.vision**) is a startup company that is developing the Mojo Lens. These smart contact lenses are essentially flexible displays which feature AR. The prototype, first demonstrated in January 2020, includes a 14,000 pixel-per-inch display with eye tracking, image stabilization, and a custom wireless radio. An external battery pack provides power to the contact lens and handles sensor data sent to the display. The lens remains under development and will require FDA approval before going to market.

Augmented Reality Examples

POM Transportation

- The Skully AR-1 motorcycle helmet (**www.facebook.com/skullytechnologies**) provides a heads-up display on the front face shield of the helmet. This shield displays basic information such as temperature, driving directions, and a real time 180-degree rear view to riders. By using Bluetooth connectivity, riders can make calls, send texts, and play music by giving voice commands.

POM Manufacturing

- For simulation purposes, Airbus (**www.airbus.com**) deployed an AR model of a new aircraft, allowing designers and engineers to view various components, potential upgrades, and sensors, before going into production. With the AR model, Airbus gave its employees the opportunity to make important design changes before beginning production.

- BMW (**www.bmw.com**) is speeding up its vehicle concept and prototype engineering processes by as much as 12 months using a new AR application. Engineers and designers use AR goggles that allow the real-world, physical vehicle body to be overlaid with true-to-scale holographic 3D models. This process helps in assessing different concept variations and assembly procedures for future vehicles without the need for many test models. People at different locations around the world can use multi-user mode to review designs and concepts together.

POM Cargo Management

- The International Air Transport Association (IATA; **www.iata.org**), whose 290 airlines supply 82 percent of the world's air traffic, deployed industrial technology company Atheer's AR headsets to employees working in cargo management. The system allowed air cargo employees to have instant access to clear and consistent working instructions for key tasks, such as accepting cargo as ready for air carriage. The instructions are delivered directly into the field of view of warehouse cargo handlers and updated wirelessly. The IATA reported a 30 percent improvement in cargo handling speed and a 90 percent reduction in errors.

HRM POM Training

- In Porsche's (**www.porsche.com**) assembly plant in Leipzig, Germany, equipment experts guide employees through their AR glasses and teach them on the job.

POM MKT Customer Service

- Vuforia Chalk is an AR tool that helps customers repair appliances with real-time virtual assistance. Users point their smartphone cameras toward the appliance and remote tech support workers draw on customers' screens to guide them through the repair steps.

MKT Grocery Shopping

- Dent Reality (**www.dentreality.com**) provides an in-store app that provides directions to customers so that they can locate any product. As customers use this app, store employees can focus on other tasks rather than directing or taking customers to products.

MKT Advertising

- AR in marketing and advertising creates a better buying experience for customers and increases their level of engagement. Many advertising campaigns use AR technologies. Consider the Starbucks AR campaign called "Everylove on Every Cup." Using AR, the retailer turned every Starbucks cup into a Valentine's Day card. By using a dedicated Starbucks AR app to scan their cups, users could watch the design come to life.

- At Universal Studios Orlando, park visitors can engage directly with the dinosaurs of the Jurassic Park franchise by using a mobile app. Visitors stand on a Hollywood star to trigger the app and a variety of dinosaurs come up to investigate them.

- With the AMC app, movie posters can do more than just basic advertising. Posters have an AR symbol at the top to indicate that the poster is scannable. Once the poster is recognized by the app, moviegoers can either watch the film's trailer or buy tickets to see the movie. The app also works on images in magazines and news articles.

MKT **Retail**   Retailers are using AR to improve the buyer's experience by bridging the gap between the perception of a product and the actual product. For instance, with AR buyers can know the size and look of the product in a realistic way.

- Augment (**www.augment.com**) is a SaaS platform where users can visualize their products in 3D in a real environment using mobile phones and tablets.
- Yihaodian (owned by Walmart) is the largest Chinese online grocery store. The grocer has placed physical images of stocked grocery shelves on walls and other surfaces in urban public areas in China. Passersby can scan codes under the images with a mobile device to purchase corresponding groceries online.
- NexTech AR Solutions (**www.nextechar.com**) provides a try-it-on feature that can be added to existing digital storefronts. The feature uses the camera on a customer's smartphone or desktop device to enable shoppers to digitally put on eyewear, jewelry, and clothing to see how these items look.
- Warby Parker (**www.warbyparker.com**) has a proprietary try-it-on feature in its app so customers can see how different styles of eyewear will look on them.
- Sephora (**www.sephora.com**) allows customers to try on makeup with its Virtual Artist 3D live experience.
- Google Lens allows users to scan QR codes and objects through their smartphone cameras. Google Lens's Style Match feature provides consumers the capability to identify pieces of clothing or furniture and view similar designs available online and through e-commerce platforms.
- Walmart provides an AR price checking tool for customers that allows them to scan physical products to display up-to-date information that includes the product name, how much the item costs, customer reviews from Walmart.com, and other valuable information.

Entertainment

- Dance Reality guides users through detailed steps and timing of countless dance styles by placing virtual footprints on the floor in front of them.

Education

- Textbooks are being printed on clickable paper, which is an interactive print solution that bridges the traditional offline–online gap. Pages contain multiple hotspots; each hotspot links to one or multiple sources, instantly taking readers from two-dimensional printed content to online, multichannel content.
- Magic Leap's Lumin operating system allows multiple wearers to share in a digital experience, such as a dissection or historical map or event. Also, students can use Magic Leap's computer-aided design application to collaborate on 3D designs.
- Numerous AR apps can identify objects in a user's sight, instantaneously presenting relevant information. For instance, if you walk past an old building, you might effortlessly learn about its history and appearance, dating back to its first construction. Imagine if you were looking at the White House, the Louvre, Westminster Abbey, and many other historical sites.
- BBC's Civilisations (**www.bbc.co.uk**) lets users hold, spin, and view X-rays of ancient artifacts while listening to historical narrations.
- The World Wildlife Fund's (**www.worldwildlife.org**) Free Rivers app transforms users' tabletops into natural landscapes, allowing users to digitally manipulate entire ecosystems to better understand how water flow impacts habitats.

Travel

- If someone is looking for a destination in an unfamiliar city, he or she could ask Google Glass for directions, and the device will overlay their vision with a graphic display of a street map, with the route to their destination highlighted.

- Translation between languages is particularly important in travel. For example, if a traveler takes an image of any foreign street sign, menu, or label, Google Translate provides an instantaneous translation. Travelers can also access subtitles while conversing across a language barrier.

Healthcare

- AccuVein (**www.accuvein.com**) helps doctors and nurses locate patients' veins more easily.
- Philips's Azurion (**www.usa.philips.com**) image-guided therapy platform, built specifically for the HoloLens 2, provides surgeons with real-time patient data and 3D imagery as they operate.
- SyncThink (**www.syncthink.com**) has developed eye-tracking technology to diagnose concussions and balance disorders.
- New developments in AR are helping the more than 3.4 million visually impaired individuals in the United States. For example, the OrCam (**www.orcam.com**) MyEye allows the user to be able to read text without asking others for help. The device snaps a picture of any text from any surface and relays the information to the user via a small earpiece.

  Float's (**www.gowithfloat.com**) Cydalion app works in indoor environments. It scans the surrounding area and provides audio navigation feedback to the visually impaired person wearing it. Currently, the app uses a Tango device on a lanyard or vest and bone conduction headphones. Tango is the AR platform developed by Google. It uses computer vision to enable smartphones to detect their position relative to the world around them without using GPS or other external signals.

- Smart glasses such as the Solos (**www.solos-wearables.com**) and Everysight Raptor (**www.everysight.com**) provide cyclists with data on speed, power, and heart rate, along with navigation instructions.

Virtual Reality Examples

HRM **Training**

- One increasingly common area of potential for VR is training. Traditional flight simulators, which physically duplicate the cockpits of various types of aircraft, have been used to train pilots for more than 80 years. The simulator is mounted on a platform that allows the cockpit to move as an airplane would. The model uses video displays that allows pilots to look out over a landscape or runway and other technologies that closely mimick actual flight with respect to motion, visualizations, communications, and air traffic. Pilots use simulators for initial pilot training (e.g., converting to a new type of aircraft) and recurrent commercial pilot training.

  Flight simulators enable students to interact with an aircraft cockpit, save fuel and wear-and-tear on the aircraft and engines, and can replicate hazardous conditions and system failures without putting any real-life passengers or crew at risk. However, they can cost over $12 million each.

  VR is changing the way that pilots are trained. In April 2019, the U.S. Air Force launched a pilot training class with 30 students using VR headsets and biometric sensors instead of traditional flight simulators. Thirteen students were certified in four months, where the usual pilot training system takes about one year. Students fully immersed themselves in a cockpit using an HTC Vive VR headset while sensors monitored heart rate and pupil measurement. The sensors gave flight instructors an accurate reading of how immersed students actually were in the learning experience. These readings were not available in traditional flight simulators.

  The VR system significantly lowered costs. Another advantage was that VR enabled the flight program to change one cockpit for another, taking just 10 seconds for a student to transition from one type of aircraft to another. Students could also analyze each of their flights because they had been captured and uploaded into the VR simulator. The VR flight training cost $1,000 per unit (headset and AI software) in contrast to the multi-million-dollar cost of a traditional flight simulator.

- `HRM` Walmart is using more than 17,000 Oculus Go headsets in stores to train staff on new technology, customer service, and regulatory compliance. The retailer also uses VR to test whether workers have the skills for middle management.

- `HRM` Farmers Insurance has developed a VR training program that uses AI-powered skills. The insurer also has a VR tool with 500 simulated damage combinations and scenarios to help staff practice home damage assessments.

- `HRM` Walmart's VR training includes the "Avoid, Deny, Defend" method developed at Texas State University, which outlines actions to take such as escaping, protecting yourself, or preparing to fight in response to an active shooter. Following the shooting at a Walmart in El Paso, Texas, Walmart got feedback from employees at the store about the VR training. The associates asserted that the training saved lives. Significantly, the employee feedback was unsolicited.

- `HRM` Firefighters can combat virtual wildfires with VR platforms such as FLAIM Trainer (**www.flaimsystems.com**) or TargetSolutions (**www.targetsolutions.com**).

- `HRM` Fidelity Investments (**www.fidelity.com**) is using VR to build workplace relationships among new employees who are working remotely as a result of the COVID-19 pandemic. Fidelity has also created a VR conference room to foster collaboration among its remote employees.

`MKT` Retail

- Macy's (**www.macys.com**) is offering a VR experience across 90 of its stores where customers provide the dimensions of a room and the retailer lays out the virtual space. Customers can then pick their pieces, design the room, including wall color and flooring, and put on the VR goggles to see how the room would appear.

  Macy's noted that in three pilot stores, VR-influenced furniture sales increased by more than 60 percent versus non-VR furniture sales, while returns decreased to less than two percent. Macy's VR service also enables the retailer to offer a full range of furniture in a much smaller space.

`POM` Engineering

- Engineers use VR in three-dimensional computer-aided design. For example, the automotive, aerospace, and ground transportation industries use VR in their product development, engineering, and manufacturing processes.

Architectural design

- Architects use VR during the design process to actually "see" the projects before they are built, thereby giving the architect a sense of scale and proportion. VR models also eliminate the need to make physical miniatures of projects and enable clients to experience the project before and during construction.

`MKT` Entertainment

- Disney released a VR experience titled Disney Movies VR (**www.disneymoviesvr.com**), free for download. The experience allows users to interact with the characters and worlds from the Disney, Marvel, and Lucasfilm universes.

- Many companies use omnidirectional cameras (also known as 360-degree or VR cameras) by GoPro, Nokia, Samsung, Ricoh, and Nikon. These cameras record in all directions, a process called VR photography. Films produced by VR cameras permit the audience to view an entire environment in every scene. In a notable example, Hyundai used VR cameras in its 2017 Super Bowl commercial, which virtually reunited service members overseas with their families at the game.

- Video games are rapidly incorporating VR, particularly with the emergence of VR headsets. In August 2020, *PC Magazine* picked the top VR video games of 2020, which included *Astro Bot Rescue Mission*, *Beat Saber*, *Budget Cuts*, *Danger Goat*, *Everybody's Golf*, *Far Point*, and others.

- In 2016, *Pokémon Go* placed virtual creatures all over the world for players to view through their smartphone screens, as if the creatures were standing in front of them in the real world. The game has been downloaded over 1 billion times and has generated billions in revenue for the developers.

Education

- In a collaboration with IBM Research, Rensselaer Polytechnic Institute offers students studying Chinese an interesting option: a 360-degree virtual environment that teleports them to the busy streets of Beijing or a crowded Chinese restaurant. Students can haggle with street vendors or order food. The environment is equipped with different capabilities to respond to the students in real time.
- Many K-12 programs are using headsets from Oculus, HTC, and Google Cardboard to send students on virtual field trips, tour the solar system, and walk through the Jurassic period.

MKT Real Estate

- The real estate industry relies heavily on customers visualizing themselves in a new home. Customers can take virtual tours of properties thanks to companies such as Matterport (**www.matterport.com**).

MKT Travel

- Companies in the retail travel industry such as CruiseAbout (**www.cruiseabout.co.nz**) and Flight Centre (**www.flightcentre.com.au**) use VR to enable customers to view cruise ship cabins and hotel rooms before booking their trips.

Healthcare

- Virtually Better (**www.virtuallybetter.com**) has developed Bravemind in collaboration with the University of Southern California's Institute of Creative Technologies. Bravemind provides two virtual environments: Iraq and Afghanistan.

  Therapists can recreate difficult memories at a pace that patients can handle. They customize the experience based on the patient's history to include explosions, firefights, insurgent attacks, and roadside bombs. The virtual experience includes sound effects such as weapon discharges and radio chatter, as well as vibrations designed to mimic engine rumbling and explosions. Bravemind also uses a scent machine to create smells appropriate to the experience such as diesel fuel, garbage, and gunpowder.
- **HRM** Medical Realities (**www.medicalrealities.com**) uses VR modules to help train health-care practitioners. The firm's platform covers a variety of training scenarios, including a physician's office and the operating room, as well as medical school education such as dissecting VR cadavers.

Mixed Reality Examples

Health Care

- A research project at Imperial College Healthcare Trust in London is using Microsoft's mixed-reality headset, HoloLens, to plan plastic surgery. The system can identify which tissue and veins can be used in reconstructive operations.
- Medical services such as 3D4Medical (**www.3d4medical.com**) and Echopixel (**www.echopixel.com**) use existing medical image datasets to create mixed-reality environments of patient-specific anatomy, allowing students and physicians to view and dissect images just as they would a real-world, physical object. These services also help physicians explain medical conditions to patients.

Entertainment

- Monster Park brings Jurassic Park dinosaurs into any landscape you desire.

- Lowe's (**www.lowes.com**), IKEA (**www.ikea.com**), Wayfair (**www.wayfair.com**), Sotheby's (**www.sothebys.com**), and other home-product retailers use MR that allows customers to see how their products will look like in their homes and whether the products will fit into specific rooms and spaces.

- Honeywell has developed a mixed-reality simulation tool to train its industrial employees using Microsoft HoloLens.
- Organizations can use headsets to help guide staff through complicated tasks such as fixing a particular piece of machinery or diagnosing and repairing an automobile.

Holograms

- Startup 8i (**www.8i.com**) has created a lifelike hologram of John Hamm for the Sundance Film Festival and a Buzz Aldrin hologram for the South by Southwest (SXSW) Conference. Analysts anticipate that the company's Holo app will have many more applications for musicians, brands, and celebrities. The public can download the Holo app to their phones to create their own 3D animations.

TG 1.5 The Central Processing Unit

The **central processing unit** performs the actual computation or "number crunching" inside any computer. The CPU is a **microprocessor** (e.g., Intel's Core i3, i5, and i7 chips with more to come) made up of millions of microscopic transistors embedded in a circuit on a silicon wafer, or *chip*. For this reason, microprocessors are commonly referred to as chips.

As shown in **Figure TG 1.2**, the microprocessor has different parts, which perform different functions. The **control unit** sequentially accesses program instructions, decodes them, and controls the flow of data to and from the arithmetic logic unit, the registers, the caches, primary storage, secondary storage, and various output devices. The **arithmetic logic unit (ALU)** performs the mathematical calculations and makes logical comparisons. The registers are high-speed storage areas that store very small amounts of data and instructions for short periods.

> **Author Lecture Videos** are available exclusively in *WileyPLUS*.
> **Apply the Concept** activities are available in the Appendix and in *WileyPLUS*.

How the CPU Works

In the CPU, inputs enter and are stored until they are needed. At that point, they are retrieved and processed, and the output is stored and then delivered somewhere. **Figure TG 1.3** illustrates this process, which works as follows:

- The inputs consist of data and brief instructions about what to do with the data. These instructions come into the CPU from random access memory (RAM). Data might be entered by the user through the keyboard, for example, or read from a data file in another part of the computer. The inputs are stored in registers until they are sent to the next step in the processing.
- Data and instructions travel in the chip through electrical pathways called *buses*. The

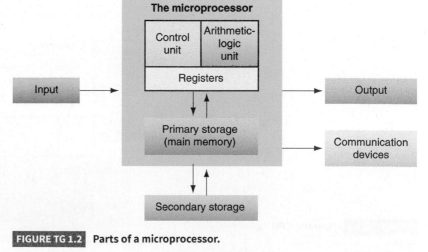

FIGURE TG 1.2 Parts of a microprocessor.

size of the bus—analogous to the width of a highway—determines how much information can flow at any time.

- The control unit directs the flow of data and instructions within the chip.
- The ALU receives the data and instructions from the registers and makes the desired computation. These data and instructions have been translated into **binary form**—that is, only 0s and 1s. A "0" or a "1" is called a **bit**. The CPU can process only binary data. All types of data, such as letters, decimal numbers, photographs, music, and so on, can be converted to a binary representation, which can then be processed by the CPU.
- The data in their original form and the instructions are sent to storage registers and then are sent back to a storage place outside the chip, such as the computer's hard drive. Meanwhile, the transformed data go to another register and then on to other parts of the computer (e.g., to the monitor for display or to storage).

Intel offers excellent demonstrations of how CPUs work. Search the Web for "Intel" with "Explore the Curriculum" to find their demos. This cycle of processing, known as a *machine instruction cycle*, occurs billions of times per second.

Advances in Microprocessor Design

Historically, improvements in chip designs occurred at an increasing rate, as described by **Moore's law**. In 1965, Gordon Moore, a cofounder of Intel Corporation, predicted that microprocessor complexity would double approximately every 18 months. His prediction was amazingly accurate for some 45 years. The advances predicted from Moore's law arose mainly from the following innovations:

- Producing increasingly miniaturized transistors. For example, the Intel i9 chip has approximately 50 billion transistors.
- Placing multiple processors on a single chip. Chips with more than one processor are called *multicore* chips. For example, the most powerful Intel i9 chip contains 10 cores.
- Three-dimensional (3D) chips require less power than two-dimensional chips while improving performance. These chips are particularly valuable in handheld devices because they extend the device's battery life.

Moore's law has been slowing down because it is becoming increasing difficult to place transistors even more close together on chips. As a result, chip manufacturing plants (called fabrication plants, or *fabs*) have taken longer to build and have become much more expensive. For example, Intel's newest fab, designed to build 10-nanometer chips, was delayed. The fab began delivering chips in 2019, five years after the previous generation of chips. (A *nanometer* is one-billionth of a meter. Ten nanometers represents the distance between transistors on a

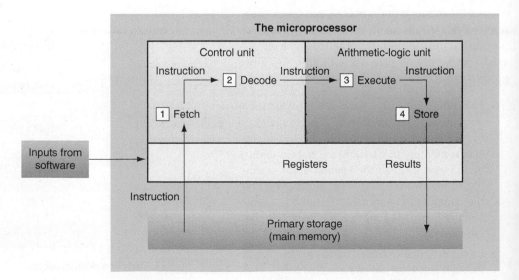

FIGURE TG 1.3 How the CPU works.

chip.) In addition to the delay, the cost of a fab is expected to reach $16 billion or more by 2022. Not coincidentally, only three companies are planning to manufacture the next generation of chips, down from eight in 2010 and 25 in 2002.

In addition to increased speed and performance, Moore's law has had an impact on cost. For example, in 1997, a desktop computer with a Pentium II microprocessor, 64 megabytes of random access memory (RAM), a 4-gigabyte hard drive, and a 17-inch monitor cost $4,000. In late 2020, a desktop computer with an Intel i9 processor, 32 gigabytes of RAM, a 2-terabyte hard drive plus 512 gigabytes of solid-state storage, and a 27-inch touchscreen cost approximately $1,900. Significantly, the 2020 desktop is far faster, has 500 times more RAM, and has 500 times more hard drive storage (without counting the solid-state storage) than the 1997 desktop, for 45 percent of the cost.

Two developments are making the slowing of Moore's law less problematic: graphics processing units and quantum computing. *Graphics processing units* (GPUs) were invented by NVIDIA (**www.nvidia.com**) in 1999. Traditional central processing units (CPUs) are composed of a limited number of cores with a large amount of cache memory. As a result, CPUs can manage a few tasks at one time and are effective at serial processing (one task at a time).

In contrast, GPUs consist of hundreds of cores and can manage thousands of tasks simultaneously. Therefore, GPUs are effective at parallel processing (many tasks at once), meaning that they break down complex problems into thousands or millions of separate tasks and work them out at once. GPUs are particularly suited for computer graphics, image processing, and artificial intelligence applications.

A new computing paradigm has emerged, called *quantum computing*. Classical computers manipulate bits (0s and 1s) to perform operations. In contrast, quantum computers use quantum bits, or qubits. Quantum computers also use 0s and 1s, but qubits have a third state called *superposition*. That is, superposition allows qubits to represent a one or a zero, or any linear combination of a one and a zero, at the same time. Superposition enables quantum computers to process exponentially more data than classical computers.

For example, let's say we want to search for a particular name in a telephone book. With one classical computer, we would start at the beginning and search the phone book sequentially until we found the name we wanted. With two classical computers, we could search the phone book twice as fast because one computer would start at the beginning and one would start at the end until one or the other found the correct name. With three classical computers, we would search the phone book three times as fast, and so on. If we search the phone book with a quantum computer, it would examine all the names in the book simultaneously, finding the correct name instantaneously.

Quantum computers are an emerging technology and the race is on to develop these machines. For example, on September 29, 2020 D-Wave (**www.dwavesys.com**) launched its 5,000-qubit quantum computing platform that purportedly handles 1 million variables. D-Wave calls the new system Advantage and is making it available to business customers over the Internet via the company's quantum cloud service.

Computer Memory

The amount and type of memory that a computer possesses has a great deal to do with its general utility. A computer's memory also determines the types of programs that the computer can run, the work it can perform, its speed, and its cost. There are two basic categories of computer memory. The first is *primary storage*. It is called "primary" because it stores small amounts of data and information that the CPU will use immediately. The second category is *secondary storage*, which stores much larger amounts of data and information (e.g., an entire software program) for extended periods.

Memory Capacity.   As you have seen, CPUs process only binary units—0s and 1s—which are translated through computer languages into bits. A particular combination of bits represents a certain alphanumeric character or a simple mathematical operation. Eight bits are needed to represent any one of these characters. This eight-bit string is known as a **byte**. The storage capacity of a computer is measured in bytes. Bits typically are used as units of measure only for telecommunications capacity, as in how many million bits per second can be sent through a particular medium.

The hierarchy of terms used to describe memory capacity is as follows:

- *Kilobyte. Kilo* means "one thousand," so a kilobyte (KB) is approximately 1,000 bytes. To be more precise, a kilobyte is 1,024 bytes. Computer designers find it convenient to work with powers of 2: 1,024 is 2 to the 10th power, and 1,024 is close enough to 1,000 that for *kilobyte* people use the standard prefix *kilo*, which means exactly 1,000 in familiar units such as the kilogram or kilometer.
- *Megabyte.* Mega means "one million," so a megabyte (MB) is approximately 1 million bytes. Most personal computers have hundreds of megabytes of RAM.
- *Gigabyte.* Giga means "one billion," so a gigabyte (GB) is approximately 1 billion bytes.
- *Terabyte.* A terabyte is approximately 1 trillion bytes. The storage capacity of modern personal computers can be several terabytes.
- *Petabyte.* A petabyte is approximately 1,000 terabytes.
- *Exabyte.* An exabyte is approximately 1,000 petabytes.
- *Zettabyte.* A zettabyte is approximately 1,000 exabytes.

To get a feel for these amounts, consider the following example: If your computer has one terabyte of storage capacity on its hard drive (a type of secondary storage), it can store approximately 1 trillion bytes of data. If the average page of text contains about 2,000 bytes, then your hard drive could store approximately 10 percent of all the print collections of the Library of Congress. That same terabyte can store 70 hours of standard-definition compressed video.

Primary Storage.   **Primary storage**, or main memory, as it is sometimes called, stores three types of information for very brief periods of time: (1) data to be processed by the CPU, (2) instructions for the CPU as to how to process the data, and (3) operating system programs that manage various aspects of the computer's operation. Primary storage takes place in chips mounted on the computer's main circuit board, called the *motherboard*. These chips are located as close as physically possible to the CPU chip. As with the CPU, all the data and instructions in primary storage have been translated into binary code.

The four main types of primary storage are (1) register, (2) cache memory, (3) random access memory (RAM), and (4) read-only memory (ROM).

Registers are part of the CPU. They have the least capacity, storing extremely limited amounts of instructions and data only immediately before and after processing.

Cache memory is a type of high-speed memory that enables the computer to temporarily store blocks of data that are used more often and that a processor can access more rapidly than main memory (RAM). Cache memory is physically located closer to the CPU than RAM. Blocks that are used less often remain in RAM until they are transferred to cache; blocks used infrequently remain in secondary storage. Cache memory is faster than RAM because the instructions travel a shorter distance to the CPU.

Random access memory (RAM) is the part of primary storage that holds a software program and small amounts of data for processing. Compared with the registers, RAM stores more information and is located farther away from the CPU. However, compared with secondary storage, RAM stores less information and is much closer to the CPU.

RAM is temporary and, in most cases, *volatile*—that is, RAM chips lose their contents if the current is lost or turned off, as from a power surge, brownout, or electrical noise generated by lightning or nearby machines.

Most of us have lost data at one time or another because of a computer crash or a power failure. What is usually lost is whatever is in RAM, the cache, or the registers at the time, because these types of memory are volatile. Therefore, you need greater security when you are storing certain types of critical data or instructions. Cautious computer users frequently save data to nonvolatile memory (secondary storage). Most modern software applications also have autosave functions.

Read-only memory is the place—actually, a type of chip—where certain critical instructions are safeguarded. ROM is nonvolatile, so it retains these instructions when the power to the computer is turned off. The read-only designation means that these instructions can only be read by the computer and cannot be changed by the user. An example of ROM is the instructions needed to start or boot the computer after it has been shut off.

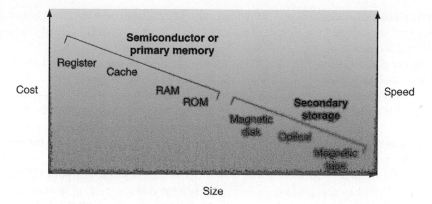

FIGURE TG 1.4 Primary memory compared with secondary storage.

Secondary Storage.

Secondary storage is designed to store very large amounts of data for extended periods. Secondary storage has the following characteristics:

- It is nonvolatile.
- It takes more time to retrieve data from it than from RAM.
- It is cheaper than primary storage (see **Figure TG 1.4**).
- It can use a variety of media, each with its own technology.

One secondary storage medium, **magnetic tape**, is kept on a large open reel or in a smaller cartridge or cassette. Although this is an old technology, it remains popular because it is the cheapest storage medium, and it can handle enormous amounts of data. As a result, many organizations (e.g., the U.S. Government Social Security Administration) use magnetic tape for archival storage. The downside is that it is the slowest method for retrieving data because all the data are placed on the tape sequentially. This process means that the system might have to run through the majority of the tape before it comes to the desired piece of data.

Magnetic disks (or hard drives or fixed disk drives) are the most commonly used mass storage devices because of their low cost, high speed, and large storage capacity. Hard disk drives read from, and write to, stacks of rotating (at up to 15,000 rpm) magnetic disk platters mounted in rigid enclosures and sealed against environmental and atmospheric contamination (see **Figure TG 1.5**). These disks are permanently mounted in a unit that may be internal or external to the computer.

Solid-state drives (SSDs) are data storage devices that serve the same purpose as a hard drive and store data in memory chips. Whereas hard drives have moving parts, SSDs do not. SSDs use the same interface with the computer's CPU as hard drives and are therefore a seamless replacement for hard drives. SSDs offer many advantages over hard drives. They use less power, are silent and faster, and produce about one-third the heat of a hard drive. The major disadvantage of SSDs is that they cost more than hard drives.

Unlike magnetic media, **optical storage devices** do not store data through magnetism. Rather, a laser reads the surface of a reflective plastic platter. Optical disk drives are slower than magnetic hard drives, but they are less fragile and less susceptible to damage from contamination.

iStock.com/Homiel

iStock.com/krzyscin

FIGURE TG 1.5 Traditional hard drives are less expensive, but solid-state drives are faster and are more reliable.

Optical disks can also store a great deal of information, both on a routine basis and when combined into storage systems. Types of optical disks include compact disk read-only memory and digital video disk.

Compact disk read-only memory (CD-ROM) storage devices have high capacity, low cost, and high durability. However, because a CD-ROM is a read-only medium, it cannot be written on. *CD-R* can be written to, but once this is done, what was written on it cannot be changed later. That is, CD-R is writable, which CD-ROM is not, but it is not rewritable, which *CD-RW* (compact disk, rewritable) is. There are applications about which not being rewritable is a plus, because it prevents some types of accidental data destruction. CD-RW adds rewritability to the recordable compact disk market.

The digital video disk *(DVD)* is a 5-inch disk with the capacity to store about 135 minutes of digital video. DVDs can also perform as computer storage disks, providing storage capabilities of 17 gigabytes. DVD players can read current CD-ROMs, but current CD-ROM players cannot read DVDs. The access speed of a DVD drive is faster than that of a typical CD-ROM drive.

Blu-ray disks can store 50 gigabytes per layer. Development of Blu-ray technology is ongoing, with multilayered disks capable of storing up to 100 gigabytes.

The various disk technologies are under pressure from on-demand, streaming services over the Internet. As the bandwidth of the Internet increases, so will the pressure on disk technologies.

Flash memory devices (or *memory cards*) are nonvolatile electronic storage devices that contain no moving parts and use 30 times less battery power than hard drives. Flash devices are also smaller and more durable than hard drives. The trade-offs are that flash devices store less data than hard drives. Flash devices are used with digital cameras, handheld and laptop computers, telephones, music players, and video game consoles.

One popular flash memory device is the **thumb drive** (also called *memory stick*, *jump drive*, or *flash drive*). These devices fit into Universal Serial Bus (USB) ports on personal computers and other devices, and they can store many gigabytes. Thumb drives have replaced magnetic floppy disks for portable storage.

Before you go on...

1. Decisions about hardware focus on what three factors?
2. What are the overall trends in hardware?
3. Define hardware and list the major hardware components.
4. Describe the different types of computers.
5. Distinguish between human data-input devices and source-data automation.
6. Briefly describe how a microprocessor functions.
7. Distinguish between primary storage and secondary storage.

What's in IT for me?

For All Business Majors

The design of computer hardware has profound impacts for businesspeople. Personal and organizational success can depend on an understanding of hardware design and a commitment to knowing where it is going and what opportunities and challenges hardware innovations will bring. Because these innovations are occurring so rapidly, hardware decisions both at the individual level and at the organizational level are difficult.

At the *individual level*, most people who have a home or office computer system and want to upgrade it, or people who are contemplating their first computer purchase, are faced with the decision of *when* to buy as much as *what* to buy and at what cost. At the *organizational level*, these same issues plague IS professionals. However, they are more complex and costly. Most organizations have many different computer systems in place at the same time. Innovations may come to different classes of computers at different times or rates. Therefore, managers must decide when old hardware *legacy systems* still have a productive role in the organization and when they should be replaced. A legacy system is an old computer system or application that continues to be used, typically because it still functions for the users' needs, even though newer technology is available.

Summary

TG1.1 Identify the major hardware components of a computer system.

Modern computer systems have six major components: the central processing unit (CPU), primary storage, secondary storage, input technologies, output technologies, and communications technologies.

TG1.2 Discuss strategic issues that link hardware design to business strategy.

Strategic issues linking hardware design to business strategy include the following: How do organizations keep up with the rapid price/performance advancements in hardware? How often should an organization upgrade its computers and storage systems? How can organizations measure benefits gained from price/performance improvements in hardware?

TG1.3 Describe the various types of computers in the computer hierarchy.

Supercomputers are the most powerful computers, designed to handle intensive computational demands. Organizations use mainframes for centralized data processing and managing large databases. Microcomputers are small, complete, general purpose computers. Laptop or notebook computers are small, easily transportable computers. Tablet computers are complete computers contained entirely in a flat touchscreen that uses a stylus, digital pen, fingertip, or soft (virtual) keyboards as input devices. Wearable computers are miniature computers that people wear under, with, or on top of their clothing.

TG1.4 Differentiate the various types of input and output technologies and their uses.

The two main types of input devices are human data-entry devices and source-data automation devices. *Human data-entry* devices require a certain amount of human effort to input data. Examples are keyboard, mouse, pointing stick, trackball, joystick, touchscreen, stylus, and voice recognition. *Source-data automation* devices input data with minimal human intervention. These technologies gather data at the source of a transaction or other event. Bar code readers are an example of source-data automation.

TG1.5 Describe the design and functioning of the central processing unit.

The CPU consists of the arithmetic logic unit, which performs the calculations; the registers, which store minute amounts of data and instructions immediately before and after processing; and the control unit, which controls the flow of information on the microprocessor chip. After processing, the data in their original form and the instructions are sent back to a storage location outside the chip.

Technology Guide Glossary

arithmetic logic unit (ALU) Portion of the CPU that performs the mathematical calculations and makes logical comparisons.

augmented reality (AR) A live, direct or indirect, view of a physical, real-world environment whose elements are enhanced by computer-generated sensory input such as sound, video, graphics, or GPS data.

binary form The form in which data and instructions can be read by the CPU—only 0s and 1s.

bit Short for *binary digit* (0s and 1s), the only data that a CPU can process.

byte An eight-bit string of data, needed to represent any one alphanumeric character or simple mathematical operation.

cache memory A type of high-speed memory that enables the computer to temporarily store blocks of data that are used more often and that a processor can access more rapidly than main memory (RAM).

central processing unit (CPU) Hardware that performs the actual computation or "number crunching" inside any computer.

control unit Portion of the CPU that controls the flow of information.

fat clients Computers that offer full functionality without having to connect to a network.

flash memory devices Nonvolatile electronic storage devices that are compact, are portable, require little power, and contain no moving parts.

gesture recognition An input method that interprets human gestures, in an attempt for computers to begin to understand human body language.

laptop computers (notebook computers) Small, easily transportable, lightweight microcomputers.

magnetic disks (or hard drives or fixed disk drives) A form of secondary storage on a magnetized disk divided into tracks and sectors that provide addresses for various pieces of data.

magnetic tape A secondary storage medium on a large open reel or in a smaller cartridge or cassette.

mainframes Relatively large computers used in large enterprises for extensive computing applications that are accessed by thousands of users.

microcomputers The smallest and least expensive category or general-purpose computers, also called micros, personal computers, or PCs.

microprocessor The CPU, made up of millions of transistors embedded in a circuit on a silicon wafer or chip.

Moore's law Prediction by Gordon Moore, an Intel cofounder, that microprocessor complexity would double approximately every two years.

notebook computer See **laptop computers**.

optical storage devices A form of secondary storage in which a laser reads the surface of a reflective plastic platter.

primary storage (also called main memory) High-speed storage located directly on the motherboard that stores data to be processed by the CPU, instructions telling the CPU how to process the data, and operating system programs.

random access memory (RAM)   The part of primary storage that holds a software program and small amounts of data when they are brought from secondary storage.

read-only memory (ROM)   Type of primary storage in which certain critical instructions are safeguarded; the storage is nonvolatile and retains the instructions when the power to the computer is turned off.

registers   High-speed storage areas in the CPU that store very small amounts of data and instructions for short periods.

secondary storage   Technology that can store very large amounts of data for extended periods.

server   Computers that support networks, enabling users to share files, software, and other network devices.

solid-state drives (SSDs)   Data storage devices that serve the same purpose as a hard drive and store data in memory chips.

thin client   A computer that does not offer the full functionality of a *fat client*.

thumb drive   Storage device that fits into the USB port of a personal computer and is used for portable storage.

virtual reality (VR)   A term that describes a realistic, three-dimensional, computer-generated environment that replicates sight, touch, hearing, and in some cases, smell.

wearable computer   A miniature computer worn by a person allowing the users to multitask.

Discussion Questions

1. What factors affect the speed of a microprocessor?

2. If you were the CIO of a firm, what factors would you consider when selecting secondary storage media for your company's records (files)?

3. Given that Moore's law has proved itself over the past two decades, speculate on what chip capabilities will be in 10 years. What might your desktop PC be able to do?

4. If you were the CIO of a firm, how would you explain the workings, benefits, and limitations of using thin clients as opposed to fat clients?

5. Where might you find embedded computers at home, at school, or at work?

6. You are the CIO of your company, and you have to develop an application of strategic importance to your firm. What are the advantages and disadvantages of using open-source software?

7. What does the statement "hardware is useless without software" mean?

Problem-Solving Activities

1. Access the websites of the major chip manufacturers—for example, Intel (**www.intel.com**) and Advanced Micro Devices (**www.amd.com**)—and obtain the latest information regarding new and planned chips. Compare performance and costs across these vendors. Be sure to take a close look at the various multicore chips.

Software

TECHNOLOGY GUIDE OUTLINE	LEARNING OBJECTIVES
TG 2.1 **Software Issues**	TG 2.1 Discuss the major software issues that confront modern organizations.
TG 2.2 **Systems Software**	TG 2.2 Describe the general functions of the operating system.
TG 2.3 **Application Software**	TG 2.3 Identify the major types of application software.

Introduction

As you begin this Technology Guide, you might be wondering, "Why do I have to know anything about software?" There are several reasons why you will benefit from understanding the basics of software. First, regardless of your major (and future functional area in an organization), you will be using different types of software throughout your career. Second, you will have input concerning the software that you will use. In this capacity, you will be required to answer many questions, such as:

- Does my software help me do my job?
- Is this software easy to use?
- Do I need more functionality in my hardware or software, and if so, what functionality would be most helpful to me?

Third, you will have input into decisions when your functional area or organization upgrades or replaces its software. Some organizations will allocate the software budget to functional areas or departments. In such cases, you might be responsible for making software decisions (at least locally) yourself. MIS employees will act as advisors, but you will provide important input into such decisions.

Computer hardware is only as effective as the instructions you give it. Those instructions are contained in **software**. The importance of computer software cannot be overestimated. The first software applications for computers in business were developed in the early 1950s. At that time, software was less costly. Today, software comprises a much larger percentage of the cost of modern computer systems; the price of hardware has dramatically decreased while both the complexity and the price of software have dramatically increased.

The ever-increasing complexity of software has also increased the potential for errors, or *bugs*. Large applications today may contain millions of lines of computer code, written by hundreds of people over the course of several years. Thus, the potential for errors is huge, and testing and debugging software is expensive and time consuming.

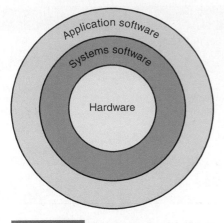

FIGURE TG 2.1 **Systems software serves as an intermediary between hardware and functional applications.**

In spite of these overall trends—increasing complexity, cost, and numbers of defects—software has become an everyday feature of our business and personal lives. Your examination of software begins with definitions of some fundamental concepts. Software consists of **computer programs**, which are sequences of instructions for the computer. The process of writing, or coding, programs is called **programming**. Individuals who perform this task are called *programmers*.

Computer programs include **documentation**, which is a written description of the program's functions. Documentation helps the user operate the computer system, and it helps other programmers understand what the program does and how it accomplishes its purpose. Documentation is vital to a business organization. Without it, the departure of a key programmer or user could deprive the organization of the knowledge of how the program is designed and functions.

The computer can do nothing until it is instructed by software. Computer hardware, by design, is general purpose. Software enables the user to instruct the hardware to perform specific functions that provide business value. There are two major types of software: systems software and application software. **Figure TG 2.1** illustrates the relationship among hardware, systems software, and application software.

TG 2.1 Software Issues

The importance of software in computer systems has brought new issues to the forefront for organizational managers. These issues include software defects (bugs), licensing, open systems, and open-source software.

Software Defects

All too often, computer program code is inefficient, poorly designed, and riddled with errors. The Software Engineering Institute (SEI) at Carnegie Mellon University in Pittsburgh defines good software as usable, reliable, defect-free, cost-effective, and maintainable. As our dependence on computers and networks increases, the risks associated with software defects are becoming more serious.

The SEI maintains that, on average, professional programmers make between 100 and 150 errors in every 1,000 lines of code they write. Fortunately, the software industry recognizes this problem. Unfortunately, however, the problem is enormous, and the industry is taking only initial steps to resolve it. One critical step is better design and planning at the beginning of the development process (discussed in Chapter 13).

Software Licensing

Many people routinely copy proprietary software. However, making copies without the manufacturer's explicit permission—a practice known as *piracy*—is illegal. The Business Software Alliance (BSA; **www.bsa.org**), a nonprofit trade association dedicated to promoting a safe and legal digital world, collects, investigates, and acts on software piracy tips. The BSA has calculated that piracy costs software vendors around the world billions of dollars annually. Most of the tips the BSA receives come from current and past employees of offending companies.

To protect their investment, software vendors must prevent their products from being copied and distributed by individuals and other software companies. A company can copyright its software, which means that the U.S. Copyright Office grants the company the exclusive legal right to reproduce, publish, and sell that software.

The number of computing devices in organizations continues to grow, and businesses continue to decentralize, so IS managers are finding it increasingly difficult to supervise their software assets. In fact, the majority of chief information officers (CIOs) are not confident that their companies are in compliance with software licensing agreements. For example, one medium-sized company was fined $10,000 for unknowingly using Microsoft Exchange mailbox licenses that had not been purchased. Worse, the company was also fined $100,000 for not having the necessary licenses for Autodesk, Inc.'s AutoCAD design software.

To help companies manage their software licenses, new firms have arisen that specialize in tracking software licenses for a fee. For example, Cherwell (**www.cherwell.com**) will track and manage a company's software licenses to ensure that a client company is in compliance with U.S. copyright laws.

Open Systems

The **open systems** concept refers to a group of computing products that work together. In an open system, the same operating system with compatible software is installed on all computers that interact within an organization. A complementary approach is to employ application software that will run across all computer platforms. Where hardware, operating systems, and application software are all designed as open systems, users can purchase the best software, called *best of breed*, for a job without worrying whether it will run on particular hardware.

Open-Source Software

Organizations today are increasingly selecting open-source software rather than proprietary software. **Proprietary software** is purchased software that has restrictions on its use, copying, and modification. Companies that develop proprietary software spend money and time developing their products, which they then sell in the marketplace. This software is labeled *proprietary* because the developer keeps the source code—the actual computer instructions—private (just as Coca-Cola does with its soft drink formula). Therefore, companies that purchase the software can use it in their operations, but they cannot change the source code themselves.

In contrast, the source code for **open-source software** is available at no cost to both developers and users. This software is distributed with license terms that ensure that its source code will always be available for all users.

Open-source software is produced by worldwide "communities" of developers who write and maintain the code. Inside each community, however, only a small group of developers, called *core developers*, is allowed to modify the code directly. All the other developers must submit their suggested changes to the core developers.

There are advantages to implementing open-source software in an organization. According to OpenSource (**www.opensource.org**), open-source development produces high-quality, reliable, low-cost software. This software is also flexible, meaning that the code can be changed to meet users' needs. In many cases, open-source software can be more reliable than proprietary software. Because the code is available to many developers, more bugs are discovered early and quickly, and they are fixed immediately. Technical support for open-source software is also available from firms that offer products derived from the software. An example is Red Hat (**www.redhat.com**), a major Linux vendor that supplies solutions to problems associated with open-source technology. Specifically, Red Hat provides education, training, and technical support for a fee.

Open-source software, however, has disadvantages. The major drawback is that companies that use open-source software depend on the continued goodwill of an army of volunteers for enhancements, bug fixes, and so on, even if they have signed a contract that includes support. Some companies will not accept this risk, although as a practical matter the support community for Linux, Apache, and Firefox is not likely to disappear. Furthermore, organizations that do not have in-house technical experts will have to purchase maintenance-support contracts from a third party. Open-source software also poses questions concerning ease of use, the time and expense needed to train users, and compatibility with existing systems either within or outside the organization.

There are many examples of open-source software, including the GNU (GNU's Not UNIX) suite of software (**www.gnu.org**) developed by the Free Software Foundation (**www.fsf .org**), the Linux operating system (**www.linux.com**), Apache web server (**www.apache.org**), sendmail SMTP (Send Mail Transport Protocol) e-mail server, the Perl programming language (**www.perl.org**), and the Firefox browser from Mozilla (**www.mozilla.com**). In fact, more than 150,000 open-source projects are under way at SourceForge (**www.sourceforge.net**), the popular open-source hosting site.

Open-source software is moving to the mainstream, as you see by the many major companies that use this type of software. For example, Japan's Shinsei Bank (**www.shinseibank .com/english/**) uses Linux on its servers, SugarCRM (**www.sugarcrm.com**) for certain customer relationship management tasks, and MySQL (**www.mysql.com**) open-source database management software. Furthermore, the *Los Angeles Times* uses Alfresco (**www.alfresco.com**) to manage some of the images and video for its website.

TG 2.2 | Systems Software

Author Lecture Videos are available exclusively in *WileyPLUS.*
Apply the Concept activities are available in the Appendix and in *WileyPLUS.*

Systems software is a set of instructions that serves primarily as an intermediary between computer hardware and application programs. Systems software performs many functions.

- It controls and supports the computer system and its information-processing activities.
- It enables computer systems to perform self-regulatory functions by loading itself when the computer is first turned on.
- It provides commonly used sets of instructions for all applications.
- It helps users and IT personnel program, test, and debug their own computer programs.
- It supports application software by directing the computer's basic functions.

The major type of systems software with which we are concerned is the operating system. The **operating system (OS)** is the "director" of your computer system's operations. It supervises the overall operation of the computer by monitoring the computer's status, scheduling operations, and managing input and output processes. Well-known desktop operating systems include Microsoft Windows (**www.microsoft.com**), Apple Mac OS X (**www.apple.com**), and Linux (**www.linux.com**). When a new version with new features is released, the developers often give the new version a new designation. For example, in mid-2020, the current version of Windows was Windows 10, and the latest version of the MacOS was Catalina.

The operating system also provides an interface between the user and the hardware. This user interface hides the complexity of the hardware from the user. That is, you do not have to know how the hardware actually operates; you simply have to know what the hardware will do and what you need to do to obtain the desired results.

The ease or difficulty of the interaction between the user and the computer is determined to a large extent by the **graphical user interface (GUI)**. The GUI allows users to directly control the hardware by manipulating visible objects (such as icons) and actions that replace complex commands. Microsoft Windows provides a widely recognized GUI.

GUI technology incorporates features such as virtual reality, head-mounted displays, speech input (user commands) and output, pen and gesture recognition, animation, multimedia, artificial intelligence, and cellular/wireless communication capabilities. These new interfaces, called *natural user interfaces* (NUIs), will combine social, haptic, and touch-enabled gesture-control interfaces. (A *haptic interface* provides tactile feedback through the sense of touch by applying forces, vibrations, or motions to the user.)

A **social interface** guides the user through computer applications by using cartoon-like characters, graphics, animation, and voice commands. The cartoon-like characters can be puppets, narrators, guides, inhabitants, or *avatars* (computer-generated human-like figures).

Social interfaces are hard to create without being corny. For example, the assistant "Clippy" was so annoying to users of Microsoft Office 97 that it was eliminated from Office 2003 and all subsequent versions.

- *Motion control gaming consoles* are another type of interface. In November 2020 Microsoft released its Xbox Series X and Sony released its PlayStation 5. These consoles track your movements without a physical controller, offer voice recognition, and accommodate multiple players.
- The Leap Motion Controller is a motion-sensing, matchbox-sized device placed on a physical desktop. Using two cameras, the device "observes" an area up to a distance of about three feet. It precisely tracks fingers or items such as a pen that cross into the observed area. The Leap can perform tasks such as navigating a website, using pinch-to-zoom gestures on maps, performing high-precision drawing, and manipulating complex three-dimensional visualizations. The smaller observation area and higher resolution of the device differentiates it from the Microsoft Kinect, which is more suitable for whole-body tracking in a space the size of a living room.

Touch-enabled gesture-control interfaces enable users to browse through photos, "toss" objects around a screen, "flick" to turn the pages of a book, play video games, and watch movies. Examples of this type of interface are Microsoft Surface and the Apple iPhone.

TG 2.3 Application Software

Application software is a set of computer instructions that provides specific functionality to a user. This functionality may be broad, such as general word processing, or narrow, such as an organization's payroll program. Essentially, an application program applies a computer to a certain need. As you will see, modern organizations use many different software applications.

Application software may be developed in-house by the organization's information systems personnel, or it may be commissioned from a software vendor. Alternatively, the software can be purchased, leased, or rented from a vendor that develops applications and sells them to many organizations. This "off-the-shelf" software may be a standard package, or it may be customizable. Special-purpose programs or "packages" can be tailored for a specific purpose, such as inventory control and payroll. A **package**, or **software suite**, is a group of programs with integrated functions that has been developed by a vendor and is available for purchase in a prepackaged form. Microsoft Office is a well-known example of a package or software suite.

General-purpose, off-the-shelf application programs designed to help individual users increase their productivity are referred to as **personal application software**. **Table TG 2.1** lists some of the major types of personal application software.

Speech-recognition software, also called *voice recognition*, is an input technology, rather than strictly an application, that enables users to provide input to systems software and application software. As the name suggests, this software recognizes and interprets human speech, either one word at a time (*discrete speech*) or in a conversational stream (*continuous speech*). Advances in processing power, new software algorithms, and better microphones have enabled developers to design extremely accurate speech-recognition software. Experts predict that, in the near future, voice recognition systems will be built into almost every device, appliance, and machine that people use. Applications for voice recognition technology abound.

TABLE TG 2.1   **Personal Application Software**

Category of Personal Application Software	Major Functions	Examples
Spreadsheets	Use rows and columns to manipulate primarily numerical data; useful for analyzing financial information and for what-if and goal-seeking analyses	Microsoft Excel Corel Quattro Pro Apple iWork Numbers
Word processing	Allow users to manipulate primarily text with many writing and editing features	Microsoft Word Apple iWork Pages
Desktop publishing	Extend word processing software to allow production of finished, camera-ready documents, which may contain photographs, diagrams, and other images combined with text in different fonts	Microsoft Publisher QuarkXPress Adobe
Data management	Allow users to store, retrieve, and manipulate related data	Microsoft Access FileMaker Pro
Presentation	Allow users to create and edit graphically rich information to appear on electronic slides	Microsoft PowerPoint Apple iWork Keynote
Graphics	Allow users to create, store, and display or print charts, graphs, maps, and drawings	Adobe PhotoShop Corel DRAW
Personal information management	Allow users to create and maintain calendars, appointments, to-do lists, and business contacts	Google Calendar Microsoft Outlook
Personal finance	Allow users to maintain checkbooks, track investments, monitor credit cards, and bank and pay bills electronically	Quicken Microsoft Money
Web authoring	Allow users to design websites and publish them on the Web	Microsoft FrontPage Adobe Dreamweaver
Communications	Allow users to communicate with other people over any distance	Novell Groupwise

Before you go on...

1. What does the statement "hardware is useless without software" mean?
2. What are the differences between systems software and application software?
3. What is open-source software, and what are its advantages? Can you think of any disadvantages?
4. Describe the functions of the operating system.

What's in IT for me?

ACCT For the Accounting Major

Accounting application software performs the organization's accounting functions, which are repetitive and performed in high volumes. Each business transaction (e.g., a person hired, a paycheck processed, an item sold) produces data that must be captured. Accounting applications capture these data and then manipulate them as necessary. Accounting applications adhere to relatively standardized procedures, handle detailed data, and have a historical focus (i.e., what happened in the past).

FIN For the Finance Major

Financial application software provides information about the firm's financial status to persons and groups inside and outside the firm. Financial applications include forecasting, funds management, and control applications. Forecasting applications predict and project the firm's future activity in the economic environment. Funds management applications use cash flow models to analyze expected cash flows. Control applications enable managers to monitor their financial performance, typically by providing information about the budgeting process and performance ratios.

MKT For the Marketing Major

Marketing application software helps management solve problems that involve marketing the firm's products. Marketing software includes marketing research and marketing intelligence applications. Marketing applications provide information about the firm's products and competitors, its distribution system, its advertising and personal selling activities, and its pricing strategies. Overall, marketing applications help managers develop strategies that combine the four major elements of marketing: product, promotion, place, and price.

POM For the Production/Operations Management Major

Managers use production/operations management (POM) application software for production planning and as part of the physical production system. POM applications include production, inventory, quality, and cost software. These applications help management operate manufacturing facilities and logistics. Materials requirements planning (MRP) software is also widely used in manufacturing. This software identifies which materials will be needed, how much will be needed, and the dates on which they will be needed. This information enables managers to be proactive.

HRM For the Human Resources Management Major

Human resources management application software provides information concerning recruiting and hiring, education and training, maintaining the employee database, termination, and administering benefits. HRM applications include workforce planning, recruiting, workforce management, compensation, benefits, and environmental reporting subsystems (e.g., equal employment opportunity records and analysis, union enrollment, toxic substances, and grievances).

MIS For the MIS Major

If your company decides to develop its own software, the MIS function is responsible for managing this activity. If the company decides to buy software, the MIS function deals with software vendors in analyzing their products. The MIS function is also responsible for upgrading software as vendors release new versions.

Summary

TG2.1 Discuss the major software issues that confront modern organizations.

Computer program code often contains errors. The industry recognizes the enormous problem of software defects, and steps are being taken to resolve this issue. Software licensing is another issue for organizations and individuals. Copying proprietary software is illegal. Software vendors copyright their software to protect it from being copied. As a result, companies must license vendor-developed software to be able to use it. Organizations must also decide between open-source software and proprietary software. Each type of software has its pros and cons that must be carefully considered.

TG2.2 Describe the general functions of the operating system.

Operating systems manage the actual computer resources (i.e., the hardware). They schedule and process applications; manage and protect memory; manage the input and output functions and hardware; manage data and files; and provide security, fault tolerance, graphical user interfaces, and windowing.

TG2.3 Identify the major types of application software.

The major types of application software are spreadsheet, data management, word processing, desktop publishing, graphics, multimedia, communications, speech recognition, and groupware. Software suites combine several types of application software (e.g., word processing, spreadsheet, and data management) into an integrated package.

Technology Guide Glossary

application software   The class of computer instructions that directs a computer system to perform specific processing activities and provide functionality for users.

computer programs   The sequences of instructions for the computer, which comprise software.

documentation   Written description of the functions of a software program.

graphical user interface (GUI)   Systems software that allows users to have direct control of the hardware by manipulating visible objects (such as icons) and actions, which replace command syntax.

open-source software   Software made available in source-code form at no cost to developers.

open systems   Computing products that work together by using the same operating system with compatible software on all the computers that interact in an organization.

operating system (OS)   The main system control program, which supervises the overall operations of the computer, allocates CPU time and main memory to programs, and provides an interface between the user and the hardware.

package   Common term for an integrated group of computer programs developed by a vendor and available for purchase in prepackaged form.

personal application software   General-purpose, off-the-shelf application programs that support general types of processing, rather than being linked to any specific business function.

programming   The process of writing or coding software programs.

proprietary software   Software that has been developed by a company and has restrictions on its use, copying, and modification.

social interface   A user interface that guides the user through computer applications by using cartoon-like characters, graphics, animation, and voice commands.

software   A set of computer programs that enable the hardware to process data.

software suite   See **package**.

speech-recognition software   Software that recognizes and interprets human speech, either one word at a time (discrete speech) or in a stream (continuous speech).

systems software   The class of computer instructions that serve primarily as an intermediary between computer hardware and application programs; provides important self-regulatory functions for computer systems.

Discussion Questions

1. You are the CIO of your company, and you have to develop an application of strategic importance to your firm. What are the advantages and disadvantages of using open-source software?

2. Describe how hardware and software are synergistic.

Problem-Solving Activities

1. A great deal of free software is available over the internet. Go to **https://100-downloads.com/programs/internet**, and observe all the software available for free. Would you feel safe downloading a software program from this site onto your computer? Why or why not?

2. Enter the IBM website (**www.ibm.com**) and perform a search on the term "software." Click on the drop box for Products and notice how many software products IBM produces. Is IBM only a hardware company?

Cloud Computing

TECHNOLOGY GUIDE OUTLINE	LEARNING OBJECTIVES
TG 3.1 Introduction	TG 3.1 Describe the evolution of the IT function.
TG 3.2 The Basics of Cloud Computing	TG 3.2 Define cloud computing and its key characteristics.
TG 3.3 Different Types of Clouds	TG 3.3 Describe each of the four types of clouds.
TG 3.4 Cloud Computing Services	TG 3.4 Explain the operational model of each of the three types of cloud services.
TG 3.5 The Benefits of Cloud Computing	TG 3.5 Identify the key benefits of cloud computing.
TG 3.6 Concerns and Risks with Cloud Computing	TG 3.6 Discuss the concerns and risks associated with cloud computing.
TG 3.7 The "Big Three" Cloud Computing Vendors	TG. 3.7 Describe the pros and cons for each of the Big Three cloud computing vendors.
TG 3.8 Web Services and Service-Oriented Architecture	TG 3.8 Explain the role of Web services in building a firm's IT applications, providing examples.

We devote this Technology Guide to a vital topic: cloud computing. A working knowledge of cloud computing will enhance your appreciation of what technology can and cannot do for a business. It will also enable you to make an immediate contribution by analyzing how your organization manages its IT assets. Going further, you will be using these computing resources in your career, and you will have input into decisions about how your department and organization can best use them. Cloud computing can also be extremely valuable if you decide to start your own business.

We present many examples of how the cloud can be used for business purposes. The cloud can also provide you with personal applications. Therefore, this guide can help you plan for your own use of the cloud. For a more detailed discussion of how you can use the cloud, see the section titled IT's Personal: "The Cloud."

TG 3.1 | Introduction

You were introduced to the concept of IT infrastructure in Chapter 1. Recall that an organization's *IT infrastructure* consists of IT components—hardware, software, networks, and databases—and IT services—developing information systems, managing security and risk, and managing

Author Lecture Videos are available exclusively in *WileyPLUS*.
Apply the Concept activities are available in the Appendix and in *WileyPLUS*.

data. (It is helpful to review Figure 1.3 of Chapter 1 here.) The organization's IT infrastructure is the foundation for all of the information systems that the organization uses.

The Evolution of Modern Information Technology Infrastructure

Modern IT infrastructure has evolved through several stages since the early 1950s, when firms first began to apply information technology to business applications. These stages are as follows:

- *Stand-alone mainframes*: Organizations initially used mainframe computers in their engineering and accounting departments. The mainframe was typically housed in a secure area, and only MIS personnel had access to it.

- *Mainframe and dumb terminals*: Forcing users to go to wherever the mainframe was located was time consuming and inefficient. As a result, firms began placing so-called dumb terminals—essentially electronic typewriters with limited processing power—in user departments. This arrangement enabled users to input computer programs into the mainframe from their departments, a process called *remote job entry.*

- *Stand-alone personal computers*: In the late 1970s, the first personal computers appeared. The IBM PC's debut in 1981 legitimized the entire personal computer market. Users began bringing personal computers to the workplace to improve their productivity—for example, by using spreadsheet and word processing applications. These computers were not initially supported by the firm's MIS department. However, as the number of personal computers increased dramatically, organizations decided to support these devices, and they established policies as to which PCs and software they would support.

- *Local area networks (client/server computing)*: When personal computers are networked, individual productivity increases. For this reason, organizations began to connect personal computers to local area networks (LANs) and then connected these LANs to the mainframe, a type of processing known as *client/server computing.*

- *Enterprise computing*: In the early 1990s, organizations began to use networking standards to integrate different kinds of networks throughout the firm, thereby creating enterprise computing. As the Internet became widespread after 1995, organizations began using the TCP/IP networking protocol to integrate different types of networks. All types of hardware were networked, including mainframes, personal computers, smartphones, printers, and many others. Software applications and data now flow seamlessly throughout the enterprise and between organizations.

- *Cloud computing and mobile computing*: Today, organizations and individuals can use the power of cloud computing. As you will see in this Technology Guide, cloud computing provides access to a shared pool of computing resources, including computers, storage, applications, and services, over a network, typically the Internet.

Keep in mind that the computing resources in each stage can be cumulative. For example, most large firms still use mainframe computers (in addition to all the other types of computing resources) as large servers to manage operations that involve millions of transactions per day.

On-Premise Computing

To appreciate the impacts of cloud computing, you first need to understand traditional IT departments in organizations and the challenges they face. Traditionally, organizations have used **on-premise computing.** That is, they own their IT infrastructure (their software, hardware, networks, and data management) and maintain it in their data centers.

On-premise computing incurs expenses for IT infrastructure, the expert staffs needed to build and maintain complex IT systems, physical facilities, software licenses, hardware, and staff training and salaries. Despite all of this spending, organizations, however, typically do not use their infrastructure to its full capacity. The majority of these expenses are typically applied to maintaining the existing IT infrastructure, with the remainder being allocated to developing new systems. As a result, on-premise computing can actually inhibit an organization's ability to respond quickly and appropriately to today's rapidly changing business environments.

As you will see in the next section, cloud computing can help organizations manage the problems that traditional IT departments face with on-premise computing. In the next section we define cloud computing and describe its essential characteristics.

Before you go on...

1. Describe the stages in the evolution of today's IT infrastructure.
2. Describe the challenges that traditional IT departments face.

TG 3.2 The Basics of Cloud Computing

Information technology departments have always been tasked to deliver useful IT applications to business users. For a variety of reasons, today's IT departments are facing increased challenges in delivering useful applications. As you study cloud computing, you will learn how it can help organizations manage the problems that occur in traditional IT departments. You will also discover why so many organizations are using cloud computing.

Author Lecture Videos are available exclusively in *WileyPLUS*.
Apply the Concept activities are available in the Appendix and in *WileyPLUS*.

What Is Cloud Computing?

We define **cloud computing** as a type of computing that delivers convenient, on-demand, pay-as-you-go access for multiple customers to a shared pool of configurable computing resources (e.g., servers, networks, storage, applications, and services) that can be rapidly and easily accessed over the Internet. Cloud computing allows customers to acquire resources at any time and then delete them the instant they are no longer needed.

Cloud native is the name of an approach to building applications and services specifically for a cloud computing environment. The term also refers to the characteristics of those apps and services. Cloud-native applications tend to be developed to operate in containers and are deployed as a collection of microservices. See Chapter 13 and recall that microservices are the individual functions within an application.

With cloud computing, setting up and maintaining an IT infrastructure need no longer be a challenge for an organization. Businesses do not have to scramble to meet the evolving needs of developing applications. Cloud computing also reduces upfront capital expenses and operational costs, and it enables businesses to better use their infrastructure and to share it from one project to the next. In general, cloud computing eases the difficult tasks of procuring, configuring, and maintaining hardware and software environments. It allows enterprises to get their applications up and running faster, with easier manageability and less maintenance. It also enables IT to adjust IT resources (e.g., servers, storage, and networking) more rapidly to meet fluctuating and unpredictable business demand.

Significantly, cloud computing is often a key ingredient in an organization's digital transformation. Let's take a look at Guinness World Records.

People from anywhere on the globe can apply online for a record attempt at Guinness World Records (GWR; **www.guinnessworldrecords.com**). Any attempt must be measurable and repeatable. Would-be record breakers must provide evidence, which usually includes video, photos, and witness statements.

In 2019, the volume of the data coming in from the public has increased from 500 megabytes per month to 4 terabytes. The organization receives some 50,000 applications per year.

The organization has changed from being a publishing house that produces its iconic book of feats to a creative consultancy that works with brands on marketing campaigns.

The book remains the core of GWR's business and it allows the organization to engage in marketing efforts.

When working with brands, GWR helps create records-based marketing initiatives. For example, LG Electronics came to Guinness with what it believed was the most stable washing machine on the market. LG needed proof of reduced vibrations and noise levels.

GWR created an attempt for the tallest house of cards built in 12 hours. Professional card stacker Bryan Berg subsequently built a 3.3-meter-high tower of cards, consisting of 48 levels, on an LG washing machine spinning at 1,000 revolutions per minute. GWR and LG felt that the record attempt successfully demonstrated the stability of the washing machine.

GWR's move from publishing house to creative consultancy was supported by its digital transformation program. In its transformation, GWR migrated its IT infrastructure to an Amazon Web Services cloud-computing platform. AWS enabled GWR to introduce a standard records management platform, which integrates all the records from GWR's global business units. Further, AWS enabled GWR to deploy a digital asset management system that controls all the evidence relating to record attempts as well as the videos that GWR produces for its marketing clients.

Cloud Computing Characteristics

The cloud computing phenomenon has several important characteristics. We take a closer look at them in this section.

Cloud Computing Provides On-Demand Self-Service.   A customer can access needed computing resources automatically. This characteristic gives customers *elasticity* and *flexibility.* That is, customers can increase (scale up) or decrease (scale down) the amount of computing they need.

For example, during the Christmas buying season retailers need much more computational capacity than at other times of the year. By using cloud computing, they can scale up before Thanksgiving (and Black Friday) and scale down after New Year's. That is, they scale up during peak periods of business activity and scale down at other times.

Consider Canadian video game and entertainment software retailer EB Games (**www .ebgames.ca**), which opened its first store in Australia in 1997. By 2020, the retailer operated over 550 brick-and-mortar stores across Australia and New Zealand.

In 2010, EB began online operations, which grew rapidly. Initially, the firm purchased its own hardware to manage the increasing demand for its online offerings. However, the hardware was unable to scale up to meet the demand. Accordingly, EB shifted its online operations to Amazon Web Services.

By using cloud computing, the retailer was able to move faster with new projects, reduce its IT infrastructure costs, improve its user experience, and manage peak demand as well as daily operations. EB was also able to move to a continuous delivery model for new IT services. The firm went from deploying new features about once per month to multiple deployments per week.

Cloud Computing Encompasses the Characteristics of Grid Computing.
Grid computing pools various hardware and software components to create a single IT environment with shared resources. Grid computing shares the processing resources of many geographically dispersed computers across a network.

- Grid computing enables organizations to use their computing resources more efficiently.
- Grid computing provides fault tolerance and redundancy, meaning that there is no single point of failure, so the failure of one computer will not stop an application from executing.
- Grid computing makes it easy to *scale up*—that is, to access increased computing resources (i.e., add more servers)—to meet the processing demands of complex applications.
- Grid computing makes it easy to *scale down* (remove computers) if extensive processing is not needed.

Consider Oxford (United Kingdom) University's Digital Mammogram National Database project. The project aims to improve breast cancer screening and reduce the rate of errone-ous diagnoses. The users of the system are radiologists, doctors, and technicians who want to query, retrieve, process, and store patients' breast images and diagnostic reports. These images tend to be large, requiring fast access, high quality, and rigid privacy.

The system uses a large distributed database that runs on a grid computing system. The grid is formed in a collaborative way, by sharing resources (CPU cycles and data) among differ-ent organizations. The database contains digital mammographies with explanatory notes and comments about each image. Because medical and university sites have different equipment, the images and reports are standardized before they are stored in the database.

The system enables individual medical sites to store, process, and manage mammograms as digital images and to enable their use through data mining and sharing of these mammog-raphy archives. Radiologists can collaborate on diagnoses without being in the same physical location.

With this system in place, the institutions involved have improved their collaboration, resulting in quicker and more accurate diagnoses. By pooling their resources, each institution gained access to a much larger and more sophisticated set of resources, without increasing their costs proportionately.

Cloud Computing Encompasses the Characteristics of Utility Computing.
In **utility computing,** a service provider makes computing resources and infra-structure management available to a customer as needed. The provider then charges the customer for its specific usage rather than a flat rate. Utility computing enables companies to efficiently meet fluctuating demands for computing power by lowering the costs of owning the hardware infrastructure.

Cloud Computing Uses Broad Network Access.
The cloud provider's computing resources are available over a network, accessed with a Web browser, and they are configured so that they can be used with any computing device.

Cloud Computing Pools Computing Resources.
The provider's computing resources are available to serve multiple customers. These resources are dynamically assigned and reassigned according to customer demand.

Cloud Computing Often Occurs on Virtualized Servers.
Cloud computing providers have placed hundreds or thousands of networked servers inside massive data centers called **server farms** (see **Figure TG 3.1**). Recall that a *server* is a computer that supports networks, thus enabling users to share files, software, and other network devices. Server farms require massive amounts of electrical power, air-conditioning, backup generators, and security. They also need to be located fairly close to fiber-optic communications links (**Figure TG 3.2**).

Going further, Gartner estimates that typical usage rates on servers are very low, generally from 5 to 10 percent. That is, most of the time, organizations are using only a small percentage of their total computing capacity. Chief information officers (CIOs) tolerate this inefficiency to make certain that they can supply sufficient computing resources to users in case demand should spike. To alleviate this problem, companies and cloud comput-ing providers are turning to virtualization.

Server virtualization uses software-based partitions to cre-ate multiple virtual servers—called *virtual machines*—on a single physical server. The major benefit of this system is that each server no longer has to be dedicated to a particular task. Multi-ple applications can run instead on a single physical server, with each application running within its own software environment.

Divine Images/F64/Media Bakery

FIGURE TG 3.1 A server farm. Notice the ventilation in the racks and ceiling.

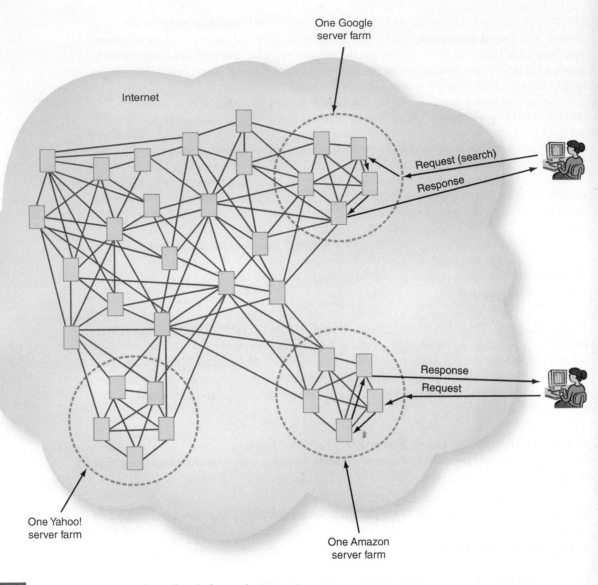

FIGURE TG 3.2   **Organizational server farms in relation to the Internet.**

As a result, virtualization enables companies to increase server usage. Companies can also realize cost savings in two areas. First, they do not have to buy additional servers to meet peak demand. Second, they reduce their utility costs because they are using less energy. The following example illustrates the benefits of virtualization for the city of Yawata in Kyoto, Japan.

The city of Yawata in Kyoto Prefecture, Japan, is very active in developing its networked city government. Deployed in 2002, the city's information system was designed to support the daily operations of the city. Since that time, the system has functioned as an IT service for city employees and members of the public.

Over a decade later, the city's continuing efforts to develop a more advanced digital community resulted in an increasing number of physical servers, with accompanying increases in power consumption. The rise in power usage was a particular problem as the city has a strong commitment to eco-friendliness.

To reduce hardware expenses, the city was running multiple applications on a single physical server, an approach that sometimes caused server availability issues. To make the system more secure and stable, the city wanted to have an individual dedicated server for each application.

The city decided to implement a server virtualization solution and realized a number of benefits. First, the city reduced its number of physical servers from 12 to 4. This reduction led to decreases in power consumption, which has helped the city reduce its environmental impact.

Second, each application now runs on a single virtual machine. This means that server availability has markedly increased, each app runs more efficiently, and the entire system is more stable. Third, by virtualizing its data center, the city is able to address future server resource needs without having to add additional physical servers.

In the next section, you learn about the various ways in which customers (individuals and organizations) can implement cloud computing. Specifically, you read about public clouds, private clouds, hybrid clouds, and vertical clouds.

Before you go on...

1. Describe the characteristics of cloud computing.
2. Define server virtualization.

TG 3.3   Different Types of Clouds

There are three major types of cloud computing that companies provide to customers or groups of customers: public clouds, private clouds, and hybrid clouds. A fourth type of cloud computing is called vertical clouds (**Figure TG 3.3**).

Public Cloud

Public clouds are shared, easily accessible, multicustomer IT infrastructures that are available nonexclusively to any entity in the general public (individuals, groups, and organizations). Public cloud vendors provide applications, storage, and other computing resources as services over the Internet. These services may be free or offered on a pay-per-usage model. Sambatech is an example of a young company using the public cloud.

International media companies such as Viacom (**www.viacom.com**), Bloomberg (**www.bloomberg.com**), and ESPN (**www.espn.com**) rely on Sambatech to deliver video content to

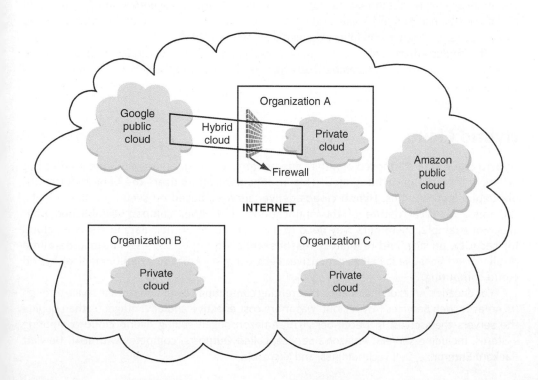

FIGURE TG 3.3 Public clouds, private clouds, and hybrid clouds.

online viewers across Latin America. As a result of its rapid growth, Samba decided to use cloud computing. The firm's chief technology officer noted that buying and managing complex IT (i.e., on-premise computing) was never part of the company's strategy.

Samba turned to Rackspace (**www.rackspace.com**), a public cloud provider, to help it with its huge IT capacity demands. In 2009, Samba needed Rackspace to host about 1 terabyte of data. In 2015, Rackspace hosted over 100 terabytes of Samba's data. Furthermore, when Samba needs additional processing power—to deliver videos for a new marketing campaign, or to coincide with a large sporting event—Rackspace provides that power quickly and affordably.

Private Cloud

Private clouds (also known as *internal clouds* or *corporate clouds*) are IT infrastructures that can be accessed only by a single entity or by an exclusive group of related entities that share the same purpose and requirements, such as all of the business units within a single organization. Private clouds provide IT activities and applications as a service over an intranet within an enterprise. Enterprises adopt private clouds to ensure system and data security. For this reason, these systems are implemented behind the corporate firewall. As an example of a private cloud, let's take a look at the National Security Agency (NSA; **www.nsa.gov**).

The NSA was running out of storage space for hundreds of different databases that contain information needed to run the agency as well as to produce intelligence on foreign matters. As a result, NSA analysts had to access many different databases to do their jobs. Questions that spanned more than one database had to be manually integrated by the analyst. The agency had to consolidate its databases to make its analysts more efficient and effective.

At first, the NSA decided to simply add more storage capacity. However, this approach actually added to the problem, so the agency decided to implement a private cloud. By putting all its different databases into one private cloud, analysts had to interface with only one system, making their jobs much easier.

The private cloud contains data that the agency acquires and uses for its missions. The cloud has strict security protocols and strong encryption, as well as a distributed architecture across multiple geographic areas. The cloud also provides a way to track every instance of every individual accessing data as specific as a single word or name in a file. This tracking includes when the data arrived, who can access them, who did access them, who downloaded them, copied them, printed them, forwarded them, modified them, or deleted them. Furthermore, if the data have legal requirements, such as they must be purged after five years, a notice will automatically tell NSA staff that the data need to be purged. One agency staff member noted that if the NSA had had this ability at the time, it is unlikely that U.S. soldier Bradley Manning would have succeeded in obtaining classified documents in 2010.

After implementation of the private cloud, analysts can perform tasks in minutes that once took days, overall data management costs have decreased, and the security of the data has been greatly enhanced.

Hybrid Cloud

Hybrid clouds are composed of public and private clouds that remain unique entities but are nevertheless tightly integrated. This arrangement offers users the benefits of multiple deployment models. Hybrid clouds deliver services based on security requirements, the mission-critical nature of the applications, and other company-established policies. For example, customers may need to maintain some of their data in a private cloud for security, privacy, and regulatory reasons while storing other, less-sensitive data in a public cloud because it is less expensive. Let's examine Amazon's deployment of hybrid cloud computing.

For decades, Amazon maintained that renting computing power and storage space through its Amazon Web Services (AWS) cloud was more cost effective and advantageous than buying the servers themselves. In December 2019, Amazon began selling hybrid cloud computing systems, including servers. Amazon's service, called Outposts, competes with IBM, Hewlett Packard Enterprise, Dell Technologies, and Microsoft.

With Outposts, Amazon customers purchase its servers, plus software that integrates those servers with Amazon's machines in its cloud. Outposts is a *hybrid cloud*, which is the ability to use cloud services for some applications, on-site servers for mission-critical applications, and a common interface to integrate all these applications.

Amazon entered this market because approximately 80 percent of organizations operate their software applications in corporate data centers (called on-premise computing) for security, regulatory, or practical reasons. For instance, Disney (**www.disney.com**) hosts video streaming and animation software on AWS. For Disney animators working in the Los Angeles area, a delay of more than 10 milliseconds between touching a stylus to the screen and seeing the mark itself made the rendering software useless. *Rendering* is an extremely computer-intensive process of generating a digital image from a physical picture of model. Amazon's main West Coast data center, more than 1,000 miles to the north in Oregon, could not resolve the problem due to speed-of-light considerations. As a result, Disney's use of AWS hybrid cloud computing provided the solution.

There are many other examples of organizations using Outposts. For example, Verizon Communications is testing Outposts to manage a new service designed to enable faster 5G browsing speeds, starting with customers in Chicago. Fox Corporation is using Outposts to help power its production facilities and modernize its video systems.

All firms in the hybrid cloud computing space offer specially assigned teams that deliver their products directly to customers' data centers. There, the customers' IT personnel can just plug the servers in, link them to a cloud vendor account, download software updates, and begin operations. If a server fails, the cloud vendor will mail the customer a new server and a return box for the defective one.

Multiple Clouds (Multiclouds)

Multicloud environments are the most common approach to cloud computing. Global security firm McAfee's (**www.mcafee.com**) 2019 Cloud Adoption and Risk Report had a surprising finding. The firm asked 1,400 IT professionals in 11 countries to estimate the total number of cloud services in use in their organization. Respondents came up with an average of 31 cloud services. When McAfee investigated further, the actual average figure was almost 2,000 services.

Let's distinguish between hybrid clouds and multiclouds. *Hybrid cloud* has traditionally meant the combination of private (either on-premise or hosted in a colocation facility) and public cloud infrastructure, with orchestration tools used to deploy workloads and manage the balance between the two. *Colocation* means that a cloud vendor either rents out an entire facility to a customer or when the vendor rents out servers within a data center to a customer. For instance, a customer employs public cloud resources for regular or episodic increases of computing and/or storage requirements.

In contrast, multicloud describes how organizations use multiple cloud providers to meet different technical or business requirements. With multicloud environments, customers use cloud-native applications built from containers and microservices using component services from different cloud providers.

There are several reasons for using multiclouds. One of the most common reasons is the desire to avoid being locked into a particular cloud vendor's infrastructure, add-on services, and pricing model. Cloud-native applications based on containers and microservices are designed to be portable between clouds, but providers will generally try to make their platforms difficult to leave with specific functions and services that differentiate them from their competitors. Another reason for avoiding vendor lock-in is so that organizations can take advantage of best-of-breed solutions.

Organizations can also minimize latency by choosing a cloud provider with data centers that are geographically close to their customers. The reason is that network performance degrades as the number of network transmissions between servers increases.

Data governance requirements, such as the European Union's General Data Protection Regulation, will often require customer data to be held in particular locations. Unless organizations are willing to deploy and operate their own on-premise data centers, these firms will have to take a multicloud approach.

All cloud vendors suffer outages. Therefore, organizations are reluctant to run their entire workloads in one vendor's cloud because they run the risk of a mission-critical application becoming unavailable. Multiclouds provide better security, failover, and disaster recovery; that is, resilience. *Failover* occurs when standby servers automatically take over when a server fails.

Vertical Clouds

A **vertical cloud** is a set of cloud computing services optimized for use in a particular industry. Unlike organizations that can use general-purpose cloud computing services, those within certain industries often have more specific information technology requirements involving security, compliance, and other issues. Vertical cloud computing vendors offer services that help their customers meet those unique requirements.

Many industries use vertical cloud computing services, such as healthcare, financial services, manufacturing, government, utilities, oil and gas, and others. For example, healthcare organizations must ensure data privacy in accordance with the Health Insurance Portability and Accountability Act (HIPAA). Therefore, these organizations might prefer a cloud provider that offers HIPAA-compliant services, as well as services for electronic medical records and other applications unique to the healthcare industry. See CareCloud Corporation (**www.carecloud.com**) for example. There are a number of specialized vertical cloud vendors. In addition, some of the major public cloud vendors also offer industry-specific services. For example, Amazon Web Services provides AWS GovCloud (**https://aws.amazon.com/govcloud-us/**), a service tailored specifically for U.S. government agencies that have sensitive operations and strict regulatory requirements.

Before you go on...

1. What is a public cloud?
2. What is a private cloud?
3. What is a hybrid cloud?
4. What is a vertical cloud?

TG 3.4   Cloud Computing Services

Cloud computing services are based on three models: infrastructure-as-a-service (IaaS), platform-as-a-service (PaaS), and software-as-a-service (SaaS). These models represent the three types of computing generally required by consumers: infrastructure to run software and store data (IaaS), platforms to develop applications (PaaS), and software applications to process their data (SaaS). **Figure TG 3.4** illustrates the differences among the three models.

As you examine the figure from left to right, note that the customer manages the service less and less, and the vendor manages it more and more.

Although each model has its distinctive features, all three share certain characteristics. First, customers rent them instead of buying them. This arrangement shifts IT from a capital expense to an operating expense. Second, vendors are responsible for maintenance, administration, capacity planning, troubleshooting, and backups. Finally, obtaining additional computing resources—that is, scale from the cloud—is usually fast and easy. Examples are more storage from an IaaS vendor, the ability to handle more PaaS projects, and more users of a SaaS application.

Infrastructure as a Service

With the **infrastructure-as-a-service (IaaS)** model, cloud computing providers offer remotely accessible servers, networks, and storage capacity. They supply these resources on demand from their large resource pools, which are located in their data centers. We can think of IaaS as a domain for systems administrators, as IaaS allows clients to migrate their physical or

ON-PREMISE SOFTWARE	INFRASTRUCTURE-AS-A-SERVICE	PLATFORM-AS-A-SERVICE	SOFTWARE-AS-A-SERVICE
CUSTOMER MANAGES { Applications Data Operating system Servers Virtualization Storage Networking	**CUSTOMER MANAGES** { Applications Data Operating system **VENDOR MANAGES** { Servers Virtualization Storage Networking	**CUSTOMER MANAGES** { Applications Data **VENDOR MANAGES** { Operating system Servers Virtualization Storage Networking	**VENDOR MANAGES** { Applications Data Operating system Servers Virtualization Storage Networking
Examples	Amazon, IBM, Google, Microsoft, Rackspace	Microsoft Windows Azure, Google App Engine, Force.com	Salesforce.com, Google Apps, Dropbox, Apple iCloud, Box.net

FIGURE TG 3.4 **Comparison of on-premise software, infrastructure-as-a-service, platform-as-a-service, and software-as-a-service.**

hardware infrastructure to the cloud. Examples include Amazon Elastic Compute Cloud, Google Compute Engine, Rackspace, and many others.

IaaS customers are often technology companies with IT expertise. These companies want access to computing power, but they do not want to be responsible for installing or maintaining it. Companies use the infrastructure to run software or simply to store data.

To deploy their applications, IaaS users install their operating system and their application software on the cloud computing provider's computers. They can deploy any software on this infrastructure, including different operating systems, applications, and development platforms. Each user is responsible for maintaining their operating system and application software. Cloud providers typically bill IaaS services on a utility computing basis—that is, the cost reflects the amount of resources the user consumes.

Cloud data management is an important application of IaaS. *Cloud data management* is the practice of storing a company's data on an offsite server that is typically owned by a vendor who specializes in cloud data hosting. Cloud data management offers many benefits to clients, which include:

- *Improved security*. Improved security results first from reduced risk of data loss due to device damage or hardware failure. Second, cloud vendors typically employ very advanced security measures and practices.

- *Scalability and savings*. Cloud vendors allow users to add and subtract storage and computing power as needed, which results in cost savings.

- *Governed access*. Cloud vendors enable all authorized users to access the data they need from wherever they are, a process called *data democratization*. Such access supports a collaborative work culture.

- *Automated backups, disaster recovery, and updates*. Cloud vendors provide automated data backups that speed up the process of disaster recovery after emergencies. For example, if a ransomware attack encrypted a firm's data, the cloud vendor would enable the client to restore data and continue business operations. In addition, cloud vendors update applications automatically, ensuring that the client does not have to pause work while the in-house IT group updates applications.

- *Improved data quality*. Cloud data management solutions help companies remove data silos and create a single source of truth for every data point. Data remains clean, consistent, and current. *Single source of truth* is a concept ensuring that everyone in an organization bases business decisions on the same data.

- *Sustainability*. Cloud data management enables organizations to reduce the carbon footprint created by their own IT facilities and to provide telecommuting options to their employees.

Let's look at an example. Southern Water (**www.southernwater.co.uk**) is a utility that used cloud data management to remove data silos. The utility manages the supply of water and waste management to 4.5 million people in southeastern England. The utility's assets include 83 water treatment plants, 8,700 miles of water mains, 2,375 pumping stations, and approximately 2,500 miles of sewers. The utility employs 3,000 people and 1,500 contractors.

The utility's data is varied and complex, with some of the data concerning assets that are 200 years old (i.e., some of the water mains in the area date back to the early 19th century). The company has 80,000 sensors that gather data every 15 minutes. Its call center staff deal with thousands of customer calls, generating audio data that is analyzed to provide better customer service.

In the past, Southern Water had groups of people in individual departments managing data. The data from many of the utility's essential business processes were isolated in departmental spreadsheets and Microsoft Access databases. If the utility had ignored this problem, it would have caused additional costs and difficulties in the future, a situation called technical debt. *Technical debt* refers to the implied cost of additional rework caused by choosing an easy solution now instead of using a better approach that would take longer.

Southern Water transformed its approach to data management to improve decision making. This process involved transitioning to a Microsoft Azure cloud-based data management solution and placing all its data workers into a centralized team. With the transition, the utility gained access to a cloud-based analytics solution that delivered significant savings. In just one instance, Southern Water was able to integrate pump data to assess pump efficiency when many pumps are named differently. Also, the team gained a better understanding of the entire organization's data, which helped to improve data literacy throughout the organization.

Platform as-a-Service

In the **platform-as-a-service (PaaS)** model, customers rent servers, operating systems, storage, a database, software development technologies such as Java and .NET, and network capacity over the Internet. We can think of PaaS as a domain for software developers. PaaS helps software developers build, test, deploy, maintain, and manage every step of the development lifecycle of applications. Examples include Amazon Web Services Elastic Beanstalk, Microsoft Azure, Cloud Foundry, and many others.

The PaaS model allows the customer to both run existing applications and to develop and test new applications. PaaS offers customers several advantages, including the following.

- Application developers can develop and run their software solutions on a cloud platform without the cost and complexity of buying and managing the underlying hardware and software layers.
- Underlying computing and storage resources automatically scale to match application demand.
- Operating system features can be upgraded frequently.
- Geographically distributed development teams can work together on software development projects.
- PaaS services can be provided by diverse sources located throughout the world.
- Initial and ongoing costs can be reduced by the use of infrastructure services from a single vendor rather than maintaining multiple hardware facilities that often perform duplicate functions or suffer from incompatibility problems.

Novartis International AG (**www.novartis.com**), a pharmaceutical company based in Basel, Switzerland, has used PaaS to improve its performance. The company employs approximately 100,000 people in 140 countries and has core businesses in pharmaceuticals, vaccines and diagnostics, and consumer health.

Novartis needed an alternative to its systems development process. The process was inflexible, expensive, and delivered new functionality much too slowly. These problems meant that the company was limited in the number of new development projects it could undertake. Novartis needed to reduce its systems development effort and cost while delivering systems with the required functionality more quickly.

As a result, Novartis turned to Dell Boomi AtomSphere (**www.boomi.com**). Using this PaaS product, Novartis was able to reduce development efforts and deliver twice the amount of new functionality in one-sixth the time than was possible earlier.

Software-as-a-Service

With the **software-as-a-service (SaaS)** delivery model, cloud computing vendors provide software that is specific to their customers' requirements. We can think of SaaS as a domain for end users or business clients. That is, users and clients can run SaaS programs on their own data. Examples include Google Apps, Salesforce, Dropbox, and numerous others.

SaaS is the most widely used service model, and it provides a broad range of software applications. SaaS providers typically charge their customers a monthly or yearly subscription fee.

SaaS applications reside in the cloud instead of on a user's hard drive or in a data center. The host manages the software and the infrastructure that runs this software and stores the customer's data. The customers do not control either the software, beyond the usual configuration settings, or the infrastructure, beyond changing the resources they use, such as the amount of disk space required for their data. This process eliminates the need to install and run the application on the user's computers, thereby simplifying maintenance and support.

What differentiates SaaS applications from other applications is their ability to scale. As a result, applications can run on as many servers as is necessary to meet changing demands. This process is transparent to the user.

To reduce the risk of an infrastructure outage, SaaS providers regularly back up all of their customers' data. Customers can also back up their data on their own storage hardware.

To understand how SaaS operates, consider Mary Kay (**www.marykay.com**). The cosmetics giant implemented Oracle's Taleo cloud-based recruitment software in the United States, China, and Brazil. Before 2014, Mary Kay did not have an applicant tracking system. The company's recruiting process was performed with Microsoft Excel spreadsheets and Access databases. Recruiters at Mary Kay lacked visibility on the manual system. If someone applied for a job in two different departments, a recruiter from each department would often call the applicant without realizing that the other recruiter had also contacted the applicant.

Taleo provides Mary Kay with a centralized repository for tracking internal and external job candidates. The software also automated processes such as job applications, onboarding, and forms. Taleo also integrates with LinkedIn, providing instant access to LinkedIn profiles and candidate records with a single click. Furthermore, Taleo can fill in forms with LinkedIn credentials.

A subset of SaaS is the *desktop-as-a-service* (DaaS) model, also known as a *cloud desktop* or *desktop in the cloud.* In this model, a SaaS provider hosts a software environment for a desktop personal computer, including productivity and collaboration software—spreadsheets, word processing programs, and so on—such as Google Apps, Microsoft 365, and other products. The DaaS model can be financially advantageous for consumers because they do not need to purchase a fully configured personal computer, or fat client. This model also makes the PC environment simpler to deploy and administer.

Functions-as-a-Service

Functions-as-a-service (FaaS or XaaS) is a category of cloud computing services that provides a platform allowing customers to develop, run, and manage applications' functions without the complexity of building and maintaining the infrastructure typically associated with developing and deploying an app. These functions are triggered by a given event.

Functions-as-a-service are a good choice for real-time (event-driven) actions. Suppose an organization needs daily sales data to help manage inventory. Every time a customer buys an item, that transaction is added to a database table. An FaaS function would trigger a function within that database table, process the data from the transaction, and either display it to a manager or even trigger another function to order more of that product.

There can be confusion between FaaS and serverless computing. *Serverless computing* is a cloud computing execution model in which the cloud vendor runs the server and dynamically manages the allocation of machine resources. That is, customers do not need to be concerned with a server configuration when deploying an application. With this model, customers shift more of the responsibilities for running an application.

For example, suppose an organization needed to deploy an e-commerce application. It would be easier to build and deploy just one application that did all the work of presenting products, managing the shopping cart, and configuring the payment system. If the firm deployed such a complex system with so many embedded functions, it would be much more manageable to keep all the business logic within one single cloud platform.

In this case, serverless computing would be the best way to go. Even if the company's e-commerce store grows, the serverless computing service will scale the application to meet the demand. Further, the application will always be running and ready to process new orders. Another example would be if an organization needed to run a mission-critical database.

IT's Personal: "The Cloud"

This Technology Guide defines the cloud as distributed computing services, and it presents many examples of how the cloud can be used for both personal and business purposes. This IT's Personal is intended to help you differentiate between the business and personal applications of the cloud and to help you plan for your own use of the cloud.

First, you need to understand that there is no single "cloud." Rather, almost all businesses refer to their Internet-based services as "cloud services." Basically, anything you do over the Internet that you used to do on a local computer is a form of cloud computing. When you store files on Dropbox, create a document using Google Docs, or use iCloud to store purchases or sync documents, you are using cloud-based services that are intended for personal use.

Infrastructure-as-a-service is an important application of the cloud for personal purposes. Dropbox is one of the most prominent companies in this area. In the past, users had to carry around a USB drive, a CD, an external hard drive, or (back in the day) floppy disks to store their personal information. Today, users can employ Dropbox for this purpose. At the time of this writing, a free Dropbox account offered 2 GB of online storage. Not only does Dropbox offer you a place to store your files (eliminating the need for a personal infrastructure of removable storage), but it also provides synchronization across computers and access from mobile devices.

Software-as-a-service has been a popular option for quite some time. For example, Google Docs offers Internet-based word processing, spreadsheet, presentation, forms, and drawing tools.

Microsoft's Office 365 product also offers these services and allows you to use a computer program without having to install it on your computer or mobile device. You simply access the entire program (and your saved files) over the Internet.

Google has combined a couple of these cloud services with Google Drive, a service that offers the same services as Dropbox in addition to Google Docs' online editing and file-sharing capabilities. Google Drive encompasses SaaS because of the added benefit of Google Docs. It is very likely that one day Google will merge virtualization, infrastructure, and software into a single cloud-based service. If this technology becomes available, then all you will need as a consumer is an Internet-connected device, and you will be able to store, access, edit, and share your files from the cloud. You will also be able to choose apps to run on your "virtual machine" much the way you currently purchase applications for your mobile devices from a vendor-approved store.

So, what is the point? Simply, cloud-based services are here to stay. The rise of ubiquitous Internet access has engendered a new world of possibilities.

A word of caution, however. Along with its seemingly endless possibilities, cloud computing raises many critical security and privacy issues. Because your files, apps, and editing capability will no longer be stored on a local machine, they are only as safe as the company to which you have entrusted them makes them. So, when you select a cloud provider, make sure you choose wisely!

Before you go on...

1. Describe infrastructure-as-a-service.
2. Describe platform-as-a-service.
3. Describe software-as-a-service.
4. Describe function-as-a-service.

Author Lecture Videos are available exclusively in *WileyPLUS*.
Apply the Concept activities are available in the Appendix and in *WileyPLUS*.

TG 3.5   The Benefits of Cloud Computing

Cloud computing offers benefits for both individuals and organizations. It allows companies to increase the scale and power of their IT and the speed at which it can be deployed and accessed. It eliminates administrative problems and it operates across locations, devices, and organizational boundaries.

Nearly half of the respondents in a recent CIO economic impact survey indicated that they evaluate cloud computing options first—before traditional IT approaches—before making any new IT investments. IBM predicts that the global cloud computing market will grow 22 percent annually to $241 billion by 2020. Next we examine three major benefits that cloud computing provides to individuals and organizations.

Benefit 1: Cloud Computing Has a Positive Impact on Employees

Cloud computing enables companies to provide their employees with access to all the information they need no matter where they are, what device they are using, or with whom they are working. Consider this example.

The attorneys of one multistate law firm needed to access documents and data on a constant basis. Since 2000, the firm's data volume had expanded from 30 gigabytes to more than 40 terabytes. Moreover, all of these data have to be stored and accessed securely. In the past, attorneys often had to manually copy case-relevant data onto external hard drives and USB devices, and then ship these devices back and forth among themselves and the firm's headquarters. These processes were nonsecure, time-consuming, and expensive.

To address these needs, the law firm turned to cloud computing for data storage, offsite disaster recovery, and multisite access within a highly secure public cloud. Rather than maintaining a massive inventory of extra storage as required by its old IT infrastructure, the firm can now increase storage capacity on demand. The cloud provides attorneys with constant access through encrypted communication channels. Furthermore, the cloud facilitates collaboration among distributed teams of attorneys, thereby increasing their overall productivity. The cloud environment has made the firm's attorneys much more efficient and the firm's IT expenses have declined by 60 percent.

Benefit 2: Cloud Computing Can Save Money

Over time, the cost of building and operating an on-premise IT infrastructure will typically be more expensive than adopting the cloud computing model. Cloud providers purchase massive amounts of IT infrastructure (e.g., hardware and bandwidth) and gain cost savings by buying in large quantity. As a result, these providers continually take advantage of Moore's law (discussed in Technology Guide 1). For example, the Amazon cloud, known as Amazon Web Services, has reduced its prices many times over the last 10 years.

As a result, cloud computing can reduce or eliminate the need to purchase hardware, build and install software, and pay software licensing fees. The organization pays only for the computing resources it needs, and then only when it needs them. This pay-for-use model provides greater flexibility and it eliminates or reduces the need for significant capital expenditures.

Let's consider the United States General Services Administration (GSA; **www.gsa.gov**). In 2010, the agency began a multiyear strategy to migrate core agency information systems to the cloud. In the first phase of the strategy, the GSA migrated 17,000 employees to Google Apps, making it the first federal agency to move basic e-mail and collaboration services entirely into a cloud environment. The GSA notes that the migration saves the agency approximately $3 million per year.

In the second phase of the strategy, the GSA worked with **Salesforce.com** (**www.salesforce.com**) to implement cloud-based software that made it easier for GSA employees to collaborate on projects, share and manage case files, find internal subject-matter experts, and capture new ideas. In one instance, employees used the software to generate 640 ideas in 30 days to streamline GSA business processes, an initiative that eventually saved the agency $5 million per year.

The GSA also established a rapid application development platform (discussed in Chapter 13) in the cloud. Within six months, GSA's IT department developed and delivered more than 100 enterprise applications that replaced more than 1,700 legacy applications. The new applications lowered the total cost of ownership by 92 percent.

And the bottom line? The GSA spent $593 million on IT in fiscal year 2014, nearly $100 million less than it spent the previous year.

Benefit 3: Cloud Computing Can Improve Organizational Flexibility and Competitiveness

Cloud computing allows organizations to use only the amount of computing resources they need at a given time. Therefore, companies can efficiently scale their operations up or down as needed to meet rapidly changing business conditions. Cloud computing is also able to deliver computing services faster than the on-premise computing can. Let's take a closer look at cloud gaming.

With 2.4 billion online gamers worldwide, the online-gaming industry is network- and data-intensive. Network traffic from online gaming is forecast to grow 900 percent by 2022, and gaming-related data reached 568 petabytes in 2020. To put that number in context, 1 petabyte is equal to 3.4 years of 24/7 high-definition video recording.

The gaming industry must manage enormous amounts of computational capacity and storage. Further, the industry must manage new technologies such as augmented reality, virtual reality, and multiplayer gaming that require even more computation and storage. As a result, online gaming has moved to the cloud and is now referred to as cloud gaming, or gaming-as-a-service (GaaS). Many vendors offer cloud gaming, including Microsoft xCloud (**https://www.xbox.com/en-US/xbox-game-pass/cloud-gaming**), Apple Arcade (**https://www .apple.com/apple-arcade**), Google Stadia (**https://stadia.google.com**), and Amazon's Prime Gaming (**https://gaming.amazon.com**).

Gaming providers process gaming data in two ways: cloud processing and edge computing. With cloud processing, vendors send gaming data for processing in the cloud and the results are sent back to the gamer's device for play. This process does eliminate the need for intensive computing that would normally occur on the gamer's desktop, laptop, smartphone, or tablet, but data transmission can cause delays while playing the game.

As a result, some providers employ edge computing. With *edge computing*, providers group individual gamers according to location and process data in servers close to the gamers' locations, thus routing traffic over shorter distances. The benefit is reduced network latency (delay), which improves the user experience.

Most gaming accounts contain personally identifiable information such as the player's name, birthday, address, mobile number, e-mail address, and a linked credit card. As a result, cloud computing enables providers to enforce two-factor authentication, requiring users to verify their identity before logging on via a time-sensitive code sent to a mobile number or e-mail. For even greater security, some providers use an authentication app that generates a QR code that can be scanned within the game. Gamers' user names are stored in the app and a new code is generated for each login.

And the bottom line? Cloud gaming is growing rapidly, valued at $1.1 billion in 2019 and expected to grow to $7 billion by 2025. The use of cloud computing has transformed the user experience largely because cloud-gaming vendors can embrace new technologies such as augmented reality and virtual reality.

Before you go on...

1. Describe how cloud computing can help organizations expand the scope of their business operations.
2. Describe how cloud computing can help organizations respond quickly to market changes.

TG 3.6 | Concerns and Risks with Cloud Computing

Gartner predicted that cloud computing would grow at an annual rate of 19 percent through the year 2016. Even if this prediction was accurate, however, cloud computing would still account for less than 5 percent of total worldwide IT spending that year. Why is this percentage so low? The reason is that there are serious concerns with cloud computing. These concerns fall into six categories: legacy IT systems, reliability, privacy, security, the legal and regulatory environment, and criminal use of cloud computing.

Author Lecture Videos are available exclusively in *WileyPLUS*.
Apply the Concept activities are available in the Appendix and in *WileyPLUS*.

Concern 1: Legacy IT Systems

Historically, organizational IT systems have accumulated a diversity of hardware, operating systems, and applications. When bundled together, these systems are called "legacy spaghetti." These systems cannot easily be transferred to the cloud because they must first be untangled and simplified. Furthermore, many IT professionals have vested interests in various legacy systems, and they resist efforts to exchange these systems for cloud computing.

Concern 2: Reliability

Many skeptics contend that cloud computing is not as reliable as a well-managed, on-premise IT infrastructure. Although cloud providers are improving the redundancy and reliability of their offerings, outages still occur. Consider the examples of Google and CenturyLink.

In June 2019, a Google Cloud outage caused portions of the Internet to go offline. The outage also blocked access to the tools that Google needed to fix the problem, which occurred when Google began what should have been a routine configuration change. These changes are maintenance events intended for a few servers in one geographic region. When such an event happens, Google routinely reroutes jobs that those servers are running to other machines or just pauses those jobs until the maintenance is finished. Unfortunately, Google's software cancelled network control jobs in multiple locations, leading to the outage.

Google engineers were aware of the problem within two minutes. However, they were not able to diagnose the problem for hours because the outage prevented them from accessing the necessary tools.

In August 2020, U.S. Internet service provider CenturyLink (**www.centurylink.com**) suffered a major technical outage after a misconfiguration in one of its data centers. The outage was serious enough to cause an overall 3.5 percent drop in global Internet traffic. CenturyLink engineers took seven hours to fix the problem.

Concern 3: Privacy

Privacy advocates have criticized cloud computing for posing a major threat to privacy because the providers control, and thus lawfully or unlawfully monitor, the data and communication stored between the user and the host company. For example, AT&T and Verizon collaborated with the NSA to use cloud computing to record more than 10 million phone calls between American citizens. Providers could also accidentally or deliberately alter or even delete some of that information.

Using a cloud computing provider also complicates data privacy because of the extent to which cloud processing and cloud storage are used to implement cloud services. The point is that customer data may not remain on the same system or in the same data center. This situation can lead to legal concerns over jurisdiction.

There have been efforts to address this problem by integrating the legal environment. One example is the U.S.-EU Safe Harbor, a streamlined process for U.S. companies to comply with the European Union directive on the protection of personal data.

Concern 4: Security

Critics also question how secure cloud computing really is. Because the characteristics of cloud computing can differ widely from those of traditional IT architectures, providers need to reconsider the effectiveness and efficiency of traditional security mechanisms. Security issues include access to sensitive data, data segregation (among customers), privacy, error exploitation, recovery, accountability, malicious insiders, and account control.

The security of cloud computing services is a contentious issue that may be delaying the adoption of this technology. Security issues arise primarily from the unease of both the private and public sectors with the external management of security-based services. The fact that providers manage these services provides great incentive for them to prioritize building and maintaining strong security services.

Another security issue involves the control over who is able to access and use the information stored in the cloud. (Recall our discussion of least privilege in Chapter 4.) Many organizations exercise least-privilege controls effectively with their on-premise IT infrastructures. Some cloud computing environments, in contrast, cannot exercise least-privilege controls effectively. This problem occurs because cloud computing environments were originally designed for individuals or groups, not for hierarchical organizations in which some people have both the right and the responsibility to exercise control over other people's private information. To address this problem, cloud computing vendors are working to incorporate administrative, least-privilege functionality into their products. In fact, many have already done so.

Consider Panama City, Florida, as an example. Panama City was one of the first cities in the United States to adopt Google Apps for Government. The city was searching for a way to gain visibility into who was using Google Apps and how users were collaborating both inside and outside the city's IT domain. Furthermore, the city had to have the ability to control and enforce data-sharing policies where necessary. The city decided to adopt Cisco CloudLock (**https:// www.cisco.com/c/en/us/products/security/cloudlock/index.html**).

CloudLock provides a security system to protect its clients' information assets located in public cloud applications like Google Apps. CloudLock provides key data management issues such as the following:

- Data inventory: How many information assets exist and what are their types?
- Which information assets are shared with the public or over the Internet?
- Who has access to what information asset and what information asset is accessible to whom?

Using CloudLock, Panama City was able to notify data owners of policy violations or exposed documents containing potentially sensitive information, change or revoke excessive privilege, and audit permissions changes. Furthermore, the city's IT manager was able to designate department leaders to manage their respective organizational unit's data policies and usage by giving them access to the CloudLock application.

Concern 5: The Regulatory and Legal Environment

There are numerous legal and regulatory barriers to cloud computing, many of which involve data access and transport. For example, the European Union prohibits consumer data from being transferred to nonmember countries without the consumers' prior consent and approval. Companies located outside the European Union can overcome this restriction by demonstrating that they provide a "safe harbor" for the data. Some countries, such as Germany, have enacted even more restrictive data export laws. Cloud computing vendors are aware of these regulations and laws, and they are working to modify their offerings so that they can assure customers and regulators that data entrusted to them are secure enough to meet all of these requirements.

To obtain compliance with regulations such as the Federal Information Security Management Act (FISMA), the Health Insurance Portability and Accountability Act (HIPAA), and the Sarbanes–Oxley Act in the United States; the Data Protection Directive in the European Union; and the credit card industry's Payment Card Industry's Data Security Standard (PCI DSS), cloud computing customers may have to adopt hybrid deployment modes that are typically more expensive and may offer restricted benefits. This process is how, for example, Google is able to "manage and meet additional government policy requirements beyond FISMA," and Rackspace (**www.rackspace.com**) is able to claim PCI compliance. FISMA requires each federal agency to develop, document, and implement a program to provide information security for the information and information systems that support the operations of the agency, including those provided by contractors. PCI DSS is a set of requirements designed to ensure that all companies that process, store, or transmit credit card information maintain a secure environment.

Concern 6: Criminal Use of Cloud Computing

Cloud computing makes available a well-managed, generally reliable, scalable global infrastructure that is, unfortunately, as well suited to illegal computing activities as it is to legitimate business activities. We look here at a number of possible illegal activities.

The huge amount of information stored in the cloud makes it an attractive target for data thieves. Also, the distributed nature of cloud computing makes it very difficult to catch criminals.

Cloud computing makes immense processing power available to anyone. Criminals using cloud computing have access to encryption technology and anonymous communication channels that make it difficult for authorities to detect their activities. When law enforcement pursues criminals, the wrongdoers can rapidly shut down computing resources in the cloud, thus greatly decreasing the chances that there will be any clues left for forensic analysis. When criminals no longer need a machine and shut it down, other clients of cloud vendors immediately reuse the storage and computational capacity allocated to that machine. Therefore, the criminal information is overwritten by data from legitimate customers. It is nearly impossible to recover any data after the machine has been *de-provisioned*.

Criminals are registering for an account (with assumed names and stolen credit cards, of course) with a cloud vendor and "legitimately" using services for illegal purposes. For example, criminals use Gmail or the text-sharing website Pastebin (**www.pastebin.com**) to plan crimes and share stolen information. Another example is that criminals use cloud computing in brute-force password cracking (see Chapter 4). Although such uses are prohibited by most company's terms-of-service agreements, policing the cloud is expensive and not very rewarding for cloud providers.

Many cloud vendors offer geographical diversity—that is, virtual machines that are located in different physical locations around the world. Criminals can use this feature in transnational attacks. Such attacks place political and technical obstacles in the way of authorities seeking to trace a cyberattack back to its source.

Another weakness exploited by criminals arises from the Web-based applications, or SaaS offerings, provided by cloud vendors. With millions of users commingling on tens of thousands of servers, a criminal can easily mix in among legitimate users.

Even more complicated for authorities and victims, cyberattacks can originate within cloud programs that we use and trust. For example, researchers at the security firm F-Secure reported that they had detected several phishing sites hosted within Google Docs. What made the attacks possible is a feature within Google's spreadsheet system that lets users create Web-based forms, with titles such as "Webmail Account Upgrade" and "Report a Bug." These forms, located on a Google server, were authenticated with Google's encryption certificate. Significantly, they requested sensitive information such as the user's full name, username, Google password, and so on, according to the F-Secure researchers.

Before you go on...

1. Discuss the various risks of cloud computing.

2. In your opinion, which risk is the greatest? Support your answer.

TG 3.7 The "Big Three" Cloud Computing Vendors

The "Big Three" public IaaS and PaaS cloud vendors are Amazon Web Services (AWS), Microsoft Azure, and Google Cloud Platform. According to Synergy Research Group (**www.srgresearch. com**), AWS is the global market leader for public IaaS and PaaS with 33 percent of this market, followed by Azure at 18 percent, Google at 9 percent, and Alibaba at 5 percent. Other leading public cloud vendors include VMware Cloud, IBM Cloud, and Oracle Cloud. Let's take a closer look at the Big Three cloud vendors.

All of the Big Three American cloud vendors offer largely similar services. For example, all three offer managed services around popular container services such as Kubernetes and all three offer excellent networking capabilities with automated server load balancing and connectivity to on-premise systems.

All three support relational databases, NoSQL databases, and data warehouses. Specifically, Amazon offers its Relational Database Service, DynamoDB (NoSQL), as well as Redshift, the firm's data warehouse product. Microsoft offers its Azure SQL Database, DocumentDB (NoSQL), and Azure Data Warehouse. For relational database support, Google offers Cloud SQL and Cloud Spanner. For NoSQL database support, Google offers Cloud Bigtable, Cloud Firestore, Firebase Realtime Database, and Cloud Memorystore. For data warehouse support, Google offers Cloud Bigtable.

All three vendors support serverless computing. AWS Lambda, Azure serverless computing, and Google Cloud serverless computing are event-driven, serverless computing platforms that run code in response to events and automatically manage the computing resources required by that code.

Prices for the three vendors are roughly comparable, particularly because AWS shifted from by-the-hour to by-the-second pricing in 2017, bringing it into line with Azure and Google. Overall, prices have been decreasing as the three compete with each other.

The three vendors offer slightly different pricing models, discounts, and make frequent price cuts. Not all customers pay the sticker price, especially at the enterprise level, where volume discounts can be negotiated. All three vendors offer free introductory tiers, allowing customers to try their services before they buy.

The key question is: What differentiates each of these cloud providers? Selecting one cloud vendor over the others depends on the individual customer and the workloads that the customer operates. Often, organizations use multiple cloud providers within different parts of their operations or for different use cases.

Amazon Web Services

Strengths. The key strength for AWS is the breadth and depth of its services, offering more than 175 services across compute, storage, database, analytics, networking, mobile, developer tools, management tools, the Internet of Things, security, and others.

Compute. AWS's main offering is its Elastic Compute Cloud (EC2), which can be customized with a large number of options. Amazon also provides related services such as Elastic Beanstalk for app deployment, the EC2 Container service, and AWS Lambda.

Storage. AWS storage includes its Simple Storage Service (S3), Elastic Block Storage, Elastic File System, and Import/Export large volume data transfer service. AWS also offers Glacier archive backup and Storage Gateway, which integrates with on-premise computing environments.

Hybrid options. AWS Outposts is Amazon's hybrid cloud computing product. As noted in Section TG 3.3, Outposts is a fully managed service where the vendor delivers pre-configured servers to a client's premises, and the client can run AWS services in its data center.

Machine Learning.   Amazon deployed SageMaker to simplify the adoption of machine learning. SageMaker is a fully managed service that enables developers and data scientists to quickly build, train, and deploy machine learning models. AWS offers a broad set of off-the-shelf machine-learning services for use cases such as image recognition (AWS Rekognition), text-to-speech deep learning models (Polly), and the engine that powers Alexa (Lex).

Customer base.   High-profile customers are a strong point of AWS. Major customers include Netflix, which decided to close all of its data centers in a final transition to the cloud in 2016; AstraZeneca; Airbnb; Financial Times; Dow Jones; Nasdaq; Nike; Pfizer; and others.

Pros and cons.   Amazon ranks highly on platform configuration options, monitoring and policy features, security, and reliability. Its partner ecosystem and general product strategy are market leading and its AWS Marketplace has a large number of third-party software services.

In the past, Amazon has been dismissive of the benefits of hybrid cloud computing. As noted in Section TG 3.3, though, the company is now competing in this area with its product, Outposts. Another problem is that certain organizations may not want to contribute to Amazon's revenue and profits, as the giant company continues to expand and compete in a growing number of industries, such as health care and finance. In fact, some boards of directors in potentially threatened industry verticals have directed their IT groups to avoid the use of AWS where possible.

Microsoft Azure

Strengths.   Azure is popular with executives who have long-standing relationships with Microsoft. Microsoft also seamlessly integrates Azure with Office 365 and Teams.

Compute.   Azure's offering is centered around its Virtual Machines, with other tools such as Cloud Services and Resource Manager to help deploy applications in the cloud.

Storage.   Microsoft offers its Azure Storage service, Azure Blob (binary large object) block storage, as well as Table, Queue, and File storage. Azure also offers Site Recovery, Import Export, and Azure Backup. A *binary large object (blob)* is a collection of binary data stored as a single entity in a database management system. Blobs are typically images, audio, or other multimedia objects.

Hybrid options.   Microsoft is an established vendor for hybrid deployments with Azure. Azure provides customers with the hardware and software required to deploy Azure public cloud services from a customer's data center with a shared management portal.

Machine Learning.   Microsoft's Azure Machine Learning enables developers to write, test, and deploy machine learning algorithms.

Customer base.   Microsoft customers include Ford, NBC News, Easyjet, and others. One of Microsoft's highest-profile customer wins occurred in late 2019, when it signed the $10 billion U.S. Department of Defense Joint Enterprise Defense Infrastructure (JEDI) contract. In February 2020, a federal judge ordered a temporary block on the JEDI cloud contract in response to a suit filed by Amazon. Despite the Department of Defense reaffirming Microsoft as the winner of the JEDI contract in September 2020, Amazon's lawsuit continued.

Pros and cons.   The biggest attraction for Azure is if Microsoft already has a strong presence within an organization and can easily play a role in helping these companies transition to the cloud. Azure integrates well with key Microsoft on-premise systems such as Windows Server, System Center, and Active Directory.

One of Azure's problems, though, has been a series of outages over the years, including a major global outage in May 2019. Zeus Kerravala (**www.zkresearch.com**) found that, through

2018 to May 2019, AWS and Google had comparable levels of IaaS downtime. During that same period of time, Azure had five times the outage rate of its two major competitors. Gartner analyst Lydia Leong recommended consider disaster recovery capabilities other than Azure for critical applications hosted in the cloud.

Google Cloud Platform

Strengths.   Although all three vendors are strong in machine learning, Google excels in this area. Google also has expertise with open-source technologies, particularly with containers. The reason is that Google played a leading role in the development of Kubernetes for orchestration and the Istio service mesh, which are becoming industry standard technologies.

Kubernetes orchestration allows organizations to build application services that span multiple containers, schedule containers across a cluster, and scale those containers. Kubernetes orchestration eliminates many of the manual processes involved in deploying and scaling containerized applications.

Istio is an open-source, independent service mesh that provides the fundamentals for an organization to operate a distributed microservice architecture. Istio reduces the complexity of managing microservice deployments by providing a uniform method to secure, connect, and monitor microservices, as well as a method to control how microservices share data with one another.

Compute.   Google's scalable Compute Engine delivers virtual machines in the company's data centers. The virtual machines are quick to start up, come with persistent disk storage, offer consistent performance, and are highly customizable depending on the needs of the customer.

Storage.   Google offers Cloud Storage for objects and blobs as well as for archival storage. Its Persistent Disk and Local SSD provides storage for virtual machines and containers. Firestore offers scalable file storage and Cloud Storage for Firebase provides scalable storage for user-generated content from apps. Google Data Transfer Services for fast offline, online, or cloud-to-cloud data transfer.

Hybrid options.   Google's hybrid offering Anthos, enables customers to build and manage hybrid applications in customers' data centers or in Google's cloud. Built on open-source technologies including Kubernetes, Istio, and Knative, Anthos provides consistency between on-premise and cloud environment. Knative is an open-source community project that adds components for deploying, operating, and managing serverless, cloud-native applications on Kubernetes.

Significantly, Anthos not only allows organizations to run applications on-premise and in Google's public cloud, but also to manage workloads running on third-party clouds such as AWS and Azure. This feature gives customers the freedom to deploy, run, and manage their applications on the cloud(s) of their choice, without requiring administrators and developers to learn new and different environments.

Machine Learning.   Google offers a one-stop-shop AI platform, which enables machine learning developers and data scientists to build and deploy models based on the firm's open source TensorFlow deep learning library.

Customer base.   Google has not had quite the same level of enterprise success as its two main competitors but does have notable customers. Spotify completed its migration to Google Cloud Platform in 2018, and United Kingdom bank HSBC has also chosen Google for its analytics and machine learning capabilities. Note that HSBC is also taking a multi-cloud approach, partnering with all three cloud vendors for different tasks.

Pros and cons.   Google has a good track record with innovative cloud-native companies and a solid standing in the open-source community. The company has strengths in Big Data and analytics applications, machine learning, and cloud-native applications. Google's market strategy has focused on smaller, innovative projects at large organizations, rather than becoming a strategic cloud partner.

Google has struggled to break into the enterprise market. In addition, Google has the smallest footprint of global instances of the big three and has no presence in China, one of the world's largest markets. AWS and Azure have regions in mainland China that are owned and operated by Chinese third-party partners. AWS's partners are Beijing Sinnet Technology and Ningxia Western Cloud Data Technology, and Azure has partnered with 21Vianet.

Before you go on...

1. Describe the similarities among the Big Three cloud computing vendors.
2. What is the single biggest advantage for each of the Big Three cloud computing vendors? Support your choice.
3. What is the single biggest disadvantage for each of the Big Three cloud computing vendors? Support your choice.

TG 3.8 Web Services and Service-Oriented Architecture

Thus far we have explained how cloud computing can deliver a variety of functionality to users in the form of services (think IaaS, PaaS, and SaaS). We conclude by examining Web services and service-oriented architecture.

Web services are applications delivered over the Internet (the cloud) that MIS professionals can select and combine through almost any device, from personal computers to mobile phones. By using a set of shared standards, or protocols, these applications permit different systems to "talk" with one another—that is, to share data and services—without requiring human beings to translate the conversations. Web services have enormous potential because they can be employed in a variety of environments: over the Internet, on an intranet inside a corporate firewall, or on an extranet set up by business partners. They can also perform a wide variety of tasks, from automating business processes to integrating components of an enterprisewide system to streamlining online buying and selling.

Web services provide numerous benefits for organizations:

- The organization can use the existing Internet infrastructure without having to implement any new technologies.
- Organizational personnel can access remote or local data without having to understand the complexities of this process.
- The organization can create new applications quickly and easily.

The collection of Web services that are used to build a firm's IT applications constitutes a **service-oriented architecture**. Businesses accomplish their processes by executing a series of these services. One of the major benefits of Web services is that they can be reused across an organization in other applications. For example, a Web service that checks a consumer's credit could be used with a service that processes a mortgage application or a credit card application.

Author Lecture Videos are available exclusively in *WileyPLUS*.
Apply the Concept activities are available in the Appendix and in *WileyPLUS*.

Web services are based on four key protocols: XML, SOAP, WSDL, and UDDI. **Extensible markup language (XML)** is a computer language that makes it easier to exchange data among a variety of applications and to validate and interpret these data. XML is a more powerful and flexible markup language than **hypertext markup language (HTML)**. HTML is a page-description language for specifying how text, graphics, video, and sound are placed on a web page document. HTML was originally designed to create and link static documents composed primarily of text (**Figure TG 3.5**). Today, however, the Web is much more social and interactive, and many web pages have multimedia elements, such as images, audio, and video. To integrate these rich media into web pages, users had to rely on third-party plug-in applications such as Flash, Silverlight, and Java. Unfortunately for users, these add-ons require both additional programming and extensive computer processing.

The next evolution of HTML, called **HTML5**, solves this problem by enabling users to embed images, audio, and video directly into a document without the add-ons. HTML5 also makes it easier for web pages to function across different display devices, including mobile devices and desktops. HTML5 supports offline data storage for apps that run over the Web. Web pages will execute more quickly, and they will resemble smartphone apps. HTML5 is used in a number of Internet platforms, including Apple's Safari browser, Google Chrome, and Mozilla Firefox. Google's Gmail and Google Reader also use HTML5. Websites listed as "iPad ready" are using HTML5 extensively. Examples of such sites are CNN, the *New York Times*, and CBS.

Where HTML is limited to describing how data should be presented in the form of web pages, XML can present, communicate, and store data. For example, in XML a number is not simply a number. The XML tag also specifies whether the number represents a price, a date,

(a) html

```
<!DOCTYPE HTML PUBLIC "-//W3C//DTD XHTML 1.0 Transitional//EN" http://www.wiley.com/college/gisslen/0470179961/video/
video111
<html xmlns="http://www.wiley.com/college/rainer/0470179061/video/video111.html"><head>
<meta http-equiv="content-Type" content="text/html; charset=ISO-8859-1">
<title>CSS Text Wrapper</title>
<link type="text/css" rel="stylesheet" href="css/stylesheet.css">
</head><body id="examples">


<div id="container">
        <div class="wrapper">
                <div class="ex">
                        <script type="text/javascript">shapewrapp
er("15","7.5,141,145|22.5,89,89|37.5,68,69|52.5,46,50|67.5,3
height: 15px; width: 39px;"></div><div style="float: left; clear: left; height: 15px; width: 27px;"></div><div style="float:
15px; width: 4px;"></div><div style="float: left; clear: left; height: 15px; width: 6px;"></div><div style="float:
right; cle
width: 43px;"></div><div style="float: left; clear: left; height: 15px; width: 57px;"></div><div style="float: right; clear:
                        <span style="font-size: 13px;" class="c">
```

(b) XML

```
<feature numbered="no" xml:id="c08-fea-0001">
    <titleGroup>
        <title type="featureName">OPENING CASE</title>
        <title type="main">Tiger Tans and Gifts</title>
    </titleGroup>
    <section xml:id="c08-sec-0002">
        <p>
            <blockFixed onlyChannels="print" type="graphic">
                <mediaResource alt="p0310" copyright="John Wiley &amp; Sons, Inc." eRights="yes"
                    href="urn:x-wiley:9781118443590:media:rainer9781118443590c08:p0310" pRights="yes"/>
            </blockFixed>
            Lisa Keiling owns & tanning salon in Wedowee, Alabama, that does very well from January to May....
        </p>
    </section>
</feature>
```

FIGURE TG 3.5 (a) Screenshot of an HTML wrapper. This wrapper gives instructions on how to open a video associated with this book. (b) Example of XML tagging.

or a ZIP code. Consider this example of XML, which identifies the contact information for Jane Smith.

```
<contact-info>
<name>Jane Smith</name>
<company>AT&T</company>
<phone>(212) 555-4567</phone>
</contact-info>
```

Simple object access protocol (SOAP) is a set of rules that define how messages can be exchanged among different network systems and applications through the use of XML. These rules essentially establish a common protocol that allows different Web services to interoperate. For example, Visual Basic clients can use SOAP to access a Java server. SOAP runs on all hardware and software systems.

The *Web services description language (WSDL)* is used to create the XML document that describes the tasks performed by the various Web services. Tools such as VisualStudio.Net automate the process of accessing the WSDL, reading it, and coding the application to reference the specific Web service.

Universal description, discovery, and integration (UDDI) allows MIS professionals to search for needed Web services by creating public or private searchable directories of these services. In other words, UDDI is the registry of descriptions of Web services.

Examples of Web services abound. As one example, the Food and Nutrition Service (FNS) within the U.S. Department of Agriculture (USDA) uses Amazon Web Services successfully. The FNS administers the department's nutrition assistance programs. Its mission is to provide children and families in need with improved access to food and a healthier diet through its food assistance programs and comprehensive nutrition education efforts.

The Supplemental Nutrition Assistance Program, or SNAP, is the cornerstone of the USDA's nutrition assistance mission. More than 47 million people—most of them children—receive SNAP benefits each month. To help recipients, in 2010 the FNS created a Web application called the SNAP Retail Locator. Faced with limited budget and time to implement the solution, the FNS selected Amazon Web Services to host the application. As its name suggests, the SNAP Retail Locator, which receives 30,000 visitors each month, helps SNAP recipients find the closest SNAP-authorized store and also provides driving directions to the store. The application has been available 100 percent of the time since it was launched. By employing Amazon, the FNS also saved 90 percent of the cost it would have incurred had it hosted the application on-premises.

Before you go on...

1. What are Web services?
2. What is a service-oriented architecture?

What's in IT for me?

For All Business Majors

As with hardware (see Technology Guide 1), the design of enterprise IT architectures has profound impacts for businesspeople. Personal and organizational success can depend on an understanding of cloud computing and a commitment to knowing the opportunities and challenges they will bring.

At the organizational level, cloud computing has the potential to make the organization function more efficiently and effectively, while saving the organization money. Web services and SOA make the organization more flexible when deploying new IT applications.

At the individual level, you might use cloud computing yourself if you start your own business. Remember that cloud computing provides startup companies with world-class IT capabilities at a very low cost.

Summary

TG3.1 Describe the evolution of the information technology function.

- Stand-alone mainframes: Organizations initially used mainframe computers in their engineering and accounting departments. The mainframe was typically housed in a secure area and only MIS personnel had access to it.

- Mainframe and dumb terminals: Firms placed dumb terminals in user departments. This arrangement enabled users to input computer programs into the mainframe from their departments.

- Stand-alone personal computers: In the late 1970s, users began bringing personal computers to the workplace to improve their productivity. These computers were not initially supported by the MIS department, but organizations eventually decided to support the computers.

- Local area networks (client/server computing): Organizations began to connect personal computers to local area networks (LANs) and then connected these LANs to the mainframe, a type of processing known as *client/server computing.*

- Enterprise computing: In the early 1990s, organizations began to use networking standards to integrate different kinds of networks throughout the firm, thereby creating enterprise computing. As the Internet became widespread after 1995, organizations began using the TCP/IP networking protocol to integrate different types of networks. All types of hardware were networked, including mainframes, personal computers, smartphones, printers, and many others. Software applications and data now flow seamlessly throughout the enterprise and between organizations.

- Cloud computing and mobile computing: Today, organizations and individuals can use the power of cloud computing. Cloud computing provides access to a shared pool of computing resources, including computers, storage, applications, and services, over a network, typically the Internet.

TG3.2 Define cloud computing and its key characteristics.

Cloud computing is a type of computing that delivers convenient, on-demand, pay-as-you-go access for multiple customers to a shared pool of configurable computing resources (e.g., servers, networks, storage, applications, and services) that can be rapidly and easily accessed over the Internet.

The essential *characteristics* of cloud computing include the following:

- Cloud computing provides on-demand self-service.
- Cloud computing includes the characteristics of grid computing.
- Cloud computing includes the characteristics of utility computing.
- Cloud computing uses broad network access.
- Cloud computing pools computing resources.
- Cloud computing typically occurs on virtualized servers.

TG3.3 Describe each of the four types of clouds.

Public clouds are shared, easily accessible, multicustomer IT infrastructures that are available nonexclusively to any entity in the public (individuals, groups, and organizations). *Private clouds* (also known as *internal clouds* or *corporate clouds*) are IT infrastructures that are accessible only by a single entity, or by an exclusive group of related entities that share the same purpose and requirements, such as all the business units within a single organization. *Hybrid clouds* are composed of public and private clouds that remain unique entities but are bound together, offering the benefits of multiple deployment models. *Vertical clouds* serve specific industries.

TG3.4 Explain the operational model of each of the three types of cloud services.

With the *infrastructure-as-a-service* model, cloud computing providers offer remotely accessible servers, networks, and storage capacity. In the *platform-as-a-service* model, customers rent servers, operating systems, storage, a database, software development technologies such as Java and .NET, and network capacity over the Internet. With the *software-as-a-service* delivery model, cloud computing vendors provide software that is specific to their customers' requirements.

TG3.5 Identify the key benefits of cloud computing.

The benefits of cloud computing include making individuals more productive, facilitating collaboration, mining insights from data, developing and hosting applications, cost flexibility, business scalability, improved usage of hardware, market adaptability, and product and service customization.

TG3.6 Discuss the concerns and risks associated with cloud computing.

Cloud computing does raise concerns and have risks, which include "legacy spaghetti," cost, reliability, privacy, security, and the regulatory and legal environment.

TG3.7 Describe the pros and cons for each of the Big Three cloud computing vendors.

Amazon. Amazon ranks highly on platform configuration options, monitoring and policy features, security, and reliability. Its partner ecosystem and general product strategy are market leading, and its AWS Marketplace has a large number of third-party software services.

In the past, Amazon has been dismissive of the benefits of hybrid cloud computing. As noted in Section TG 3.3, though, the company is now competing in this area with its product Outposts. Another problem is that certain organizations may not want to contribute to Amazon revenue and profits, as the giant company continues to expand and compete in a growing number of industries, such as health care and finance. In fact, some boards of directors in potentially threatened industry verticals have directed their IT groups to avoid the use of AWS where possible.

Microsoft. The biggest attraction for Azure is if Microsoft already has a strong presence within an organization and therefore can easily play a role in helping these companies transition to the cloud. Azure integrates well with key Microsoft on-premise systems such as Windows Server, System Center, and Active Directory.

One of Azure's problems, though, has been a series of outages over the years, including a major global outage in May 2019. Gartner analyst Lydia Leong recommended consider disaster recovery capabilities other than Azure for critical applications hosted in the cloud. Note: AWS had its last major outage in 2017 and Google Cloud last had a major outage of its own in November 2019.

Google. Google has a good track record with innovative cloud-native companies and a solid standing in the open-source community. The company has strengths in Big Data and analytics applications, machine learning, and cloud-native applications. Google's market strategy has focused on smaller, innovative projects at large organizations, rather than becoming a strategic cloud partner.

Google has struggled to break into the enterprise market. In addition, Google has the smallest footprint of global instances of the big three and has no presence in China, one of the world's largest markets. AWS and Azure have regions in mainland China which are owned and operated by Chinese third-party partners. AWS's partners are Beijing Sinnet Technology and Ningxia Western Cloud Data Technology, and Azure has partnered with 21Vianet.

TG3.8 Explain the role of Web services in building a firm's IT applications, providing examples.

Web services are applications delivered over the Internet that MIS professionals can select and combine through almost any device, from personal computers to mobile phones. A *service-oriented architecture* makes it possible for MIS professionals to construct business applications using Web services.

Technology Guide Glossary

cloud computing   A technology in which tasks are performed by computers physically removed from the user and accessed over a network, in particular the Internet.

extensible markup language (XML)   A computer language that makes it easier to exchange data among a variety of applications and to validate and interpret these data.

functions-as-a-Service (XaaS)   A category of cloud computing services that provides a platform allowing customers to develop, run, and manage applications functions without the complexity of building and maintaining the infrastructure typically associated with developing and deploying an app.

grid computing   A technology that applies the unused processing resources of many geographically dispersed computers in a network to form a virtual supercomputer.

HTML5   A page-description language that makes it possible to embed images, audio, and video directly into a document without add-ons. Also makes it easier for web pages to function across different display devices, including mobile devices as well as desktops. It supports the storage of data offline.

hybrid clouds   Clouds composed of public and private clouds that remain unique entities but are bound together, offering the benefits of multiple deployment models.

hypertext markup language (HTML)   A page-description language for specifying how text, graphics, video, and sound are placed on a web page document.

infrastructure-as-a-service (IaaS)   A model with which cloud computing providers offer remotely accessible servers, networks, and storage capacity.

on-premise computing   A model of IT management in which companies own their IT infrastructure (their software, hardware, networks, and data management) and maintain it in their data centers.

platform-as-a-service (PaaS)   A model in which customers rent servers, operating systems, storage, a database, software development technologies such as Java and .NET, and network capacity over the Internet.

private clouds (also known as *internal clouds* or *corporate clouds*)   IT infrastructures that are accessible only by a single entity or by an exclusive group of related entities that share the same purpose and requirements, such as all the business units within a single organization.

public clouds   Shared, easily accessible, multicustomer IT infrastructures that are available nonexclusively to any entity in the general public (individuals, groups, and organizations).

server farms   Massive data centers, which may contain hundreds of thousands of networked computer servers.

server virtualization   A technology that uses software-based partitions to create multiple virtual servers (called *virtual machines*) on a single physical server.

service-oriented architecture   An IT architecture that makes it possible to construct business applications using Web services.

software-as-a-service (SaaS)   A delivery model in which cloud computing vendors provide software that is specific to their customers' requirements.

utility computing   A technology whereby a service provider makes computing resources and infrastructure management available to a customer as needed.

vertical cloud   A set of cloud computing services optimized for use in a particular industry.

Web services   Applications delivered over the Internet that IT developers can select and combine through almost any device, from personal computers to mobile phones.

Discussion Questions

1. What is the value of server farms and virtualization to any large organization?

2. If you were the chief information officer of a firm, how would you explain the workings, benefits, and limitations of cloud computing?

3. What is the value of cloud computing to a small organization?

4. What is the value of cloud computing to an entrepreneur who is starting a business?

Problem-Solving Activities

1. Investigate the status of cloud computing by researching the offerings of the following vendors: Dell (**www.dell.com**), Oracle (**www.oracle.com**), IBM (**www.ibm.com**), Alibaba (**www.alibaba.com**) and Tencent (**www.tencent.com**). Compare Alibaba and Tencent with American cloud vendors.

Apply the Concept Activities

Apply the Concept 1.1

LEARNING OBJECTIVE 1.1

Identify the reasons why being an informed user of information systems is important in today's world.

STEP 1: Background (Here is what you are learning.)

Section 1.1 discussed how businesses are utilizing modern technologies to become more productive by connecting to their customers, suppliers, partners, and other parties. Those connections, however, do not exist simply to support the businesses. Do you realize how connected you are? Computers and information systems have become an essential feature of our everyday lives. Most of you have a cell phone within reach and have looked at it within the past 5 minutes. No longer is a phone just a phone; rather, it is your connection to family, friends, shopping, driving directions, entertainment (games, movies, music, etc.), and much more.

When you embark on your career, you likely will have to interface with information systems to post transactions and search for or record information. Accomplishing these tasks will require you to work effectively with computers, regardless of the industry in which you find yourself employed.

STEP 2: Activity (Here is what you do.)

Visit the websites of three local businesses: a bank, a dentist, and a retail shop. Examine their information to see if you can determine what types of information systems they use to support their operations. It is likely that you will find some similarities and differences among the three. Also, see if they have any open positions. If they do, what technical skills do these positions require? Summarize your findings in a paragraph or two.

STEP 3: Deliverable (Here is what you turn in.)

Based on your research, identify five reasons why it is important for you to be an informed user of information technology. Reference your summarized findings to support your reasoning. Submit this list to your instructor, but also keep it in mind. You have just looked into the real world (your local world, in fact) and identified a reason for taking this course!

Apply the Concept 1.2

LEARNING OBJECTIVE 1.2

Classify the activities supported by various types of computer-based information systems in an organization.

STEP 1: Background

Section 1.2 discussed the various functional areas in which you most likely will be employed and the different IS that support them. It should be no surprise that these are the majors from which you can choose in most colleges of business. The four major functional areas are marketing and sales, finance and accounting, manufacturing, and human resources. Often, these areas will use the same database and networks within a company, but they will use them to support their specific needs. This activity will help you develop a solid understanding of the role of IS within the different functional areas.

STEP 2: Activity

Review the section material that describes the major functions of the four major functional areas. Then, review the basic functions of the following types of information systems: transaction processing, management information, and decision support.

After you have acquired a solid understanding of the functional areas and information systems that support them, you are ready to move forward with the activity!

STEP 3: Deliverable

Create a table like the one shown below, and classify the activities supported by various types of computer-based information systems. To assist you, we have prefilled one item in each type of system. After you complete your chart, submit it to your professor.

	Transaction Processing	Management Information System	Decision Support System
Marketing and Sales	Enter Sales Data		
Accounting and Finance			
Human Resources			Comply with EEOC
Manufacturing		Inventory Reporting	

Apply the Concept 1.3

LEARNING OBJECTIVE 1.3

Discuss ways in which information technology can affect managers and nonmanagerial workers.

STEP 1: Background

Section 1.3 demonstrated that the essential reason businesses use information systems is to add value to their daily activities. In fact, IS have radically transformed the nature of both managerial and nonmanagerial work. Managers employ IT to instantly track information that previously was available only in monthly reports. Support staff can view calendars and schedules for all employees and can schedule meetings more easily. Sales representatives can view current product information while visiting with clients. This list does not even scratch the surface of the countless ways technology has added value to modern businesses.

STEP 2: Activity

Consider the restaurant industry. You have probably visited some "old-school" restaurants where your order is written down on a piece of paper and never entered into a computer system for preparation. You have most likely also been to a very modern restaurant where you

enter your own order with a tablet, smartphone, or other piece of technology. Visit http://www
.wiley.com/go/rainer/IS9e/applytheconcept and watch the two videos about using the restaurant table as the menu and ordering system.

STEP 3: Deliverable

Imagine that you are a manager in each type of restaurant. How does working without technology impact how you do your job? How does adding the technology change your performance? Based on your thoughts from Step 2, imagine that you are explaining to your friend the ways that restaurants could benefit from IT. Prepare a paragraph or two that will discuss the ways that the traditional job of a restaurant manager and other employees has been changed by IT.

Apply the Concept 1.4

LEARNING OBJECTIVE 1.4

Identify positive and negative societal effects of the increased use of information technology.

STEP 1: Background

As you have just read, the increased use of IS has had a significant impact on society. Section 1.4 focused on three areas—quality-of-life improvements, robotics, and health care—to spark your interest in the ways our lives are being touched. Unfortunately, the technologies that provide quality-of-life improvements can also create economic and political problems. For example, robots that help streamline production also eliminate jobs. Similarly, health care improvements raise concerns regarding shared data and privacy violations.

STEP 2: Activity

Conduct a Web search for "technology and work–life balance." Look for programs, articles, research, suggestions, and other materials that help you understand the positive and negative effects of the increased use of information technologies.

STEP 3: Deliverable

Create a table that identifies the positive and negative effects for the following areas: quality of life, robotics, health care, and work–life balance. Set your table up as in the example below, and submit it to your instructor.

	Positive	Negative
Quality of Life		
Robotics		
Health care		
Work–Life Balance		

Apply the Concept 2.1

LEARNING OBJECTIVE 2.1

Discuss ways in which information systems enable cross-functional business processes and business processes for a single functional area.

STEP 1: Background

This chapter defines a business process as an ongoing collection of related activities that create a product or a service of value to the organization, its business partners, and/or its customers. Normally, we do not see everything that goes into a process; rather, we observe only the results of the process. For example, when you shop at a grocery store, you see stocked shelves. However, the inventory-management processes that operate to keep the shelves stocked—as well as the information systems that support those processes—remain essentially invisible.

STEP 2: Activity

Visit http://www.wiley.com/go/rainer/IS9e/applytheconcept and click on the link provided for Section 2.1. This link will take you to a YouTube video that focuses on workflow and business process management in a health care environment. As you watch the video, look for the ways that information systems enable cross-functional business processes and make the flow of data much easier and quicker for everyone involved.

STEP 3: Deliverable

Based on the video from Step 2, write a brief description of how information systems enable both cross-functional business processes and business processes for a single functional area. Submit your description to your instructor.

Apply the Concept 2.2

LEARNING OBJECTIVE 2.2

Compare and contrast business process reengineering (BPR) and business process management (BPM) to determine the advantages and disadvantages of each.

STEP 1: Background

One of the most difficult decisions related to business processes is whether they need to be reengineered or simply managed. Reengineering business processes is a "clean-slate" approach in which you build completely new processes to accomplish current tasks. In contrast, managing these processes involves making current processes more efficient. Put simply, reengineering is radical, whereas management is incremental.

STEP 2: Activity

Consider the many processes involved in getting you (as a student) accepted, enrolled, registered, housed, fed, and, ultimately, educated. Do you recall the processes you went through to accomplish these tasks? Did any of these processes strike you as inefficient?

STEP 3: Deliverable

Imagine that you are a student representative on a committee whose task is to consider reengineering or modifying (managing) these business processes. Prepare a written statement for the committee that will compare and contrast BPR and BPM to determine the advantages and disadvantages of each strategy. Make a recommendation as to which one your university should follow, and present your recommendation to your instructor.

Apply the Concept 2.3

LEARNING OBJECTIVE 2.3

Identify effective IT responses to different kinds of business pressures.

STEP 1: Background

Businesses face immense pressures today from every angle imaginable. The market is constantly shifting, technology becomes obsolete almost as quickly as it is implemented, society expects businesses to take more responsibility for the communities their work impacts, and legal compliance is required. Businesses increasingly employ cutting-edge technologies to navigate these difficult waters.

STEP 2: Activity

Pick one business pressure from each of the three broad categories presented in the chapter: Market, Technology, and Societal/Political/Legal. Now search for a real-world business story related to each of the pressures you have chosen.

STEP 3: Deliverable

After you have selected your three examples, identify an effective IT response to each one. Feel free to use the responses listed in the chapter. For each example, explain why you feel this is an appropriate response to the business pressure you have identified.

Perhaps there is a response outlined in the story you found. If so, determine whether the response was truly effective in dealing with the business pressure. Your submission should follow the outline below:

Broad Category: _____

Business Pressure: _____

IT Response: _____

Description: _____

Apply the Concept 2.4

LEARNING OBJECTIVE 2.4

Describe the strategies that organizations typically adopt to counter Porter's five competitive forces.

STEP 1: Background

This section has exposed you to Porter's five forces model, which explains how various forces can affect an organization. The threat of entry of new competitors, bargaining power of suppliers, bargaining power of customers, threat of substitute products or services, and rivalry among existing firms in the industry all have an impact on the organization's success. Based on this model, the chapter presents five strategies for competitive advantage: cost leadership, differentiation, innovation, operational effectiveness, and customer orientation.

Walmart is a worldwide company that focuses on a cost-leadership strategy. Review the ways Walmart uses the five forces (or controls them) to maintain their position as a global cost leader. Although it may be somewhat easy to perform this exercise with a global giant like Walmart, it is very difficult to apply these concepts to small businesses.

STEP 2: Activity

Visit your favorite restaurant and ask to speak to the manager. Asking only a few questions, evaluate whether the manager has a grasp of the five forces model. Do not ask anything specifically about Porter. Rather, inquire about rivals, substitutes, customers' bargaining power, suppliers' power, and so on. A good manager should be familiar with these concepts regardless of whether he or she uses the term *Porter's five forces*. Finally, ask the manager what strategy he or she uses. Then, try to classify that strategy as a cost leadership, differentiation, innovation, operational effectiveness, or customer orientation strategy.

STEP 3: Deliverable

Identify which of the five forces are at work based on the manager's feedback. Then, describe the strategies that *could* help deal with these particular forces, and explain *if* this is what the restaurant is currently attempting to do. If it is not, then explain what they should do differently. Your submission will have two parts: (1) a definition of the forces and (2) a description of the strategies at play in response to those forces.

Apply the Concept 3.1

LEARNING OBJECTIVE 3.1

Describe ethics, its three fundamental tenets, and the four categories of ethical issues related to information technology.

STEP 1: Background

As you begin your career, you need to be aware of the current trends affecting the four areas of concern presented in Section 3.1. Privacy (what people know about you), property (who owns the data about you), accuracy (are the data about you accurate), and accessibility (who can access your data) are major topics in today's high-tech world. They are especially important in the migration to electronic health records, mobile wallets, social media, and government-run databases, to name a few.

STEP 2: Activity

Visit http://www.wiley.com/go/rainer/IS9e/applytheconcept and read the article posted from Forbes magazine that was posted in November 2013. The article describes an unusual (or not-so-unusual) action on the part of Goldman Sachs. It seems they decided that their junior bankers should have weekends off!

Understand that it isn't illegal to require your employees to work weekends, nor is it illegal to give them time off. It also isn't illegal to work people 75 hours a week. Many of the talking points in this article focus expressly on ethics. An employer is trying to do the "right" thing, and they have used a new standard to define "right."

STEP 3: Deliverable

Summarize the article for your professor. In your summary, make certain to define ethics and to describe how the three fundamental tenets of ethics (responsibility, liability, and accountability) played a role in Goldman Sachs' decision. Finally (not from the article), discuss how these same bankers deal with the four areas of ethical concern with regard to your financial information.

Apply the Concept 3.2

LEARNING OBJECTIVE 3.2

Discuss at least one potential threat to the privacy of the data stored in each of three places that store personal data.

STEP 1: Background

Section 3.2 has defined privacy as the right to be left alone and to be free of unreasonable personal intrusions. Information privacy is the right to determine when, and to what extent, information about you can be gathered and/or communicated to others. And, where our data are concerned, we are in control, right? If so, then why do people always seem to fear that "Big Brother" is spying on us and violating our privacy? The law generally assigns a higher priority to society's right to access information than to an individual's right to privacy.

The 2002 movie *Minority Report* presented a future in which a special police unit could predict when and where crimes were going to occur before they actually did. This unit could arrest "criminals" before they committed a crime. Along these same lines, a 2008 movie titled *Eagle Eye* focused on a highly intelligent computer system that chose to abide by the Constitution even if it meant having the president of the United States assassinated.

STEP 2: Activity

Movie night! If you have not seen the two films noted in Step 1, then schedule a movie night and watch them from the perspective of privacy and information security. Discuss the movies with your friends, and obtain their thoughts on these issues. If you don't have time to watch the movies, then visit http://www.wiley.com/go/rainer/IS9e/applytheconcept to read a synopsis of both films on IMDb.com.

STEP 3: Deliverable

After considering the plots in these movies, prepare a paper identifying three types of storage options you use for storing personal data. For each location, discuss at least one potential threat to your personal privacy that arises from storing your information there. Make them major threats . . . on the scale of the movies. Consider just how far your seemingly innocent decisions can take you! Present your paper to the class and submit it to your instructor.

Apply the Concept 4.1

LEARNING OBJECTIVE 4.1

Identify the five factors that contribute to the increasing vulnerability of information resources and specific examples of each factor.

STEP 1: Background

Section 4.1 has taught you about the importance of information security, particularly when you are conducting business over the Web. It is important to note that a chain is only as strong as its weakest link. Therefore, although you may have been careful to maintain security across your network, if your business partners have not done so as well, then as your information passes over their networks it will be at risk.

STEP 2: Activity

Visit http://www.wiley.com/go/rainer/IS9e/applytheconcept and click on the link to VeriSign's website. As you read this page, keep in mind that VeriSign is in the business of protecting websites and Web users, which is something we all appreciate. In fact, it is likely that you feel some level of comfort when you see the VeriSign symbol on an e-commerce site.

STEP 3: Deliverable

After reading the article, compose a brief memo from VeriSign to a potential client. Identify the five factors that contribute to the increasing vulnerability of information resources and provide examples of how VeriSign can help protect the client's digital assets against these threats. Submit your memo to your instructor.

Apply the Concept 4.2

LEARNING OBJECTIVE 4.2

Compare and contrast human mistakes and social engineering, along with specific examples of each one.

STEP 1: Background

Sensitive information is generally stored in a safe location, both physically and digitally. However, as you have just read, this information is often vulnerable to unintentional threats that result from careless mistakes. As one example, employees frequently use USB (flash) drives to take information home. Although these actions are perfectly legal, the USB drive makes it easy to lose the information or to copy it onto unauthorized machines. In fact, any device that stores information can become a threat to information security—backup drives, CDs, DVDs, and even printers! Printers? Because people can "copy" information? Not quite. Continue the activity to find out more.

STEP 2: Activity

Visit http://www.wiley.com/go/rainer/IS9e/applytheconcept and click on the link provided for Apply the Concept 4.2. You will find an article about how the hard drive in a printer sometimes stores images of all the documents that have been copied. In the past, when these printers were discarded, their hard drives were not erased, leaving medical records, police reports, and other private information in a vulnerable state.

STEP 3: Deliverable

Compare and contrast human mistakes and social engineering using the example above. How might someone make a mistake with a printer? How might someone use social engineering to access or create copies of personal information? Put your thoughts into a report and submit it to your instructor.

Apply the Concept 4.3

LEARNING OBJECTIVE 4.3

Discuss the 10 types of deliberate attacks.

STEP 1: Background

Unfortunately there are many people who take advantage of others. Fraud, espionage, information extortion, identity theft, cyberterrorism, spamming, phishing, and many other deliberate acts have created a world where we must always confirm the identity of the people with whom we share information.

STEP 2: Activity

Visit http://www.wiley.com/go/rainer/IS9e/applytheconcept and click on the links provided for Apply the Concept 4.3. The link will take you to a video about foreign lotteries and a website the U.S. Postal Service provides to help people realize when they are being scammed. This type of scam has taken advantage of many people who are not aware that such scams exist. After watching the video, search the Web for other fraudulent activities that involve Craigslist, eBay, and any other sites you find.

STEP 3: Deliverable

Imagine you are the owner of a site such as Craigslist. Draft a memo to your users—both buyers and sellers—explaining your intention to run a "clean" site where all parties are safe. In your memo, discuss the 10 types of deliberate attacks that you want your users to be aware of as they conduct business on your site. Submit your memo to your instructor.

Apply the Concept 4.4

LEARNING OBJECTIVE 4.4

Describe the three risk mitigation strategies and provide examples of each one in the context of owning a home.

STEP 1: Background

Section 4.4 discussed at length the ways businesses deal with risk. Risk management is so important that companies frequently assign an entire department to oversee risk analysis and mitigation. When companies address risk, they have three basic methods from which to choose: risk acceptance, risk limitation, and risk transference. Significantly, we do the same thing when it comes to our personal assets.

Like businesses, homeowners face intentional and unintentional threats. To mitigate against these threats, almost all homeowners take certain actions. These actions reflect, among other things, where your home is located. For example, a home on the beach is much more susceptible to hurricanes than is a home in Nebraska. However, the home in Nebraska is (perhaps) more susceptible to tornadoes than is the home on the beach.

STEP 2: Activity

Imagine that you own your home. What risks do you need to manage? What property do you need to assess? What is the probability that any asset will be compromised? (*Note:* You will need to assess the risk to each asset.) What are the costs associated with each asset being compromised?

STEP 3: Deliverable

In a document, define the three risk management strategies and provide an example of each one in the context of owning a home. Submit your document to your instructor.

Apply the Concept 4.5

LEARNING OBJECTIVE 4.5

Identify the three major types of controls that organizations can use to protect their information resources and provide an example of each one.

STEP 1: Background

Security controls are designed to protect all components of an information system, including data, software, hardware, and networks. Because there are so many diverse threats, organizations utilize layers of controls. One security feature discussed in this chapter is public key encryption. This feature requires a public key and a private key. The public key is shared and is used to encrypt a message that only the individual's private key can decrypt.

STEP 2: Activity

Visit http://www.wiley.com/go/rainer/IS9e/applytheconcept and click on the link provided for Apply the Concept 4.5. The link will take you to an article about the 2004 movie *National Treasure*. Watching the actual film is preferable, but you may not have access to it. For this activity, reading about it will suffice. In this movie, Ben Gates (played by Nicholas Cage) steals one of our nation's most sacred documents—the Declaration of Independence. In the process, you see how the thief breaches all three of the major types of controls.

STEP 3: Deliverable

Identify the three major types of controls that the National Archives employs—and that Gates ultimately penetrates—and provide examples of them from the movie. Prepare a document with the three types of controls and examples from the movie and submit it to your instructor.

Apply the Concept 5.1

LEARNING OBJECTIVE 5.1

Discuss ways that common challenges in managing data can be addressed using data governance.

STEP 1: Background

The amount of data we create today is absolutely mind-boggling. Dell EMC is a global company that focuses on helping organizations manage their data. Recently, the company sponsored a study to determine exactly how big the "digital universe" actually is and to envision its projected growth. There are some amazing findings in this study that point to a dramatic growth in data and an increase in virtual data centers. In the future, it will be possible to run your information systems in data centers that do not operate on your premises.

STEP 2: Activity

Visit http://www.wiley.com/go/rainer/IS9e/applytheconcept and click on the link provided for Apply the Concept 5.1. Watch this video and consider how the trends it presents relate to the challenges discussed in this section. Now imagine that your parents own their own business. It is successful, but it is also struggling under pressure to upgrade IT services for its employees and customers. How could you help them to look ahead to the future rather than keeping the status quo?

STEP 3: Deliverable

Write an e-mail to your parents to explain how data and data management are likely to evolve over the next 10 years. Describe the common challenges they face and discuss how data governance can help address these issues. Also, based on the video, highlight the qualities they should look for in new employees. Finally, identify the types of training they should provide for their current employees.

   Submit your e-mail to your instructor.

Apply the Concept 5.2

LEARNING OBJECTIVE 5.2

Discuss the advantages and disadvantages of relational databases.

STEP 1: Background

This section has introduced you to the advantages and disadvantages of using a relational database. This is one of those concepts that cannot really be appreciated until you work through the process of designing a database. Even though very few people go on to become database administrators, it is still valuable to have some understanding of how a database is built and administered. In this activity, you will be presented with a scenario, and you will then apply the concepts you have just read about. In the process, you will develop a solid foundation to discuss the advantages and disadvantages of relational databases.

STEP 2: Activity

You are employed as the coordinator of multiple ongoing projects within a company. Your responsibilities include keeping track of the company's commercial projects, its employees, and the employees' participation in each project. Usually, a project will have multiple team members, but some projects have not been assigned to any team members. For each project, the company must keep track of the project's title, description, location, estimated budget, and due date.

   Each employee can be assigned to one or more projects. Some employees can also be on leave and therefore will not be working on any assignments. Project leaders usually need to know the following information about their team members: name, address, phone number, Social Security number, highest degree attained, and expertise (for example, IS, accounting, marketing, finance).

   Your manager has instructed you to present an overview of the advantages and disadvantages of a database that would support the company's efforts to manage the data described in this scenario. At a minimum, you should define the tables and the relationships among the key variables to provide structure to the information that would be included in the database.

STEP 3: Deliverable

Using the relational database design you created in Step 2, prepare a discussion of the advantages and disadvantages of this database. How will it benefit the company? What additional challenges might it create?

Submit your design and your discussion to your instructor.

Apply the Concept 5.3

LEARNING OBJECTIVE 5.3

Define Big Data and its basic characteristics.

STEP 1: Background

This section describes Big Data as an ongoing phenomenon that is providing businesses with access to vast amounts of information. The key "ingredients" that make the Big Data phenomenon a reality are volume, velocity, and variety.

STEP 2: Activity

TIBCO (www.tibco.com) is a company that provides a real-time event-processing software platform that brings customers and vendors together in a very interactive and engaging way. It uses vast amounts of data (volume), in real time (velocity), from multiple sources (variety) to bring this solution to its customers. Visit http://www.wiley.com/go/rainer/IS9e/applytheconcept and click on the link provided for Apply the Concept 5.3. As you view this video, watch carefully for the three "ingredients" mentioned above.

STEP 3: Deliverable

Write a review on the video from Step 2. In your review, define Big Data and discuss its basic characteristics relative to the video. Also in your review, note the functional areas of an organization referred to in the video.

Submit your review to your instructor.

Apply the Concept 5.4

LEARNING OBJECTIVE 5.4

Explain the elements necessary to successfully implement and maintain data warehouses.

STEP 1: Background

A set of general ingredients is required for organizations to effectively utilize the power of data marts and data warehouses. Figure 5.4 presents this information. Health care as an industry has not been centralized for many business, legal, and ethical reasons. However, the overall health implications of a centralized data warehouse are unimaginable.

STEP 2: Activity

Visit http://www.wiley.com/go/rainer/IS9e/applytheconcept and read the article in *HealthTech* magazine from July 11, 2018, titled "Fitbit Pushes into the Clinical Space to Make Medicine More Personal." As you read the article, think about how Fitbit and Google are using data warehouses. (The term *warehouse* is not used, but the concept is applicable.)

STEP 3: Deliverable

To demonstrate that you recognize the environmental factors necessary to implement and maintain a data warehouse, imagine that the date is exactly five years in the future. Write a blog post titled "Data from Gadgets Like Fitbit Changed How Medical Data Was Used." In your article, imagine that all of the ingredients necessary in the environment have come together. Discuss what the environment was like in 2018 and how things have changed today with devices like the Apple Watch and Fitbit.

    Be aware that there is no right or wrong answer to this exercise. The objective is for you to recognize the necessary environment for a successful data warehouse implementation. The health care–related example simply provides a platform to accomplish this task.

Apply the Concept 5.5

LEARNING OBJECTIVE 5.5

Describe the benefits and challenges of implementing knowledge management systems in organizations.

STEP 1: Background

As you have learned in this text, data are captured, stored, analyzed, and shared to create knowledge within organizations. This knowledge is exposed in meetings when colleagues are interpreting the information they received from the latest report, in employee presentations, in e-mail among coworkers, and in numerous other scenarios. The problem many organizations face is that there are massive amounts of knowledge that are created and shared, but this information is not stored in a centralized, searchable format.

STEP 2: Activity

Visit http://www.wiley.com/go/rainer/IS9e/applytheconcept and click on the links provided for Apply the Concept 5.5. They will take you to two YouTube videos: *Discover What You Know* by user Ken Porter and *Lee Bryant—Knowledge Management* by user UsNowFilm. Both videos illustrate the importance of capturing knowledge within an organization so it can be shared with the right person at the right time to support effective decision making.

STEP 3: Deliverable

Write a short paragraph or two to discuss the benefits and challenges faced by companies when they attempt to implement a knowledge management system. How many of these elements are technical and how many are social? Also, discuss the ways that companies can use technologies to help capture and share knowledge.

    Submit this essay to your instructor.

Apply the Concept 5.6

LEARNING OBJECTIVE 5.6

Understand the processes of querying a relational database, entity-relationship modeling, and normalization and joins.

STEP 1: Background

It is very important that you understand the connections among entities, attributes, and relationships. This section has defined each of these terms for you. Typically, entities are described by their attributes, and they are related to other entities. For example, if "student name" is the entity, then age, gender, country of origin, marital status, and other demographic data are the attributes (characteristics) of that particular student. That student is also related to other entities such as financial information, major, and course information.

STEP 2: Activity

An entity–relationship model is one of the most challenging aspects of designing a database because you have to (1) understand the rules that govern how processes work and (2) be able to define and describe these rules in a picture. This section has provided you with the necessary tools to draw a basic ER model.

Imagine the following scenario. You are designing a database for your local police department to keep track of traffic violations. The department has provided you with the following rules:

- Each officer can write multiple tickets.
- Each ticket will list only one officer.
- Each ticket will list only one driver.
- Drivers can receive multiple tickets.

STEP 3: Deliverable

Using the tools described in this section, demonstrate that you understand the process of ER modeling by drawing and submitting an ER model for the scenario provided in Step 2.

Apply the Concept 6.1

LEARNING OBJECTIVE 6.1

Compare and contrast the major types of networks.

STEP 1: Background

Section 6.1 has introduced you to the different types of networks that connect businesses around the world. These networking capabilities enable modern organizations to operate over many geographic locations. Frequently, a company's headquarters are located in one city with various branches in other countries. In addition, employees often work from home rather than commute to a physical office. The computer network is the technology that allows all of this to happen. For a network to function, a few components are required. In this activity, you will place these components in the appropriate places to create a computer network.

STEP 2: Activity

Consider the following company, called JLB TechWizards, and the following potential network components:

1. Headquarters: JLB TechWizards manufactures, sells, and services computer equipment. The company's headquarters, located in Chicago, house several key functions, including marketing, accounting, HR, and manufacturing. Each office has a number of PCs that connect to the main server. All offices share data and printers.

2. Salesforce: The company has technicians who service equipment sold within the United States. Each technician has a laptop that must connect to the database at headquarters about three hours each day to check inventory, enter repairs, and place orders. Technicians are constantly on the road and they need to be able to check inventory whether they are in a hotel or at a customer site. In addition, each evening the technicians must log on to check for updates and to post their daily activities.

3. Employees from home: JLB TechWizards has a number of employees who work from home part-time on flex time. These employees must have a fast, secure connection because some of them are dealing with financial data stored in the main computer and its databases at headquarters. They all live within 20 miles of their workplace.

STEP 3: Deliverable

Use the description of JLB TechWizards presented above to compare and contrast the types of networks discussed in this section. Explain how these networks will or will not meet the needs of each situation. A table may be useful to present this information, but it is not required. Create a Word document with your description and explanations and submit it to your instructor.

Apply the Concept 6.2

LEARNING OBJECTIVE 6.2

Describe the wireline communications media and transmission technologies.

STEP 1: Background

Section 6.2 covers network channels, protocols, and other network fundamentals. These computer networks enable businesses to receive and share information with customers, suppliers, and employees. Made up of several possible cable types and protocols, they are quite literally the backbone of modern businesses.

STEP 2: Activity

Imagine that you work in the billing department of a midsized hospital. Recently, your supervisor stated that team effectiveness had not declined at all due to COVID and that they had decided to repurpose the billing department office space. You would now begin to work from home permanently and would be reimbursed for setting up your home office and for your home Internet connection. The only requirement is that you finalize the same number of bills each day from home as you did in the office. You can schedule your own time as long as your work gets done.

Visit http://www.wiley.com/go/rainer/IS9e/applytheconcept to watch a few videos about telecommuting.

STEP 3: Deliverable

Describe the wireline communication media and the transmission technologies (protocols) that you will need to be able to telecommute. Your description should (at a minimum) include the home Internet connection, use of the Web, and connections within the office. It should also describe the protocols that operate to support these connections. Submit your description to your instructor.

Apply the Concept 6.3

LEARNING OBJECTIVE 6.3

Describe the most common methods for accessing the Internet.

STEP 1: Background

Section 6.3 has explained the difference between the Internet and the World Wide Web. Although many people use these terms interchangeably, they are very different. Most computers today are continuously connected to the Internet, though they are not always accessing the Web. Offices and other places of employment typically set up an Internet connection via a local area network (LAN). However, at home you have several options to consider.

STEP 2: Activity

Visit http://www.wiley.com/go/rainer/IS9e/applytheconcept and watch the YouTube videos listed there. These videos go into a little more detail about the types of connections mentioned in Table 6.2. You will learn about advantages, disadvantages, and things to consider for the different methods of connecting to the Internet.

STEP 3: Deliverable

Imagine that your parents are "technologically challenged" (some of you may not have to imagine). They have just bought a house at the beach and they are getting ready to set up an Internet connection. At home, there is only one provider, so DSL versus cable versus cellular versus satellite is not an issue. However, there are several options at the beach and your parents do not know where to begin.

Compose an e-mail to your parents that describes the most common methods for accessing the Internet to help them develop criteria for making their choice.

Apply the Concept 6.4

LEARNING OBJECTIVE 6.4

Explain the impact that discovery network applications have had on business and everyday life.

STEP 1: Background

Section 6.4 has introduced you to the discovery aspect of networks, specifically the Web. Search engines (of all kinds) open up doors of knowledge for anyone with a question. Translation tools allow you to even discover your answer from other languages. These, however, are very broad tools. Portals help by focusing your search within a narrow realm of information. They also push very specific information to you rather than waiting on you to request everything.

STEP 2: Activity

Before there were online search tools, there was the library card catalog. It was a method of organizing information in a library so that you could easily retrieve the information you needed. Today, research is handled very differently. Visit http://www.wiley.com/go/rainer/IS9e/applytheconcept to watch a video about the use of the "old-school" library card catalog.

STEP 3: Deliverable

Search the Web for the book referenced in the YouTube video linked above. Use multiple search engines (such as google.com, yahoo.com, or bing.com), some meta search engines (such as dogpile.com or excite.com), and your school's library system. Make note of the amount of and type of information you are able to find in just a few minutes about the book referenced in the YouTube video above. Write a paragraph that compares your experience to the card catalog system.

Now think even bigger. If discovery applications have made this much impact on something as simple as finding a book (or information on the book), how much bigger is the impact on business and everyday life? Prepare a second paragraph that discusses the latter question.

Submit both paragraphs to your instructor.

Apply the Concept 6.5

LEARNING OBJECTIVE 6.5

Explain the impact that communication network applications have had on business and everyday life.

STEP 1: Background

Section 6.5 has introduced you to the communication aspect of networks that have radically changed the way humans interact with each other. Most of these methods of communication are even available on our mobile devices now via a cellular connection. Such drastic changes have brought about many struggles and possibilities for businesses.

STEP 2: Activity

The methods that we use to communicate today vary greatly from just 50 years ago. Visit http://www.wiley.com/go/rainer/IS9e/applytheconcept to watch a YouTube video about how communication has changed. While it only goes up to 1965, you will still recognize the situations and the uses of improved communications.

STEP 3: Deliverable

Consider the various uses of communications in the video (work, personal, military, emergency, etc.). How do our modern technologies such as Internet, video, mobile, and text impact what is possible on these types of communication? Create a list of the ways that the technologies discussed in this section have changed the way we communicate on a personal level, at work, in emergencies, and in military situations and give a brief explanation of each. Discuss at least three changes for each area of communication. Submit your answers to your professor.

Apply the Concept 6.6

LEARNING OBJECTIVE 6.6

Explain the impact that collaboration network applications have had on business and everyday life.

STEP 1: Background

As you have seen, collaboration tools impact people inside and outside the organization. Some collaboration tools allow geographically separated employees to work together, while some allow those across the hall to work more effectively. Other tools just allow larger groups to brainstorm and be creative. The big idea here is that there is synergy created when people are able to work together via digital tools that overcome time and space.

STEP 2: Activity

Brightidea provides a suite of products that touches on many of the topics in the chapter. Visit http://www.wiley.com/go/rainer/IS9e/applytheconcept and watch the YouTube video that introduces the company. Then click the second link to visit the Brightidea website. There are several case studies, videos, and product explanations that will help you understand what this product offers.

STEP 3: Deliverable

As you peruse Brightidea's website, look for evidence that the software supports the topics discussed in this section: workflow, virtual collaboration, crowdsourcing, and teleconferencing. Prepare a set of presentation slides (use any tool at your disposal or at your instructor's request) that discusses the impact that collaboration network applications (such as Brightidea's products) have had on businesses. Present your slides to your class and professor.

Apply the Concept 6.7

LEARNING OBJECTIVE 6.7

Explain the impact that educational network applications have had on business and everyday life.

STEP 1: Background

Imagine that you are an expert in math. Someone hands you a piece of chalk and a small chalkboard and gives you a task of creating an educational experience to share your knowledge with other people. You would probably create a traditional classroom. Now imagine that you are not handed chalk, but are given the Internet, video capabilities, file sharing, collaboration, tools, and more! Imagine the possibilities!

STEP 2: Activity

Visit http://www.wiley.com/go/rainer/IS9e/applytheconcept and view the first video, and then visit the website about Brightspace. Be sure to look at the video about how technology has changed education. Brightspace (you may have heard it called by its former name, Desire-2Learn) is a learning management system that several schools use as a platform to offer educational activities using the digital tools available today. This platform can be used to offer e-learning experiences, distance learning opportunities, or fully virtual classrooms.

There are many discussions about how these educational network applications impact an individual's everyday life. Single parents are able to go to school using educational network applications. Working professionals are able to pursue graduate degrees online. But what about the impact on businesses?

STEP 3: Deliverable

Many organizations use these tools to facilitate mandatory training or for onboarding new employees. Visit http://www.wiley.com/go/rainer/IS9e/applytheconcept and view the second link about Brightspace's enterprise offerings. Research their site to create and discuss a list of five ways that educational network applications impact businesses.

Apply the Concept 7.1

LEARNING OBJECTIVE 7.1

Describe the six common types of electronic commerce.

STEP 1: Background

Today, there are many companies that specialize in making e-commerce a reality for small businesses. Amazon, Yahoo!, PayPal, and other entities offer services that provide everything a small business needs to sell products and accept payment over the Internet. In fact, many consumers prefer that their transactions go through these larger global companies because they trust these companies' security.

STEP 2: Activity

Visit http://www.wiley.com/go/rainer/IS9e/applytheconcept and click on the link provided for Apply the Concept 7.1. This link will take you to PayPal's website. Click on the business link at the top of the page. You will find that PayPal offers easy solutions for both businesses and customers.

STEP 3: Deliverable

Create and submit a table that lists and describes the six common types of e-commerce. Which ones are supported by PayPal and which are not? For the second group, can you explain why they are not supported? Should PayPal move into these areas of e-commerce as well?

Apply the Concept 7.2

LEARNING OBJECTIVE 7.2

Describe the various online services of business-to-consumer (B2C) commerce, along with specific examples of each.

STEP 1: Background

At this point in your "buying" career, you have probably purchased something online, visited an auction site (and possibly won a bid), and engaged in some form of online banking. Your generation is very comfortable with the retail side of e-commerce. While you were engaging in B2C e-commerce, you probably created an account with a few vendors and received some e-mail advertisements. No doubt you have also received some pop-up ads promoting products during your Internet searches. Another aspect of modern business that has changed is that companies now want you to do their advertising for them. The text refers to this development as viral marketing.

STEP 2: Activity

Imagine that you and some friends decide to start a new online thrift store. To become a member, an individual has to donate to the thrift. For every 10 items a person donates, he or she is awarded a two-month membership. However, you have no IT platform for e-commerce. After some research, you determine that Shopify is your best provider. Shopify is an e-commerce platform that enables individuals and businesses to create online stores.

Visit http://www.wiley.com/go/rainer/IS9e/applytheconcept and click on the link provided for Apply the Concept 7.2. This link will take you to Shopify's website. Near the top of the page, you will see a link to "Examples" of other providers. Look through the examples to identify ideas you would like to incorporate into your store.

STEP 3: Deliverable

After reviewing the Shopify site, prepare a presentation or a document that describes the various online services of B2C commerce provided by Shopify. Provide specific examples of services that attracted your attention and discuss how you would apply these services to your store.

Apply the Concept 7.3

LEARNING OBJECTIVE 7.3

Describe the three business models for business-to-business electronic commerce.

STEP 1: Background

Section 7.3 describes forward auctions, reverse auctions, and exchanges. Forward auctions are used when a seller is trying to reach several buyers, and reverse auctions are used when a buyer is soliciting from several sellers. In an exchange, both buyers and sellers come to a central website to quickly and easily establish a B2B relationship. Some of these websites or exchanges are for materials involved in manufacturing a product; others involve materials that help run the business.

STEP 2: Activity

Visit http://www.wiley.com/go/rainer/IS9e/applytheconcept and click on the link provided for Apply the Concept 7.3. This link will take you to one of the horizontal exchanges (an exchange for many buyers and sellers across industries) listed in the section. As you examine the available products, you should get a better understanding of the breadth of a horizontal exchange.

STEP 3: Deliverable

Describe the three business models for B2B e-commerce by comparing and contrasting them to Globalsource. Submit your description to your professor.

Apply the Concept 7.4

LEARNING OBJECTIVE 7.4

Discuss the ethical and legal issues related to electronic commerce, along with examples.

STEP 1: Background

Amazon.com is the world's largest online retailer. In fact, it is one of a kind in many ways. It competes with Apple, Google, Microsoft, and Walmart, some of the biggest names in the tech and retail universe (online and in-store).

However, for many years there was a huge controversy surrounding Amazon. Specifically, the retailer did not collect sales tax in all states. A recent Supreme Court decision in 2017 has changed that.

STEP 2: Activity

Read the article in the *Los Angeles Times* titled "Small retailers who sold through Amazon are facing a tax time bomb" from May 1, 2019. What do you think about the Supreme Court decision and California's subsequent actions?

STEP 3: Deliverable

Take a little time to consider this controversy. Then, create a list of arguments for and against California's new requirements. Make certain your argument identifies both the ethical and legal aspects of this issue.

Apply the Concept 8.1

LEARNING OBJECTIVE 8.1

Identify advantages and disadvantages of each of the four main types of wireless transmission media.

STEP 1: Background

As stated in this section, mobile communication has changed our world more rapidly and dramatically than any other technology. Although several wireless transmission media are available, rarely will one technology meet all of a business's needs by itself. Vislink is a global technology firm that collects and delivers high-quality video broadcasts. These broadcasts are utilized in sports, news, law enforcement, and other areas. Although Vislink specializes in video, they rely on multiple mobile transmission media to obtain live feeds from multiple locations. Rajant is one of the providers that Vislink has utilized for their wireless media.

STEP 2: Activity

Visit http://www.wiley.com/go/rainer/IS9e/applytheconcept and click on the link provided for Apply the Concept 8.1. There are three links. One will take you to Vislink's website, another to Rajant's website, and the last to a YouTube video in which Vislink demonstrates how they can provide a live video feed to law enforcement agencies using Rajant's wireless mesh network.

STEP 3: Deliverable

As you watch the video, listen for the wireless transmission media they mention and pay attention to how many of them are discussed in this section of the book. Write and submit a summary of your findings that highlights the advantages and disadvantages of the transmission media types and explains why they were or were not used in the product that Vislink and Rajant demonstrated.

Apply the Concept 8.2

LEARNING OBJECTIVE 8.2

Explain how businesses can use technology employed by short-range, medium-range, and long-range networks, respectively.

STEP 1: Background

Many cellular phones today, including both Apple and Android devices, contain multiple radios. These include cellular, Bluetooth, Wi-Fi, infrared, GPS, and NFC chips. With all of these radios embedded in a small mobile device, the possibilities of connectivity are nearly endless because one device can utilize short-range, mid-range, and wide-range connectivity.

STEP 2: Activity

Visit http://www.wiley.com/go/rainer/IS9e/applytheconcept and view the video demonstration by Serial IO. There is also a link to their website, where you will find several examples of wireless products intended for business use. Although most of these products are short-range devices, you must assume they will be connected to some mid-range and/or wide-range wireless network. In fact, these devices support Windows, Mac, Android, iOS, BlackBerry, and other platforms.

STEP 3: Deliverable

Based on the video and the Serial IO website, create and submit a table to explain how businesses can use the technologies employed by short-range, medium-range, and long-range networks to achieve their business purposes.

Apply the Concept 8.3

LEARNING OBJECTIVE 8.3

Provide a specific example of how each of the five major m-commerce applications can benefit a business.

STEP 1: Background

Section 8.3 introduced you to five of the most popular mobile commerce applications. These applications are location-based applications, financial services, intrabusiness applications, accessing information, and telemetry. Although you may not have had experience with each of these, it is likely that you have experienced some.

STEP 2: Activity

Read (or reread) the section and consider the following questions related to your personal experiences with mobile commerce: Do you use a mobile wallet? Has using a mobile wallet replaced your traditional wallet? What location-based services do you allow on your mobile device? Do you freely share your location, or are you more private? What type of intrabusiness applications do you utilize as an employee or customer of an organization? What type of information do you access on a regular basis? Do you utilize any telemetry information (such as a wireless connection to your vehicle computer to record information on your mobile phone)?

STEP 3: Deliverable

Based on your answers to the questions in Step 2, build a table that provides a brief discussion of how each of the five major m-commerce applications benefit businesses and provide your personal experiences with each.

Apply the Concept 8.4

LEARNING OBJECTIVE 8.4

Describe the Internet of Things, along with examples of how organizations can utilize the Internet of Things.

STEP 1: Background

Section 8.4 has introduced the concept of the Internet of Things (IoT) and provided several examples. There is no doubt that the IoT will continue to grow and shape our lives. Many industries will change from reactive (correcting problems after they happen) to proactive (acting to prevent problems before they happen based on IoT data).

STEP 2: Activity

Visit http://www.wiley.com/go/rainer/IS9e/applytheconcept and watch the YouTube video. It describes examples of personal applications of IoT and professional uses of IoT. After watching the video, let your mind wander into the future to a time when everything is connected via the

IoT—not just the devices mentioned in the video (like your car) but also your coffee pot, bed, clothes, closet door, front door, toothbrush, and so much more.

STEP 3: Deliverable

Write a paragraph or two to first describe the IoT, and then provide current examples of how it has impacted your life and is currently making a difference for businesses and industries. Finally, provide a few ideas of how the IoT will shape the future.

Apply the Concept 9.1

LEARNING OBJECTIVE 9.1

Describe five Web 2.0 tools and the two major types of Web 2.0 sites.

STEP 1: Background

This section differentiates Web 1.0, which consists of places to visit, from Web 2.0, where users interact and share information. Whether or not you have thought of these media in these terms, you are familiar with these differences. No doubt you are much more accustomed to Web 2.0, and businesses have begun to integrate information sharing into their public sites.

STEP 2: Activity

Visit http://www.wiley.com/go/rainer/IS9e/applytheconcept and click on the link for Apply the Concept 9.1. This video provides a valuable overview of Web 2.0 technologies. Take notes of the various features that Web 2.0 makes available, and then click on the second link. This link will take you to a CNN Money Web page that provides a rank-order list of the Fortune 500 companies. Visit the websites of the top 10 firms and identify the Web 2.0 technologies they employ on their site.

STEP 3: Deliverable

Create a table that displays the following information about 5 of the top 10 companies on the CNN Money rankings:

- The company's name
- The company's rank
- The industry (e.g., retail, consulting services, communications)
- A description of the Web 2.0 technologies/applications that each company uses
- A description of the Web 2.0 tools the company does not use

Submit your table to your professor.

Apply the Concept 9.2

LEARNING OBJECTIVE 9.2

Describe the benefits and risks of social commerce to companies.

STEP 1: Background

Collaborative consumption has been fueled by social networks because it allows owners to share their goods with those who would rather rent something than permanently own it. Sharing also makes items cheaper to own because the cost of ownership is spread across many users. The sharing economy has changed drastically in recent years as companies like Uber and Airbnb continue to gain in popularity, and social media has driven this rise.

STEP 2: Activity

Visit https://davidbuckingham.net/ and read his 2017 critique, "Media and the Sharing Economy." Now think about how you can apply these lessons to bike sharing. Look up a company called Citi Bike.

STEP 3: Deliverable

Many of these companies, including Citi Bike, got their start in big cities. Why do you think they started in such heavily populated areas? What advantages would a collaborative consumption business model have in a heavily populated area? What disadvantages would they face? In what ways might a college campus be a prime location to introduce users to collaborative consumption services? Create a table that compares the advantages and disadvantages of collaborative consumption for the biking industry. Submit your table to your instructor.

Apply the Concept 9.3

LEARNING OBJECTIVE 9.3

Identify the methods used for shopping socially.

STEP 1: Background

Section 9.3 defines shopping socially as taking the key aspects of social networks (e.g., groups, reviews, discussions) and applying them to shopping. This phenomenon is not new. People have shopped socially for years, through general conversation.

Today, most consumers conduct a lot of research before they make a purchase by reading reviews posted by other customers. Recently, however, the validity of these reviews has been questioned. As you learn about social shopping, you should also become aware of the potential fraud that takes place online.

STEP 2: Activity

Visit http://www.wiley.com/go/rainer/IS9e/applytheconcept and click on the link for Apply the Concept 9.3. This link will take you to an article from the *New York Times* and one from the *Denver Post*. Both articles deal with the issue of falsified recommendations and ratings. Talk to some of your classmates about this topic and record their feedback. How did they respond to the fact that product ratings may not be legitimate? Ask them the following questions:

- What star rating do you rely on when you are considering a product?
- Do you read reviews or simply notice the number of stars?
- If you read reviews, do you read only the good ones, only the bad ones, or a mixture of both?
- Do you rely on reviews more than a third-party organization such as Consumer Reports?

STEP 3: Deliverable

Considering the material you have read and your conversations with your classmates, identify various methods of shopping socially and discuss the role that trust plays in each method. Prepare a paper or presentation for your professor documenting what you have learned.

Apply the Concept 9.4

LEARNING OBJECTIVE 9.4

Discuss innovative ways to use social networking sites for advertising and market research.

STEP 1: Background

Section 9.4 presented the major uses of social computing in advertising and market research. Social advertising is simply a way of presenting information to potential customers via a social platform. Social market research makes use of these same social platforms to examine the ongoing communication between the company and its customer community for information that the company can use to improve products or services.

STEP 2: Activity

Visit http://www.wiley.com/go/rainer/IS9e/applytheconcept and find the two links. First, read the article called "20 Companies You Should Be Following on Social Media." Some of these companies are not specifically related to advertising or market research, but you will still enjoy learning about them. Next, read the article on Digimind.com about the innovative ways people are using social media as a rich pool of information.

STEP 3: Deliverable

After reviewing the examples in the articles linked in Step 2, prepare a discussion of the top three innovative ways that these companies are using social networking for advertising and the top three innovative ways that companies are using the information available on social networks as a mechanism for learning about their customers. Submit your discussion to your instructor.

Apply the Concept 9.5

LEARNING OBJECTIVE 9.5

Describe how social computing improves customer service.

STEP 1: Background

Social customer relationship management involves using social networks to maintain customer loyalty. One company that employs this strategy quite skillfully is ZAGG (Zealous About Great Gadgets; www.zagg.com). ZAGG makes and sells accessories for mobile devices such as smartphones and tablets. To help sell its products, the company has developed one of the best social customer relationship management plans around.

When ZAGG develops a new product, it not only posts notes about the product on its social networking page, but it also involves customers in the process. For example, when ZAGG was releasing its ZAGGFolio for the iPad, the company allowed fans to vote on the colors of the new product.

ZAGG is also proficient at monitoring the social network for product-related issues. It is not uncommon for a customer to complain and then receive feedback from a ZAGG employee. Not only does the company retain that individual customer, but it also develops a sense of trust with all of its customers, who are confident they would receive the same treatment.

STEP 2: Activity

Visit http://www.wiley.com/go/rainer/IS9e/applytheconcept and click on the link to ZAGG's website. At the bottom of the page you will find a link to all of the company's social networks. Visit their Facebook page and review their timeline. Search for customer complaints and for how the company deals with them. Did you find a customer representative present on the social networking site? Does the site offer any competitions? Polls? Give-aways? Can you reverse-engineer the company's social customer relationship management methodology?

STEP 3: Deliverable

Imagine that you are a marketing manager, and you have been selected to present a report to the president to describe how social computing improves customer service. Create the outline that you would use to make your points and present it to the class and to your instructor.

Apply the Concept 9.6

LEARNING OBJECTIVE 9.6

Discuss different ways in which human resource managers make use of social computing.

STEP 1: Background

Social human resource management is redefining the ways we search and apply for jobs and make hiring decisions. Going digital was a natural step, but it was also an awkward one. When position announcements went from the bulletin board and local newspaper to Monster.com, the number of positions and applicants exploded. We are so connected today that it is impossible to go back. After you graduate, you will no doubt use social networks to find and apply for jobs.

STEP 2: Activity

Visit LinkedIn, a professional social network. Create a profile that includes the college you currently attend. Connect to your classmates as they also complete this activity. You never know when you will need to call on one of these individuals.

Next, search the Web for "job search websites," and see which ones will allow you to connect with your LinkedIn profile. As you connect with these professional sites, consider the differences between a professional and a personal social network.

STEP 3: Deliverable

In a paper, discuss the various ways in which human resources managers can make use of social computing and how you can best present yourself online. Present your paper to your instructor.

Apply the Concept 10.1

LEARNING OBJECTIVE 10.1

Explain the purpose of transaction processing systems.

STEP 1: Background

Section 10.1 has explained that transaction processing systems (TPS) capture data and then automatically transmit those data to the various functional area systems. Most TPS are designed based on an organization's existing processes. To better understand how a TPS operates, you should consider the flow of data through the student application process.

STEP 2: Activity

Visit http://www.wiley.com/go/rainer/IS9e/applytheconcept and click on the link provided for Apply the Concept 10.1. This link will take you to a Web page that describes the process of creating data flow diagrams (DFDs). The page uses the example of a college student application to demonstrate the flow of data through a university. Review this description and identify the transactions that take place throughout the process.

STEP 3: Deliverable

Consider your student application process. Are there any pieces of your application that you feel were handled differently than the example described? Prepare a short description of the application process described in the video and discuss the purpose of the TPS for this process.

Apply the Concept 10.2

LEARNING OBJECTIVE 10.2

Explain the types of support that information systems can provide for each functional area of the organization.

STEP 1: Background

Section 10.2 introduced you to the concept of functional area information systems (FAIS). As you can see, every area of business has processes in place that define how data are stored, analyzed, applied, and distributed across the area. For example, inventory management is easy to manage with a computer system because it involves simply keeping track of your materials and products. However, when you integrate inventory management with production and operations management (POM), you have a very effective functional system that supports the internal production line.

STEP 2: Activity

Visit http://www.wiley.com/go/rainer/IS9e/applytheconcept and click on the link provided for Apply the Concept 10.2. You will be directed to four websites that present real-world examples of the information systems discussed in this section. Read over them, and look for any specific material that you can tie back into the concepts covered in the chapter.

STEP 3: Deliverable

Prepare a report that explains the types of support the IS reviewed in Step 2 can provide for each functional area within an organization. Submit your report to your instructor.

Apply the Concept 10.3

LEARNING OBJECTIVE 10.3

Identify advantages and drawbacks to businesses implementing an enterprise resource planning system.

STEP 1: Background

Section 10.3 explained that enterprise resource planning (ERP) works toward removing information silos within an organization by implementing a single system to support all of the functional areas. One example of an ERP system is SAP Business One. SAP is an industry-leading ERP company. In this activity, you will consider the advantages and drawbacks of using an ERP such as SAP.

STEP 2: Activity

Visit http://www.wiley.com/go/rainer/IS9e/applytheconcept and click on the link provided for Apply the Concept 10.3. This link will take you to a YouTube video titled *SAP-Business-One.wmv* by user angeltechdotit. As you watch the video, consider how many departments the representative would have to contact to find the information that SAP Business One can present in just a few moments. If this organization operated out of silos, the representative would have to take extensive notes, visit multiple departments, and call the customer back at a later time with the answers.

STEP 3: Deliverable

After considering how complicated it would be for OEC to handle the customer's requests without an ERP, identify the advantages and drawbacks to OEC of using the SAP Business One ERP. Submit your thoughts to your professor.

Apply the Concept 10.4

LEARNING OBJECTIVE 10.4

Describe the three main business processes supported by ERP systems.

STEP 1: Background

We have discussed reports that you can receive from TPS, FAIS, and ERP systems earlier in this chapter. In particular, these reports truly are the power of an ERP. Getting the right information to the right person at the right time to make the right decision is the underlying purpose for installing and utilizing an ERP. Recall from earlier in the text that managers need IT decision-support tools because decisions are becoming more complex, there is less time to make decisions, there are more options, and the costs of making incorrect decisions are increasing.

STEP 2: Activity

Visit http://www.wiley.com/go/rainer/IS9e/applytheconcept and click on the link provided for Apply the Concept 10.4. This link will take you to a YouTube video titled *Phoebus ERP— Customized Dashboard*. This video will introduce you to the dashboard tool provided by Phoebus, which individual users can customize to provide the specific information they need. This type of dashboard pulls together the many reports you have learned about in this chapter. As you watch the video, look for examples of the three major types of processes (procurement, fulfillment, and production) that are supported by ERP systems as discussed in this section.

STEP 3: Deliverable

Discuss the three major types of processes and the ways that an ERP can support them. Use what you learned in the dashboard video to discuss the types of information that could be presented in a dashboard to support these processes.

Apply the Concept 11.1

LEARNING OBJECTIVE 11.1

Identify the primary functions of both customer relationship management (CRM) and collaborative CRM strategies.

STEP 1: Background

Section 11.1 introduced the concept of a CRM system, and it suggested that it is better to focus on relationships than on transactions. The idea is that relationships create transactions, so if you grow the relationship, you keep the customers (and the transactions)!

STEP 2: Activity

Visit http://www.wiley.com/go/rainer/IS9e/applytheconcept and click on the link provided for Apply the Concept 11.1. This link will take you to a YouTube video that illustrates how Recreational Equipment Incorporated (REI) uses CRM to service their customers.

STEP 3: Deliverable

In a report, identify the primary functions of both customer relationship management (CRM) and collaborative CRM strategies. What are REI's approaches to CRM? Can you make any suggestions to help them improve? Submit your report to your professor.

Apply the Concept 11.2

LEARNING OBJECTIVE 11.2

Describe how businesses might utilize applications of each of the two major components of operational CRM systems.

STEP 1: Background

Section 11.2 introduced you to the concept of customer-facing and customer-touching CRM applications, the two major components of operational CRM systems. Many organizations use a combination of both types of systems to establish, develop, and maintain relationships with consumers. This activity will help you to see these systems in action when you do business on a website or in a brick-and-mortar business.

STEP 2: Activity

Visit a physical store where you like to shop (or recall a recent visit and discuss it with some friends), and visit the store's website. Make certain to select a company that has both an Internet site and a physical store so you can compare the two channels.

As you walked through the store, did you notice any cues that could tie a customer to a CRM? Did the business have a customer loyalty program? Are there any significant advantages to joining the program? Is the in-store membership tied to anything online? If so, how? Or, does the store seem to have separate in-store and online memberships?

STEP 3: Deliverable

After considering the points mentioned in Step 2, describe how businesses might utilize both the customer-facing and customer-touching applications of a CRM to integrate the online and traditional shopping experiences. Prepare a report and submit it to your instructor.

Apply the Concept 11.3

LEARNING OBJECTIVE 11.3

Explain the advantages and disadvantages of mobile CRM systems, on-demand CRM systems, open-source CRM systems, social CRM systems, and real-time CRM systems.

STEP 1: Background

Section 11.3 has outlined different CRM systems—not operational or analytical, but, instead, the different ways you can actually implement a CRM system. For example, you can run mobile CRM, open-source CRM, on-demand CRM (cloud), and more. You will have most—if not all—of these options with any system you plan to implement!

STEP 2: Activity

Visit http://www.wiley.com/go/rainer/IS9e/applytheconcept and click on the links provided for Apply the Concept 11.3. One link will take you to a YouTube video that describes an on-demand CRM system (Salesforce). Another will take you to a video that highlights an open-source CRM

(Sugar CRM). The final link will illustrate a hybrid approach, Sales Cloud (mobile-cloud CRM). Watch these videos, paying special attention to the advantages and disadvantages of each approach. The advantages will be easy to spot (these are promotional videos). The disadvantages of each one will become obvious as you compare the advantages of the others because you may notice particular functions that system one cannot perform but the others can.

STEP 3: Deliverable

Build a table that highlights the advantages and disadvantages of each approach. Do the differences reside in the capabilities of the software or in the user experience? Submit your table to your instructor.

Apply the Concept 11.4

LEARNING OBJECTIVE 11.4

Describe the three components and the three flows of a supply chain.

STEP 1: Background

Section 11.4 focused on supply chain flows, materials, and "positions" (upstream, internal, and downstream). It is important to understand how products move in the supply chain because data move along with them every step of the way. In fact, the data that travel with materials and products are more important to the efficiency of the operation than the products themselves!

STEP 2: Activity

Visit http://www.wiley.com/go/rainer/IS9e/applytheconcept and click on the link provided for Apply the Concept 11.4. This link will take you to a YouTube video titled *Module 1: What Is Supply Chain Management? (ASU-WPC-SCM)* by user W. P. Carey School. As you watch the video, consider the data that would be transferred with each product movement within the bottled water supply chain. Certain types of data, such as inventory updates, shipment information, quality checks, and supplier information, would deal just with the bottled water itself. In addition, there will be HR information, employee data, and machine data from the internal organization as well as from all of the suppliers!

STEP 3: Deliverable

Using the example you learned about in Step 2, describe the three components and the three flows of a water bottle supply chain in a report. Submit your report to your instructor.

Apply the Concept 11.5

LEARNING OBJECTIVE 11.5

Identify popular strategies to solving different challenges of supply chains.

STEP 1: Background

Section 11.5 explained that managing a supply chain is not a simple task because consumer demand is so uncertain. Although organizations can forecast demand with some accuracy, actual demand almost inevitably will differ from the organizations' predictions. To manage demand fluctuations, organizations are moving toward JIT (just-in-time) inventory models. These data must be shared in a timely fashion if organizations are to remain flexible and capable of adapting to consumer demand.

STEP 2: Activity

Visit http://www.wiley.com/go/rainer/IS9e/applytheconcept and click on the links provided for Apply the Concept 11.5. The first link will take you to an article that examines how the bullwhip effect wreaks havoc on the supply chain, and the second will take you to an activity in which you will manage a supply chain for beer. This latter task might not sound difficult until you consider that there are serious timing issues due to the perishable nature of the product. The simulation begins with your supply chain in equilibrium, but it then suddenly shifts. Your job is to put things back in order!

As you work through the simulation, pay attention to how much information needs to be shared across the supply chain to make the entire operation function smoothly.

STEP 3: Deliverable

Based on your experience, discuss how the popular strategies for dealing with supply chain challenges (building inventory, JIT inventory, vendor-managed inventory) would or would not work for this product. Write a report and submit it to your instructor.

Apply the Concept 11.6

LEARNING OBJECTIVE 11.6

Explain the utility of each of the three major technologies that support supply chain management.

STEP 1: Background

Electronic data interchange (EDI) is defined in this section as a communication standard that enables business partners to exchange routine documents, such as purchasing orders, electronically. You should understand the need for electronic sharing of information if you completed the activity in Apply the Concept 11.6. That activity required you to manage a supply chain on your own. Imagine the challenge of performing this function without being able to share data electronically!

STEP 2: Activity

Visit http://www.wiley.com/go/rainer/IS9e/applytheconcept and click on the links provided for Apply the Concept 11.6. The link will take you to a YouTube video titled *What is EDI* by user Hitek Equipment. You will also link to an article that defines EDI and discusses some of its standards.

As you watch the video, pay attention to the important components that are necessary to share information between two organizations. Then, consider the fact that suppliers rarely operate in only a single supply chain. In fact, suppliers typically have multiple customers, which means they are sharing information with many organizations via EDI.

STEP 3: Deliverable

Based on the content of this section and the video you watched in Step 2, explain the utility of each of the three major technologies (EDI, extranets, and corporate portals) that support supply chain management. In other words, how might these technologies interact to enable the participating parties to exchange data? Put your explanation in a report and submit it to your instructor.

Apply the Concept 12.1

LEARNING OBJECTIVE 12.1

Use a decision support framework to demonstrate how technology supports managerial decision making at each phase of the decision-making process.

STEP 1: Background

If you look back through this section, you will see that Henry Mintzberg's 1973 book, *The Nature of Managerial Work*, was referenced when the three basic roles of a manager were presented. This text focuses on the decisional role because that is the one that is most supported by information systems. However, Mintzberg's work goes well beyond the decisional role.

STEP 2: Activity

Visit http://www.wiley.com/go/rainer/IS9e/applytheconcept and click on the link provided for Apply the Concept 12.1. The link will take you to a YouTube video titled *Data-Driven Decision Making* by user Minnetonka Schools. This video mentions a strategic plan, operational control, and decisional control. As you view the video, make certain to watch for these key points, and pay special attention to how they are supported by data.

STEP 3: Deliverable

Write a short paper (a couple of paragraphs is plenty) for your professor that will identify the phases in the decision-making process for Minnetonka Schools. Be sure to demonstrate how technology supports their decision making in each phase.

Apply the Concept 12.2

LEARNING OBJECTIVE 12.2

Describe each phase of the business analytics process.

STEP 1: Background

In this section you learned that BA is a concept that encompasses everything from the collection, analysis, and dissemination of data to the technology tools that enable this process to take place. In particular, organizations use BA to support the following:

- Specific departmental needs
- Organizational change

STEP 2: Activity

There are several companies that provide data management and BA tools to help make decisions. Two of these companies are Avitas and Intricity. Visit http://www.wiley.com/go/rainer/IS9e/applytheconcept to watch a short YouTube video about BA by each of these companies. While you watch, look for examples of how their tools support departments, enterprises, and/or organizational change.

STEP 3: Deliverable

Write a short description of how Avitas and Intricity help users work through the BA process (see Figure 12.3). Try to show how the process is supported, but also be aware that there might be gaps. Make note of any areas for improvement as well, if you find any.

Apply the Concept 12.3

LEARNING OBJECTIVE 12.3

Describe each of the various analytics tools and examples of their uses.

STEP 1: Background

This section explained that data are more abundant today than ever before. One thing we are learning is that there is much we can know that we do not know. In fact, there are many questions we are not even aware we should be asking! For such questions, we use multidimensional analysis and data-mining tools to extract valuable insights from the data. When we know the questions, we frequently employ decision support systems to run sensitivity, what-if, or goal-seeking analysis.

STEP 2: Activity

Consider your university. Various departments focus on teaching, student academic support, financial aid, admissions, recruitment, administration, and much more. Each of these departments has its special purpose, but overall the enterprise exists to support student learning.

Visit your university's website, and look for these various functions. What can you learn about their purpose? Based on this knowledge, what can you imply about the types of BA applications they might use?

STEP 3: Deliverable

Within the context of higher education, describe the various tools and provide an example of how each could be used to support your campus. Submit your response to your instructor.

Apply the Concept 12.4

LEARNING OBJECTIVE 12.4

Provide a definition and a use case example for predictive analytics.

STEP 1: Background

According to the text, predictive analytics attempts to detect patterns that can be used to predict, or forecast, future events. While trends change, when you look at them over time, they can show periods of growth and decline. This information is invaluable to managers who are required to make decisions about resource allocation to prepare for the future.

STEP 2: Activity

Imagine that you work for a fast-food restaurant. You have been there for a long time, but the new boss is just figuring things out. Last week, your boss stopped you and asked for some help planning labor for various times of the day and days of the week. Obviously, once the crowd arrives it is too late to bring in more labor. But the restaurant cannot afford to keep a full staff all of the time. What kind of analytics could help?

STEP 3: Deliverable

Put together a short report for your boss that defines predictive analytics and explains how you intend to use them in the restaurant. Use the example above to give context to the solution. Discuss ways that data from past weeks, months, and years can help inform patterns that can be used to determine labor needs for the future.

Apply the Concept 12.5

LEARNING OBJECTIVE 12.5

Provide a definition and a use case example for descriptive analytics, predictive analytics, and prescriptive analytics.

STEP 1: Background

Section 12.5 discusses descriptive, predictive, and prescriptive analytics. Descriptive analytics describe what has happened, predictive analytics predict what might happen, and prescriptive analytics prescribe probabilities to future outcomes based on future activities.

STEP 2: Activity

Visit http://www.wiley.com/go/rainer/IS9e/applytheconcept and click on the link provided for Apply the Concept 12.5. This link will take you to a video that describes prescriptive analytics to help a rock climber determine the best path to the top based on certain decisions. While this is a simple example, it illustrates the need to think past the next choice and to see how this choice will impact the overall probability of reaching the desired outcome.

STEP 3: Deliverable

Based on the video and any of your own Web research, describe and give examples of how a rock climber might use descriptive analytics, predictive analytics, and prescriptive analytics to determine the best path to the goal.

Apply the Concept 12.6

LEARNING OBJECTIVE 12.6

Identify and discuss two examples of presentation tools.

STEP 1: Background

Visual aids have been around for a long time. In fact, most of our communication is through visual aids. Letters represent sounds and from them, we can put together words and meaning. Additionally, today a growing number of messages are sent primarily using emojis! Liking pictures and images on Instagram or similar platform is a regular activity for many people. Sharing data is no different. Graphs and charts have been used for years to help viewers quickly grasp the meaning of data.

STEP 2: Activity

Imagine that you manage a children's clothing store. Each month you make decisions on products, quantities, prices, timing of sales, and much more. What kind of information do you think you would you like to see? Sales by department? Sales over time? Product line comparisons? What else?

STEP 3: Deliverable

Sketch an example of a dashboard that would provide at least six visual aids to understand the data you might want to see as a clothing store manager.

Apply the Concept 13.1

LEARNING OBJECTIVE 13.1

Discuss the different cost–benefit analyses that companies must take into account when formulating an IT strategic plan.

STEP 1: Background

You may not realize it, but you perform cost–benefit analyses all the time. Imagine that you want to go to the beach for the weekend, but you decide not to because you would have to drive eight hours each way and therefore would not get to spend much time there. In this case, the costs outweigh the benefits. However, if you could extend your stay another day, then the benefits might outweigh the costs. The difficulty in this example is that the benefits are difficult to measure. A cost–benefit analysis is designed to quantify all of the key elements, and sometimes there are subjective benefits for which there are no clear-cut numerical values.

STEP 2: Activity

Visit http://www.wiley.com/go/rainer/IS9e/applytheconcept and click on the links provided for Apply the Concept 13.1. You will watch three short videos that offer a financial explanation for net present value (NPV), return on investment (ROI), and break-even analysis. The business case approach is not a financial approach, and it does not require further explanation.

STEP 3: Deliverable

Imagine you are creating a website to sell promotional items. You have no experience developing a site, so you will have to pay someone to do this for you. You research this service and discover that the site you have in mind will cost $3,500. (For this example, assume there are no monthly hosting fees.) This design will last five years, after which you will need to update it. You anticipate that you can make $500 in year 1, $750 in year 2, $750 in year 3, $1,000 in year 4, and $1,500 in year 5 from the site. Calculate the NPV, ROI, and break-even analysis for this case, and discuss which metric is most helpful. Also, explain how a business case analysis would be helpful beyond what the numbers provide. Prepare a document with your figures and present it to your instructor.

Apply the Concept 13.2

LEARNING OBJECTIVE 13.2

Discuss the four business decisions that companies must make when they acquire new applications.

STEP 1: Background

Section 13.2 discusses the many options available to acquire information systems. One of the more popular methods is software-as-a-service (SaaS). SaaS is popular because it eliminates the need for the company purchasing the software to maintain the hardware on which the software will run. They simply need an Internet connection to access the software from the host company.

STEP 2: Activity

Visit http://www.wiley.com/go/rainer/IS9e/applytheconcept and click on the links provided for Apply the Concept 13.2. There are two videos linked there that illustrate SaaS. As you watch these videos, consider the types of hardware that are required on both sides of the relationship. Also, give some thought to the legal nature of the relationship, given that the data will likely reside with the service provider.

STEP 3: Deliverable

Imagine that a company has decided to use an SaaS model to acquire a new piece of software. Prepare a paper discussing the four business decisions they have made in light of this type of acquisition. Submit your paper to your instructor.

Apply the Concept 13.3

LEARNING OBJECTIVE 13.3

Enumerate the primary tasks and the importance of each of the six processes involved in the systems development life cycle.

STEP 1: Background

The systems development life cycle uses a very systematic approach in which each stage builds on work completed at an earlier stage. It is an excellent model to follow, assuming that the right decisions are made at each stage of the SDLC and are appropriately communicated to the next stage of the SDLC.

STEP 2: Activity

Visit http://www.wiley.com/go/rainer/IS9e/applytheconcept and watch the video titled *Software Development Life Cycle*, which is linked to Apply the Concept 13.3. The video conveys a realistic (though perhaps a bit pessimistic) view of how poor communication can severely damage the software-development process.

STEP 3: Deliverable

After watching the video, build an outline that specifies the primary tasks and the importance of each of the six processes involved in the SDLC. Make certain to discuss the importance of communication from one step to the next.

Apply the Concept 13.4

LEARNING OBJECTIVE 13.4

Describe alternative development methods and the tools that augment development methods.

STEP 1: Background

The systems development life cycle is a very thorough method of development. However, it is also very time consuming and expensive. Section 13.4 discusses several alternative methods. Joint application design, rapid application development, and agile development are used in conjunction with several tools for systems development.

STEP 2: Activity

Visit http://www.wiley.com/go/rainer/IS9e/applytheconcept and click on the link provided for Apply the Concept 13.4. This link will take you to a Vimeo about prototyping. Imagine that you are a developer of iPhone apps. At lunch the other day, someone mentioned a very cool idea for a new camera app that would enable users to take pictures simply by opening the app and saying "click" rather than having to push a button.

Describe the idea to a couple of friends to develop a list of user needs and preferences. From this list, make a sketch of the app. Then let the same people review your design and make suggestions. Use the second set of suggestions to create your "final" drawings of the app.

STEP 3: Deliverable

Write a short report documenting the alternative development methods you have used and how the tools discussed in this section might help you to actually develop your app. Be sure to mention how you might use different tools at different stages of development.

Apply the Concept 14.1

LEARNING OBJECTIVE 14.1

Explain the potential value and the potential limitations of artificial intelligence.

STEP 1: Background

This section introduced you to several applications of artificial intelligence. One of these applications was the Google self-driving car. This innovation presents a scenario in which technology could potentially greatly enhance the safety of motorists, pedestrians, and passengers. However, there are also significant risks posed by turning over the keys to the computer.

STEP 2: Activity

Visit YouTube and watch the video titled *Self-Driving Car Test: Steve Mahan* that introduces the Google self-driving car. Although this innovation is very exciting, it can also be very scary! While you are watching the video, imagine the advantages and disadvantages of this type of intelligent system. Would it function best as a "pilot" or a very helpful "copilot"?

STEP 3: Deliverable

Build a table that displays both the potential value (advantages) and the potential limitations (disadvantages) of artificial intelligence for different scenarios illustrated in the example below.

	Advantages	Disadvantages
Tired driver		
Distracted driver (texting)		
Sick/stressed driver		
Ambulance driver		
School bus driver		
Soccer mom, minivan driver		

Apply the Concept 14.2

LEARNING OBJECTIVE 14.2

Provide use case examples of expert systems, machine learning systems, deep learning systems, and neural networks.

STEP 1: Background

Throughout much of human history, expertise was transferred from a master to an apprentice through years of training. Only after the apprentice had mastered all of the "tricks of the trade" was he or she considered ready to perform on his or her own. We still employ a similar system for doctors, who must participate in a residency program under the guidance of the resident doctor before they can begin their own practice. This approach is not appropriate, however, for many non–life-threatening situations. In some cases, being able to make an expert decision is simply a matter of having access to the experts' knowledge and experiences. If this knowledge can be captured in a computer-based information system, then it can be distributed for other people to use in similar scenarios. Although this sounds great, there are many challenges to developing this type of system.

STEP 2: Activity

Visit http://www.wiley.com/go/rainer/IS9e/applytheconcept and watch the YouTube video linked for Apply the Concept 14.2. This video will show you a short demonstration of an expert cooking system. The video mentions that you are responsible for building and testing an expert system, but that is not part of this activity. As you watch the video, pay particular attention to the miscommunication between the cook and the computer. You will find this interaction to be quite comical.

STEP 3: Deliverable

Based on the video and material in this section, provide examples of the benefits, applications, and limitations of using artificial intelligence in the world of cooking. Create a Word document to submit to your instructor.

Apply the Concept 14.3

LEARNING OBJECTIVE 14.3

Describe the structure of a neural network and discuss how that structure contributes to the purpose of neural networks in machine learning.

STEP 1: Background

This section describes the structure of a neural network using terms such as nodes, synapses, weights, biases, and functions. This structure parallels the structure of the human brain, allowing computer systems to recognize patterns and create a means for identifying and predicting the future.

STEP 2: Activity

Reread the section examples about the convolutional neural networks. Pay special attention to the portion regarding the mistakes the system made. The system appeared to be learning and doing a good job identifying wolves and huskies. But in the end, it was not accurate at all.

STEP 3: Deliverable

Imagine a scenario where artificial intelligence is used to identify potential thieves. The system is given a series of videos, some of which include theft and some of which do not. What kind of potential problems do you anticipate? What limitations could exist in the outcomes? Answer these questions in an email to your instructor.

Apply the Concept 14.4

LEARNING OBJECTIVE 14.4

Provide use case examples (other than the ones in the text) of computer vision, natural language processing, robotics, image recognition, and intelligent agents.

STEP 1: Background

This section presented many interesting examples of AI. However, there are new technologies being developed each day. As hard as authors try, the time it takes to print a textbook always leaves us a few months behind the latest and greatest examples of technology.

STEP 2: Activity

Use your favorite search engine and look up each of the use cases presented in the text (computer vision, natural language processing, robotics, speech recognition, and intelligent agents) and see what companies are making headlines in these areas.

STEP 3: Deliverable

Build a table like the one below and include the new examples you have discovered.

Technology	Company	Product/Progress
Computer Vision		
Natural Language Processing		
Robotics		
Speech Recognition		
Intelligent Agents		

Apply the Concept 14.5

LEARNING OBJECTIVE 14.5

Provide use case examples (other than the ones in the text) of artificial intelligence applications in accounting, finance, marketing, production and operations management, human resource management, and management information systems.

STEP 1: Background

This section presented many interesting examples of the functional use of artificial intelligence. However, as is stated in Apply the Concept from Section 14.4, new technologies are being developed each day. As hard as authors try, the time it takes to print a textbook always leaves us a few months behind the latest and greatest examples of technology.

STEP 2: Activity

Use your favorite search engine and look up each of the use cases presented in the text (accounting, finance, marketing, production and operations management, human resource management, and management information systems) and see what companies are making headlines in these areas.

STEP 3: Deliverable

Build a table like the one below and include the new examples you have discovered.

Technology	Company	Product/Progress
Accounting		
Finance		
Marketing		
Production and Operations Management		
Human Resource Management		
Management Information Systems		

Apply the Concept Technology Guide 1.1

LEARNING OBJECTIVE TG 1.1

Identify the major hardware components of a computer system.

STEP 1: Background

At a basic level, a computer is a computer, just like an automobile is an automobile. The purpose of the automobile drives its size, design, build, price, and much more. Similarly, the purpose of a computer dictates its build requirements, storage capability, and price.

STEP 2: Activity

Imagine a colleague has been asked to create high-quality training videos for internal purposes. The project will take 6 months to complete and she has been given a $1,500 budget for purchasing any needed equipment. After searching, she finds out that a 4K webcam will cost $150 and a high-quality USB microphone will cost $125. This leaves $1,225 for a new computer. Think of which features will be most important for your colleague's uses and how they will function in conjunction with the webcam and microphone.

STEP 3: Deliverable

Review the definitions of central processing and primary and secondary storage that are detailed in this tech guide. Then visit Dell's website and customize a computer that would meet your friend's needs and stay within the budget. Write a memo to your professor describing your selection with a justification for the choices.

Apply the Concept Technology Guide 1.2

LEARNING OBJECTIVE TG 1.2

Discuss strategic issues that link hardware design to business strategy.

STEP 1: Background

In the modern business environment, computer hardware components are inextricably linked to business strategy. Put simply, computers are tools that allow businesses to automate some transactions and make others more efficient. As technology evolves, businesses need to evolve the ways they use that technology to execute their business strategies. The generally accepted rule is that technology should *not* drive business strategy, but business strategy *must* consider how the organization can implement new types of hardware to achieve its goals.

STEP 2: Activity

Consider Lowe's (www.lowes.com). A large home improvement warehouse store might seem very distant from the use of information technology. However, in 2011 Lowe's made significant improvements to its customer experience by implementing a type of hardware. What hardware is that? The answer is—smartphones.

Visit http://www.wiley.com/go/rainer/IS9e/applytheconcept and click on the link provided for Apply the Concept TG 1.2. This link will take you to a *U.S. News and World Report* article that discusses how Lowe's implemented smartphone technology for their employees and their customers.

STEP 3: Deliverable

Discuss strategic issues that link hardware design to business strategy, using the Lowe's case to illustrate these links. Put your discussion in a Word document and submit it to your professor.

Apply the Concept Technology Guide 1.3

LEARNING OBJECTIVE TG 1.3

Describe the various types of computers in the computer hierarchy.

STEP 1: Background

All computers require processing power and storage capability. But as you move along the computer hierarchy, that processing and storage can sometimes be distributed to another location. We refer to this as fat and thin clients.

STEP 2: Activity

You are an inventory manager for a local tire shop. You have well over 2,000 SKUs that you are responsible for. Inventory management has been managed on paper by keeping up with invoices for items in stock and receipts of items sold. Monthly reconciliation has been sufficient, but now upper management is seeking daily clarity on inventory and there is a need for an up-to-date system.

STEP 3: Deliverable

Search the Web for inventory management software and review the type of computers that are used in the specific inventory management system. It is likely that it will have some type of server, desktop PC, and mobile devices. Prepare a list of those and describe each one relative to the computer hierarchy.

Apply the Concept Technology Guide 1.4

LEARNING OBJECTIVE TG 1.4

Differentiate the various types of input and output technologies and their uses.

STEP 1: Background

Computers in and of themselves are not very useful to us. They are usually boxes that make some noise and create some heat. However, it is our ability to interact with their power that makes them invaluable to us. Input and output technologies allow us to engage with the processing power of the computer and all the "knowledge" of the Internet to be able to make decisions.

STEP 2: Activity

Traditional input and output technologies have relied heavily on keyboards, mice, and flat displays. However, this is changing rapidly. New technologies are allowing for more virtual interaction that is changing what is possible with computers.

STEP 3: Deliverable

Search the Web for virtual and augmented reality. As you read about them, consider the different forms of input and output technologies. Prepare a table that describes these innovative tools for interacting with a computer.

Apply the Concept Technology Guide 2.1

LEARNING OBJECTIVE TG 2.1

Discuss the major software issues that confront modern organizations.

STEP 1: Background

Today's organizations deal with many decisions when it comes to technology. Will it meet our needs? Will it be flexible enough to meet our needs in the future? Will there be support for problems? Will it be user-friendly? Can we afford it? Will the licensing change in the future? Is there some technology that will make this useless in the next three to five years? These are just a few of the questions that will be considered when looking at software.

STEP 2: Activity

Imagine that you are meeting with your boss about a new software package for the human resources department of your organization. A focus group has created a list of user requirements for the new system to be functional and supportive, and your boss is meeting with them next week.

STEP 3: Deliverable

Help prepare a list of questions that the boss should discuss concerning the software from an administrative perspective. Remember, the group has focused on what they "want and need," not necessarily what is best for the organization (or what is feasible).

Apply the Concept Technology Guide 2.2

LEARNING OBJECTIVE TG 2.2

Describe the general functions of the operating system.

STEP 1: Background

There are a lot of computing terms that are commonly used in the wrong way. For example, most of the time when people say they have a "PC," they are referring to a computer that runs some version of the Microsoft Windows OS. This was even used in the Mac versus PC commercials that Apple ran a few years ago. In reality, though, a PC is just a personal computer and could run any operating system.

STEP 2: Activity

Operating systems are a necessary part of the computer. Without them, the computer will not function. Imagine that you are helping your friend pick out a computer. He just wants to pick out the color, shape, and size of the computer, but you are trying to help him understand the differences in computers.

STEP 3: Deliverable

One major difference is the type of operating system. Write a paragraph that describes what an operating system does and why it is important to be careful about your selection.

Apply the Concept Technology Guide 2.3

LEARNING OBJECTIVE TG 2.3

Differentiate between the two major types of software.

STEP 1: Background

There are two types of software (systems and application), two general ways of obtaining software licenses (proprietary versus open-source), and two general types of uses (traditional versus mobile). You should be sufficiently familiar with software to be able to categorize programs that you use.

STEP 2: Activity

Visit http://www.wiley.com/go/rainer/IS9e/applytheconcept and click on the link for Apply the Concept TG 2.3. This link will take you to CNET's Download.com. At this website, you should immediately notice one of the categories mentioned above. At the time of this writing, the site automatically recognized the type of computer operating system on the user's computer. For example, this author is writing on a Mac, and the system recognized the Mac OS and defaulted to the Mac software page. Review the available software and differentiate between the operating systems and the applications. Within applications, differentiate by method of obtaining a license—some you have to pay for, and some are available by open-source or freeware licensing.

STEP 3: Deliverable

Build a table that differentiates between the two major types of software. To complete this task, list 10 applications you reviewed on the website mentioned in Step 2. Use the template provided below. Turn your completed table in to your instructor.

Application	Operating System	Licensing

Apply the Concept Technology Guide 3.1

LEARNING OBJECTIVE TG 3.1

Describe the problems that modern information technology departments face.

STEP 1: Background

This section discussed the evolution of computer infrastructure over time. Early computing models were called "terminal to host." Today we have "cloud," or "distributed computing," models available. A knowledge of how infrastructure models have changed can help you understand the challenges confronting modern IT departments.

STEP 2: Activity

Review the evolution of IT infrastructure as presented in this section. It is likely that all businesses today have some form of a local area network (LAN) in the client/server model of computing. Beginning with that stage, consider the problems that modern IT departments face as their systems evolve.

Imagine that your boss has asked your advice on moving from traditional LAN computing, in which each department operates a separate network, toward enterprise or cloud computing. What type of challenges could you help your boss anticipate?

STEP 3: Deliverable

Write a letter to your boss (your instructor) that describes the problems that modern IT departments must address as they evolve toward enterprise and cloud computing.

Apply the Concept Technology Guide 3.2

LEARNING OBJECTIVE TG 3.2

Describe the key characteristics and advantages of cloud computing.

STEP 1: Background

One of the more popular virtual servers is a virtual Web server offered by Web hosting companies. Historically, someone would simply purchase and share space on a server that would host his or her files. However, many people today need dedicated servers that guarantee performance for their consumers.

STEP 2: Activity

Visit http://www.wiley.com/go/rainer/IS9e/applytheconcept and click on the link provided for Apply the Concept TG 3.2. This link will take you to a case study on an offshore drilling company, Seadrill, that migrated from in-house data centers to a virtual private cloud data center. As you review the site, focus carefully on the advantages and concerns mentioned in the case study.

STEP 3: Deliverable

In a Word document, describe the key characteristics and advantages of cloud computing for Seadrill. Submit your document to your instructor.

Apply the Concept Technology Guide 3.3

LEARNING OBJECTIVE TG 3.3

Identify a use case scenario for each of the four types of clouds.

STEP 1: Background

This section describes four types of clouds: public, private, hybrid, and vertical. The common feature among all four types is that resources are hosted remotely and made available to a wide range of devices over high-speed Internet connections. All four types display the basic features of the cloud that were presented in earlier sections. However, the applications of these features differ for each type.

STEP 2: Activity

Refer to the Boeing example presented in this section. Boeing employs a hybrid cloud. As you have seen, there are many possible strategies for utilizing the cloud. Imagine a use case scenario for Boeing for each type of cloud.

STEP 3: Deliverable

Build a table that identifies a use case scenario for each of the four types of clouds for Boeing.

Apply the Concept Technology Guide 3.4

LEARNING OBJECTIVE TG 3.4

Explain the operational model of each of the three types of cloud services.

STEP 1: Background

Infrastructure-as-a-service, platform-as-a-service, and software-as-a-service are relatively new processing models made available by the rise in dependable, high-speed Internet access and powerful "host-computer" processing capabilities. The three cloud models are differentiated by how users employ them and which services providers offer with each one.

STEP 2: Activity

Review the material in this section. For each operational model, consider who owns the infrastructure, the operating systems, and the applications.

STEP 3: Deliverable

In a Word document, explain the operational model for each of the three types of cloud services by highlighting the differences in who is responsible for the infrastructure, the operating systems, and the applications for each model. Submit your document to your instructor.

Apply the Concept Technology Guide 3.5

LEARNING OBJECTIVE TG 3.5

Identify the key benefits of cloud computing.

STEP 1: Background

This section has outlined the benefits that are driving many organizations to transition to cloud computing. Productivity, cost reductions, collaboration, more robust data mining, flexibility, and scope expansion are just the beginning. Cloud computing is a powerful tool that is changing the ways we do business.

STEP 2: Activity

Visit the Amazon Web Services (AWS) site (www.aws.amazon.com) and learn about the variety of cloud computing services Amazon provides. This site contains video of several customer testimonials. As you watch them, look for common benefits the various customers receive from cloud computing.

STEP 3: Deliverable

Based on the video and the material in this section, identify the key benefits of cloud computing that Amazon offers its business customers. Detail these benefits in a memo to your boss (instructor).

Apply the Concept Technology Guide 3.6

LEARNING OBJECTIVE TG 3.6

Discuss the concerns and risks associated with cloud computing.

STEP 1: Background

This section discussed why the risks associated with cloud computing outweigh the benefits for some organizations. The statistics provided early on that cloud computing will remain a small portion of IT spending reflect concerns regarding these risks.

STEP 2: Activity

Visit http://www.wiley.com/go/rainer/IS9e/applytheconcept and click on the link provided for TG 3.6. This link will take you to an article that addresses some of the risks of cloud computing that senior managers need to consider. As you read the article, try to organize the managers' thoughts according to the concerns presented in this section: legacy systems, costs, reliability, security, privacy, and regulatory and legal environment. Imagine you have just overheard a conversation about how wonderful cloud computing is that mentioned all of the positives and none of the negatives. How would you respond?

STEP 3: Deliverable

Based on the material contained in this section and the information conveyed in the article, write a response to the above scenario that discusses the concerns and risks associated with cloud computing.

Apply the Concept Technology Guide 3.7

LEARNING OBJECTIVE TG 3.7

Explain the role of Web services in building a firm's IT applications and provide examples.

STEP 1: Background

Web services allow companies to increase functionality with minimal effort by using standard protocols to access and share data. The advantage of using Web services is that they standardize the Web platform. Using the same Web protocols that allow you to access any website makes sharing data much easier.

STEP 2: Activity

Imagine you work for a bank and you want to display some financial data on your intranet to keep your employees up to date on major market trends. One option is to gather data, perform an analysis, build and share charts and graphs, and then keep everything current. This probably sounds like a lot of work. But, suppose someone else had done all of the work for you?

Visit http://www.wiley.com/go/rainer/IS9e/applytheconcept and click on the link provided for Apply the Concept TG 3.7. This link will take you to a website that discusses the available "widgets" (another name for an embeddable Web service) that businesses can select to display on their sites. Review the available information and consider how it would help you add content to your bank's intranet with minimal effort.

STEP 3: Deliverable

Write a summary that explains the role of Web services in building a firm's IT applications. Include a few examples based on the options you viewed in Step 2.

Company Index